Citroën C4

Owners Workshop Manual

Peter T Gill

(5576 - 416 - 3Y1)

Models covered

Hatchback & Coupe
Petrol: 1.4 litre (1360cc) & 1.6 litre (1587cc & 1598cc)
Turbo-diesel: 1.6 litre (1560cc) & 2.0 litre (1997cc) DOHC

Does NOT cover 1.6 litre THP turbo or 2.0 litre petrol engines, or 2.0 litre SOHC diesel engines
Does NOT cover 'BioFlex' models, C4 Picasso or Grand Picasso, or revised Citroën C4 'II' range introduced January 2011

A book in the **Haynes Owners Workshop Manual Series**

ISBN **978 1 78521 375 5**

British Library Cataloguing in Publication Data
A catalogue record for this book is available from the British Library.

Haynes Group Limited
Haynes North America, Inc

www.haynes.com

Disclaimer

There are risks associated with automotive repairs. The ability to make repairs depends on the individual's skill, experience and proper tools. Individuals should act with due care and acknowledge and assume the risk of performing automotive repairs.

The purpose of this manual is to provide comprehensive, useful and accessible automotive repair information, to help you get the best value from your vehicle. However, this manual is not a substitute for a professional certified technician or mechanic.

This repair manual is produced by a third party and is not associated with an individual vehicle manufacturer. If there is any doubt or discrepancy between this manual and the owner's manual or the factory service manual, please refer to the factory service manual or seek assistance from a professional certified technician or mechanic.

Even though we have prepared this manual with extreme care and every attempt is made to ensure that the information in this manual is correct, neither the publisher nor the author can accept responsibility for loss, damage or injury caused by any errors in, or omissions from, the information given.

Contents

Contents

The Citroën C4 was introduced into the UK in October 2004. At its launch, the C4 was offered with a choice of 1.4 (1360cc), 1.6 (1587cc) and 2.0 litre (1997cc) petrol engines, or 1.6 litre (1560cc) and 2.0 litre (1997cc) turbo-diesel engines. In September 2008 a new 1.6 litre (1598cc) petrol engine was introduced, including a turbo version. It was available in two body styles – a 3-door Coupe and 5-door Hatchback.

The engines fitted to the C4 range are all versions of the well-proven units, which have appeared in many Peugeot/Citroën vehicles over the years, with the 1.6 litre HDi engine developed in a joint venture with the Ford Motor Co.

The engine is mounted transversely at the front of vehicle, with the transmission mounted on its left-hand end. All engines are fitted with a manual transmission as standard (an automatic transmission is available on certain engines).

All models have fully independent front suspension, incorporating shock absorbers, coil springs and an anti-roll bar. The rear beam axle has a built-in anti-roll bar, with separate shock absorbers and coil spring.

A wide range of standard and optional equipment is available within the range to suit most tastes, including central locking, electric windows, and front, side and curtain airbags. An air conditioning system is available on all models.

Provided that regular servicing is carried out in accordance with the manufacturer's recommendations, the vehicle should prove reliable and very economical. The engine compartment is well designed, and most of the items requiring frequent attention are easily accessible.

Citroën C4 manual

The aim of this manual is to help you get the best value from your vehicle. It can do so in several ways. It can help you decide what work must be done (even should you choose to get it done by a garage). It will also provide information on routine maintenance and servicing, and give a logical course of action and diagnosis when random faults occur. However, it is hoped that you will use the manual by tackling the work yourself. On simpler jobs it may even be quicker than booking the car into a garage and going there twice, to leave and collect it. Perhaps most important, a lot of money can be saved by avoiding the costs a garage must charge to cover its labour and overheads.

The manual has drawings and descriptions to show the function of the various components so that their layout can be understood. Tasks are described and photographed in a clear step-by-step sequence.

References to the 'left' and 'right' of the vehicle are in the sense of a person in the driver's seat facing forward.

Acknowledgements

Thanks are due to Draper Tools Limited and Auto Service Tools Limited (asttools.co.uk) who provided some of the workshop tools, and to all those people at Sparkford who helped in the production of this manual.

We take great pride in the accuracy of information given in this manual, but vehicle manufacturers make alterations and design changes during the production run of a particular vehicle of which they do not inform us. No liability can be accepted by the authors or publishers for loss, damage or injury caused by any errors in, or omissions from, the information given.

Working on your car can be dangerous. This page shows just some of the potential risks and hazards, with the aim of creating a safety-conscious attitude.

General hazards

Scalding

• Don't remove the radiator or expansion tank cap while the engine is hot.

• Engine oil, transmission fluid or power steering fluid may also be dangerously hot if the engine has recently been running.

Burning

• Beware of burns from the exhaust system and from any part of the engine. Brake discs and drums can also be extremely hot immediately after use.

Crushing

• When working under or near a raised vehicle, always supplement the jack with axle stands, or use drive-on ramps. ***Never venture under a car which is only supported by a jack.***

• Take care if loosening or tightening high-torque nuts when the vehicle is on stands. Initial loosening and final tightening should be done with the wheels on the ground.

Fire

• Fuel is highly flammable; fuel vapour is explosive.

• Don't let fuel spill onto a hot engine.

• Do not smoke or allow naked lights (including pilot lights) anywhere near a vehicle being worked on. Also beware of creating sparks (electrically or by use of tools).

• Fuel vapour is heavier than air, so don't work on the fuel system with the vehicle over an inspection pit.

• Another cause of fire is an electrical overload or short-circuit. Take care when repairing or modifying the vehicle wiring.

• Keep a fire extinguisher handy, of a type suitable for use on fuel and electrical fires.

Electric shock

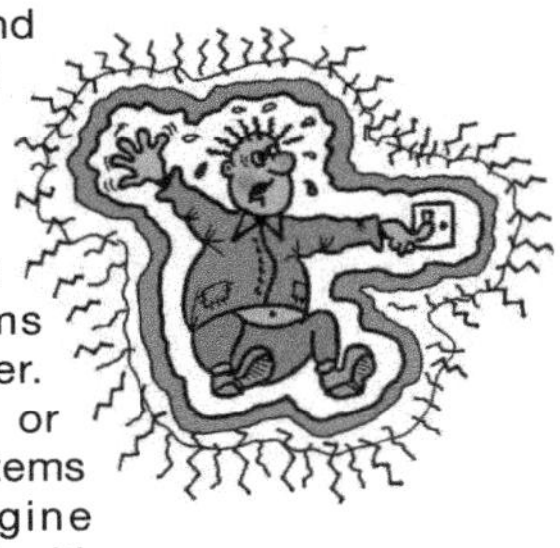

• Ignition HT and Xenon headlight voltages can be dangerous, especially to people with heart problems or a pacemaker. Don't work on or near these systems with the engine running or the ignition switched on.

• Mains voltage is also dangerous. Make sure that any mains-operated equipment is correctly earthed. Mains power points should be protected by a residual current device (RCD) circuit breaker.

Fume or gas intoxication

• Exhaust fumes are poisonous; they can contain carbon monoxide, which is rapidly fatal if inhaled. Never run the engine in a confined space such as a garage with the doors shut.

• Fuel vapour is also poisonous, as are the vapours from some cleaning solvents and paint thinners.

Poisonous or irritant substances

• Avoid skin contact with battery acid and with any fuel, fluid or lubricant, especially antifreeze, brake hydraulic fluid and Diesel fuel. Don't syphon them by mouth. If such a substance is swallowed or gets into the eyes, seek medical advice.

• Prolonged contact with used engine oil can cause skin cancer. Wear gloves or use a barrier cream if necessary. Change out of oil-soaked clothes and do not keep oily rags in your pocket.

• Air conditioning refrigerant forms a poisonous gas if exposed to a naked flame (including a cigarette). It can also cause skin burns on contact.

Asbestos

• Asbestos dust can cause cancer if inhaled or swallowed. Asbestos may be found in gaskets and in brake and clutch linings. When dealing with such components it is safest to assume that they contain asbestos.

Special hazards

Hydrofluoric acid

• This extremely corrosive acid is formed when certain types of synthetic rubber, found in some O-rings, oil seals, fuel hoses etc, are exposed to temperatures above 4000C. The rubber changes into a charred or sticky substance containing the acid. *Once formed, the acid remains dangerous for years. If it gets onto the skin, it may be necessary to amputate the limb concerned.*

• When dealing with a vehicle which has suffered a fire, or with components salvaged from such a vehicle, wear protective gloves and discard them after use.

The battery

• Batteries contain sulphuric acid, which attacks clothing, eyes and skin. Take care when topping-up or carrying the battery.

• The hydrogen gas given off by the battery is highly explosive. Never cause a spark or allow a naked light nearby. Be careful when connecting and disconnecting battery chargers or jump leads.

Air bags

• Air bags can cause injury if they go off accidentally. Take care when removing the steering wheel and trim panels. Special storage instructions may apply.

Diesel injection equipment

• Diesel injection pumps supply fuel at very high pressure. Take care when working on the fuel injectors and fuel pipes.

Warning: Never expose the hands, face or any other part of the body to injector spray; the fuel can penetrate the skin with potentially fatal results.

Remember...

DO

• Do use eye protection when using power tools, and when working under the vehicle.

• Do wear gloves or use barrier cream to protect your hands when necessary.

• Do get someone to check periodically that all is well when working alone on the vehicle.

• Do keep loose clothing and long hair well out of the way of moving mechanical parts.

• Do remove rings, wristwatch etc, before working on the vehicle – especially the electrical system.

• Do ensure that any lifting or jacking equipment has a safe working load rating adequate for the job.

DON'T

• Don't attempt to lift a heavy component which may be beyond your capability – get assistance.

• Don't rush to finish a job, or take unverified short cuts.

• Don't use ill-fitting tools which may slip and cause injury.

• Don't leave tools or parts lying around where someone can trip over them. Mop up oil and fuel spills at once.

• Don't allow children or pets to play in or near a vehicle being worked on.

The following pages are intended to help in dealing with common roadside emergencies and breakdowns. You will find more detailed fault finding information at the back of the manual, and repair information in the main chapters.

If your car won't start and the starter motor doesn't turn

- ☐ If it's a model with automatic transmission, make sure the selector is in the P or N position.
- ☐ Open the bonnet and make sure that the battery terminals are clean and tight.
- ☐ Switch on the headlights and try to start the engine. If the headlights go very dim when you're trying to start, the battery is probably flat. Try jump starting using another car.

If your car won't start even though the starter motor turns as normal

- ☐ Is there fuel in the tank?
- ☐ Is there moisture on electrical components under the bonnet? Switch off the ignition, and then wipe off any obvious dampness with a dry cloth. Spray a water-repellent aerosol product (WD-40 or equivalent) on ignition and fuel system electrical connectors like those shown in the photos. Pay special attention to the ignition coils wiring connector. (Note that diesel engines do not normally suffer from damp.)

A Remove the plastic cover and check the condition and security of the battery connections.

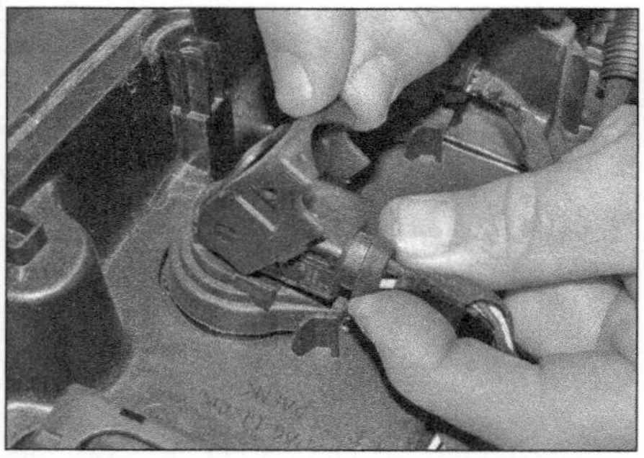

B Check that the ignition system (as applicable) wiring connectors are securely connected (VTi petrol model shown).

C Check the camshaft sensor wiring connectors are securely connected (VTi petrol model shown).

Check that electrical connections are secure (with the ignition switched off) and spray them with a water dispersant spray like WD-40 if you suspect a problem due to damp.

D Remove the cover and check that all fuses are still in good condition and none have blown.

Jump starting

HAYNES HiNT ***Jump starting will get you out of trouble, but you must correct whatever made the battery go flat in the first place. There are three possibilities:***

1 The battery has been drained by repeated attempts to start, or by leaving the lights on.

2 The charging system is not working properly (alternator drivebelt slack or broken, alternator wiring fault or alternator itself faulty).

3 The battery itself is at fault (electrolyte low, or battery worn out).

When jump-starting a car, observe the following precautions:

✓ Before connecting the booster battery, make sure that the ignition is switched off.

Caution: Remove the key in case the central locking engages when the jump leads are connected

✓ Ensure that all electrical equipment (lights, heater, wipers, etc) is switched off.

✓ Take note of any special precautions printed on the battery case.

✓ Make sure that the booster battery is the same voltage as the discharged one in the vehicle.

✓ If the battery is being jump-started from the battery in another vehicle, the two vehicles MUST NOT TOUCH each other.

✓ Make sure that the transmission is in neutral (or PARK, in the case of automatic transmission).

HAYNES HiNT ***Budget jump leads can be a false economy, as they often do not pass enough current to start large capacity or diesel engines. They can also get hot.***

1 Unclip the plastic cover and connect the red jump lead to the positive (+) battery terminal.

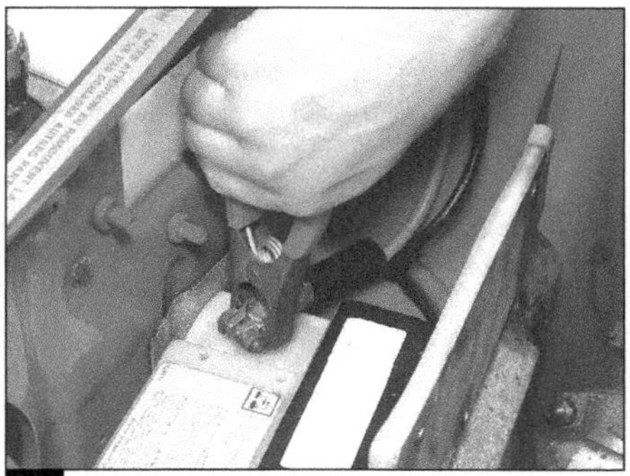

2 Connect the other end of the red jump lead to the positive (+) terminal of the booster battery.

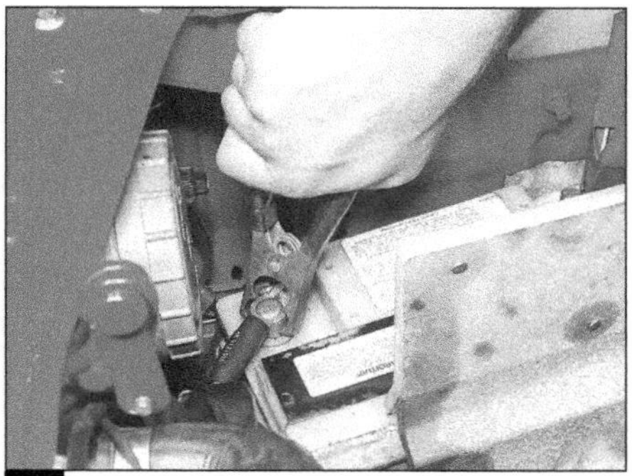

3 Connect one end of the black jump lead to the negative (-) terminal of the booster battery.

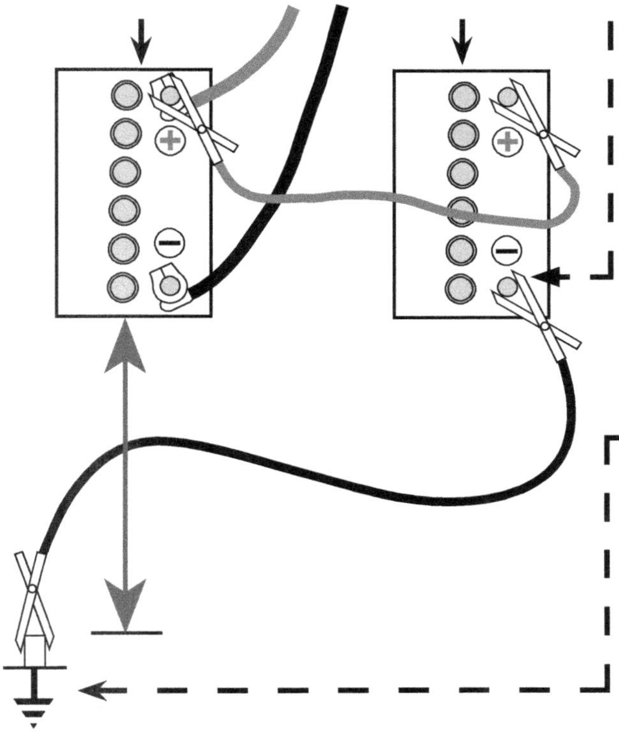

4 Connect the other end of the black jump lead negative (-) terminal to the metal casting bracket on the front of the cylinder head.

5 Make sure that the jump leads will not come in to contact with the cooling fan, drivebelts or any other moving parts on the engine.

6 Start the engine, then with the engine running at fast idle speed, disconnect the jump leads in the reverse order of connection, ie, negative (black) lead first. Securely refit the plastic cover to the battery positive terminal when completed.

Identifying leaks

Puddles on the garage floor or drive, or obvious wetness under the bonnet or underneath the car, suggest a leak that needs investigating. It can sometimes be difficult to decide where the leak is coming from, especially if an engine undershield is fitted. Leaking oil or fluid can also be blown rearwards by the passage of air under the car, giving a false impression of where the problem lies.

Warning: Most automotive oils and fluids are poisonous. Wash them off skin, and change out of contaminated clothing, without delay.

HAYNES HiNT *The smell of a fluid leaking from the car may provide a clue to what's leaking. Some fluids are distinctively coloured. It may help to remove the engine undershield, clean the car carefully and to park it over some clean paper overnight as an aid to locating the source of the leak. Remember that some leaks may only occur while the engine is running.*

Sump oil

Engine oil may leak from the drain plug...

Oil from filter

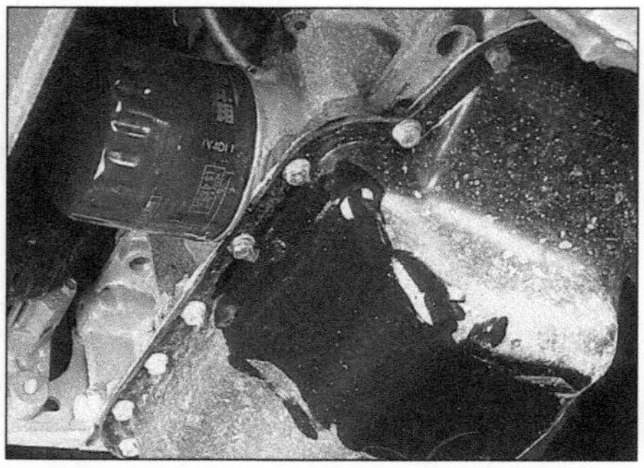

...or from the base of the oil filter.

Gearbox oil

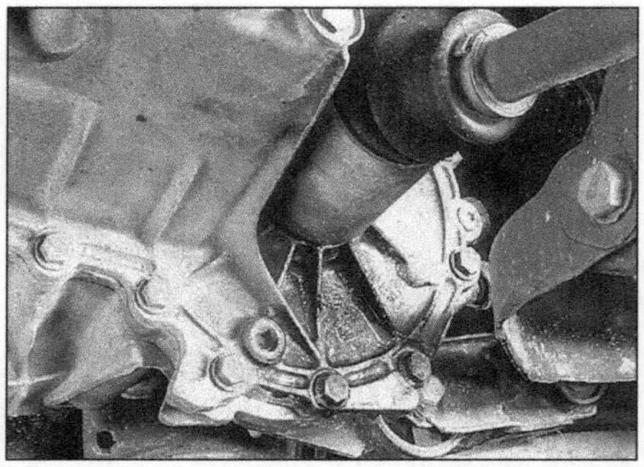

Gearbox oil can leak from the seals at the inboard ends of the driveshafts.

Antifreeze

Leaking antifreeze often leaves a crystalline deposit like this.

Brake fluid

A leak occurring at a wheel is almost certainly brake fluid.

Power steering fluid

Power steering fluid may leak from the pipe connectors on the steering rack.

Towing

When all else fails, you may find yourself having to get a tow home – or of course you may be helping somebody else. Long-distance recovery should only be done by a garage or breakdown service. For shorter distances, DIY towing using another car is easy enough, but observe the following points:

☐ Use a proper tow-rope – they are not expensive. The vehicle being towed must display an ON TOW sign in its rear window.

☐ Always turn the ignition key to the 'on' position when the vehicle is being towed, so that the steering lock is released, and that the direction indicator and brake lights work.

☐ The towing eye is kept inside the spare wheel (see *Wheel changing*). To fit the eye, unclip the access cover from the relevant bumper and screw the eye firmly into position **(see illustrations)**.

☐ Before being towed, release the handbrake and select neutral on the transmission.

Caution: On models with automatic transmission, do not tow the car at speeds in excess of 30 mph or for a distance greater than 30 miles. If towing speeds/ distances are to exceed these limits, then the car must be towed with its front wheels off the ground.

☐ Note that greater-than-usual pedal pressure will be required to operate the brakes, since the vacuum servo unit is only operational with the engine running.

☐ The driver of the car being towed must keep the tow-rope taut at all times to avoid snatching.

☐ Make sure that both drivers know the route before setting off.

☐ Only drive at moderate speeds and keep the distance towed to a minimum. Drive smoothly and allow plenty of time for slowing down at junctions.

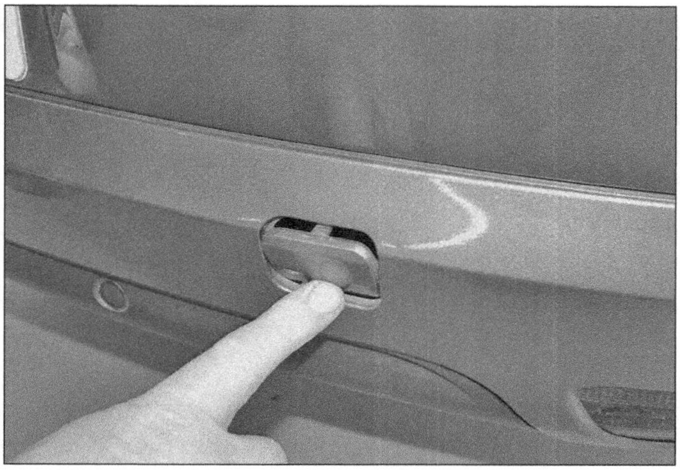

Unclip the access cover from the rear bumper ...

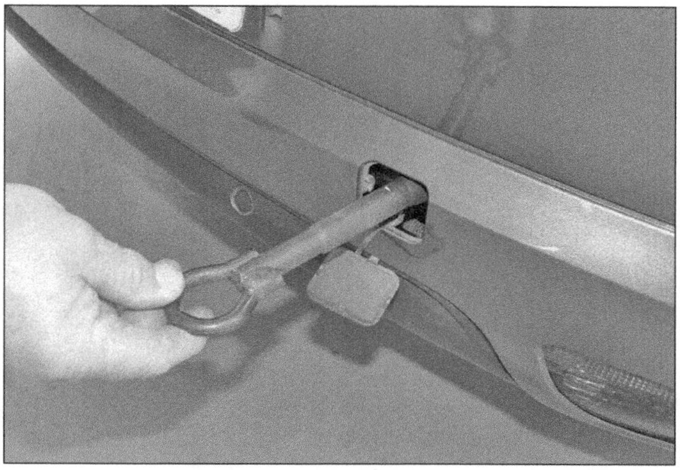

... then screw the towing eye in securely (use wheel brace through eye to tighten)

Unclip the cover from the front bumper ...

... and then fit the towing eye to the front of the vehicle

Wheel changing

***Warning:** Do not change a wheel in a situation where you risk being hit by another vehicle. On busy roads, try to stop in a lay-by or a gateway. Be wary of passing traffic while changing the wheel – it is easy to become distracted by the job in hand.*

Preparation

- ☐ When a puncture occurs, stop as soon as it is safe to do so.
- ☐ Park on firm level ground, if possible, and well out of the way of other traffic.
- ☐ Use hazard warning lights if necessary.
- ☐ If you have one, use a warning triangle to alert other drivers of your presence.
- ☐ Apply the handbrake and engage first or reverse gear (or Park on models with automatic transmission).
- ☐ If the ground is soft, use a flat piece of wood to spread the load under the foot of the jack.
- ☐ Place a chock against the wheel diagonally opposite the wheel to be removed, or use a large stone (or similar) to stop the car rolling.

Changing the wheel

1 The spare wheel and tools are stored in the luggage compartment, lift up the floor panel/carpet. Release the retaining strap (where fitted) and remove the tool kit from the centre of the spare wheel. Unscrew the centre fastener and remove the spare wheel.

2 On models with steel wheels, remove the wheel trim/hub cap. On models with alloy wheels, unclip the plastic centre cover, using the plastic tool provided in the tool kit.

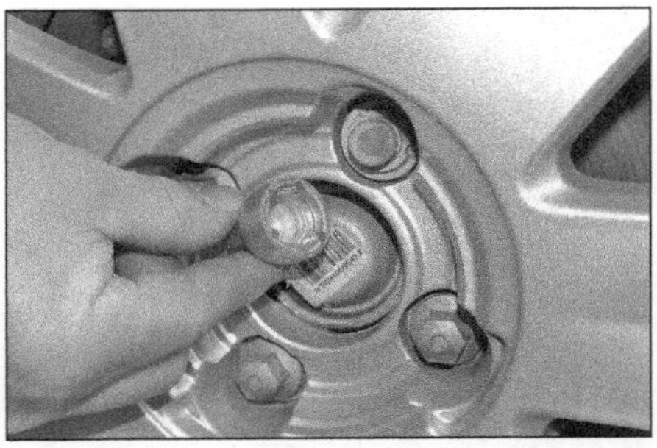

3 Where anti-theft wheel bolts are fitted, unscrew the anti-theft bolt using the special tool provided – normally stored in the passenger glovebox or toolkit.

4 With the vehicle still on the ground, use the tool provided to slacken each wheel bolt by half a turn.

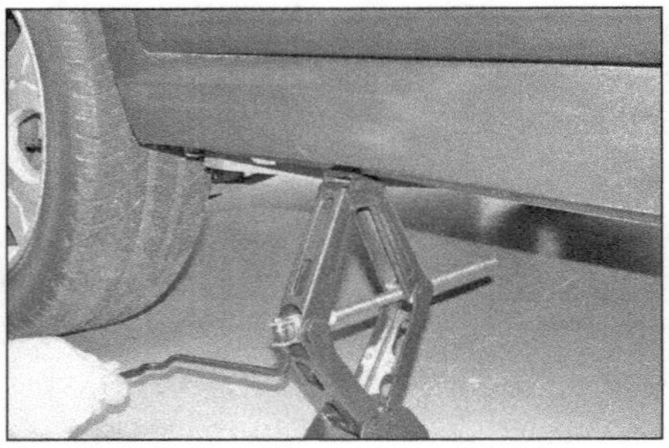

5 Make sure the jack is located on firm ground, and engage the jack head correctly with the sill. Then raise the jack until the wheel is raised clear of the ground.

6 Unscrew the wheel bolts and remove the wheel. Place the wheel under the vehicle sill in case the jack fails.

7 Fit the spare wheel and screw in the bolts. Lightly tighten the bolts with the wheel brace then lower the car to the ground.

8 Securely tighten the wheel bolts in a diagonal sequence then refit the wheel trim/ hub cap/wheel bolt covers (as applicable). Stow the punctured wheel and tools back in the boot, and secure them in position.

Finally . . .

- ☐ Remove the wheel chock.
- ☐ Check the tyre pressure on the wheel just fitted. If it is low, or if you don't have a pressure gauge with you, drive slowly to the next garage and inflate the tyre to the correct pressure.
- ☐ The wheel bolts should be slackened and retightened to the specified torque at the earliest possible opportunity (see Chapter 1A, Specifications or Chapter 1B, Specifications).
- ☐ Have the damaged tyre or wheel repaired as soon as possible, or another puncture will leave you stranded.

Introduction

There are some very simple checks which need only take a few minutes to carry out, but which could save you a lot of inconvenience and expense.

These checks require no great skill or special tools, and the small amount of time they take to perform could prove to be very well spent, for example;

☐ Keeping an eye on tyre condition and pressures, will not only help to stop them wearing out prematurely, but could also save your life.

☐ Many breakdowns are caused by electrical problems. Battery-related faults are particularly common, and a quick check on a regular basis will often prevent the majority of these.

☐ If your car develops a brake fluid leak, the first time you might know about it is when your brakes don't work properly. Checking the level regularly will give advance warning of this kind of problem.

☐ If the oil or coolant levels run low, the cost of repairing any engine damage will be far greater than fixing the leak, for example.

Underbonnet check points

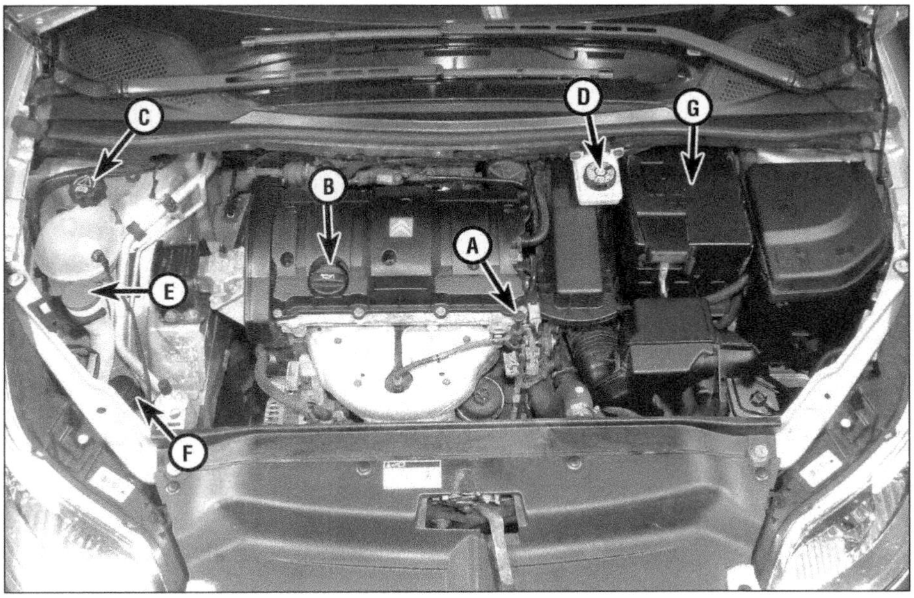

◀ 1.6 litre petrol engine (TU5 engine shown)

A *Engine oil level dipstick*
B *Engine oil filler cap*
C *Coolant expansion tank*
D *Brake (and clutch) fluid reservoir*
E *Screen washer fluid reservoir*
F *Power steering fluid reservoir*
G *Battery*

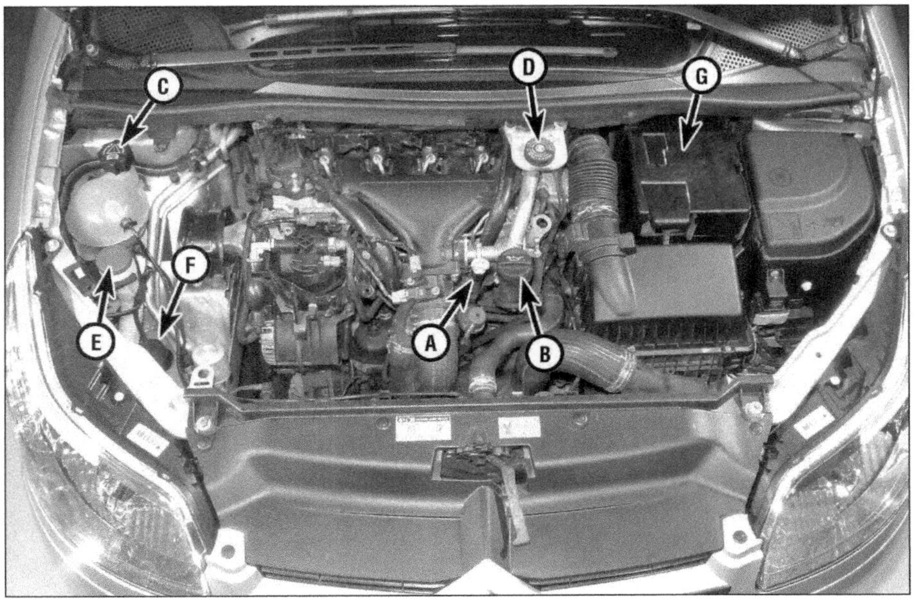

◀ 2.0 litre diesel engine

A *Engine oil level dipstick*
B *Engine oil filler cap*
C *Coolant expansion tank*
D *Brake (and clutch) fluid reservoir*
E *Screen washer fluid reservoir*
F *Power steering fluid reservoir*
G *Battery*

Engine oil level

Before you start

✔ Make sure that your car is on level ground.
✔ Check the oil level before the car is driven, or at least 5 minutes after the engine has been switched off.

> **HAYNES HiNT** ***If the oil is checked immediately after driving the vehicle, some of the oil will remain in the upper engine components, resulting in an inaccurate reading on the dipstick.***

The correct oil

Modern engines place great demands on their oil. It is very important that the correct oil for your car is used (see *Lubricants and fluids*).

Car care

- If you have to add oil frequently, you should check whether you have any oil leaks. Place some clean paper under the car overnight, and check for stains in the morning. If there are no leaks, the engine may be burning oil.
- Always maintain the level between the upper and lower dipstick marks (see photo 3). If the level is too low severe engine damage may occur. Oil seal failure may result if the engine is overfilled by adding too much oil.

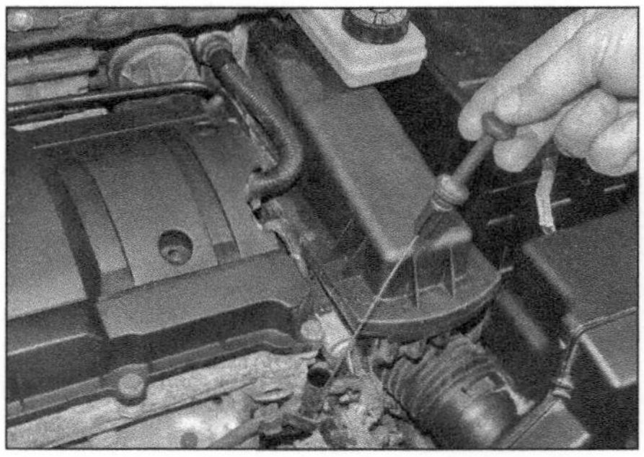

1 The dipstick is located at the front of the engine (see *Underbonnet check points*); the dipstick is often brightly coloured or has a picture of an oil-can on the top for identification. Withdraw the dipstick (1.6 litre TU5 petrol engine shown).

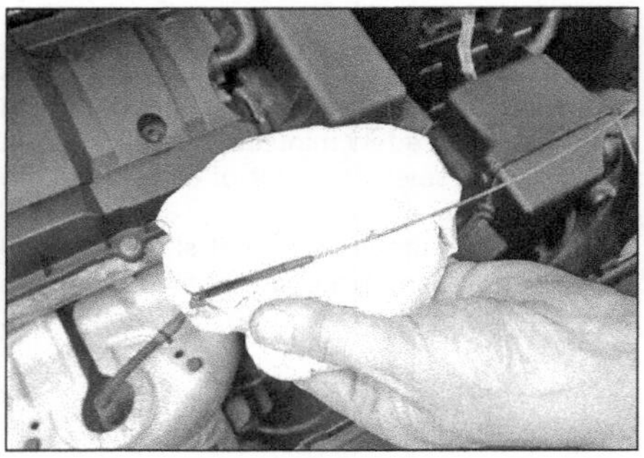

2 Using a clean rag or paper towel, remove all oil from the dipstick. Insert the clean dipstick into the tube as far as it will go, then withdraw it again.

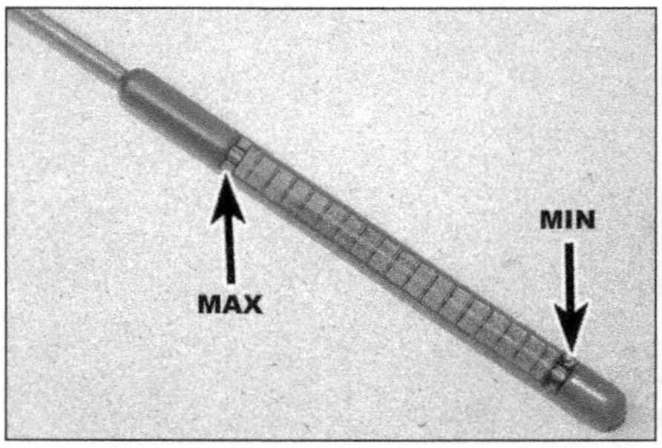

3 Note the oil level on the end of the dipstick, which should be between the upper (MAX) mark and lower (MIN) mark. Approximately 1.0 litre of oil will raise the level from the lower mark to the upper mark.

4 Oil is added through the filler cap. Unscrew the cap and top-up the level; a funnel may help to reduce spillage. Add the oil slowly, checking the level on the dipstick often. Don't overfill (see *Car care*).

Coolant level

⚠ ***Warning: DO NOT attempt to remove the expansion tank pressure cap when the engine is hot, as there is a very great risk of scalding.***
Warning: Do not leave open containers of coolant about, as it is poisonous.

Car care

- Adding coolant should not be necessary on a regular basis. If frequent topping-up is required, it is likely there is a leak. Check the radiator, all hoses and joint faces for signs of staining or wetness, and rectify as necessary.
- It is important that antifreeze is used in the cooling system all year round, not just during the winter months. Don't top-up with water alone, as the antifreeze will become too diluted.

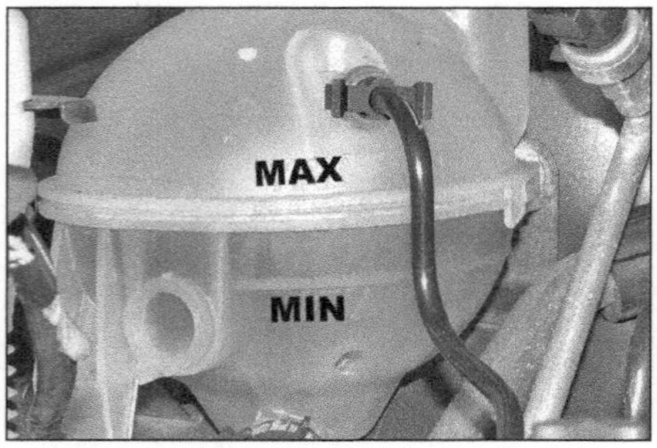

1 The coolant level must be checked with the engine cold; the coolant level should be between the MAX and MIN marks on the expansion tank.

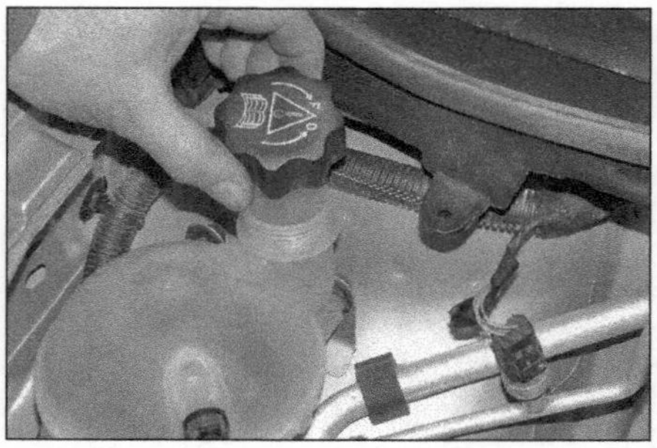

2 If topping-up is necessary, remove the pressure cap (see *Warning*) from the expansion tank, which is located on the right-hand side rear of the engine compartment.

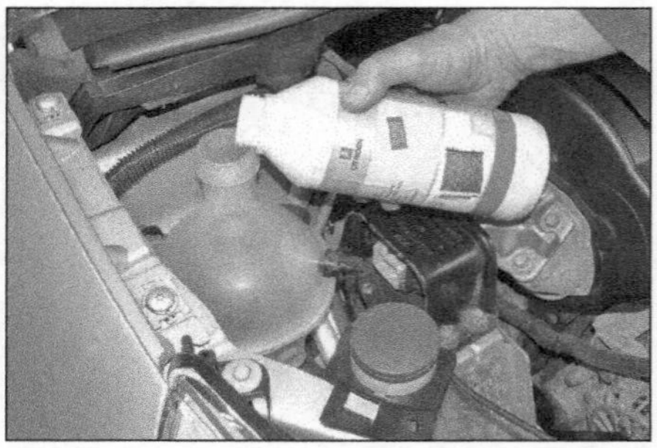

3 Add a mixture of water and antifreeze to the expansion tank until the coolant level is between the level marks. Once the level is correct, securely refit the cap.

Brake (and clutch) fluid level

Warning: Brake fluid can harm your eyes and damage painted surfaces, so use extreme caution when handling and pouring it.

Warning: Do not use fluid that has been standing open for some time, as it absorbs moisture from the air, which can cause a dangerous loss of braking effectiveness.

Before you start

✔ Make sure that your car is on level ground.

Safety first!

● If the reservoir requires repeated topping-up this is an indication of a fluid leak somewhere in the system, which should be investigated immediately.

● If a leak is suspected, the car should not be driven until the braking system has been checked. Never take any risks where brakes are concerned.

1 The upper (MAX) fluid level marking is on the side of the upper reservoir, which is located at the rear of the engine compartment.

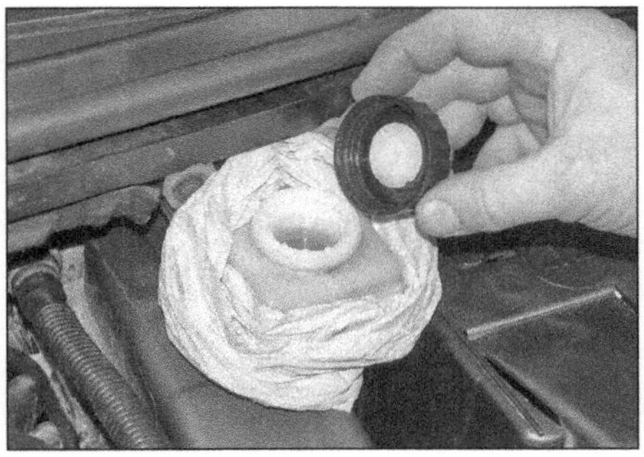

2 If topping-up is necessary, first wipe clean the area around the filler cap with a clean cloth, then unscrew the cap and remove it along with the rubber diaphragm.

3 Carefully add fluid, avoiding spilling it on the surrounding paintwork. Use only the specified hydraulic fluid. After filling to the correct level, refit the diaphragm and cap, and tighten it securely. Wipe off any spilt fluid.

Power steering fluid level

Before you start

✔ Park the vehicle on level ground.
✔ Set the steering wheel straight-ahead.
✔ The engine should be cold and turned off.

Safety first!

● The need for frequent topping-up indicates a leak, which should be investigated immediately.

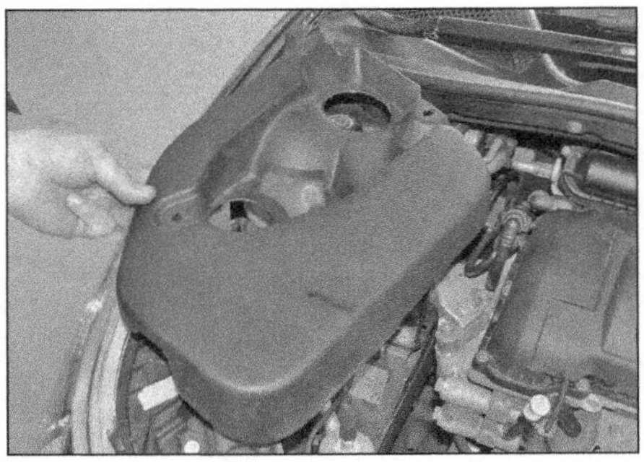

1 The fluid reservoir is on the right-hand side of the engine compartment, behind the right-hand headlight, below the coolant reservoir. Unclip the plastic cover and clean the area around the reservoir cap.

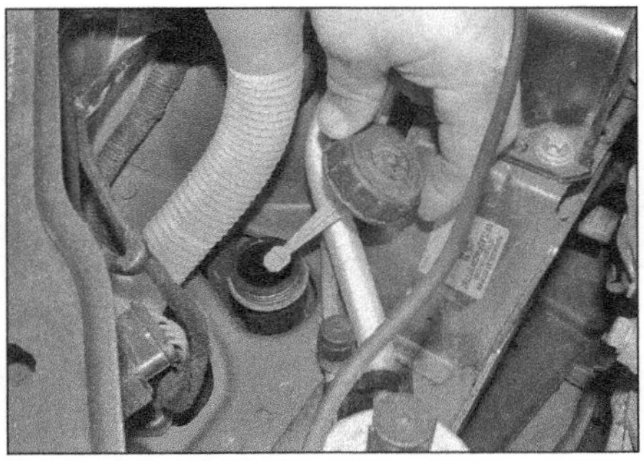

2 Unscrew the cap from the power steering fluid reservoir.

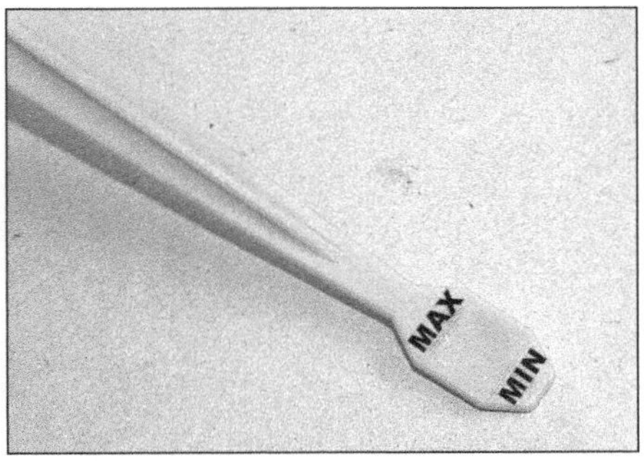

3 Check the fluid level is up to the upper (MAX) level indicator on the dipstick. Top-up the reservoir with the specified type of the fluid, using a funnel. Once the level is between the level marks, securely refit the reservoir cap. Do not overfill the reservoir.

Screen washer fluid level

● Screenwash additives not only keep the windscreen clean during foul weather, they also prevent the washer system freezing in cold weather – which is when you are likely to need it most. Don't top-up using plain water as the screenwash will become too diluted, and will freeze during cold weather.

⚠ ***Warning: On no account use coolant antifreeze in the washer system, as this may damage the paintwork.***

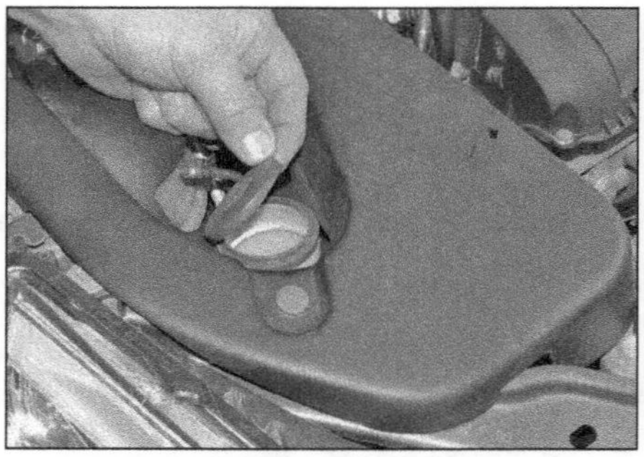

1 The washer fluid reservoir is located in the right-hand front corner of the engine compartment. To check the fluid level, open the cap and look down the filler neck.

2 If topping-up is necessary, add water and a screenwash additive in the quantities recommended on the bottle.

Wiper blades

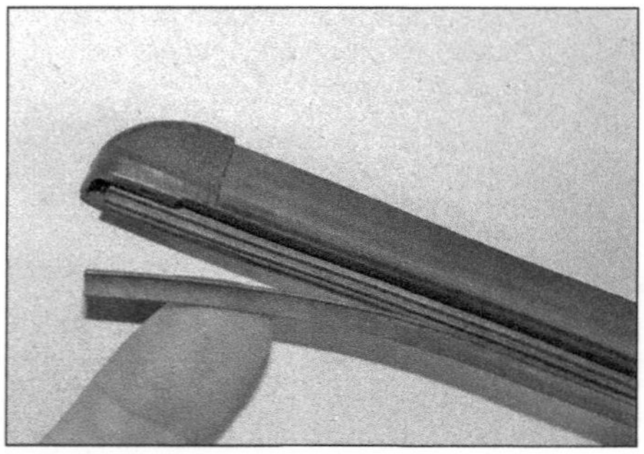

1 Check the condition of the wiper blades: if they are cracked or show signs of deterioration, or if the glass swept area is smeared, renew them. For maximum clarity of vision, wiper blades should be renewed annually.

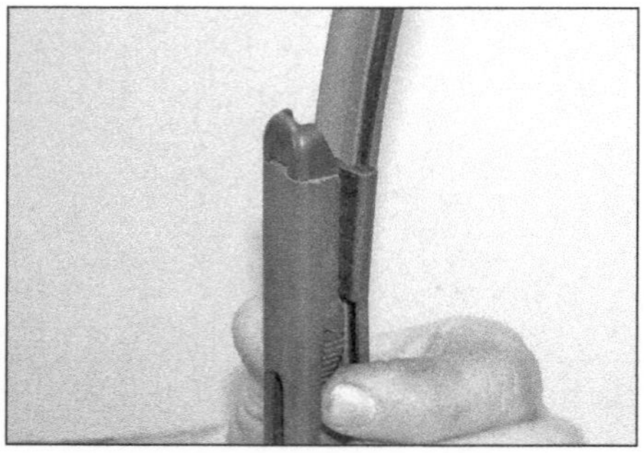

2 To remove a windscreen wiper blade, turn the ignition on, then turn the ignition off, and press the wiper switch stalk down once. This places the arms in the 'service' position. Lift the wiper from the screen and squeeze the lower ends of the retaining clip together ...

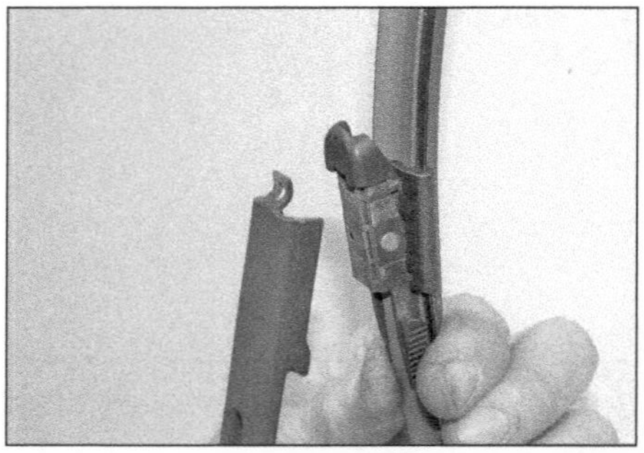

3 ... and disengage the blade by unhooking it from the end of the wiper arm, taking care not to allow the wiper arm to spring back and damage the windscreen. When completed, return the blades to the park position by pressing the wiper switch stalk again.

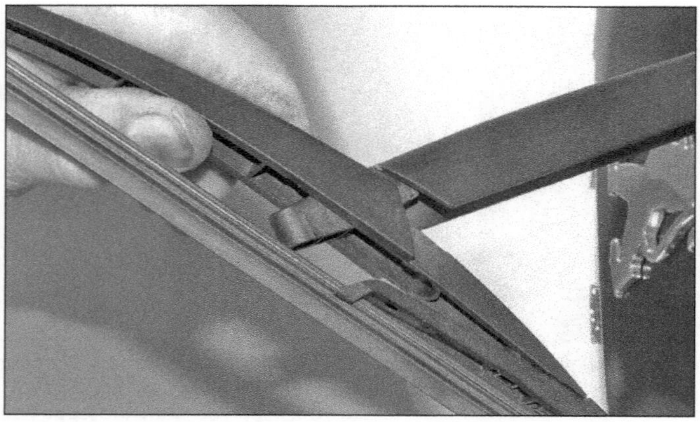

4 To remove the rear wiper blade, tilt the wiper blade ...

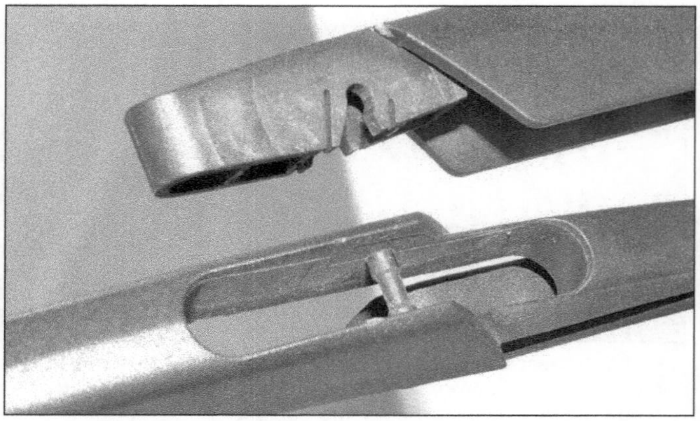

5 ... and then unclip it from the arm, taking care not to allow the arm to spring back and damage the rear screen.

Battery

Caution: Before carrying out any work on the vehicle battery, read the precautions given in 'Safety first!' at the start of this manual.

✔ Make sure that the battery tray is in good condition, and that the clamp is tight. Corrosion on the tray, retaining clamp and the battery itself can be removed with a solution of water and baking soda. Thoroughly rinse all cleaned areas with water. Any metal parts damaged by corrosion should be covered with a zinc-based primer, and then painted.

✔ Periodically (approximately every three months), check the charge condition of the battery, as described in Chapter 5A, Section 3.

✔ If the battery is flat, and you need to jump start your vehicle, see *Roadside repairs*.

HAYNES HiNT

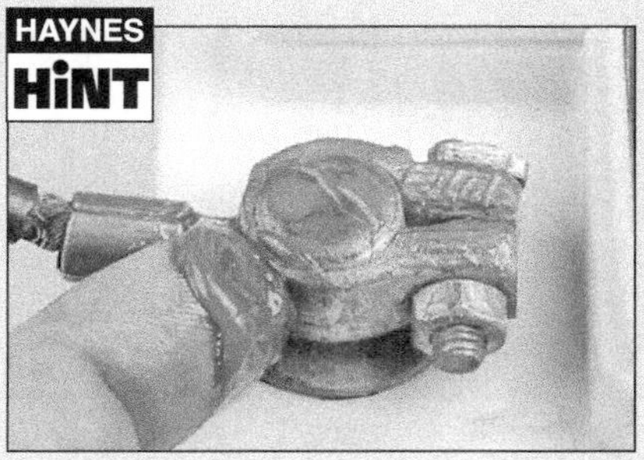

Battery corrosion can be kept to a minimum by applying a layer of petroleum jelly to the clamps and terminals after they are reconnected.

1 Lift the plastic cover to gain access to the battery positive terminal, which is located on the left-hand side of the engine compartment. The exterior of the battery should be inspected periodically for damage such as a cracked case or cover.

2 Check the battery lead clamps for tightness to ensure good electrical connections, and check the leads for signs of damage.

3 If corrosion (white, fluffy deposits) is evident, remove the cables from the battery terminals, clean them with a small wire brush, then refit them. Automotive stores sell a tool for cleaning the battery post …

4 … as well as the battery cable clamps.

Bulbs and fuses

✔ Check all external lights and the horn. Refer to Chapter 12, Section 2 for details if any of the circuits are found to be inoperative.

✔ Visually check all accessible wiring connectors, harnesses and retaining clips for security, and for signs of chafing or damage.

HAYNES HiNT ***If you need to check your brake lights and indicators unaided, back up to a wall or garage door and operate the lights. The reflected light should show if they are working properly.***

1 If a single indicator light, brake light, sidelight or headlight has failed, it is likely that a bulb has blown, and will need to be renewed. Refer to Chapter 12, Section 5 for details. If both brake lights have failed, it is possible that the switch has failed (see Chapter 9, Section 17).

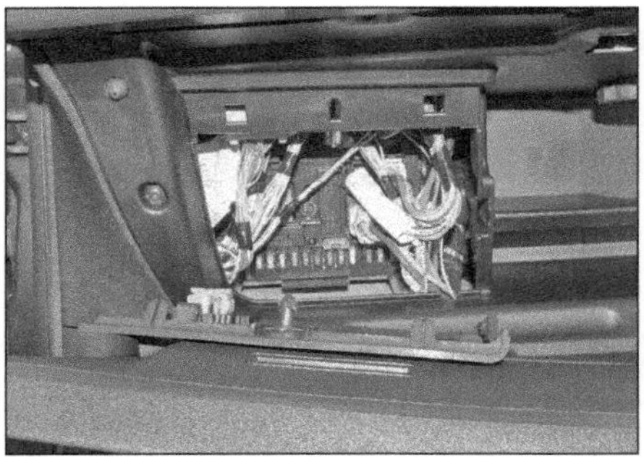

2 If more than one indicator or tail light has failed, it is likely that either a fuse has blown or that there is a fault in the circuit. Fuses are located behind a cover in the glovebox. Open the glovebox, rotate the screw fastener to lower the cover.

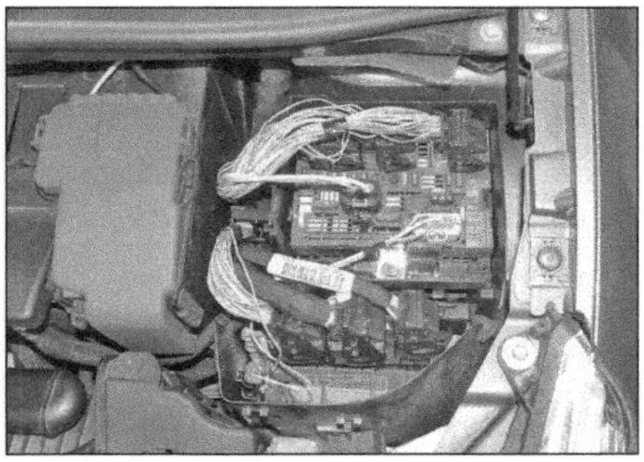

3 Additional fuses and relays are located in the left-hand side of the engine compartment fusebox. To renew a blown fuse, simply pull it out and fit a new fuse of the correct rating (see *Wiring diagrams*). If the fuse blows again, it is important that you find out why – a complete checking procedure is given in Chapter 12, Section 2.

Tyre condition and pressure

It is very important that tyres are in good condition, and at the correct pressure - having a tyre failure at any speed is highly dangerous.
Tyre wear is influenced by driving style - harsh braking and acceleration, or fast cornering, will all produce more rapid tyre wear. As a general rule, the front tyres wear out faster than the rears. Interchanging the tyres from front to rear ("rotating" the tyres) may result in more even wear. However, if this is completely effective, you may have the expense of replacing all four tyres at once!
Remove any nails or stones embedded in the tread before they penetrate the tyre to cause deflation. If removal of a nail does reveal that the tyre has been punctured, refit the nail so that its point of penetration is marked. Then immediately change the wheel, and have the tyre repaired by a tyre dealer.
Regularly check the tyres for damage in the form of cuts or bulges, especially in the sidewalls. Periodically remove the wheels, and clean any dirt or mud from the inside and outside surfaces. Examine the wheel rims for signs of rusting, corrosion or other damage. Light alloy wheels are easily damaged by "kerbing" whilst parking; steel wheels may also become dented or buckled. A new wheel is very often the only way to overcome severe damage.
New tyres should be balanced when they are fitted, but it may become necessary to re-balance them as they wear, or if the balance weights fitted to the wheel rim should fall off. Unbalanced tyres will wear more quickly, as will the steering and suspension components. Wheel imbalance is normally signified by vibration, particularly at a certain speed (typically around 50 mph). If this vibration is felt only through the steering, then it is likely that just the front wheels need balancing. If, however, the vibration is felt through the whole car, the rear wheels could be out of balance. Wheel balancing should be carried out by a tyre dealer or garage.

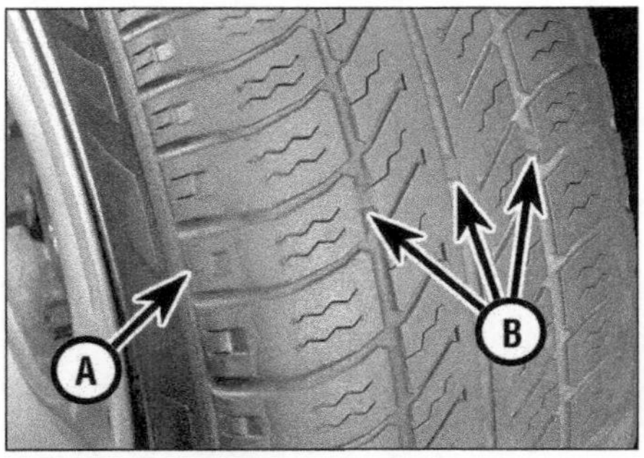

1 ***Tread Depth - visual check***
The original tyres have tread wear safety bands (B), which will appear when the tread depth reaches approximately 1.6 mm. The band positions are indicated by a triangular mark on the tyre sidewall (A).

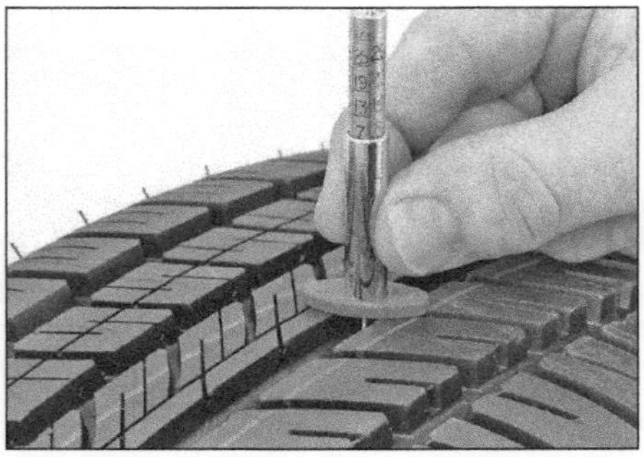

2 ***Tread Depth - manual check***
Alternatively, tread wear can be monitored with a simple, inexpensive device known as a tread depth indicator gauge.

3 ***Tyre Pressure Check***
Check the tyre pressures regularly with the tyres cold. Do not adjust the tyre pressures immediately after the vehicle has been used, or an inaccurate setting will result.

Tyre tread wear patterns

Shoulder Wear

Underinflation (wear on both sides)
Under-inflation will cause overheating of the tyre, because the tyre will flex too much, and the tread will not sit correctly on the road surface. This will cause a loss of grip and excessive wear, not to mention the danger of sudden tyre failure due to heat build-up.
Check and adjust pressures
Incorrect wheel camber (wear on one side)
Repair or renew suspension parts
Hard cornering
Reduce speed!

Centre Wear

Overinflation
Over-inflation will cause rapid wear of the centre part of the tyre tread, coupled with reduced grip, harsher ride, and the danger of shock damage occurring in the tyre casing.
Check and adjust pressures

If you sometimes have to inflate your car's tyres to the higher pressures specified for maximum load or sustained high speed, don't forget to reduce the pressures to normal afterwards.

Uneven Wear

Front tyres may wear unevenly as a result of wheel misalignment. Most tyre dealers and garages can check and adjust the wheel alignment (or "tracking") for a modest charge.
Incorrect camber or castor
Repair or renew suspension parts
Malfunctioning suspension
Repair or renew suspension parts
Unbalanced wheel
Balance tyres
Incorrect toe setting
Adjust front wheel alignment
Note: *The feathered edge of the tread which typifies toe wear is best checked by feel.*

Lubricants and fluids

Engine

Petrol models:	
ET3 and TU5 (non-VTi) engines	Multigrade engine oil, viscosity SAE 10W/40, 5W/40, 5W/30 or 0W/30 to ACEA A3 and API SJ/SL specification*
EP6 (VTi) engines	Multigrade engine oil, viscosity SAE 5W/30 or 0W/30 to ACEA A3 and API SJ/SL specification*
Diesel models:	
Without particulate filter	Multigrade engine oil, viscosity SAE 10W/40, 5W/40, 5W/30 or 0W/30 to ACEA B3 and API CD/CF specification*
With particulate filter	Multigrade engine oil, viscosity SAE 10W/40, 5W/40 or 5W/30 to ACEA C2 and API CD/CF specification*

Cooling system

All models	Glysantin G33 or RevkoGel 2000

Transmission

Manual	ESSO EZL848 or TOTAL H6965 gear oil (SAE 75W-80W)
Automatic:	
AL4	LT 71141 ATF (automatic transmission fluid)
AM6:	
Euro 4 engine	Esso JWS 3309 ATF (automatic transmission fluid)
Euro 5 engine **(do not use Esso JWS 3309 ATF)**	AW-1 ATF (automatic transmission fluid)

Braking and clutch system

All models	Hydraulic fluid to DOT 4

Power steering (electro-pump assembly)

All models	Total Fluide DA

Particulate filter additives (diesel models)

All models	Eolys DPX42 or Eolys 176

** Due to the extended service intervals Citroën specify, it is essential that semi-synthetic or fully-synthetic engine oil be used.*

Tyre pressures

Note: *The make of tyres, the sizes and the pressures for each vehicle are given on a label attached to the driver's door A-pillar* ***(see illustration)****. On models with a space-saver spare wheel, a separate pressure is given for the spare tyre, and care must be taken not to misread the sticker; the space-saver wheel is inflated to a much higher pressure than the standard tyres (typically 60 psi). On models with a space-saver spare wheel, note that the spare is for temporary use only; whilst the spare is fitted, the vehicle should not be driven at speeds in excess of 50 mph.*
Note: *Pressures on the label apply to original-equipment tyres listed, and may vary if any other makes or type of tyre is fitted; check with the tyre manufacturer or supplier for correct pressures if necessary.*
Note: *Tyre pressures must always be checked with the tyres cold to ensure accuracy.*

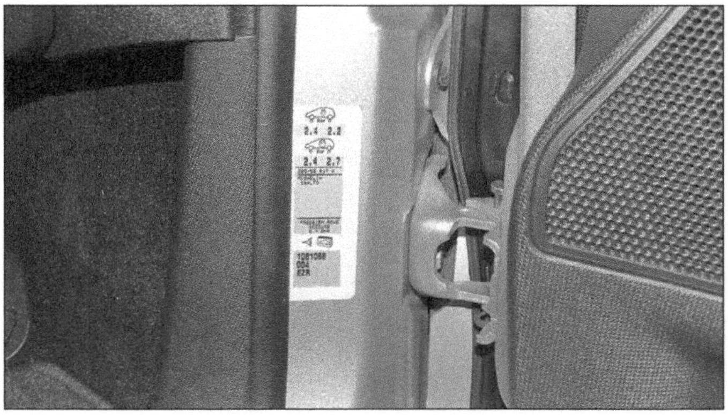

Driver's door A-pillar label

Chapter 1 Part A: Routine maintenance and servicing – petrol models

Contents

Degrees of difficulty

Easy, suitable for novice with little experience	**Fairly easy,** suitable for beginner with some experience	**Fairly difficult,** suitable for competent DIY mechanic	**Difficult,** suitable for experienced DIY mechanic	**Very difficult,** suitable for expert DIY or professional

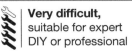

Lubricants and fluids	Refer to *Lubricants and fluids*

Capacities

Note: *All values are approximate.*

Engine oil

Including filter:	
1.4 litre (ET3)	3.75 litres
1.6 litre:	
Non-VTi engine (TU5)	3.25 litres
VTi engine (EP6)	4.25 litres
Difference between MAX and MIN dipstick marks	1.2 litres

Cooling system

1.4 litre (ET3)	5.8 litres
1.6 litre:	
Non-VTi engine (TU5):	
Manual transmission	6.2 litres
Automatic transmission	6.7 litres
VTi engine (EP6):	
Manual transmission	6.0 litres
Automatic transmission	6.2 litres

Transmission

Manual transmissions:	
Drain and refill:	
5-speed transmission:	
MA5	2.0 litres
BE4/5	1.9 litres
Automatic transmission (AL4):	
Drain and refill	4.5 litres
Total capacity, including torque converter	6.0 litres

Power-assisted steering

All models	0.85 litres

Fuel tank

All models	60 litres

Engine

Auxiliary drivebelt tension with belt tensioning tool (non-VTi engines) – see text:	
Without air conditioning:	
New belt	87 SEEM units
Used belt	61 SEEM units
With air conditioning:	
New belt	120 SEEM units

Cooling system

Antifreeze mixture:	
50% antifreeze	Protection down to –37°C
55% antifreeze	Protection down to –45°C

Note: *Refer to antifreeze manufacturer for latest recommendations.*

Ignition system

Spark plugs:	
1.4 litre (ET3)	Bosch VR8SE
1.6 litre:	
Non-VTi engine (TU5)	Bosch FR8ME or FR8SE0
VTi engine (EP6)	NGK PLZKBR7A-G or Beru 12ZR 6SP03
Electrode gap:	
1.4 litre (ET3) and 1.6 litre non-VTi engines (TU5)	0.90 mm
1.6 litre VTi engine (EP6)	0.95 mm

Brakes

Brake pad friction material minimum thickness	2.0 mm

Tyre pressures	See *Lubricants, fluids and tyre pressures*

Remote control battery

Type	CR1620
Volts	3V

Torque wrench settings

	Nm	lbf ft
Alternator mounting/tensioner bolts	20	15
Automatic transmission (AL4):		
Fluid drain plug	33	24
Fluid filler plug	24	18
Fluid level plug:		
To RPO 9855 (hexagonal)	24	18
From RPO 9856 (socket key)	9	7
Manual transmission:		
MA5:		
Drain plug	33	24
Filler/level plug	25	18
BE4/5:		
Drain plug	35	26
Filler/level plug	22	16
Oil filter cap/cover	25	18
Roadwheel bolts	90	66
Spark plugs	23	17
Sump drain plug	30	22

Underbonnet view (1.6 litre non-VTi model shown)

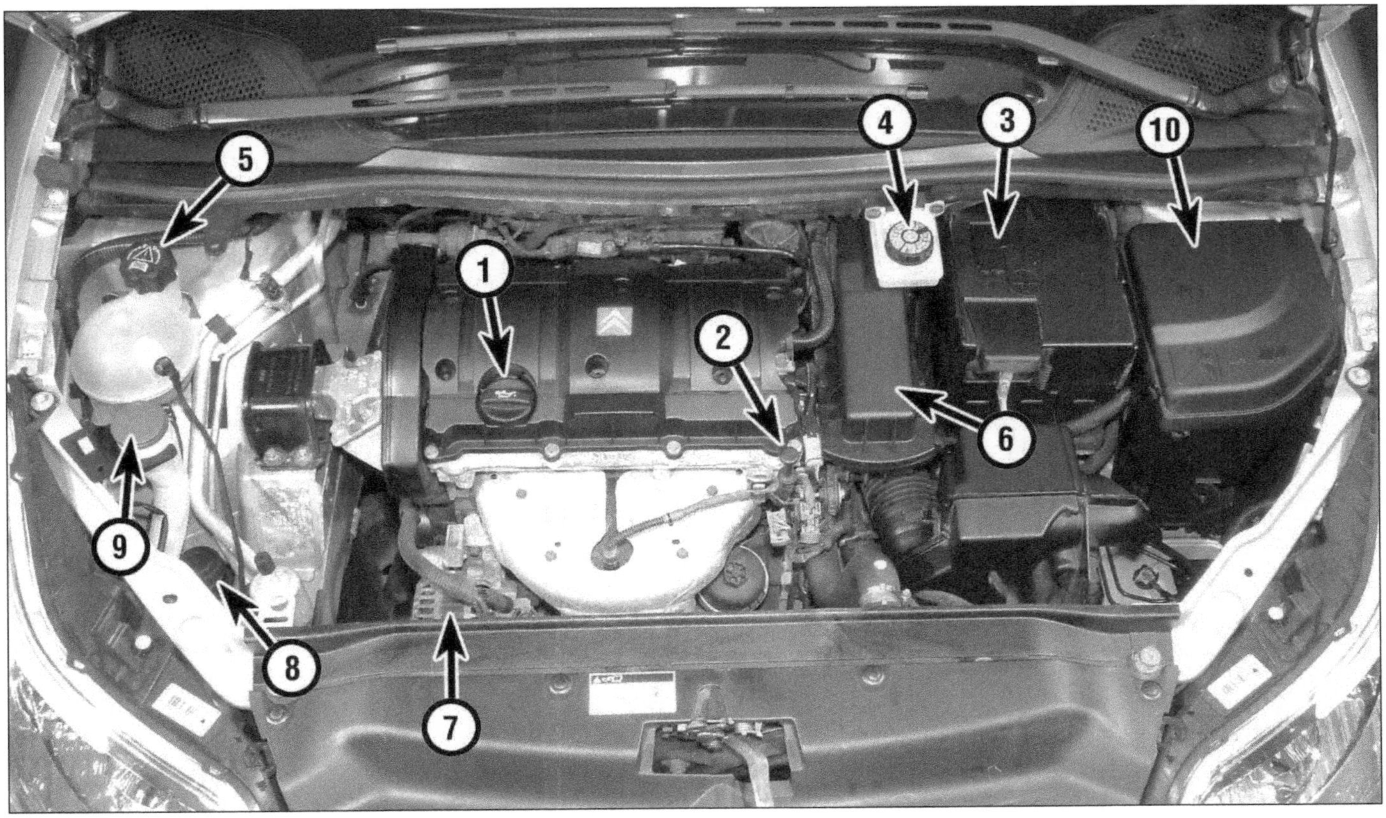

1 Engine oil filler cap
2 Engine oil level dipstick
3 Battery
4 Brake/clutch fluid reservoir
5 Coolant expansion tank
6 Air filter housing
7 Alternator
8 Power steering fluid reservoir
9 Washer fluid reservoir
10 Fuse/electrical box

Front underbody view

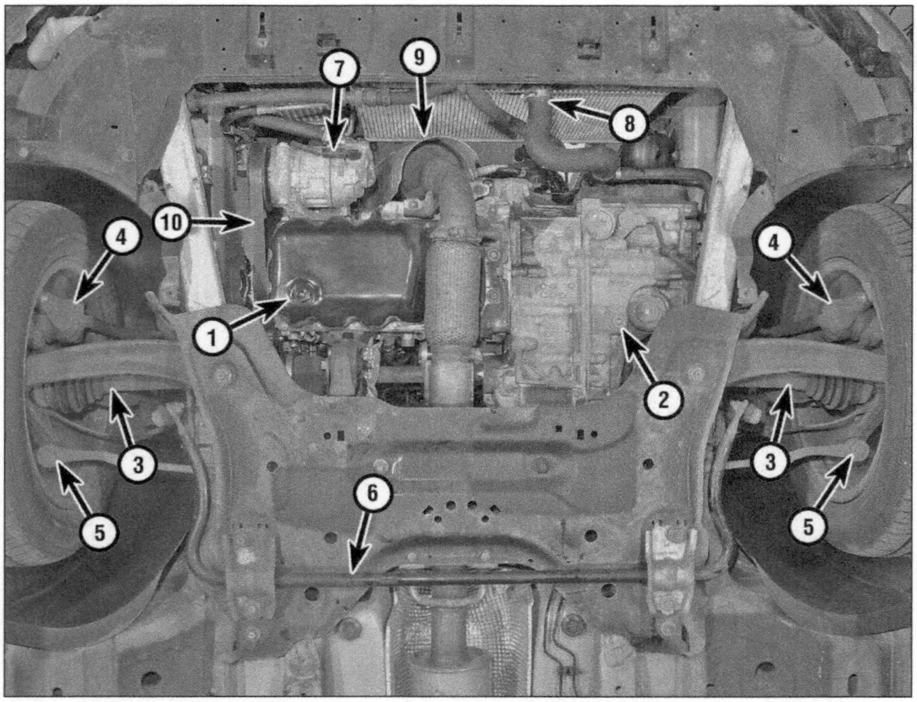

1 Engine oil drain plug
2 Automatic transmission level/drain plug
3 Driveshaft
4 Brake caliper
5 Track rod balljoint
6 Anti-roll bar
7 Air conditioning compressor
8 Radiator bottom hose
9 Catalytic converter
10 Auxiliary belt

Rear underbody view

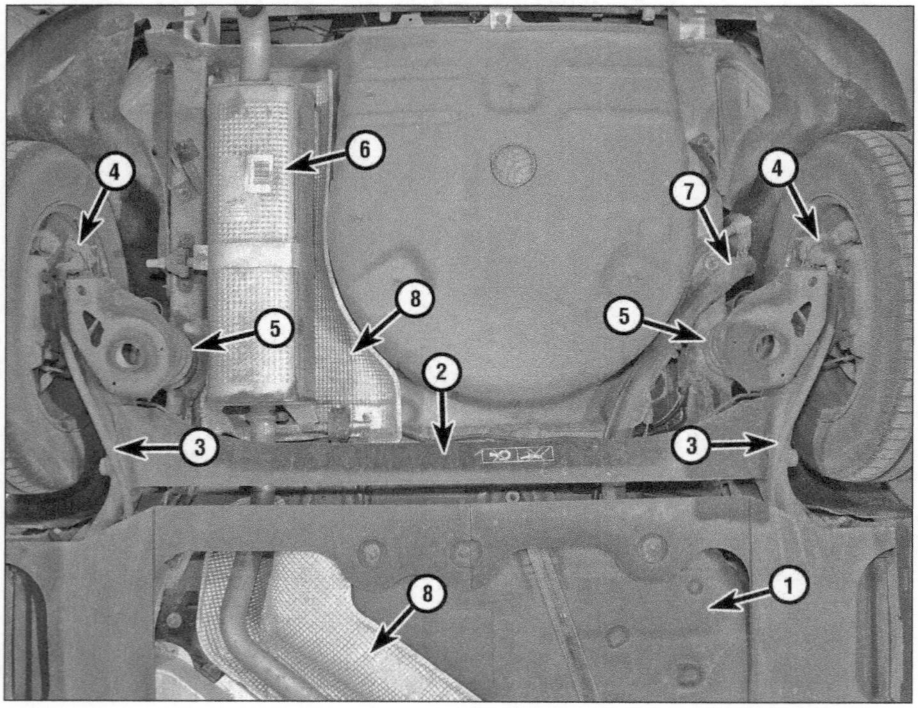

1 Fuel tank
2 Beam axle
3 Handbrake cable
4 Brake caliper
5 Coil spring
6 Exhaust rear silencer
7 Fuel filler neck
8 Heat shields

Note: *This maintenance schedule is a guide recommended by Haynes for servicing your own vehicle. Check with your local dealer for the manufacturer's maintenance schedule.*

1 The maintenance intervals in this manual are provided with the assumption that you, not the dealer, will be carrying out the work. These are the minimum maintenance intervals recommended by us for vehicles driven daily. If you wish to keep your vehicle in peak condition at all times, you may wish to perform some of these procedures more often. We encourage frequent maintenance, because it enhances the efficiency, performance and resale value of your vehicle.

2 If the vehicle is driven in dusty areas, used to tow a trailer, or driven frequently at slow speeds (idling in traffic) or on short journeys, more frequent maintenance intervals are recommended.

3 When the vehicle is new, it should be serviced by a dealer service department (or other workshop recognised by the vehicle manufacturer as providing the same standard of service) in order to preserve the warranty. The vehicle manufacturer may reject warranty claims if you are unable to prove that servicing has been carried out as and when specified, using only original equipment parts or parts certified to be of equivalent quality.

4 All Citroën models are equipped with a service indicator function incorporated into the mileage recorder, which will indicate the mileage until the next service is due. However, Citroën point out that: 'Due to the relationship between time and mileage, some operating conditions will make annual service more suitable'.

Every 250 miles or weekly

- ☐ Refer to *Weekly checks*

Every 10 000 miles or 12 months – whichever comes first

- ☐ Renew the engine oil and filter (Section 3)
- ☐ Check all underbonnet components for fluid leaks (Section 4)
- ☐ Check the condition of the driveshaft joints and rubber gaiters (Section 5)
- ☐ Lubricate all hinges and locks (Section 6)
- ☐ Carry out a road test (Section 7)
- ☐ Reset the service interval indicator (Section 8)

Every 20 000 miles or 2 years – whichever comes first

- ☐ Check and renew the pollen filter (Section 9)
- ☐ Check the condition of the auxiliary drivebelt (Section 10)
- ☐ Check the condition of the brake pads and discs (Section 11)
- ☐ Check the operation of the handbrake (Section 12)
- ☐ Check the steering and suspension components (Section 13)
- ☐ Check the coolant antifreeze concentration (Section 14)
- ☐ Check the exhaust system (Section 15)
- ☐ Check the seat belt condition (Section 16)
- ☐ Check the airbag system (Section 17)

Every 40 000 miles or 4 years – whichever comes first

- ☐ Renew the timing belt – non-VTi engines (Section 18).

Note: *Although the normal interval for timing belt renewal is 80 000 miles, it is strongly recommended that the interval is reduced to 40 000 miles, especially on vehicles which are subjected to intensive use, ie, mainly short journeys or a lot of stop-start driving. The actual belt renewal interval is therefore very much up to the individual owner, but bear in mind that severe engine damage will result if the belt breaks.*

- ☐ Renew the brake fluid (Section 19)

Note: *The hydraulic clutch shares its fluid reservoir with the braking system, and will also need to be bled.*

- ☐ Renew the spark plugs (Section 20)
- ☐ Renew the air filter element (Section 21)
- ☐ Check the manual transmission oil level (Section 22)
- ☐ Check the automatic transmission fluid level (Section 23)
- ☐ Check the exhaust emissions (Section 24)
- ☐ Renew the coolant (Section 25)
- ☐ Renew the remote control battery (Section 26)

Every 15 years

- ☐ Renew the airbags and seat belt pretensioners (Section 27)

1 General information

1 This Chapter is designed to help the home mechanic maintain his/her vehicle for safety, economy, long life and peak performance.

2 The Chapter contains a master maintenance schedule, followed by Sections dealing specifically with each task in the schedule. Visual checks, adjustments, component renewal and other helpful items are included. Refer to the accompanying illustrations of the engine compartment and the underside of the vehicle for the locations of the various components.

3 Servicing your vehicle in accordance with the mileage/time maintenance schedule and the following Sections will provide a planned maintenance programme, which should result in a long and reliable service life. This is a comprehensive plan, so maintaining some items but not others at the specified service intervals will not produce the same results.

4 As you service your vehicle, you will discover that many of the procedures can – and should – be grouped together, because of the particular procedure being performed, or because of the close proximity of two otherwise-unrelated components to one another. For example, if the vehicle is raised for any reason, the exhaust can be inspected at the same time as the suspension and steering components.

5 The first step in this maintenance programme is to prepare you before the actual work begins. Read through all the Sections relevant to the work to be carried out, then make a list and gather together all the parts and tools required. If a problem is encountered, seek advice from a parts specialist, or a dealer service department.

2 Routine maintenance

1 If, from the time the vehicle is new, the routine maintenance schedule is followed closely, and frequent checks are made of fluid levels and high-wear items, as suggested throughout this manual, the engine will be kept in relatively good running condition, and the need for additional work will be minimised.

2 It is possible that there will be times when the engine is running poorly due to the lack of regular maintenance. This is even more likely if a used vehicle, which has not received regular and frequent maintenance checks, is purchased. In such cases, additional work may need to be carried out, outside of the regular maintenance intervals.

3 If engine wear is suspected, a compression test (refer to Chapter 2A or 2B) will provide valuable information regarding the overall performance of the main internal components. Such a test can be used as a basis to decide on the extent of the work to be carried out. If, for example, a compression test indicates serious internal engine wear, conventional maintenance as described in this Chapter will not greatly improve the performance of the engine, and may prove a waste of time and money, unless extensive overhaul work (Chapter 2E) is carried out first.

4 The following series of operations are those often required to improve the performance of a generally poor-running engine:

Primary operations

a) Clean, inspect and test the battery (See 'Weekly checks').
b) Check all the engine-related fluids (See 'Weekly checks').
c) Check the condition and tension of the auxiliary drivebelt (Section 10).
d) Renew the spark plugs (Section 20).
e) Check the condition of the air filter element, and renew if necessary (Section 21).
f) Check the condition of all hoses, and check for fluid leaks (Section 4).

5 If the above operations do not prove fully effective, carry out the following operations:

Secondary operations

All items listed under *Primary operations*, plus the following:

a) Check the charging system (Chapter 5A, Section 5).
b) Check the ignition system (Chapter 5B, Section 2).
c) Check the fuel system (Chapter 4A).

Every 10 000 miles or 12 months

3 Engine oil and filter renewal

Note: *A suitable hexagon or square-section wrench may be required to undo the sump drain plug. These wrenches can be obtained from most motor factors or your Citroën dealer.*

1 Frequent oil and filter changes are the most important preventative maintenance procedures which can be undertaken by the DIY owner. As engine oil ages, it becomes diluted and contaminated, which leads to premature engine wear.

2 Before starting this procedure, gather together all the necessary tools and materials. Also make sure that you have plenty of clean rags and newspapers handy, to mop-up any spills. Ideally, the engine oil should be warm, as it will drain better, and more built-up sludge will be removed with it. Take care, however, not to touch the exhaust or any other hot parts of the engine when working under the vehicle. To avoid any possibility of scalding, and to protect yourself from possible skin irritants and other harmful contaminants in used engine oils, it is advisable to wear gloves when carrying out this work. Access to the underside of the vehicle will be greatly improved if it can be raised on a lift, driven onto ramps, or jacked up and supported on axle stands (see *Jacking and vehicle support*). Whichever method is chosen, make sure that the vehicle remains level, or if it is at an angle, that the drain plug is at the lowest point.

3 Undo the fasteners and remove the plastic engine undershield from below the engine compartment.

4 Slacken the drain plug about half a turn **(see illustrations)**. Position the draining container under the drain plug, and then remove the plug completely. If possible, try to keep the plug pressed into the sump while

3.4a Sump drain plug on 1.6 litre non-VTi engine ...

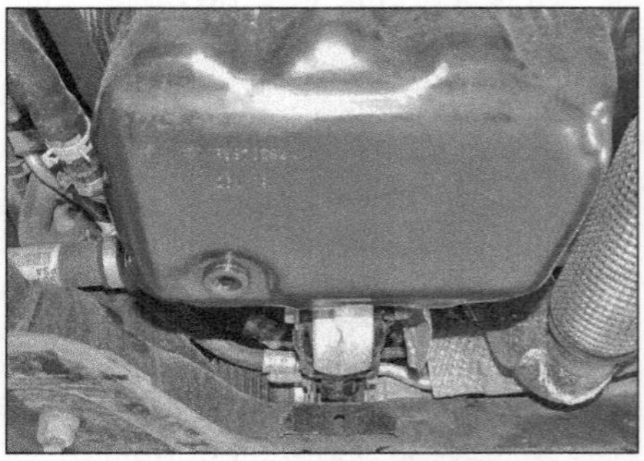

3.4b ... and on 1.6 litre VTi engine

HAYNES HiNT

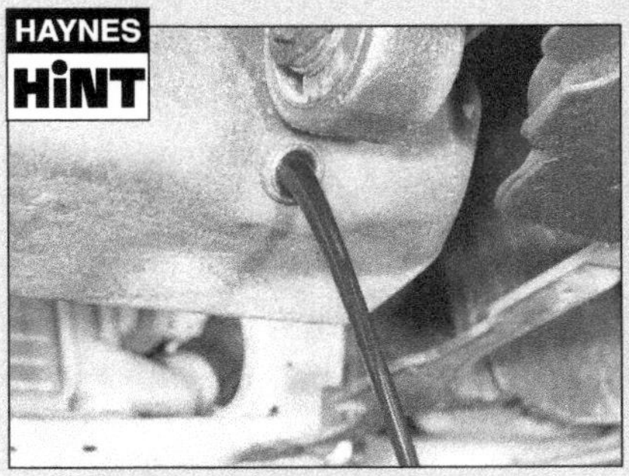

As the drain plug releases from the sump threads, move it away sharply, so the stream of oil issuing from the sump runs into the container, not up your sleeve.

3.8a Slacken the filter cover ...

3.8b ... and unscrew the filter plastic cover

unscrewing it by hand the last couple of turns **(see Haynes Hint)**. Recover the sealing ring from the drain plug.

5 Allow some time for the old oil to drain, noting that it may be necessary to reposition the container as the oil flow slows to a trickle.

6 After all the oil has drained, wipe off the drain plug with a clean rag, and fit a new sealing washer. Clean the area around the drain plug opening, and refit the plug, tightening it to the specified torque.

7 Move the container into position under the oil filter, which is located on the front of the cylinder block.

8 The filter element is contained within a filter cover. Using a socket or spanner, slacken and remove the filter cover from above **(see illustrations)**. Be prepared for fluid spillage, and recover the O-ring seal from the cover.

9 Pull the filter element from the filter cover.

10 Use a clean rag to remove all oil, dirt and sludge from the inside and outside of the filter cover.

11 Fit the new O-ring seal to the filter cover, insert the new filter element, then apply a little clean engine oil to the seal, and fit it to the filter cover **(see illustrations)**.

12 Refit the filter/cover to the housing and tighten the cover to the specified torque.

13 Remove the old oil and all tools from under the car, then lower the car to the ground (if applicable).

14 Remove the dipstick, and then unscrew the oil filler cap from the cylinder head cover. Fill the engine, using the correct grade and type of oil (see *Lubricants and fluids*). An oil can spout or funnel may help to reduce spillage. Pour in half the specified quantity of oil first, and then wait a few minutes for the oil to run to the sump. Continue adding oil a small quantity at a time until the level is up to the lower mark on the dipstick. Refit the filler cap.

15 Start the engine and run it for a few minutes; check for leaks around the oil filter seal and the sump drain plug. Note that there may be a delay of a few seconds before the oil pressure warning light goes out when the engine is first started, as the oil circulates through the engine oil galleries and the new oil filter before the pressure builds-up.

16 Refit the engine undershield (where applicable), and secure it in place with the screw fasteners.

17 Switch off the engine, and wait a few minutes for the oil to settle in the sump once more. With the new oil circulated and the filter completely full, recheck the level on the dipstick, and add more oil as necessary.

18 Dispose of the used engine oil safely, with reference to *General repair procedures*.

3.11a Renew the O-ring seal to the cover ...

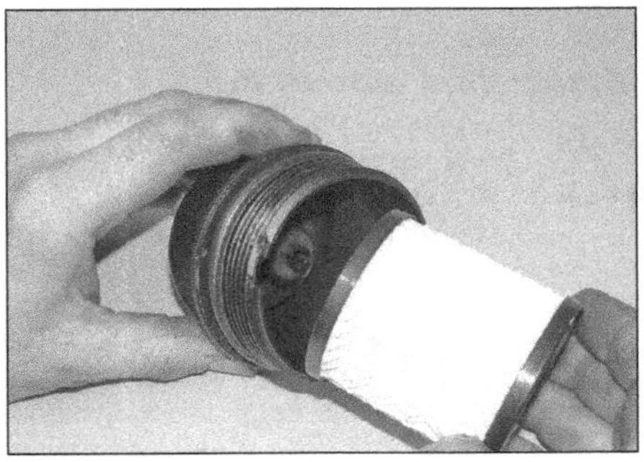

3.11b ... insert the new filter into the cap ...

3.11c ... then apply a little clean oil to the seal ...

3.11d ... and refit the oil filter and cover

4 Hose and fluid leak check

Cooling system

Warning: Refer to the safety information given in 'Safety first!' and Chapter 3, Section 1 before disturbing any of the cooling system components.

1 Carefully check the radiator and heater coolant hoses along their entire length. Renew any hose which is cracked, swollen or which shows signs of deterioration. Cracks will show up better if the hose is squeezed. Pay close attention to the clips that secure the hoses to the cooling system components. Hose clips that have been overtightened can pinch and puncture hoses, resulting in cooling system leaks.

2 Inspect all the cooling system components

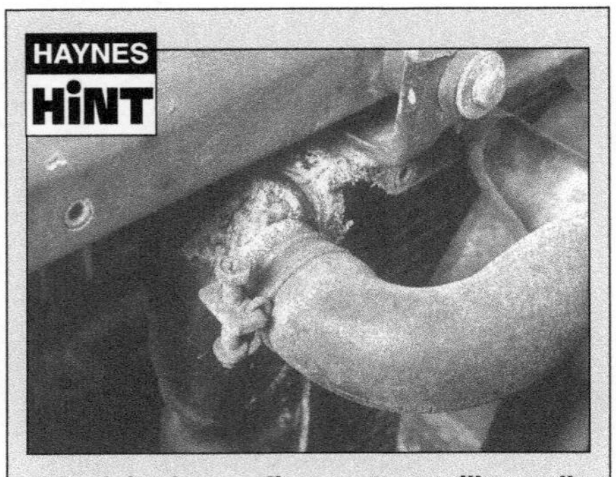

A leak in the cooling system will usually show up as white- or antifreeze-coloured deposits on the area adjoining the leak.

(hoses, joint faces, etc) for leaks **(see Haynes Hint)**.

3 Where any problems of this nature are found on system components, renew the component or gasket with reference to Chapter 3.

Fuel

⚠ *Warning: Refer to the safety information given in 'Safety first!' and Chapter 4A, Section 1, before disturbing any of the fuel system components.*

4 Check all fuel lines at their connections to the injection pump, injectors and fuel filter, depending on engine.

5 Examine each fuel hose/pipe along its length for splits or cracks. Check for leakage from the union nuts and examine the unions between the metal fuel lines and the fuel filter (where applicable). Also check the area around the fuel injectors for signs of leakage.

6 To identify fuel leaks between the fuel tank and the engine bay, the vehicle should raised and securely supported on axle stands. Inspect the fuel tank and filler neck for punctures, cracks and other damage. The connection between the filler neck and tank is especially critical. Sometimes a rubber filler neck or connecting hose will leak due to loose retaining clamps or deteriorated rubber.

7 Carefully check all rubber hoses and metal fuel lines leading away from the fuel tank. Check for loose connections, deteriorated hoses, kinked lines, and other damage. Pay particular attention to the vent pipes and hoses, which often loop up around the filler neck and can become blocked or kinked, making tank filling difficult. Follow the fuel supply and return lines to the front of the vehicle, carefully inspecting them all the way for signs of damage or corrosion. Renew damaged sections as necessary.

Engine oil

8 Inspect the area around the camshaft cover, cylinder head, oil filter and sump joint faces. Bear in mind that, over a period of time, some very slight seepage from these areas is to be expected – what you are really looking for is any indication of a serious leak caused by gasket failure. Engine oil seeping from the base of the timing chain cover or the transmission bellhousing may be an indication of crankshaft or intake camshaft oil seal failure. Should a leak be found, renew the failed gasket or oil seal by referring to the appropriate Chapters in this manual.

Air conditioning refrigerant

⚠ *Warning: Refer to the safety information given in 'Safety first!' and Chapter 3, Section 11, regarding the dangers of disturbing any of the air conditioning system components.*

9 The air conditioning system is filled with a liquid refrigerant, which is retained under high pressure. If the air conditioning system is opened and depressurised without the aid of specialised equipment, the refrigerant will immediately turn into gas and escape into the atmosphere. If the liquid comes into contact with your skin, it can cause severe frostbite. In addition, the refrigerant contains substances which are environmentally damaging; for this reason, it should not be allowed to escape into the atmosphere.

10 Any suspected air conditioning system leaks should be immediately referred to a Citroën dealer or air conditioning specialist. Leakage will be shown up as a steady drop in the level of refrigerant in the system.

11 Note that water may drip from the condenser drain hose, underneath the car, immediately after the air conditioning system has been in use. This is normal, and should not be cause for concern.

Brake (and clutch) fluid

⚠ *Warning: Refer to the safety information given in 'Safety first!' and Chapter 9, Section 2, regarding the dangers of handling brake fluid.*

12 With reference to Chapter 9, Section 10, examine the area surrounding the brake pipe unions at the master cylinder for signs of leakage. Check the area around the base of fluid reservoir for signs of leakage caused by seal failure. Also examine the brake pipe unions at the ABS hydraulic unit.

13 If fluid loss is evident, but the leak cannot be pinpointed in the engine bay, the brake calipers and underbody brake lines and should be carefully checked with the vehicle raised and supported on axle stands. Leakage of fluid from the braking system is a serious fault that must be rectified immediately.

14 Check for leakage around the hydraulic fluid line connections to the clutch master cylinder at the bulkhead, and to the clutch slave cylinder bolted to the side of the transmission bellhousing.

15 Brake/clutch hydraulic fluid is a toxic substance with a watery consistency. New fluid is almost colourless, but it becomes darker with age and use.

Unidentified fluid leaks

16 If there are signs that a fluid of some description is leaking from the vehicle, but you cannot identify the type of fluid or its exact origin, remove the engine undershield, park the vehicle overnight and slide a large piece of card underneath it. Providing that the card is positioned in roughly in the right location, even the smallest leak will show up on the card. Not only will this help you to pinpoint the exact location of the leak, it should be easier to identify the fluid from its colour. Bear in mind, though, that the leak may only be occurring when the engine is running!

Vacuum hoses

17 Although the braking system is hydraulically operated, the brake servo unit amplifies the effort you apply at the brake pedal, by making use of the vacuum created by the engine intake manifold (ET3 and TU5 engines), or a vacuum pump (EP6 engines), see Chapter 9, Section 12 or 21. Vacuum is ported to the servo by means of a large-bore hose. Any leaks that develop in this hose will reduce the effectiveness of the braking system.

18 In addition, many of the underbonnet components, particularly the emission control components, are driven by vacuum supplied from the vacuum pump (EP6 engines), via narrow-bore hoses. A leak in a vacuum hose means that air is being drawn into the hose (rather than escaping from it) and this makes leakage very difficult to detect. One method is to use an old length of vacuum hose as a kind of stethoscope – hold one end close to (but not in) your ear and use the other end to probe the area around the suspected leak. When the end of the hose is directly over a vacuum leak, a hissing sound will be heard clearly through the hose. Care must be taken to avoid contacting hot or moving components, as the engine must be running when testing in this manner. Renew any vacuum hoses that are found to be defective.

5 Driveshaft gaiter and CV joints check

1 With the vehicle raised and securely supported on stands (see *Jacking and vehicle support*), turn the steering onto full lock, then slowly rotate the roadwheel. Inspect the condition of the outer constant velocity (CV) joint gaiters, squeezing the gaiters to open out the folds **(see illustration)**. Check for signs of cracking, splits or deterioration of the gaiter, which may allow the grease to escape, and lead to water and grit entry into the joint. Also check the security and condition of the retaining clips. Repeat these checks on the inner CV joints. If any damage or deterioration is found, the gaiters should be renewed (see Chapter 8, Section 3).

5.1 Check the driveshaft gaiters for signs of damage or deterioration

8.2 Service indicator trip/reset button (arrowed)

2 At the same time, check the general condition of the CV joints themselves by first holding the driveshaft and attempting to rotate the wheel. Repeat this check by holding the inner joint and attempting to rotate the driveshaft. Any appreciable movement indicates wear in the joints, wear in the driveshaft splines, or a loose driveshaft retaining nut.

6 Hinge and lock lubrication

1 Work around the vehicle, and lubricate the hinges of the bonnet, doors and tailgate with a small amount of general-purpose oil.
2 Lightly lubricate the bonnet release mechanism and exposed section of inner cable with a smear of grease.
3 Check carefully the security and operation of all hinges, latches and locks, adjusting them where required. Check the operation of the central locking system (if fitted).
4 Check the condition and operation of the tailgate struts, renewing them if either is leaking or no longer able to support the tailgate securely when raised.

7 Road test

Instruments and electrical equipment

1 Check the operation of all instruments and electrical equipment.
2 Make sure that all instruments read correctly, and switch on all electrical equipment in turn to check it functions properly. Check the function of the heating, air conditioning and automatic climate control systems.

Steering and suspension

3 Check for any abnormalities in the steering, suspension, handling or road 'feel'.
4 Drive the vehicle, and check that there are no unusual vibrations or noises.
5 Check that the steering feels positive, with no excessive 'sloppiness', or roughness, and check for any suspension noises when cornering, or when driving over bumps. Check that the power steering system operates correctly.

Drivetrain

6 Check the performance of the engine, clutch, transmission and driveshafts.
7 Listen for any unusual noises from the engine, clutch (manual transmission) and transmission.
8 Make sure the engine idles smoothly, and that there is no hesitation when accelerating.
9 On manual transmissions, check that the clutch action is smooth and progressive, that the drive is taken up smoothly, and that the pedal travel is not excessive. Also listen for any noises when the clutch pedal is depressed. Check that all gears can be engaged smoothly, without noise, and that the gear lever action is smooth and not abnormally vague or 'notchy'.
10 On automatic transmission models, make sure that all gearchanges occur smoothly, without snatching, and without an increase in engine speed between changes. Check that all the gear positions can be selected with the vehicle at rest. If any problems are found, they should be referred to a Citroën dealer.
11 Listen for a metallic clicking sound from the front of the vehicle, as the vehicle is driven slowly in a circle with the steering on full lock. Carry out this check in both directions. If a clicking noise is heard, this indicates wear in a driveshaft joint; in which case, refer to Chapter 8, Section 2.

Braking system

12 Make sure that the vehicle does not pull to one side when braking, and that the wheels do not lock when braking hard.
13 Check that there is no vibration through the steering when braking.
14 Check that the handbrake operates correctly, without excessive movement of the lever, and that it holds the vehicle on a slope.
15 Test the operation of the brake servo unit as follows. With the engine off, depress the footbrake four or five times to exhaust the vacuum. Start the engine, holding the brake pedal depressed. As the engine starts, there should be a noticeable 'give' in the brake pedal as vacuum builds-up. Allow the engine to run for at least two minutes, and then switch it off. If the brake pedal is depressed now, it should be possible to detect a hiss from the servo as the pedal is depressed. After about four or five applications, no further hissing should be heard, and the pedal should feel considerably firmer.

8 Resetting the service indicator

1 The instrument cluster mileage recorder incorporates a service interval indicator. When the vehicle is started, the unit displays the mileage until the next service, or the mileage covered since the service was due. The service indicator is manually reset to zero after the vehicle has been serviced. The indicator can also be reset at any time using the Citroën diagnostic tool.
2 To manually reset the mileage to zero, carry out the following procedure:

a) Switch off the ignition.
b) Press and hold down the trip/reset button on the instrument panel ***(see illustration)****.*
c) While the trip/reset button is held down, switch on the ignition.
d) Keep the trip/reset button pressed until zero appears and the maintenance symbol disappears.
e) Release the trip/reset button and switch off the ignition.

3 Switch on the ignition – the distance remaining until (or covered since) the next service is due will flash in the display.

Every 20 000 miles or 2 years

9 Pollen filter check and renewal

9.2 Remove the sound insulation material

9.3a Pull the filter cover (arrowed) ...

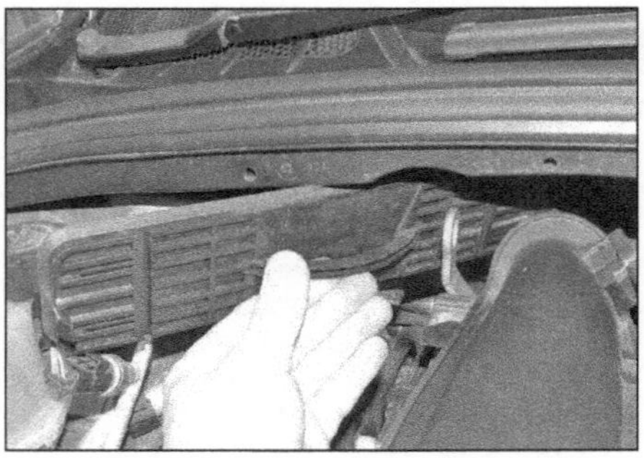

9.3b ... and withdraw it from the bulkhead

9.4 Slide the pollen filter out from the bulkhead

1 Open the bonnet; the pollen filter is positioned in the right-hand rear of the engine compartment.

2 Prise up the centre pins, lever out the complete plastic expanding rivets, and then remove the sound insulation trim covering the pollen filter cover **(see illustration)**.

3 Grasp the filter plastic cover and pull it, to release it from the bulkhead **(see illustrations)**.

4 Slide the filter out, noting its fitted position **(see illustration)**.

5 Check the condition of the filter, and renew it if dirty.

6 Wipe clean the inside of the housing and fit the pollen filter element, making sure that it is correctly seated.

7 Refit the pollen filter cover.

8 Refit the sound insulation trim, secure it in place with the plastic rivets and close the bonnet.

10 Auxiliary drivebelt check and renewal

Note: *For non-VTi models, Citroën specify the use of a special electronic tool (SEEM C.TRONIC type 105.5 belt tension measuring tool) to correctly set the auxiliary drivebelt tension. If access to this equipment cannot be obtained, an approximate setting can be achieved using the method described below. If this method is used, the tension should be checked using the special electronic tool at the earliest opportunity.*

1 All models are equipped with a single, multi-ribbed auxiliary drivebelt, which is used to drive the alternator and where fitted, an air conditioning compressor, from the crankshaft pulley. The belt tension is adjusted either manually, or by means of an automatic spring-loaded tensioner mechanism.

Check

2 Apply the handbrake, slacken the front right-hand roadwheel bolts, and then jack up the front of the car and support it on axle stands (see *Jacking and vehicle support*). Remove the right-hand front roadwheel.

3 Remove the fixings securing the wheel arch liner to the body, and then manoeuvre the liner out from underneath the wing.

4 Using a suitable socket and extension bar fitted to the crankshaft sprocket bolt, rotate the crankshaft so that the entire length of the drivebelt can be examined. Examine the drivebelt for cracks, splitting, fraying or damage **(see illustration)**. Check also for signs of glazing (shiny patches) and for separation of the belt plies. Renew the belt if worn or damaged.

5 If the condition of the belt is satisfactory, on non-VTi models, check the drivebelt tension as described below. **Note:** *On models with an automatic tensioner fitted, there is no need to check the drivebelt tension.*

6 Refit the wheel arch liner and roadwheel, and then lower the vehicle to the ground. Tighten the wheel bolts to the specified torque.

Non-VTi engines without air conditioning

7 If not already done, proceed as described in paragraphs 2 and 3.

8 On 1.4 litre models, slacken both the alternator upper and lower mounting bolts, whilst on 1.6 litre models it is only necessary to slacken the lower mounting bolt **(see illustration)**.

10.4 Check the condition of the auxiliary belt

9 Back off the adjuster bolt, which is positioned at the top of the alternator on 1.6 litre models, and at the lower rear of the alternator on 1.4 litre models. Relieve the tension in the drivebelt, and then slip the drivebelt from the pulleys. **Note:** *If the belt is going to be re-used, mark the direction of rotation on the belt prior to removal. This will ensure it is refitted the correct way around.*

10 If the belt is being renewed, ensure that the correct type is used. If the original belt is being refitted, use the mark made on removal to ensure it is fitted the correct way around.

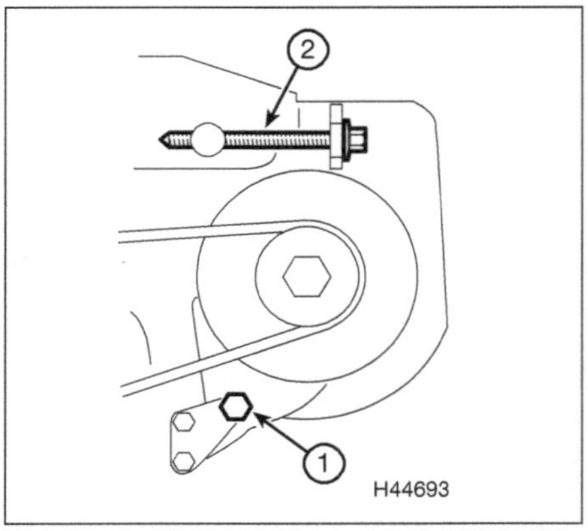

10.8 Auxiliary belt adjustment (models without air conditioning)

1 Alternator pivot bolt 2 Adjuster bolt

11 Fit the belt around the pulleys, and take up the slack in the belt by tightening the adjuster bolt. Tension the drivebelt as described in the following paragraphs.

Tensioning

12 If not already done, proceed as described in paragraphs 2 and 3.
13 If the special measuring tool is available, fit the measuring equipment to the 'lower run' of the belt, approximately midway between the crankshaft and alternator pulley. The belt tension should be set to the figure given in the Specifications at the start of this Chapter.
14 If the measuring tool is not available, the belt should be tensioned so that, under firm thumb pressure, there is about 5.0 mm of free movement at the mid-point between the pulleys on the lower belt run.
Caution: Correct tensioning of the drivebelt will ensure it has a long life. A belt that is too slack will slip and squeal. Beware of overtightening, as this can cause wear in the alternator bearings.
15 To adjust the belt tension, with the mounting bolt(s) just slackened, turn the adjuster bolt until the correct tension is achieved.
16 Rotate the crankshaft a couple of times, recheck the tension, and then tighten the alternator mounting bolt(s) to the specified torque.
17 Refit the wheel arch liner, securing it in position with the plastic expanding rivets.
18 Refit the roadwheel, and then lower the vehicle to the ground. Tighten the wheel bolts to the specified torque.

Non-VTi engines with air conditioning (manually-adjusted tensioner)

19 If not already done, proceed as described in paragraphs 2 and 3.
20 Slacken the tensioner pulley bracket bolts and rotate the adjuster bolt to release the tension in the belt, then remove the belt from the pulleys **(see illustration)**. **Note:** *If the belt is to be re-used, mark the direction of rotation on the belt prior to removal. This will ensure it is refitted the correct way around.*
21 If the belt is being renewed, ensure that the correct type is used. If the original belt is being refitted, use the mark made on removal to ensure it is fitted the correct way around. Fit the drivebelt around the pulleys in the following order:

a) Air conditioning compressor.
b) Crankshaft.
c) Alternator.
d) Idler roller
e) Manual tensioner pulley.

22 Ensure that the ribs on the belt are correctly engaged with the grooves in the pulleys, and that the drivebelt is correctly routed. Tension the belt as follows.

Tensioning

23 If not already done, proceed as described in paragraphs 2 and 3.
24 If the special measuring tool is available, fit the measuring equipment to the belt, approximately midway between the crankshaft and air conditioning compressor pulleys. Check the belt tension is as given in the Specifications at the start of this Chapter.
25 If the measuring tool is not available, the belt should be tensioned so that, under firm thumb pressure, there is about 5.0 mm of free movement at the mid-point between the crankshaft and air conditioning compressor pulleys.
Caution: Correct tensioning of the drivebelt will ensure it has a long life. A belt that is too slack will slip and squeal. Beware of overtightening, as this can cause wear in the alternator bearings.
26 To adjust the tension, rotate the adjuster bolt until the correct tension is achieved. Once the belt is correctly tensioned, tighten the tensioner pulley bracket bolts to the specified torque. Rotate the crankshaft a couple of times and recheck the tension.
27 When the belt is correctly tensioned, refit the wheel arch liner.
28 Refit the roadwheel, and then lower the vehicle to the ground; tighten the wheel bolts to the specified torque.

Non-VTi engines with air conditioning (automatic spring-loaded tensioner)

29 If not already done, proceed as described in paragraphs 2 and 3.
30 Rotate the tensioner pulley clockwise, away from the drivebelt, using a spanner on the tensioner pulley retaining bolt.
31 Once the tension is released, disengage the belt from all the pulleys, noting its correct routing. Remove the drivebelt from the engine compartment. **Note:** *If the belt is to be re-used, mark the direction of rotation on the belt prior to removal. This will ensure it is refitted the correct way around.*
32 If the belt is being renewed, ensure that the correct type is used. If the original belt is being refitted, use the mark made on removal to ensure it is fitted the correct way around. Fit the drivebelt around the pulleys in the following order:

a) Air conditioning compressor.
b) Crankshaft.
c) Alternator.
d) Idler roller
e) Automatic tensioner pulley.

33 Ensure that the ribs on the belt are correctly engaged with the grooves in the pulleys, and that the drivebelt is correctly routed.
Caution: Do not allow the tensioner pulley to spring forcefully onto the belt as this could result in damage.
34 Refit the wheel arch liner, securing it in position with the retaining plastic expanding rivets.
35 Refit the roadwheel, and then lower the vehicle to the ground; tighten the wheel bolts to the specified torque.

VTi engines

36 If not already done, proceed as described in paragraphs 2 and 3.
37 Move the tensioner pulley away from the drivebelt, using a spanner on the tensioner arm. Rotate the tensioner arm clockwise away from the belt. When the notch at the top

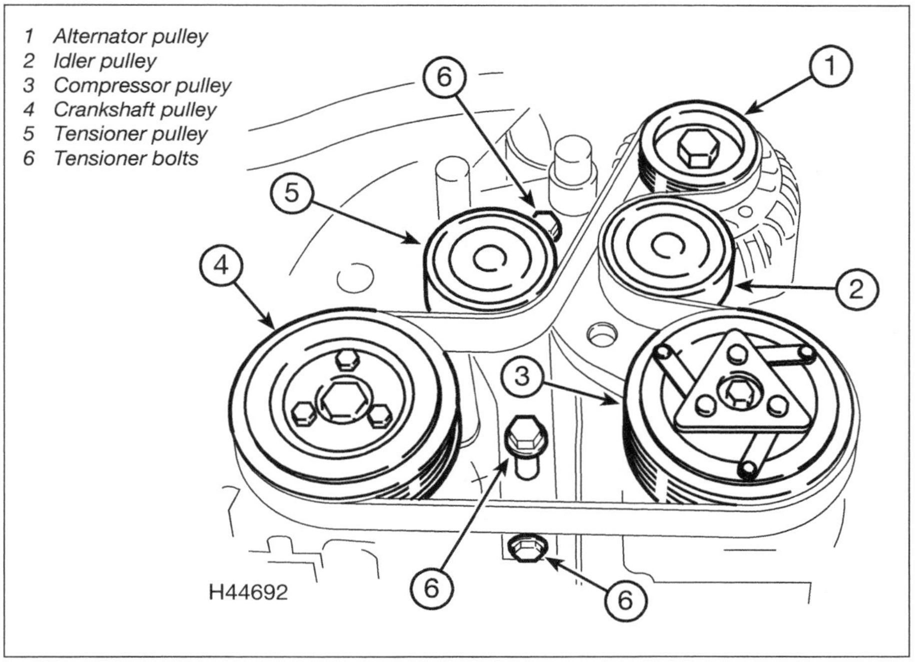

10.20 Auxiliary belt routing and adjustment (models with air conditioning)

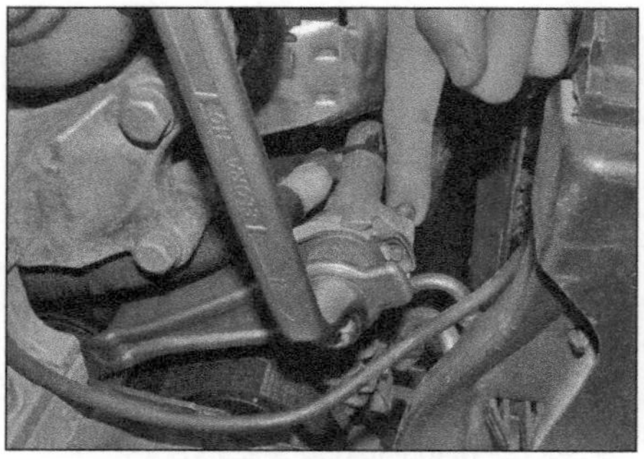

10.37a Turn the tensioner arm clockwise ...

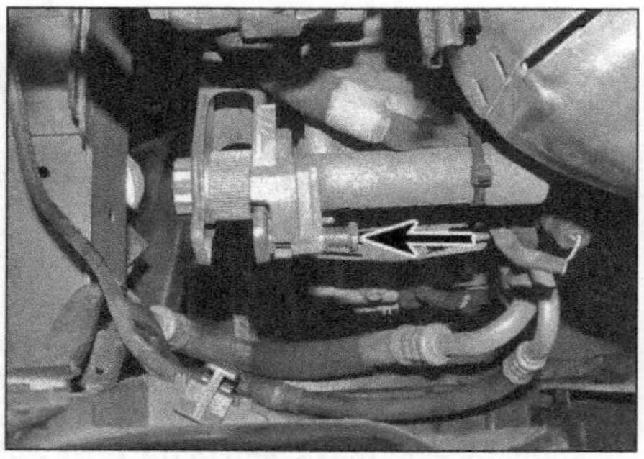

10.37b ... and then push the locking pin (arrowed) into position

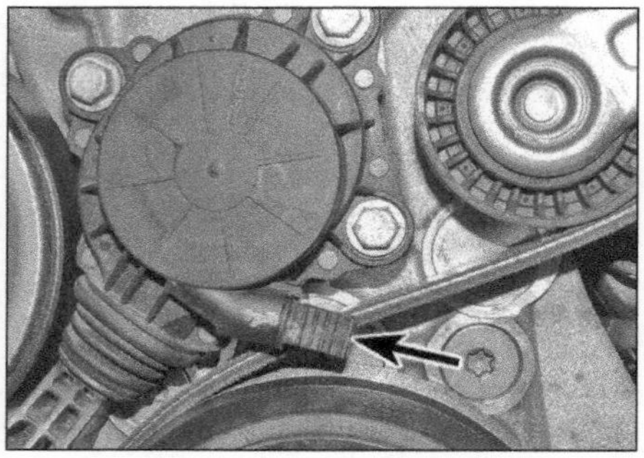

10.38a Pull out the spring (arrowed) ...

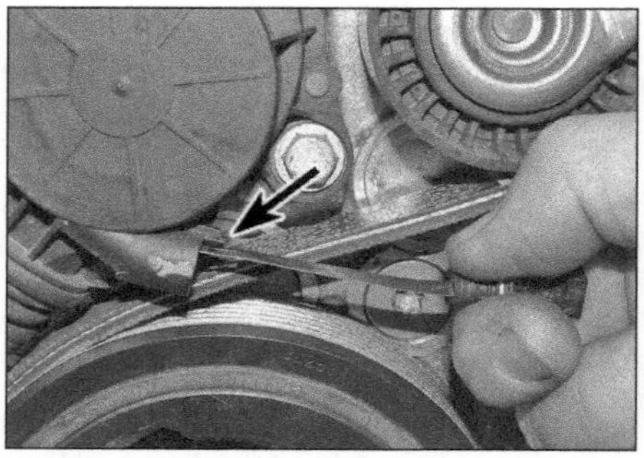

10.38b ... and lock it onto the locating peg (arrowed)

10.39 Remove the belt from the pulleys

of the arm is aligned with the spring-loaded pin, push the pin to the stop and release the tension on the spanner **(see illustrations)**.

38 Once the tension arm is secured in the released position, reach under the wheel arch and pull out the spring locking tab from the friction wheel drive and secure it on the locating peg on the friction wheel housing **(see illustrations)**. **Note:** *This needs to be released to allow removal of the belt from the crankshaft pulley.*

39 Working under the wheel arch, disengage the belt from all the pulleys, noting its correct routing. Remove the drivebelt from the engine **(see illustration)**. **Note:** *If the belt is going to be re-used, mark the direction of rotation on the belt prior to removal. This will ensure it is refitted the correct way around.*

Refitting and tensioning

40 If the belt is being renewed, ensure that the correct type is used. If the original belt is being refitted, use the mark made on removal to ensure it is fitted the correct way around. Fit the drivebelt around the pulleys in the following order **(see illustration)**:

a) Alternator.
b) Air conditioning compressor (where applicable).
c) Crankshaft.
d) Automatic tensioner pulley.

41 Ensure that the ribs on the belt are correctly engaged with the grooves in the pulleys

42 Hold the tensioner in place with the spanner, release the spring-loaded pin, and then slowly allow the tensioner pulley to rotate anti-clockwise and act against the belt. The belt is automatically tensioned by the spring-loaded tensioner.

Caution: Do not allow the tensioner pulley to spring forcefully onto the belt as this could result in damage.

43 Refit the wheel arch liner.

44 Refit the roadwheel, and then lower the vehicle to the ground; tighten the wheel bolts to the specified torque.

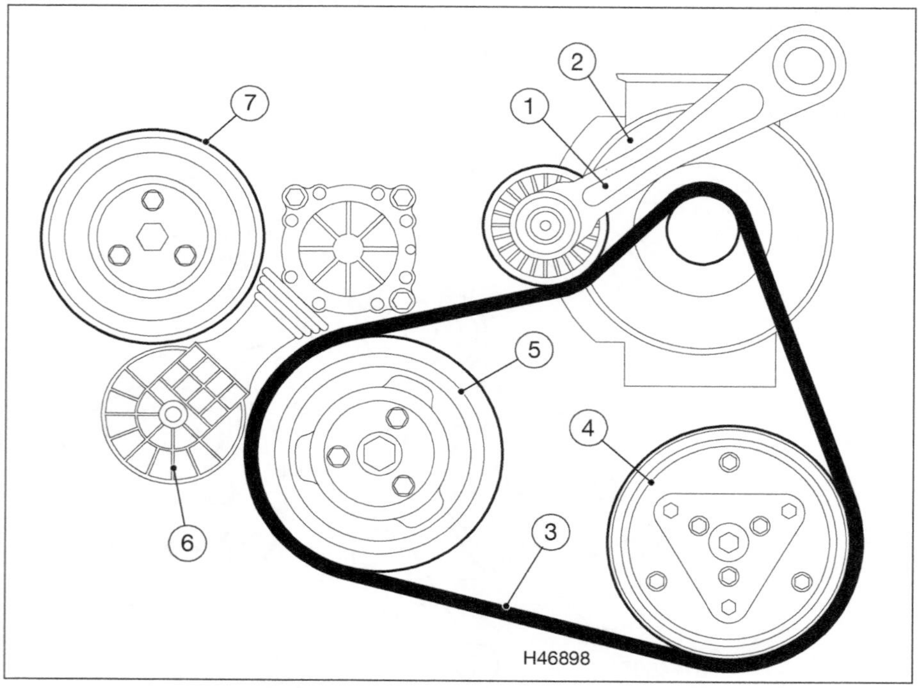

10.40 Auxiliary belt routing and adjustment (with air conditioning)

1 Automatic tensioner
2 Alternator
3 Auxiliary belt
4 Compressor pulley
5 Crankshaft pulley
6 Driving friction wheel
7 Coolant pump pulley

11 Brake pad wear and disc check

1 The work described in this Section should be carried out at the specified intervals, or whenever a defect is suspected in the braking system. Any of the following

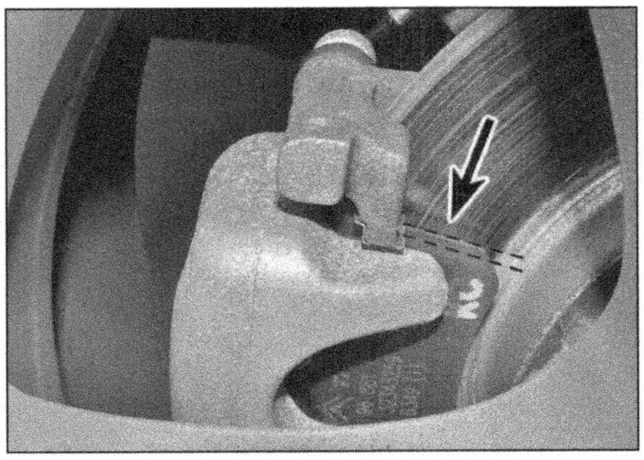

11.3 Checking brake pad thickness through alloy wheels

symptoms could indicate a potential brake system defect:

a) The vehicle pulls to one side when the brake pedal is depressed.
b) The brakes make squealing, scraping or dragging noises when applied.
c) Brake pedal travel is excessive, or pedal feel is poor.
d) The brake fluid requires repeated topping-up. Note that, because the hydraulic clutch shares the same fluid as the braking system, this problem could be due to a leak in the clutch system.

Front disc brakes

2 Chock the rear wheels then loosen the front wheel bolts. Jack up the front of the vehicle, and support it on axle stands (see *Jacking and vehicle support*).
3 For better access to the brake calipers, remove the wheels **(see illustration)**.
4 Look through the inspection window in the caliper, and check that the thickness of the friction lining material on each of the pads is not less than the recommended minimum thickness given in the Specifications **(see Haynes hint)**. Bear in mind that the lining material is normally bonded to a metal backing plate. To differentiate between the metal and the lining material, it is helpful to turn the disc slowly at first – the edge of the disc can then be identified, with the lining material on each pad either side of it, and the backing plates behind.
5 If it is difficult to determine the exact thickness of the pad linings, or if you are at all concerned about the condition of the pads, then remove them from the calipers for further inspection (refer to Chapter 9, Section 4).
6 Check the other caliper in the same way.
7 If any one of the brake pads has worn down to, or below, the specified limit, all four pads at that end of the car must be renewed as a set **(see illustration)**. If the pads on one side are significantly more worn than the other, this may indicate that the caliper pistons have partially seized – refer to the brake pad renewal procedure in Chapter 9, Section 4, and push the pistons back into the caliper to free them.
8 Measure the thickness of the discs with a micrometer, if available, to make sure that they still have service life remaining. Do not be fooled by the lip of rust which often forms on the outer edge of the disc, which may make the disc appear thicker than it really is – scrape off the loose rust if necessary, without scoring the disc friction (shiny) surface.

HAYNES HiNT

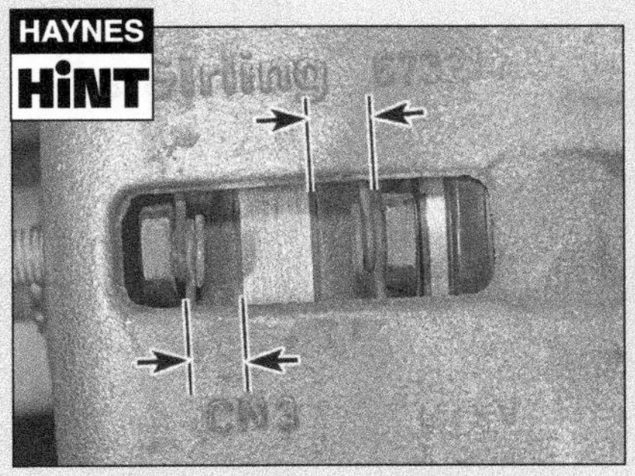

For a quick check, the thickness of the friction material on each brake pad can be measured through the aperture in the caliper body.

9 If any disc is thinner than the specified minimum thickness, renew both (refer to Chapter 9, Section 6).
10 Check the general condition of the discs. Look for excessive scoring and discolouration caused by overheating. If these conditions exist, remove the relevant disc and have it resurfaced or renewed (refer to Chapter 9, Section 6).
11 Make sure that the transmission is in neutral. Spin the wheel, and check that the brake is not binding. Some drag is normal with a disc brake, but it should not require any great effort to turn the wheel – also, on front brakes, do not confuse brake drag with resistance from the transmission.
12 Before refitting the wheels, check all brake lines and hoses (refer to Chapter 9, Section 3). In particular, check the flexible hoses in the vicinity of the calipers, where they are subjected to most movement. Bend them slightly between the fingers (but do not actually bend them double, or the casing may be damaged) and check that this does not reveal previously hidden cracks, cuts or splits.
13 On completion, refit the wheels and lower the car to the ground. Tighten the wheel bolts to the specified torque.

Rear disc brakes

14 Loosen the rear wheel bolts then chock the front wheels. Jack up the rear of the car, and support it on axle stands. Release the handbrake and remove the rear wheels.
15 The procedure for checking the rear brakes is much the same as described in paragraphs 2 to 13 above. Check that the rear brakes are not binding, noting that transmission resistance is not a factor on the rear wheels. Abnormal effort may indicate that the handbrake needs adjusting – see Chapter 9, Section 14.

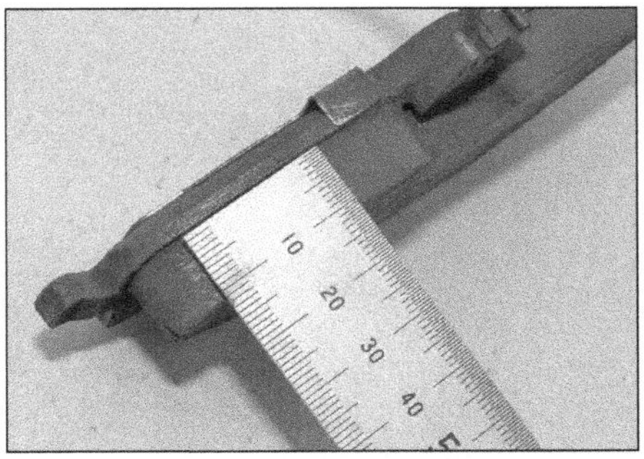

11.7 Check the thickness of the brake pad friction material

12 Handbrake check and adjustment

1 To check the handbrake adjustment, apply normal moderate pressure and pull the handbrake lever to the fully applied position, counting the number of clicks emitted from the handbrake ratchet mechanism. If adjustment is correct, there should be 2 clicks before the brakes begins to apply, and no more than 6 before the handbrake is fully applied. If this is not the case, adjust as described in Chapter 9, Section 14.

13 Steering and suspension check

Front suspension and steering

1 Raise the front of the vehicle, and securely support it on axle stands (see *Jacking and vehicle support*).
2 Visually inspect the balljoint dust covers and the steering gear gaiters for splits **(see illustration)**, chafing or deterioration. Any wear of these components will cause loss of lubricant, together with dirt and water entry, resulting in rapid deterioration of the balljoints or steering gear.
3 Grasp the roadwheel at the 12 o'clock and 6 o'clock positions, and try to rock it **(see**

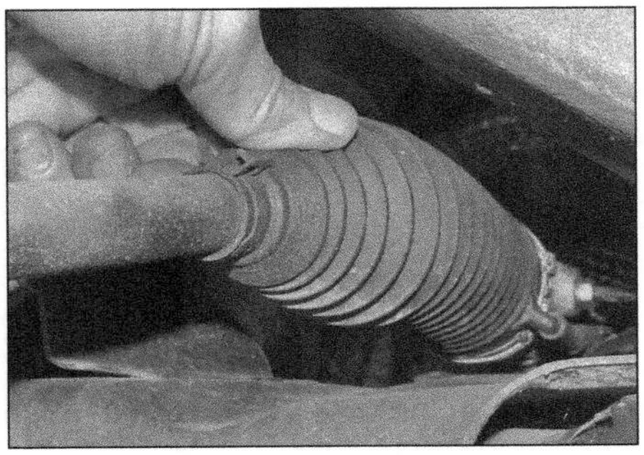

13.2 Check the steering rack gaiters for signs of damage or deterioration

13.3 Check for wear in the hub bearings by grasping the wheel and trying to rock it ...

13.4 ... and checking for wear in the steering rack and balljoints

illustration). Very slight free play may be felt, but if the movement is appreciable, further investigation is necessary to determine the source. Continue rocking the wheel while an assistant depresses the footbrake. If the movement is now eliminated or significantly reduced, it is likely that the hub bearings are at fault. If the free play is still evident with the footbrake depressed, then there is wear in the suspension joints or mountings.

4 Now grasp the wheel at the 9 o'clock and 3 o'clock positions, and try to rock it as before **(see illustration)**. Any movement felt now may again be caused by wear in the hub bearings or the steering track rod balljoints. If the inner or outer balljoint is worn, the visual movement will be obvious.

5 Using a large screwdriver or flat bar, check for wear in the suspension mounting bushes by levering between the relevant suspension component and its attachment point. Some movement is to be expected as the mountings are made of rubber, but excessive wear should be obvious. Also check the condition of any visible rubber bushes, looking for splits, cracks or contamination of the rubber.

6 With the car standing on its wheels, have an assistant turn the steering wheel back-and-forth about an eighth of a turn each way. There should be very little, if any, lost movement between the steering wheel and roadwheels. If this is not the case, closely observe the joints and mountings previously described, but in addition, check the steering column universal joints for wear, and the steering gear itself.

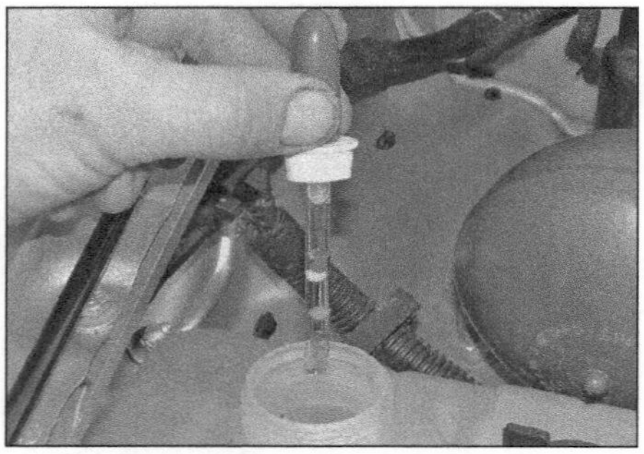

14.3 Check the antifreeze concentration with a hydrometer

Suspension strut/ shock absorber

7 Check for any signs of fluid leakage around the suspension strut/shock absorber body, or from the rubber gaiter around the piston rod. Should any fluid be noticed, the suspension strut/shock absorber is defective internally, and should be renewed. **Note:** *Suspension struts/shock absorbers should always be renewed in pairs on the same axle, or the handling of the vehicle will be adversely affected.*

8 The efficiency of the suspension strut/shock absorber may be checked by bouncing the vehicle at each corner. Generally speaking, the body will return to its normal position and stop after being depressed. If it rises and returns on a rebound, the suspension strut/shock absorber is probably suspect. Examine also the suspension strut/shock absorber upper and lower mountings for any signs of wear.

14 Coolant antifreeze concentration check

1 The cooling system should be filled with the recommended antifreeze and corrosion protection fluid. Over a period of time, the concentration of fluid may be reduced due to topping-up (this can be avoided by topping-up with the correct antifreeze mixture) or fluid loss. If loss of coolant has been evident, it is important to make the necessary repair before adding fresh fluid. The exact mixture of antifreeze-to-water that you should use depends on the relative weather conditions. The mixture should contain at least 40% antifreeze, but not more than 70%. Consult the mixture ratio chart on the antifreeze container before adding coolant. Use antifreeze which meets the vehicle manufacturer's specifications.

2 With the engine cold, carefully remove the cap from the expansion tank. If the engine is not completely cold, place a cloth rag over the cap before removing it, and remove it slowly to allow any pressure to escape.

3 Antifreeze checkers are available from car accessory shops. Draw some coolant from the expansion tank and observe how many plastic balls are floating in the checker **(see illustration)**. Usually, 2 or 3 balls must be floating for the correct concentration of antifreeze, but follow the manufacturer's instructions.

4 If the concentration is incorrect, it will be necessary to either withdraw some coolant and add antifreeze, or alternatively drain the old coolant and add fresh coolant of the correct concentration.

15 Exhaust system check

1 With the engine cold, check the complete exhaust system, from its starting point at the engine to the end of the tailpipe. If necessary, raise the front and rear of the vehicle and support it on axle stands (see *Jacking and vehicle support*). Remove any engine undershields as necessary for full access to the exhaust system.

2 Check the exhaust pipes and connections for evidence of leaks, severe corrosion, and damage. Make sure that all brackets and mountings are in good condition and that all relevant nuts and bolts are tight **(see**

illustrations). Leakage at any of the joints or in other parts of the system will usually show up as a black sooty stain in the vicinity of the leak.

3 Rattles and other noises can often be traced to the exhaust system, especially the brackets and rubber mountings. Try to move the pipes and silencers. If the components are able to come into contact with the body or suspension parts, secure the system with new mountings. Otherwise separate the joints (if possible) and twist the pipes as necessary to provide additional clearance.

15.2a Check the condition of the exhaust rubber mountings at the front ...

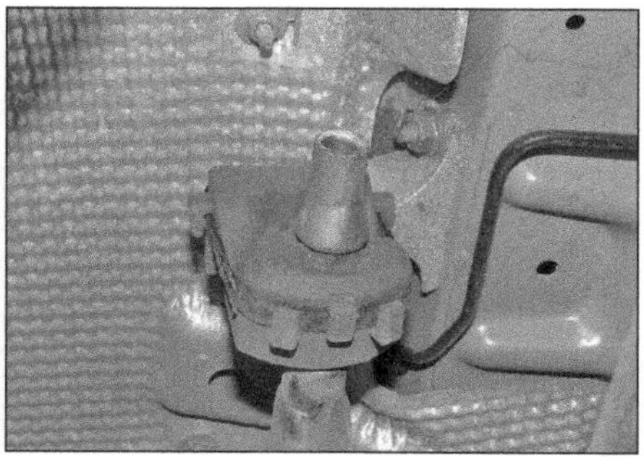

15.2b ... and the mountings along the length of the exhaust system

16 Seat belt condition check

1 Working on each seat belt in turn, carefully examine the seat belt webbing for cuts, or for any signs of serious fraying or deterioration. Pull the belt all the way out, and examine the full extent of the webbing.

2 Fasten and unfasten the belt, ensuring that the locking mechanism holds securely, and releases properly when intended. Check also that the retracting mechanism operates correctly when the belt is released.

3 Check the security of all seat belt mountings and attachments which are accessible from inside the vehicle without removing any trim or other components.

4 Check the function of the seat belt reminder lamp.

17 Airbag system check

1 The following work can be carried out by the home mechanic, however, if an electronic fault is apparent, it will be necessary to take the car to a Citroën dealer or specialist, who will have the necessary diagnostic equipment to extract fault codes from the system.

2 Turn the ignition switch to the drive position (ignition warning lights on), and check that the airbag warning light is illuminated for approximately 6 seconds. After this period the light should go out, indicating that the system has been checked and is functioning correctly.

3 If the warning light remains on or refuses to light, have the system checked by a Citroën dealer or specialist.

4 Visually examine the steering wheel centre pad, knee airbag and the passenger airbag modules for external damage. Also check the exterior of the front seats around the side airbag locations. If damage is evident, consult a Citroën dealer or specialist.

5 In the interests of safety, make sure that there are no loose items inside the car, which could be thrown onto the airbag modules in the event of an accident.

Every 40 000 miles or 4 years

18 Timing belt renewal (non-VTi engines)

1 Refer to Chapter 2A, Section 6, for the removal and refitting procedure.

19 Brake fluid renewal

⚠ ***Warning: Brake hydraulic fluid can harm your eyes and damage painted surfaces, so use extreme caution when handling and pouring it. Do not use fluid that has been standing open for some time, as it absorbs moisture from the air. Excess moisture can cause a dangerous loss of braking effectiveness.***

Note: *A hydraulic clutch shares its fluid reservoir with the braking system, and will also need to be bled (see Chapter 6, Section 2).*

1 The procedure is similar to that for the bleeding of the hydraulic system as described in Chapter 9, Section 2, except that the brake fluid reservoir should be emptied by siphoning, using a clean ladle or similar before starting, and allowance should be made for the old fluid to be expelled when bleeding a section of the circuit.

2 Working as described in Chapter 9, Section 2, open the first bleed screw in the sequence, and pump the brake pedal gently until nearly all the old fluid has been emptied from the master cylinder reservoir.

3 Top-up to the MAX level with new fluid **(see illustration)**, and continue pumping until only the new fluid remains in the reservoir, and new fluid can be seen emerging from the bleed screw. Tighten the screw, and top the reservoir level up to the MAX level line.

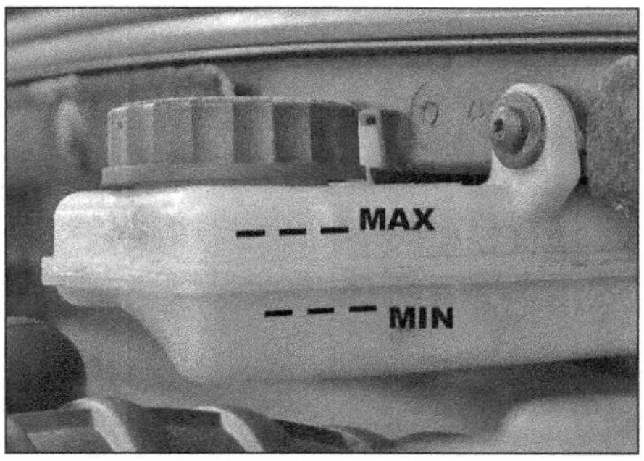

19.3 Brake/clutch fluid level markings

4 Work through all the remaining bleed screws in the sequence until new fluid can be seen at all of them. Be careful to keep the master cylinder reservoir topped-up to above the MIN level at all times, or air may enter the system and increase the length of the task.

5 When the operation is complete, check that all bleed screws are securely tightened, and that their dust caps are refitted. Wash off all traces of spilt fluid, and recheck the master cylinder reservoir fluid level.

6 Check the operation of the brakes before taking the car on the road.

20 Spark plug renewal

1 The correct functioning of the spark plugs is vital for the correct running and efficiency of the engine. It is essential that the plugs fitted are appropriate for the engine (see Specifications). If this type is used and the engine is in good condition, the spark plugs should not need attention between scheduled renewal intervals. Spark plug cleaning is rarely

20.3a Unscrew the spark plug ...

20.3b ... and remove it from the cylinder head

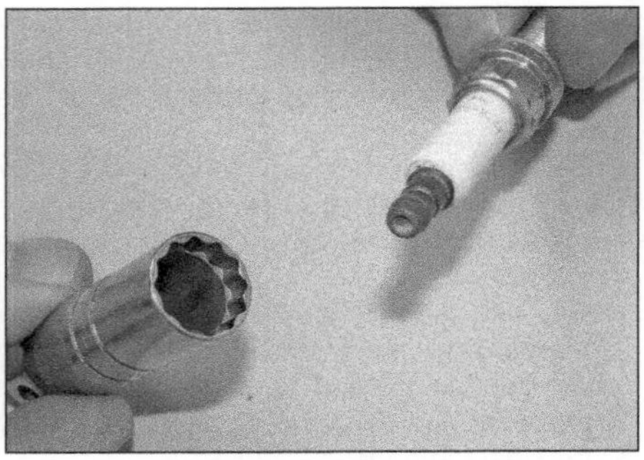

20.3c On VTi models a special socket may be required

necessary, and should not be attempted unless specialised equipment is available, as damage can easily be caused to the firing ends.

2 To gain access to the spark plugs, remove the ignition HT coils as described in Chapter 5B, Section 3.

3 Unscrew the plugs using a spark plug spanner, suitable box spanner or a deep socket and extension bar **(see illustrations)**. Keep the socket aligned with the spark plug – if it is forcibly moved to one side, the ceramic insulator may be broken off. As each plug is removed, examine it as follows.

4 Examination of the spark plugs will give a good indication of the condition of the engine **(see illustration)**. If the insulator nose of the spark plug is clean and white, with no deposits, this is indicative of a weak mixture or too hot a plug (a hot plug transfers heat away from the electrode slowly, a cold plug transfers heat away quickly).

5 If the tip and insulator nose are covered with hard black-looking deposits, then this is indicative that the mixture is too rich. Should the plug be black and oily, and then it is likely that the engine is fairly worn, as well as the mixture being too rich.

6 If the insulator nose is covered with light tan to greyish-brown deposits, then the mixture is correct and it is likely that the engine is in good condition.

7 The spark plug electrode gap is of considerable importance as, if it is too large or too small, the size of the spark and its efficiency will be seriously impaired. The gap should be set to the value given in the Specifications at the beginning of this Chapter. **Note:** *The electrode gap on multi-electrode spark plugs cannot be adjusted.*

8 To set the gap on single-electrode plugs, measure the gap with a feeler blade, and then bend open, or closed, the outer plug electrode until the correct gap is achieved **(see illustration)**. The centre electrode should never be bent, as this may crack the insulator and cause plug failure, if nothing worse. If using feeler blades, the gap is correct when the appropriate-size blade is a firm sliding fit.

9 Special spark plug electrode gap adjusting tools are available from most motor accessory shops, or from spark plug manufacturers.

10 Before fitting the spark plugs, check that the threaded connector sleeves are tight, and that the plug exterior and threads are clean **(see Haynes Hint)**.

11 Remove the rubber hose (if used), and tighten the plug to the specified torque using the spark plug socket and a torque wrench **(see illustration)**. Refit the remaining spark plugs in the same manner.

12 Refit the ignition HT coil as described in Chapter 5B, Section 3.

20.4 Examine the spark plugs to check the condition of the engine (see text)

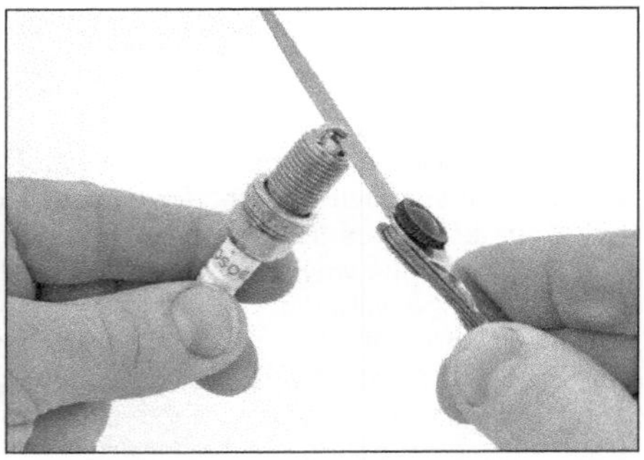

20.8 Measure the spark plug electrode gap with a feeler gauge

HAYNES HiNT

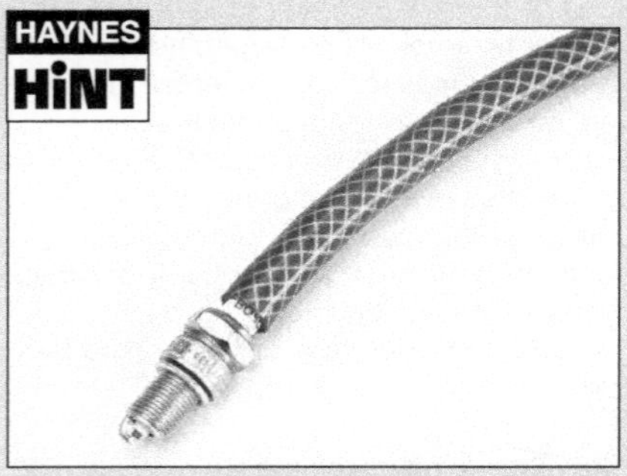

It is very often difficult to insert spark plugs into their holes without cross-threading them. To avoid this possibility, fit a short length of 8 mm internal diameter rubber hose over the end of the spark plug. The flexible hose acts as a universal joint to help align the plug with the plug hole. Should the plug begin to cross-thread, the hose will slip on the spark plug, preventing thread damage to the cylinder head.

20.11 Use a torque wrench to tighten the spark plugs

21 Air filter element renewal

Non-VTi engines

1 Remove the scuttle panel lower grille panel from the back of the engine compartment, as described in Chapter 11, Section 22.

2 Remove the air cleaner assembly as described in Chapter 4A, Section 2.

3 With the air cleaner assembly on the bench, undo the screws securing the air cleaner upper cover to the lower housing. Lift off the

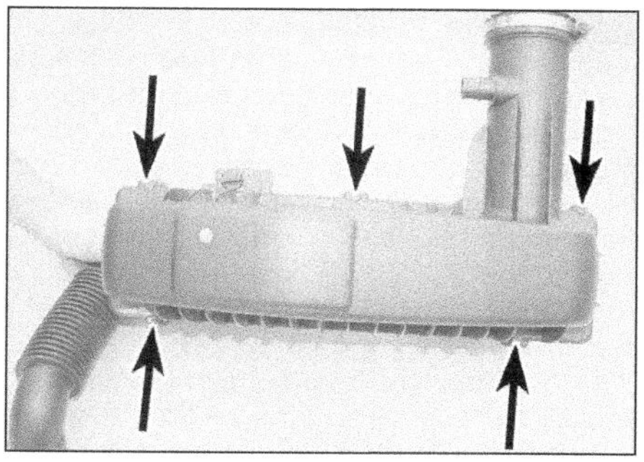
21.3a Undo the retaining screws (arrowed) ...

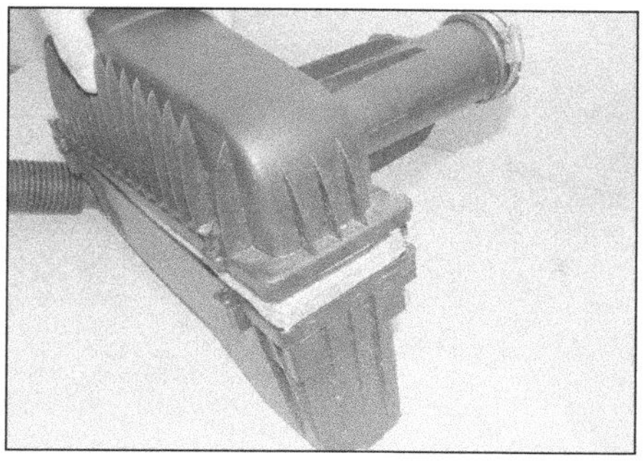
21.3b ... remove the upper cover ...

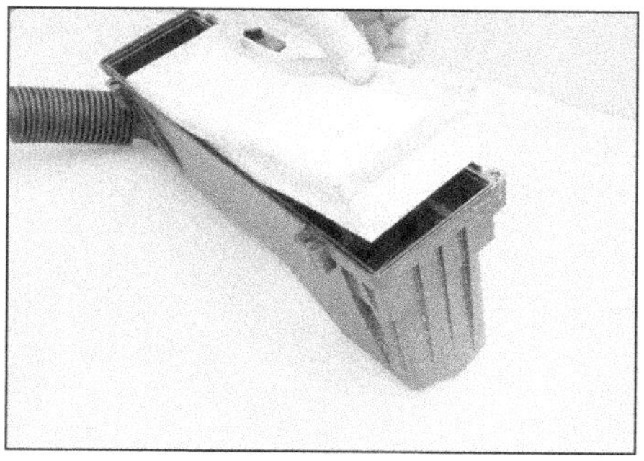
21.3c ... and remove the air filter element

upper cover and remove the air filter element, noting its fitted position **(see illustrations)**.

4 Wipe clean the inside of the air cleaner housing then fit the new element, ensuring it is correctly located, as noted on removal.

5 Locate the upper cover to the lower housing correctly and securely tighten the retaining screws.

6 Refit the scuttle lower grille panel, as described in Chapter 11, Section 22.

VTi engines

7 If required, to make access easier, remove the scuttle panel lower grille panel from the back of the engine compartment, as described in Chapter 11, Section 22.

8 Undo the securing bolt from the rear of the camshaft cover **(see illustration)**.

9 Undo the retaining screws from around the air cleaner upper housing, lift the front of the upper housing and withdraw it from the rear of the engine compartment **(see illustrations)**.

10 Lift the air filter element from the housing, noting its fitted position **(see illustration)**.

11 Wipe clean the inside of the housing then fit the new element, ensuring it is correctly located, as noted on removal.

12 Locate the upper part of the housing correctly and securely tighten the retaining screws and centre bolt in the camshaft cover.

13 If removed, refit the scuttle lower grille panel, as described in Chapter 11, Section 22.

22 Manual transmission oil level check

Note: *There is no specific recommendation in the manufacturer's schedule to check the oil level on 6-speed transmissions. They are described as 'Lubricated for life'. However, we consider it prudent to check the oil level, as a leak from the driveshaft oil seal or sealing washer could cause expensive damage. On these transmissions, there is also no level plug. If it is suspected the oil level is low, drain and refill the transmission as described in Chapter 7A, Section 2.*

Note: *On later 5-speed transmissions there is also no filler/level plug fitted. These transmissions do not require regular maintenance and are filled for life. If the transmission develops a leak or is removed for other work, the oil needs to be completely drained and refilled with the correct amount of oil. Refer to Chapter 7A, Section 2.*

21.8 Undo the retaining bolt ...

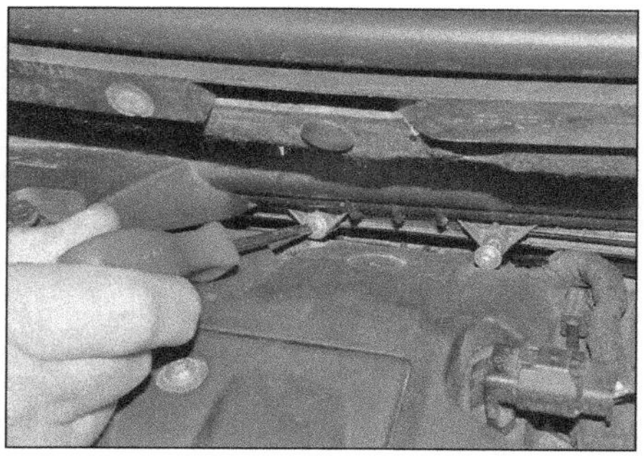
21.9a ... undo the retaining screws ...

21.9b ... and remove the upper housing

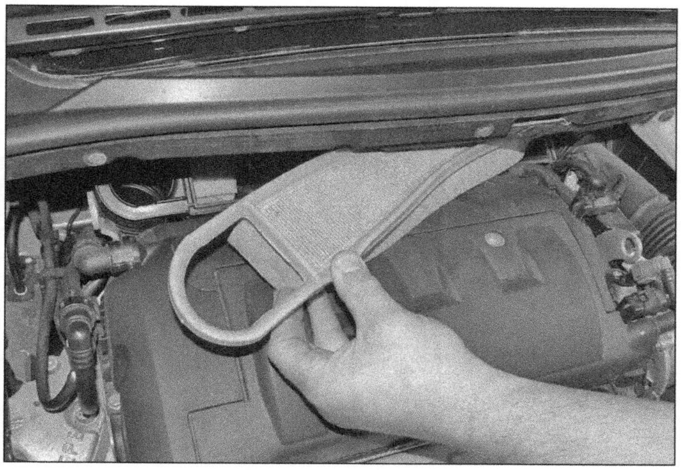
21.10 Remove the air filter element from the lower housing

22.3 Remove the inner wheel arch liner

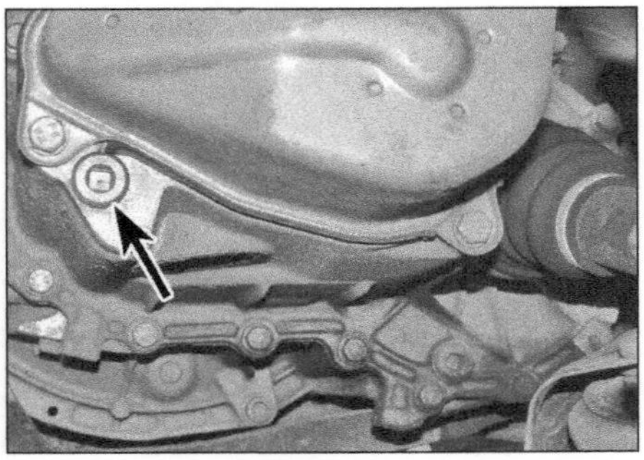

22.4a Fluid level/filler plug (arrowed) – MA transmission

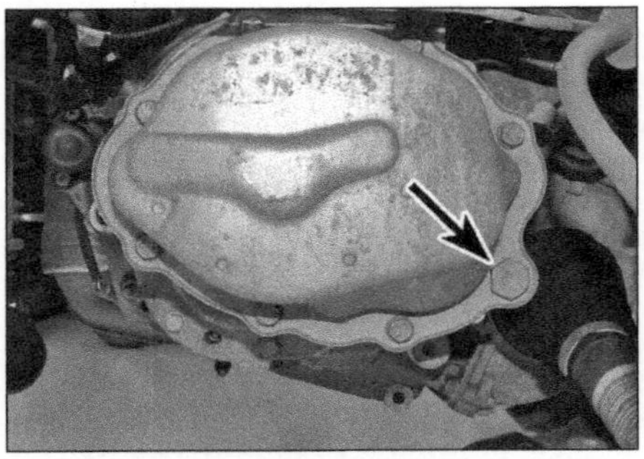

22.4b Fluid level/filler plug (arrowed) – BE4/5 transmission

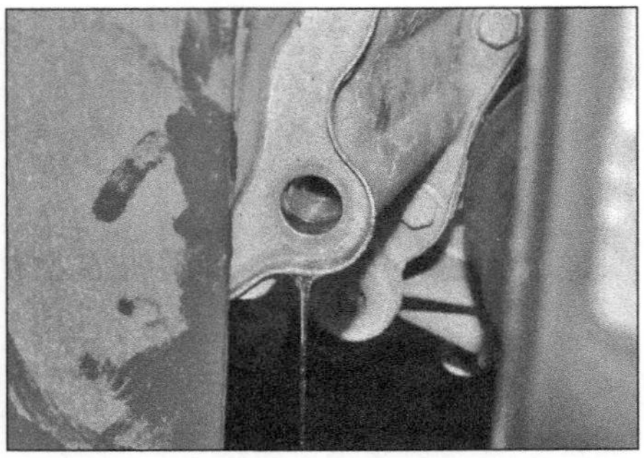

22.5 Add oil until a continuous trickle emerges from the plug hole

Note: *A suitable square-section wrench may be required to undo the transmission filler/level plug on some models. These wrenches can be obtained from most motor factors or your Citroën dealer. A new sealing washer will be required for the transmission filler/level plug when refitting.*

Early 5-speed transmissions

1 Take the car on a short journey to warm the transmission up to normal operating temperature. Position the car over an inspection pit, or alternatively jack up the front and rear of the car and support on axle stands (see *Jacking and vehicle support*). Whichever method is used, make sure that the car is level for checking the fluid level later.

2 The oil level must be checked at least 5 minutes after the engine has been switched off. If the oil is checked immediately after driving the car, some of the oil will remain distributed around the transmission, resulting in an inaccurate level reading.

3 Remove the left-hand front wheel, and then release the fasteners and remove the wheel arch liner **(see illustration)**.

4 Wipe clean the area around the filler/level plug, which is on the left-hand end of the transmission. Unscrew the plug and clean it; discard the sealing washer **(see illustrations)**.

5 The oil level should reach the lower edge of the filler/level hole. A certain amount of oil will have gathered behind the filler/level plug, and will trickle out when it is removed; this does not necessarily indicate that the level is correct. To ensure that a true level is established, wait until the initial trickle has stopped, then add oil as necessary until a trickle of new oil can be seen emerging **(see illustration)**. The level will be correct when the flow ceases; use only good-quality oil of the specified type (see *Lubricants and fluids*).

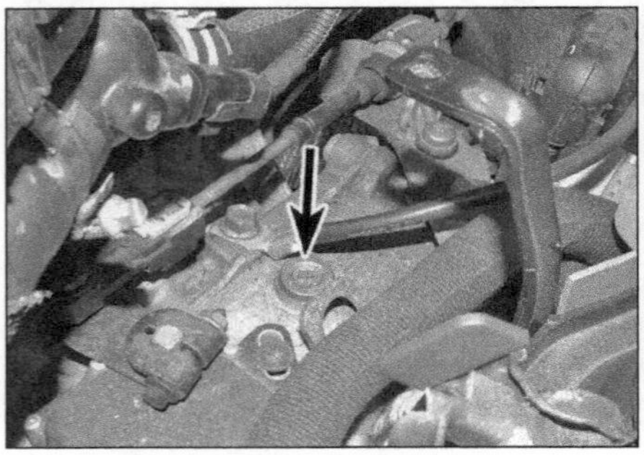

23.2 Transmission filler plug – AL4 transmission

23.5 Remove the square-drive (8 mm) plug to check level – AL4 transmission

6 Filling the transmission with oil is an extremely awkward operation; above all, allow plenty of time for the oil level to settle properly before checking it. If a large amount is added to the transmission, and a large amount flows out on checking the level, refit the filler/level plug and take the vehicle on a short journey so that the new oil is distributed fully around the transmission components, then recheck the level when it has settled again.

7 If the transmission has been overfilled so that oil flows out as soon as the filler/level plug is removed, Check that the car is completely level (front-to-rear and side-to-side), allow the surplus to drain off into a container.

8 When the level is correct, fit a new sealing washer to the filler/level plug. Refit the plug, tightening it to the specified torque setting. Wash off any spilt oil then refit the wheel arch liner, securing it in position with the fasteners. Refit the roadwheel and tighten to the specified torque setting.

9 Frequent need for topping-up indicates a leak, which should be found and corrected before it becomes serious.

23 Automatic transmission fluid level check

Note: *The transmission unit is equipped with a fluid wear sensor to inform the driver when the fluid needs renewing (the ECU flashes the Sport and Snow mode indicator lights when fluid renewal is necessary). Every time the transmission unit is topped-up, this sensor should be adjusted to compensate for the new fluid being added, however this can only be done using the Citroën diagnostic test box. Adding fluid without adjusting the sensor will not cause any problems but will mean the sensor is giving an inaccurate reading, resulting in fluid renewal being recommended earlier than is necessary.*

1 Take the vehicle on a short journey, to warm the transmission up to normal operating temperature, and then park the vehicle on level ground. Firmly apply the handbrake and place the selector lever in the P position.

2 Wipe clean the area around the filler plug, which is situated on the top of the transmission, directly beneath the battery. Remove the battery and battery tray/box as described in Chapter 5A, Section 4, then unscrew the filler plug from the transmission and recover the sealing washer **(see illustration)**.

3 Carefully add 0.5 litre of the specified type of fluid to the transmission via the filler plug aperture. Fit a new sealing washer to the filler plug then refit the plug, tightening it to the specified torque.

4 Undo the screws and remove the engine undershield – where fitted.

5 Position a suitable container under the drain/level plug arrangement, situated on the base of the transmission **(see illustration)**. **Note:** *The drain/level plug is in two parts,* *the first plug with an 8 mm square drive is the level plug, and then inside the housing is the second part of the plug (8 mm Allen key), which is the drain plug.*

Caution: Do not remove the drain plug by mistake.

6 Refit the battery and battery tray/box as described in Chapter 5A, Section 4.

7 Start the engine and allow it to idle. With the engine running, slacken and remove the level plug and sealing washer. Note the vehicle must be kept completely level for this procedure (front-to-rear and side-to-side).

> ⚠ ***Warning: The fluid will be hot, take precautions against scalding.***

8 If there is sufficient fluid in the transmission unit, fluid should trickle out the centre of the drain plug before slowing to a drip. **Note:** *If no fluid trickles out, or just a few drips appear when the plug is removed, the fluid level is too low. Refit the level plug then switch off the engine. Add a further 0.5 litre of fluid to the transmission then refit the filler plug and repeat the check.*

9 Once the flow of fluid stops, the level is correct. Fit a new sealing washer to the level plug then refit the plug and tighten it to the specified torque. Switch off the engine.

24 Emissions control systems check

1 This check specified by Citroën involves checking the engine management system by plugging an electronic tester into the system diagnostic socket to check the electronic control unit (ECU) memory for faults (see Chapter 4A, Section 5).

2 In reality, if the vehicle is running correctly and the engine management warning light on the instrument panel is functioning normally, then this check need not be carried out.

25 Coolant renewal

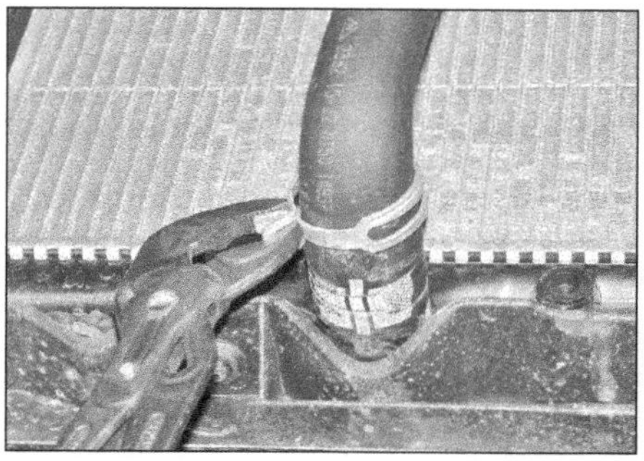

25.4 Squeeze together the tabs to release the hose clamp

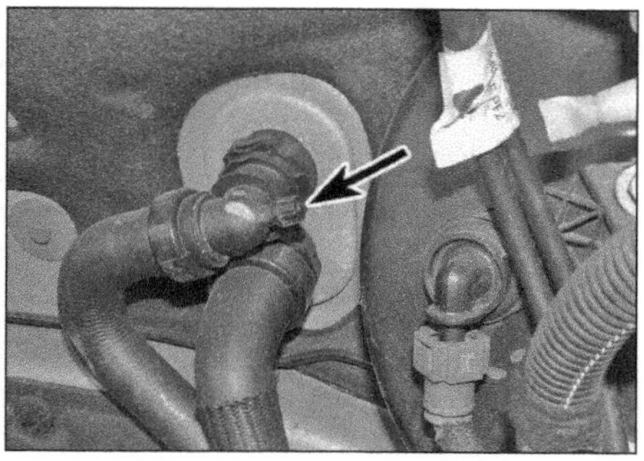

25.5a Undo the bleed screw from the heater hose union (arrowed) ...

25.5b ... and the bleed screw (arrowed) on the coolant housing – VTi engines

25.5c Bleed screw (arrowed) on the coolant housing – early non-VTi engines

> ***Warning: Do not allow antifreeze to come in contact with your skin or painted surfaces of the vehicle. Flush contaminated areas immediately with plenty of water. Don't store new coolant, or leave old coolant lying around, where it's accessible to children or pets – they're attracted by its sweet smell. Ingestion of even a small amount of coolant can be fatal. Wipe up garage-floor and drip pan spills immediately. Keep antifreeze containers covered, and repair cooling system leaks as soon as they're noticed.***

> ***Warning: Never remove the expansion tank filler cap when the engine is running, or has just been switched off, as the cooling system will be hot, and the consequent escaping steam and scalding coolant could cause serious injury.***

> ⚠ ***Warning: Wait until the engine is cold before starting these procedures.***

Cooling system draining

1 With the engine completely cold, remove the expansion tank filler cap. Turn the cap anti-clockwise, wait until any pressure remaining in the system is released, then unscrew it and lift it off.

2 Chock the rear wheels, and then raise the front of the vehicle and support it on axle stands (see *Jacking and vehicle support*). Undo the retaining bolts/nuts and remove the engine undershield.

3 Position a suitable container beneath the coolant hoses at the lower part of the radiator.

4 Release the retaining clip and disconnect the lower hose, allowing the coolant to drain into the container **(see illustration)**.

5 To assist draining, remove the cooling system bleed cap/screw (as applicable) from the heater matrix outlet hose union on the engine compartment bulkhead and, on some models, the bleed screw and sealing washer from the top of the coolant housing on the left-hand end of the cylinder head **(see illustrations)**. In order to improve access to the bleed screw on the heater union, remove the air filter housing and air ducts, as described in Chapter 4A, Section 2.

6 If the coolant has been drained for a reason other than renewal, then provided it is clean and less than four years old, it can be re-used, though new fresh coolant would be recommended.

7 Refit the radiator hose and secure it with the hose clamp.

8 Refit the engine undershield, and then lower the vehicle to the ground.

Cooling system flushing

9 If coolant renewal has been neglected, or if the antifreeze mixture has become diluted, then in time, the cooling system may gradually lose efficiency, as the coolant passages become restricted due to rust, scale deposits, and other sediment. The cooling system efficiency can be restored by flushing the system clean.

10 The radiator should be flushed separately from the engine, to avoid excess contamination.

Radiator flushing

11 Disconnect the top and bottom hoses and any other relevant hoses from the radiator (see Chapter 3, Section 4).

12 Insert a garden hose into the radiator top inlet. Direct a flow of clean water through the radiator, and continue flushing until clean water emerges from the radiator bottom outlet.

13 If after a reasonable period, the water still does not run clear, the radiator can be flushed with a good proprietary cleaning agent. It is important that their manufacturer's instructions are followed carefully. If the contamination is particularly bad, insert the hose in the radiator bottom outlet, and reverse-flush the radiator.

Engine flushing

14 To flush the engine, remove the thermostat (see Chapter 3, Section 5). If the radiator top hose has been disconnected, temporarily reconnect the hose. **Note:** *This may not be possible on some models, as the thermostat may be part of the coolant housing on the end of the cylinder head.*

15 With the bottom hose disconnected from the radiator, insert a garden hose into the coolant housing. Direct a clean flow of water through the engine, and continue flushing until clean water emerges from the radiator bottom hose.

16 When flushing is complete, refit the thermostat and reconnect the hoses (see Chapter 3, Section 5).

Cooling system filling

17 Before attempting to fill the cooling system, make sure that all hoses and clips are in good condition, and that the clips are tight. Note that an antifreeze mixture must be used all year round, to prevent corrosion of the engine components (see following sub-Section).

18 Make sure that the air conditioning (A/C) or automatic climate control (ACC) is switched off. This is to prevent the air conditioning system starting the radiator cooling fan before the engine is at normal temperature when refilling the system.

19 Remove the expansion tank filler cap and remove the cooling system bleed screws (see paragraph 5).

20 Citroën recommend the use of a 'header tank' when refilling the cooling system, to reduce the possibility of air being trapped in the system. Although Citroën dealers use a special header tank which screws onto the expansion tank, the same effect can be achieved by using a suitable 1.0 litre bottle, with a seal between the bottle and the expansion tank **(see illustration)**.

21 Fit the header tank to the expansion tank and slowly fill the system whilst observing the bleed holes. Coolant will emerge from each of the bleed holes in turn, starting with the heater matrix hose. As soon as coolant free from air bubbles emerges from the heater matrix hose outlet, securely refit the cap/screw (as applicable) then watch the bleed hole on the coolant housing. Once coolant free from air bubbles emerges from the housing hole, refit the bleed screw and sealing washer and tighten securely.

22 Continue to fill the cooling system until bubbles stop appearing in the expansion tank. Help to bleed the air from the system by repeatedly squeezing the radiator bottom hose.

23 When no more bubbles appear, ensure the header tank is full (at least 1.0 litre of coolant) then start the engine. Run the engine at a fast idle speed (do not exceed 2000 rpm) until the cooling fan cuts in and out TWICE, then when the fan has stopped for the second time, switch the engine off.

Caution: The coolant will be hot. Take great care not to scald yourself.

24 Allow the engine to cool, and then remove the 'header tank' from the reservoir. Wash off any spilt coolant with cold water.

25 When the engine has cooled, check the coolant level with reference to *Weekly checks*. Top-up the level if necessary, and refit the expansion tank cap.

Antifreeze mixture

26 The antifreeze should always be renewed at the specified intervals. This is necessary not only to maintain the antifreeze properties, but also to prevent corrosion, which would otherwise occur as the corrosion inhibitors become progressively less effective.

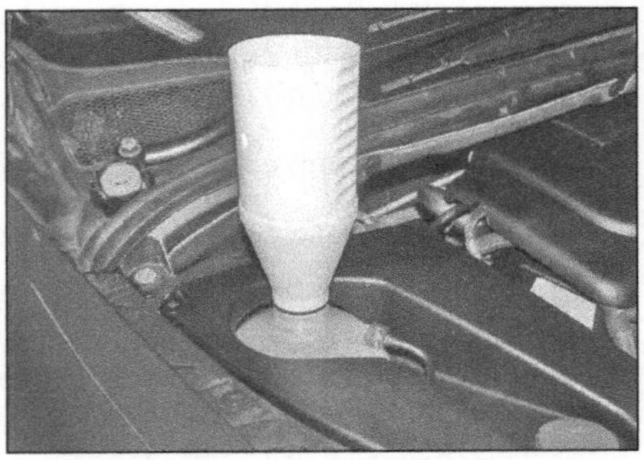

25.20 Using a 1.0 litre plastic bottle as a header tank

27 Always use an ethylene glycol based antifreeze, which is suitable for use in mixed-metal cooling systems.

28 Before adding antifreeze, the cooling system should be completely drained, preferably flushed, and all hoses checked for condition and security.

29 After filling with antifreeze, a label should be attached to the expansion tank, stating the type and concentration of antifreeze used, and the date installed. Any subsequent topping-up should be made with the same type and concentration of antifreeze.

Caution: Do not use engine antifreeze in the windscreen/tailgate washer system, as it will damage the vehicle paintwork. A screen wash additive should be added to the washer system in the quantities stated on the bottle.

26 Remote control battery renewal

1 Refer to Chapter 11, Section 17, for the renewal of the remote control battery.

Every 15 years

27 Airbags and seat belt pretensioners renewal

1 Citroën recommend that the airbags and seat belt pretensioners be renewed regardless of their condition within fifteen years. Refer to Chapter 12, Section 22 for airbag renewal, and Chapter 11, Section 24 for seat belt pretensioner renewal.

Chapter 1 Part B:
Routine maintenance and servicing – diesel models

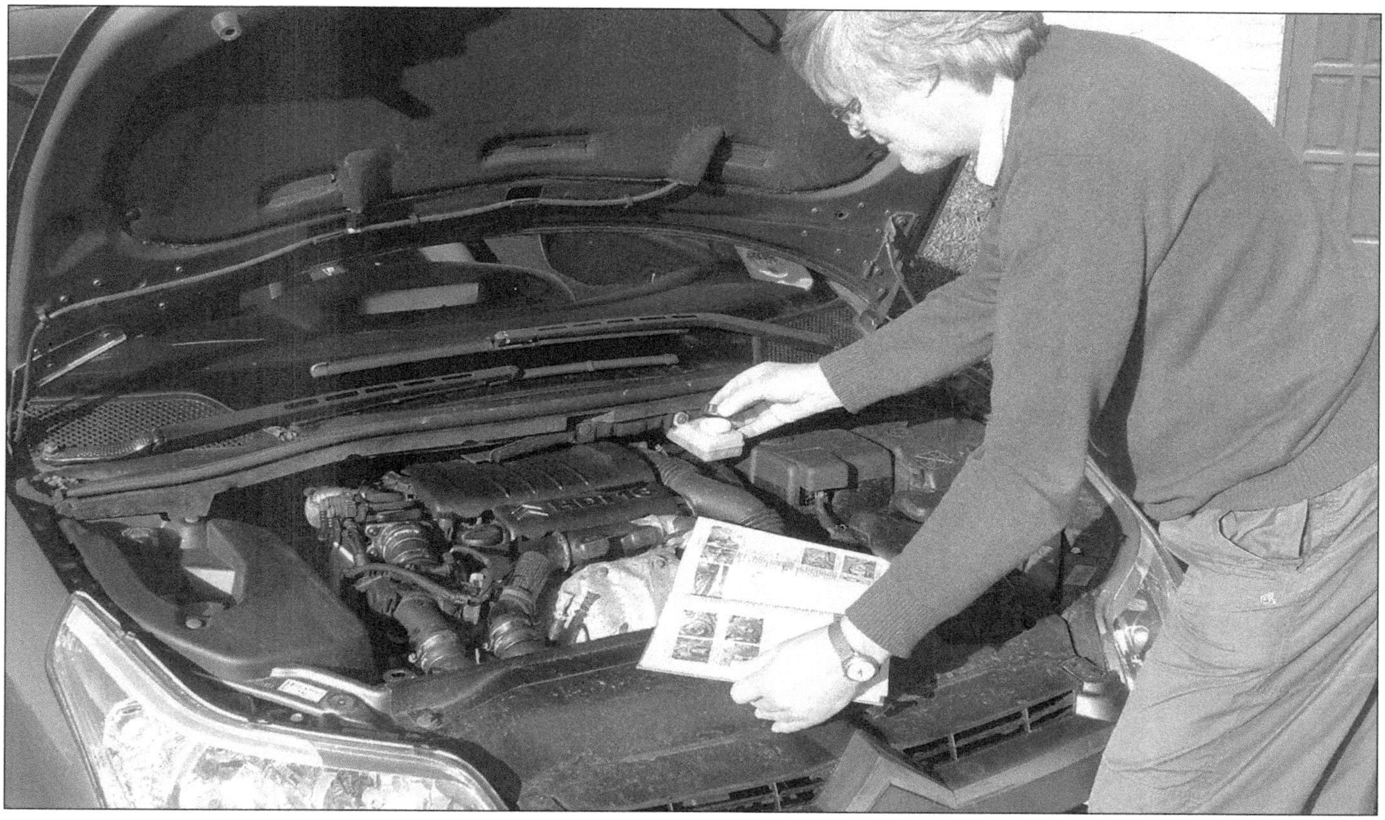

Contents

Degrees of difficulty

Easy, suitable for novice with little experience	**Fairly easy,** suitable for beginner with some experience	**Fairly difficult,** suitable for competent DIY mechanic	**Difficult,** suitable for experienced DIY mechanic	**Very difficult,** suitable for expert DIY or professional

Lubricants and fluids	Refer to *Lubricants and fluids*

Capacities

Note: *All values are approximate.*

Engine oil

Drain and refill, with filter change:	
1.6 litre engines	3.75 litres
2.0 litre engines	5.25 litres
Between dipstick MAX and MIN markings:	
1.6 litre engines	1.5 litres
2.0 litre engines	2.0 litres

Cooling system

1.6 litre engines	6.5 litres
2.0 litre engines:	
Manual transmission	9.0 litres
Automatic transmission	10.0 litres

Transmission

Manual transmission:	
Drain and refill:	
5-speed transmission (BE4/5)	1.9 litres
6-speed transmission (ML6C):	
Without cooling fins on the transmission casing	2.6 litres
With cooling fins on the transmission casing	1.9 litres
Automatic transmission (AM6):	
Drain and refill	3.0 litres
Total capacity, including torque converter	7.0 litres

Power-assisted steering

All models	0.85 litres

Fuel tank

All models	60 litres

Cooling system

Antifreeze mixture:*	
50% antifreeze	Protection down to -37°C
55% antifreeze	Protection down to -45°C

* **Note:** *Refer to antifreeze manufacturer for latest recommendations.*

Brakes

Brake pad friction material minimum thickness	2.0 mm

Tyre pressures	See *Lubricants, fluids and tyre pressures*

Remote control battery

Type	CR1620
Volts	3V

Torque wrench settings

Torque wrench settings	Nm	lbf ft
Automatic transmission (AM6):		
Drain/overflow plug	48	35
Level plug (centre of drain/overflow plug)	7	5
Filler plug	40	30
Engine oil sump drain plug:		
1.6 litre engines	25	18
2.0 litre engines	34	25
Manual transmission:		
BE4/5:		
Filler/level plug	22	16
Drain plug	35	26
ML6C:		
Drain plug	30	22
Oil filter cap	25	18
Wheel bolts	90	66

Note: *This maintenance schedule is a guide recommended by Haynes for servicing your own vehicle. Check with your local dealer for the manufacturer's maintenance schedule.*

1 The maintenance intervals in this manual are provided with the assumption that you will be carrying out the work yourself. These are the minimum maintenance intervals recommended by ourselves for vehicles driven daily, based on the schedule produced by the manufacturer. If you wish to keep your vehicle in peak condition at all times, you may wish to perform some of these procedures more often. We encourage frequent maintenance, because it enhances the efficiency, performance and resale value of your vehicle.

2 If the vehicle is driven in dusty areas, used to tow a trailer, or driven frequently at slow speeds (idling in traffic) or on short journeys, more frequent maintenance intervals are recommended.

3 When the vehicle is new, it should be serviced by a dealer service department (or other workshop recognised by the vehicle manufacturer as providing the same standard of service) in order to preserve the warranty. The vehicle manufacturer may reject warranty claims if you are unable to prove that servicing has been carried out as and when specified, using only original equipment parts or parts certified to be of equivalent quality.

4 All Citroën models are equipped with a service indicator function incorporated into the mileage recorder, which will indicate the mileage until the next service is due. However, Citroën point out that, 'due to the relationship between time and mileage, some operating conditions will make annual service more suitable'.

Every 250 miles or weekly

- ☐ Refer to *Weekly checks*

Every 10 000 miles or 12 months – whichever comes first

- ☐ Renew the engine oil and filter (Section 3)
- ☐ Check all underbonnet components for fluid leaks (Section 4)
- ☐ Check the steering and suspension components (Section 5)
- ☐ Check the condition of the driveshaft joints and rubber gaiters (Section 6)
- ☐ Lubricate all hinges and locks (Section 7)
- ☐ Drain the fuel filter (Section 8)
- ☐ Reset the service interval indicator (Section 9)

Every 20 000 miles or 2 years – whichever comes first

- ☐ Check the condition of the brake pads and discs (Section 10)
- ☐ Check the operation of the handbrake (Section 11)
- ☐ Check the seat belt condition (Section 12)
- ☐ Check the airbag system (Section 13)
- ☐ Carry out a road test (Section 14)
- ☐ Check the coolant antifreeze concentration (Section 15)
- ☐ Check the exhaust system (Section 16)
- ☐ Check the condition of the auxiliary drivebelt (Section 17)
- ☐ Check and renew the pollen filter (Section 18)

Every 40 000 miles or 4 years – whichever comes first

- ☐ Renew the brake fluid (Section 19)

Note: *The hydraulic clutch shares its fluid reservoir with the braking system, and will also need to be bled.*

- ☐ Renew the coolant (Section 20)
- ☐ Renew the air filter element (Section 21)
- ☐ Check the manual transmission oil level (Section 22)
- ☐ Check the automatic transmission fluid level (Section 23)
- ☐ Renew the fuel filter (Section 8)
- ☐ Renew the remote control battery (Section 24)

Every 80 000 miles or 8 years – whichever comes first

- ☐ Check the particulate filter fluid (Section 25)
- ☐ Renew the particulate filter (Section 26)
- ☐ Timing belt renewal (Section 27)

Note: *The interval recommended by Citroën is 150 000 miles or 10 years. However, It is strongly recommended that the interval be reduced on vehicles that are subjected to intensive use, ie, mainly short journeys or a lot of stop-start driving. The actual belt renewal interval is very much up to the individual owner, but bear in mind that severe engine damage will result if the belt breaks.*

Every 15 years

- ☐ Renew the airbags and seat belt pretensioners (Section 28)

Front underbody view

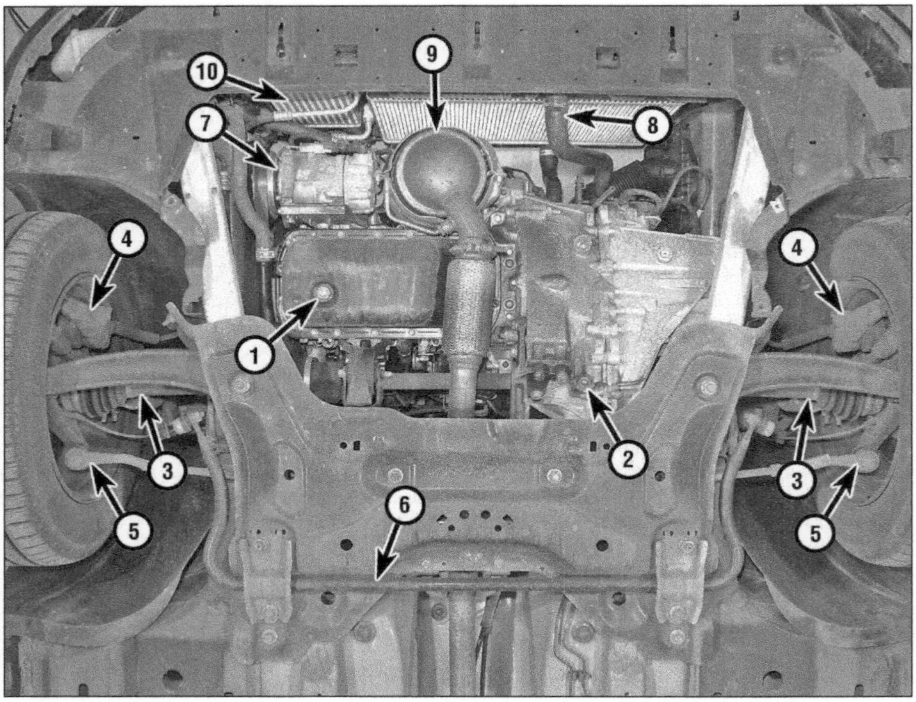

1 Engine oil drain plug
2 Manual transmission drain plug
3 Driveshaft
4 Brake caliper
5 Track rod balljoint
6 Anti-roll bar
7 Air conditioning compressor
8 Radiator bottom hose
9 Catalytic converter
10 Intercooler

Rear underbody view

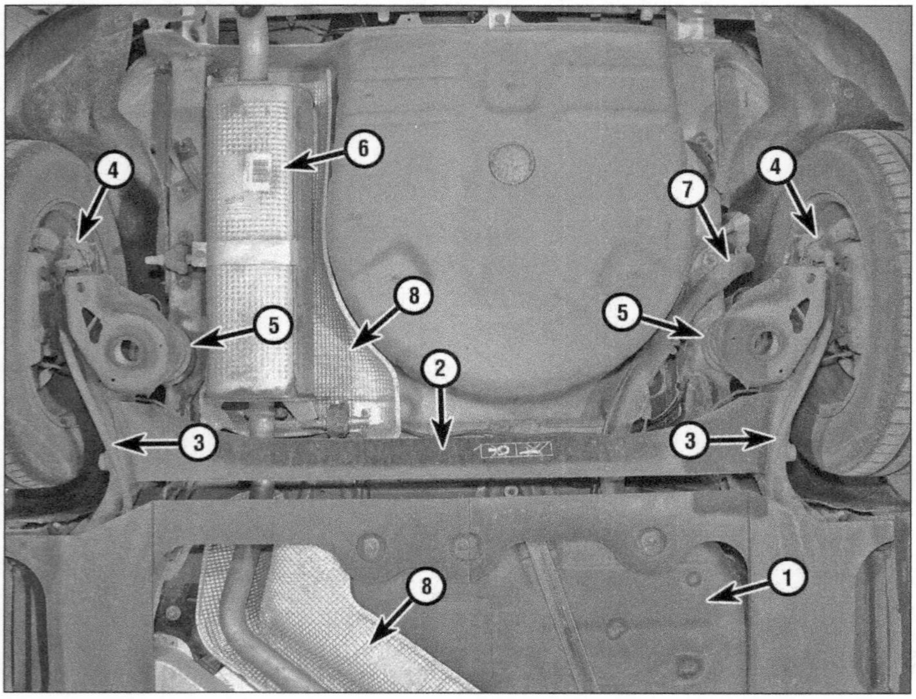

1 Fuel tank
2 Beam axle
3 Handbrake cable
4 Brake caliper
5 Coil spring
6 Exhaust rear silencer
7 Fuel filler neck
8 Heat shields

Underbonnet view (2.0 litre model shown)

1 Engine oil filler cap
2 Engine oil level dipstick
3 Battery
4 Brake/clutch fluid reservoir
5 Oil filter cap
6 Coolant expansion tank
7 Fuel priming hand pump
8 Alternator
9 Power steering fluid reservoir
10 Washer fluid reservoir
11 Fuse/electrical box

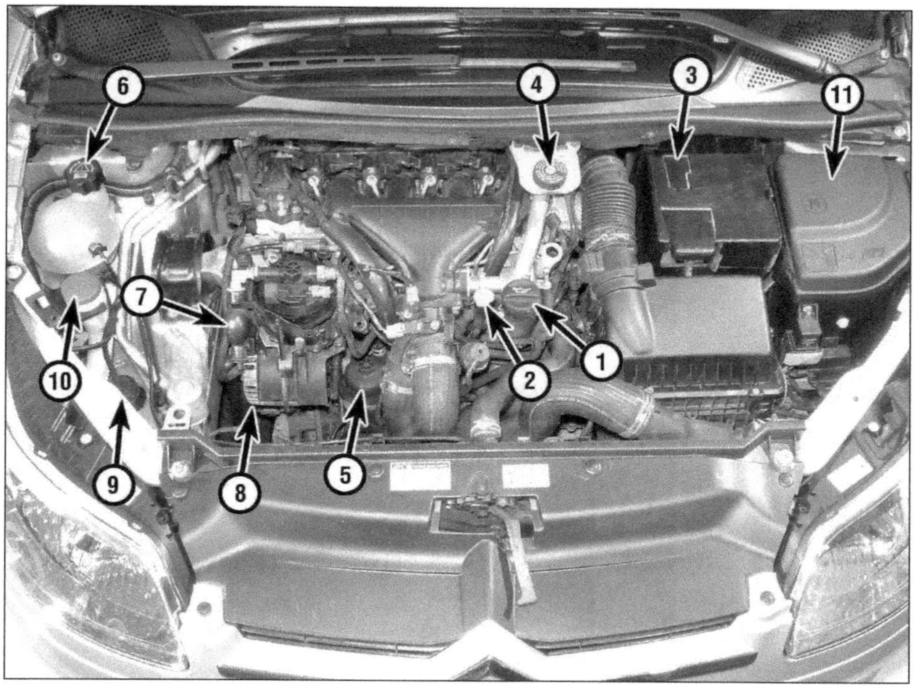

Maintenance procedures

1 General information

1 This Chapter is designed to help the home mechanic maintain his/her vehicle for safety, economy, long life and peak performance.
2 The Chapter contains a master maintenance schedule, followed by Sections dealing specifically with each task in the schedule. Visual checks, adjustments, component renewal and other helpful items are included. Refer to the accompanying illustrations of the engine compartment and the underside of the vehicle for the locations of the various components.
3 Servicing your vehicle in accordance with the mileage/time maintenance schedule and the following Sections will provide a planned maintenance programme, which should result in a long and reliable service life. This is a comprehensive plan, so maintaining some items, but not others, at the specified service intervals will not produce the same results.
4 As you service your vehicle, you will discover that many of the procedures can – and should – be grouped together, because of the particular procedure being performed, or because of the close proximity of two otherwise-unrelated components to one another. For example, if the vehicle is raised for any reason, the exhaust system could be inspected at the same time as the suspension and steering components.
5 The first step in this maintenance programme is to prepare yourself before the actual work begins. Read through all the Sections relevant to the work to be carried out, then make a list and gather together all the parts and tools required. If a problem is encountered, seek advice from a parts specialist, or a dealer service department.

2 Routine maintenance

1 If, from the time the vehicle is new, the routine maintenance schedule is followed closely, and frequent checks are made of fluid levels and high-wear items, as suggested throughout this manual, the engine will be kept in relatively good running condition, and the need for additional work will be minimised.
2 It is possible that there will be times when the engine is running poorly due to the lack of regular maintenance. This is even more likely if a used vehicle, which has not received regular and frequent maintenance checks, is purchased. In such cases, additional work may need to be carried out, outside of the regular maintenance intervals.
3 If engine wear is suspected, a compression test (refer to Chapter 2C or 2D) will provide valuable information regarding the overall performance of the main internal components. Such a test can be used as a basis to decide on the extent of the work to be carried out. If, for example, a compression test indicates serious internal engine wear, conventional maintenance as described in this Chapter will not greatly improve the performance of the engine, and may prove a waste of time and money, unless extensive overhaul work (Chapter 2E) is carried out first.
4 The following series of operations are those most often required to improve the performance of a generally poor-running engine:

Primary operations

a) Clean, inspect and test the battery ('Weekly checks' and Chapter 5A)
b) Check all the engine-related fluids ('Weekly checks').
c) Check the condition and tension of the auxiliary drivebelt (Section 17).
d) Check the condition of the air filter element, and renew if necessary (Section 21).
e) Check the condition of all hoses, and check for fluid leaks (Section 4).

5 If the above operations do not prove fully effective, carry out the following secondary operations:

Secondary operations

a) Check the charging system (Chapter 5A, Section 5).
b) Check the fuel system (Chapter 4B).

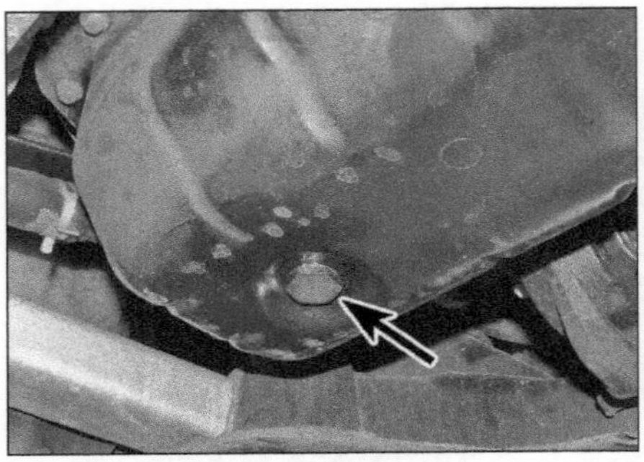

3.5a Engine oil drain plug on 1.6 litre engines ...

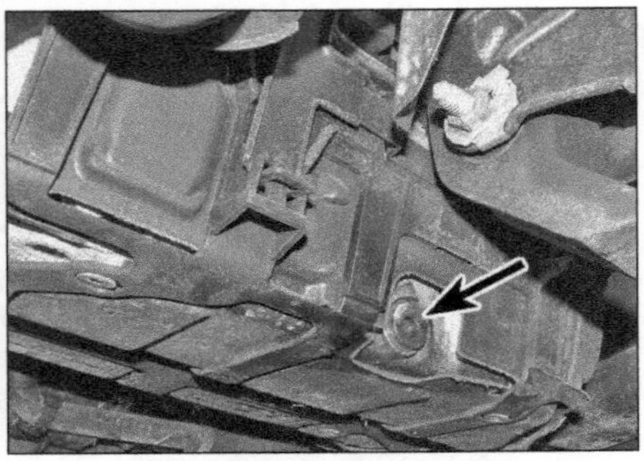

3.5b ... and on 2.0 litre engines

HAYNES HiNT

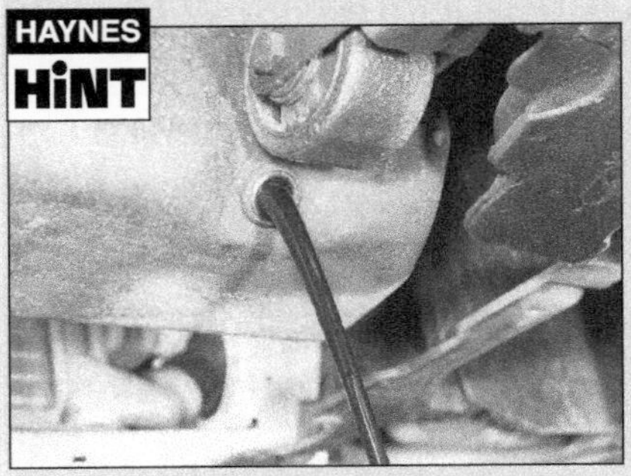

As the drain plug releases from the sump threads, move it away sharply, so the stream of oil issuing from the sump runs into the container, not up your sleeve.

Every 10 000 miles or 12 months

3 Engine oil and filter renewal

Note: *A suitable square-section wrench may be required to undo the sump drain plug on certain models. These wrenches can be obtained from most motor factors or your Citroën dealer.*

1 Frequent oil changes are the most important preventative maintenance the DIY home mechanic can give the engine, because ageing oil becomes diluted and contaminated, which leads to premature engine wear.

2 Before starting this procedure, gather together all the necessary tools and materials. Also make sure that you have plenty of clean rags and newspapers handy, to mop-up any spills. Ideally, the engine oil should be warm, as it will drain better, and more built-up sludge will be removed with it. Take care, however, not to touch the exhaust or any other hot parts of the engine when working under the vehicle. To avoid any possibility of scalding, and to protect yourself from possible skin irritants and other harmful contaminants in used engine oils, it is advisable to wear gloves when carrying out this work.

3 Access to the filter and drain plug will be greatly improved if the front of the vehicle is raised and support securely on axle stands (see *Jacking and vehicle support*).

4 Undo the fasteners and remove the engine undershield.

5 Slacken the plug about half a turn **(see illustrations)**. Position the draining container under the drain plug, then remove the plug completely – recover the sealing washer **(see Haynes Hint)**.

6 Allow some time for the old oil to drain, noting that it may be necessary to reposition the container as the oil flow slows to a trickle.

7 The oil filter is of a separate disposable paper element contained under a plastic cap, which is screwed into a housing on the front of the cylinder block **(see illustrations)**.

8 On 1.6 litre engines, remove the air intake hoses from the front left-hand corner of the engine compartment to access the oil filter cap **(see illustrations)**.

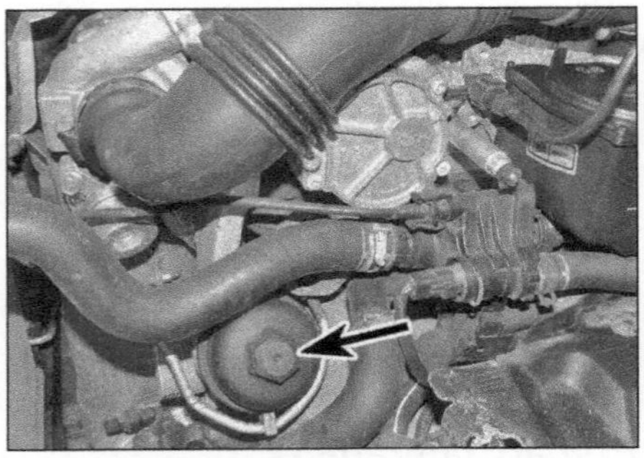

3.7a Engine oil filter location on 1.6 litre engines ...

3.7b ... and on 2.0 litre engines

3.8a Release the securing clips ...

3.8b ... and remove the air intake ducting ...

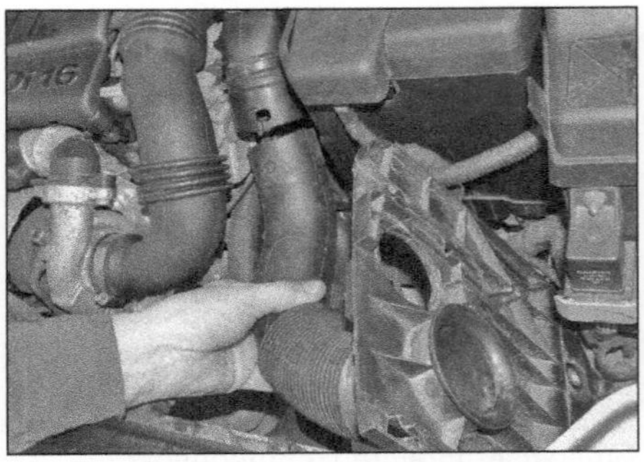

3.8c ... from the front of the engine compartment

3.9a Slacken the engine oil filter cover ...

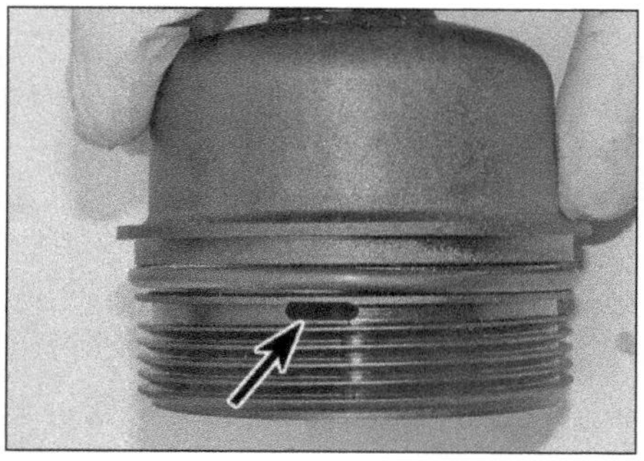

3.9b ... until the vent hole (arrowed) is uncovered

3.10 Fit a new sealing washer to the drain plug

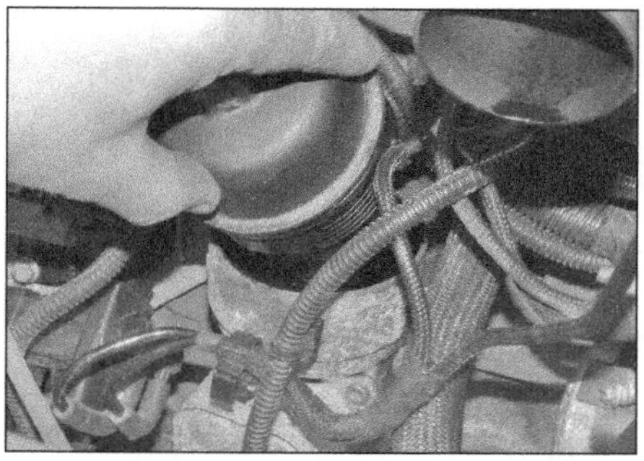

3.11 Unscrew the oil filter plastic cover

3.13 Renew the O-ring seal ...

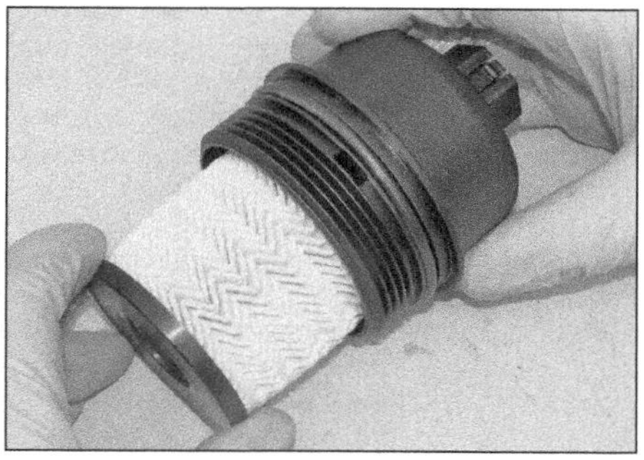

3.14a ... insert the new filter into the cap ...

9 Using a socket or spanner, slacken the oil filter plastic cap a couple of turns to allow the oil in the filter housing to drain into the sump **(see illustrations)**. Do not completely remove at this stage.

10 After all the oil has drained, wipe off the drain plug with a clean rag. Clean the area around the drain plug opening, and refit the plug with a new sealing washer **(see illustration)**. Tighten the plug to the specified torque.

11 The oil filter plastic cap can now be unscrewed the rest of the way by hand **(see illustration)**. Use a rag to catch any oil spillage as the filter is removed.

12 Lift the oil filter plastic cap away, depending on model the paper filter element may stay in the lower part of the housing or will stay in the cap as it is removed. Remove the paper element from the filter housing, if required.

13 Use a clean rag to remove all oil and dirt from inside the filter cap and housing, and then remove the O-ring seal from the cap **(see illustration)**. A new seal should be supplied with the new filter.

14 Fit a new O-ring seal to the cap, and fit the new paper element to the cap. On 1.6 litre engines, fit the element to the housing, ensuring the lug on the base of the element locates correctly in the corresponding hole in the housing. Lightly lubricate the O-ring seal with clean engine oil **(see illustrations)**.

15 Screw the cap into place by hand, and then tighten it to the specified torque.

16 Lower the vehicle to the ground, then

3.14b ... then apply a little clean oil to the seal

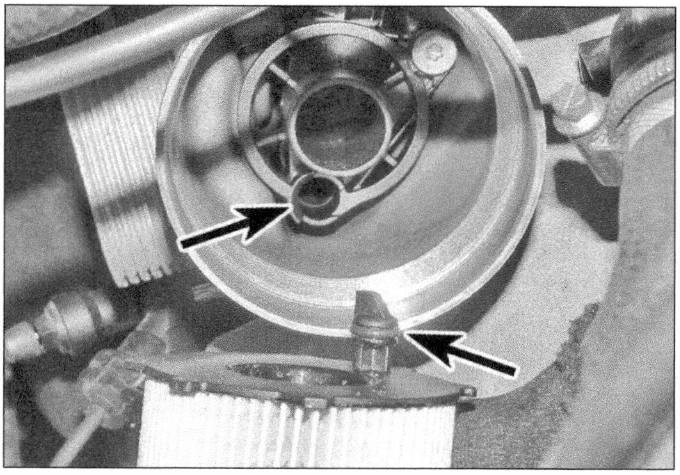

3.14c Ensure the filter locating peg (arrowed) locates into the corresponding hole in the housing (arrowed)

remove the oil filler cap and withdraw the level dipstick from the tube **(see illustrations)**.

17 Fill the engine, using the correct oil (see *Lubricants and fluids*). An oil can spout or funnel may help to reduce spillage. Pour in half the specified quantity of oil first (see Specifications), and then wait a few minutes for the oil to run to the sump. Continue adding oil a small quantity at a time until the level is up to the lower mark on the dipstick. Adding a further 1.5 litres (approx.) will bring the level up to the upper mark on the dipstick **(see illustration)**. Insert the dipstick, and refit the filler cap when completed.

18 Start the engine and run it for a few minutes; check for leaks around the oil filter seal and the sump drain plug. Note that there may be a delay of a few seconds before the oil pressure warning light goes out when the engine is first started, as the oil circulates through the engine oil galleries and the new oil filter before the pressure builds-up.

19 Switch off the engine, and wait a few minutes for the oil to settle in the sump once more. With the new oil circulated and the filter completely full, recheck the level on the dipstick, and add more oil as necessary. When completed, refit the engine undershield.

20 Dispose of the used engine oil safely, in accordance with the guidance given in *General repair procedures*.

3.16a Remove the oil filler cap ...

3.16b ... and the oil level dipstick – 1.6 litre engines

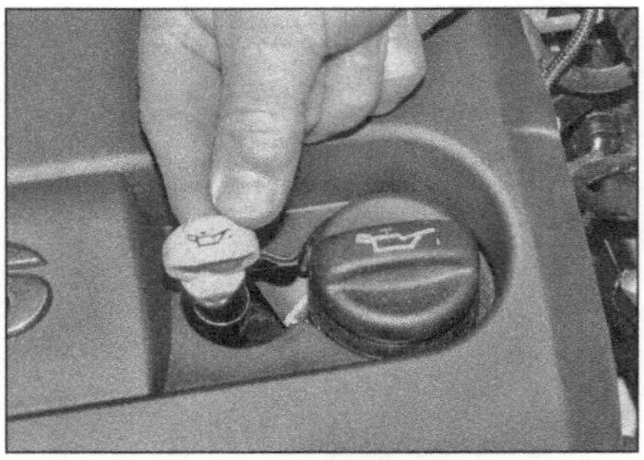

3.16c The oil level dipstick – 2.0 litre engines

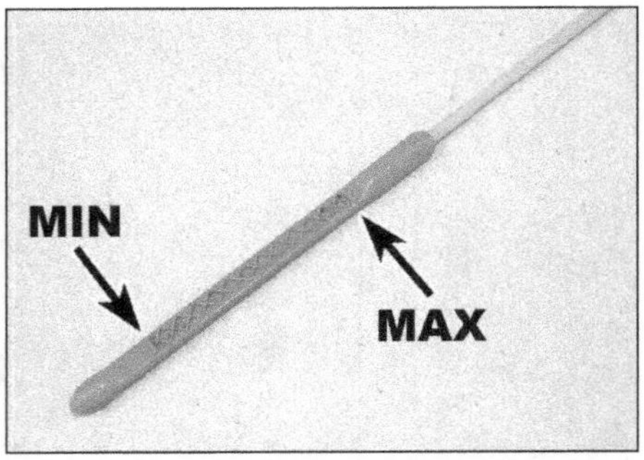

3.17 Upper and lower dipstick markings (arrowed)

4 Hose and fluid leak check

Cooling system

Warning: Refer to the safety information given in 'Safety first!' and Chapter 3, Section 1 before disturbing any of the cooling system components.

1 Carefully check the radiator and heater coolant hoses along their entire length. Renew any hose that is cracked, swollen or which shows signs of deterioration. Cracks will show up better if the hose is squeezed. Pay close attention to the clips that secure the hoses to the cooling system components. Hose clips that have been overtightened can pinch and puncture hoses, resulting in cooling system leaks.

2 Inspect all the cooling system components (hoses, joint faces, etc) for leaks. Where any problems of this nature are found on system components, renew the component or gasket with reference to Chapter 3 **(see Haynes hint)**.

Fuel system

Warning: Refer to the safety information given in 'Safety first!' and Chapter 4B, Section 2 before disturbing any of the fuel system components.

3 Diesel leaks are easier to spot than petrol, but can be difficult to pinpoint unless the leakage is significant and hence easily visible. Fuel tends to spread, especially in a hot engine bay. Small drips can spread before you get a chance to identify the point of leakage. If you suspect that there is a fuel leak from the area of the engine bay, leave the vehicle overnight then start the engine from cold, with the bonnet open. Metal components tend to shrink when they are cold, and rubber seals and hoses tend to harden, so any leaks will be more apparent whilst the engine is warming-up from a cold start.

4 Check all fuel lines at their connections to the fuel rail, fuel pressure regulator, fuel filter, fuel cooler and especially the return hoses on top of the injectors. Examine each rubber fuel hose along its length for splits or cracks. Check for leakage from the crimped joints between rubber and metal fuel lines. Examine the unions between the metal fuel lines and the fuel filter housing. Also check the area around the fuel injectors for signs of O-ring leakage.

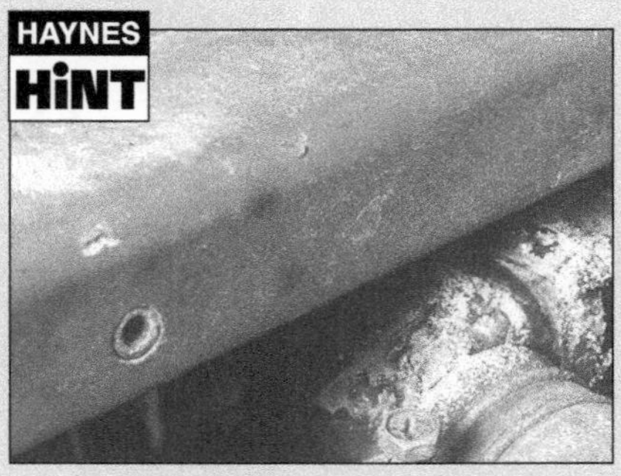

A leak in the cooling system will usually show up as white- or antifreeze-coloured deposits on the area adjoining the leak.

5 To identify fuel leaks between the fuel tank and the engine bay, the vehicle should be raised and securely supported on axle stands (see *Jacking and vehicle support*). Inspect the fuel tank and filler neck for punctures, cracks and other damage. The connection between the filler neck and tank is especially critical. Sometimes a rubber filler neck or connecting hose will leak due to loose retaining clamps or deteriorated rubber.

6 Carefully check all rubber hoses and metal fuel lines leading away from the fuel tank. Check for loose connections, deteriorated hoses, kinked lines, and other damage. Pay particular attention to the vent pipes and hoses, which often loop up around the filler neck and can become blocked or kinked, making tank filling difficult. Follow the fuel supply and return lines to the front of the vehicle, carefully inspecting them all the way for signs of damage or corrosion. Renew damaged sections as necessary.

Engine oil

7 Inspect the area around the camshaft cover, cylinder head, oil filter and sump joint faces. Bear in mind that, over a period of time, some very slight seepage from these areas is to be expected – what you are really looking for is any indication of a serious leak caused by gasket failure. Engine oil seeping from the base of the timing belt cover or the transmission bellhousing may be an indication of crankshaft or transmission input shaft oil seal failure. Should a leak be found, renew the failed gasket or oil seal by referring to the appropriate Chapters in this manual.

Automatic transmission fluid

8 Where applicable, check the hoses leading to the transmission fluid cooler at the front of the engine bay for leakage. Look for deterioration caused by corrosion and damage from grounding, or debris thrown up from the road surface. Automatic transmission fluid is a thin oil and is usually red in colour.

Air conditioning refrigerant

Warning: Refer to the safety information given in 'Safety first!' and Chapter 3, Section 11 regarding the dangers of disturbing any of the air conditioning system components.

9 The air conditioning system is filled with a liquid refrigerant, which is retained under high pressure. If the air conditioning system is opened and depressurised without the aid of specialised equipment the refrigerant will immediately turn into gas and escape into the atmosphere. If the liquid comes into contact with your skin, it can cause severe frostbite. In addition, the refrigerant contains substances which are environmentally damaging; for this reason, it should not be allowed to escape into the atmosphere in an uncontrolled fashion.

10 Any suspected air conditioning system leaks should be immediately referred to a Citroën dealer or air conditioning specialist. Leakage will be shown up as a steady drop in the level of refrigerant in the system.

11 Note that water may drip from the condenser drain pipe, underneath the car, immediately after the air conditioning system has been in use. This is normal, and should not be cause for concern.

Brake (and clutch) fluid

Warning: Refer to the safety information given in 'Safety first!' and Chapter 9, Section 2 regarding the dangers of handling brake fluid.

12 With reference to Chapter 9, Section 10, examine the area surrounding the brake/clutch pipe unions at the master cylinder for signs of leakage. Check the area around the base of fluid reservoir, for signs of leakage caused by seal failure. Also examine the brake pipe unions at the ABS hydraulic unit.

13 If fluid loss is evident, but the leak cannot be pinpointed in the engine bay, the brake calipers and underbody brake lines should be carefully checked with the vehicle raised and supported on axle stands (see *Jacking and vehicle support*). Leakage of fluid from the braking system is a serious fault that must be rectified immediately.

14 Brake/clutch hydraulic fluid is a toxic substance with a watery consistency. New fluid is almost colourless, but it becomes darker with age and use.

Unidentified fluid leaks

15 If there are signs that a fluid of some description is leaking from the vehicle, but you cannot identify the type of fluid or its exact origin, park the vehicle overnight and slide a large piece of card underneath it. Providing that the card is positioned in roughly the right location, even the smallest leak will show up on the card. Not only will this help you to pinpoint the exact location of the leak, it should be easier to identify the fluid from its colour. Bear in mind, though, that the leak may only be occurring when the engine is running!

Vacuum hoses

16 Although the braking system is hydraulically operated, the brake servo unit amplifies the effort applied at the brake pedal by making use of the vacuum supplied by the vacuum pump, driven by the engine. Vacuum is ported to the servo by means of a large-bore hose. Any leaks that develop in this hose will reduce the effectiveness of the braking system, and may affect the running of the engine.

17 In addition, a number of the underbonnet components, particularly the turbocharger control components, are driven by vacuum supplied from the vacuum pump via narrow-bore hoses. A leak in a vacuum hose means that air is being drawn into the hose (rather than escaping from it) and this makes leakage very difficult to detect. One method is to use an old length of vacuum hose as a kind of stethoscope – hold one end close to (but not in) your ear and use the other end to probe the area around the suspected leak. When the end of the hose is directly over a vacuum leak, a hissing sound will be heard clearly through the hose. Care must be taken to avoid contacting hot or moving components, as the engine must be running, when testing in this manner. Renew any vacuum hoses that are found to be defective.

5 Steering and suspension components check

Front suspension and steering

1 Raise the front of the vehicle, and securely support it on axle stands (see *Jacking and vehicle support*).

2 Visually inspect the balljoint dust covers and the steering rack-and-pinion gaiters for splits **(see illustration)**, chafing or deterioration. Any wear of these components will cause loss of lubricant, together with dirt and water entry, resulting in rapid deterioration of the balljoints or steering gear.

3 Check the power steering fluid hoses for chafing or deterioration, and the pipe and hose unions for fluid leaks. Also check for signs of fluid leakage under pressure from the steering gear rubber gaiters, which would indicate failed fluid seals within the steering gear.

4 Grasp the roadwheel at the 12 o'clock and 6 o'clock positions, and try to rock it **(see illustration)**. Very slight free play may be felt, but if the movement is appreciable, further investigation is necessary to determine the source. Continue rocking the wheel while an assistant depresses the footbrake. If the movement is now eliminated or significantly reduced, it is likely that the hub bearings are at fault. If the free play is still evident with the footbrake depressed, then there is wear in the suspension joints or mountings.

5 Now grasp the wheel at the 9 o'clock and 3 o'clock positions, and try to rock it as before **(see illustration)**. Any movement felt now may again be caused by wear in the hub bearings or the steering track rod balljoints. If the outer

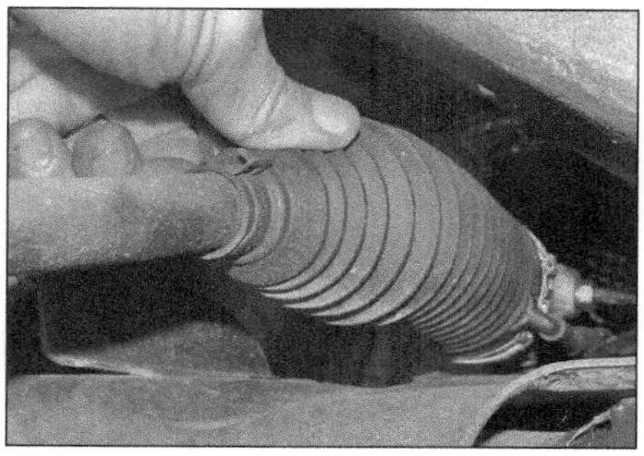

5.2 Check the steering rack gaiters for signs of damage or deterioration

5.4 Check for wear in the hub bearings by grasping the wheel and trying to rock it ...

5.5 ... and checking for wear in the steering rack and balljoints

6.1 Check the driveshaft gaiters for signs of damage or deterioration

balljoint is worn, the visual movement will be obvious. If the inner joint is suspect, it can be felt by placing a hand over the rack-and-pinion rubber gaiter and gripping the track rod. If the wheel is now rocked, movement will be felt at the inner joint if wear has taken place.

6 Using a large screwdriver or flat bar, check for wear in the suspension mounting bushes by levering between the relevant suspension component and its attachment point. Some movement is to be expected, as the mountings are made of rubber, but excessive wear should be obvious. Also check the condition of any visible rubber bushes, looking for splits, cracks or contamination of the rubber.

7 With the car standing on its wheels, have an assistant turn the steering wheel back-and-forth, about an eighth of a turn each way. There should be very little, if any, lost movement between the steering wheel and roadwheels. If this is not the case, closely observe the joints and mountings previously described. In addition, check the steering column universal joints for wear, and also check the rack-and-pinion steering gear itself.

8 The front suspension mountings should be checked for tightness.

Rear suspension

9 Chock the front wheels, then jack up the rear of the vehicle and support securely on axle stands (see *Jacking and vehicle support*).

10 Working as described previously for the front suspension, check the rear hub bearings, the suspension bushes and the strut or shock absorber mountings (as applicable) for wear.

8.1 Remove the air intake hose from above the filter

11 The rear suspension mountings should be checked for tightness.

Shock absorber

12 Check for any signs of fluid leakage around the shock absorber bodies, or from the rubber gaiters around the piston rods. Should any fluid be noticed, the shock absorber is defective internally, or the rubber gaiter is split, and may need renewing. **Note:** *Shock absorbers should always be renewed in pairs on the same axle.*

6 Driveshaft joints and gaiters check

1 With the front of the vehicle raised and securely supported on stands, turn the steering onto full lock then slowly rotate the roadwheel. Inspect the condition of the outer constant velocity (CV) joint rubber gaiters while squeezing the gaiters to open out the folds **(see illustration)**. Check for signs of cracking, splits or deterioration of the rubber, which may allow the grease to escape and lead to water and grit entry into the joint. Also check the security and condition of the retaining clips. Repeat these checks on the inner CV joints. If any damage or deterioration is found, the gaiters should be renewed as described in Chapter 8, Section 3.

2 At the same time check the general condition of the CV joints themselves by first holding the driveshaft and attempting to rotate the wheel. Repeat this check by holding the inner joint and attempting to rotate the driveshaft. Any appreciable movement indicates wear in the joints, wear in the driveshaft splines or a loose driveshaft retaining nut.

7 Hinges and locks lubrication

1 Work around the vehicle and lubricate the hinges of the bonnet, doors and tailgate with a light machine oil.

2 Lightly lubricate the two bonnet release locks with a smear of grease.

3 Check carefully the security and operation of all hinges, latches and locks. Check that the central locking system operates correctly.

4 Check the condition and operation of the bonnet and tailgate/boot lid struts, renewing them if either is leaking or no longer able to support the bonnet/tailgate/boot lid.

8 Fuel filter draining and renewal

Draining

1 The purpose of this operation is to purge the filter assembly of any accumulated water. Remove the plastic cover on the top of the engine. On 1.6 litre engines, also remove the air intake hose from the air filter lower housing **(see illustration)**.

2 Place a container underneath the filter, then slacken the fuel filter drain screw, and operate the hand priming pump a few times until all water or impurities cease to run out **(see illustrations)**. Tighten the drain screw.

3 Start the engine and run it at a fast idle speed (less than 2000 rpm) for 30 seconds. Refit the engine cover.

Renewal

1.6 litre engines

4 To make access easier, remove the battery cover and battery as described in Chapter 5A, Section 4.

5 Unclip the plastic trim cover from the top of the engine **(see illustration)**.

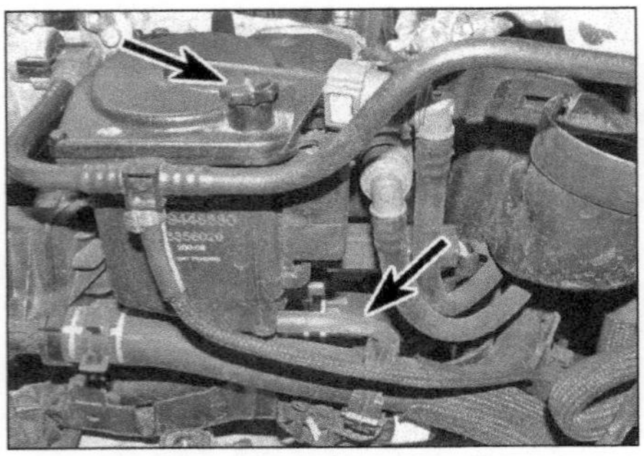

8.2a Vent screw and water drain hose (arrowed) – 1.6 litre engines

8.2b Bleed screw and water drain hose (arrowed) – 2.0 litre engines

8.5 Unclip the engine trim cover

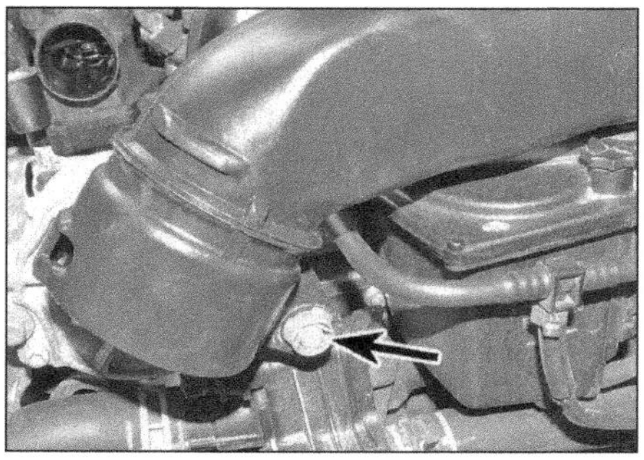

8.7a Release from the locating lug (arrowed) ...

8.7b ... and remove the air intake hose

8.8 Unscrew the brake fluid reservoir and move it to one side

6 Remove the air intake hoses from the front left-hand corner of the engine compartment to access the fuel filter **(see illustrations 3.8a, 3.8b and 3.8c)**.

7 Remove the upper part of the air filter housing as described in Section 21. Also release the air intake hose from its locating peg and unclip it from the air filter lower housing **(see illustrations)**

8 Undo the two retaining screws and move the brake fluid upper reservoir to one side **(see illustration).** Do not disconnect any pipes/hoses.

9 Disconnect the wiring connector from the fuel heater at the rear of the filter **(see illustration)**

8.9 Disconnect the wiring connector (arrowed)

8.10 Release the securing clips and disconnect the fuel lines (arrowed)

10 Place rags beneath the filter housing, and then disconnect the fuel pipes from the fuel filter, noting their fitted positions **(see illustration)**. Plug the openings to prevent contamination.

11 Release the retaining clip and lift the filter from the bracket on the end of the cylinder head **(see illustrations)**. As the filter is withdrawn, disconnect the wiring connector from the base of the fuel filter and disconnect the drain tube.

12 Release the clip and detach the fuel heater from the side of the filter assembly **(see illustrations)**.

13 Clip the fuel heater into place on the new filter. Fit the new filter into place, remove the plugs and reconnect the pipes, and the wiring plug.

14 Refit the upper part of the filter housing, air intake hoses and battery.

2.0 litre engines

15 Disconnect the battery negative lead (refer to precautions in Chapter 5A, Section 1), then remove the plastic cover from the top of the engine.

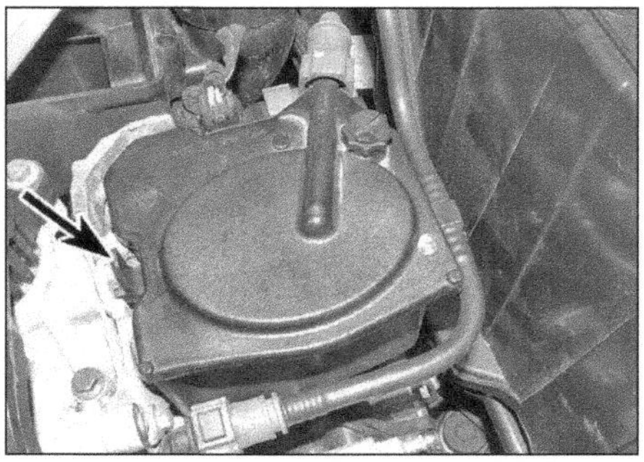

8.11a Release the clip (arrowed) ...

8.11b ... and slide the filter upwards from the mounting bracket

8.11c Disconnect the wiring connector and the drain tube (arrowed)

8.12a Release the clip (arrowed) ...

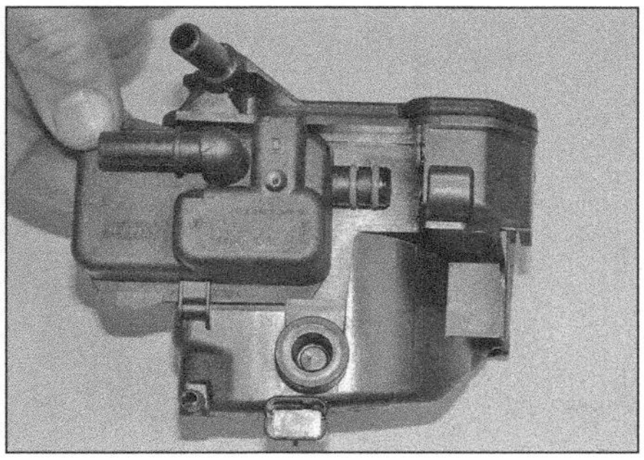

8.12b ... and slide the heater from the filter body

8.16 Slacken the drain screw at the base of the filter

8.17a Depress the release buttons, disconnect the fuel pipes and the wiring plug (arrowed)

8.17b Plug the ends to prevent contamination

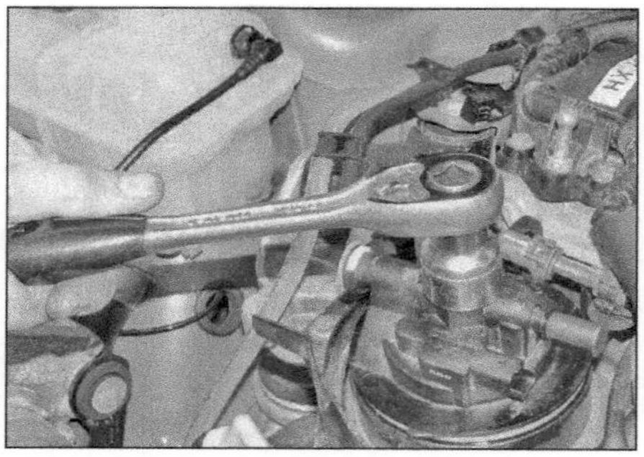

8.18 Use a socket to unscrew the filter head ...

8.19 ... then lift out the filter element

8.21a Renew the O-ring seal ...

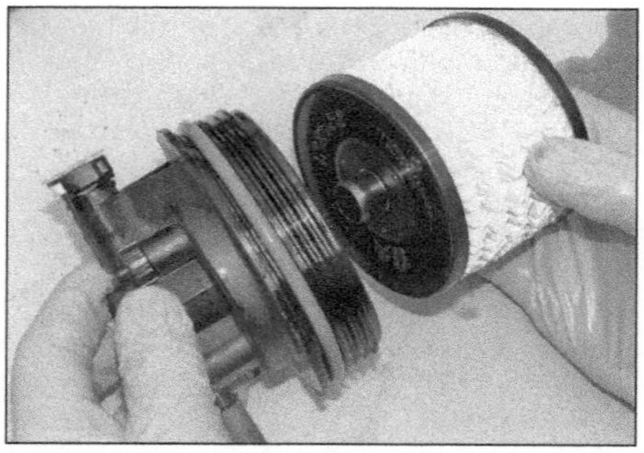

8.21b ... insert the new filter element into the filter head ...

16 Slacken the drain screw at the base of the filter and allow the filter to drain **(see illustration)**.

17 Thoroughly clean the area around the fuel pipe connectors, then disconnect the pipes and wiring connector (where applicable) at the top of the filter assembly **(see illustrations)**. Plug the openings to prevent contamination.

18 Using a 27 mm socket, unscrew the filter head **(see illustration)**.

19 Lift the filter head, and extract the filter element **(see illustration)**. Discard the seal on the filter head – a new one must be fitted.

20 Thoroughly clean the filter housing chamber using clean, lint-free rags.

21 Fit the new seal and filter element into the filter head, and then lubricate the new seal using clean fuel, and fit it in place on the filter head **(see illustrations)**.

22 Refit the filter head and tighten it until the filter head touches the stop **(see illustrations)**.

23 Remove the protective plugs, and then reconnect the fuel pipes/wiring plug to the filter housing.

All engines

24 Reconnect the battery negative lead (refer to precautions in Chapter 5A, Section 1).

25 Bleed the fuel system as described in Chapter 4B, Section 3.

8.22a ... and then refit the fuel filter housing ...

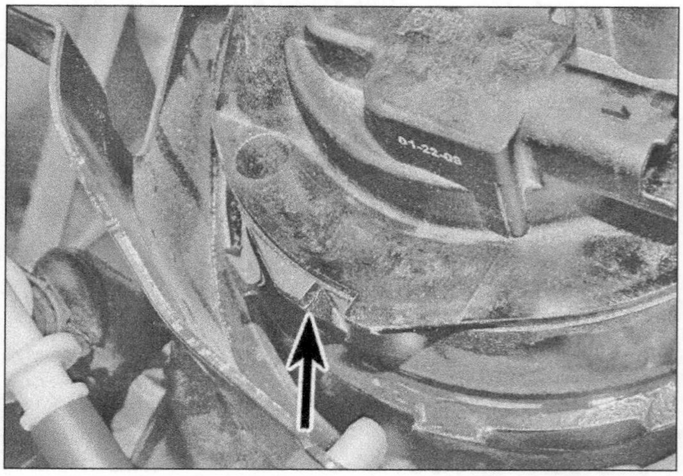

8.22b ... tighten filter head until it reaches the stop (arrowed)

9 Resetting the service indicator

1 The instrument cluster mileage recorder incorporates a service interval indicator. When the vehicle is started, the unit displays the mileage until the next service, or the mileage covered since the service was due. The service indicator is manually reset to zero after the vehicle has been serviced. The indicator can also be reset at any time using the Citroën diagnostic tool.

2 To manually reset the mileage to zero, carry out the following procedure:

a) *Switch off the ignition.*
b) *Press and hold down the trip/reset button on the instrument panel* ***(see illustration)****.*
c) *While the trip/reset button is held down, switch on the ignition.*
d) *Keep the trip/reset button pressed until zero appears and the maintenance symbol disappears.*
e) *Release the trip/reset button and switch off the ignition.*

3 Switch on the ignition – the distance remaining until (or covered since) the next service is due will flash in the display.

9.2 Service indicator trip/reset button (arrowed)

Every 20 000 miles or 2 years

10 Brake pad wear and disc check

1 The work described in this Section should be carried out at the specified intervals, or whenever a defect is suspected in the braking system. Any of the following symptoms could indicate a potential brake system defect:

a) *The vehicle pulls to one side when the brake pedal is depressed.*
b) *The brakes make squealing, scraping or dragging noises when applied.*
c) *Brake pedal travel is excessive, or pedal feel is poor.*
d) *The brake fluid requires repeated topping-up. Note that, because the hydraulic clutch shares the same fluid as the braking system, this problem could be due to a leak in the clutch system.*

Front disc brakes

2 Chock the rear wheels then loosen the front wheel bolts. Jack up the front of the vehicle, and support it on axle stands (see *Jacking and vehicle support*).

3 For better access to the brake calipers, remove the wheels **(see illustration)**.

4 Look through the inspection window in the caliper, and check that the thickness of the friction lining material on each of the pads is not less than the recommended minimum thickness given in the Specifications **(see Haynes hint)**. Bear in mind that the lining material is normally bonded to a metal backing plate. To differentiate between the metal and the lining material, it is helpful to turn the disc slowly at first – the edge of the disc can then be identified, with the lining material on each pad either side of it, and the backing plates behind.

5 If it is difficult to determine the exact thickness of the pad linings, or if you are at all concerned about the condition of the pads, then remove them from the calipers for further inspection (refer to Chapter 9, Section 4).

6 Check the other caliper in the same way.

7 If any one of the brake pads has worn down to, or below, the specified limit, *all four* pads at that end of the car must be renewed as a set **(see illustration)**. If the pads on one side are significantly more worn than the other, this may indicate that the caliper pistons have partially seized – refer to the brake pad renewal procedure in Chapter 9, Section 4, and push the pistons back into the caliper to free them.

8 Measure the thickness of the discs with a micrometer, if available, to make sure that they still have service life remaining. Do not be fooled by the lip of rust which often forms on the outer edge of the disc, which may make the disc appear thicker than it really is – scrape off the loose rust if necessary, without scoring the disc friction (shiny) surface.

9 If any disc is thinner than the specified minimum thickness, renew both (refer to Chapter 9, Section 6).

10 Check the general condition of the discs. Look for excessive scoring and discolouration caused by overheating. If these conditions exist, remove the relevant disc and have it resurfaced or renewed (refer to Chapter 9, Section 6).

11 Make sure that the transmission is in neutral. Spin the wheel, and check that the brake is not binding. Some drag is normal with a disc brake, but it should not require any great effort to turn the wheel – also, do not confuse brake drag with resistance from the transmission.

12 Before refitting the wheels, check all brake lines and hoses (refer to Chapter 9, Section 3). In particular, check the flexible hoses in the vicinity of the calipers, where they are subjected to most movement. Bend them between the fingers (but do not actually bend them double, or the casing may be damaged) and check that this does not reveal previously hidden cracks, cuts or splits.

13 On completion, refit the wheels and lower the car to the ground. Tighten the wheel bolts to the specified torque.

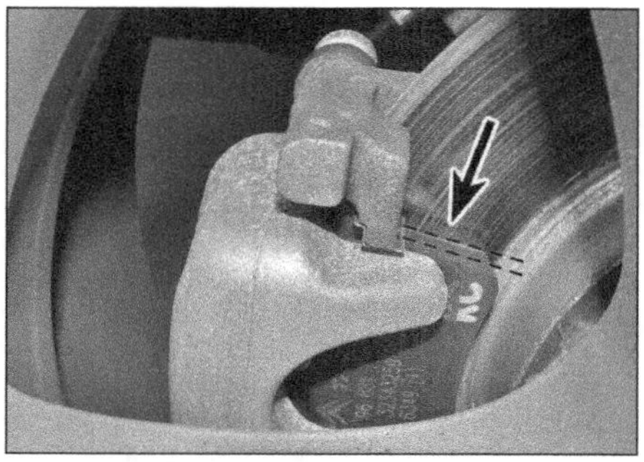

10.3 Checking brake pad thickness through alloy wheels

HAYNES HiNT

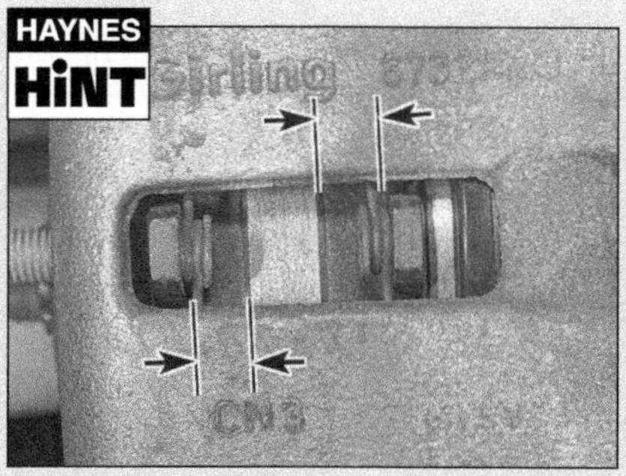

For a quick check, the thickness of the friction material on each brake pad can be measured through the aperture in the caliper body.

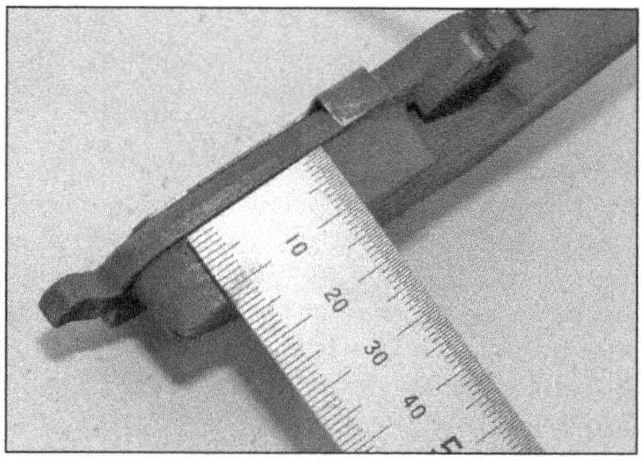

10.7 Check the thickness of the brake pad friction material

Rear disc brakes

14 Loosen the rear wheel bolts then chock the front wheels. Jack up the rear of the car, and support it on axle stands. Release the handbrake and remove the rear wheels.

15 The procedure for checking the rear brakes is much the same as described in paragraphs 2 to 13 above. Check that the rear brakes are not binding, noting that transmission resistance is not a factor on the rear wheels. Abnormal effort may indicate that the handbrake needs adjusting – see Chapter 9, Section 14.

11 Handbrake check and adjustment

1 To check the handbrake adjustment, apply normal moderate pressure and pull the handbrake lever to the fully applied position, counting the number of clicks emitted from the handbrake ratchet mechanism. If adjustment is correct, there should be 2 clicks before the brakes begins to apply, and no more than 6 before the handbrake is fully applied. If this is not the case, adjust as described in Chapter 9, Section 14.

12 Seat belt condition check

1 Working on each seat belt in turn, carefully examine the seat belt webbing for cuts, or for any signs of serious fraying or deterioration. Pull the belt all the way out, and examine the full extent of the webbing.

2 Fasten and unfasten the belt, ensuring that the locking mechanism holds securely, and releases properly when intended. Check also that the retracting mechanism operates correctly when the belt is released.

3 Check the security of all seat belt mountings and attachments, which are accessible from inside the vehicle without removing any trim or other components.

4 Check the function of the seat belt reminder lamp.

13 Airbag system check

1 The following work can be carried out by the home mechanic, however, if an electronic fault is apparent, it will be necessary to take the car to a Citroën dealer or specialist who will have the necessary diagnostic equipment to extract fault codes from the system.

2 Turn the ignition switch to the drive position (ignition warning lights on), and check that the airbag warning light is illuminated for approximately 6 seconds. After this period the light should go out, indicating that the system has been checked and is functioning correctly.

3 If the warning light remains on or refuses to light, have the system checked by a Citroën dealer or specialist.

4 Visually examine the steering wheel centre pad, knee airbag and the passenger airbag modules for external damage. Also check the exterior of the front seats around the side airbag locations. If damage is evident, consult a Citroën dealer or specialist.

5 In the interests of safety, make sure that there are no loose items inside the car, which could be thrown onto the airbag modules in the event of an accident.

14 Road test

Instruments and electrical equipment

1 Check the operation of all instruments and electrical equipment.

2 Make sure that all instruments read correctly, and switch on all electrical equipment in turn to check that it functions properly. Check the function of the heating, air conditioning and automatic climate control systems.

Steering and suspension

3 Check for any abnormalities in the steering, suspension, handling or road 'feel'.

4 Drive the vehicle, and check that there are no unusual vibrations or noises.

5 Check that the steering feels positive, with no excessive 'sloppiness', or roughness, and check for any suspension noises when cornering, or when driving over bumps. Check that the power steering system operates correctly.

Drivetrain

6 Check the performance of the engine, clutch (manual transmission), transmission and driveshafts.

7 Listen for any unusual noises from the engine, clutch (manual transmission) and transmission.

8 Make sure that the engine runs smoothly when idling, and that there is no hesitation when accelerating.

9 On manual transmission models, check that the clutch action is smooth and progressive, that the drive is taken up smoothly, and that the pedal travel is not excessive. Also listen for any noises when the clutch pedal is depressed. Check that all gears can be engaged smoothly, without noise, and that the gear lever action is smooth and not abnormally vague or 'notchy'.

10 On automatic transmission models, make sure that all gearchanges occur smoothly without snatching, and without an increase in engine speed between changes. Check that all the gear positions can be selected with the vehicle at rest. If any problems are found, they should be referred to a Citroën dealer.

11 Listen for a metallic clicking sound from the front of the vehicle, as the vehicle is driven slowly in a circle with the steering on full lock. Carry out this check in both directions. If a clicking noise is heard, this indicates wear in a driveshaft joint, in which case, refer to Chapter 8, Section 2.

Braking system

12 Make sure that the vehicle does not pull to one side when braking, and that the wheels do not lock when braking hard.

13 Check that there is no vibration through the steering when braking.

14 Check that the handbrake operates correctly, without excessive movement of the lever, and that it holds the vehicle stationary on a slope.

15 Test the operation of the brake servo unit as follows. With the engine off, depress the footbrake four or five times to exhaust the vacuum, and then start the engine while holding the brake pedal depressed. As the engine starts, there should be a noticeable 'give' in the brake pedal as vacuum builds-up. Allow the engine to run for at least two minutes, and then switch it off. If the brake pedal is now depressed again, it should be possible to detect a 'hiss' from the servo as the pedal is depressed. After about four or five applications, no further hissing should be heard, and the pedal should feel considerably harder.

15 Coolant antifreeze concentration check

1 The cooling system should be filled with the recommended antifreeze and corrosion protection fluid. Over a period of time, the concentration of fluid may be reduced due to topping-up (this can be avoided by topping-up with the correct antifreeze mixture) or fluid loss. If loss of coolant has been evident, it is important to make the necessary repair before adding fresh fluid. The exact mixture of antifreeze-to-water that you should use depends on the relative weather conditions. The mixture should contain at least 40% antifreeze, but not more than 70%. Consult the mixture ratio chart on the antifreeze container before adding coolant. Use antifreeze, which meets the vehicle manufacturer's specifications.

2 With the engine cold, carefully remove the cap from the expansion tank. If the engine is not completely cold, place a cloth rag over the cap before removing it, and remove it slowly to allow any pressure to escape.

3 Antifreeze checkers are available from car accessory shops. Draw some coolant from the expansion tank and observe how many plastic balls are floating in the checker **(see**

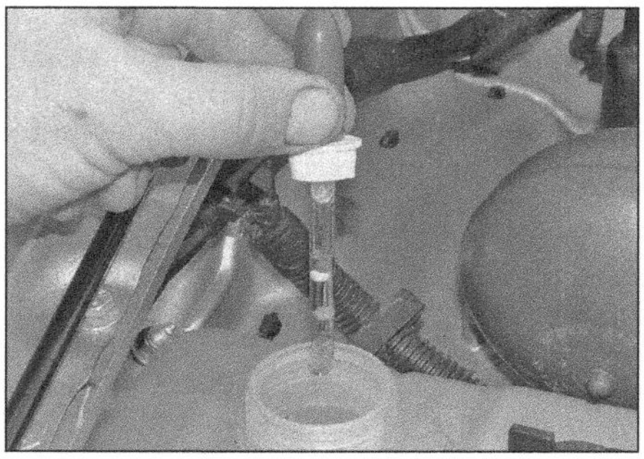

15.3 Check the antifreeze concentration with a hydrometer

illustration). Usually, 2 or 3 balls must be floating for the correct concentration of antifreeze, but follow the manufacturer's instructions.

4 If the concentration is incorrect, it will be necessary to either withdraw some coolant and add antifreeze, or alternatively drain the old coolant and add fresh coolant of the correct concentration.

16 Exhaust system check

1 With the engine cold, check the complete exhaust system, from its starting point at the engine to the end of the tailpipe. If necessary, raise the front and rear of the vehicle and support it on axle stands (see *Jacking and vehicle support*). Remove any engine undershields as necessary for full access to the exhaust system.

2 Check the exhaust pipes and connections for evidence of leaks, severe corrosion, and damage. Make sure that all brackets and mountings are in good condition and that all relevant nuts and bolts are tight **(see illustrations)**. Leakage at any of the joints or in other parts of the system will usually show up as a black sooty stain in the vicinity of the leak.

3 Rattles and other noises can often be traced to the exhaust system, especially the brackets and rubber mountings. Try to move the pipes and silencers. If the components are able to come into contact with the body or suspension parts, secure the system with new mountings. Otherwise separate the joints (if possible) and twist the pipes as necessary to provide additional clearance.

17 Auxiliary drivebelt check and renewal

1 On all engines, a single, multi-grooved auxiliary drivebelt is used to transmit drive from the crankshaft pulley to the alternator and the refrigerant compressor. The drivebelt is tensioned automatically by a spring-loaded tensioner pulley.

Check

2 For better access to the drivebelt, chock the rear wheels then jack up the front of the car and support it on axle stands (see *Jacking and vehicle support*). Remove the right-hand front roadwheel, and then remove the plastic liner from under the right-hand wheel arch to expose the crankshaft pulley.

3 Using a suitable socket and extension bar fitted to the crankshaft pulley bolt, rotate the crankshaft so that the entire length of the drivebelt(s) can be examined. Examine the drivebelt for cracks, splitting, fraying, or other damage **(see illustration)**. Check also for signs of glazing (shiny patches) and for separation of the belt plies.

16.2a Check the condition of the exhaust rubber mountings at the front ...

16.2b ... and the mountings along the length of the exhaust system

17.3 Check the condition of the auxiliary belt

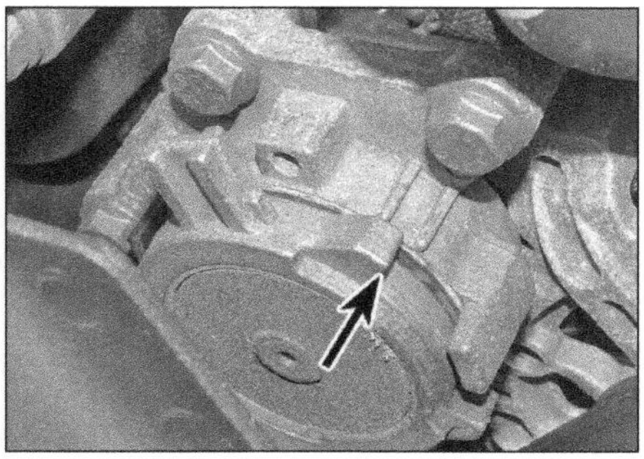

17.6 The alignment lug (arrowed) must be between the two lines on the housing

Renewal

1.6 litre engines

4 If not already done, proceed as described in paragraphs 2 and 3.

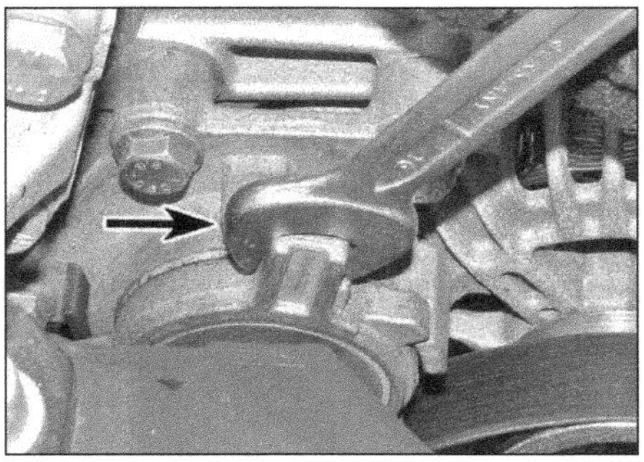

17.7 Rotate the tensioner arm clockwise, then lock it in place by inserting a 4 mm drill into the hole (hidden behind spanner) in the tensioner body (arrowed)

5 If the belt is to be refitted, mark its direction of normal rotation with a pen.

6 The automatic tensioner has markings, which align with each other when the belt is in serviceable condition. If the small lug is outside these lines then the belt will need to be renewed **(see illustration)**.

7 Using an open-ended spanner, reach down and rotate the tensioner arm clockwise to release the belt tension. Insert a 4 mm drill bit or rod into the hole in the tensioner body, so that the tensioner arm rests against it, and locks it in this position **(see illustration)**. It is usefull to have a small mirror available to enable the alignment of the locking holes to be more easily seen in the limited space available.

8 Manoeuvre the belt from the pulleys **(see illustration)**. Take the opportunity to check

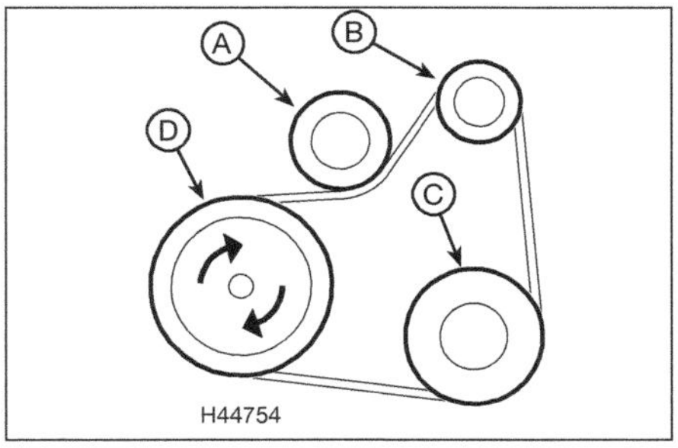

17.8 Auxiliary belt routing and adjustment (with air conditioning)

A Automatic tensioner
B Alternator pulley
C Air conditioning compressor pulley
D Crankshaft pulley

17.15 Insert a 4 mm drill bit/rod through the holes in the tensioner (arrowed)

the tensioner and idler pulleys spin freely, with no signs of roughness or slack.

9 Refit the belt around the pulleys, ensuring that the ribs on the belt are correctly engaged with the grooves in the pulleys, and the drivebelt is correctly routed. If refitting a used belt, use the marks made on removal to ensure it is fitted the correct way around.

Caution: Do not allow the tensioner pulley to spring forcefully onto the belt as this could result in damage.

10 Using an open-ended spanner, hold the tensioner arm so that the locking drill bit/rod can be removed, then release the pressure on the spanner so that the automatic tensioner takes up the slack in the drivebelt.

11 Refit the wheel arch liner and roadwheel, and then lower the vehicle to the ground.

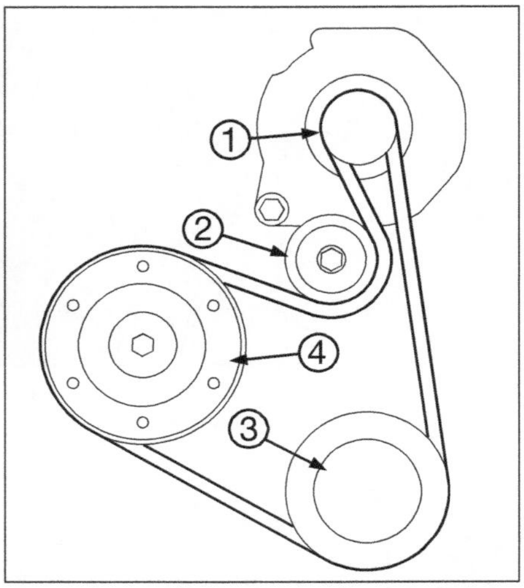

17.17 Auxiliary belt routing and adjustment (with air conditioning)

1 *Alternator pulley*
2 *Tensioner pulley bolt*
3 *Air conditioning compressor pulley*
4 *Crankshaft pulley*

2.0 litre engines

12 If not already done, proceed as described in paragraphs 2 and 3.

13 If the belt is to be refitted, mark its direction of normal rotation with a pen.

14 Using a spanner on the centre bolt, rotate the tensioner pulley, and slacken the belt.

15 Lock the tensioner in this position using a 4.0 mm drill bit through the holes in the tensioner **(see illustration)**.

16 Manoeuvre the belt from the pulleys. Take the opportunity to check the tensioner and idler pulleys spin freely, with no signs of roughness or slack.

17 Begin refitting by placing the belt on the pulleys, ensuring it's correctly located in grooves of the pulleys **(see illustration)**.

18 Hold the tensioner in place with the spanner, remove the locking drill bit, and slowly allow the tensioner pulley to rotate anti-clockwise and act against the belt. The belt is automatically tensioned by the spring-loaded tensioner.

19 Refit the wheel arch liner and roadwheel, and then lower the vehicle to the ground.

18 Pollen filter check and renewal

1 Open the bonnet and the pollen filter is positioned in the right-hand rear of the engine compartment.

2 Prise up the centre pins, lever out the complete plastic expanding rivets, and then remove the sound insulation trim covering the pollen filter cover **(see illustration)**.

3 Grasp the filter plastic cover and pull it, to release it from the bulkhead **(see illustrations)**.

4 Slide the filter out, noting its fitted position **(see illustration)**.

5 Check the condition of the filter, and renew it if dirty.

6 Wipe clean the inside of the housing and fit the pollen filter element, making sure that it is correctly seated.

7 Refit the pollen filter cover.

8 Refit the sound insulation trim, secure it in place with the plastic rivets and close the bonnet.

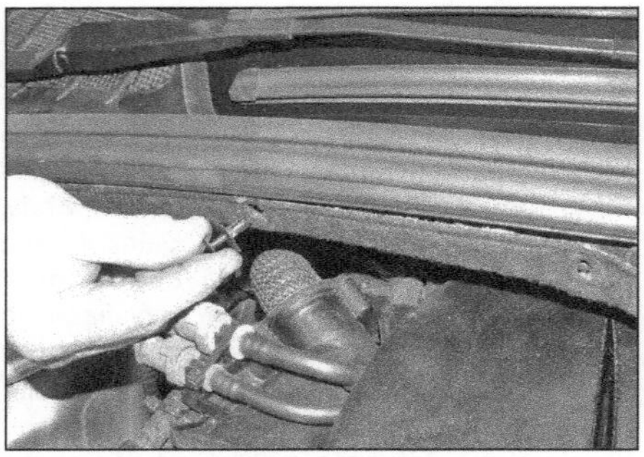

18.2a Remove the retaining clips ...

18.2a ... and the sound insulation material

18.3a Pull the filter cover (arrowed) ...

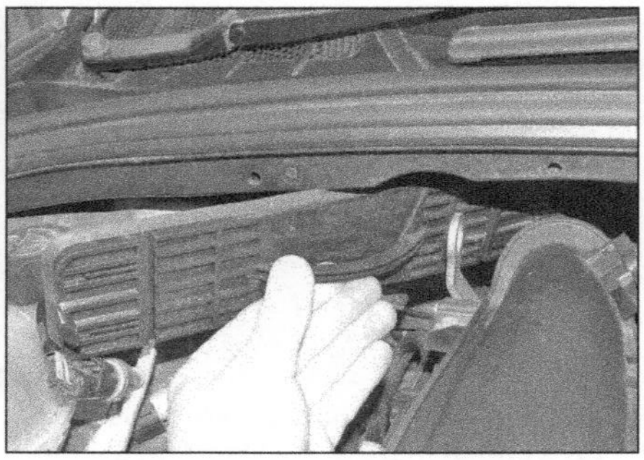

18.3b ... and withdraw it from the bulkhead

18.4 Slide the pollen filter out from the bulkhead

Every 40 000 miles or 2 years

19 Brake fluid renewal

Warning: Brake hydraulic fluid can harm your eyes and damage painted surfaces, so use extreme caution when handling and pouring it. Do not use fluid that has been standing open for some time, as it absorbs moisture from the air. Excess moisture can cause a dangerous loss of braking effectiveness.

Note: *A hydraulic clutch shares its fluid reservoir with the braking system, and will also need to be bled (see Chapter 6, Section 2).*

1 The procedure is similar to that for the bleeding of the hydraulic system as described in Chapter 9, Section 2, except that the brake fluid reservoir should be emptied by siphoning, using a clean ladle or similar before starting, and allowance should be made for the old fluid to be expelled when bleeding a section of the circuit.

2 Working as described in Chapter 9, Section 2, open the first bleed screw in the sequence, and pump the brake pedal gently until nearly all the old fluid has been emptied from the master cylinder reservoir.

3 Top-up to the MAX level with new fluid **(see illustration)**, and continue pumping until only the new fluid remains in the reservoir, and new fluid can be seen emerging from the bleed screw. Tighten the screw, and top the reservoir level up to the MAX level line.

4 Work through all the remaining bleed screws in the sequence until new fluid can be seen at all of them. Be careful to keep the master cylinder reservoir topped-up to above the MIN level at all times, or air may enter the system and increase the length of the task.

5 When the operation is complete, check that all bleed screws are securely tightened, and that their dust caps are refitted **(see illustration)**. Wash off all traces of spilt fluid, and recheck the master cylinder reservoir fluid level.

6 Check the operation of the brakes before taking the car on the road.

20 Coolant renewal

Warning: Do not allow antifreeze to come in contact with your skin or painted surfaces of the vehicle. Flush contaminated areas immediately with plenty of water. Don't store new coolant, or leave old coolant lying around, where it's accessible to children or pets – they're attracted by its sweet smell. Ingestion of even a small amount of coolant can be fatal. Wipe up garage-floor and drip pan spills immediately. Keep antifreeze containers covered, and repair cooling system leaks as soon as they're noticed.

Warning: Never remove the expansion tank filler cap when the engine is running, or has just been switched off, as the cooling system will be hot, and the consequent escaping steam and scalding coolant could cause serious injury.

Warning: Wait until the engine is cold before starting these procedures.

Cooling system draining

1 With the engine completely cold, remove the expansion tank filler cap. Turn the cap anti-clockwise, wait until any pressure remaining in the system is released, then unscrew it and lift it off.

2 Chock the rear wheels, and then raise the front of the vehicle and support it on axle stands (see *Jacking and vehicle support*). Undo the retaining bolts/nuts and remove the engine undershield.

3 Position a suitable container beneath the radiator lower hose outlet at the lower centre of the radiator.

4 Release the retaining clip and disconnect the radiator lower hose **(see illustration)**. Be prepared for coolant spillage.

1.6 litre engines

5 Open the bleed screws; there are two bleed screws, one on the heater hose at the bulkhead connection and one on the top of the thermostat housing at the left-hand side of the cylinder head **(see illustrations)**. **Note:**

19.3 Brake/clutch fluid level markings

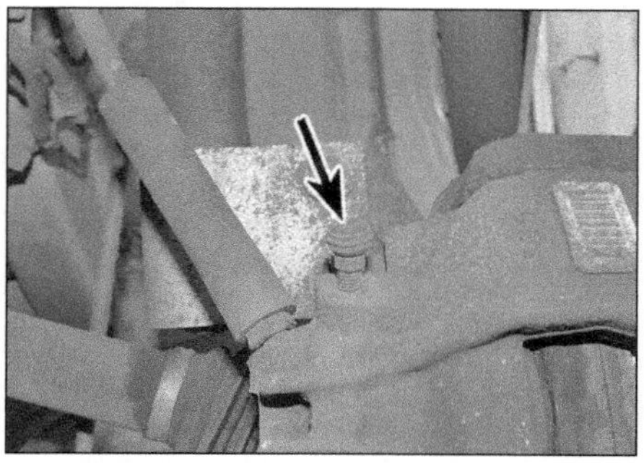

19.5 Make sure dust cap (arrowed) is refitted to bleed screw

20.4 Squeeze together the tabs to release the hose clamp

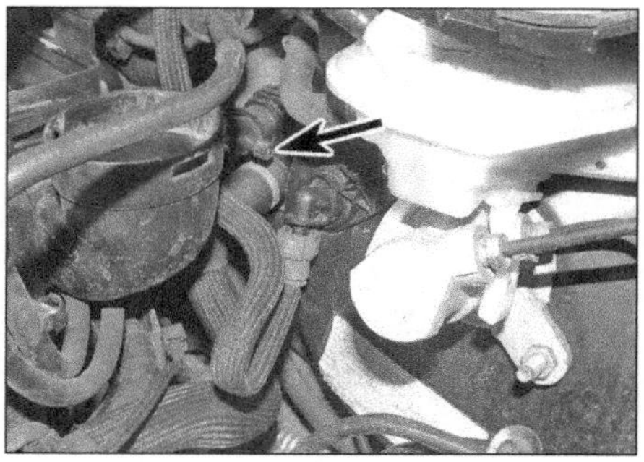

20.5a Undo the bleed screw from the heater hose union (arrowed) ...

20.5b ... and the bleed screw (arrowed) on the coolant housing – early models

20.5c ... later models have a return pipe (arrowed) to the reservoir

20.6 Prise out the retaining clip (arrowed) and pull out the coolant drain plug

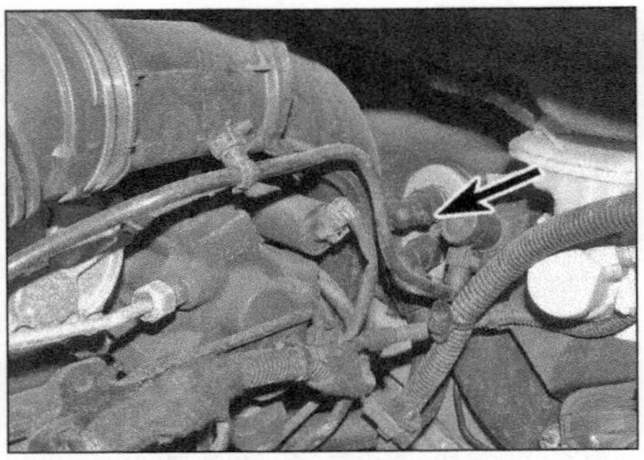

20.9a Undo the bleed screw from the heater hose union (arrowed)

20.9b ... and the bleed screw (arrowed) on the coolant housing – early models

On later models there is no bleed screw on the thermostat housing; the return pipe to the reservoir fits in its place.

6 To drain the cylinder block, pull out the clip and remove the plug located in the coolant housing at the rear of the engine **(see illustration)**. The plug must be refitted with a new clip and O-ring.

7 Once the coolant has finished draining, refit the plug, and reconnect the bottom hose. If the coolant has been drained for a reason other than renewal, then provided it is clean and less than two years old, it can be re-used, though this is not always recommended.

8 Refit the engine undershield, and then lower the vehicle to the ground.

2.0 litre engine

9 Open the bleed screws; there are two bleed screws, one on the heater hose at the bulkhead connection and one on the top of the thermostat housing at the left-hand side of the cylinder head **(see illustrations)**. **Note:** *On later models there is no bleed screw on the thermostat housing; the return pipe to the reservoir fits in its place.*

10 Although a cylinder block drain plug is fitted to the rear of the cylinder block, access to the plug is extremely limited. We found it impossible to undo the plug with the engine fitted **(see illustration)**.

11 Once the coolant has finished draining, refit the plug, and reconnect the bottom hose. If the coolant has been drained for a reason other than renewal, then provided it is clean and less than two years old, it can be re-used, though this is not always recommended.

12 Refit the undershield, and then lower the vehicle to the ground.

Cooling system flushing

13 If coolant renewal has been neglected, or if the antifreeze mixture has become diluted, then in time, the cooling system may gradually lose efficiency, as the coolant passages become restricted due to rust, scale deposits, and other sediment. The cooling system efficiency can be restored by flushing the system clean.

14 The radiator should be flushed separately from the engine, to avoid excess contamination.

Radiator flushing

15 Disconnect the top and bottom hoses and any other relevant hoses from the radiator (see Chapter 3, Section 4).

16 Insert a garden hose into the radiator top inlet. Direct a flow of clean water through the radiator, and continue flushing until clean water emerges from the radiator bottom outlet.

17 If after a reasonable period, the water still does not run clear, the radiator can be flushed with a good proprietary cleaning agent. It is important that their manufacturer's instructions are followed carefully. If the contamination is particularly bad, insert the hose in the radiator bottom outlet, and reverse-flush the radiator.

Engine flushing

18 To flush the engine, remove the thermostat (see Chapter 3, Section 5). If the radiator top hose has been disconnected, temporarily reconnect the hose. **Note:** *This may not be possible on some models, as the thermostat may be part of the coolant housing on the end of the cylinder head.*

19 With the bottom hose disconnected from the radiator, insert a garden hose into the coolant housing. Direct a clean flow of water through the engine, and continue flushing until clean water emerges from the radiator bottom hose.

20 When flushing is complete, refit the thermostat and reconnect the hoses (see Chapter 3, Section 5).

Cooling system filling

21 Before attempting to fill the cooling system, make sure that all hoses and clips are in good condition, and that the clips are tight. Note that an antifreeze mixture must be used all year round, to prevent corrosion of the engine components (see following sub-Section).

22 Make sure that the air conditioning (A/C) or automatic climate control (ACC) is switched off. This is to prevent the air conditioning system starting the radiator cooling fan before the engine is at normal temperature when refilling the system.

23 Remove the expansion tank filler cap and remove the cooling system bleed screws (see paragraphs 5 or 9).

24 Citroën recommend the use of a 'header tank' when refilling the cooling system, to reduce the possibility of air being trapped in the system. Although Citroën dealers use a special header tank which screws onto the expansion tank, the same effect can be achieved by using a suitable 1.0 litre bottle, with a seal between the bottle and the expansion tank **(see illustration)**.

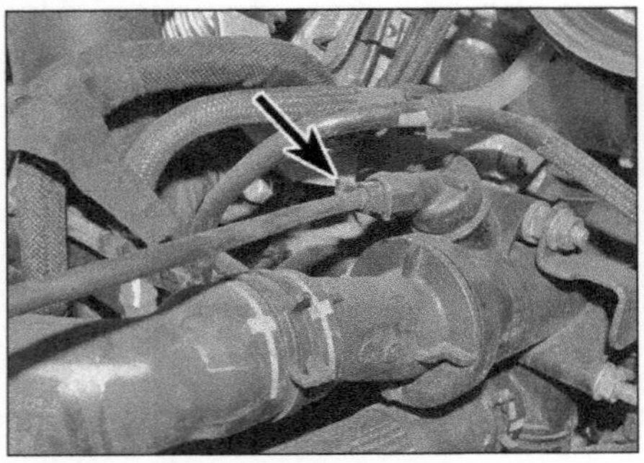

20.9c ... later models have a return pipe (arrowed) to the reservoir

20.10 Access to the cylinder block drain plug (arrowed) is limited

20.24 Using a 1.0 litre plastic bottle as a header tank

25 Fit the header tank to the expansion tank and slowly fill the system whilst observing the bleed holes. Coolant will emerge from each of the bleed holes in turn, starting with the heater matrix hose. As soon as coolant free from air bubbles emerges from the heater matrix hose outlet, securely refit the cap/screw (as applicable) then watch the bleed hole on the coolant housing. Once coolant free from air bubbles emerges from the housing hole, refit the bleed screw and sealing washer and tighten securely.

26 Continue to fill the cooling system until bubbles stop appearing in the expansion tank. Help to bleed the air from the system by repeatedly squeezing the radiator bottom hose.

27 When no more bubbles appear, ensure the header tank is full (at least 1.0 litre of coolant) then start the engine. Run the engine at a fast idle speed (do not exceed 2000 rpm) until the cooling fan cuts in and out TWICE, then when the fan has stopped for the second time, switch the engine off.

Caution: The coolant will be hot. Take great care not to scald yourself.

28 Allow the engine to cool, and then remove the 'header tank' from the reservoir. Wash off any spilt coolant with cold water.

29 When the engine has cooled, check the coolant level with reference to *Weekly checks*. Top-up the level if necessary, and refit the expansion tank cap.

Antifreeze mixture

30 The antifreeze should always be renewed at the specified intervals. This is necessary not only to maintain the antifreeze properties, but also to prevent corrosion, which would otherwise occur as the corrosion inhibitors become progressively less effective.

31 Always use an ethylene glycol based antifreeze, which is suitable for use in mixed-metal cooling systems.

32 Before adding antifreeze, the cooling system should be completely drained, preferably flushed, and all hoses checked for condition and security.

33 After filling with antifreeze, a label should be attached to the expansion tank, stating the type and concentration of antifreeze used, and the date installed. Any subsequent topping-up should be made with the same type and concentration of antifreeze.

Caution: Do not use engine antifreeze in the windscreen/tailgate washer system, as it will cause damage to the vehicle paintwork. A screenwash additive should be added to the washer system in the quantities stated on the bottle.

21 Air filter element renewal

1.6 litre engines

1 Pull the plastic cover upwards from the top of the engine **(see illustration 8.5)**.

2 Slacken the securing clips from each end of the air intake ducting to the turbocharger, release the breather tube clips and remove the air ducting **(see illustrations)**.

21.2a Slacken the air cleaner retaining clip (arrowed) ...

21.2b ... and the retaining clip (arrowed) on the turbo ...

21.2c ... release the securing clip ...

21.2d ... and remove the air intake hose

21.3 Disconnect the wiring connector

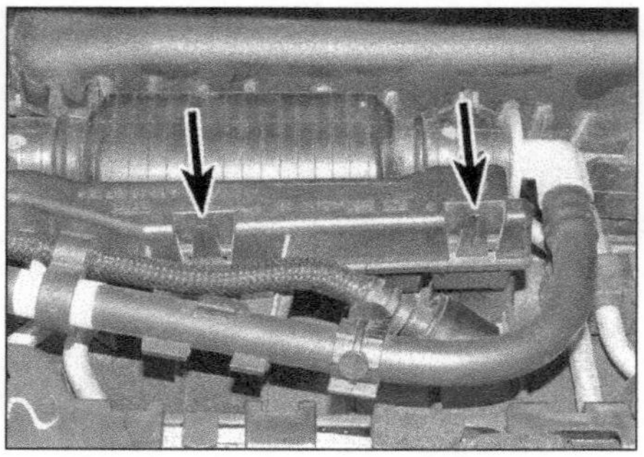
21.4a Release the two locking clips (arrowed) ...

21.4b ... and move the priming pump to one side

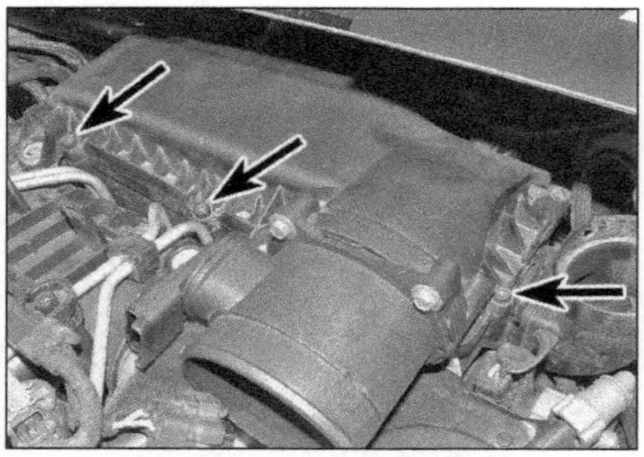
21.5a Undo the retaining screws (arrowed) ...

21.5b ... and remove the upper housing

21.6 Remove the air filter element

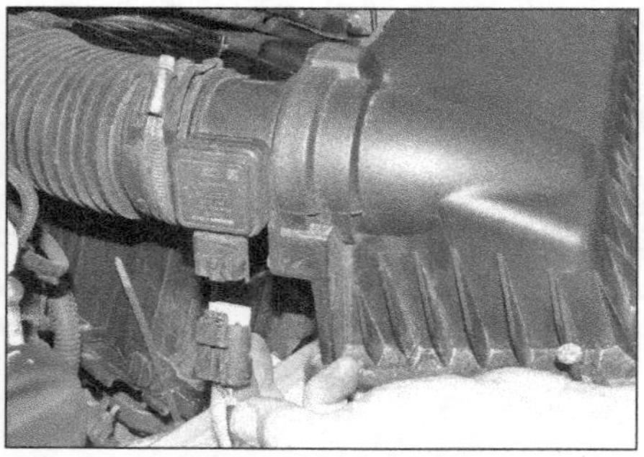
21.10 Disconnect the wiring connector

3 Disconnect the wiring plug connector from the mass airflow sensor **(see illustration)**.

4 Release the retaining clips and move the fuel priming pump to one side to access the air filter cover retaining screws **(see illustration)**.

5 Undo the air filter cleaner cover retaining screws, and lift the cover from air filter housing **(see illustrations)**.

6 Note which way round the air filter element is fitted, and then lift it out from the housing **(see illustration)**.

7 Wipe clean the inner surfaces of the cover and main housing, then locate the new element in the housing, making sure that the sealing lip is correctly engaged with the edge of the housing.

8 Refit the filter cover/intake ducting assembly, ensuring the rear edge of the cover engages correctly with the rear of the filter housing.

9 Connect the wiring plug to the airflow sensor, and then refit the plastic cover to the top of the engine.

2.0 litre engines

10 Disconnect the mass airflow sensor wiring plug **(see illustration)**.

11 Slacken the securing clip from the air intake ducting and disconnect it from the upper part of the air filter housing **(see illustration)**.

12 Undo the 4 retaining screws, and lift the cover from place **(see illustration)**.

13 Lift the air filter element from place, noting which way around it's fitted **(see illustration)**.

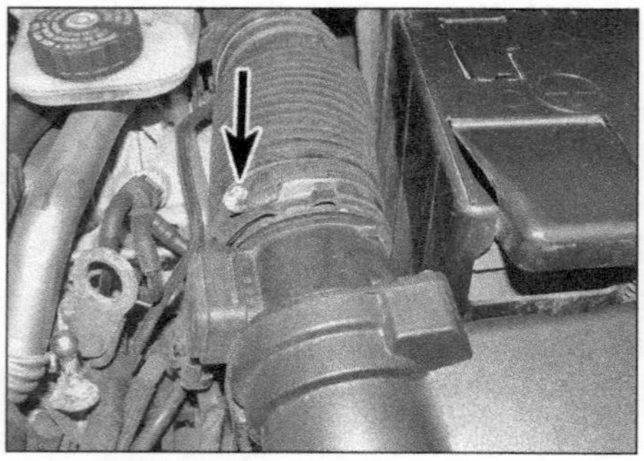
21.11 Slacken the air cleaner retaining clip (arrowed) ...

21.12 Undo the retaining screws (arrowed), remove the upper housing

21.13 ... and withdraw the air filter element

22.3 Remove the inner wheel arch liner

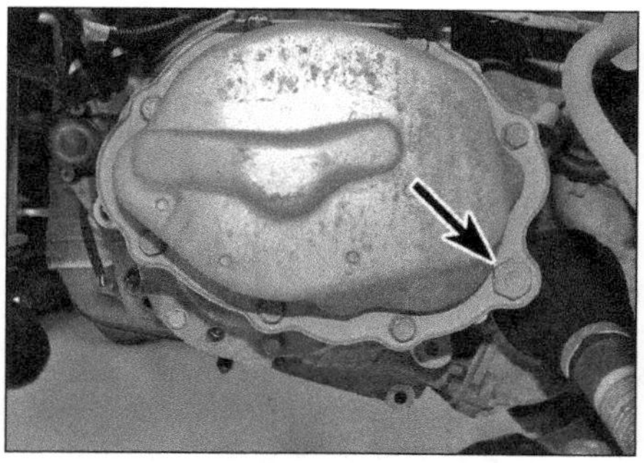

22.4 Fluid level/filler plug (arrowed) – BE4/5 transmission

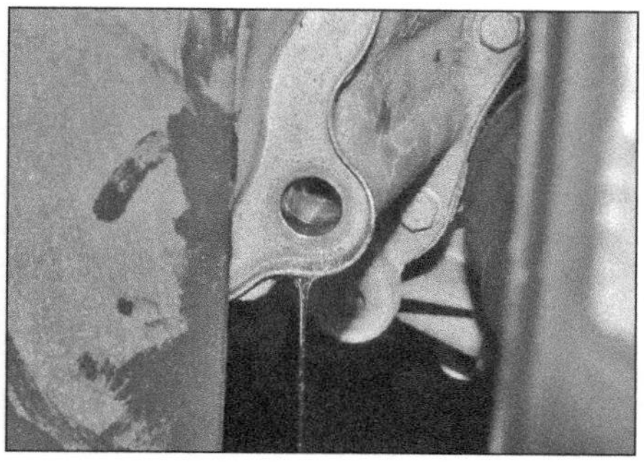

22.5 Add oil until a continuous trickle emerges from the plug hole

14 Wipe clean the inner surfaces of the cover and main housing, then locate the new element in the housing, making sure that the sealing lip is correctly engaged with the edge of the housing.
15 Refit the cover, and secure it with the screws.
16 Reconnect the mass airflow sensor wiring plug.

22 Manual transmission oil level check

Note: *There is no specific recommendation in the manufacturer's schedule to check the oil level on 6-speed transmissions. They are described as 'Lubricated for life'. However, we consider it prudent to check the oil level, as a leak from the driveshaft oil seal or sealing washer could cause expensive damage. On these transmissions, there is also no level plug. If it is suspected the oil level is low, drain and refill the transmission as described in Chapter 7A, Section 2.*
Note: *On later 5-speed transmissions there is also no filler/level plug fitted. These transmissions do not require regular maintenance and are filled for life. If the transmission develops a leak or is removed for other work, the oil needs to be completely drained and refilled with the correct amount of oil. Refer to Chapter 7A, Section 2.*
Note: *A suitable square-section wrench may be required to undo the transmission filler/level plug on some models. These wrenches can be obtained from most motor factors or your Citroën dealer. A new sealing washer will be required for the transmission filler/level plug when refitting.*

Early 5-speed transmissions

1 Take the car on a short journey to warm the transmission up to normal operating temperature. Position the car over an inspection pit, or alternatively jack up the front and rear of the car and support on axle stands (see *Jacking and vehicle support*). Whichever method is used, make sure that the car is level for checking the fluid level later.
2 The oil level must be checked at least 5 minutes after the engine has been switched off. If the oil is checked immediately after driving the car, some of the oil will remain distributed around the transmission, resulting in an inaccurate level reading.
3 Remove the left-hand front wheel, and then release the fasteners and remove the wheel arch liner **(see illustration)**.
4 Wipe clean the area around the filler/level plug, which is on the left-hand end of the transmission. Unscrew the plug and clean it; discard the sealing washer **(see illustration)**.
5 The oil level should reach the lower edge of the filler/level hole. A certain amount of oil will have gathered behind the filler/level plug, and will trickle out when it is removed; this does not necessarily indicate that the level is correct. To ensure that a true level is established, wait until the initial trickle has stopped, then add oil as necessary until a trickle of new oil can be seen emerging **(see illustration)**. The level will be correct when the flow ceases; use only good-quality oil of the specified type (see *Lubricants and fluids*).
6 Filling the transmission with oil is an extremely awkward operation; above all, allow plenty of time for the oil level to settle properly before checking it. If a large amount is added to the transmission, and a large amount flows out on checking the level, refit the filler/level plug and take the vehicle on a short journey so that the new oil is distributed fully around the transmission components, then recheck the level when it has settled again.
7 If the transmission has been overfilled so that oil flows out as soon as the filler/level plug is removed, Check that the car is completely level (front-to-rear and side-to-side), allow the surplus to drain off into a container.
8 When the level is correct, fit a new sealing washer to the filler/level plug. Refit the plug, tightening it to the specified torque setting. Wash off any spilt oil then refit the wheel arch liner, securing it in position with the fasteners. Refit the roadwheel and tighten to the specified torque setting.
9 Frequent need for topping-up indicates a leak, which should be found and corrected before it becomes serious.

23 Automatic transmission fluid level check

Note: *The transmission unit is equipped with a fluid wear sensor to inform the driver when the fluid needs renewing (the ECU flashes the Sport and Snow mode indicator lights when fluid renewal is necessary). Every time the transmission unit is topped-up, this sensor should be adjusted to compensate for the new fluid being added, however this can only be done using the Citroën diagnostic test box. Adding fluid without adjusting the sensor will not cause any problems but will mean the sensor is giving an inaccurate reading, resulting in fluid renewal being recommended earlier than is necessary.*
1 Take the vehicle on a short journey, to warm the transmission up to normal operating temperature, and then park the vehicle on level ground. Firmly apply the handbrake and place the selector lever in the P position.
2 Wipe clean the area around the filler plug, which is situated on the top of the transmission, directly beneath the battery. Remove the battery and battery tray/box as described in Chapter 5A, Section 4, then unscrew the filler plug from the transmission and recover the sealing washer **(see illustration)**.
3 Carefully add 0.5 litre of the specified type of fluid to the transmission via the filler plug aperture. Fit a new sealing washer to the filler

23.2 Transmission filler plug – AM6 transmission

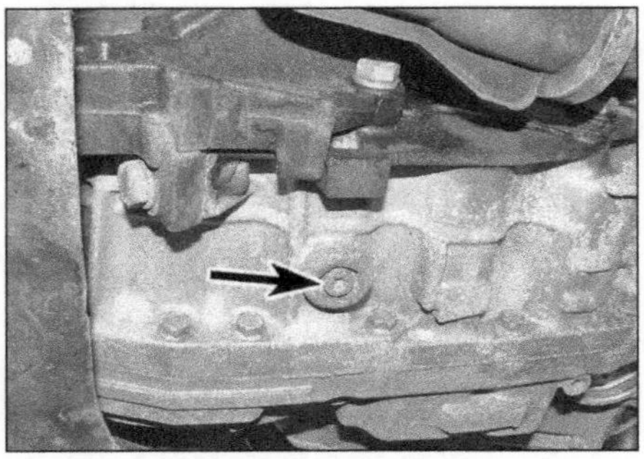

23.5 The level plug is the smaller plug (arrowed) – AM6 transmission

plug then refit the plug, tightening it to the specified torque.

4 Undo the screws and remove the engine undershield – where fitted.

5 Position a suitable container under the drain/level plug arrangement, situated on the base of the transmission **(see illustration)**. **Note:** *The drain/level plug is in two parts, the smaller plug in the centre of the drain plug is the level plug.*

Caution: Do not remove the drain plug by mistake.

6 Refit the battery and battery tray/box as described in Chapter 5A, Section 4.

7 Start the engine and allow it to idle. With the engine running, slacken and remove the level plug and sealing washer. Note the vehicle must be kept completely level for this procedure (front-to-rear and side-to-side).

Warning: The fluid will be hot, take precautions against scalding.

8 If there is sufficient fluid in the transmission unit, fluid should trickle out the centre of the drain plug before slowing to a drip. **Note:** *If no fluid trickles out, or just a few drips appear when the plug is removed, the fluid level is too low. Refit the level plug then switch off the engine. Add a further 0.5 litre of fluid to the transmission then refit the filler plug and repeat the check.*

9 Once the flow of fluid stops, the level is correct. Fit a new sealing washer to the level plug then refit the plug and tighten it to the specified torque. Switch off the engine.

24 Remote control battery renewal

1 Refer to Chapter 11, Section 17, for the renewal of the remote control battery.

Every 80 000 miles or 8 years

25 Particulate filter fluid check

1 Eolys 176 and DPX42 fluid is an additive used on vehicles equipped with a particulate filter incorporated into the exhaust system.

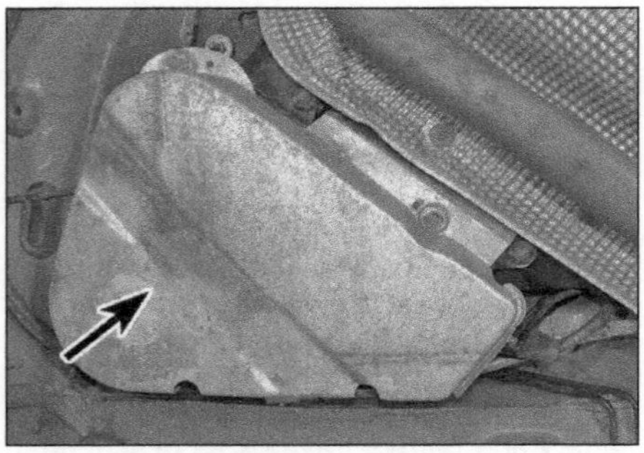

25.1 Particle filter additive fluid tank

Over a period of time, the soot produced by the engine will clog the filter. When the filter requires cleaning, the engine management system injects a small quantity of fuel into the combustion chamber after combustion has taken place. The unburnt fuel enters the exhaust system, where it ignites, and burns the soot deposits from the particulate filter. In order to lower the temperature at which the soot is burnt, Eolys fluid is added to the fuel in the tank. The fluid is stored in a separate tank adjacent to the fuel tank **(see illustration)**, and added to the main fuel tank. Every time the fuel tank is filled, the system computes how much Eolys fluid to add. Eventually the level of fluid will fall below a minimum level and a warning light will illuminate on the instrument cluster.

2 If the system runs out of fluid, the particulate filter will be unable to purge, causing its blockage, and premature failure. Unfortunately, the process of checking the level, replenishing the Eolys fluid tank and resetting the engine management values requires access to Citroën diagnostic equipment, and therefore must be entrusted to a Citroën dealer or suitably-equipped specialist. Failure to reset the ECU values will prevent the filter cleaning process from occurring.

26 Particulate filter renewal

Renewal of the particulate filter is described in Chapter 4B, Section 18.

27 Timing belt renewal

Refer to Chapter 2C, Section 7 for 1.6 litre engines or Chapter 2D, Section 7 for 2.0 litre engines.

Every 15 years

28 Airbags and seat belt pretensioners renewal

1 Citroën recommends that the airbags and seat belt pretensioners be renewed regardless of their condition within fifteen years. Refer to Chapter 12, Section 22 for airbag renewal, and Chapter 11, Section 24 for seat belt pretensioner renewal.

Chapter 2 Part A:
Non-VTi petrol engines in-car repair procedures

Contents

Degrees of difficulty

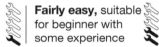

Easy, suitable for novice with little experience	**Fairly easy,** suitable for beginner with some experience	**Fairly difficult,** suitable for competent DIY mechanic	**Difficult,** suitable for experienced DIY mechanic	**Very difficult,** suitable for expert DIY or professional

Specifications

Engine (general)

Capacity:	
1.4 litre engine	1360cc
1.6 litre engine	1587cc
Designation:	
1.4 litre engine	ET3J4
1.6 litre engine	TU5JP4
Engine codes:*	
1.4 litre engine	KFU
1.6 litre engine	NFU
Bore:	
1.4 litre engine	75.00 mm
1.6 litre engine	78.50 mm
Stroke:	
1.4 litre engine	77.00 mm
1.6 litre engine	82.00 mm
Direction of crankshaft rotation	Clockwise (viewed from right-hand side of vehicle)
No 1 cylinder location	At transmission end of the block
Compression ratio	11.1 : 1
Emission standard	Euro 4
Maximum power output:	
1.4 litre engine	65 kW (90 hp) @ 5250 rpm
1.6 litre engine	80 kW (110 hp) @ 5800 rpm
Maximum torque output:	
1.4 litre engine	133 Nm @ 4250 rpm
1.6 litre engine	147 Nm @ 4000 rpm

** The engine code is situated on front, left-hand end of the cylinder block.*

Camshafts

Drive	Toothed belt

Valves

Valve clearances	Hydraulic adjusters

Lubrication system

Oil pump type	Gear type, chain-driven off the crankshaft
Minimum oil pressure at 80°C:	
1000 rpm	1.5 bars
2000 rpm	3.0 bars
4000 rpm	4.0 bars
Oil pressure warning switch operating pressure	0.8 bars

Torque wrench settings

Torque wrench settings	Nm	lbf ft
Battery tray retaining bolts/nuts	20	15
Big-end bearing cap nuts:*		
1.4 litre engine:		
Stage 1	30	22
Stage 2	Angle-tighten a further 45°	
1.6 litre engine	40	30
Camshaft bearing housing to cylinder head	10	7
Camshaft sprocket retaining bolt(s):		
1.4 litre engine:		
Exhaust sprocket retaining bolt	45	33
Intake sprocket retaining bolt:		
Stage 1	20	15
Stage 2	60	44
Intake sprocket retaining bolt cover	40	30
1.6 litre engine	45	33
Crankshaft oil seal housing bolts	8	6
Crankshaft pulley retaining bolts	25	18
Crankshaft sprocket retaining bolt:*		
Stage 1	40	30
Stage 2	Angle-tighten a further 45°	
Cylinder head bolts:		
1.4 litre engine:		
Stage 1	15	11
Stage 2	25	18
Stage 3	Angle-tighten a further 200°	
1.6 litre engine:		
Stage 1	20	15
Stage 2	Angle-tighten a further 260°	
Cylinder head cover bolts	10	7
Driveplate bolts*	67	49
Engine-to-transmission bolts:		
Manual transmission:		
MA5	45	33
BE4/5	54	40
Automatic transmission	52	38
Engine/transmission left-hand mounting:		
Mounting centre nut	65	48
Mounting-to-bracket nuts	30	22
Mounting bracket-to-body bolts	19	14
Mounting bracket-to-manual transmission nuts	25	18
Mounting bracket-to-automatic transmission nuts	40	30
Engine/transmission rear mounting:		
Mounting link-to-mounting bracket bolt	55	41
Mounting link-to-subframe bolt	40	30
Mounting support plate-to-sump bolts	20	15
Engine/transmission right-hand mounting:		
Support bracket:to engine	45	33
Mounting bracket to support bracket	60	44
Mounting bolts to body	60	44
Flywheel bolts*	70	52
Intake sprocket retaining bolt:		
Stage 1	20	15
Stage 2	60	44
Main bearing cap bolts (1.6 litre engine):		
Stage 1	20	15
Stage 2	Angle-tighten a further 49°	
Main bearing ladder casting (1.4 litre engine):		
M11 bolts:		
Stage 1	20	15
Stage 2	Angle-tighten a further 44°	
M6 bolts	8	6

Torque wrench settings (continued)

	Nm	lbf ft
Oil filter	25	18
Oil filter housing to engine block (1.6 litre engine)	10	7
Oil pressure switch	20	15
Oil pump retaining bolts	9	7
Piston oil jet spray tube bolts	10	7
Roadwheel bolts	90	66
Sump drain plug	30	22
Sump retaining nuts and bolts	8	6
Timing belt cover bolts	8	6
Timing belt tensioner pulley nut:		
1.4 litre engine	20	15
1.6 litre engine	22	16

** Do not re-use*

1 General information

How to use this Chapter

1 This Chapter describes those repair procedures that can reasonably be carried out on the petrol engine while it remains in the car. If the engine has been removed from the car and is being dismantled, as described in Chapter 2E, any preliminary dismantling procedures can be ignored.

2 Note that, while it may be possible physically to overhaul items such as the piston/connecting rod assemblies while the engine is in the car, such tasks are not normally carried out as separate operations. Usually, several additional procedures (not to mention the cleaning of components and of oilways) have to be carried out. For this reason, all such tasks are classed as major overhaul procedures, and are described in Chapter 2E.

3 Chapter 2E describes the removal of the engine/transmission from the vehicle, and the full overhaul procedures that can then be carried out.

Petrol engine description

4 The petrol engines in this Chapter are from the TU and ET series, and are well-proven engines, which have been fitted to many previous Peugeot and Citroën vehicles. 1.4 and 1.6 litre double overhead camshaft (DOHC) 16-valve, in-line four cylinder engines are fitted, being mounted transversely at the front of the car with the transmission attached to the left-hand end.

5 Both 1.4 and 1.6 litre engines have similar cylinder heads and repair procedures are identical, except in the area of the hydraulic followers. On the 1.6 litre, the camshaft operates directly on the hydraulic followers which are located in the cylinder head beneath the camshaft. On the 1.4 litre, the valves are operated by roller rocker arms between the camshaft and the tops of the valves – one end of the rocker arm is clipped to the hydraulic follower and the other end rests on top of the valve stem. The valve clearances are self-adjusting by means of hydraulic followers in the cylinder head.

6 The crankshaft runs in five main bearings. Thrustwashers are fitted to No 2 main bearing (upper half) to control crankshaft endfloat.

7 The connecting rods rotate on horizontally split bearing shells at their big ends. The pistons are attached to the connecting rods by gudgeon pins, which are an interference fit in the connecting rod small-end eyes. The aluminium-alloy pistons are fitted with three piston rings – two compression rings and an oil control ring.

8 On 1.4 litre engines, the cylinder block is made of aluminium, and wet liners are fitted to the cylinder bores. Sealing O-rings are fitted at the base of each liner, to prevent the escape of coolant into the sump.

9 On 1.6 litre engines, the cylinder block is made from cast-iron, and the cylinder bores are an integral part of the cylinder block. On this type of engine, the cylinder bores are sometimes referred to as having dry liners.

10 The intake and exhaust valves are each closed by coil springs, and operate in guides pressed into the cylinder head; the valve seat inserts are also pressed into the cylinder head, and can be renewed separately if worn.

11 The camshafts are driven by a timing belt, and operate the 16 valves. The camshafts rotate directly in the cylinder head and are retained by a one-piece bearing housing. The belt also drives the coolant pump.

12 Lubrication is by means of an oil pump, which is driven (via a chain and sprocket) off the right-hand end of the crankshaft. It draws oil through a strainer located in the sump, and then forces it through an externally mounted filter into galleries in the cylinder block/crankcase. From there, the oil is distributed to the crankshaft (main bearings) and camshaft. The big-end bearings are supplied with oil via internal drillings in the crankshaft, while the camshaft bearings also receive a pressurised supply. On 1.6 litre engines, piston cooling oil spray jets are fitted to spray oil on the underside of each piston. The camshaft lobes and valves are lubricated by splash, as are all other engine components.

Operations with engine in car

13 The following work can be carried out with the engine in the car:

a) Compression pressure – testing.
b) Cylinder head cover – removal and refitting.
c) Timing belt covers – removal and refitting.
d) Timing belt – removal, refitting and adjustment.
e) Timing belt tensioner and sprockets – removal and refitting.
f) Camshaft oil seals – renewal.
g) Camshafts and rocker arms/followers – removal, inspection and refitting.
h) Cylinder head – removal and refitting.
i) Cylinder head and pistons – decarbonising.
j) Sump – removal and refitting.
k) Oil pump – removal, overhaul and refitting.
l) Crankshaft oil seals – renewal.
m) Engine/transmission mountings – inspection and renewal.
n) Flywheel/driveplate – removal, inspection and refitting.

2 Compression test – description and interpretation

1 When engine performance is down, or if misfiring occurs which cannot be attributed to the ignition or fuel systems, a compression test can provide diagnostic clues as to the engine's condition. If the test is performed regularly, it can give warning of trouble before any other symptoms become apparent.

2 The engine must be fully warmed-up to normal operating temperature, the battery must be fully charged. The aid of an assistant will also be required.

3 Remove the ignition HT coil assembly (see Chapter 5B, Section 3) then remove the spark plugs (see Chapter 1A, Section 20).

4 Fit a compression tester to the No 1 cylinder spark plug hole – the type of tester which screws into the plug thread is to be preferred.

5 Have the assistant hold the throttle wide open, and crank the engine on the starter motor; after one or two revolutions, the compression pressure should build-up to a maximum figure, and then stabilise. Record the highest reading obtained.

6 Repeat the test on the remaining cylinders, recording the pressure in each.

7 All cylinders should produce very similar pressures; a difference of more than 2 bars between any two cylinders indicates a fault. Note that the compression should build-up quickly in a healthy engine; low compression on the first stroke, followed by gradually increasing pressure on successive strokes, indicates worn piston rings. A low compression reading on the first stroke, which does not build-up during successive strokes, indicates leaking valves or a blown head gasket (a cracked head could also be the cause). Deposits on the undersides of the valve heads can also cause low compression.

8 Although Citroën do not specify exact compression pressures, as a guide, any cylinder pressure of below 10 bars can be considered as less than healthy. Refer to a Citroën dealer or other specialist if in doubt as to whether a particular pressure reading is acceptable.

9 If the pressure in any cylinder is low, carry out the following test to isolate the cause. Introduce a teaspoonful of clean oil into that cylinder through its spark plug hole, and repeat the test.

10 If the addition of oil temporarily improves the compression pressure, this indicates that bore or piston wear is responsible for the pressure loss. No improvement suggests that leaking or burnt valves, or a blown head gasket, may be to blame.

11 A low reading from two adjacent cylinders is almost certainly due to the head gasket having blown between them; the presence of coolant in the engine oil will confirm this.

12 If one cylinder is about 20 percent lower than the others and the engine has a slightly rough idle; a worn camshaft lobe could be the cause.

13 If the compression reading is unusually high, the combustion chambers are probably coated with carbon deposits. If this is the case, the cylinder head should be removed and decarbonised.

14 On completion of the test, refit the spark plugs and ignition HT coil (see Chapter 1A, Section 20 and Chapter 5B, Section 3).

3 Engine assembly/valve timing holes – general information and usage

Note: *Do not attempt to rotate the engine whilst the crankshaft/camshaft are locked in position. If the engine is to be left in this state for a long period of time, it is a good idea to place warning notices inside the vehicle, and in the engine compartment. This will reduce the possibility of the engine being accidentally cranked on the starter motor, which is likely to cause damage with the locking pins in place.*

1 On 1.4 and 1.6 litre models, timing holes are drilled in the camshaft sprockets and in the rear of the flywheel/driveplate. The holes are used to ensure that the crankshaft and camshafts are correctly positioned when assembling the engine (to prevent the possibility of the valves contacting the pistons when refitting the cylinder head), or refitting the timing belt. When the timing holes are aligned with access holes in the cylinder head and the front of the cylinder block, suitable diameter bolts/pins can be inserted to lock both the camshaft and crankshaft in position, preventing them from rotating. Proceed as follows.

2 Remove the timing belt upper cover as described in Section 5.

3 Turn the crankshaft until the holes in the camshaft sprockets align with the corresponding holes in the cylinder head. The crankshaft can be turned by using a spanner on the crankshaft sprocket bolt, noting that it should always be rotated in a clockwise direction (viewed from the right-hand end of the engine).

4 With the camshaft sprocket holes correctly positioned, insert a 6 mm diameter stud or pin, 90 mm long, welded to a length of weld rod bent to the appropriate shape, through the hole in the front left-hand flange of the cylinder block, and locate it in the timing hole in the rear of the flywheel/driveplate **(see illustrations)**. A purpose-made Citroën tool No 0132-QY is available from dealers. Note that it may be necessary to rotate the crankshaft slightly to get the holes to align.

5 With the crankshaft correctly positioned, insert suitable bolts or pins through the timing holes in the camshaft sprockets, and locate them in the holes in the cylinder head **(see illustrations)**. **Note:** *The holes on all engines is 8 mm diameter except for the intake camshaft sprocket hole on 1.4 litre engines which is 5 mm.*

6 The crankshaft and camshaft are now locked in position, preventing unnecessary rotation.

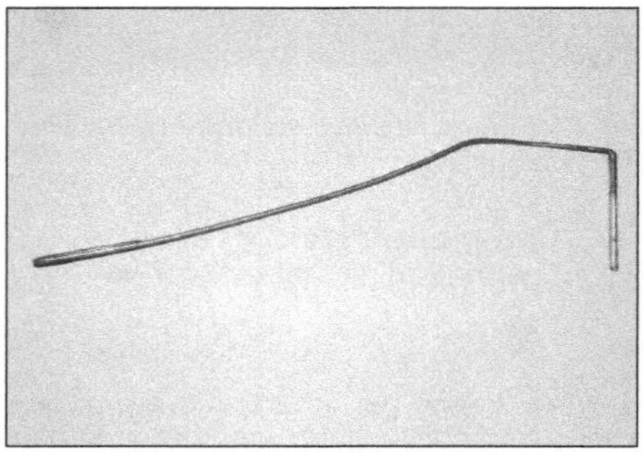

3.4a Weld a 90 mm length of 6 mm rod/stud to a length of weld rod ...

3.4b ... and insert it into the hole in the cylinder block flange (arrowed)

3.5a Use suitable bolts/pins (arrowed) to lock the camshaft sprockets in position (1.6 litre engine)

3.5b Lock the camshaft sprockets in position using 5 mm and 8 mm diameter drill bits/bolts (1.4 litre engine)

4 Cylinder head cover – removal and refitting

Removal

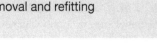

1 Disconnect the battery (refer to precautions in Chapter 5A, Section 1), and remove the ignition coil as described in Chapter 5B, Section 3.

2 Working in a spiral pattern, progressively and evenly slack the cylinder head cover bolts, and remove the covers. Recover the gaskets.

Refitting

3 Carefully clean the cylinder head and cover mating surfaces, and remove all traces of oil.

4 Check the condition of the cover's composite gasket, and re-use it if undamaged. If it is damaged, a repair may be effected using silicone sealing compound.

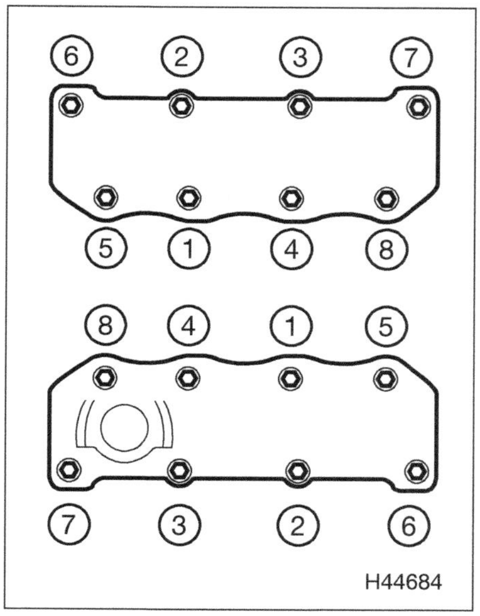

4.5 Cylinder head cover bolts tightening sequence

5 Refit the cover(s) and tighten the bolts in sequence **(see illustration)**.
6 Refit the ignition coils (Chapter 5B, Section 3).
7 Reconnect the battery.

5 Timing belt covers – removal and refitting

1 Firmly apply the handbrake, and then jack up the front of the vehicle and support it on axle stands (see *Jacking and vehicle support*). Undo the bolts/nuts and remove the engine undershield.

Removal

Upper cover

2 Position a trolley jack under the engine, with a block of wood between the jack head and the sump to prevent damage. Raise the jack to take the weight of the engine.
3 Slacken the right-hand engine mounting bolts, and then remove the mounting and brackets from the end of the engine **(see illustrations)**.

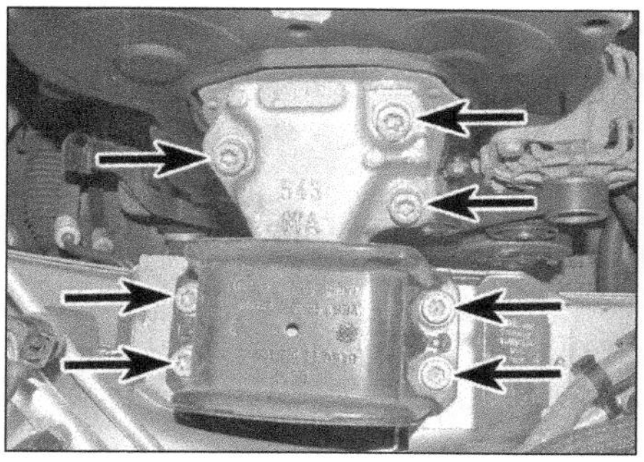

5.3a Undo the bolts (arrowed) securing the mounting and bracket ...

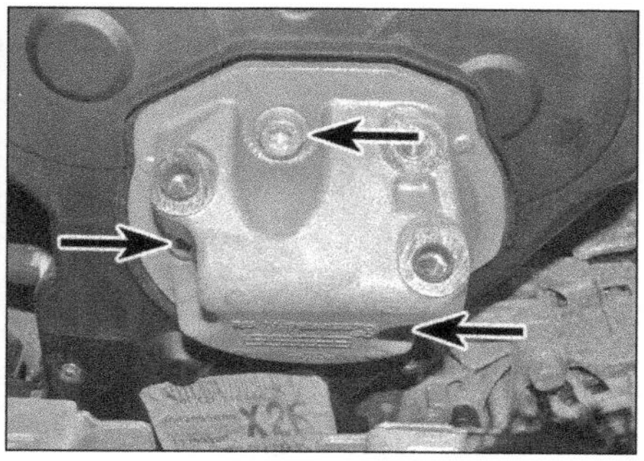

5.3b ... and the bolts (arrowed) securing the bracket to the engine

4 Slacken the two lower bolts, then undo the five upper bolts and remove the upper timing belt cover **(see illustration)**.

Lower cover

5 Remove the upper cover as described previously.
6 Remove the auxiliary drivebelt as described in Chapter 1A, Section 10.
7 Undo the three crankshaft pulley retaining bolts and remove the pulley, noting which way round it is fitted **(see illustrations)**.
8 Slacken and remove the retaining bolts then remove the lower cover from the engine **(see illustration)**.

Inner cover

9 Remove the camshaft sprockets and tensioner pulley as described in Section 7.
10 Undo the bolts and remove the inner cover **(see illustration)**.

Refitting

Upper cover

11 Refitting is the reverse of removal.

Lower cover

12 Locate the lower cover over the timing belt sprocket, and tighten its retaining bolts.
13 Fit the pulley to the end of the crankshaft, ensuring it is fitted the correct way round, and tighten its bolts to the specified torque.
14 Refit the upper cover as described above.
15 Refit and tension the auxiliary drivebelt as described in Chapter 1A, Section 10.

Inner cover

16 Refitting is a reversal of removal.

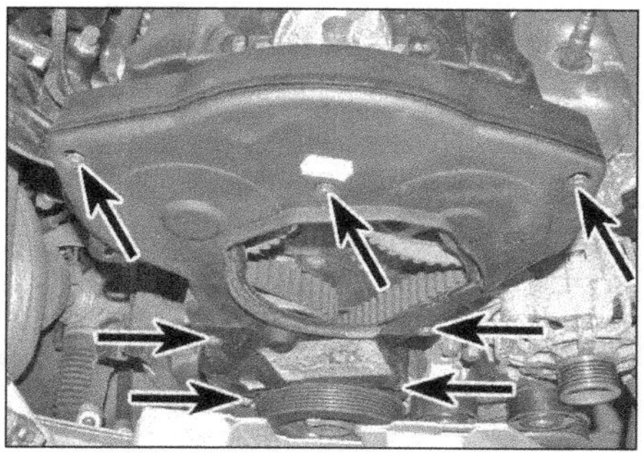

5.4 Undo the screws (arrowed) and remove the upper timing belt cover

5.7a Undo the retaining bolts (arrowed) ...

5.7b ... and remove the crankshaft pulley

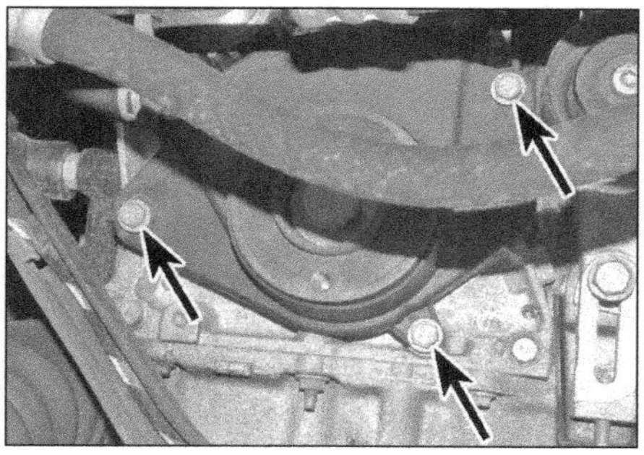

5.8 Unscrew the bolts (arrowed) and remove the timing belt lower cover

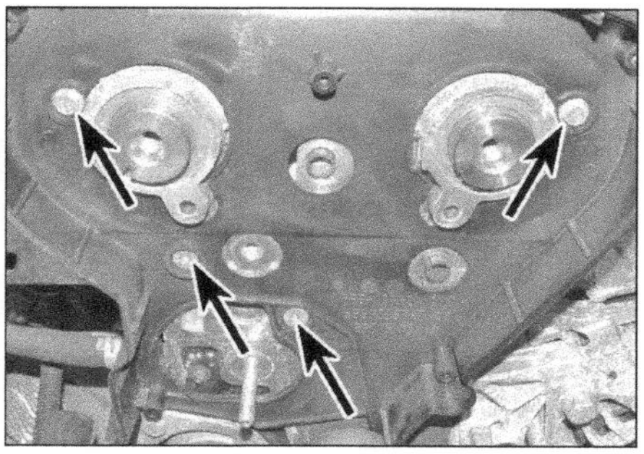

5.10 Undo the bolts (arrowed) and remove the inner cover (1.6 litre engine)

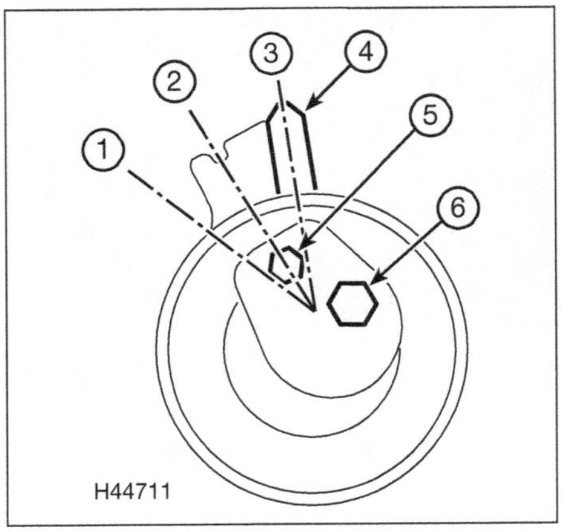

6.7 Timing belt tensioner

1 *Minimum tension position*
2 *Normal tension position*
3 *Maximum tension position*
4 *Index arm*
5 *Hole for hexagonal key*
6 *Tensioner pulley nut*

6 Timing belt – general information, removal and refitting

General information

1 The timing belt drives the camshafts and coolant pump from a toothed sprocket on the front of the crankshaft. If the belt breaks or slips in service, the pistons are likely to hit the valve heads, resulting in extensive (and expensive) damage.

2 The timing belt should be renewed at the specified intervals, or earlier if it is contaminated with oil or if it is at all noisy in operation (a 'scraping' noise due to uneven wear).

3 If the timing belt is being removed, it is a wise precaution to check the condition of the coolant pump at the same time (check for signs of coolant leakage). This may avoid the need to remove the timing belt again at a later stage, should the coolant pump fail.

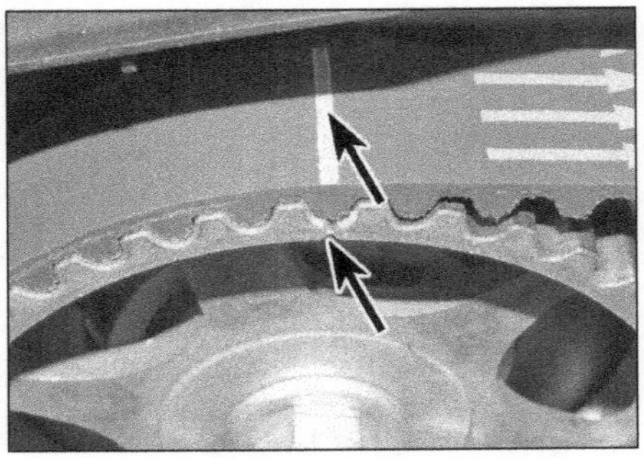

6.11 Note the timing belt marks which correspond to the camshaft sprockets and crankshaft sprocket

Removal

4 Disconnect the battery (refer to precautions in Chapter 5A, Section 1).

5 Align the engine assembly/valve timing holes as described in Section 3, and lock both the camshaft sprockets and the flywheel/driveplate in position.

Caution: Do not attempt to rotate the engine whilst the locking tools are in position.

6 Remove the timing belt lower cover as described in Section 5.

7 Slacken the timing belt tensioner pulley retaining nut and, using a hexagonal key, rotate the pulley clockwise until the index arm is in the minimum tension position **(see illustration)**. Temporarily tighten the tensioner pulley nut in this position.

8 If the timing belt is to be re-used, use white paint or similar to mark the direction of rotation on the belt (if markings do not already exist). Slip the belt off the sprockets.

9 Check the timing belt carefully for any signs of uneven wear, splitting, or oil contamination. Pay particular attention to the roots of the teeth. Renew the belt if there is the slightest doubt about its condition. If the engine is undergoing an overhaul, and has covered more than 40 000 miles with the existing belt fitted, renew the belt as a matter of course, regardless of its apparent condition. The cost of a new belt is nothing when compared to the cost of repairs should the belt break in service. If signs of oil contamination are found, trace the source of the oil leak, and rectify it. Wash

7.4 Use an open-ended spanner to counterhold the camshaft whilst slackening the bolt

down the engine timing belt area and all related components, to remove all traces of oil.

10 Prior to refitting, thoroughly clean the timing belt sprockets. Check that the tensioner pulley rotates freely, without any sign of roughness. If necessary, renew the tensioner pulley as described in Section 7. Make sure that the locking tools are still in place, as described in Section 3.

Refitting

11 Manoeuvre the timing belt into position, ensuring that the arrows on the belt are pointing in the direction of rotation (clockwise, when viewed from the right-hand end of the engine). Note that there are three marks on a new belt, which correspond to marks on the crankshaft and camshaft sprockets **(see illustration)**.

12 Do not twist the timing belt sharply while refitting it. Fit the belt over the crankshaft and camshaft sprockets aligning the marks on the belt with those on the crankshaft and camshaft sprockets. Make sure that the 'front run' of the belt is taut – ie, ensure that any slack is on the tensioner pulley side of the belt. Fit the belt over the coolant pump sprocket and tensioner pulley. Ensure that the belt teeth are seated centrally in the sprockets.

13 Insert the hexagonal key on the tensioner pulley, slacken the pulley nut and rotate the key to bring the index arm to the maximum tension position **(see illustration 6.7)**. Tighten the tensioner roller nut securely.

14 Remove the camshaft and crankshaft locking tools, and rotate the crankshaft 4

7.8a Remove the retaining bolt and washer ...

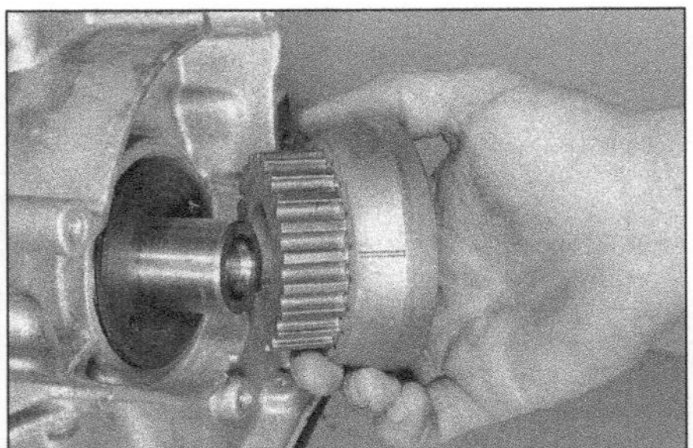

7.8b ... then slide off the crankshaft sprocket

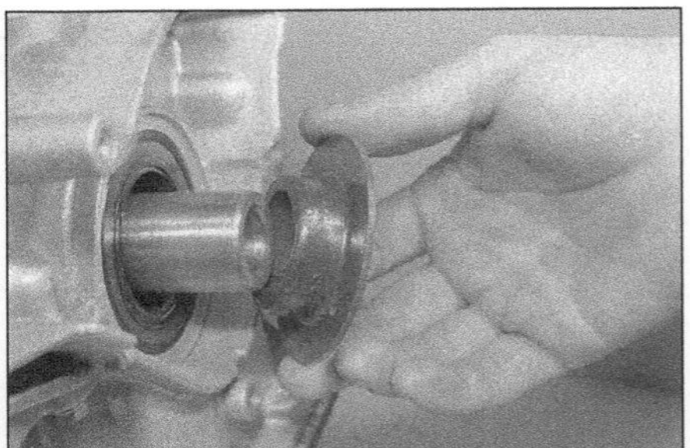

7.9 Remove the Woodruff key and flanged spacer (where fitted) from the crankshaft

complete revolutions clockwise, and refit the crankshaft locking tool.

15 Insert the hexagon key in the tensioner, slacken the nut and rotate the tensioner using the key, until the index arm is in the normal tension position **(see illustration 6.7)**. Tighten the tensioner nut to the specified torque.

16 Remove the crankshaft locking tool, and rotate the crankshaft two complete revolutions clockwise. Check the position of the tensioner index arm – it should be no more than 2.0 mm away from the normal tension position. If it is not, repeat the belt fitting procedure from Paragraph 11.

17 The remainder of refitting is a reversal of removal.

7 Timing belt tensioner and sprockets – removal, inspection and refitting

Removal

Camshaft sprockets

1 Remove the cylinder head covers as described in Section 4.

2 Remove the timing belt as described in Section 6.

3 Withdraw the crankshaft and camshaft locking tools, and using a spanner or socket on the crankshaft pulley bolt, rotate the crankshaft backwards (anti-clockwise) 90°. This is to prevent any accidental contact between the pistons and valves.

4 Using an open-ended spanner on the square section to counterhold the camshaft, undo the sprocket retaining bolt **(see illustration)**.

Caution: Do not attempt to use the sprocket locking pin to prevent the sprocket from rotating whilst the bolt is slackened.

5 With the retaining bolt removed, slide the sprocket off the end of the camshaft. Note that the key is integral with the sprocket. Examine the camshaft oil seals for signs of oil leakage and, if necessary, renew it as described in Section 8.

Crankshaft sprocket

6 Remove the timing belt as described in Section 6.

7 Slacken the crankshaft sprocket bolt. To prevent crankshaft rotation on manual transmission models, select top gear, and have an assistant apply the brakes firmly. If the engine has been removed from the vehicle or the vehicle is equipped with an automatic transmission unit, it will be necessary to lock the flywheel/driveplate (see Section 14).

Caution: Do not be tempted to use the flywheel/driveplate locking pin to prevent the crankshaft from rotating; temporarily remove the locking pin prior to slackening the pulley bolt, then refit it once the bolt has been slackened.

8 Unscrew the retaining bolt and washer, then slide the sprocket off the end of the crankshaft **(see illustrations)**.

9 If the Woodruff key is a loose fit in the crankshaft, remove it and store it with the sprocket for safekeeping. If necessary, also slide the flanged spacer (where fitted) off the end of the crankshaft **(see illustration)**. Examine the crankshaft oil seal for signs oil leakage and, if necessary, renew as described in Section 13.

Tensioner pulley

10 Remove the lower timing belt cover (see Section 5).

11 Lock the camshaft and crankshaft at TDC on No 1 cylinder as described in Section 3.

12 Slacken and remove the timing belt tensioner pulley retaining nut, and slide the pulley off its mounting stud. Examine the mounting stud for signs of damage and, if necessary, renew it.

Inspection

13 Clean the sprockets thoroughly, and renew any that show signs of wear, damage or cracks.

14 Clean the tensioner assembly, but do not use any strong solvent which may enter the pulley bearing. Check that the pulley rotates freely about its hub, with no sign of stiffness or of free play. Renew the tensioner pulley if there is any doubt about its condition, or if there are any obvious signs of wear or damage.

15 Inspect the timing belt (see Section 6). Renew the belt is there is any doubt about its condition.

Refitting

Camshaft sprocket

16 Refit the locating pin (where removed) then locate the sprocket on the end of the camshaft. Ensure that the locating pin is correctly engaged with the sprocket and the cut-out in the camshaft end. Note that on 1.6 litre engines, the exhaust sprocket is marked E and the intake sprocket marked A **(see illustrations)**.

17 Refit the sprocket retaining bolt and washer. Tighten the bolt to the specified torque, whilst retaining the sprocket/camshaft with the method used on removal.

18 Realign the timing hole in the camshaft sprocket (see Section 3) with the corresponding hole in the cylinder head, and refit the locking pin.

19 Rotate the crankshaft 90° in the normal direction of rotation (clockwise), until the crankshaft locking pin can be inserted.

20 Refit the timing belt as described in Section 6. Refit the cylinder head covers as described in Section 4.

Crankshaft sprocket

21 Locate the Woodruff key in the crankshaft end, then slide on the flanged spacer (where fitted) aligning its slot with the Woodruff key.

22 Align the crankshaft sprocket slot with the Woodruff key, and slide it onto the end of the crankshaft.

23 Temporarily remove the locking pin from the rear of the flywheel/driveplate, and then refit the crankshaft sprocket retaining bolt and washer. Tighten the bolt to the specified torque, whilst preventing crankshaft rotation using the method employed on removal. Refit the locking pin to the rear of the flywheel/driveplate.

24 Refit the timing belt as described in Section 6.

Tensioner pulley

25 Refit the tensioner pulley to its mounting stud, ensuring the cut-out aligns with the pin **(see illustration)**, and fit the retaining nut.

26 Ensure that the 'front run' of the belt is taut – ie, ensure that any slack is on the pulley side of the belt. Check that the belt is centrally located on all its sprockets. Rotate the pulley anti-clockwise to remove all free play from

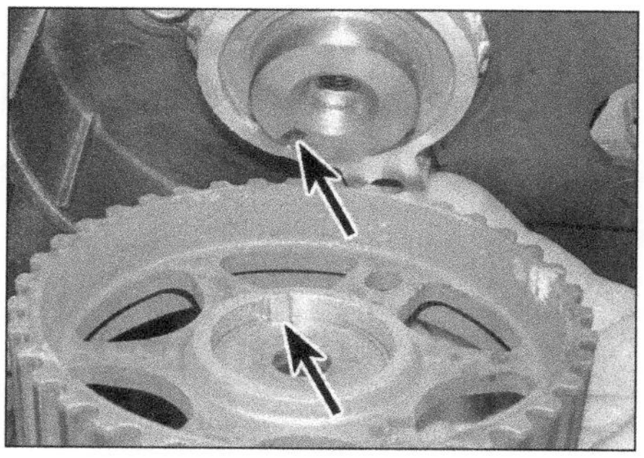

7.16a The locating pin must engage with the slot (arrowed)

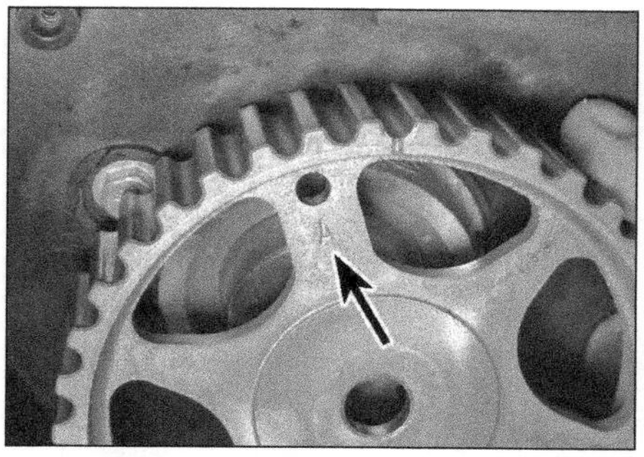

7.16b On 1.6 litre engines, the intake sprocket is marked A (arrowed) and the exhaust E

7.25 The cut-out aligns the locating pin (arrowed)

the timing belt, and then tighten the pulley retaining nut securely.

27 Tension the timing belt as described in Section 6.

28 Once the belt is correctly tensioned, refit the timing belt covers as described in Section 5.

8 Camshaft oil seals – renewal

Note: *If the camshaft oil seal has been leaking, check the timing belt for signs of oil contamination; the belt must be renewed if signs of oil contamination are found. Ensure that all traces of oil are removed from the sprockets and surrounding area before the new belt is fitted.*

1 Remove the camshaft sprocket as described in Section 7.

2 Punch or drill two small holes opposite each other in the oil seal. Screw a self-tapping screw into each, and pull on the screws with pliers to extract the seal. Alternatively, carefully prise the seal out using a flat-bladed screwdriver **(see illustration)**.

3 Clean the seal housing, and polish off any burrs or raised edges, which may have caused the seal to fail in the first place.

4 Lubricate the lips of the new seal with clean engine oil, and drive it into position until it seats on its locating shoulder. Use a suitable tubular drift, such as a socket, which bears only on the hard outer edge of the seal. Take care not to damage the seal lips during fitting. Note that the seal lips should face inwards.

5 Refit the camshaft sprocket as described in Section 7.

9 Camshafts and followers – removal, inspection and refitting

General information

1 The cylinder head does not have to be removed for this procedure, as the camshafts and followers can be removed upwards from the top of the cylinder head. The valves are operated by followers, which incorporate

8.2 Carefully prise the camshaft oil seal out with a flat-bladed screwdriver

hydraulic compensator units between the camshaft and the top of the valves.

Removal

2 Remove the camshaft sprockets as described in Section 7. Undo the screws and securing the inner timing cover to the cylinder head.

3 Starting from the outside, working in a spiral pattern, progressively and evenly slacken the camshaft bearing housing retaining bolts, and lift the housing from the cylinder head **(see illustration)**.

4 Identify each camshaft for position – the intake camshaft is at the rear and the exhaust camshaft is at the front of the cylinder head. Also note the TDC position of each camshaft for correct refitting.

5 Remove the camshafts by pressing on the transmission ends to release the opposite ends from their bearings. Withdrawn the camshafts from the cylinder head and slide the oil seals from the ends.

6 Obtain 16 small, clean plastic containers, and number them intake 1 to 8 and exhaust 1 to 8; alternatively divide a large container into 16 compartments and number each compartment accordingly. On 1.6 litre engines, use a rubber sucker to withdraw each follower in turn, and place it in its respective container. On 1.4 litre engines, withdraw each rocker arm complete with hydraulic follower, and place it in its respective container **(see illustrations)**. Don't interchange the followers since the wear rate will be much increased.

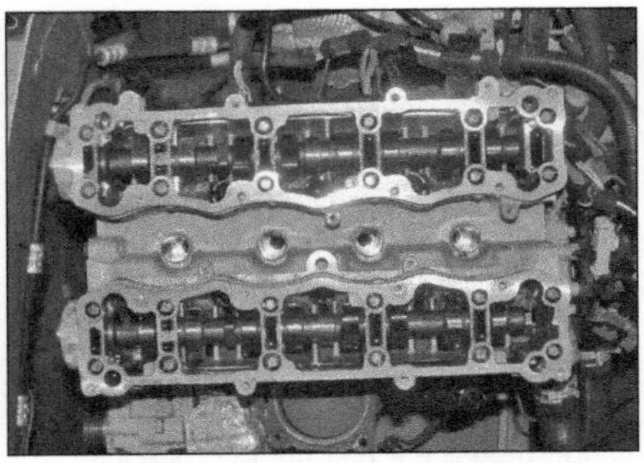

9.3 Evenly and progressively slacken the camshaft housing retaining bolts

Inspection

7 Examine the camshaft bearing surfaces and cam lobes for signs of wear ridges and scoring. Renew the camshaft if any of these conditions are apparent. Examine the condition of the bearing surfaces, both on the camshaft journals and in the cylinder head/bearing housing. If the head bearing surfaces are worn excessively, the cylinder head will need to be renewed. If the necessary measuring equipment is available, camshaft bearing journal wear can be checked by direct measurement, noting that No 1 journal is at the transmission end of the head.

8 Examine the hydraulic follower surfaces, which contact the camshaft lobes for wear ridges and scoring. Renew any follower where these conditions are apparent. If a follower bearing surface is badly scored, also examine the corresponding lobe on the camshaft for wear, as it is likely that both will be worn **(see illustration)**. Renew any components as necessary.

Refitting

9 Before commencing refitting, remove all traces of oil from the bearing housing retaining bolts holes in the cylinder head, using a clean rag. Also ensure that both the cylinder head and bearing housing mating faces are clean and free from oil.

10 Liberally oil the cylinder head hydraulic follower bores and the followers. Carefully refit the followers to the cylinder head; ensuring that each follower is refitted to its original bore.

9.6a Remove the rocker arms complete with hydraulic lifter ...

9.6b ... and keep them in a clean container

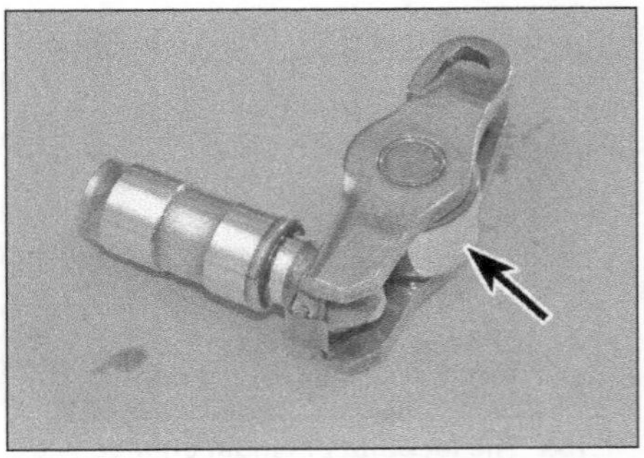

9.8 Check the roller surface (arrowed) on the rocker arm

9.10a Refit the rocker arm and hydraulic lifter ...

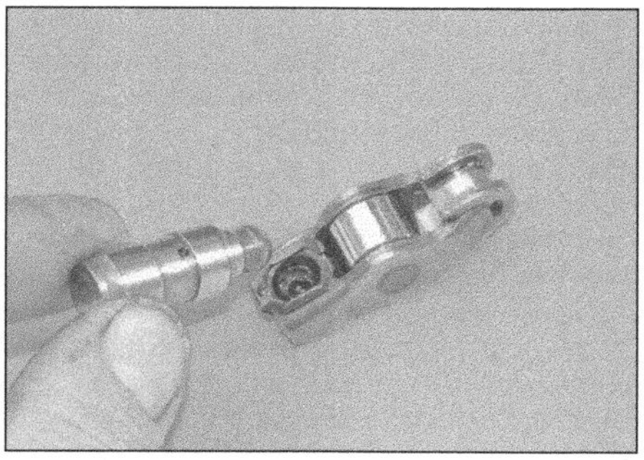

9.10b ... making sure the hydraulic lifter is clipped into the rocker arm securely

9.11 Position the intake camshaft locking notch at the 7 o'clock position and the exhaust camshaft at 8 o'clock (arrowed)

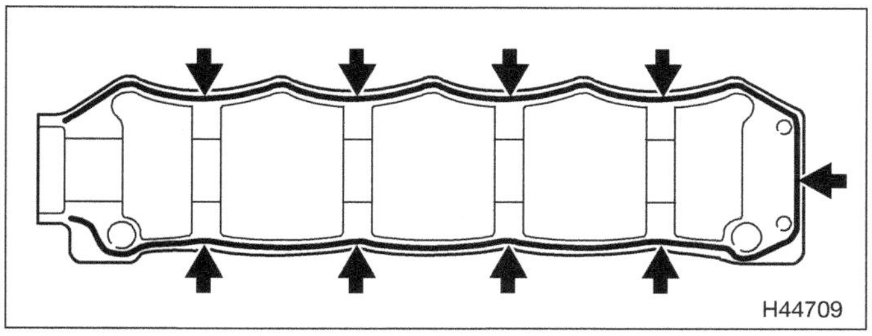

9.12 Apply a bead of silicone sealant to the cylinder head mating surface (arrowed)

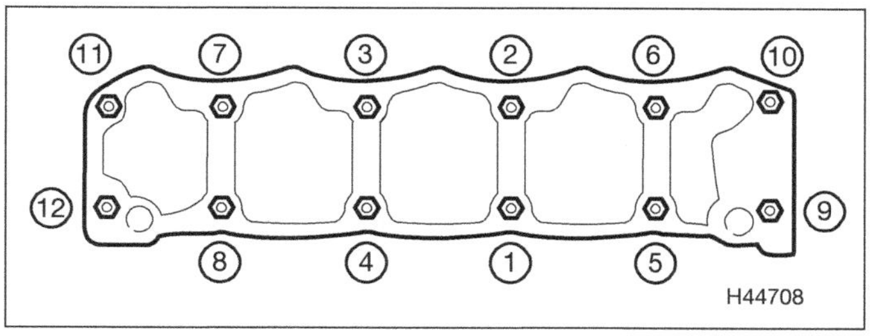

9.13 Camshaft bearing housing bolts tightening sequence

Some care will be required to enter the followers squarely into their bores. Check that each follower rotates freely. On the 1.4 litre engine, make sure the rocker arms are clipped to the hydraulic follower securely **(see illustrations).**

11 Liberally oil the camshaft bearings in the cylinder head and the camshaft lobes, and then refit the camshafts to the cylinder head in the previously-noted positions. The locating notch in the right-hand end of the camshafts should be positioned at the 7 o'clock position on the intake camshaft, and the 8 o'clock position on the exhaust camshaft **(see illustration)**.

12 Apply a bead of silicone-based jointing compound around the perimeter of the mating faces and around the retaining bolt hole locations **(see illustration)**.

13 Refit the bearing housing, and tighten the bolts progressively, in sequence, to the specified torque **(see illustration)**.

14 Fit new oil seals with reference to Section 8.

15 Ensure that the lower edge of the inner timing belt cover engages correctly with the upper edge of the crankshaft oil seal housing **(see illustration)**.

16 Refit the camshaft sprockets as described in Section 7.

10 Cylinder head – removal and refitting

Note: *Ensure the engine is cold before removing the cylinder head.*

Removal

1 Disconnect the battery (refer to precautions in Chapter 5A, Section 1).

2 Drain the cooling system as described in Chapter 1A, Section 25.

3 Remove the ignition HT coil assembly (see Chapter 5B, Section 3) then remove the spark plugs (see Chapter 1A, Section 20).

4 Remove the cylinder head covers as described in Section 4.

5 Align the engine assembly/valve timing holes as described in Section 3, and lock both the camshaft sprockets and flywheel/driveplate in position.

Caution: Do not attempt to rotate the engine whilst the tools are in position.

6 Note that the following text assumes that the cylinder head will be removed with both intake and exhaust manifolds attached; this is easier, but makes it a bulky and heavy assembly to handle. If it is wished to remove the manifolds first, proceed as described in Chapter 4A, Section 13 (intake) and Section 14 (exhaust).

7 Carry out the following operations as described in Chapter 4A:

a) Disconnect the exhaust system front pipe from the manifold. Disconnect or release the oxygen sensor wiring.

b) Remove the air cleaner housing and intake duct assembly.

c) Disconnect the fuel feed and return hoses from the fuel rail (plug all openings, to prevent loss of fuel and entry of dirt into the fuel system).

d) Note their fitted positions, then disconnect the relevant electrical connectors and vacuum/breather hoses from the intake manifold.

e) Where necessary unbolt the support bracket from the intake manifold.

9.15 Ensure the lower edge of the inner timing belt cover engages correctly (arrowed)

8 Remove the timing belt inner cover as described in Section 5.

9 Undo the mounting bolt and remove the upper section of the oil dipstick guide tube. Note their fitted positions, then slacken the retaining clips, and disconnect the coolant hoses from the cylinder head. Likewise, note the routing, and then disconnect all electrical connectors from the cylinder head.

10 Remove the camshafts as described in Section 9.

11 Working in the **reverse** of the tightening sequence **(see illustration 10.29)**, progressively slacken the cylinder head bolts by half a turn at a time, until all bolts can be unscrewed by hand.

10.15 On 1.4 litre engines, clamp the cylinder liners in position before rotating the crankshaft (clamps arrowed)

12 On 1.4 litre engines, the joint between the cylinder head, gasket and cylinder block/crankcase must now be broken without disturbing the wet liners. To break the joint, obtain two stout screwdrivers, which fit into the cylinder head bolt holes. Gently 'rock' the cylinder head free towards the front of the car. Do not try to swivel the head on the cylinder block/crankcase; it is located by dowels, as well as by the tops of the liners. **Note:** *If care is not taken and the liners are moved, there is also a possibility of the bottom seals being disturbed, causing leakage after refitting the head.* When the joint is broken, lift the cylinder head away; seek assistance if possible, as it is a heavy assembly, especially if it is being removed complete with the manifolds.

13 On 1.6 litre engines, lift the cylinder head away; seek assistance if possible, as it is a heavy assembly, especially if it is being removed complete with the manifolds.

14 Remove the gasket from the top of the cylinder block; noting its fitted position and the two locating dowels in the block. If the locating dowels are a loose fit, remove them and store them with the head for safekeeping. Do not discard the gasket – on some models it will be needed for identification purposes (see paragraphs 20 and 21).

Caution: On 1.4 litre engines, do not attempt to rotate the crankshaft with the cylinder head removed, otherwise the wet liners may be displaced.

15 Operations that require the rotation of the crankshaft (eg, cleaning the piston crowns) should only be carried out on 1.4 litre engines once the cylinder liners are firmly clamped in position **(see illustration)**. In the absence of the special Citroën liner clamps, the liners can be clamped in position using large flat washers positioned underneath suitable-length bolts. Alternatively, the original head bolts could be temporarily refitted, with suitable spacers fitted to their shanks.

16 If the cylinder head is to be dismantled for overhaul, refer to Chapter 2E, Section 6.

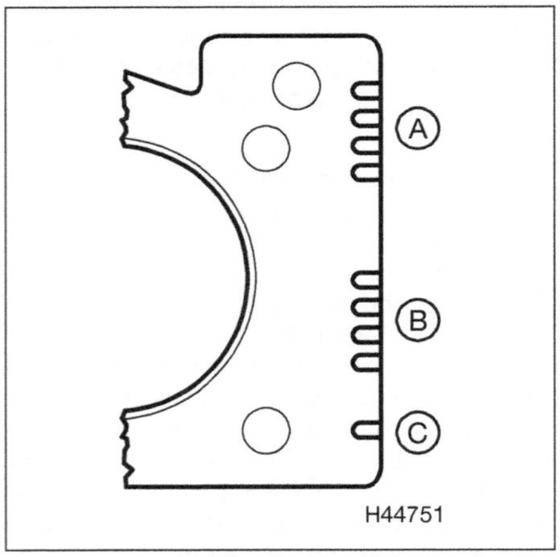

10.21 Cylinder head gasket identification markings

A Engine type identification cut-out locations
B Gasket manufacturer identification cut-out locations
C Gasket thickness identification cut-out locations

Preparation for refitting

17 The mating faces of the cylinder head and cylinder block/crankcase must be perfectly clean before refitting the head. Use a hard plastic or wood scraper to remove all traces of gasket and carbon; also clean the piston crowns. **Note:** *On 1.4 litre engines, clamp the liners in position before turning the crankshaft (see paragraph 15).* Take particular care during the cleaning operations, as aluminium alloy is easily damaged. Also, make sure that the carbon is not allowed to enter the oil and water passages – this is particularly important for the lubrication system, as carbon could block the oil supply to the engine's components. Using adhesive tape and paper, seal the water, oil and bolt holes in the cylinder block/crankcase. To prevent carbon entering the gap between the pistons and bores, smear a little grease in the gap. After cleaning each piston, use a small brush to remove all traces of grease and carbon from the gap, and then wipe away the remainder with a clean rag. Clean all the pistons in the same way.

18 Check the mating surfaces of the cylinder block/crankcase and the cylinder head for nicks, deep scratches and other damage. If slight, they may be removed carefully with a file, but if excessive, machining may be the only alternative to renewal.

19 If warpage of the cylinder head gasket surface is suspected, use a straight-edge to check it for distortion. Refer to Chapter 2E, Section 7 if necessary.

20 When purchasing a new cylinder head gasket, it is essential that a gasket of the correct thickness be obtained. On some models only one thickness of gasket is available, so this is not a problem. On other models, there are two different thicknesses available – the standard gasket, and a slightly thicker 'repair' gasket (+ 0.2 mm). The gaskets can be identified as described in the following paragraph, using the cut-outs on the left-hand end of the gasket.

21 With the gasket fitted the correct way up on the cylinder block, there will be a single or double cut-out at the rear of the left-hand side of the gasket identifying the engine type (eg, TU5J engine). In the centre of the gasket there will likely be another series of between 0 and 4 cut-outs, identifying the manufacturer of the gasket and whether or not it contains asbestos (these cut-outs are of little importance). The important cut-out location is at the front of the gasket; on the standard gasket there will be no cut-out in this position, whereas on the thicker 'repair' gasket there will be a single cut-out **(see illustration)**. Identify the gasket type, and ensure that the new gasket obtained is of the correct thickness. If there is any doubt as to which gasket is fitted, take the old gasket along to your Citroën dealer, and have him confirm the gasket type.

22 Check the condition of the cylinder head bolts, and particularly their threads, whenever they are removed. Wash the bolts in suitable solvent, and wipe them dry. Check each for any sign of visible wear or damage, renewing any bolt if necessary. Measure the length of each bolt, from the underside of its head to the bolt end, to check for stretching **(see illustration)**. On the 1.4 litre engine, the maximum length for the bolts is 118.6 mm and they can only be re-used twice. On 1.6 litre engines, the maximum length for the bolts is 122.6 mm. Although Citroën do not actually specify that the bolts must be renewed, it is strongly recommended that the bolts should be renewed as a complete set, regardless of their apparent condition, whenever they are disturbed.

23 On 1.4 litre engines, prior to refitting the cylinder head, check the cylinder liner protrusion as described Chapter 2E, Section 11.

Refitting

24 Wipe clean the mating surfaces of the cylinder head and cylinder block/crankcase. Check that the two locating dowels are in position at each end of the cylinder block/

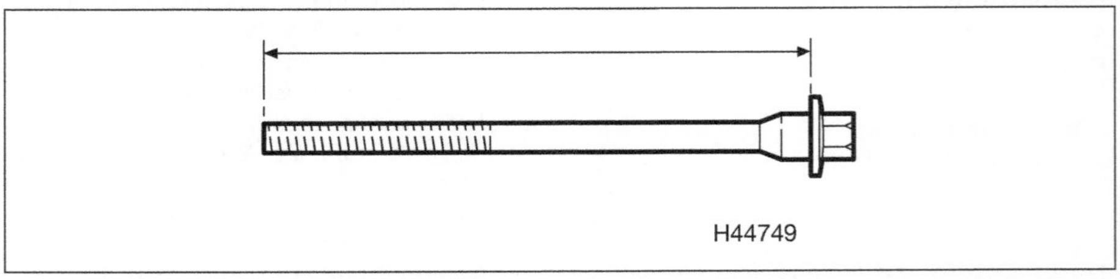

10.22 Measure the bolt length from the underside of the bolt head to the end of the bolt

10.24 Ensure the locating dowels (arrowed) are in position then fit the new head gasket

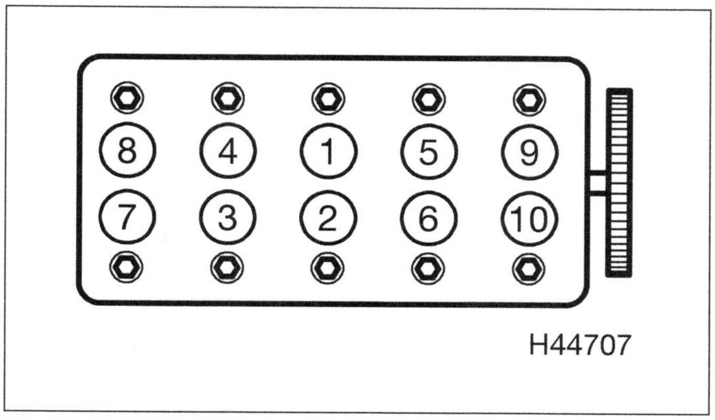

10.29 Cylinder head bolt tightening sequence

crankcase surface and, if necessary, remove the cylinder liner clamps **(see illustration)**.

25 Position a new gasket on the cylinder block/crankcase surface, ensuring that its identification cut-outs are at the left-hand end of the gasket, and the side marked TOP is uppermost.

26 Check that the flywheel/driveplate and camshaft sprockets are still correctly locked in position with their respective tools then, with the aid of an assistant, carefully refit the cylinder head assembly to the block, aligning it with the locating dowels. Ensure that the inner timing cover lower edge engages correctly with the upper edge of the crankshaft oil seal housing.

27 Lubricate the threads and underside of the heads of the cylinder head bolts lightly with clean engine oil.

28 Carefully enter each bolt into its relevant hole (*do not drop them in*) and screw in, by hand only, until finger-tight.

29 Working progressively and in the sequence shown, tighten the cylinder head bolts to their Stage 1 torque setting, using a torque wrench and suitable socket **(see illustration)**.

30 Once all the bolts have been tightened to their Stage 1 setting, working again in the given sequence, angle-tighten the bolts through the specified Stage 2 and 3 torque/angle, using a socket and extension bar. It is recommended that an angle-measuring gauge be used during the final stage of the tightening, to ensure accuracy. If a gauge is not available, use white paint to make alignment marks between the bolt head and cylinder head prior to tightening; the marks can then be used to check that the bolt has been rotated through the correct angle during tightening.

31 Refit the timing belt inner cover as described in Section 5. Reconnect the all wiring plugs to the cylinder head and manifold.

32 Refit the camshafts with reference to Section 9.

33 Working as described in the Chapter 4A, carry out the following tasks:

a) *Refit all disturbed wiring, hoses and control cable(s) to the intake manifold and fuel system components.*
b) *Reconnect the exhaust system front pipe to the manifold and reconnect the oxygen sensor wiring connector.*
c) *Refit the air cleaner and intake duct.*

34 Refit the cylinder head covers as described in Section 4.

35 Refit the spark plugs and install the ignition HT coil (see Chapter 1A, Section 20 and Chapter 5B, Section 3).

36 On completion, reconnect the battery (refer to precautions in Chapter 5A, Section 1), and refill the cooling system as described in Chapter 1A, Section 25.

11 Sump – removal and refitting

Removal

1 Firmly apply the handbrake, and then jack up the front of the vehicle and support it on axle stands (see *Jacking and vehicle support*). Undo the screws and remove the engine undershield.

2 Drain the engine oil, then clean and fit new sealing washer to the oil drain plug. Fit the oil drain plug and tighten it to the specified torque. If the engine is nearing its service interval when the oil and filter are due for renewal, it is recommended that the filter is also removed, and a new one fitted. After reassembly, the engine can then be refilled with fresh oil. Refer to Chapter 1A, Section 3 for further information.

3 Remove the exhaust system front pipe as described in Chapter 4A, Section 15.

4 Undo the three retaining bolts and remove the mounting support plate from the rear of the sump **(see illustration).**

5 Progressively slacken and remove all the sump nuts and bolts/nuts and where applicable, position the wiring harness guide clear of the sump **(see illustrations)**.

11.4 Remove the mounting bracket (arrowed)

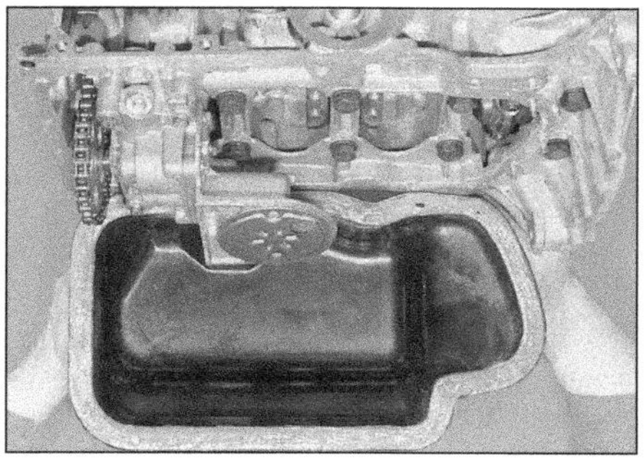

11.5a Undo the nuts and bolts, then remove the sump from the engine (1.4 litre engine)

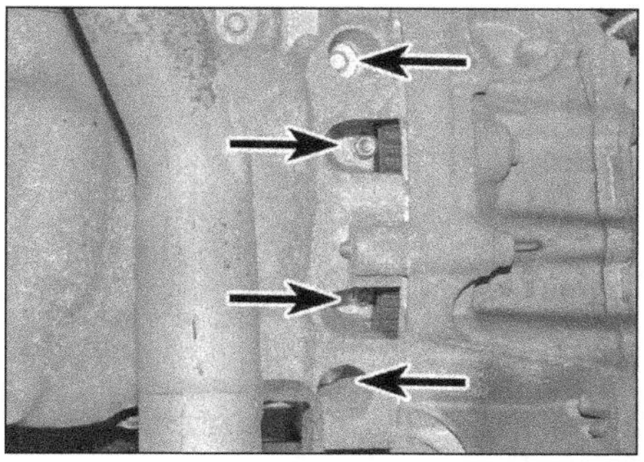

11.5b Access to the sump end bolts/nuts is through holes in the casing (arrowed) (1.6 litre engine)

12.2 Unscrew the three bolts securing the oil pump in position

13.2 Use a screwdriver to lever out the crankshaft right-hand oil seal

14.2 Use a tool to lock the flywheel ring gear and prevent rotation

6 Break the joint by striking the sump with the palm of your hand, then lower and withdraw the sump from under the car. On 1.6 litre engines, recover the gasket.

7 While the sump is removed, take the opportunity to check the oil pump pick-up/ strainer for signs of clogging or splitting. If necessary, remove the pump as described in Section 12, and clean or renew the strainer.

Refitting

8 Clean all traces of sealant from the mating surfaces of the cylinder block/crankcase and sump, and then use a clean rag to wipe out the sump and the engine's interior.

9 Ensure that the sump and cylinder block/ crankcase mating surfaces are clean and dry, then on 1.4 litre engines, apply a coating of suitable sealant to the sump mating surface. On 1.6 litre engines, if the gasket is undamaged, refit it to the sump. If required, fit a new sump gasket.

10 Offer up the sump and locate it on its studs. Locate the wiring harness guide back in position then refit the sump retaining nuts and bolts. Tighten the nuts and bolts evenly and progressively to the specified torque.

11 Refit the exhaust front pipe as described in Chapter 4A, Section 15 and refit the engine undershield.

12 Refill the engine with the correct grade of oil, with reference to Chapter 1A, Section 3.

12 Oil pump – removal, inspection and refitting

Removal

1 Remove the sump (see Section 11).

2 Slacken and remove the three bolts securing the oil pump in position **(see illustration)**. Disengage the pump sprocket from the chain, and remove the oil pump. If the locating dowel for the pump is a loose fit in the cylinder block, remove and store it with the bolts for safekeeping.

Inspection

3 Examine the oil pump sprocket for signs of damage and wear, such as chipped or missing teeth. If the sprocket is worn, the pump assembly must be renewed, as the sprocket is not available separately. It is also recommended that the chain and drive sprocket, fitted to the crankshaft, are renewed at the same time. On 1.4 litre engines, renewal of the chain and drive sprocket is an involved operation requiring the removal of the main bearing ladder, and therefore cannot be carried out with the engine still fitted to the vehicle. On 1.6 litre engines, the oil pump drive sprocket and chain can be removed with the engine still in the vehicle, once the crankshaft sprocket has been removed and the crankshaft oil seal housing has been unbolted.

4 Slacken and remove the bolts securing the strainer cover to the pump body, and then lift off the strainer cover. Remove the relief valve piston and spring (and guide pin – 1.6 litre engines only), noting which way round they are fitted.

5 Examine the pump rotors and body for signs of wear ridges and scoring. If worn, the complete pump assembly must be renewed.

6 Examine the relief valve piston for signs of wear or damage, and renew if necessary. The condition of the relief valve spring can only be measured by comparing it with a new one; if there is any doubt about its condition, it should also be renewed. Both the piston and spring are available individually.

7 Thoroughly clean the oil pump strainer with a suitable solvent, and check it for signs of clogging or splitting. If the strainer is damaged, the strainer and cover assembly must be renewed.

8 Locate the relief valve spring, piston and (where fitted) the guide pin in the strainer cover, then refit the cover to the pump body. Align the relief valve piston with its bore in the pump. Refit the cover retaining bolts, tightening them securely.

Refitting

9 Ensure that the locating dowel is in position, and then engage the pump sprocket with its drive chain. Locate the pump on its dowel, and refit the pump retaining bolts, tightening them to the specified torque setting.

10 Refit the sump as described in Section 11.

13 Crankshaft oil seals – renewal

Right-hand oil seal

1 Remove the crankshaft sprocket and flanged spacer (where fitted) as described in Section 7.

2 Make a note of the correct fitted depth of the seal in its housing then carefully punch or drill two small holes opposite each other in the seal. Screw a self-tapping screw into each, and pull on the screws with pliers to extract the seal. Alternatively, the seal can be levered out of position using a suitable flat-bladed screwdriver, taking great care not to damage the crankshaft/oil pump drivegear shoulder or seal housing **(see illustration)**.

3 Clean the seal housing, and polish off any burrs or raised edges, which may have caused the seal to fail in the first place.

4 Lubricate the lips of the new seal with clean engine oil, and carefully locate the seal on the end of crankshaft. Note that its sealing lip must face inwards. Take care not to damage the seal lips during fitting.

5 Using a suitable tubular drift (such as a socket), which bears only on the hard outer edge of the seal, tap the seal into position, to the same depth in the housing as the original was prior to removal. The inner face of the seal must be flush with the inner wall of the crankcase.

6 Wash off any traces of oil, and then refit the crankshaft sprocket as described in Section 7.

Left-hand oil seal

7 Remove the flywheel/driveplate (see Section 14).

8 Make a note of the correct fitted depth of the seal in its housing. Punch or drill two small holes opposite each other in the seal. Screw a self-tapping screw into each, and pull on the screws with pliers to extract the seal.

9 Clean the seal housing, and polish off any burrs or raised edges, which may have caused the seal to fail in the first place.

10 Lubricate the lips of the new seal with

clean engine oil, and carefully locate the seal on the end of the crankshaft.

11 Using a suitable tubular drift, which bears only on the hard outer edge of the seal, drive the seal into position, to the same depth in the housing as the original was prior to removal.

12 Wash off any traces of oil, and then refit the flywheel/driveplate as described in Section 14.

14 Flywheel/driveplate – removal, inspection and refitting

Flywheel

Removal

1 Remove the transmission as described in Chapter 7A, Section 7, and then remove the clutch assembly as described in Chapter 6, Section 6.

2 Prevent the flywheel from turning by locking the ring gear teeth **(see illustration)**. Alternatively, bolt a strap between the flywheel and the cylinder block/crankcase.

Caution: Do not attempt to lock the flywheel in position using the locking pin described in Section 3.

3 Slacken and remove the flywheel retaining bolts.

4 Remove the flywheel. Do not drop it, as it is very heavy. If the locating dowel is a loose fit in the crankshaft end, remove and store it with the flywheel for safekeeping.

Inspection

5 If the flywheel's clutch mating surface is deeply scored, cracked or otherwise damaged, the flywheel must be renewed. However, it may be possible to have it surface-ground. If required, seek the advice of a Citroën dealer or engine-reconditioning specialist.

6 If the ring gear is badly worn or has missing teeth, it must be renewed. The temperature to which the new ring gear must be heated for installation is critical and, if not done accurately, the hardness of the teeth will be destroyed. This job is best left to a Citroën dealer or engine reconditioning specialist.

Refitting

7 Clean the mating surfaces of the flywheel and crankshaft.

8 If the new flywheel retaining bolts are not supplied with their threads already pre-coated, apply a suitable thread-locking compound to the threads of each bolt.

9 Ensure that the locating dowel is in position. Offer up the flywheel, locating it on the dowel, and fit the retaining bolts.

10 Lock the flywheel using the method employed on dismantling, and then tighten the retaining bolts evenly and progressively to the specified torque.

11 Refit the clutch as described in Chapter 6, Section 6. Remove the locking tool, and refit the transmission as described in Chapter 7A, Section 7.

Driveplate

Removal

12 Remove the transmission as described in Chapter 7B, Section 9.

13 Prevent the driveplate from turning by locking the ring gear teeth with a similar arrangement to that for the flywheel **(see illustration 14.2)**. Alternatively, bolt a strap between the driveplate and the cylinder block/crankcase.

Caution: Do not attempt to lock the driveplate in position using the locking pin described in Section 3.

14 Slacken and remove the driveplate retaining bolts and remove the outer spacer plate and torque converter mounting plate.

15 Remove the driveplate and inner spacer plate from the end of the crankshaft. If the locating dowel is a loose fit in the crankshaft end, remove and store it with the driveplate for safekeeping. **Note:** *The inner and outer spacer plates are different and are not interchangeable.*

Inspection

16 Inspect the driveplate and torque converter mounting plate for signs of wear or damage. If damage is found, the worn component must be renewed (it is not possible to renew the driveplate ring gear separately).

Refitting

17 Ensure all mating surfaces are clean and dry.

18 Remove any traces of locking compound from the threads of the driveplate bolts and apply a small amount of fresh locking compound (Citroën recommend Loctite Frenbloc) to the bolt threads.

19 Ensure that the locating dowel is in position then refit the inner spacer plate, driveplate, torque converter mounting plate and outer spacer plate. Ensure all components are correctly located on the dowel then fit the retaining bolts.

20 Lock the driveplate using the method employed on dismantling, and then tighten the retaining bolts evenly and progressively to the specified torque.

21 Refit the transmission as described in Chapter 7B, Section 9.

15.5 Remove the plastic trim cover

15 Engine/transmission mountings – inspection and renewal

Inspection

1 If improved access is required, raise the front of the car and support it on axle stands (see *Jacking and vehicle support*). Undo the retaining bolts/nuts and remove the engine undershield.

2 Check the mounting rubber to see if it is cracked, hardened or separated from the metal at any point; renew the mounting if any such damage or deterioration is evident.

3 Check that all the mounting's fasteners are securely tightened; use a torque wrench to check if possible.

4 Using a large screwdriver or a crowbar, check for wear in the mounting by carefully levering against it to check for free play. Where this is not possible, enlist the aid of an assistant to move the engine/transmission back-and-forth, or from side-to-side, while you watch the mounting. While some free play is to be expected even from new components, excessive wear should be obvious. If excessive free play is found, check first that the fasteners are secure, and then renew any worn components as described below.

Renewal

Right-hand mounting

5 Release all the retaining clips and remove the plastic trim from above the right-hand engine mounting **(see illustration)**. If not already done, undo the retaining bolts/nuts and remove the engine undershield.

6 Place a jack beneath the engine, with a block of wood on the jack head. Raise the jack until it is supporting the weight of the engine.

7 Undo the bolts securing the engine mounting to the body and the support bracket **(see illustration)**.

8 If required, undo the bolts and remove the support bracket from the engine. Where applicable, release the wiring loom and fuel lines from the retaining clips as it is removed.

9 Check for signs of wear or damage on all components, and renew as necessary.

10 On reassembly, refit the support bracket

15.7 Right-hand engine mounting upper bolts (arrowed)

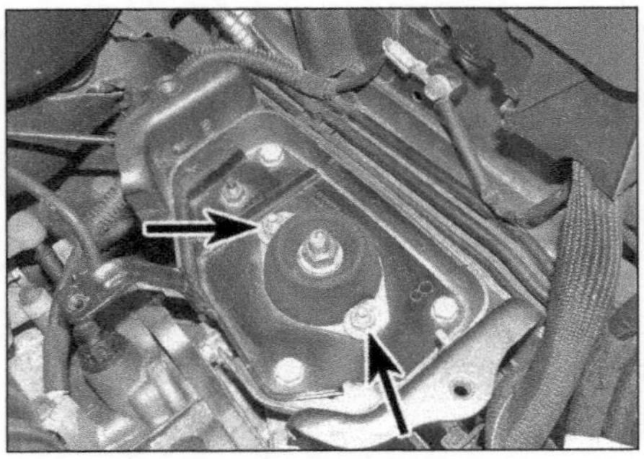

15.15 Undo the left-hand transmission mounting securing nuts (arrowed) ...

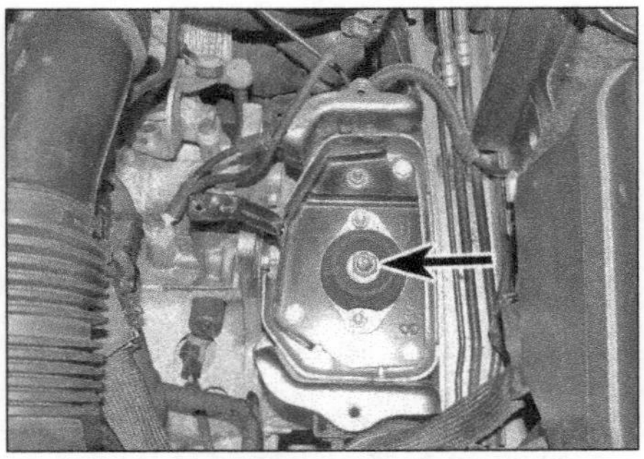

15.16 ... and the mounting centre nut (arrowed)

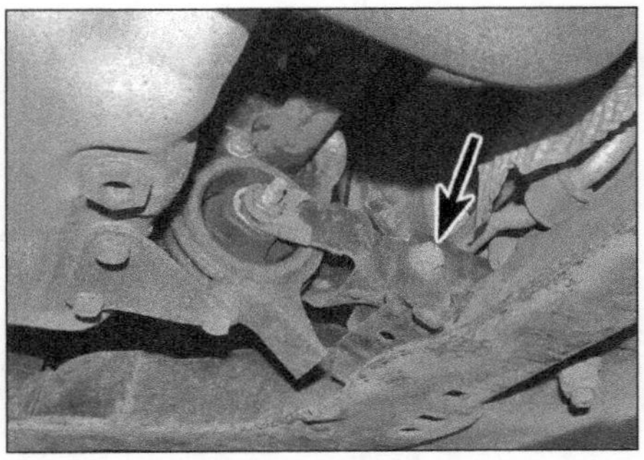

15.22 Undo the rear link-to-subframe mounting bolt (arrowed) ...

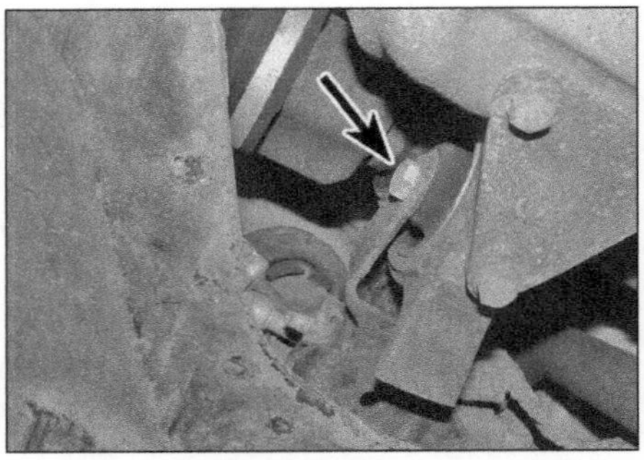

15.23 ... and the lower link-to-mounting bracket bolt (arrowed)

to the engine, tightening the bolts to the specified torque.

11 Install the mounting and mounting bracket and tighten its retaining bolts to the specified torque setting.

12 Remove the jack from underneath the engine and refit the engine undershield.

Left-hand mounting

13 Remove the battery, and battery tray/box as described in Chapter 5A, Section 4.

14 If not already done, undo the retaining bolts/nuts and remove the engine undershield. Place a jack beneath the transmission, with a block of wood on the jack head. Raise the jack until it is supporting the weight of the transmission.

15 Slacken and remove the mounting's two upper retaining nuts **(see illustration)**.

16 Undo the centre retaining nut and remove the mounting from the transmission mounting bracket **(see illustration)**.

17 Check carefully for signs of wear or damage on all components, and renew them where necessary.

18 Refit the mounting to the mounting bracket and tighten it to the specified torque.

19 Fit the mounting nuts to the bracket on the transmission and tighten the retaining nuts to the specified torque.

20 Refit the engine undershield, remove the jack from underneath the transmission, and then refit the battery as described in Chapter 5A, Section 4.

Lower engine torque link

21 Firmly apply the handbrake, and then jack up the front of the vehicle and support it securely on axle stands (see *Jacking and vehicle support*). If not already done, undo the retaining bolts/nuts and remove the engine undershield.

22 Unscrew and remove the bolt securing the rear mounting link to the subframe **(see illustration)**.

23 Remove the bolt securing the rear mounting link to the driveshaft inner bearing bracket at the rear of the cylinder block **(see illustration)**, and then remove the mounting torque reaction link.

24 To remove the intermediate bearing housing assembly it will first be necessary to remove the right-hand driveshaft as described in Chapter 8, Section 2.

25 With the driveshaft removed, undo the retaining bolts and remove the bearing housing/mounting from the rear of the cylinder block.

26 Check carefully for signs of wear or damage on all components, and renew them where necessary. The rubber bush fitted to the driveshaft bearing housing is available as a separate item on some models, check with your local dealer for availability of parts. If available, the rubber bush can be pressed out of the bearing housing, noting its fitted position, and then a new one pressed back into place.

27 On reassembly, fit the bearing housing assembly to the rear of the cylinder block, and tighten its retaining bolts securely. Refit the driveshaft as described in Chapter 8, Section 2.

28 Refit the rear mounting torque reaction link, and tighten both its bolts to their specified torque settings.

29 Refit the engine undershield, and then lower the vehicle to the ground.

Chapter 2 Part B:
VTi petrol engines in-car repair procedures

Contents

Degrees of difficulty

Easy, suitable for novice with little experience	**Fairly easy,** suitable for beginner with some experience	**Fairly difficult,** suitable for competent DIY mechanic	**Difficult,** suitable for experienced DIY mechanic	**Very difficult,** suitable for expert DIY or professional

Specifications

Engine (general)

Designation	EP6
Engine code*	5FW
Capacity	1598 cc
Bore	77.00 mm
Stroke	85.80 mm
Direction of crankshaft rotation	Clockwise (viewed from the right-hand side of vehicle)
No 1 cylinder location	At the transmission end of the block
Compression ratio	11.0 : 1
Maximum power output	88 kW (120 hp) @ 6000 rpm
Maximum torque output	160 Nm @ 4250 rpm

** The engine code is stamped on the lower left-hand end of the cylinder block/lower casing, below the oil filter housing.*

Camshafts

Drive	Chain

Lubrication system

Oil pump type	Gear type, chain-driven off the crankshaft
Minimum oil pressure at 80°C (with correct oil level):	
1000 rpm	2.0 bar
2000 rpm	3.0 bar
4000 rpm	3.2 bar
Oil pressure warning switch operating pressure	0.5 bar

Torque wrench settings

Torque wrench settings	Nm	lbf ft
Big-end bearing bolts:*		
Stage 1	5	4
Stage 2	15	11
Stage 3	Angle-tighten a further 130°	
Camshaft sprocket centre bolts (intake and exhaust):		
Stage 1	20	15
Stage 2	Angle-tighten a further 180°	
Crankshaft pulley centre hub bolt:		
Stage 1	50	37
Stage 2	Angle-tighten a further 180°	
Crankshaft pulley-to-centre hub bolts (3)	28	21
Cylinder head bolts:*		
Main bolts (10):		
Stage 1	30	22
Stage 2	Angle-tighten a further 90°	
Stage 3	Angle-tighten a further 90°	
Timing chain end bolts (2):		
Stage 1	15	11
Stage 2	Angle-tighten a further 90°	
Stage 3	Angle-tighten a further 90°	
Small bolt at rear of head (1):		
Stage 1	25	18
Stage 2	Angle-tighten a further 30°	
Cylinder head cover bolts	9	7
Driveplate retaining bolts:*		
Stage 1	8	6
Stage 2	30	22
Stage 3	Angle-tighten a further 90°	
Engine mountings:		
Left-hand engine/transmission mounting:		
Upper support plate to body bolts/nut	20	15
Flexible bush centre nut	65	48
Flexible bush to upper plate nuts	30	22
Rear lower engine mounting:		
Connecting link-to-mounting bracket bolt	40	30
Connecting link-to-subframe bolt	40	30
Mounting bracket-to-engine bolts	60	44
Right-hand engine/transmission mounting:		
Mounting bracket to support bracket	60	44
Rubber mounting to body	60	44
Support bracket to engine	55	41
Engine-to-transmission bolts:		
Manual transmission	54	40
Automatic transmission:	52	38
Flywheel retaining bolts:*		
Stage 1	8	6
Stage 2	30	22
Stage 3	Angle-tighten a further 90°	
Main bearing bolts:		
Stage 1	30	22
Stage 2	Angle-tighten a further 150°	
Main bearing outer housing/ladder bolts	9	7
Oil filter cap	25	18
Oil filter housing to cylinder block	10	7
Oil gallery caps on cylinder block	35	26
Oil pump-to-engine bolts:		
Stage 1	10	7
Stage 2	25	18
Oil pump sprocket bolt:		
Stage 1	5	4
Stage 2	Angle-tighten a further 90°	
Roadwheels	90	66
Sump baffle plate bolts	10	7
Sump drain plug	30	22
Sump retaining bolts	12	9
Timing chain guide securing bolts	25	18
Timing chain tensioner	75	55
Timing control solenoid valves (2) securing bolts	9	7
Variable timing actuator	8	6

** Do not re-use*

1 General information

How to use this Chapter

This Chapter describes those repair procedures that can reasonably be carried out on the engine while it remains in the car. If the engine has been removed from the car and is being dismantled as described in Chapter 2E, any preliminary dismantling procedures can be ignored.

Note that, while it may be possible physically to overhaul items such as the piston/connecting rod assemblies while the engine is in the car, such tasks are not usually carried out as separate operations. Usually, several additional procedures (not to mention the cleaning of components and oilways) have to be carried out. For this reason, all such tasks are classed as major overhaul procedures, and are described in Chapter 2E.

Chapter 2E describes the removal of the engine/transmission unit from the vehicle, and the full overhaul procedures that can then be carried out.

EP series engine

The engine is of in-line four-cylinder, double-overhead camshaft, 16-valve type, mounted transversely at the front of the car. The clutch and transmission are attached to its left-hand end.

The engine is of conventional 'dry-liner' type, and the cylinder block is cast in aluminium.

The crankshaft runs in five main bearings. Thrustwashers are fitted to No 2 main bearing cap, to control crankshaft endfloat.

The connecting rods rotate on horizontally split bearing shells at their big ends. The pistons are attached to the connecting rods by gudgeon pins. The gudgeon pins are an interference fit in the connecting rod small-end eyes. The aluminium alloy pistons are fitted with three piston rings – two compression rings and an oil control ring.

The camshafts are driven by a chain, and operate sixteen valves by rocker arms located beneath each cam lobe. The valve clearances are self-adjusting by means of hydraulic followers in the cylinder head. The camshafts run in bearing cap housings, which are bolted to the top of the cylinder head. The intake and exhaust valves are each closed by coil springs, and operate in guides pressed into the cylinder head. The engine has a variable valve timing arrangement which has two electrovalves: one for the exhaust camshaft and one for the intake camshaft; these are positioned at the timing chain end at the front and rear of the cylinder head. Also an eccentric shaft actuator is fitted to the left-hand rear of the cylinder head and this alters the intake valve opening and closing.

At the time of writing, there was no procedure available for the removal of the camshafts and valve assembly. The timing components: camshafts, bearings, rockers, followers, springs, valves and valve seals cannot be renewed individually. Citroën recommend that if there is any damage to any of these components that the complete cylinder head assembly be renewed.

Caution: Work on the intake valve spring mechanism is prohibited as a considerable risk of injury may occur.

The coolant pump is driven by a friction wheel, via the auxiliary belt and located in the right-hand end, at the rear of the cylinder block.

Lubrication is by means of an oil pump, which is chain driven off the crankshaft right-hand end. It draws oil through a strainer located in the sump, and then forces it through an externally mounted filter into galleries in the cylinder block/crankcase. From there, the oil is distributed to the crankshaft (main bearings) and camshaft. The big-end bearings are supplied with oil via internal drillings in the crankshaft; the camshaft bearings also receive a pressurised supply. The camshaft lobes and valves are lubricated by splash, as are all other engine components.

Throughout the manual, it is often necessary to identify the engines not only by their type and cubic capacity, but also by their engine code. The engine code consists of three digits (eg, 5FW). The code is stamped on a plate attached to the front, left-hand end of the cylinder block, or stamped directly onto the front face of the cylinder block, on the machined surface located just to the left of the oil filter (next to the crankcase vent hose union).

Operations with engine in car

The following work can be carried out with the engine in the car:

a) Compression pressure – testing.
b) Cylinder head covers – removal and refitting.
c) Crankshaft pulley – removal and refitting.
d) Timing chain – removal, refitting and adjustment.
e) Timing chain tensioner and sprockets – removal and refitting.
f) Cylinder head – removal and refitting.
g) Cylinder head and pistons – decarbonising.
h) Sump – removal and refitting.
i) Oil pump – removal, overhaul and refitting.
j) Crankshaft oil seals – renewal.
k) Engine/transmission mountings – inspection and renewal.
l) Flywheel/driveplate – removal, inspection and refitting.

2 Compression test – description and interpretation

1 When engine performance is down, or if misfiring occurs which cannot be attributed to the ignition or fuel systems, a compression test can provide diagnostic clues as to the engine's condition. If the test is performed regularly, it can give warning of trouble before any other symptoms become apparent.

2 The engine must be fully warmed-up to normal operating temperature and the battery must be fully charged. The aid of an assistant will also be required.

3 Remove the ignition HT coil assembly (see Chapter 5B, Section 3) then remove the spark plugs (see Chapter 1A, Section 20).

4 Fit a compression tester to the No 1 cylinder spark plug hole – the type of tester which screws into the plug thread is to be preferred.

5 Have the assistant hold the throttle wide open, and crank the engine on the starter motor; after one or two revolutions, the compression pressure should build-up to a maximum figure, and then stabilise. Record the highest reading obtained.

6 Repeat the test on the remaining cylinders, recording the pressure in each.

7 All cylinders should produce very similar pressures; a difference of more than 2 bars between any two cylinders indicates a fault. Note that the compression should build-up quickly in a healthy engine; low compression on the first stroke, followed by gradually increasing pressure on successive strokes, indicates worn piston rings. A low compression reading on the first stroke, which does not build-up during successive strokes, indicates leaking valves or a blown head gasket (a cracked head could also be the cause). Deposits on the undersides of the valve heads can also cause low compression.

8 Although Citroën do not specify exact compression pressures, as a guide, any cylinder pressure of below 10 bars can be considered as less than healthy. Refer to a Citroën dealer or other specialist if in doubt as to whether a particular pressure reading is acceptable.

9 If the pressure in any cylinder is low, carry out the following test to isolate the cause. Introduce a teaspoonful of clean oil into that cylinder through its spark plug hole, and repeat the test.

10 If the addition of oil temporarily improves the compression pressure, this indicates that bore or piston wear is responsible for the pressure loss. No improvement suggests that leaking or burnt valves, or a blown head gasket, may be to blame.

11 A low reading from two adjacent cylinders is almost certainly due to the head gasket having blown between them; the presence of coolant in the engine oil will confirm this.

12 If one cylinder is about 20 percent lower than the others and the engine has a slightly rough idle; a worn camshaft lobe could be the cause.

13 If the compression reading is unusually high, the combustion chambers are probably coated with carbon deposits. If this is the case, the cylinder head should be removed and decarbonised.

14 On completion of the test, refit the spark plugs and ignition HT coil (see Chapter 1A, Section 20 and Chapter 5B, Section 3).

3 Engine assembly/valve timing holes – general information and usage

Note: *Special tools are required to lock the camshafts in position.*

1 Each camshaft has flats on the transmission end to accommodate the locking tools. The special tools are bolted down to the top of the cylinder head, locking the camshafts in position **(see illustrations)**.

2 A timing hole is drilled in the lower cylinder block; when the timing hole is aligned with the corresponding hole in the flywheel, the pin can be inserted to lock the crankshaft in position, preventing it from rotating **(see illustration)**.

3 This ensures that the camshafts and crankshaft are correctly positioned when assembling the engine (to prevent the possibility of the valves contacting the pistons when refitting the cylinder head), or refitting the timing chain. To set the engine in the timing position, proceed as follows.

4 Undo the retaining bolts and remove the cylinder head cover (see Section 4).

5 Using a socket and extension bar fitted to the crankshaft pulley centre hub bolt, turn the crankshaft in the normal direction of rotation until the hole in the flywheel aligns with the hole in the lower part of the cylinder block. When the timing hole is aligned correctly the pistons should be halfway down the cylinders. **Note:** *Do not attempt to rotate the engine whilst the crankshaft/camshafts are locked in position. If the engine is to be left in this state for a long period of time, it is a good idea to place suitable warning notices inside the vehicle, and in the engine compartment. This will reduce the possibility of the engine being accidentally cranked on the starter motor, which is likely to cause damage with the locking rods/tool in place.*

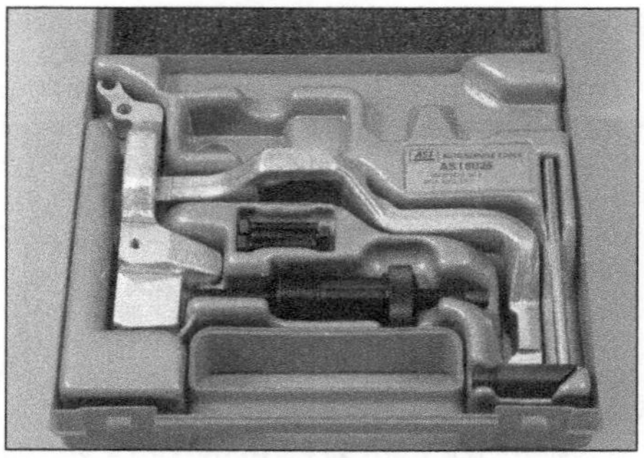

3.1a Special tools like these from Auto Service Tools Limited are needed ...

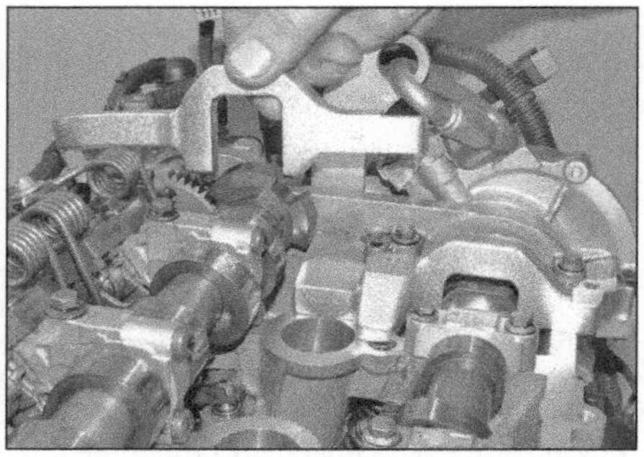

3.1b ... to lock the camshafts in position

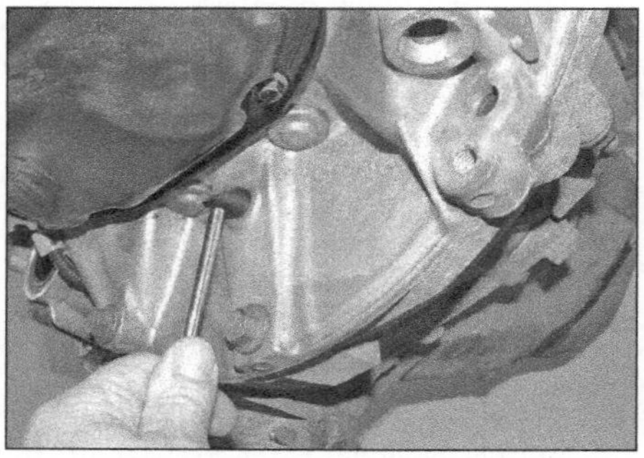

3.2 When the timing hole is aligned with the hole in the flywheel, the pin can be inserted to lock the crankshaft in position

3.6 Bolt the special tool over the camshafts to lock them in position

6 With the flats on the camshafts correctly positioned, fit the special tools over the camshafts to lock them in position on the cylinder head **(see illustration)** and insert the flywheel positioning tool **(see illustration 3.2)**.

7 The crankshaft and camshafts are now locked in position, preventing rotation.

4 Cylinder head cover – removal and refitting

Removal

1 Remove the battery cover and disconnect the battery. **Note:** *Wait 15 minutes after switching off the ignition before disconnecting the battery, to ensure that the ECU's memory is stored.*

2 Remove the air filter housing and air intake hoses as described in Chapter 4A, Section 2.

3 Undo the two retaining screws and unclip the plastic cover from the front of the cylinder head cover **(see illustration)**.

4 Remove the ignition coils as described in Chapter 5B, Section 3.

5 Release the wiring loom from across the front of the cylinder head cover, including the earth connection **(see illustration)**.

6 Disconnect the wiring connectors from the two camshaft position sensors in the transmission end of the cylinder head cover **(see illustration)**.

7 Slide the wiring loom bracket from the end

4.3 Remove the cylinder head cover

4.5 Disconnect the earth cable

4.6 Disconnect the camshaft sensors

4.7 Unclip the wiring harness bracket

4.8 Unclip the breather pipe

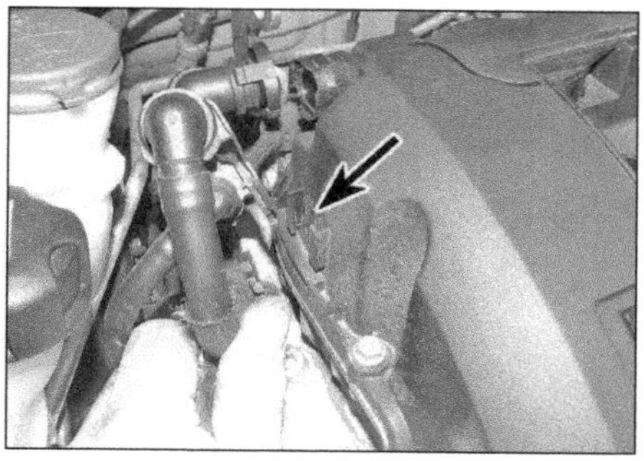

4.9 Release the clip from the camshaft cover

4.10 Two inner camshaft cover retaining bolts – arrowed

4.11 Remove the camshaft cover

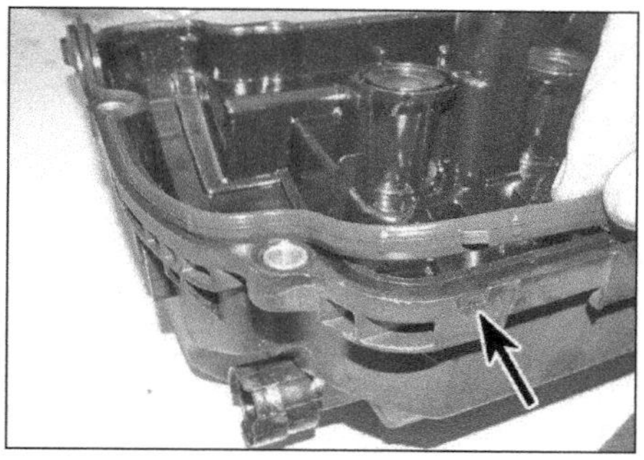

4.13 Clip the rubber gasket into the cover

of the cylinder head cover upwards and move it to one side **(see illustration)**.

8 Disconnect the breather pipe from the right-hand rear of the cylinder head cover **(see illustration)**.

9 Unclip the fuel pipes from the right-hand rear of the cylinder head cover and move them to one side **(see illustration)**.

10 Progressively unscrew the bolts securing the cylinder head cover to the cylinder head. Noting the two bolts in the centre of the cylinder head cover **(see illustration)**.

11 Remove the cylinder head cover and gaskets **(see illustration)**.

Refitting

12 Thoroughly clean the surfaces of the covers and cylinder head.

13 Fit new gaskets and locate the cover on the head **(see illustration)**. Insert all the retaining bolts and finger-tighten them.

14 Progressively tighten the bolts to the correct torque setting.

15 The remainder of refitting is a reversal of removal. Refer to Chapter 4A, Section 2 and Chapter 5B, Section 3 if required.

5 Crankshaft pulley – removal and refitting

Removal

1 Remove the auxiliary drivebelt (Chapter 1A, Section 10)

2 If required, to prevent the crankshaft turning whilst the pulley retaining bolts are being slackened on manual transmission models, select 5th gear and have an assistant apply the brakes firmly. On automatic transmission models it will be necessary to remove the starter motor (Chapter 5A, Section 10) and lock the driveplate with a suitable tool. If the engine has been removed from the vehicle, lock the flywheel ring gear as described in Section 12. Do not attempt to lock the pulley by inserting a bolt/drill through the timing hole. If the locking pin is in position, temporarily remove it prior to slackening the pulley bolt, then refit it once the bolt has been slackened.

3 Undo the three crankshaft pulley retaining bolts and remove the pulley from the centre hub on the end of the crankshaft **(see illustrations)**.

5.3a Undo the retaining bolts ...

5.3b ... and remove the crankshaft pulley

Refitting

4 Locate the pulley on the hub on the end of the crankshaft, refit the three retaining bolts and tighten them to the specified torque.

5 Refit and tension the auxiliary drivebelt as described in Chapter 1A, Section 10.

6 Timing chain assembly – general information, removal and refitting

General information

1 The timing chain drives the camshafts from a toothed sprocket on the end of the crankshaft.

2 The chain should be renewed if the sprocket or chain is worn, indicated by excessive lateral play between the links, and excessive noise

6.4a Insert the tool into the cylinder head where the chain tensioner fits

6.4b Screw the threaded centre part of the tool in until it contacts the timing chain guide and hand-tighten

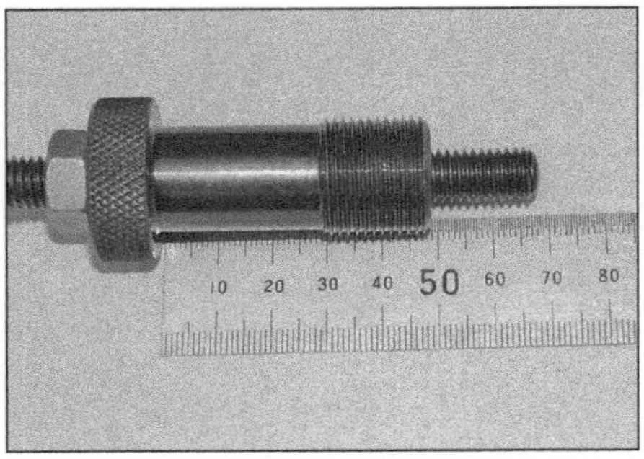

6.4c Make sure the length does not exceed 68 mm

6.8 Hold the camshafts in position and slacken the camshaft sprocket/dephaser unit retaining bolts

in operation. It is wise to renew the chain in any case if the engine is to be dismantled for overhaul. Note that the rollers on a very badly worn chain may be slightly grooved. To avoid future problems, if there is any doubt at all about the condition of the chain, renew it.

3 The timing chain and guides are removed as a complete assembly and are withdrawn out through the top of the cylinder head.

4 To check the wear of the timing chain a special tool is required **(see illustration 3.1a)**. Insert the tool into the cylinder head where the tensioner fits, and tighten the outer part (see paragraph 11). Run the threaded centre part of the tool in until it contacts the timing chain guide and tighten to 0.6 Nm/0.4 lbf ft (finger-tight). Lock the nut on the centre thread and remove the special tool. Check the length of the tool to make sure that it does not exceed 68 mm **(see illustrations)**.

6.11 Remove the timing chain tensioner

Removal

5 Remove the cylinder head cover, as described in Section 4.

6 Set the engine valve timing and lock in position, as described in Section 3.

7 Slacken the crankshaft pulley centre hub retaining bolt. To prevent the crankshaft turning whilst the bolt is being slackened on manual transmission models, select 5th gear and have an assistant apply the brakes firmly. On automatic transmission models it will be necessary to remove the starter motor (Chapter 5A, Section 10) and lock the driveplate with a suitable tool. If the engine has been removed from the vehicle, lock the flywheel ring gear as described in Section 12. Do not attempt to lock the pulley by inserting a bolt/drill through the timing hole. If the locking pin is in position, temporarily remove it prior to slackening the bolt, then refit it once the bolt has been slackened.

8 Hold the camshafts in position with an open-ended spanner on the flats on the camshaft, and then slacken the camshaft sprocket/dephaser unit retaining bolts **(see illustration)**.

9 Remove the crankshaft pulley, as described in Section 5.

10 Remove the throttle housing unit from the intake manifold, as described in Chapter 4A, Section 11.

11 Slacken and remove the timing chain tensioner from the rear of the cylinder head **(see illustration)**. Before the tensioner is removed, make sure the camshafts and crankshaft are locked in position as described in Section 3.

12 Undo the two retaining bolts and remove the chain guide/anti-knock pad from the top of the cylinder head **(see illustration)**.

13 Position a trolley jack under the engine, placing a block of wood between the jack head and the sump. Take the weight of the engine, undo the bolts/nuts and remove the right-hand engine mounting and bracket **(see illustration)**.

6.12 Remove the guide/anti-knock pad from the cylinder head

6.13 Remove the engine mounting bracket

6.14a Remove the upper guide securing bolts ...

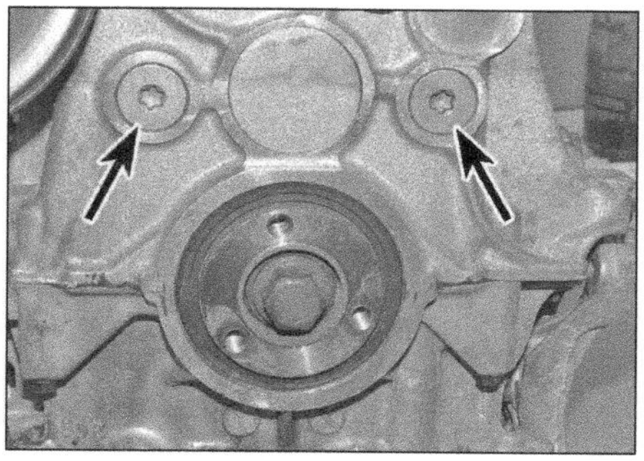

6.14b ... and the two lower securing bolts – arrowed

6.15a Remove the crankshaft hub retaining bolt ...

6.15b ... and then withdraw the hub

6.17a Undo the retaining bolts ...

6.17b ... then remove the intake ...

6.17c ... and exhaust camshaft sprockets

14 Slacken and remove the timing chain guide retaining bolts **(see illustrations)**.

15 Remove the crankshaft pulley centre bolt and hub **(see illustrations)**.

16 Withdraw the dipstick and remove it from the dipstick tube. The dipstick goes down through the chain guide; if this is not removed it will prevent the timing chain assembly from being withdrawn out through the cylinder head.

17 Undo the retaining bolts and remove the camshaft sprocket/dephaser units from the ends of the camshafts, keeping the timing chain held in position **(see illustrations)**. **Note:** *The camshafts are marked IN for intake and EX for exhaust.*

18 Withdraw the timing chain and guide assembly out through the top of the cylinder head, complete with crankshaft sprocket **(see illustrations)**.

19 Check the timing chain assembly carefully for any signs of wear. Renew it if there is the slightest doubt about its condition. If the engine is undergoing an overhaul, it is advisable to renew the chain as a matter of course, regardless of its apparent condition.

Refitting

20 Before refitting, thoroughly clean the crankshaft sprockets. The sprockets are a compression fit between the pulley centre hub and the crankshaft. The mating faces need to be clean and free from any oil when assembling, use a dry product like brake cleaner or similar.

21 Check the camshaft sprocket/dephaser units are in the rest position **(see illustration)**. If these are not aligned the sprocket/dephaser unit will need to be renewed.

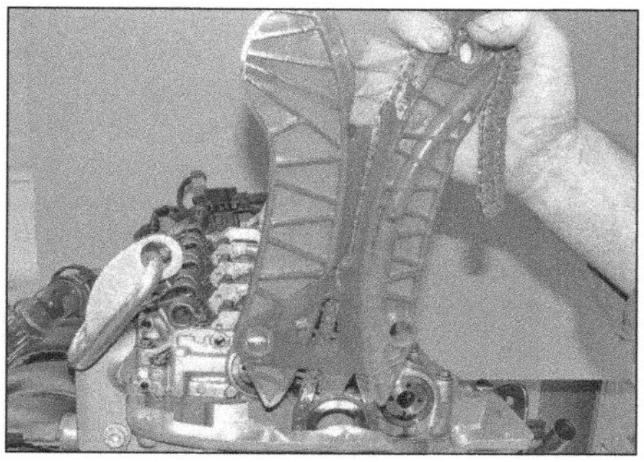

6.18a Withdraw the timing chain guide assembly ...

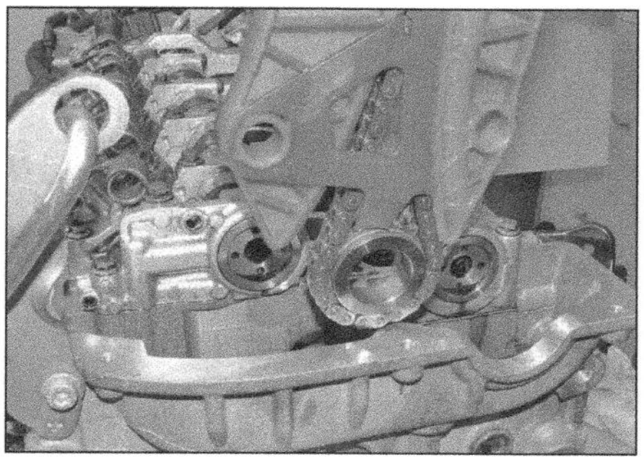

6.18b ... complete with crankshaft sprocket

6.21 Check the alignment marks are in position – arrowed

6.22 Lower the sprocket into position

6.26 Refit the camshaft sprockets

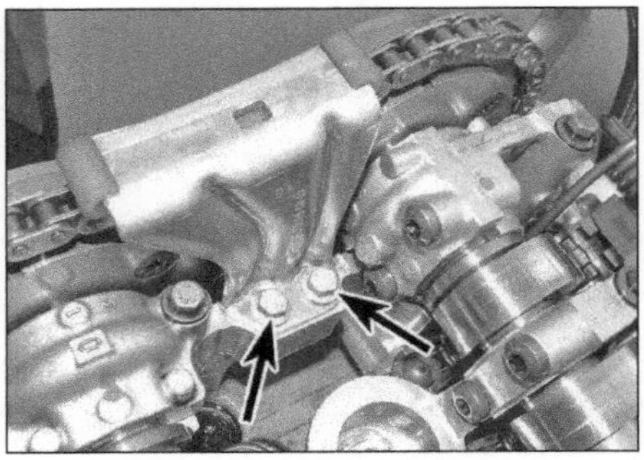
6.27 Refit the guide/anti-knock pad securing bolts – arrowed

22 Lower the timing chain assembly down through the top of the cylinder head, complete with crankshaft sprocket **(see illustration)**.

23 Refit the crankshaft pulley hub; making sure it locates correctly with the crankshaft sprockets. Tighten the bolt to the torque setting specified, preventing the crankshaft from turning as carried out for removal.

24 Refit the timing chain guide retaining bolts and renew the seals/washer.

25 Check that the camshafts and crankshaft are still locked in correct position as described in Section 3.

26 Refit the camshaft sprocket/dephaser units to the ends of the camshafts and tighten to the correct torque setting. Make sure the timing chain is located correctly around the sprockets **(see illustration)**. **Note:** *The camshaft sprockets are marked IN for intake and EX for exhaust.*

27 Refit the chain guide/anti-knock pad to the top of the cylinder head **(see illustration)**.

28 Refit the timing chain tensioner and tighten to the specified torque setting.

29 Remove the camshaft and crankshaft locking tools, and rotate the crankshaft four complete revolutions clockwise (viewed from the right-hand end of the engine). Realign the engine valve timing holes and refit the locking tools, to check the timing is still aligned. If required, refer to Section 3 to check timing mark alignment is correct. When correct remove the timing locking tools from the engine.

Caution: Do not attempt to rotate the engine whilst the locking tools are in position.

30 Refit the right-hand engine mounting with reference to Section 13.

31 Refit the throttle housing unit, as described in Chapter 4A, Section 11.

32 Refit the crankshaft pulley, as described in Section 5.

33 Refit the camshaft cover with reference to Section 4.

34 Refit the engine oil dipstick and reconnect the battery lead.

7 Camshafts and valve assembly – general information

Warning: Work on the intake valve spring mechanism has a considerable risk of injury.

Due to the complexity of the intake camshaft variable lift springs, it is not recommended that the home mechanic carry out this work. Citroën use special tools to tension the springs as they are removed and refitted.

8 Cylinder head – removal and refitting

Note: *The cylinder head cannot be dismantled without the use of special tools (see Section 7); this procedure is for just the removal and refitting of the cylinder head.*

Removal

1 Disconnect the battery (see Chapter 5A, Section 4). **Note:** *Wait 15 minutes after switching off the ignition before disconnecting the battery, to ensure that the ECU's memory is stored.*

2 Apply the handbrake, then jack up the front of the vehicle and support it on axle stands (see *Jacking and vehicle support*). Undo the nuts/bolts and remove the engine undershield. For improved access, remove the bonnet as described in Chapter 11, Section 8.

3 Drain the cooling system as described in Chapter 1A, Section 25.

4 Disconnect the pipe from the vacuum pump, release the securing clip and move the pipe to one side **(see illustration)**.

5 Disconnect the wiring connectors from the thermostat, temperature sensor in the coolant housing and oil pressure sensor on the end of the cylinder head **(see illustrations)**.

6 Disconnect the wiring connectors from the two camshaft position sensors in the transmission end of the cylinder head cover **(see illustration)**.

8.4 Disconnect the vacuum pipe

8.5a Disconnect the thermostat wiring connector

8.5b Disconnect the oil pressure sensor and temperature sensor wiring connector

8.6 Disconnect the camshaft sensor wiring connectors

8.7 Unclip the wiring harness mounting bracket

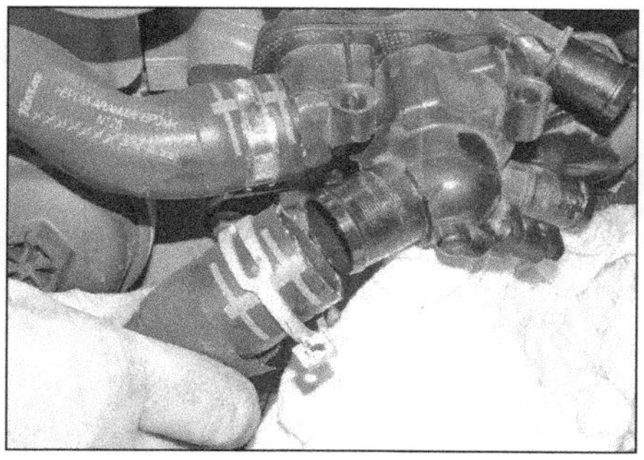

8.8 Disconnect the coolant hoses

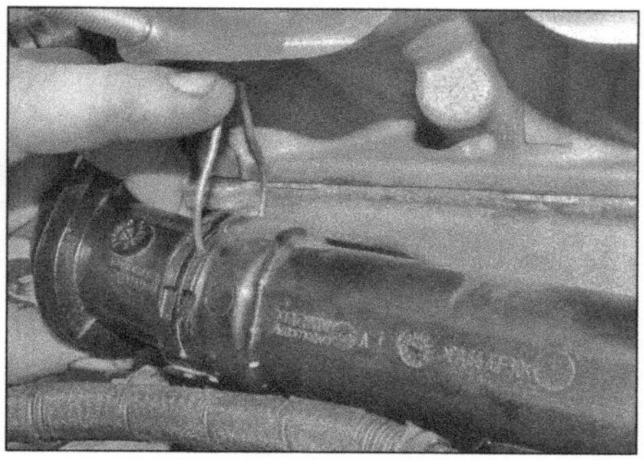

8.9 Release the securing clip at the rear of the housing

8.10 Withdraw the housing from the cylinder head

8.11a Undo the retaining bolts (arrowed) ...

8.11b ... and withdraw the actuator from the cylinder head using an Allen key

7 Slide the wiring loom bracket upwards from the end of the cylinder head cover and move it to one side **(see illustration)**.

8 Disconnect the four coolant hoses from the thermostat housing **(see illustration)**.

9 Release the retaining clip at the rear of the cylinder head, where the thermostat housing joins the pipe to the coolant pump **(see illustration)**.

10 Undo the retaining bolts and remove the thermostat housing from the cylinder head, and withdraw it from the coolant pump feed pipe **(see illustration)**.

11 Disconnect the wiring connector from the eccentric shaft actuator at the left-hand rear of the cylinder head. Undo the actuator retaining bolts and then remove it from the cylinder head by using a 4 mm Allen key, and turning the centre shaft anti-clockwise, while withdrawing the actuator from the cylinder head **(see illustrations)**.

12 Remove the intake manifold and exhaust manifold/catalytic converter, with reference to Chapter 4A, Section 13 and 14.

13 Remove the timing chain assembly, as described in Section 6.

14 If not already done, undo the retaining bolts and remove the mounting bracket from the right-hand end of the cylinder head. Release the wiring loom and fuel pipes from the securing clips where required **(see illustration)**.

15 Disconnect the wiring connectors from the intake and exhaust variable timing electrovalves at the front and rear of the cylinder head at the timing chain end **(see illustrations)**.

8.14 Remove the engine mounting bracket

8.15a Disconnect the exhaust electrovalve connector ...

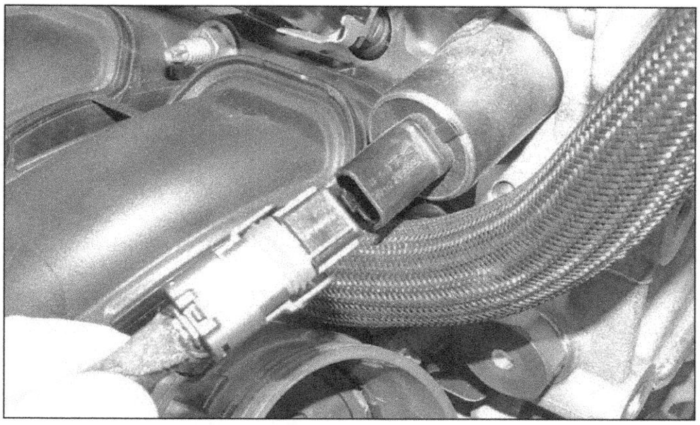

8.15b ... and the intake electrovalve connector

8.16 Cylinder head securing bolt – arrowed

8.17 Cylinder head securing bolts – arrowed

16 Slacken and remove the cylinder head bolt at the right-hand rear of the cylinder head **(see illustration)**.

17 Slacken and remove the two cylinder head bolts at the timing chain end of the cylinder head **(see illustration)**.

18 Progressively slacken and remove the remaining ten cylinder head bolts starting from the middle and spiralling outwards.

19 With all the cylinder head bolts removed, the joint between the cylinder head and gasket, and the cylinder block/crankcase must now be broken. Carefully 'rock' the cylinder head free towards the front of the car. Do not try to swivel the head on the cylinder block/ crankcase; it is located in place by dowels. When the joint is broken, lift the cylinder head away. Use a hoist or seek assistance if possible, as it is a heavy assembly. Remove the gasket from the top of the block, noting the two locating dowels. If the locating dowels are a loose fit, remove them and store them with the head for safekeeping. Do not discard the gasket; it will be needed for identification purposes.

Preparation for refitting

20 The mating faces of the cylinder head and cylinder block/crankcase must be perfectly clean before refitting the head. Use a hard plastic or wooden scraper to remove all traces of gasket and carbon and also clean the piston crowns. Make sure that the carbon is not allowed to enter the oil and water passages – this is particularly important for the lubrication system, as carbon could block the oil supply to the engine's components. Using adhesive tape and paper, seal the water, oil and bolt holes in the cylinder block/crankcase. To prevent carbon entering the gap between the pistons and bores, smear a little grease in the gap. After cleaning each piston, use a small brush to remove all traces of grease and carbon from the gap, and then wipe away the remainder with a clean rag. Clean all the pistons in the same way.

8.22 Cylinder head thickness markings – arrowed

21 Check the mating surfaces of the cylinder block/crankcase and the cylinder head for nicks, deep scratches and other damage. If slight, they may be removed carefully with a file, but if excessive, machining may be the only alternative to renewal. If warpage of the cylinder head gasket surface is suspected, use a straight-edge to check it for distortion. Refer to Chapter 2E, Section 7 if necessary.

22 Obtain a new cylinder head gasket before starting the refitting procedure. There are different thicknesses available – check the old head gasket for markings on the rear right-hand side of the gasket **(see illustration)**. Note that modifications to the cylinder head gasket material, type, and manufacturer are constantly taking place; seek the advice of a Citroën dealer as to the latest recommendations.

23 Due to the stress that the cylinder head bolts are under, it is highly recommended that they be renewed along with the washers, regardless of their apparent condition.

Refitting

24 Wipe clean the mating surfaces of the cylinder head and cylinder block/crankcase. Check that the two locating dowels are in position at each end of the cylinder block/ crankcase surface.

25 Position a new gasket on the cylinder block/crankcase surface.

26 Check that the crankshaft pulley and camshaft sprockets are still at their locked positions (see Section 3).

27 With the aid of an assistant, carefully lower the cylinder head assembly onto the block, aligning it with the locating dowels.

28 Apply a smear of grease to the threads, and to the underside of the heads, of the cylinder head bolts. Citroën recommend the use of Molykote G Rapid Plus (available from your Citroën dealer); in the absence of the specified grease, any good-quality high melting-point grease may be used.

29 Carefully enter each of the new bolts and washers into their relevant hole (do not drop them in) and then screw them in finger-tight.

30 Working progressively tighten the main ten cylinder head bolts starting from the middle and spiraling outwards. Then tighten the two bolts at the timing chain end of the cylinder head and the one at the rear of the head. Tighten all the cylinder head bolts to their Stage 1 torque setting.

31 Once all the bolts have been tightened to their Stage 1 torque setting, proceed to tighten them through the remaining stages as given in the Specifications. It is recommended that an angle-measuring gauge be used for the angle-tightening stages, however, if a gauge is not available, use white paint to make alignment marks between the bolt head and cylinder head prior to tightening; the marks can then be used to check that the bolt has rotated sufficiently. Each step must be completed in one movement without stopping.

32 The remainder of the refitting procedure is a reversal of removal, referring to the relevant Chapters or Sections as required. On completion, refill the cooling system as described in Chapter 1A, Section 25. Initialise the engine management ECU as follows. Start the engine and run to normal temperature. Carry out a road test during which the following procedure should be made. Engage

9.4 Undo the two bolts – arrowed

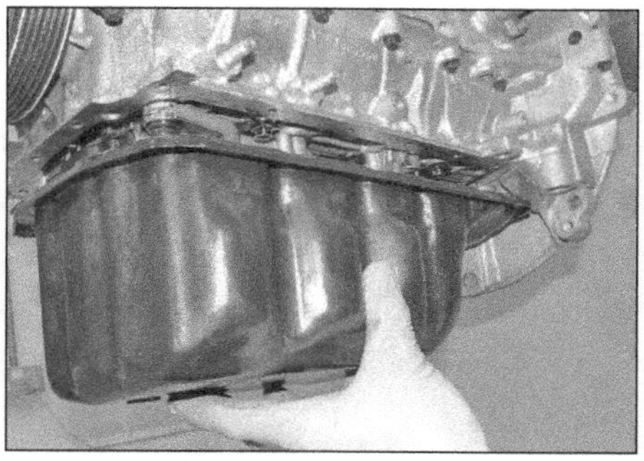

9.6 Remove the sump

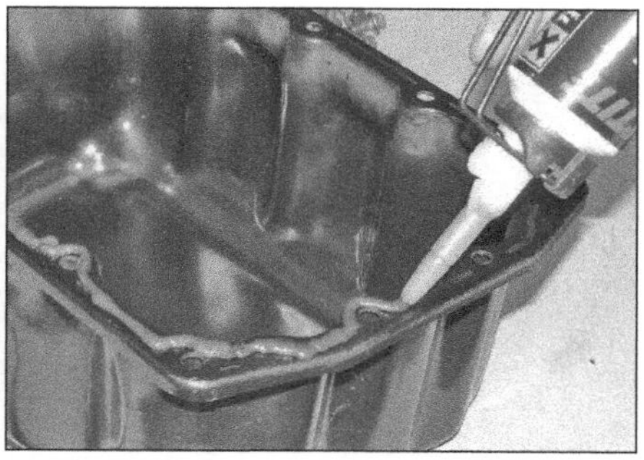

9.10 Apply a thin bead of RTV sealant to the sump mating surface

third gear and stabilise the engine at 1000 rpm. Now accelerate fully to 3500 rpm. **Note:** *This is the procedure for manual transmission models; consult your dealer for automatic models.*

9 Sump – removal and refitting

Removal

1 Apply the handbrake, then jack up the front of the vehicle and support it on axle stands (see *Jacking and vehicle support*). Undo the screws and remove the engine undershield (if fitted).

2 Drain the engine oil, then clean and fit new sealing washer to the oil drain plug. Fit the oil drain plug and tighten it to the specified torque. If the engine is nearing its service interval when the oil and filter are due for renewal, it is recommended that the filter is also removed, and a new one fitted. After reassembly, the engine can then be refilled with fresh oil. Refer to Chapter 1A, Section 3 for further information.

3 Withdraw the engine oil dipstick from the guide tube.

4 Where fitted, undo the two retaining bolts and remove the mounting plate from the rear of the sump **(see illustration)**.

5 Progressively slacken and remove all the sump retaining bolts. Make a note of the fitting position of the bolts, as they may be different lengths. This will avoid the possibility of installing the bolts in the wrong locations on refitting.

6 Break the joint by striking the sump with the palm of your hand. Lower the sump, and withdraw it from underneath the vehicle **(see illustration)**. While the sump is removed, take the opportunity to check the oil pump pick-up/strainer for signs of clogging or splitting. If necessary, remove the pump as described in Section 10, and clean or renew the strainer. If required, unbolt the oil baffle plate from the bottom of the main bearing ladder, noting which way round it is fitted.

Refitting

7 Where removed, refit the baffle plate to the main bearing ladder and tighten the bolts securely.

8 Where removed, refit the oil pump and pick-up/strainer with reference to Section 10.

9 Clean all traces of sealant/gasket from the mating surfaces of the main bearing ladder and sump, and then use a clean rag to wipe out the sump and the engine's interior.

10 Ensure that the sump mating surfaces are clean and dry, and then apply a thin coating of suitable sealant to the sump mating surface **(see illustration)**.

11 Refit the sump onto the main bearing ladder, and insert the bolts and finger-tighten them at this stage, so that it is still possible to move the sump. Make sure the bolts are refitted in their correct locations.

12 Refit the mounting plate to the rear of the sump and tighten all the retaining bolts.

13 Check that the oil drain plug is tightened securely, then refit the engine undershield (where applicable) and lower the vehicle to the ground.

14 Refit the dipstick and refill the engine with oil as described in Chapter 1A, Section 3.

10 Oil pump – removal, inspection and refitting

Removal

1 Remove the sump as described in Section 9.

2 Unclip the cover from the oil pump drive sprocket **(see illustration)**.

3 Slacken and remove the drive sprocket retaining bolt, withdraw the sprocket from the drive chain **(see illustration)**.

4 Undo the oil pump retaining bolts and withdraw the pump from the bottom of main bearing ladder **(see illustration)**.

Inspection

5 At the time of writing, checking specifications for the oil pump were not available, however, clean the pump and inspect it for damage and excessive wear.

6 Thoroughly clean the oil pump strainer with a suitable solvent, and check it for signs of clogging or splitting. If the strainer is damaged, the strainer and cover assembly must be renewed.

7 If the oil pump drive chain needs renewing, the timing chain assembly will need to be removed first as described in Section 6. The chain is around a sprocket on the end of

10.2 Unclip the cover ...

10.3 ... and undo the sprocket retaining bolt

10.4 Undo the oil pump housing retaining bolts

10.7 Oil pump drive chain sprocket – arrowed

11.2 Check the depth of the fitted oil seal

the crankshaft, at the rear of the crankshaft sprocket for the timing chain **(see illustration)**.

Refitting

8 Clean the mating surfaces of the oil pump and main bearing ladder/cylinder block and fit the retaining bolts. Tighten to the specified torque setting.

9 Locate the sprocket onto the pump making sure it is located correctly in the drive chain. Tighten the sprocket retaining bolt securely.

10 Refit the sprocket cover to the end of the oil pump.

11 Refit the sump as described in Section 9.

11.5 Locate the oil seal and fitting sleeve over the end of the crankshaft

12 Before starting the engine, prime the oil pump as follows. Disconnect the fuel injector wiring connectors, and then turn the engine over on the starter motor until the oil pressure warning light goes out. Reconnect the injector wiring on completion.

11 Crankshaft oil seals – renewal

Right-hand oil seal

1 Remove the crankshaft pulley, with reference to Section 5.

2 Check the depth of the seal in the engine casing before removing **(see illustration)**.

3 Punch or drill two small holes opposite each other in the seal. Screw a self-tapping screw into each, and pull on the screws with pliers to extract the seal **(see illustrations 11.10a and 11.10b)**. Alternatively, the seal can be levered out of position. Use a flat-bladed screwdriver, and take great care not to damage the crankshaft shoulder or seal housing.

4 Clean the seal housing, and polish off any burrs or raised edges, which may have caused the seal to fail in the first place.

5 Lubricate the lips of the new seal with clean engine oil, and carefully locate the seal on the end of the crankshaft. The new seal will normally be supplied with a plastic fitting sleeve to protect the seal lips as the seal is fitted. If so, lubricate the fitting sleeve and locate it over the end of the crankshaft **(see illustration)**.

6 Fit the new seal using a suitable tubular drift, which bears only on the hard outer edge of the seal. Tap the seal into position, to the same depth in the housing as the original **(see illustration)**.

7 Wash off any traces of oil, and then refit the crankshaft pulley as described in Section 5.

Left-hand oil seal

8 Remove the flywheel/driveplate and crankshaft timing plate, as described in Section 12.

9 Make a note of the correct fitted depth of the seal in its housing **(see illustration 11.2)**.

10 Punch or drill two small holes opposite each other in the seal. Screw a self-tapping screw into each, and pull on the screws with pliers to extract the seal **(see illustrations)**.

11 Clean the seal housing, and polish off any burrs or raised edges that may have

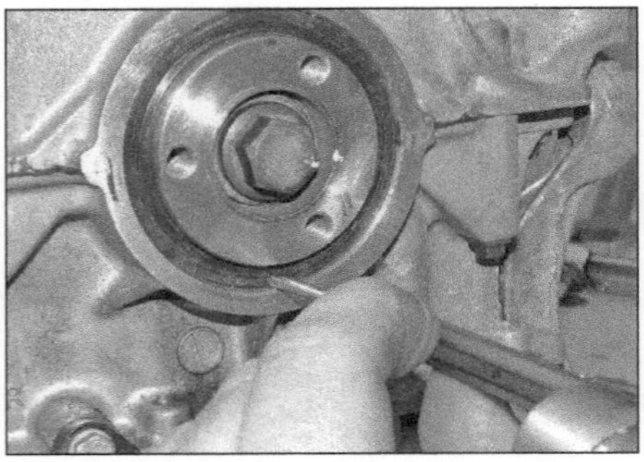

11.6 Tap the seal squarely into position

11.10a Drill a hole ...

11.10b ... then use a self-tapping screw and pliers to extract the oil seal

caused the seal to fail in the first place **(see illustration)**.

12 Lubricate the lips of the new seal with clean engine oil, and carefully locate the seal on the end of the crankshaft. The new seal will normally be supplied with a plastic fitting sleeve to protect the seal lips as the seal is fitted. If so, lubricate the fitting sleeve and locate it over the end of the crankshaft **(see illustrations)**.

13 Before driving the seal fully into position, put a small amount of sealer at each side of the seal, where the upper and lower crankcases meet **(see illustration)**. Drive the seal into position, to the same depth in the housing as the original.

14 Clean off any excess sealer or oil and then refit the crankshaft timing plate and flywheel/driveplate as described in Section 12.

11.11 Clean out the recess

11.12a The new oil seal comes with a protective sleeve ...

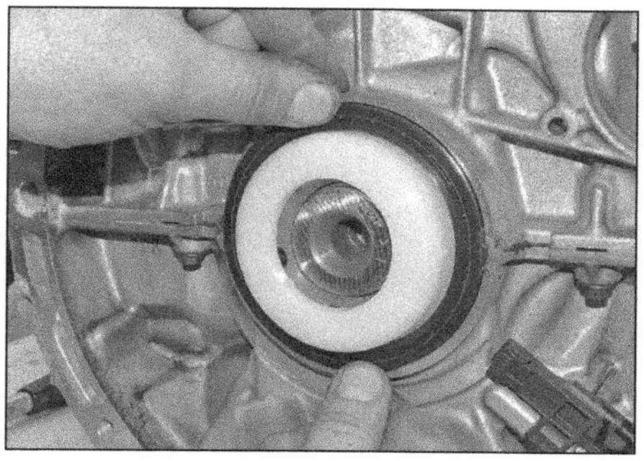

11.12b ... which fits over the end of the crankshaft

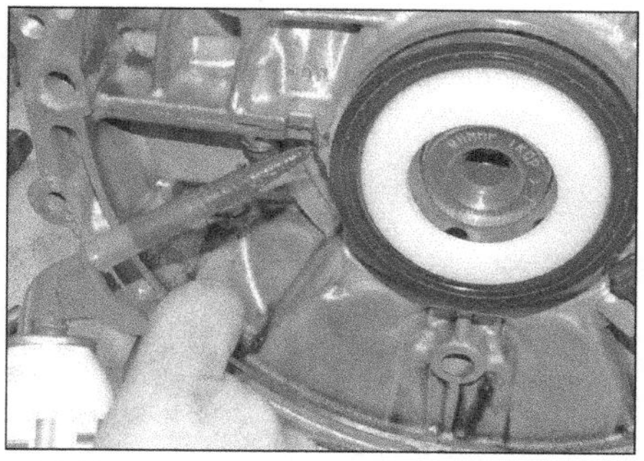

11.13 Apply a small amount of sealer at the casing joints

12 Flywheel/driveplate – removal, inspection and refitting

Removal

Flywheel

1 Remove the transmission as described in Chapter 7A, Section 7, then remove the clutch assembly as described in Chapter 6, Section 6.

2 Prevent the crankshaft from turning by locking the flywheel with a wide-bladed screwdriver between the ring gear teeth and the transmission casing. Alternatively, bolt a strap between the flywheel and the cylinder block/crankcase **(see illustration)**. Do not attempt to lock the flywheel in position using the crankshaft pulley locking pin described in Section 3.

3 Slacken and remove the flywheel retaining bolts, and remove the flywheel from the end of the crankshaft **(see illustrations)**. Be careful not to drop it; it is heavy. If the flywheel locating dowel is a loose fit in the crankshaft end, remove it and store it with the flywheel for safekeeping. Discard the flywheel bolts; new ones must be used on refitting.

4 If required, remove the crankshaft TDC timing plate from the end of the crankshaft **(see illustration)**.

Driveplate

5 Remove the transmission as described in Chapter 7B, Section 9. Lock the driveplate as described in paragraph 2. Mark the relationship between the torque converter plate and the driveplate, and slacken all the driveplate retaining bolts.

6 Remove the retaining bolts, along with the torque converter plate and (where fitted) the two shims (one fitted on each side of the torque converter plate). Note that the shims are of different thickness, the thicker one being on the outside of the torque converter plate. Discard the driveplate retaining bolts; new ones must be used on refitting.

7 Remove the driveplate from the end of the crankshaft. If the locating dowel is a loose fit in the crankshaft end, remove it and store it with the driveplate for safekeeping.

8 If required remove the crankshaft TDC timing plate from the end of the crankshaft.

Inspection

9 On models with manual transmission, examine the flywheel for scoring of the clutch face, and for wear or chipping of the ring gear

12.2 Use a tool to lock the flywheel ring gear and prevent rotation

12.3a Slacken the securing bolts ...

12.3b ... and remove the flywheel

12.4 Remove the TDC timing plate from the crankshaft

teeth. If the clutch face is scored, the flywheel may be surface-ground, but renewal is preferable. Seek the advice of a Citroën dealer or engine reconditioning specialist to see if machining is possible. If the ring gear is worn or damaged, the flywheel must be renewed, as it is not possible to renew the ring gear separately.

10 On models with automatic transmission, check the torque converter driveplate carefully for signs of distortion. Look for any hairline cracks around the bolt holes or radiating outwards from the centre, and inspect the ring gear teeth for signs of wear or chipping. If any sign of wear or damage is found, the driveplate must be renewed.

11 Check the crankshaft TDC timing plate for any damage; make sure that none of the teeth around the circumference of the disc are bent.

Refitting

Flywheel

12 Clean the mating surfaces of the flywheel and crankshaft. Remove any remaining locking compound from the threads of the crankshaft holes, using the correct-size tap, if available.

13 If the new flywheel retaining bolts are not supplied with their threads pre-coated, apply a suitable thread-locking compound to the threads of each bolt.

14 If removed, refit the crankshaft TDC timing plate to the end of the crankshaft.

15 Ensure the locating dowel is in position. Offer up the flywheel, locating it on the dowel, and fit the new retaining bolts.

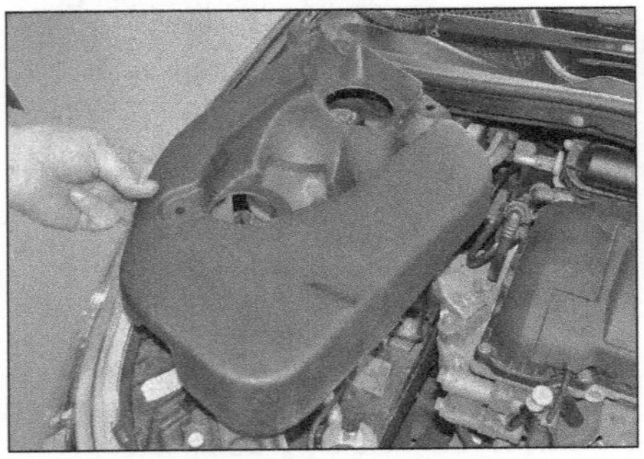

13.5 Remove the plastic trim cover

13.8 Removing the engine mounting bracket

16 Lock the flywheel using the method employed on dismantling, and tighten the retaining bolts to the specified torque and angle.

17 Refit the clutch as described in Chapter 6, Section 6. Remove the flywheel locking tool, and refit the transmission as described in Chapter 7A, Section 7.

Driveplate

18 Carry out the operations described above in paragraphs 12 and 13, substituting 'driveplate' for all references to the flywheel.

19 If removed, refit the crankshaft TDC timing plate to the end of the crankshaft.

20 Locate the driveplate on its locating dowel.

21 Offer up the torque converter plate, with the thinner shim positioned behind the plate and the thicker shim on the outside, and align the marks made prior to removal.

22 Fit the new retaining bolts, and then lock the driveplate using the method employed on dismantling. Tighten the retaining bolts to the specified torque wrench setting and angle.

23 Remove the driveplate locking tool, and refit the transmission as described in Chapter 7B, Section 9.

13 Engine/transmission mountings – inspection and renewal

Inspection

1 If improved access is required, raise the front of the car and support it on axle stands (see *Jacking and vehicle support*). Undo the retaining bolts/nuts and remove the engine undershield.

2 Check the mounting rubber to see if it is cracked, hardened or separated from the metal at any point; renew the mounting if any such damage or deterioration is evident.

3 Check that all the mounting's fasteners are securely tightened; use a torque wrench to check if possible.

4 Using a large screwdriver or a crowbar, check for wear in the mounting by carefully levering against it to check for free play. Where this is not possible, enlist the aid of an assistant to move the engine/transmission back-and-forth, or from side-to-side, while you watch the mounting. While some free play is to be expected even from new components, excessive wear should be obvious. If excessive free play is found, check first that the fasteners are secure, and then renew any worn components as described below.

Renewal

Right-hand mounting

5 Release all the retaining clips and remove the plastic trim from above the right-hand engine mounting **(see illustration)**. If not already done, undo the retaining bolts/nuts and remove the engine undershield.

6 Place a jack beneath the engine, with a block of wood on the jack head. Raise the jack until it is supporting the weight of the engine.

7 Undo the bolts securing the engine mounting to the body and the support bracket **(see illustration)**.

8 If required, undo the bolts and remove the support bracket from the engine **(see illustration)**. Where applicable, release the wiring loom and fuel lines from the retaining clips as it is removed.

9 Check for signs of wear or damage on all components, and renew as necessary.

10 On reassembly, refit the support bracket to the engine, tightening the bolts to the specified torque.

11 Install the mounting and mounting bracket and tighten its retaining bolts to the specified torque setting.

12 Remove the jack from underneath the engine and refit the engine undershield.

Left-hand mounting

13 Remove the battery, and battery tray/box as described in Chapter 5A, Section 4.

14 If not already done, undo the retaining bolts/nuts and remove the engine undershield. Place a jack beneath the transmission, with a block of wood on the jack head. Raise the jack until it is supporting the weight of the transmission.

15 Slacken and remove the mounting's two upper retaining nuts, noting their fitted position **(see illustration)**.

16 Undo the centre retaining nut and remove

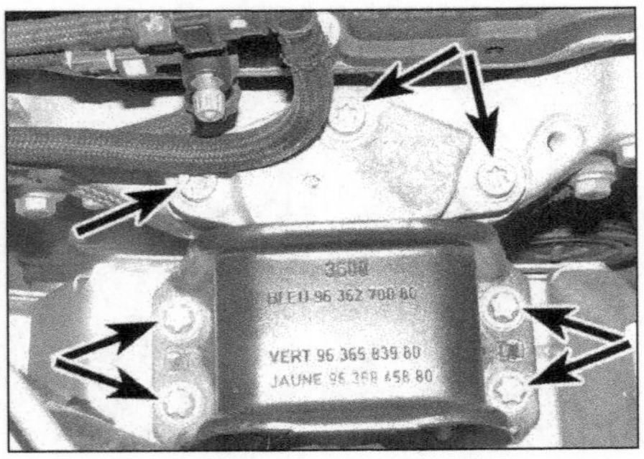

13.7 Right-hand engine mounting upper bolts (arrowed)

13.15 Undo the left-hand transmission mounting securing nuts (arrowed) ...

13.16 ... and the mounting centre nut (arrowed)

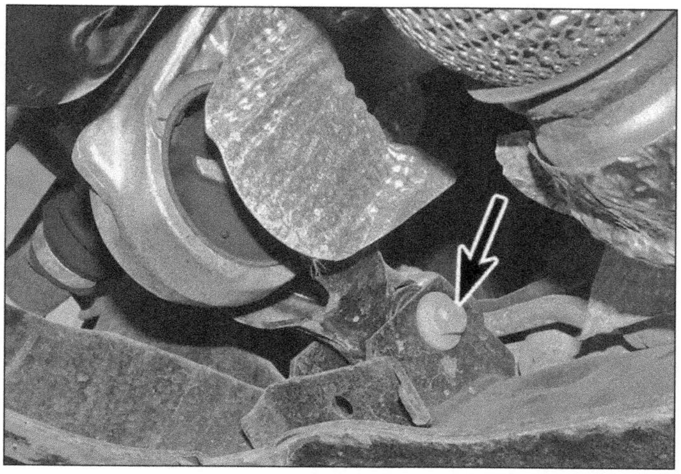

13.22 Undo the rear link-to-subframe mounting bolt (arrowed) ...

the mounting from the bracket above the transmission housing **(see illustration)**.

17 Check carefully for signs of wear or damage on all components, and renew them where necessary.

18 Refit the mounting to the mounting bracket and tighten it to the specified torque.

19 Fit the mounting nuts to the bracket on the transmission and tighten the retaining nuts to the specified torque.

20 Remove the jack from underneath the transmission, refit the engine undershield, and then refit the battery as described in Chapter 5A, Section 4.

Lower engine torque link

21 Firmly apply the handbrake, and then jack up the front of the vehicle and support it securely on axle stands (see *Jacking and vehicle support*). If not already done, undo the retaining bolts/nuts and remove the engine undershield.

22 Unscrew and remove the bolt securing the rear mounting link to the subframe **(see illustration)**.

23 Remove the bolt securing the rear mounting link to the driveshaft inner bearing bracket at the rear of the cylinder block **(see illustration)**, and then remove the mounting torque reaction link.

24 To remove the intermediate bearing housing assembly it will first be necessary to remove the right-hand driveshaft as described in Chapter 8, Section 2.

25 With the driveshaft removed, undo the retaining bolts and remove the bearing housing/mounting from the rear of the cylinder block.

26 Check carefully for signs of wear or damage on all components, and renew them where necessary. The rubber bush fitted to the driveshaft bearing housing is available as a separate item on some models, check with your local dealer for availability of parts. If available, the rubber bush can be pressed out of the bearing housing, noting its fitted position, and then a new one pressed back into place.

27 On reassembly, fit the bearing housing assembly to the rear of the cylinder block, and tighten its retaining bolts securely. Refit the driveshaft as described in Chapter 8, Section 2.

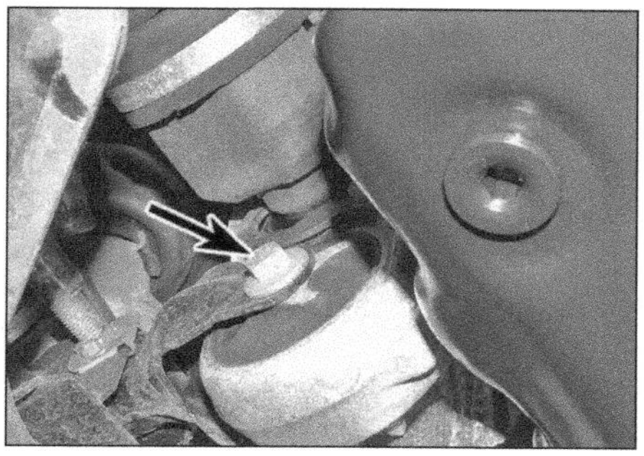

13.23 ... and the lower link-to-mounting bracket bolt (arrowed)

28 Refit the rear mounting torque reaction link, and tighten both its bolts to their specified torque settings.

29 Refit the engine undershield, and then lower the vehicle to the ground.

Chapter 2 Part C:
1.6 litre diesel engines in-car repair procedures

Contents

Degrees of difficulty

Easy, suitable for novice with little experience	**Fairly easy,** suitable for beginner with some experience	**Fairly difficult,** suitable for competent DIY mechanic	**Difficult,** suitable for experienced DIY mechanic	**Very difficult,** suitable for expert DIY or professional

Specifications

General

Designation:	
Without intercooler	DV6TED4
With intercooler	DV6ATED4
Engine codes:*	
DV6ATED4 (without particulate filter)	9HX
DV6TED4:	
Without particulate filter	9HY
With particulate filter	9HZ
Capacity	1560 cc
Bore	75.0 mm
Stroke	88.3 mm
Direction of crankshaft rotation	Clockwise (viewed from the right-hand side of vehicle)
No 1 cylinder location	At the transmission end of block
Maximum power output:	
9HX	66 kW (90hp) @ 4000 rpm
9HY and 9HZ	80 kW (110 hp) @ 4000 rpm
Maximum torque output:	
9HX	215 Nm @ 1750 rpm
9HY and 9HZ	240 Nm @ 1750 rpm
Compression ratio	18.0 :1
Emissions standard:	
9HX and 9HY	Euro 4
9HZ	Euro 3

** The engine code is stamped on a plate attached to the front of the cylinder block.*

Compression pressures (engine hot, at cranking speed)

Normal (new engine)	20 ± 5 bar
Minimum	15 bar
Maximum difference between any two cylinders	5 bar

Cylinder head gasket

Gasket thickness:	
1 notch	1.35 mm
2 notch	1.25 mm
3 notch	1.30 mm
4 notch	1.40 mm
5 notch	1.45 mm
Piston protrusion (gasket required):	
0.685 to 0.734 mm	1 notch
0.533 to 0.634 mm	2 notch
0.635 to 0.684 mm	3 notch
0.735 to 0.784 mm	4 notch
0.785 to 0.886 mm	5 notch

Cylinder head bolts

Maximum length (measured under head)	149 mm

Camshaft

Drive:	
Intake camshaft	Toothed belt from crankshaft
Exhaust camshaft	Chain-drive from intake camshaft
Number of teeth	19
Length:	
Intake camshaft	401.0 ± 0.15 mm
Exhaust camshaft	389.0 ± 0.5 mm
Endfloat	0.195 to 0.300 mm

Lubrication system

Oil pump type	Gear-type, driven directly by the right-hand end of the crankshaft, by two flats machined along the crankshaft journal
Minimum oil pressure at 80°C:	
1000 rpm	1.3 bar
4000 rpm	3.5 bar

Torque wrench settings

	Nm	lbf ft
Ancillary drivebelt tensioner roller	20	15
Big-end bolts:*		
Stage 1	10	7
Stage 2	Slacken 180°	
Stage 3	30	22
Stage 4	Angle-tighten a further 140°	
Camshaft bearing caps	10	7
Camshaft cover/bearing ladder:		
Studs	10	7
Bolts	10	7
Camshaft position sensor bolt	5	4
Camshaft sprocket:		
Stage 1	20	15
Stage 2	Angle-tighten a further 50°	
Coolant outlet housing bolts	7	5
Crankshaft position/speed sensor bolt	5	4
Crankshaft pulley/sprocket bolt:*		
Stage 1	35	26
Stage 2	Angle-tighten a further 190 °	
Cylinder head bolts:		
Stage 1	20	15
Stage 2	40	30
Stage 3	Angle-tighten a further 260°	
Cylinder head cover/manifold	10	7
EGR valve	10	7

Torque wrench settings (continued)	Nm	lbf ft
Engine mountings:		
Left-hand engine/transmission mounting:		
Mounting bracket to transmission	55	41
Mounting to bracket	60	44
Rear engine/transmission mounting:		
Connecting link to mounting assembly	60	44
Connecting link-to-subframe nut/bolt	60	44
Mounting to engine	60	44
Right-hand engine mounting:		
Mounting to body	60	44
Mounting to support bracket	60	44
Support bracket to engine	55	41
Engine-to-transmission fixing bolts	54	40
Flywheel bolts:*		
Dual mass flywheel:		
Stage 1	25	18
Stage 2	Fully slacken	
Stage 3	8	6
Stage 4	30	22
Stage 5	Angle-tighten a further 90°	
Normal flywheel:		
Stage 1	25	18
Stage 2	Fully slacken	
Stage 3	8	6
Stage 4	17	13
Stage 5	Angle-tighten a further 75°	
Fuel pump sprocket	50	37
Main bearing ladder outer seam bolts:		
Stage 1	5	4
Stage 2	10	7
Main bearing ladder to cylinder block:		
Stage 1	10	7
Stage 2	Slacken 180°	
Stage 3	30	22
Stage 4	Angle-tighten a further 140°	
Piston oil jet spray tube bolt	20	15
Oil filter cover	25	18
Oil pick-up pipe	10	7
Oil pressure switch	32	24
Oil pump to cylinder block	10	7
Sump drain plug	25	18
Sump bolts/nuts	12	9
Timing belt idler pulley	35	26
Timing belt tensioner pulley	25	18
Timing chain tensioner	10	7
Vacuum pump:		
Stage 1	18	13
Stage 2	Angle-tighten a further 5°	

** Do not re-use*

1 General information

How to use this Chapter

This Chapter describes the repair procedures that can reasonably be carried out on the engine whilst it remains in the vehicle. If the engine has been removed from the vehicle and is being dismantled as described in Chapter 2E, any preliminary dismantling procedures can be ignored.

Note that, while it may be possible physically to overhaul items such as the piston/connecting rod assemblies while the engine is in the car, such tasks are not usually carried out as separate operations. Usually, several additional procedures are required (not to mention the cleaning of components and oilways); for this reason, all such tasks are classed as major overhaul procedures, and are described in Chapter 2E.

Chapter 2E describes the removal of the engine/transmission from the car, and the full overhaul procedures that can then be carried out.

DV series engines

The 1.6 litre DV series engine is the result of development collaboration between Peugeot/Citroën and Ford. The engine is of double overhead camshaft (DOHC) 16-valve design. The direct injection, turbocharged, four-cylinder engine is mounted transversely, with the transmission mounted on the left-hand side.

A toothed timing belt drives the intake camshaft, high-pressure fuel pump and coolant pump. The intake camshaft drives the exhaust camshaft via a chain. The camshafts operate the intake and exhaust valves via rocker arms, which are supported at their pivot ends by hydraulic self-adjusting tappets. The camshafts are supported by bearings machined directly in the cylinder head and camshaft bearing housing.

The high-pressure fuel pump supplies fuel to the fuel rail, and subsequently to the electronically controlled injectors, which inject the fuel direct into the combustion chambers. This design differs from the previous type where an injection pump supplies the fuel at high pressure to each injector. The earlier, conventional type injection pump required fine calibration and timing, and these functions are now completed by the high-pressure pump, electronic injectors and engine management ECU.

The crankshaft runs in five main bearings of the usual shell type. Endfloat is controlled by thrustwashers either side of No 2 main bearing.

The pistons are selected to be of matching weight, and incorporate fully floating gudgeon pins retained by circlips.

Repair operations precaution

The engine is a complex unit with numerous accessories and ancillary components. The design of the engine compartment is such that every conceivable space has been utilised, and access to virtually all of the engine components is extremely limited. In many cases, ancillary components will have to be removed, or moved to one side, and wiring, pipes and hoses will have to be disconnected or removed from various cable clips and support brackets.

When working on this engine, read through the entire procedure first, look at the car and engine at the same time, and establish whether you have the necessary tools, equipment, skill and patience to proceed. Allow considerable time for any operation, and be prepared for the unexpected.

Because of the limited access, many of the engine photographs appearing in this Chapter were, by necessity, taken with the engine removed from the vehicle.

Warning: It is essential to observe strict precautions when working on the fuel system components of the engine, particularly the high-pressure side of the system. Before carrying out any engine operations that entail working on, or near, any part of the fuel system, refer to the special information given in Chapter 4B, Section 2.

Operations with engine in vehicle

a) Compression pressure – testing.
b) Cylinder head cover – removal and refitting.
c) Crankshaft pulley – removal and refitting.
d) Timing belt covers – removal and refitting.
e) Timing belt – removal, refitting and adjustment.
f) Timing belt tensioner and sprockets – removal and refitting.
g) Camshaft oil seal – renewal.
h) Camshaft, rocker arms and hydraulic tappets – removal, inspection and refitting.
i) Sump – removal and refitting.
j) Oil pump – removal and refitting.
k) Crankshaft oil seals – renewal.
l) Engine/transmission mountings – inspection and renewal.
m) Flywheel – removal, inspection and refitting.

2 Compression and leakdown tests – description and interpretation

Compression test

Note: *A compression tester specifically designed for diesel engines must be used for this test.*

1 When engine performance is down, or if misfiring occurs which cannot be attributed to the fuel system, a compression test can provide diagnostic clues as to the engine's condition. If the test is performed regularly, it can give warning of trouble before any other symptoms become apparent.

2 A compression tester specifically intended for diesel engines must be used, because of the higher pressures involved. The tester is connected to an adapter, which screws into the glow plug or injector hole. On this engine, an adapter suitable for use in the glow plug holes will be required, so as not to disturb the fuel system components. It is unlikely to be worthwhile buying such a tester for occasional use, but it may be possible to borrow or hire one – if not, have the test performed by a garage.

3 Unless specific instructions to the contrary are supplied with the tester, observe the following points:

a) The battery must be in a good state of charge, the air filter must be clean, and the engine should be at normal operating temperature.
b) All the glow plugs should be removed as described in Chapter 5C, Section 2 before starting the test.
c) The wiring connectors on the engine management system ECU (located in the plastic box next to the battery) must be disconnected.

4 The compression pressures measured are not so important as the balance between cylinders. Values are given in the Specifications.

5 The cause of poor compression is less easy to establish on a diesel engine than on a petrol one. The effect of introducing oil into the cylinders ('wet' testing) is not conclusive, because there is a risk that the oil will sit in the swirl chamber or in the recess on the piston crown instead of passing to the rings. However, the following can be used as a rough guide to diagnosis.

6 All cylinders should produce very similar pressures; any difference greater than that specified indicates the existence of a fault. Note that the compression should build-up quickly in a healthy engine; low compression on the first stroke, followed by gradually increasing pressure on successive strokes, indicates worn piston rings. A low compression reading on the first stroke, which does not build-up during successive strokes, indicates leaking valves or a blown head gasket (a cracked head could also be the cause). Deposits on the undersides of the valve heads can also cause low compression.

7 A low reading from two adjacent cylinders is almost certainly due to the head gasket having blown between them; the presence of coolant in the engine oil will confirm this.

8 If the compression reading is unusually high, the cylinder head surfaces, valves and pistons are probably coated with carbon deposits. If this is the case, the cylinder head should be removed and decarbonised (see Chapter 2E, Section 7).

Leakdown test

9 A leakdown test measures the rate at which compressed air fed into the cylinder is lost. It is an alternative to a compression test, and in many ways it is better, since the escaping air provides easy identification of where pressure loss is occurring (piston rings, valves or head gasket).

10 The equipment needed for leakdown testing is unlikely to be available to the home mechanic. If poor compression is suspected, have the test performed by a suitably-equipped garage.

3 Engine assembly/valve timing holes – general information and usage

Note: *Do not attempt to rotate the engine whilst the crankshaft and camshaft are locked in position. If the engine is to be left in this state for a long period of time, it is a good idea to place suitable warning notices inside the vehicle, and in the engine compartment. This will reduce the possibility of the engine being accidentally cranked on the starter motor, which is likely to cause damage with the locking pins in place.*

1 Timing holes or slots are located only in the crankshaft pulley flange and camshaft sprocket hub. The holes/slots are used to position the pistons halfway up the cylinder bores. This will ensure that the valve timing is maintained during operations that require removal and refitting of the timing belt. When the holes/slots are aligned with their corresponding holes in the cylinder block and cylinder head, suitable diameter bolts/pins can be inserted to lock the crankshaft and camshaft in position, preventing rotation.

2 Note that the HDi type fuel system used on these engines does not have a conventional diesel injection pump, but instead uses a high-pressure fuel pump. Although it may be argued that timing of the fuel pump is irrelevant because it merely pressurises the fuel in the fuel rail, Citroën include this procedure for engines fitted with a Bosch high-pressure fuel pump, using the same timing rod/pin used

3.9 Insert a 5.0 mm drill bit/bolt through the round hole in the sprocket flange, into the hole in the oil pump housing (lower timing belt cover removed for clarity)

3.10a Insert an 8.0 mm drill bit/bolt through the hole in the camshaft sprocket (early model sprocket) ...

3.10b ... and into the corresponding hole in the cylinder head (later model sprocket)

for crankshaft sprocket timing. **Note:** *On the Bosch pump, the drive sprocket is keyed to the shaft*. In addition, note that the hole in the fuel pump sprocket only aligns correctly with the hole in the mounting bracket every 12 revolutions of the crankshaft (or every 6 revolutions of the camshaft sprocket).

3 To align the engine assembly/valve timing holes, proceed as follows.

4 Chock the rear wheels then jack up the front of the vehicle and support it on axle stands (see *Jacking and vehicle support*). Remove the right-hand front roadwheel.

5 To gain access to the crankshaft pulley, to enable the engine to be turned, the wheel arch plastic liner must be removed. The liner is secured by several plastic expanding rivets/nut/screws. To remove the rivets, push in the centre pins a little, and then prise the clips from place. Remove the liner from under the front wing. The crankshaft can then be turned using a suitable socket and extension bar fitted to the pulley bolt.

6 Remove the upper and lower timing belt covers as described in Section 6.

7 Temporarily refit the crankshaft pulley bolt, remove the crankshaft locking tool, then turn the crankshaft until the timing hole in the camshaft sprocket hub is aligned with the corresponding hole in the cylinder head. Note that the crankshaft must always be turned in a clockwise direction (viewed from the right-hand side of vehicle). Use a small mirror so that the position of the sprocket hub timing slot can be observed. When the slot is aligned with the corresponding hole in the cylinder head, the camshaft is positioned correctly.

8 Remove the crankshaft drivebelt pulley as described in Section 5.

9 Insert a 5 mm diameter bolt, rod or drill through the hole in crankshaft sprocket flange and into the corresponding hole in the oil pump housing **(see illustration)**, if necessary, carefully turn the crankshaft either way until the rod enters the timing hole in the block.

10 Insert an 8 mm bolt, rod or drill through the hole in the camshaft sprocket hub and into engagement with the cylinder head. Note that a modified 3-segment camshaft sprocket is fitted to later models **(see illustrations)**.

11 If using this procedure during refitting of the timing belt, insert a 5 mm diameter bolt, rod or drill through the hole in the fuel pump sprocket and into the corresponding hole in the cylinder head **(see illustration)**. **Note:** *On some engines, a hole is provided at the 5 o'clock position for locking purposes only, however, the timing hole is at the 12 o'clock position.* Note the comment in paragraph 2 – if the fuel pump sprocket holes are not aligned during removal of the timing belt, it is of no consequence, however it is important to align the holes during the refitting procedure. If timing alignment alone is being checked there is no need to check alignment of the pump sprocket.

12 The crankshaft and camshaft are now locked in position, preventing unnecessary rotation.

4 Cylinder head cover/intake manifold – removal and refitting

Removal

1 To make access easier, remove the scuttle panel lower grille panel as described in Chapter 11, Section 22.

2 Pull the plastic engine cover upwards to release the locating pegs from the rubber mountings on top of the cylinder head cover **(see illustration)**.

3 Remove the air intake hoses, then unscrew the air filter housing upper cover bolts and remove the filter element as described in Chapter 1B, Section 21. Pull the air filter lower housing from its rubber mountings.

4 Disconnect the wiring plugs from the top of each injector, undo the guide bolts, then make sure all wiring harnesses are freed from any retaining brackets on the cylinder head cover/intake manifold **(see illustration)**. Disconnect any vacuum pipes as necessary, having first noted their fitted positions.

5 Remove the EGR heat exchanger as described in Chapter 4C, Section 2.

6 Depress the release buttons and disconnect

3.11 Insert a 5.0 mm drill bit/bolt through the round hole in the fuel pump sprocket flange, into the hole in the cylinder head

4.2 Pull the plastic cover upwards to release the rubber mountings

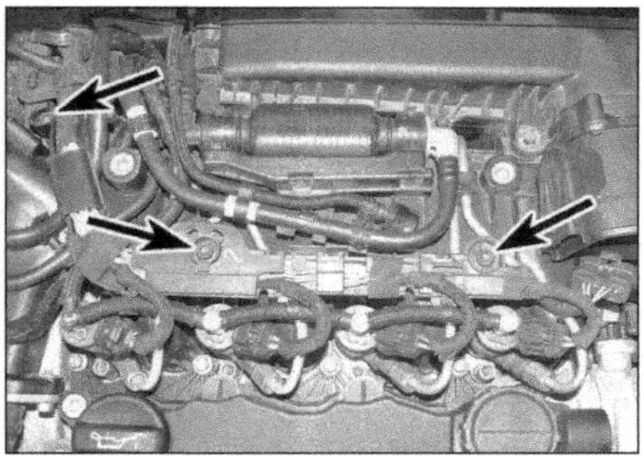

4.4 Undo the Allen screws (arrowed) and position the wiring harness/guide to one side

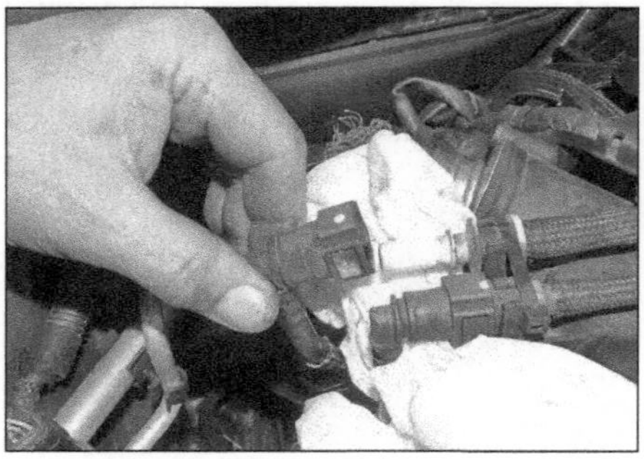

4.6 Depress the release buttons and disconnect the fuel feed and return hoses

4.7a Slacken the left-hand turbocharger outlet hose bolt, undo the right-hand bolt (arrowed) ...

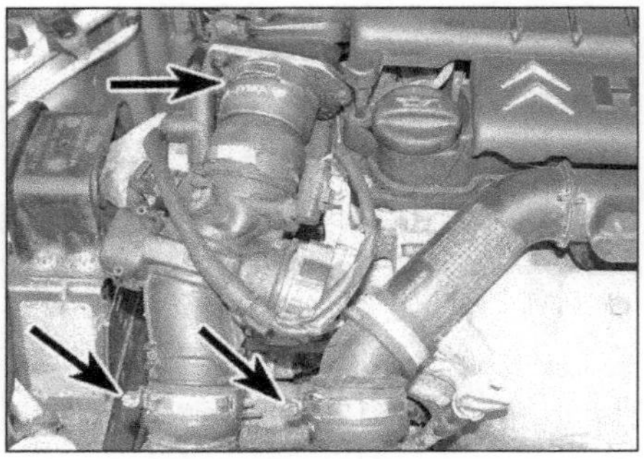

4.7b ... then slacken the hose clamps (arrowed) ...

4.7c ... disconnect the wiring plugs ...

4.7d ... and undo the securing bolts (2 bolts arrowed)

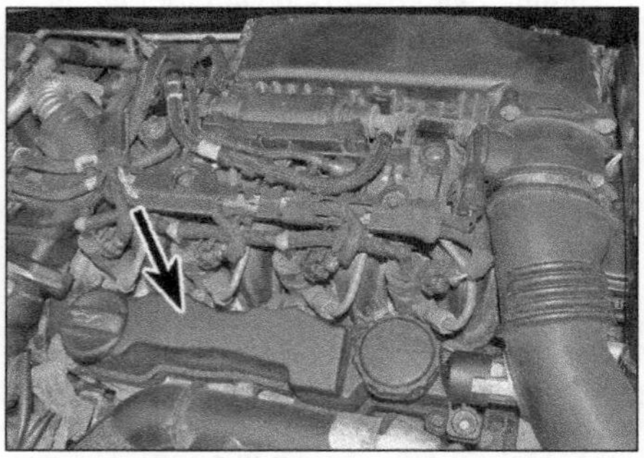

4.8 Undo the bolts and remove the oil separator (arrowed)

the fuel feed and return hoses at the right-hand end of the cylinder head, then disconnect the fuel temperature sensor wiring plug, and move the pipe/priming bulb assembly to the rear **(see illustration)**.

7 Release the clamps, undo the bolts and remove the intake ducting between the turbocharger and the intake manifold. Make a note of their fitted positions, and then disconnect the various wiring plugs, as the assembly is withdrawn **(see illustrations)**.

8 Undo the retaining bolts and remove the oil separator from the top of the cylinder head **(see illustration)**. Recover the rubber seal.

9 Prise out the retaining clips and disconnect the fuel return pipes from the injectors, then undo the unions and remove the high-pressure fuel pipes from the injectors and the common fuel rail at the rear of the cylinder head – counterhold the unions with a second spanner **(see illustrations)**. Plug the openings to prevent dirt ingress.

10 Undo the 2 bolts securing the cylinder head cover/intake manifold. Lift the assembly away **(see illustration)**. Recover the manifold rubber seals.

Refitting

11 Refitting is a reversal of removal, bearing in mind the following points:

a) *Examine the seals for signs of damage and deterioration, and renew if necessary. Smear a little clean engine oil on the manifold seals.*
b) *Renew the fuel injector high-pressure pipes – see Chapter 4B, Section 11.*
c) *Refit the air intake hoses and filter element – see Chapter 1B, Section 21.*
d) *Refit the scuttle panel – see Chapter 11, Section 22.*

5 Crankshaft pulley – removal and refitting

Removal

1 Remove the auxiliary drivebelt as described in Chapter 1B, Section 17.

2 To lock the crankshaft, working underneath the engine, insert Citroën/Peugeot tool No 0194-C into the hole in the right-hand face of the engine block casting over the lower

4.9a Prise out the clip and pull the return hose from the top of each injector

4.9b Use a second spanner to hold the injector port whilst slackening the fuel pipe unions

4.10 Undo the 2 remaining bolts (arrowed) and pull the cover/manifold upwards

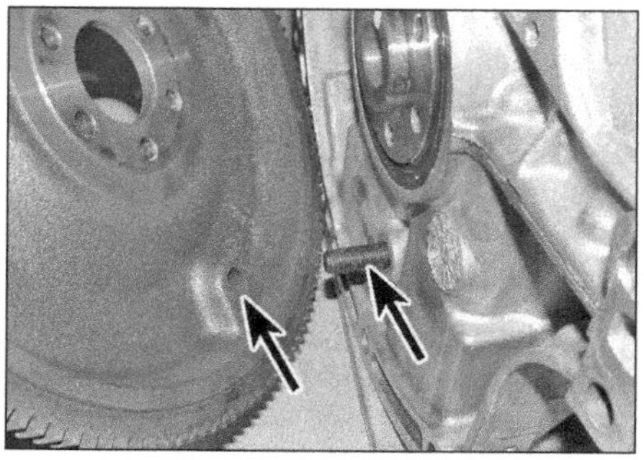

5.2 The locking pin/bolt (arrowed) must locate in the hole in the flywheel (arrowed) to prevent rotation

section of the flywheel. Rotate the crankshaft until the tool engages in the corresponding hole in the flywheel. In the absence of the Citroën tool, insert a 12 mm rod or drill into the hole **(see illustration)**. **Note:** *The hole in the casting and the hole in the flywheel are provided purely to lock the crankshaft whilst the pulley bolt is undone, it does not position the crankshaft at TDC.*

3 Using a suitable socket and extension bar, unscrew the retaining bolt, remove the washer, then slide the pulley off the end of the crankshaft **(see illustrations)**. If the pulley is tight fit, it can be drawn off the crankshaft using a suitable puller. If a puller is being used, refit the pulley retaining bolt without the washer to avoid damaging the crankshaft as the puller is tightened.

Caution: Do not touch the outer magnetic sensor ring of the sprocket with your fingers, or allow metallic particles to come into contact with it.

5.3a Undo the retaining bolt ...

5.3b ... and remove the crankshaft pulley

Refitting

4 Refit the pulley to the end of the crankshaft, making sure the locating lug on the end of the crankshaft aligns with the slot in the rear of the pulley **(see illustration)**.

5 Thoroughly clean the threads of the pulley retaining bolt, then apply a coat of locking compound to the bolt threads. Citroën recommend the use of Loctite (available from your Citroën dealer); in the absence of this, any good-quality locking compound may be used.

6 Refit the crankshaft pulley retaining bolt and washer. Tighten the bolt to the specified torque, and then through the specified angle, preventing the crankshaft from turning using the method employed on removal.

5.4 Crankshaft sprocket alignment lug (arrowed)

7 Refit and tension the auxiliary drivebelt as described in Chapter 1B, Section 17.

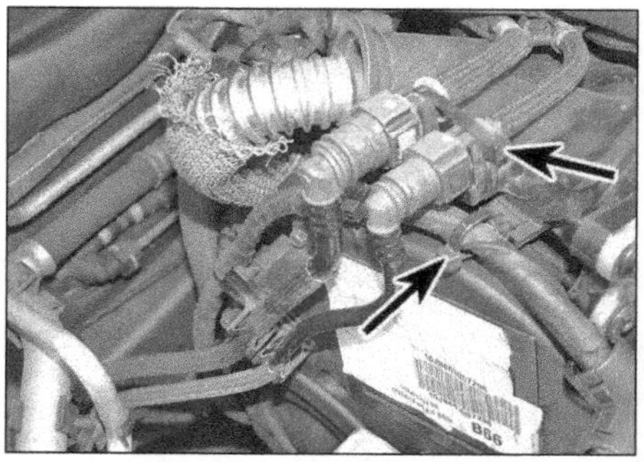

6.4 Unclip the fuel pipes (arrowed) and the wiring harness (arrowed)

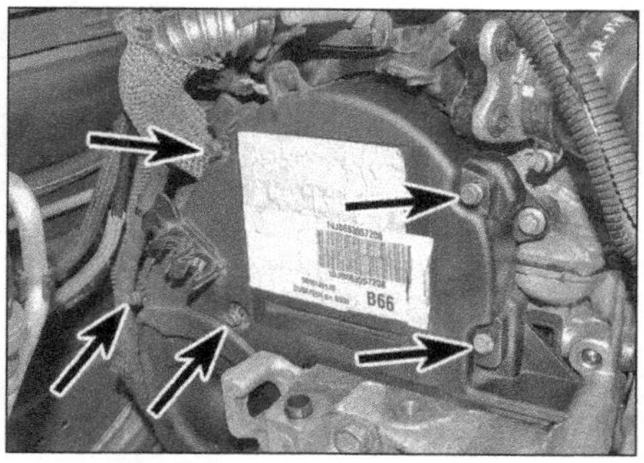

6.5a Undo the upper cover securing bolts (arrowed) ...

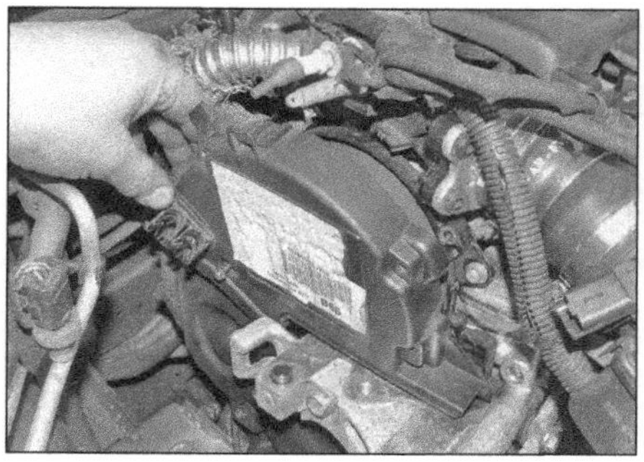

6.5b ... and remove it from over the timing belt

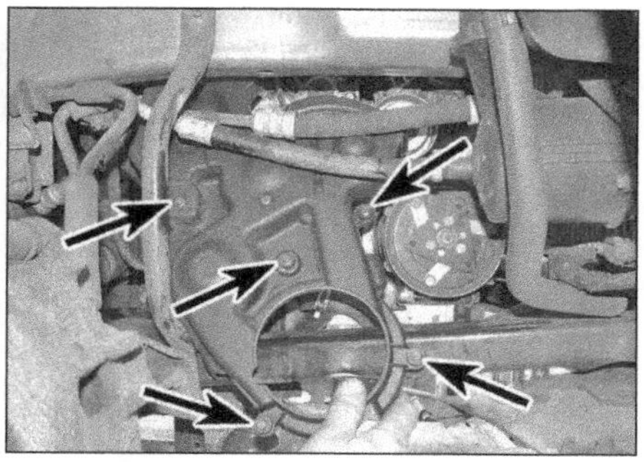

6.8 Timing belt lower cover retaining bolts (arrowed)

6 Timing belt covers – removal and refitting

Warning: Refer to the precautionary information contained in Section 1 before proceeding.

Removal

Upper cover

1 Disconnect the battery (refer to precautions in Chapter 5A, Section 1).

2 Remove the scuttle panel lower grille panel as described in Chapter 11, Section 22.

3 Support the engine and remove the right-hand engine mounting as described in Section 17.

4 Release the retaining clips and unclip the fuel pipes and wiring harness from the upper cover **(see illustration)**.

5 Undo the five screws and remove the timing belt upper cover **(see illustrations)**.

Lower cover

6 Remove the upper cover as described previously.

7 Remove the crankshaft pulley as described in Section 5.

8 Remove the auxiliary drivebelt tensioner locking tool (where applicable), then undo the five bolts and remove the lower cover **(see illustration)**.

Refitting

9 Refitting of all the covers is a reversal of the relevant removal procedure, ensuring that each cover section is correctly located, and that the cover retaining bolts are securely tightened. Ensure that all disturbed hoses are reconnected and retained by their relevant clips.

7 Timing belt – removal, inspection, refitting and tensioning

General

1 The timing belt drives the intake camshaft, high-pressure fuel pump, and coolant pump from a toothed sprocket on the end of the crankshaft. If the belt breaks or slips in service, the pistons are likely to hit the valve heads, resulting in expensive damage.

2 The timing belt should be renewed at the specified intervals, or earlier if it is contaminated with oil, or at all noisy in operation (a 'scraping' noise due to uneven wear).

3 If the timing belt is being removed, it is a wise precaution to check the condition of the coolant pump at the same time (check for signs of coolant leakage). This may avoid the need to remove the timing belt again at a later stage should the coolant pump fail.

Removal

4 Chock the rear wheels then jack up the front of the vehicle and support it on axle stands (see *Jacking and vehicle support*). Remove the front right-hand roadwheel, wheel arch liner (to expose the crankshaft pulley), and the engine undershield. The wheel arch liner is secured by several plastic expanding rivets/plastic clips. Pull the centre pins out a little then prise the rivets from place. The engine undershield is retained by several bolts/nuts.

5 Remove the auxiliary drivebelt as described in Chapter 1B, Section 17.

6 Remove the upper and lower timing belt covers, as described in Section 6.

7 Refer to Chapter 4B, Section 18 and disconnect the front exhaust pipe at the flexible section.

8 Position a trolley jack under the engine, and using a block of wood on the jack head, take the weight of the engine.

9 Undo the bolts/nut and remove the right-hand engine mounting and support bracket as described in Section 17.

10 Undo the screw and remove the crankshaft position sensor adjacent to the crankshaft sprocket flange, and move it to one side **(see illustration)**.

11 Undo the retaining screw and remove the timing belt protection bracket, again adjacent to the crankshaft sprocket flange **(see illustration)**.

12 Lock the crankshaft and camshaft in the correct position as described in Section 3. If necessary, temporarily refit the crankshaft pulley bolt to enable the crankshaft to be rotated. At this stage, it is of no consequence whether the fuel pump sprocket aligns correctly with the hole in the pump mounting bracket.

13 Insert a hexagon key into the belt tensioner pulley centre, slacken the pulley bolt, and allow the tensioner to rotate, relieving the belt tension **(see illustration)**. With the belt slack, temporarily tighten the pulley bolt.

14 Note its routing, then remove the timing belt from the sprockets.

Inspection

15 Renew the belt as a matter of course, regardless of its apparent condition. The cost of a new belt is nothing compared with the cost of repairs should the belt break in service. If signs of oil contamination are found, trace the source of the oil leak and rectify it. Wash down the engine timing belt area and all related components, to remove all traces of oil. Check that the tensioner and idler pulleys rotate freely without any sign of roughness, and also check that the coolant pump pulley rotates freely. Due to the complexity of this procedure, it is recommended that the tensioner and idler pulleys be renewed when fitting a new timing belt **(see illustration)**.

Refitting and tensioning

16 Commence refitting by ensuring that the crankshaft and camshaft timing pins are still in position correctly. Also, where a Bosch high-pressure fuel pump is fitted, locate and lock the fuel pump sprocket in its correct position as described in Section 3.

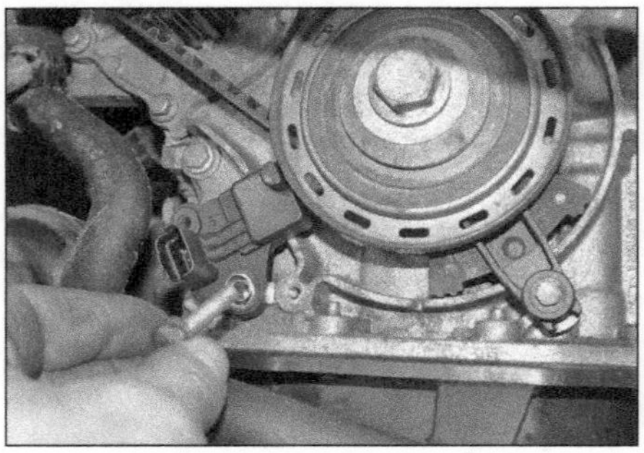

7.10 Undo the bolt and remove the crankshaft position sensor

7.11 Remove the timing belt protection bracket bolt (arrowed)

7.13 Slacken the bolt and allow the tensioner to rotate, relieving the tension on the belt

7.15 Tensioner and idler pulleys

7.17a Feed the timing belt around the crankshaft sprocket first ...

7.17b ... and then finally around the tensioner pulley

17 Locate the timing belt on the crankshaft sprocket then, keeping it taut, locate it around the idler pulley, camshaft sprocket, high-pressure pump sprocket, coolant pump sprocket, and the tensioner pulley **(see illustrations)**. If the timing belt has directional arrows on it, make sure that they point in the direction of normal engine rotation.

18 Refit the timing belt protection bracket and tighten the retaining bolt securely.

19 Slacken the tensioner pulley bolt and, using a hexagonal key, rotate the tensioner anti-clockwise, which moves the index arm clockwise, until the index arm is aligned as shown **(see illustration)**.

20 Remove the camshaft and crankshaft and fuel pump timing pins and, using a socket on the crankshaft pulley bolt, crankshaft clockwise 6 complete revolutions. Align the camshaft and crankshaft timing holes and check that the timing pins can be inserted, then remove them. There is no requirement to check the fuel pump sprocket alignment, as it will only be aligned after 12 complete revolutions.

21 Check that the tensioner index arm is still aligned between the edges of the area shown **(see illustration 7.19)**. If it is not, remove and belt and begin the refitting process again.

22 The remainder of refitting is a reversal of removal. Tighten all fasteners to the specified torque where given.

8 Timing belt sprockets and tensioner – removal and refitting

Camshaft sprocket

Removal

1 Remove the timing belt as described in Section 7.

2 Remove the locking tool from the camshaft sprocket/hub. Slacken the sprocket hub retaining bolt. To prevent the camshaft rotating as the bolt is slackened, a sprocket holding tool will be required. In the absence of the special Citroën tool, an acceptable substitute can be fabricated at home **(see Tool Tip)**. Do not attempt to use the engine assembly/valve timing locking tool to prevent the sprocket from rotating whilst the bolt is slackened.

3 Remove the sprocket hub retaining bolt, and slide the sprocket and hub off the end of the camshaft.

7.17c Timing belt routing

7.19 The index arm must align with the lug (arrowed)

HAYNES HiNT

A sprocket holding tool can be made from two lengths of steel strip bolted together to form a forked end. Drill holes and insert bolts in the ends of the fork to engage with the sprocket spokes.

4 Clean the camshaft sprocket thoroughly, and renew it if there are any signs of wear, damage or cracks.

Refitting

5 Refit the camshaft sprocket to the camshaft **(see illustration)**.

6 Refit the sprocket hub retaining bolt. Tighten the bolt to the specified torque, preventing the camshaft from turning as during removal.

7 Align the engine assembly/valve timing slot in the camshaft sprocket hub with the hole in the cylinder head and refit the timing pin to lock the camshaft in position.

8.5 Ensure the lug on the sprocket hub engages with the slot on the end of the camshaft (arrowed)

8.11a Slide the sprocket from the crankshaft ...

8.11b ... and recover the Woodruff key

8.17 Insert a suitable drill bit through the sprocket into the hole in the backplate

8 Fit the timing belt around the pump sprocket and camshaft sprocket, and tension the timing belt as described in Section 7.

Crankshaft sprocket

Removal

9 Remove the timing belt as described in Section 7.

10 Check that the engine assembly/valve timing holes are still aligned as described in Section 3, and the camshaft sprocket and flywheel are locked in position.

11 Slide the sprocket off the end of the crankshaft and collect the Woodruff key **(see illustrations)**.

12 Examine the crankshaft oil seal for signs of oil leakage and, if necessary, renew it as described in Section 14.

13 Clean the crankshaft sprocket thoroughly, and renew it if there are any signs of wear, damage or cracks. Recover the crankshaft locating key.

Refitting

14 Refit the key to the end of the crankshaft, then refit the crankshaft sprocket (with the flange facing the crankshaft pulley).

15 Fit the timing belt around the crankshaft sprocket, and tension the timing belt as described in Section 7.

Fuel pump sprocket

HAYNES HiNT

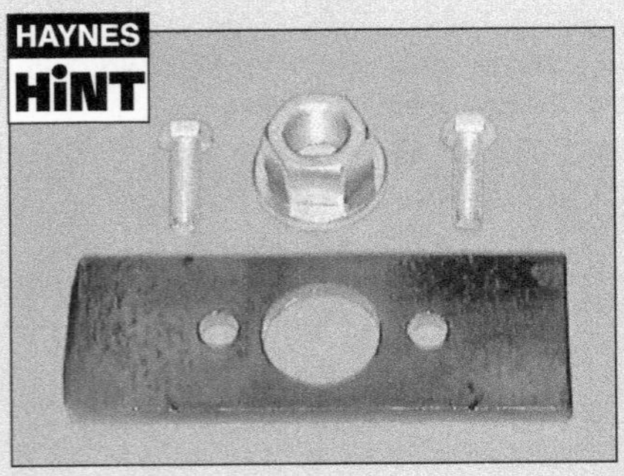

Make a sprocket releasing tool from a short strip of steel. Drill two holes in the strip to correspond with the two holes in the sprocket. Drill a third hole just large enough to accept the flats of the sprocket retaining nut.

Removal

16 Remove the timing belt as described in Section 7.

17 Using a suitable socket, undo the pump sprocket retaining nut. The sprocket can be held stationary by inserting a suitably-sized locking pin, drill or rod through the hole in the sprocket, and into the corresponding hole in the backplate **(see illustration)**, or by using a suitable forked tool engaged with the holes in the sprocket **(see Tool Tip in paragraph 2)**. **Note:** *On some engines, a hole is provided at the 5 o'clock position for locking purposes only, however, the timing position hole is at the 12 o'clock position.*

18 The pump sprocket is a taper fit on the pump shaft and it will be necessary to make up another tool to release it from the taper **(see Tool Tip)**.

19 On late models where the sprocket is keyed to the shaft, unscrew the retaining nut and remove the sprocket, then recover the Woodruff key. On early models where the sprocket is not keyed to the shaft, partially unscrew the sprocket retaining nut, then fit the home-made tool, and secure it to the sprocket with two suitable bolts. Prevent the sprocket from rotating as before, and unscrew the sprocket retaining nut. The nut will bear against the tool, as it is undone, forcing the sprocket off the shaft taper. Once the taper is released, remove the tool, unscrew the nut fully, and remove the sprocket from the pump shaft.

20 Clean the sprocket thoroughly, and renew it if there are any signs of wear, damage or cracks.

8.25 Remove the tensioner retaining bolt

Refitting

21 Refit the Woodruff key (later models only) then refit the pump sprocket and retaining nut, and tighten the nut to the specified torque. Prevent the sprocket rotating as the nut is tightened using the sprocket holding tool.

22 Fit the timing belt around the pump sprocket, and tension the timing belt as described in Section 7.

Coolant pump sprocket

23 The coolant pump sprocket is integral with the pump, and cannot be removed. Coolant pump removal is described in Chapter 3, Section 8.

Tensioner pulley

Removal

24 Remove the timing belt as described in Section 7.

25 Remove the tensioner pulley retaining bolt, and remove the pulley from the cylinder block **(see illustration)**.

26 Clean the tensioner pulley, but do not use any strong solvent, which may enter the pulley bearings. Check that the pulley rotates freely, with no sign of stiffness or free play. Renew the pulley if there is any doubt about its condition, or if there are any obvious signs of wear or damage.

27 Examine the pulley locating stud for signs of damage.

Refitting

28 Refit the tensioner pulley to the cylinder block making sure it is positioned over the locating stud **(see illustration)**, and then fit the retaining bolt.

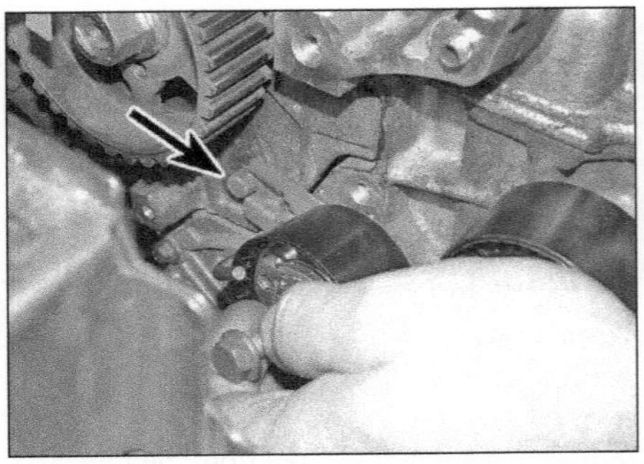

8.28 Make sure the tensioner is fitted to the lug (arrowed) on the engine casing

8.31 Undo the timing belt idler pulley retaining nut

29 Refit the timing belt as described in Section 7.

Idler pulley

Removal

30 Remove the timing belt as described in Section 7.
31 Undo the retaining nut and withdraw the idler pulley from the engine **(see illustration)**.
32 Clean the idler pulley, but do not use any

9.5 Vacuum pump bolts (arrowed)

strong solvent which may enter the bearings. Check that the pulley rotates freely, with no sign of stiffness or free play. Renew the idler pulley if there is any doubt about its condition, or if there are any obvious signs of wear or damage.

Refitting

33 Locate the idler pulley on the engine, and fit the retaining nut. Tighten the nut to the specified torque.
34 Refit the timing belt (see Section 7).

9.7 Timing belt inner, upper cover bolts (arrowed)

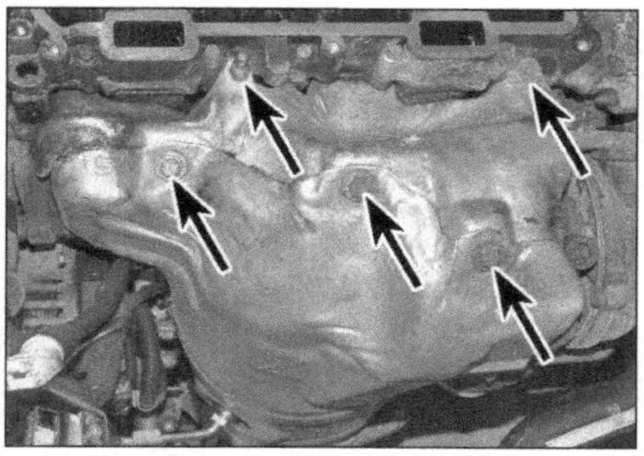

9.9a Undo the bolts (arrowed) and remove the rear section of the heat shield

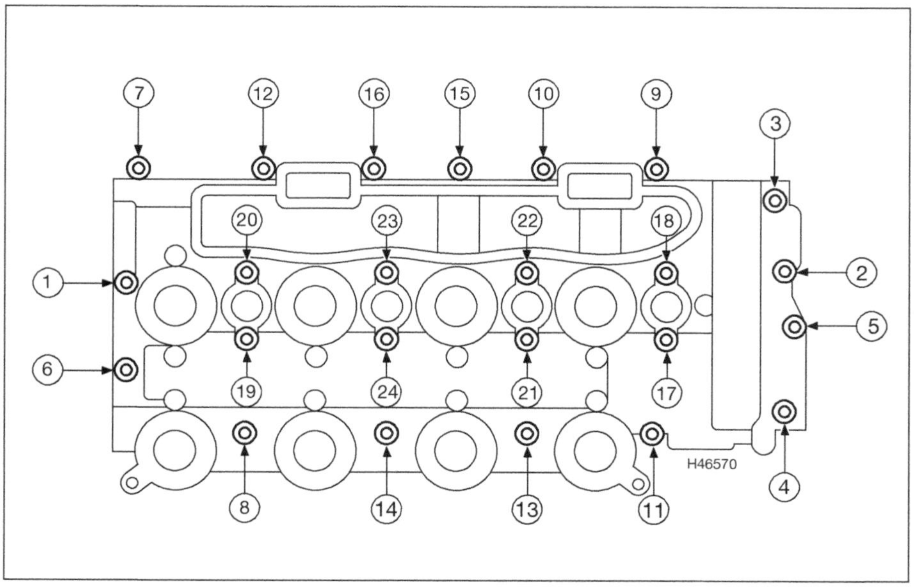

9.9b Camshaft cover/bearing ladder bolt slackening sequence

9 Camshafts, rocker arms and hydraulic tappets – removal, inspection and refitting

Removal

1 Remove the cylinder head cover/manifold as described in Section 4.
2 Remove the injectors as described in Chapter 4B, Section 11.
3 Remove the camshaft sprocket as described in Section 8.
4 Refit the right-hand engine mounting, but only tighten the bolts moderately; this will keep the engine supported during the camshaft removal.
5 Undo the bolts and remove the vacuum pump. Recover the pump O-ring seals **(see illustration)**.
6 Remove the fuel filter (see Chapter 1B, Section 8), then undo the bolts and remove the fuel filter mounting bracket.
7 Release the wiring harness clips, then undo the 3 bolts and remove the timing belt inner, upper cover **(see illustration)**.
8 Disconnect the wiring plug, unscrew the retaining bolt, and remove the camshaft position sensor from the camshaft cover/bearing ladder.
9 Undo the 5 bolts and remove the upper rear section of the turbocharger heat shield, then working gradually and evenly, slacken and remove the bolts securing the camshaft cover/bearing ladder to the cylinder head in sequence **(see illustrations)**. Lift the cover/ladder from position complete with the camshafts.
10 Undo the retaining bolts and remove the bearing caps. Note their fitted positions, as they must be refitted into their original positions **(see illustration)**. Note that the bearing caps are marked A for intake, and E for exhaust, and 1 to 4 from the flywheel end of the cylinder head.
11 Undo the bolts securing the chain tensioner assembly to the camshaft cover/bearing ladder, and then lift the camshafts, chain and tensioner from place **(see**

9.10 Bearing caps are numbered 1 to 4 from the flywheel end – A for intake, and E for exhaust (arrowed)

9.11a Undo the tensioner bolts (arrowed) ...

9.11b ... then lift the camshafts, chain and tensioner from place

9.21 Refit the hydraulic tappets ...

illustrations). Discard the camshaft oil seal.

12 Obtain 16 small, clean plastic containers, and number them 1 to 8 intake and 1 to 8 exhaust; alternatively, divide a larger container into 16 compartments.

13 Lift out each rocker arm. Place the rocker arms in their respective positions in the box or containers.

14 A compartmentalised container filled with engine oil is now required to retain the hydraulic tappets while they are removed from the cylinder head. Withdraw each hydraulic follower and place it in the container, keeping them each identified for correct refitting. The tappets must be totally submerged in the oil to prevent air entering them.

Inspection

15 Inspect the cam lobes and the camshaft bearing journals for scoring or other visible evidence of wear. Once the surface hardening of the cam lobes has been eroded, wear will occur at an accelerated rate. **Note:** *If these symptoms are visible on the tips of the camshaft lobes, check the corresponding rocker arm, as it will probably be worn as well.*

16 Examine the condition of the bearing surfaces in the cylinder head and camshaft bearing housing. If wear is evident, the cylinder head and bearing housing will both have to be renewed, as they are a matched assembly.

17 Inspect the rocker arms and tappets for scuffing, cracking or other damage and renew any components as necessary. Also check the condition of the tappet bores in the cylinder head. As with the camshafts, any wear in this area will necessitate cylinder head renewal.

9.22 ... and rocker arms to their original locations

Refitting

18 Thoroughly clean the sealant from the mating surfaces of the cylinder head and camshaft bearing housing. Use a suitable liquid gasket dissolving agent (available from Citroën dealers) together with a soft putty knife; do not use a metal scraper or the faces will be damaged. As there is no conventional gasket used, the cleanliness of the mating faces is of the utmost importance. Prise out the oil injector oil seals from the camshaft bearing housing.

19 Clean off any oil, dirt or grease from both components and dry with a clean lint-free cloth. Ensure that all the oilways are completely clean.

20 Liberally lubricate the hydraulic tappet bores in the cylinder head with clean engine oil.

9.23 Align the marks on the sprockets with the centre of the black-coloured chain links (arrowed). There must be 12 link pins between the sprocket marks

21 Insert the hydraulic tappets into their original bores in the cylinder head unless they have been renewed **(see illustration)**.

22 Lubricate the rocker arms and place them over their respective tappets and valve stems **(see illustration)**.

23 Engage the timing chain around the camshaft sprockets, aligning the black-coloured links with the marked teeth on the camshaft sprockets **(see illustration)**. If the black colouring has been lost, there must be 12 chain link pins between the marks on the sprockets.

24 Fit the chain tensioner between the upper and lower runs of the chain, then lubricate the bearing surfaces with clean engine oil, and fit the camshafts into position on the underside of the camshaft cover/bearing ladder. Refit the bearing caps to their original positions and tighten the retaining bolts to the specified torque **(see**

9.24a Assemble the chain tensioner between the upper and lower runs of the chain ...

9.24b ... and lower the camshafts, chain and tensioner into position

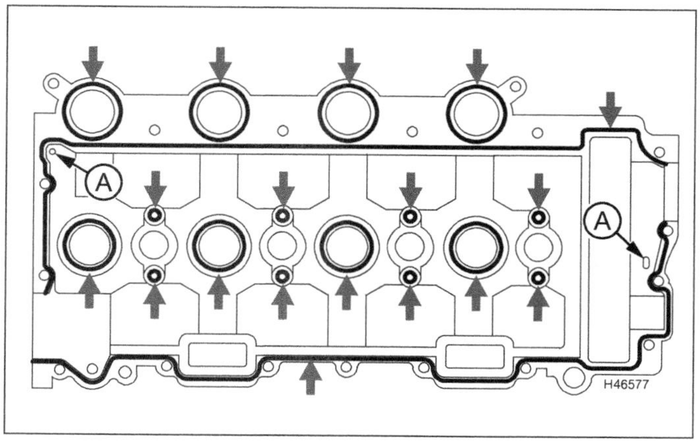

9.25 **Apply sealant to the camshaft cover/bearing ladder as indicated by the heavy black lines. Ensure sealant does not enter the tensioner oil holes – marked A**

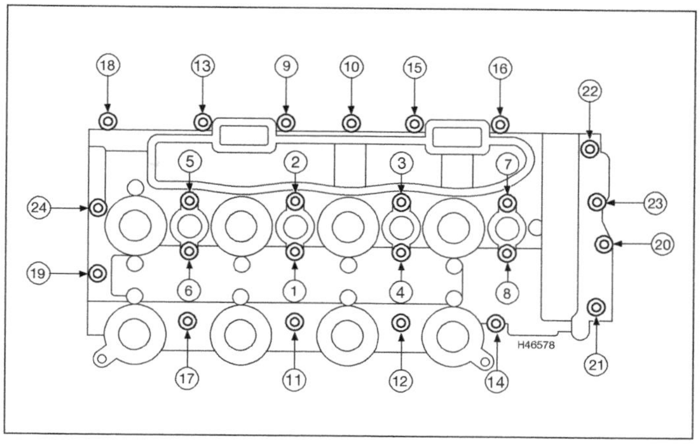

9.26 **Camshaft cover/bearing ladder bolt tightening sequence**

illustrations). Tighten the tensioner retaining bolts to the specified torque.

25 Apply a thin bead of sealant to the mating surface of the camshaft cover/bearing ladder as shown. Citroën recommend the use of Autojoint Noir **(see illustration)**. Do not allow the sealant to obstruct the oil channels for the hydraulic chain tensioner.

26 Check that the black-coloured links on the chain are still aligned with the marks on the camshaft sprockets, then refit the camshaft cover/bearing ladder, and gradually and evenly tighten the retaining bolts until the cover/ ladder is in contact with the cylinder head, then tighten the bolts to the specified torque in sequence **(see illustration)**. **Note:** *Ensure the cover/ladder is correctly located by checking the bores of the vacuum pump and camshaft oil seal at each end of the cover/ladder.*

27 Fit a new camshaft oil seal as described in Section 14.

28 Refit the camshaft sprocket, and tighten the retaining bolt finger-tight.

29 Using a spanner on the camshaft sprocket bolt, rotate the camshafts approximately 40 complete revolutions clockwise. Check the black-coloured links on the chain still align with the marks on the camshaft sprockets.

30 If the marks still align, refit the camshaft sprocket as described in Section 8.

31 Refit and adjust the camshaft position sensor as described in Chapter 4B, Section 12.

32 Press the new oil seals into the bearing housing, using a tube/socket of approximately 20 mm outside diameter, ensuring the inner lip of the seal fits around the injector guide tube **(see illustrations)**. Refit the injectors as described in Chapter 4B, Section 11.

33 Refit the cylinder head cover/manifold as described in Section 4.

10 Cylinder head – removal and refitting

Removal

1 Chock the rear wheels then jack up the front of the vehicle and support it on axle stands (see *Jacking and vehicle support*). Remove the front right-hand roadwheel, the engine undershield, and the front wheel arch liner. The undershield is secured by several screws, and the wheel arch liner is secured by several plastic expanding rivets/nuts/plastic clips. Push the centre pins in a little, then prise the rivet from place.

2 Disconnect the battery (refer to precautions in Chapter 5A, Section 1).

3 Drain the cooling system as described in Chapter 1B, Section 20.

4 Remove the camshafts, rocker arms and hydraulic tappets as described in Section 9.

5 Remove the turbocharger as described in Chapter 4B, Section 16.

6 Remove the glow plugs as described in Chapter 5C, Section 2.

7 Undo the upper mounting bolts, and pivot the alternator away from the engine, undo the oil dipstick guide tube bolt, then undo the bolts securing the alternator/power steering pump mounting bracket to the cylinder head/ block.

8 Undo the coolant outlet housing (left-hand end of the cylinder head) retaining bolts, slacken the two bolts securing the housing support bracket to the top of the transmission bellhousing, and move the outlet housing away from the cylinder head a little **(see illustration)**. There is no need to disconnect the hoses.

9 Disconnect the high-pressure fuel pipe from the common rail to the pump, and disconnect the fuel supply and return hoses. Remove the bracket at the rear of the pump, then undo the

9.32a **Fit the new seal around a 20 mm outside diameter socket ...**

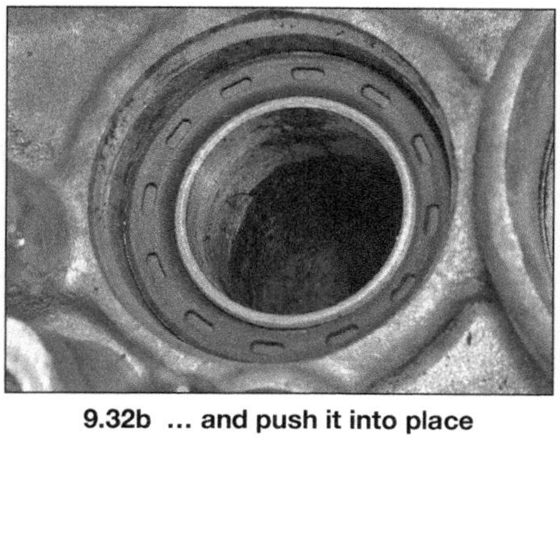

9.32b **... and push it into place**

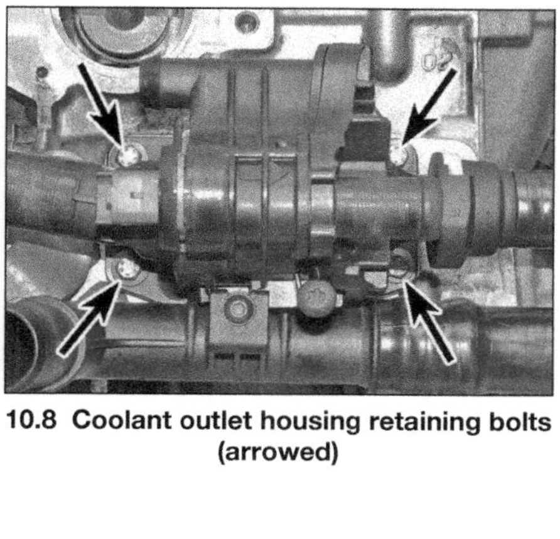

10.8 **Coolant outlet housing retaining bolts (arrowed)**

10.9a Remove the high-pressure pipe (arrowed) ...

10.9b ... and the bracket (arrowed)

10.9c Pump mounting bracket upper nut and lower mounting bolt (arrowed)

bolt/nut and remove the pump and mounting bracket as an assembly **(see illustrations)**. Note that a new high-pressure pipe must be fitted – see Chapter 4B, Section 9.

10 Working in the **reverse** of the sequence shown **(see illustration 10.32)** undo the cylinder head bolts.

11 Release the cylinder head from the cylinder block and location dowels by rocking it. The Citroën tool for doing this consists simply of two metal rods with 90-degree angled ends **(see illustration)**. Do not prise between the mating faces of the cylinder head and block, as this may damage the gasket faces.

12 Lift the cylinder head from the block, and recover the gasket.

13 If necessary, remove the exhaust manifold with reference to Chapter 4B, Section 14.

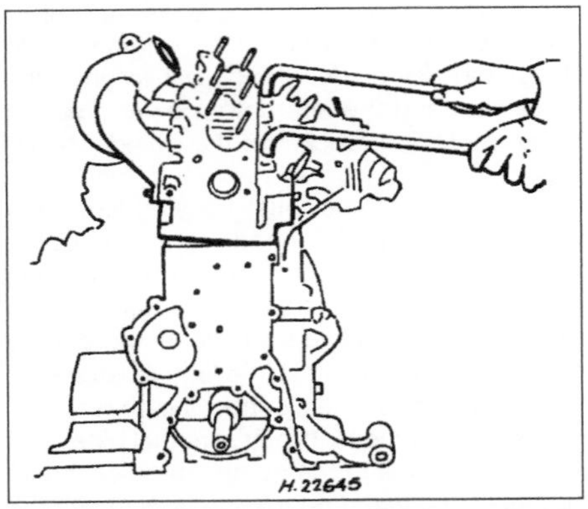

10.11 Free the cylinder head using angled rods

Preparation for refitting

14 The mating faces of the cylinder head and cylinder block must be perfectly clean before refitting the head. Citroën recommend the use of a scouring agent for this purpose, but acceptable results can be achieved by using a hard plastic or wood scraper to remove all traces of gasket and carbon.

15 The same method can be used to clean the piston crowns. Take particular care to avoid scoring or gouging the cylinder head/ cylinder block mating surfaces during the cleaning operations, as aluminium alloy is easily damaged. Make sure that the carbon is not allowed to enter the oil and water passages – this is particularly important for the lubrication system, as carbon could block the oil supply to the engine's components. Using adhesive tape and paper, seal the water, oil and bolt holes in the cylinder block. To prevent carbon entering the gap between the pistons and bores, smear a little grease in the gap. After cleaning each piston, use a small brush to remove all traces of grease and carbon from the gap, and then wipe away the remainder with a clean rag.

16 Check the mating surfaces of the cylinder block and the cylinder head for nicks, deep scratches and other damage. If slight, they may be removed carefully with a file, but if excessive, machining may be the only alternative to renewal. If warpage of the cylinder head gasket surface is suspected, use a straight-edge to check it for distortion. Refer to Chapter 2E, Section 7 if necessary.

17 Thoroughly clean the threads of the cylinder head bolt holes in the cylinder block. Ensure that the bolts run freely in their threads, and that all traces of oil and water are removed from each bolt hole. If required, pull the oil feed non-return valve from the cylinder head, and check the ball moves freely. Push a new valve into place if necessary **(see illustrations)**.

Gasket selection

18 Remove the crankshaft timing pin, then turn the crankshaft until pistons 1 and 4 are at TDC (Top Dead Centre). Position a dial test indicator (dial gauge) on the cylinder block adjacent to the rear of No 1 piston, and zero it on the block face. Transfer the probe to the crown of No 1 piston (10.0 mm in from the rear edge), and then slowly turn the crankshaft back-and-forth past TDC, noting the highest reading on the indicator. Record this reading as protrusion A.

19 Repeat the check described in paragraph 18, this time 10.0 mm in from the front edge of the No 1 piston crown. Record this reading as protrusion B.

20 Add protrusion A to protrusion B, then divide the result by 2 to obtain an average reading for piston No 1.

21 Repeat the procedure described in paragraphs 18 to 20 on piston 4, then turn the crankshaft through 180° and carry out the procedure on the piston Nos 2 and 3 **(see illustration)**. Check that there is a maximum difference of 0.07 mm protrusion between any two pistons.

22 If a dial test indicator is not available,

10.17a Pull the non-return valve from the cylinder head ...

10.17b ... and push a new one into place

10.21 Measure the piston protrusion using a DTI gauge

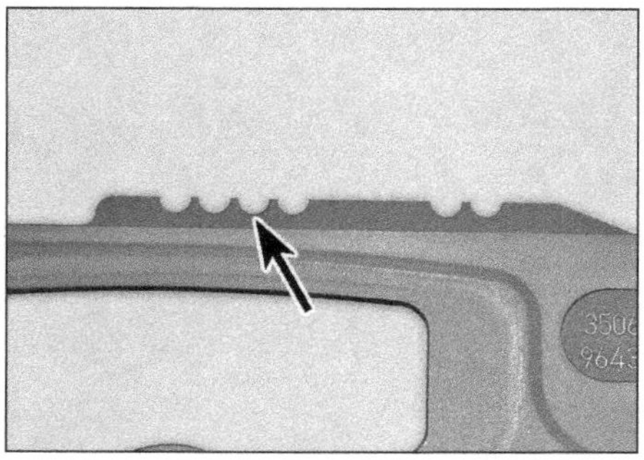

10.23 Cylinder head gasket thickness identification notches (arrowed)

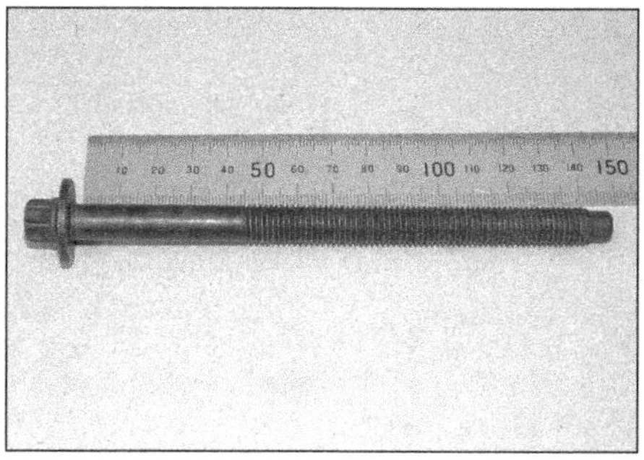

10.24 Measure the length from under the bolt head to its end

10.27 Ensure the gasket locates over the dowels (arrowed)

piston protrusion may be measured using a straight-edge and feeler blades or Vernier calipers. However, this is much less accurate, and cannot therefore be recommended.

23 Note the greatest piston protrusion measurement, and use this to determine the correct cylinder head gasket from the following table. The series of notches/holes on the side of the gasket are used for thickness identification **(see illustration)**.

Piston protrusion	Gasket identification
0.685 to 0.734 mm	*1 notch*
0.533 to 0.634 mm	*2 notch*
0.635 to 0.684 mm	*3 notch*
0.735 to 0.784 mm	*4 notch*
0.785 to 0.886 mm	*5 notch*

Head bolt examination

24 Carefully examine the cylinder head bolts for signs of damage to the threads or head, and for any sign of corrosion. If the bolts are in a satisfactory condition, measure the length of each bolt from the underside of the head to the end of the shank. The bolts may be re-used providing that the measured length does not exceed 149.0 mm **(see illustration)**. **Note:** *Considering the stress to which the cylinder head bolts are subjected, it is highly recommended that they be all renewed, regardless of their apparent condition.*

Refitting

25 Turn the crankshaft and position Nos 1 and 4 pistons at TDC, then turn the crankshaft a quarter turn (90°) anti-clockwise.

26 Thoroughly clean the surfaces of the cylinder head and block.

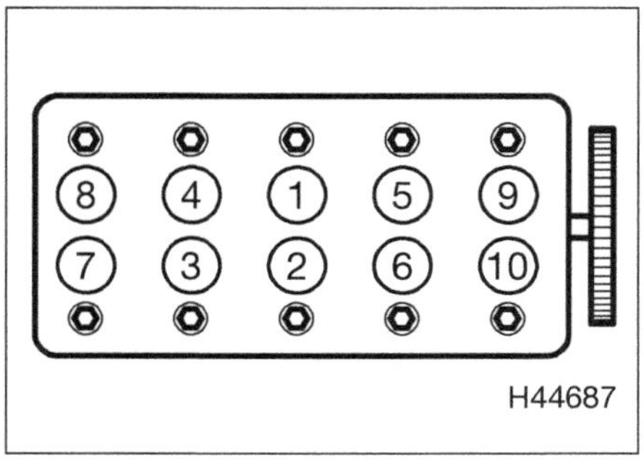

10.32 Cylinder head bolt tightening sequence

27 Make sure that the locating dowels are in place, then fit the correct gasket the right way round on the cylinder block **(see illustration)**.

28 If necessary, refit the exhaust manifold to the cylinder head as described in Chapter 4B, Section 14.

29 Carefully lower the cylinder head onto the gasket and block, making sure that it locates correctly onto the dowels.

30 Apply a smear of grease to the threads, and to the underside of the heads, of the cylinder head bolts. Citroën recommend the use of Molykote G Rapid Plus (available from your Citroën dealer); in the absence of the specified grease, any good-quality high melting-point grease may be used.

31 Carefully insert the cylinder head bolts into their holes (*do not drop them in*) and initially finger-tighten them.

32 Working progressively and in sequence, tighten the cylinder head bolts to their Stage 1 torque setting, using a torque wrench and suitable socket **(see illustration)**.

33 Once all the bolts have been tightened to their Stage 1 torque setting, working again in the specified sequence, tighten each bolt to the specified Stage 2 setting. Finally, angle-tighten the bolts through the specified Stage 3 angle. It is recommended that an angle-measuring gauge be used during this stage of tightening, to ensure accuracy. **Note:** *Retightening of the cylinder head bolts after running the engine is not required*.

34 Refit the hydraulic tappets, rocker arms, and camshaft housing (complete with camshafts) as described in Section 9.

35 Refit the timing belt as described in Section 7.

36 The remainder of refitting is a reversal of removal, noting the following points.

a) *Use a new seal when refitting the coolant outlet housing.*
b) *When refitting a cylinder head, it is good practice to renew the thermostat.*
c) *Refit the camshaft position sensor and set the air gap with reference to Chapter 4B, Section 12.*
d) *Tighten all fasteners to the specified torque where given.*
e) *Refill the cooling system as described in Chapter 1B, Section 20.*
f) *The engine may run erratically for the first few miles, until the engine management ECU relearns its stored values.*

11 Sump – removal and refitting

Removal

1 Drain the engine oil, then clean and refit the engine oil drain plug, tightening it securely. If the engine is nearing the service interval when the oil and filter are due for renewal, it is recommended that the filter is also removed, and a new one fitted. After reassembly, the engine can then be refilled with fresh oil. Refer to Chapter 1B, Section 3 for further information.

2 Chock the rear wheels then jack up the front of the vehicle and support it on axle stands (see *Jacking and vehicle support*). Undo the screws and remove the engine undershield.

3 Remove the exhaust front pipe as described in Chapter 4B, Section 18.

4 Where necessary, disconnect the wiring connector from the oil temperature sender unit, which is screwed into the sump.

5 Progressively slacken and remove all the sump retaining bolts/nuts. Since the sump bolts vary in length, remove each bolt in turn, and store it in its correct fitted order by pushing it through a clearly marked cardboard template. This will avoid the possibility of installing the bolts in the wrong locations on refitting.

6 Try to break the joint by striking the sump with the palm of your hand, then lower and withdraw the sump from under the car. If the sump is stuck (which is quite likely) use a putty knife or similar, carefully inserted between the sump and block. Ease the knife along the joint until the sump is released. While the sump is removed, take the opportunity to check the oil pump pick-up/strainer for signs of clogging or splitting. If necessary, remove the pump as described in Section 12, and clean or renew the strainer.

Refitting

7 Clean all traces of sealant from the mating surfaces of the cylinder block/crankcase and

11.8 Apply a bead of sealant to the sump or crankcase mating surface. Ensure the sealant is applied on the inside of the retaining bolt holes

sump, and then use a clean rag to wipe out the sump and the engine's interior.

8 On engines where the sump was fitted without a gasket, ensure that the sump mating surfaces are clean and dry, then apply a thin coating of suitable sealant to the sump or crankcase mating surface **(see illustration)**.

9 Offer up the sump to the cylinder block/crankcase. Refit its retaining bolts/nuts, ensuring that each bolt is screwed into its original location. Tighten the bolts evenly and progressively to the specified torque setting **(see illustration)**.

10 Where necessary, align the air conditioning compressor with its mountings on the sump, and insert the retaining bolts. Securely tighten the compressor retaining bolts, then refit the drivebelt as described in Chapter 1B, Section 17.

11.9 Refit the sump and tighten the bolts

11 Reconnect the wiring connector to the oil temperature sensor (where fitted).

12 Lower the vehicle to the ground, then refill the engine with oil as described in Chapter 1B, Section 3.

12 Oil pump – removal, inspection and refitting

Removal

1 Remove the sump as described in Section 11.

2 Remove the crankshaft sprocket as described in Section 8. Recover the locating key from the crankshaft.

3 Disconnect the wiring plug, undo the bolts and remove the crankshaft position sensor, located on the right-hand end of the cylinder block.

12.4 Oil pick-up tube Allen screws (arrowed)

4 Undo the three Allen screws and remove the oil pump pick-up tube from the pump/block **(see illustration)**. Discard the oil seal; a new one must be fitted.

5 Undo the 8 bolts, and remove the oil pump **(see illustration)**.

Inspection

6 Undo and remove the Torx bolts securing the cover to the oil pump **(see illustration)**. Examine the pump rotors and body for signs of wear and damage. If worn, the complete pump must be renewed.

7 Remove the circlip, and extract the cap, valve piston and spring, noting which way around they are fitted **(see illustrations)**. The condition of the relief valve spring can only be measured by comparing it with a new one; if there is any doubt about its condition, it should also be renewed.

12.5 Oil pump retaining bolts (arrowed)

12.6 Undo the Torx bolts and remove the pump cover

12.7a Remove the circlip ...

12.7b ... cap ...

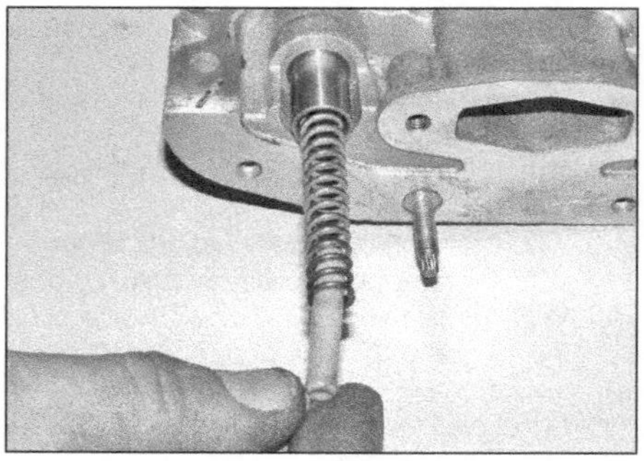

12.7c ... spring ...

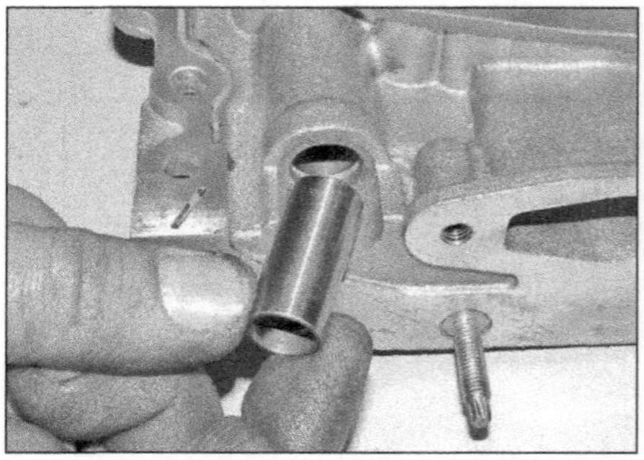

12.7d ... and piston

12.11 Apply a bead of sealant to the cylinder block mating surface

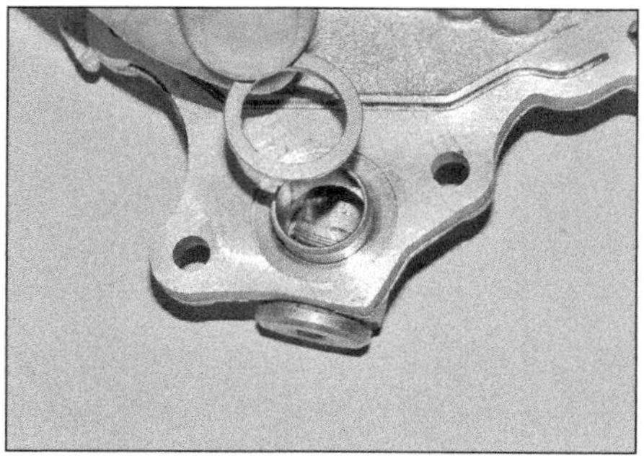

12.12a Fit a new seal ...

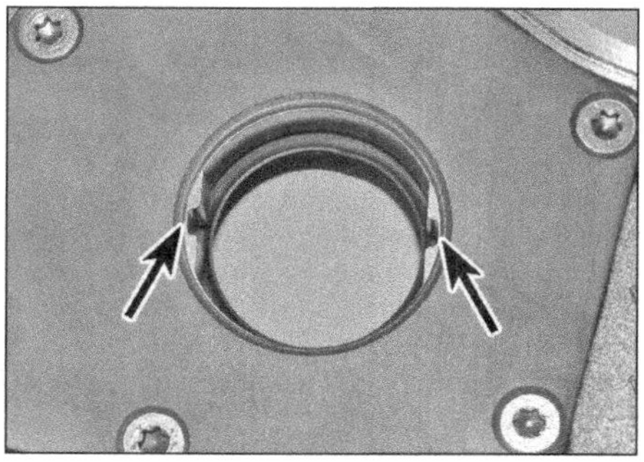

12.12b ... align the pump gear flats (arrowed) ...

12.12c ... with those of the crankshaft (arrowed)

8 Refit the relief valve piston and spring, and then secure them in place with the circlip.
9 Refit the cover to the oil pump, and tighten the Torx bolts securely.

Refitting

10 Remove all traces of sealant, and thoroughly clean the mating surfaces of the oil pump and cylinder block.
11 Apply a 4 mm wide bead of silicone sealant to the mating face of the cylinder block **(see illustration)**. Ensure that no sealant enters any of the holes in the block.
12 With a new oil seal fitted, refit the oil pump over the end of the crankshaft, aligning the flats in the pump drivegear with the flats machined in the crankshaft **(see illustrations)**. Note that new oil pumps are supplied with the oil seal already fitted, and a seal protector sleeve. The sleeve fits over the end of the crankshaft to protect the seal as the pump is fitted.
13 Install the oil pump bolts and tighten them to the specified torque.
14 Refit the oil pick-up tube to the pump/cylinder block using a new O-ring seal. Ensure the oil dipstick guide tube is correctly refitted.
15 Refit the Woodruff key to the crankshaft, and slide the crankshaft sprocket into place.
16 The remainder of refitting is a reversal of removal.

13 Oil cooler – removal and refitting

Removal

1 Chock the rear wheels then jack up the front of the vehicle and support it on axle stands (see *Jacking and vehicle support*). Undo the retaining bolts/nuts and remove the engine undershield.
2 The oil cooler is fitted to the front of the oil filter housing. Drain the coolant as described in Chapter 1B, Section 20.
3 Drain the engine oil as described in Chapter 1B, Section 3, or be prepared for fluid spillage.
4 Undo the 5 bolts/stud and remove the oil cooler. Recover the O-ring seals **(see illustrations)**.

Refitting

5 Fit new O-ring seals into the recesses in the oil filter housing, and refit the cooler. Tighten the bolts securely.
6 Refill or top-up the cooling system and engine oil level as described in Chapter 1B, Section 20 and 3, or *Weekly checks* (as applicable). Start the engine, and check the oil cooler for signs of leakage.

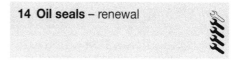

14 Oil seals – renewal

Crankshaft

Right-hand oil seal

1 Remove the crankshaft sprocket and Woodruff key as described in Section 8.
2 Measure and note the fitted depth of the oil seal.
3 Pull the oil seal from the housing using a screwdriver. Alternatively, drill a small hole in the oil seal, and use a self-tapping screw and a pair of pliers to remove it **(see illustration)**.
4 Clean the oil seal housing and the crankshaft sealing surface.
5 The seal has a Teflon lip and must not be oiled or marked. The new seal should be supplied with a protector sleeve, which fits over the end of the crankshaft to prevent any damage to the seal lip. With the sleeve in place, press the seal (open end first) into the pump to the previously-noted

13.4a Undo the oil cooler bolts/stud (arrowed)

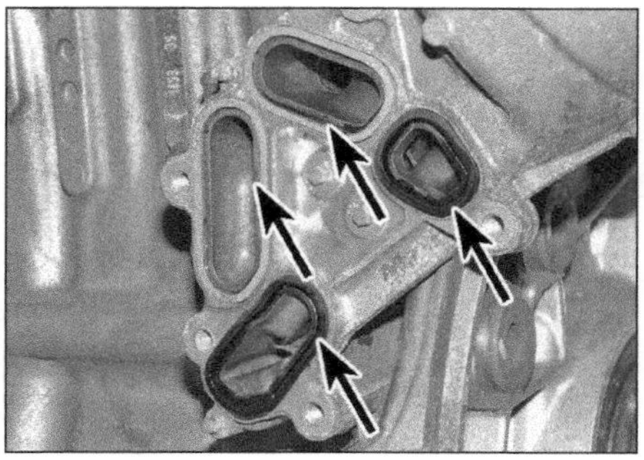

13.4b Renew the O-ring seals (arrowed)

14.3 Take great care not to mark the crankshaft whilst levering out the oil seal

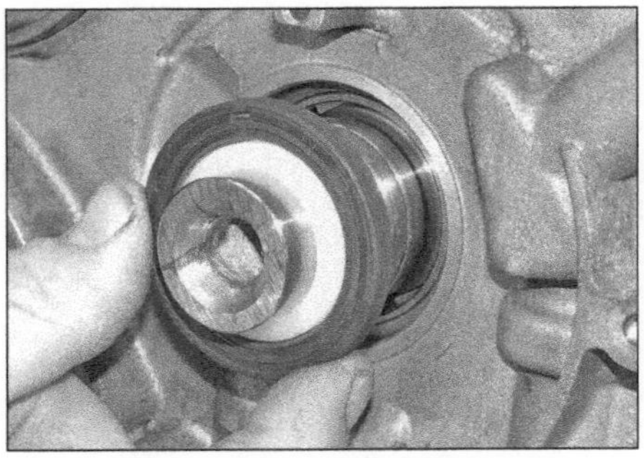

14.5a Slide the seal and protective sleeve over the end of the crankshaft ...

14.16 Drill a hole, insert a self-tapping screw, and pull the seal from place using pliers

depth, using a suitable tube or socket **(see illustrations)**.

6 Where applicable, remove the plastic sleeve from the end of the crankshaft.

7 Refit the timing belt crankshaft sprocket as described in Section 8.

Left-hand oil seal

8 Remove the flywheel, as described in Section 16.

9 Measure and note the fitted depth of the oil seal.

10 Pull the oil seal from the housing using a screwdriver. Alternatively, drill a small hole in the oil seal, and use a self-tapping screw and a pair of pliers to remove it **(see illustration 14.3)**.

11 Clean the oil seal housing and the crankshaft sealing surface.

12 The seal has a Teflon lip and must not be oiled or marked. The new seal should be supplied with a protector sleeve, which fits over the end of the crankshaft to prevent any damage to the seal lip **(see illustration)**. With the sleeve in place, press the seal (open end first) into the housing to the previously-noted depth, using a suitable tube or socket.

13 Where applicable, remove the plastic sleeve from the end of the crankshaft.

14 Refit the flywheel, as described in Section 16.

15.3 The oil pressure switch is located on the front face of the cylinder block (arrowed)

14.5b ... and press the seal into place

14.18 Fit the protective sleeve and seal over the end of the camshaft

Camshaft

15 Remove the camshaft sprocket as described in Section 8. In principle there is no need to remove the timing belt completely, but remember that if the belt has been contaminated with oil, it must be renewed.

16 Pull the oil seal from the housing using a hooked instrument. Alternatively, drill a small hole in the oil seal and use a self-tapping screw and a pair of pliers to remove it **(see illustration)**.

15.5 The oil level sensor is located on the rear face of the cylinder block (arrowed)

14.12 Slide the seal and protective sleeve over the left-hand end of the crankshaft

17 Clean the oil seal housing and the camshaft sealing surface.

18 The seal has a Teflon lip and must not be oiled or marked. The new seal should be supplied with a protector sleeve, which fits over the end of the camshaft to prevent any damage to the seal lip **(see illustration)**. With the sleeve in place, press the seal (open end first) into the housing, using a suitable tube or socket, which bears only of the outer edge of the seal.

19 Refit the camshaft sprocket as described in Section 8.

20 Where necessary, fit a new timing belt with reference to Section 7.

15 Oil pressure switch and level sensor – removal and refitting

Removal

Oil pressure switch

1 The oil pressure switch is located at the front of the cylinder block, adjacent to the oil dipstick guide tube. Note that on some models, access to the switch may be improved if the vehicle is jacked up and supported on axle stands, then undo the bolts/nuts and remove the engine undershield so that the switch can be reached from underneath (see *Jacking and vehicle support*).

2 Remove the protective sleeve from the wiring plug (where applicable), and then disconnect the wiring from the switch.

3 Unscrew the switch from the cylinder block, and recover the sealing washer **(see illustration)**. Be prepared for oil spillage, and if the switch is to be left removed from the engine for any length of time, plug the hole in the cylinder block.

Oil level sensor

4 The oil level sensor is located at the rear of the cylinder block. Jack up the front of the vehicle and support it securely on axle stands (see *Jacking and vehicle support*). Undo the retaining bolts/nuts and remove the engine undershield.

5 Reach up between the driveshaft and the cylinder block, and disconnect the sensor wiring plug **(see illustration)**.

6 Using an open-ended spanner, unscrew the sensor and withdraw it from position.

Refitting

Oil pressure switch

7 Examine the sealing washer for any signs of damage or deterioration, and if necessary renew.
8 Refit the switch, complete with washer, and tighten it to the specified torque.
9 Refit the engine undershield, and lower the vehicle to the ground.
10 Check the engine oil level, and top-up as required (see *Weekly checks*).
11 Check for correct operation of the warning light, and for signs of oil leaks once the engine has been started and warmed-up to normal operating temperature.

Oil level sensor

12 Smear a little silicone sealant on the threads and refit the sensor to the cylinder block, tightening it securely.
13 Reconnect the sensor wiring plug.
14 Refit the engine undershield, and lower the vehicle to the ground.
15 Check the engine oil level, and top-up as required (see *Weekly checks*).
16 Check for correct operation of the warning light, and for signs of oil leaks once the engine has been started and warmed-up to normal operating temperature.

16 Flywheel – removal, inspection and refitting

Removal

1 Remove the transmission as described in Chapter 7A, Section 7, then remove the clutch assembly as described in Chapter 6, Section 6.
2 Prevent the flywheel from turning by locking the ring gear teeth **(see illustration)**. Alternatively, bolt a strap between the flywheel and the cylinder block/crankcase. Do not attempt to lock the flywheel in position using the crankshaft pulley locking tool described in Section 3. Insert a 12 mm diameter rod or drill bit through the hole in the flywheel cover casting, and into a slot in the flywheel.
3 Make alignment marks between the flywheel and crankshaft to aid refitting. Slacken and remove the flywheel retaining bolts, and remove the flywheel from the end of the crankshaft. Be careful not to drop it; it is heavy. If the flywheel locating dowel (where fitted) is a loose fit in the crankshaft end, remove it and store it with the flywheel for safekeeping. Discard the flywheel bolts; new ones must be used on refitting.

Inspection

4 Examine the flywheel for scoring of the clutch face, and for wear or chipping of the ring gear teeth. If the clutch face is scored, the flywheel may be surface-ground, but renewal is preferable. Seek the advice of a Citroën dealer or engine reconditioning specialist to see if machining is possible. If the ring gear is worn or damaged, the flywheel must be renewed, as it is not possible to renew the ring gear separately.

Refitting

5 Clean the mating surfaces of the flywheel and crankshaft. Remove any remaining locking compound from the threads of the crankshaft holes, using the correct size of tap, if available.
6 If the new flywheel retaining bolts are not supplied with their threads already pre-coated, apply a suitable thread-locking compound to the threads of each bolt.

Engines with normal flywheel

7 Ensure that the locating dowel is in position. Offer up the flywheel, locating it on the dowel (where fitted), and fit the new retaining bolts. Where no locating dowel is fitted, align the previously-made marks to ensure the flywheel is refitted in its original position.
8 Lock the flywheel using the method employed on dismantling, and tighten the retaining bolts to the specified torque **(see illustration)**.

Engines with dual mass flywheel

9 The dual mass flywheel is designed to reduce harshness and vibration in the action of the engine, clutch and transmission. With this type of flywheel, two flywheel centralising tools are needed (available from Citroën dealers). These are screwed into two opposite flywheel bolt holes in the crankshaft. As the tools are screwed down, their conical shape centralises the flywheel with regard to the crankshaft.
10 With the flywheel centralised, fit the new bolts into the remaining flywheel holes, then lock the flywheel using the same method employed on dismantling, and tighten the bolts to the specified torque.
11 Remove the two centralising tools, fit the new bolts and tighten them to the specified torque.

All models

12 Refit the clutch as described in Chapter 6, Section 6. Remove the flywheel locking tool, and refit the transmission as described in Chapter 7A, Section 7.

17 Engine/transmission mountings – inspection and renewal

Inspection

1 If improved access is required, chock the rear wheels then jack up the front of the car and support it on axle stands (see *Jacking and vehicle support*). Undo the retaining bolts/nuts and remove the engine undershield.
2 Check the mounting rubbers to see if they are cracked, hardened or separated from the metal at any point; renew the mounting if any such damage or deterioration is evident.
3 Check that all the mountings fasteners are securely tightened; use a torque wrench to check if possible.
4 Using a large screwdriver or a crowbar, check for wear in each mounting by carefully levering against it to check for free play. Where this is not possible, enlist the aid of an assistant to move the engine/transmission back-and-forth, or from side-to-side, while you watch the mounting. While some free play is to be expected even from new components, excessive wear should be obvious. If excessive free play is found, check first that the fasteners are correctly secured, and then renew any worn components as described below.

Renewal

Right-hand mounting

5 Release all the retaining clips and remove the plastic trim from above the right-hand engine mounting **(see illustration)**. If not

16.2 Using a tool to lock the flywheel ring gear and prevent rotation

16.8 Flywheel retaining Torx bolts

17.5 Remove the plastic trim cover

17.7a Undo the upper bolts (arrowed) ...

17.7b ... and withdraw the engine mounting

17.8 Engine mounting bracket retaining bolts (arrowed)

already done, undo the retaining bolts/nuts and remove the engine undershield.

6 Place a jack beneath the engine, with a block of wood on the jack head. Raise the jack until it is supporting the weight of the engine.

7 Undo the bolts securing the engine mounting to the body and the support bracket **(see illustrations)**.

8 If required, undo the four bolts securing the support bracket to the cylinder head **(see illustration)**.

9 Check all components carefully for signs of wear or damage, and renew as necessary.

10 Where removed, refit the support bracket to the cylinder head, and tighten the bolts securely.

11 Refit the mounting to the body and support bracket, and then tighten the bolts to the specified torque.

12 Remove the jack from underneath the engine and refit the engine undershield.

Left-hand mounting

13 Remove the battery and battery tray as described in Chapter 5A, Section 4.

14 If not already done, undo the retaining bolts/nuts and remove the engine undershield. Place a jack beneath the transmission, with a block of wood on the jack head. Raise the jack until it is supporting the weight of the transmission.

15 Slacken and remove the mounting's two upper retaining nuts **(see illustration)**.

16 Undo the centre retaining nut and remove the mounting from the transmission mounting bracket.

17 Check carefully for signs of wear or damage on all components, and renew them where necessary.

18 Refit the mounting to the mounting bracket and tighten it to the specified torque.

19 Fit the mounting nuts to the bracket on the transmission and tighten the retaining nuts to the specified torque.

20 Remove the jack from underneath the transmission, refit the engine undershield, and then refit the battery as described in Chapter 5A, Section 4.

Lower engine torque link

21 Firmly apply the handbrake, and then jack up the front of the vehicle and support it securely on axle stands (see *Jacking and vehicle support*). If not already done, undo the retaining bolts/nuts and remove the engine undershield.

22 Unscrew and remove the bolt securing the rear mounting link to the subframe **(see illustration)**.

23 Remove the bolt securing the rear mounting link to the driveshaft inner bearing bracket at the rear of the cylinder block **(see illustration)**, and then remove the mounting torque reaction link.

24 To remove the intermediate bearing housing/mounting assembly it will first be necessary to remove the right-hand driveshaft as described in Chapter 8, Section 2.

25 With the driveshaft removed, undo the retaining bolts and remove the bearing housing/ mounting from the rear of the cylinder block.

26 Check carefully for signs of wear or damage on all components, and renew them where necessary. The rubber bush fitted to the driveshaft bearing housing is available as a separate item on some models, check with your local dealer for availability of parts. If available, the rubber bush can be pressed out of the bearing housing, noting its fitted position, and then a new one pressed back into place.

27 On reassembly, fit the bearing housing assembly to the rear of the cylinder block, and tighten its retaining bolts securely. Refit the driveshaft as described in Chapter 8, Section 2.

28 Refit the rear mounting torque reaction link, and tighten both its bolts to their specified torque settings.

29 Refit the engine undershield, and then lower the vehicle to the ground.

17.15 Left-hand transmission mounting

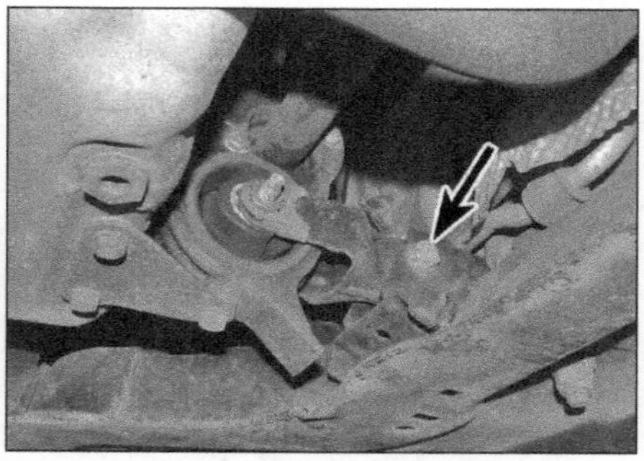

17.22 Undo the rear link-to-subframe mounting bolt (arrowed) ...

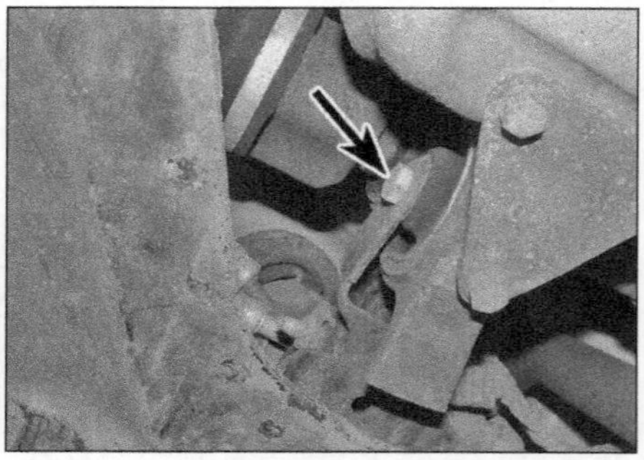

17.23 ... and the lower link-to-mounting bracket bolt (arrowed)

Chapter 2 Part D:
2.0 litre diesel engine in-car repair procedures

Contents

Degrees of difficulty

Easy, suitable for novice with little experience	**Fairly easy,** suitable for beginner with some experience	**Fairly difficult,** suitable for competent DIY mechanic	**Difficult,** suitable for experienced DIY mechanic	**Very difficult,** suitable for expert DIY or professional

Specifications

General

Designation	DW10BTED4
Engine code*	RHF or RHR
Capacity	1997 cc
Bore	85.00 mm
Stroke	88.00 mm
Direction of crankshaft rotation	Clockwise (viewed from the right-hand side of vehicle)
No 1 cylinder location	At the transmission end of block
Maximum power output:	
RHR	100 kW (134 hp) @ 4000 rpm
RHF	103 kW (138 hp) @ 4000 rpm
Maximum torque output	320 Nm @ 1750 rpm
Compression ratio	18.0 : 1
Emissions standard:	
RHR	Euro 4
RHF	Euro 5

** The engine code is stamped on a plate attached to the front of the cylinder block.*

Compression pressures (engine hot, at cranking speed)

Normal (new engine)	20 ± 5 bar
Maximum difference between any two cylinders	5 bar

Cylinder head gasket

Gasket thickness:	
1 hole	1.25 mm
2 hole	1.30 mm
3 hole	1.35 mm
4 hole	1.40 mm
Piston protrusion (gasket required):	
0.55 to 0.60 mm	1 notch
0.61 to 0.65 mm	2 notch
0.66 to 0.70 mm	3 notch
0.71 to 0.75 mm	4 notch

Cylinder head bolts

Maximum length (measured under head):	
Early models with loose washer	134.5 mm ± 0.05 mm
Later models without washer	129.0 mm ± 0.05 mm

Camshaft

Drive	Toothed belt

Lubrication system

Oil pump type	Gear-type, chain-driven off the crankshaft right-hand end
Minimum oil pressure @ 110°C:	
2000 rpm	2.0 bar
4000 rpm	4.0 bar
Oil pressure warning switch operating pressure	0.8 bar

Torque wrench settings

	Nm	lbf ft
Big-end bearing cap nuts:*		
Stage 1	20	15
Stage 2	Angle-tighten a further 70°	
Camshaft bearing housing bolts	10	7
Camshaft position sensor bolt	6	4
Camshaft sprocket bolt:		
Stage 1	20	15
Stage 2	Angle-tighten a further 60°	
Clutch bellhousing closure plate	18	13
Coolant outlet housing	18	13
Crankshaft pulley bolt:		
Stage 1	70	52
Stage 2	Angle-tighten a further 60°	
Crankshaft right-hand oil seal housing bolts	14	10
Crankshaft sensor bolt	7	5
Cylinder head bolts:		
Stage 1	20	15
Stage 2	60	44
Stage 3	Slacken 360° (in sequence)	
Stage 4	20	15
Stage 5	60	44
Stage 6	Angle-tighten a further 220° ± 5°	
Cylinder head cover bolts	10	7
Driveplate bolts:*		
Stage 1	20	15
Stage 2	66	49
Engine mountings:		
Left-hand engine/transmission mounting:		
Bracket-to-transmission bolts	60	44
Bracket-to-transmission nut	55	41
Mounting to body/bracket	60	44
Rear engine mounting/torque rod bolts/nuts	60	44
Right-hand engine mounting bolts/nuts	60	44
Engine-to-transmission bolts:		
Manual transmission	55	41
Automatic transmission	60	44
Exhaust manifold nuts	25	18
Flywheel bolts*	50	37
High-pressure fuel pump bolts	20	15
Main bearing cap bolts:		
Stage 1	25	18
Stage 2	Angle-tighten a further 60°	
Oil filter cap	25	18
Oil pressure switch	32	24
Oil level sensor	27	20
Oil pump mounting bolts	16	12
Piston oil jet spray tube bolt	10	7
Sump bolts	16	12
Sump drain plug	34	25
Timing belt idler pulley bolt	56	41
Timing belt tensioner	21	15
Timing chain tensioner bolts	6	4
Vacuum pump (brakes)	9	7

** Do not re-use.*

1 General information

How to use this Chapter

This Chapter describes the repair procedures that can reasonably be carried out on the engine while it remains in the vehicle. If the engine has been removed from the vehicle and is being dismantled as described in Chapter 2E, any preliminary dismantling procedures can be ignored.

Note that, while it may be possible physically to overhaul items such as the piston/connecting rod assemblies while the engine is in the car, such tasks are not usually carried out as separate operations. Usually, several additional procedures are required (not to mention the cleaning of components and oilways); for this reason, all such tasks are classed as major overhaul procedures, and are described in Chapter 2E.

Chapter 2E describes the removal of the engine/transmission from the car, and the full overhaul procedures that can then be carried out.

DW engines

This engine is based on the well-proven DW10 SOHC direct injection engine, which has appeared in many Peugeot and Citroën vehicles. In particular, the cylinder block components are very similar but the remainder of the engine has been completely redesigned. The engine is of double overhead camshaft (DOHC) 16-valve design. The turbocharged, four-cylinder engine is mounted transversely, with the transmission mounted on the left-hand side.

A toothed timing belt drives the exhaust camshaft, and coolant pump. The exhaust camshaft drives the intake camshaft via a chain at the timing belt end. The camshafts operate the intake and exhaust valves via rocker arms, which are supported at their pivot ends by hydraulic self-adjusting tappets. The camshafts are supported by bearings machined directly in the cylinder head and camshaft bearing housing.

The high-pressure fuel pump is driven from the left-hand end of the exhaust camshaft. The high-pressure fuel pump supplies fuel to the fuel rail, and subsequently to the electronically-controlled injectors that inject the fuel directly into the combustion chambers. This design differs from the previous type where an injection pump supplies the fuel at high pressure to each injector. The earlier conventional type injection pump required fine calibration and timing, and these functions are now completed by the high-pressure pump, electronic injectors and engine management ECU.

The crankshaft runs in five main bearings of the usual shell type. Endfloat is controlled by thrustwashers either side of No 2 main bearing.

The pistons are selected to be of matching weight, and incorporate fully-floating gudgeon pins retained by circlips.

The oil pump is chain-driven from the right-hand end of the crankshaft.

Throughout the manual it is often necessary to identify the engines not only by their cubic capacity, but also by their engine code. The engine code consists of three letters (eg, RHR). The code is stamped on a plate attached to the front of the cylinder block.

Repair operations precaution

The engine is a complex unit with numerous accessories and ancillary components. The design of the engine compartment is such that every conceivable space has been utilised, and access to virtually all of the engine components is extremely limited. In many cases, ancillary components will have to be removed, or moved to one side, and wiring, pipes and hoses will have to be disconnected or removed from various cable clips and support brackets.

When working on this engine, read through the entire procedure first, look at the car and engine at the same time, and establish whether you have the necessary tools, equipment, skill and patience to proceed. Allow considerable time for any operation, and be prepared for the unexpected. Any major work on these engines is not for the faint-hearted!

Because of the limited access, many of the engine photographs appearing in this Chapter were, by necessity, taken with the engine removed from the vehicle.

Warning: It is essential to observe strict precautions when working on the fuel system components of the engine, particularly the high-pressure side of the system. Before carrying out any engine operations that entail working on, or near, any part of the fuel system, refer to the special information given in Chapter 4B, Section 2.

Operations with engine in vehicle

a) Compression pressure – testing.
b) Cylinder head cover(s) – removal and refitting.
c) Crankshaft pulley – removal and refitting.
d) Timing belt covers – removal and refitting.
e) Timing belt/chain – removal, refitting and adjustment.
f) Timing belt tensioner and sprockets – removal and refitting.
g) Camshaft oil seal – renewal.
h) Camshafts, rocker arms and hydraulic tappets – removal, inspection and refitting.
i) Sump – removal and refitting.
j) Oil pump – removal and refitting.
k) Crankshaft oil seals – renewal.
l) Engine/transmission mountings – inspection and renewal.
m) Flywheel/driveplate – removal, inspection and refitting.

2 Compression and leakdown tests – description and interpretation

Compression test

Note: *A compression tester specifically designed for diesel engines must be used for this test.*

1 When engine performance is down, or if misfiring occurs which cannot be attributed to the fuel system, a compression test can provide diagnostic clues as to the engine's condition. If the test is performed regularly, it can give warning of trouble before any other symptoms become apparent.

2 A compression tester specifically intended for diesel engines must be used, because of the higher pressures involved. The tester is connected to an adapter that screws into the glow plug or injector hole. On these engines, an adapter suitable for use in the glow plug holes will be required, so as not to disturb the fuel system components. It is unlikely to be worthwhile buying such a tester for occasional use, but it may be possible to borrow or hire one – if not, have the test performed by a garage.

3 Unless specific instructions to the contrary are supplied with the tester, observe the following points:

a) The battery must be in a good state of charge, the air filter must be clean, and the engine should be at normal operating temperature.
b) All the glow plugs should be removed as described in Chapter 5C, Section 2 before starting the test.
c) The wiring connector on the engine management system ECU must be disconnected.

4 The compression pressures measured are not so important as the balance between cylinders. Values are given in the Specifications.

5 The cause of poor compression is less easy to establish on a diesel engine than on a petrol one. The effect of introducing oil into the cylinders ('wet' testing) is not conclusive, because there is a risk that the oil will sit in the swirl chamber or in the recess on the piston crown instead of passing to the rings. However, the following can be used as a rough guide to diagnosis.

6 All cylinders should produce very similar pressures; any difference greater than that specified indicates the existence of a fault. Note that the compression should build-up quickly in a healthy engine; low compression on the first stroke, followed by gradually increasing pressure on successive strokes, indicates worn piston rings. A low compression reading on the first stroke, which does not build-up during successive strokes, indicates leaking valves or a blown head gasket (a cracked head could also be the cause). Deposits on the undersides of the valve heads can also cause low compression.

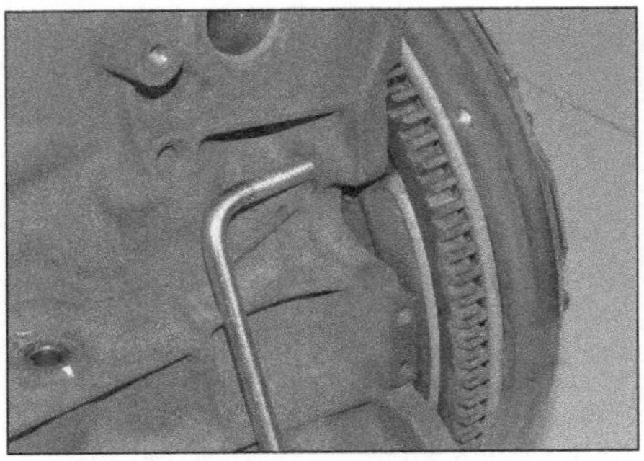

3.7a The tool fits through the hole in the cylinder block flange ...

3.7b ... and into a hole in the rear of the flywheel

3.8 Fit the tool through the hole in the exhaust camshaft sprocket, into the timing hole in the cylinder head

7 A low reading from two adjacent cylinders is almost certainly due to the head gasket having blown between them; the presence of coolant in the engine oil will confirm this.
8 If the compression reading is unusually high, the cylinder head surfaces, valves and pistons are probably coated with carbon deposits. If this is the case, the cylinder head should be removed and decarbonised (see Chapter 2E, Section 7).

Leakdown test

9 A leakdown test measures the rate at which compressed air fed into the cylinder is lost. It is an alternative to a compression test, and in many ways it is better, since the escaping air provides easy identification of where pressure loss is occurring (piston rings, valves or head gasket).
10 The equipment needed for leakdown testing is unlikely to be available to the home mechanic. If poor compression is suspected, have the test performed by a suitably-equipped garage.

3 Engine assembly/valve timing holes – general information and usage

Note: *Do not attempt to rotate the engine whilst the crankshaft and camshaft are locked in position. If the engine is to be left in this state for a long period of time, it is a good idea to place suitable warning notices inside the vehicle, and in the engine compartment. This will reduce the possibility of the engine being accidentally cranked on the starter motor, which is likely to cause damage with the locking pins in place.*
1 Timing holes or slots are located only in the flywheel/driveplate and camshaft sprocket hub. The holes/slots are used to align the crankshaft and camshaft at the TDC position for Nos 1 and 4. This will ensure that the valve timing is maintained during operations that require removal and refitting of the timing belt. When the holes/slots are aligned with their corresponding holes in the cylinder block and cylinder head, suitable diameter bolts/pins can be inserted to lock the crankshaft and camshaft in position, preventing rotation. Note that with the timing holes aligned, No 4 piston is at TDC on its compression stroke.
2 To align the engine assembly/valve timing holes, proceed as follows.
3 Chock the rear wheels then jack up the front of the vehicle and support it on axle stands (see *Jacking and vehicle support*). Remove the right-hand front roadwheel.
4 To gain access to the crankshaft pulley, to enable the engine to be turned, the wheel arch plastic liner must be removed. The liner is secured by several plastic expanding rivets. To remove the rivets, push in the centre pins a little, and then prise the clips from place. Remove the liner from under the front wing. Where necessary, unclip the coolant hoses from under the wing to improve access further. The crankshaft can then be turned using a suitable socket and extension bar fitted to the pulley bolt.
5 Remove the upper timing belt cover as described in Section 6.
6 Turn the crankshaft until the timing hole in the camshaft sprocket is aligned with the corresponding hole in the cylinder head. Note that the crankshaft must always be turned in a clockwise direction (viewed from the right-hand side of vehicle). Use a small mirror so that the position of the sprocket timing slot can be observed. When the slot is aligned with the corresponding hole in the cylinder head, the camshaft is positioned correctly.
7 Insert Citroën tool No (-).0188.X or an 8 mm diameter bolt, rod or drill through the hole in the left-hand flange of the cylinder block by the starter motor; if necessary, carefully turn the crankshaft either way until the rod enters the timing hole in the flywheel/driveplate **(see illustrations)**. Note that if a bolt/rod/drill bit is used, it must be flat (not tapered at all) at the end. If improved access is required, remove the starter motor as described in Chapter 5A, Section 10.
8 Insert the 8 mm bolt, rod or drill through the hole in the camshaft sprocket hub and into engagement with the cylinder head **(see illustration)**.
9 The crankshaft and camshaft are now locked in position, preventing unnecessary rotation.

4.3 Undo the bolt and remove the camshaft position sensor (arrowed)

4 Cylinder head cover/intake manifold – removal and refitting

Removal

1 Remove the plastic cover from the top of the engine. The cover simply pulls up from its rubber mountings.
2 The cylinder head cover is integral with the intake manifold. Begin by disconnecting any wiring connectors and releasing the wiring harness from the timing belt upper cover.
3 Disconnect the wiring plug, and then unscrew the camshaft position sensor from the cover **(see illustration)**.
4 Undo the bolts securing the upper timing belt cover to the cylinder head cover/intake manifold **(see illustration)**.
5 Disconnect the wiring connectors and

4.4 Undo the upper cover bolt

4.5a Disconnect the wiring connectors ...

4.5b ... and disconnect the air intake hoses

4.6 Release the clips (arrowed) and detach the injector wiring harness duct

disconnect the air intake hose(s) from the front of the intake manifold **(see illustrations)**.

Siemens fuel system

6 Disconnect the injectors' wiring plugs, and then detach the harness duct from the intake manifold/cover and position it to one side **(see illustration)**.

7 Disconnect the crankcase ventilation hoses from the intake manifold/cover, then release the clamp and disconnect the EGR pipe from the intake manifold **(see illustrations)**.

8 Release the glow plugs' wiring harness from the 2 clips on the rear of the cover.

9 Slacken the clamps and disconnect the intake hoses from the manifold.

10 Unclip the fuel temperature sensor from the underside of the manifold.

11 Undo the manifold/cover retaining bolts in the **reverse** of the sequence shown in illustration 4.22. Check around the manifold/cover for any wiring or hoses, and then remove the manifold/cover and discard the gaskets. New gaskets must be used on refitting.

Delphi fuel system

12 Disconnect the breather hose from across the rear of the intake manifold/cover **(see illustration)**.

13 Disconnect the breather hose from left-hand rear of the intake manifold/cover **(see illustration)**.

14 Release the retaining clip and disconnect the EGR pipe **(see illustration)**.

15 Unclip the fuel pipes from under the side of the intake manifold **(see illustration)**.

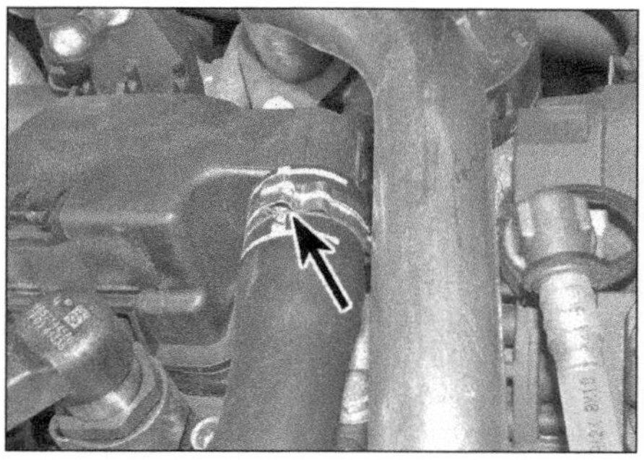

4.7a Release the clamps and disconnect the breather hose (arrowed) from the cylinder head cover ...

4.7b ... the EGR pipe from the intake manifold ...

4.7c ... then slide out the locking clip and disconnect the breather hose from the rear of the cylinder head cover

4.12 Disconnect the breather hose

4.13 Disconnect the breather hose from the cover

4.14 Release the EGR pipe securing clip (arrowed)

4.15 Unclip the fuel pipes (arrowed) from under the manifold

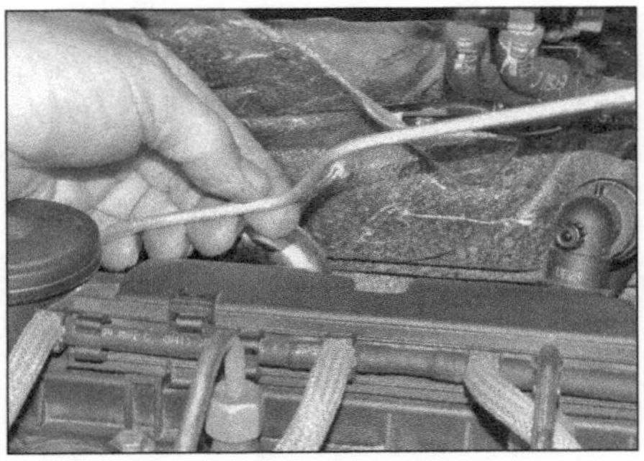

4.16 Unclip the vacuum pipe from the rear of the cover

4.17 Remove the fuel return hoses

4.18 Unbolt the mounting bracket from the cover

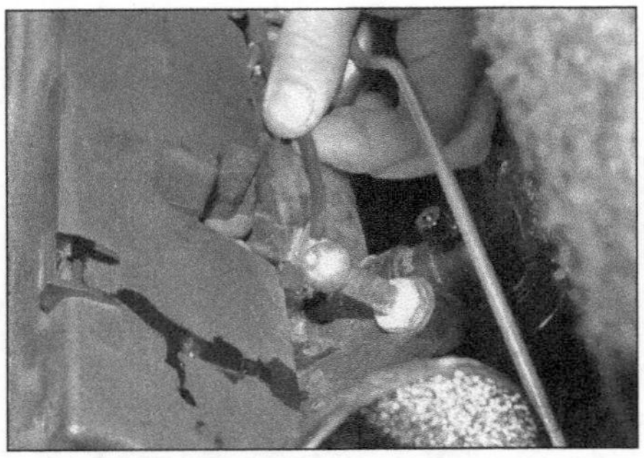

4.19 Unclip the glow plug wiring from the rear of the cover

4.20 Remove the intake manifold/cover from the engine

16 Disconnect the vacuum hose and unclip the vacuum pipe from the rear of the cylinder head cover **(see illustration)**.

17 Disconnect the fuel return pipes from the injectors and the fuel pump, and then detach the harness duct from the intake manifold/cover and position it to one side **(see illustration)**.

18 Unbolt the mounting bracket from the right-hand rear of the cylinder head **(see illustration)** to access the cylinder head cover retaining bolt.

19 Release the glow plugs' wiring harness from the 2 clips on the rear of the cover **(see illustration)**.

20 Undo the manifold/cover retaining bolts in the **reverse** of the sequence shown in illustration 4.22. Check around the manifold/cover for any wiring or hoses, and then remove the manifold/cover and discard the gaskets. New gaskets must be used on refitting **(see illustration)**.

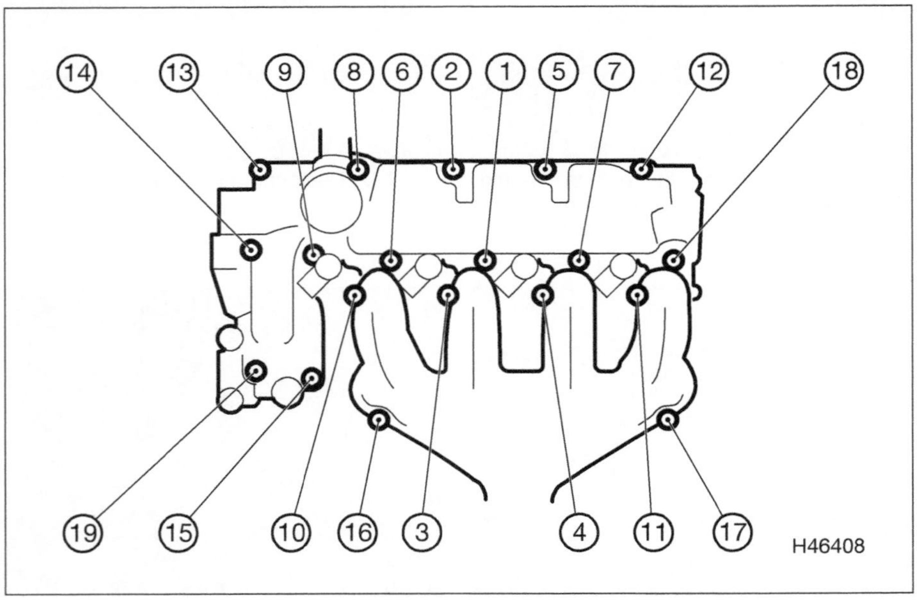

4.22 Intake manifold/cylinder head cover bolt tightening sequence

55 mm bolt is fitted in position 14 *70 mm bolts are fitted in positions 16 and 17*

Refitting

21 Clean the sealing surfaces of the manifold/cover and the cylinder head.

22 Fit the new seals to the intake manifold/cover, and then fit it to the cylinder head. Use a little petroleum jelly on the manifold O-rings to ease reassembly. Tighten the bolts to the specified torque in sequence **(see illustration)**.

23 The remainder of refitting is a reversal of removal, noting the following points:

a) *Tighten all fasteners to their specified torque.*

b) *Before refitting the timing belt upper cover, adjust the camshaft position sensor air gap as described in Chapter 4B, Section 12.*

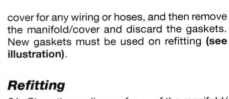

5 Crankshaft pulley – removal and refitting

Removal

1 Remove the auxiliary drivebelt as described in Chapter 1B, Section 17.

2 Position the camshaft and crankshaft as described in Section 3. **Note:** *It is essential that the crankshaft and camshaft timing pins are in place as described in Section 3. This is because on these engines, the crankshaft sprocket has a wider keyway to allow it to rotate a little independently of the crankshaft during the belt tensioning procedure. Failure to lock the crankshaft and camshaft could result in the timing being lost.*

3 To prevent crankshaft turning whilst the pulley retaining bolt is being slackened, the flywheel/driveplate ring gear can be locked using (Citroën tool No (-).0188.F) or a suitable tool made from steel angle. Remove the starter motor as described in Chapter 5A, Section 10, and bolt the tool to the bellhousing flange so it engages with the ring gear teeth **(see**

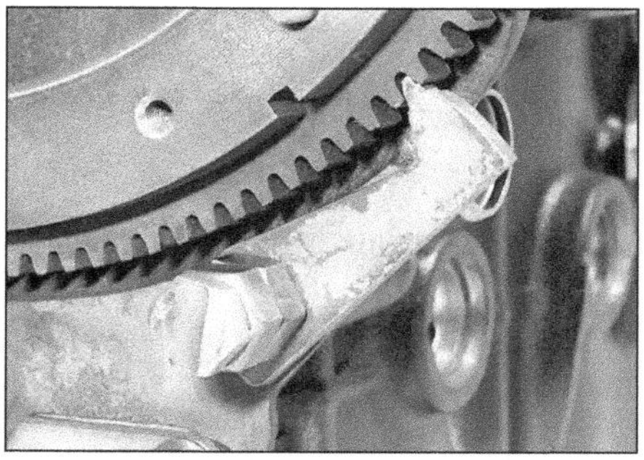

5.3 Use a fabricated tool similar to this to lock the flywheel ring gear and prevent crankshaft rotation

5.4 Undo the bolt and remove the crankshaft pulley

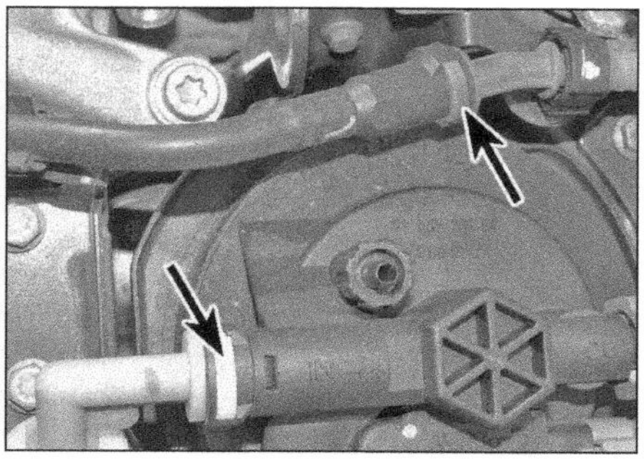

6.4 Depress the clips and disconnect the fuel pipes (arrowed)

illustration). *Do not* attempt to lock the pulley by only inserting a bolt/drill through the timing hole.

4 Using a suitable socket and extension bar, unscrew the retaining bolt, remove the washer, then slide the pulley off the end of the crankshaft **(see illustration)**. If the pulley is a tight fit, it can be drawn off the crankshaft using a suitable puller. If a puller is being used, refit the pulley retaining bolt without the washer, to avoid damaging the crankshaft as the puller is tightened.

Refitting

5 Ensure the camshaft and crankshaft are positioned at TDC as described previously, and the flywheel/driveplate ring gear is locked in position, as described in paragraph 3.

6 Thoroughly clean the threads of the pulley retaining bolt, then apply a coat of locking compound to the bolt threads. Citroën recommend the use of Loctite (available from your Citroën dealer); in the absence of this, any good-quality locking compound may be used.

7 Refit the crankshaft pulley retaining bolt and washer. Tighten the bolt to the specified torque, then through the specified angle.

8 Remove the crankshaft, camshaft and flywheel/driveplate locking tools.

9 Refit and tension the auxiliary drivebelt as described in Chapter 1B, Section 17.

6 **Timing belt covers –** removal and refitting

Warning: Refer to the precautionary information contained in Section 1 before proceeding.

Removal

Upper cover

1 Pull up the plastic cover from the top of the engine, then undo the screws and remove the engine undershield.

2 Position a trolley jack under the engine, and using a piece of wood on the jack head, support the weight of the engine.

3 Undo the bolts and remove the right-hand engine mounting and support bracket – see Section 17.

4 At the connections at the right-hand end of the cylinder head, disconnect the fuel supply and return hose quick-release fittings using a small screwdriver to press down and release the locking clip **(see illustration)**. Cover the open unions to prevent dirt entry, using small plastic bags, or fingers cut from clean rubber gloves.

5 Release the two fuel hoses from the retaining clips at the right-hand end of the cylinder head.

6 Move the electrical harness to one side, then undo the screws/nut and remove the upper timing belt cover **(see illustration)**.

Lower cover

7 Remove the upper cover as described previously.

8 Remove the crankshaft pulley as described in Section 5.

9 Undo the bolt and position the crankshaft sensor to one side **(see illustration)**.

10 Carefully pull the crankshaft sensor signal disc from the crankshaft **(see illustration)**. If the disc is reluctant to move, screw in two 6.0 mm bolts into the threaded holes in the disc and force it from place.

11 Undo the bolts and remove the lower timing belt cover.

Refitting

12 Refitting of all the covers is a reversal of the relevant removal procedure, ensuring that each cover section is correctly located, and that the cover retaining bolts are securely tightened. Ensure that all disturbed hoses are reconnected and retained by their relevant clips.

7 **Timing belt** – removal, inspection, refitting and tensioning

General

1 The timing belt drives the exhaust camshaft and coolant pump from a toothed sprocket on the end of the crankshaft. If the belt breaks or

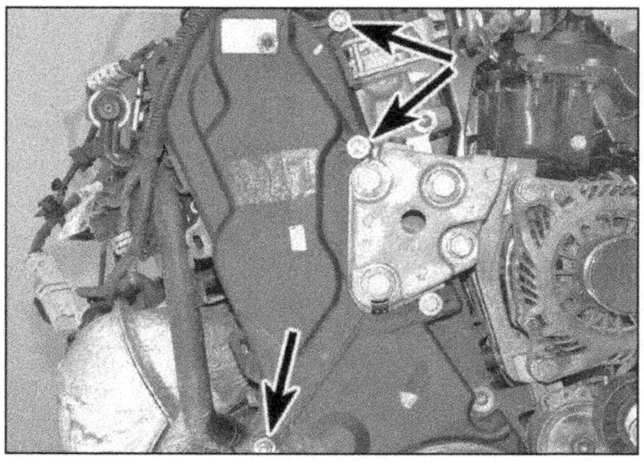

6.6 Upper timing belt fasteners (arrowed)

6.9 Crankshaft position sensor bolt (arrowed)

6.10 Sensor signal disc

7.12 Position the crankshaft sprocket so that equal gaps exists each side of the key (arrowed)

slips in service, the pistons are likely to hit the valve heads, resulting in expensive damage.

2 The timing belt should be renewed at the specified intervals, or earlier if it is contaminated with oil or at all noisy in operation (a 'scraping' noise due to uneven wear).

3 If the timing belt is being removed, it is a wise precaution to check the condition of the coolant pump at the same time (check for signs of coolant leakage). This may avoid the need to remove the timing belt again at a later stage should the coolant pump fail.

Removal

4 Chock the rear wheels then jack up the front of the vehicle and support it on axle stands (see *Jacking and vehicle support*). Remove the front right-hand roadwheel, wheel arch liner (to expose the crankshaft pulley), and the engine undershield. The wheel arch liner is secured by several plastic expanding rivets, or push-in clips. Push the centre pins in a little then prise the rivet from place. Undo the retaining screws and remove the engine undershield.

5 Remove the crankshaft pulley as described in Section 5, then use 6.0 mm bolts to draw the sensor disc from the end of the crankshaft **(see illustration 6.10)**.

6 Remove the upper and lower timing belt covers as described in Section 6.

7 Ensure the engine is positioned at TDC as described in Section 3, with the camshaft and crankshaft locking tools described in place.

8 Loosen the bolt on the tensioner pulley, and turn the tensioner clockwise to release the tension on the timing belt. Use an Allen key in the hole provided, to turn the tensioner bracket against the spring tension. Retighten the bolt sufficiently to hold the tensioner in its released position; do not fully-tighten the bolt in this position.

7.14 Timing belt routing

9 Mark the timing belt with an arrow to indicate its running direction as a reference for refitting. Remove the belt from the sprockets.

Inspection

10 Renew the belt as a matter of course, regardless of its apparent condition. The cost of a new belt is nothing compared with the cost of repairs should the belt break in service. If signs of oil contamination are found, trace the source of the oil leak and rectify it. Wash down the engine timing belt area and all related components, to remove all traces of oil. Check that the tensioner and idler pulleys rotate freely without any sign of roughness, and also check that the coolant pump rotates freely. If necessary, renew these items.

Refitting and tensioning

11 Commence refitting by ensuring that the TDC timing pins are still in position correctly.

12 Centre the crankshaft sprocket by inserting Citroën tool (-).0188.AH either side of the crankshaft key, and into the keyway in the sprocket. In the absence of the tool, position the sprocket centrally, ensuring a gap exists each side of the key **(see illustration)**.

13 Fit the timing belt to the camshaft sprocket. Citroën technicians use a clip to retain the belt on the sprocket; if necessary, use a plastic cable-tie to hold it.

14 Continue to fit the belt in the following order, keeping the belt taut as it's fitted around the idler pulley and the crankshaft sprocket **(see illustration)**:

a) Idler pulley.
b) Crankshaft sprocket.
c) Coolant pump sprocket.
d) Tensioner pulley.

15 Remove the tool/cable-tie securing the belt to the camshaft sprocket, and the crankshaft sprocket centring tool.

16 Slacken the tensioner pulley retaining bolt, then using an Allen key, rotate the tensioner anti-clockwise until the index pointer is aligned with the lower, outside edge of the reference plate **(see illustrations)**. Tighten the tensioner pulley retaining bolt to the specified torque.

17 Ensure the crankshaft/flywheel ring gear locking tool is still in place, then refit the lower timing belt cover, sensor disc and crankshaft pulley, and tighten the retaining bolt to 70 Nm (52 lbf ft).

18 Remove the camshaft sprocket and crankshaft locking/timing tools.

19 Rotate the crankshaft 10 times in the normal direction of rotation, and refit the camshaft sprocket and crankshaft locking/timing tools.

20 With the flywheel ring gear locked, slacken the crankshaft pulley bolt.

21 Slacken the timing belt tensioner retaining bolt, then use an Allen key to rotate the tensioner clockwise until the index pointer aligns with the notch in the reference plate **(see illustration)**. Tighten the tensioner pulley bolt to the specified torque.

22 Tighten the crankshaft pulley bolt to 70 Nm (52 lbf ft), at this stage.

23 Remove the camshaft sprocket and crankshaft/flywheel ring gear locking/aligning tools, and rotate the crankshaft 2 complete revolutions in the normal direction of rotation (clockwise).

24 Check that the camshaft sprocket and crankshaft/flywheel aligning tools can still be inserted, and that the tensioner index pointer is still aligned with the notch in the reference

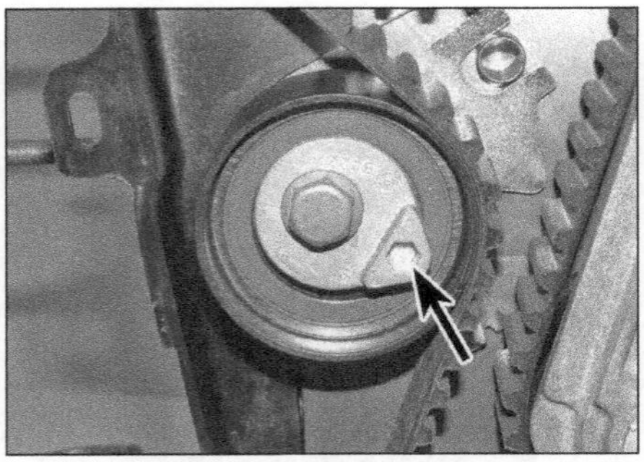

7.16a Use an Allen key in the tensioner (arrowed)

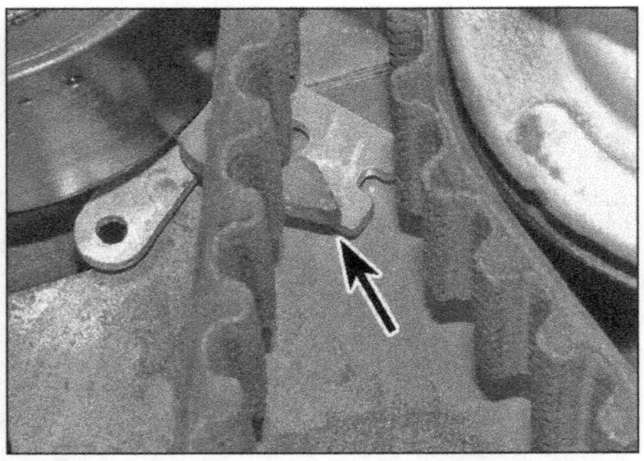

7.16b Rotate the tensioner anti-clockwise until the index pointer is aligned with the lower edge of the reference plate (arrowed)

7.21 Align the index pointer with the notch in the reference plate

plate. If necessary, repeat the tensioning procedure until the pointer and notch align.

25 Lock the flywheel ring gear using the previously described tool and undo the crankshaft pulley bolt.

26 Refit the crankshaft sensor. Tighten the retaining bolt securely.

27 Apply a little thread-locking compound to the threads, then tighten the crankshaft pulley retaining bolt to the specified torque.

28 Remove the camshaft sprocket and crankshaft/flywheel ring gear locking/aligning tools.

29 The remainder of refitting is a reversal of removal.

8 Timing belt sprockets and tensioner – removal and refitting

Camshaft sprocket

Removal

1 Remove the timing belt as described in Section 7.

2 Remove the locking tool from the camshaft sprocket, then slacken the sprocket retaining bolt. To prevent the camshaft rotating as the bolt is slackened, Citroën technicians use tool No 6016-T. In the absence of this tool, fabricate a substitute as described **(see Tool Tip)**. *Do not* attempt to use the camshaft sprocket locking tool to prevent the sprocket from rotating whilst the bolt is slackened. **Note:** *Take care not to damage the sensor signal disc integral with the sprocket.*

3 Remove the bolt, and slide the sprocket from the camshaft. If the Woodruff key is a loose fit in the camshaft, remove it for safekeeping. Examine the camshaft oil seal for signs of oil leakage and, if necessary, renew it as described in Section 14.

4 Clean the camshaft sprocket thoroughly, and renew it if there are any signs of wear, damage or cracks.

Refitting

5 Where applicable, refit the Woodruff key to the end of the camshaft, and then refit the camshaft sprocket and hub.

HAYNES HiNT

To make a sprocket holding tool, obtain two lengths of steel strip about 6.0 mm thick by about 30 mm wide or similar, one 600 mm long, the other 200 mm long (all dimensions approximate). Bolt the two strips together to form a forked end, leaving the bolt slack so that the shorter strip can pivot freely. At the other end of each 'prong' of the fork, drill a suitable hole and fit a nut and bolt to engage with the spokes or holes in the sprocket. It may be necessary to cut-off or grind the side slightly to allow them to fit in the sprocket holes.

6 Refit the sprocket retaining bolt and washer. Tighten the bolt to the specified torque, preventing the camshaft from turning as during removal.

7 Align the timing slot in the camshaft sprocket with the hole in the cylinder head and refit the tool locking the camshaft in position.

8 Refit the timing belt as described in Section 7.

Crankshaft sprocket

Removal

9 Remove the timing belt as described in Section 7.

10 Slide the sprocket off the end of the crankshaft and collect the Woodruff key **(see illustrations)**.

11 Examine the crankshaft oil seal for signs of oil leakage and, if necessary, renew it as described in Section 14.

12 Clean the crankshaft sprocket thoroughly, and renew it if there are any signs of wear, damage or cracks.

8.10a Slide off the crankshaft pulley ...

8.10b ... and recover the Woodruff key

Refitting

13 Refit the Woodruff key to the end of the crankshaft, and then refit the crankshaft sprocket (with the flange nearest the cylinder block).

14 Refit the timing belt as described in Section 7.

Coolant pump sprocket

15 The coolant pump sprocket is integral with the pump, and cannot be removed.

Tensioner pulley

Removal

16 Remove the timing belt as described in Section 7.

17 Remove the tensioner pulley retaining bolt, and slide the pulley off its mounting stud.

18 Clean the tensioner pulley, but do not use any strong solvent that may enter the pulley bearings. Check that the pulley rotates freely, with no sign of stiffness or free play. Renew the pulley if there is any doubt about its condition, or if there are any obvious signs of wear or damage.

Refitting

19 Refit the tensioner pulley, and insert the retaining bolt.

20 Refit the timing belt as described in Section 7.

Idler pulley

Removal

21 Remove the timing belt as described in Section 7.

22 Undo the retaining bolt and withdraw the idler pulley from the engine.

23 Clean the idler pulley, but do not use any strong solvent, which may enter the bearings. Check that the pulley rotates freely, with no sign of stiffness or free play. Renew the idler pulley if there is any doubt about its condition, or if there are any obvious signs of wear or damage.

Refitting

24 Locate the idler pulley on the engine, and fit the retaining bolt. Tighten the bolt to the specified torque.

25 Fit the timing belt around the idler pulley, and tension the timing belt as described in Section 7.

9 Camshafts, rocker arms and hydraulic tappets – removal, inspection and refitting

Removal

1 Remove the cylinder head cover as described in Section 4.

2 Remove the camshaft sprocket as described in Section 8.

3 Slacken the retaining clamps and disconnect the air intake hose from the left-hand end of the cylinder head. Remove the intercooler air

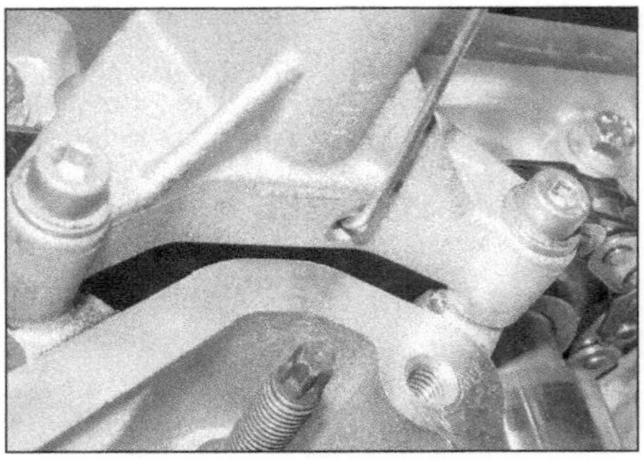

9.8 Lift up the upper chain guide rail and insert a 2.0 mm diameter rod/drill bit into the hole in the tensioner body

duct from the left-hand end of the cylinder head.

4 Remove the air cleaner assembly, high-pressure fuel pump, and fuel injectors.

5 Refit the right-hand engine mounting, but only tighten the bolts moderately; this will keep the engine supported during the camshaft removal.

6 Disconnect the vacuum pipe from the brake vacuum pump on the left-hand end of the cylinder head.

7 Remove the vacuum pump from the cylinder head with reference to Chapter 9, Section 20.

8 Compress the timing chain tensioner and insert a 2.0 mm drill bit into the tensioner body to lock the piston in the compressed state **(see illustration)**.

9 Undo the bolts and remove the timing chain tensioner **(see illustration)**.

10 Working in a spiral pattern from the outside to the inside, progressively loosen the camshaft bearing cap housing bolts until they can be removed.

11 Withdraw the bearing cap housing from the cylinder head. The housing is likely to be initially tight to release, as it is located by two dowels on the forward facing side of the cylinder head. If necessary, very carefully prise up the housing using a screwdriver inserted in the slotted lug adjacent to each dowel location. Once the bearing housing is free, lift it squarely from the cylinder head. The camshaft will rise up slightly under the pressure of the valve springs – be careful it doesn't tilt and jam in the cylinder head or bearing housing section.

12 Check that the camshafts and chain are marked in relation to each other – the chain should have two black or copper links that align with marks on the teeth. If necessary, mark the chain and teeth with dabs of paint. The marks on the teeth are the most important as they determine the valve timing, however the chain links can be marked as they are 7 links (inclusive) apart **(see illustrations)**.

9.12b ... the mark on the sprockets is a dot and a line

9.9 Undo the tensioner retaining bolts (arrowed)

13 Simultaneously, lift the camshafts and chain from the cylinder head. Release the camshafts from the chain.

14 Either get sixteen small, clean plastic containers, and number them 1 to 16, or divide a larger container into sixteen compartments.

15 Lift out each rocker arm and release it from the spring clip on the tappet **(see illustration)**. Place the rocker arms in their respective positions in the box or containers.

16 A compartmentalised container filled with engine oil is now required to retain the hydraulic tappets while they are removed from the cylinder head. Using a rubber sucker, withdraw each hydraulic tappet and place it in the container, keeping them each identified for correct refitting. The tappets must be totally submerged in the oil to prevent air entering them.

Inspection

17 Inspect the cam lobes and the camshaft bearing journals for scoring or other visible evidence of wear. Once the surface hardening of the cam lobes has been eroded, wear will occur at an accelerated rate. **Note:** *If these symptoms are visible on the tips of the camshaft lobes, check the corresponding rocker arm, as it will probably be worn as well.*

18 Examine the condition of the bearing surfaces in the cylinder head and camshaft bearing housing. If wear is evident, the cylinder head and bearing housing will both have to be renewed, as they are a matched assembly.

9.15 Lift out the rocker arms with the hydraulic tappets

9.12a The coloured links on the chain (arrowed) align with the marks on the camshaft sprockets ...

19 Inspect the rocker arms and tappets for scuffing, cracking or other damage and renew any components as necessary. Also check the condition of the tappet bores in the cylinder head. As with the camshafts, any wear in this area will necessitate cylinder head renewal.

Refitting

20 Thoroughly clean the sealant from the mating surfaces of the cylinder head and camshaft bearing housing. Use a suitable liquid gasket dissolving agent (available from Citroën dealers) together with a soft putty knife; do not use a metal scraper or the faces will be damaged. As there is no conventional gasket used, the cleanliness of the mating faces is of the utmost importance.

21 Clean off any oil, dirt or grease from both components and dry with a clean lint-free cloth. Ensure that all the oilways are completely clean.

22 To prevent any possibility of the valves contacting the pistons as the camshaft is refitted, remove the locking pin/drill from the flywheel/driveplate and turn the crankshaft a quarter turn in the *opposite* direction to normal rotation (ie, anti-clockwise), to position all the pistons at mid-stroke.

23 Liberally lubricate the hydraulic tappet bores in the cylinder head with clean engine oil.

24 Insert the hydraulic tappets into their original bores in the cylinder head unless they have been renewed **(see illustration)**.

9.24 Insert the tappets and rocker arms into their original locations

9.27 **Position the camshafts so the mark on the intake camshaft (arrowed) is in the 12 o'clock position**

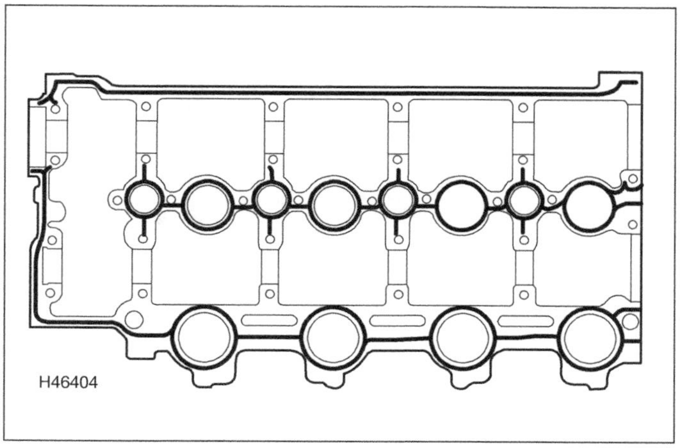

9.32a **Apply a thin bead of sealant as indicated by the heavy black line**

25 Lubricate the rocker arms and place them over their respective tappets and valve stems. Ensure that the ends of the rocker arms engage with the spring clips on the tappets.
26 Lubricate the camshaft bearing journals in the cylinder head sparingly with oil, taking care not to allow the oil to spill over onto the camshaft bearing housing contact areas.
27 Engage the camshafts with the chain, making sure that the coloured links are aligned with the marked teeth, fit the tensioner between the chain runs, and then lower them into position. The longer exhaust camshaft must go at the rear of the cylinder head. Rotate the camshaft so the mark on the intake camshaft is in the 12 o'clock position **(see illustration)**.
28 Fit a new camshaft oil seal as described in Section 14.
29 Refit the camshaft sprocket, lightly tighten the retaining bolt, and then fit the camshaft sprocket locking tool. Turn the crankshaft 45° clockwise and re-insert the crankshaft locking pin/drill.
30 Check the marks on the camshaft sprockets still align with the coloured links on the chain.
31 Ensure that the mating faces of the cylinder head and camshaft bearing housing are clean and free of any oil or grease.

9.32b **We inserted a tapered rod (arrowed) into the tensioner oil supply hole to prevent any sealant from entering**

32 Sparingly apply a bead of sealant (Loctite 518) to the mating face of the camshaft bearing housing, taking care not to allow the product to contaminate the camshaft bearing journal areas **(see illustrations)**.
33 Lower the housing into place, then insert and tighten the camshaft bearing housing bolts to the specified torque, in sequence **(see illustration)**.
34 Refit the chain tensioner, tighten the retaining bolts to the specified torque, then pull out the locking pin and allow the tensioner to act upon the chain.
35 The remainder of refitting is a reversal of removal.

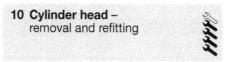

10 Cylinder head – removal and refitting

Note: *This is an involved procedure, and it is suggested that the Section is read thoroughly before starting work. To aid refitting, make notes on the locations of all relevant brackets and the routing of hoses and cables before removal.*

Removal

1 Chock the rear wheels then jack up the front of the vehicle and support it on axle stands (see *Jacking and vehicle support*). Remove the front right-hand roadwheel, the engine undershield, and the front wheel arch liner. The undershield is secured by several screws, and the wheel arch liner is secured by several plastic expanding rivets. Push the centre pins in a little, and then prise the rivet from place.
2 Remove the battery (see Chapter 5A, Section 4).
3 Drain the cooling system as described in Chapter 1B, Section 20.
4 Remove the camshafts, rocker arms and hydraulic tappets as described in Section 9.
5 Remove the timing chain pad at the

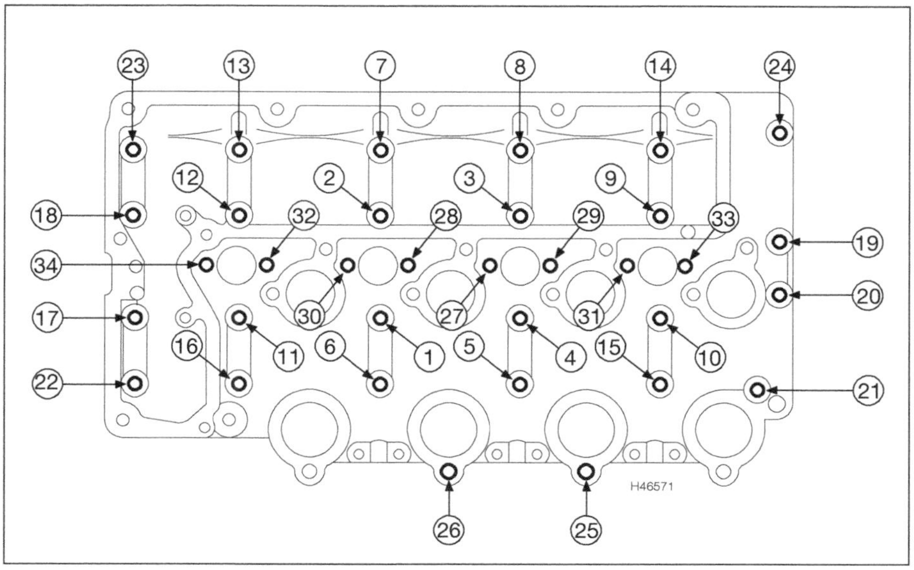

9.33 **Camshaft bearing cap housing bolts tightening sequence**

10.5 Remove the timing chain pad from the cylinder head

10.8 Undo the bracket upper bolt (arrowed)

right-hand side of the cylinder head **(see illustration)**.

6 Remove the fuel filter and bracket.

7 Remove the common (fuel) rail as described in Chapter 4B, Section 10.

8 Remove the uppermost bolt securing the engine mounting support bracket to the right-hand end of the cylinder head **(see illustration)**, then temporarily refit the mounting to support the engine whilst the cylinder head is being removed.

9 Note their fitted positions and routing, then disconnect all coolant and vacuum hoses from the cylinder head.

10 Undo the bolts/studs securing the coolant outlet housing to the left-hand end of the cylinder head. Pull the housing away from the cylinder head **(see illustration)**.

11 Remove the turbocharger and exhaust manifold as described in Chapter 4B, Section 16 and Section 14.

12 Progressively slacken the cylinder head bolts, in the **reverse** order to that shown for tightening **(see illustration 10.33)**. A Torx socket will be required for this.

13 When all the bolts are loose, unscrew them fully and remove them from the cylinder head.

14 Release the cylinder head from the cylinder block and location dowels by rocking it. The Citroën tool for doing this consists simply of two metal rods with 90-degree angled ends. Do not prise between the mating faces of the cylinder head and block, as this may damage the gasket faces.

15 Lift the cylinder head from the block, and recover the gasket.

Preparation for refitting

16 The mating faces of the cylinder head and cylinder block must be perfectly clean before refitting the head. Citroën recommend the use of a scouring agent for this purpose, but acceptable results can be achieved by using a hard plastic or wood scraper to remove all traces of gasket and carbon. The same method can be used to clean the piston crowns. Take particular care to avoid scoring or gouging the cylinder head/cylinder block mating surfaces during the cleaning operations, as aluminium alloy is easily damaged. Make sure that the carbon is not allowed to enter the oil and water passages – this is particularly important for the lubrication system, as carbon could block the oil supply to the engine's components. Using adhesive tape and paper, seal the water, oil and bolt holes in the cylinder block. To prevent carbon entering the gap between the pistons and bores, smear a little grease in the gap. After cleaning each piston, use a small brush to remove all traces of grease and carbon from the gap, and then wipe away the remainder with a clean rag.

17 Check the mating surfaces of the cylinder block and the cylinder head for nicks, deep scratches and other damage. If slight, they may be removed carefully with a file, but if excessive, machining may be the only alternative to renewal. If warpage of the cylinder head gasket surface is suspected, use a straight-edge to check it for distortion. Refer to Chapter 2E, Section 7 if necessary.

18 Thoroughly clean the threads of the cylinder head bolt holes in the cylinder block. Ensure that the bolts run freely in their threads, and that all traces of oil and water are removed from each bolt hole. If possible, use a M12 x 150 tap to clean out the threads.

Gasket selection

19 Turn the crankshaft until pistons 1 and 4 are at TDC (Top Dead Centre). Position a dial test indicator (dial gauge) on the cylinder block adjacent to the rear of No 1 piston, and zero it on the block face **(see illustration)**. Transfer the probe to the crown of No 1 piston (10.0 mm in from the rear edge), and then slowly turn the crankshaft back-and-forth past TDC, noting the highest reading on the indicator. Record this reading as protrusion A.

20 Repeat the check described in paragraph 19, this time 10.0 mm in from the front edge of the No 1 piston crown. Record this reading as protrusion B.

21 Add protrusion A to protrusion B, then divide the result by 2 to obtain an average reading for piston No 1.

22 Repeat the procedure described in paragraphs 19 to 21 on piston 4, then turn the crankshaft through 180° and carry out the procedure on the piston Nos 2 and 3. Check that there is a maximum difference of 0.07 mm protrusion between any two pistons.

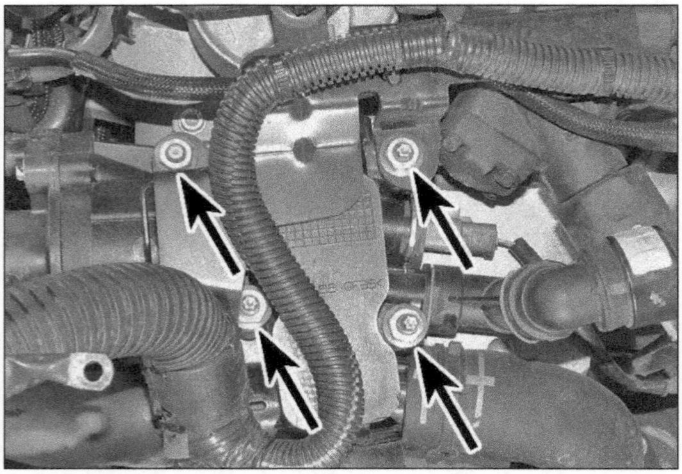
10.10 Undo the nuts (arrowed) and remove the coolant outlet housing

10.19 Zero the DTI on the gasket face

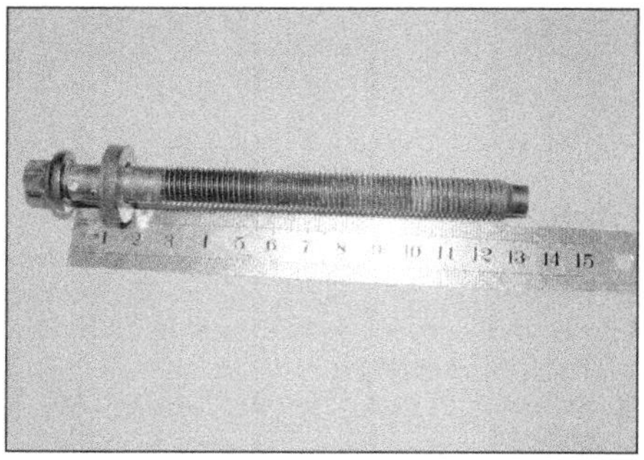

10.25 Measure the length of the cylinder head bolts from under the bolt head, not the washer

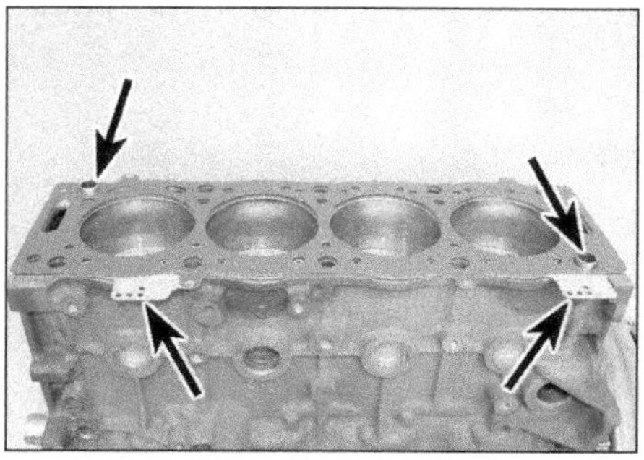

10.28 Fit the new gasket over the dowels, with the thickness identification holes at the front (arrowed)

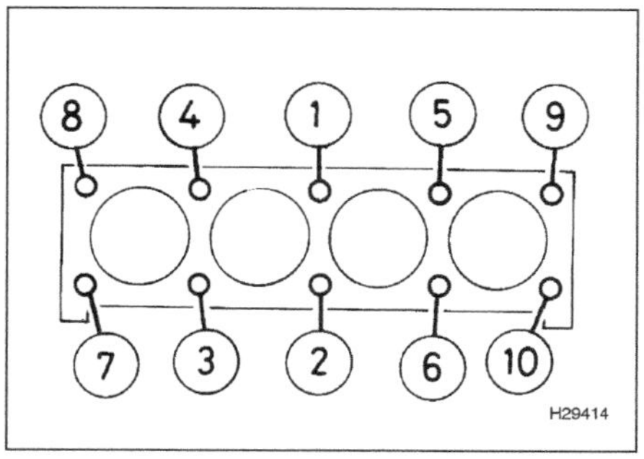

10.33 Cylinder head bolt tightening sequence

23 If a dial test indicator is not available, piston protrusion may be measured using a straight-edge and feeler blades or Vernier calipers. However, this is much less accurate, and cannot therefore be recommended.

24 Note the greatest piston protrusion measurement, and use this to determine the correct cylinder head gasket from the following table. The series of holes on the front side of the gasket are used for thickness identification.

Piston protrusion	Gasket identification
0.55 to 0.60 mm	*1 hole*
0.61 to 0.65 mm	*2 holes*
0.66 to 0.70 mm	*3 holes*
0.71 to 0.75 mm	*4 holes*

Head bolt examination

25 Carefully examine the cylinder head bolts for signs of damage to the threads or head, and for any sign of corrosion. If the bolts are in a satisfactory condition, measure the length of each bolt from the underside of the head to the end of the shank. Two different types of bolts may be fitted:

a) The older type have a washer which is loose on the top of the bolt ***(see illustration)****; on these bolts, they may be re-used providing that the measured length from beneath the bolt head to the very end of the bolt, does not exceed 134.5 mm ± 0.05 mm.*

b) The newer type have a washer which is part of the bolt head; on these bolts, they may be re-used providing that the measured length from beneath the bolt head to the very end of the bolt, does not exceed 129.0 mm ± 0.05 mm.

Note: *Considering the stress to which the cylinder head bolts are subjected, it is highly recommended that they are all renewed, regardless of their apparent condition.*

Refitting

26 Turn the crankshaft and position Nos 1 and 4 pistons at TDC, then turn the crankshaft a quarter turn (90°) anti-clockwise.

27 Thoroughly clean the surfaces of the cylinder head and block.

28 Make sure that the locating dowels are in place, then fit the correct gasket the right way round on the cylinder block **(see illustration)**.

29 If necessary, refit the exhaust manifold with reference to Chapter 4B, Section 14.

30 Carefully lower the cylinder head onto the gasket and block, making sure that it locates correctly onto the dowels.

31 Apply a light smear of grease to the threads, and to the underside of the heads, of the cylinder head bolts. Citroën recommend the use of Molykote G Rapid Plus (available from your Citroën dealer); in the absence of the specified grease, any good-quality high melting-point grease may be used.

32 Carefully insert the cylinder head bolts into their holes *(do not drop them in)* and initially finger-tighten them.

33 Working progressively and in sequence, tighten the cylinder head bolts to their Stage 1 torque setting, using a torque wrench and suitable socket **(see illustration)**.

34 Once all the bolts have been tightened to their Stage 1 torque setting, working again in the specified sequence, tighten each bolt following the Stages given in the Specifications. Finally, angle-tighten the bolts through the specified Stage 6 angle. It is recommended that an angle-measuring gauge be used during this stage of tightening, to ensure accuracy. **Note:** *Retightening of the cylinder head bolts after running the engine is not required.*

11.4 Insulation shield fitted around the sump

35 The remainder of refitting is a reversal of removal, noting the following points.

a) Use a new seal when refitting the coolant outlet housing.

b) Refit the camshaft position sensor and set the air gap with reference to Chapter 4B, Section 12.

c) Tighten all fasteners to the specified torque where given.

d) Refill the cooling system as described in Chapter 1B, Section 20.

e) The engine may run erratically for the first few miles, until the engine management ECU relearns its stored values.

11 Sump – removal and refitting

Removal

1 Drain the engine oil, then clean and refit the engine oil drain plug, tightening it securely. If the engine is nearing its service interval when the oil and filter are due for renewal, it is recommended that the filter is also removed, and a new one fitted. After reassembly, the engine can then be refilled with fresh oil. Refer to Chapter 1B, Section 3 for further information.

2 Chock the rear wheels then jack up the front of the vehicle and support it on axle stands (see *Jacking and vehicle support*). Undo the retaining bolts/nuts and remove the engine undershield.

3 On models with air conditioning, where the compressor is mounted onto the side of the sump, remove the drivebelt as described in Chapter 1B, Section 17. Unbolt the compressor, and position it clear of the sump. Support the weight of the compressor by tying it to the vehicle, to prevent any excess strain being placed on the compressor lines. Do not disconnect the refrigerant lines from the compressor (refer to the warnings given in Chapter 3, Section 11).

4 Where fitted, undo the retaining bolts, release the retaining clips and remove the sump insulation shield **(see illustration)**.

5 Slacken the clamps, undo the bolts and

11.5 Remove the charge air pipe securing bolts (arrowed)

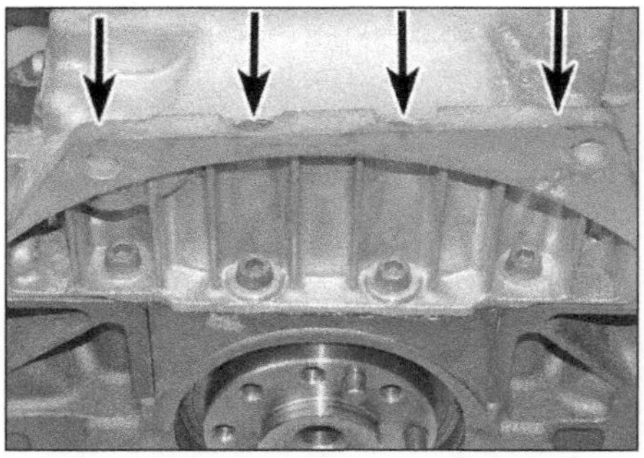

11.7b ... access to the sump end bolts is through the holes (arrowed)

remove the charge air pipe from under the sump **(see illustration)**.

6 Where necessary, disconnect the wiring connector from the oil temperature sender unit, which is screwed into the sump.

7 Progressively slacken and remove all the sump retaining bolts **(see illustrations)**. Since the sump bolts vary in length, remove each bolt in turn, and store it in its correct fitted order by pushing it through a clearly marked cardboard template. This will avoid the possibility of installing the bolts in the wrong locations on refitting.

8 Try to break the joint by striking the sump with the palm of your hand, then lower and withdraw the sump from under the car. If the sump is stuck (which is quite likely) use a putty knife or similar carefully inserted between the sump and block. Ease the knife along the joint until the sump is released. While the sump is removed, take the opportunity to check the oil pump pick-up/strainer for signs of clogging or splitting. If necessary, remove the pump as described in Section 12, and clean or renew the strainer.

Refitting

9 Clean all traces of sealant/gasket from the mating surfaces of the cylinder block/crankcase and sump, and then use a clean rag to wipe out the sump and the engine's interior.

10 Ensure that the sump mating surfaces are clean and dry, then apply a thin coating of suitable sealant (E10 – available from Citroën dealers) to the sump or crankcase mating surface **(see illustration)**.

11 Offer up the sump to the cylinder block/crankcase. Refit its retaining bolts, ensuring

11.7a Undo the 2 bolts securing the sump to the transmission (arrowed) ...

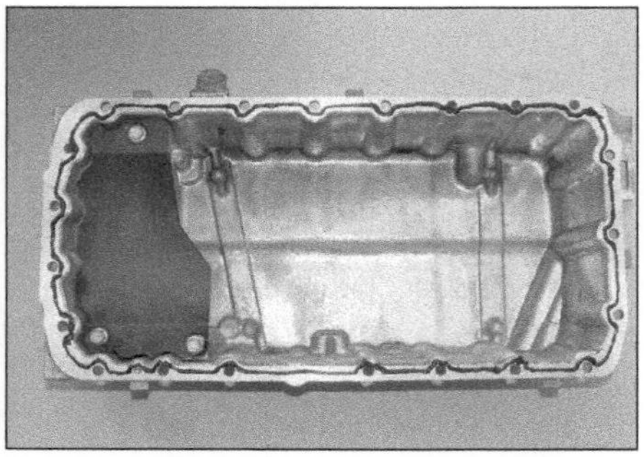

11.10 Apply a bead of sealant around the inside of the bolt holes

that each bolt is screwed into its original location. Tighten the bolts evenly and progressively to the specified torque setting.

12 The remainder of refitting is a reversal of removal, remembering to refill the engine with oil as described in Chapter 1B, Section 3.

12.4 Oil level pipe bracket bolt (arrowed)

12.5b ... undo the pump mounting bolts (arrowed), slide the assembly from the crankshaft ...

12 Oil pump – removal, inspection and refitting

Removal

1 Remove the timing belt as described in Section 7, then slide off the crankshaft sprocket. Recover the Woodruff key from the end of the crankshaft.

2 Remove the sump as described in Section 11.

3 Undo the retaining bolts and remove the front cover and crankshaft seal. Note the original locations of the cover screws – they are different lengths.

4 Undo the bolt securing the oil level pipe **(see illustration)**.

5 Pull out the key from the end of the crankshaft sprocket, then undo the pump mounting bolts, slide the pump, chain and crankshaft sprocket from the end of the engine **(see illustrations)**. Recover the O-ring between the sprocket and crankshaft.

Inspection

6 Examine the oil pump sprocket for signs of damage and wear, such as chipped or missing teeth. If the sprocket is worn, the pump assembly must be renewed, since the sprocket is not available separately. It is also recommended that the chain and drive sprocket, fitted to the crankshaft, be renewed at the same time.

7 Undo the retaining screws and remove the

12.5a Remove the sprocket key ...

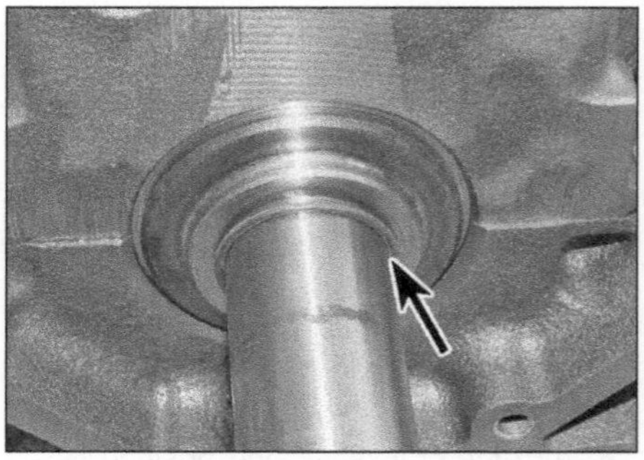

12.5c ... and recover the O-ring between the sprocket and the crankshaft (arrowed)

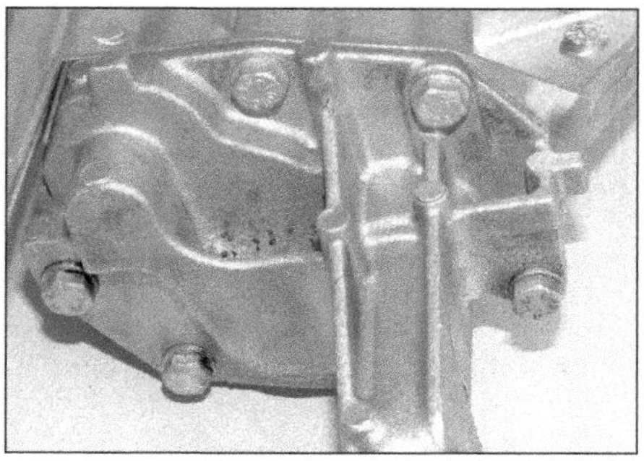

12.7 Oil pump cover screws

cover from the oil pump **(see illustration)**. Note the location of any identification marks on the inner and outer rotors for refitting.

8 Unscrew the plug and remove the pressure relief valve, spring and plunger, clean out and check the condition of the components **(see illustration)**.

9 Examine the pump rotors and body for signs of wear ridges or scoring. If worn, the complete pump assembly must be renewed.

10 Examine the relief valve piston for signs of wear or damage, and renew if necessary. The condition of the relief valve spring can only be measured by comparing it with a new one; if there is any doubt about its condition, it should also be renewed. Both the piston and spring are available individually.

11 Thoroughly clean the oil pump strainer with a suitable solvent, and check it for signs of clogging or splitting. If the strainer is damaged, the strainer and cover assembly must be renewed.

12 Locate the relief valve spring and piston in the strainer cover. Refit the cover to the pump body, aligning the relief valve plunger with its bore in the pump. Refit the baffle plate (where fitted) and the cover retaining bolts, and tighten them securely.

13 Prime the pump by filling it with clean engine oil before refitting.

Refitting

14 Before refitting the oil pump, ensure the mating faces of the pump and engine block are completely clean.

15 Fit the O-ring to the end of the crankshaft **(see illustration)**.

13.2 Oil cooler retaining bolts (arrowed)

12.8 Oil pressure relief valve plug

16 Engage the drive chain with the oil pump and crankshaft sprockets, then slide the crankshaft sprocket into place (aligning the slot in the sprocket with the keyway in the crankshaft) as the pump is refitted. Refit the crankshaft key.

17 Refit the mounting bolts and tighten them to the specified torque. Note that the front, left-hand bolt is slightly longer than the others.

18 Apply a 3 mm bead of sealant to the oil seal housing flange. Refit the housing and tighten the bolts to the specified torque.

19 Fit a new oil seal to the carrier as described in Section 14.

20 Refit the bolt securing the oil level pipe.

21 The remainder of refitting is a reversal of removal.

13 Oil cooler – removal and refitting

Note: *New sealing rings will be required on refitting – check for availability prior to commencing work.*

Removal

1 The cooler is fitted to the oil filter housing on the front of the cylinder block. Access is from under the vehicle. Undo the retaining bolts/nuts and remove the engine undershield. To further improve access, undo the mounting bolts and move the air conditioning compressor to one side. Suspend the compressor using wire or straps. There is no need to disconnect the refrigerant pipes.

14.3a Drill a small hole in the seal ...

12.15 Fit the O-ring to the end of the crankshaft

2 Undo the 4 retaining bolts and detach the cooler from the housing **(see illustration)**. Recover the sealing rings and be prepared for coolant/oil spillage.

Refitting

3 Refitting is a reversal of removal, bearing in mind the following points:

a) Use new sealing rings.

b) Tighten the cooler mounting bolts securely.

c) Refit the engine undershield.

d) On completion lower the car to the ground. Check and if necessary top-up the oil and coolant levels, then start the engine and check for signs of oil or coolant leakage.

14 Oil seals – renewal

Crankshaft

Right-hand oil seal

1 Remove the crankshaft sprocket as described in Section 8.

2 Measure and note the fitted depth of the oil seal.

3 Pull the oil seal from the housing using a hooked instrument. Alternatively, drill a small hole in the oil seal, and use a self-tapping screw and a pair of pliers to remove it **(see illustrations)**.

14.3b ... insert a self-tapping screw and pull out the seal

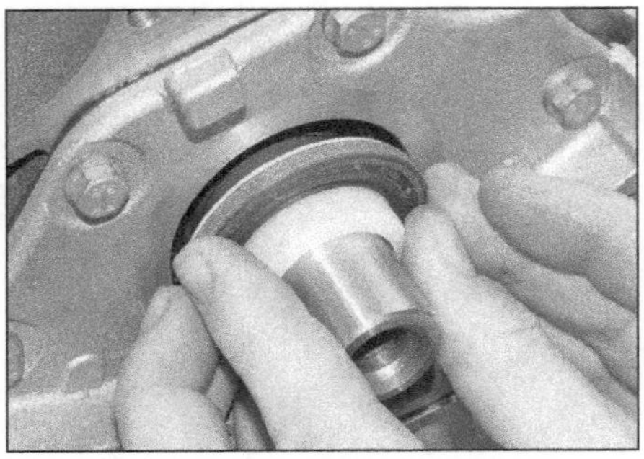

14.5a Locate the new seal and guide over the end of the crankshaft ...

14.5b ... then drive the seal home until it's flush with housing

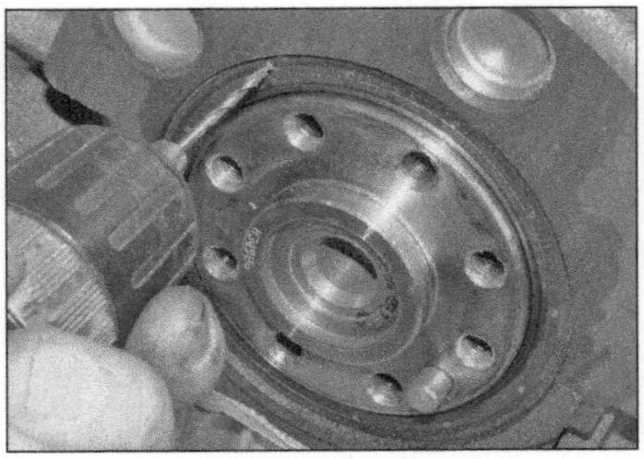

14.10a Drill a hole in the seal ...

14.10b ... then insert a self-tapping screw and pull out the seal

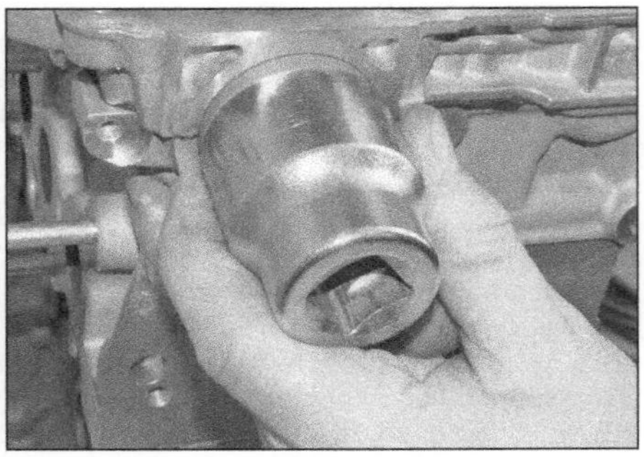

14.19a Use a socket or similar to drive the seal into place ...

14.19b ... until it's flush with the casing surface

4 Clean the oil seal housing and the crankshaft sealing surface.
5 Press the new seal into the housing (open end first) to the previously-noted depth, using a suitable tube or socket. A piece of thin plastic or tape wound around the front of the crankshaft is useful to prevent damage to the oil seal as it is fitted. Note that special tools to guide the seal onto the crankshaft and drive it into place may be available from Citroën **(see illustrations)**.
6 Where applicable, remove the plastic or tape from the end of the crankshaft.
7 Refit the crankshaft sprocket as described in Section 8.

Left-hand oil seal

8 Remove the flywheel/driveplate, as described in Section 16.
9 Measure and note the fitted depth of the oil seal.
10 Pull the oil seal from the housing using a hooked instrument. Alternatively, drill a small hole in the oil seal, and use a self-tapping screw and a pair of pliers to remove it **(see illustrations)**.
11 Clean the oil seal housing and the crankshaft sealing surface.
12 Press the new seal into the housing (open end first) to the previously-noted depth, using a suitable tube or socket. A piece of thin plastic or tape wound around the end of the crankshaft is useful to prevent damage to the oil seal as it is fitted.
13 Where applicable, remove the plastic or tape from the end of the crankshaft.
14 Refit the flywheel/driveplate, as described in Section 16.

Camshaft

15 Remove the camshaft sprocket as described in Section 8. In principle there is no need to remove the timing belt completely, but remember that if the belt has been contaminated with oil, it must be renewed.
16 Pull the oil seal from the housing using a hooked instrument. Alternatively, drill a small hole in the oil seal and use a self-tapping screw and a pair of pliers to remove it **(see illustration 14.3b)**.
17 Clean the oil seal housing and the camshaft sealing surface.
18 Fit it over the end of the camshaft, open end first. Note that the seal must not be oiled prior to fitting. A piece of thin plastic or tape wound around the end of the camshaft is useful to prevent damage to the oil seal as it is fitted.
19 Press the seal into the housing until it is flush with the end face of the cylinder head. Use an M10 bolt (screwed into the end of the camshaft), washers and a suitable tube or socket that bears only on the outer edge of the seal to press it into position **(see illustrations)**.
20 Refit the camshaft sprocket as described in Section 8.
21 Where necessary, fit a new timing belt with reference to Section 7.

15 Oil pressure switch and level sensor – removal and refitting

Removal

Oil pressure switch

1 The oil pressure switch is located at the front of the cylinder block, in the lower part of the oil filter housing **(see illustration)**. Note that on some models, access to the switch may be improved if the vehicle is jacked up and supported on axle stands, then undo the bolts/nuts and remove the engine undershield so that the switch can be reached from underneath (see *Jacking and vehicle support*).
2 Remove the protective sleeve from the

15.1 Oil pressure warning light switch (arrowed)

15.2 Disconnect the wiring plug from the switch

15.5 Oil level sensor (arrowed) at the front of the engine

wiring plug (where applicable), and then disconnect the wiring from the switch **(see illustration)**.

3 Unscrew the switch from the filter housing, and recover the sealing washer. Be prepared for oil spillage, and if the switch is to be left removed from the engine for any length of time, plug the hole in the cylinder block.

Oil level sensor

4 The oil level sensor is located at the front of the engine, at the transmission end of the sump. Jack up the front of the vehicle and support it securely on axle stands (see *Jacking and vehicle support*). Undo the retaining bolts/nuts and remove the engine undershield.

5 Reach up and disconnect the sensor wiring plug **(see illustration)**.

6 Using an open-ended spanner, unscrew the sensor and withdraw it from position.

Refitting

Oil pressure switch

7 Examine the sealing washer for any signs of damage or deterioration, and if necessary renew.

8 Refit the switch, complete with washer, and tighten it to the specified torque.

9 Refit the engine undershield, and lower the vehicle to the ground.

10 Check the engine oil level, and top-up as required (see *Weekly checks*).

11 Check for correct operation of the warning light, and for signs of oil leaks once the engine has been started and warmed-up to normal operating temperature.

Oil level sensor

12 Smear a little silicone sealant on the threads and refit the sensor to the sump, tightening it securely.

13 Reconnect the sensor wiring plug.

14 Refit the engine undershield, and lower the vehicle to the ground.

15 Check the engine oil level, and top-up as required (see *Weekly checks*).

16 Check for correct operation of the warning light, and for signs of oil leaks once the engine has been started and warmed-up to normal operating temperature.

16 Flywheel/driveplate – removal, inspection and refitting

Removal

Flywheel

1 Remove the transmission as described in Chapter 7A, Section 7, then remove the clutch assembly as described in Chapter 6, Section 6.

2 Prevent the flywheel from turning by locking the ring gear teeth **(see illustration 5.3)**. Alternatively, bolt a strap between the flywheel and the cylinder block/crankcase. *Do not* attempt to lock the flywheel in position using the crankshaft pulley locking tool described in Section 3.

3 Slacken and remove the flywheel retaining bolts, and remove the flywheel from the end of the crankshaft **(see illustration)**. Be careful not to drop it; it is heavy. If the flywheel locating dowel is a loose fit in the crankshaft end, remove it and store it with the flywheel for safe-keeping. Discard the flywheel bolts; new ones must be used on refitting.

16.3 Flywheel retaining bolts

Driveplate

4 Remove the transmission as described in Chapter 7B, Section 9. Lock the driveplate as described in paragraph 2 of this Section. Mark the relationship between the torque converter plate and the driveplate, and slacken all the driveplate retaining bolts.

5 Remove the retaining bolts, along with the torque converter plate and the two shims (one fitted on each side of the torque converter plate). Note that the shims are of different thickness, the thicker one being on the outside of the torque converter plate. Discard the driveplate retaining bolts; new ones must be used on refitting.

6 Remove the driveplate from the end of the crankshaft. If the locating dowel is a loose fit in the crankshaft end, remove it and store it with the driveplate for safekeeping.

Inspection

7 On models with manual transmission, examine the flywheel for scoring of the clutch face, and for wear or chipping of the ring gear teeth. If the clutch face is scored, the flywheel may be surface-ground, but renewal is preferable. Seek the advice of a Citroën dealer or engine reconditioning specialist to see if

16.11 Note the locating dowel and the corresponding hole (arrowed)

machining is possible. If the ring gear is worn or damaged, the flywheel must be renewed, as it is not possible to renew the ring gear separately.

8 On models with automatic transmission, check the torque converter driveplate carefully for signs of distortion. Look for any hairline cracks around the bolt holes or radiating outwards from the centre, and inspect the ring gear teeth for signs of wear or chipping. If any sign of wear or damage is found, the driveplate must be renewed.

Refitting

Flywheel

9 Clean the mating surfaces of the flywheel and crankshaft. Remove any remaining locking compound from the threads of the crankshaft holes, using the correct size of tap, if available.

10 If the new flywheel retaining bolts are not supplied with their threads already pre-coated, apply a suitable thread-locking compound to the threads of each bolt.

11 Ensure that the locating dowel is in position. Offer up the flywheel, locating it on the dowel, and fit the new retaining bolts **(see illustration)**.

12 Lock the flywheel using the method employed on dismantling, and tighten the retaining bolts to the specified torque.

13 Refit the clutch as described in Chapter 6, Section 6. Remove the flywheel locking tool, and refit the transmission as described in Chapter 7A, Section 7.

Driveplate

14 Carry out the operations described above in paragraphs 9 and 10, substituting 'driveplate' for all references to the flywheel.

15 Locate the driveplate on its locating dowel.

16 Offer up the torque converter plate, with the thinner shim positioned behind the plate and the thicker shim on the outside, and align the marks made prior to removal.

17 Fit the new retaining bolts, then lock the driveplate using the method employed on dismantling. Tighten the retaining bolts to the specified torque wrench setting.

18 Remove the driveplate locking tool, and refit the transmission (see Chapter 7B, Section 9).

17 Engine/transmission mountings – inspection and renewal

Inspection

1 If improved access is required, chock the rear wheels then jack up the front of the car and support it on axle stands (see *Jacking and vehicle support*). Undo the retaining bolts/nuts and remove the engine undershield.

2 Check the mounting rubbers to see if they are cracked, hardened or separated from the metal at any point; renew the mounting if any such damage or deterioration is evident.

3 Check that all the mountings fasteners are securely tightened; use a torque wrench to check if possible.

4 Using a large screwdriver or a crowbar, check for wear in each mounting by carefully levering against it to check for free play. Where this is not possible, enlist the aid of an assistant to move the engine/transmission back-and-forth, or from side-to-side, while you watch the mounting. While some free play is to be expected even from new components, excessive wear should be obvious. If excessive free play is found, check first that the fasteners are correctly secured, and then renew any worn components as described below.

Renewal

Right-hand mounting

5 Release all the retaining clips and remove the plastic trim from above the right-hand engine mounting **(see illustration)**. If not already done, undo the retaining bolts/nuts and remove the engine undershield.

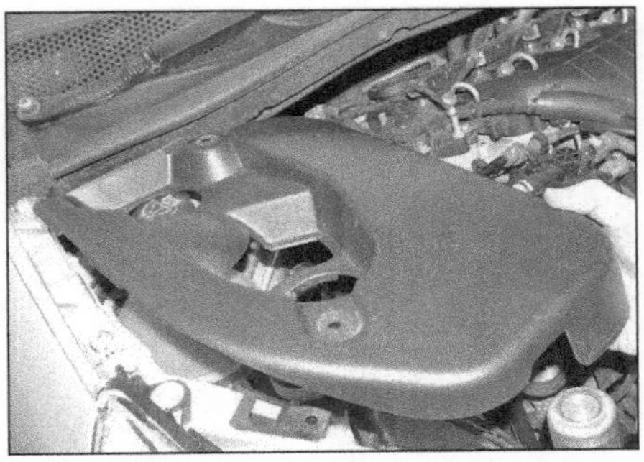

17.5 Remove the plastic trim cover

6 Place a jack beneath the engine, with a block of wood on the jack head. Raise the jack until it is supporting the weight of the engine.

7 Unclip the hoses from across the top of the mounting bracket and move them to one side. Then undo the bolts securing the engine mounting to the body and the support bracket **(see illustration)**.

8 If required, undo the bolts securing the support bracket to the cylinder head.

9 Check all components carefully for signs of wear or damage, and renew as necessary.

10 Where removed, refit the support bracket to the cylinder head, and tighten the bolts securely.

11 Refit the mounting to the body and support bracket, and then tighten the bolts to the specified torque. Refit the hoses back into position in their retaining clips.

12 Remove the jack from underneath the engine and refit the engine undershield.

Left-hand mounting

13 Remove the battery and battery tray as described in Chapter 5A, Section 4.

14 If not already done, undo the retaining bolts/nuts and remove the engine undershield. Place a jack beneath the transmission, with a block of wood on the jack head. Raise the jack until it is supporting the weight of the transmission.

15 Slacken and remove the mounting's two upper retaining nuts **(see illustration)**.

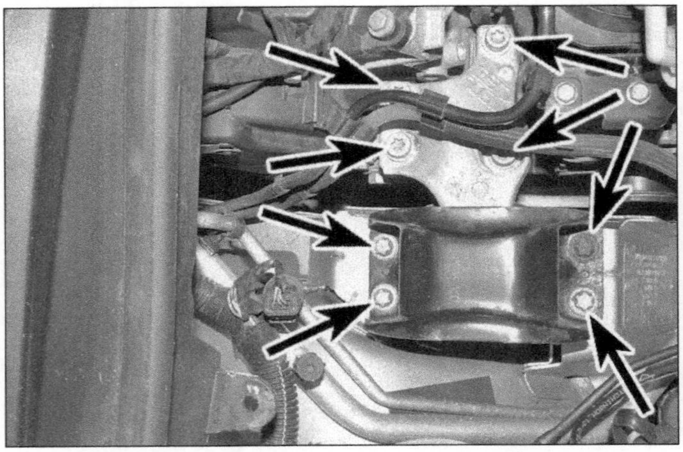

17.7 Right-hand engine mounting retaining bolts (arrowed)

17.15 Undo the left-hand transmission mounting securing nuts (arrowed) ...

17.16 ... and the mounting centre nut (arrowed)

17.22 Undo the rear link-to-subframe mounting bolt (arrowed) ...

16 Undo the centre retaining nut and remove the mounting from the transmission mounting bracket **(see illustration)**.

17 Check carefully for signs of wear or damage on all components, and renew them where necessary.

18 Refit the mounting to the mounting bracket and tighten it to the specified torque.

19 Fit the mounting nuts to the bracket on the transmission and tighten the retaining nuts to the specified torque.

20 Remove the jack from underneath the transmission, refit the engine undershield, and then refit the battery as described in Chapter 5A, Section 4.

Lower engine torque link

21 Firmly apply the handbrake, and then jack up the front of the vehicle and support it securely on axle stands (see *Jacking and vehicle support*). If not already done, undo the retaining bolts/nuts and remove the engine undershield.

22 Unscrew and remove the bolt securing the rear mounting link to the subframe **(see illustration)**.

23 Remove the bolt securing the rear mounting link to the driveshaft inner bearing bracket at the rear of the cylinder block **(see illustration)**, and then remove the mounting torque reaction link.

24 To remove the intermediate bearing housing/mounting assembly it will first be necessary to remove the right-hand driveshaft as described in Chapter 8, Section 2.

25 With the driveshaft removed, undo the retaining bolts and remove the bearing housing/mounting from the rear of the cylinder block.

26 Check carefully for signs of wear or damage on all components, and renew them where necessary. The rubber bush fitted to the driveshaft bearing housing is available as a separate item on some models, check with your local dealer for availability of parts. If available, the rubber bush can be pressed out of the bearing housing, noting its fitted position, and then a new one pressed back into place.

27 On reassembly, fit the bearing housing assembly to the rear of the cylinder block, and tighten its retaining bolts securely. Refit the driveshaft as described in Chapter 8, Section 2.

28 Refit the rear mounting torque reaction link, and tighten both its bolts to their specified torque settings.

29 Refit the engine undershield, and then lower the vehicle to the ground.

17.23 ... and the lower link-to-mounting bracket bolt (arrowed)

Chapter 2 Part E:
Engine removal and overhaul procedures

Contents

Degrees of difficulty

Easy, suitable for novice with little experience	**Fairly easy,** suitable for beginner with some experience	**Fairly difficult,** suitable for competent DIY mechanic	**Difficult,** suitable for experienced DIY mechanic	**Very difficult,** suitable for expert DIY or professional

Specifications

Engine identification

Petrol engines

1.4 litre engine:	
Designation	ET3J4
Engine code	KFU
1.6 litre engine:	
Non-VTi engine:	
Designation	TU5JP4
Engine code	NFU
VTi engine:	
Designation	EP6
Engine code	5FW

Diesel engines

1.6 litre engine:	
Designation	DV6TED4 or DV6ATED4
Engine codes:	
DV6TED4	9HV, 9HY or 9HZ
DV6ATED4	9HX
2.0 litre engine:	
Designation	DW10BTED4
Engine codes	RHF or RHR

Cylinder block

Cylinder bore diameter:	
Petrol engines:	
1.4 litre	75.00 mm (nominal)
1.6 litre	78.50 mm (nominal)
Diesel engines:	
1.6 litre (reboring not possible)	75.00 mm (nominal)
2.0 litre	85.00 mm (nominal)
Liner protrusion (1.4 litre petrol engines):	
Standard	0.03 to 0.10 mm
Maximum difference between two cylinders	0.05 mm

Cylinder head

Maximum gasket face distortion	0.05 mm
New cylinder head height:	
Petrol engines:	
1.4 litre	111.20 mm
1.6 litre	N/A
Diesel engines:	
1.6 litre	124.0 ± 0.05 mm
2.0 litre	133.0 ± 0.05 mm
Minimum cylinder head height after machining:	
Petrol engines:	
1.4 litre	111.0 mm
1.6 litre	N/A
Diesel engines:	
1.6 litre	N/A
2.0 litre	132.60 mm
Valve head-to-cylinder head measurement (diesel engines):	
1.6 litre	N/A
2.0 litre	0.20 mm (maximum)

Valves

	Intake	Exhaust
Valve head diameter:		
Petrol engines:		
1.4 litre	36.7 mm	29.4 mm
1.6 litre	N/A	N/A
Diesel engines:		
1.6 litre	N/A	N/A
2.0 litre	35.6 mm	33.8 mm
Valve stem diameter:		
Petrol engines:		
1.4 litre	6.965 to 6.980 mm	6.945 to 6.960 mm
1.6 litre	N/A	N/A
Diesel engines:		
1.6 litre	5.485 +0.0 -0.015 mm	5.475 +0.0 -0.015 mm
2.0 litre	5.978 ± 0.009 mm	5.968 ± 0.009 mm

Pistons

Piston diameter:	
Petrol engines:	
1.4 litre	74.950 mm (nominal)
1.6 litre	78.455 mm (nominal)
Diesel engines:	
1.6 litre	74.945 mm (nominal)
2.0 litre	N/A

Check with your Citroën dealer or engine specialist regarding piston oversizes

Piston ring end gaps

Petrol engines:	
Top compression ring	0.20 to 0.45 mm
Second compression ring	0.30 to 0.50 mm
Oil control ring	0.30 to 0.50 mm
Diesel engines:	
1.6 litre:	
Top compression ring	0.15 to 0.25 mm
Second compression ring	0.30 to 0.50 mm
Oil control ring	0.35 to 0.55 mm
2.0 litre:	
Top compression ring	0.20 to 0.35 mm
Second compression ring	0.80 to 1.00 mm
Oil control ring	0.25 to 0.50 mm

Crankshaft

Endfloat:	
Petrol engines	0.07 to 0.27 mm
Diesel engines:	
1.6 litre	0.10 to 0.30 mm (thrustwasher thickness 2.40 ± 0.05 mm)
2.0 litre	0.07 to 0.32 mm
Maximum bearing journal out-of-round (all models)	0.007 mm

Torque wrench settings

1.4 and 1.6 litre non-VTi petrol engines

Refer to Chapter 2A Specifications

1.6 litre VTi petrol engines

Refer to Chapter 2B Specifications

1.6 litre diesel engines

Refer to Chapter 2C Specifications

2.0 litre diesel engines

Refer to Chapter 2D Specifications

1 General information

Included in this Chapter are details of removing the engine/transmission from the car and general overhaul procedures for the cylinder head, cylinder block/crankcase and all other engine internal components.

The information given ranges from advice concerning preparation for an overhaul and the purchase of parts, to detailed step-by-step procedures covering removal, inspection, renovation and refitting of engine internal components.

After Section 5, all instructions are based on the assumption that the engine has been removed from the car. For information concerning in-car engine repair, as well as the removal and refitting of those external components necessary for full overhaul, refer to Chapter 2A, 2B, 2C or 2D, as applicable and to Section 5. Ignore any preliminary dismantling operations that are no longer relevant once the engine has been removed from the car.

Apart from torque wrench settings, which are given at the beginning of Chapter 2A, 2B, 2C or 2D, all specifications relating to engine overhaul are at the beginning of this Chapter.

2 Engine overhaul – general information

1 It is not always easy to determine when, or if, an engine should be completely overhauled, as a number of factors must be considered.

2 High mileage is not necessarily an indication that an overhaul is needed, while low mileage does not preclude the need for an overhaul. Frequency of servicing is probably the most important consideration. An engine, which has had regular and frequent oil and filter changes, as well as other required maintenance, should give many thousands of miles of reliable service. Conversely, a neglected engine may require an overhaul very early in its life.

3 Excessive oil consumption is an indication that piston rings, valve seals and/or valve guides are in need of attention. Make sure that oil leaks are not responsible before deciding that the rings and/or guides are worn. Perform a compression test, as described in Chapter 2A, 2B, 2C or 2D (as applicable), to determine the likely cause of the problem.

4 Check the oil pressure with a gauge fitted in place of the oil pressure switch, and compare it with that specified. If it is extremely low, the main and big-end bearings, and/or the oil pump, are probably worn out.

5 Loss of power, rough running, knocking or metallic engine noises, excessive valve gear noise, and high fuel consumption may also point to the need for an overhaul, especially if they are all present at the same time. If a complete service does not remedy the situation, major mechanical work is the only solution.

6 A full engine overhaul involves restoring all internal parts to the specification of a new engine. During a complete overhaul, the pistons and the piston rings are renewed. New main and big-end bearings are generally fitted; if necessary, the crankshaft may be reground, to compensate for wear in the journals. The valves are also serviced as well, since they are usually in less-than-perfect condition at this point. While the engine is being overhauled, other components, such as the starter and alternator, can be overhauled as well. Always pay careful attention to the condition of the oil pump when overhauling the engine, and renew it if there is any doubt as to its serviceability. The end result should be an as-new engine that will give many trouble-free miles.

7 Critical cooling system components such as the hoses, thermostat and water pump should be renewed when an engine is overhauled. The radiator should be checked carefully, to ensure that it is not clogged or leaking. Also, it is a good idea to renew the oil pump whenever the engine is overhauled.

8 Before beginning the engine overhaul, read through the entire procedure, to familiarise yourself with the scope and requirements of the job. Overhauling an engine is not difficult if you follow carefully all of the instructions, have the necessary tools and equipment, and pay close attention to all specifications. It can, however, be time-consuming. Plan on the car being off the road for a minimum of two weeks, especially if parts must be taken to an engineering works for repair or reconditioning. Check on the availability of parts and make sure that any necessary special tools and equipment are obtained in advance. Most work can be done with typical hand tools, although a number of precision measuring tools are required for inspecting parts to determine if they must be renewed. Often the engineering works will handle the inspection of parts and offer advice concerning reconditioning and renewal.

9 Always wait until the engine has been completely dismantled, and until all components (especially the cylinder block/crankcase and the crankshaft) have been inspected, before deciding what service and repair operations must be performed by an engineering works. The condition of these components will be the major factor to consider when determining whether to overhaul the original engine, or to buy a reconditioned unit. Do not, therefore, purchase parts or have overhaul work done on other components until they have been thoroughly inspected. As a general rule, time is the primary cost of an overhaul, so it does not pay to fit worn or sub-standard parts.

10 As a final note, to ensure maximum life and minimum trouble from a reconditioned engine, everything must be assembled with care, in a spotlessly clean environment.

3 Engine removal – methods and precautions

1 If you have decided that the engine must be removed for overhaul or major repair work, several preliminary steps should be taken.

2 Locating a suitable place to work is extremely important. Adequate workspace, along with storage space for the car, will be needed. Engine/transmission removal is extremely complicated and involved on these vehicles. It must be stated, that unless the vehicle can be positioned on a ramp, or raised and supported on axle stands over an inspection pit, it will be more difficult to carry out the work involved.

3 Cleaning the engine compartment and engine/transmission before beginning the removal procedure will help keep tools clean and organised.

4 An engine hoist or A-frame will also be necessary. Make sure the equipment is rated in excess of the weight of the engine. Safety is of primary importance, considering the potential hazards involved in lifting the engine/transmission out of the car.

5 The help of an assistant is essential. Apart

from the safety aspects involved, there are many instances when one person cannot simultaneously perform all of the operations required during engine/transmission removal.

6 Plan the operation ahead of time. Before starting work, arrange for the hire of or obtain all of the tools and equipment you will need. Some of the equipment necessary to perform engine/transmission removal and installation safely and with relative ease (in addition to an engine hoist) is as follows: a heavy duty trolley jack, complete sets of spanners and sockets (see *Tools and working facilities*), wooden blocks, and plenty of rags and cleaning solvent for mopping-up spilled oil, coolant and fuel. If the hoist must be hired, make sure that you arrange for it in advance, and perform all of the operations possible without it beforehand. This will save you money and time.

7 Plan for the car to be out of use for quite a while. An engineering machine shop or engine reconditioning specialist will be required to perform some of the work, which cannot be accomplished without special equipment. These places often have a busy schedule, so it would be a good idea to consult them before removing the engine, in order to accurately estimate the amount of time required to rebuild or repair components that may need work.

8 During the engine/transmission removal procedure, it is advisable to make notes of the locations of all brackets, cable-ties, earthing points, etc, as well as how the wiring harnesses, hoses and electrical connections are attached and routed around the engine and engine compartment. An effective way of doing this is to take a series of photographs of the various components before they are disconnected or removed; the resulting photographs will prove invaluable when the engine/transmission is refitted.

9 The engine can be removed complete with the transmission as an assembly. Remove the front bumper, crossmember and radiator panel, and then the assembly is removed from the front of the vehicle.

10 Always be extremely careful when removing and refitting the engine/transmission. Serious injury can result from careless actions. Plan ahead and take your time, and a job of this nature, although major, can be accomplished successfully.

4 Engine – removal and refitting

Note: *Such is the complexity of the power unit arrangement on these vehicles, and the variations that may be encountered according to model and optional equipment fitted, the following should be regarded as a guide to the work involved, rather than a step-by-step procedure. Where differences are encountered, or additional component disconnection or removal is necessary, make notes of the work involved as an aid to refitting.*

Removal

1 Remove the battery and battery support tray (see Chapter 5A, Section 4). Wait five minutes, and then disconnect the engine wiring harness plugs at the fusebox or ECU depending on model **(see illustration)**. Release the wiring harness from the retaining clips on the timing cover at the right-hand end of the engine (where applicable).

2 Apply the handbrake, then jack up the front of the vehicle and support it on axle stands (see *Jacking and vehicle support*). Remove both front roadwheels. Undo the retaining bolts/nuts and remove the engine undershield, also release the securing clips and remove the front wheel arch liners.

3 Where fitted, remove the plastic covers from the top of the engine. On diesel engines, the engine cover simply pulls up from place.

4 Drain the cooling system with reference to Chapter 1A, Section 25 or Chapter 1B, Section 20.

5 Drain the transmission oil/fluid as described in Chapter 7A, Section 2 or Chapter 7B, Section 2. Refit the drain and filler plugs, and tighten them to their specified torque settings.

6 If the engine is to be dismantled, drain the engine oil and remove the oil filter as described in Chapter 1A, Section 3 or Chapter 1B, Section 3. Clean and refit the drain plug, tightening it securely.

7 Refer to Chapter 8, Section 2 and remove both front driveshafts.

8 Remove the front bumper and bumper bar as described in Chapter 11, Section 6. Also, remove the headlamps (see Chapter 12, Section 7).

9 Refer to Chapter 1A, Section 10 or Chapter 1B, Section 17 and remove the auxiliary drivebelt.

10 Remove the radiator/cooling fan and front panel assembly as described in Chapter 3, Section 4 and 6. On air conditioned models, tie the condenser to one side. Do not disconnect the refrigerant pipes.

11 Undo the securing bolts and remove the front panel lower crossmember and side rails **(see illustrations)**.

12 On turbo diesel engines, remove the air hoses leading from the intercooler to the turbocharger located on the right-hand side of the radiator (1.6 litre engines) and left-hand side of radiator (2.0 litre engines), and to the intake manifold.

13 Remove the air cleaner housing and ducting, then remove the exhaust system with reference to Chapter 4A, Section 2 and 15 or Chapter 4B, Section 4 and 18.

14 Note their fitted positions and harness routing, then disconnect all wiring plugs from the transmission. If necessary label the connectors as they are unplugged. On diesel models, undo the nut and remove the heater control box (still connected) from the front left-hand corner of the engine compartment.

15 Disconnect the hose from the vacuum pump on the left-hand end of the cylinder head (diesel models) or the brake servo unit vacuum pipe (petrol models) – see Chapter 9, Section 20

16 Disconnect the fuel feed and return hoses. Plug the end of the hoses to prevent dirt ingress.

17 Disconnect the selector cable(s) from the transmission as described in Chapter 7A, Section 3 or Chapter 7B, Section 4.

18 On manual transmission models, unbolt the clutch slave cylinder, then tie it to one side, without disconnecting the fluid pipe (see Chapter 6, Section 4). Use an elastic band around the cylinder to prevent the piston from coming out.

19 From underneath the vehicle, slacken and remove the nuts and bolts securing the rear engine mounting connecting link to the mounting assembly and subframe,

4.1 Disconnect the ECU wiring plugs

4.11a Remove the front panel lower crossmember ...

4.11b ... and the side rails

and remove the connecting link. Refer to Chapter 2A, 2B, 2C or 2D.

20 On models with air conditioning, refer to Chapter 3, Section 12 and unbolt the compressor from the engine. Do not disconnect the refrigerant lines. Support or tie the compressor to one side.

21 Using a hoist attached to the lifting eyes on the cylinder head, take the weight of the engine and transmission.

22 Remove the right-hand and left-hand engine mountings and support brackets as described in Chapter 2A, 2B, 2C or 2D.

23 Completely pull out the wire retaining clips and disconnect the heater hoses at the engine compartment bulkhead.

24 Make a final check to ensure all wiring; hoses and brackets that would prevent the removal of the assembly have been disconnected.

25 Move the engine/transmission forwards and out from the front of the vehicle. Enlist the help of an assistant during this procedure, as it may be necessary to tilt and twist the assembly slightly to clear the body panels and adjacent components. Move the unit clear of the car and lower it to the ground.

Separation

26 With the engine/transmission assembly removed, support the assembly on suitable blocks of wood on a workbench (or failing that, on a clean area of the workshop floor).

27 Undo the retaining bolts, and remove the flywheel lower cover plate (where fitted) from the transmission.

28 Slacken and remove the retaining bolts, and remove the starter motor from the transmission.

29 Disconnect any remaining wiring connectors at the transmission, then move the main engine wiring harness to one side.

30 On automatic transmission models, locate the access hole at the lower rear of the cylinder block, then turn the crankshaft by means of a socket on the crankshaft pulley bolt until one of the three torque converter retaining nuts is accessible through the access hole. Undo the accessible torque converter bolt, then turn the crankshaft as necessary and undo the remaining two bolts.

31 Ensure that both engine and transmission are adequately supported, then slacken and remove the remaining bolts securing the transmission housing to the engine. Note the correct fitted positions of each bolt (and the relevant brackets) as they are removed, to use as a reference on refitting. On diesel models, the left-hand catalytic converter mounting stud must be removed to access the front transmission-to-engine bolt **(see illustration)**.

32 Carefully withdraw the transmission from the engine, ensuring that the weight of the transmission is not allowed to hang on the input shaft while it is engaged with the clutch friction disc (manual transmission models) or that the torque converter does not slip from the input shaft (automatic transmission models).

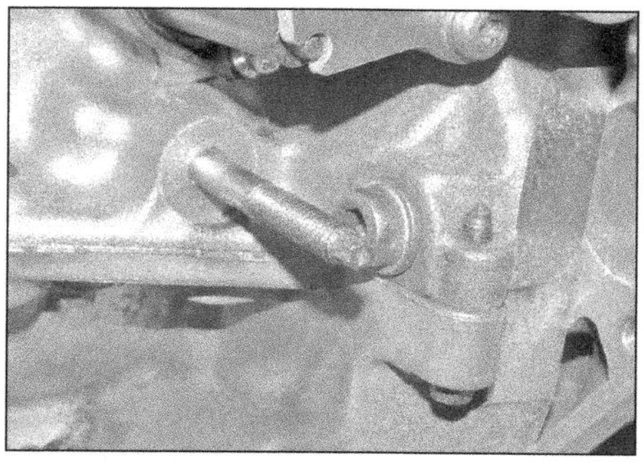

4.31 The stud must be removed to access the front transmission-to-engine bolt

33 If they are loose, remove the locating dowels from the engine or transmission, and keep them in a safe place.

Refitting

34 If the engine and transmission have not been separated, perform the operations described below from paragraph 41 onwards.

35 Apply a smear of high melting-point grease (Citroën recommend the use of Molykote BR2 plus – available from your Citroën dealer) to the splines of the transmission input shaft. Do not apply too much; otherwise there is a possibility of the grease contaminating the clutch friction disc. **Note:** *On late models, Citroën recommend no grease be applied.*

36 On automatic transmission models, prior to reconnection it is necessary to make a simple tool to align the torque converter with the driveplate as the transmission is refitted. To make the tool, carry out the following:

a) Obtain a bolt of the same size as the torque converter retaining bolts, but long enough to extend through the access hole in the cylinder block when the transmission is refitted.

b) Cut the head off the bolt and cut a slot (to enable it to be unscrewed) in the plain end. Check that the tool will slide easily through the torque converter retaining bolt hole in the driveplate.

c) Turn the engine crankshaft so that one of the torque converter retaining bolt holes in the driveplate is aligned with the access hole in the cylinder block. Screw the alignment tool (finger-tight only) into one of the retaining bolt holes in the torque converter. Turn the torque converter so that the alignment tool is in approximately the correct position, relative to the cylinder block access hole. As the transmission is refitted, the alignment tool will pass through the retaining bolt hole in the driveplate and through the access hole. It can then be unscrewed with a screwdriver and the first torque converter retaining bolt fitted in its place.

d) Check that the torque converter support bush fitted to the centre of the crankshaft is in good condition, and in place.

37 Ensure that the locating dowels are correctly positioned in the engine or transmission, and then carefully offer the transmission to the engine until the locating dowels are engaged. On manual transmission models, ensure that the weight of the transmission is not allowed to hang on the input shaft as it is engaged with the clutch friction disc. On automatic transmission models, ensure the torque converter studs engage correctly with the corresponding holes in the driveplate.

38 Refit the transmission housing-to-engine bolts, ensuring that all the necessary brackets are correctly positioned, and tighten them securely.

39 Refit the starter motor, and securely tighten its retaining bolts.

40 Refit the lower flywheel cover plate (where fitted) to the transmission, and securely tighten the bolts.

41 Reconnect the hoist and lifting tackle to the engine lifting brackets. With the aid of an assistant, lift the assembly into the engine compartment, taking care not to damage surrounding components.

42 Refit the right-hand engine mounting and support bracket, but leave the bolts finger-tight at this stage.

43 Working on the left-hand mounting, refit the mounting to the transmission and finger-tighten.

44 Remove the hoist.

45 From underneath the vehicle, refit the rear mounting connecting link and finger-tighten the bolts.

46 Rock the engine to settle it on its mountings, then go around and tighten all the mounting nuts and bolts to their specified torque settings.

47 The remainder of the refitting procedure is a direct reversal of the removal sequence, with reference to the relevant chapters and noting the following points:

a) Ensure that the wiring loom is correctly routed and retained by all the relevant retaining clips; all connectors should be correctly and securely reconnected.

b) Prior to refitting the driveshafts to the transmission, renew the driveshaft oil seals as described in Chapter 7A, Section 4 or Chapter 7B, Section 6.

c) Ensure that all coolant hoses are correctly reconnected, and securely retained by their retaining clips.

d) Refill the engine and transmission with the correct quantity and type of lubricant.

e) Refill the cooling system as described in Chapter 1A, Section 25 or Chapter 1B, Section 20.

f) Initialise the engine management ECU as follows. Start the engine and run to normal temperature. Carry out a road test during which the following procedure should be made. Engage third gear and stabilise the engine at 1000 rpm. Now accelerate fully to 3500 rpm. **Note:** *This is the procedure for manual transmission models; consult your dealer for automatic models.*

5 Engine overhaul – dismantling sequence

1 It is much easier to dismantle and work on the engine if it is mounted on a portable engine stand. These stands can often be hired from a tool hire shop. Before the engine is mounted on a stand, the flywheel/driveplate should be removed, so that the stand bolts can be tightened into the end of the cylinder block/crankcase.

2 If a stand is not available, it is possible to dismantle the engine with it blocked up on a sturdy workbench, or on the floor. Be extra careful not to tip or drop the engine when working without a stand.

3 If you are going to obtain a reconditioned engine, all the external components must be removed first, to be transferred to the new engine (just as they will if you are doing a complete engine overhaul yourself). These components include the following:

a) Ancillary unit mounting brackets (oil filter, starter, alternator, power steering pump, etc)
b) Thermostat and housing (Chapter 3, Section 5).
c) Dipstick tube/sensor.
d) All electrical switches and sensors.
e) Intake and exhaust manifolds – where applicable.
f) Ignition coils and spark plugs – as applicable (Chapter 5B, Section 3 and Chapter 1A, Section 20).
g) Flywheel/driveplate (Chapter 2A, 2B, 2C or 2D).

Note: *When removing the external components from the engine, pay close attention to details that may be helpful or important during refitting. Note the fitted position of gaskets, seals, spacers, pins, washers, bolts, and other small items.*

4 If you are obtaining a 'short' engine (which consists of the engine cylinder block/crankcase, crankshaft, pistons and connecting rods all assembled), then the cylinder head, sump, oil pump, and timing chain/belt will have to be removed also.

5 If you are planning a complete overhaul, the engine can be dismantled, and the internal components removed, in the order given below, referring to Chapter 2A, 2B, 2C or 2D unless otherwise stated.

a) Intake and exhaust manifolds – where applicable (Chapter 4A or 4B).
b) Timing chains/belts, sprockets and tensioner(s).
c) Cylinder head.
d) Flywheel/driveplate.
e) Sump.
f) Oil pump.
g) Piston/connecting rod assemblies (Section 9).
h) Crankshaft (Section 10).

6 Before beginning the dismantling and overhaul procedures, make sure that you have all of the correct tools necessary. Refer to *Tools and working facilities* for furtherinformation.

6 Cylinder head – dismantling

Note: *At the time of writing, there was no procedure available for the removal of the camshafts and valve assembly on the VTi petrol engines. The timing components: camshafts, bearings, rockers, followers, springs, valves and valve seals cannot be renewed individually. Citroën recommend that if there is any damage to any of these components that the complete cylinder head assembly be renewed.*

Note: *New and reconditioned cylinder heads are available from the manufacturer, and from engine overhaul specialists. Be aware that some specialist tools are required for the dismantling and inspection procedures, and new components may not be readily available. It may therefore be more practical and economical for the home mechanic to purchase a reconditioned head, rather than dismantle, inspect and recondition the original head.*

1 Remove the cylinder head as described in Chapter 2A, 2C or 2D (as applicable).

2 If not already done, remove the intake and the exhaust manifolds with reference to Chapter 4A or 4B. Remove any remaining brackets or housings as required.

3 Remove the camshafts, hydraulic followers and rockers (as applicable) as described in Chapter 2A, 2C or 2D.

4 If not already done on petrol models, remove the spark plugs as described in Chapter 1A, Section 20.

5 If not already done on diesel models, remove the glow plugs as described in Chapter 5C, Section 2.

6 On all models, using a valve spring compressor, compress each valve spring in turn until the split collets can be removed. Release the compressor, and lift off the spring retainer, spring and, where fitted, the spring seat. Using a pair of pliers, carefully extract the valve stem oil seal from the top of the guide. On 16-valve engines, the valve stem oil seal also forms the spring seat and is deeply recessed in the cylinder head. It is also a tight fit on the valve guide making it difficult to remove with pliers or a conventional valve stem oil seal removal tool. It can be easily removed, however, using a self-locking nut of suitable diameter screwed onto the end of a bolt and locked with a second nut. Push the nut down onto the top of the seal; the locking portion of the nut will grip the seal allowing it to be withdrawn from the top of the valve guide. Access to the valves is limited, and it may be necessary to make up an adapter out of metal tube – cut out a 'window' so that the valve collets can be removed **(see illustrations).**

7 If, when the valve spring compressor is screwed down, the spring retainer refuses to free and expose the split collets, gently tap the top of the tool, directly over the retainer, with a light hammer. This will free the retainer.

8 Withdraw the valve from the combustion chamber. Remove the valve stem oil seal from the top of the guide, then lift out the spring seat where fitted.

9 It is essential that each valve is stored together with its collets, retainer, spring, and

6.6a Compress the valve spring using a spring compressor ...

6.6b ... then extract the collets and release the spring compressor

6.6c Remove the spring retainer ...

6.6d ... followed by the valve spring ...

6.6e ... and the spring seat (not all models)

spring seat. The valves should also be kept in their correct sequence, unless they are so badly worn that they are to be renewed. If they are going to be kept and used again, place each valve assembly in a labelled polythene bag or similar small container **(see illustration)**. Note that No 1 valve is nearest to the transmission (flywheel/driveplate) end of the engine.

7 Cylinder head and valves - cleaning and inspection

Note: *At the time of writing, there was no procedure available for the removal of the camshafts and valve assembly on the VTi petrol engines. The timing components: camshafts, bearings, rockers, followers, springs, valves and valve seals cannot be renewed individually. Citroën recommend that if there is any damage to any of these components that the complete cylinder head assembly be renewed.*

1 Thorough cleaning of the cylinder head and valve components, followed by a detailed inspection, will enable you to decide how much valve service work must be carried out during the engine overhaul. **Note:** *If the engine has been severely overheated, it is best to assume that the cylinder head is warped – check carefully for signs of this.*

Cleaning

2 Scrape away all traces of old gasket material from the cylinder head.

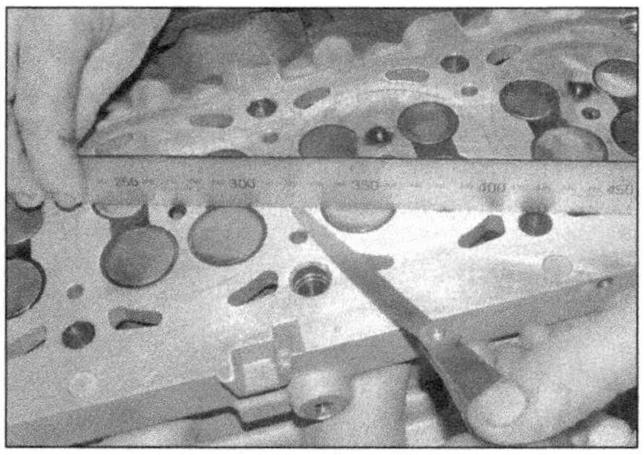

7.5 Check the cylinder head gasket surface for distortion

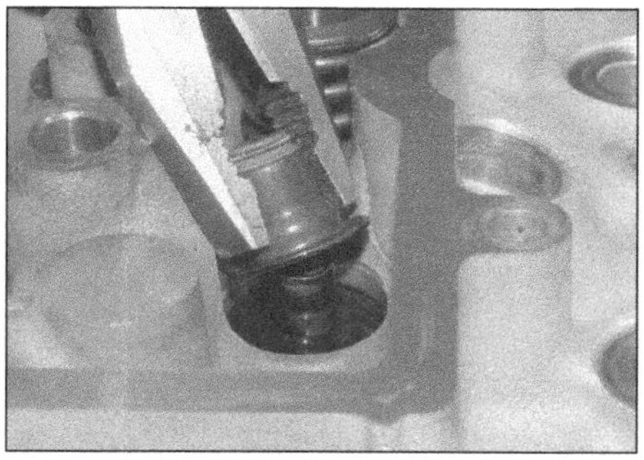

6.6f Use a pair of pliers to remove the valve stem oil seal. On some models the spring seat is integral with the seal

3 Scrape away the carbon from the combustion chambers and ports, then wash the cylinder head thoroughly with paraffin or a suitable solvent.

4 Scrape off any heavy carbon deposits that may have formed on the valves, then use a power-operated wire brush to remove deposits from the valve heads and stems.

Inspection

Note: *Be sure to perform all the following inspection procedures before concluding that the services of a machine shop or engine overhaul specialist are required. Make a list of all items that require attention.*

Cylinder head

5 Inspect the head very carefully for cracks, evidence of coolant leakage, and other damage. If cracks are found, a new cylinder head should be obtained. Use a straight-edge and feeler blade to check that the cylinder head gasket surface is not distorted **(see illustration)**. If it is, it may be possible to have it machined, provided that the cylinder head height is not significantly reduced.

6 Examine the valve seats in each of the combustion chambers. If they are severely pitted, cracked, or burned, they will need to be renewed or recut by an engine overhaul specialist. If they are only slightly pitted, this can be removed by grinding-in the valve heads and seats with fine valve grinding compound, as described below. If in any doubt, have the cylinder head inspected by an engine overhaul specialist.

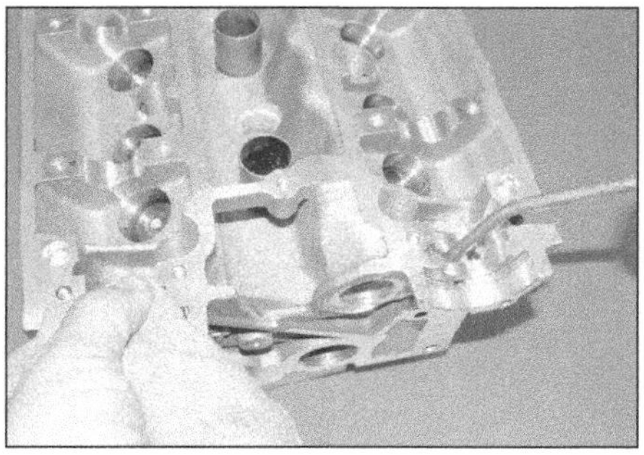

7.9a Apply compressed air to the oil feed bore of the intake camshaft, seal the bore in the exhaust camshaft bore with a rag ...

6.9 Place each valve and its associated components in a labelled bag

7 Check the valve guides for wear by inserting the relevant valve, and checking for side-to-side motion of the valve. A very small amount of movement is acceptable. If the movement seems excessive, remove the valve. Measure the valve stem diameter (see below), and renew the valve if it is worn. If the valve stem is not worn, the wear must be in the valve guide, and the guide must be renewed. The renewal of valve guides is best carried out by a Citroën dealer or engine overhaul specialist, who will have the necessary tools available. Where no valve stem diameter is specified, seek the advice of a Citroën dealer on the best course of action.

8 If renewing the valve guides, the valve seats should be recut or reground only after the guides have been fitted.

9 Where applicable, examine the camshaft oil supply non-return valve in the oil feed bore at the timing belt/chain end of the cylinder head. Check that the valve is not loose in the cylinder head and that the ball is free to move within the valve body. If the valve is a loose fit in its bore, or if there is any doubt about its condition, it should be renewed. The non-return valve can be removed (assuming it is not loose), using compressed air, such as that generated by a tyre foot pump. Place the pump nozzle over the oil feed bore of the camshaft bearing journal and seal the corresponding oil feed bore with a rag. Apply the compressed air and the valve will be forced out of its location in the underside of the cylinder head **(see illustrations)**. Fit

7.9b ... and the camshaft oil supply non-return valve will be ejected from the underside of the cylinder head

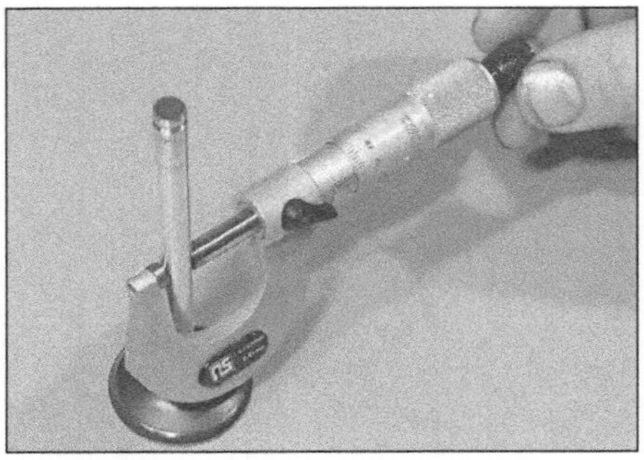

7.11 Measure the valve stem diameter with a micrometer

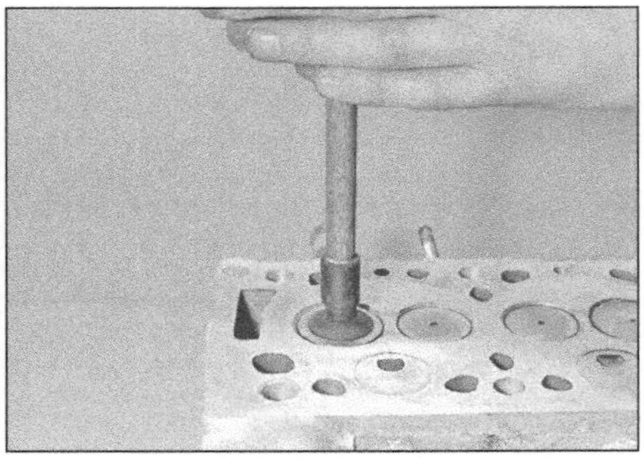

7.14 Grinding-in a valve

the new non-return valve to its bore on the underside of the head ensuring it is fitted the correct way. Oil should be able to pass upwards through the valve to the camshafts, but the ball in the valve should prevent the oil from returning back to the cylinder block. Use a thin socket or similar to push the valve fully into position.

Valves

10 Examine the head of each valve for pitting, burning, cracks, and general wear. Check the valve stem for scoring and wear ridges. Rotate the valve, and check for any obvious indication that it is bent. Look for pits or excessive wear on the tip of each valve stem. Renew any valve that shows any such signs of wear or damage.

11 If the valve appears satisfactory at this stage, measure the valve stem diameter at several points using a micrometer **(see illustration)**. Any significant difference in the readings obtained indicates wear of the valve stem. Should any of these conditions be apparent, the valve must be renewed.

12 If the valves are in satisfactory condition, they should be ground (lapped) into their respective seats, to ensure a smooth, gas-tight seal. If the seat is only lightly pitted, or if it has been recut, fine grinding compound only should be used to produce the required finish. Coarse valve-grinding compound should not be used, unless a seat is badly burned or deeply pitted. If this is the case, the cylinder head and valves should be inspected by an expert, to decide whether seat recutting, or even the renewal of the valve or seat insert (where possible) is required.

13 Valve grinding is carried out as follows. Place the cylinder head upside-down on a bench.

14 Smear a trace of (the appropriate grade of) valve-grinding compound on the seat face, and press a suction grinding tool onto the valve head **(see illustration)**. With a semi-rotary action, grind the valve head to its seat, lifting the valve occasionally to redistribute the grinding compound. A light spring placed under the valve head will greatly ease this operation.

15 If coarse grinding compound is being used, work only until a dull, matt even surface is produced on both the valve seat and the valve, then wipe off the used compound, and repeat the process with fine compound. When a smooth unbroken ring of light grey matt finish is produced on both the valve and seat, the grinding operation is complete. Do not grind-in the valves any further than absolutely necessary, or the seat will be prematurely sunk into the cylinder head.

16 When all the valves have been ground-in, carefully wash off all traces of grinding compound using paraffin or a suitable solvent, before reassembling the cylinder head.

Valve components

17 Examine the valve springs for signs of damage and discoloration. No minimum free length is specified by Citroën, so the only way of judging valve spring wear is by comparison with a new component.

18 Stand each spring on a flat surface, and check it for squareness. If any of the springs are damaged, distorted or have lost their tension, obtain a complete new set of springs. It is normal to renew the valve springs as a matter of course if a major overhaul is being carried out.

19 Renew the valve stem oil seals regardless of their apparent condition.

8 Cylinder head – reassembly

1 Working on the first valve assembly, refit the spring seat then dip the new valve stem oil seal in fresh engine oil. Locate the seal on the valve guide and press the seal firmly onto the guide using a suitable socket **(see illustrations)**. Note that on diesel engines, the seal is integral with the lower spring seat.

2 Lubricate the stem of the first valve, and insert it in the guide **(see illustration)**.

3 Locate the valve spring on top of its seat, and then refit the spring retainer.

4 Compress the valve spring, and locate the split collets in the recess in the valve stem. Release the compressor, then repeat the procedure on the remaining valves. Ensure that each valve is inserted into its original location. If new valves are being fitted, insert them into the locations to which they have been ground.

5 With all the valves installed, support the cylinder head and, using a hammer and interposed block of wood, tap the end of each valve stem to settle the components.

8.1a Locate the valve stem oil seal on the valve guide ...

8.1b ... and press the seal firmly onto the guide using a suitable socket

8.1c On some models, the valve stem oil seal is integral with the spring seat

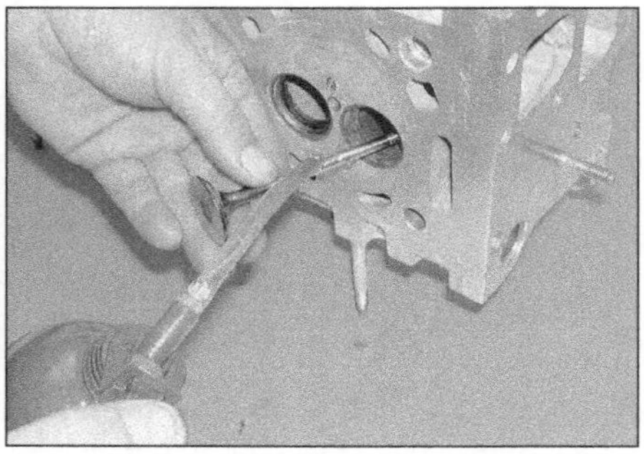

8.2 Lubricate the stem of the valve and insert it into the guide

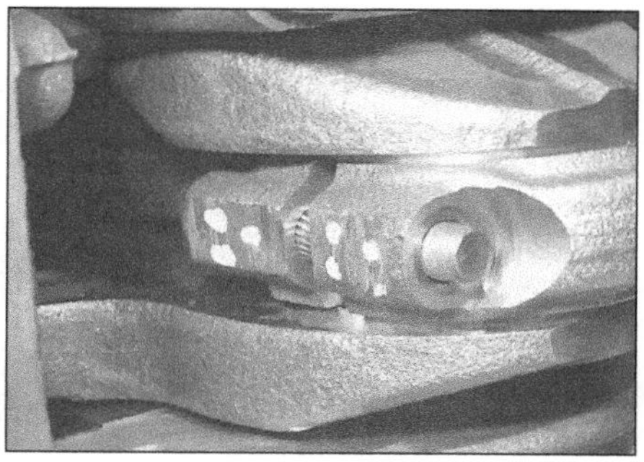

9.3 Connecting rod and big-end bearing cap identification marks (No 3 shown)

9.5 Remove the big-end bearing shell and cap

9.6 To protect the crankshaft journals, tape over the connecting rod stud threads

6 Refit the camshafts, hydraulic followers and rocker arms (as applicable) as described in Chapter 2A, 2C or 2D.
7 Refit any remaining components using the reverse of the removal sequence and with new seals or gaskets as necessary.
8 The cylinder head can then be refitted as described in Chapter 2A, 2C or 2D.

9 Piston/connecting rod assembly – removal

Note: *On diesel engines and VTi petrol engines, the main bearing ladder must be removed before the piston/connecting rods.*
1 Remove the cylinder head, sump and oil pump as described in Chapter 2A, 2B, 2C or 2D.
2 If there is a pronounced wear ridge at the top of any bore, it may be necessary to remove it with a scraper or ridge reamer, to avoid piston damage during removal. Such a ridge indicates excessive wear of the cylinder bore.
3 Using quick-drying paint, mark each connecting rod and big-end bearing cap with its respective cylinder number on the flat machined surface provided; if the engine has been dismantled before, note carefully any identifying marks made previously **(see illustration)**. Note that No 1 cylinder is at the transmission (flywheel) end of the engine.
4 Turn the crankshaft to bring pistons 1 and 4 to BDC (Bottom Dead Centre). Remove the main bearing ladder, as described in Section 10.
5 Unscrew the nuts or bolts, as applicable, from No 1 piston big-end bearing cap. Take off the cap, and recover the bottom half bearing shell **(see illustration)**. If the bearing shells are to be re-used, tape the cap and the shell together.
6 Where applicable, to prevent the possibility of damage to the crankshaft bearing journals, tape over the connecting rod stud threads **(see illustration)**.
7 Using a hammer handle, push the piston up through the bore, and remove it from the top of the cylinder block. Recover the bearing shell, and tape it to the connecting rod for safekeeping.
8 Loosely refit the big-end cap to the connecting rod, and secure with the nuts/bolts – this will help to keep the components in their correct order.
9 Remove number 4 piston assembly in the same way.
10 Turn the crankshaft through 180° to bring pistons 2 and 3 to BDC (Bottom Dead Centre), and remove them in the same way.

10 Crankshaft – removal

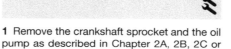

1 Remove the crankshaft sprocket and the oil pump as described in Chapter 2A, 2B, 2C or 2D (as applicable).
2 Remove the pistons and connecting rods, as described in Section 9. If no work is to be done on the pistons and connecting rods, there is no need to remove the cylinder head, or to push the pistons out of the cylinder bores. The pistons should just be pushed far enough up the bores so that they are positioned clear of the crankshaft journals. **Note:** *On diesel engines and VTi petrol engines, the main bearing ladder must be removed before the piston/connecting rods.*
3 Check the crankshaft endfloat as described in Section 13, then proceed as follows.

Non-VTi petrol engine

1.4 litre

4 Work around the outside of the cylinder block, and unscrew all the small (M6) bolts securing the main bearing ladder to the base of the cylinder block. Note the correct fitted depth of both the left- and right-hand crankshaft oil seals in the cylinder block/main bearing ladder.
5 Working in a diagonal sequence, evenly and progressively slacken the ten large (M11) main bearing ladder retaining bolts by a turn at a time. Once all the bolts are loose, remove them from the ladder.
6 With all the retaining bolts removed, carefully lift the main bearing ladder casting away from the base of the cylinder block. Recover the lower main bearing shells, and tape them to their respective locations in the casting. If the two locating dowels are a loose fit, remove them and store them with the casting for safekeeping.
7 Lift out the crankshaft, and discard both the oil seals. Remove the oil pump drive chain from the end of the crankshaft. Where necessary, slide off the drive sprocket, and recover the Woodruff key.
8 Recover the upper main bearing shells, and store them along with the relevant lower bearing shell. Also recover the two thrustwashers (one fitted either side of No 2 main bearing) from the cylinder block.

1.6 litre

9 Unbolt and remove the crankshaft left- and right-hand oil seal housings from each end of the cylinder block, noting the correct fitted locations of the locating dowels. If the locating dowels are a loose fit, remove them and store them with the housings for safekeeping.
10 Remove the oil pump drive chain, and slide the drive sprocket off the end of the crankshaft. Remove the Woodruff key, and store it with the sprocket for safekeeping.
11 The main bearing caps should be numbered 1 to 5 from the transmission (flywheel/driveplate) end of the engine. If not, mark them accordingly using a centre-punch or paint.
12 Unscrew and remove the main bearing cap retaining bolts, and withdraw the caps. Recover the lower main bearing shells, and tape them to their respective caps for safekeeping.
13 Carefully lift out the crankshaft, taking care not to displace the upper main bearing shell.
14 Recover the upper bearing shells from the cylinder block, and tape them to their respective caps for safekeeping. Remove the thrustwasher halves from the side of No 2 main bearing, and store them with the bearing cap.

VTi petrol engine

15 Work around the outside of the cylinder block, and unscrew all the small bolts securing the main bearing ladder to the base of the cylinder block. Note the correct fitted depth of the left-hand crankshaft oil seal in the cylinder block/main bearing ladder.
16 Working in a diagonal sequence, evenly and progressively slacken the large main bearing ladder retaining bolts by a turn at a time. Once all the bolts are loose, remove them from the ladder.
17 With all the retaining bolts removed, carefully lift the main bearing ladder casting away from

10.21 On diesel engines, prise up the two caps to expose the main bearing bolts at the flywheel end

the base of the cylinder block. Recover the lower main bearing shells, and tape them to their respective locations in the casting. If the two locating dowels are a loose fit, remove them and store them with the casting for safekeeping.

18 Undo the big-end bolts and remove the pistons/connecting rods as described in Section 9. Lift out the crankshaft, and discard both the oil seals.

19 Recover the upper main bearing shells, and store them along with the relevant lower bearing shell. Also recover the two thrustwashers (one fitted either side of No 2 main bearing) from the cylinder block.

Diesel engine

1.6 litre

20 Work around the outside of the cylinder block, and unscrew all the small bolts securing the main bearing ladder to the base of the cylinder block. Note the correct fitted depth of the left-hand crankshaft oil seal in the cylinder block/main bearing ladder.

21 Working in a diagonal sequence, evenly and progressively slacken the large main bearing ladder retaining bolts by a turn at a time. Once all the bolts are loose, remove them from the ladder. **Note:** *Prise up the two caps at the flywheel end of the ladder to expose the two end main bearing bolts* ***(see illustration)****.*

22 With all the retaining bolts removed, carefully lift the main bearing ladder casting away from the base of the cylinder block. Recover the lower main bearing shells, and tape them to their respective locations in the casting. If the two locating dowels are a loose fit, remove them and store them with the casting for safekeeping.

23 Undo the big-end bolts and remove the pistons/connecting rods as described in Section 9. Lift out the crankshaft, and discard both the oil seals.

24 Recover the upper main bearing shells, and store them along with the relevant lower bearing shell. Also recover the two thrustwashers (one fitted either side of No 2 main bearing) from the cylinder block.

2.0 litre

25 Slacken and remove the retaining bolts, and remove the oil seal housing from the right-hand (timing belt) end of the cylinder block **(see illustration)**.

10.25 Remove the oil seal housing from the right-hand end of the cylinder block

26 Remove the oil pump drive chain, and slide the drive sprocket and spacer (where fitted) off from the crankshaft. Remove the Woodruff key, and store it with the sprocket for safekeeping **(see illustrations)**.

10.26a Remove the oil pump drive chain ...

10.26b ... then slide off the drive sprocket ...

10.26c ... and remove the Woodruff key from the crankshaft

27 The main bearing caps should be numbered 1 to 5, starting from the transmission (flywheel) end of the engine **(see illustration)**. If not, mark them accordingly using a centre-punch. Also note the correct fitted depth of the crankshaft oil seal in the bearing cap.

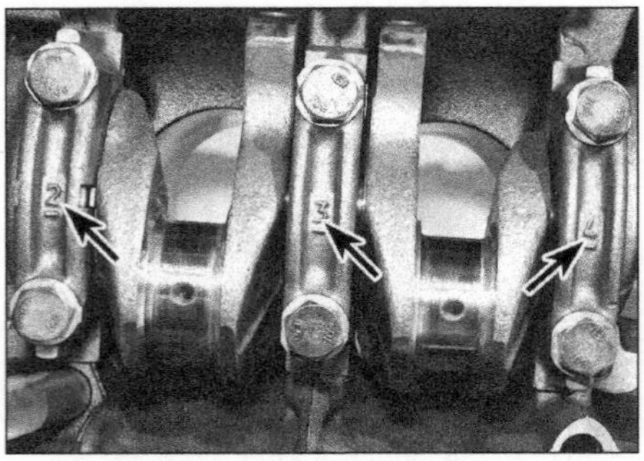

10.27 Main bearing cap identification markings (arrowed)

28 Slacken and remove the main bearing cap retaining bolts, and lift off each bearing cap. Recover the lower bearing shells, and tape them to their respective caps for safekeeping. Also recover the lower thrustwasher halves from the side of No 2 main bearing cap **(see illustration)**. Remove the sealing strips from the sides of No 1 main bearing cap, and discard them.

10.28 Note the thrustwasher (arrowed) fitted to the No 2 main bearing cap

29 Undo the big-end bolts and remove the pistons/connecting rods as described in Section 9. Lift out the crankshaft, and discard the left-hand (flywheel end) oil seal **(see illustration)**.

10.29 Lift out the crankshaft

30 Recover the upper bearing shells from the cylinder block, and tape them to their respective caps for safekeeping **(see illustration)**. Remove the upper thrustwasher halves from the side of No 2 main bearing, and store them with the lower halves.

11 Cylinder block/crankcase – cleaning and inspection

Cleaning

1 Remove all external components and electrical switches/sensors from the block. For complete cleaning, the core plugs should ideally be removed **(see illustration)**. Drill a small hole in the plugs, and then insert a self-tapping screw into the hole. Pull out the plugs by pulling on the screw with a pair of grips, or by using a slide hammer.

2 On 1.4 litre petrol engines, remove the cylinder liners – see paragraph 18.

3 Where applicable, undo the retaining bolts and remove the piston oil jet spray tubes (there is one for each piston) from inside the cylinder block **(see illustration)**.

4 Scrape all traces of gasket from the cylinder block/crankcase, and from the main bearing ladder/caps (as applicable), taking care not to damage the gasket/sealing surfaces.

5 Remove all oil gallery plugs (where fitted). The plugs are usually very tight – they may have to be drilled out, and the holes retapped. Use new plugs when the engine is reassembled.

6 If any of the castings are extremely dirty, all should be steam-cleaned.

7 After the castings are returned, clean all oil holes and oil galleries one more time. Flush all internal passages with warm water until the water runs clear. Dry thoroughly, and apply a light film of oil to all mating surfaces, to prevent rusting. If you have access to compressed air, use it to speed up the drying process, and to blow out all the oil holes and galleries.

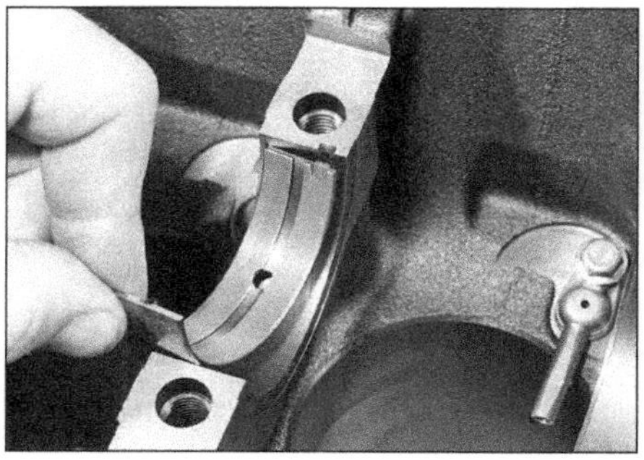

10.30 Remove the upper main bearing shells

Warning: Wear eye protection when using compressed air.

8 If the castings are not very dirty, you can do an adequate cleaning job with hot (as hot as you can stand), soapy water and a stiff brush. Take plenty of time, and do a thorough job. Regardless of the cleaning method used, be sure to clean all oil holes and galleries very thoroughly, and to dry all components well. On cast-iron block engines, protect the cylinder bores as described above, to prevent rusting.

9 All threaded holes must be clean, to ensure accurate torque readings during reassembly. To clean the threads, run the correct-size tap into each of the holes to remove rust, corrosion, thread sealant or sludge, and to restore damaged threads **(see illustration)**. If possible, use compressed air to clear the holes of debris produced by this operation.

10 Apply suitable sealant to the new oil gallery plugs, and insert them into the holes in the block. Tighten them securely. Also apply suitable sealant to new core plugs, and drive them into the block using a tube or socket.

11 Where applicable, clean the threads of the piston oil jet retaining bolts, and apply a drop of thread-locking compound (Citroën recommend Loctite Frenetanch) to each bolt threads. Refit the piston oil jet spray tubes to the cylinder block, and tighten the retaining bolts to the specified torque setting.

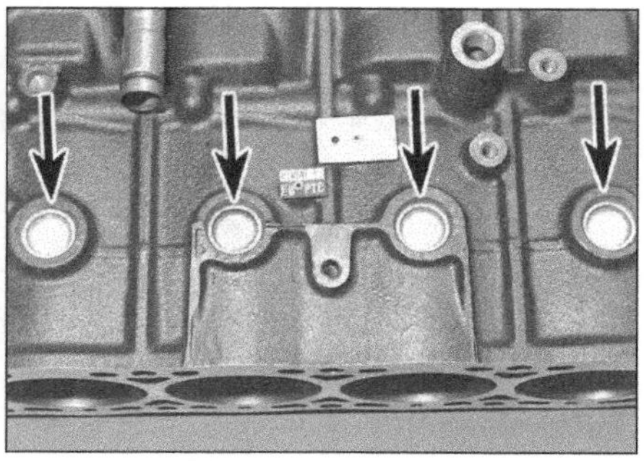

11.1 Cylinder block core plugs (arrowed)

12 If the engine is not going to be reassembled right away, cover it with a large plastic bag to keep it clean; protect all mating surfaces and the cylinder bores as described above, to prevent rusting.

Inspection

Cast-iron cylinder block

13 Visually check the castings for cracks and corrosion. Look for stripped threads in the threaded holes. If there has been any history of internal water leakage, it may be worthwhile having an engine overhaul specialist check the cylinder block/crankcase with special equipment. If defects are found, have them repaired if possible, or renew the assembly.

14 Check each cylinder bore for scuffing and scoring. Check for signs of a wear ridge at the top of the cylinder, indicating that the bore is excessively worn.

15 If the necessary measuring equipment is available, measure the bore diameter of each cylinder at the top (just under the wear ridge), centre, and bottom of the cylinder bore, parallel to the crankshaft axis.

16 Next, measure the bore diameter at the same three locations, at right angles to the crankshaft axis. Compare the results with the figures given in the Specifications. If there is any doubt about the condition of the cylinder

11.3 Piston oil jet spray tube (arrowed) in the cylinder block

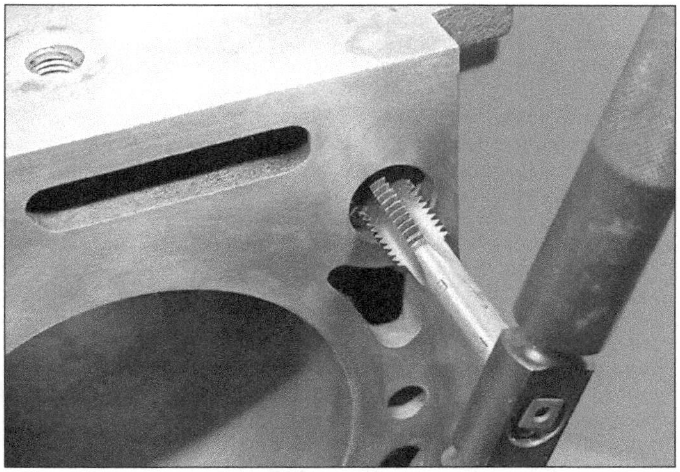

11.9 Use a suitable tap to clean the cylinder block threaded holes

11.18a On aluminium block engines, remove each liner ...

11.18b ... and recover the bottom O-ring seal (arrowed)

12.2 Remove the piston rings with the aid of a feeler gauge

bores, seek the advice of a Citroën dealer or suitable engine reconditioning specialist.

17 At the time of writing, it was not clear whether oversize pistons were available for all models. Consult your Citroën dealer or engine specialist for the latest information on piston availability. If oversize pistons are available, then it may be possible to have the cylinder bores rebored and fit the oversize pistons. If oversize pistons are not available, and the bores are worn, renewal of the block seems to be the only option.

Aluminium cylinder block

18 Remove the liner clamps (where used), and then use a hardwood drift to tap out each liner from the inside of the cylinder block. When all the liners are released, tip the cylinder block/crankcase on its side and remove each liner from the top of the block. As each liner is removed, stick masking tape on its left-hand (transmission side) face, and write the cylinder number on the tape. No 1 cylinder is at the transmission (flywheel/driveplate) end of the engine. Remove the sealing ring from the base of each liner, and discard **(see illustrations)**.

19 Check each cylinder liner for scuffing and scoring. Check for signs of a wear ridge at the top of the liner, indicating that the bore is excessively worn.

20 Take the liners to a Citroën dealer or engine reconditioning specialist and have their bores measured to determine if renewal is necessary. If it is, the dealer or specialist will be able to advise you regarding piston/liner availability.

21 Prior to installing the liners, check the liner protrusion as follows. Thoroughly clean the mating surfaces of the liner and cylinder block. Insert the liners into the block, without a sealing ring, ensuring each one is correctly seated; if the original liners are being refitted, ensure the liners are fitted in their original locations. With all four liners correctly installed, use a dial gauge (or a straight-edge and feeler blade) to check that the protrusion of each liner above the upper surface of the cylinder block is within the limits given in the Specifications. The maximum difference between any two liners must not be exceeded. **Note:** *If new liners are being fitted, it is permissible to interchange them to bring the difference in protrusion within limits. Remember to keep each piston with its respective liner.* If liner protrusion is not within the specified limits, seek the advice of a Citroën dealer or engine reconditioning specialist before proceeding with the engine rebuild.

22 Once the protrusions have been checked, remove the liners from the block and fit a new sealing ring carefully to the base of each liner. Lubricate the base of each liner with a smear of oil to aid installation.

23 Insert each liner into the cylinder block, taking care not to damage the O-ring, and press it home as far as possible by hand. Using a hammer and a block of wood, tap each liner lightly but fully onto its locating shoulder. If the original liners are being refitted, use the marks made on removal to ensure that each is refitted the correct way round, and is inserted into its original bore.

24 Wipe clean, then lightly oil all exposed liner surfaces, to prevent rusting. Where necessary, clamp the liners back in position.

12 Piston/connecting rod assembly – inspection

1 Before the inspection process can begin, the piston/connecting rod assemblies must be cleaned, and the original piston rings removed from the pistons.

2 Carefully expand the old rings over the top of the pistons. The use of two or three old feeler blades will be helpful in preventing the rings dropping into empty grooves **(see illustration)**. Be careful not to scratch the piston with the ends of the ring. The rings are brittle, and will snap if they are spread too far. They are also very sharp – protect your hands and fingers. Note that the third ring incorporates an expander. Always remove the rings from the top of the piston. Keep each set of rings with its piston if the old rings are to be re-used.

3 Scrape away all traces of carbon from the top of the piston. A hand-held wire brush (or a piece of fine emery cloth) can be used, once the majority of the deposits have been scraped away.

4 Remove the carbon from the ring grooves in the piston, using an old ring. Break the ring in half to do this (be careful not to cut your fingers – piston rings are sharp). Be careful to remove only the carbon deposits – do not remove any metal, and do not nick or scratch the sides of the ring grooves.

5 Once the deposits have been removed, clean the piston/connecting rod assembly with paraffin or a suitable solvent, and dry thoroughly. Make sure that the oil return holes in the ring grooves are clear.

6 If the pistons and cylinder bores are not damaged or worn excessively, and if the cylinder block does not need to be re-bored (where possible), the original pistons can be refitted. Normal piston wear shows up as even vertical wear on the piston thrust surfaces, and slight looseness of the top ring in its groove. New piston rings should always be used when the engine is reassembled.

7 Carefully inspect each piston for cracks around the skirt, around the gudgeon pin holes, and at the piston ring 'lands' (between the ring grooves).

8 Look for scoring and scuffing on the piston skirt, holes in the piston crown, and burned areas at the edge of the crown. If the skirt is scored or scuffed, the engine may have been suffering from overheating, and/or abnormal combustion, which caused excessively high operating temperatures. The cooling and lubrication systems should be checked thoroughly. Scorch marks on the sides of the pistons show that blow-by has occurred. A hole in the piston crown, or burned areas at the edge of the piston crown, indicates that abnormal combustion (pre-ignition, knocking, or detonation) has been occurring. If any of the above problems exist, the causes must be investigated and corrected, or the damage will occur again. The causes may include incorrect ignition/injection pump timing, or a faulty injector (as applicable).

9 Corrosion of the piston, in the form of pitting, indicates that coolant has been leaking into the combustion chamber and/or the crankcase. Again, the cause must be corrected, or the problem may persist in the rebuilt engine.

10 On engines with wet liners, it is not possible to renew the pistons separately; pistons are only supplied with piston rings and

12.15a Prise out the circlip ...

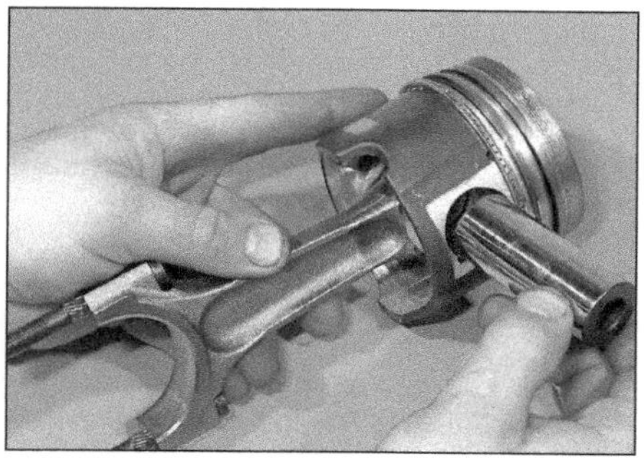

12.15b ... and withdraw the gudgeon pin

a liner, as a part of a matched assembly (see Section 11). On iron-block engines, pistons can be purchased from a Citroën dealer or engine reconditioning specialist.

11 Examine each connecting rod carefully for signs of damage, such as cracks around the big-end and small-end bearings. Check that the rod is not bent or distorted. Damage is highly unlikely, unless the engine has been seized or badly overheated. Detailed checking of the connecting rod assembly can only be carried out by a Citroën dealer or engine specialist with the necessary equipment.

12 The connecting rod big-end cap bolts/nuts must be renewed whenever they are disturbed. Although Citroën do not specify that the bolts must also renewed, it is recommended that the nuts and bolts are renewed as a complete set.

Petrol engines

13 On petrol engines, the gudgeon pins are an interference fit in the connecting rod small-end bearing. Therefore, piston and/or connecting rod renewal should be entrusted to a Citroën dealer or engine repair specialist, who will have the necessary tooling to remove and install the gudgeon pins.

Diesel engines

14 On diesel engines, the gudgeon pins are of the floating type, secured in position by two circlips. On these engines, the pistons and connecting rods can be separated as described in the following paragraphs.

15 Using a small flat-bladed screwdriver, prise out the circlips, and push out the gudgeon pin **(see illustrations)**. Hand pressure should be sufficient to remove the pin. Identify the piston and rod to ensure correct reassembly. Discard the circlips – new ones must be used on refitting.

16 Examine the gudgeon pin and connecting rod small-end bearing for signs of wear or damage. Wear can be cured by renewing both the pin and bush (where possible) or connecting rod. Bush renewal, however, is a specialist job – press facilities are required, and the new bush must be reamed accurately.

17 The connecting rods themselves should not be in need of renewal, unless seizure or some other major mechanical failure has occurred. Check the alignment of the connecting rods visually, and if the rods are not straight, take them to an engine overhaul specialist for a more detailed check.

18 Examine all components, and obtain any new parts from your Citroën dealer. If new pistons are purchased, they will be supplied complete with gudgeon pins and circlips. Circlips can also be purchased individually.

19 Position the piston as shown **(see illustration)**.

20 Ensure the piston and connecting rod are correctly positioned then apply a smear of clean engine oil to the gudgeon pin. Slide it into the piston and through the connecting rod small-end. Check that the piston pivots freely on the rod, then secure the gudgeon pin in position with two new circlips. Ensure that each circlip is correctly located in its groove in the piston.

13.2 The crankshaft endfloat can be checked with a dial gauge ...

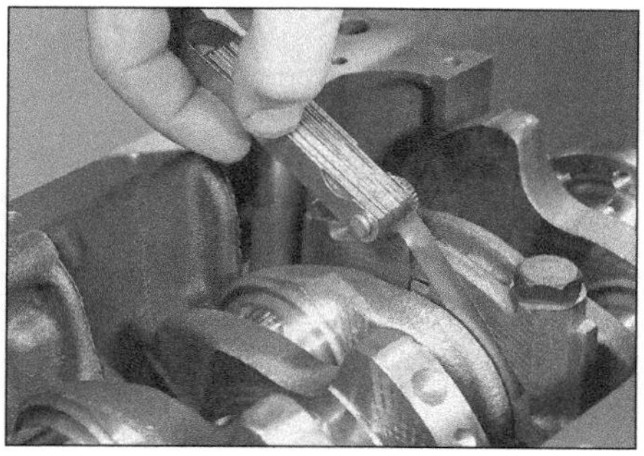

13.3 ... or with feeler gauges

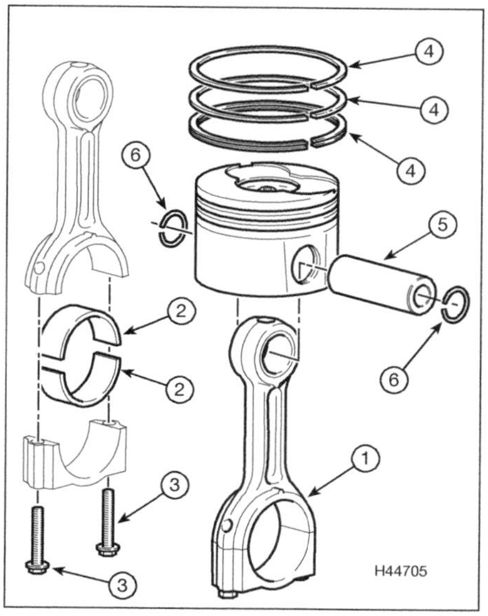

12.19 Piston and connecting rod assembly (diesel engine)

1 Connecting rod	*4 Piston rings*
2 Big-end shells	*5 Gudgeon pin*
3 Big-end bolt	*6 Circlips*

13 Crankshaft – inspection

Checking endfloat

1 If the crankshaft endfloat is to be checked, this must be done when the crankshaft is still installed in the cylinder block/crankcase, but is free to move (see Section 10).

2 Check the endfloat using a dial gauge in contact with the end of the crankshaft. Push the crankshaft fully one way, and then zero the gauge. Push the crankshaft fully the other way, and check the endfloat. The result can be compared with the specified amount, and will give an indication as to whether new thrustwashers are required **(see illustration).**

3 If a dial gauge is not available, feeler blades can be used. First push the crankshaft fully towards the flywheel end of the engine, and then use feeler blades to measure the gap between the web of No 2 crankpin and the thrustwasher **(see illustration)**.

Inspection

4 Clean the crankshaft using paraffin or a suitable solvent, and dry it, preferably with compressed air if available. Be sure to clean the oil holes with a pipe cleaner or similar probe, to ensure that they are not obstructed.

Warning: Wear eye protection when using compressed air.

5 Check the main and big-end bearing journals for uneven wear, scoring, pitting and cracking.

6 Big-end bearing wear is accompanied by

distinct metallic knocking when the engine is running (particularly noticeable when the engine is pulling from low speed) and some loss of oil pressure.

7 Main bearing wear is accompanied by severe engine vibration and rumble – getting progressively worse as engine speed increases – and again by loss of oil pressure.

8 Check the bearing journal for roughness by running a finger lightly over the bearing surface. Any roughness (which will be accompanied by obvious bearing wear) indicates that the crankshaft requires regrinding (where possible) or renewal.

9 Check the oil seal contact surfaces at each end of the crankshaft for wear and damage. If the seal has worn a deep groove in the surface of the crankshaft, consult an engine overhaul specialist; repair may be possible, but otherwise a new crankshaft will be required.

10 Take the crankshaft to a Citroën dealer or engine reconditioning specialist to have it measured for journal wear. If excessive wear is evident, they will be able to advise you with regard to regrinding the crankshaft and supplying new bearing shells.

11 If the crankshaft has been reground, check for burrs around the crankshaft oil holes (the holes are usually chamfered, so burrs should not be a problem unless regrinding has been carried out carelessly). Remove any burrs with a fine file or scraper, and thoroughly clean the oil holes as described previously.

12 At the time of writing, it was not clear whether Citroën produce undersize bearing shells for all of these engines. On some engines, if the crankshaft journals have not already been reground, it may be possible to have the crankshaft reconditioned, and to fit undersize shells. If no undersize shells are available and the crankshaft has worn beyond the specified limits, it will have to be renewed. Consult your Citroën dealer or engine specialist for further information on parts availability.

14 Main and big-end bearings – inspection

1 Even though the main and big-end bearings should be renewed during the engine overhaul, the old bearings should be retained for close examination, as they may reveal valuable information about the condition of the engine. The bearing shells are graded by thickness, the grade of each shell being indicated by the colour code marked on it.

2 Bearing failure can occur due to lack of lubrication, the presence of dirt or other foreign particles, overloading the engine, or corrosion **(see illustration)**. Regardless of the cause of bearing failure, the cause must be corrected (where applicable) before the engine is reassembled, to prevent it from happening again.

3 When examining the bearing shells, remove them from the cylinder block/crankcase, the main bearing ladder/caps (as appropriate), the connecting rods and the connecting rod big-end bearing caps. Lay them out on a clean surface in the same general position as their location in the engine. This will enable you to match any bearing problems with the corresponding crankshaft journal. Do not touch any shell's bearing surface with your fingers while checking it, or the delicate surface may be scratched.

4 Dirt and other foreign matter gets into the engine in a variety of ways. It may be left in the engine during assembly, or it may pass through filters or the crankcase ventilation system. It may get into the oil, and from there into the bearings. Metal chips from machining operations and normal engine wear are often present. Abrasives are sometimes left in engine components after reconditioning, especially when parts are not thoroughly cleaned using the proper cleaning methods. Whatever the source, these foreign objects often end up embedded in the soft bearing material, and are easily recognised. Large particles will not embed in the bearing, and will score or gouge the bearing and journal. The best prevention for this cause of bearing failure is to clean all parts thoroughly, and keep everything spotlessly clean during engine assembly. Frequent and regular engine oil and filter changes are also recommended.

5 Lack of lubrication (or lubrication breakdown) has a number of interrelated causes. Excessive heat (which thins the oil), overloading (which squeezes the oil from the bearing face) and oil leakage (from excessive bearing clearances, worn oil pump or high engine speeds) all contribute to lubrication breakdown. Blocked oil passages, which usually are the result of misaligned oil holes in a bearing shell, will also oil-starve a bearing, and destroy it. When lack of lubrication is the cause of bearing failure, the bearing material is wiped or extruded from the steel backing of the bearing. Temperatures may increase to the point where the steel backing turns blue from overheating.

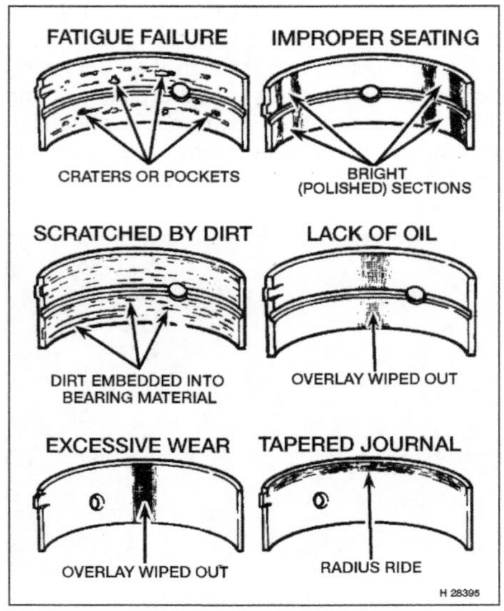

14.2 Typical bearing failures

6 Driving habits can have a definite effect on bearing life. Full-throttle, low-speed operation (labouring the engine) puts very high loads on bearings, tending to squeeze out the oil film. These loads cause the bearings to flex, which produces fine cracks in the bearing face (fatigue failure). Eventually, the bearing material will loosen in pieces, and tear away from the steel backing.

7 Short-distance driving leads to corrosion of bearings, because insufficient engine heat is produced to drive off the condensed water and corrosive gases. These products collect in the engine oil, forming acid and sludge. As the oil is carried to the engine bearings, the acid attacks and corrodes the bearing material.

8 Incorrect bearing installation during engine assembly will lead to bearing failure as well. Tight-fitting bearings leave insufficient bearing running clearance, and will result in oil starvation. Dirt or foreign particles trapped behind a bearing shell result in high spots on the bearing, which lead to failure.

9 Do not touch any shell's bearing surface with your fingers during reassembly; there is a risk of scratching the delicate surface, or of depositing particles of dirt on it.

10 As mentioned at the beginning of this Section, the bearing shells should be renewed as a matter of course during engine overhaul; to do otherwise is false economy.

15 Engine overhaul – reassembly sequence

1 Before reassembly begins, ensure that all new parts have been obtained, and that all necessary tools are available. Read through the entire procedure to familiarise yourself with the work involved, and to ensure that all items necessary for reassembly of the engine are at hand. In addition to all normal tools and materials, thread-locking compound will be needed. A tube of suitable liquid sealant will also be required for the joint faces that are fitted without gaskets. It is recommended that Citroën's own product(s) be used, which are specially formulated for this purpose; the relevant product names are quoted in the text of each Section where they are required.

2 In order to save time and avoid problems, engine reassembly can be carried out in the following order, referring to Chapter 2A, 2B, 2C or 2D unless otherwise stated:

a) Crankshaft (see Section 17).
b) Piston/connecting rod assemblies (See Section 18).
c) Oil pump.
d) Sump.
e) Flywheel/driveplate.
f) Cylinder head.
g) Injection pump and mounting bracket – diesel engine (Chapter 4B, Section 9).
h) Timing chain/belt tensioner pulley(s) and sprockets, and timing chain/belt.
i) Engine external components.

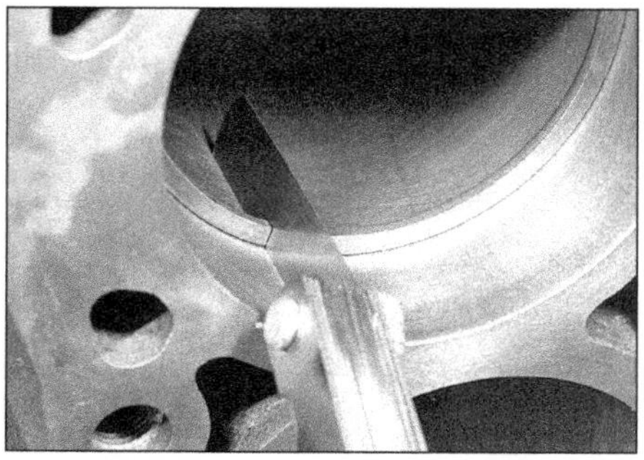

16.5 Measure the piston rings end gaps with a feeler gauge

3 At this stage, all engine components should be absolutely clean and dry, with all faults repaired. The components should be laid out (or in individual containers) on a completely clean work surface.

16 Piston rings – refitting

1 Before fitting new piston rings, the ring end gaps must be checked as follows.

2 Lay out the piston/connecting rod assemblies and the new piston ring sets, so that the ring sets will be matched with the same piston and cylinder during the end gap measurement and subsequent engine reassembly.

3 Insert the top ring into the first cylinder, and push it down the bore using the top of the piston. This will ensure that the ring remains square with the cylinder walls. Position the ring near the bottom of the cylinder bore, at the lower limit of ring travel. Note that the top and second compression rings are different. The second ring can be identified by its taper; on petrol engines it also has a step on its lower surface. On diesel engines, the top ring has a chamfer on its upper/outer edge.

4 Measure the end gap using feeler blades.

5 Repeat the procedure with the ring at the top of the cylinder bore, at the upper limit of its travel **(see illustration)**, and compare the measurements with the figures given in the Specifications. If the end gaps are incorrect, check that you have the correct rings for your engine and for the cylinder bore size.

6 Repeat the checking procedure for each ring in the first cylinder, and then for the rings in the remaining cylinders. Remember to keep rings, pistons and cylinders matched up.

7 Once the ring end gaps have been checked and if necessary corrected, the rings can be fitted to the pistons.

8 Fit the oil control ring expander (where fitted) then install the ring. The ring gap should be positioned 180° from the expander gap.

9 The second and top rings are different and can be identified from their cross-sections; the top ring is symmetrical whilst the second ring is tapered. Fit the second ring, ensuring its identification (TOP) marking is facing

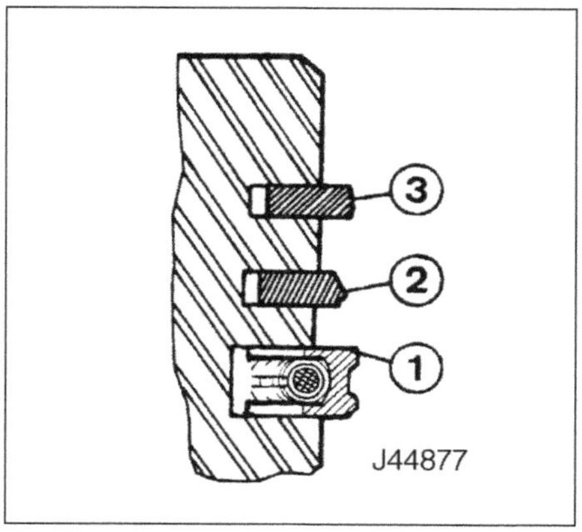

16.9a Piston ring fitting diagram (typical)

1 Oil control ring
2 Second compression ring
3 Top compression ring

upwards, and then install the top ring **(see illustrations)**. Arrange the second and top ring end gap so they are equally spaced 120° apart. **Note:** *Always follow any instructions supplied with the new piston ring sets – different manufacturers may specify different procedures. Do not mix up the top and second compression rings, as they have different cross-sections.*

17 Crankshaft – refitting

Selection of bearing shells

1 Have the crankshaft inspected and measured by a Citroën dealer or engine reconditioning specialist. They will be able to carry out any regrinding/repairs, and supply suitable main and big-end bearing shells.

Crankshaft refitting

Note: *New main bearing cap/lower crankcase bolts must be used when refitting the crankshaft.*

2 Where applicable, ensure that the oil spray jets are fitted to the bearing locations in the cylinder block.

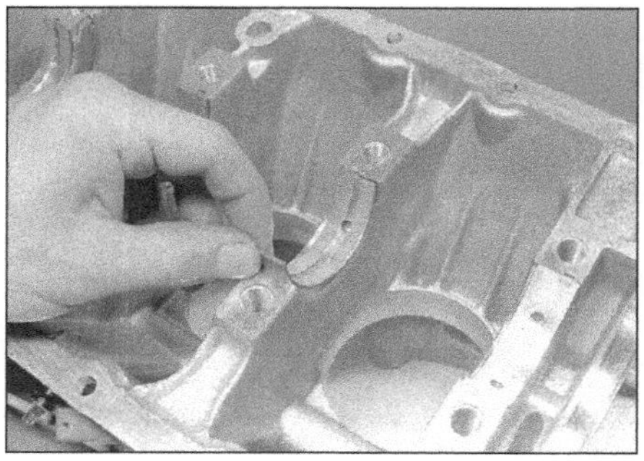

17.5 Fit the grooved bearing shells to No 2 and 4 main bearings (non-VTi petrol engines)

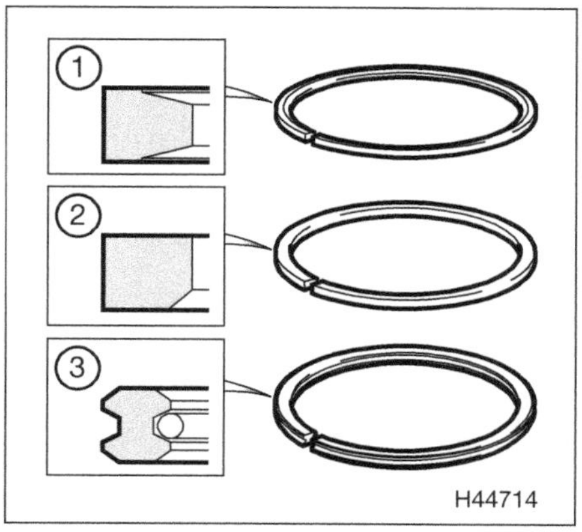

16.9b Piston rings (diesel engine)

1 Top compression ring
2 Second compression ring
3 Oil control ring

1.4 litre non-VTi petrol engine

3 Using a little grease, stick the upper thrustwashers to each side of the No 2 main bearing upper location; ensure that the oilway grooves on each thrustwasher face outwards (away from the block).

4 Clean the backs of the bearing shells, and the bearing locations in both the cylinder block/crankcase and the main bearing ladder/bearing caps.

5 Press the bearing shells into their locations, ensuring that the tab on each shell engages in the notch in the cylinder block/crankcase or main bearing ladder/bearing cap. Take care not to touch any shell's bearing surface with your fingers. Note that the grooved bearing shells, both upper and lower, are fitted to numbers 2 and 4 main bearings **(see illustration)**.

6 Liberally lubricate each bearing shell in the cylinder block/crankcase with clean engine oil.

7 Refit the Woodruff key, then slide on the oil pump drive sprocket, and locate the drive chain on the sprocket **(see illustration)**. Lower the crankshaft into position so that numbers 2 and 3 cylinder crankpins are at TDC; numbers 1 and 4 cylinder crankpins will be at BDC, ready for fitting No 1 piston. Check the crankshaft endfloat as described in Section 13.

17.7 Fit the oil pump drive chain and sprocket

17.8 Apply a thin film of sealant to the cylinder block mating surface

17.10 Tighten the ten main bearing bolts to the specified torque

8 Thoroughly degrease the mating surfaces of the cylinder block/crankcase and the main bearing ladder. Apply a thin bead of suitable sealant to the cylinder block, mating surface of the main bearing ladder casting, then spread to an even film **(see illustration)**.

9 Ensure the locating dowels are in position then lubricate the lower bearing shells with clean engine oil. Refit the main bearing ladder to the cylinder block, ensuring that the lower bearings remain correctly fitted.

10 Install the main bearing ladder retaining bolts, and tighten them all by hand only. Working in a spiral pattern from the centre bolts outwards, evenly and progressively tighten the bolts to the specified Stage 1 torque wrench setting. Once all the bolts have been tightened to the Stage 1 setting, working in the same sequence, angle-tighten the bolts through the specified Stage 2 angle using a socket and extension bar. It is recommended that an angle-measuring gauge is used during this stage of the tightening, to ensure accuracy **(see illustration)**. If a gauge is not available, use a dab of white paint to make alignment marks between the bolt head and casting prior to tightening; the marks can then be used to check that the bolt has been rotated sufficiently during tightening.

11 Refit all the smaller bolts securing the main bearing ladder to the base of the cylinder block, and tighten them to the specified torque. Check that the crankshaft rotates freely.

12 Refit the piston/connecting rod assemblies to the crankshaft as described in Section 18.

13 Ensuring that the drive chain is correctly located on the sprocket, refit the oil pump and sump as described in Chapter 2A, Section 12 and 11.

14 Fit two new crankshaft oil seals, referring to Chapter 2A, Section 13.

15 Refit the flywheel/driveplate, referring to Chapter 2A, Section 14.

16 Refit the cylinder head (where removed) and also refit the crankshaft sprocket and timing belt.

1.6 litre non-VTi petrol engine

17 Using a little grease, stick the upper thrustwashers to each side of the No 2 main bearing upper location. Ensure that the oilway grooves on each thrustwasher face outwards (away from the cylinder block) **(see illustration)**.

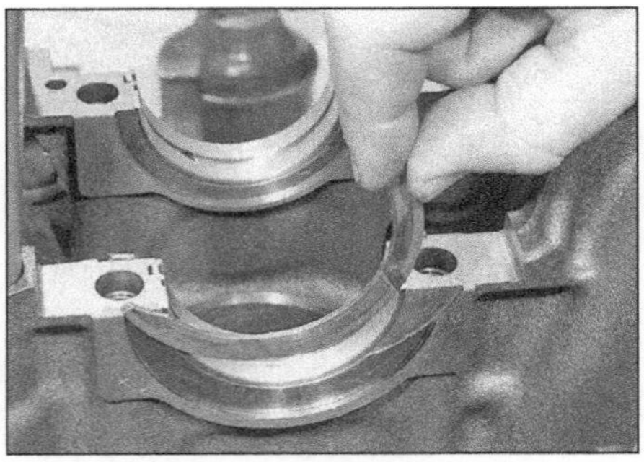

17.17 Fit the thrustwashers to either side of the No 2 main bearing, with the oilway grooves facing outwards

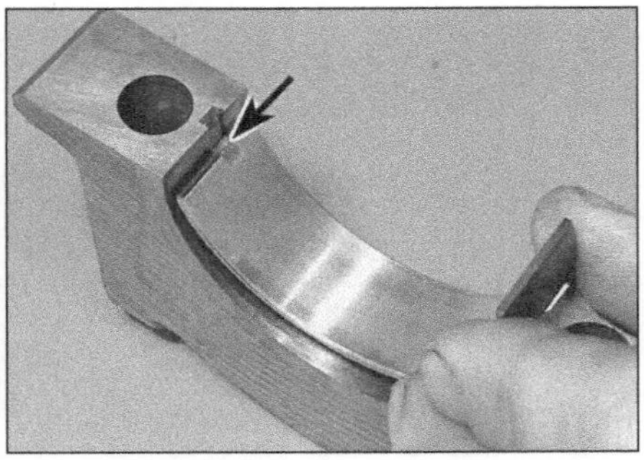

17.18 Ensure the tab (arrowed) is located in the cut-out when fitting the bearing shells

18 Place the bearing shells in their locations as described in paragraphs 4 and 5 **(see illustration)**. If new shells are being fitted, ensure that all traces of protective grease are cleaned off using paraffin. Wipe dry the shells and connecting rods with a lint-free cloth. Liberally lubricate each bearing shell in the cylinder block/crankcase and cap with clean engine oil.

19 Lower the crankshaft into position so that numbers 2 and 3 cylinder crankpins are at TDC; numbers 1 and 4 cylinder crankpins will be at BDC, ready for fitting No 1 piston. Check the crankshaft endfloat as described in Section 13.

20 Lubricate the lower bearing shells in the main bearing caps with clean engine oil. Make sure that the locating lugs on the shells engage with the corresponding recesses in the caps.

21 Fit the main bearing caps to their correct locations, ensuring that they are fitted the correct way round (the bearing shell lug recesses in the block and caps must be on the same side).

22 Lightly lubricate the threads and the underside of the heads of the main bearing cap bolts with engine oil then refit the bolts. Working in a spiral sequence from the centre bolts outwards, tighten the main bearing cap bolts evenly and progressively to the specified Stage 1 torque wrench setting. Once all the bolts have been tightened to the Stage 1 setting, working in the same sequence, angle-tighten the bolts through the specified Stage 2 angle, using a socket and extension bar. It is recommended that an angle-measuring gauge be used during this stage of the tightening, to ensure accuracy. If a gauge is not available, use a dab of white paint to make alignment marks between the bolt head and casting prior to tightening; the marks can then be used to check that the bolt has been rotated sufficiently during tightening.

23 Check that the crankshaft rotates freely.

24 Refit the piston/connecting rod assemblies to the crankshaft as described in Section 18.
25 Refit the Woodruff key to the crankshaft groove, and slide on the oil pump drive sprocket. Locate the drive chain on the sprocket.
26 Ensure that the mating surfaces of right-hand (timing belt end) oil seal housing and cylinder block are clean and dry. Note the correct fitted depth of the oil seal then, using a large flat-bladed screwdriver, lever the seal out of the housing.
27 Apply a smear of suitable sealant to the oil seal housing mating surface, and make sure that the locating dowels are in position. Slide the housing over the end of the crankshaft, and into position on the cylinder block. Tighten the housing retaining bolts securely.
28 Repeat the operations in paragraphs 26 and 27, and fit the left-hand (flywheel/driveplate end) oil seal housing.
29 Fit new crankshaft oil seals, referring to Chapter 2A, Section 13.
30 Ensuring that the chain is correctly located on the drive sprocket, refit the oil pump and sump.
31 Refit the flywheel/driveplate, referring to Chapter 2A, Section 14.
32 Refit the cylinder head (where removed) and install the crankshaft sprocket and timing belt.

1.6 litre VTi petrol engines

33 Clean the backs of the bearing shells in both the cylinder block/crankcase and the main bearing ladder. If new shells are being fitted, ensure that all traces of protective grease are cleaned off using paraffin. Wipe dry the shells with a lint-free cloth.
34 Press the bearing shells into their locations, ensuring that the tab on each shell engages in the notch in the cylinder block/crankcase and bearing ladder. Take care not to touch any shell's bearing surface with your fingers. Note that the upper bearing shells all have a grooved surface, whereas the lower shells have a plain bearing surface.
35 Liberally lubricate each bearing shell in the cylinder block with clean engine oil then lower the crankshaft into position.
36 Insert the thrustwashers to either side of No 2 main bearing upper location and push them around the bearing journal until their edges are horizontal.
37 Ensure that the oilway grooves on each thrustwasher face outwards (away from the cylinder block).
38 Thoroughly degrease the mating surfaces of the cylinder block and the crankshaft bearing cap housing/main bearing ladder.
39 Apply a thin bead of RTV sealant to the bearing cap housing mating surface. Citroën recommend the use of Loctite Autojoint Noir for this purpose.
40 Lubricate the lower bearing shells with clean engine oil, then refit the bearing cap housing, ensuring that the shells are not displaced, and that the locating dowels engage correctly.
41 Install the large and small crankshaft bearing cap housing/ladder retaining bolts, and screw them in until they are just making contact with the housing.
42 Working in a spiral sequence, tighten all the main bearing bolts to the Stage 1 torque setting given in Chapter 2B Specifications.
43 Using an angle tightening gauge, tighten all bolts to their Stage 2 setting, working in the same sequence.
44 With the bearing cap housing in place, check that the crankshaft rotates freely.
45 Refit the piston/connecting rod assemblies to the crankshaft as described in Section 18.
46 Refit the oil pump and sump, referring to Chapter 2B, Section 10 and 9.
47 Fit a new crankshaft left-hand oil seal, then refit the flywheel as described in Chapter 2A, Section 11 and 12.
48 Where removed, refit the crankshaft sprocket and timing belt.

1.6 litre diesel engine

49 Place the bearing shells in their locations. If new shells are being fitted, ensure that all traces of protective grease are cleaned off using paraffin. Wipe dry the shells with a lint-free cloth. The upper bearing shells all have a grooved surface, whereas the lower shells have a plain surface. On these engines, it's essential that the lower bearing shells are centrally located in the bearing cap housing/ladder. To ensure this use Citroën tool No 0194-QZ positioned over the housing/ladder, and insert the bearing shells through the slots in the tool **(see illustration)**.

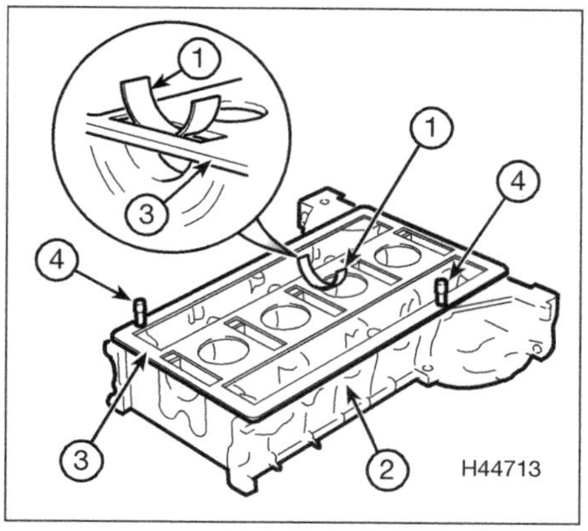

17.49 Main bearing shell refitment (diesel engine)

1 Bearing shell
2 Main bearing ladder
3 Citroën tool
4 Aligning pins

50 Liberally lubricate each bearing shell in the cylinder block with clean engine oil then lower the crankshaft into position.
51 Insert the thrustwashers to either side of No 2 main bearing upper location and push them around the bearing journal until their edges are horizontal **(see illustration)**. Ensure that the oilway grooves on each thrustwasher face outwards (away from the bearing journal).
52 Thoroughly degrease the mating surfaces of the cylinder block and the crankshaft bearing cap housing. Apply a thin bead of RTV sealant to the bearing cap housing mating surface **(see illustration)**. Citroën recommend the use of Loctite Autojoint Noir for this purpose.
53 Lubricate the lower bearing shells with clean engine oil, then refit the bearing cap housing, ensuring that the shells are not displaced, and that the locating dowels engage correctly.
54 Install the ten large diameter and sixteen smaller diameter crankshaft bearing cap housing retaining bolts, and screw them in until they are just making contact with the housing.
55 Working in sequence, tighten the bolts to the torque settings given in Chapter 2C Specifications **(see illustration)**.

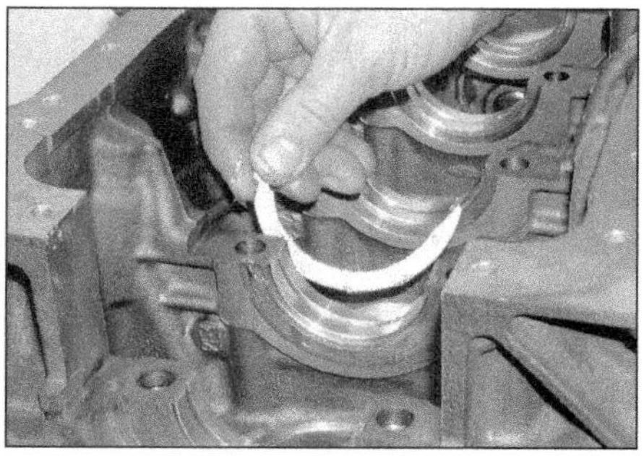

17.51 Place the thrustwashers each side of the No 2 bearing upper location

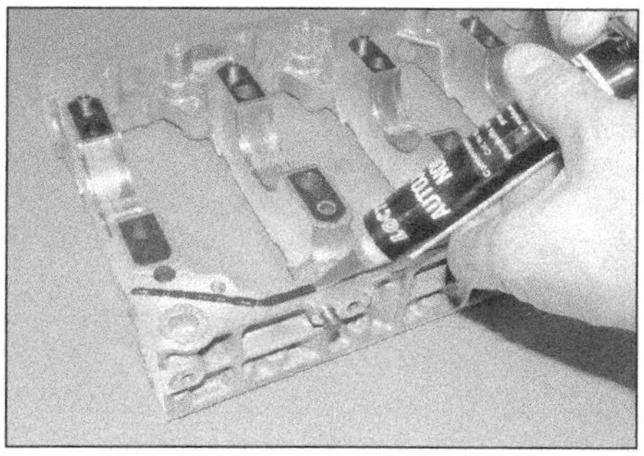

17.52 Apply a thin bead of RTV sealant to the bearing cap housing mating surface

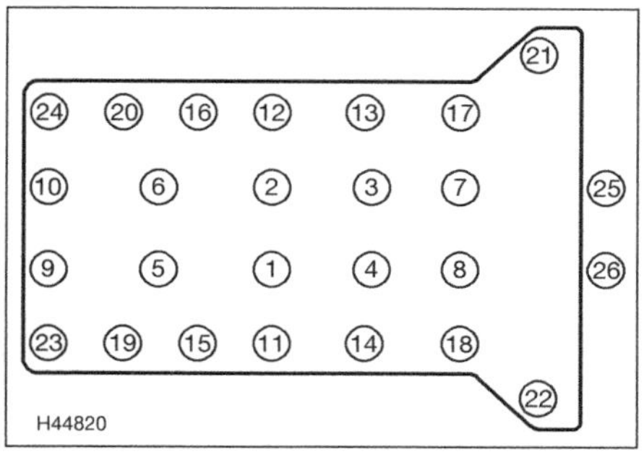

17.55 Main bearing ladder bolts tightening sequence (diesel engine)

17.62a Ensure the grooved main bearing shells are fitted to the cylinder block ...

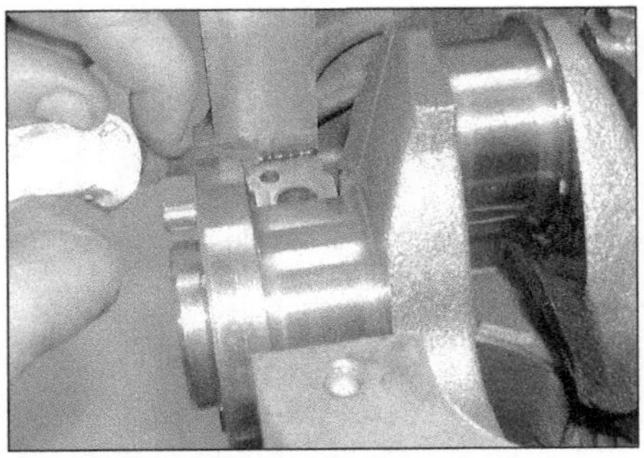

17.66 Apply sealant to the No 1 main bearing cap mating face on the cylinder block, around the sealing strip holes and in the corners

56 With the bearing cap housing in place, check that the crankshaft rotates freely.
57 Refit the piston/connecting rod assemblies to the crankshaft as described in Section 18.
58 Refit the oil pump and sump, as described in Chapter 2C, Section 12 and 11.
59 Fit a new crankshaft left-hand oil seal, then refit the flywheel, as described in Chapter 2C, Section 14 and 16.
60 Refit the cylinder head (where removed) and also refit the crankshaft sprocket and timing belt.

2.0 litre diesel engine

61 Using a little grease, stick the thrustwashers to each side of No 2 main bearing upper location and bearing cap **(see illustration 17.51)**. Ensure that the oilway grooves on each thrustwasher face outwards (away from the cylinder block).
62 Place the bearing shells in their locations **(see illustrations)**. If new shells are being fitted, ensure that all traces of protective grease are cleaned off using paraffin. Wipe dry the shells and connecting rods with a lint-free cloth. Liberally lubricate each bearing shell in the cylinder block/crankcase and cap with clean engine oil.
63 Lower the crankshaft into position so that Nos 2 and 3 cylinder crankpins are at TDC; Nos 1 and 4 cylinder crankpins will be at BDC, ready for fitting No 1 piston. Check the crankshaft endfloat, referring to Section 13.
64 Lubricate the lower bearing shells in the main bearing caps with clean engine oil. Make sure that the locating lugs on the shells engage with the corresponding recesses in the caps.
65 Fit main bearing caps Nos 2 to 5 to their correct locations, ensuring that they are fitted the correct way round (the bearing shell tab recesses in the block and caps must be on the same side) **(see illustration)**. Ensure the thrustwashers remain correctly fitted to No 2 bearing cap then refit the bearing cap bolts, tightening them only lightly at this stage.
66 Apply a small amount of sealant to the No 1 main bearing cap mating face on the cylinder block, around the sealing strip holes **(see illustration)**.
67 Locate the tab of each sealing strip over the pins on the base of No 1 bearing cap, and press the strips into the bearing cap grooves. It is now necessary to obtain two thin metal strips, of 0.25 mm thickness or less, in order to prevent the strips moving when the cap is being fitted. Citroën garages use the tool shown, which acts as a clamp. Metal strips (such as old feeler blades) can be used, provided all burrs that may damage the sealing strips are first removed **(see illustrations)**.
68 Where applicable, oil both sides of the metal strips, and hold them on the sealing strips. Fit the No 1 main bearing cap, insert the bolts loosely, and then carefully pull out the metal strips in a horizontal direction, using a pair of pliers **(see illustration)**.
69 Working in sequence **(see illustration)**, tighten the main bearing cap bolts evenly and progressively to the specified Stage 1 torque wrench setting. Once all the bolts have been

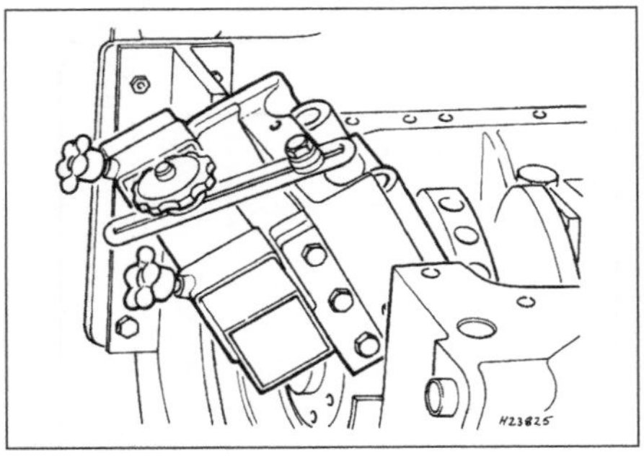

17.67b Using the Citroën tool to fit the No 1 main bearing cap

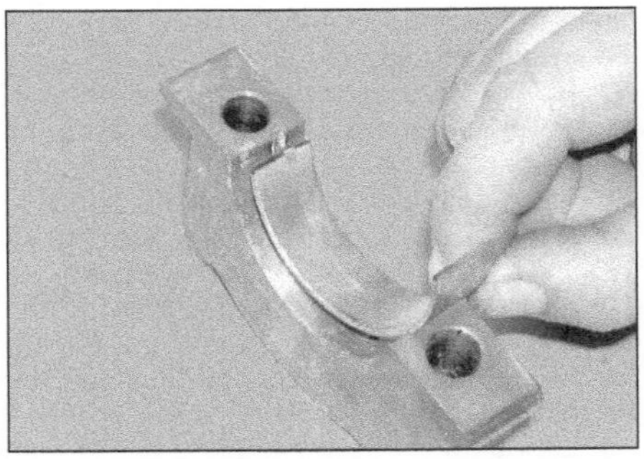

17.62b ... and the plain bearing shells are fitted to the bearing caps

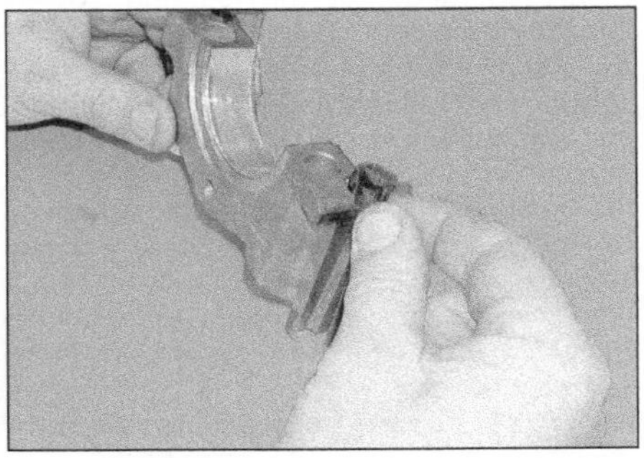

17.67a Fit the sealing strips to each side of No 1 main bearing cap, ensuring they are correctly engaged

17.68 Using 2 metal strips to hold the sealing strips in place as the bearing cap is fitted

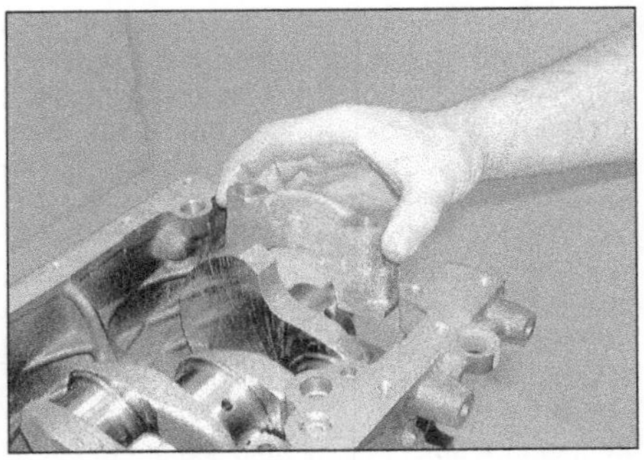

17.65 Fit the No 2 to 5 bearing caps and install the bolts

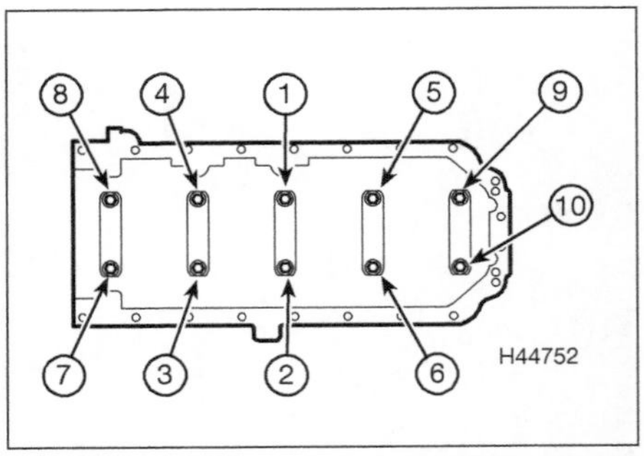

17.69 Main bearing cap bolt tightening sequence

tightened to the Stage 1 setting, working in the specified sequence, angle-tighten the bolts through the specified Stage 2 angle, using a socket and extension bar. It is recommended that an angle-measuring gauge be used during this stage of the tightening, to ensure accuracy. If a gauge is not available, use a dab of white paint to make alignment marks between the bolt head and casting prior to tightening; the marks can then be used to check that the bolt has been rotated sufficiently during tightening.

70 Check that the sealing strips protrude slightly from above the cylinder block/ crankcase mating surface by approximately 1 mm. If not, remove the bearing cap again and refit; the seals are supplied the correct length and should not be cut. Also check that the crankshaft rotates freely.

71 Fit a new crankshaft left-hand (flywheel end) oil seal as described in Chapter 2D, Section 14.

72 Refit the piston/connecting rod assemblies to the crankshaft as described in Section 18.

73 Fit a new sealing ring (where fitted) the crankshaft then refit the Woodruff key and slide on the oil pump drive sprocket and spacer. Locate the drive chain on the sprocket.

74 Ensure that the mating surfaces of the right-hand (timing belt end) oil seal housing and cylinder block are clean and dry. Note the correct fitted depth of the oil seal then, using a large flat-bladed screwdriver, lever the old seal out of the housing.

75 Apply a smear of suitable sealant to the oil seal housing mating surface. Ensure that the locating dowels are in position, and then slide the housing over the end of the crankshaft and into position on the cylinder block. Tighten the housing retaining bolts to the specified torque.

76 Fit a new crankshaft right-hand (timing belt end) oil seal as described in Chapter 2D, Section 14.

77 Ensuring that the drive chain is correctly located on the sprocket, refit the oil pump and sump as described in Chapter 2D, Section 12 and 11.

78 Refit the flywheel as described in Chapter 2D, Section 16.

79 Refit the cylinder head (where removed) and also refit the crankshaft sprocket and timing belt.

18 Piston/connecting rod assembly – refitting

Note: *New big-end cap nuts/bolts must be used on refitting.*

1 Note that the following procedure assumes that, the cylinder liners (1.4 litre petrol engines) are in position in the cylinder block/crankcase as described in Section 11, and that the crankshaft and main bearing ladder/caps are in place.

2 Clean the backs of the bearing shells, and the bearing locations in both the connecting rod and bearing cap.

All except 1.6 litre diesel engine

3 Press the bearing shells into their locations, ensuring that the tab on each shell engages in the notch in the connecting rod and cap. Take care not to touch any shell's bearing surface with your fingers **(see illustration)**.

All engines

4 Lubricate the cylinder bores, the pistons and piston rings, then lay out each piston/connecting rod assembly in its respective position.

5 Start with assembly No 1. Make sure that the piston rings are still spaced as described in Section 16, and then clamp them in position with a piston ring compressor.

6 Insert the piston/connecting rod assembly into the top of cylinder number 1; ensuring the piston is correctly positioned as follows.

a) On petrol engines, ensure that the arrow on the piston crown is pointing towards the timing belt/chain end of the engine.

b) On 1.6 litre diesel engines, ensure that the DIST mark or arrow on the piston crown is towards the timing belt end of the engine.

c) On 2.0 litre diesel engines, ensure that the valve recesses on the piston crown are towards the rear of the cylinder block.

7 Once the piston is correctly positioned, using a block of wood or hammer handle against the piston crown, tap the assembly into the cylinder until the piston crown is flush with the top of the cylinder **(see illustration)**.

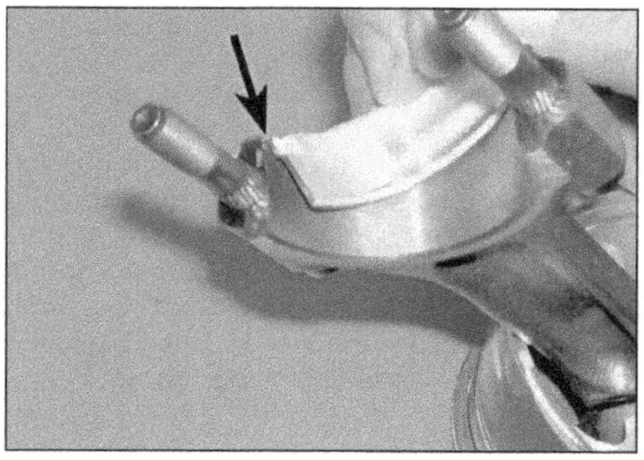

18.3 Ensure the bearing shell tab (arrowed) locates correctly in the cut-out

All except 1.6 litre diesel engine

8 Ensure that the bearing shell is still correctly installed. Liberally lubricate the crankpin and both bearing shells. Taking care not to mark the cylinder bores, pull the piston/connecting rod assembly down the bore and onto the crankpin. Refit the big-end bearing cap and fit the new nuts, tightening them finger-tight at first **(see illustration)**. Note that the faces with the identification marks must match (which means that the bearing shell locating tabs abut each other).

9 Tighten the bearing cap retaining nuts evenly and progressively to the specified torque setting.

1.6 litre diesel engine

10 On these engines, the connecting rod is made in one piece, and the big-end bearing cap is 'cracked' off. This ensures that the cap fits onto the connecting rod only in one position, and with maximum rigidity. Consequently, there are no locating notches for the bearing shells to fit into.

11 To ensure that the big-end bearing shells are centrally located in the connecting rod and cap, two special tools are available from Citroën. These half-moon shaped tools are pressed in from either side of the rod/cap and locate the shell exactly in the centre **(see illustration)**. Fit the shells into the connecting

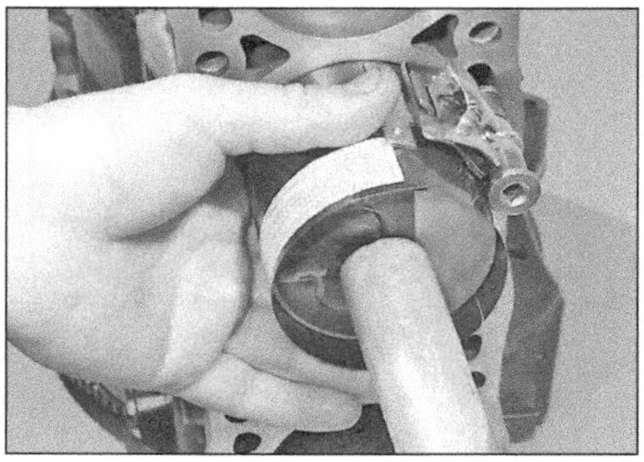

18.7 Tap the piston into the bore using a hammer handle

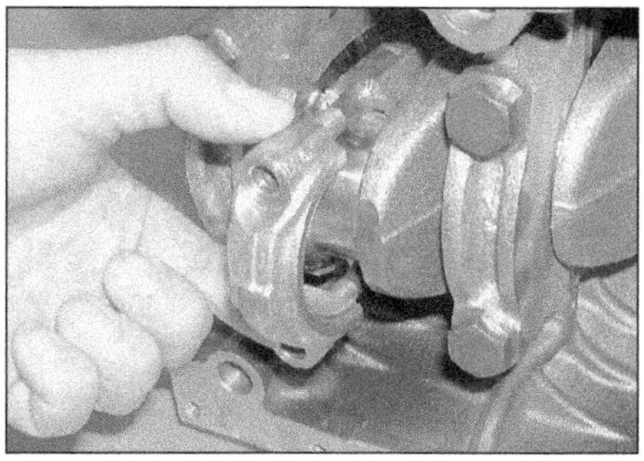

18.8 Fit the big-end bearing cap, ensuring it is fitted the right way around, and screw on the new nuts

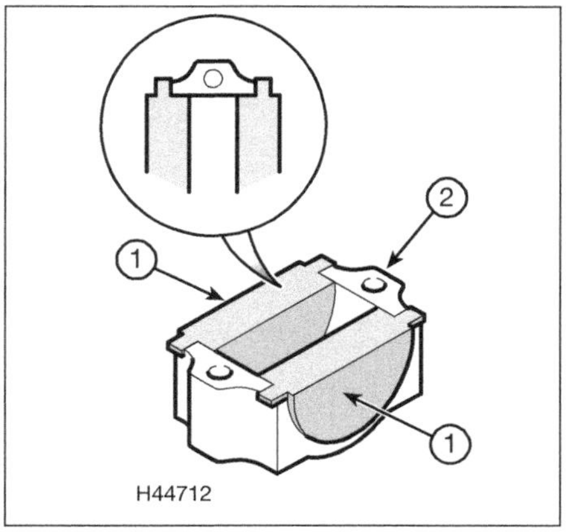

18.11 Big-end bearing shell positioning (1.6 litre diesel engine)

1 Tool No 0194-P 2 Bearing shell

rods and big-end caps and lubricate them with plenty of clean engine oil.

12 Pull the connecting rods and pistons down the bores and onto the crankshaft journals. Fit the big-end caps – they will only fit properly one way round (see paragraph 10), and insert the new bolts.

13 Tighten the bolts to the Stage 1 torque setting, then slacken them 180° (Stage 2). Tighten the bolts to the Stage 3 setting, followed by the Stage 4 angle-tightening setting.

All engines

14 Once the bearing cap retaining nuts have been correctly tightened, rotate the crankshaft. Check that it turns freely; some stiffness is to be expected if new components have been fitted, but there should be no signs of binding or tight spots.

15 Refit the cylinder head and oil pump as described in Chapter 2A, 2B, 2C or 2D (as applicable).

19 Engine – initial start-up after overhaul

1 With the engine refitted in the vehicle, double-check the engine oil and coolant levels. Make a final check that everything has been reconnected, and that there are no tools or rags left in the engine compartment.

Petrol engine models

2 Remove the spark plugs (Chapter 1A, Section 20) and disable the fuel system by disconnecting the wiring connectors from the fuel injectors, referring to Chapter 4A, Section 12 for further information.

3 Turn the engine on the starter until the oil pressure warning light goes out. Refit the spark plugs, and reconnect the wiring.

Diesel engine models

4 On the models covered in this Manual, the oil pressure warning light is linked to the STOP warning light, and is not illuminated when the ignition is initially switched on. Therefore it is not possible to check the oil pressure warning light when turning the engine on the starter motor.

5 Prime the fuel system (refer to Chapter 4B, Section 3).

6 Fully depress the accelerator pedal, turn the ignition key to position M, and wait for the preheating warning light to go out.

All models

7 Start the engine, noting that this may take a little longer than usual, due to the fuel system components having been disturbed.

8 While the engine is idling, check for fuel, water and oil leaks. Don't be alarmed if there are some odd smells and smoke from parts getting hot and burning off oil deposits.

9 Assuming all is well; keep the engine idling until hot water is felt circulating through the top hose, then switch off the engine.

10 After a few minutes, recheck the oil and coolant levels as described in *Weekly checks*, and top-up as necessary.

11 Note that there is no need to retighten the cylinder head bolts once the engine has first run after reassembly.

12 If new pistons, rings or crankshaft bearings have been fitted, the engine must be treated as new, and run-in for the first 500 miles. Do not operate the engine at full-throttle, or allow it to labour at low engine speeds in any gear. It is recommended that the oil and filter be changed at the end of this period.

Chapter 3
Cooling, heating and ventilation systems

Contents

Degrees of difficulty

Easy, suitable for novice with little experience	**Fairly easy,** suitable for beginner with some experience	**Fairly difficult,** suitable for competent DIY mechanic	**Difficult,** suitable for experienced DIY mechanic	**Very difficult,** suitable for expert DIY or professional

Specifications

General

Maximum system pressure	1.4 bars
Engine coolant temperature sensor resistance (approx):	
Petrol engines:	
20°C	6100 ohms
80°C	620 ohms
Diesel engines:	
60°C	1266 ohms
80°C	642 ohms

Thermostat

Start of opening temperature:	
Petrol models:	
Non-VTi engines	89°C
VTi engines	82°C
Diesel engine	83°C

Air conditioning compressor oil

Quantity	120 cc
Type	SP10

Compressor

All engines except 1.6 litre non-VTi	SD 6C 12
1.6 litre non-VTi engines	SD 6V 12

Refrigerant

Quantity:	
Petrol models	450 ± 25 g
Diesel models:	
Up to RPO number 10553	670 ± 25 g
From RPO number 10554	450 ± 25 g
Type	R134a

Torque wrench settings

	Nm	lbf ft
Air conditioning compressor mounting bolts:		
Petrol engines	25	18
Diesel engines:		
1.6 litre engine	25	18
2.0 litre engine	35	26
Coolant outlet housing	10	7
Coolant pump:		
Non-VTi petrol engines:		
Upper bolt	16	12
Lower bolt	8	6
VTi petrol engines	10	7
Diesel engines:		
1.6 litre engine	10	7
2.0 litre engine	16	12
Coolant pump friction wheel assembly bolts (VTi petrol engines)	8	6
Coolant temperature sensor (non-VTi petrol engines)	16	12

1 General information and precautions

1 The cooling system is of pressurised type, comprising a coolant pump driven by the timing belt or auxiliary belt on VTi petrol engines, an aluminium radiator, an expansion tank, an electric cooling fan, a thermostat, a heater matrix, and all associated hoses and switches.

2 The system functions as follows. Cold coolant in the bottom of the radiator passes through the bottom hose to the coolant pump, where it is pumped around the cylinder block and head passages. After cooling the cylinder bores, combustion surfaces and valve seats, the coolant reaches the underside of the thermostat, which is initially closed. The coolant passes through the heater, and is returned via the cylinder block to the coolant pump.

3 When the engine is cold, the coolant circulates only through the cylinder block, cylinder head, and heater. When the coolant reaches a predetermined temperature, the thermostat opens, and the coolant passes through the top hose to the radiator. As the coolant passes down through the radiator, it is cooled by the inrush of air when the car is in forward motion. The airflow is supplemented by the action of the electric cooling fan when necessary. Upon reaching the bottom of the radiator, the coolant has now cooled, and the cycle is repeated.

4 On models with automatic transmission, a proportion of the coolant is recirculated through the transmission fluid cooler mounted on the transmission. On models fitted with an engine oil cooler, the coolant is also passed through the oil cooler.

5 The operation of the electric cooling fan(s) is controlled by the engine management control unit.

Warning: Do not attempt to remove the expansion tank filler cap, or to disturb any part of the cooling system, while the engine is hot, as there is a high risk of scalding. If the expansion tank filler cap must be removed before the engine and radiator have fully cooled (even though this is not recommended), the pressure in the cooling system must first be relieved. Cover the cap with a thick layer of cloth to avoid scalding, and slowly unscrew the filler cap until a hissing sound is heard. When the hissing has stopped, indicating that the pressure has reduced, slowly unscrew the filler cap until it can be removed; if more hissing sounds are heard, wait until they have stopped before unscrewing the cap. At all times keep well away from the filler cap opening, and protect your hands.

Warning: Do not allow antifreeze to come into contact with your skin, or with the painted surfaces of the vehicle. Rinse off spills immediately, with plenty of water. Never leave antifreeze lying around in an open container, or in a puddle in the driveway or on the garage floor. Children and pets are attracted by its sweet smell, but antifreeze can be fatal if ingested.

2.4 Slacken the upper hose retaining clip (arrowed)

Warning: If the engine is hot, the electric cooling fan(s) may start rotating even if the engine is not running. Be careful to keep your hands, hair, and any loose clothing well clear when working in the engine compartment.

Warning: Refer to Section 11 for precautions to be observed when working on models equipped with air conditioning.

2 Cooling system hoses – disconnection and renewal

Note: *Refer to the warnings given in Section 1 of this Chapter before proceeding. Hoses should only be disconnected once the engine has cooled sufficiently to avoid scalding.*

1 If the checks described in the hose and fluid leak check in Chapter 1A, Section 4 or Chapter 1B, Section 4 reveal a faulty hose, it must be renewed as follows.

2 First drain the cooling system (see Chapter 1A, Section 25 or Chapter 1B, Section 20). If the coolant is not due for renewal, it may be re-used, providing it is collected in a clean container.

3 To disconnect a hose, proceed as follows, according to the type of hose connection.

Conventional connections

4 On conventional connections, the clips used to secure the hoses in position may be either standard worm-drive clips **(see illustration)**, spring clips or disposable crimped types. The crimped type of clip is not designed to be re-used and should be updated with a worm-drive type on reassembly.

5 To disconnect a hose, release the retaining clips and move them along the hose, clear of the relevant inlet/outlet. Carefully work the hose free. The hoses can be removed with

2.5 Release the retaining clip and move it along the hose

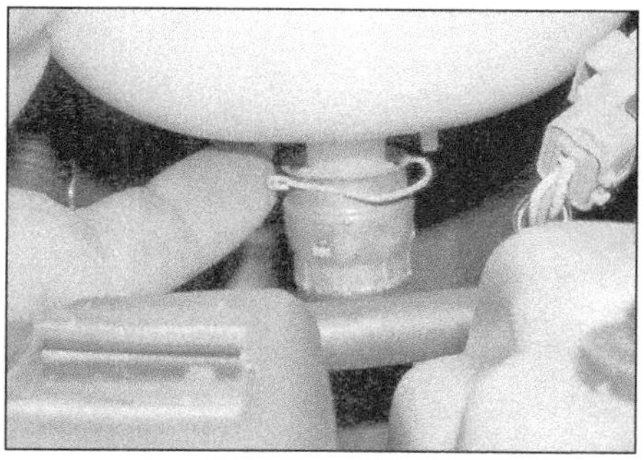

2.12 Where click-fit connectors are used, prise out the circlip then disconnect the hose

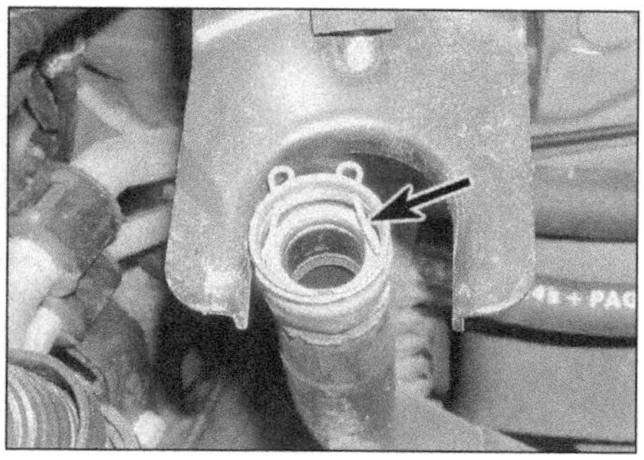

2.13 Ensure the sealing ring and circlip (arrowed) are correctly fitted to the hose union before reconnecting a connector

relative ease when new – on an older car they may have stuck **(see illustration)**.

6 If a hose proves to be difficult to remove, try to release it by rotating its ends before attempting to free it. Gently prise the end of the hose with a blunt instrument (such as a flat-bladed screwdriver), but do not apply too much force, and take care not to damage the pipe stubs or hoses. Note in particular that the radiator inlet stub is fragile; do not use excessive force when attempting to remove the hose. If all else fails, cut the hose with a sharp knife, then slit it so that it can be peeled off in two pieces. Although this may prove expensive if the hose is otherwise undamaged, it is preferable to buying a new radiator. Check first, however, that a new hose is readily available.

7 When fitting a hose, first slide the clips onto the hose, and then work the hose into position. If crimped-type clips were originally fitted, use standard worm-drive clips when refitting the hose.

8 Work the hose into position, checking that it is correctly routed, and then slide each clip back along the hose until it passes over the flared end of the relevant inlet/outlet, before tightening the clip securely.

9 Refill the cooling system (see Chapter 1A, Section 25 or Chapter 1B, Section 20).

10 Check thoroughly for leaks as soon as possible after disturbing any part of the cooling system.

Click-fit connections

Note: *New sealing ring should be used when reconnecting the hose.*

11 On certain models, some cooling system hoses are secured in position with click-fit connectors where the hose is retained by a large circlip.

12 To disconnect this type of hose fitting, carefully prise the wire clip out of position then disconnect the hose connection **(see illustration)**. Once the hose has been disconnected, refit the wire clip to the hose union. Inspect the hose unit sealing ring for signs of damage or deterioration and renew if necessary.

13 On refitting, ensure that the sealing ring is in position and the wire clip is correctly located in the groove in the union **(see illustration)**. Lubricate the sealing ring with a smear of soapy water, to ease installation, and then push the hose into its union until it is heard to click into position.

14 Ensure the hose is securely retained by the wire clip then refill the cooling system as described in Chapter 1A, Section 25 or Chapter 1B, Section 20.

15 Check thoroughly for leaks as soon as possible after disturbing any part of the cooling system.

3.2 Remove the plastic trim cover

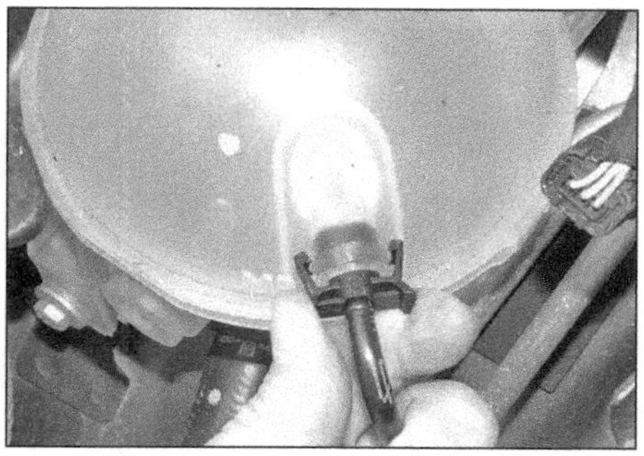

3.3a Squeeze the clips to disconnect the coolant pipe ...

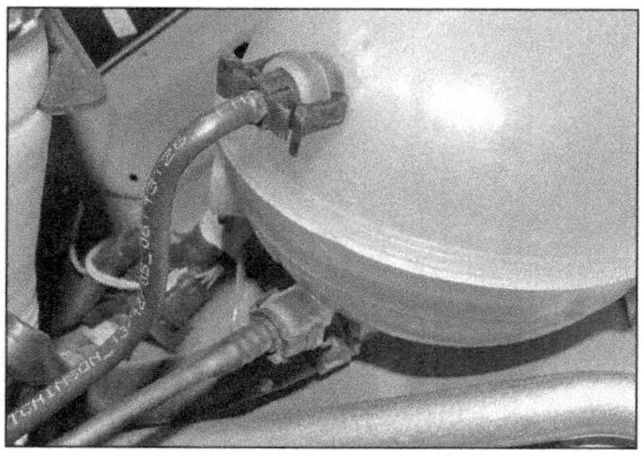

3.3b ... some models have a lower pipe also

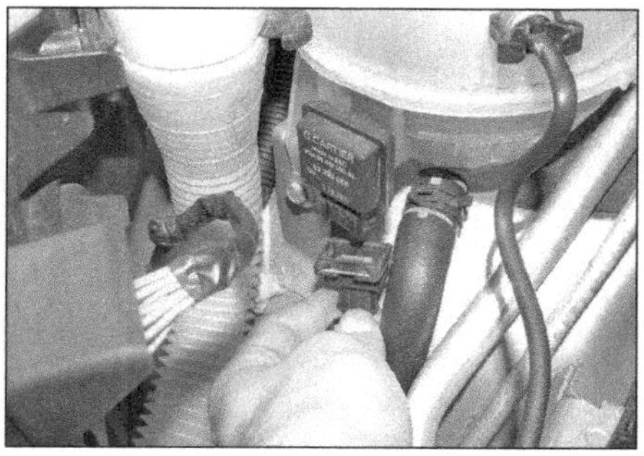

3.4 Disconnect the sensor wiring connector

3 Coolant expansion tank – removal and refitting

Removal

1 Referring to Chapter 1A, Section 25 or Chapter 1B, Section 20, drain the cooling system sufficiently to empty the contents of the expansion tank. Do not drain any more coolant than is necessary.

2 Release the retaining clips and remove the plastic trim from above the coolant expansion tank **(see illustration)**.

3 Squeeze together the collar, and then pull the plastic hose(s) from the expansion tank **(see illustrations)**. On some models, the hoses may be secured by expanding clamps.

4 Disconnect the level sensor wiring plug – where fitted **(see illustration)**.

5 Unscrew the mounting bolt and free the tank

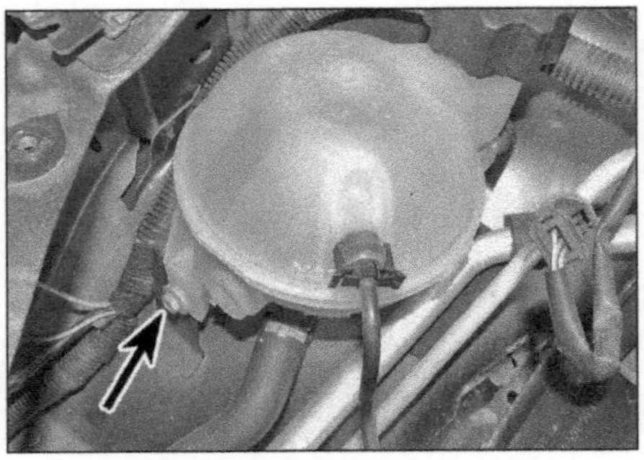

3.5 Coolant reservoir mounting bolt (arrowed)

from its mount **(see illustration)**. Withdraw the expansion tank from the mounting rubbers in the inner wing panel.

6 Slacken the clip and disconnect the remaining hose from the bottom of the expansion tank **(see illustration)**, as it is removed.

Refitting

7 Refitting is the reverse of removal, ensuring the hoses are securely reconnected. On completion, top-up the coolant level as described in *Weekly checks*.

4 **Radiator** – removal, inspection and refitting

Note: *If leakage is the reason for removing the radiator, bear in mind that minor leaks can often be cured using a radiator sealant with the radiator still in position.*

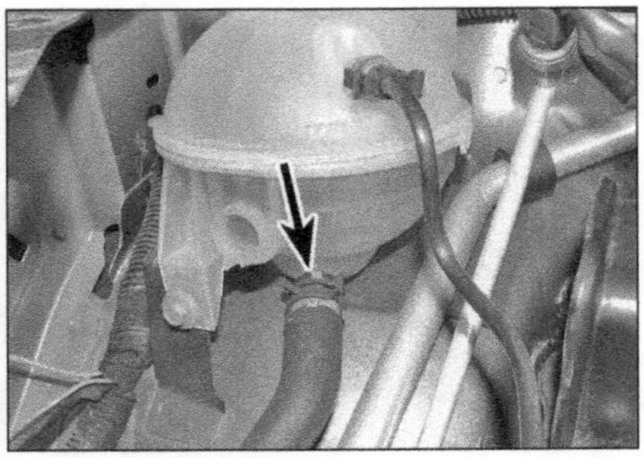

3.6 Release the coolant hose securing clip (arrowed)

Removal

1 Drain the cooling system (see Chapter 1A, Section 25 or Chapter 1B, Section 20).

2 Remove the front bumper as described in Chapter 11, Section 6.

3 Release the retaining clips and disconnect the upper and lower coolant hoses from the radiator **(see illustrations)**. The lower hose may have already been removed to drain the cooling system, see paragraph 1.

4 On models with AL4 automatic transmissions, disconnect the transmission cooler hose from the lower part of the radiator **(see illustration)**.

5 Squeeze together the collar, then pull the plastic hose to disconnect it from the top of the radiator **(see illustration)**.

6 Slacken and remove the retaining screws securing the radiator upper mounting brackets to the front panel. Move the radiator away from the front panel and unclip both brackets from the top of the radiator **(see illustration)**.

7 Carefully lift the radiator out of position, taking care not to damage the radiator fins.

Inspection

8 If the radiator has been removed due to suspected blockage, reverse-flush it as described in Chapter 1A, Section 25 or Chapter 1B, Section 20. Clean dirt and debris from the radiator fins, using an airline (in which case, wear eye protection) or a soft brush. Be careful, as the fins are sharp, and easily damaged.

9 If necessary, a radiator specialist can perform a 'flow test' on the radiator, to establish whether an internal blockage exists.

10 A leaking radiator must be referred to a specialist for permanent repair. Do not attempt to weld or solder a leaking radiator, as damage to the plastic components may result.

11 Inspect the condition of the radiator mounting rubbers, and renew them if necessary. Check the radiator lower mounting rubbers are in position, before refitting.

Refitting

12 Refitting is a reversal of removal, bearing in mind the following points:

*a) Ensure that the lower lugs on the radiator are correctly engaged with the mounting rubbers in the body panel **(see illustration)**.*

4.3a Disconnect the upper hose retaining clip (arrowed) ...

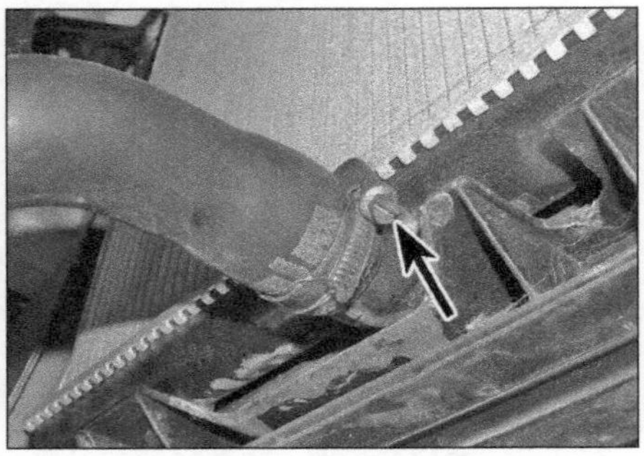

4.3b ... and the lower radiator hose retaining clip (arrowed)

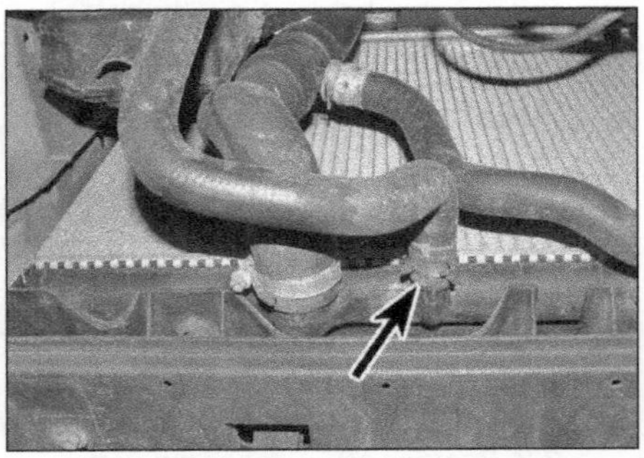

4.4 Cooler hose (arrowed) on the AL4 automatic transmission

4.5 Squeeze the clips to disconnect the coolant pipe from the top of the radiator

4.6 Radiator upper mounting screws (arrowed)

4.12 Locate the radiator locating pegs in the rubber mountings (arrowed)

b) Reconnect the hoses with reference to Section 2, using new sealing rings where applicable.
c) On completion, refill the cooling system as described in Chapter 1A, Section 25 or Chapter 1B, Section 20.

5 Thermostat – removal, testing and refitting

5.9 Unclip the wiring loom mounting bracket

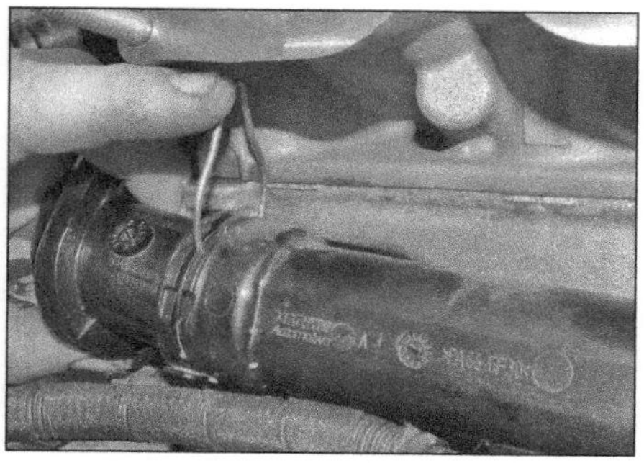

5.10 Release the securing clip from the rear of the coolant housing

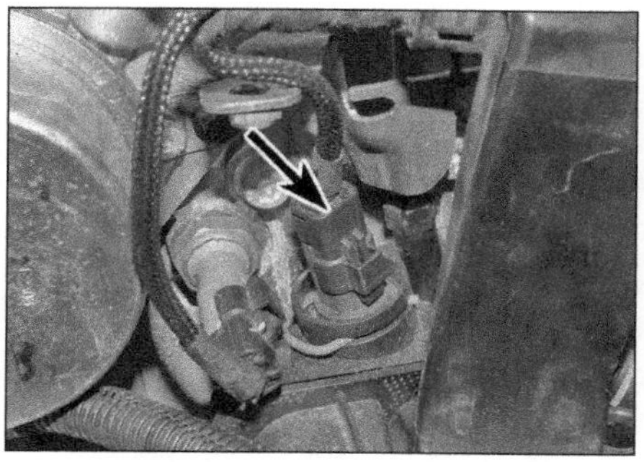

5.11a Disconnect the temperature sensor wiring connector (arrowed) ...

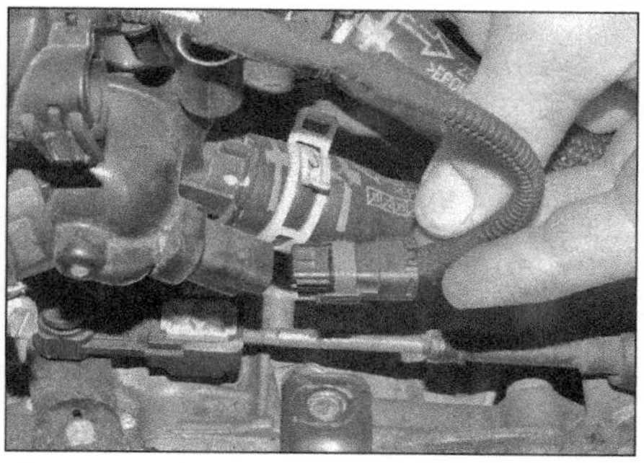

5.11b ... and the electronically-controlled thermostat

Removal

1 The thermostat is located in the coolant outlet housing on the left-hand end of the cylinder head. On all later models the thermostat is integral with the housing, requiring removal of the complete housing. On early non-VTi petrol engines and early 2.0 litre diesel engines the thermostat can be removed without having to remove the complete housing.
2 Drain the cooling system (see Chapter 1A, Section 25 or Chapter 1B, Section 20).
3 To make access easier remove the air cleaner ducting as described in Chapter 4A, Section 2 or Chapter 4B, Section 4, and also the battery as described in Chapter 5A, Section 4.

Petrol models

Non-VTi engines up to RPO No 10436

4 Disconnect the top hose from the front of the coolant housing.
5 Unscrew the two retaining bolts, and then remove the thermostat from the front of the coolant housing. Recover the gasket/seal a new one will be required for refitting.

Non-VTi engines from RPO No 10437

6 Disconnect the wiring connector from the temperature sensor in the top of the coolant housing.
7 Note the fitted position of the hoses, and then disconnect them from the coolant housing.
8 Unscrew the four retaining bolts, and then remove the housing, recover the gasket/seal a new one will be required for refitting. **Note:** *The thermostat is part of the coolant housing.*

VTi engines

9 Disconnect the wiring connectors from the camshaft position sensors and oil pressure sensor on the end of the cylinder head. Slide the wiring loom bracket upwards, disconnect it from the end of the cylinder head and move it to one side **(see illustration)**.
10 Release the retaining clip at the rear of the cylinder head, where the thermostat housing joins the pipe around the rear of the engine to the coolant pump **(see illustration)**.
11 Disconnect the wiring connectors from the temperature sensor in the top of the coolant housing and the electronically-controlled thermostat connector at the bottom of the coolant housing **(see illustrations)**.
12 Note the fitted position of the hoses, and then disconnect them from the coolant housing **(see illustration)**.
13 Unscrew the two retaining bolts at the bottom of the housing and the retaining nut at the top of the housing, then remove the housing. Recover the gasket/seal, a new one will be required for refitting. **Note:** *The coolant housing will need to be disengaged from the coolant pipe at the rear of the engine on removal.*

Diesel models

1.6 litre engines

14 Disconnect the wiring connector from the temperature sensor in the coolant housing **(see illustration)**.
15 Note the fitted position of the hoses, and then disconnect them from the coolant housing.
16 Unscrew the four retaining bolts, and then remove the housing from the left-hand end of the cylinder head. Recover the gasket/seal a new one will be required for refitting.

2.0 litre engines up to RPO No 10289

17 Unclip the wiring loom from the mounting bracket, and then remove the mounting bracket to access the coolant housing **(see illustration)**.

5.12 Note the position of the hoses before removal

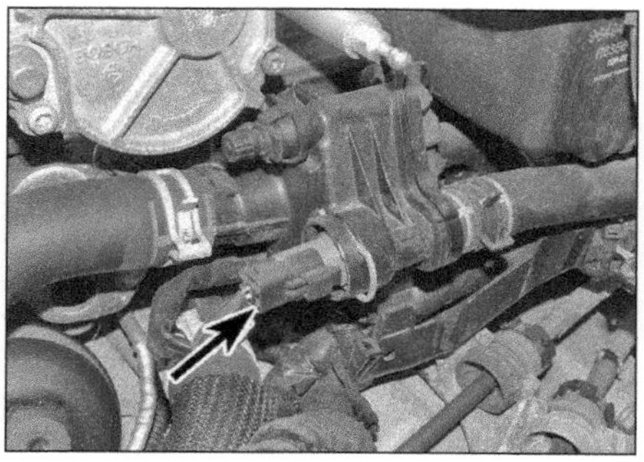

5.14 Disconnect the temperature sensor wiring connector (arrowed)

5.17 Unclip the wiring loom from the bracket

5.23 Thermostat housing retaining nuts (arrowed)

18 Disconnect the top hose from the front of the coolant housing.

19 Unscrew the three retaining bolts, and then remove the thermostat housing from the front of the coolant housing. Recover the gasket/seal a new one will be required for refitting.

2.0 litre engines from RPO No 10290

20 Unclip the wiring loom from the mounting bracket, and then remove the mounting bracket to access the coolant housing **(see illustration 5.17)**.

21 Disconnect the wiring connector from the temperature sensor in the coolant housing.

22 Note the fitted position of the hoses, and then disconnect them from the coolant housing.

23 Unscrew the retaining bolts, and then remove the housing from the left-hand end of the cylinder head **(see illustration)**. Recover the gasket/seal a new one will be required for refitting.

Testing

24 A rough test of the thermostat may be made by suspending it with a piece of string in a container full of water. Heat the water to bring it to the boil – the thermostat must open by the time the water boils. If not, renew it.

25 If a thermometer is available, the precise opening temperature of the thermostat may be determined; compare with the figures given in the Specifications. The opening temperature may also be marked on the thermostat.

26 A thermostat which fails to close as the water cools must also be renewed.

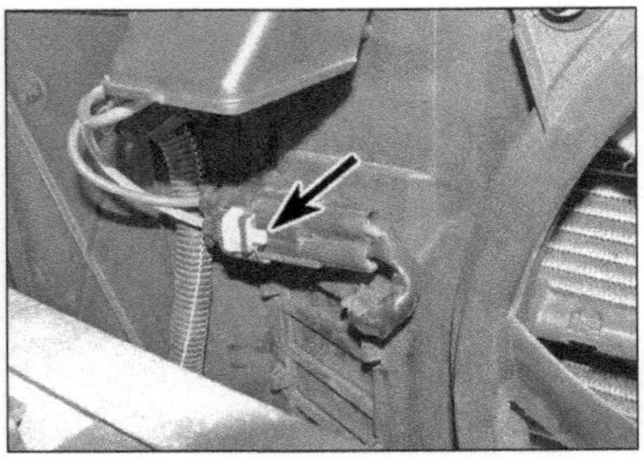

6.2 Release the securing clip (arrowed)

6.4a Undo the four cooling fan bolts (arrowed) ...

Refitting

27 Refitting is a reversal of removal, bearing in mind the following points.

a) Renew the coolant housing gasket/seal.
b) Make sure all wiring connectors are fitted securely.
c) On completion, refill the cooling system as described in Chapter 1A, Section 25 or Chapter 1B, Section 20.

6 Electric cooling fan and resistor – removal and refitting

Removal

1 Remove the front bumper as described in Chapter 11, Section 6.

Cooling fan

2 Release the locking clip, then disconnect the fan wiring plug connector and release it from the securing clip on the radiator front panel **(see illustration)**.

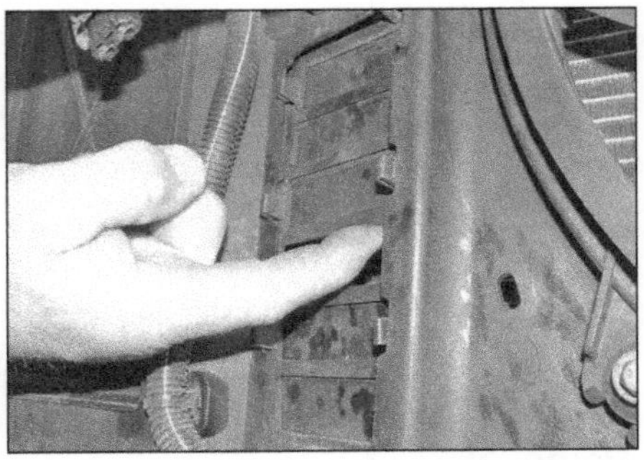

6.3 Unclip the louvered vent panel

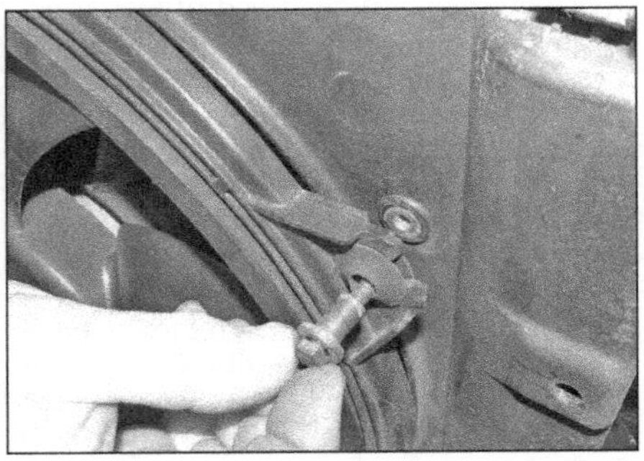

6.4b ... noting the collars fitted to the bolts for refitting

3 Unclip the louvered vent panel from the radiator front panel to allow for the wiring to be withdrawn **(see illustration)**.

4 Slacken and remove the four bolts and washers securing the cooling fan to the radiator front panel. Recover the collar from the rear of each mounting rubber **(see illustrations)**.

5 Remove the cooling fan from the front panel, and withdraw the fan and wiring out from the front panel **(see illustrations)**.

Cooling fan resistor

6 The cooling fan resistor is fitted to the radiator front panel and is located next to the cooling fan.

7 Unclip the plastic cover from the front panel **(see illustration)**.

8 Disconnect the two wiring connectors

6.5a Remove the fan from the front panel

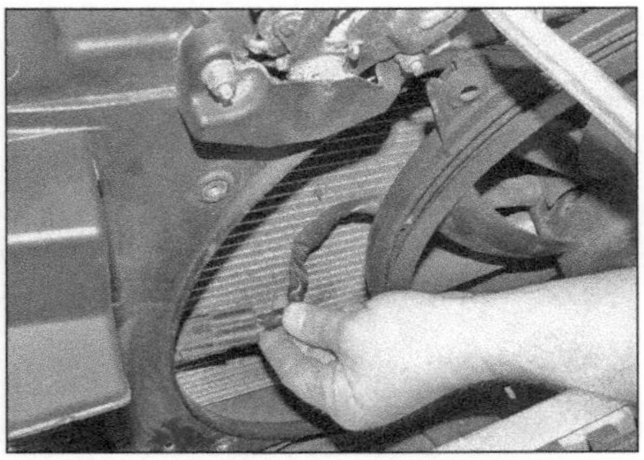

6.5b ... and withdraw the wiring connector from the front panel

6.7 Unclip the plastic cover from the resistor

from the fan control resistor, note the locking clip has to be released on the lower connector before it can be disconnected **(see illustrations)**.

9 Undo the retaining screw, and then remove the resistor from the front panel **(see illustrations)**.

Refitting

10 Refitting is a reversal of removal.

7 Cooling system electrical sensors – general information, removal and refitting

General information

1 The coolant temperature sensor is fitted to the coolant housing on the left-hand end of the cylinder head (see Section 5). The coolant temperature gauge and the cooling fan are all operated by the engine management ECU using the signal supplied by this sensor.

2 On VTi petrol models, there is a second wiring connector on the lower part of the coolant housing, this is for the electronically-controlled thermostat. The thermostat is integral with the housing, requiring removal of the complete housing, see Section 5.

3 To make access easier remove the air cleaner ducting as described in Chapter 4A, Section 2 or Chapter 4B, Section 4, and also the battery as described in Chapter 5A, Section 4.

Removal

Note: *Ensure the engine is cold before removing a temperature sensor.*

4 Partially drain the cooling system to just below the level of the sensor (as described in Chapter 1A, Section 25 or Chapter 1B, Section 20). Alternatively, have ready a suitable bung to plug the sensor aperture whilst the sensor is removed. If this method is used, take great care not to damage the switch aperture or use anything that will allow foreign matter to enter the cooling system.

5 Disconnect the wiring connector from the sensor **(see illustrations)**.

6 On all later models the sensor is clipped in place; prise out the sensor retaining circlip then remove the sensor and sealing ring from the housing **(see illustrations)**. If the system has not been drained, plug the sensor aperture to prevent further coolant loss.

7 On early non-VTi petrol engines and early 2.0 litre diesel engines (see Section 5) the sensors are screwed into the housing. Unscrew the sensor and recover the sealing washer (where applicable). If the system has not been drained, plug the sensor aperture to prevent further coolant loss.

6.8a Disconnect the wiring connectors ...

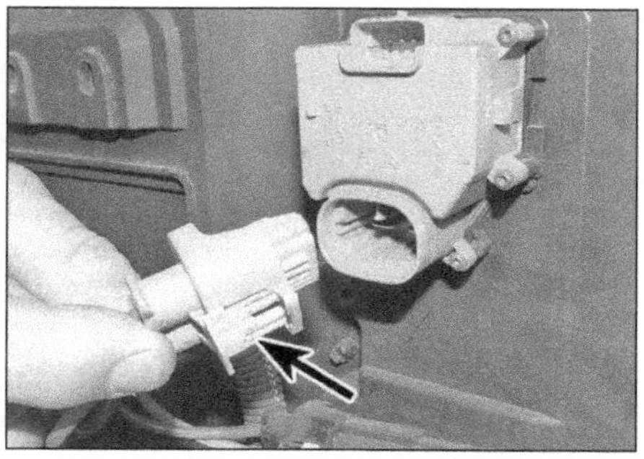

6.8b ... release the securing clip (arrowed)

6.9a Undo the retaining screw ...

6.9b ... and remove the cooling fan resistor

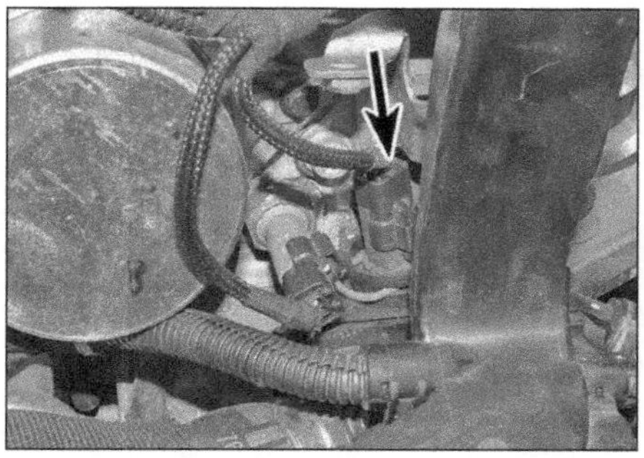

7.5a Temperature sensor wiring connector (arrowed) – 1.6 litre VTi petrol engines

7.5b Temperature sensor wiring connector (arrowed) – 1.6 litre diesel engines

7.5c Temperature sensor wiring connector (arrowed) – 2.0 litre diesel engines

7.6a Prise out the sensor securing clip ...

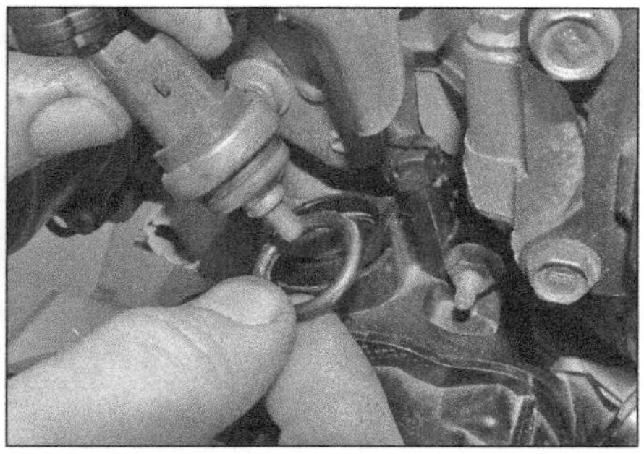

7.6b ... and pull out the sensor and seal from the housing

Refitting

8 Where the sensor is clipped in place, fit a new sealing ring to the sensor. Push the sensor firmly into the housing and secure it in position with the circlip, ensuring it is correctly located in the housing groove.

9 Where the sensor is screwed into the housing, if the sensor was originally fitted with sealing compound, clean the threads thoroughly, and coat them with fresh sealing compound. If the sensor was originally fitted using a sealing washer, use a new sealing washer. Fit the sensor and tighten securely.

10 Reconnect the wiring connector then refit any components removed from access. Refit the air cleaner and if removed, refit the battery.

11 Top-up the cooling system as described in *Weekly checks*.

8 Coolant pump – removal and refitting

Belt-driven pump

1 Drain the cooling system (see Chapter 1A, Section 25 or Chapter 1B, Section 20).

8.3a Remove the coolant pump ...

8.3b ... and recover the sealing ring – non-VTi petrol engines

Non-VTi petrol models

2 Remove the timing belt as described in Chapter 2A, Section 6.

3 Slacken and remove the retaining bolts from the coolant pump, and then withdraw it from the cylinder block. Recover the pump sealing ring/gasket (as applicable) and discard it; a new one must be used on refitting **(see illustrations)**. **Note:** *The sealing ring may not be available separately from the pump – check with your Citroën dealer.*

VTi petrol models

4 Slacken the coolant pump pulley retaining bolts **(see illustration)**; do not remove the bolts completely at this point.

5 Remove the auxiliary drivebelt as described in Chapter 1A, Section 10.

6 Undo the retaining bolts and remove the friction wheel drive from the cylinder block **(see illustrations)**.

7 The pulley bolts can now be completely removed and withdraw the pulley from the coolant pump **(see illustration)**.

8.4 Slacken the coolant pump pulley securing bolts (arrowed)

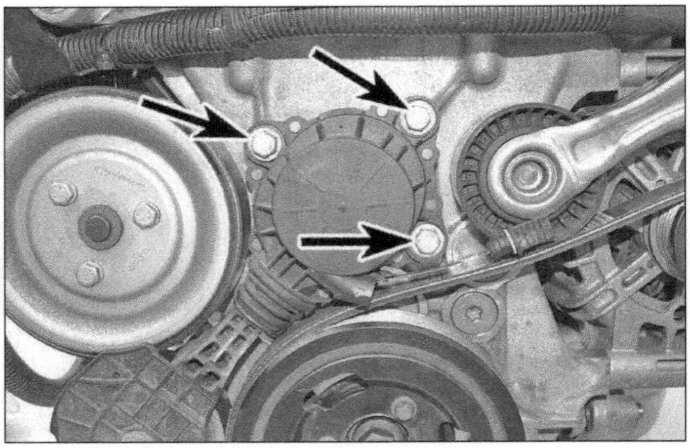

8.6a Undo the retaining bolts (arrowed) ...

8.6b ... and remove the friction wheel drive unit

8.7 Remove the coolant pump pulley

8.8a Undo the coolant pump bolts (arrowed) ...

8.8b ... and remove the coolant pump

8 Undo the coolant pump securing bolts, and then withdraw it from the cylinder block **(see illustrations)**.

Diesel models

9 Remove the timing belt as described in Chapter 2C, Section 7 (1.6 litre engines) or Chapter 2D, Section 7 (2.0 litre engines).

10 Slacken and remove the retaining bolts from the coolant pump, and then withdraw it from the cylinder block. Recover the pump sealing ring/gasket (as applicable) and discard it; a new one must be used on refitting **(see illustration)**. **Note:** *The sealing ring may not be available separately from the pump – check with your Citroën dealer.*

All models

11 Ensure that the pump and cylinder block/housing mating surfaces are clean and dry.

12 Fit the new sealing ring/gasket (as applicable) to the pump, and then refit the pump assembly, tightening its retaining bolts securely.

13 On diesel engines, refit the timing belt as described in Chapter 2C, Section 7 or Chapter 2D, Section 7.

14 On non-VTi petrol engines, refit the timing belt as described in Chapter 2A, Section 6.

15 On VTi petrol engines, refit the friction wheel drive to the cylinder block and refit the auxiliary drivebelt as described in Chapter 1A, Section 10.

16 Refill the cooling system as described in Chapter 1A, Section 25 or Chapter 1B, Section 20 (as applicable).

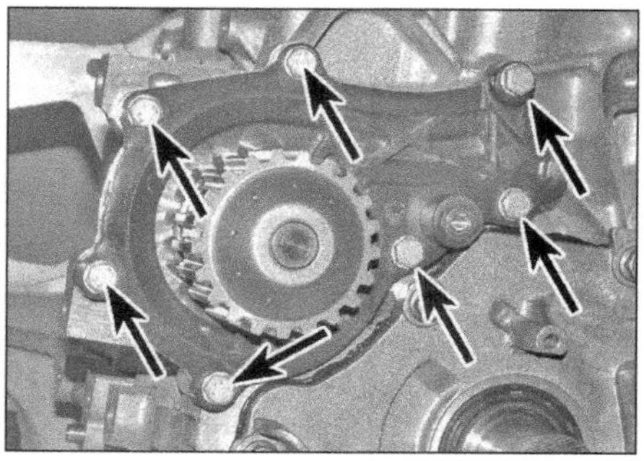

8.10 Undo the coolant pump bolts (arrowed) – 1.6 litre diesel engines

9 Heating and ventilation system – general information

Note: *Refer to Section 11 for information on the air conditioning side of the system.*

Manually-controlled system

1 The heating/ventilation system consists of a four-speed blower motor (housed behind the facia), face level vents in the centre and at each end of the facia, and air ducts to the front footwells.

2 The control unit is located in the facia, and the controls operate flap valves to deflect and mix the air flowing through the various parts of the heating/ventilation system. The flap valves are contained in the air distribution housing, which acts as a central distribution unit, passing air to the various ducts and vents.

3 Cold air enters the system through the grille in the scuttle. If required, the airflow is boosted by the blower, and then flows through the various ducts, according to the settings of the controls. Stale air is expelled through ducts at the rear of the vehicle. If warm air is required, the cold air is passed over the heater matrix, which is heated by the engine coolant.

4 A recirculation button enables the outside air supply to be closed off, while the air inside the vehicle is recirculated. This can be useful to prevent unpleasant odours entering from outside the vehicle, but should only be used briefly, as the recirculated air inside the vehicle will soon become stale.

9.9 Vehicle diagnostic plug connector (arrowed)

5 On some diesel engine models an electric heater is fitted into the heater housing. When the coolant temperature is cold, the heater warms the air before it enters the heater matrix. This quickly increases the temperature of the heater matrix on cold starts, resulting in warm air being available to heat the vehicle interior soon after start-up.

Automatic climate control

6 A fully automatic electronic climate control system was offered as an option on some models. The main components of the system are exactly the same as those described for the manual system, the only major difference being that the temperature and distribution flaps in the heating/ventilation housing are operated by electric motors rather than cables.

7 The operation of the system is controlled by the electronic control module (which is incorporated in the blower motor assembly) along with the following sensors.

a) *The passenger compartment sensor – informs the control module of the temperature of the air inside the passenger compartment.*
b) *Evaporator temperature sensor – informs the control module of the evaporator temperature.*
c) *Heater matrix temperature sensor – informs the control module of the heater matrix temperature.*

8 Using the information from the above sensors, the control module determines the appropriate settings for the heating/ventilation system housing flaps to maintain the passenger compartment at the desired setting on the control panel.

9 If the system develops a fault, the vehicle should be taken to a Citroën dealer. A complete test of the system can then be carried out, using a special electronic diagnostic test unit, which is simply plugged into the system's diagnostic connector. This is located below the ashtray, in the front of the centre console **(see illustration)**.

10.2a Unclip the trim covers ...

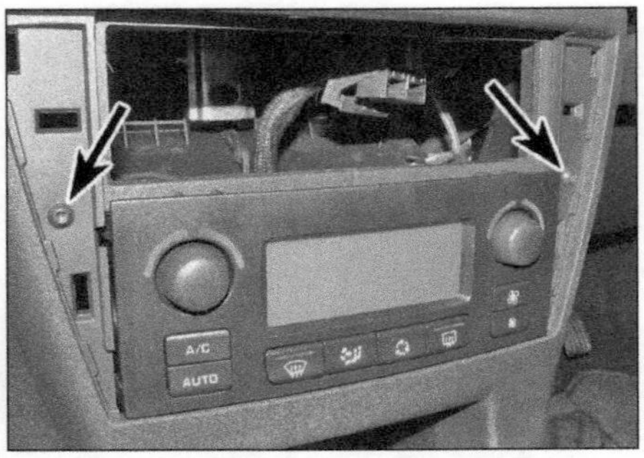

10.2b ... and remove the retaining screws (arrowed)

10.3 Remove the ashtray

10.4a Unclip the trim from around the gear lever – manual models

10.4b Unclip the trim from around the gear lever – automatic models

10.5a Unclip the lower part of the trim ...

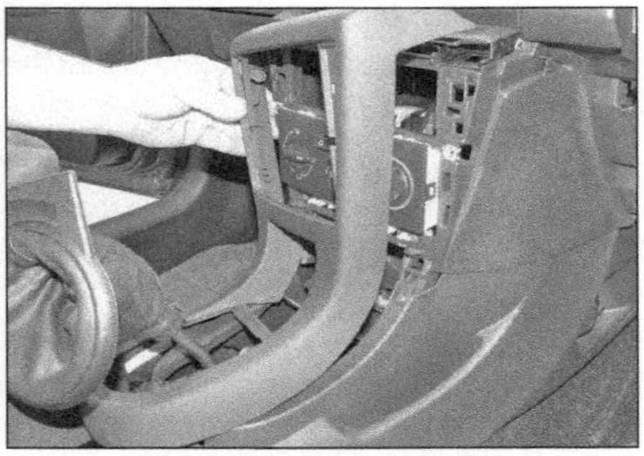

10.5b ... and then release the trim from the centre of the facia

10 Heater/ventilation components – removal and refitting

Control panel

1 Remove the audio unit from the facia, as described in Chapter 12, Section 17.

2 Carefully unclip the two trim panels from each side of the heater control panel and undo the retaining screws **(see illustrations)**.

3 Unclip the ashtray from the front of the centre console **(see illustration)**.

4 Release the retaining clips and remove the gear lever gaiter/trim from the front trim panel **(see illustrations)**.

5 Carefully unclip the lower part of the front trim panel and remove it from the facia and around the heater control panel **(see illustrations)**.

Manually-operated system

6 Remove the glovebox assembly, as described in Chapter 11, Section 27.

7 Release the retaining clips and remove the trim panel from the lower part of the steering column **(see illustration)**.

8 Slacken the retaining screws and disconnect the directional control (blue) cable from the right-hand side of the heater housing **(see illustrations)**.

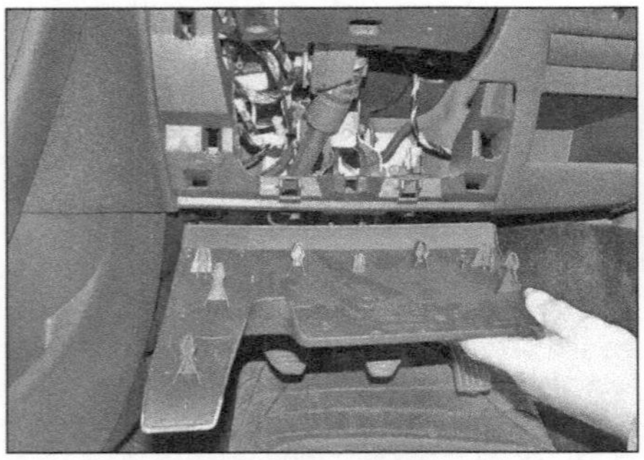

10.7 Unclip the driver's side lower facia trim

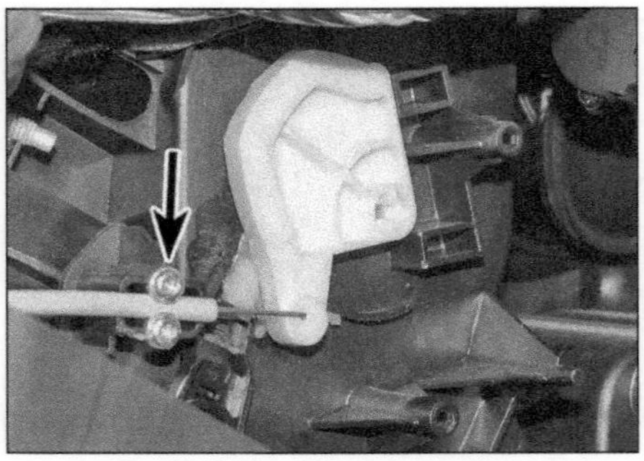

10.8a Slacken the retaining screws (arrowed) ...

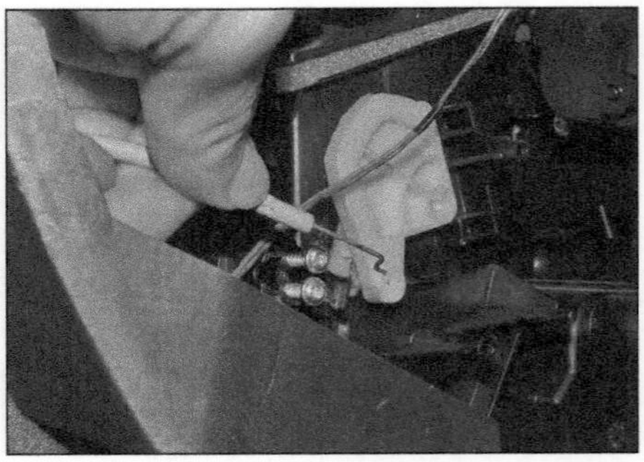

10.8b ... and release the direction control cable from the control lever

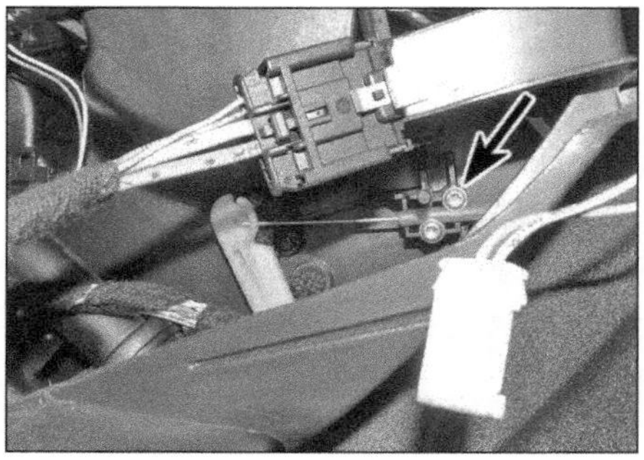

10.9 Temperature control cable retaining screws (arrowed)

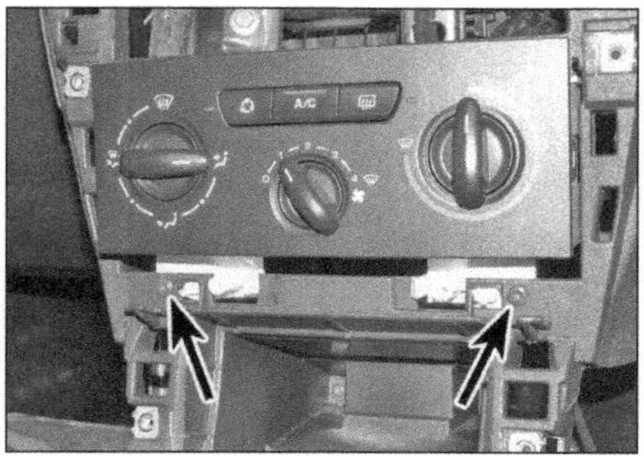

10.10a Undo the two retaining screws (arrowed) ...

10.10b ... and remove the heater control panel

10.11 Disconnect the wiring connectors

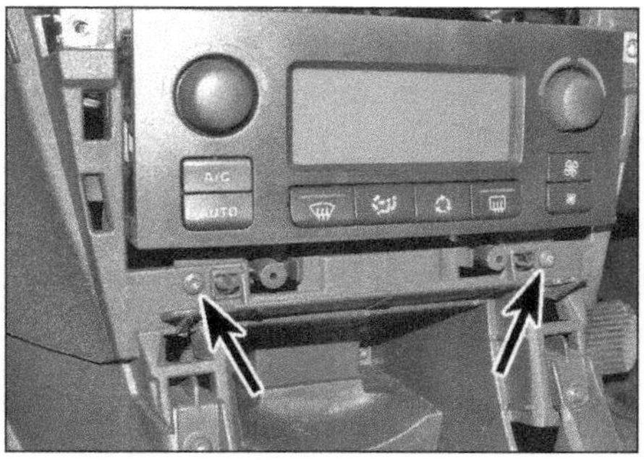

10.13a Undo the retaining screws (arrowed) ...

10.13b ... and remove the heater control panel

9 Slacken the retaining screws and disconnect the temperature control (red) cable from the left-hand side of the heater housing **(see illustration)**.

10 Undo the two retaining screws, release the upper retaining clips and tilt the control panel to manoeuvre it out from the facia **(see illustrations)**.

11 Disconnect the two wiring connectors from the rear of the control panel **(see illustration)**, and then withdraw the heater control panel, complete with cables from the facia. Note the routing of the cables as they are withdrawn through the facia.

12 Refitting is the reverse of removal. Ensure the control cables are correctly reconnected and securely held by the retaining clips; check the operation of the control knobs before refitting the trim panels and glovebox assembly.

Automatic climate system

13 Undo the two retaining screws, release the upper retaining clips and tilt the control panel to manoeuvre it out from the facia **(see illustrations)**.

14 Disconnect the wiring connectors from the rear of the control panel **(see illustration)**, and then withdraw the heater control panel from the facia.

15 Refitting is the reverse of removal. Check the operation of the controls before refitting the trim panels.

Control cables

16 Remove the manually-operated system control panel as described previously in this Section.

17 Before disconnecting the cables from the rear of the control panel note their fitted position **(see illustration)**.

10.14 Disconnect the wiring connectors

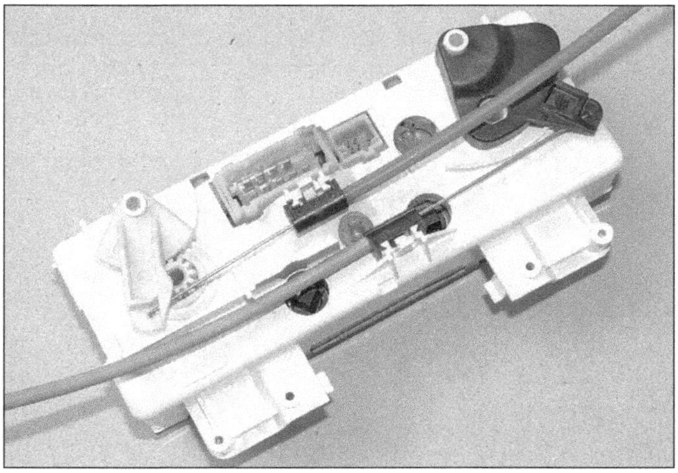

10.17 Note the fitted position of the cables

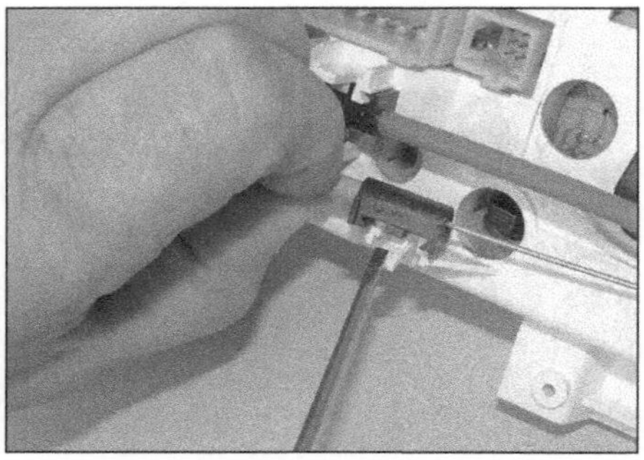

10.18a Release the securing clip ...

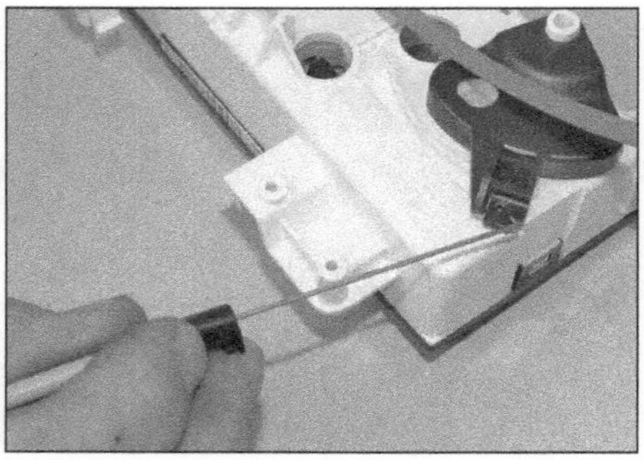

10.18b ... and release the inner cable from the operating lever

10.21 Using hose clamps to prevent the loss of fluid

18 Release the retaining clip and then detach the relevant cable from the lever on the rear of the control panel **(see illustrations)**.

19 Refitting is the reverse of removal, ensuring the cable is secured in place by its retaining clips. Check the operation of the control panel and cables.

Heater matrix

20 To improve access to the matrix unions on the bulkhead, remove the battery as described in Chapter 5A, Section 4. Where necessary also remove the air cleaner housing intake duct (see Chapter 4A, Section 2 or Chapter 4B, Section 4).

21 Drain the cooling system (see Chapter 1A, Section 25 or Chapter 1B, Section 20). Alternatively, clamp the heater matrix coolant hoses to minimise coolant loss **(see illustration)**.

22 Release the retaining clips and disconnect the coolant hoses from the heater matrix pipe unions on the engine compartment bulkhead **(see illustrations)**. On earlier models, prise out the retaining clips to release the heater hoses and on later models press on the locking clips to release the heater hoses. **Note:** *To help evacuate the heater matrix of coolant, an air gun can be used at the inlet pipe, to blow the coolant through the matrix. Catch the coolant in a container, to prevent it going over the engine compartment.*

23 Slacken and remove the screw securing the heater matrix pipe unions on the engine compartment bulkhead **(see illustrations)**.

24 Working inside the passenger side front footwell, undo the retaining screws and unclip the trim panel from the front left-hand side of the centre console in the passenger's front footwell **(see illustration)**. To gain better access, if required remove the glovebox assembly, as described in Chapter 11, Section 27.

25 Position a container or some rags beneath the heater matrix pipe union on the left-hand side of the heating/ventilation housing to catch any spilt coolant.

26 Undo the retaining screw from the two heater pipes under the facia **(see illustration)**.

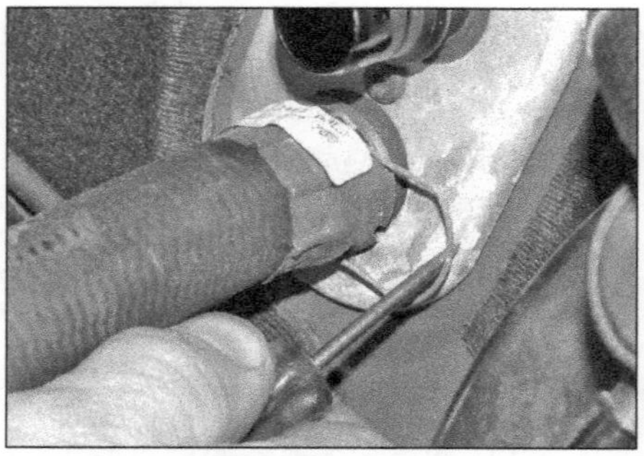

10.22a Prise out the heater hose wire retaining clip – early models ...

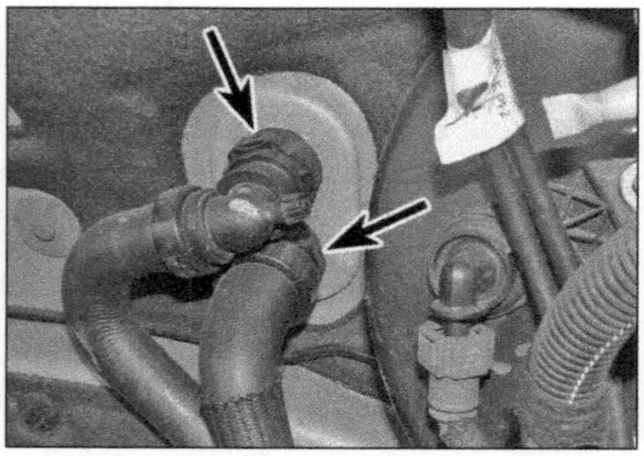

10.22b ... press in the locking clips (arrowed) to release the heater hoses – later models

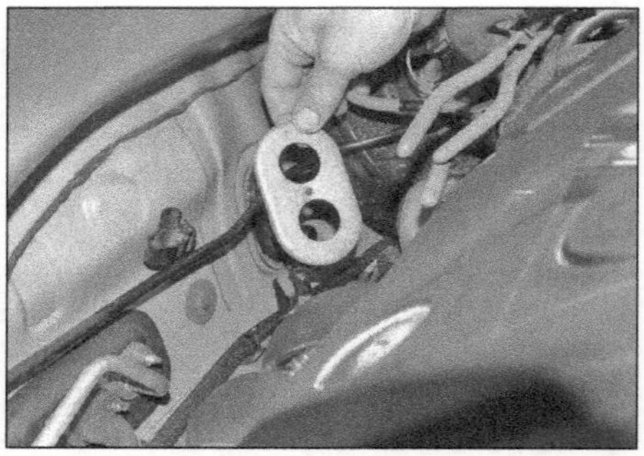

10.23a Remove the heater pipe retaining plate ...

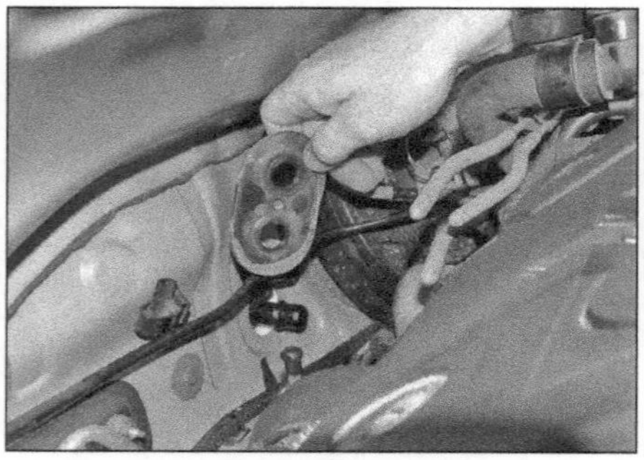

10.23b ... and bulkhead rubber seal

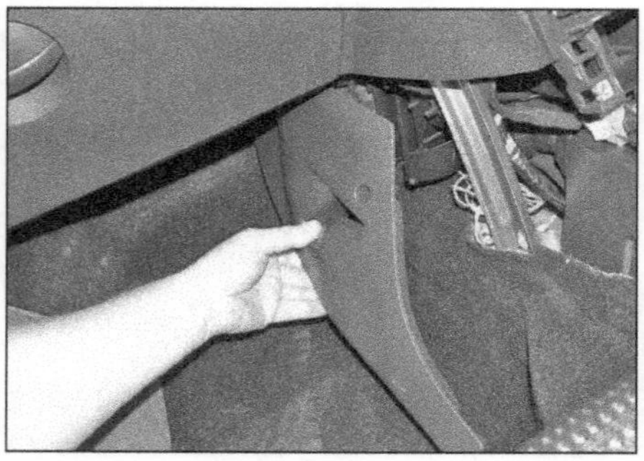

10.24 Undo the retaining screws and remove the trim panel

10.26 Undo the retaining screw (arrowed)

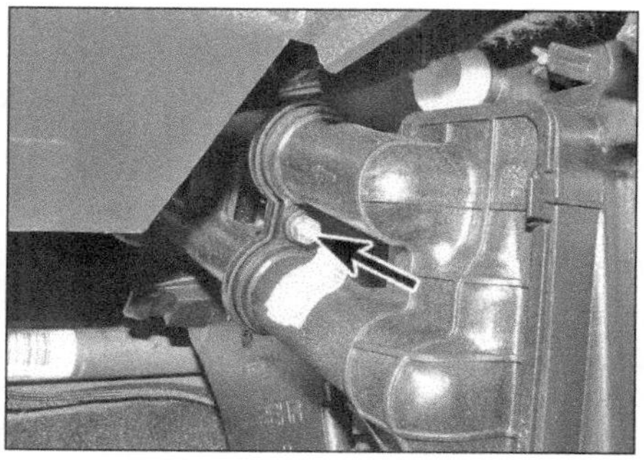

10.27 Undo the retaining bolt (arrowed)

10.29 Release the heater matrix securing clips (arrowed)

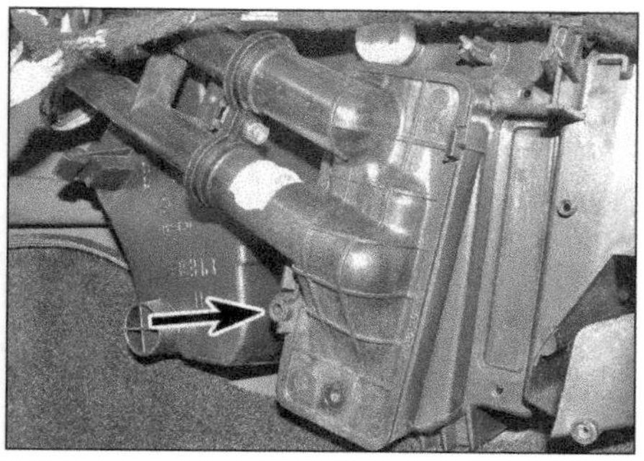

10.30 if required secure the heater matrix with a retaining screw in the position arrowed

27 Undo the retaining bolt securing the heater pipes to the matrix **(see illustration)**.

28 Carefully free the heater pipes from the matrix, catching any spilt coolant as the pipes are disconnected. Recover the sealing rings fitted to the pipe unions and discard them; new ones should be used on refitting. If required, the coolant pipes can be withdrawn from the bulkhead.

29 Release the retaining clips and slide the matrix out from the housing. Keep the matrix unions uppermost as the matrix is removed to prevent any coolant spillage **(see illustration). Note:** *On some models there may also be a retaining screw securing the heater matrix **(see illustration 10.30)**.*

30 Ease the matrix into the housing, until the retaining clips secure the heater matrix, if the retaining clips have broken, secure the matrix in place with retaining screw **(see illustration)**

31 Fit a new sealing ring to each of the pipe unions, and then manoeuvre the pipes into position and secure them to the matrix with the retaining bolt.

32 Make sure the heater pipes are located correctly at the bulkhead, and then refit the retaining screw to the upper part of the coolant pipes.

33 Working inside the engine compartment, refit the seal and retaining plate to the top end of the matrix pipes at the bulkhead.

34 Reconnect the heater coolant hoses, securing them in position with the retaining clips. Where fitted, remove the clamps from the heater hoses and refill the cooling system (see Chapter 1A, Section 25 or Chapter 1B, Section 20).

35 Refit the battery (see Chapter 5A, Section 4).

36 Working back inside the passenger side front footwell, refit the trim panel to the left-hand side of the centre console in the passenger's front footwell, and if removed refit the glovebox assembly, as described in Chapter 11, Section 27.

Heater blower motor

37 The blower motor is fitted to the top of the heating/ventilation housing, on the left-hand side **(see illustration)**.

38 On right-hand drive models, remove the glovebox (see Chapter 11, Section 27). Access to the motor can then be gained through the glovebox aperture.

10.37 Location of heater blower motor (arrowed)

39 On left-hand drive models, remove the steering column as described in Chapter 10, Section 17 to gain access to the motor.

40 Disconnect the wiring connector from the blower motor **(see illustration)**.

41 Rotate the motor anti-clockwise to free it from the housing. Manoeuvre the motor down and out from under the facia **(see illustrations)**. **Note:** *On some models there may also be a retaining screw securing the heater blower motor in place.*

42 Refitting is the reverse of removal.

Heater blower motor resistor

43 The resistor is located below the heater blower motor, in the top left-hand side of the heater housing **(see illustration)**.

44 Working inside the passenger's front

10.40 Disconnect the wiring connector

10.41a Remove the retaining screw (arrowed) – where fitted

10.41b Rotate the motor anti-clockwise to remove

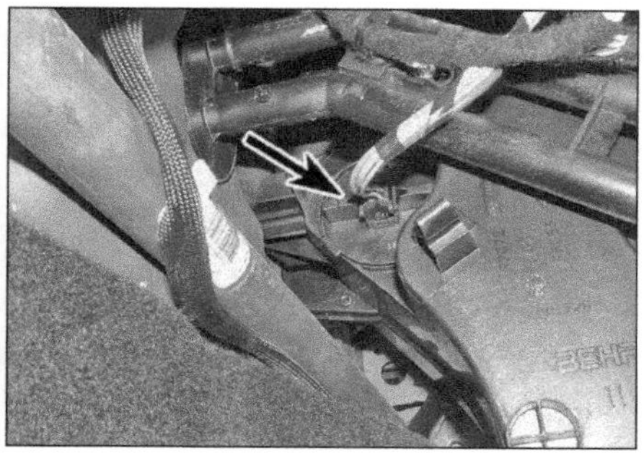

10.43 Location of blower motor resistor (arrowed)

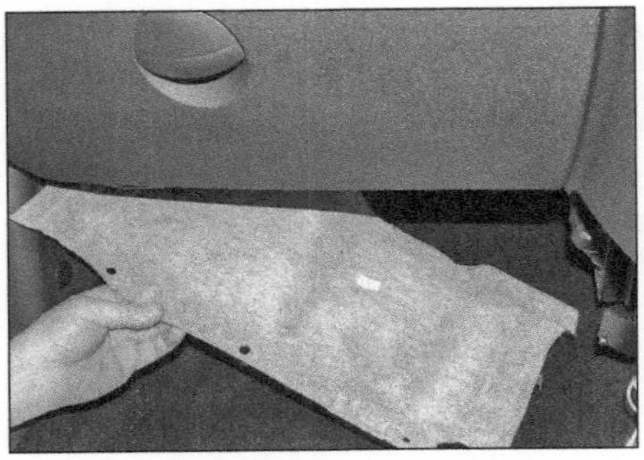

10.44 Remove the lower trim panel

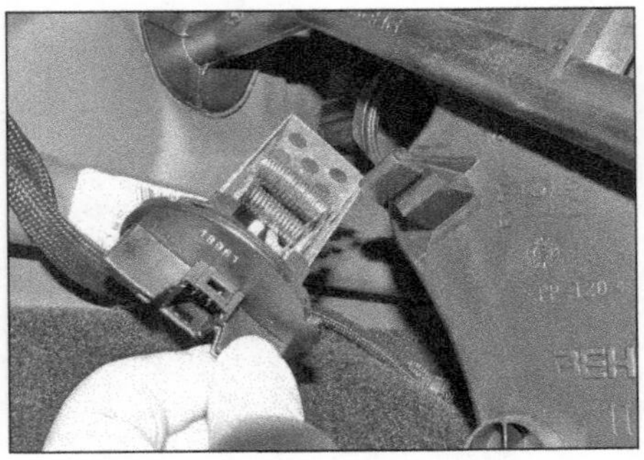

10.46 Rotate the resistor to remove

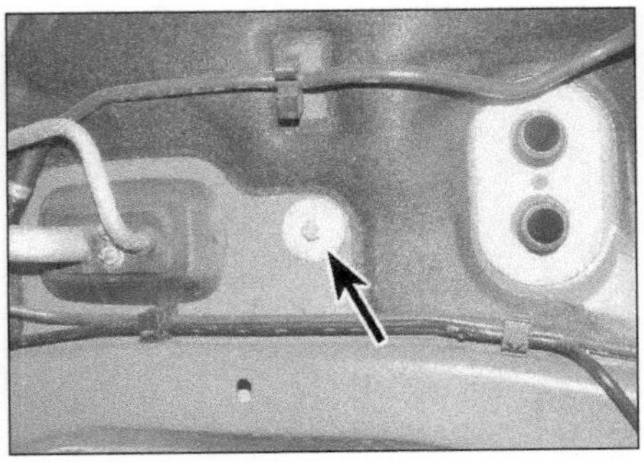

10.52 Heater/ventilation housing retaining bolt (arrowed)

footwell, release the retaining clips and remove the trim panel from under the glovebox **(see illustration)**.

45 Reach under the facia and disconnect the wiring connector from the resistor.

46 Rotate the heater resistor anti-clockwise, and withdraw it from the heater housing **(see illustration)**.

47 To refit manoeuvre the resistor into position and rotate it clockwise to secure in place in the heater housing. Connect the wiring connector and refit any components removed for access.

Housing assembly

Models without air conditioning

48 To improve access to the matrix unions on the bulkhead, remove the battery as described in Chapter 5A, Section 4. Where necessary also remove the air cleaner housing intake duct (see Chapter 4A, Section 2 or Chapter 4B, Section 4).

49 Drain the cooling system (see Chapter 1A, Section 25 or Chapter 1B, Section 20). Alternatively, working in the engine compartment, clamp the heater matrix coolant hoses to minimise coolant loss.

50 Release the retaining clips and disconnect the coolant hoses from the heater matrix pipe unions on the engine compartment bulkhead **(see illustrations 10.22a and 10.22b)**.

51 Slacken and remove the screw securing the heater matrix pipes to the bulkhead and remove the retaining plate and seal **(see illustrations 10.23a and 10.23b)**.

52 Slacken and remove the bolt securing the heating/ventilation housing to the bulkhead **(see illustration)**.

53 Remove the facia assembly as described in Chapter 11, Section 27.

54 Disconnect the wiring connectors from the heating/ventilation housing components then remove the housing assembly from the vehicle. Keep the heater matrix pipe unions uppermost as the assembly is removed to prevent coolant spillage.

55 Recover the seal and retaining plate from the heater matrix pipes, and the seal from the housing mounting. Renew the seals if they show signs of damage or deterioration.

56 Refitting is the reverse of removal ensuring the seals are in position on the pipes and housing mounting. On completion, refill the cooling system (see Chapter 1A, Section 25 or Chapter 1B, Section 20).

Models with air conditioning

Warning: Refer to Section 11 for precautions to be observed when working on models equipped with air conditioning. Do not attempt the following procedure unless the system has been professionally discharged.

57 Have the air conditioning system discharged by an air conditioning specialist and obtain some plugs to seal the air conditioning pipe unions whilst the system is disconnected.

58 Carry out the operations described in paragraphs 48 to 51.

59 Unscrew the two nuts securing the air conditioning pipe union to the bulkhead **(see illustration)**. Separate the pipes from the evaporator and quickly seal the pipe and evaporator unions to prevent the entry of moisture into the refrigerant circuit. Discard the sealing rings, new ones must be used on refitting.

Warning: Failure to seal the refrigerant pipe unions will result in the dehydrator reservoir become saturated, necessitating its renewal.

60 Remove the heating/ventilation housing assembly as described in paragraphs 52 to 55 and recover the seal from the e vaporator.

61 Ensure the bulkhead seals are correctly fitted to the evaporator, matrix pipes and housing mounting. Manoeuvre the housing assembly into position, locating the housing drain hose correctly in its hole in the floor **(see illustration)**.

62 Loosely refit the housing mounting bolt then refit the retaining plate to the heater

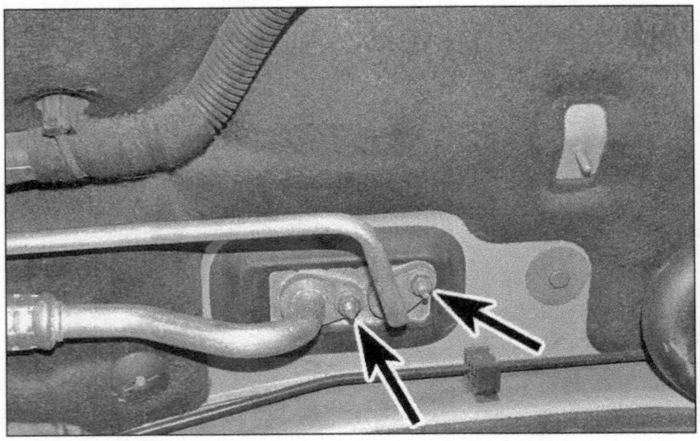

10.59 Undo the two nuts (arrowed) securing the air conditioning pipes

10.61 Heater housing drain tube (arrowed)

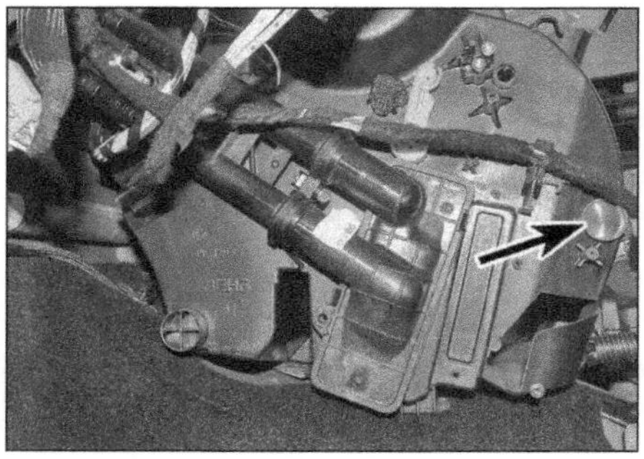

10.66 Location of interior air temperature sensor (arrowed) – where fitted

10.70 Location of additional heater (arrowed) – where fitted

10.79a Disconnect the wiring connector ...

matrix pipe and loosely install the retaining screw.

63 Lubricate the new evaporator union sealing rings with compressor oil. Remove the plugs and install the sealing rings then quickly fit the refrigerant pipe union to the evaporator. Ensure the refrigerant pipes and evaporator are correctly joined then refit the retaining nuts and tighten them securely.

64 Tighten the matrix pipe retaining screw securely and securely tighten the housing mounting bolt.

65 The remainder of refitting is the reverse of removal. On completion, refill the cooling system (see Chapter 1A, Section 25 or Chapter 1B, Section 20).

Interior air temperature sensor

66 Depending on model, there may be two air temperature sensors fitted, to the rear left- and right-hand sides of the heater housing **(see illustration)**.

67 Remove centre console as described in Chapter 11, Section 27, and then remove the trims from under the facia in each of the footwells.

68 Disconnect the wiring plug connector and then turn the sensor a quarter of a turn anti-clockwise to remove it from the heater housing.

69 Refitting is a reversal of removal.

Additional heater (diesel models)

70 Depending on model, there may be an additional heater fitted, to the rear left-hand side of the heater housing **(see illustration)**.

71 On right-hand drive models, remove the glovebox and passenger's side central kick panel as described in Chapter 11, Section 27.

72 On left-hand drive models, remove the trim panel above the pedals, undo the two fasteners and remove the trim panel at the front of the centre console, adjacent to the pedals.

73 Pull down on the locking clip to release the wiring plug connector, and then disconnect it from the heater element.

10.79b ... and undo the retaining screws (arrowed)

74 Undo the two retaining screws, and slide the heater element out from the housing.

75 Refitting is the reverse of removal.

Air control motors

76 Depending on model, there may be a number of control motors fitted to the heater housing assembly.

77 Remove the glovebox and passenger's side central kick panel to access the control motors on the left-hand side of the heater housing.

78 Remove the steering column lower trim panels and driver's side central kick panel to gain access to the control motors on the right-hand side of the heater housing.

79 Disconnect the motor wiring plug, undo the bolts, and remove the motor **(see illustrations)**.

80 Refitting is a reversal of removal.

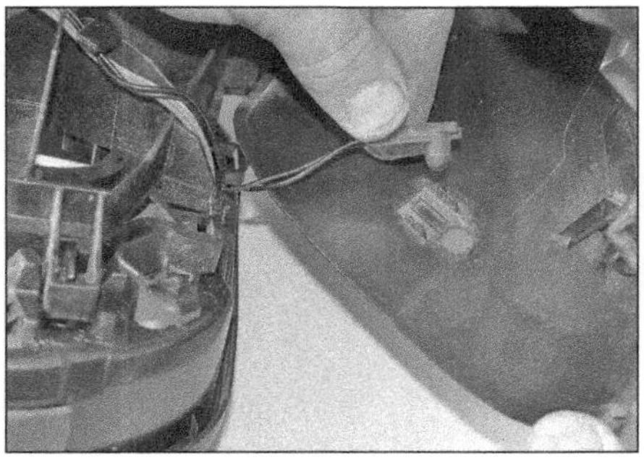

10.82a Unclip the sensor from the cover

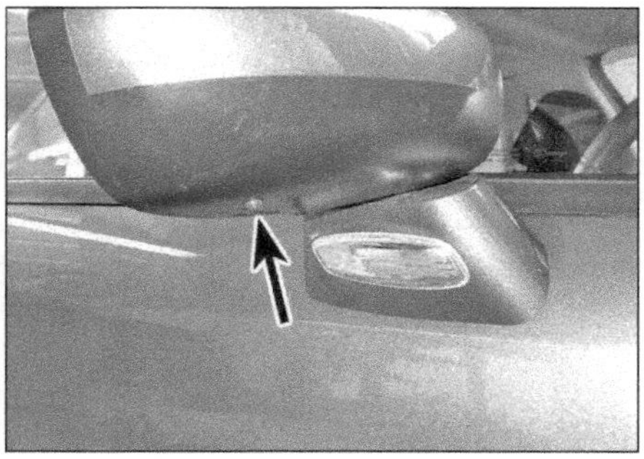

10.81 Location of ambient air temperature sensor

Ambient temperature sensor

81 The ambient temperature sensor is located on the underside of the driver's side exterior door mirror **(see illustration)**. To remove the sensor, remove the mirror upper and lower rear covers as described in Chapter 11, Section 18.

82 Unclip the sensor from the mirror housing **(see illustrations)**. To renew or remove the sensor completely, the two wires going to the sensor will need to be cut, as they go into the door wiring harness. The wires must be cut more than 30 mm away from the sensor.

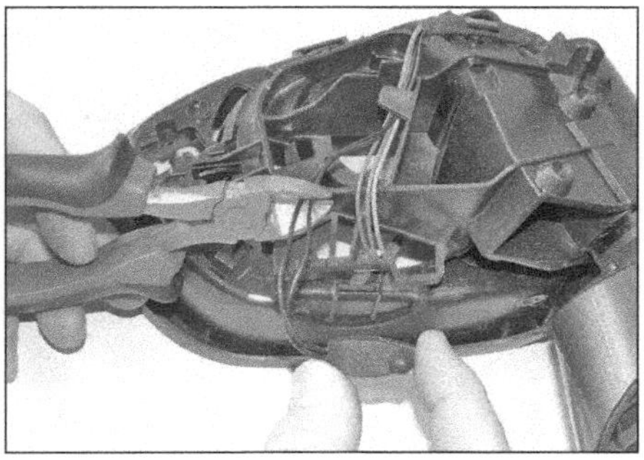

10.82b ... and cut the wires to the sensor

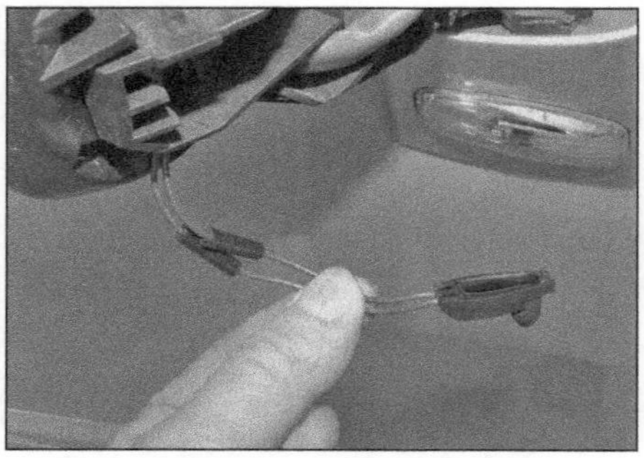

10.83 Make sure new sensor wiring is made correctly

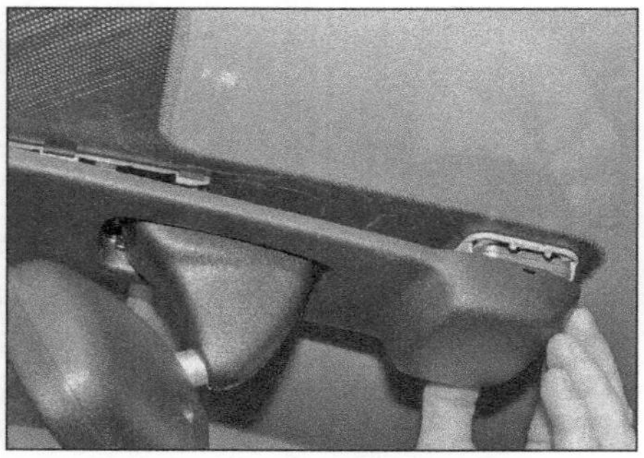

10.84 Unclip the plastic trim ...

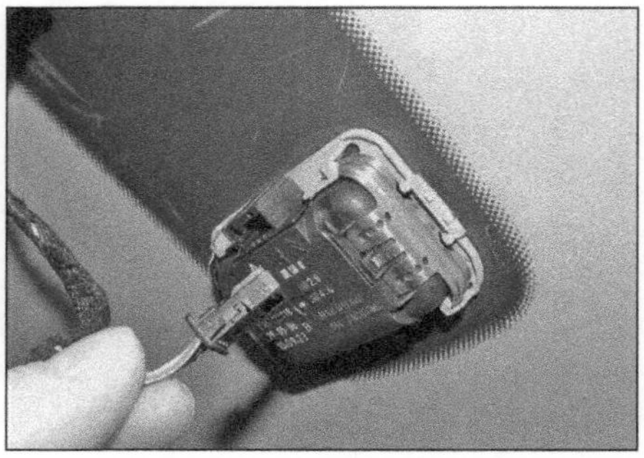

10.85a ... disconnect the wiring connector ...

83 When refitting the sensor, make sure the connections are made correctly, and insulated using a heat-shrink sleeve **(see illustration)**.

Rain sensor

84 Unclip the plastic trim from around the mirror base **(see illustration)**.

85Disconnect the wiring plug connector and then release the two securing clips one at each side of the sensor to remove it from the mounting base on the windscreen **(see illustrations)**.

86 Refitting is a reversal of removal.

Sunlight sensor

87 The sunlight sensor is built into the rear of the instrument cluster on the centre of the facia. Remove the instrument cluster as described in Chapter 12, Section 9.

11 Air conditioning system – general information and precautions

1 An air conditioning system is available on all models. It enables the temperature of incoming air to be lowered, and also dehumidifies the air, which makes for rapid demisting and increased comfort.

2 The cooling side of the system works in the same way as a domestic refrigerator. Refrigerant gas is drawn into a belt-driven compressor, and passes into a condenser mounted on the front of the radiator, where it loses heat and becomes liquid. The liquid passes through an expansion valve to an evaporator, where it changes from liquid under high pressure to gas under low pressure. This change is accompanied by a drop in temperature, which cools the evaporator. The refrigerant returns to the compressor, and the cycle begins again.

3 Air blown through the evaporator passes to the heating/ventilation housing, where it is mixed with hot air blown through the heater matrix to achieve the desired temperature in the passenger compartment.

4 The heating side of the system works in the same way as on models without air conditioning (see Section 9).

5 The operation of the system is controlled electronically by the ECU integral with the control panel. Any problems with the system should be referred to a Citroën dealer, or suitably-equipped specialist **(see illustrations)**.

Precautions

6 When an air conditioning system is fitted, it is necessary to observe special precautions whenever dealing with any part of the system, or its associated components. The refrigerant is potentially dangerous, and should only be handled by qualified persons. Uncontrolled discharging of the refrigerant is dangerous and damaging to the environment for the following reasons.

- If it is splashed onto the skin, it can cause frostbite.
- The refrigerant is heavier then air and so displaces oxygen. In a confined space, which is not adequately ventilated, this could lead to a risk of suffocation. The gas is odourless and colourless so there is no warning of its presence in the atmosphere.
- Although not poisonous, in the presence of a naked flame (including a cigarette) it forms a noxious gas that causes headaches, nausea, etc.

Warning: Never attempt to open any air conditioning system refrigerant pipe/hose union without first having the system fully discharged by an air conditioning specialist. On completion of work, have the system recharged with the correct type and amount of fresh refrigerant.

Warning: Always seal disconnected refrigerant pipe/hose unions as soon as they are disconnected. Failure to form an airtight seal on any union will result in the dehydrator reservoir become saturated, necessitating its renewal. Also renew all sealing rings disturbed.

Caution: Do not operate the air conditioning system if it is known to be short of refrigerant as this could damage the compressor.

12 Air conditioning system components – removal and refitting

Warning: Refer to the precautions given in Section 11 and have the system discharged by an air conditioning specialist before carrying out any work on the air conditioning system.

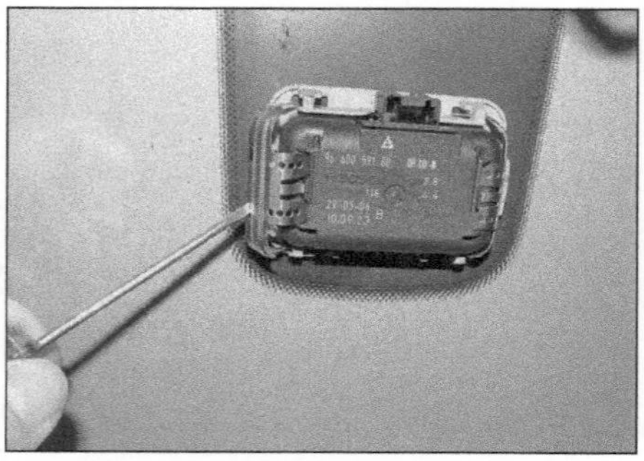

10.85b ... and unclip the sensor from the mounting bracket

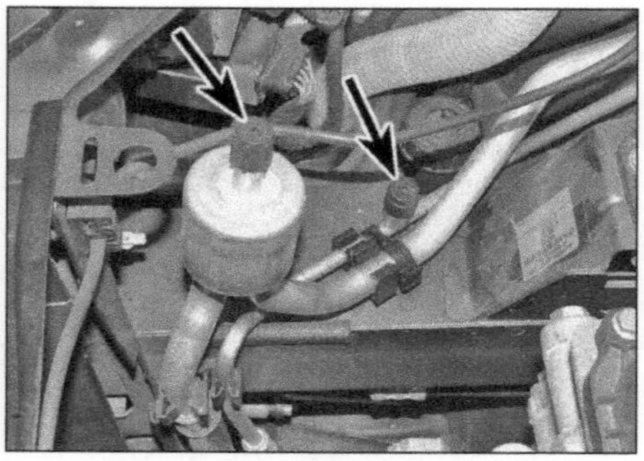

11.5a Air conditioning high- and low-pressure circuits service ports (arrowed)

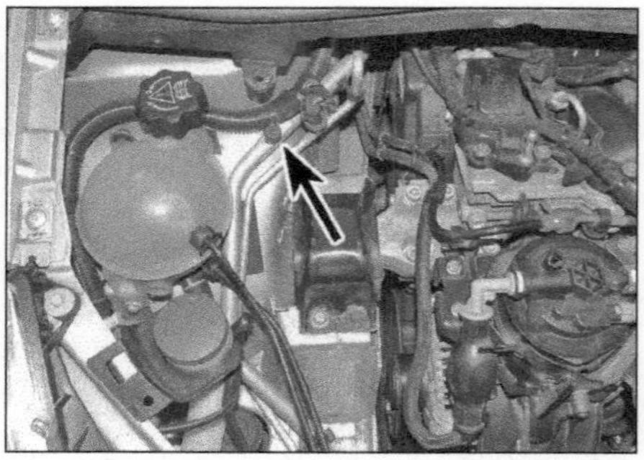

11.5b Low-pressure service port (arrowed) – some models

12.3a Disconnect the wiring connector

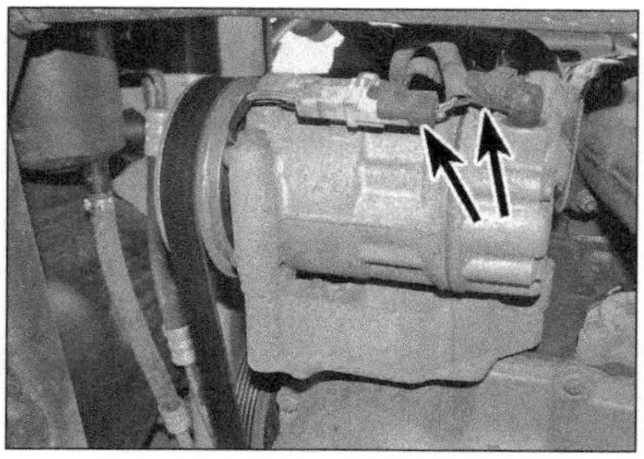

12.3b On some models there are two connectors

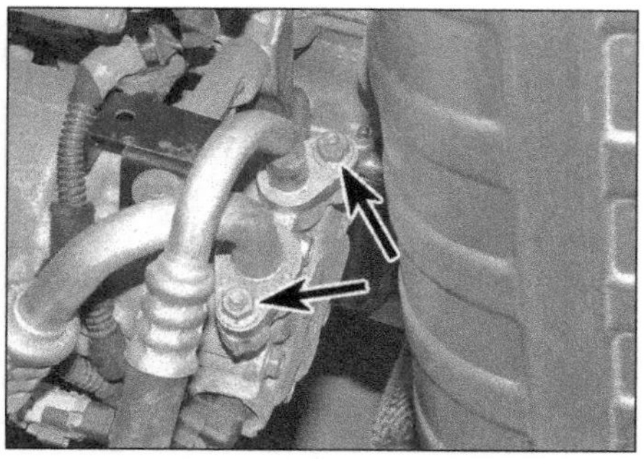

12.4 Undo the nuts (arrowed) securing the refrigerant pipes to the compressor

Compressor

1 Have the air conditioning system fully discharged and evacuated by an air conditioning specialist.

2 Remove the auxiliary drivebelt as described in Chapter 1A, Section 10 or Chapter 1B, Section 17 (as applicable).

3 Disconnect the compressor wiring connector(s), and unclip the wiring harness from the retaining clips **(see illustrations)**.

4 Unscrew the nuts securing the refrigerant pipes retaining plates to the compressor **(see illustration)**. Separate the pipes from the compressor and quickly seal the pipe and compressor unions to prevent the entry of moisture into the refrigerant circuit. Discard the sealing rings, new ones must be used on refitting.

Warning: Failure to seal the refrigerant pipe unions will result in the dehydrator reservoir become saturated, necessitating its renewal.

5 Unscrew the compressor mounting bolts and nuts then free the compressor from its mounting bracket and remove it from the engine **(see illustration)**. Take care not to lose the spacers from the compressor rear mountings (where fitted).

6 If the compressor is to be renewed, drain the refrigerant oil from the old compressor. The specialist who recharges the refrigerant system will need to add this amount of oil to the system.

7 Ensure the spacers are correctly fitted to the rear mountings then manoeuvre the compressor into position and fit the mounting bolts and nuts.

8 Tighten the compressor front (drivebelt pulley) end mounting bolts to the specified torque first then tighten the rear bolts.

9 Lubricate the new refrigerant pipe sealing rings with compressor oil. Remove the plugs and install the sealing rings then quickly fit the refrigerant pipes to the compressor. Ensure the refrigerant pipes are correctly joined then refit the retaining bolt, tighten it securely.

10 Reconnect the wiring connector then refit the auxiliary drivebelt (see Chapter 1A, Section 10 or Chapter 1B, Section 17).

11 Have the air conditioning system recharged with the correct type and amount of refrigerant by a specialist before using the system. Remember to inform the specialist which components have been renewed, so they can add the correct amount of oil.

Condenser

12 Have the air conditioning system fully discharged by an air conditioning specialist.

12.5 Remove the compressor mounting bolts (arrowed)

13 Remove the radiator as described in Section 4.

14 Undo the retaining nuts and disconnect the refrigerant pipes from the right-hand side of the condenser. Recover the O-ring seals **(see illustration)**.

Warning: Failure to seal the refrigerant pipe unions will result in the dehydrator reservoir become saturated, necessitating its renewal.

15 Move the top of the condenser to the rear and withdraw it from the engine compartment **(see illustration)**.

16 Refitting is a reversal of removal. Noting the following points:

*a) Ensure the upper and lower mounting rubbers are correctly fitted then seat the condenser in position in the front panel **(see illustrations)**.*

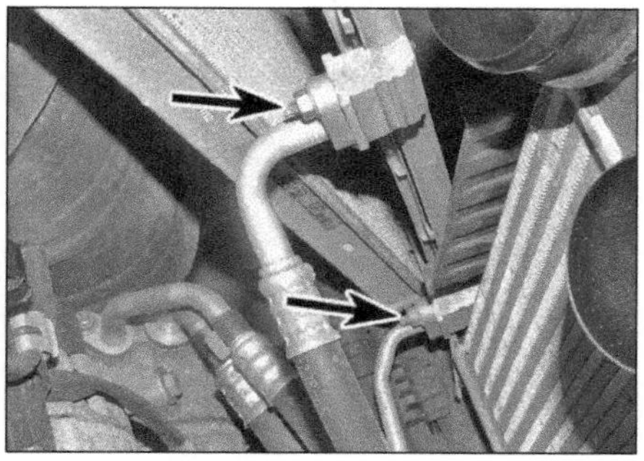

12.14 Undo the nuts (arrowed) securing the refrigerant pipes to the condenser

12.15 Removing the condenser from the engine compartment

12.16a Make sure the rubber mountings are fitted securely ...

12.16b ... and the lower pegs locate in the rubber mountings (arrowed)

12.17 Receiver/drier (arrowed) fitted to the side of the condenser

12.18 Pressure switch location (arrowed)

b) Lubricate the sealing rings with compressor oil. Remove the plugs and install the sealing rings then quickly fit the refrigerant pipes to the condenser. Securely tighten the dehydrator pipe union nut and ensure the compressor pipe is correctly joined.

c) Have the air conditioning system recharged with the correct type and amount of refrigerant by a specialist before using the system.

Receiver/drier

17 The receiver/drier is located on the left-hand side of the condenser **(see illustration)**. See paragraphs 12 to 15 to remove the condenser. The receiver/drier is not available separately; see your local dealer for further information.

Pressure switch

18 The switch is located in the high-pressure pipe on the right-hand side of the engine compartment **(see illustration)**.

19 Have the air conditioning system fully discharged by an air conditioning specialist.

20 Disconnect the wiring connector, and then unscrew the switch from the high-pressure pipe. Quickly seal the condenser union to prevent the entry of moisture into the refrigerant circuit.

⚠ ***Warning: Failure to seal the refrigerant pipe unions will result in the dehydrator reservoir become saturated, necessitating its renewal.***

21 Refitting is a reversal of removal noting the following points:

a) Lubricate the switch seal with compressor oil.

b) Have the air conditioning system recharged with the correct type and amount of refrigerant by a specialist prior to using the system.

Evaporator

22 Have the air conditioning system fully discharged and evacuated by an air conditioning specialist.

23 Remove the heating/ventilation housing as described in Section 10.

24 Note their fitted positions, and then disconnect the wiring plugs and harness from the housing.

25 Release the retaining clips, undo the screws and separate the two halves of the heater housing.

26 With the two halves of the housing separated, undo the screws, remove the pipe cover, and then slide the evaporator from the housing.

27 Refitting is a reversal of removal but have the air conditioning system recharged with the correct type and amount of refrigerant by a specialist prior to using the system.

Expansion valve

28 Have the air conditioning system fully discharged and evacuated by an air conditioning specialist.

29 Remove the sound insulation material/heat shield from the engine compartment bulkhead (where fitted).

30 Undo the nuts securing the refrigerant pipes to the connection at the engine compartment bulkhead. Plug/cover the openings to prevent contamination/saturation. Recover and discard the O-ring seals – new ones must be fitted.

⚠ ***Warning: Failure to seal the refrigerant pipe unions will result in the receiver/drier becoming saturated, necessitating its renewal.***

31 Pull the seal from around the pipes connection at the bulkhead, and then undo the 2 studs using a Torx socket, and remove the expansion valve. Recover and discard the O-ring seals – new ones must be fitted.

32 Refitting is a reversal of removal but have the air conditioning system recharged with the correct type and amount of refrigerant by a specialist prior to using the system.

Chapter 4 Part A:
Fuel and exhaust systems – petrol models

Contents

Degrees of difficulty

Easy, suitable for novice with little experience	**Fairly easy,** suitable for beginner with some experience	**Fairly difficult,** suitable for competent DIY mechanic	**Difficult,** suitable for experienced DIY mechanic	**Very difficult,** suitable for expert DIY or professional

Specifications

Engine identification

	Designation	Engine code
1.4 litre	ET3J4	KFU
1.6 litre:		
Non-VTi engine	TU5JP4	NFU
VTi engine	EP6	5FW

System type

1.4 litre models	Marelli 6LP
1.6 litre models:	
TU5JP4	Bosch ME7.4
EP6	Bosch MEV 17.4

Fuel system data

Fuel pump type	Electric, immersed in tank
Fuel pump regulated constant pressure	3.5 ± 0.2 bars
Specified idle speed	850 ± 100 rpm (not adjustable – controlled by ECU)
Idle mixture CO content	Less than 1.0% (not adjustable – controlled by ECU)

Recommended fuel

Minimum octane rating	95 RON unleaded (UK unleaded premium). Leaded/lead replacement fuel (LRP) must **not** be used

Torque wrench settings

	Nm	lbf ft
Catalytic converter-to-cylinder block bolts (VTi engine)	25	18
Exhaust manifold to catalytic converter (non-VTi engine)	40	30
Exhaust manifold-to-cylinder head nuts	25	18
Intake manifold nuts:		
M6	10	7
M8	20	15
Oxygen sensor	45	33
Roadwheel bolts	90	66

1 General information and precautions

1 The fuel supply system consists of a fuel tank, which is mounted under the rear of the car, with an electric fuel pump immersed in it, a fuel filter (depending on model), fuel feed and return lines. The fuel pump supplies fuel to the fuel rail, which acts as a reservoir for the four fuel injectors, which inject fuel into the intake tracts. The fuel filter incorporated in the feed line from the pump to the fuel rail ensures that the fuel supplied to the injectors is clean.

2 Refer to Section 5 for further information on the operation of the engine management system, and to Section 15 for information on the exhaust system.

Warning: Many of the procedures in this Chapter require the removal of fuel lines and connections, which may result in some fuel spillage. Before carrying out any operation on the fuel system, refer to the precautions given in 'Safety first!' at the beginning of this manual, and follow them implicitly. Petrol is a highly dangerous and volatile liquid, and the precautions necessary when handling it cannot be overstressed.

Caution: Residual pressure will remain in the fuel lines long after the vehicle was last used. When disconnecting any fuel line, first depressurise the fuel system as described in Section 6.

2 Air cleaner assembly and intake ducts – removal and refitting

Removal

1 To make access easier, remove the windscreen wiper arms, and then unclip the plastic scuttle panel from below the windscreen. Pull up the ends of the panel to release it from the windscreen clips. Release the plastic expanding rivets from along the front edge of the scuttle panel. Undo the two screws securing the brake/clutch master cylinder upper reservoir and move it to one side. Release the sound insulation trim from the scuttle crossmember, undo the bolt on the left-hand side of the crossmember, then release the retaining clips at the right-hand side of the crossmember to remove it from the engine compartment – refer to Chapter 11, Section 22.

VTi engines

2 Undo the retaining bolt from the top of the cam cover **(see illustration)**.

3 Slacken the retaining screws and remove the upper cover from the top of the air cleaner housing **(see illustrations)**.

4 Lift out the air filter from the lower housing **(see illustration)**.

5 Undo the two retaining screws, and remove the middle section of the air cleaner housing, releasing the air intake hose as it is removed **(see illustrations)**.

6 Undo the retaining bolt and unclip any wiring from the air ducting, then remove it from the engine compartment **(see illustrations)**.

7 Pull the lower part of the air cleaner housing upwards to release from its mountings on

2.2 Undo the retaining bolt

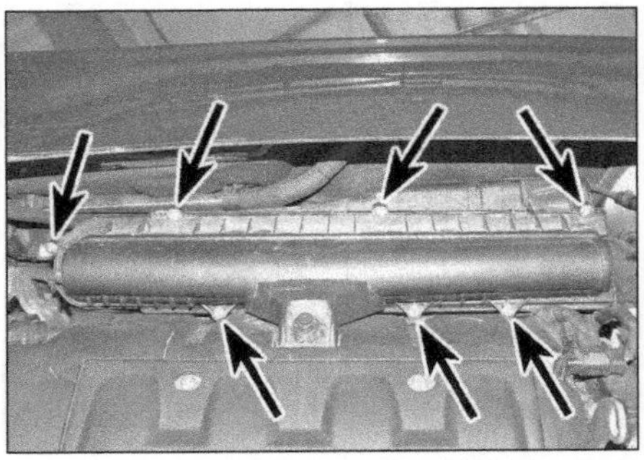

2.3a Undo the retaining screws (arrowed) ...

2.3b ... and remove the upper housing

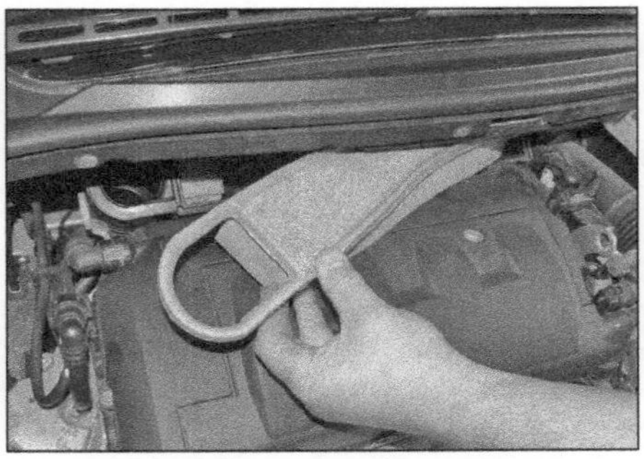

2.4 Remove the air filter element

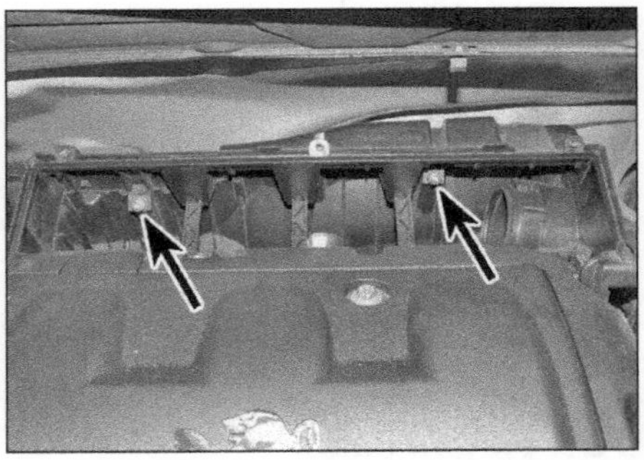

2.5a Undo the two retaining screws (arrowed) ...

2.5b ... and remove the centre section

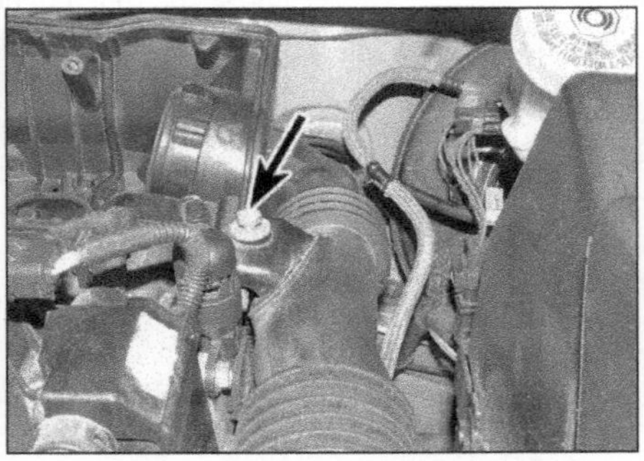

2.6a Undo the retaining bolt (arrowed) ...

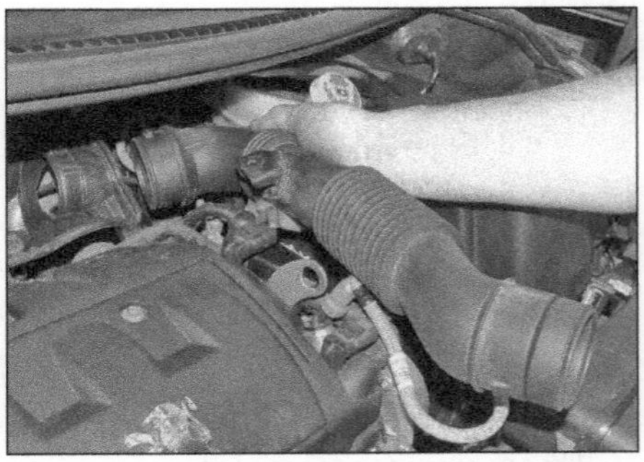

2.6b ... and remove the air ducting

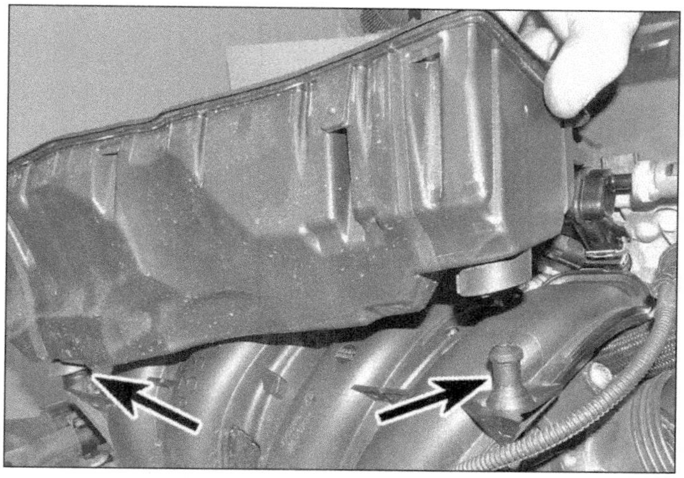

2.7a Pull the lower part of the housing up ...

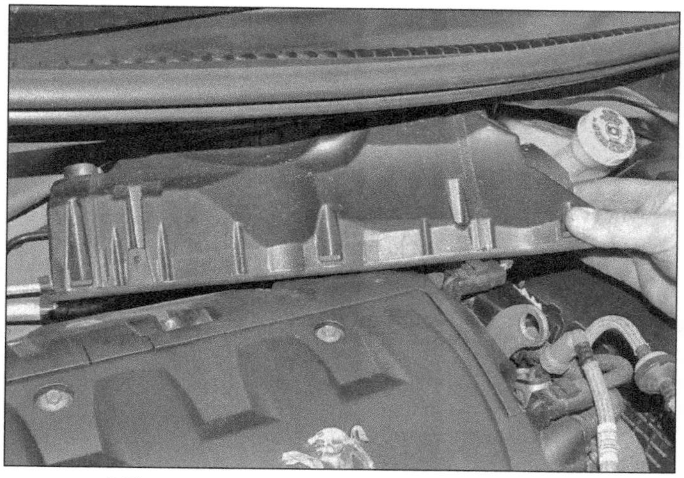

2.7b ... and out from the engine compartment

the manifold, and then turn the housing and withdraw it out from the rear of the engine compartment **(see illustrations)**.

8 To remove the resonator box, release the securing clip, and withdraw the upper part of the housing from the engine compartment. Undo the retaining clip and release the hose from the resonator housing, then release the retaining clip and withdraw the resonator housing upwards and out from the front of the engine compartment **(see illustrations)**.

Non-VTi engines

9 Remove the resonator box by releasing the securing clip, then withdraw the resonator housing upwards and release it from the plastic hose to the air cleaner housing **(see illustrations)**.

10 Slacken the retaining clip securing the air cleaner upper housing to the throttle housing **(see illustration)**.

11 Depress the sides of the quick-release fitting and detach the engine breather hose

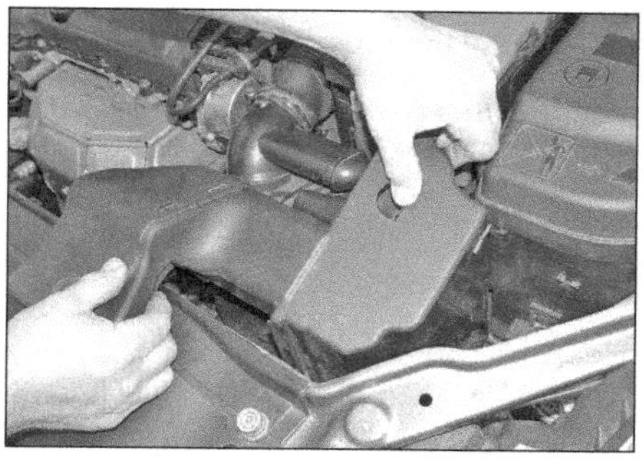

2.8a Release the securing clip ...

2.8b ... and disconnect the air intake hose

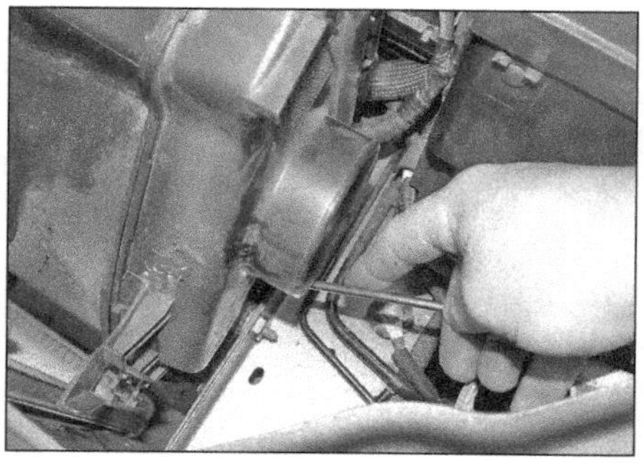

2.8c Release the retaining clip ...

2.8d ... and remove the resonator box – VTi engines

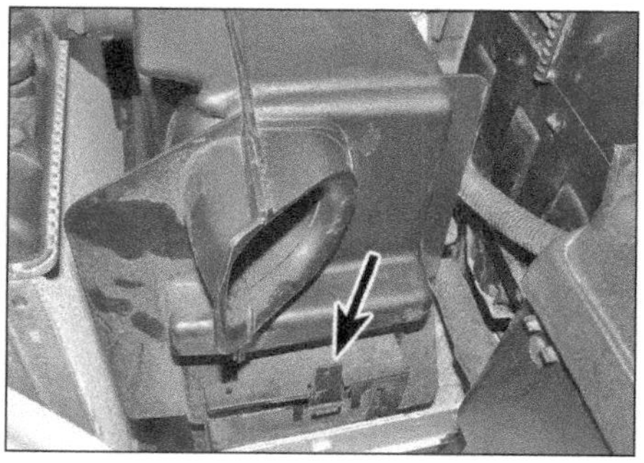

2.9a Release the retaining clip (arrowed) ...

2.9b ... and remove the resonator box – non-VTi engines

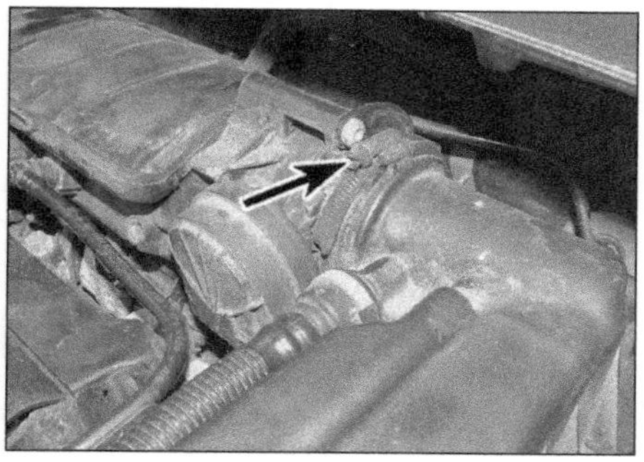

2.10 Slacken the retaining clip (arrowed ...

2.11 ... and disconnect the breather hose

2.12a Undo the retaining bolt ...

2.12b ... and release the air filter housing from its the locating position (arrowed)

from the air cleaner upper housing **(see illustration)**.

12 Slacken and remove the securing bolt at the front of the air cleaner housing, then detach the upper part of the air cleaner housing from the throttle housing, while at the same time lifting the air cleaner housing upwards to release it from the lower mounting and out of the engine compartment **(see illustrations)**.

Refitting

13 Refitting is a reversal of the removal procedure, ensuring that all hoses and ducts are properly reconnected and correctly seated and, where necessary, securely held by their retaining clips.

3 Accelerator pedal – removal and refitting

Removal

1 Release the fasteners and remove trim panel above the pedals **(see illustration)**.

2 Disconnect the accelerator pedal position sensor wiring plug from the top of the pedal **(see illustration)**.

3 Undo the three nuts and remove the pedal assembly **(see illustration)**.

Refitting

4 Refitting is a reversal of the removal procedure.

4 Unleaded petrol – general information and usage

Note: *The information given in this Chapter is correct at the time of writing. If updated information is thought to be required, check with a Citroën dealer. If traveling abroad, consult one of the motoring organisations (or a similar authority) for advice on the fuel available.*

1 The fuel recommended by *Citroën* is given in the Specifications Section of this Chapter, followed by the equivalent petrol currently on sale in the UK.

2 All models are designed to run on fuel with a minimum octane rating of 95 (RON). All models have a catalytic converter, and so must be run on unleaded fuel only. Under no circumstances should leaded/lead replacement fuel (UK 4-star/LRP) be used, as this may damage the converter.

3 Super unleaded petrol (97, 98 or 99 octane) can also be used in all models if wished, though there is no advantage in doing so.

5 Engine management system – general information

Note: *The fuel injection ECU is of the 'self-learning' type, meaning that as it operates, it also monitors and stores the settings, which give optimum engine performance under all operating conditions. When the battery is disconnected, these settings are lost and the ECU reverts to the base settings programmed into its memory at the factory. On restarting, this may lead to the engine running/idling roughly for a short while, until the ECU has relearned the optimum settings. This process is best accomplished by taking the vehicle on a road test (for approximately 15 minutes), covering all engine speeds and loads, concentrating mainly in the 2500 to 3500 rpm region.*

On all engines, the fuel injection and ignition functions are combined into a single engine management system. Bosch and Magneti Marelli manufacture the systems fitted, they are very similar to each other in most respects, the only significant differences being in the software contained in the system ECU, and specific component location according to engine type. Each system incorporates a closed-loop catalytic converter and an evaporative emission control system, and complies with the latest emission control standards. Refer to Chapter 5B for information on the ignition side of each system; the fuel side of the system operates as follows.

The fuel pump, which is situated in the fuel tank, supplies fuel from the tank to the fuel rail. The pump motor is permanently immersed in fuel, to keep it cool. The fuel rail is mounted directly above the fuel injectors and acts as a fuel reservoir.

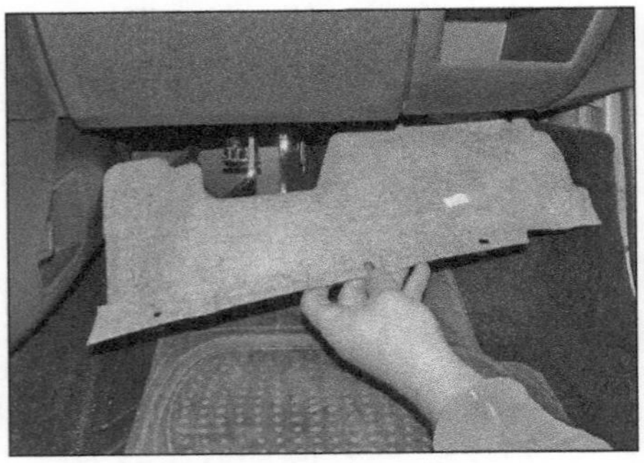

3.1 Unclip the lower trim panel

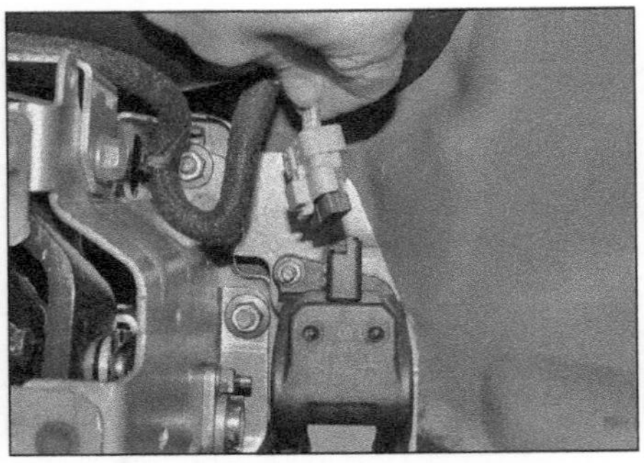

3.2 Disconnect the wiring connector

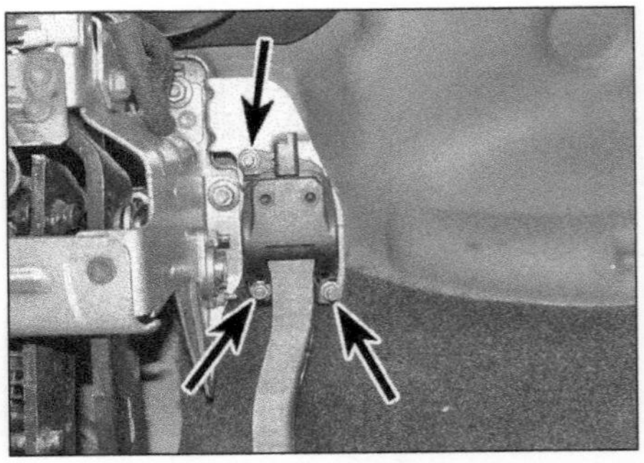

3.3 Undo the pedal retaining nuts (arrowed)

Fuel rail supply pressure is controlled by the pressure regulator, also located in the fuel tank. The regulator contains a spring-loaded valve, which lifts to allow excess fuel to recirculate within the tank when the optimum operating pressure of the fuel system is exceeded (eg, during low speed, light load cruising).

The fuel injectors are electromagnetic pintle valves, which spray atomised fuel into the intake manifold tracts under the control of the engine management system ECU. There are four injectors, one per cylinder, mounted in the intake manifold close to the cylinder head on non-VTi engines, and in the cylinder head close to the intake manifold on VTi engines. Each injector is mounted at an angle that allows it to spray fuel directly onto the back of the intake valves. The ECU controls the volume of fuel injected by varying the length of time for which each injector is held open. The fuel injection systems are of the sequential type, whereby each injector operates individually in cylinder sequence.

The electrical control system consists of the ECU, along with the following sensors:

a) Throttle potentiometer – informs the ECU of the throttle valve position, and the rate of throttle opening/closing.

b) Coolant temperature sensor – informs the ECU of engine temperature.

c) Intake air temperature sensor – informs the ECU of the temperature of the air passing through the throttle housing.

d) Oxygen sensors – inform the ECU of the oxygen content of the exhaust gases (explained in greater detail Chapter 4C).

e) Manifold pressure sensor – informs the ECU of the load on the engine (expressed in terms of intake manifold vacuum).

f) Crankshaft position sensor – informs the ECU of engine speed and crankshaft angular position.

g) Vehicle speed sensor – informs the ECU of the vehicle speed (not all models).

h) Knock sensor – informs the ECU of pre-ignition (detonation) within the cylinders (not all models).

i) Camshaft sensor – informs the ECU which cylinder is on the firing stroke on systems with sequential injection.

j) Accelerator pedal position sensor – informs the ECU of the pedal position and rate of change.

k) Throttle valve positioner motor – allows the ECU to control the throttle valve position.

l) Engine oil temperature sensor – informs the ECU of the engine oil temperature (not all models).

m) Clutch and brake pedal position sensor – informs the ECU of the pedal positions (not all models).

Signals from each of the sensors are compared by the ECU and, based on this information, the ECU selects the response appropriate to those values, and controls the fuel injectors (varying the pulse width – the length of time the injectors are held open – to provide a richer or weaker air/fuel mixture, as appropriate). The air/fuel mixture is constantly varied by the ECU, to provide the best settings for cranking, starting (with either a hot or cold engine) and engine warm-up, idle, cruising and acceleration.

The ECU also has full control over the engine idle speed, via a stepper motor (depending on model) fitted to the throttle housing. The stepper motor either controls the amount of air passing through a bypass drilling at the side of the throttle or controls the position of the throttle valve itself, depending on model. A sensor informs the ECU of the position, and rate of change, of the accelerator pedal. The ECU then controls the throttle valve by means of a throttle positioning motor integral with the throttle body – no accelerator cable is fitted. The ECU also carries out 'fine tuning' of the idle speed by varying the ignition timing to increase or reduce the torque of the engine as it is idling. This helps to stabilise the idle speed when electrical or mechanical loads (such as headlights, air conditioning, etc) are switched on and off.

The throttle housing is also fitted with an electric heating element. The heater is supplied with current by the ECU, warming the throttle housing on cold starts to help prevent icing of the throttle valve.

The exhaust and evaporative loss emission control systems are described in more detail in Chapter 4C, Section 1.

If there is any abnormality in any of the readings obtained from the coolant temperature sensor, the intake air temperature sensor or the oxygen sensor, the ECU enters its 'back-up' mode. If this happens, the erroneous sensor signal is overridden, and the ECU assumes a preprogrammed 'back-up' value, which will allow the engine to continue running, albeit at reduced efficiency. If the ECU enters this mode, the warning lamp on the instrument panel will be illuminated, and the relevant fault code will be stored in the ECU memory.

If the warning light illuminates, the vehicle should be taken to a Citroën dealer or specialist at the earliest opportunity. Once there, a complete test of the engine management system can be carried out, using a special electronic diagnostic test unit, which is plugged into the system's diagnostic connector, located under the ashtray in the centre console, in front of the gear lever **(see illustration 10.2)**.

6.2 Pressure relief valve – VTi engines

6 Fuel system – depressurisation and pressurising

Note: *Refer to the warning note in Section 1 before proceeding.*

Depressurisation

Warning: The following procedure will merely relieve the pressure in the fuel system – remember that fuel will still be present in the system components and take precautions accordingly before disconnecting any of them.

1 The fuel system referred to in this Section is defined as the tank-mounted fuel pump, the fuel filter (where fitted), the fuel injectors, the fuel rail and the pipes of the fuel lines between these components. All these contain fuel, which will be under pressure while the engine is running, and/or while the ignition is switched on. The pressure will remain for some time after the ignition has been switched off, and must be relieved in a controlled fashion when any of these components are disturbed for servicing work.

2 Some models are equipped with a pressure relief valve on the end of the fuel rail **(see illustration)**. On these models, unscrew the cap from the valve and position a container beneath the valve. Hold a wad of rag over the valve and relieve the pressure in the system by depressing the valve core with a suitable screwdriver. Be prepared for the squirt of fuel as the valve core is depressed and catch it with the rag. Hold the valve core down until no more fuel is expelled from the valve. Once the pressure is relieved, securely refit the valve cap.

3 Where no valve is fitted to the fuel rail, it will be necessary to release the pressure as the fuel pipe is disconnected. Place a container beneath the union and position a large rag around the union to catch any fuel spray, which may be expelled. Slowly release and disconnect the fuel pipe and catch any spilt fuel in the container. Plug the pipe/union to minimise fuel loss and prevent the entry of dirt into the fuel system.

Pressurising

4 After any work is carried out on the fuel system, the system should be pressurised as follows.

5 Depress the accelerator pedal fully then switch on the ignition. Hold the pedal depressed for approximately 1 second then release it. The ECU should then operate the fuel pump for between 20 and 30 seconds to refill the fuel system. Once the fuel pump stops the ignition can be switched off.

7.2 Release the fuel pump access cover

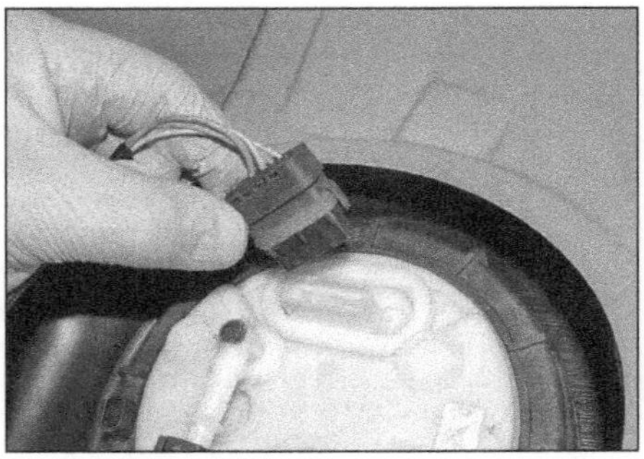

7.3 Disconnect the pump wiring plug

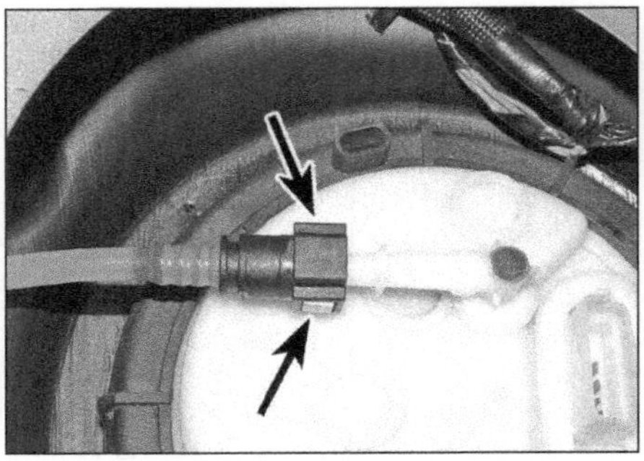

7.4a Depress the release buttons (arrowed) ...

7 Fuel pump – removal and refitting

Note: *The fuel pump is only available as a complete assembly – no components are available separately.*

Removal

1 For access to the fuel pump, tilt or remove the right-hand rear seat cushion (see Chapter 11, Section 23).

2 Using a thin blade, carefully release the plastic access cover retaining clips, and remove the cover from the floor to expose the fuel pump/sender unit **(see illustration)**.

3 Disconnect the wiring connector from the fuel pump, and tape the connector to the vehicle body, to prevent it from disappearing behind the tank **(see illustration)**.

4 Depress the retaining clips and detach the fuel pipe(s) from the top of the pump **(see illustrations)**, bearing in mind the information given in Section 6 on depressurising the fuel system. Plug the pipe end(s) to minimise fuel loss and prevent the entry of dirt. **Note:** *Depending on model, the amount of pipes to the top of the pump will vary note their fitted position, before removal.*

5 Noting the alignment marks on the tank **(see illustrations)**, pump cover and the locking ring, unscrew the ring and remove it from the tank. This is best accomplished by using a screwdriver on the raised ribs of the locking ring. Carefully tap the screwdriver to turn the ring anti-clockwise until it can be unscrewed by hand. Alternatively, a Citroën special tool is available which fits over the collar and allows it to be released using a socket ratchet and extension.

6 Carefully lift the fuel pump assembly out of the fuel tank, taking great care not to damage the fuel gauge sender unit float arm, or to spill fuel onto the interior of the vehicle **(see illustration)**. Recover the rubber sealing ring and discard it – a new one must be used on refitting.

7 If the fuel pump is going to be left out of the fuel tank for a while, screw the ring back to the top of the fuel tank to prevent it from going out of shape. Cover the access hole in the tank to prevent dirt ingress.

Refitting

8 Fit the new sealing ring to the top of the fuel tank **(see illustration)**.

9 Carefully manoeuvre the pump assembly into the fuel tank, taking care not to damage the float arm.

10 Align the notch in the top of the fuel tank with the arrows on the fuel pump cover to locate the pump assembly into position **(see illustration)**

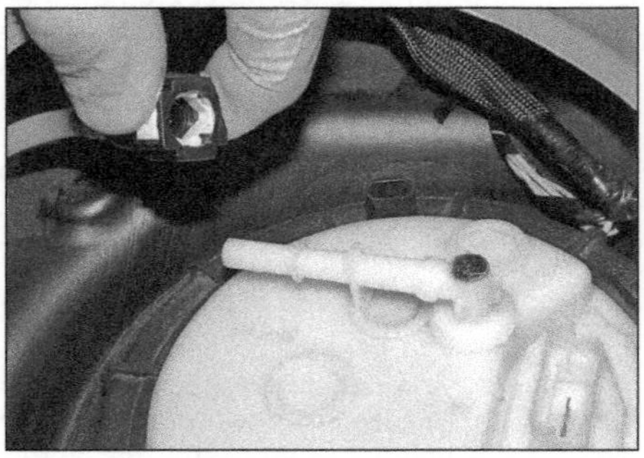

7.4b ... and disconnect the fuel pipe(s)

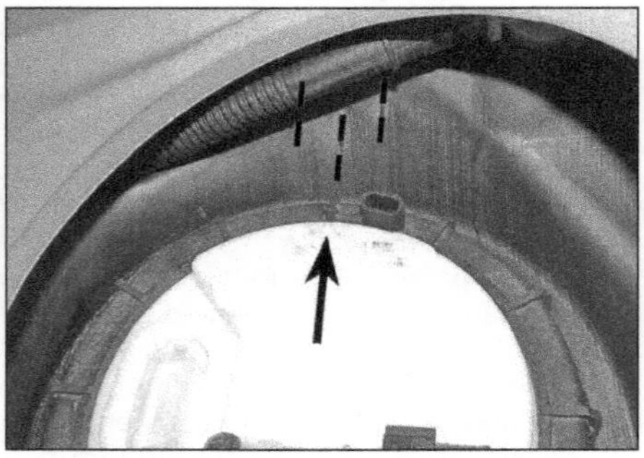

7.5a Fuel sender alignment marks (arrowed)

7.5b Using a home-made tool to slacken the collar

7.6 Lift the fuel pump assembly, taking care not to damage the float arm

7.8 Fit a new sealing ring to the top of the tank

7.10 Align the pump with the cut-out (arrowed) in the fuel tank

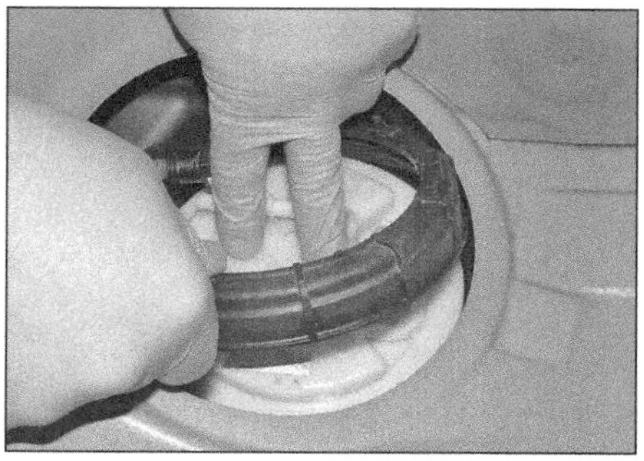

7.11 Hold the pump in position and tighten the securing ring

11 Press down on the pump and refit the locking ring, tighten it securely until its alignment mark aligns with the alignment marks on the fuel tank, as noted on removal **(see illustration)**.

12 Securely reconnect the fuel pipe(s) to the pump cover then reconnect the pump wiring connector.

13 Pressurise the fuel system (see Section 6). Start the engine and check the fuel pump feed and return hoses unions for signs of leakage.

14 If all is well, refit the plastic access cover ensuring its tabs are located correctly.

15 Refit the rear seat cushion with reference to Chapter 11, Section 23, if required.

8 Fuel gauge sender unit – removal and refitting

The fuel gauge sender unit is an integral part of the fuel pump assembly and is not available separately. Refer to Section 7 for removal and refitting details.

9 Fuel tank – removal and refitting

Note: *Refer to the warning note in Section 1 before proceeding.*

Removal

1 Before removing the fuel tank, all fuel must be drained from the tank. Since a fuel tank drain plug is not provided, it is therefore preferable to carry out the removal operation when the tank is nearly empty. Before proceeding, disconnect the battery (refer to precautions in Chapter 5A, Section 1) and siphon or hand-pump the remaining fuel from the tank.

2 Lift the rear seat cushion and remove the cover from the floor to expose the fuel pump **(see illustration 7.2)**. Disconnect the wiring connector and fuel pipe(s) from the top of the fuel pump, with reference to Section 7.

3 Chock the front wheels then jack up the rear of the vehicle and support it on axle stands (see *Jacking and vehicle support*). Remove the rear roadwheels and inner wheel arch liners.

4 Where applicable, undo the retaining screws and remove the plastic undershields from under the rear of the vehicle **(see illustration)**.

5 Unclip the fuel pipes from the side of the fuel tank **(see illustration)**. If required, disconnect the fuel pipe connections and remove the fuel pipes with the fuel tank.

6 Remove the rear shock absorbers and springs as described in Chapter 10, Section 12 and 13. This will need to be done to allow the rear axle to move downwards to allow the removal of the fuel tank.

7 Remove the rear part of the exhaust system as described in Section 15.

8 If required, undo the fasteners, and remove the heat shield from the underside of the fuel tank **(see illustration)**.

9 Undo the upper retaining bolt and the lower retaining nut from the fuel filler neck **(see illustrations)**.

10 Place a trolley jack with an interposed block of wood beneath the tank, then raise

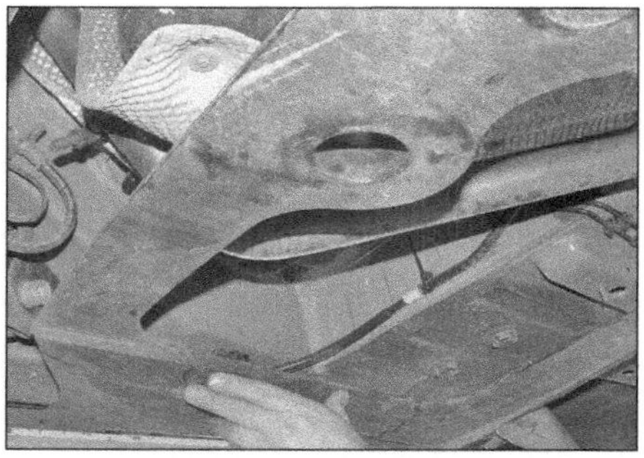

9.4 Remove the plastic undershields – where fitted

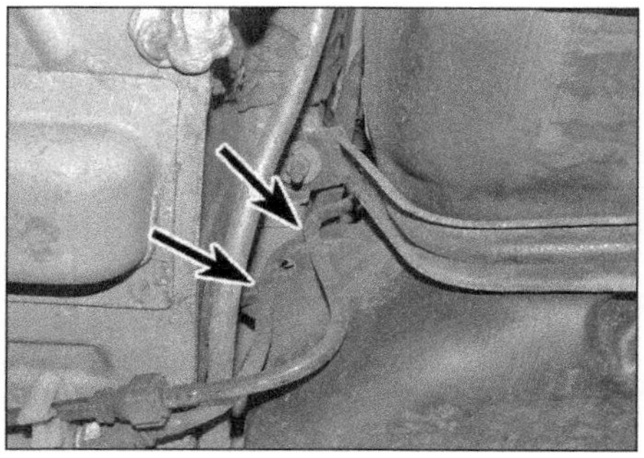

9.5 Release the fuel lines (arrowed) from the fuel tank

9.8 Remove the heat shield (arrowed)

9.9a Undo the fuel filler neck upper securing nut (arrowed) ...

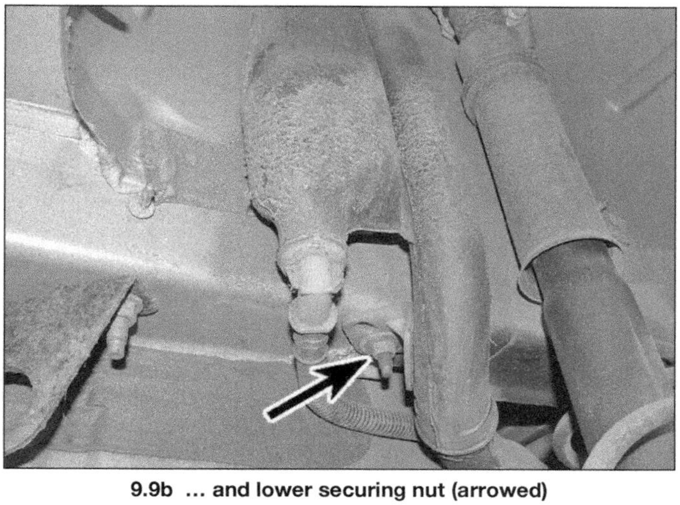

9.9b ... and lower securing nut (arrowed)

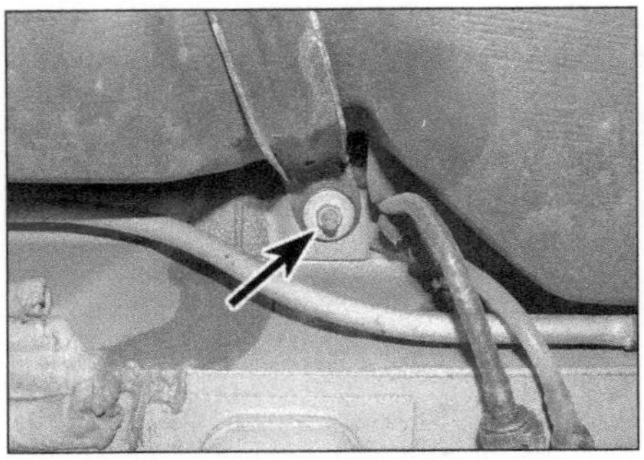

9.11a Undo the fuel tank front retaining strap nuts (arrowed) ...

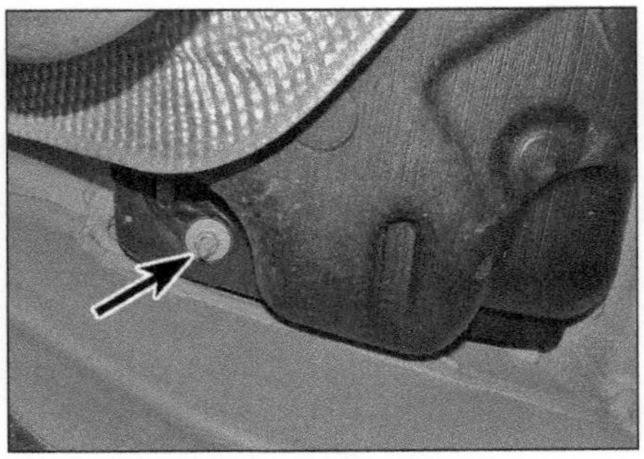

9.11b ... side securing nut ...

9.11c ... and rear retaining strap nut (arrowed)

the jack until it is supporting the weight of the tank.

11 Slacken and remove the bolts securing the fuel tank to the body **(see illustrations)**. Release the filler neck seal from the body at the filler cap aperture.

12 Slowly lower the fuel tank; ensuring the filler neck assembly is guided out of position without placing any stress on it.

13 If the tank is contaminated with sediment or water, remove the fuel pump (Section 7), and swill the tank out with clean fuel. The tank is injection-moulded from a synthetic material – if seriously damaged, it should be renewed. However, in certain cases, it may be possible to have small leaks or minor damage repaired. Seek the advice of a specialist before attempting to repair the fuel tank.

14 It is not possible to separate the filler neck from the tank. If damaged, the complete assembly must be renewed.

Refitting

15 Refitting is the reverse of the removal procedure, noting the following points:

a) *Ensure the wiring connector and fuel pipes are securely reconnected and retained by all the relevant clips. When lifting the tank back into position, take care to ensure that the pipes/wiring do not become trapped between the tank and vehicle body.*

b) *Refit the rear suspension as described in Chapter 10, Section 12 and 13.*

c) *Refit the exhaust as described in Section 15.*

d) *On completion, refill the tank with a small amount of fuel and pressurise the fuel system as described in Section 6. Check for signs of leakage prior to taking the vehicle out on the road.*

10 Engine management system – testing and adjustment

Testing

1 If a fault appears in the engine management system, first ensure that all the system wiring connectors are securely connected and free of corrosion. Ensure that the fault is not due to poor maintenance; ie, check that the air filter element is clean, the spark plugs are in good condition and correctly gapped, the cylinder compression pressures are correct and that the engine breather hoses are clear and undamaged, referring to Chapters 1A, 2A, 2B and 5B for further information.

2 If these checks fail to reveal the cause of the problem, the vehicle should be taken to a suitablyequipped Citroën dealer or specialist for testing using a diagnostic tester, which is connected into the diagnostic socket located under the ashtray in the centre console, in front of the gear lever **(see illustration)**. The tester will locate the fault quickly and simply, alleviating the need to test all the system components individually, which is a time-consuming operation that carries a risk of damaging the ECU.

Adjustment

3 Whilst it is possible to check the exhaust CO level and the idle speed, if these are found to be in need of adjustment, the car *must* be taken to a suitably equipped Citroën dealer or specialist or further testing. Neither the mixture adjustment (exhaust gas CO level) nor the idle speed is adjustable, and should either be incorrect, a fault must be present in the engine management system.

11 Throttle housing – removal and refitting

Removal

Non-VTi engines

1 The throttle housing is located on the left-hand side of the intake manifold.

2 Remove the air cleaner housing and air ducting as described in Section 2.

3 Depress the retaining clip and disconnect the wiring connector(s) from the throttle body **(see illustration)**. **Note:** *Depending on model there may be more than one connector.*

4 Undo the retaining screws and remove the throttle housing from the left-hand end of the intake manifold **(see illustration)**. Recover the sealing ring from the manifold and discard it; a new one must be used on refitting.

VTi engines

5 The throttle housing is located on the right-hand side of the intake manifold.

10.2 Diagnostic plug connector (arrowed)

11.3 Disconnect the wiring connector from the throttle housing – non-VTi engines

11.4 Undo the three retaining screws (arrowed)

11.7 Remove the air intake hose

11.8 Disconnect the wiring connector from the throttle housing – VTi engines

11.9a Undo the three retaining screws (arrowed) ...

11.9b ... and remove the throttle housing from the manifold

11.10 Fit a new seal to the intake manifold

6 Remove the upper air cleaner housing and air ducting as described in Section 2.

7 Slacken the securing clip and remove the intake hose from the throttle housing **(see illustration)**.

8 Depress the retaining clip and disconnect the wiring connector(s) from the throttle body **(see illustration)**.

9 Undo the retaining screws and remove the throttle housing from the right-hand end of the intake manifold **(see illustrations)**. Recover the sealing ring from the manifold and discard it; a new one must be used on refitting.

Refitting

10 Refitting is a reversal of the removal procedure, noting the following points:

a) *Fit a new sealing ring to the manifold **(see illustration)**, then refit the throttle housing and securely tighten its retaining screws.*

b) *Ensure all wiring is correctly routed, and that the connectors are securely reconnected.*

c) *Refit the air cleaner housing and air ducts with reference to Section 2.*

12 Engine management system components – removal and refitting

Note: *Refer to the warning note in Section 1 before proceeding.*

1 Before proceeding with removing any of the engine management system components, disconnect the battery (refer to precautions in Chapter 5A, Section 1).

Fuel rail and injectors

Note: *If a faulty injector is suspected, before condemning the injector, it is worth trying the effect of one of the proprietary injector cleaning treatments, which are available from car accessory shops.*

2 Remove the air cleaner housing and air ducting as described in Section 2.

3 Before any work is carried out on the fuel system, depressurise the system as described in Section 6.

1.4 litre non-VTi models

4 Remove the ignition HT coil as described in Chapter 5B, Section 3.

5 Depress the retaining clip and disconnect the fuel pipe from the right-hand end of the fuel rail **(see illustration)**.

6 Slacken and remove the two bolts securing the fuel rail to the cylinder head, and the nut securing the rail to the manifold **(see illustration)**.

7 Loosen the bolt securing the fuel rail centre bracket to the intake manifold, then lift off the bracket (the bracket is slotted to ease removal) **(see illustration)**.

8 Disconnect the injector wiring harness connector, and then unclip the connector from the rear of the intake manifold. Also disconnect the wiring connectors from the throttle housing and position the wiring harness clear of the manifold so that it does not hinder fuel rail removal.

9 Carefully ease the fuel rail and injector assembly out from the cylinder head and

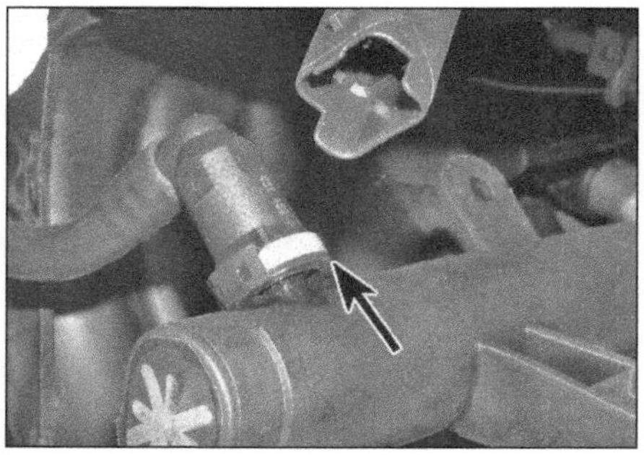

12.5 Depress the retaining clip (arrowed) to disconnect the fuel hose

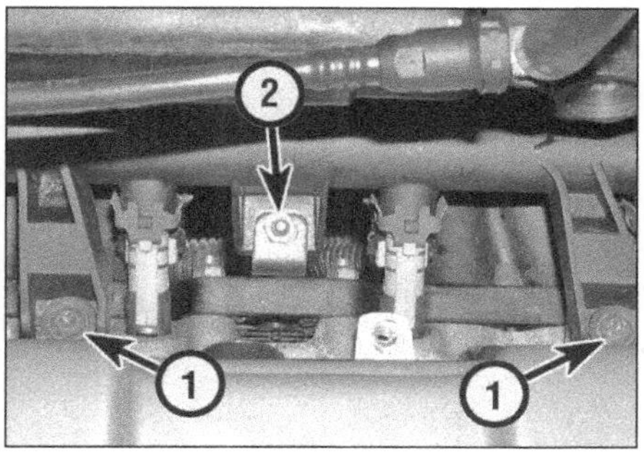

12.6 Unscrew the fuel rail mounting bolts (1) and the retaining nut (2) ...

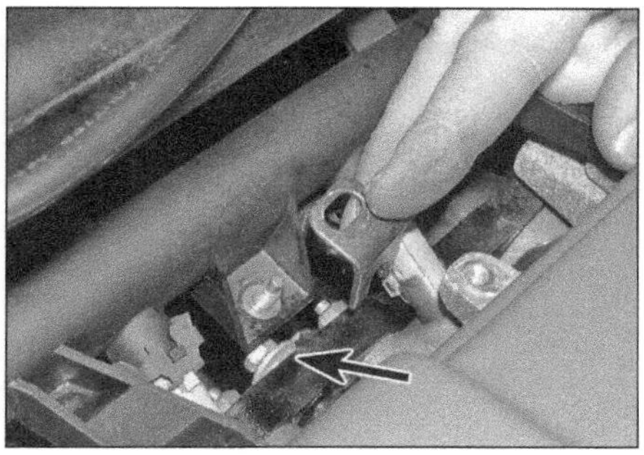

12.7 ... then slacken the bolt (arrowed) and lift off the centre bracket

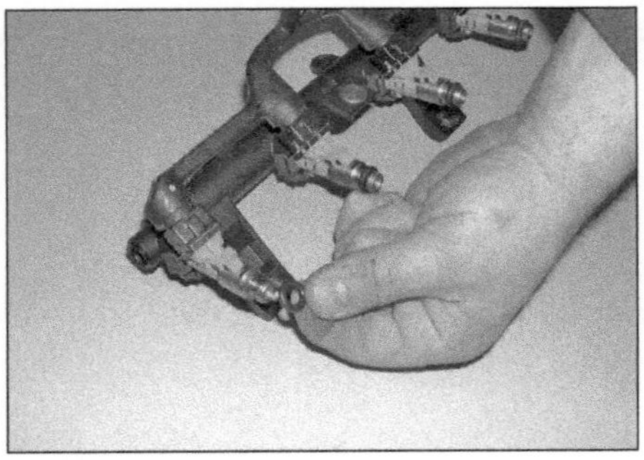

12.9 Remove the seal from the end of each injector

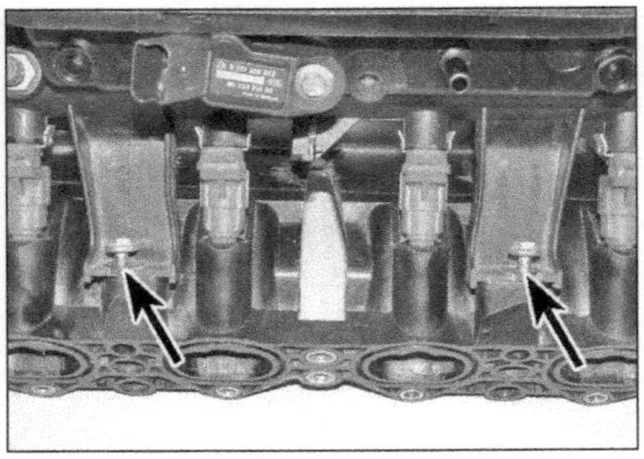

12.12 Undo the two retaining bolts (arrowed)

12.13 Slide off the retaining clip and remove the injector from the fuel rail

manoeuvre it out of position. Remove the seals from the end of each injector and discard them; they must be renewed whenever they are disturbed **(see illustration)**.

10 Refitting is a reversal of the removal procedure, noting the following points.

a) *Fit new seals to all disturbed injector unions.*
b) *Apply a smear of engine oil to the seals to aid installation, then ease the injectors and fuel rail into position ensuring that none of the seals are displaced.*
c) *On completion, pressurise the fuel system as described in Section 6. Start the engine and check for fuel leaks.*

1.6 litre non-VTi models

11 Remove the intake manifold as described in Section 13.

12 Undo the two bolts and remove the fuel rail with injectors from the manifold **(see illustration)**.

13 Disconnect the wiring connector(s) then slide out the retaining clip(s) and remove the relevant injector(s) from the fuel rail. Remove the seals from each disturbed injector and discard; all disturbed seals must be renewed **(see illustration)**.

14 Refitting is a reversal of the removal procedure, noting the following points.

a) *Fit new seals to all disturbed injector unions **(see illustration)**.*
b) *Apply a smear of engine oil to the seals to aid installation, then ease the injectors and fuel rail into position ensuring that none of the seals are displaced.*
c) *On completion, pressurise the fuel system as described in Section 6. Start the engine and check for fuel leaks.*

VTi models

15 Depress the release button and disconnect the fuel supply hose from the left-hand end of the fuel rail. **Note:** *Depressurise the system as described in Section 6, before disconnecting.*

16
Unclip the wiring loom from across the top of the cylinder head cover, and undo the two retaining bolts from the fuel rail **(see illustrations)**.

17 Carefully ease the fuel rail, complete with injectors, from the cylinder head **(see illustration)**.

18 Depress the retaining clip, and disconnect the wiring connectors from the four injectors **(see illustration)**

19 Remove the O-rings from the end of each injector **(see illustration)** and discard them; these must be renewed whenever they are disturbed.

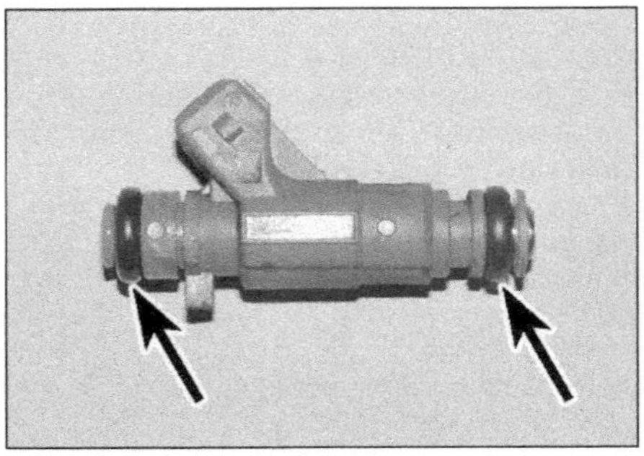

12.14 Renew all injector seals (arrowed)

12.16a Unclip the wiring loom ...

12.16b ... undo the two retaining bolts (arrowed) ...

12.17 ... then withdraw the fuel rail and injectors

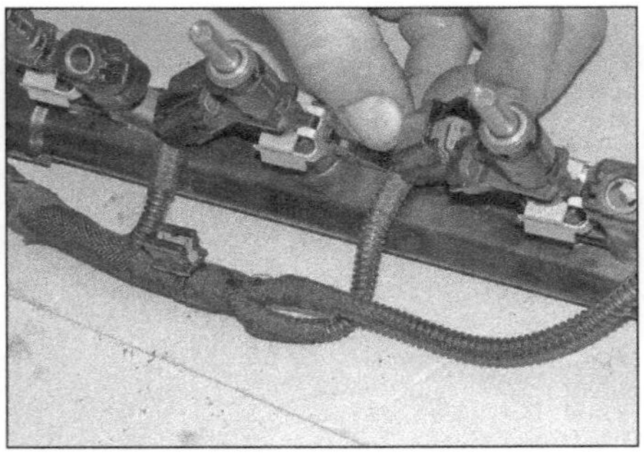

12.18 Disconnect the wiring connectors

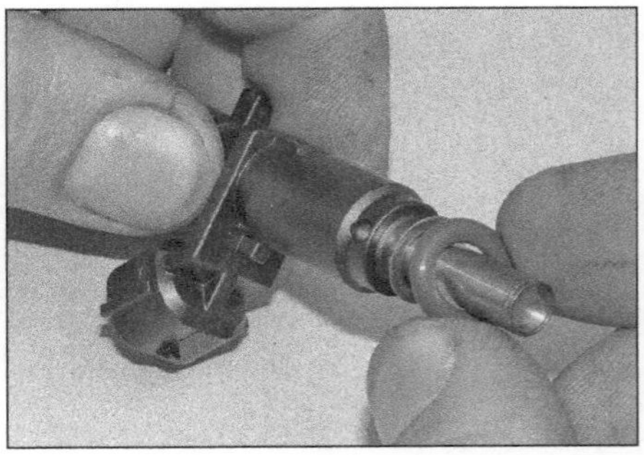

12.19 Remove the seal from the end of each injector

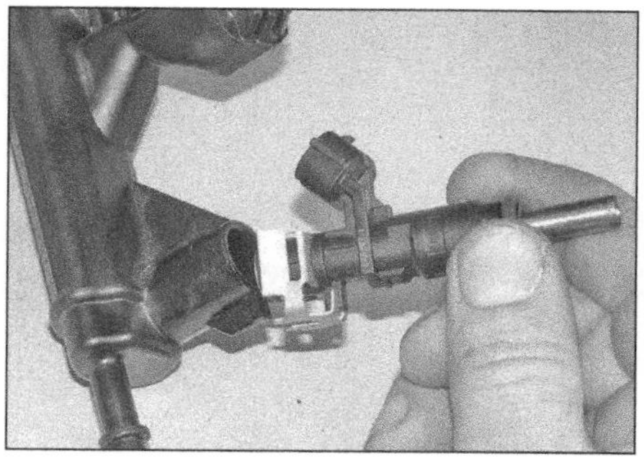

12.20 Remove the injector from the fuel rail

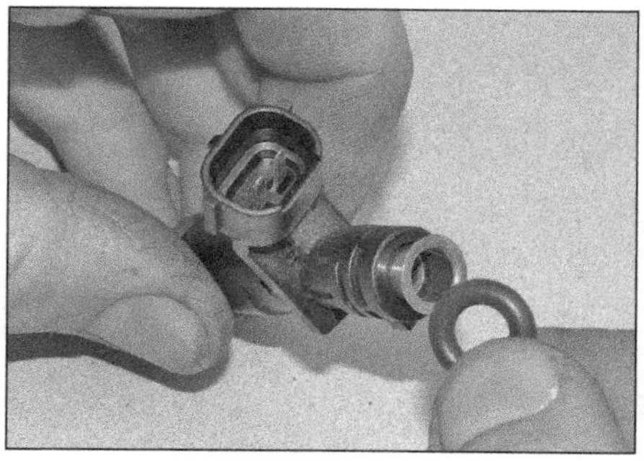

12.21 Remove the upper seal from the end of each injector

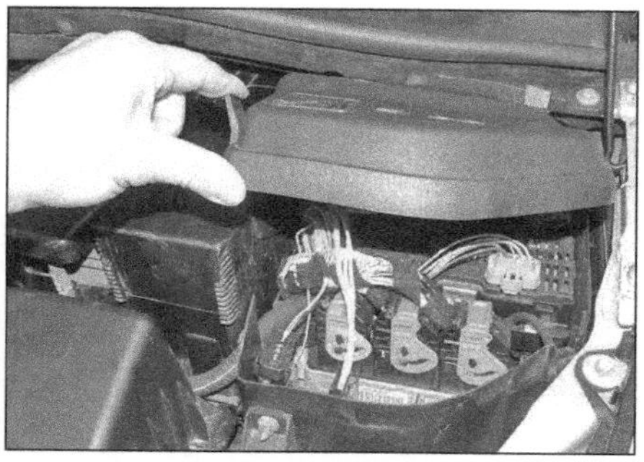

12.27 Remove the fusebox cover

20 Slide out the retaining clip and remove the relevant injector from the fuel rail **(see illustration)**.

21 Remove the upper O-ring from each disturbed injector and discard; all disturbed O-rings must be renewed **(see illustration)**.

22 Refitting is a reversal of the removal procedure, noting the following points.

a) Fit new O-rings to all disturbed injector unions.

b) Apply a smear of clean engine oil to the O-rings to aid installation then ease the injectors and fuel rail into position ensuring that none of the O-rings are displaced.

c) On completion start the engine and check for fuel leaks.

Fuel pressure regulator

23 The fuel pressure regulator is an integral part of the fuel pump assembly and is not available separately. Refer to Section 7 for removal and refitting details.

Throttle potentiometer

24 The potentiometer is an integral part of the throttle housing and is not available separately see your local dealer for availability of parts. Refer to Section 11 for removal and refitting of the throttle housing.

Electronic control unit (ECU)

Note: *If a new ECU is being fitted, the vehicle will not start until the immobiliser ECU has been matched to the engine management ECU. This can only be performed using dedicated test equipment. Consequently, entrust the procedure to a Citroën dealer or suitably-equipped specialist.*

25 Disconnect the battery (refer to precautions in Chapter 5A, Section 1).

26 The ECU is located on the left-hand side of the engine compartment, inside the engine compartment fusebox.

27 Remove the plastic cover from the top of the fusebox **(see illustration)**.

28 Release the locking clips and disconnect the wiring connectors from the top of the ECU **(see illustration)**.

29 Lift the ECU upwards and withdraw it out from the engine compartment fusebox.

30 Refitting is a reverse of the removal procedure ensuring the wiring connectors are securely reconnected.

12.28 Release the locking clips and disconnect the ECU wiring plugs

Idle speed stepper motor (early non-VTi models)

31 The idle speed stepper motor is fitted to the rear of the throttle housing.

32 Disconnect the wiring connector from the motor **(see illustration)**.

33 Slacken and remove the retaining screws then remove the motor from the throttle housing **(see illustration)**. If necessary, remove the throttle potentiometer to improve access to the motor lower screw.

34 Refitting is a reversal of the removal

12.32 Disconnect the idle speed stepper motor wiring plug (arrowed) – early non-VTi engines

12.33 Undo the retaining screws (arrowed) and remove the motor from the housing

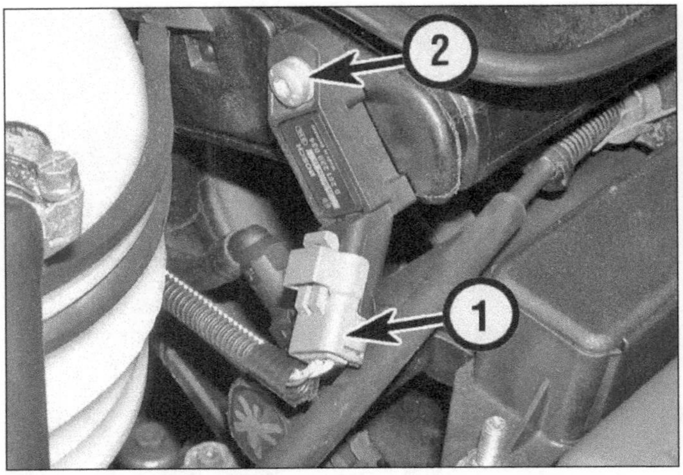

12.36a Disconnect the wiring connector (1) then undo the retaining screw (2) and remove the MAP sensor – 1.4 litre non-VTi engines

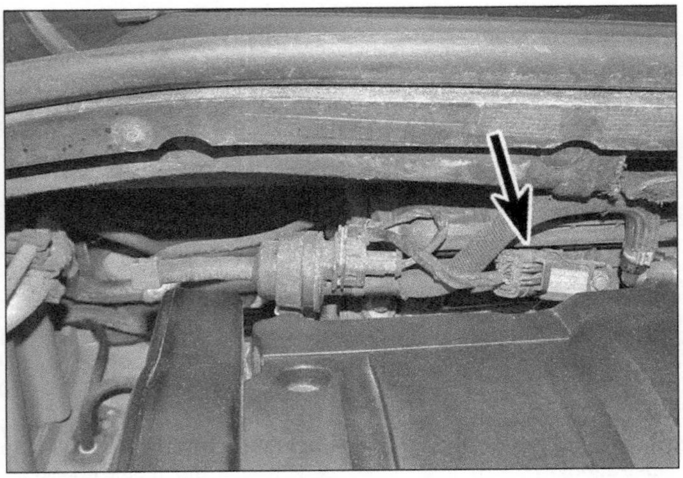

12.36b Disconnect the wiring connector (arrowed) – 1.6 litre non-VTi engines

procedure ensuring the seal is in good condition.

Manifold pressure sensor

35 The MAP sensor is mounted on the intake manifold.

36 Disconnect the wiring connector then undo the screw and remove the sensor from the manifold **(see illustrations)**.

37 Refitting is a reversal of the removal procedure ensuring the sensor seal is in good condition.

Coolant temperature sensor

38 The coolant temperature sensor is either screwed, or secured by a retaining clip, in the coolant outlet housing on the left-hand end of the cylinder head. Refer to Chapter 3, Section 7, for removal and refitting information.

Intake air temperature sensor

39 The intake air temperature sensor is integral with the throttle housing and is not available separately.

Crankshaft position sensor

Non-VTi engines

40 The crankshaft sensor is situated on the front face of the transmission clutch housing.

41 Disconnect the sensor wiring connector and unclip the wiring. Undo the retaining bolt and remove the sensor and bracket assembly from the transmission unit **(see illustrations)**.

42 Refitting is reverse of the removal procedure.

VTi engines

43 The crankshaft sensor is situated at the rear of the cylinder block, below the starter motor **(see illustration)**.

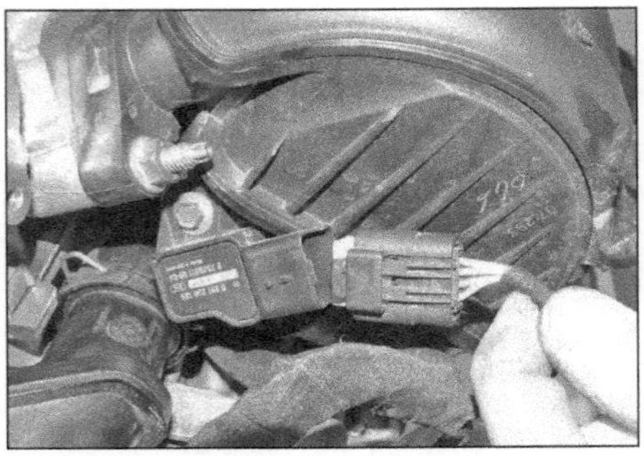

12.36c Disconnect the wiring connector – 1.6 litre VTi engines

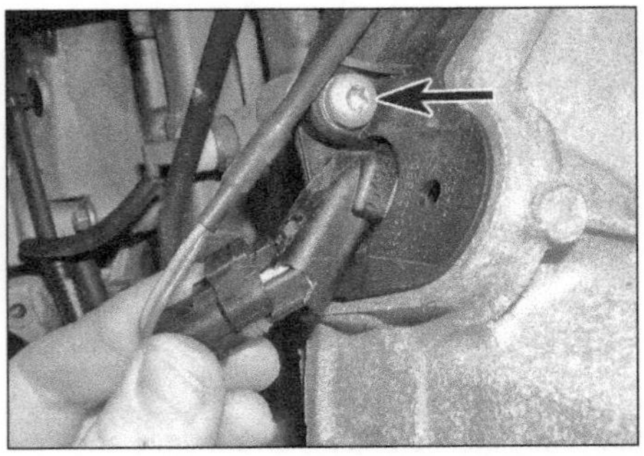

12.41a Disconnect the wiring connector, then undo the retaining screw (arrowed) ...

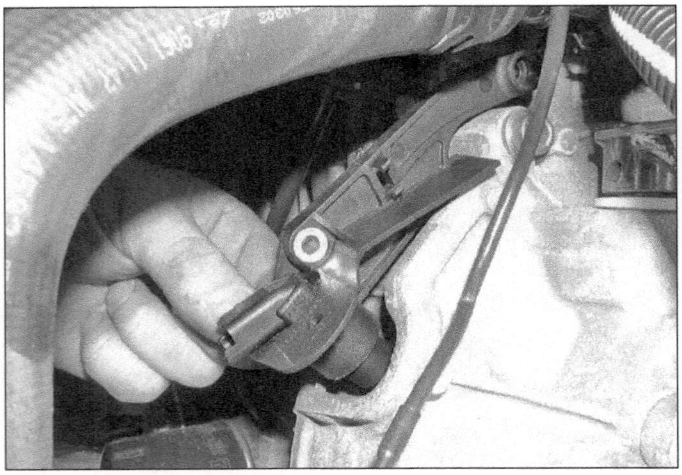

12.41b ... and remove the crankshaft sensor from the front of the transmission housing – non-VTi engines

12.43 Crankshaft position sensor (arrowed) – VTi engines

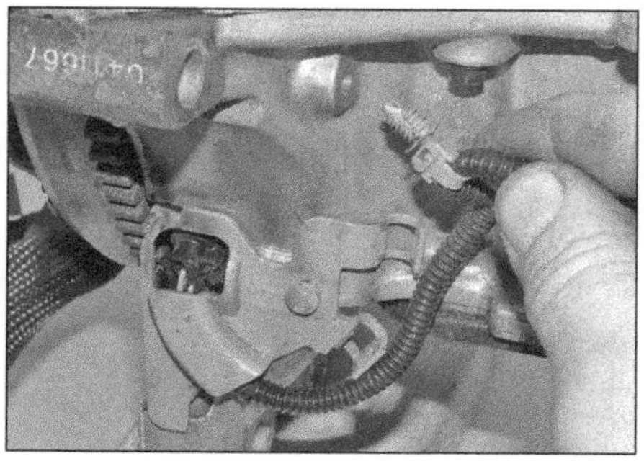

12.44a Remove the wiring clip ...

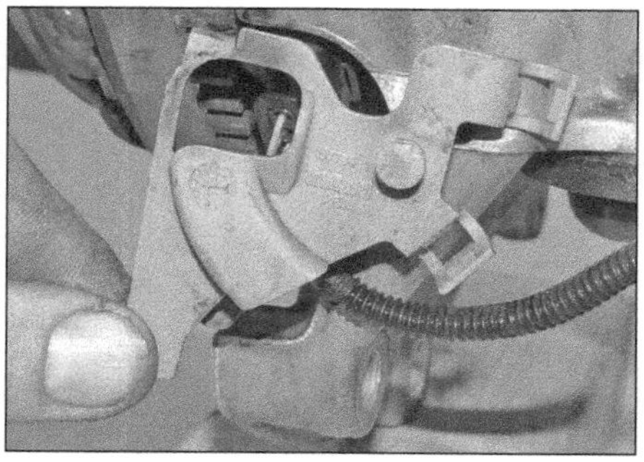

12.44b ... unclip the plastic cover ...

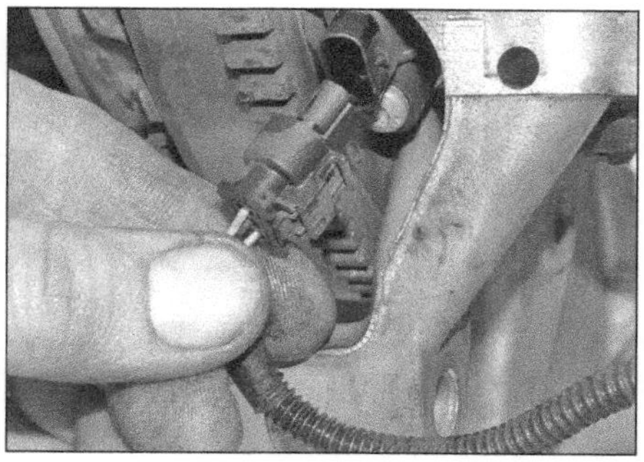

12.44c ... and disconnect the wiring connector

12.47 Remove the throttle housing heating element – 1.4 litre non-VTi engines

12.52 Camshaft position sensors (arrowed) – VTi engines

12.53a Disconnect the wiring connector ...

44 Release the securing clips for the wiring loom, unclip the plastic cover and disconnect the sensor wiring connector. Undo the retaining bolt and remove the sensor from behind the flywheel **(see illustrations)**.

45 Refitting is reverse of the removal procedure.

Throttle housing heating element

Note: *The heating element is only fitted to aluminium throttle housings. Plastic housings do not need a heater.*

46 The heating element is fitted to the top of the throttle housing.

47 Disconnect the wiring connector then unscrew the retaining screw and remove the heating element from the throttle housing **(see illustration)**.

48 Refitting is the reverse of removal.

Vehicle speed sensor

49 The ECU receives vehicle speed data from the wheel speed sensors, via the ABS ECU. Refer to Chapter 9, Section 19 for removal.

Knock sensor

50 Refer to Chapter 5B, Section 5.

Air conditioning pressure switch

51 The air conditioning pressure switch is fitted to the refrigerant pipe located on the right-hand rear of the engine compartment. Refer to Chapter 3, Section 12 for removal.

Camshaft position sensor

52 There are two camshaft position sensors located on the left-hand end of the cylinder head cover on VTi engines **(see illustration)**, and one camshaft sensor fitted to non-VTi engines.

53 Disconnect the wiring plug, then undo the bolt and remove the sensor from the cylinder head cover **(see illustrations)**.

54 Refitting is the reverse of removal ensuring the sensor seal is in good condition **(see illustration)**.

12.53b ... undo the bolt and withdraw the sensor

12.54 Renew the O-ring seal

13.3 Disconnect the pressure sensor wiring connector

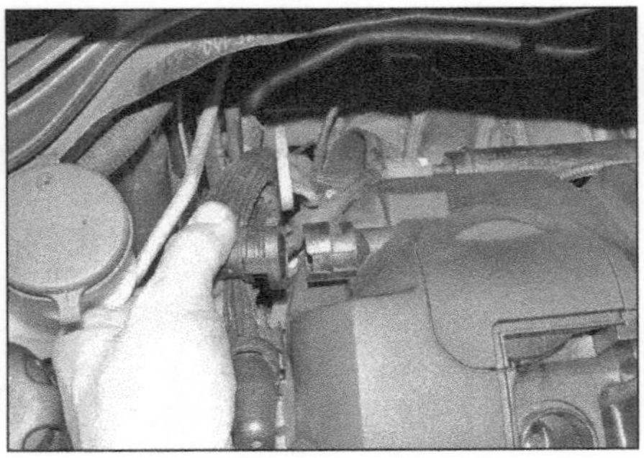

13.4 Disconnect the breather pipe

13.5 Undo the bracket mounting bolt (arrowed)

Throttle valve positioner motor

55 The throttle valve positioner motor (where fitted) is integral with the throttle body, and is not available separately.

Accelerator pedal position sensor

56 The sensor is integral with the accelerator pedal assembly – see Section 3.

13 Intake manifold – removal and refitting

Note: *Refer to the warning note in Section 1 before proceeding.*

Removal

1 Remove the fuel rail and injectors as described in Section 12.

2 Remove the throttle housing as described in Section 11.

3 Disconnect the wiring connector from the manifold pressure sensor **(see illustration)**.

4 Disconnect the breather/vacuum pipe from the cylinder head cover **(see illustration)**.

5 Undo the retaining bolt and move the purge valve to one side, disconnect the vapour pipe(s) from the intake manifold **(see illustration)**.

6 Working your way along the lower edge of the manifold, unclip the wiring loom and move it to one side, noting its fitted position **(see illustration)**.

7 On VTi models, disconnect the wiring connector from the eccentric shaft actuator at the left-hand rear of the cylinder head. Undo the actuator retaining bolts and then remove it from the cylinder head by using a 4 mm Allen key, and turning the centre shaft anti-clockwise while withdrawing the actuator from the cylinder head **(see illustrations)**.

8 Undo the retaining bolts and remove the lower mounting bracket from the intake manifold **(see illustration)**.

9 Undo the manifold retaining nuts and withdraw the manifold from the engine compartment. Recover the four manifold seals and discard them; new ones must be used on refitting **(see illustrations)**.

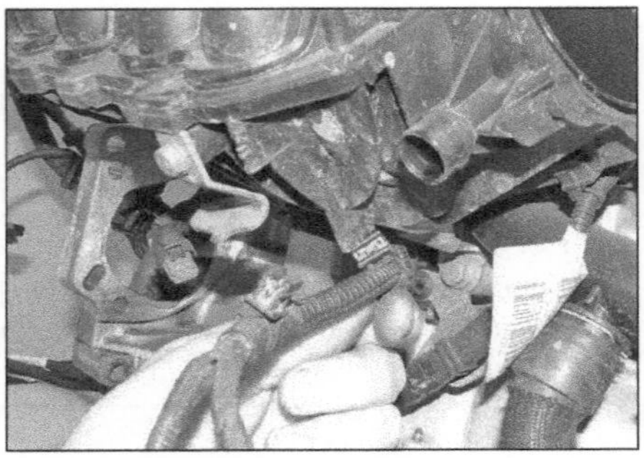

13.6 Unclip the wiring loom

13.7a Undo the retaining bolts (arrowed) ...

13.7b ... then, using an Allen key, withdraw the actuator from the cylinder head

13.8 Undo the bracket mounting bolts (arrowed)

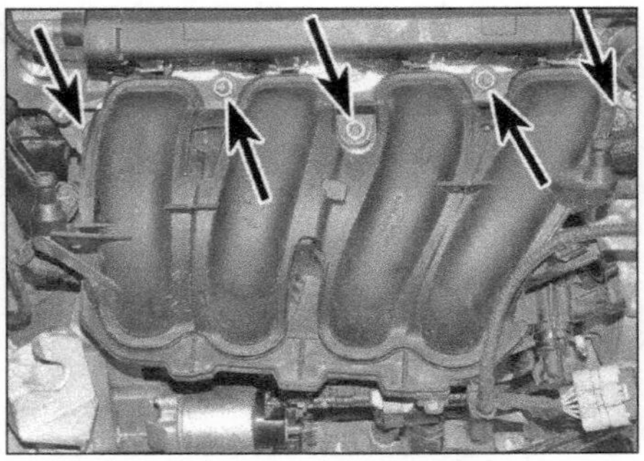

13.9a Intake manifold nuts (arrowed)

13.9b Withdraw the manifold from the head

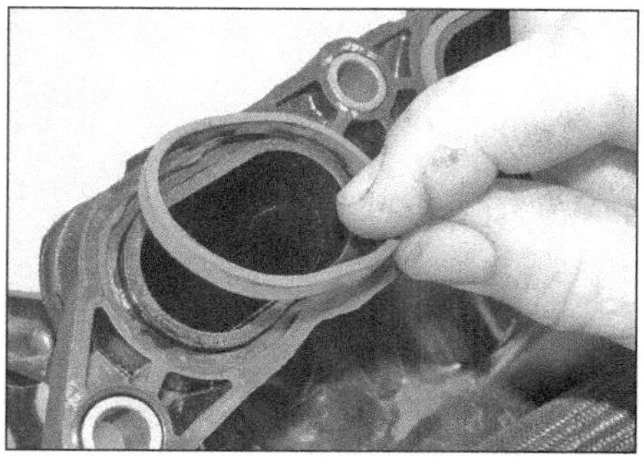

13.10 Ensure new manifold seals are fitted

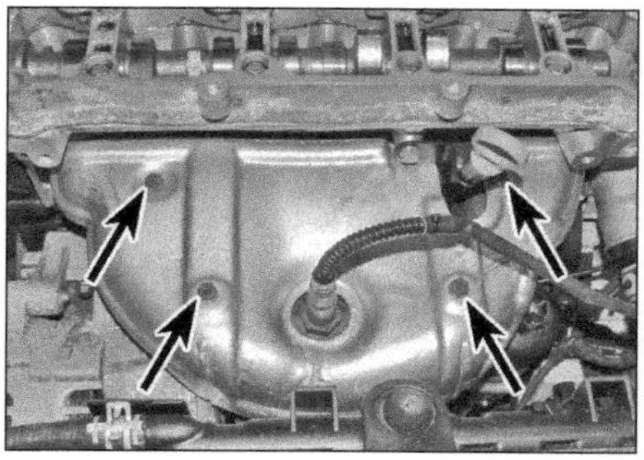

14.3a Undo the heat shield retaining bolts (arrowed) ...

14.3b ... and where applicable the dipstick mounting bolt

Refitting

10 Refitting is a reverse of the removal procedure, noting the following points:

*a) Ensure that the manifold and cylinder head mating surfaces are clean and dry, then locate the new seals in their recesses in the manifold **(see illustration)**. Refit the manifold and tighten its retaining nuts to the specified torque.*

b) Ensure that all relevant hoses are reconnected to their original positions and are securely held (where necessary) by the retaining clips.

c) Ensure the wiring is correctly routed and all connectors are securely reconnected.

14 Exhaust manifold – removal and refitting

Removal

1 Disconnect the battery (refer to precautions in Chapter 5A, Section 1).

2 Firmly apply the handbrake, and then jack up the front of the vehicle and support it on axle stands (see *Jacking and vehicle support*). Release the screws and remove the engine undershield (where fitted).

Non-VTi models

3 Slacken and remove the retaining screws and remove the shroud from the top of the exhaust manifold. It may be necessary to remove the engine lifting eye bracket from the left-hand end of the cylinder head. On early models undo the retaining bolt and remove the oil dipstick tube **(see illustrations)**.

4 On some models, a second heat shield is fitted on the underside of the manifold, above the oil filter. Undo the bolts and remove the heat shield.

5 Trace the oxygen sensors wiring back to the connectors and disconnect them.

6 Undo the nuts securing the exhaust front pipe to the manifold, and then remove the bolt securing the front pipe to its mounting bracket. Disconnect the front pipe from the manifold, and recover the gasket.

Caution: Do not place any strain on the flexible section of the exhaust front pipe; it is easily damaged.

7 Undo the retaining nuts securing the manifold to the head. Manoeuvre the manifold out of the engine compartment, and discard the manifold gasket(s).

VTi models

Note: *The exhaust manifold and catalytic converter are a complete assembly, and cannot be renewed separately.*

8 Undo the bolts and remove the heat shield from the top of the exhaust manifold **(see illustrations)**.

9 Disconnect the oxygen sensor wiring connectors and unclip them from the mounting bracket **(see illustration)**.

10 Remove the upper oxygen sensor from the top of the catalytic converter **(see illustration)**.

11 Undo the bolts and remove the heat shield from around the front of the catalytic converter **(see illustration)**.

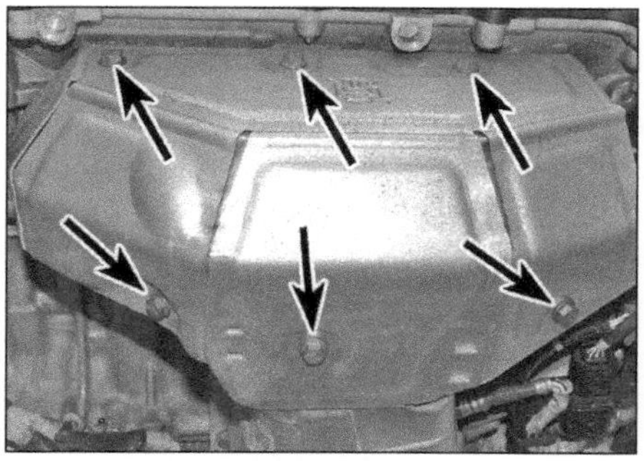

14.8a Undo the heat shield retaining bolts (arrowed) ...

14.8b ... and remove the heat shield – VTi engines

14.9 Disconnect the sensor wiring connectors

14.10 Remove the oxygen sensor ...

14.11 ... and then the lower heat shield

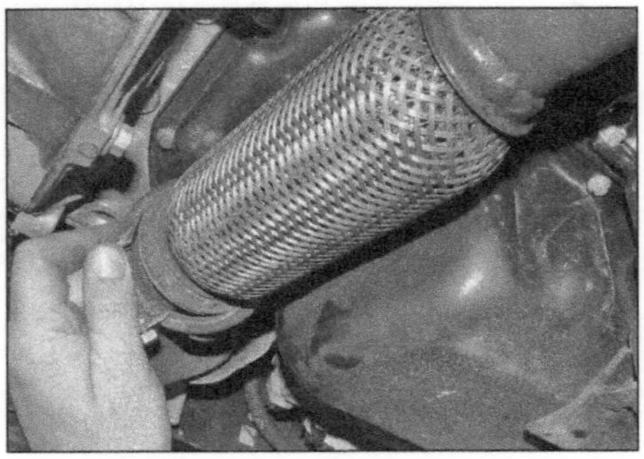

14.12 Undo the clamp from the front pipe

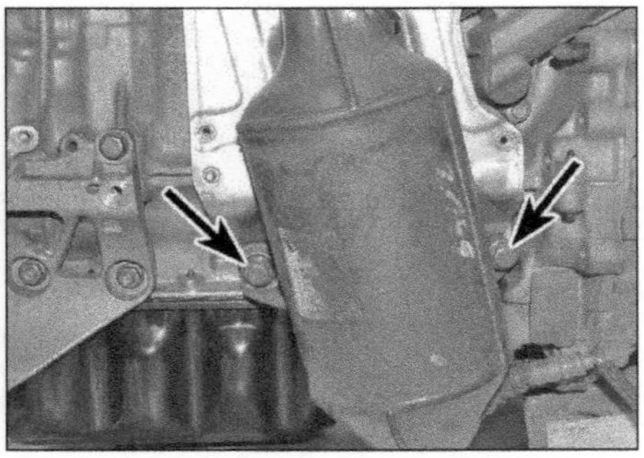

14.13 Undo the catalytic converter mounting bolts (arrowed)

14.15 Remove the exhaust manifold

14.17 Manifold gasket has built-in heat shield – VTi engines

12 Working underneath the vehicle, undo the retaining clamp bolt and disconnect the front exhaust pipe from the bottom of the catalytic converter **(see illustration)**.

13 Undo the two mounting bolts from each side of the catalytic converter **(see illustration)**.

14 If necessary to gain better access, remove the radiator and fan assembly as described in Chapter 3.

15 Undo the manifold-to-cylinder head nuts, and manoeuvre the manifold from the vehicle **(see illustration)**. **Note:** *The lower oxygen sensor can remain fitted to the lower part of the catalytic converter; make sure the wiring is disconnected.*

16 Remove the manifold gasket/heat shield and discard, as a new one will be required for refitting.

Refitting

17 Refitting is the reverse of the removal procedure, noting the following points:

a) Examine all the exhaust manifold studs for signs of damage and corrosion; remove all traces of corrosion, and repair or renew any damaged studs.

b) Ensure that the manifold and cylinder head sealing faces are clean and flat, and fit the new manifold gasket/heat shield ***(see illustration)****. Tighten the manifold retaining nuts to the specified torque.*

c) Reconnect the front pipe to the catalytic converter.

d) Where necessary (on non-VTi models), renew the oil dipstick tube O-ring.

15 Exhaust system – general information, removal and refitting

General information

1 The system is either a three or four-piece section exhaust, depending on model. On VTi engines, the catalytic converter is part of the exhaust manifold, see Section 14.

2 The system is suspended throughout its entire length by rubber mountings, and supported by a rubber-mounting block where the front pipe goes over the front subframe.

3 To remove the system or part of the system, first jack up the front or rear of the car and support it on axle stands (see *Jacking and vehicle support*). Alternatively, position the car over an inspection pit or on car ramps. Undo the retaining bolts/nuts and remove the engine undershield.

Removal

Catalytic converter/front pipe

Note: *On VTi engines, the catalytic converter/front pipe is part of the exhaust manifold, see Section 14.*

4 Apply the handbrake, then jack up the front of the vehicle and support it on axle stands (see *Jacking and vehicle support*). Undo the securing bolts/nuts and remove the engine undershield. Disconnect the battery, (refer to precautions in Chapter 5A, Section 1).

5 Place a sheet of thick cardboard over the rear of the radiator to protect it from accidental damage.

6 Trace the wiring back from the oxygen sensors to their wiring connectors **(see illustration)**. Disconnect the connectors and free the wiring from all its clips and ties so the sensors are free to be removed with the front pipe.

7 Undo the bolt securing the exhaust to the support bracket to the underside of the transmission casing **(see illustration)**.

8 Undo the nuts securing the catalytic converter/front pipe flange joint to the manifold, separate the flange joint and collect the gasket.

9 Slacken and remove the two nut(s) securing the front pipe flange joint to the intermediate pipe **(see illustration)**. Withdraw the catalytic

15.6 Disconnect the oxygen sensor wiring connectors (arrowed)

15.7 Undo the exhaust support bracket bolt (arrowed)

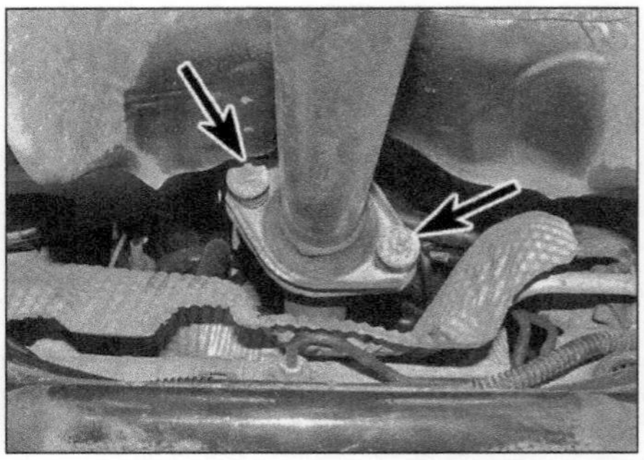

15.9 Front pipe-to-middle pipe retaining clamp bolts (arrowed)

15.10 Flexible pipe-to-catalytic converter retaining clamp (arrowed)

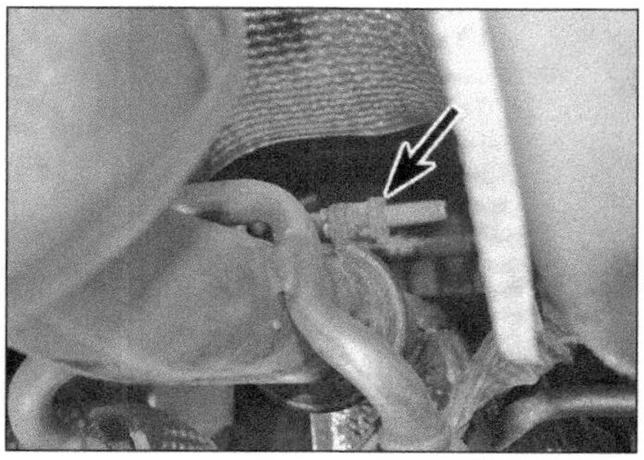

15.11 Front flexible pipe-to-middle pipe retaining clamp bolt (arrowed)

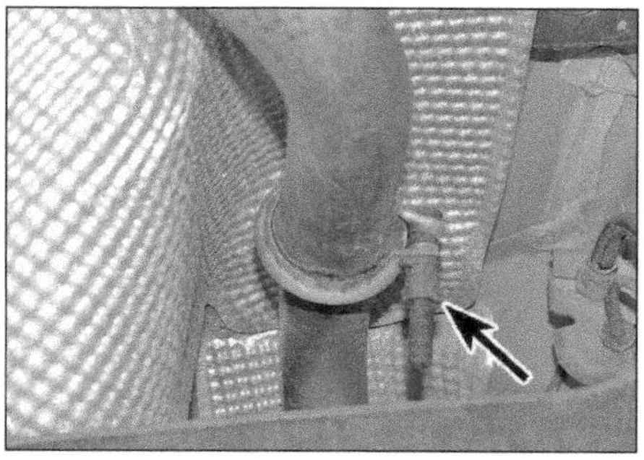

15.13 Middle pipe-to-rear silencer retaining clamp (arrowed)

converter/front pipe from underneath the vehicle. Recover the gasket.

Front flexible pipe

10 Undo the exhaust clamp retaining nut and disconnect the front of the flexible pipe from the front pipe/catalytic converter **(see illustration)**.

11 Undo the exhaust clamp retaining nut and disconnect the rear of the flexible pipe from where it goes over the subframe to the intermediate pipe **(see illustration)**. The flexible pipe can now be withdrawn from under the vehicle.

Intermediate pipe/silencer

12 Undo the exhaust clamp retaining nut and disconnect the front of the intermediate pipe from the rear of the flexible pipe where it goes over the subframe **(see illustration 15.11)**.

13 Undo the exhaust clamp retaining nut and disconnect the rear of the intermediate pipe from the front of the rear silencer **(see illustration)**.

14 The intermediate pipe/silencer can now be released from the rubber mountings and withdrawn from under the vehicle **(see illustrations)**.

Rear silencer

15 Undo the retaining clamp bolt and disconnect the rear exhaust silencer from the intermediate pipe **(see illustration 15.13)**.

16 The rear silencer can now be released from the rubber mountings and withdrawn from under the rear of the vehicle **(see illustrations)**. If required, undo the retaining

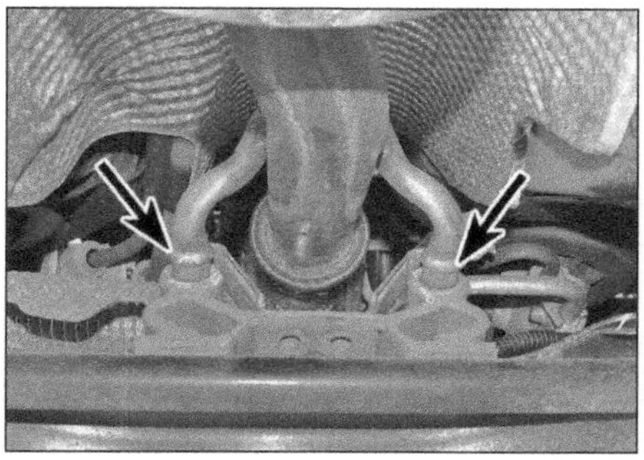

15.14a Exhaust front rubber mounting block (arrowed) ...

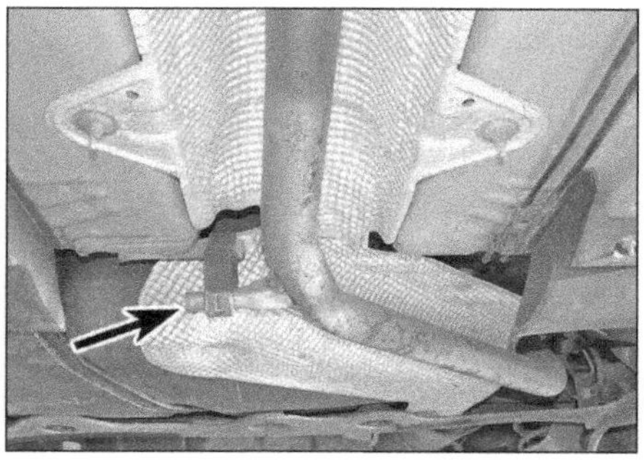

15.14b ... and centre rubber mounting (arrowed)

nuts and remove the mounting rubbers from the vehicle floor panel.

Heat shield(s)

17 The heat shields are secured to the underside of the body by various nuts and fasteners. If a shield is being removed to gain access to a component located behind it, remove the retaining nuts and/or fastener, exhaust mountings and manoeuvre the shield out of position **(see illustration)**. On some models it may be necessary to free the exhaust system from its mountings to gain the clearance necessary to remove the larger heat shield.

Refitting

18 Each section is refitted by reversing the removal sequence, noting the following points:

a) Ensure that all traces of corrosion have been removed from the flanges and renew all necessary gaskets.

b) Inspect the rubber mountings for signs of damage or deterioration, and renew as necessary.

c) Where joints are secured together by a clamping ring, apply a smear of exhaust system jointing paste to the flange joint to ensure a gas-tight seal. Insert the bolt through the clamping ring and fit the washer.

d) Prior to tightening the exhaust system fasteners, ensure that all rubber mountings are correctly located, and that there is adequate clearance between the exhaust system and vehicle underbody.

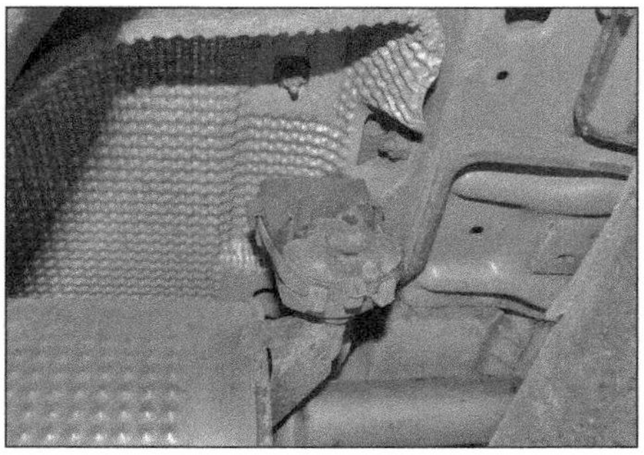

15.16a Rear silencer mounting rubber ...

15.16b ... and mounting block at the left-hand side of the silencer

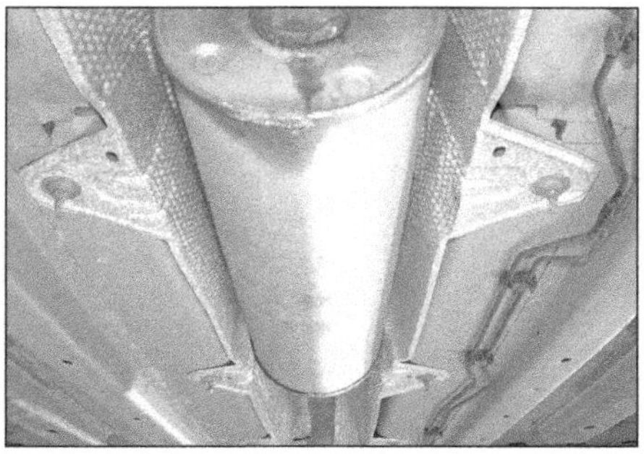

15.17 Heat shields have various fasteners, depending on model

Chapter 4 Part B:
Fuel and exhaust systems – diesel models

Contents

Section number

Degrees of difficulty

Easy, suitable for novice with little experience	**Fairly easy,** suitable for beginner with some experience	**Fairly difficult,** suitable for competent DIY mechanic	**Difficult,** suitable for experienced DIY mechanic	**Very difficult,** suitable for expert DIY or professional

Specifications

Engine identification

1.6 litre engine:	
Designation	DV6TED4 or DV6ATED4
Engine codes:	
DV6TED4	9HV, 9HY or 9HZ
DV6ATED4	9HX
2.0 litre engine:	
Designation	DW10BTED4
Engine codes	RHF or RHR

General

System type	HDi (high-pressure diesel injection) with full electronic control, direct injection and turbocharger
Designation:	
1.6 litre engines	Bosch EDC 16 C34
2.0 litre engines:	
RHF	Delphi DCM 3,4
RHR	Siemens SID 803 or Delphi DCM 3,4
Firing order	1-3-4-2 (No 1 at flywheel end)
Fuel system operating pressure	200 to 1800 bars (according to engine speed)

Injectors

Type	Electromagnetic or Piezo

Turbocharger

Type:	
1.6 litre engines	MHI – TD025S2 or Garrett GT1544V
2.0 litre engines	Garrett GT1749V
Boost pressure (approximate):	
1.6 litre engines	0.9 bar @ 3500 rpm
2.0 litre engines	1.0 bar @ 4000 rpm

Torque wrench settings

	Nm	lbf ft
Camshaft position sensor bolt	6	4
Common rail mounting bolts	23	17
Engine knock sensor	20	15
Exhaust manifold nuts:		
1.6 litre engines	20	15
2.0 litre engines	25	18
Exhaust system fasteners:		
Catalytic converter-to-manifold nuts	40	30
Clamping ring nuts	20	15
Fuel filter water sensor	25	18
Fuel injector clamp bolts/nuts:		
1.6 litre engines:		
Stage 1	4	3
Stage 2	Angle-tighten a further 65°	
2.0 litre engines:		
Siemens:		
Stage 1	4	3
Stage 2	Angle-tighten a further 45°	
Delphi:		
Stage 1	4	3
Stage 2	Angle-tighten a further 77°	
Fuel pipe unions:		
1.6 litre engines	25	18
2.0 litre engines:		
Stage 1	23	17
Stage 2	30	22
Fuel pressure regulator:		
Screw-in type	28	20
With retaining screws:		
Stage 1	3	2
Stage 2	Slacken 180°	
Stage 3	2	1
Stage 4	3	2
Stage 5	6	4
Fuel temperature sensor (Delphi systems)	15	11
High-pressure fuel pump mounting bolts:		
1.6 litre engines	25	18
2.0 litre engines:		
Siemens	20	15
Delphi:		
2 lower bolts	20	15
1 upper bolt (from engine side)	8	6
High-pressure fuel pump rear mounting bolts/nut (8 mm)	17	13
High-pressure fuel pump sprocket nut	50	37
Intake manifold bolts	10	7
Turbocharger mounting bolts/nuts	25	18
Turbocharger oil feed pipe banjo bolts:		
1.6 litre engines	30	20
2.0 litre engines:		
Engine pipe to cylinder block	40	30
All other connections	25	18
Turbocharger oil return pipe bolts:		
1.6 litre engines	30	20
2.0 litre engines	10	7

1 General information and system operation

The fuel system consists of a rear-mounted fuel tank with an immersed level sensor, a fuel pump, a fuel filter with integral water separator, a fuel cooler mounted under the car (depending on model), and an electronically-controlled high-pressure diesel injection (HDi) system, together with a single turbocharger.

The exhaust system is conventional, but to meet the latest emission levels an unregulated catalytic converter and an exhaust gas recirculation system are fitted to all models. On some 2.0 litre models, there is also a pre-cat, which is fitted directly to the exhaust manifold. Also, an exhaust emission particulate filter may be fitted – refer to Chapter 4C, Section 1, for further details.

The HDi system (generally known as a 'common rail' system) derives its name from the fact that a common rail, or fuel reservoir, is used to supply fuel to all the fuel injectors. Instead of an in-line or distributor type injection pump, which distributes the fuel directly to each injector, a high-pressure pump is used, which generates a very high fuel pressure (up to 1800 bar at high engine speed) in the common rail. The common rail stores fuel, and maintains a constant fuel pressure with the aid of a pressure control valve. Each injector is supplied with high-pressure fuel from the common rail, and the injectors are individually controlled via signals from the system electronic control module (ECU). The injectors are electronically operated.

In addition to the various sensors used on models with a conventional fuel injection pump; common rail systems also have a fuel pressure sensor. The fuel pressure sensor allows the ECU to maintain the required fuel pressure, via the pressure control valve.

System operation

For the purposes of describing the operation of a common rail injection system, the components can be divided into three sub-systems; the low-pressure fuel system, the high-pressure fuel system and the electronic control system.

Low-pressure fuel system

The low-pressure fuel system consists of the following components:

a) Fuel tank.
b) Fuel pump.
c) Fuel cooler.
d) Fuel heater (not all models).
e) Fuel filter/water trap.
f) Low-pressure fuel lines.

The low-pressure system (fuel supply system) is responsible for supplying clean fuel to the high-pressure fuel system.

High-pressure fuel system

The high-pressure fuel system consists of the following components:

a) High-pressure fuel pump with pressure control valve.
b) High-pressure fuel common rail.
c) Fuel injectors.
d) High-pressure fuel lines.

After passing through the fuel filter, the fuel reaches the high-pressure pump, which forces it into the common rail. As diesel fuel has certain elasticity, the pressure in the common rail remains constant, even though fuel leaves the rail each time one of the injectors operates. Additionally, a pressure control valve mounted on the high-pressure pump ensures that the fuel pressure is maintained within preset limits.

The pressure control valve is operated by the ECU. When the valve is opened, fuel is returned from the high-pressure pump to the tank, via the fuel return lines, and the pressure in the common rail falls. To enable the ECU to trigger the pressure control valve correctly, the pressure in the common rail is measured by a fuel pressure sensor.

The electronically controlled fuel injectors are operated individually, via signals from the ECU, and each injector injects fuel directly into the relevant combustion chamber. The fact that high fuel pressure is always available allows very precise and highly flexible injection in comparison to a conventional injection pump: for example combustion during the main injection process can be improved considerably by the pre-injection of a very small quantity of fuel.

Electronic control system

The electronic control system consists of the following components:

a) Electronic control module (ECU).
b) Crankshaft speed/position sensor.
c) Camshaft position sensor.
d) Accelerator pedal position sensor.
e) Coolant temperature sensor.
f) Fuel temperature sensor.
g) Airflow meter.
h) Fuel pressure sensor.
i) Fuel injectors.
j) Fuel pressure control valve.
k) Preheating control module.
l) EGR solenoid valve.
m) Air temperature sensor.
n) Atmospheric pressure sensor – integral with the ECU.
o) Intake manifold pressure sensor.

The information from the various sensors is passed to the ECU, which evaluates the signals. The ECU contains electronic 'maps' which enable it to calculate the optimum quantity of fuel to inject, the appropriate start of injection, and even pre- and post-injection fuel quantities, for each individual engine cylinder under any given condition of engine operation.

Additionally, the ECU carries out monitoring and self-diagnostic functions. Any faults in the system are stored in the ECU memory, which enables quick and accurate fault diagnosis using appropriate diagnostic equipment (such as a suitable fault code reader).

2 High-pressure diesel injection system – special information

Warnings and precautions

1 It is essential to observe strict precautions when working on the fuel system components, particularly the high-pressure side of the system. Before carrying out any operations on the fuel system, refer to the precautions given in *Safety first!* at the beginning of this manual, and to the following additional information.

- Do not carry out any repair work on the high-pressure fuel system unless you are competent to do so, have all the necessary tools and equipment required, and are aware of the safety implications involved.
- Before starting any repair work on the fuel system, wait at least 30 seconds after switching off the engine to allow the fuel circuit pressure to reduce.
- Never work on the high-pressure fuel system with the engine running.
- Keep well clear of any possible source of fuel leakage, particularly when starting the engine after carrying out repair work. A leak in the system could cause an extremely high-pressure jet of fuel to escape, which could result in severe personal injury.
- Never place your hands or any part of your body near to a leak in the high-pressure fuel system.
- Do not use steam cleaning equipment or compressed air to clean the engine or any of the fuel system components.

Procedures and information

2 Strict cleanliness must be observed at all times when working on any part of the fuel system. This applies to the working area in general, the person doing the work, and the components being worked on.

3 Before working on the fuel system components, they must be thoroughly cleaned with a suitable degreasing fluid. Specific cleaning products may be obtained from Citroën dealers. Alternatively, a suitable brake cleaning fluid may be used. Cleanliness is particularly important when working on the fuel system connections at the following components:

a) Fuel filter.
b) High-pressure fuel pump.
c) Common rail.
d) Fuel injectors.
e) High-pressure fuel pipes.

4 After disconnecting any fuel pipes or components, the open union or orifice must be immediately sealed to prevent the entry of dirt or foreign material. Plastic plugs and caps in various sizes are available in packs from motor factors and accessory outlets, and are

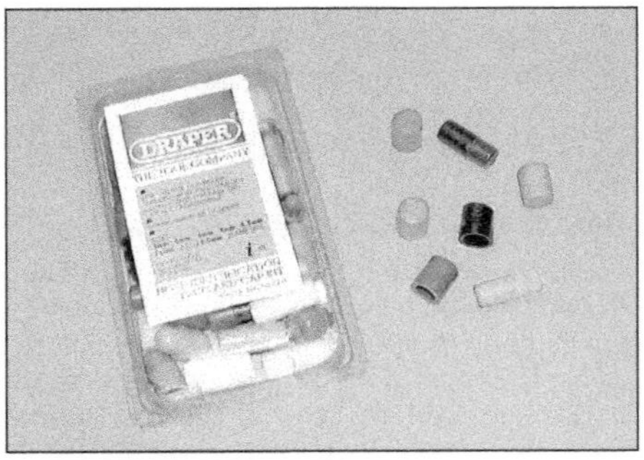

2.4 Typical plastic plug and cap set for sealing disconnected fuel pipes and components

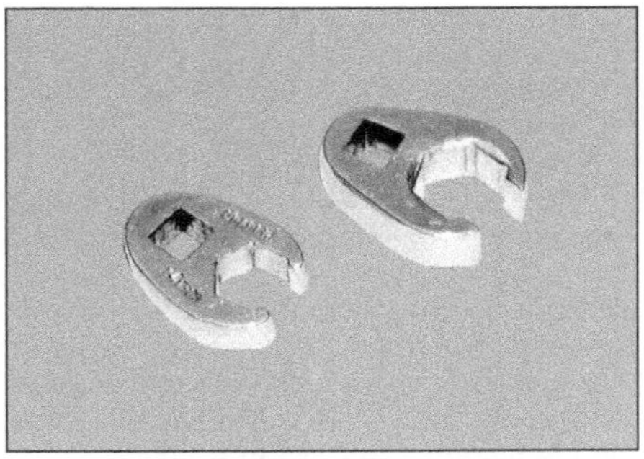

2.7 Two crow-foot adapters will be necessary for tightening the fuel pipe unions

particularly suitable for this application **(see illustration)**. Fingers cut from disposable rubber gloves should be used to protect components such as fuel pipes, fuel injectors and wiring connectors, and can be secured in place using elastic bands. Suitable gloves of this type are available at no cost from most petrol station forecourts.

5 Whenever any of the high-pressure fuel pipes are disconnected or removed, new pipes must be obtained for refitting.

6 On the completion of any repair on the high-pressure fuel system, Citroën recommend the use of a leak-detecting compound. This is a powder which is applied to the fuel pipe unions and connections, and turns white when dry. Any leak in the system will cause the product to darken indicating the source of the leak.

7 The torque wrench settings given in the Specifications must be strictly observed when tightening component mountings and connections. This is particularly important when tightening the high-pressure fuel pipe unions. To enable a torque wrench to be used on the fuel pipe unions, two Citroën crow-foot adapters are required. Suitable alternatives are available from motor factors and accessory outlets **(see illustration)**.

3 Fuel system – priming and bleeding

1 Should the fuel supply system be disconnected between the fuel tank and high-pressure pump, it is necessary to prime the fuel system. This is achieved by operating the hand-priming pump until resistance is felt **(see illustrations)**.

3.1a Hand-priming pump – 1.6 litre engines

3.1b Hand-priming pump (arrowed) – 2.0 litre engines

2 If vehicle will still not run, it may be necessary to connect a suitable hose (special Citroën hose No 444-T may be available) from the fuel filter outlet pipe to the fuel return pipe and forcing fuel through the filter into the return system. If the suitable hose is not available, it will suffice to connect a length of hose to the filter outlet, with the other end of the hose in a suitable container. The method of forcing the fuel through differs according to engine type:

- *1.6 litre engines. Operate the hand priming pump for approximately 2 minutes.*
- *2.0 litre engines. Operate the hand priming pump for approximately 1 minute.*

3 Turn the ignition key on and operate the starter until the engine starts.

4 Air cleaner assembly – removal and refitting

Removal

1 To make access easier, remove the windscreen wiper arms, and then unclip the plastic scuttle panel from below the windscreen. Pull up the ends of the panel to release it from the windscreen clips. Release the plastic expanding rivets from along the front edge of the scuttle panel. Undo the two screws securing the brake/clutch master cylinder upper reservoir and move it to one side. Release the sound insulation trim from the scuttle crossmember, undo the bolt on the left-hand side of the crossmember, then release the retaining clips at the right-hand side of the crossmember to remove it from the engine compartment – refer to Chapter 11, Section 22.

2 Remove the air filter element as described in Chapter 1B, Section 21.

1.6 litre engines

3 Pull the air filter lower housing upwards from the rubber mounting grommets **(see illustrations)**.

2.0 litre engines

4 Depress the retaining clip and lift the lower part of the air cleaner upwards to release it from the mounting bracket **(see illustration)**.

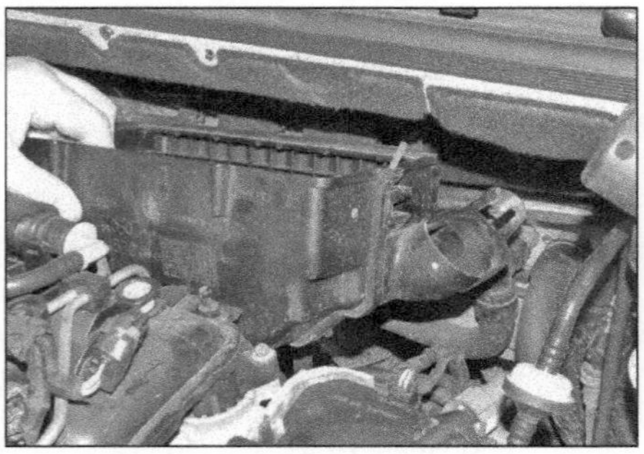

4.3a Withdraw the lower part of the housing ...

4.3b ... noting the rubber mountings (arrowed) are still in place

4.4 Release the securing clips (arrowed)

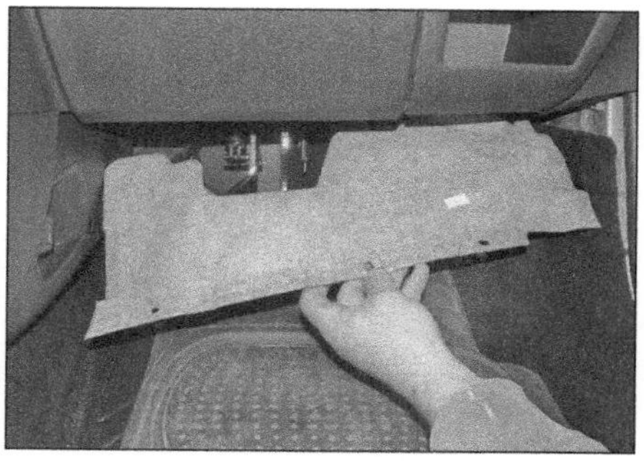

5.1 Remove the lower trim panel

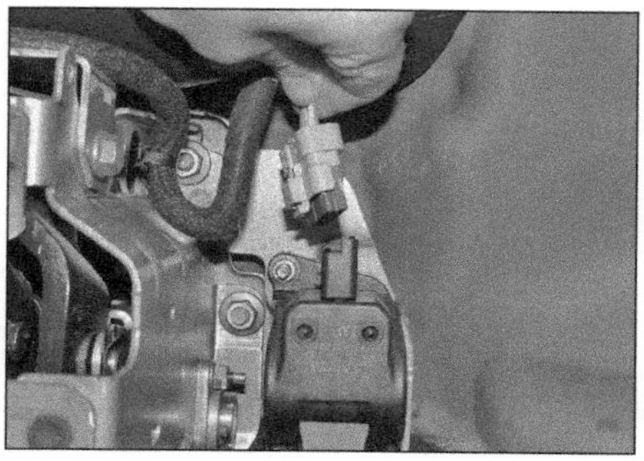

5.2 Disconnect the wiring connector

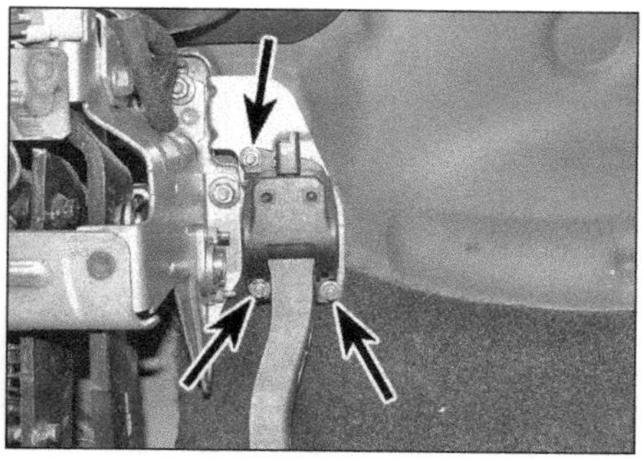

5.3 Undo the three retaining nuts (arrowed)

Refitting

5 Refitting is a reverse of the removal procedure. Examine the condition of the seals and retaining clips, and renew if necessary.

5 Accelerator pedal – removal and refitting

Removal

1 Release the fasteners and remove trim panel above the pedals **(see illustration)**.

2 Disconnect the accelerator pedal position sensor wiring plug from the top of the pedal **(see illustration)**.

3 Undo the three nuts and remove the pedal assembly **(see illustration)**.

Refitting

4 Refitting is a reversal of the removal procedure.

6 Fuel lift pump – removal and refitting

Note: *The fuel pump is only available as a complete assembly – no components are available separately.*

Removal

1 For access to the fuel pump, tilt or remove the right-hand rear seat cushion (see Chapter 11, Section 23).

2 Using a thin blade, carefully release the plastic access cover retaining clips, and remove the cover from the floor to expose the fuel pump/sender unit **(see illustration)**.

3 Disconnect the wiring connector from the fuel pump, and tape the connector to the vehicle body, to prevent it from disappearing behind the tank **(see illustration)**.

4 Depress the retaining clips and detach the fuel pipe(s) from the top of the pump **(see illustrations)**, bearing in mind the information given in Section 2 on warnings and precautions to be taken with the fuel system before disconnecting. Plug the pipe end(s) to minimise fuel loss and prevent the entry of dirt. **Note:** *Depending on model, the amount of pipes to the top of the pump will vary note their fitted position, before removal.*

5 Noting the alignment marks on the tank **(see illustrations)**, pump cover and the locking ring, unscrew the ring and remove it from the

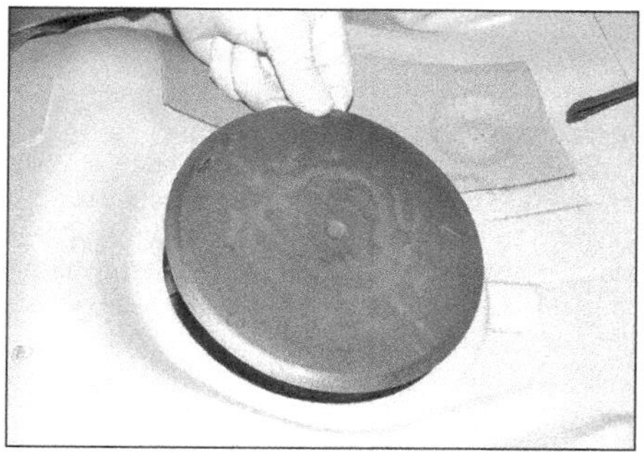

6.2 Release the fuel pump access cover

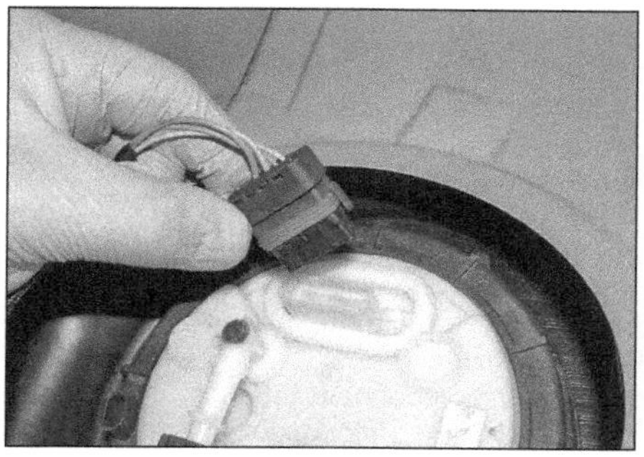

6.3 Disconnect the pump wiring plug

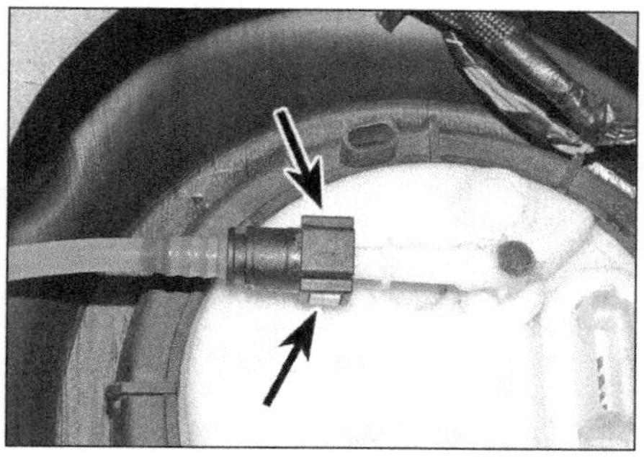

6.4a Depress the release buttons (arrowed) ...

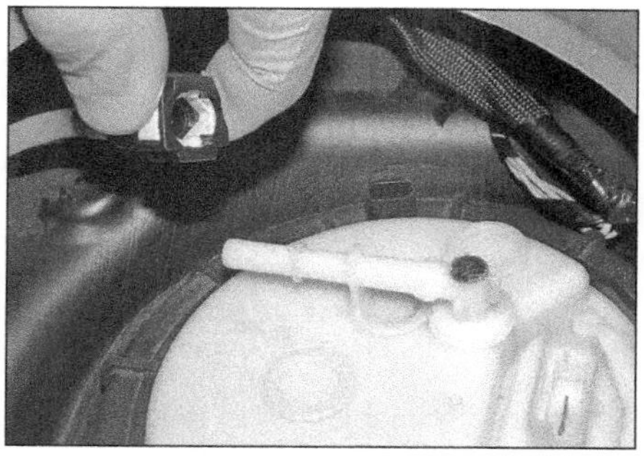

6.4b ... and disconnect the fuel pipe(s)

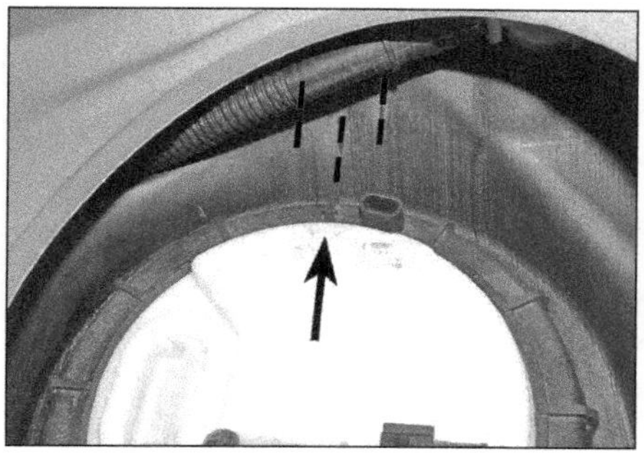

6.5a Fuel sender alignment marks (arrowed)

6.5b Using a home-made tool to slacken the collar

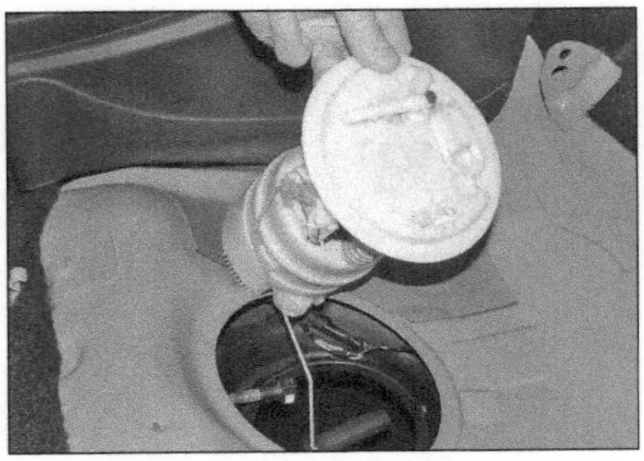

6.6 Lift the fuel pump assembly, taking care not to damage the float arm

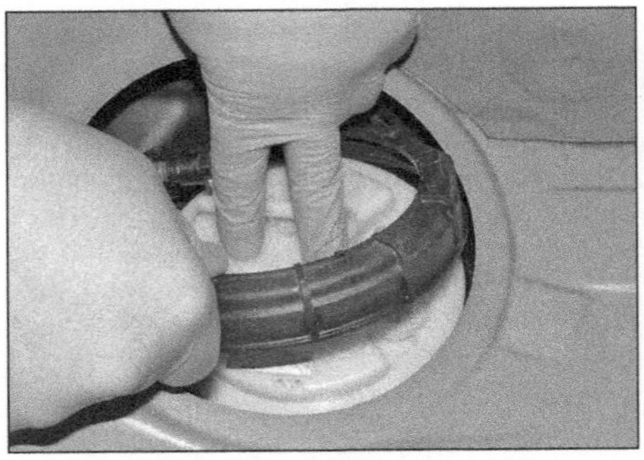

6.11 Hold the pump in position and tighten the securing ring

tank. This is best accomplished by using a screwdriver on the raised ribs of the locking ring. Carefully tap the screwdriver to turn the ring anti-clockwise until it can be unscrewed by hand. Alternatively, a Citroën special tool is available which fits over the collar and allows it to be released using a socket ratchet and extension.

6 Carefully lift the fuel pump assembly out of the fuel tank, taking great care not to damage the fuel gauge sender unit float arm, or to spill fuel onto the interior of the vehicle **(see illustration)**. Recover the rubber sealing ring and discard it – a new one must be used on refitting.

7 If the fuel pump is going to be left out of the fuel tank for a while, screw the ring back to the top of the fuel tank to prevent it from going out of shape. Cover the access hole in the tank to prevent dirt ingress.

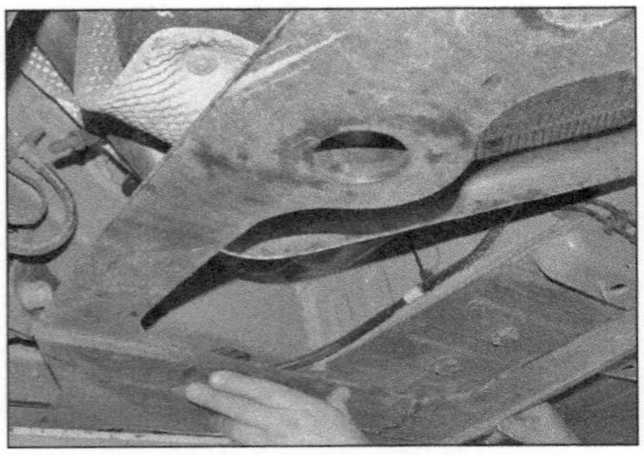

8.5 Remove the plastic undershields – where fitted

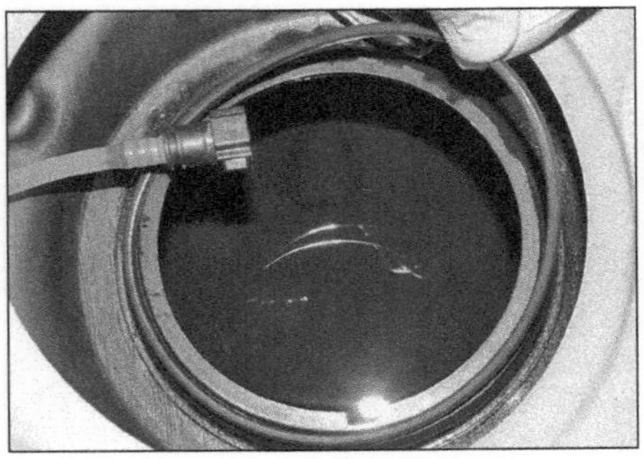

6.8 Fit a new sealing ring to the top of the tank

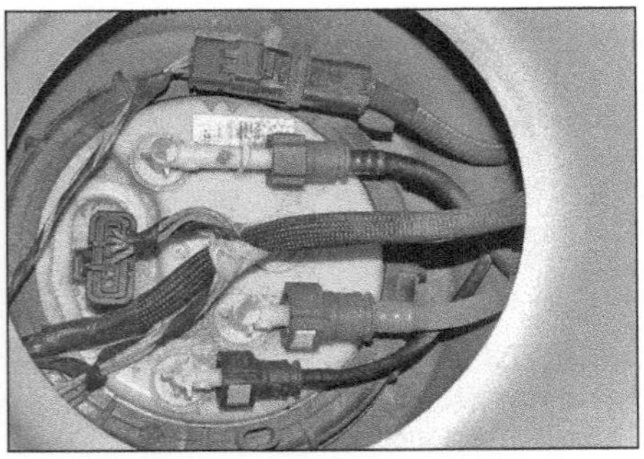

6.12 Fuel pipes and wiring connections – 2.0 litre model shown

Refitting

8 Fit the new sealing ring to the top of the fuel tank **(see illustration)**.

9 Carefully manoeuvre the pump assembly into the fuel tank, taking care not to damage the float arm.

10 Align the notch in the top of the fuel tank with the arrows on the fuel pump cover to locate the pump assembly into position **(see illustration)**

11 Press down on the pump and refit the locking ring, tighten it securely until its alignment mark aligns with the alignment marks on the fuel tank, as noted on removal **(see illustration)**.

12 Securely reconnect the fuel pipe(s) to the pump cover then reconnect the pump wiring connector **(see illustration)**.

13 Prime the fuel system (see Section 3).

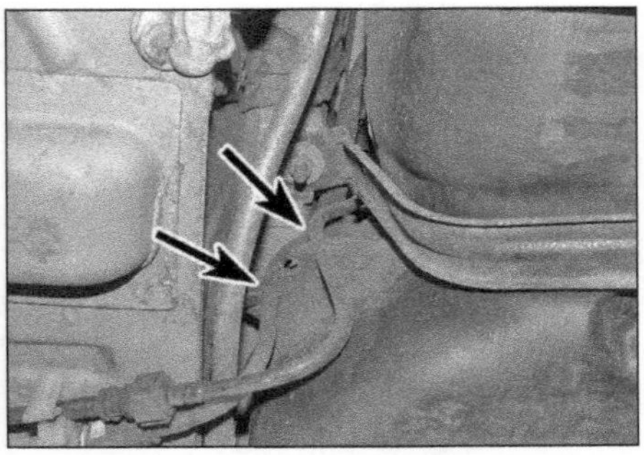

8.6 Release the fuel lines (arrowed) from the fuel tank

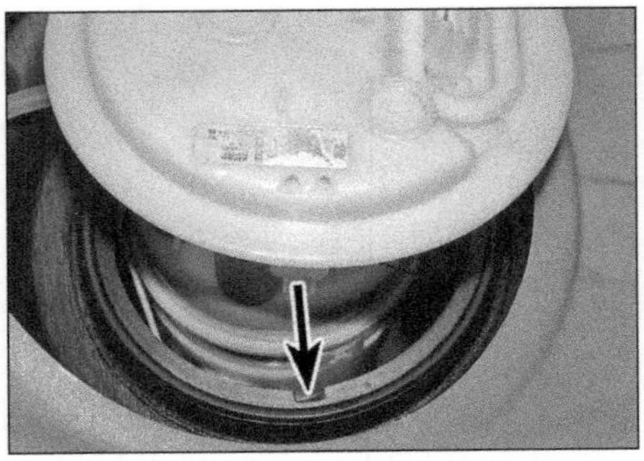

6.10 Align the pump with the cut-out (arrowed) in the fuel tank

Start the engine and check the fuel pump feed and return hoses unions for signs of leakage.

14 If all is well, refit the plastic access cover ensuring its tabs are located correctly.

15 Refit the rear seat cushion with reference to Chapter 11, Section 23, if required.

7 Fuel gauge sender unit – removal and refitting

The fuel gauge sender unit is an integral part of the fuel lift pump assembly and is not available separately. Refer to Section 6 for removal and refitting details.

8 Fuel tank and cooler – removal and refitting

Fuel tank

Note: *Refer to the warnings and precautions in Section 2 before proceeding.*

1 Before removing the fuel tank, all fuel must be drained from the tank. Since a fuel tank drain plug is not provided, it is therefore preferable to carry out the removal operation when the tank is nearly empty. Before proceeding, disconnect the battery (refer to precautions in Chapter 5A, Section 1), and then siphon or hand-pump the remaining fuel from the tank.

2 Remove the rear seat cushion and, using a flat blade, carefully release the access cover retaining clips and remove the cover from the floor to expose the fuel pump **(see illustration 6.2)**.

3 Disconnect the wiring connectors and fuel pipes from the top of the fuel sender/pump assembly, with reference to Section 6 of this Chapter. Plug the pipe end(s) to minimise fuel loss and prevent the entry of dirt. Note the fitted position of the fuel pipes for refitting.

4 Chock the front wheels then jack up the rear of the vehicle and support it on axle stands (*see Jacking and vehicle support*). Remove the rear roadwheels and right-hand inner wheel arch liner.

5 Where applicable, undo the retaining screws and remove the plastic undershields from under the rear of the vehicle **(see illustration)**.

8.10a Undo the fuel filler neck upper securing nut (arrowed) ...

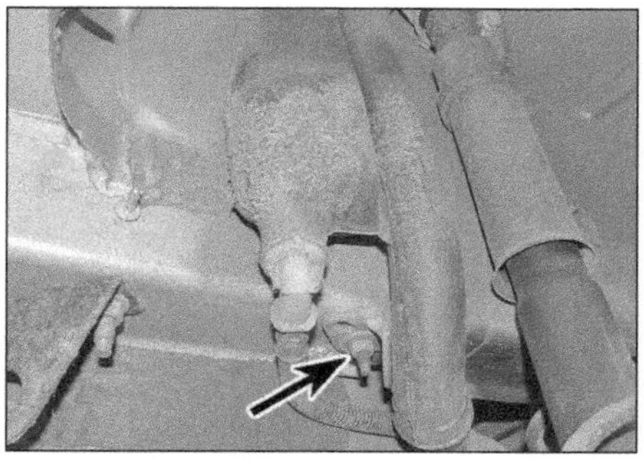

8.10b ... and lower securing nut (arrowed)

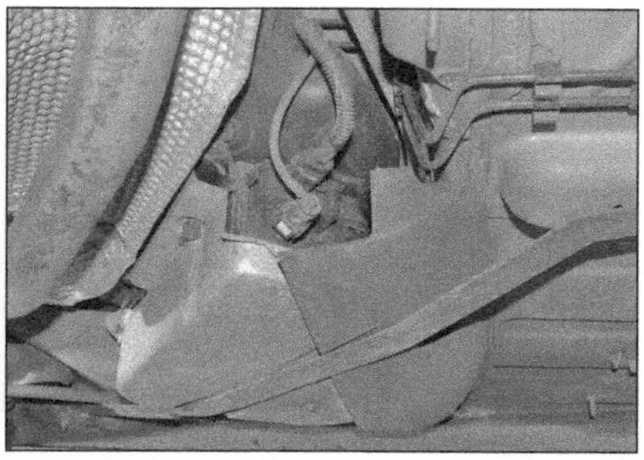

8.11 Disconnect the fuel pipe and wiring connector from the additive tank (where fitted)

6 Unclip the fuel pipes from the side of the fuel tank **(see illustration)**. If required, disconnect the fuel pipe connections and remove the fuel pipes with the fuel tank.

7 Remove the rear shock absorbers and springs as described in Chapter 10, Section 12 and 13. This will need to be done to allow the rear axle to move downwards to allow the removal of the fuel tank.

8 Remove the rear part of the exhaust system as described in Section 18.

9 If required, undo the fasteners, and remove the heat shield from the underside of the fuel tank.

10 Undo the upper retaining bolt and the lower retaining nut from the fuel filler neck **(see illustrations)**.

11 On models with particulate filter, disconnect the wiring connector and hose(s) from the additive tank, and remove the securing strap from across the bottom of the additive tank **(see illustration)**.

12 Place a trolley jack with an interposed block of wood beneath the tank, then raise the jack until it is supporting the weight of the tank.

13 Slacken and remove the bolts securing the fuel tank to the body **(see illustrations)**. Release the filler neck seal from the body at the filler cap aperture.

14 Slowly lower the fuel tank; ensuring the filler neck assembly is guided out of position without placing any stress on it.

15 If the tank is contaminated with sediment or water, remove the fuel pump (Section 6), and swill the tank out with clean fuel. The tank is injection-moulded from a synthetic material – if seriously damaged, it should be renewed. However, in certain cases, it may be possible to have small leaks or minor damage repaired. Seek the advice of a specialist before attempting to repair the fuel tank.

16 It is not possible to separate the filler neck from the tank. If damaged, the complete assembly must be renewed.

17 Refitting is the reverse of the removal procedure, noting the following points:

a) Ensure the wiring connectors and fuel pipes are securely reconnected and retained by all the relevant clips. When lifting the tank back into position, take care to ensure that the pipes/wiring do not become trapped between the tank and vehicle body.

b) Refit the rear suspension as described in Chapter 10, Section 12 and 13.

c) Refit the exhaust as described in Section 18.

d) On completion, refill the tank with a small amount of fuel and prime the fuel system as described in Section 3. Check for signs of leakage prior to taking the vehicle out on the road.

Fuel cooler

Note: *The fuel cooler is not fitted to all models.*

18 The fuel cooler is located under the right-hand side of the vehicle **(see illustration)**. Jack up the rear of the vehicle, and support it on axle stands (see *Jacking and vehicle support*).

19 Where fitted, undo the fasteners and remove the plastic undershield from the right-hand underside of the vehicle.

20 Working underneath the vehicle, undo the retaining nut, and release the cooler bracket from the locating holes **(see illustration)**.

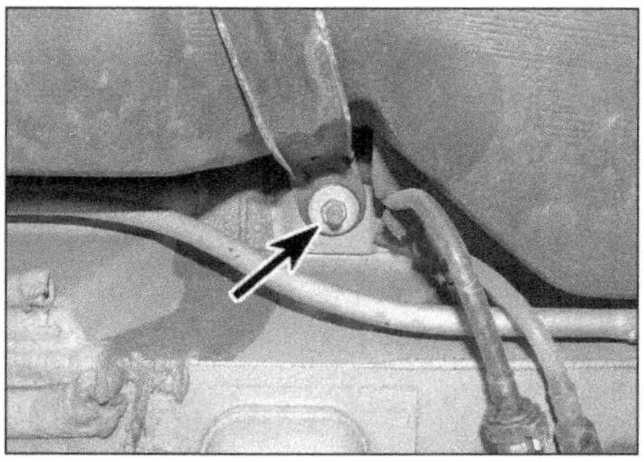

8.13a Undo the fuel tank front retaining strap nuts (arrowed) ...

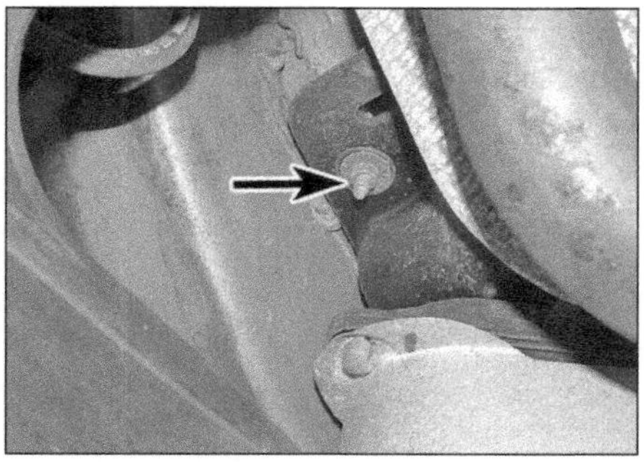

8.13b ... side securing nut (arrowed) ...

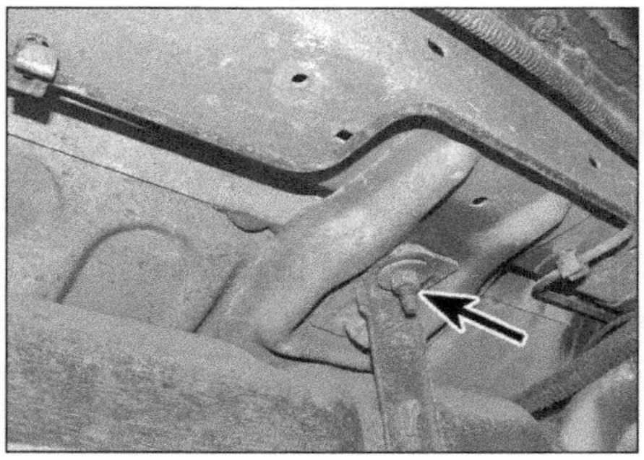

8.13c ... and rear retaining strap nut (arrowed)

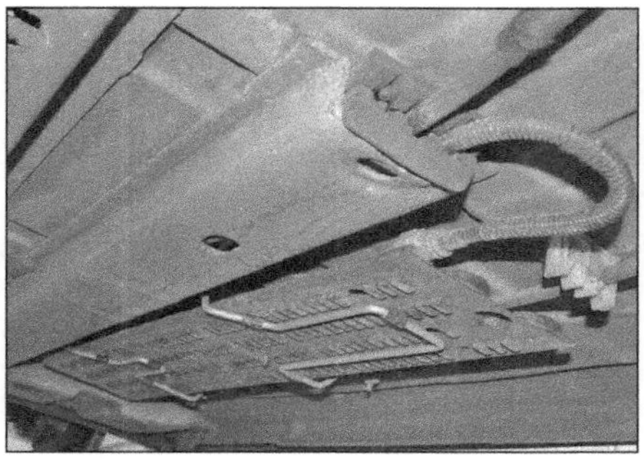

8.18 Fuel cooler fitted under floor panel

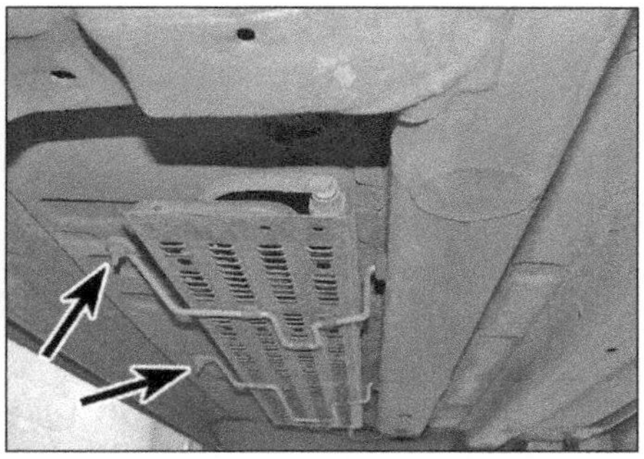

8.20 Undo the nuts (arrowed) securing the fuel cooler

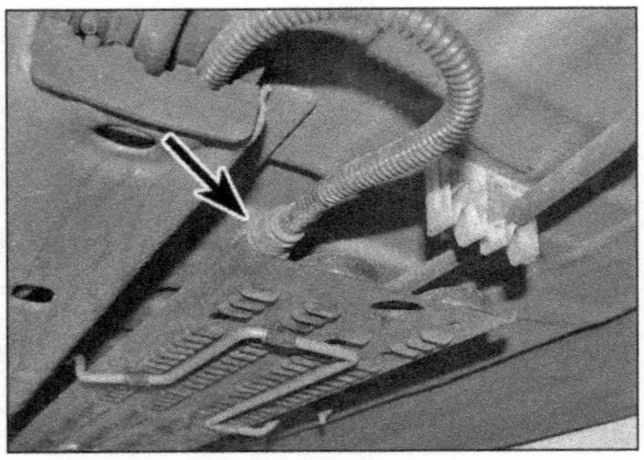

8.21 Depress the release button (arrowed) and disconnect the hoses

21 Release the pipes from the clips on the vehicle underside, then depress the release buttons and disconnect the fuel feed and return hoses from each end of the cooler. Be prepared for fuel spillage, and plug the hose and cooler openings to prevent dirt ingress **(see illustration)**.

22 Refitting is a reversal of removal.

9 High-pressure fuel pump – removal and refitting

Warning: Refer to the information contained in Section 2 before proceeding.

Note: *A new fuel pump-to-common rail high-pressure fuel pipe will be required for refitting.*

Removal

1.6 litre engines

1 Disconnect the battery (refer to precautions in Chapter 5A, Section 1) and remove the timing belt as described in Chapter 2C, Section 7. After removal of the timing belt, temporarily refit the right-hand engine mounting but do not fully-tighten the bolts.

2 Remove the air cleaner assembly as described in Section 4.

TOOL TiP 1

A sprocket holding tool can be made from two lengths of steel strip bolted together to form a forked end. Bend the ends of the strip through 90° to form the fork 'prongs'.

TOOL TiP 2

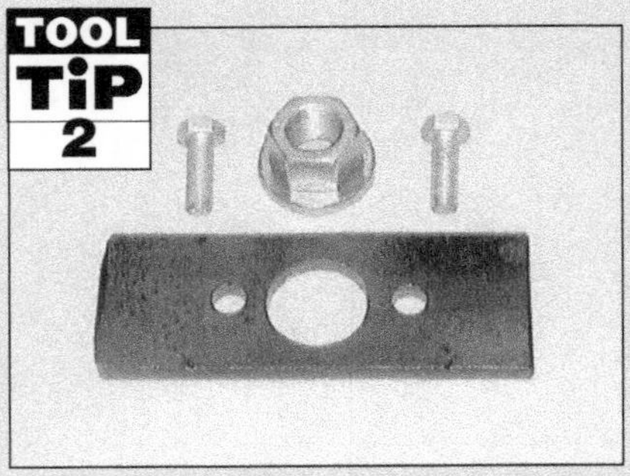

Make a sprocket releasing tool from a short strip of steel. Drill two holes in the strip to correspond with the two holes in the sprocket. Drill a third hole just large enough to accept the flats of the sprocket retaining nut.

3 Remove the EGR heat exchanger/cooler as described in Chapter 4C, Section 2.

4 Undo the bolts/nuts and remove the 3 support brackets above the fuel common rail and the high-pressure pump **(see illustrations)**.

5 Undo the union nuts and remove the high-pressure fuel pipe between the fuel common rail and the high-pressure pump. Plug the openings to prevent contamination.

6 Disconnect the wiring plug from the high-pressure fuel pump.

7 Depress the release buttons and disconnect the fuel supply and return hoses from the pump. Note that the hoses may have a release button on each side of the fitting. Plug the openings to prevent contamination.

8 Hold the pump sprocket stationary, and loosen the centre nut securing it to the pump shaft **(see Tool Tip)**.

9 The fuel pump sprocket is a taper fit on the pump shaft and it will be necessary to make up a tool to release it from the taper **(see Tool Tip)**. Partially unscrew the sprocket retaining nut, fit the home-made tool, and secure it to the sprocket with two 7.0 mm bolts and nuts. Prevent the sprocket from rotating as before, and screw down the nuts, forcing the sprocket off the shaft taper. Once the taper is released, remove the tool, unscrew the nut fully, and remove the sprocket from the pump shaft.

10 Undo the three bolts, and remove the pump from the mounting bracket.

Caution: The high-pressure fuel pump is manufactured to extremely close tolerances and must not be dismantled in any way. Do not unscrew the fuel pipe male union on the rear of the pump, or attempt to remove the sensor, piston de-activator switch, or the seal on the pump shaft. No parts for the pump are available separately and if the unit is in any way suspect, it must be renewed.

11 Undo the bolts securing the bracket to the rear of the pump (where fitted), then undo the 3 bolts and pull the pump from the inner timing cover.

2.0 litre engines

12 Disconnect the battery (refer to precautions in Chapter 5A, Section 1).

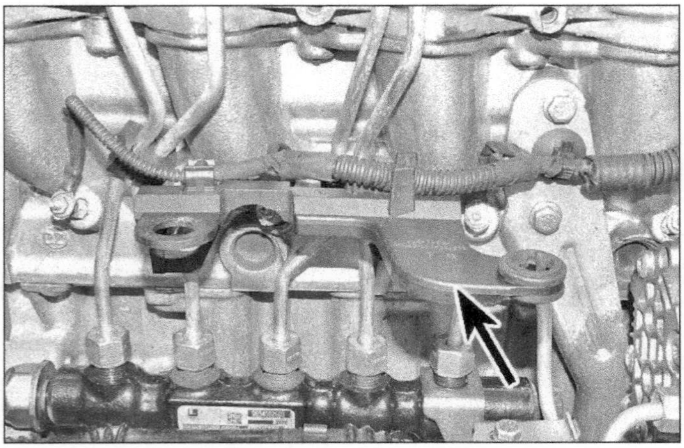

9.4a Remove the air filter support bracket (arrowed) ...

9.4b ... and the brackets around the fuel pump (arrowed)

9.14a Undo the turbo intake duct securing bolt (arrowed) ...

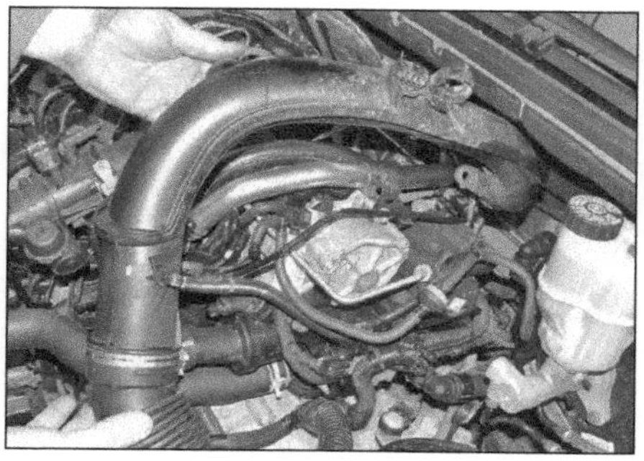

9.14b ... and withdraw the ducting from the engine compartment

9.15a Unclip the wiring loom ...

9.15b ... and then undo the bracket retaining nuts (arrowed)

9.16 Unscrew the high-pressure fuel pipe (arrowed)

13 Remove the plastic cover from the top of the engine.

14 Undo the retaining bolts and securing clip and remove the turbocharger intake duct from the engine compartment **(see illustrations)**.

15 Release the retaining clips and unclip the wiring loom from the mounting bracket at the end of the cylinder head, and then remove the mounting bracket **(see illustrations)**.

16 Thoroughly clean the high-pressure fuel pipe unions on the fuel pump and common rail. Using an open-ended spanner, unscrew the union nuts securing the high-pressure fuel pipe to the fuel pump and common rail. Counterhold the unions on the pump and common rail with a second spanner, while unscrewing the union nuts. Withdraw the high-pressure fuel pipe and plug or cover the open unions to prevent dirt entry **(see illustration)**. Note that a new high-pressure fuel pipe will be required for refitting. **Note:** *The fuel lines must be renewed every time they are removed, as it is possible for minute metal particles to enter them as a result of tightening the union nuts. If these particles enter the fuel injectors, fuel at high pressure can enter the combustion chambers unrestricted.*

17 Disconnect the fuel supply and return hoses from the high-pressure pump **(see illustration)**. Plug the openings to prevent contamination.

18 Note their fitted positions, and disconnect the wiring plugs from the pump. Move the wiring harness to one side.

19 Undo the 3 bolts and withdraw the fuel pump from the cylinder head **(see illustrations)**. Note on Delphi fuel pumps the upper bolt is accessed from the cylinder head side of the fuel pump.

Caution: The high-pressure fuel pump is manufactured to extremely close tolerances and must not be dismantled in any way. Do not unscrew the fuel pipe male union on the rear of the pump, or attempt to remove the pressure control valve, piston de-activator switch, or the seal on the pump shaft. No parts for the pump are available separately and if the unit is in any way suspect, it must be renewed.

Refitting

20 Refitting is a reversal of removal, noting the following points:

a) *Always renew the pump-to-common rail high-pressure pipe.*

b) *Renew the fuel pump drive seal.*

c) *With everything reassembled and reconnected, and observing the precautions listed in Section 2, start the engine and allow it to idle. Check for leaks at the high-pressure fuel pipe unions with the engine idling. If satisfactory, increase the engine speed to 3000 rpm and check again for leaks.*

d) *Take the car for a short road test and check for leaks once again on return. If any leaks are detected, obtain and fit another new high-pressure fuel pipe.* ***Do not*** *attempt to cure even the slightest leak by further tightening of the pipe unions.*

9.17 Disconnect the fuel hoses (arrowed) from the pump

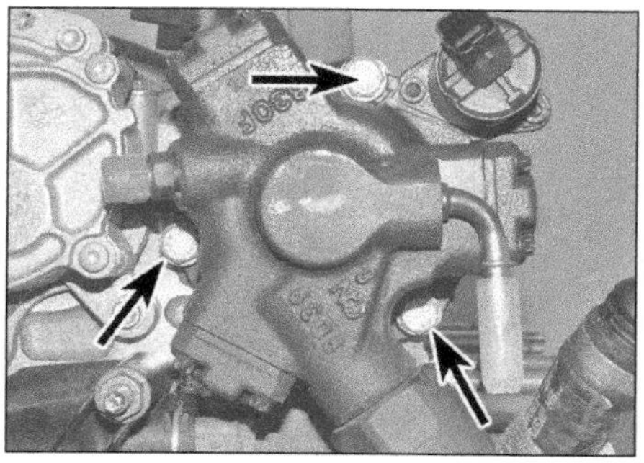

9.19a Unscrew the three bolts (arrowed) and remove the pump

9.19b Delphi fuel pumps have a mounting bolt (arrowed) on the cylinder head side of the pump

10.6 Undo the bolts (arrowed) and move the coolant pump outlet assembly aside

10.8 The pressure sensor is located at the end of the accumulator rail (arrowed)

10.9 Accumulator rail mounting bolt/stud (arrowed)

10 Common rail – removal and refitting

Warning: Refer to the information contained in Section 2 before proceeding.

Note: *A complete new set of high-pressure fuel pipes will be required for refitting.*

Removal

1 Disconnect the battery (refer to precautions in Chapter 5A, Section 1).

2 Remove the plastic cover from the top of the engine.

1.6 litre engines

3 Remove the cylinder head cover/intake manifold as described in Chapter 2C, Section 4.

4 Drain the cooling system as described in Chapter 1B, Section 20.

5 Remove the EGR heat exchanger/cooler as described in Chapter 4C, Section 2.

6 Undo the 2 mounting bolts, slacken the clamps, and move the coolant pump outlet assembly aside **(see illustration)**.

7 Clean around the pipe, then undo the unions and remove the high-pressure pipe from the common rail to the high-pressure pump. Plug the openings to prevent contamination.

8 Disconnect the pressure sensor wiring plug from the common rail **(see illustration)**.

9 Unscrew the two rail mounting bolts and manoeuvre it from place **(see illustration)**.

Note: *Citroën insist that the fuel pressure sensor on the common rail must not be removed.*

Caution: Do not attempt to remove the four high-pressure fuel pipe male unions from the common rail. These parts are not available separately and if disturbed are likely to result in fuel leakage on reassembly.

2.0 litre engines

10 Disconnect the engine breather hose from the cylinder head cover.

11 Remove the air filter assembly, as described in Section 4.

12 Remove the cylinder head cover/intake manifold as described in Chapter 2D, Section 4.

13 Move the oil filler neck to one side.

14 Thoroughly clean all the high-pressure fuel pipe unions on the common rail, fuel pump and injectors. Using an open-ended spanner, unscrew the union nuts securing the high-pressure fuel pipe to the fuel pump and common rail. Counterhold the unions on the pump and common rail (where applicable) with a second spanner, while unscrewing the union nuts. Withdraw the high-pressure fuel pipe and plug or cover the open unions to prevent dirt entry **(see illustrations)**.

15 Again using two spanners, hold the unions and unscrew the union nuts securing the high-pressure fuel pipes to the fuel injectors and common rail **(see illustration)**. Withdraw the high-pressure fuel pipes and plug or cover the open unions to prevent dirt entry.

16 Undo the 2 mounting nuts and manoeuvre the common rail from position. Recover the mounting spacers. Disconnect the sensor wiring plug(s) as the common rail is withdrawn. **Note:** *Citroën insist that the fuel pressure sensor on the common rail must not be removed.*

Refitting

17 Locate the common rail in position, refit and finger-tighten the mounting bolts/nuts.

18 Reconnect the common rail wiring plug(s).

19 Fit the new pump-to-rail high-pressure pipe, and only finger-tighten the unions at first, then tighten the unions to the specified torque setting. Use a second spanner to counterhold the union screwed into the pump body.

20 Fit the new set of rail-to-injector high pressure pipes, and finger-tighten the unions. If it's not possible to fit the new pipes to the injector unions, remove and refit the injectors as described in Section 11, and then try again.

21 Tighten the common rail mounting bolts/nuts to the specified torque.

22 Tighten the rail-to-injector pipe unions to the specified torque setting. Use a second spanner to counterhold the injector unions.

23 The remainder of refitting is a reversal of removal, noting the following points:

a) *Ensure all wiring connectors and harnesses are correctly refitting and secured.*

b) *Reconnect the battery, referring to precautions in Chapter 5A, Section 1.*

10.14a Unscrew the unions from the rail ...

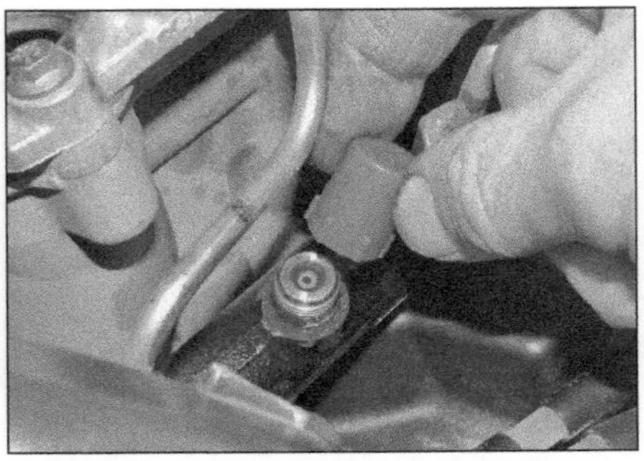
10.14b ... and plug the ends to prevent contamination

10.15 Counterhold the injector with a second spanner whilst slackening the pipe union

c) Observing the precautions listed in Section 2, start the engine and allow it to idle. Check for leaks at the high-pressure fuel pipe unions with the engine idling. If satisfactory, increase the engine speed to 3000 rpm and check again for leaks. Take the car for a short road test and check for leaks once again on return.

If any leaks are detected, obtain and fit additional new high-pressure fuel pipes as required. ***Do not*** *attempt to cure even the slightest leak by further tightening of the pipe unions.*

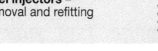

11 Fuel injectors – removal and refitting

Warning: Refer to the information contained in Section 2 before proceeding.

Removal

1 Remove the plastic cover from the top of the engine, and disconnect the battery (refer to precautions in Chapter 5A, Section 1).

1.6 litre engines

Note: *The following procedure describes the removal and refitting of the injectors as a complete set, however each injector may be removed individually if required. New copper washers, upper seals, and a high-pressure fuel pipe will be required for each disturbed injector when refitting.*

2 Remove the EGR heat exchanger/cooler as described in Chapter 4C, Section 2.

3 Undo the bolts, slacken the clamps and remove the air intake ducting assembly from between the turbocharger and the intake manifold. Note their fitted positions, and disconnect the various wiring plugs as the assembly is withdrawn **(see illustrations)**.

4 Disconnect the injector wiring plugs.

5 Undo the bolts and move aside the wiring harness support bracket **(see illustration)**.

6 Release the manual fuel priming pump and its support.

7 Extract the retaining circlip and disconnect the leak-off pipe from each fuel injector **(see illustration)**.

8 Clean the area around the high-pressure fuel pipes between the injectors and the common rail, then unscrew the pipe unions. Use a second spanner to counterhold the union screwed into the injector body **(see illustration)**. The injectors' screwed-in unions must not be allowed to move. Remove the bracket above the common rail unions, and then remove the pipes. Plug the openings in the common rail and injectors to prevent dirt ingress.

9 Unscrew the injector retaining nuts, and carefully pull or lever the injector from place. If necessary, use an open-ended spanner and twist the injector to free it from position **(see illustrations)**. Do not lever against or pull on the solenoid housing at the top of the injector. Note down the injectors position – if the injectors are to be re-used, they must be refitted to their original locations. If improved access is required, undo the bolts and remove the oil separator housing from the front of the cylinder head cover.

10 Remove the copper washer and the upper seal from each injector, or from the cylinder head if they remained in place during injector removal. New copper washers and upper seals will be required for refitting. Cover the injector hole in the cylinder head to prevent dirt ingress.

11 Examine each injector visually for any signs of obvious damage or deterioration. If any defects are apparent, renew the injector(s). Note down the 8-digit injector classification number – this may be needed during the refitting procedure if the ECU has been renewed **(see illustrations 11.19a and 11.9b)**.

Caution: The injectors are manufactured to extremely close tolerances and must not be dismantled in any way. Do not unscrew the fuel pipe union on the side of the injector,

11.3a Intake ducting securing clamps (arrowed) ...

11.3b ... and retaining bolts (arrowed)

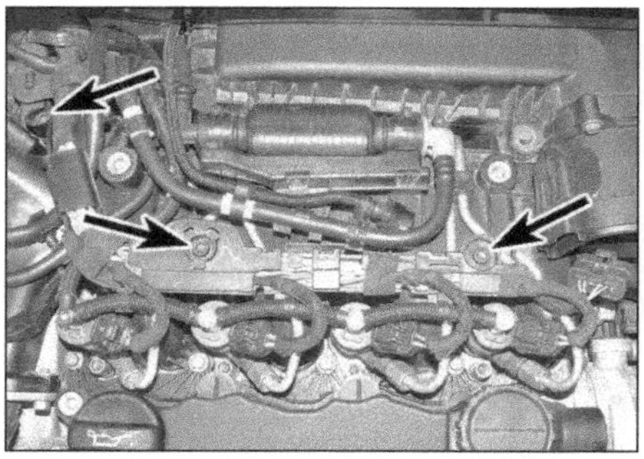

11.5 Wiring harness support bracket bolts (arrowed)

11.7 Prise out the clip and pull the return pipe from each injector

11.8 Use a second spanner to counterhold the high-pressure pipe union nuts

11.9a Injector retaining nuts (arrowed)

11.9b Use a spanner to twist the injector and free it from position

11.13 Disconnect the injector wiring plugs

11.15a Prise down the lower edge of the retaining clip (shown with the hose disconnected for clarity) ...

11.15b ... then pull the hose from the injector

11.16a Cover the intake ports to prevent anything being dropped inside

11.16b Undo the injector retaining nuts

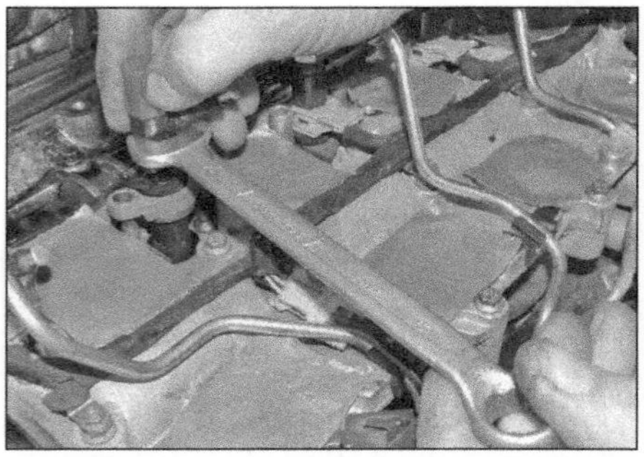

11.17a Use a spanner to slightly twist the injector ...

or separate any parts of the injector body. Do not attempt to clean carbon deposits from the injector nozzle or carry out any form of ultrasonic or pressure testing.

2.0 litre engines

Note: *New copper washers, upper seals, studs and a high-pressure fuel pipe will be required for each disturbed injector when refitting.*

12 Remove the intake manifold/cylinder head cover as described in Chapter 2D, Section 4.

13 Disconnect the wiring plugs from the injectors **(see illustration)**.

14 Thoroughly clean all the high-pressure fuel pipe unions on the fuel injectors and common rail. Using two open-ended spanners, unscrew the union nuts securing the high-pressure fuel pipes to the fuel injectors and common rail. Withdraw the high-pressure fuel pipes and plug or cover the open unions on the injectors and common rail to prevent dirt entry. Note that a new high-pressure fuel pipe will be required for each removed injector when refitting.

15 On Siemens systems, release the retaining clip and disconnect the leak-off pipe from each fuel injector **(see illustrations)**.

16 Cover the intake ports in the cylinder head, then progressively and evenly, slacken and remove the injector retaining nuts **(see illustrations)**.

17 Carefully pull the injectors upwards from the cylinder head **(see illustrations)**. Note down the injectors' position – if the injectors are to be re-used, they must be refitting to their original locations.

18 Remove the lower copper washer and upper seal from each injector.

19 Examine each injector visually for any signs of obvious damage or deterioration. If any defects are apparent, renew the injector(s). Note down the injector classification number – this may be needed during the refitting procedure if the ECU has been renewed **(see illustrations)**.

Caution: The injectors are manufactured to extremely close tolerances and must not be dismantled in any way. Do not unscrew the fuel pipe union on the side of the injector, or separate any parts of the injector body. Do not attempt to clean carbon deposits from the injector nozzle or carry out any form of ultrasonic or pressure testing.

20 If the injectors are in a satisfactory condition, plug the fuel pipe union (if not already done) and suitably cover the electrical element and the injector nozzle.

11.17b ... and then free it from its position in the cylinder head

11.19a Note the Bosch injector classification number ...

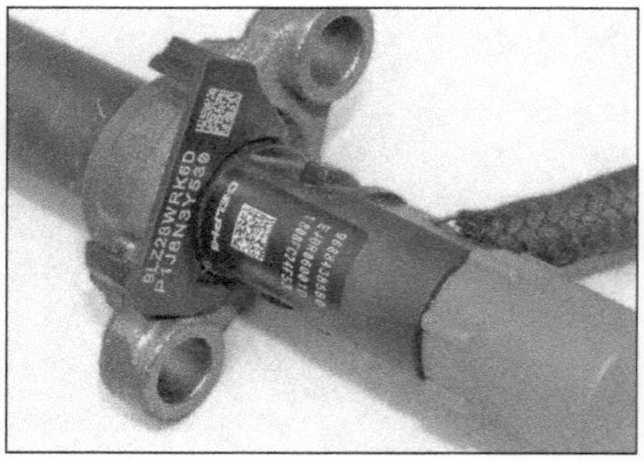

11.19b ... and the Delphi injector classification number

11.21a Unscrew the old injector retaining studs ...

11.21b ... and fit new studs

11.22 Make sure the injector recess (arrowed) is clean

Refitting

21 Unscrew the injector retaining studs from the cylinder head and renew **(see illustrations)**.

22 Clean out the injector recess in the cylinder head and make sure it is free from any dirt **(see illustration)**

23 Locate a new upper seal in the cylinder head, and place a new copper washer down the injector recess in the cylinder head **(see illustrations)**.

24 Where fitted, refit the injector clamp locating dowels to the cylinder head.

25 Ensure the injector clamps are in place over their respective circlips on the injector bodies, and then fit the injectors into place in the cylinder head. If the original injectors are being refitted, ensure they are fitted into their original positions **(see illustrations)**.

26 Fit the injector retaining bolts/nuts, but only finger-tighten them at this stage **(see illustration)**. When tightening the nuts/bolts, ensure the clamps stay horizontal.

27 Working on one fuel injector at a time, remove the blanking plugs from the fuel pipe unions on the common rail and the relevant injector. Locate a new high-pressure fuel pipe over the unions and screw on the union nuts **(see illustration)**. Take care not to cross-thread the nuts or strain the fuel pipes as they are fitted. Once the union nut threads have started, finger-tighten the nuts to the ends of the threads.

28 When all the fuel pipes are in place, tighten the injector clamp retaining nuts/bolts to the specified torque and angle **(see illustration)**.

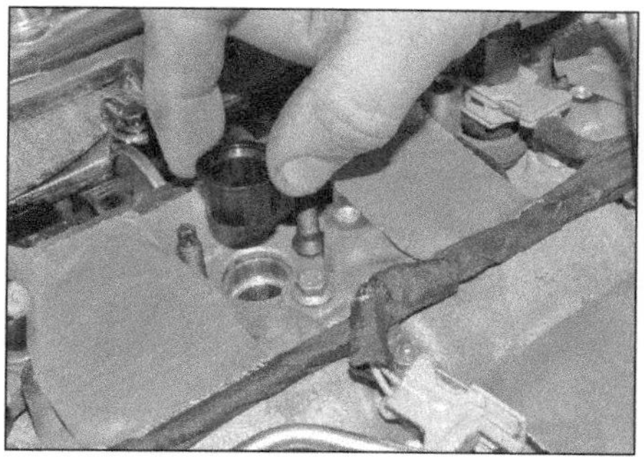

11.23a Fit a new upper seal ...

11.23b ... and use a length of wire to guide the new sealing washer into place

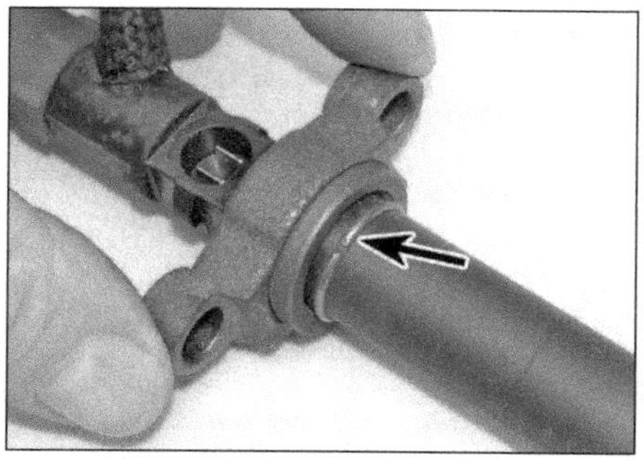

11.25a Ensure the circlip (arrowed) is in place (where applicable) ...

11.25b ... then fit the injectors into their original positions

11.26 Fit new injector securing nuts

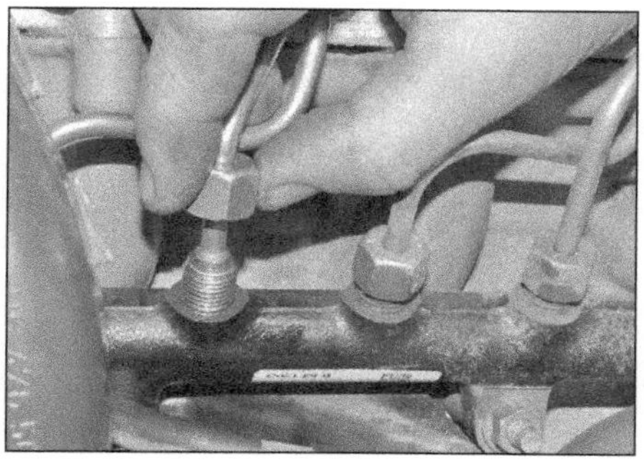

11.27 Screw the high-pressure fuel pipes to the fuel rail

11.28 Using an angle gauge to tighten the injector securing nuts

11.29 Using a crow-foot adapter to tighten the injector pipes

12.2 Vehicle diagnostic socket (arrowed)

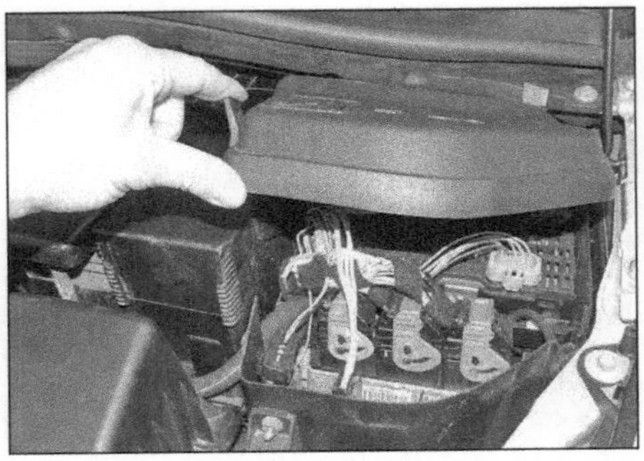

12.6 Remove the fusebox cover

29 Using an open-ended spanner, hold each fuel pipe union in turn and tighten the union nut to the specified torque using a torque wrench and crow-foot adapter **(see illustration)**. Tighten all the disturbed union nuts in the same way.

30 If new injectors have been fitted, their classification numbers must be programmed into the engine management ECU using dedicated diagnostic equipment/scanner. If this equipment is not available, entrust this task to a Citroën dealer or suitably-equipped repairer. Note that it should be possible to drive the vehicle, albeit with reduced performance/increased emissions, to a repairer for the numbers to be programmed.

31 The remainder of refitting is a reversal of removal, noting the following points:

a) *Ensure all wiring connectors and harnesses are correctly refitting and secured.*
b) *Reconnect the battery, referring to precautions in Chapter 5A, Section 1.*
c) *Observing the precautions listed in Section 2, start the engine and allow it to idle. Check for leaks at the high-pressure fuel pipe unions with the engine idling. If satisfactory, increase the engine speed to 3000 rpm and check again for leaks. Take the car for a short road test and check for leaks once again on return. If any leaks are detected, obtain and fit additional new high-pressure fuel pipes as required.* ***Do not*** *attempt to cure even the slightest leak by further tightening of the pipe unions.*

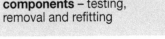

12 Electronic control system components – testing, removal and refitting

Testing

1 If a fault is suspected in the electronic control side of the system, first ensure that all the wiring connectors are securely connected and free of corrosion. Ensure that the suspected problem is not of a mechanical nature, or due to poor maintenance; ie, check that the air filter element is clean, the engine breather hoses are clear and undamaged, and that the cylinder compression pressures are correct.

2 If these checks fail to reveal the cause of the problem, the vehicle should be taken to a Citroën dealer or suitably-equipped garage for testing. A diagnostic socket is located in the centre console inside the armrest storage compartment **(see illustration)** to which a fault code reader or other suitable test equipment can be connected. By using the code reader or test equipment, the engine management ECU (and the various other vehicle system ECUs) can be interrogated, and any stored fault codes can be retrieved. This will allow the fault to be quickly and simply traced, alleviating the need to test all the system components individually, which is a time-consuming operation that carries a risk of damaging the ECU.

Removal and refitting

3 Before carrying out any of the following procedures, disconnect the battery (refer to precautions in Chapter 5A, Section 1). Reconnect the battery on completion of refitting.

Electronic control unit (ECU)

Note: *If a new ECU is being fitted, the vehicle will not start until the immobiliser ECU has been matched to the engine management ECU. This can only be performed using dedicated test equipment. Consequently, entrust the procedure to a Citroën dealer or suitably-equipped specialist.*

4 Disconnect the battery (refer to precautions in Chapter 5A, Section 1).

5 The ECU is located on the left-hand side of the engine compartment, inside the engine compartment fusebox.

6 Remove the plastic cover from the top of the fusebox **(see illustration)**.

7 Release the locking clips and disconnect the wiring connectors from the top of the ECU **(see illustration)**.

8 Lift the ECU upwards and withdraw it out from the engine compartment fusebox.

9 Refitting is a reverse of the removal procedure ensuring the wiring connectors are securely reconnected.

Crankshaft speed/position sensor

10 The crankshaft position sensor is located adjacent to the crankshaft pulley on the right-hand end of the engine. Slacken the right-hand front roadwheel bolts, and then jack the front of the vehicle up and support it on axle stands (see *Jacking and vehicle support*). Remove the right-hand front roadwheel.

11 Push in the centre pins a little, then prise out the rivets and remove the wheel arch liner.

12 Disconnect the sensor wiring plug **(see illustration)**.

13 Undo the bolt and remove the sensor.

14 Refitting is a reversal of removal, tightening the sensor retaining bolt securely.

Camshaft position sensor – 1.6 litre engines

15 The camshaft position sensor is mounted on the right-hand end of the cylinder head cover, directly behind the camshaft sprocket.

16 Remove the upper timing belt cover, as described in Chapter 2C, Section 6.

12.7 Release the locking clips and disconnect the ECU wiring plugs

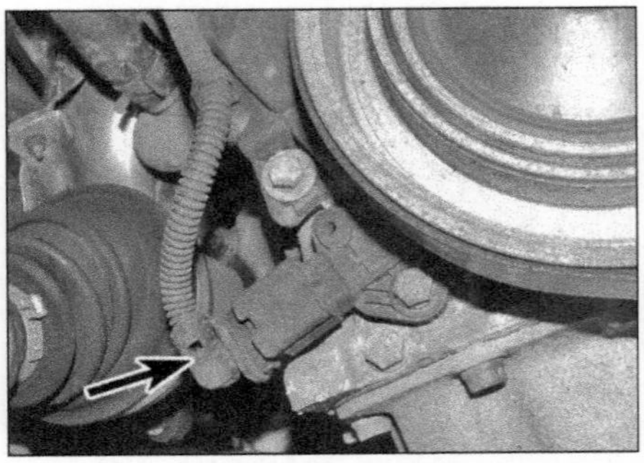

12.12 Disconnect the crankshaft position sensor wiring plug (arrowed)

17 Unplug the sensor wiring connector.
18 Undo the bolt and pull the sensor from position **(see illustration)**.
19 Upon refitting, position the sensor so that the air gap between the sensor end and the webs of the signal wheel is 1.2 mm, measured with feeler gauges **(see illustrations)**. If a new sensor is being fitted, position it so the nipple of the sensor is just in contact with the camshaft signal wheel. Tighten the sensor retaining bolt to the specified torque.
20 The remainder of refitting is a reversal of removal.

Camshaft position sensor – 2.0 litre engines

Note: *The camshaft position sensor is mounted on the right-hand end of the cylinder head cover, directly behind the camshaft sprocket.*
21 Remove the plastic cover from the top of the engine.
22 Disconnect the sensor wiring plug **(see illustration)**.
23 Undo the retaining bolt and remove the sensor **(see illustration)**.
24 To refit and adjust the sensor position, locate the sensor on the cylinder head cover and loosely refit the retaining bolt.
25 When refitting a used sensor, insert a 8.5 mm drill bit in between the sensor and the timing belt cover to get the sensor in position **(see illustration)**. Tighten the retaining bolt securely.
26 When fitting a new sensor, slide the sensor into position until the plastic nipple on the tip of the sensor just comes into contact with the spoke on the camshaft sprocket. Tighten the retaining bolt securely. Note that, depending on the position of the camshaft sprocket, it may need to be rotated slightly to get one of the spokes on sprocket to align with the hole for the sensor.

Accelerator pedal position sensor

27 The pedal sensor is integral with the accelerator pedal assembly. Refer to Section 5 of this Chapter for the pedal removal procedure.

Coolant temperature sensor

28 Refer to Chapter 3, Section 7.

12.23 Withdraw the sensor from the cover

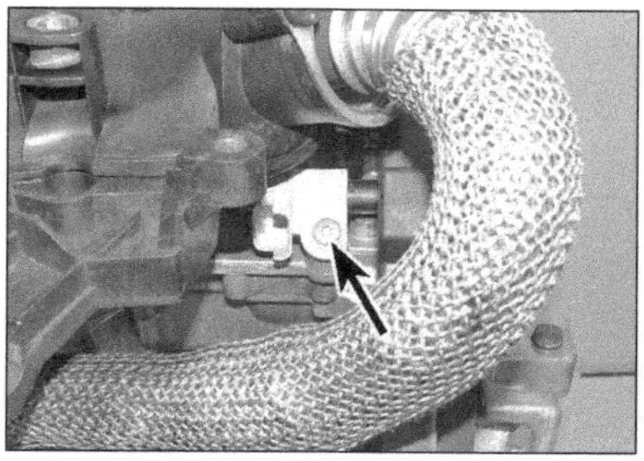
12.18 Undo the camshaft sensor retaining bolt (arrowed) – 1.6 litre engine

12.19b ... must be 1.2 mm measured with a feeler gauge

Fuel temperature sensor – 1.6 litre engines

Warning: Refer to the information contained in Section 2 before proceeding.

29 The sensor is clipped in to the plastic fuel manifold at the right-hand rear end of the cylinder head. To remove the sensor, disconnect the wiring plug, and then unclip the sensor from the manifold. Be prepared for fuel spillage **(see illustration)**.
30 Refitting is a reversal of removal. Observing the precautions listed in Section 2, start the engine and allow it to idle. Check for leaks at the fuel temperature sensor with the engine idling. If satisfactory, increase the engine speed to 4000 rpm and check again for leaks. Take the car for a short road test and check for leaks once again on return. If any leaks are detected, obtain and fit a new sensor.

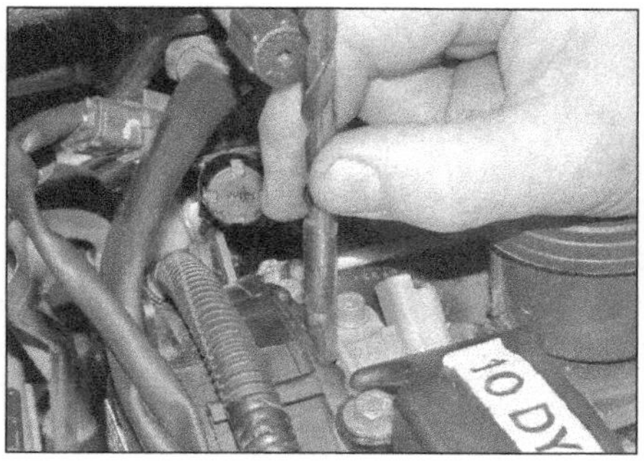

12.25 Using an 8.5 mm drill bit to measure the position of the sensor

12.19a The gap between the end of the used sensor and signal wheel (arrowed) ...

12.22 Disconnect the wiring connector

Fuel temperature sensor – 2.0 litre engines (Siemens)

Warning: Refer to the information contained in Section 2 before proceeding.

31 The fuel temperature sensor (where fitted) is located in the fuel supply pipe between the fuel filter and the high-pressure pump, in the vicinity of the common rail.
32 Disconnect the fuel temperature sensor wiring connector.
33 Thoroughly clean the area around the sensor and its location.
34 Suitably protect the components below the sensor and have plenty of clean rags handy. Be prepared for considerable fuel spillage.
35 Release the retaining clips and detach the sensor from the fuel pipes.
36 Refit the sensor to the fuel pipes, ensuring the clips fully engage.

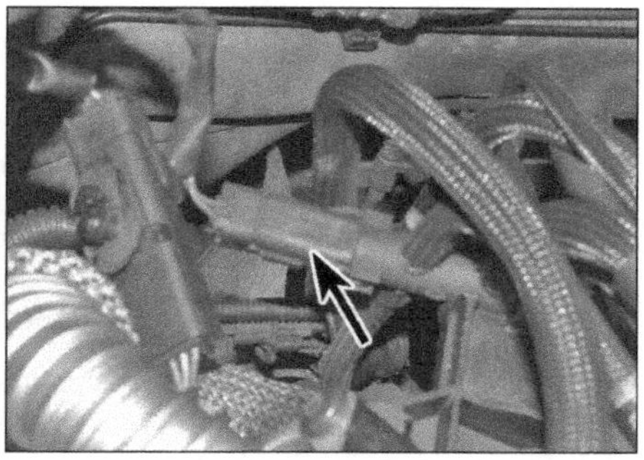
12.29 Fuel temperature sensor (arrowed) – 1.6 litre engine

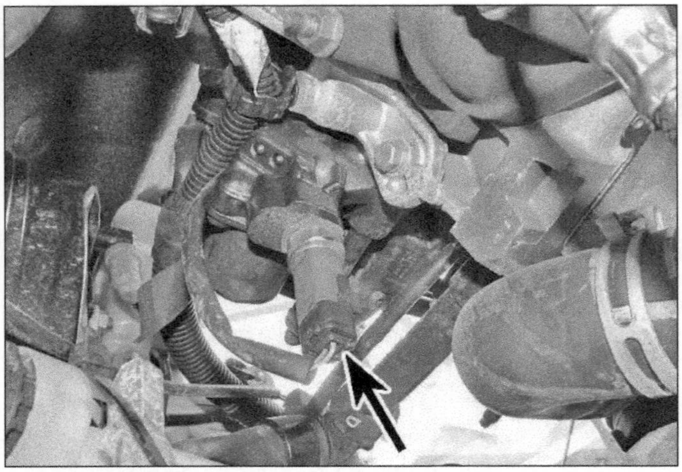

12.39 Delphi fuel temperature sensor (arrowed) – 2.0 litre engine

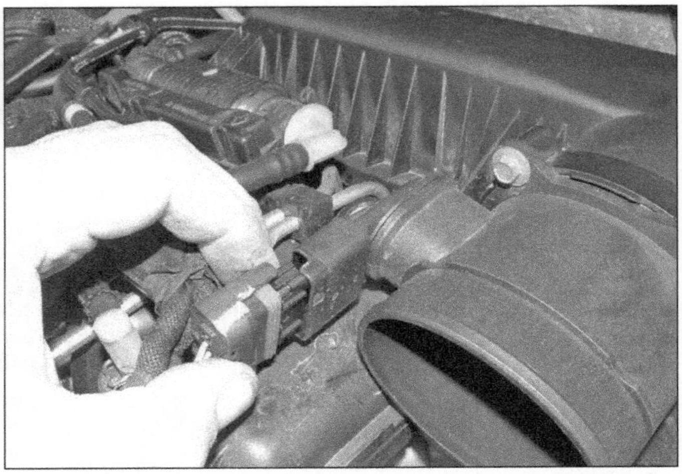

12.47a Disconnect the airflow meter wiring plug connector – 1.6 litre engine

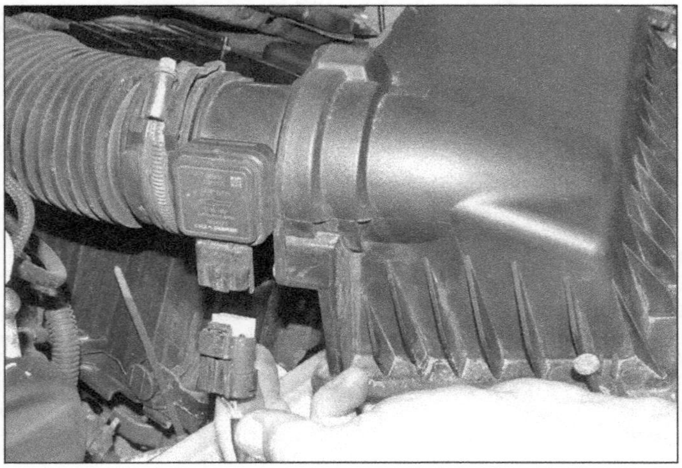

12.47b Disconnect the airflow meter wiring plug connector – 2.0 litre engine

12.52 Delphi fuel pressure regulator (arrowed) – 2.0 litre engine

37 Reconnect the sensor wiring plug.

38 Observing the precautions listed in Section 2, start the engine and allow it to idle. Check for leaks at the fuel temperature sensor with the engine idling. If satisfactory, increase the engine speed to 4000 rpm and check again for leaks. Take the car for a short road test and check for leaks once again on return. If any leaks are detected, obtain and fit a new sensor.

Fuel temperature sensor – 2.0 litre engines (Delphi)

39 The fuel temperature sensor is located in the high-pressure fuel pump **(see illustration)**.

40 Disconnect the fuel temperature sensor wiring connector.

41 Thoroughly clean the area around the sensor and its location.

42 Suitably protect the components below the sensor and have plenty of clean rags handy. Be prepared for considerable fuel spillage.

43 Undo the sensor and remove it from the fuel pump.

44 Refitting is a reversal of removal, tightening the sensor to the specified torque.

45 Observing the precautions listed in Section 2, start the engine and allow it to idle. Check for leaks at the fuel temperature sensor with the engine idling. If satisfactory, increase the engine speed to 4000 rpm and check again for leaks. Take the car for a short road test and check for leaks once again on return. If any leaks are detected, obtain and fit a new sensor.

Airflow meter

46 The airflow meter is located in the intake ducting from the air cleaner housing.

47 Disconnect the meter wiring plug **(see illustrations)**.

48 Slacken the retaining clips and disconnect the air intake ducting from either side of the airflow meter. Suitably plug or cover the turbocharger intake duct, using clean rag to prevent any dirt or foreign material from entering.

49 Undo the retaining screws and disconnect the airflow meter from the air cleaner cover.

50 Refitting is reverse of the removal procedure.

Fuel pressure sensor

51 The fuel pressure sensor is integral with the common rail, and is not available separately. Citroën insist that the sensor is not removed from the rail.

Fuel pressure regulator

52 The fuel pressure regulator is located in the high-pressure fuel pump **(see illustration)**. Depending on fuel system, the regulator may be screwed into the fuel pump or it may have two retaining screws securing it to the fuel pump.

53 Disconnect the wiring connector from the fuel pressure regulator.

54 Thoroughly clean the area around the sensor and its location.

55 Suitably protect the components below the sensor and have plenty of clean rags handy. Be prepared for considerable fuel spillage.

56 Depending on type fitted, either unscrew the regulator and remove it from the fuel pump

14.2a Undo the exhaust manifold nuts, recover the spacers, and remove the manifold

14.2b Recover the manifold gasket - 1.6 litre engine

14.2c Exhaust manifold - 2.0 litre engine

or undo the two retaining screws and remove the regulator from the pump.

57 Refitting is a reversal of removal, tightening the sensor to the specified torque.

58 Observing the precautions listed in Section 2, start the engine and allow it to idle. Check for leaks at the fuel temperature sensor with the engine idling. If satisfactory, increase the engine speed to 4000 rpm and check again for leaks. Take the car for a short road test and check for leaks once again on return. If any leaks are detected, obtain and fit a new sensor.

EGR solenoid valve

59 Refer to Chapter 4C, Section 2.

Vehicle speed sensor

60 The engine management ECU receives the vehicle speed signal from the wheel speed sensors via the ABS ECU. Refer to Chapter 9, Section 19 for wheel speed sensor removal.

13 Intake manifold – removal and refitting

1 The intake manifold is integral with the cylinder head cover. For the removal and refitting procedure, refer to Chapter 2C, Section 4, for 1.6 litre engines and Chapter 2D, Section 4, for 2.0 litre engines.

14 Exhaust manifold – removal and refitting

Removal

1 Remove the turbocharger as described in Section 16.

2 Undo the retaining nuts, recover the spacers (where fitted), and remove the manifold. Recover the gasket **(see illustrations)**.

Refitting

3 Refitting is a reverse of the removal procedure, bearing in mind the following points:

a) *Ensure that the manifold and cylinder head mating faces are clean, with all traces of old gasket removed.*

b) *Use new gaskets when refitting the manifold to the cylinder head.*

c) *Tighten the exhaust manifold retaining nuts to the specified torque, starting with the ones at the centre and then working your way to the outer ones.*

15 Turbocharger – description and precautions

1 A turbocharger is fitted to increase engine efficiency by raising the pressure in the intake manifold above atmospheric pressure. Instead of the air simply being sucked into the cylinders, it is forced in.

2 Energy for the operation of the turbocharger comes from the exhaust gas. The gas flows through a specially shaped housing (the turbine housing) and, in so doing, spins the turbine wheel. The turbine wheel is attached to a shaft, at the end of which is another vaned wheel known as the compressor wheel. The compressor wheel spins in its own housing, and compresses the intake air on the way to the intake manifold.

3 Boost pressure (the pressure in the intake manifold) is limited by a wastegate, which diverts the exhaust gas away from the turbine wheel in response to a pressure-sensitive actuator. The turbocharger incorporates a variable intake nozzle to improve boost pressure at low engine speeds.

4 The turbo shaft is pressure-lubricated by an oil feed pipe from the main oil gallery. The shaft 'floats' on a cushion of oil. A drain pipe returns the oil to the sump.

Precautions

5 The turbocharger operates at extremely high speeds and temperatures. Certain precautions must be observed, to avoid premature failure of the turbo, or injury to the operator.

- Do not operate the turbo with any of its parts exposed, or with any of its hoses removed. Foreign objects falling onto the rotating vanes could cause excessive damage, and (if ejected) personal injury.
- Do not race the engine immediately after start-up, especially if it is cold. Give the oil a few seconds to circulate.
- Always allow the engine to return to idle speed before switching it off – do not blip the throttle and switch off, as this will leave the turbo spinning without lubrication.
- Allow the engine to idle for several minutes before switching off after a high-speed run.
- Observe the recommended intervals for oil and filter changing, and use a reputable oil of the specified quality. Neglect of oil changing, or use of inferior oil, can cause carbon formation on the turbo shaft, leading to subsequent failure.

16 Turbocharger – removal, inspection and refitting

Removal

1 Chock the rear wheels then jack up the front of the vehicle and support it on axle stands (see *Jacking and vehicle support*). Undo the screws and remove the engine undershield.

2 Disconnect the battery, (refer to precautions in Chapter 5A, Section 1).

1.6 litre engines

3 Place a sheet of thick cardboard over the rear of the radiator to protect it from accidental damage.

4 Slacken the clamps, undo the bolts, and remove the air ducts to and from the turbocharger and intake manifold **(see illustrations 11.3a and 11.3b)**. Note their fitted positions and disconnect the various wiring plugs, as the assembly is withdrawn.

5 Disconnect the vacuum hose from the turbocharger wastegate control assembly **(see illustration)**.

16.5 Disconnect the vacuum pipe from the wastegate control assembly (arrowed)

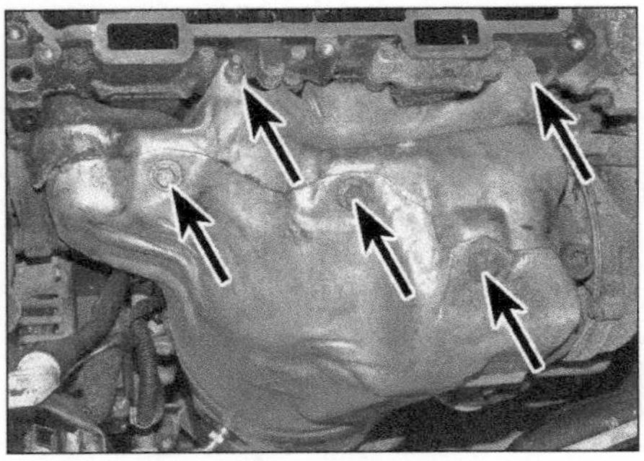

16.6 Undo the bolts and remove the turbocharger heat shield (arrowed)

16.8 Turbocharger oil supply and return pipes (arrowed)

16.10 Undo the 3 nuts (arrowed – one hidden) and remove the support bracket bolt (arrowed)

6 Undo the mounting bolts **(see illustration)**, and remove the heat shield from above turbocharger.

7 Remove the catalytic converter/particulate filter (where applicable) as described in Section 18.

8 Undo the oil supply pipe banjo bolts and recover the sealing washers **(see illustration)**.

9 Slacken the retaining clip and disconnect the oil return pipe from the turbocharger and cylinder block.

10 Unscrew the four nuts, and the nut securing the support bracket, then remove the turbocharger from the exhaust manifold **(see illustration)**.

2.0 litre engines

11 Remove the air cleaner assembly as described in Section 4.

12 Working underneath the vehicle, undo the retaining bolts and remove the crossbar that is bolted to the front subframe. Then undo the rear lower engine torque link bolts and remove the torque link mounting from under the vehicle. Move the lower part of the engine forwards and wedge a block of wood (approx 75 mm thick) between the transmission and the subframe **(see illustrations)**.

13 Undo the retaining clamp and disconnect the exhaust front pipe from the pre-catalyst **(see illustration)**.

14 Where applicable undo the retaining bolts and remove the heat shield from over the pre-catalyst **(see illustration)**. Note on some models the heat shield is removed with the pre-catalyst.

16.12a Undo the crossbar retaining bolts (one side shown)

16.12b Remove the rear lower mounting torque link

16.13 Exhaust flexible pipe-to-pre-catalyst securing clamp (arrowed)

16.14 Pre-catalyst heat shield can be removed on some models

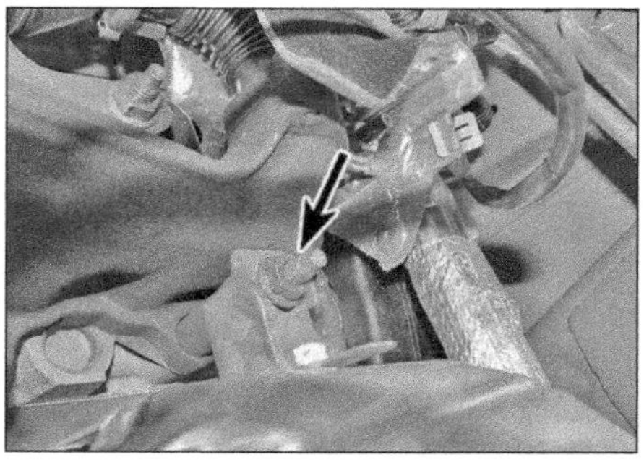
16.15a Undo the upper mounting bracket (arrowed) ...

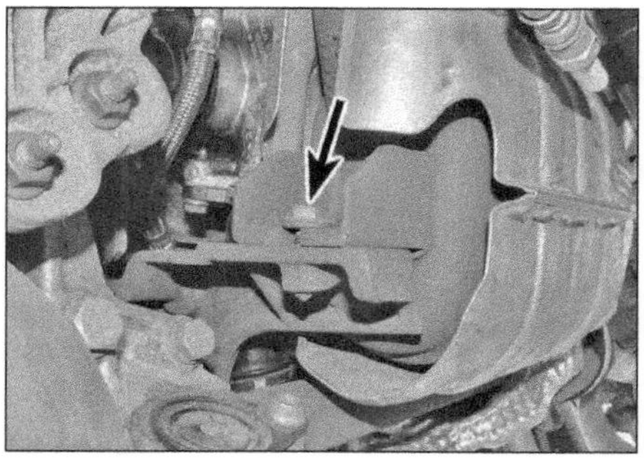
16.15b ... and the mounting bolt (arrowed) on the left-hand side

16.16a Slacken the clamp (arrowed) securing the pre-cat to the turbo ...

16.16b ... and then withdraw the pre-cat from under the vehicle

16.16c The clamp is self-slackening

16.18 Remove the air intake and outlet ducts (arrowed)

15 Undo the pre-catalyst mounting bolts/nuts, remove the pre-catalyst support bracket at the right-hand upper end, undo the mounting bolt at the left-hand end **(see illustrations)**.

16 Slacken the clamp securing the pre-catalyst to the turbocharger, and remove the pre-catalyst **(see illustrations)**. Note the clamp is self-slackening; as the bolt is slackened it will open up to release from the flange, discard as a new one will be required for refitting.

17 Depending on model, it may be necessary to disconnect the wiring connector from the gas temperature sensor fitted in the top of the pre-catalyst.

18 Undo the retaining bolts and disconnect the turbocharger air intake and outlet ducts **(see illustration)**.

19 Disconnect the vacuum pipe and wiring plug from the turbocharger control valve **(see illustration)**.

20 Disconnect the oil supply and return pipes from the engine cylinder block **(see illustrations)**. Tape over the openings.

21 Remove the support bracket beneath the turbocharger **(see illustration)**.

22 Undo the nuts/bolt securing the turbocharger to the exhaust manifold, lift the assembly slightly, then lower the turbocharger downwards from position **(see illustration)**.

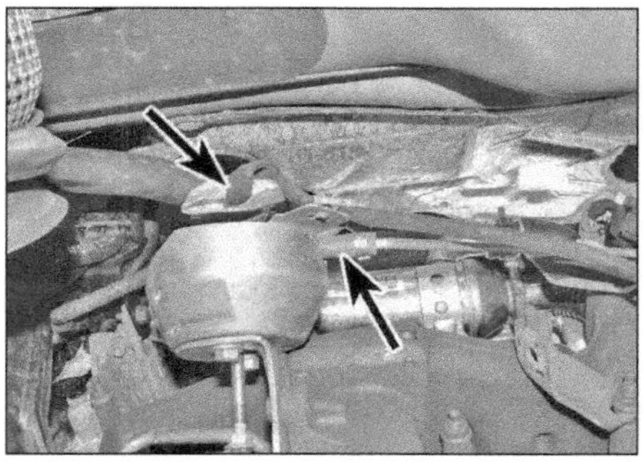
16.19 Disconnect the wiring connector and the vacuum pipe (arrowed)

16.20a Disconnect the turbocharger oil supply pipe (arrowed) ..

16.20b ... and the return pipe (arrowed)

16.21 Turbocharger lower mounting bracket bolt (arrowed)

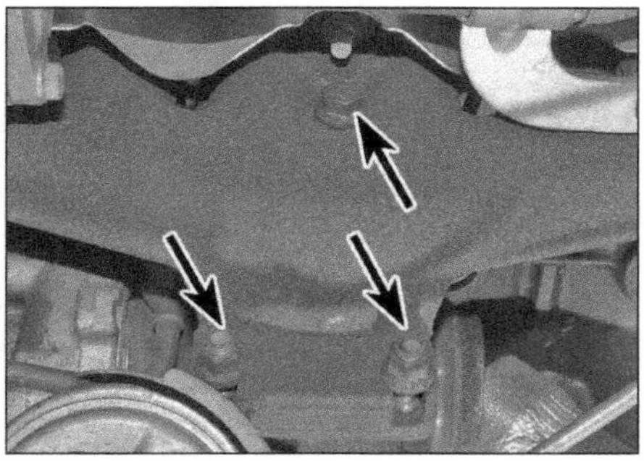
16.22 Turbocharger upper mounting nuts and bolt (arrowed)

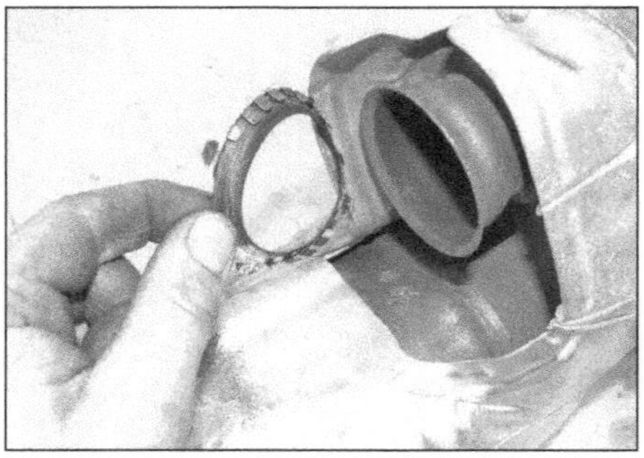

16.27a Unclip the old inner sealing washer from the old clamp

Inspection

23 With the turbocharger removed, inspect the housing for cracks or other visible damage.

24 Spin the turbine or the compressor wheel to verify that the shaft is intact and to feel for excessive shake or roughness. Some play is normal, since in use the shaft is 'floating' on a film of oil. Check that the wheel vanes are undamaged.

25 If oil contamination of the exhaust or induction passages is apparent, it is likely that turbo shaft oil seals have failed.

26 No DIY repair of the turbo is possible and none of the internal or external parts are available separately. If the turbocharger is suspect in any way a complete new unit must be obtained. Do not attempt to dismantle the turbocharger control assemblies.

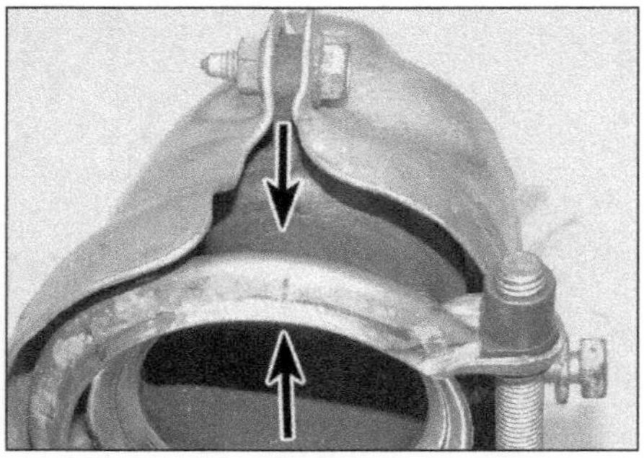

16.27b Fit the alignment mark on the new clamp (arrowed) with the upper flange of the pre-cat

Refitting

27 Refitting is a reverse of the removal procedure, bearing in mind the following points:

a) *Renew the turbocharger retaining nuts and gaskets.*

b) *When fitting the new clamp to the pre-catalyst, align the clamp on the flange **(see illustrations)**.*

c) *If a new turbocharger is being fitted, change the engine oil and filter. Also renew the filter in the oil feed pipe.*

d) *Prime the turbocharger by injecting clean engine oil through the oil feed pipe union before reconnecting the union.*

17 Intercooler – removal and refitting

Removal

1 Remove the front bumper as described in Chapter 11, Section 6.

1.6 litre models

2 The intercooler is located at the front of the engine compartment, on the right-hand side of the radiator.

3 Slacken the retaining clips and disconnect the air intake and outlet hoses from the top of the intercooler **(see illustration)**.

4 Unclip the coolant reservoir overflow pipe to the radiator from the cross panel and move it to one side **(see illustration)**.

5 Undo the upper retaining bolts, and then lift the intercooler, releasing it from its lower mountings in the radiator front panel **(see illustrations)**.

6 If required, undo the two bolts (one at each side) securing the radiator front panel to the vehicle body **(see illustration)**, and then carefully pull the panel forwards to allow more room for the removal of the intercooler.

2.0 litre models

7 The intercooler is located at the front of the engine compartment, on the left-hand side of the radiator.

8 Remove the air cleaner assembly as described in Section 4. Release the retaining

17.3 Remove the upper hose clamps (arrowed) from the intercooler

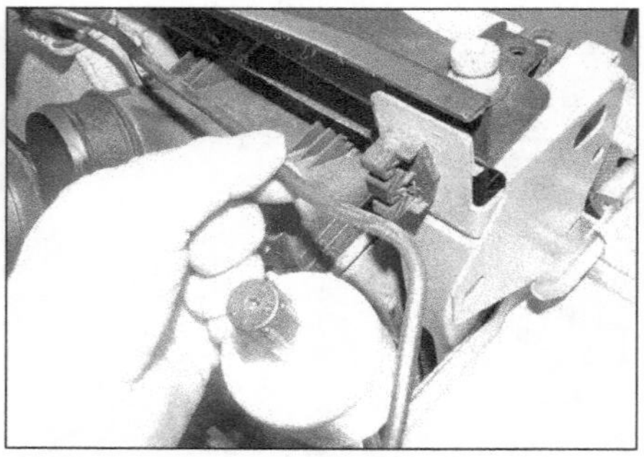

17.4 Unclip the coolant overflow pipe from the retaining clip

17.5a Undo the mounting bolts (arrowed) ...

17.5b ... and withdraw the intercooler from the engine compartment – 1.6 litre engines

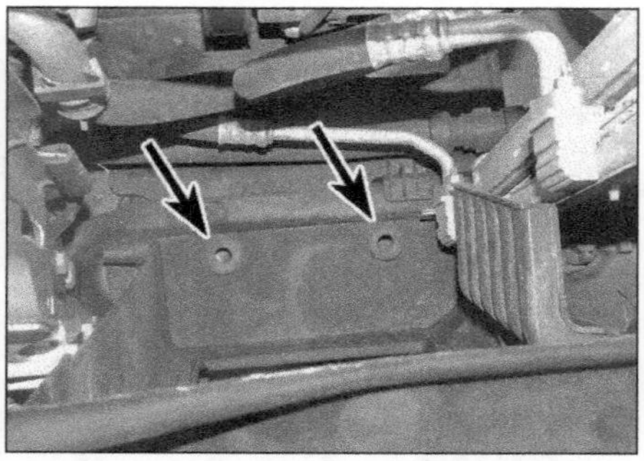

17.5c Make sure the lower mounting rubbers are still in place

17.6 Undo the front panel outer retaining bolts (one side arrowed)

clips and remove the air intake scoop from the front of the crossmember **(see illustrations)**.

9 Slacken the retaining clip and disconnect the upper air hose from the top of the intercooler **(see illustration)**.

10 Slacken the retaining clip and disconnect the lower air hose from the base of the intercooler **(see illustration)**. To make access easier, undo the retaining bolts/nuts and remove the engine undershield.

11 Undo the upper retaining screw, then lift the intercooler, releasing it from its lower mountings in the radiator front panel **(see illustrations)**.

17.8a Release the retaining clips ...

17.8b ... and remove the air intake ducting

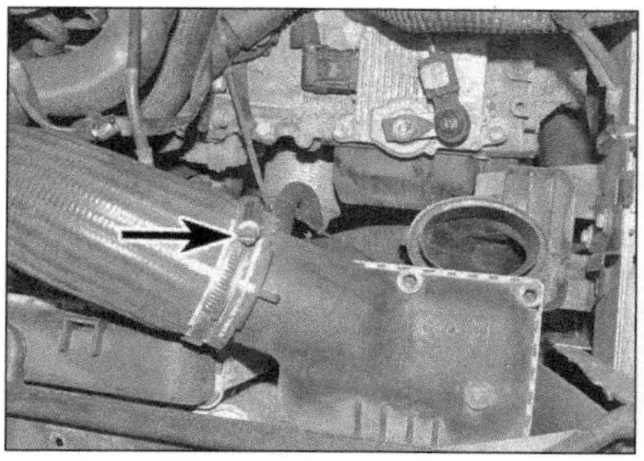

17.9 Release the intercooler upper hose retaining clip (arrowed) ...

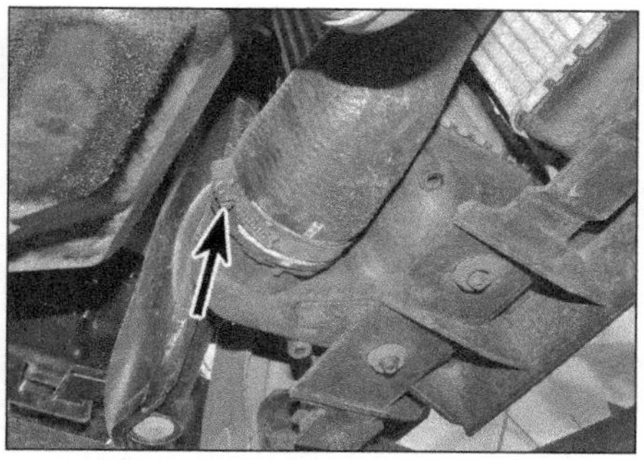

17.10 ... and lower hose retaining clip (arrowed) – 2.0 litre engines

17.11a Undo the mounting bolt (arrowed) ...

17.11b ... and withdraw the intercooler from the lower rubber mountings (arrowed)

Refitting

12 Refitting is a reversal of removal.

18 Exhaust system – general information and component renewal

General information

1 According to model, the exhaust system consists of either three or four sections. Three-section systems consist of a catalytic converter, an intermediate pipe, and a rear silencer. Four-section systems consist of a pre-catalyst after the turbocharger, followed by a catalytic converter, particulate filter (not all models), intermediate pipe, and rear silencer.

2 The exhaust joints are of either the spring-loaded ball type (to allow for movement in the exhaust system) or clamp-ring type.

3 The system is suspended throughout its entire length by rubber mountings.

Removal

4 Each exhaust section can be removed individually, or alternatively, the complete system can be removed as a unit.

5 To remove the system or part of the system, first jack up the front or rear of the car, and support it on axle stands (see *Jacking and vehicle support*). Alternatively, position the car over an inspection pit, or on car ramps.

Catalytic converter/particulate filter – 1.6 litre engines

6 Undo the retaining bolts/nuts and remove the engine undershield.

7 Unscrew the pressure take-off unions from the side and base of the assembly **(see illustrations)**.

8 Disconnect the sensor wiring plug on the side of the catalytic converter.

9 Undo the bolts and remove the heat shield from the catalytic converter/particulate filter.

10 Slacken the retaining clamps joining the catalytic converter to the turbocharger and exhaust pipe. Take care not to damage the flexible section of the front exhaust pipe **(see illustration)**.

11 Slacken the clamp securing the catalytic converter to the turbocharger.

12 Undo the 2 nuts securing the catalytic

18.7a Unscrew the pressure take-off union from the side of the catalyst/filter ...

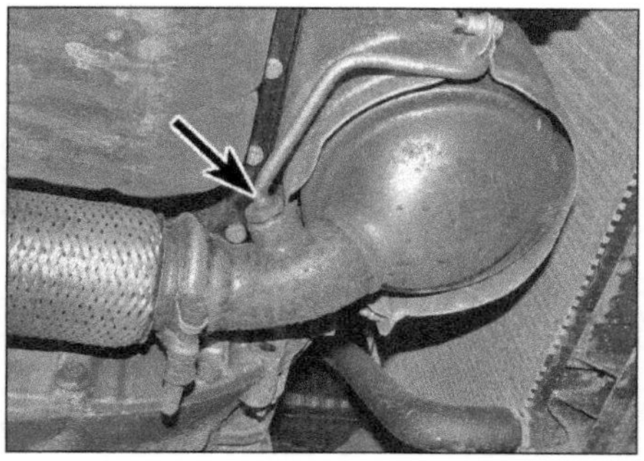

18.7b ... and the one at the base

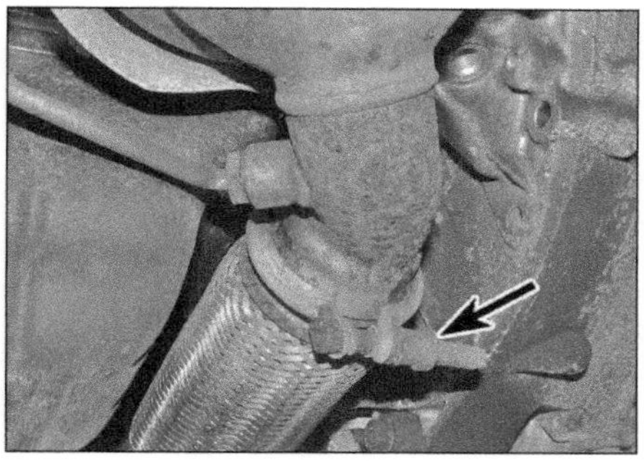

18.10 Exhaust flexible pipe-to-catalyst/filter clamp (arrowed)

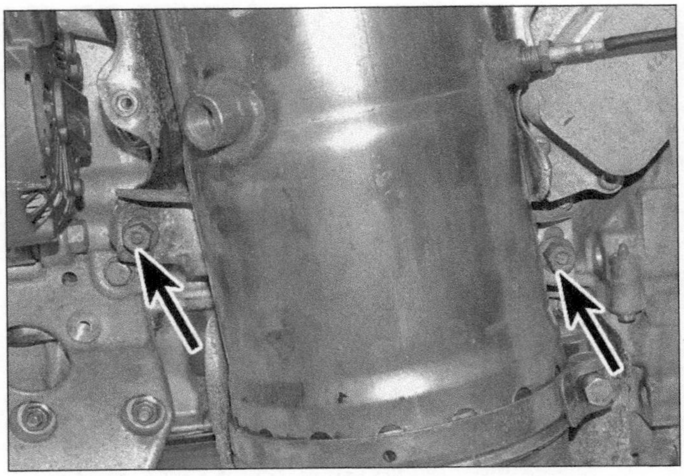

18.12 Catalytic converter/particulate filter retaining nuts (arrowed)

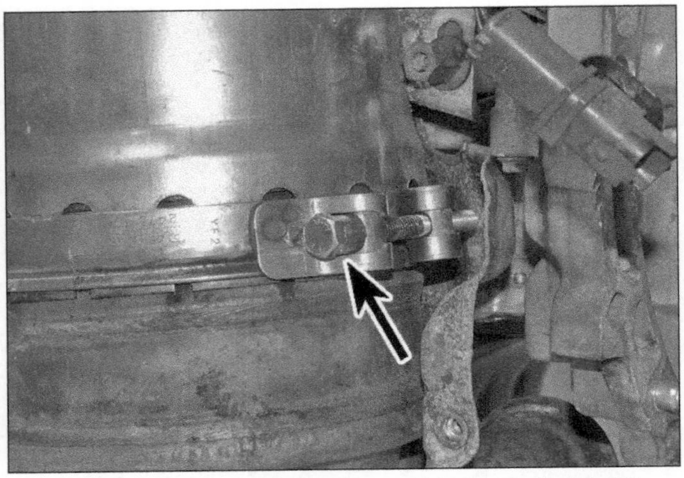

18.13 Undo the clamp (arrowed) and slide the particulate filter from the catalytic converter

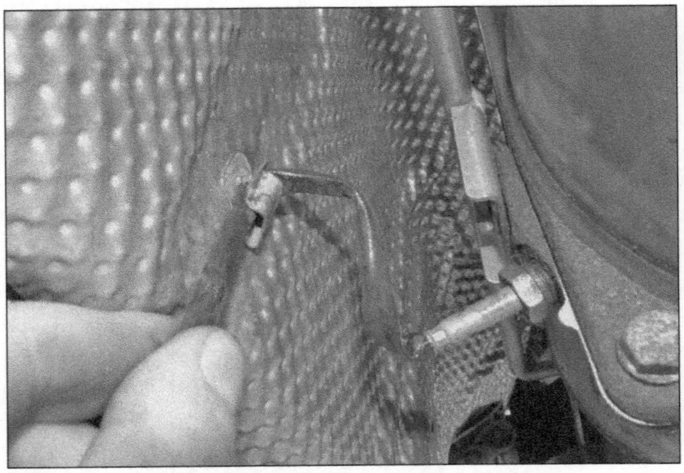

18.14 Unclip the wiring from the heat shield

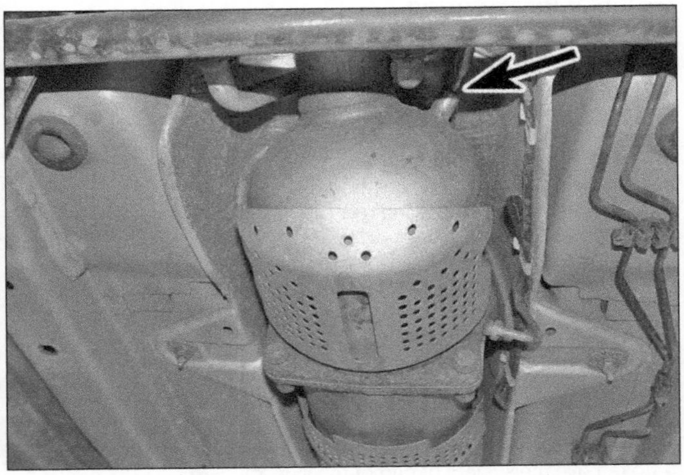

18.15a Unscrew the pressure take-off union (arrowed) from the front of the catalyst/particulate filter ...

converter to the cylinder block and manoeuvre it down and out of the engine compartment **(see illustration)**.

13 If required, note its fitted position, then slacken the clamp and detach the particulate filter from the base of the catalytic converter **(see illustration)**.

Catalytic converter/particulate filter – 2.0 litre engines

14 Trace the wire back and disconnect the temperature sensor wiring connector from the particulate filter **(see illustration)**.

15 Carefully unscrew the pressure pipes and disconnect them from the catalytic converter **(see illustrations)**. Undo the securing bolt on the side of the catalytic converter, and then fasten the pipes to one side to prevent any damage.

16 Undo the front pipe retaining clamp on the pre-catalyst **(see illustration)**.

17 Undo the rear clamp bolt and pull the

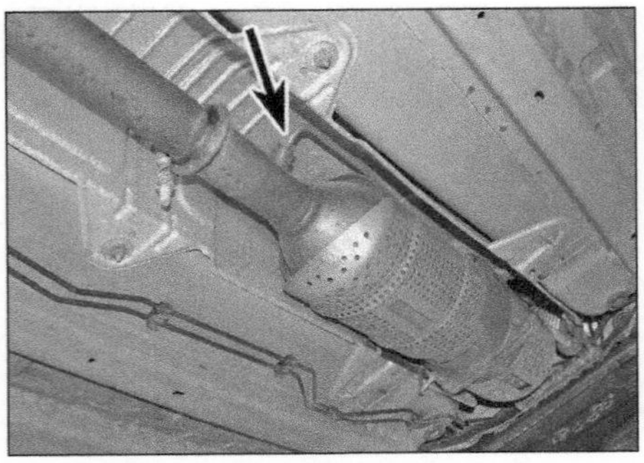

18.15b ... and the one at the rear (arrowed) of the catalyst/particulate filter

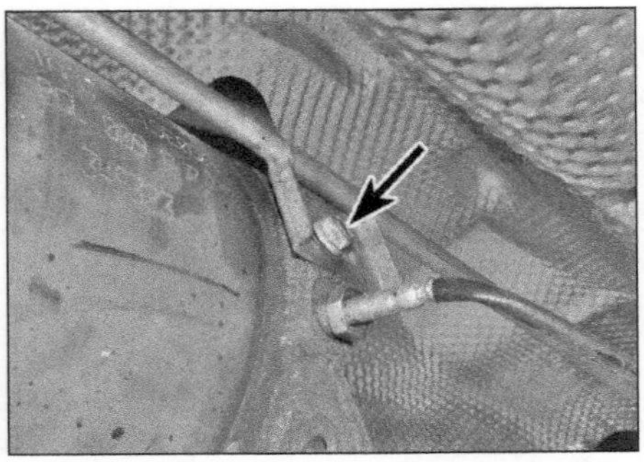

18.15c Undo the pipe retaining bracket bolt (arrowed)

18.16 Exhaust pipe-to-pre-catalyst clamp (arrowed)

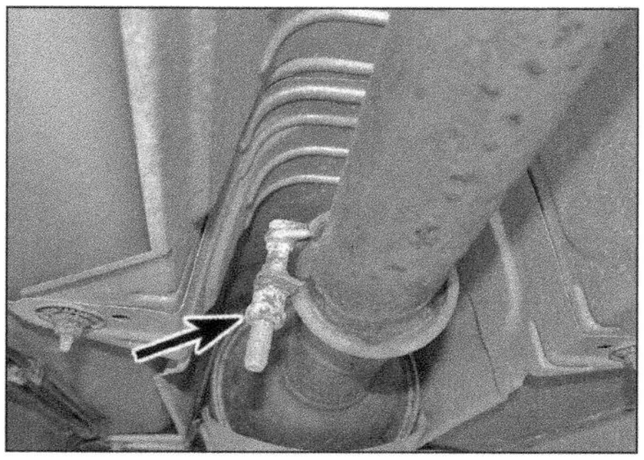

18.17a Undo the exhaust securing clamp (arrowed) ...

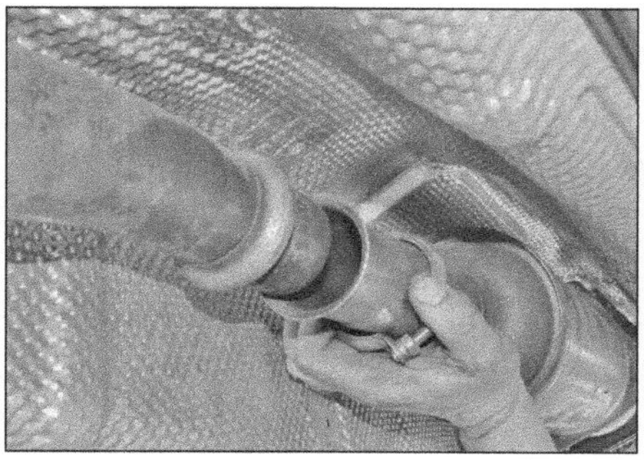

18.17b ... and slide the catalyst/particulate filter from the intermediate pipe ...

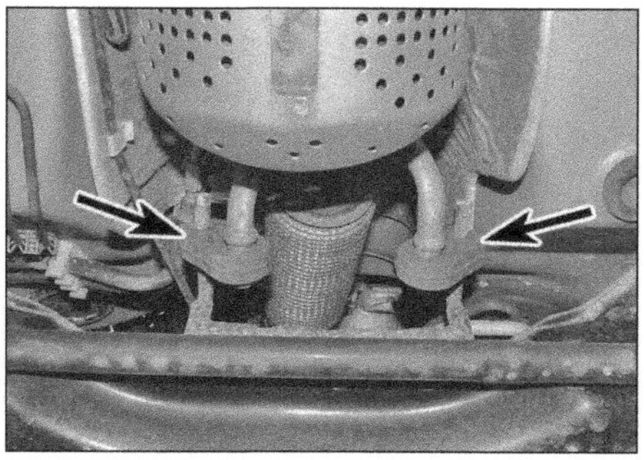

18.17c ... releasing it from the front rubber mountings (arrowed)

exhaust apart, slide the catalytic converter/particulate filter from the rubber mountings as it is removed from under the vehicle **(see illustrations)**.

18 It is possible to separate the particulate filter from the catalytic converter. With the assembly on a bench, undo the four bolts/nuts and separate the two halves. Discard the gasket, as a new one will be required for refitting **(see illustration)**.

Pre-catalytic converter – 2.0 litre engines

19 The pre-catalyst removal procedure is described within the turbocharger removal procedure – see Section 16.

Intermediate pipe

20 Slacken the clamping ring bolts, and disengage both clamps from the flange joints at each end of the pipe.

21 Release the pipe from its mounting rubbers and remove it from underneath the vehicle **(see illustration)**. Alternatively, undo the nuts securing the mounting bracket to the vehicle body.

Rear silencer

22 Slacken the rear silencer clamping ring bolts, and disengage the clamp from the flange joint.

23 Unhook the rear silencer from its mounting rubbers, and remove it from the vehicle **(see illustrations)**. Alternatively, undo the nuts/bolts securing the mounting bracket to the vehicle body.

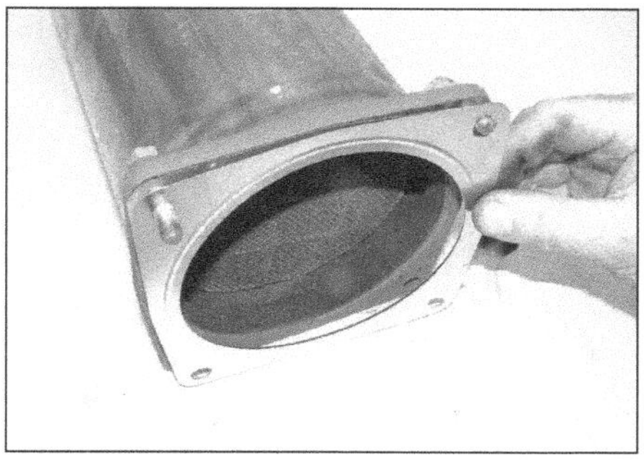

18.18 Fit a new gasket between the catalyst and the particulate filter

Heat shield(s)

24 The heat shields are secured to the underside of the body by various fasteners. Each shield can be removed once the relevant exhaust section has been removed **(see illustration)**. If a shield is being removed to gain access to a component located behind it, it may prove sufficient in some cases to remove the fasteners and simply lower the shield, without disturbing the exhaust system.

Refitting

25 Each section is refitted by reversing the removal sequence, noting the following points:

a) Ensure that all traces of corrosion have been removed from the flanges, and renew all necessary gaskets.

b) Inspect the rubber mountings for signs of damage or deterioration, and renew as necessary.

c) On joints secured together by a clamping ring, apply a smear of exhaust system jointing paste to the flange joint, to ensure a gas-tight seal. Tighten the clamping ring nuts evenly and progressively, so that the clearance between the clamp halves remains equal on either side.

d) Prior to tightening the exhaust system fasteners, ensure that all rubber mountings are correctly located, and that there is adequate clearance between the exhaust system and vehicle underbody.

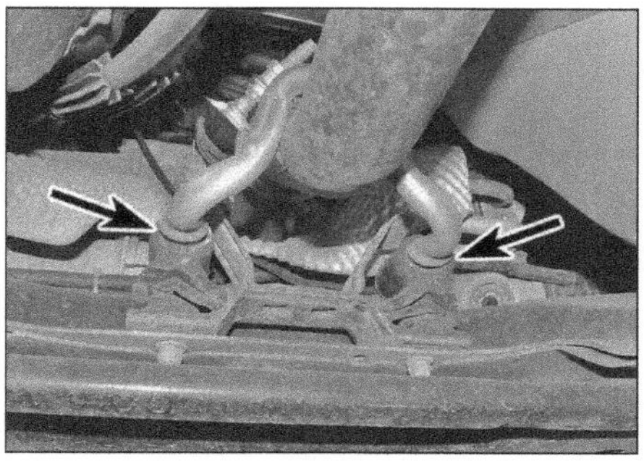

18.21 Exhaust system front mounting bracket (arrowed)

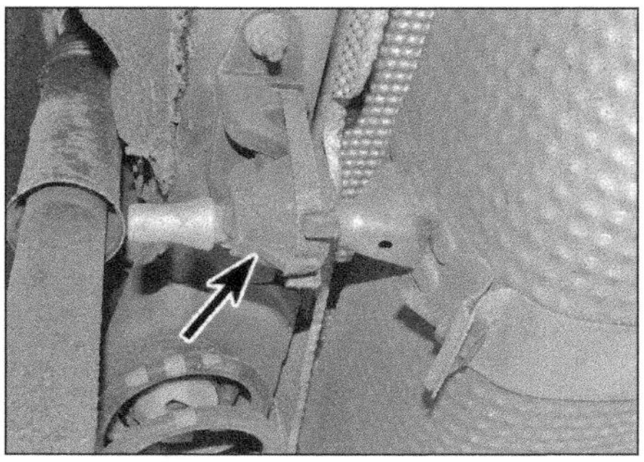

18.23a Exhaust rear silencer side rubber mounting (arrowed) ...

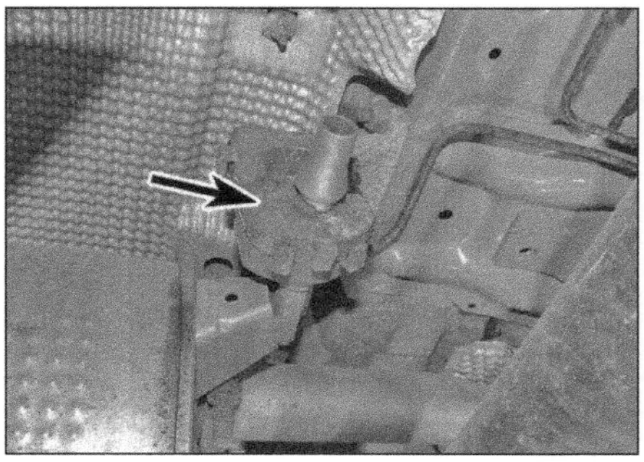

18.23b ... and front rubber mounting (arrowed)

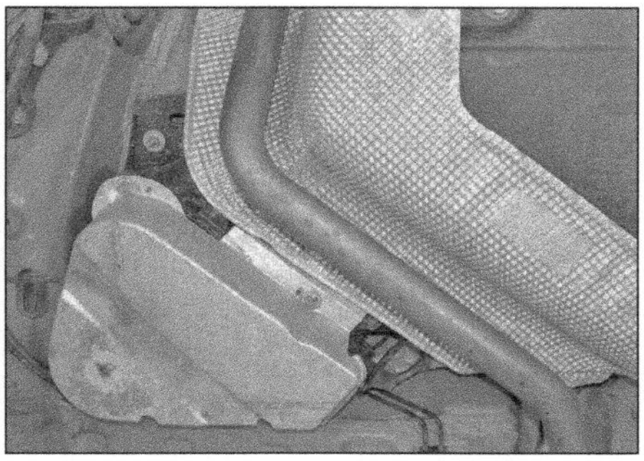

18.24 Heat shields have various fasteners

Notes

Chapter 4 Part C:
Emission control systems

Contents

Degrees of difficulty

Easy, suitable for novice with little experience	**Fairly easy,** suitable for beginner with some experience	**Fairly difficult,** suitable for competent DIY mechanic	**Difficult,** suitable for experienced DIY mechanic	**Very difficult,** suitable for expert DIY or professional

1 General information

The emission control systems are as follows.

Petrol engines

All petrol engines use unleaded petrol and also have various other features built into the fuel system to help minimise harmful emissions. In addition, all engines are equipped with the crankcase emission control system described below. All engines are also equipped with a catalytic converter and an evaporative emission control system.

Crankcase emission control

To reduce the emission of unburned hydrocarbons from the crankcase into the atmosphere, the engine is sealed and the blow-by gases and oil vapour are drawn from inside the crankcase, through a wire mesh oil separator, into the intake tract to be burned by the engine during normal combustion.

Under all conditions the gases are forced out of the crankcase by the (relatively) higher crankcase pressure; if the engine is worn, the raised crankcase pressure (due to increased blow-by) will cause some of the flow to return under all manifold conditions.

Exhaust emission control

To minimise the amount of pollutants which escape into the atmosphere, a catalytic converter is fitted in the exhaust system. Where a catalytic converter is fitted, the system is of the closed-loop type, in which oxygen (lambda) sensors in the exhaust system provides the fuel injection/ignition system ECU with constant feedback, enabling the ECU to adjust the mixture to provide the best possible conditions for the converter to operate.

The oxygen sensors have a heating element built-in that is controlled by the ECU through the oxygen sensor relay to quickly bring the sensor's tip to an efficient operating temperature. The sensor's tip is sensitive to oxygen and sends the ECU a varying voltage depending on the amount of oxygen in the exhaust gases; if the intake air/fuel mixture is too rich, the exhaust gases are low in oxygen so the sensor sends a low-voltage signal, the voltage rising as the mixture weakens and the amount of oxygen rises in the exhaust gases. Peak conversion efficiency of all major pollutants occurs if the intake air/fuel mixture is maintained at the chemically correct ratio for the complete combustion of petrol of 14.7 parts (by weight) of air to 1 part of fuel (the 'stoichiometric' ratio). The sensor output voltage alters in a large step at this point, the ECU using the signal change as a reference point and correcting the intake air/fuel mixture accordingly by altering the fuel injector pulse width.

Evaporative emission control

To minimise the escape into the atmosphere of unburned hydrocarbons, an evaporative emission control system is fitted to models equipped with a catalytic converter. The fuel tank filler cap is sealed and a charcoal canister is mounted behind the wheel arch liner under the right-hand side front wing to collect the petrol vapours generated in the tank when the car is parked. It stores them until they can be cleared from the canister (under the control of the fuel injection/ignition system ECU) via the purge valve into the intake tract to be burned by the engine during normal combustion.

To ensure that the engine runs correctly when it is cold and/or idling and to protect the catalytic converter from the effects of an over-rich mixture, the purge control valve is not opened by the ECU until the engine has warmed-up, and the engine is under load; the valve solenoid is then modulated on and off to allow the stored vapour to pass into the intake tract.

Diesel engines

All diesel engines are designed to meet strict emission requirements and are equipped with a crankcase emission control system and a catalytic converter. To further reduce exhaust emissions, all diesel engines are also fitted with an exhaust gas recirculation (EGR) system. Additionally, some diesel models may be equipped with a particulate emission filter, which uses porous silicon carbide substrate to trap particulates of carbon as the exhaust gases pass through.

Crankcase emission control

Refer to the description for petrol engines.

Exhaust emission control

To minimise the level of exhaust pollutants released into the atmosphere, a catalytic converter is fitted in the exhaust system of all models.

The catalytic converter consists of a canister containing a fine mesh impregnated with a catalyst material, over which the hot exhaust gases pass. The catalyst speeds up the oxidation of harmful carbon monoxide, un-burnt hydrocarbons and soot, effectively reducing the quantity of harmful products released into the atmosphere via the exhaust gases.

Exhaust gas recirculation system

This system is designed to recirculate small quantities of exhaust gas into the intake tract, and therefore into the combustion process. This process reduces the level of oxides of nitrogen present in the final exhaust gas, which is released into the atmosphere.

The volume of exhaust gas recirculated is controlled by the system electronic control unit.

A vacuum-operated valve is fitted to the exhaust manifold, to regulate the quantity of exhaust gas recirculated. The valve is operated by the vacuum supplied by the solenoid valve.

Particulate filter system

The particulate filter is combined with the catalytic converter in the exhaust system on some models, and its purpose it to trap particles of carbon (soot) as the exhaust gases pass through, in order to comply with latest emission regulations.

The filter can be automatically regenerated (cleaned) by the system's ECU on-board the vehicle. The engine's high-pressure injection system is utilised to inject fuel into the exhaust gases during the post-injection period; this causes the filter temperature to increase sufficiently to oxidise the particulates, leaving an ash residue. The regeneration period is automatically controlled by the on-board ECU. Subsequently, at the correct service interval the filter must be removed from the exhaust system, and renewed.

To assist the combustion of the trapped carbon (soot) during the regeneration process, a fuel additive (cerium-based Eolys) is automatically mixed with the diesel fuel in the fuel tank. The additive is stored in a container attached to the left-hand side of the fuel tank, and the ECU regulates the amount of additive to send to the fuel tank by means of an additive injector located on the top of the fuel tank.

2 Emission control systems (petrol engines) – testing and component renewal

Crankcase emission control

1 The components of this system require no attention other than to check that the hose(s) are clear and undamaged at regular intervals.

Evaporative emission control

2 If the system is thought to be faulty, disconnect the hoses from the charcoal canister and purge control valve and check that they are clear by blowing through them. If the purge control valve or charcoal canister is thought to be faulty, they must be renewed.

Charcoal canister

3 The charcoal canister (where fitted) is located under the right-hand side front wing, under the inner wing liner at the rear of the wing panel. To gain access, slacken the right-hand front roadwheel bolts, jack up the front of the car and support it on axle stands. Remove the roadwheel, release the centre pins then prise out the plastic expanding rivets **(see illustration)**, and remove the wheel arch liner.

4 Gently prise the canister from its three retaining support mountings and lower it from the top rear corner of the wheel arch.

5 Identify the location of the two hoses then depress the quick-release button and disconnect hoses from the purge valve and the canister **(see illustration)**. Disconnect the wiring plug connector from the purge valve.

6 Refitting is a reverse of the removal procedure ensuring that the hoses are correctly reconnected.

Purge solenoid valve

7 The purge valve is located under the intake manifold, disconnect the wiring connector and unclip the valve from the retaining bracket.

Exhaust emission control

8 The performance of the catalytic converter can only be checked by measuring the exhaust gases, using a good quality, carefully calibrated exhaust gas analyser.

9 If the CO level at the tailpipe is too high, the vehicle should be taken to a Citroën dealer or specialist so that the complete fuel injection and ignition systems, including the oxygen sensor, can be thoroughly checked using the special diagnostic equipment. Once these have been checked and are known to be free from faults, the fault must be in the catalytic converter, which must be renewed as described in Chapter 4A, Section 15.

Catalytic converter renewal

10 Refer to Chapter 4A, Section 15 for the removal and refitting procedure.

Oxygen sensor renewal

Note: *The oxygen sensor is delicate and will not work if it is dropped or knocked, if its power supply is disrupted, or if any cleaning materials are used on it.*

11 Trace the wiring back from the oxygen sensor(s), which are located before and after the catalytic converters **(see illustrations)**. Disconnect both wiring connectors and free the wiring from any relevant retaining clips or ties.

12 Unscrew the sensor from the exhaust system front pipe/manifold and remove it, along with its sealing washer **(see illustration)**.

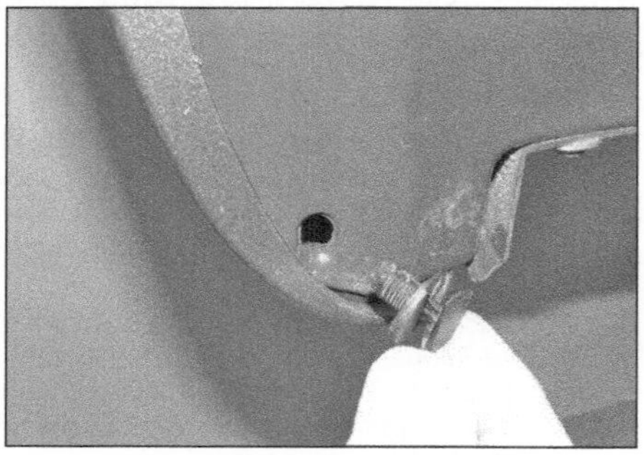

2.3 Release the plastic retaining clips

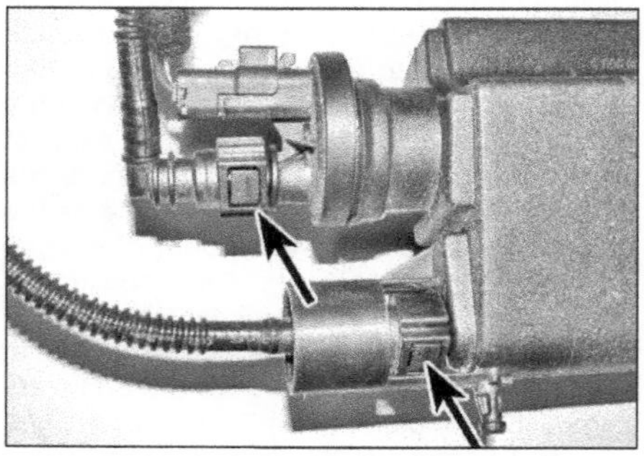

2.5 Depress the quick-release buttons, and disconnect the hoses (arrowed)

2.11a Oxygen (lambda) sensors – non-VTi petrol engines

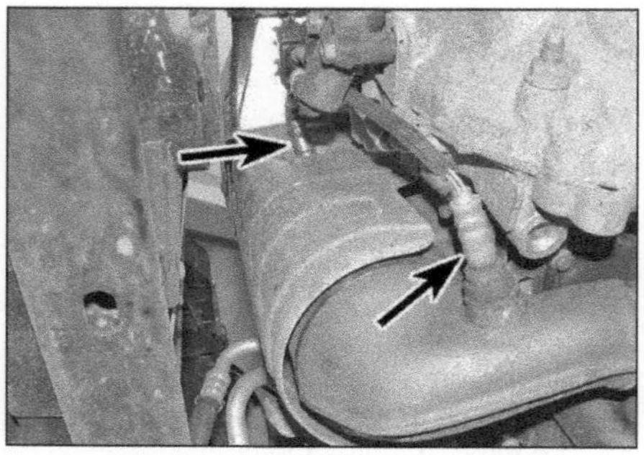

2.11b Oxygen (lambda) sensors – VTi petrol engines

2.12 Removing the upper sensor – VTi petrol engines

13 Refitting is a reverse of the removal procedure using a new sealing washer. Prior to installing the sensor apply a smear of high temperature grease to the sensor threads. Ensure that the sensor is securely tightened, and that the wiring is correctly routed and in no danger of contacting either the exhaust system or engine.

3 Emission control systems (diesel engines) - testing and component renewal

Crankcase emission control

1 The components of this system require no attention other than to check that the hose(s) are clear and undamaged at regular intervals.

Exhaust emission control

2 The performance of the catalytic converter can be checked only by measuring the exhaust gases, using a good quality, carefully calibrated exhaust gas analyser.

3 If the catalytic converter is thought to be faulty, before assuming the catalytic converter is faulty, it is worth checking the problem is not due to a faulty injector. Refer to your Citroën dealer for further information.

Catalytic converter renewal

4 Refer to Chapter 4B, Section 18.

Exhaust gas recirculation system

5 Testing of the system should ideally be entrusted to a Citroën dealer since a vacuum pump and vacuum gauge are required.

EGR valve renewal

6 Disconnect the battery, (refer to precautions in Chapter 5A, Section 1).

7 To make access easier, remove the windscreen wiper arms, and then unclip the plastic scuttle panel from below the windscreen. Pull up the ends of the panel to release it from the windscreen clips. Release the plastic expanding rivets from along the front edge of the scuttle panel. Undo the two screws securing the brake/clutch master cylinder upper reservoir and move it to one side. Release the sound insulation trim from the scuttle crossmember, undo the bolt on the left-hand side of the crossmember, then release the retaining clips at the right-hand side of the crossmember to remove it from the engine compartment – refer to Chapter 11, Section 22.

8 The EGR valve is located at the rear of the cylinder head, bolted to the left-hand end of the heat exchanger. On 1.6 litre models, the EGR valve can be removed separately from the heat exchanger. On 2.0 litre models, the EGR valve and heat exchanger have to be removed as one complete unit.

1.6 litre engine

9 Remove the air cleaner housing and air ducting, as described in Chapter 4B, Section 4, and then remove the heat shield from over the EGR valve.

10 Slacken and remove the securing clamp from between the heat exchanger and EGR valve **(see illustration)**. It may be necessary to undo the heat exchanger mounting bracket nuts and move it to one side.

11 Disconnect the wiring connector from the top of the EGR valve.

12 There are two bolts securing the EGR valve, undo the bolts and remove the valve **(see illustration)**. Discard the metal gasket from the valve, and the O-ring seal from the pipe – new ones must be fitted.

13 Refitting is a reversal of removal.

2.0 litre engine

14 Remove the plastic engine cover by lifting it up at the front of the engine, and then pull it to the front of the vehicle to release it from the rear mountings **(see illustration)**.

15 Release the retaining clips and remove the breather pipe from across the rear of the cylinder head cover **(see illustration)**.

16 Drain the cooling system as described in Chapter 1B, Section 20, and then disconnect the coolant hoses from the EGR heat exchanger at the rear of the cylinder head **(see illustrations)**

17 Working down the right-hand rear of the engine, disconnect the wiring connectors and unbolt the mounting bracket from the rear of

3.10 EGR heat exchanger-to-valve clamp (arrowed)

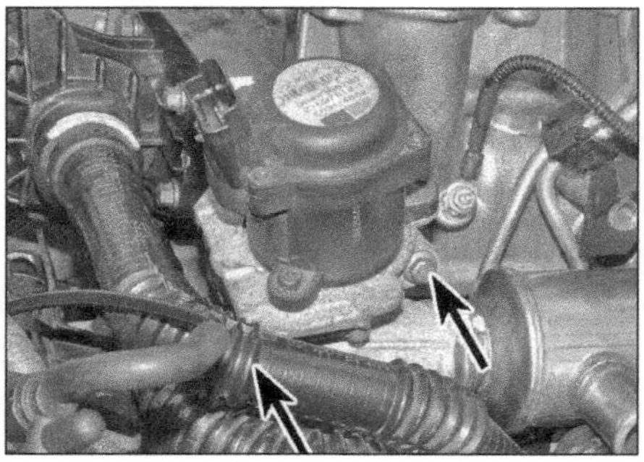

3.12 EGR valve mounting bolts (arrowed – one hidden)

3.14 Unclip the upper engine trim cover – 2.0 litre diesel engines

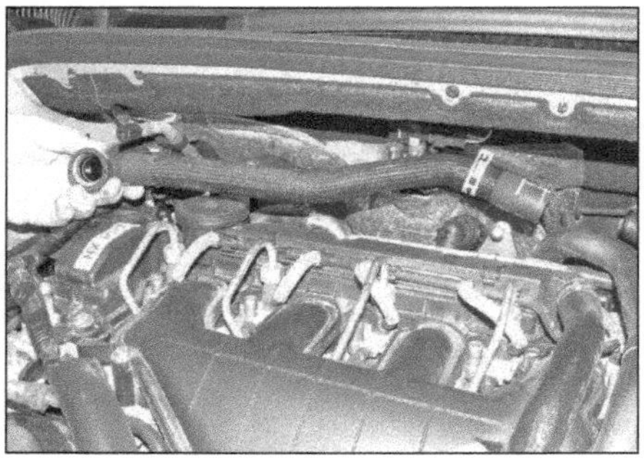

3.15 Remove the breather hose

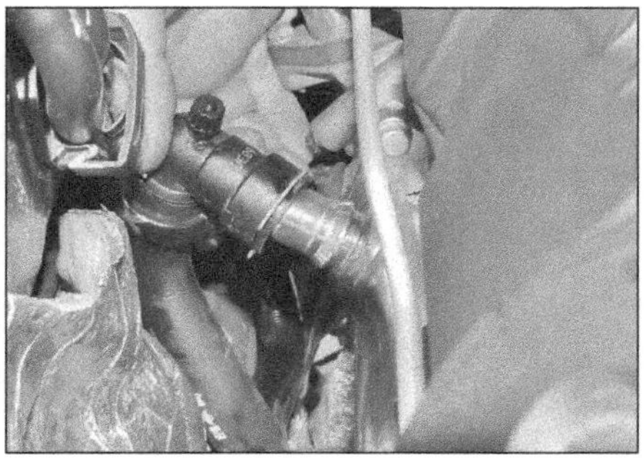

3.16a Release the retaining clip and remove the hose

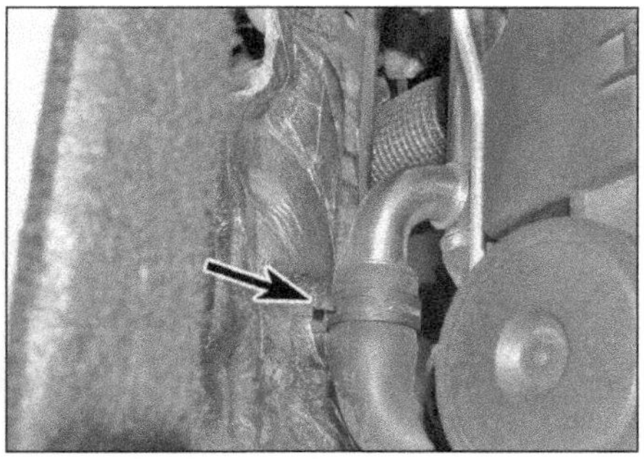

3.16b Release the hose clamp (arrowed)

3.17a Disconnect the wiring connector ...

3.17b ... and undo the bracket securing bolts

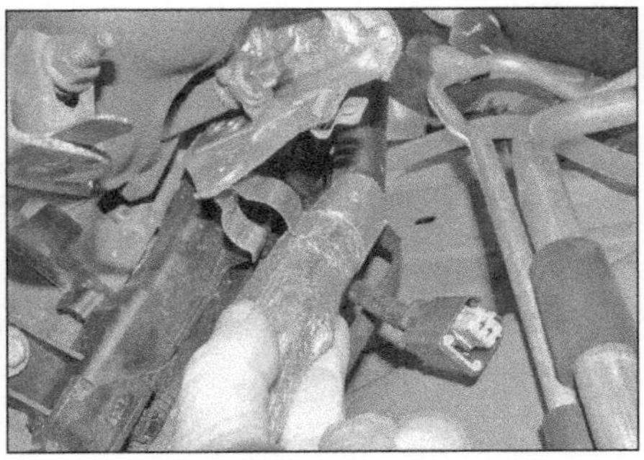

3.18a Unclip the hose from the heat shield ...

the cylinder head **(see illustrations)**. Move the mounting bracket and valve to one side.

18 Unclip the coolant hose from the retaining clip on the side of the heat shield, and then undo the retaining nut and remove the heat shield from above the manifold **(see illustrations)**.

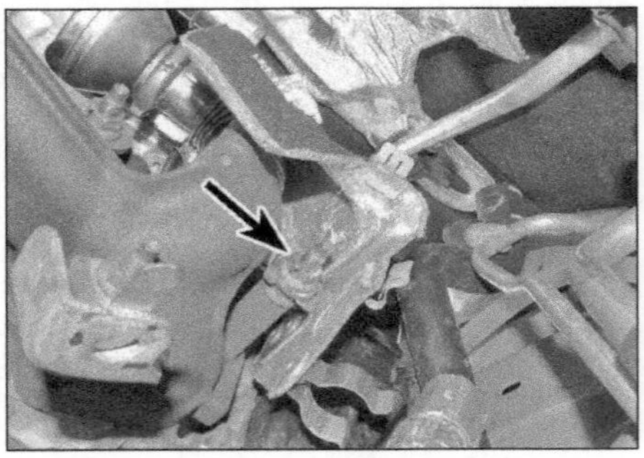

3.18b ... and undo the securing nut (arrowed)

19 Undo the retaining bolts and then release the heat exchanger pipe collar, and remove the elbow from the right-hand rear of the exhaust manifold **(see illustration)**.

3.19 Remove the cooler pipe elbow

20 Disconnect the wiring connector from the top of the EGR valve (and vacuum pipe where fitted) **(see illustration)**.

21 Undo the retaining bolts and release the EGR pipe from the top of the valve housing **(see illustration)**.

22 Undo the retaining nut from the heat exchanger lower mounting bracket **(see illustration)**.

23 Undo the retaining bolt from the EGR valve housing lower mounting bracket **(see illustration)**.

24 Undo the two retaining bolts from the top of the EGR valve housing and then lift out the EGR valve complete with heat exchanger from the rear of the engine **(see illustrations)**.

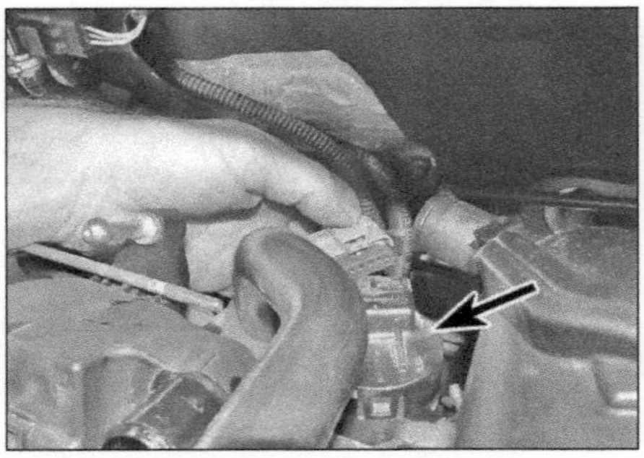

3.20 Disconnect the wiring connector from the EGR valve (arrowed)

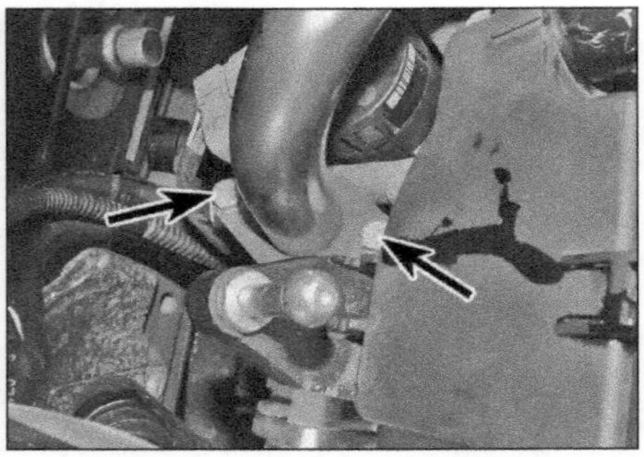

3.21 Undo the EGR pipe retaining bolts (arrowed)

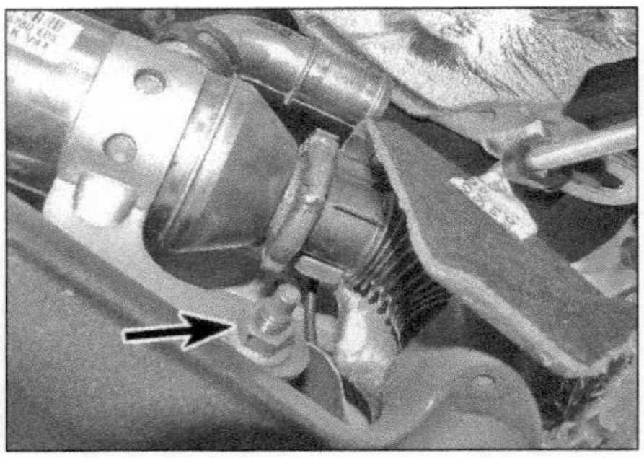

3.22 Undo the EGR cooler lower mounting bracket nut (arrowed)

3.23 EGR valve housing lower mounting bolt (arrowed)

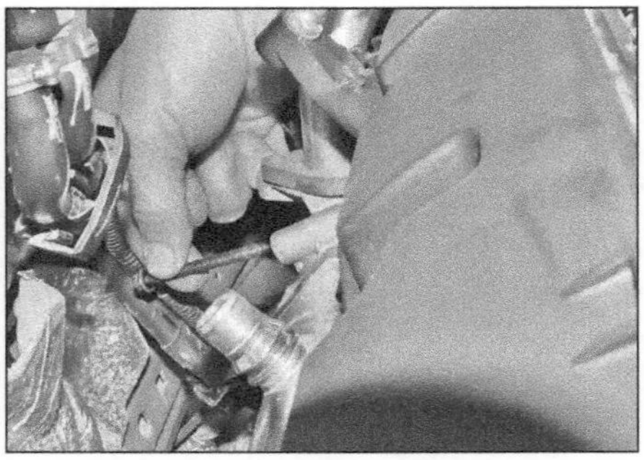

3.24a Remove the EGR valve housing mounting bolts ...

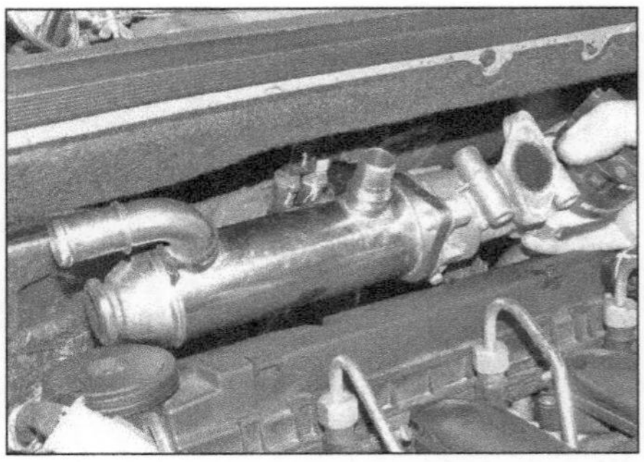

3.24b ... and remove the EGR cooler

3.25 Cooler-to-EGR valve housing securing bolts (arrowed)

3.31 EGR cooler-to-pipe clamp (arrowed)

25 To remove the EGR solenoid valve and housing from the heat exchanger, undo the two retaining bolts **(see illustration)**.

26 Refitting is a reversal of removal.

EGR heat exchanger renewal

Note: *The following procedure is for 1.6 litre diesel engines, for 2.0 litre diesel models, see EGR valve renewal, paragraphs 14 to 26.*

27 Disconnect the battery, (refer to precautions in Chapter 5A, Section 1).

28 Drain the cooling system (see Chapter 1B, Section 20). Alternatively, fit hose clamps to the hoses connected to the EGR heat exchanger.

29 Remove the air cleaner housing and air ducting, as described in Chapter 4B, Section 4, and then remove the heat shield from over the EGR valve.

30 Slacken and remove the securing clamp from between the heat exchanger and EGR valve **(see illustration 3.10)**. It may be necessary to undo the heat exchanger mounting bracket nuts and move it to one side.

31 Slacken and remove the securing clamp from between the heat exchanger and EGR pipe **(see illustration)**.

32 Loosen the clips and disconnect the coolant hoses from the EGR heat exchanger **(see illustration)**.

33 If not already done, undo the heat exchanger mounting bracket nuts and remove the heat exchanger from the rear of the engine.

34 Refitting is a reversal of removal.

Particulate filter

Fuel additive system

35 It is possible to check the fuel additive pump delivery pressure, but this should be made by a Citroën dealer or specialist.

Fuel additive reservoir renewal

Note: *Ideally, the additive reservoir should be empty before removing it, otherwise take precautions against spillage.*

⚠ ***Warning: Wear protective gloves and eye protection when handling the reservoir.***

36 To remove the fuel additive reservoir, chock the front wheels then jack up the rear of the vehicle and support on axle stands (see *Jacking and vehicle support*). The reservoir is attached to the left-hand side of the fuel tank.

37 Remove the undershields from beneath the fuel tank/additive reservoir **(see illustration)**.

38 Disconnect the wiring from the level sensor on the reservoir **(see illustration)**.

39 Note the location of the additive pipes on the reservoir, then depress the release buttons and disconnect them. Tape over or plug the openings to prevent dirt ingress.

40 Release the fasteners for the reservoir and carefully remove it from under the vehicle.

41 Have a suitable container available to catch spilled additive, undo the two retaining screws and detach the reservoir.

42 Refitting is a reversal of removal.

43 Have the reservoir refilled by a Citroën dealer or specialist.

Particulate filter

44 Renewal of the particulate filter is described in Chapter 4B, Section 18.

Pressure differential sensor

45 This sensor measures the pressure at the entrance and exit of the particulate filter, and is located in the engine compartment **(see illustration)**. It is fitted to the left-hand rear of the engine compartment on a mounting bracket below the brake master cylinder.

3.32 Release the coolant hose retaining clamps (arrowed)

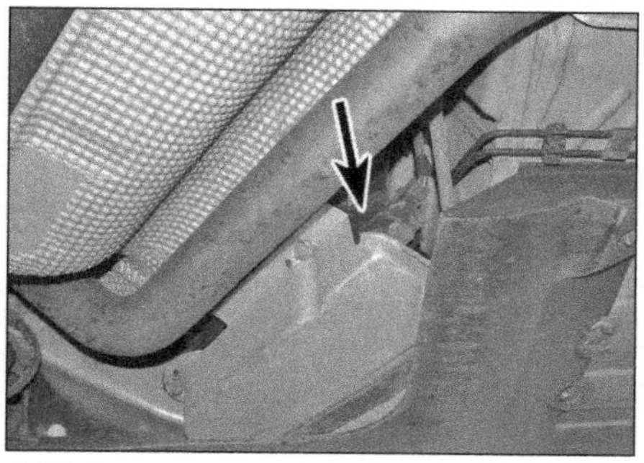

3.37 Fuel additive tank reservoir (arrowed)

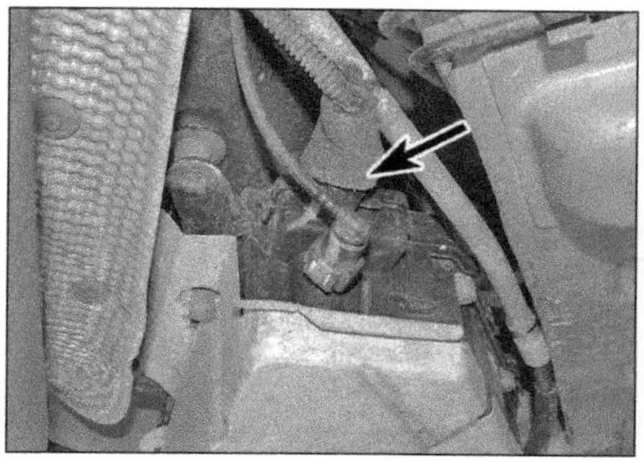

3.38 Disconnect the wiring connector (arrowed)

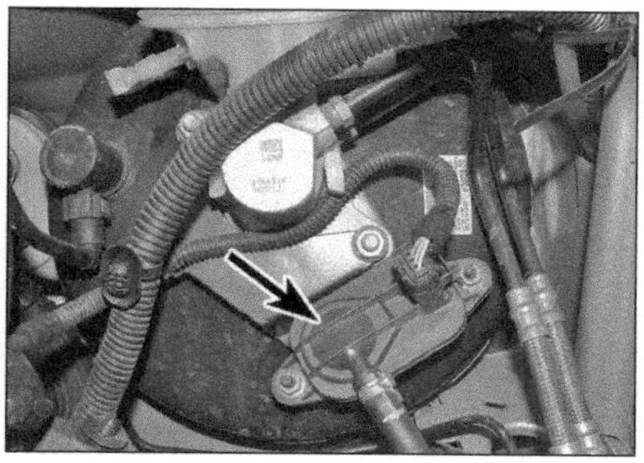

3.45 The pressure differential sensor (arrowed) is located on a bracket below the brake master cylinder

46 Remove the battery and battery tray as described in Chapter 5A, Section 4.

47 Note the fitted position of the hoses, and then disconnect the hoses and wiring connectors from the pressure sensor.

48 Undo the mounting nuts and remove the sensor from the mounting bracket.

4 Catalytic converter – general information and precautions

1 The catalytic converter is a reliable and simple device which needs no maintenance in itself, but there are some facts of which an owner should be aware if the converter is to function properly for its full service life.

Petrol models

a) DO NOT use leaded petrol or LRP – the lead will coat the precious metals, and will eventually destroy the converter.

b) Always keep the ignition and fuel systems well maintained to the service schedule.

c) If the engine develops a misfire, do not drive the car at all (or at least as little as possible) until the fault is cured.

d) DO NOT push- or tow-start the car – this will soak the catalytic converter in unburned fuel, causing it to overheat when the engine does start.

e) DO NOT switch off the ignition at high engine speeds.

f) DO NOT use fuel or engine oil additives – these may contain substances harmful to the catalytic converter.

g) DO NOT continue to use the car if the engine burns oil to the extent of leaving a visible trail of blue smoke.

h) Remember that the catalytic converter operates at very high temperatures. DO NOT, therefore, park the car in dry undergrowth, over long grass or piles of dead leaves after a long run.

i) Remember that the catalytic converter is FRAGILE – do not strike it with tools.

j) In some cases a sulphurous smell (like that of rotten eggs) may be noticed from the exhaust. This is common to many catalytic converter-equipped cars and once the car has covered a few thousand miles the problem should disappear.

k) If the converter is no longer effective it must be renewed.

Diesel models

2 Refer to parts f, g, h and i of the petrol models information given above.

Chapter 5 Part A:
Starting and charging systems

Contents

Degrees of difficulty

Easy, suitable for novice with little experience	**Fairly easy,** suitable for beginner with some experience	**Fairly difficult,** suitable for competent DIY mechanic	**Difficult,** suitable for experienced DIY mechanic	**Very difficult,** suitable for expert DIY or professional

Specifications

System type	12 volt, negative earth
Battery	
Type	Low maintenance or 'maintenance-free' sealed for life
Charge condition:	
Poor	12.5 volts
Normal	12.6 volts
Good	12.7 volts
Alternator	
Type	Valeo, Denso, Bosch, Magneti Marelli or Mitsubishi (depending on model)
Rating:	
Petrol models	70, 80, 90 or 120 amp
Diesel models	150 amp
Starter motor	
Type	Valeo, Bosch, Ducellier, Mitsubishi or Iskra (depending on model)

Torque wrench settings

	Nm	lbf ft
Alternator mounting bolts:		
Petrol engines	40	30
Diesel engines:		
1.6 litre:		
Front upper bolt	40	30
Rear bolts	49	36
2.0 litre:		
Front bolts	40	30
Rear upper bolt	49	36
Rear lower bolt	40	30
Auxiliary belt idler roller-to-mounting bracket (1.6 litre diesel)	45	33
Auxiliary belt tensioner-to-cylinder block bolt (diesel engines):		
1.6 litre	20	15
2.0 litre	43	32
Oil level sensor	27	20
Oil pressure switch:		
All petrol engines	30	22
Diesel engines:		
1.6 litre	20	15
2.0 litre	32	24
Starter motor:		
Petrol engines	35	26
Diesel engines:		
1.6 litre	20	15
2.0 litre	35	26

1 General information and precautions

General information

The engine electrical system consists mainly of the charging and starting systems. Because of their engine-related functions, these components are covered separately from the body electrical devices such as the lights, instruments, etc (which are covered in Chapter 12). On petrol engine models refer to Chapter 5B, Section 1 for information on the ignition system, and on diesel models refer to Chapter 5C, Section 1 for information on the preheating system.

The electrical system is of the 12 volt negative earth type.

The battery is of the low maintenance or 'maintenance-free' (sealed for life) type and is charged by the alternator, which is belt-driven from the crankshaft pulley.

The starter motor is of the pre-engaged type incorporating an integral solenoid. On starting, the solenoid moves the drive pinion into engagement with the flywheel ring gear before the starter motor is energised. Once the engine has started, a one-way clutch prevents the motor armature being driven by the engine until the pinion disengages from the flywheel.

Precautions

Further details of the various systems are given in the relevant Sections of this Chapter. While some repair procedures are given, the usual course of action is to renew the component concerned.

It is necessary to take extra care when working on the electrical system to avoid damage to semi-conductor devices (diodes and transistors), and to avoid the risk of personal injury. In addition to the precautions given in *Safety first!* at the beginning of this manual, observe the following when working on the system:

- Always remove rings, watches, etc, before working on the electrical system. Even with the battery disconnected, capacitive discharge could occur if a component's live terminal is earthed through a metal object. This could cause a shock or nasty burn.
- Do not reverse the battery connections. Components such as the alternator, electronic control units, or any other components having semi-conductor circuitry could be irreparably damaged.
- If the engine is being started using jump leads and a slave battery, connect the batteries positive-to-positive and negative-to-negative (see *Jump starting*). This also applies when connecting a battery charger.
- Never disconnect the battery terminals, the alternator, any electrical wiring or any test instruments when the engine is running.
- Do not allow the engine to turn the alternator when the alternator is not connected.
- Never 'test' for alternator output by 'flashing' the output lead to earth.
- Never use an ohmmeter of the type incorporating a hand-cranked generator for circuit or continuity testing.
- Always ensure that the battery negative lead is disconnected when working on the electrical system.
- Before using electric-arc welding equipment on the car, disconnect the battery, alternator and components such as the fuel injection/ignition electronic control unit to protect them from the risk of damage.

2 Electrical fault finding – general information

Refer to Chapter 12, Section 2.

3 Battery – testing and charging

Testing

Standard and low maintenance battery

1 If the vehicle covers a small annual mileage, it is worthwhile checking the specific gravity of the electrolyte every three months to determine the state of charge of the battery. Use a hydrometer to make the check and compare the results with the following table. Note that the specific gravity readings assume an electrolyte temperature of 15°C; for every 10°C below 15°C subtract 0.007. For every 10°C above 15°C add 0.007.

	Above 25°C	Below 25°C
Fully-charged	1.210 to 1.230	1.270 to 1.290
70% charged	1.170 to 1.190	1.230 to 1.250
Discharged	1.050 to 1.070	1.110 to 1.130

2 If the battery condition is suspect, first check the specific gravity of electrolyte in each cell. A variation of 0.040 or more between any cells indicates loss of electrolyte or deterioration of the internal plates.

3 If the specific gravity variation is 0.040 or more, the battery should be renewed. If the cell variation is satisfactory but the battery is discharged, it should be charged as described later in this Section.

Maintenance-free battery

4 In cases where a 'sealed for life' maintenance-free battery is fitted, topping-up and testing of the electrolyte in each cell is not possible. The condition of the battery can therefore only be tested using a battery condition indicator or a voltmeter.

5 Certain models may be fitted with a 'Delco' type maintenance-free battery, with a built-in charge condition indicator. The indicator is located in the top of the battery casing, and indicates the condition of the battery from its colour **(see illustration)**. If the indicator shows green, then the battery is in a good state of charge. If the indicator shows black, then the battery requires charging, as described later in this Section. If the indicator shows blue, then the electrolyte level in the battery is too low to allow further use, and the battery should be renewed.

Caution: Do not attempt to charge, load or jump start a battery when the indicator shows clear/yellow.

All battery types

6 If testing the battery using a voltmeter, connect the voltmeter across the battery and compare the result with those given in the Specifications under 'charge condition'. The test is only accurate if the battery has not been subjected to any kind of charge for the previous six hours. If this is not the case, switch on the headlights for 30 seconds, then wait four to five minutes before testing the battery after switching off the headlights. All other electrical circuits must be switched off, so check that the doors and tailgate are fully shut when making the test.

7 If the voltage reading is less than 12.2 volts, then the battery is discharged, whilst a reading of 12.2 to 12.4 volts indicates a partially discharged condition.

8 If the battery is to be charged, remove it from the vehicle (Section 4) and charge it as described later in this Section.

Charging

Note: *The following is intended as a guide only. Always refer to the manufacturer's recommendations (often printed on a label attached to the battery) before charging a battery.*

Standard and low maintenance battery

9 Charge the battery at a rate of 3.5 to 4 amps and continue to charge the battery at this rate until no further rise in specific gravity is noted over a four hour period.

10 Alternatively, a trickle charger charging at the rate of 1.5 amps can safely be used overnight.

11 Specially rapid 'boost' charges which are claimed to restore the power of the battery in 1 to 2 hours are not recommended, as they can cause serious damage to the battery plates through overheating.

12 While charging the battery, note that the temperature of the electrolyte should never exceed 38°C.

Maintenance-free battery

13 This battery type takes considerably longer to fully recharge than the standard type, the time taken being dependent on the extent of discharge, but it can take anything up to three days.

14 A constant voltage type charger is required to be set, when connected, to 13.9 to 14.9 volts with a charger current below 25 amps. Using this method, the battery should be usable within three hours, giving a voltage reading of 12.5 volts, but this is for a partially discharged battery and, as mentioned, full charging can take considerably longer.

15 If the battery is to be charged from a fully discharged state (condition reading less than 12.2 volts), have it recharged by your Citroën dealer or local automotive electrician, as the charge rate is higher and constant supervision during charging is necessary.

4 Battery and tray – removal and refitting

Note: *The audio unit fitted as standard equipment by Citroën is equipped with an anti-theft system, to deter thieves. If the power source is disconnected, the unit will automatically recode itself as long as it is still fitted to the correct vehicle. If the unit is removed it will not operate in another vehicle.*

Note: *Prior to disconnecting the battery, wait 15 minutes after switching off the ignition to allow the vehicle's ECUs to store all learned values in their memories.*

Removal

Battery

1 Prior to disconnecting the battery, close all windows and the sunroof (where fitted), and ensure that the vehicle alarm system is deactivated (see Owner's Handbook or Chapter 12, Section 20).

2 The battery is located on the left-hand side rear of the engine compartment.

3 To make access easier and depending on model, release the fasteners and remove the air intake ducting from the front left-hand side of the engine compartment, with reference to Chapter 4A, Section 2 or Chapter 4B, Section 4.

4 Unclip the battery positive terminal cover, then lift up the red quick-release lever and disconnect the positive lead from the battery **(see illustration)**.

5 On VTi petrol engines, unclip the red plastic cover from the additional fuses on top of the battery cover. Release the securing clips and slide the additional fuse link assembly

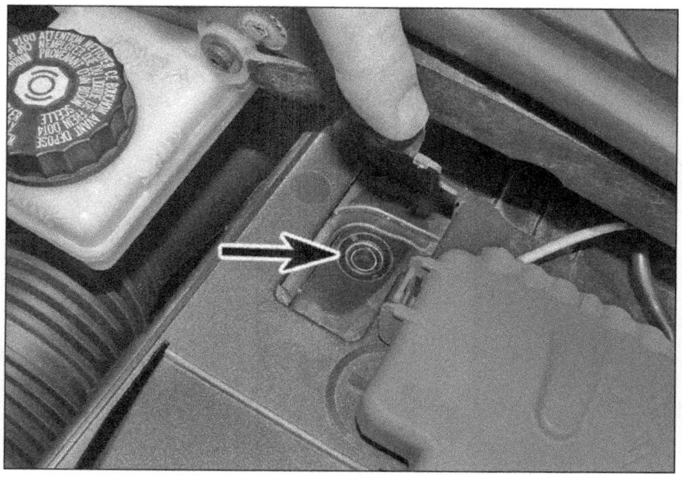

3.5 Battery charge condition indicator (arrowed)

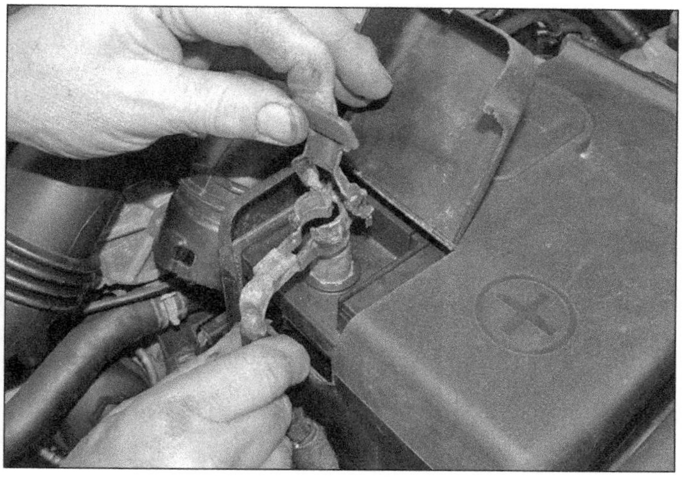

4.4 Lift up the quick-release lever and disconnect the positive lead

4.5a Unclip the red cover from the top of the battery ...

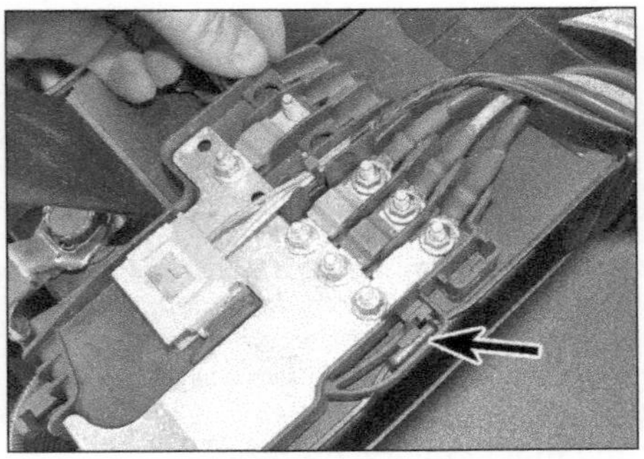

4.5b ... release the securing clip (arrowed) ...

4.5c ... and the lower securing clip ...

4.5d ... then slide the fused link assembly upwards

4.6a Remove the cover from the battery ...

upwards and away from the battery cover **(see illustrations)**.

6 Withdraw the battery cover upwards, releasing it from the lower plastic inner tray and remove it from the battery **(see illustrations)**.

7 Lift up the green quick-release lever and disconnect the negative terminal connector from the rear of the battery **(see illustration).**

8 On diesel models, lift out the corrugated insulator from around the battery **(see illustration)**

9 Unscrew the securing bolt and remove the battery retaining clamp **(see illustration)**.

10 The battery can now be lifted out of the engine compartment **(see illustration)**.

11 If required, on diesel models, lift out the corrugated insulator from the base of the battery tray **(see illustration)**

4.6b ... releasing it from the locating peg (arrowed)

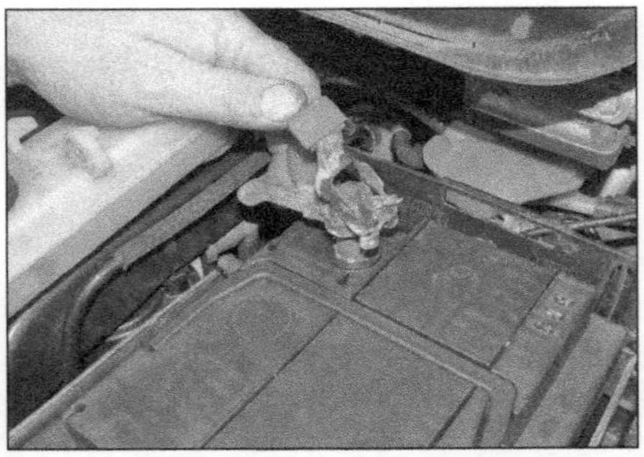

4.7 Lift up the green quick-release lever and disconnect the negative lead

4.8 On diesel models remove the corrugated insulator

4.9 Release the securing clamp bolt (arrowed) ...

4.10 ... and then lift out the battery

4.11 If required, remove the corrugated insulator from the tray – diesel engines

4.12 Remove the ECU from the rear of the battery tray – AL4 automatic transmission

4.13a Undo the two retaining nuts (arrowed) ...

4.13b ... and lift out the battery plastic inner tray

Battery tray

12 On models with AL4 automatic transmission fitted, undo the two retaining nuts and remove the transmission ECU from the rear of the battery tray **(see illustration)**. Alternatively, slide out the securing clip and disconnect the wiring connector, leaving the ECU attached to the battery tray.

13 Undo the two securing nuts and withdraw the plastic battery inner tray from the engine compartment **(see illustrations)**. Where applicable, note the fitted position of any wiring loom securing clips, and disconnect them from the plastic battery tray as it is removed.

14 Slacken the left-hand front roadwheel bolts, then jack up the front of the vehicle and support it securely on axle stands (see *Jacking and vehicle support*). Remove the left-hand front road wheel.

15 Release the various fasteners and remove the wheel arch liner from under the front wing **(see illustration)**.

16 Working inside the engine compartment, undo the fasteners securing the metal battery tray to the inner wing panel, including the one on the outside from under the wheel arch **(see illustrations)**.

17 Note the fitted position of the wiring loom securing clips, and disconnect them from the metal battery tray **(see illustrations).**

18 Carefully move aside all cables and hoses, and then lift the metal battery tray out of the engine compartment **(see illustration).**

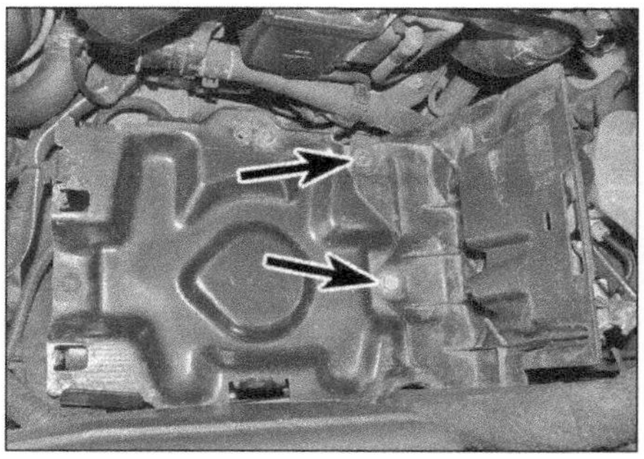

4.13c Undo the securing screw and bolt (arrowed) to remove the rear plastic shield

4.15 Remove the inner wheel arch liner

4.16a Undo the battery tray fasteners (arrowed) ...

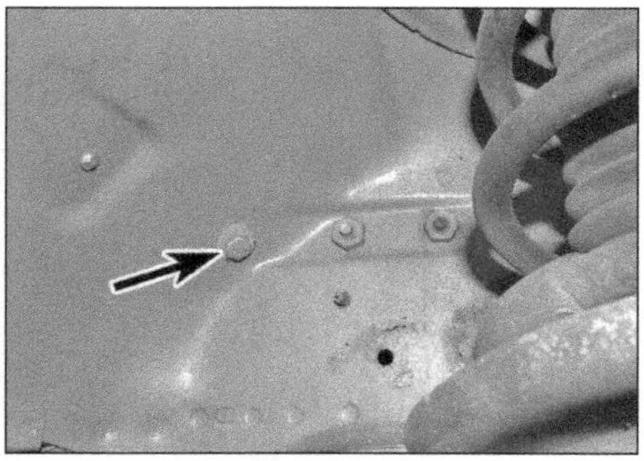

4.16b ... including the bolt (arrowed) inside the inner wing

4.17a Release the wiring clips at the rear ...

4.17b ... and at the front of the battery tray ...

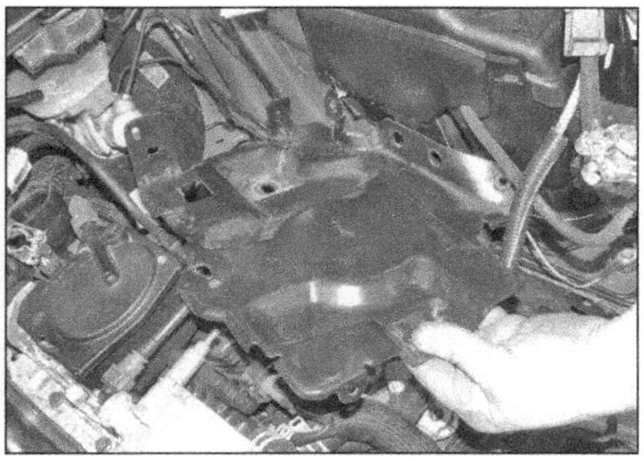

4.18 ... and then lift the battery tray out from the engine compartment

Refitting

19 Refitting is a reversal of removal, but smear petroleum jelly on the terminals after reconnecting the leads, and reconnect the negative lead first, and positive the lead last.

20 With the battery reconnected, switch on the ignition and wait at least 1 minute before starting the engine. This will allow the vehicle electronic systems and control units to stabilise. Also refer to Chapter 12, Section 20 on models with the anti-theft alarm system.

21 On models with a sunroof, after reconnecting the battery, re-initialise the sunroof mechanism as follows:

a) Turn the switch to the maximum partial-opening position (3rd position to the right).
b) Keep the control switch pressed in. The sunroof will reach the maximum partially-open position, then close slightly.
c) Release the switch within 6 seconds.
d) Press the switch within 6 seconds. The sunroof starts to close after 4 seconds from the switch being pressed, then opens completely, then closes completely.

5 Charging system – testing

Note: *Refer to the warnings given in 'Safety first!' and in Section 1 of this Chapter before starting work.*

1 If the ignition warning light fails to illuminate when the ignition is switched on, first check the alternator wiring connections for security. If satisfactory, check that the warning light bulb has not blown, and that the bulbholder is secure in its location in the instrument panel. If the light still fails to illuminate, check the continuity of the warning light feed wire from the alternator to the bulbholder. If all is satisfactory, the alternator is at fault and should be renewed or taken to an auto-electrician for testing and repair.

2 If the ignition warning light illuminates when the engine is running, stop the engine and check that the drivebelt is correctly fitted and tensioned (see Chapter 1A, Section 10 or Chapter 1B, Section 17) and that the alternator connections are secure. If all is so far satisfactory, have the alternator checked by an auto-electrician for testing and repair.

3 If the alternator output is suspect even though the warning light functions correctly, the regulated voltage may be checked as follows.

4 Connect a voltmeter across the battery terminals and start the engine.

5 Increase the engine speed until the voltmeter reading remains steady; the reading should be approximately 12 to 13 volts, and no more than 14 volts.

6 Switch on as many electrical accessories as possible (eg, the headlights, heated rear window and heater blower), and check that the alternator maintains the regulated voltage of around 13 to 14 volts.

7 If the regulated voltage is not as stated, the fault may be due to worn brushes, weak brush springs, a faulty voltage regulator, a faulty diode, a severed phase winding or worn or damaged slip-rings. The alternator should be renewed or taken to an auto-electrician for testing and repair.

6 Alternator drivebelt – removal, refitting and tensioning

Refer to the procedure given for the auxiliary drivebelt in Chapter 1A, Section 10 or Chapter 1B, Section 17.

7 Alternator – removal and refitting

Removal

1 Disconnect the battery (see Section 4).

2 Remove the auxiliary drivebelt as described in Chapter 1A, Section 10 or Chapter 1B, Section 17. On some models, it may be necessary to undo the bolts and remove the auxiliary drivebelt idler pulley bracket bolts, which obscures the lower alternator mounting bolt.

Diesel models

3 On 1.6 litre engines, slacken the retaining clips and remove the intercooler air intake hoses, to gain better access to the alternator **(see illustration)**.

4 On 2.0 litre engines, undo the three retaining screws, unclip the filter drain tube and remove the plastic fuel spillage shield from above the alternator **(see illustration)**.

5 Remove the rubber cover from the alternator terminal, then unscrew the retaining nut and disconnect the wiring from the rear of the alternator **(see illustrations)**. Prise out the retaining clip to release the wiring harness routed around the end of the alternator.

6 Where an auxiliary drivebelt tensioner is fitted, undo the three bolts and remove it

7.3 Remove the air intake hoses from the intercooler – 1.6 litre diesel engines

7.4 Remove the plastic shield from above the alternator

7.5a Remove the rubber cover and undo the securing nut (arrowed) ...

7.5b ... then disconnect the alternator wiring and plug ...

7.5c ... release the wiring loom (arrowed) from the rear of the alternator

7.6 Undo the auxiliary drivebelt tensioner bolts (arrowed)

7.7 Undo the auxiliary drivebelt pulley bolt (arrowed) – 1.6 litre diesel engines

7.8a Alternator right-hand mounting bolts (arrowed) ...

from the alternator mounting bracket **(see illustration)**.

7 Where an elasticated auxiliary drivebelt is fitted, undo the idler roller retaining bolt and remove it from the alternator mounting bracket **(see illustration)**. **Note:** *The idler roller retaining bolt is also the alternator lower bolt.*

8 Unscrew the alternator mounting bolts **(see illustrations)**. Manoeuvre the alternator away from its mounting brackets and out from the engine compartment.

Petrol models

9 Remove the rubber cover from the alternator terminal, then unscrew the retaining nut and disconnect the wiring from the rear of the alternator **(see illustrations)**. If required, prise out the retaining clip to release the wiring harness routed around the end of the alternator.

10 On VTi engines, undo the alternator upper two securing bolts and remove the auxiliary belt automatic tensioner **(see illustrations)**.

11 Unscrew the lower nut(s) and/or mounting bolt(s), or undo the nut securing the adjuster bolt bracket to the alternator (as applicable). Note that, where a long through-bolt is used to secure the alternator in position, the bolt does not need to be fully removed; the alternator can be disengaged from the bolt once it has been slackened sufficiently. On some models, it may be necessary to remove the drivebelt idler/tensioner pulley to gain access to the

7.8b ... and left-hand mounting bolts (arrowed)

7.9a Disconnect the wiring connector ...

7.9b ... prise out the rubber cover ...

7.9c ... and undo the retaining nut

7.9d Release the wiring securing clip (arrowed) – VTi petrol engines

7.10a Undo the upper two bolts (arrowed) ...

7.10b ... and remove the automatic tensioner

alternator mounting nuts and bolts (depending on specification).

12 Manoeuvre the alternator away from its mounting brackets and out from the engine compartment.

Refitting

13 Refitting is a reversal of removal, tensioning the auxiliary drivebelt as described in Chapter 1A, Section 10 or Chapter 1B, Section 17, and ensuring that the alternator mountings are securely tightened. Note that on diesel models, one of the bolts acts as a centraliser and should be tightened first **(see illustration)**.

8 Alternator brushes, regulator and drive pulley – inspection and renewal

Note: *If the alternator is thought to be suspect, check on the cost of repairs before proceeding, as it may prove more economical to obtain a new or exchange alternator. The alternator fitted may vary slightly, depending on model and age; the model shown in the following sequence is for a Valeo type alternator.*

Brushes and regulator

1 Remove the alternator as described in Section 7.

2 Unscrew the nuts/screws securing the cover to the rear of the alternator **(see illustration)**.

3 Using a screwdriver, lever off the cover, and remove it from the rear of the alternator.

7.13 On some models, the upper bolt acts as a centraliser

8.2 Undo the screw/nuts (arrowed) and remove the cover from the alternator

8.4 Undo the bolts (arrowed) and remove the regulator/brush pack

8.7 Check the condition of the slip-rings

4 Unscrew and remove the three retaining screws, and remove the regulator/brush holder from the rear of the alternator **(see illustration)**.

5 Check the brushes for excessive wear and damage. No specifications for brush length are given by Citroën. If the brushes are suspect, renew them along with the regulator as a complete assembly.

6 If the brushes are in good condition, clean them and check that they move freely in their holders.

7 Wipe clean the alternator slip-rings, and check them for signs of scoring or burning **(see illustration)**. It may be possible to have the slip-rings renovated by an electrical specialist.

8 Use a paper clip to restrain the brushes, then refit the regulator/brush holder assembly and securely tighten the retaining screws **(see illustration)**.

9 Refit the cover, then insert and tighten the retaining screws/nuts.

10 Refit the alternator with reference to Section 7.

8.8 Use a screwdriver to push back the brushes against the springs, then insert a thin rod (arrowed) to hold them in place

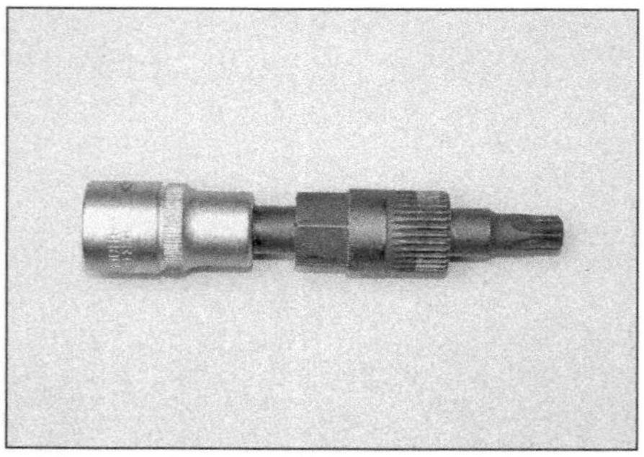

8.13a A special tool is required to remove the alternator pulley

8.13b Insert the central Torx bit into the end of the alternator shaft, unscrew the pulley ...

8.13c ... and remove the pulley from the shaft

Drive pulley

11 The alternator drive pulley is fitted with a one-way clutch to reduced wear and stress on the auxiliary drivebelt. In order to remove the pulley, a special tool will be required to hold the alternator shaft whilst unscrewing the pulley. This tool should be available from auto electrical specialists/automotive tool specialists.

12 Prise the plastic cap from the pulley.

13 Insert the special tool into the splines of the pulley, engaging the central Torx bit with the alternator shaft **(see illustrations)**. Unscrew the pulley anti-clockwise whilst holding the shaft with the Torx bit, and remove the pulley.

14 Fit the pulley to the alternator shaft, and tighten it securely using the special tool.

9 Starting system – testing

Note: *Refer to the precautions given in 'Safety first!' and in Section 1 of this Chapter before starting work.*

1 If the starter motor fails to operate when the ignition key is turned to the appropriate position, the following possible causes may be to blame.

a) The engine immobiliser is faulty.
b) The battery is faulty.
c) The electrical connections between the switch, solenoid, battery and starter motor are somewhere failing to pass the necessary current from the battery through the starter to earth.
d) The solenoid is faulty.
e) The starter motor is mechanically or electrically defective.

2 To check the battery, switch on the headlights. If they dim after a few seconds, this indicates that the battery is discharged – recharge (see Section 3) or renew the battery. If the headlights glow brightly, operate the ignition switch and observe the lights. If they dim, then this indicates that current is reaching the starter motor, therefore the fault must lie in the starter motor. If the lights continue to glow brightly (and no clicking sound can be heard from the starter motor solenoid), this indicates that there is a fault in the circuit or solenoid – see following paragraphs. If the starter motor turns slowly when operated, but the battery is in good condition, then this indicates that either the starter motor is faulty, or there is considerable resistance somewhere in the circuit.

3 If a fault in the circuit is suspected, disconnect the battery leads (including the earth connection to the body), the starter/solenoid wiring and the engine/transmission earth strap – located on the top of the transmission housing **(see illustration)**. Thoroughly clean the connections and reconnect the leads and wiring, then use a voltmeter or test lamp to check that full battery voltage is available at the battery positive lead connection to the solenoid, and that the earth is sound. Smear petroleum jelly around the battery terminals to prevent corrosion – corroded connections are amongst the most frequent causes of electrical system faults.

9.3 Engine/transmission earth strap connection (arrowed)

4 If the battery and all connections are in good condition, check the circuit by disconnecting the wire from the solenoid blade terminal. Connect a voltmeter or test lamp between the wire end and a good earth (such as the battery negative terminal), and check that the wire is live when the ignition switch is turned to the 'start' position. If it is, then the circuit is sound – if not the circuit wiring can be checked as described in Chapter 12, Section 2.

5 The solenoid contacts can be checked by connecting a voltmeter or test lamp between the battery positive feed connection on the starter side of the solenoid, and earth. When the ignition switch is turned to the 'start' position, there should be a reading or lighted bulb, as applicable. If there is no reading or lighted bulb, the solenoid is faulty and should be renewed.

6 If the circuit and solenoid are proved sound, the fault must lie in the starter motor. In this event, it may be possible to have the starter motor overhauled by a specialist, but check on the cost of spares before proceeding, as it may prove more economical to obtain a new or exchange motor.

10.5 Vacuum reservoir retaining bolt (arrowed)

10 Starter motor – removal and refitting

Removal

1 Disconnect the battery (see Section 4).

2 So that access to the motor can be gained both from above and below, apply the handbrake then jack up the front of the vehicle and support it on axle stands (see *Jacking and vehicle support*). Undo the retaining bolts/nuts and remove the engine undershield.

3 Remove the battery and the battery tray as described in Section 4.

4 Remove the air cleaner housing and air ducting as described in Chapter 4A, Section 2 or Chapter 4B, Section 4.

1.6 litre diesel engines

5 Undo the retaining bolt and remove the vacuum reservoir from below the starter motor, on the rear of the engine **(see illustration)**.

6 Disconnect the wiring connectors from the starter motor solenoid, and where fitted, recover the washers under the nuts **(see illustrations)**.

7 Release the wiring loom from the retaining clips, and then if required, undo the bolt securing the wiring loom support plate above the starter motor **(see illustration)**.

8 Undo the three mounting bolts (two at the rear of the motor, and one which comes through

10.6a Undo the two nuts (arrowed) and disconnect the starter motor wiring – early models

10.6b Undo the nut and wiring connector (arrowed) from the starter motor – later models

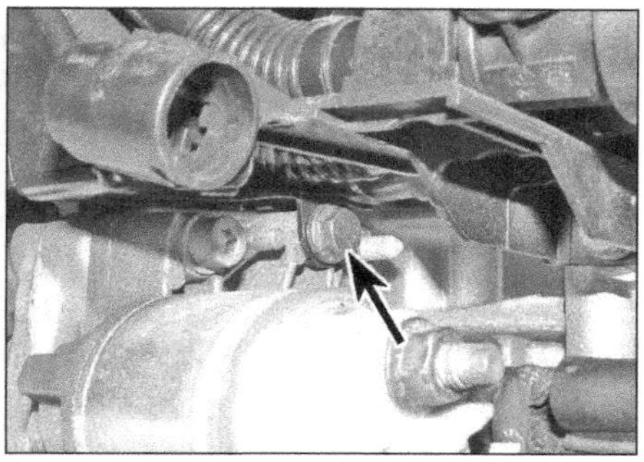

10.7 Undo the bolt (arrowed) securing the wiring loom support plate

10.8 Starter motor mounting bolts (arrowed) – 1.6 litre diesel engines

10.9 Remove the starter motor

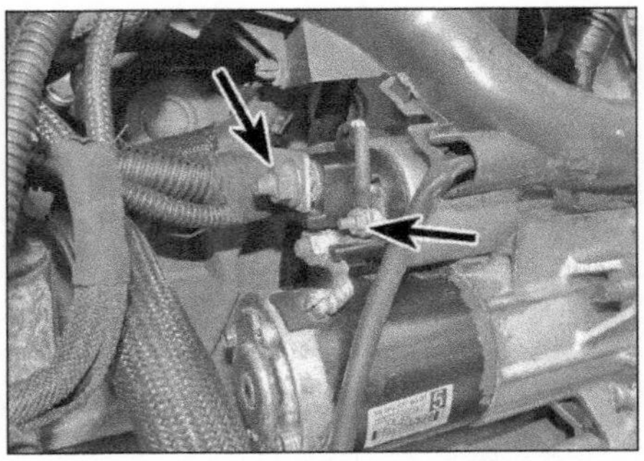

10.10 Disconnect the starter motor wiring (arrowed)

from the top of the transmission housing), supporting the starter motor as the bolts are withdrawn. Recover the washers from under the bolt heads and note the locations of any wiring or hose brackets secured by the bolts **(see illustration)**.

9 Manoeuvre the starter motor out from underneath the engine; recover the locating dowel(s) from the motor/transmission so that they do not get lost **(see illustration)**.

2.0 litre diesel engines

10 Disconnect the wiring connectors from the starter motor solenoid, and where fitted, recover the washers under the nuts **(see illustration)**.

11 Undo the three mounting bolts, supporting the starter motor as the bolts are withdrawn. Recover the washers from under the bolt heads and note the locations of any wiring or hose brackets secured by the bolts **(see illustration)**.

12 Manoeuvre the starter motor out from the front of the engine; recover the locating dowel(s) from the motor/transmission so that they do not get lost **(see illustration)**.

All petrol engines

13 On non-VTi engines, remove the intake manifold as described in Chapter 4A, Section 13.

14 Slacken and remove the retaining nut(s) and disconnect the wiring from the starter motor solenoid. Recover the washers under the nuts **(see illustrations 10.6a and 10.6b)**.

15 Where applicable, release the wiring loom from the retaining clips, then undo the bolt securing the wiring loom support plate above the starter motor **(see illustrations 10.7)**.

16 Undo the three mounting bolts (two at the rear of the motor, and one which comes through from the top of the transmission housing), supporting the motor as the bolts are withdrawn. Recover the washers from under the bolt heads and note the locations of any wiring or hose brackets secured by the bolts **(see illustration 10.8)**.

17 Manoeuvre the starter motor out from underneath the engine and recover the locating dowel(s) from the motor/transmission (as applicable) **(see illustration 10.9)**.

Refitting

18 Refitting is a reversal of removal, ensuring that the locating dowel(s) are correctly positioned. Also make sure that any wiring or hose brackets are in place under the bolt heads as noted prior to removal.

11 Starter motor – testing and overhaul

If the starter motor is thought to be suspect, it should be removed from the vehicle and taken to an auto-electrician for testing. Most auto-electricians will be able to supply and fit brushes at a reasonable cost. However, check on the cost of repairs before proceeding, as it may prove more economical to obtain a new or exchange motor.

12 Ignition switch – removal and refitting

The ignition switch is integral with the steering column lock, and can be removed as described in Chapter 10, Section 18.

13 Oil pressure warning light switch – removal and refitting

Removal

1 The switch is fitted at the front of the cylinder block, in the following locations:

- *Petrol engines: Screwed into the left-hand end of the cylinder head.*
- *1.6 litre diesel engines: Adjacent to the oil dipstick guide tube on the front of the cylinder block*
- *2.0 litre diesel engines: Screwed into the base of the oil filter housing at the front of the engine*

Note that on some models access to the switch may be improved if the vehicle is jacked up and supported on axle stands, and the engine undershield removed (where fitted), so that the switch can be reached from underneath (see *Jacking and vehicle support*).

2 Remove the protective sleeve from the wiring plug (where applicable), and then disconnect the wiring from the switch **(see illustration)**.

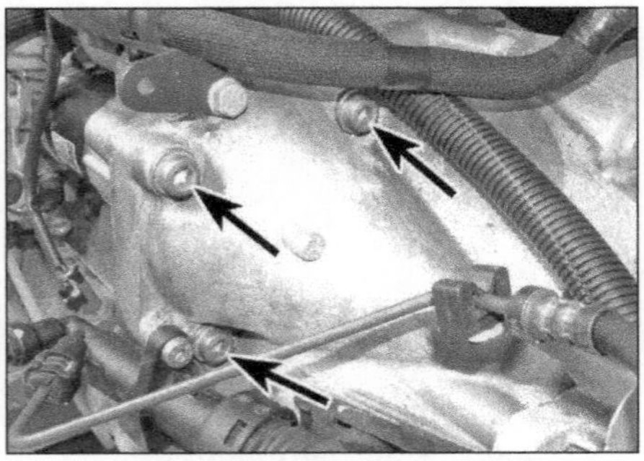

10.11 Starter motor mounting bolts (arrowed) – 2.0 litre diesel engines

10.12 Remove the starter motor

13.2 Disconnect the wiring connector from the oil pressure switch

13.3a Unscrew the switch (arrowed) from the end of the cylinder head – VTi petrol engines

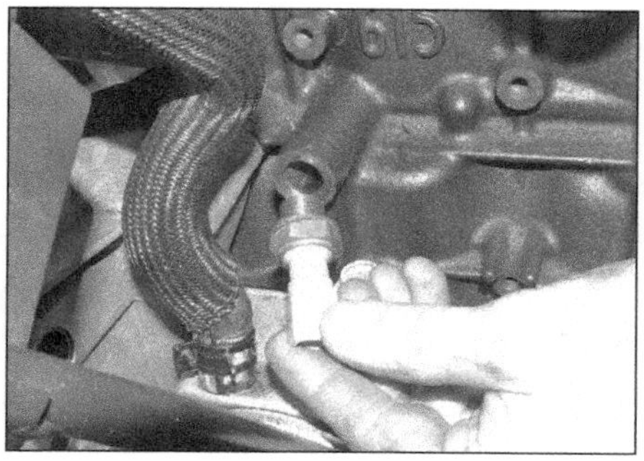

13.3b Unscrew the switch from the cylinder block – 1.6 litre diesel engines

13.3c Unscrew the switch (arrowed) – 2.0 litre diesel engines

3 Unscrew the switch from the cylinder head/block, and recover the sealing washer **(see illustrations)**. Be prepared for oil spillage, and if the switch is to be left removed from the engine for any length of time, plug the hole in the cylinder block.

Refitting

4 Examine the sealing washer for signs of damage or deterioration and if necessary renew.

5 Refit the switch, complete with washer, and tighten it securely. Reconnect the wiring connector.

6 Lower the vehicle to the ground and then check the oil level. If necessary, top-up the engine oil as described in *Weekly checks*.

14 Oil level sensor – removal and refitting

1 The sensor is fitted in the following locations **(see illustrations)**:

- *Non-VTi petrol engines: Screwed into the front side of the cylinder block, adjacent to the oil filter housing.*
- *VTi petrol engines: Screwed into the rear lower part of the cylinder block, at the centre.*
- *1.6 litre diesel engines: Screwed into the rear lower part of cylinder block, at the centre.*
- *2.0 litre diesel engines: Screwed into the front upper edge of the sump below the starter motor.*

2 So that access to the sensor can be gained from below, apply the handbrake then jack up the front of the vehicle and support it on axle stands (see *Jacking and vehicle support*). Undo the retaining bolts/nuts and remove the engine undershield.

3 The removal and refitting procedure is as described for the oil pressure switch in Section 13.

14.1a Disconnect the wiring connector from the oil level sensor

14.1b Oil level sensor (arrowed) – 2.0 litre diesel engines

Chapter 5 Part B: Ignition system – petrol models

Contents

Section number

Degrees of difficulty

Easy, suitable for novice with little experience	**Fairly easy,** suitable for beginner with some experience	**Fairly difficult,** suitable for competent DIY mechanic	**Difficult,** suitable for experienced DIY mechanic	**Very difficult,** suitable for expert DIY or professional

Specifications

General

System type	Static (distributorless) ignition system controlled by engine management ECU
Firing order	1-3-4-2 (No 1 cylinder at transmission end)
Spark plugs	See Chapter 1A Specifications
Ignition timing	Controlled by engine management ECU

Torque wrench setting

Torque wrench setting	Nm	lbf ft
Knock sensor securing bolt	20	15

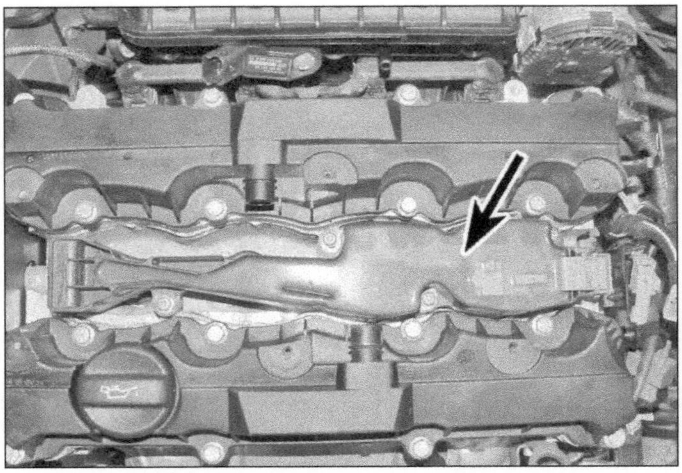

1.2a Single unit ignition coil fitted (arrowed) – non-VTi engines

1.2b Individual ignition coils fitted (arrowed) – VTi engines

1 Ignition system – general information

The ignition system is integrated with the fuel injection system to form a combined engine management system under the control of one ECU (see Chapter 4A, Section 5 for further information). The ignition side of the system is of the static (distributorless) type, consisting of the ignition coils and spark plugs.

On non-VTi engines, the ignition coils are housed in a single unit mounted directly above the spark plugs **(see illustration)**. On VTi engines there are four separate coils, fitted directly onto the top each spark plug **(see illustration)**. The coils are integral with the spark plug caps and are pushed directly onto the top of the spark plugs, one for each plug. This removes the need for any HT leads connecting the coils to the plugs.

Under the control of the ECU, the ignition coils operate on the 'wasted spark' principle, ie, each plug sparks twice for every cycle of the engine, once during the compression stroke and once during the exhaust stroke. The spark voltage is greatest in the cylinder which is under compression; in the cylinder on its exhaust stroke the compression is low and this produces a very weak spark which has no effect on the exhaust gases.

2.2 Vehicle diagnostic plug connector (arrowed)

The ECU uses its inputs from the various sensors to calculate the required ignition advance setting and coil charging time, depending on engine temperature, load and speed. At idle speeds, the ECU varies the ignition timing to alter the torque characteristic of the engine, enabling the idle speed to be controlled. This system operates in conjunction with the idle speed control motor – see Chapter 4A, Section 5 for additional details.

A knock sensor is also incorporated into the ignition system. Mounted onto the cylinder block, the sensor detects the high-frequency vibrations caused when the engine starts to pre-ignite, or 'pink'. Under these conditions, the knock sensor sends an electrical signal to the ECU, which in turn retards the ignition advance setting in small steps until the 'pinking' ceases.

2 Ignition system – testing

Warning: Voltages produced by an electronic ignition system are considerably higher than those produced by conventional ignition systems. Extreme care must be taken when working on the system with the ignition switched on. Persons with surgically implanted cardiac pacemaker devices should keep well clear of the ignition circuits, components and test equipment.

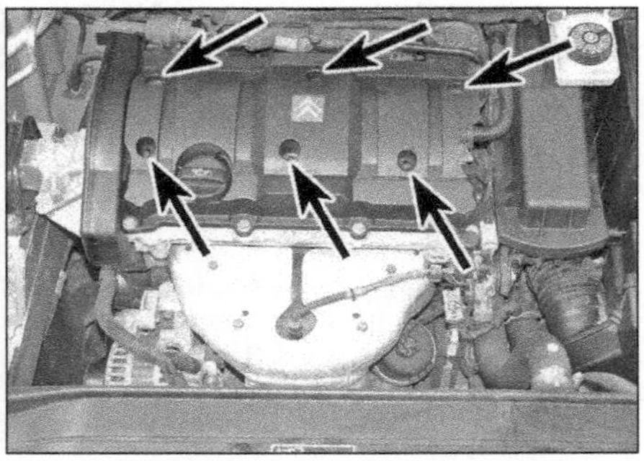

3.1 Remove the upper cover retaining screws (arrowed)

If a fault appears in the engine management (fuel injection/ignition) system, first ensure that the fault is not due to a poor electrical connection or poor maintenance; ie, check that the air cleaner filter element is clean, the spark plugs are in good condition and correctly gapped, that the engine breather hoses are clear and undamaged. If the engine is running very roughly, check the compression pressures and the valve clearances.

If these checks fail to reveal the cause of the problem the vehicle should be taken to a suitably-equipped Citroën dealer or specialist for testing. A wiring block diagnostic connector is incorporated in the engine management circuit into which a special electronic diagnostic tester can be plugged **(see illustration)**. The tester will locate the fault quickly and simply alleviating the need to test all the system components individually, which is a time-consuming operation that carries a high risk of damaging the ECU.

The only ignition system checks which can be carried out by the home mechanic are those described in Chapter 1A, Section 20 relating to the spark plugs.

3 Ignition coil unit – removal, testing and refitting

Removal

Non-VTi engines

1 Undo the six screws and remove the plastic coil pack cover from the top of the engine between the two camshaft covers **(see illustration)**.

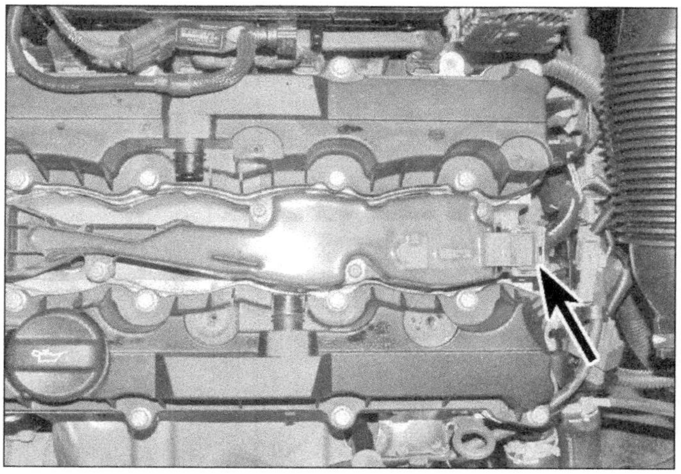

3.2 Disconnect the wiring connector (arrowed)

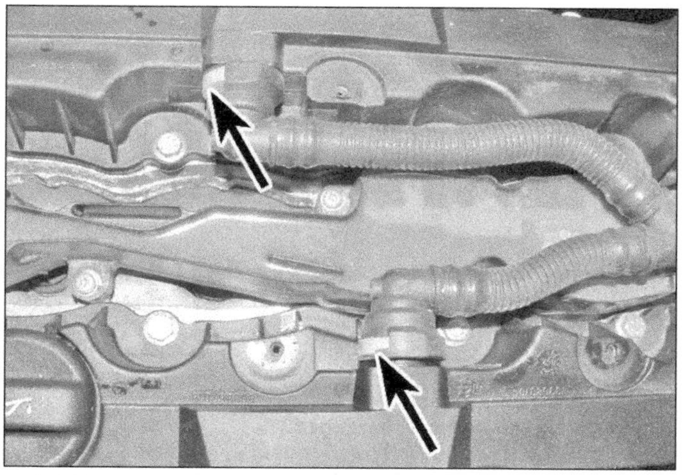

3.3 Depress the clips (arrowed) and disconnect the breather pipes

2 Disconnect the wiring plug from the left-hand end of the ignition coil unit **(see illustration)**.

3 Depress the clips and remove the two breather pipes from between the camshaft covers **(see illustration)**.

4 Undo the four mounting screws securing the coil pack **(see illustration)**.

5 Lift the ignition coil unit upwards and at the same time carefully ease the HT extension pillars away from the tops of the spark plugs. Lift the unit off the plugs and withdraw it from the engine.

VTi engines

6 Undo the two retaining screws and unclip the front of the plastic cover from the cylinder head cover **(see illustrations)**.

7 Release the locking lever and disconnect the wiring connectors from the top of the ignition coil units **(see illustrations)**.

8 Lift the coil unit upwards, off the spark plugs and from its location in the cylinder head cover **(see illustration)**.

Testing

9 The circuitry arrangement of the ignition coil unit on these engines is such that testing of an individual coil in isolation from the remainder of the engine management system is unlikely to prove effective in diagnosing a particular

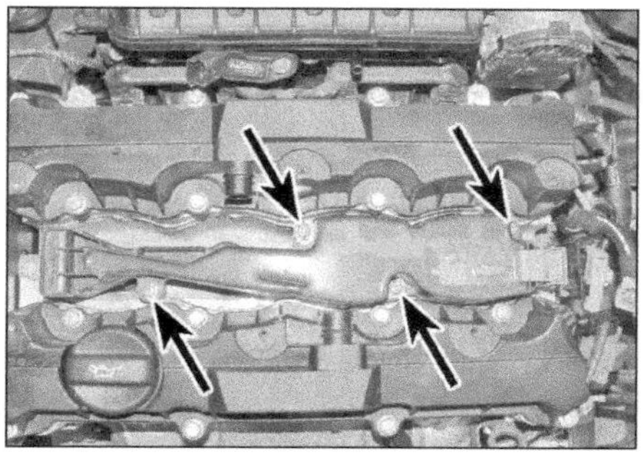

3.4 Undo the four retaining screws (arrowed)

3.6a Undo the retaining screws (arrowed) ...

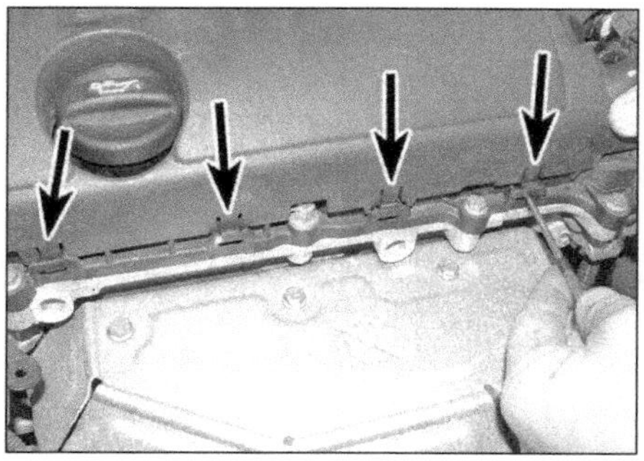

3.6b ... release the retaining clips (arrowed) ...

3.6c ... and remove the upper cover

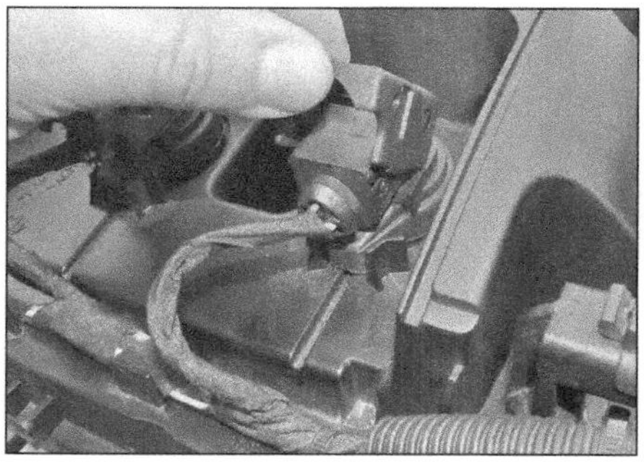

3.7a Release the locking clip ...

3.7b ... disconnect the wiring connector ...

3.8 ... and withdraw the ignition coil

fault. Should there be any reason to suspect a faulty individual coil, the engine management system should be tested by a Citroën dealer or specialist using diagnostic test equipment (see Section 2).

Refitting

10 Refitting is a reversal of the relevant removal procedure ensuring the wiring connectors are securely reconnected.

4 Ignition timing – checking and adjustment

1 There are no timing marks on the flywheel or crankshaft pulley. The timing is constantly being monitored and adjusted by the engine management ECU, and nominal values cannot be given. Therefore, it is not possible for the home mechanic to check the ignition timing.

2 The only way in which the ignition timing can be checked is using special electronic test equipment, connected to the engine management system diagnostic connector, see Section 2.

5 Knock sensor – removal and refitting

Removal

1 The knock sensor is screwed into the rear face of the cylinder block.

2 Firmly apply the handbrake, and then jack up the front of the vehicle and support it securely on axle stands (see *Jacking and vehicle support*). Undo the retaining bolts/nuts and remove the engine undershield.

3 Depending on type of knock sensor fitted, either trace the wiring back from the sensor to its wiring connector, and disconnect it from the main loom or disconnect the wiring connector directly from the sensor **(see illustration)**.

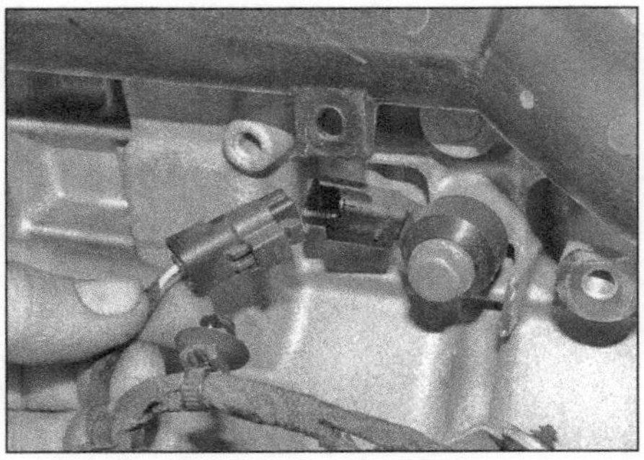

5.3 Disconnect the knock sensor wiring plug

4 Undo the sensor securing bolt and remove the sensor from the cylinder block.

Refitting

5 Refitting is a reversal of the removal procedure, ensuring that the securing bolt for the knock sensor is tightened to the specified torque.

Chapter 5 Part C:
Pre/post-heating system – diesel models

Contents

Degrees of difficulty

Easy, suitable for novice with little experience	**Fairly easy,** suitable for beginner with some experience	**Fairly difficult,** suitable for competent DIY mechanic	**Difficult,** suitable for experienced DIY mechanic	**Very difficult,** suitable for expert DIY or professional

Specifications

Preheating system

Preheating period at ambient temperatures of (approximate values):

-30°C	20 seconds
-10°C	5 seconds
0°C	0.5 seconds
18°C	0 seconds

Post-heating system

Post-heating period at ambient temperatures of (approximate values):

-30°C	3 minutes
-10°C	3 minutes
0°C	1 minutes
18°C	30 seconds
40°C	0 seconds

Torque wrench settings

	Nm	lbf ft
Glow plugs:		
1.6 litre engines	10	7
2.0 litre engines	22	16

1 Pre/post-heating system – description and testing

Description

1 To assist cold starting, diesel engines are fitted with a preheating system, which consists of four glow plugs (one per cylinder), a glow plug relay unit, a facia-mounted warning lamp, the engine management ECU, and the associated electrical wiring.

2 The glow plugs are miniature electric heating elements, encapsulated in a metal case with a probe at one end and electrical connection at the other. Each combustion chamber has one glow plug threaded into it, with the tip of the glow plug probe positioned directly in line with incoming spray of fuel from the injectors. When the glow plug is energised, it heats up rapidly, causing the fuel passing over the glow plug probe to be heated to its optimum temperature, ready for combustion. In addition, some of the fuel passing over the glow plugs is ignited and this helps to trigger the combustion process.

3 The preheating system begins to operate as soon as the ignition key is switched to the second position, but only if the engine coolant temperature is below 20° C and the engine is turned at more than 70 rpm for 0.2 seconds. A facia-mounted warning lamp informs the driver that preheating is taking place. The lamp extinguishes when sufficient preheating has taken place to allow the engine to be started, but power will still be supplied to the glow plugs for a further period until the engine is started. If no attempt is made to start the engine, the power supply to the glow plugs is switched off after 10 seconds, to prevent battery drain and glow plug burn-out.

4 With the electronically controlled diesel injection systems fitted to models in this manual, the glow plug relay unit is controlled by the engine management system ECU, which determines the necessary preheating time based on inputs from the various system sensors. The system monitors the temperature of the intake air, and then alters the preheating time (the length for which the glow plugs are supplied with current) to suit the conditions.

5 Post-heating takes place after the ignition key has been released from the 'start' position, but only if the engine coolant temperature is below 20°C, the injected fuel flow is less than a certain rate, and the engine speed is less than 2000 rpm. The glow plugs continue to operate for a maximum of 60 seconds, helping to improve fuel combustion whilst the engine is warming-up, resulting in quieter, smoother running and reduced exhaust emissions.

2.2 Undo the nuts securing the glow plug connections (arrowed)

2.4a Unscrew the glow plugs (arrowed) ...

Testing

6 If the system malfunctions, testing is ultimately by substitution of known good units, but some preliminary checks may be made as follows.

7 Connect a voltmeter or 12 volt test lamp between the glow plug supply cable and earth (engine or vehicle metal). Make sure that the live connection is kept clear of the engine and bodywork.

8 Have an assistant switch on the ignition, and check that voltage is applied to the glow plugs. Note the time for which the warning light is lit, and the total time for which voltage is applied before the system cuts out. Switch off the ignition.

9 Compare the results with the information given in the Specifications. Warning light time will increase with lower temperatures and decrease with higher temperatures.

10 If there is no supply at all, the control module or associated wiring is at fault.

11 To gain access to the glow plugs for further testing, remove the following components, according to model:

- *1.6 litre engine: Remove the cylinder head cover/manifold assembly as described in Chapter 2C, Section 4.*
- *2.0 litre engine: Working as described in Chapter 4C, Section 3, undo the bolts and move the EGR heat exchanger and valve assembly to one side.*

12 Disconnect the main supply cable and the interconnecting wire or strap from the top of the glow plugs. Be careful not to drop the nuts and washers.

13 Use a continuity tester or a 12 volt test lamp connected to the battery positive terminal to check for continuity between each glow plug terminal and earth. The resistance of a glow plug in good condition is very low (less than 1 ohm), so if the test lamp does not light or the continuity tester shows a high resistance, the glow plug is certainly defective.

14 If an ammeter is available, the current draw of each glow plug can be checked. After an initial surge of 15 to 20 amps, each plug should draw 12 amps. Any plug that draws much more or less than this is probably defective.

15 As a final check, the glow plugs can be removed and inspected as described in the following Section. On completion, refit any components removed for access.

2 Glow plugs – removal, inspection and refitting

Caution: If the preheating system has just been energised, or if the engine has been running, the glow plugs will be very hot.

Removal

1 Ensure the ignition is turned off. To gain access to the glow plugs, remove the components described in Section 1, paragraph 11, according to engine.

2 Unscrew the nuts from the glow plug terminals, and recover the washers **(see illustration)**.

3 Where applicable, carefully move any obstructing pipes or wires to one side to enable access to the relevant glow plug(s).

4 Unscrew the glow plug(s) and remove from the cylinder head **(see illustrations)**.

Inspection

5 Inspect each glow plug for physical damage. Burnt or eroded glow plug tips can be caused by a bad injector spray pattern. Have the injectors checked if this sort of damage is found.

6 If the glow plugs are in good physical condition, check them electrically using a 12 volt test lamp or continuity tester as described in the previous Section.

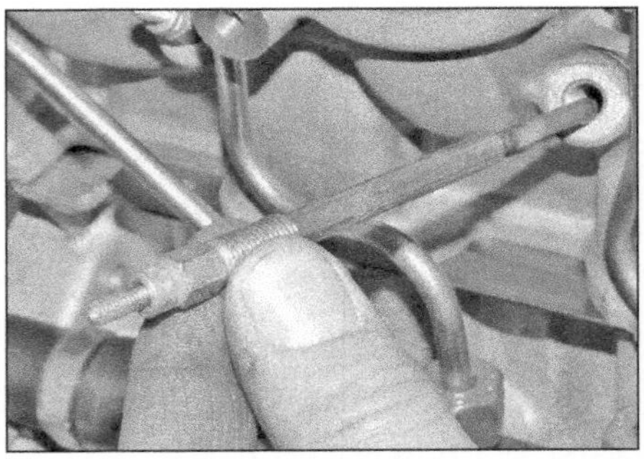

2.4b ... and remove them from the cylinder head

7 The glow plugs can be energised by applying 12 volts to them to verify that they heat up evenly and in the required time. Observe the following precautions.

- *Support the glow plug by clamping it carefully in a vice or self-locking pliers. Remember it will become red-hot.*
- *Make sure that the power supply or test lead incorporates a fuse or overload trip to protect against damage from a short circuit.*
- *After testing, allow the glow plug to cool for several minutes before attempting to handle it.*

8 A glow plug in good condition will start to glow red at the tip after drawing current for 5 seconds or so. Any plug that takes much longer to start glowing, or which starts glowing in the middle instead of at the tip is defective.

Refitting

9 Refit by reversing the removal operations. Apply a smear of copper-based anti-seize compound to the plug threads and tighten the glow plugs to the specified torque. Do not overtighten, as this can damage the glow plug element.

10 Refit any components removed for access.

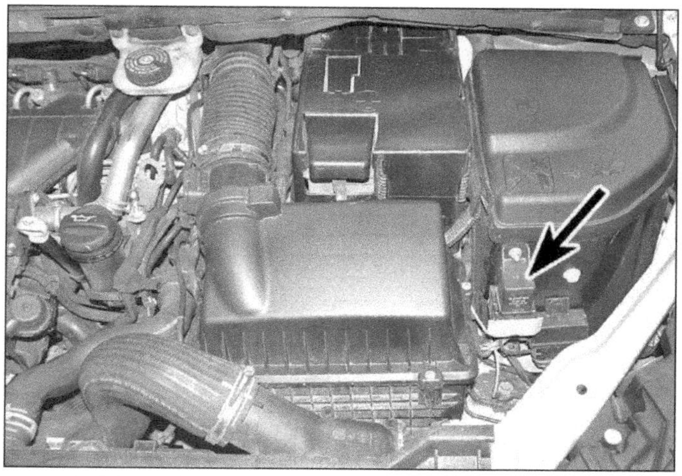

3.1 Location of the pre/post-heating relay (arrowed)

3.3 Remove the air ducting cover – 1.6 litre diesel engines

3 Pre/post-heating system relay unit – removal and refitting

Removal

1 The unit is located on the left-hand front side of the engine compartment where it is mounted just in front of the fuse/relay box **(see illustration)**.

2 Disconnect the battery (see precautions in Chapter 5A, Section 1).

3 On 1.6 litre engines, release the retaining clip and slide the air ducting cover from the front left-hand corner of the engine compartment **(see illustration)**.

4 Slide out the wiring connector locking clip and disconnect the wiring connector from the relay unit, then undo the securing nut and remove the relay unit from the front of the engine compartment fusebox **(see illustration)**.

Refitting

5 Refitting is a reversal of removal, ensuring that the wiring connector is correctly connected.

3.4 Release the wiring connector (arrowed) and undo the mounting nut

Chapter 6
Clutch

Contents

Degrees of difficulty

Easy, suitable for novice with little experience	**Fairly easy,** suitable for beginner with some experience	**Fairly difficult,** suitable for competent DIY mechanic	**Difficult,** suitable for experienced DIY mechanic	**Very difficult,** suitable for expert DIY or professional

Specifications

Type

All models	Single dry disc with diaphragm spring, hydraulic operation

Friction disc diameter

Petrol engines:	
Non-VTi	200 mm
VTi	228 mm
Diesel engines:	
DV6TED	228mm
DV6ATED	235mm
DW10BTED	235mm

Torque wrench settings

	Nm	lbf ft
Clutch slave cylinder bolts (5-speed)	19	14
Clutch slave cylinder/release bearing bolts (6-speed)	10	7
Pressure plate retaining bolts	20	15

1 General information

The clutch consists of a friction disc, a pressure plate assembly, and a release bearing; all of these components are contained in the large cast-aluminium alloy bellhousing, sandwiched between the engine and the transmission. The release mechanism is hydraulic, operated by a master cylinder and a slave cylinder, which on some models is part of the thrust bearing inside the bellhousing. The hydraulic master cylinder is located in the bulkhead, directly behind the brake pedal, and the clutch fluid reservoir is shared with the brake fluid reservoir on top of the brake master cylinder.

The friction disc is fitted between the engine flywheel and the clutch pressure plate, and is allowed to slide on the transmission input shaft splines.

The pressure plate assembly is bolted to the engine flywheel. When the engine is running, drive is transmitted from the crankshaft, via the flywheel, to the friction disc (these components being clamped securely together by the pressure plate assembly) and from the friction disc to the transmission input shaft.

To interrupt the drive, the spring pressure must be relaxed by the hydraulically operated release mechanism. Depressing the clutch pedal operates the master cylinder, which in turn, through the hydraulic system, presses the release bearing against the pressure plate spring fingers. This causes the springs to deform and releases the clamping force on the pressure plate. When the pedal is released the diaphragm spring forces the pressure plate into contact with the friction linings on the friction plate. The friction disc is now firmly sandwiched between the pressure plate and the flywheel, thus transmitting engine power to the transmission.

The clutch pedal is connected to the clutch master cylinder by a short pushrod. The master cylinder is mounted on the engine side of the bulkhead in front of the driver and receives its hydraulic fluid supply from the brake master cylinder reservoir. Depressing the clutch pedal moves the piston in the master cylinder forwards, so forcing hydraulic fluid through the clutch hydraulic pipe to the slave cylinder.

On 5-speed models, the piston in the slave cylinder moves forward on the entry of the fluid and actuates the clutch release fork by means of a short pushrod. The release fork pivots on its mounting stud, and the other end of the fork then presses the release bearing against the pressure plate spring fingers. This causes the springs to deform and releases the clamping force on the pressure plate.

On 6-speed models, the slave cylinder is part of the release bearing, and when the fluid is pushed through the system the release bearing moves forward against the pressure plate spring fingers. This causes the springs to deform and releases the clamping force on the pressure plate.

On all models the clutch operating mechanism is self-adjusting, and no manual adjustment is required.

2 Clutch hydraulic system – bleeding

Warning: Hydraulic fluid is poisonous; wash off immediately and thoroughly in the case of skin contact, and seek immediate medical advice if any fluid is swallowed or gets into the eyes. Certain types of hydraulic fluid are inflammable, and may ignite when allowed into contact with hot components; when servicing any hydraulic system, it is safest to assume that the fluid IS inflammable, and to take precautions against the risk of fire as though it is petrol that is being handled. Hydraulic fluid is also an effective paint stripper, and will attack plastics. If any is spilt, it should be washed off immediately, using copious quantities of clean water. When topping-up or renewing the fluid, always use the recommended type, and ensure that it comes from a freshly opened sealed container.

1 Obtain a clean container, a suitable length of rubber or clear plastic tubing that is a tight fit over the bleed screw on the clutch slave cylinder, and a tin of the specified hydraulic fluid. The help of an assistant will also be required. If a one-man do-it-yourself bleeding kit for bleeding the brake hydraulic system is available, this can be used quite satisfactorily for the clutch also. Full information on the use of these kits may be found in Chapter 9, Section 2.

2 Remove the air cleaner intake ducting from the front left-hand side of the engine compartment (see Chapter 4A, Section 2 or Chapter 4B, Section 4), to access the clutch bleed screw.

3 Remove the filler cap from the brake master cylinder reservoir, and if necessary top-up the fluid. Keep the reservoir topped-up during subsequent operations.

4 On 5-speed transmissions, remove the dust cap from the slave cylinder bleed screw, located on the lower front facing side of the transmission **(see illustration)**.

5 On 6-speed transmissions, remove the dust cap from the bleed screw at the hydraulic connection, located on the lower front facing side of the transmission **(see illustration)**.

6 Connect one end of the bleed tube to the bleed screw, and insert the other end of the tube in the jar containing sufficient clean hydraulic fluid to keep the end of the tube submerged **(see illustration)**.

7 Open the bleed screw half a turn and have your assistant depress the clutch pedal and then slowly release it. Continue this procedure until clean hydraulic fluid, free from air bubbles, emerges from the tube. Now tighten the bleed screw at the end of a downstroke. Make sure that the brake master cylinder reservoir is checked frequently to ensure that the level does not drop too far, allowing air into the system.

8 Check the operation of the clutch pedal. After a few strokes it should feel normal. Any sponginess would indicate air still present in the system.

9 On completion remove the bleed tube and refit the dust cover. Top-up the master cylinder reservoir if necessary and refit the cap. Fluid expelled from the hydraulic system should now be discarded, as it will be contaminated with moisture, air and dirt, making it unsuitable for further use.

2.4 Remove the dust cap from the bleed screw – 5-speed transmission

2.5 Remove the dust cap (arrowed) from the bleed screw – 6-speed transmission

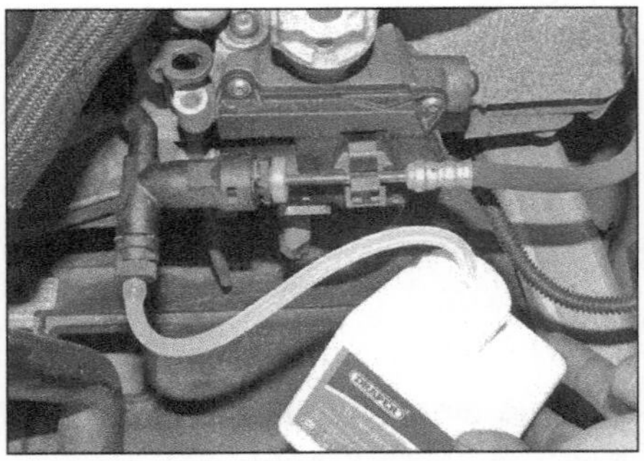

2.6 Air bleed bottle connected to bleed screw

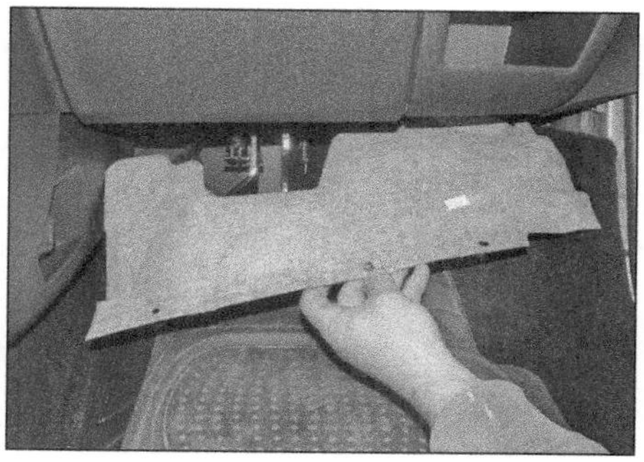

3.1 **Unclip the trim panel from under the facia**

3.2 **Release the end of the pushrod from the pedal**

3.4 **Location of clutch master cylinder (arrowed)**

3 Clutch master cylinder – removal and refitting

Note: *Before starting work, refer to the note at the beginning of Section 2 concerning the dangers of hydraulic fluid.*

Removal

1 Working inside the driver's footwell, prise up the centre pins, lever out the complete expanding plastic rivets, and remove the trim panel above the pedals **(see illustration)**. Disconnect the interior light from the trim as it is removed.

2 Release the securing clips, and then prise the master cylinder pushrod end from the pedal pin **(see illustration)**. Press on the securing clips to free the pushrod from the pedal.

3 To minimise hydraulic fluid loss, remove the brake master cylinder reservoir filler cap then tighten it down onto a piece of polythene to obtain an airtight seal.

4 Working inside the engine compartment, down the back of the engine, place absorbent rags under the clutch master cylinder pipe connections in the engine compartment and be prepared for hydraulic fluid loss **(see illustration)**.

5 Release the master cylinder hydraulic pressure pipe and supply pipe from there retaining clips on the engine compartment bulkhead, then prise out the retaining wire clips and disconnect the pipes from the master cylinder **(see illustration)**. Suitably plug or cap the pipe end to prevent further fluid loss and dirt entry.

6 Rotate the master cylinder 45 degrees clockwise, and remove it from the bulkhead **(see illustration)**.

Refitting

7 Refitting the master cylinder is the reverse sequence to removal, bearing in mind the following points.

a) Ensure all retaining clips are correctly refitted.

b) Remove the piece of polythene from the top of the reservoir.

c) Bleed the clutch hydraulic system as described in Section 2.

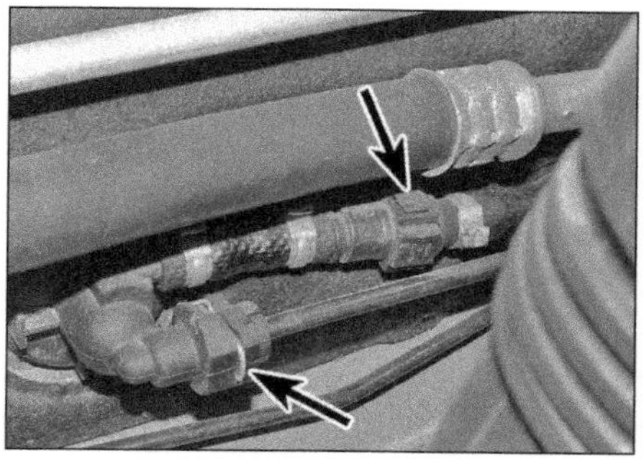

3.5 **Release the clips (arrowed), and disconnect the pipes from the master cylinder**

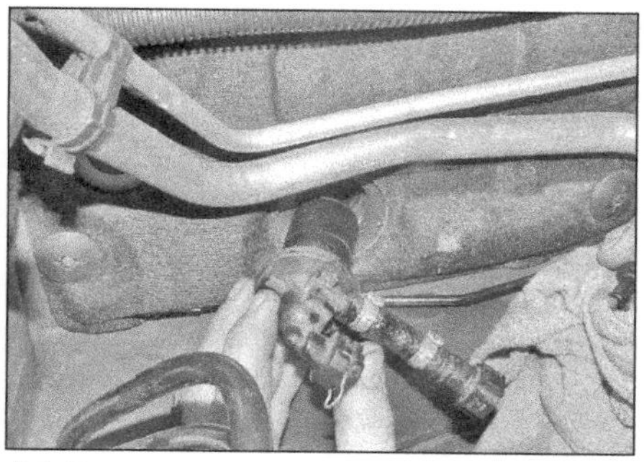

3.6 **Turn the master cylinder 45° clockwise, and remove it from the bulkhead**

4 Clutch slave cylinder – removal and refitting

Note: *Before starting work, refer to the note at the beginning of Section 2 concerning the dangers of hydraulic fluid.*

Removal

5-speed transmissions

1 To minimise hydraulic fluid loss, remove the brake master cylinder reservoir filler cap then tighten it down onto a piece of polythene to obtain an airtight seal.

2 Remove the air cleaner intake ducting from the front left-hand side of the engine compartment (see Chapter 4A, Section 2 or Chapter 4B, Section 4), to access the clutch slave cylinder.

3 Place absorbent rags under the clutch slave cylinder located on the lower front facing side of the transmission. Be prepared for hydraulic fluid loss.

4 Where necessary for access, release the wiring harness from the retaining clips and move the harness clear of the slave cylinder.

5 Lever out the retaining clip a little, and then disconnect the hydraulic pipe from the side of the slave cylinder **(see illustration)**. Suitably plug or cap the pipe end to prevent further fluid loss and dirt entry.

6 Undo the two retaining bolts and remove the cylinder from the transmission housing **(see illustration)**.

6-speed transmissions

7 On 6-speed transmissions, the clutch slave cylinder is part of the release bearing

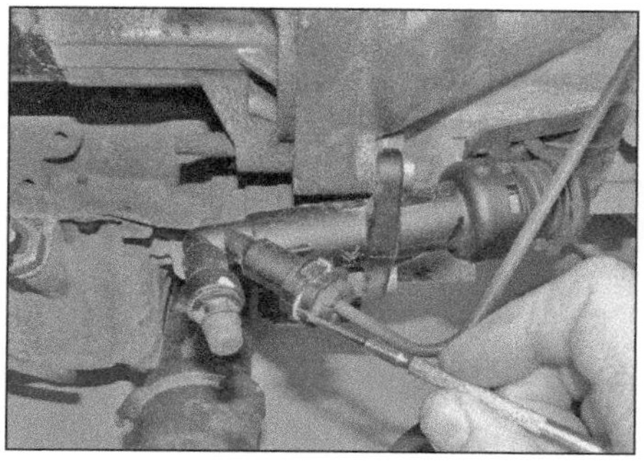

4.5 **Lever out the hydraulic pipe retaining clip**

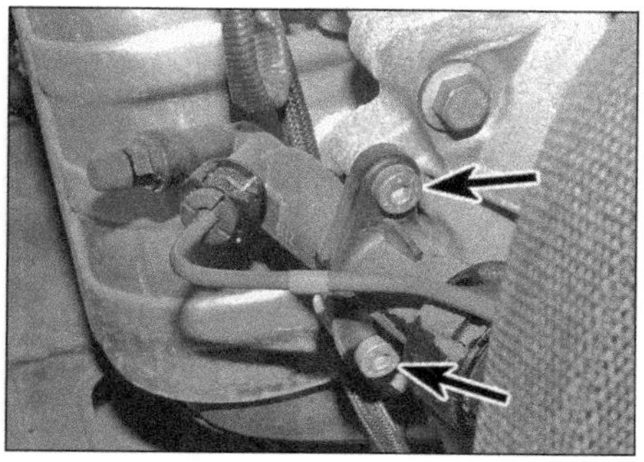

4.6 **Undo the two bolts (arrowed) and remove the clutch slave cylinder**

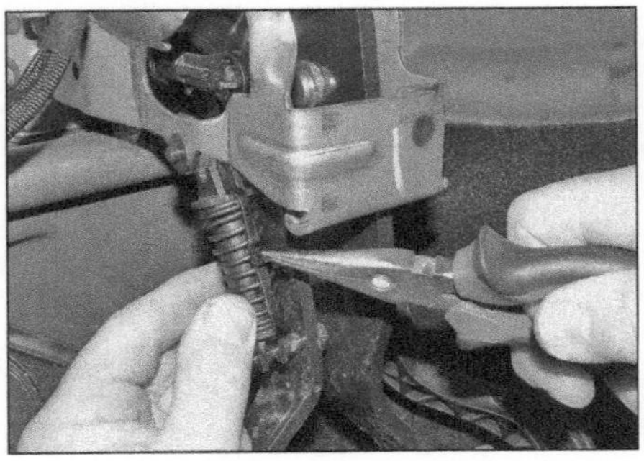

5.3 Use a cable-tie to secure the spring assembly together

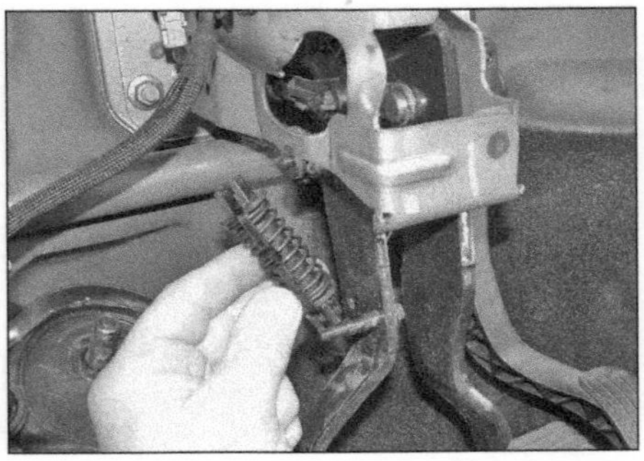

5.4 Withdraw the spring assembly out from the pedal

5.5 Pedal pivot bolt retaining nut (arrowed)

assembly. Refer to Section 7 for the removal and refitting procedure.

Refitting

8 Refitting the slave cylinder is the reverse sequence to removal, bearing in mind the following points.

a) *Apply a little Molykote BR2 Plus grease to the end of the slave cylinder pushrod.*
b) *Remove the piece of polythene from the top of the reservoir.*
c) *Bleed the clutch hydraulic system as described in Section 2.*

5 Clutch pedal – removal and refitting

Removal

1 Release the securing clips and remove the trim panel from above the driver's pedals **(see illustration 3.1)**.
2 Release the securing clips, and then using a flat-bladed screwdriver, prise the master cylinder pushrod end from the pedal pin **(see illustration 3.2)**.
3 Fasten a cable-tie around the clutch pedal return spring to prevent it coming apart when removed **(see illustration)**.
4 Move the clutch pedal and remove the clutch return spring from the locating pegs **(see illustration)**.
5 Undo the nut from the clutch pedal pivot bolt and withdraw the bolt **(see illustration)**. Do not withdraw the bolt completely, as it is also the brake pedal pivot bolt.
6 Remove the clutch pedal from the pedal bracket and recover the bush (where applicable) from the pedal pivot.
7 Check the condition of the pedal, pivot bush and return spring assembly and renew any components as necessary.

Refitting

8 Lubricate the pedal pivot bolt with multipurpose grease, then locate the pedal in the bracket and insert the pivot bolt. Refit the pivot bolt nut and tighten it securely.
9 Reconnect the return spring to the pedal and pedal bracket; making sure it locates correctly **(see illustration)**. Cut the cable-tie from around the spring once it is in its fitted position.
10 Reconnect the clutch master cylinder pushrod to the clutch pedal.
11 Depress the pedal two or three times and check the operation of the clutch release mechanism.
12 Refit the facia lower trim panel and secure with the plastic clips.

6 Clutch assembly – removal, inspection and refitting

Warning: Dust created by clutch wear and deposited on the clutch components may contain asbestos, which is a health hazard. DO NOT blow it out with compressed air, nor inhale any of it. DO NOT use petrol or petroleum-based solvents to clean off the dust. Brake system cleaner or methylated spirit should be used to flush the dust into a suitable receptacle. After the clutch components are wiped clean with rags, dispose of the contaminated rags and cleaner in a sealed, marked container.

Note: *Although most friction materials no longer contain asbestos, it is safest to assume that some still do, and to take precautions accordingly.*

Removal

1 Unless the complete engine/transmission unit is to be removed from the car and separated for major overhaul (see Chapter 2E, Section 4), the clutch can be reached by removing the transmission as described in Chapter 7A, Section 7.
2 Before disturbing the clutch, use chalk or a marker pen to mark the relationship of the pressure plate assembly to the flywheel **(see illustration)**.
3 Working in a diagonal sequence, slacken the pressure plate bolts by half a turn at a time, until spring pressure is released and the bolts can be unscrewed by hand **(see illustration)**.
4 Prise the pressure plate assembly off its locating dowels, and collect the friction disc, noting which way round the disc is fitted.

Inspection

Note: *Due to the amount of work necessary to remove and refit clutch components, it is considered good practice to renew the clutch friction disc, pressure plate assembly*

5.9 Spring locating pegs (arrowed) on the pedal and mounting bracket

6.2 Mark the position of the pressure plate on the flywheel

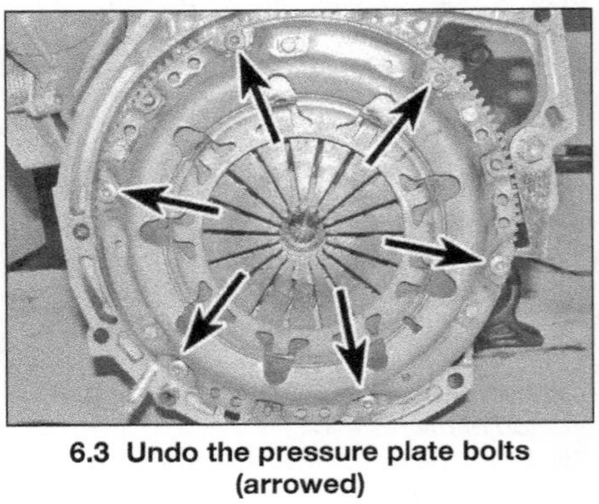

6.3 Undo the pressure plate bolts (arrowed)

6.13a Fit the disc so the spring hub assembly faces away from the flywheel

and release bearing as a matched set, even if only one of these is worn enough to require renewal. It is worth considering the renewal of the clutch components on a preventative basis if the engine and/or transmission have been removed for some other reason.

5 When cleaning clutch components, read the warning at the beginning of this Section first; remove dust using a clean, dry cloth, and working in a well-ventilated atmosphere.

6 Check the friction disc facings for signs of wear, damage or oil contamination. If the friction material is cracked, burnt, scored or damaged, or if it is contaminated with oil or grease (shown by shiny black patches), the friction disc must be renewed.

7 If the friction material is still serviceable, check that the centre boss splines are unworn, that the torsion springs are in good condition and securely fastened, and that all the rivets are tight. If any wear or damage is found, the friction disc must be renewed.

8 If the friction material is fouled with oil, this must be due to an oil leak from the crankshaft left-hand oil seal, from the sump-to-cylinder block joint, or from the transmission input shaft. Renew the seal or repair the joint, as appropriate, as described in Chapter 2A, 2B, 2C or 2D, or Chapter 7A, Section 4, before installing the new friction disc.

9 Check the pressure plate assembly for obvious signs of wear or damage; shake it to check for loose rivets or worn or damaged fulcrum rings, and check that the drive straps securing the pressure plate to the cover do not show signs (such as a deep yellow or blue discoloration) of overheating. If the diaphragm

6.18 ... then move the adjusting ring (arrowed) anti-clockwise to the stop

6.13b ... or the protruding hub away from the flywheel

spring is worn or damaged, or if its pressure is in any way suspect, the pressure plate assembly should be renewed.

10 Examine the machined bearing surfaces of the pressure plate and of the flywheel; they should be clean, completely flat, and free from scratches or scoring. If either is discoloured from excessive heat, or shows signs of cracks, it should be renewed – although minor damage of this nature can sometimes be polished away using emery paper.

11 Check that the release bearing contact surface rotates smoothly and easily, with no sign of noise or roughness. Also check that the surface itself is smooth and unworn, with no signs of cracks, pitting or scoring. If there is any doubt about its condition, the bearing must be renewed.

Refitting

12 On reassembly, ensure that the bearing surfaces of the flywheel and pressure plate are completely clean, smooth, and free from oil or grease. Use solvent to remove any protective grease from new components.

13 Fit the friction disc so that its spring hub assembly faces away from the flywheel; there may be a marking showing which way round the disc is to be refitted **(see illustrations)**.

Models with self-adjusting clutch

14 On these models, the clutch pressure plate has a pre-adjustment mechanism to compensate for wear in the friction disc (this is termed by Citroën as a self-adjusting clutch (SAC), which is slightly ambiguous as all clutches fitted to these models are essentially self-adjusting). However, this mechanism must

6.22 Centralise the friction plate on the flywheel using a clutch aligning tool

6.16 Using some threaded rod, washers and nuts, compress the spring and the pressure plate together ...

be reset before refitting the pressure plate. A new plate may be supplied preset, in which case this procedure can be ignored.

15 A large diameter bolt (M14 at least) long enough to pass through the pressure plate, a matching nut, and several large diameter washers, will be needed for this procedure. Mount the bolt head in the jaws of a sturdy bench vice, with one large washer fitted.

16 Offer the plate over the bolt, friction disc surface facing down, and locate it centrally over the bolt and washer – the washer should bear on the centre hub **(see illustration)**.

17 Fit several further large washers over the bolt, so that they bear on the ends of the spring fingers, then add the nut and tighten by hand to locate the washers.

18 The purpose of the procedure is to turn the plate's internal adjuster disc so that the three small coil springs visible on the plate's outer surface are fully compressed. Tighten the nut just fitted until the adjuster disc is free to turn. Using a pair of thin-nosed, or circlip, pliers in one of the two windows in the top surface, open the jaws of the pliers to turn the adjuster disc anti-clockwise, so that the springs are fully compressed **(see illustration)**.

19 Hold the pliers in this position, and then unscrew the centre nut. Once the nut is released, the adjuster disc will be gripped in position, and the pliers can be removed. Take the pressure plate from the vice, and it is ready to fit.

All models

20 Refit the pressure plate assembly, aligning the marks made on dismantling (if the original pressure plate is re-used), and locating the pressure plate on its three locating dowels. Fit the pressure plate bolts, but tighten them only finger-tight, so that the friction disc can still be moved.

21 The friction disc must now be centralised, so that when the transmission is refitted, its input shaft will pass through the splines at the centre of the friction disc.

22 Centralisation can be achieved by passing a screwdriver or other long bar through the friction disc and into the hole in the crankshaft; the friction disc can then be moved around until it is centred on the crankshaft hole. Alternatively, a clutch-aligning tool can be used to eliminate the guesswork; these can be obtained from most accessory shops **(see illustration)**.

23 When the friction disc is centralised, tighten the pressure plate bolts evenly and in a diagonal sequence to the specified torque setting.

24 Apply a thin smear of molybdenum disulphide grease (Citroën recommend the use of Molykote BR2 Plus – available from your dealer) to the splines of the friction disc and the transmission input shaft, and also to the release bearing bore and release fork shaft.

25 Refit the transmission as described in Chapter 7A, Section 7.

7 Clutch release mechanism – removal, inspection and refitting

Note: *Refer to the warning concerning the dangers of asbestos dust at the beginning of Section 2.*

Removal

1 Unless the complete engine/transmission unit is to be removed from the car and separated for major overhaul (see Chapter 2E, Section 4), the clutch release mechanism can be reached by removing the transmission only, as described in Chapter 7A, Section 7.

5-speed transmissions

2 With the transmission removed, squeeze together the tabs of the retaining clip and pull the release fork off the pivot ball-stud **(see illustration)**.

7.2 Squeeze the tabs of the retaining clip together and remove the release fork ...

3 Slide the release bearing off the guide tube and disengage the arms off the release fork **(see illustration)**.

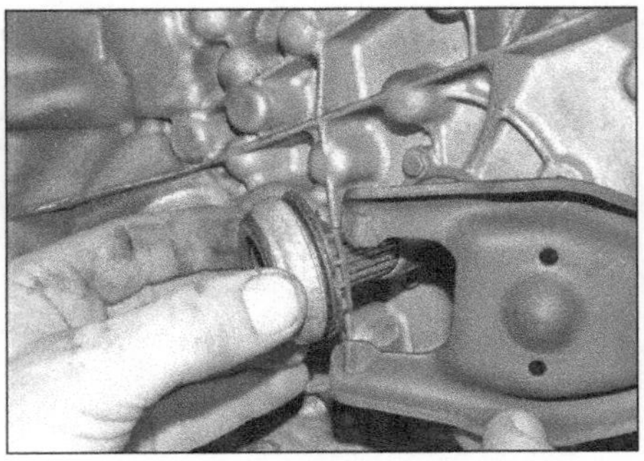

7.3 ... disengage the release bearing as the fork is removed

4 If required, recover the shim where fitted and unscrew the mounting stud from the transmission housing **(see illustrations)**.

7.4a Recover the shim ...

7.4b ... then unscrew the pivot ball-stud (arrowed)

6-speed transmissions

5 With the transmission removed, undo the three mounting bolts from inside the bellhousing **(see illustration)**.

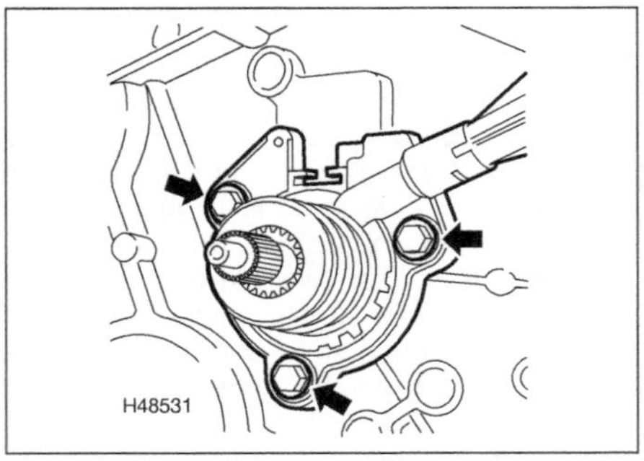

7.5 Undo the slave cylinder/release bearing retaining bolts

6 Withdraw the slave cylinder/release bearing by sliding it over the transmission input shaft.

Inspection

7 Check that the release bearing contact surface rotates smoothly and easily, with no sign of noise or roughness, and that the surface itself is smooth and unworn, with no signs of cracks, pitting or scoring. If there is any doubt about its condition, the bearing must be renewed.

8 On 5-speed transmissions, check the bearing surfaces and points of contact on the release fork and pivot ball-stud, renewing any component, which is worn or damaged.

Refitting

9 Apply a smear of molybdenum disulphide grease to the pivot ball-stud.

10 On 5-speed transmissions, insert the outer end of the release fork through the rubber boot in the side of the transmission bellhousing. Engage the arms of the release fork with the release bearing collar, then slide the release bearing onto the guide tube. Position the shim over the tabs of the pivot ball-stud clip, then push the fork over the stud, ensuring the tabs of the retaining clip engage correctly with the fork **(see illustrations)**.

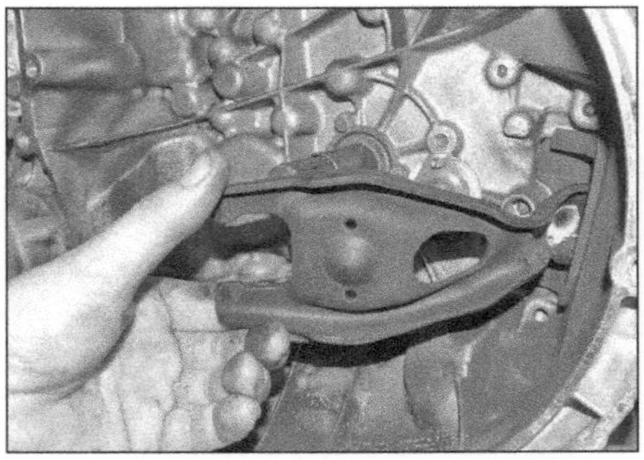

7.10a Refit the release fork into the rubber gaiter and release bearing

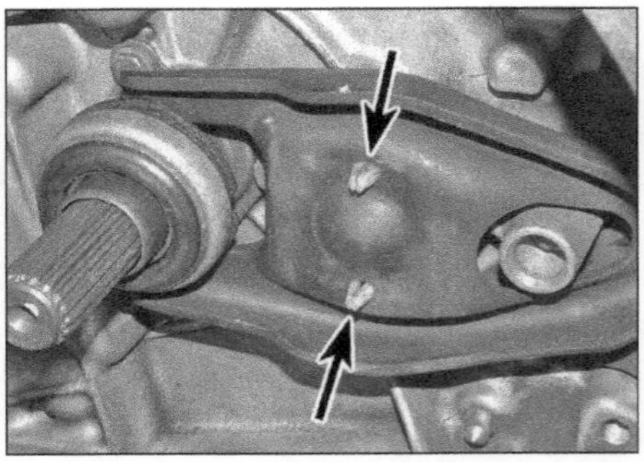

7.10b Ensure the retaining tabs (arrowed) engage correctly with the release fork

11 On 6-speed transmissions, slide the slave cylinder/release bearing over the transmission input shaft and tighten the retaining bolts to the specified torque setting.

12 Refit the transmission as described in Chapter 7A, Section 7.

Chapter 7 Part A: Manual transmission

Contents

Degrees of difficulty

Easy, suitable for novice with little experience	**Fairly easy,** suitable for beginner with some experience	**Fairly difficult,** suitable for competent DIY mechanic	**Difficult,** suitable for experienced DIY mechanic	**Very difficult,** suitable for expert DIY or professional

Specifications

General

Type	Manual, five or six forward speeds and reverse. Synchromesh on all forward speeds
Designation:	
Petrol engines:	
Non-VTi:	
1.4 litre	MA5
1.6 litre	MA5 or BE4/5
VTi	BE4/5
Diesel engines:	
1.6 litre	BE4/5
2.0 litre	ML6C
Application (transmission code):	
Petrol engines:	
Non-VTi	
1.4 litre	20 CP 42
1.6 litre	20 CP 43
VTi	20 DP 42
Diesel engine:	
1.6 litre:	
With intercooler	20 DM 75
Without intercooler	20 DM 69
2.0 litre	20 MB 01

Lubrication

Capacity	Refer to Chapter 1A or 1B
Recommended oil type	See *Lubricants and fluids*

Torque wrench settings

	Nm	lbf ft
MA5 transmission		
Clutch release bearing guide sleeve bolts	10	7
Engine-to-transmission fixing bolts	Refer to Chapter 2A	
Gearchange lever mounting nuts	8	6
Left-hand engine/transmission mounting	Refer to Chapter 2A	
Oil drain plug	33	24
Oil filler/level plug (where fitted)	25	18
Reversing light switch	25	18
Roadwheel bolts	90	66
Speedometer drive housing bolts	10	7
BE4/5 transmission		
Clutch release bearing guide sleeve bolts	15	11
Engine-to-transmission fixing bolts	Refer to Chapter 2A, 2B or 2C	
Gearchange lever mounting nuts	8	6
Left-hand engine/transmission mounting	Refer to Chapter 2A, 2B or 2C	
Neutral sensor bolt	10	7
Oil drain plug	35	26
Oil filler/level plug	22	16
Reversing light switch	25	18
Roadwheel bolts	90	66
Speedometer drive housing bolts	15	11
ML6C transmission		
Clutch release bearing guide sleeve bolts	10	7
Driveshaft seal thrust plate bolts (left-hand side)	20	15
Engine movement limiter to subframe	65	48
Engine-to-transmission fixing bolts	Refer to Chapter 2D	
Gearchange lever housing bolts	10	7
Left-hand engine/transmission mounting	Refer to Chapter 2D	
Oil drain plug	33	24
Reversing light switch	25	18
Roadwheel bolts	90	66

1 General information

1 The transmission is contained in a cast-aluminium alloy casing bolted to the engine's left-hand end, and consists of the gearbox and final drive differential – often called a transaxle.

2 Drive is transmitted from the crankshaft via the clutch to the input shaft that has a splined extension to accept the clutch friction disc, and rotates in sealed ball-bearings. From the input shaft, drive is transmitted to the output shaft, which rotates in a roller bearing at its right-hand end, and a sealed ball-bearing at its left-hand end. From the output shaft, the drive is transmitted to the differential crownwheel, which rotates with the differential case and planetary gears, thus driving the sun gears and driveshafts. The rotation of the planetary gears on their shaft allows the inner roadwheel to rotate at a slower speed than the outer roadwheel when the car is cornering.

3 The input and output shafts are arranged side-by-side, parallel to the crankshaft and driveshafts, so that their gear pinion teeth are in constant mesh. In the neutral position, the output shaft gear pinions rotate freely, so that drive cannot be transmitted to the crownwheel.

4 Three different manual transmissions are used on the models covered in this manual; non-VTI petrol engines either use the MA5 or BE4/5 transmission, VTi petrol engines use the BE4/5 transmission, 1.6 litre diesel engines use the BE4/5 and 2.0 litre diesel engines use the ML6C transmission.

5 On ML6C transmissions from 03/06, the casing was modified; this improved lubrication and lowered the oil temperature in the transmission. Cooling fins were added to the lower part of the casing to provide better cooling **(see illustration)**. These transmissions with cooling fins do not require as much oil. See specifications at the start of this Chapter.

6 On later MA5 and BE4/5 transmissions, the oil level cannot be checked, as there is no filler/level plug fitted. All later transmissions do not require regular maintenance and are filled for life. If the transmission develops a leak or is removed for other work, the oil needs to be completely drained and refilled with the correct amount of oil. The transmission will then be refilled through the vent on the top of the transmission.

7 Gear selection is via a floor-mounted lever and two cables, which pass through the floor panel to the top of the transmission housing. The selector/gearchange cables cause the appropriate selector fork to move its respective synchro-sleeve along the shaft, to lock the gear pinion to the synchro-hub. Since the synchro-hubs are splined to the output shaft, this locks the pinion to the shaft, so that drive can be transmitted. To ensure that gearchanging can be made quickly and quietly, a synchromesh system is fitted to all forward gears, consisting of baulk rings and spring-loaded fingers, as well as the gear pinions and synchro-hubs. The synchromesh cones are formed on the mating faces of the baulk rings and gear pinions.

1.5 Fins (arrowed) on lower part of transmission casing for cooling

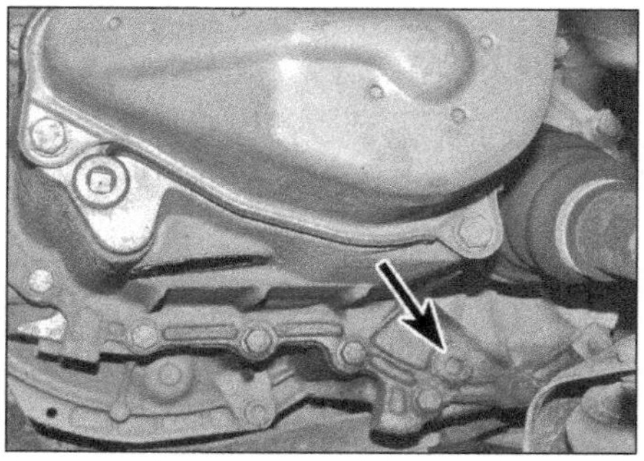

2.3a Oil drain plug (arrowed) – MA5 transmission

2.3b Oil drain plug (arrowed) – BE4/5 transmission

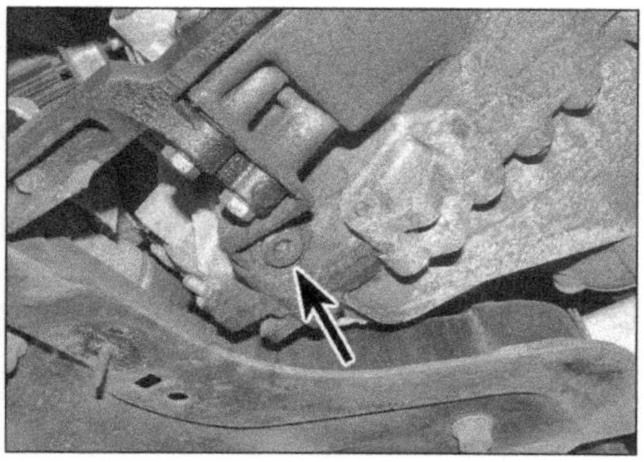

2.3c Oil drain plug (arrowed) – ML6C transmission

2 Manual transmission – draining and refilling

Note: *A suitable square section wrench may be required to undo the transmission filler/level and drain plugs on some models. These wrenches can be obtained from most motor factors or your Citroën dealer.*

1 This operation is much quicker and more efficient if the car is first taken on a journey of sufficient length to warm the engine/transmission up to normal operating temperature.

2 Park the car on level ground, switch off the ignition and apply the handbrake firmly. For improved access, jack up the front of the car and support it securely on axle stands (see *Jacking and vehicle support*). Note that on early MA5 and BE4/5 transmissions the car must be level to ensure accuracy when refilling and checking the oil level. Undo the screws and remove the engine undershield (where fitted).

3 Position a suitable container under the drain plug (situated on the final drive casing at the rear of the transmission) and unscrew the plug **(see illustrations).**

4 Allow the oil to drain completely into the container. If the oil is hot, take precautions against scalding. Clean the drain plug, being especially careful to wipe any metallic particles off the magnetic inserts. Discard the original sealing washer, as it should be renewed whenever it is disturbed.

MA5 and BE4/5 transmissions

Note: *The part number (referred to as RPO number – Replacement Parts Organisation number) can be found on a label on the driver's door A-pillar. The first five numbers are the RPO number* ***(see Haynes Hint).***

Up to RPO 9974

5 To improve access to the filler/level plug, remove the left-hand front wheel and wheel arch liner **(see illustration)**.

6 Wipe clean the area around the filler/level plug; it is situated on the left-hand end of the transmission, next to the end cover. The filler/level plug is the largest bolt among those securing the end cover to the transmission. Remove the filler/level plug from the transmission and recover the sealing washer **(see illustration)**.

7 When the oil has finished draining, clean the drain plug threads and those of the transmission casing, fit a new sealing washer and refit the drain plug, tightening it to the specified torque wrench setting. Refit the undercover (where fitted), and then check that the vehicle is level before refilling.

8 Refilling the transmission is an extremely awkward operation **(see illustration)**. Above all, allow plenty of time for the oil level to settle properly before checking it. Note that the car must be parked on flat level ground when checking the oil level.

9 Refill the transmission with the exact amount of the specified type of oil, and then check the oil level as described in Chapter 1A, Section 22 or Chapter 1B, Section 22; if the correct amount was poured

HAYNES HiNT

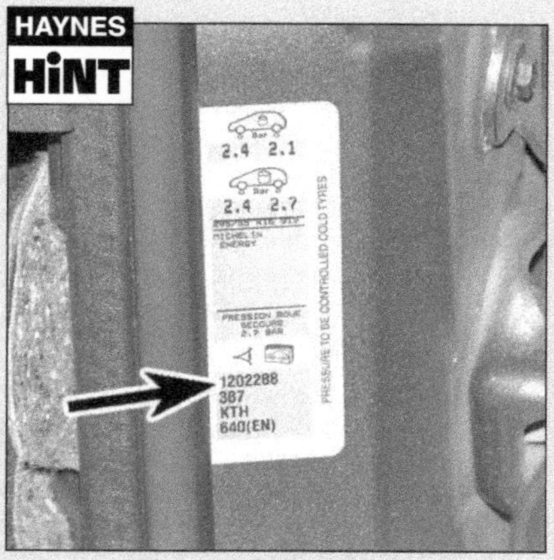

The first five numbers (arrowed) are the RPO number.

2.5 Remove the inner wheel arch liner

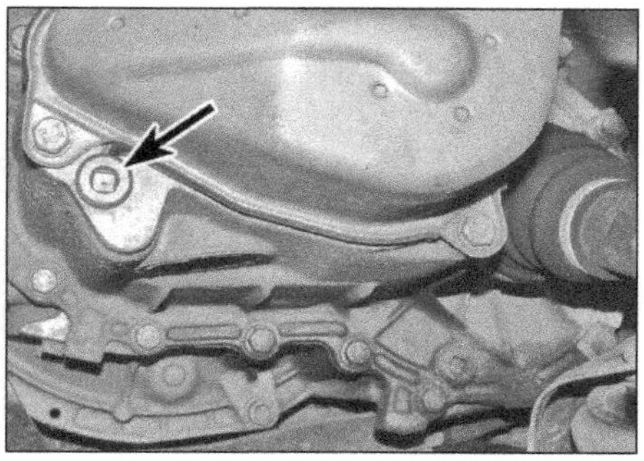

2.6a Oil filler/level plug (arrowed) – MA5 transmission

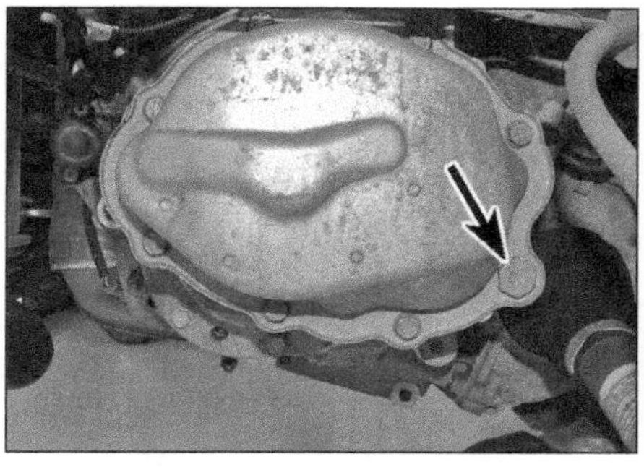

2.6b Oil filler/level plug (arrowed) – BE4/5 transmission

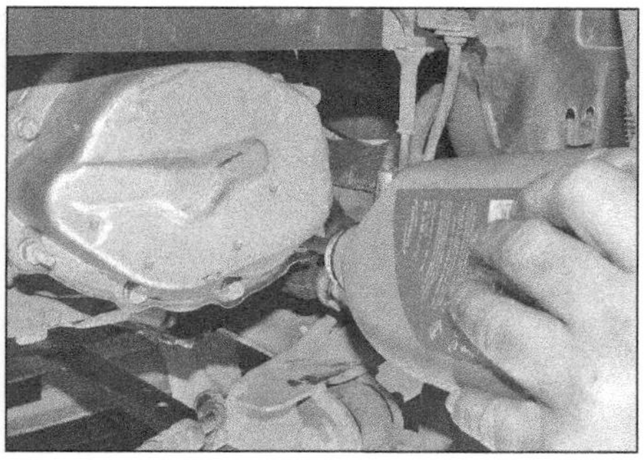

2.8 Topping-up the transmission through the wheel arch

2.13a Vent on top of transmission housing (arrowed)

2.13b Unclip the breather/vent cap and add the exact amount of fluid specified using a funnel

into the transmission and a large amount flows out on checking the level, refit the filler/ level plug and take the car on a short journey so that the new oil is distributed fully around the transmission components, then check the level again on your return.

10 Once the oil level is correct securely refit the inner cover/wheel arch liner and roadwheel; tighten to the specified torque.

From RPO 9975

Note: *The oil level cannot be checked, as there is no level plug fitted. These transmissions do not require regular maintenance and are filled for life. If the transmission develops a leak or is removed for other work, the oil needs to be completely drained and refilled with the correct amount of oil. The transmission will then be refilled through the vent/breather on the top of the transmission* ***(see illustration 2.13a)****.*

11 Remove the battery and battery tray as described in Chapter 5A, Section 4.

12 When the oil has finished draining, clean the drain plug threads and those of the transmission casing, fit a new sealing washer and refit the drain plug, tightening it to the specified torque wrench setting. Refit the undercover (where fitted) then lower the vehicle to the ground.

13 Carefully prise off the breather cap from the top of the transmission casing, and then using a funnel, add the exact amount of transmission oil specified **(see illustrations)**.

14 Clean up any spilt oil, and then refit the breather cap.

15 Refit the battery tray and battery with reference to Chapter 5A, Section 4 if required.

3.3 Disconnect the end of the cable (arrowed)

3.4a Release the locking clips (arrowed) ...

ML6C transmissions

Note: *Transmissions from 03/06 have been modified; there are cooling fins under the transmission housing to help cooling* ***(see illustration 1.5)****. These later transmissions with cooling fins do not require as much oil. See specifications at the start of this Chapter.*

Note: *The oil level cannot be checked, as there is no level plug fitted. These transmissions do not require regular maintenance and are filled for life. If the transmission develops a leak or is removed for other work, the oil needs to be completely drained and refilled with the correct amount of oil. The transmission will then be refilled through the vent/ breather on the top of the transmission* ***(see illustration 2.13a)****.*

16 Follow the procedures for MA5 and BE4/5 transmissions (from RPO 9975), as described in paragraphs 11 to 15 above.

3 Gearchange lever and cables – removal, refitting and adjustment

Removal

1 Firmly apply the handbrake, and then jack up the front of the vehicle and support it on axle stands (see *Jacking and vehicle support*).

2 Remove the centre console as described in Chapter 11, Section 26.

3 Use a screwdriver to carefully lever the cable balljoints from the bottom of the gear lever assembly **(see illustration)**.

4 Pull out the retaining clips, and then release the outer cable from the bottom of the gear lever housing **(see illustrations)**.

5 Undo the four nuts securing the gearchange lever housing to the floor and manoeuvre the lever housing assembly from the vehicle **(see illustrations)**. The gearchange lever is integral with the housing, and is not available separately.

6 Working inside the engine compartment, remove the battery and battery tray, as described in Chapter 5A, Section 4.

7 Note their fitted locations, then carefully prise the two gearchange cable balljoints from

3.4b ... and lift the cables from the mounting bracket

3.5a Undo the gear lever housing mounting nuts (arrowed) ...

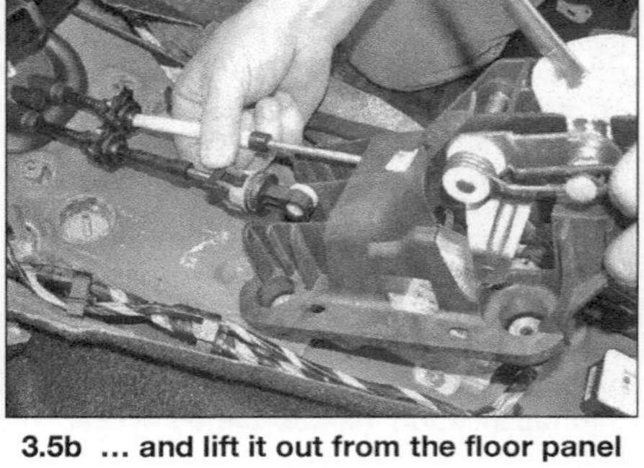

3.5b ... and lift it out from the floor panel

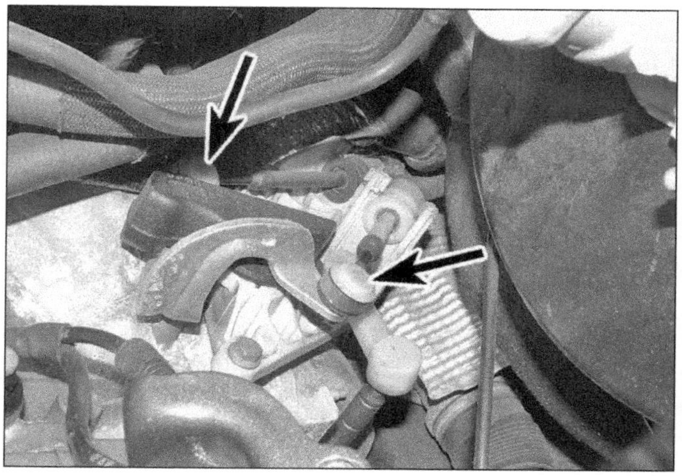

3.7 Prise the gearchange cables (arrowed) from their balljoints

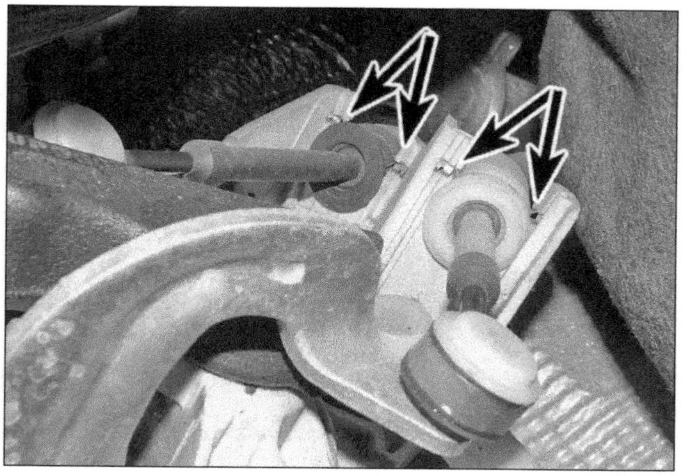

3.8 Release the locking clips (arrowed) and withdraw the cables

the selector levers on the transmission **(see illustration)**.

8 Using a small screwdriver, press down the two horseshoe-shaped retaining clips upper tangs, then lever or pull the outer cables upwards to release them from the support bracket on top of the transmission housing **(see illustration)**. Note the cables fitted position for refitting.

9 Release the cable sealing grommet from the floor, and manoeuvre the cables from the vehicle **(see illustration)**. Note on some models it may be necessary to remove the exhaust heat shield from under the vehicle to access the cable grommet.

Refitting

10 Refitting is a reversal of the removal procedure.

Adjustment

11 If not already done, remove the centre console as described in Chapter 11, Section 26.

12 Carefully prise the left-hand gear selector cable from the balljoint on the bottom of the gear lever **(see illustration)**.

13 Use a screwdriver to lever back the collar on the end of the gearchange cable to allow the orange locking clip to be withdrawn, locking the collar into position **(see illustrations)**. The gear selection cable is then in the adjustment position.

14 Using a plastic cable-tie, secure the gear lever spring in position, making sure the ends of the spring are up against the gear lever housing **(see illustration)**.

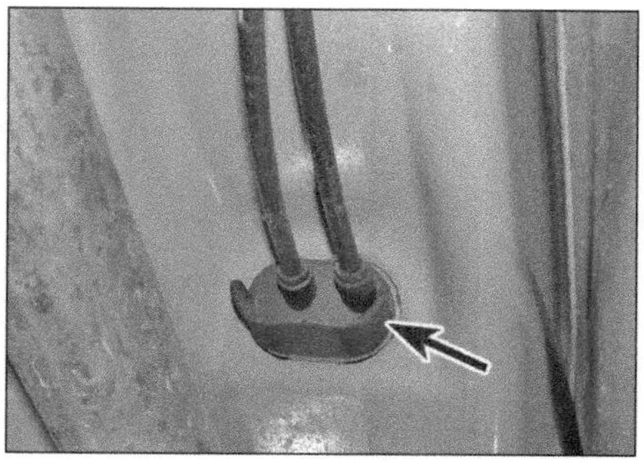

3.9 Gearchange cable rubber grommet (arrowed) fitted in floor panel

3.12 Using a screwdriver (arrowed) to lever the end of the cable off the balljoint

3.13a Keep the spring (arrowed) compressed ...

3.13b ... to allow for the locking clip (arrowed) to drop down ...

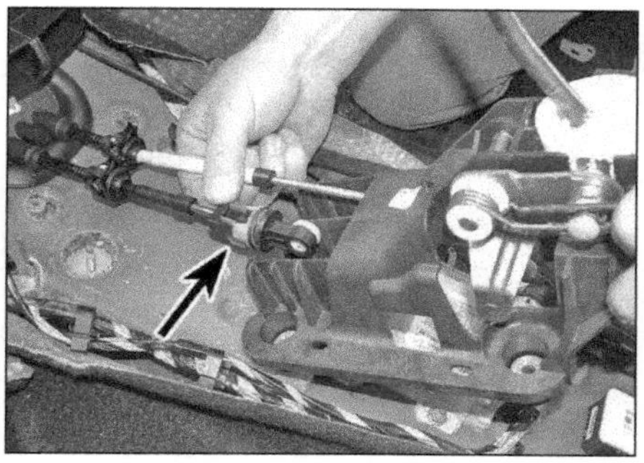

3.13c ... and keep the spring compressed

3.14 Secure the spring in place by using a cable-tie (arrowed)

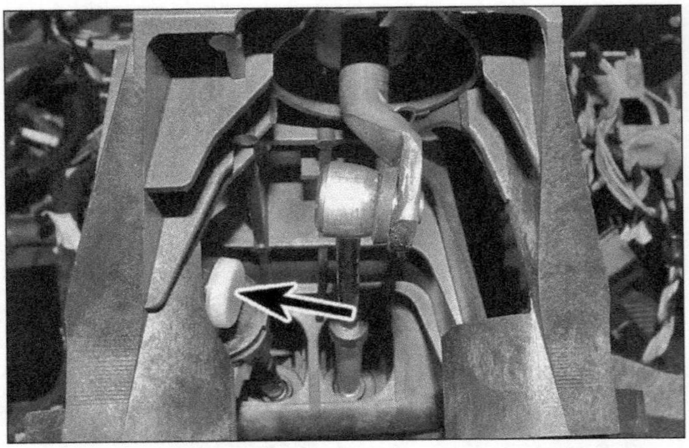

3.15 Prise the end of the gearchange cable (arrowed) from the balljoint

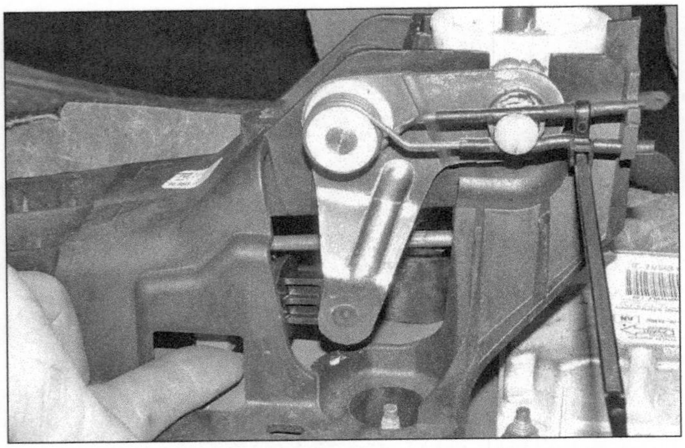

3.16 Press the locking clip upwards to reset the gearchange cable

15 With the spring secure, refit the gear selection cable balljoint back to the bottom of the gear lever **(see illustration)**.

16 Reach under the gear lever housing and push the orange locking clip upwards; the collar will then be released into the adjusted position **(see illustration)**.

17 Remove the plastic cable-tie from the gear lever spring/housing and check the operation of the gearchange lever. If all is satisfactory, refit the centre console.

4 Oil seals – renewal

Driveshaft oil seals

1 Remove the appropriate driveshaft as described in Chapter 8, Section 2.

All except left-hand side seal on ML6C transmissions

2 Carefully prise the oil seal out of the transmission, using a large flat-bladed screwdriver **(see illustration)**.

3 Remove all traces of dirt from the area around the oil seal aperture, then apply a smear of grease to the outer lip of the new oil seal. Fit the new seal into its aperture, and drive it squarely into position using a suitable tubular drift (such as a socket) which bears only on the hard outer edge of the seal until it abuts its locating shoulder. If the seal was supplied with a plastic protector sleeve, leave this in position until the driveshaft has been refitted **(see illustrations)**.

Left-hand side seal on ML6C transmissions

4 On the ML6C transmission, the passenger side oil seal is fitted to a thrust plate bolted to the differential casing **(see illustration)**.

5 Undo the four retaining bolts and remove the thrust plate, noting the fitted position of the oil seal. Remove the seal from the thrust plate **(see illustrations)**.

6 Remove all traces of dirt from around the thrust plate, and then apply a smear of grease

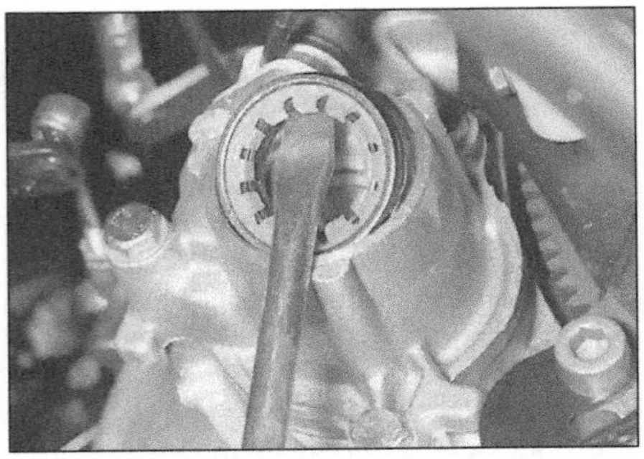

4.2 Use a large flat-bladed screwdriver to prise out the driveshaft oil seals

4.3a Fit the new seal to the transmission, noting the plastic seal protector ...

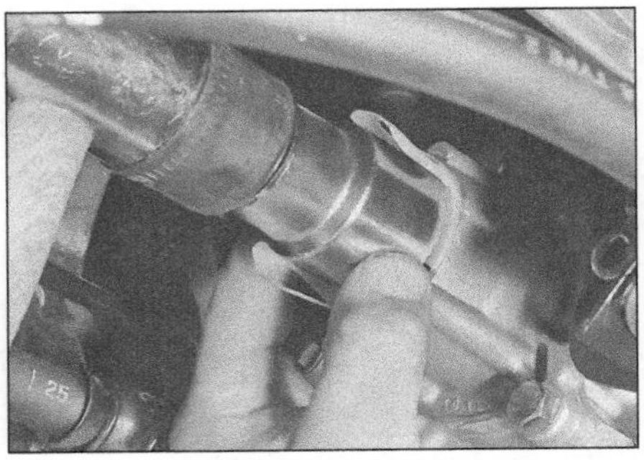

4.3b ... and tap it into position using a tubular drift/socket

4.4 Thrust plate (arrowed) on left-hand side of transmission

4.5a Remove the thrust plate from the transmission ...

4.5b ... and drift out the oil seal

4.6a Fit the new seal to the thrust plate ...

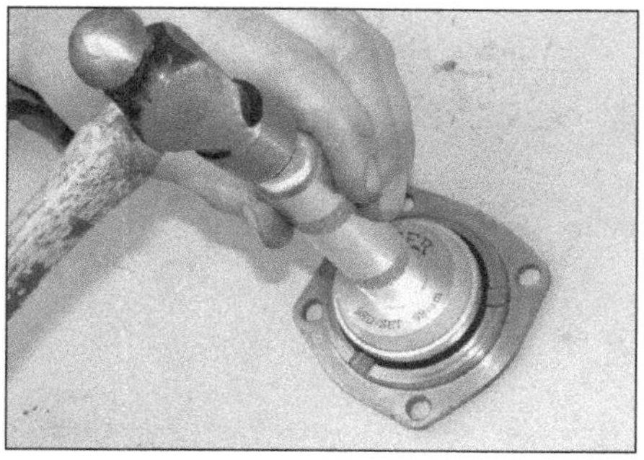

4.6b ... using a drift; make sure it is fitted squarely

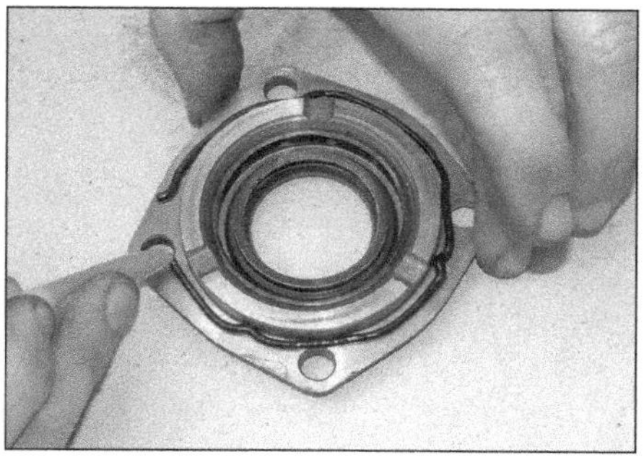

4.7 Apply a bead of sealant around the thrust plate

to the outer lip of the new oil seal. Fit the new seal into its aperture, and drive it squarely into position using a suitable tubular drift, which bears only on the hard outer edge of the seal, until it's located in the thrust plate to the position noted on removal **(see illustrations)**.

7 Apply a bead of sealant around the outer edge of the thrust plate, and then refit to the transmission casing **(see illustration).** Tighten the oil seal thrust plate bolts to the specified torque setting.

All oil seals

8 Apply a thin film of grease to the oil seal lip.

9 Refit the driveshaft as described in Chapter 8, Section 2.

Input shaft oil seal

Note: *On some transmission, the oil seal appears to be integral with the guide sleeve. Check with your Citroën parts specialist before removal.*

10 Remove the transmission as described in Section 7, and the clutch release mechanism as described in Chapter 6, Section 7.

11 Undo the three bolts (two bolts on some models) securing the clutch release bearing guide sleeve in position, and slide the guide off the input shaft, along with its sealing ring or gasket (as applicable) **(see illustrations)**. Recover any shims or thrustwashers, which have stuck to the rear of the guide sleeve, and refit them to the input shaft.

12 Where applicable, carefully lever the oil seal out of the guide using a suitable flat-bladed screwdriver **(see illustration)**.

13 Before fitting a new seal, check the input shaft's seal rubbing surface for signs of burrs, scratches or other damage, which may have caused the seal to fail in the first place. It may be possible to polish away minor faults of this sort using fine abrasive paper; however, more serious defects will require the renewal of the input shaft. Ensure that the input shaft is clean and greased, to protect the seal lips on refitting.

14 Where applicable, dip the new seal in clean oil, and fit it to the guide sleeve.

15 On transmissions where the seals are integral with the guide sleeve, lubricate the lips of the seal before refitting.

16 Fit a new sealing ring or gasket (as applicable) to the rear of the guide sleeve, then carefully slide the sleeve into position over the input shaft. Refit the retaining bolts and tighten them to the specified torque setting **(see illustration)**.

17 Take the opportunity to inspect the clutch components if not already done (Chapter 6, Section 6). Finally, refit the transmission as described in Section 7.

Selector shaft oil seal

MA5 transmissions

18 To renew the selector shaft oil seal on these models, the transmission must be dismantled. This task should therefore be entrusted to a Citroën dealer or transmission specialist.

BE4/5 transmissions

19 Park the car on level ground, apply the handbrake, slacken the left-hand front roadwheel bolts, then jack up the front of the vehicle and support it on axle stands (see *Jacking and vehicle support*). Remove the left-hand front roadwheel.

20 Using a large flat-bladed screwdriver, lever the link rod balljoint off the transmission selector shaft, and disconnect the link rod.

21 Using a large flat-bladed screwdriver, carefully prise the selector shaft seal out of the housing, and slide it off the end of the shaft.

22 Before fitting a new seal, check the selector shaft's seal rubbing surface for signs of burrs, scratches or other damage, which may have caused the seal to fail in the first place. It may be possible to polish away minor faults of this sort using fine abrasive paper; however, more serious defects will require the renewal of the selector shaft.

23 Apply a smear of grease to the new seal's outer edge and sealing lip, then carefully slide the seal along the selector rod. Press the seal fully into position in the transmission housing.

4.11a Undo the three bolts (arrowed) and remove the guide sleeve ...

4.11b ... and any shims, where fitted – BE4/5 transmission

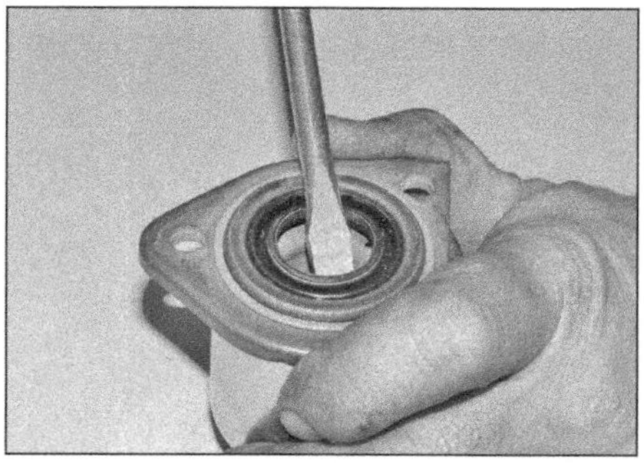

4.12 Remove the input shaft seal from the guide sleeve – BE4/5 transmission

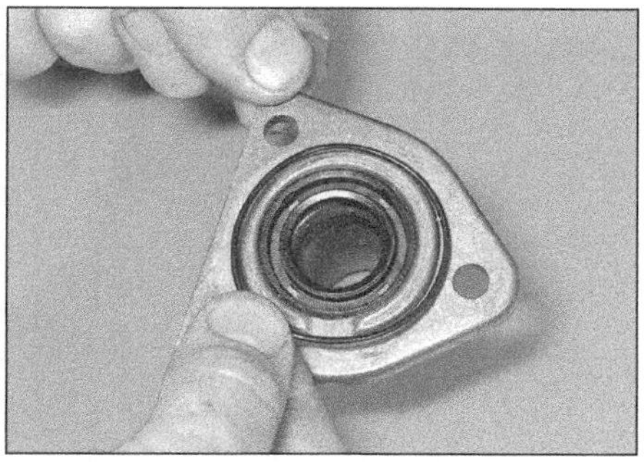

4.16 Fit a new O-ring/gasket (as applicable) to the guide sleeve – BE4/5 transmission

5.1a Location of reversing light switch – BE4/5 transmission

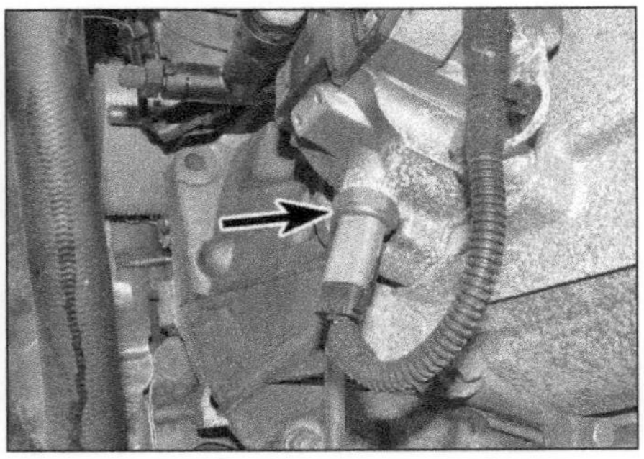

5.1b Location of reversing light switch – ML6C transmission

7.5 Remove the intercooler hose clips (arrowed) – turbo models

24 Refit the link rod to the selector shaft, ensuring that its balljoint is pressed firmly onto the shaft. Lower the car to the ground.

ML6C transmissions

25 To renew the selector shaft oil seal on these models, the transmission must be dismantled. This task should therefore be entrusted to a Citroën dealer or transmission specialist.

5 Reversing light switch – testing, removal and refitting

Testing

1 The reversing light circuit is controlled by a plunger-type switch, which is screwed into the front of the transmission housing **(see illustrations)**. If a fault develops, first ensure that the circuit fuse has not blown.

2 To test the switch, disconnect the wiring connector, and use a multimeter (set to the resistance function) or a battery-and-bulb test circuit to check that there is continuity between the switch terminals only when reverse gear is selected. If this is not the case, and there are no obvious breaks or other damage to the wires, the switch is faulty, and must be renewed.

Removal

3 Where necessary, to improve access to the switch, remove the air cleaner housing intake duct from the front left-hand side of the engine compartment (see Chapter 4A, Section 2 or Chapter 4B, Section 4).

4 Disconnect the wiring connector, and then unscrew the switch from the transmission casing along with its sealing washer.

Refitting

5 Fit a new sealing washer to the switch, then screw it back into position in the top of the transmission housing and tighten it to the specified torque setting. Refit the wiring plug, and test the operation of the circuit. Refit any components removed for access.

6 Speedometer drive – general information

The speedometer receives vehicle speed data from the engine management ECU, which is supplied by the wheel speed sensors and the ABS ECU.

7 Manual transmission – removal and refitting

Removal

1 Chock the rear wheels, then firmly apply the handbrake. Slacken both front roadwheel bolts. Jack up the front of the vehicle, and securely support it on axle stands (see *Jacking and vehicle support*). Remove both front roadwheels, and the plastic engine undershields.

2 Drain the transmission oil as described in Section 2, and then refit the drain and filler plugs (where applicable).

3 Remove both driveshafts as described in Chapter 8, Section 2.

4 In order to prevent any damage, remove the exhaust front flexible pipe as described in Chapter 4A, Section 15 or Chapter 4B, Section 18.

5 On turbocharged diesel engines, remove the air intake hoses from the top of the intercooler to prevent any damage as the engine is tilted to allow the transmission to be removed **(see illustration)**.

6 Remove the front bumper as described in Chapter 11, Section 6.

7 Undo the retaining bolts and remove the lower crossbeam from the front of the vehicle **(see illustration)**.

8 Undo the retaining bolts and remove the strengthener bar from across the front of the main subframe and the subframe side-member **(see illustration)**.

9 Remove the battery and battery tray as described in Chapter 5A, Section 4.

10 Remove the starter motor (Chapter 5A, Section 10).

11 On transmissions with external slave cylinders, detach the clutch slave cylinder from the front of the transmission as described in Chapter 6, Section 4. Note the slave cylinder can be moved to one side; there is no need to disconnect the fluid pipe from the cylinder.

12 On transmissions with integral release bearing/slave cylinder, disconnect the fluid supply pipe to the front of the transmission **(see illustration)**, as described in Chapter 6, Section 7. Plug the ends of the fluid pipes, to prevent dirt ingress.

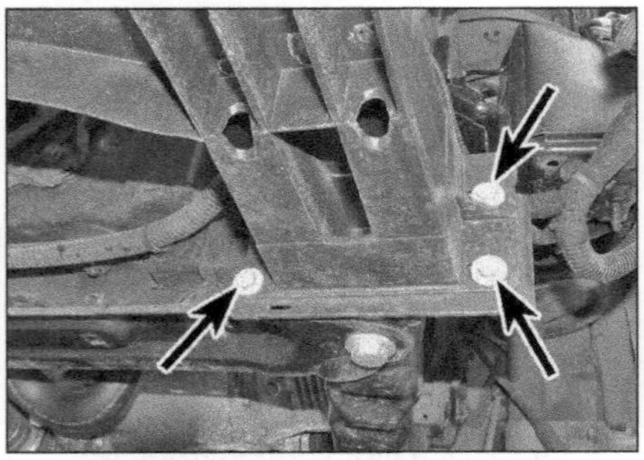

7.7 Front lower crossmember retaining bolts (arrowed)

7.8 Remove the front strengthener bar (arrowed)

7.12 Release the retaining clip (arrowed), to disconnect the fluid supply pipe

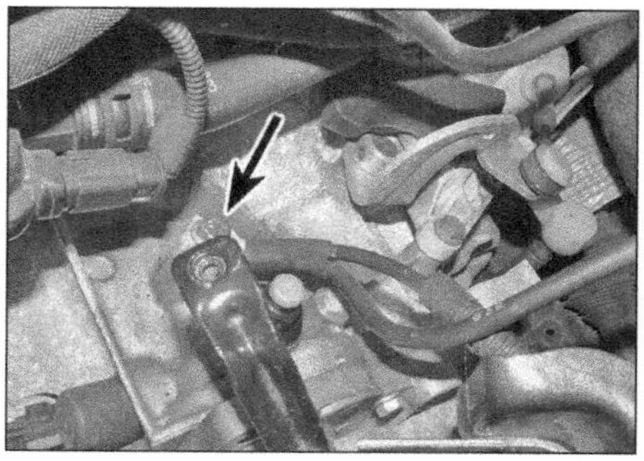

7.15 Disconnect the earth cable (arrowed) from the top of the transmission

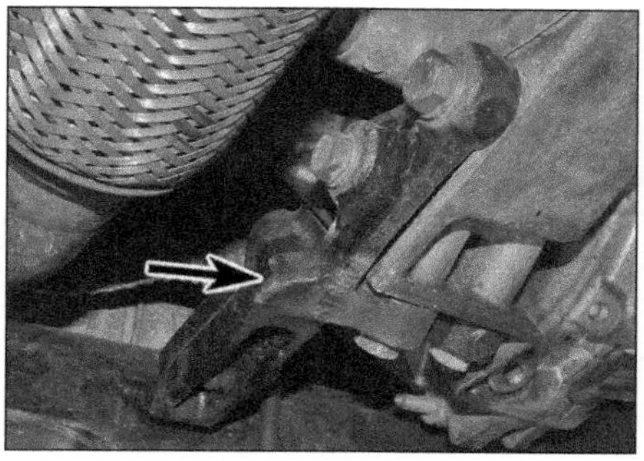

7.16 Remove the impact absorber (arrowed) from the transmission

7.20 Remove the transmission mounting – BE4/5 transmission shown

13 Disconnect the wiring connector from the reversing light switch on the upper front part of the transmission housing.
14 Disconnect the gearchange cables from the transmission and support bracket as described in Section 3.
15 Undo the retaining bolt and disconnect the earth cable from the top of the transmission housing **(see illustration)**.
16 Where fitted, undo the retaining bolts and remove the impact absorber from the rear of the differential casing **(see illustration)**.
17 Depending on model, there may be a lower cover plate fitted to the transmission. Where fitted, undo the retaining bolts, and remove the cover plate from the transmission.
18 Place a jack with a block of wood beneath the engine, to take the weight of the engine. Alternatively, attach a couple of lifting eyes to the engine, and fit a hoist or support bar to take the engine weight.
19 Place a jack and block of wood beneath the transmission, and raise the jack to take the weight of the transmission.
20 Slacken and remove the mounting bolts/nuts from the left-hand transmission mounting and remove it from the top of the transmission **(see illustration)**. Refer to Chapter 2A, 2B, 2C or 2D for further information on engine/transmission mountings.
21 Undo the retaining bolts and remove the mounting stud bracket from the top of the transmission housing.
22 Note their fitted positions, and then disconnect all wiring plugs/retaining clips from around the transmission. Note the harness routing and move the harness to one side.
23 With the jack positioned beneath the transmission taking the weight, slacken and remove the remaining bolts securing the transmission housing to the engine. Note the correct fitted positions of each bolt and the necessary brackets as they are removed, to use as a reference on refitting. With the nuts removed, slacken the studs from the top and front edge of the transmission, to allow for the removal of the transmission.
24 Make a final check that all components have been disconnected, and are positioned clear of the transmission so that they will not hinder the removal procedure.

Caution: As the engine is lowered, make sure no wiring, hoses or cables are being stretched or damaged in any way.

25 With the bolts/nuts removed, move the trolley jack and transmission to the left, to free it from its locating dowels. Lower the engine slightly to enable the transmission to be freed.

Caution: Take great care not to damage the radiator if the engine is moved – place a sheet of thick cardboard over the rear face of the radiator. On models equipped with air conditioning, care must also be taken to ensure the auxiliary drivebelt pulleys do not damage the air conditioning pipes on the right-hand side of the engine compartment.

26 Once the transmission is free, lower the jack and manoeuvre the unit out from under the car. Remove the locating dowels from the transmission or engine if they are loose, and keep them in a safe place.

Refitting

27 The transmission is refitted by a reversal of the removal procedure, bearing in mind the following points:

a) Prior to refitting, check the clutch assembly and release mechanism components (see Chapter 6, Section 6). Lubricate the release-bearing guide with a little high melting-point grease (Citroën recommend the use of Molykote BR2 Plus). Do not apply too much grease, otherwise there is a possibility of the grease contaminating the clutch friction disc, and ensure no grease is applied to the input shaft/friction disc splines.
b) Ensure that the locating dowels are correctly positioned prior to installation.
c) Tighten all nuts and bolts to the specified torque (where given).
d) Renew the driveshaft oil seals (Section 4), then refit the driveshafts (see Chapter 8, Section 2).
e) Refit the slave cylinder (see Chapter 6, Section 4).
f) On completion, refill the transmission with the specified type and quantity of lubricant, as described in Section 2.

8 Manual transmission overhaul – general information

1 Overhauling a manual transmission is a difficult and involved job for the DIY home mechanic. In addition to dismantling and reassembling many small parts, clearances must be precisely measured and, if necessary, changed by selecting shims and spacers. Internal transmission components are also often difficult to obtain, and in many instances, extremely expensive. Because of this, if the transmission develops a fault or becomes noisy, the best course of action is to have the unit overhauled by a specialist repairer, or to obtain an exchange reconditioned unit.
2 Nevertheless, it is not impossible for the more experienced mechanic to overhaul the transmission, provided the special tools are available, and the job is done in a deliberate step-by-step manner, so that nothing is overlooked.
3 The tools necessary for an overhaul include internal and external circlip pliers, bearing pullers, slide hammer, set of pin punches, dial test indicator, and possibly a hydraulic press. In addition, a large, sturdy workbench and a vice will be required.
4 During dismantling of the transmission, make careful notes of how each component is fitted, to make reassembly easier and more accurate.
5 Before dismantling the transmission, it will help if you have some idea what area is malfunctioning. Certain problems can be closely related to specific areas in the transmission, which can make component examination and renewal easier. Refer to *Fault finding* for more information.

Chapter 7 Part B:
Automatic transmission

Contents

Degrees of difficulty

Easy, suitable for novice with little experience	**Fairly easy,** suitable for beginner with some experience	**Fairly difficult,** suitable for competent DIY mechanic	**Difficult,** suitable for experienced DIY mechanic	**Very difficult,** suitable for expert DIY or professional

Specifications

General

Type:	
AL4	Automatic, four forward speeds and reverse
AM6	Automatic, six forward speeds and reverse

Lubrication

Capacity	See Chapter 1A or 1B
Recommended fluid	See *Lubricants and fluids*

Torque wrench settings

	Nm	lbf ft
AL4 transmissions		
Engine-to-transmission fixing bolts	Refer to Chapter 2A or 2B	
Engine/transmission mountings	Refer to Chapter 2A or 2B	
Fluid cooler centre bolt	42	31
Fluid drain plug	33	24
Fluid filler plug	24	18
Fluid level plug	10	7
Fluid pressure sensor bolts	9	7
Input shaft speed sensor bolt	10	7
Multifunction switch retaining bolts	10	7
Roadwheel bolts	90	66
Torque converter-to-driveplate nuts:		
Stage 1	10	7
Stage 2	30	22
AM6 transmission		
Electronic control unit retaining bolts	25	18
Engine-to-transmission fixing bolts	Refer to Chapter 2D	
Engine/transmission mountings	Refer to Chapter 2D	
Fluid cooler centre bolt	36	27
Fluid drain plug	47	35
Fluid filler plug	39	29
Fluid level plug	9	7
Roadwheel bolts	90	66
Selector lever nut	20	15
Torque converter-to-driveplate nuts:		
Stage 1	20	15
Stage 2	Slacken 100°	
Stage 3	30	22

1 General information

1 Certain models are offered with the option of a four- or six-speed electronically controlled automatic transmission, consisting of a torque converter, an epicyclic geartrain, and hydraulically operated clutches and brakes. The unit is controlled by the electronic control unit (ECU) via the electrically operated solenoid valves in the hydraulic block within the transmission unit. The transmission also has three optional driving modes: manual, sport and snow; the mode buttons are situated on the left-hand side of the selector lever and the mode indicator lights are incorporated in the instrument panel.

2 The normal mode is the standard mode for driving in which the transmission shifts up at relatively low engine speeds to combine reasonable performance with economy. If the transmission unit is switched into sport mode, the transmission will shift up only at high engine speeds, giving improved acceleration and overtaking performance. In snow mode, the transmission will select 2nd gear when the vehicle pulls away from a standing start; this helps maintain traction on slippery surfaces. In manual mode, the gears are selected by the driver, giving a sequential gearchange.

3 The torque converter provides a fluid coupling between the engine and transmission, which acts as an automatic clutch, and also provides a degree of torque multiplication when accelerating.

4 The epicyclic geartrain provides either of the four forward or one reverse gear ratios, according to which of its component parts are held stationary or allowed to turn. The components of the geartrain are held or released by brakes and clutches, which are controlled by the ECU via the electrically operated solenoid valves in the hydraulic unit. A fluid pump within the transmission provides the necessary hydraulic pressure to operate the brakes and clutches.

5 Driver control of the transmission is by a selector lever and a single cable that goes to the top of the transmission housing.

1.6a Use a screwdriver to release ...

1.6b ... the locking lever (arrowed), to move it out of P (park) position

The transmission has a 'drive' position that provides automatic changing throughout the range of all gear ratios, and is the one to select for normal driving. An automatic kickdown facility shifts the transmission down a gear if the accelerator pedal is fully depressed.

6 On most models, the selector lever is equipped with a shift-lock function. This prevents the selector lever being moved from the P position unless the brake pedal is depressed **(see illustrations)**.

7 Due to the complexity of the automatic transmission, any repair or overhaul work must be left to a Citroën dealer with the necessary special equipment for fault diagnosis and repair. The contents of the following Sections are therefore confined to supplying general information, and any service information and instructions that can be used by the owner.

Note: *The automatic transmission unit is of the 'auto-adaptive' type. This means that it takes into account your driving style and modifies the transmission shift points to provide optimum performance and economy to suit. When the battery is disconnected, the transmission will lose its memory and will resort to one of its many base shift programmes. The transmission will then relearn the optimum shift points when the vehicle is driven a few miles. During these first few miles of driving, there maybe a noticeable difference in performance whilst the transmission adapts to your individual style.*

2 Automatic transmission fluid – draining and refilling

Note: *A suitable square section wrench may be required to undo the transmission filler plug. These wrenches can be obtained from most motor factors or your Citroën dealer.*

Note: *The transmission unit is equipped with a fluid wear sensor to inform the driver when the fluid needs renewing (the ECU flashes the sport and snow mode indicator lights when fluid renewal is necessary). If the transmission unit is drained and refilled with new fluid, this sensor should be reset. This can only be done using the Citroën diagnostic equipment.*

Draining

1 This operation is much quicker and more efficient if the car is first taken on a journey of sufficient length to warm the engine/transmission up to normal operating temperature.

2 Park the car on level ground, switch off the ignition and apply the handbrake firmly. For improved access, jack up the front of the car and support it securely on axle stands (see *Jacking and vehicle support*). Undo the screws and remove the engine/transmission undershield (where fitted).

3 Position a suitable container under the drain plug, situated on the base of the transmission. Unscrew the drain plug and recover the sealing washer **(see illustrations)**. Allow the

2.3a On AL4 transmissions, remove the outer level plug (arrowed) ...

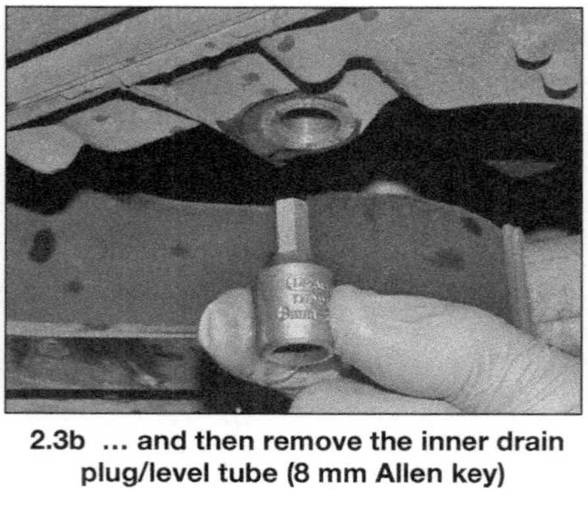

2.3b ... and then remove the inner drain plug/level tube (8 mm Allen key)

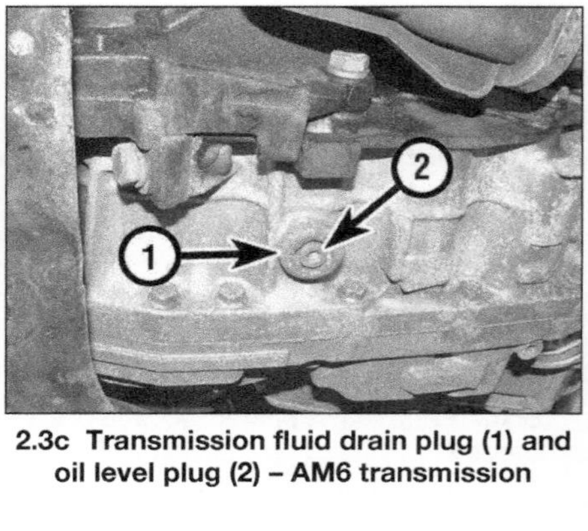

2.3c Transmission fluid drain plug (1) and oil level plug (2) – AM6 transmission

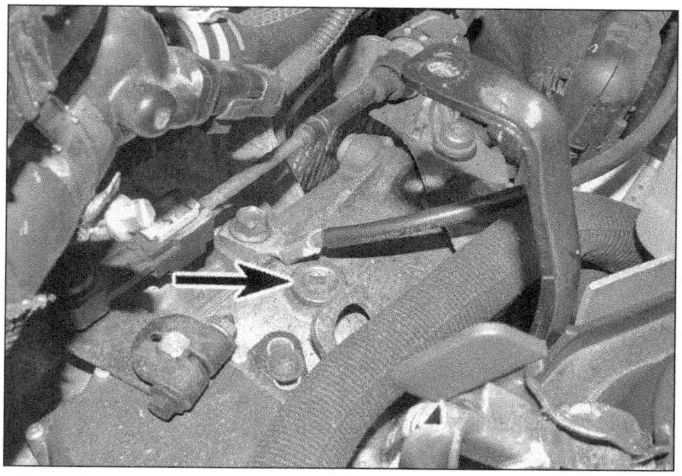

2.7a Transmission fluid filler plug (arrowed) – AL4 transmission

2.7b Transmission fluid filler plug (arrowed) – AM6 transmission

fluid to drain completely into the container. **Note:** *On AM6 transmissions the drain/level plug is in two parts, the smaller plug in the centre of the drain plug is the level plug. On AL4 transmissions the drain/level plug is also in two parts, the first plug with an 8 mm square drive is the level plug, and then inside the housing is the second part of the plug (8 mm Allen key), which is the drain plug – see Chapter 1A, Section 23 or Chapter 1B, Section 23.*

Warning: If the fluid is hot, take precautions against scalding.

4 Clean the drain plug, being especially careful to wipe off any metallic particles. Discard the sealing washer; it should be renewed whenever it is disturbed.

5 When the fluid has finished draining, clean the drain plug threads and those of the transmission casing, fit a new sealing washer and refit the drain plug, tightening it to the specified torque wrench setting. If the car was raised for the draining operation, now lower it to the ground.

Refilling

6 To improve access to the filler plug, remove air cleaner ducting (Chapter 4A, Section 2 or Chapter 4B, Section 4), and the battery and battery tray as described in Chapter 5A, Section 4.

7 Wipe clean the area around the filler plug, which is situated directly behind the transmission selector lever **(see illustrations)**. Unscrew the filler plug from the transmission and recover the sealing washer.

8 Carefully refill the transmission with the correct amount of the specified type of fluid. Fit the new sealing washer to the filler plug then refit the plug, tightening it to the specified torque. Refit the battery and tray (see Chapter 5A, Section 4) and air cleaner ducting (Chapter 4A, Section 2 or Chapter 4B, Section 4).

9 Take the vehicle on a short journey to warm the transmission up to normal operating temperature.

10 On your return, check the transmission fluid level as described in Chapter 1A, Section 23 or Chapter 1B, Section 23.

3 Selector cable – adjustment

1 To gain access to the transmission end of the selector cable, remove the battery and battery tray as described in Chapter 5A, section 4.

AL4 transmissions

2 Position the selector lever firmly against its detent in the P (park) position.

3 Unclip the yellow plastic part on the end of the cable end fitting to unlock the adjustment system **(see illustration)**.

4 Ensure that the selector lever on top of the transmission is fully forward, then press the yellow clip back into the end of the selector cable, to lock it in position.

5 Check the operation of the selector lever before refitting the battery tray and battery (see Chapter 5A, Section 4).

AM6 transmissions

6 Position the selector lever in the N (neutral) position.

7 Unclip the yellow plastic part on the end of the cable end fitting to unlock the adjustment system **(see illustration)**.

8 Ensure that the selector lever on top of the transmission is in the N (neutral) position **(see illustration)**, and then press the yellow clip back into the end of the selector cable, to lock it in position.

9 Check the operation of the selector lever before refitting the battery tray and battery (see Chapter 5A, Section 4).

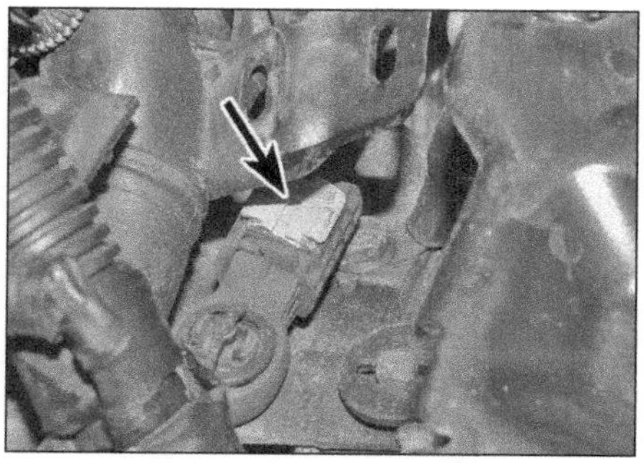

3.3 Prise up the cable locking catch (arrowed) – AL4 transmission

3.7 Prise up the cable locking catch (arrowed) – AM6 transmission

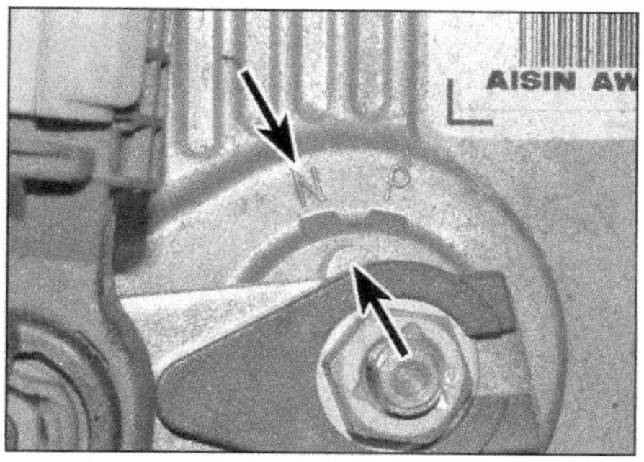

3.8 Ensure that the transmission lever shaft lug is aligned with the N on the casing (arrowed)

4.3a Squeeze the securing clips ...

4.3b ... to release the cable balljoint

4.4a Pull back on the locating peg (arrowed) ...

4 Selector lever and cable – removal and refitting

Removal

1 Firmly apply the handbrake, and then jack up the front of the vehicle and support it on axle stands (see *Jacking and vehicle support*). Position the selector lever in the P position.

2 To gain access to the transmission end of the selector cable, remove the battery and battery box/tray as described in Chapter 5A, Section 4.

3 Unclip the selector cable end fitting from the balljoint on the transmission lever **(see illustrations)**.

4 Release the outer cable sleeve from the mounting bracket on the top of the transmission housing, by pulling out the locking pin, and then lifting the cable from its location **(see illustrations)**.

5 Working inside the vehicle, remove the centre console as described in Chapter 11, Section 26.

6 To give better access, carefully pull the plastic rear air vent ducting from place **(see illustration)**.

7 Note their fitted positions and disconnect all wiring plugs from the lever housing **(see illustration)**.

8 Release the securing clips and then remove the selector cable end fitting from the balljoint on the lever **(see illustration)**.

9 Release the outer cable sleeve from the gear lever mounting bracket by pulling out the locking pin, and then lifting the cable from its location **(see illustrations 4.4a and 4.4b)**.

10 Release the cable sealing grommet from the floor, and manoeuvre the cable from the vehicle. Note on some models it may be necessary to remove the exhaust heat shield from under the vehicle, before removing the gearchange cable and grommet.

11 If required, pull the gear knob from the top of the lever and unclip the trim panel from the top of the gear lever housing **(see illustrations)**. Note the gear knob is a very tight fit on the lever; take care of injuries when removing, as the plastic sleeve on the lever has sharp edges.

12 Undo the four nuts and manoeuvre the lever housing out from inside the vehicle.

Refitting

13 Refitting is the reverse of removal, noting the following points.

a) Support the transmission selector lever when pressing the cable onto its balljoint to prevent the lever being bent.

b) Adjust the cable as described in Section 3 before refitting all components removed for access.

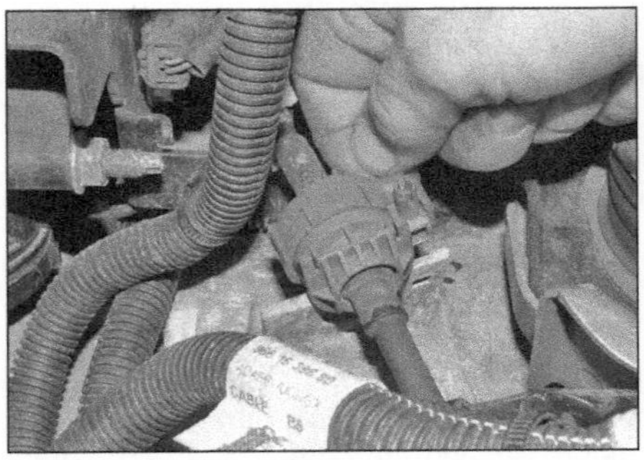
4.4b ... to release the outer cable from the transmission housing

4.6 Unclip the heater air vent ducting

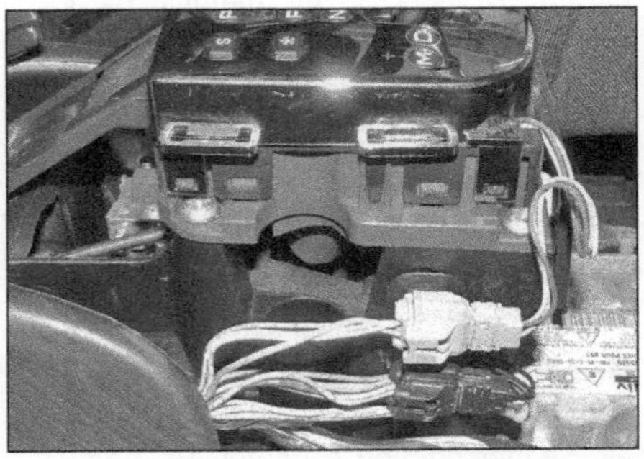
4.7 Disconnect the wiring connectors on the gear lever housing

4.8 Squeeze the securing clips to release the cable balljoint

4.11a Pull the gear knob from the lever ...

4.11b ... then unclip the trim panel from the top of the housing

5 Speedometer drive – general information

The transmissions fitted to the engines in this workshop manual do not have a speedometer drive pinion fitted. On AM6 transmissions, the speedometer receives vehicle speed data from the engine management ECU, which is supplied by the wheel speed sensors and the ABS ECU. On AL4 transmissions, the speedometer receives vehicle speed data from a sensor fitted to the rear left-hand side of the transmission housing (see Section 8).

6 Oil seals – renewal

Driveshaft oil seals

Note: *The procedure for renewing the driveshaft oil seals on automatic transmissions is similar to manual transmissions, see illustrations in Chapter 7A, Section 4 for further information.*

1 Remove the appropriate driveshaft as described in Chapter 8, Section 2.

Right-hand seal

2 Remove the O-ring from the differential sun gear shaft then carefully remove the oil seal from of the transmission, taking care not to damage the shaft or housing. To remove the seal, carefully punch or drill two small holes opposite each other into the seal. Screw a self-tapping screw into each hole and pull on the screws to extract the seal.

3 Remove all traces of dirt from the area around the oil seal aperture, then apply a smear of grease to the outer edge and sealing lip of the new oil seal. Ease the new seal onto the shaft and into its aperture, taking care not to damage its lip. Drive the seal squarely into position using a suitable tubular drift (such as a socket), which bears only on the hard outer edge of the seal.

4 Once the seal is correctly installed, fit a new O-ring to the sun gear shaft and slide along until it abuts the seal.

5 Refit the driveshaft as described in Chapter 8, Section 2.

Left-hand seal

6 Carefully prise the oil seal out of the transmission, using a large flat-bladed screwdriver.

7 Remove all traces of dirt from the area around the oil seal aperture, then apply a smear of grease to the outer lip of the new oil seal. Fit the new seal into its aperture, and drive it squarely into position using a suitable tubular drift (such as a socket), which bears only on the hard outer edge of the seal until it abuts its locating shoulder. If the seal was supplied with a plastic protector sleeve, leave this in position until the driveshaft has been refitted.

8 Apply a thin film of grease to the oil seal lip.

9 Refit the driveshaft as described in Chapter 8, Section 2.

Selector shaft oil seal

Note: *Citroën use special tools to remove (tool No 0338-N1/N2) and refit (tool No 0338-K) the selector shaft oil seal; we were able to renew the seal without the Citroën tool as follows.*

10 To gain access to the transmission selector shaft, remove the battery and battery tray as described in Chapter 5A, Section 4.

11 Position the selector lever firmly against its detent mechanism in the P position.

12 Slacken and remove the nut and clamp bolt securing the selector lever to the transmission shaft **(see illustration)**. Make alignment marks between the shaft and lever then free the lever from the shaft.

13 If required, remove the retaining clip and free the selector cable from transmission bracket **(see illustration 4.4a and 4.4b)**. Position the cable clear of the selector shaft.

14 Make alignment marks between the multifunction switch and transmission unit then unscrew the retaining bolts and remove the switch **(see illustration)**.

15 Carefully remove the oil seal from the transmission, taking care not to damage the shaft or housing. To remove the seal, carefully punch or drill two small holes opposite each other into the seal. Screw a self-tapping screw into each hole and pull on the screws to extract the seal.

16 Remove all traces of dirt from the area around the oil seal aperture, then apply a smear of grease to the outer edge and sealing lip of the new oil seal. Ease the new seal onto the shaft, taking care not to damage its lip, and press it squarely into its aperture.

17 Locate the multifunction switch back on the selector shaft. Align the marks made prior to removal then refit the switch bolts, tightening them to the specified torque.

18 Seat the selector cable in the transmission bracket and engage the selector lever with the transmission shaft. Ensure the marks made on removal are correctly aligned then refit the lever clamp bolt and nut and tighten securely.

19 Secure the selector cable in position with the retaining clip then adjust the cable as described in Section 3.

20 Refit all components removed for access.

Torque converter seal

21 Remove the transmission unit as described in Section 9.

22 Carefully slide the torque converter off the transmission shaft whilst being prepared for fluid spillage.

23 Note the correct fitted position of the seal in the housing then carefully lever it out of position, taking care not to mark the housing or shaft.

24 Remove all traces of dirt from the area

6.12 Unscrew the nut and clamp bolt (arrowed) and free the selector lever from the transmission shaft

6.14 Multifunction switch retaining screws (arrowed)

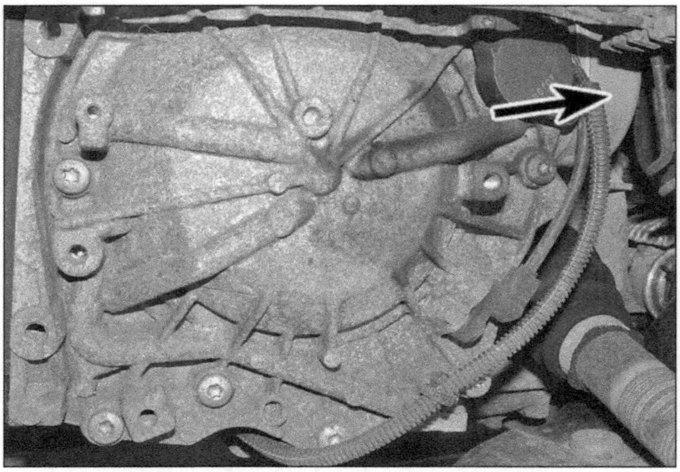

7.2 Fluid cooler (arrowed) – AL4 transmission

7.3 Fluid cooler (arrowed) – AM6 transmission

around the oil seal aperture. Ease the new seal into its aperture, ensuring its sealing lip is facing inwards, then press it squarely into position.

25 Engage the torque converter with the transmission shaft splines and slide it into position, taking care not to damage the oil seal.

26 Refit the transmission unit as described in Section 9.

7 Fluid cooler – removal and refitting

Caution: Be careful not to allow dirt into the transmission unit during this procedure.

Removal

1 To gain access to the fluid cooler, chock the rear wheels jack up the front of the vehicle and support it on axle stands (see *Jacking and vehicle support*). Remove the engine undershield and, on AL4 transmissions, remove the left-hand front wheel and inner wheel arch liner.

2 On AL4 transmissions, the fluid cooler is mounted on the rear of the transmission housing **(see illustration)**. Remove the battery and battery box as described in Chapter 5A, Section 4.

3 On AM6 transmissions, the fluid cooler is mounted on the front of the transmission housing **(see illustration)**. Remove the air cleaner intake ducting from the front left-hand corner of the engine compartment (refer to Chapter 4B, Section 4).

4 Remove all traces of dirt from around the fluid cooler before proceeding.

5 Using a hose clamp or similar, clamp both the fluid cooler coolant hoses to minimise coolant loss during subsequent operations.

6 Release the retaining clips, and disconnect both coolant hoses from the fluid cooler – be prepared for some coolant spillage **(see illustrations)**. Wash off any spilt coolant immediately with cold water, and dry the surrounding area before proceeding further.

7 On AM6 transmissions, it may be necessary to drain the transmission, as the fluid cooler is fitted to the lower part of the transmission housing. Be prepared for any spilt fluid as the cooler is removed.

8 Slacken and remove the fluid cooler centre bolt, and remove the cooler from the transmission. Remove the seal from the centre bolt, and the two seals fitted to the rear of the cooler, and discard them; new ones must be used on refitting **(see illustration)**.

Refitting

9 Lubricate the new seals with clean automatic transmission fluid, then fit the two new seals to the rear of the fluid cooler, and a new seal to the centre bolt.

10 Locate the fluid cooler on the transmission housing then refit the centre bolt. Ensure the cooler is correctly positioned then tighten the centre bolt to the specified torque setting. Note that on AM6 transmission, the tab at the top of the fluid cooler must align between the two notches on the transmission casing.

11 Reconnect the coolant hoses to the fluid cooler, and secure them in position with their retaining clips. Remove the hose clamps.

12 On AM6 transmissions, refill the automatic transmission fluid as described in Section 2, if required.

13 Refit the battery, intake ducting, wheel arch liner and roadwheel as applicable.

14 Top-up the cooling system as described in *Weekly checks* and check the transmission unit fluid level as described in Chapter 1A, Section 23 or Chapter 1B, Section 23.

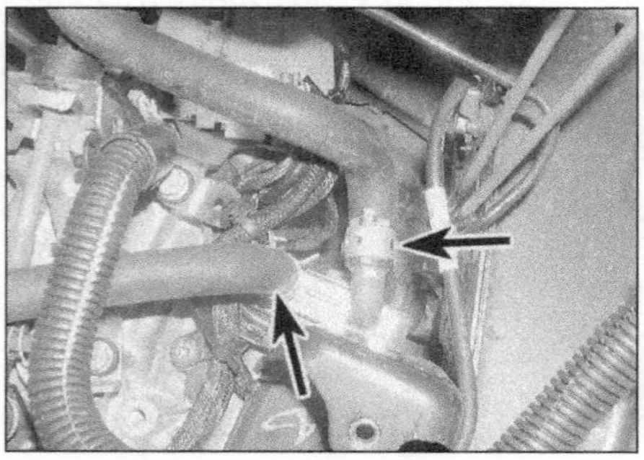

7.6a Disconnect the fluid cooler hoses (arrowed) – AL4 transmission

7.6b Disconnect the fluid cooler hoses (arrowed) – AM6 transmission

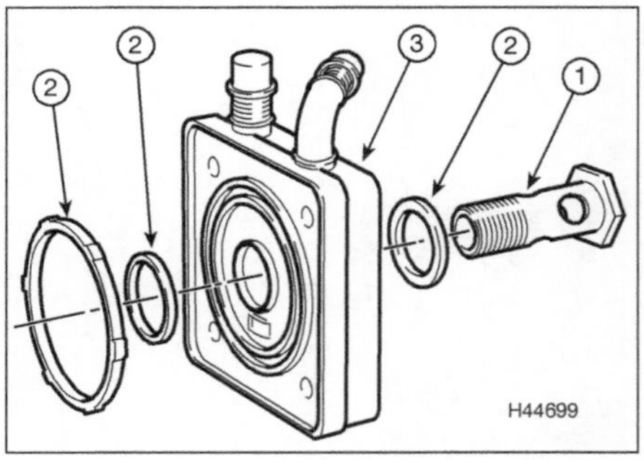

7.8 Fluid cooler – AL4 transmission

1 Bolt 2 Seals 3 Fluid cooler

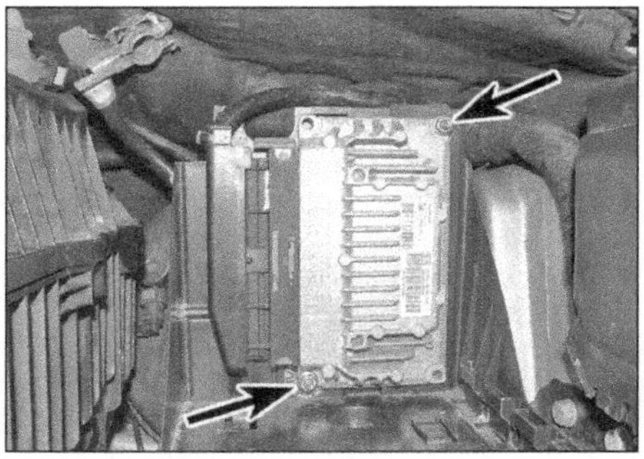

8.2a Undo the two retaining nuts ...

8.2b ... and remove the ECU from the rear of the battery tray

8.3 Slide out the locking catch to disconnect the wiring plug from the ECU

8 Transmission control system components – removal and refitting

AL4 transmissions

Electronic control unit (ECU)

Note: *The automatic transmission electronic control system relies on accurate communication between the engine management ECU and the automatic transmission ECU. If either ECU is renewed, then both ECUs must be 'initialised'. The initialisation procedure requires access to specialised electronic test equipment and so it is recommended that this operation be entrusted to a suitably-equipped Citroën dealer or specialist.*

1 Remove the battery as described in Chapter 5A, Section 4.

2 Undo the two mounting nuts and remove the ECU from the mounting plate **(see illustrations)**.

3 Slide out the locking catch and disconnect the wiring connector from the ECU **(see illustration)**.

4 Refitting is the reverse of removal, ensuring the wiring connector is securely reconnected.

Multifunction switch

Note: *The multifunction switch is slotted to allow for adjustment. Accurate adjustment requires the use an accurate multimeter – see the text later in this Section.*

5 Remove the air cleaner ducting from the front left-hand corner of the engine compartment as described in Chapter 4A, Section 2. If required, for better access, remove the battery and tray as described in Chapter 5A, Section 4.

6 Fully apply the handbrake, then turn on the ignition and place the selector lever in position N. Turn off the ignition and wait 15 mins, then disconnect the battery negative terminal.

7 Slacken and remove the nut and clamp bolt securing the selector lever to the transmission shaft **(see illustration 6.12)**. Make alignment marks between the shaft and lever then free the lever from the shaft.

8 Remove the retaining clip and free the selector cable from transmission bracket. Position the cable clear of the selector shaft.

9 Unscrew the two bolts and free the main wiring connector from the transmission unit **(see illustration)**. Cut the cable-tie securing the wiring to the connector cover then release the clips and slide the cover off the connector.

10 Trace the wiring back from the switch to the main wiring connector, freeing it from all the relevant retaining clips and ties. Carefully release the retaining clips then slide the 12-way connector out from the rear of the main connector, noting which way around it is fitted.

11 Make accurate alignment marks between the multifunction switch and transmission unit then unscrew the retaining bolts and remove the switch **(see illustration)**.

12 If required, fit new seal to transmission housing as described in Section 6.

13 Locate the multifunction switch back on the selector shaft. Align the marks made prior to removal then refit the switch bolts, tightening them to the specified torque.

14 Clip the wiring back into the main wiring connector, ensuring it is fitted the right way around. Slide the cover back onto the main connector, ensuring it is clipped securely in position, and secure the wiring to the cover with a new cable-tie. Locate the connector on the transmission unit and securely tighten its retaining bolts.

15 Reconnect the main wiring connector to the transmission unit.

16 Seat the selector cable in the transmission bracket and engage the selector lever with the transmission shaft. Ensure the marks made on removal are correctly aligned then refit the lever clamp bolt and nut, and tighten securely.

17 Secure the selector cable in position with the retaining clip, and then adjust the cable as described in Section 3, and the multifunction switch as described in the following paragraphs.

18 Slacken the switch mounting bolts and rotate the switch fully anti-clockwise as far as it will go.

19 Set the multimeter to measure ohms, and connect the meter terminals to the external switch contacts **(see illustration)**.

20 Slowly rotate the switch clockwise until the switch contacts close (the meter should register zero ohms – no resistance).

21 In this position, make an alignment mark between the switch and the transmission casing.

8.9 Transmission main wiring loom connection (arrowed)

8.11 Mark the position of the retaining screw in the elongated hole for refitting

8.19 Terminals (arrowed) to check resistance of switch

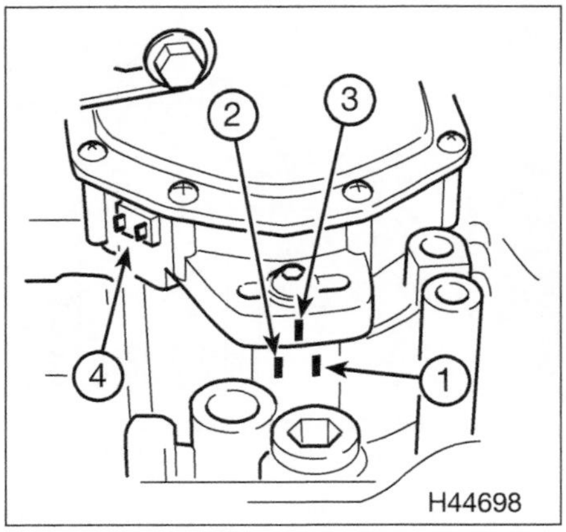

8.23 Multifunction switch adjustment

1 *1st alignment mark*
2 *2nd alignment mark*
3 *Switch body alignment mark*
4 *Switch external contacts*

22 Continue to rotate the switch clockwise until the contacts open (the meter should register infinite ohms or similar)

23 Make another alignment mark between the transmission casing and the mark made previously on the switch **(see illustration)**.

24 Rotate the switch until the alignment mark on the switch body is exactly halfway between the two marks made on the transmission casing. Tighten the switch mounting bolts to the specified torque.

25 Refit the air cleaner assembly as described in Chapter 4A, Section 2.

26 Check the selector lever operation and road test.

Fluid pressure sensor

Caution: Be careful not to allow dirt into the transmission unit during this procedure.

27 The fluid pressure sensor is located on the base of the transmission unit.

28 To gain access to the sensor, chock the rear wheels, firmly apply the handbrake then jack up the front of the vehicle and securely support it on axle stands (see *Jacking and vehicle support*).

29 Remove the air cleaner assembly as described in Chapter 4A, Section 2.

30 Unscrew the two bolts and free the main wiring connector from the rear of the transmission unit **(see illustration 8.9)**. Cut the cable-tie securing the wiring to the connector cover then release the clips and slide the cover off the connector.

31 Trace the wiring back from the sensor being removed to the main wiring connector, freeing it from all the relevant retaining clips and ties. Carefully release the retaining clips then slide the green 3-way sensor connector out from the rear of the main connector, noting which way around it is fitted.

32 Wipe clean the area around the sensor. Slacken and remove the retaining bolts then remove the sensor, along with its sealing ring **(see illustration)**. Discard the sealing ring; a new one must be used on refitting. Be prepared for fluid spillage, and plug the opening to minimise fluid loss.

8.32 The fluid pressure sensor is secured to the base of the transmission by two screws (arrowed)

33 Refitting is the reverse of removal, noting the following points.

a) *Fit a new sealing ring to the sensor and tighten the sensor bolts to the specified torque.*
b) *Ensure the sensor wiring is correctly routed and retained by all the necessary clips and ties.*
c) *Clip the sensor wiring back into the main wiring connector, ensuring it is fitted the right way around. Slide the cover back onto the main connector, ensuring it is clipped securely in position, and secure the wiring to the cover with a new cable-tie.*
d) *On completion, check the transmission fluid level as described in Chapter 1A, Section 23.*

Input shaft speed sensor

Caution: Be careful not to allow dirt into the transmission unit during this procedure.

34 The input shaft speed sensor is located on the left-hand end of the transmission unit, above the left-hand driveshaft.

35 To gain access to the sensor, chock the rear wheels jack up the front of the vehicle and support it on axle stands (see *Jacking and vehicle support*). Remove the engine undershield, left-hand front wheel and inner wheel arch liner.

36 Unscrew the two bolts and free the main wiring connector from the rear of the transmission unit **(see illustration 8.9)**. Cut the cable-tie securing the wiring to the connector cover then release the clips and slide the cover off the connector.

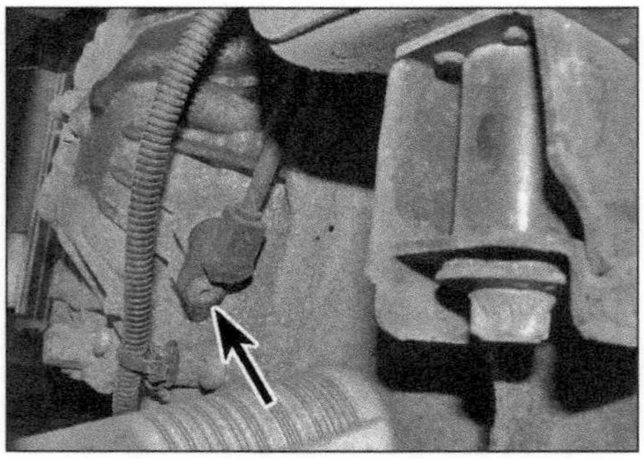

8.38a Input shaft speed sensor securing bolt (arrowed)

37 Trace the wiring back from the sensor being removed to the main wiring connector, freeing it from all the relevant retaining clips and ties. Carefully release the retaining clips then slide the yellow 3-way sensor connector out from the rear of the main connector, noting which way around it is fitted.

38 Wipe clean the area around the sensor **(see illustrations)**. Slacken and remove the retaining bolt then remove the sensor, along with its sealing ring. Discard the sealing ring; a new one must be used on refitting.

39 Refitting is the reverse of removal, noting the following points.

a) *Fit a new sealing ring to the sensor and tighten the sensor bolt to the specified torque.*
b) *Ensure the sensor wiring is correctly routed and retained by all the necessary clips and ties.*
c) *Clip the sensor wiring back into the main wiring connector, ensuring it is fitted the right way around. Slide the cover back onto the main connector, ensuring it is clipped securely in position, and secure the wiring to the cover with a new cable-tie. Secure the connector to the transmission unit with the retaining bolts.*
d) *On completion, check the transmission fluid level as described in Chapter 1A, Section 23.*

AM6 transmissions

Electronic control unit (ECU)

Note: *The automatic transmission electronic control system relies on accurate communication between the engine management ECU and the automatic transmission ECU. If either ECU is renewed, then both ECUs must be 'initialised'. The initialisation procedure requires access to specialised electronic test equipment and so it is recommended that this operation be*

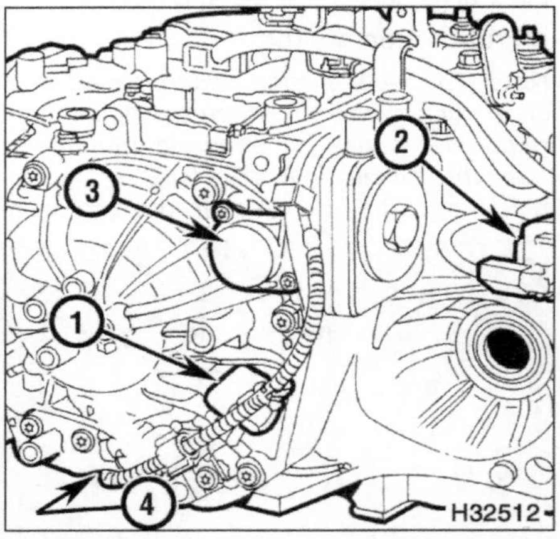

8.38b Sensor locations – AL4 transmission

1 *Input speed sensor*
2 *Output speed sensor*
3 *Fluid cooler flow control solenoid*
4 *Line pressure sensor*

8.43 Disconnect the gearchange cable

8.44a Release the securing clip ...

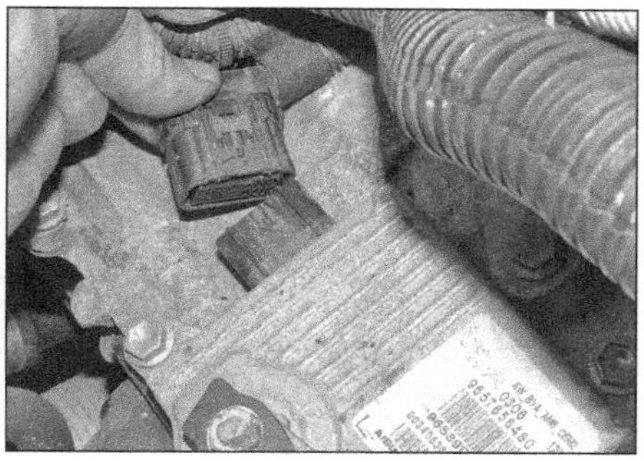

8.44b ... and disconnect the wiring connector

entrusted to a suitably-equipped Citroën dealer or specialist.

40 Remove the air cleaner ducting from the front left-hand corner of the engine compartment as described in Chapter 4B, Section 4.

41 Fully apply the handbrake, then turn on the ignition and place the selector lever in position N. Turn off the ignition and wait 15 minutes, then disconnect the battery negative terminal.

42 Squeeze together the side of the clip and pull the end of the selector cable from the balljoint on the transmission lever.

Caution: Support the selector rod and lever when slackening or tightening the securing nut, as damage can occur to the slide valve in the hydraulic block.

43 Release the securing clip and disconnect the gear selector cable from the control unit **(see illustration)**.

44 Disconnect the wiring plug connector from the control unit **(see illustrations)**.

45 Undo the 3 retaining bolts, and lift the control unit straight upwards and over the end of the selector shaft, disconnecting the control unit from the transmission internal connections as it's withdrawn **(see illustration)**.

46 If required, fit new selector seal to transmission housing as described in Section 6.

47 Check the condition of the electrical connections in the top of the transmission housing. Make sure the locating tab on the connector is secured in the notch on the transmission casing.

48 When the control unit is refitted to the top of the transmission, check the selector rod is in the neutral position **(see illustration 3.8)**, and the dot on the selector shaft is aligned with the arrow on the control unit casing.

49 With the control unit in the correct position, ensure the locating notch fits over the lug on the casing. Tighten the control unit retaining bolts to the specified torque setting.

50 The refitting is a reversal of removal. Note that if a new control unit has been fitted, it must be programmed and matched to the engine management control unit using Citroën diagnostic equipment. Entrust this task to a Citroën dealer or suitably-equipped specialist. Even after reprogramming/matching, the vehicle should be taken on an extensive road test, on a route that will allow numerous gearchanges and full use of the transmission mode settings. Initially, transmission response and gearchange quality may be less than acceptable, but should improve as the ECU control circuitry adapts to the transmission parameters.

9 Automatic transmission – removal and refitting

Removal

1 Chock the rear wheels, then firmly apply the handbrake. Slacken both front roadwheel bolts. Jack up the front of the vehicle, and securely support it on axle stands (see *Jacking and vehicle support*). Remove both front roadwheels.

2 Drain the transmission fluid as described in Section 2, and then fit a new sealing washer and tighten the drain plug to the specified torque setting.

3 Remove both driveshafts as described in Chapter 8, Section 2.

4 In order to prevent any damage, remove the exhaust front flexible pipe as described in Chapter 4A, Section 15 or Chapter 4B, Section 18.

5 Remove the air cleaner ducting from the front left-hand corner of the engine compartment as described in Chapter 4A, Section 2 or Chapter 4B, Section 4.

6 Remove the front bumper as described in Chapter 11, Section 6.

7 Undo the retaining bolts and remove the lower crossbeam from the front of the vehicle **(see illustration)**.

8 Undo the retaining bolts and remove the strengthener bar from across the front of the main subframe and the subframe side-member **(see illustration)**.

9 Remove the battery and battery tray as described in Chapter 5A, Section 4.

10 Remove the automatic transmission ECU as described in Section 8.

11 Remove the starter motor (Chapter 5A, Section 10).

12 Unclip the selector cable end fitting off the balljoint on the transmission lever. Release the securing clip then free the outer cable sleeve from its bracket and position it clear of the transmission unit **(see illustrations 4.4a and 4.4b)**.

13 Drain the cooling system or, using a hose

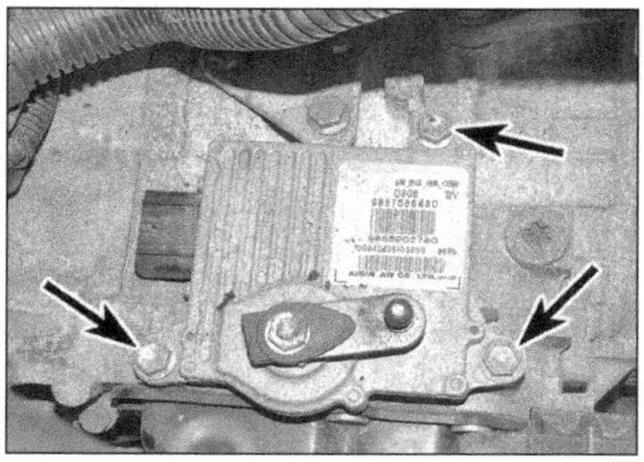

8.45 Transmission control unit mounting bolts (arrowed) – AM6 transmission

9.7 Front lower crossmember retaining bolts (arrowed)

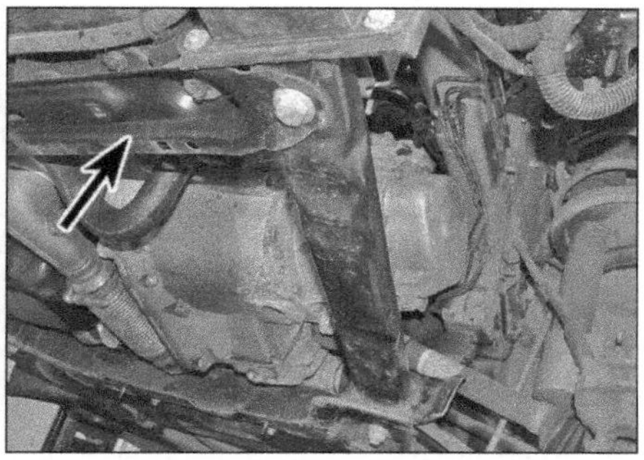

9.8 Remove the front strengthener bar (arrowed)

9.14 Release the hoses from the front of the transmission

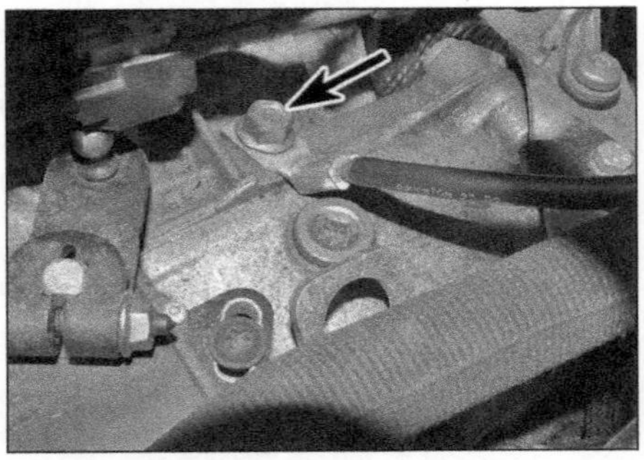

9.16 Disconnect the earth cable (arrowed) from the transmission

clamp or similar, clamp both the fluid cooler coolant hoses to minimise coolant loss. Release the retaining clips and disconnect both coolant hoses from the fluid cooler – be prepared for some coolant spillage. Wash off any spilt coolant immediately with cold water, and dry the surrounding area before proceeding further.

14 Where applicable, undo the retaining bolts and remove the mounting bracket for the coolant hoses from the front of the transmission housing **(see illustration)**, move the hoses and bracket to one side.

15 Lift the retaining clip and disconnect the main wiring connector from the transmission wiring block, located at the rear of the unit **(see illustration)**. Also disconnect the output shaft speed sensor wiring connector (located next to the main connector) then position the wiring harness clear of the transmission unit.

16 Undo the retaining bolt, and disconnect the earth cable from the top of the transmission housing **(see illustration)**. Free the wiring from any relevant retaining clips, and position it clear of the transmission.

17 Access to the torque converter retaining nuts is gained through the starter motor aperture at the rear of the cylinder block. Use a socket and extension bar to rotate the crankshaft pulley to align the first nut with the aperture. Unscrew the nut then rotate the crankshaft 120°. Remove the second nut then rotate the crankshaft another 120°. Unscrew the third and final nut and discard all three nuts; new ones must be used on refitting.

18 To ensure that the torque converter does not fall out as the transmission is removed, secure it in position using a length of metal strip

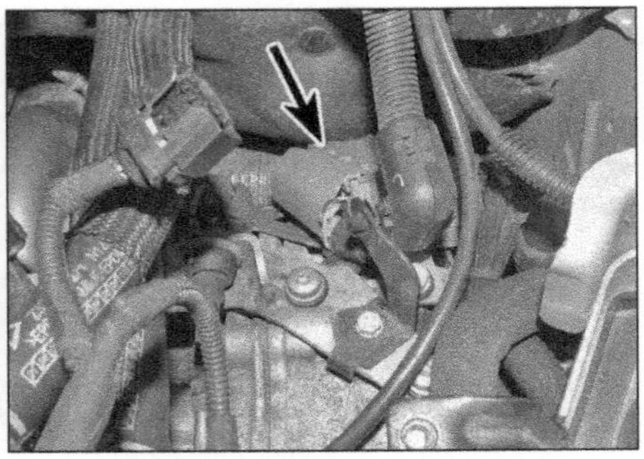

9.15 Disconnect the transmission main wiring loom connector (arrowed)

9.21 Remove the transmission mounting – AM6 transmission

bolted to one of the starter motor bolt holes.

19 Place a jack with a block of wood beneath the engine, to take the weight of the engine. Alternatively, attach a couple of lifting eyes to the engine, and fit a hoist or support bar to take the engine weight.

20 Place a jack and block of wood beneath the transmission, and raise the jack to take the weight of the transmission.

21 Slacken and remove the centre nut and washer from the left-hand engine/transmission mounting then undo the mounting bolts and remove the mounting. Unscrew the bolts securing the mounting bracket to the body and remove the bracket **(see illustration)**.

22 Slide the spacer off the mounting stud, then unscrew the stud from the top of the transmission housing and remove it along with its washer. If the mounting stud is tight, a universal stud extractor can be used to unscrew it.

23 With the jack positioned beneath the transmission taking the weight, slacken and remove the remaining bolts securing the transmission housing to the engine. Note the correct fitted positions of each bolt and the necessary brackets as they are removed to use as a reference on refitting. Make a final check that all components have been disconnected, and are positioned clear of the transmission so that they will not hinder the removal procedure.

24 With the bolts removed, move the trolley jack and transmission to the left, to free it from its locating dowels. If necessary, lower the engine slightly to enable the transmission to be freed.

25 Once the transmission is free, lower the jack and manoeuvre the unit out from under the car. Remove the locating dowels from the transmission or engine if they are loose, and keep them in a safe place.

Refitting

26 Ensure that the bush fitted to the centre of the crankshaft is in good condition, and apply a little Molykote BR2 grease to the torque converter centring pin.

Caution: Do not apply too much; otherwise there is a possibility of the grease contaminating the torque converter.

27 Ensure that the engine/transmission locating dowels are correctly positioned then raise the transmission unit into position. Align the torque converter studs with the driveplate holes then engage the transmission unit with the engine.

Caution: Do not allow the weight of the transmission unit to hang on the torque converter as the unit is installed.

28 With the transmission and engine correctly joined, refit the transmission-to-engine unit bolts and tighten them to the specified torque.

29 Screw the new nuts onto the torque converter studs, tightening them lightly only, rotating the crankshaft as necessary. Tighten all three nuts to the specified Stage 1 torque setting. Once all have been tightened to the Stage 1 torque, go around and tighten them to the specified Stage 2 and Stage 3 torque settings, where given.

30 The remainder of refitting is the reverse of removal, noting the following.

a) *Apply thread-locking fluid to the left-hand engine/transmission mounting stud threads, prior to refitting it to the transmission. Tighten the stud to the specified torque.*
b) *Tighten all nuts and bolts to the specified torque (where given).*
c) *Renew the driveshaft oil seals (Section 6), then refit the driveshafts (see Chapter 8, Section 2).*
d) *Reconnect the selector cable and adjust as described in Section 3.*
e) *On completion, check the transmission fluid level as described in Chapter 1A, Section 23 or Chapter 1B, Section 23.*

10 Automatic transmission overhaul – general information

1 In the event of a fault occurring with the transmission, it is first necessary to determine whether it is of an electrical, mechanical or hydraulic nature, and to do this special test equipment is required. It is therefore essential to have the work carried out by a Citroën dealer or specialist if a transmission fault is suspected.

2 Do not remove the transmission from the car for possible repair before professional fault diagnosis has been carried out, since most tests require the transmission to be in the vehicle.

Chapter 8
Driveshafts

Contents

Degrees of difficulty

Easy, suitable for novice with little experience	**Fairly easy,** suitable for beginner with some experience	**Fairly difficult,** suitable for competent DIY mechanic	**Difficult,** suitable for experienced DIY mechanic	**Very difficult,** suitable for expert DIY or professional

Specifications

Lubrication (overhaul only – see text)

Lubricant type/specification	Use only special grease supplied in sachets with gaiter kits – joints are otherwise pre-packed with grease and sealed

Torque wrench settings

Torque wrench settings	Nm	lbf ft
Driveshaft retaining nut	325	240
Right-hand driveshaft intermediate bearing retaining bolt	10	7
Roadwheel bolts	90	66
Suspension strut-to-hub carrier bolts	90	66

1 General information

Drive is transmitted from the differential to the front wheels by means of two solid-steel driveshafts of unequal length.

Both driveshafts are splined at their outer ends, to accept the wheel hubs, and are threaded so that each hub can be fastened by a large nut. The inner end of each driveshaft is splined, to accept the differential sun gear.

Constant velocity (CV) joints are fitted to each end of the driveshafts, to ensure that the smooth and efficient transmission of power at all suspension and steering angles. The outer constant velocity joints are of the ball-and-cage type, and the inner constant velocity joints are of the tripod type.

On the right-hand side, due to the length of the driveshaft, the inner constant velocity joint is situated approximately halfway along the shaft's length, and an intermediate support bearing is mounted in the engine/transmission rear mounting bracket. The inner end of the driveshaft passes through the bearing (which prevents any lateral movement of the driveshaft inner end) and the inner constant velocity joint outer member. On automatic transmission models, the inboard end of the right-hand driveshaft fits over a splined shaft from the transmission differential.

2 Driveshafts – removal and refitting

Removal

1 Remove the wheel trim/hub cap (as applicable) then withdraw the R-clip and remove the locking cap from the driveshaft retaining nut. Slacken the driveshaft nut with the vehicle resting on its wheels. Also slacken the wheel bolts.

2 Chock the rear wheels of the car, firmly apply the handbrake, and then jack up the front of the car and support it on axle stands (see *Jacking and vehicle support*). Remove the appropriate front roadwheel.

3 On manual transmission models drain the transmission oil as described in Chapter 7A, Section 2. On automatic transmission models there is no need to drain the fluid.

4 Unclip the wiring for the ABS wheel speed sensor, to make sure that it does not get damaged as the hub assembly is moved.

5 Slacken and remove the driveshaft retaining nut. If the nut was not slackened with the wheels on the ground (see paragraph 1), withdraw the R-clip and remove the locking

2.5a Use a screwdriver to prise out the R-clip

2.5b Using a fabricated tool to hold the front hub stationary whilst the driveshaft nut is slackened

2.7 Disconnect the track rod end

cap **(see illustration)**. Refit at least two roadwheel bolts to the front hub, tightening them securely, then have an assistant firmly depress the brake pedal to prevent the front hub from rotating, whilst you slacken and remove the driveshaft retaining nut. Alternatively, a tool can be fabricated from two lengths of steel strip (one long, one short) and a nut and bolt; the nut and bolt forming the pivot of a forked tool **(see illustration)**.

6 Undo the brake caliper guide pin or guide pin bolts and slide the caliper from the disc (refer to Chapter 9, Section 8, if required). Suspend the caliper from the suspension coil spring using a cable-tie to prevent straining the brake hose. Discard the guide pin bolts, new ones must be fitted.

2.8a Early models – bolts go in from the front, with nuts and washers to the rear

7 Undo the retaining nut and disconnect the track rod end from the stub axle **(see illustration)**.

Left-hand driveshaft

8 Slacken and remove the two bolts securing the steering hub carrier to the base of the suspension strut. Pull the hub carrier outwards to free it from the strut. **Note:** *After releasing the hub carrier, rotate the base of the strut 90° towards the rear of the vehicle to minimise the chances of damaging the rubber driveshaft gaiter* ***(see illustrations)****.*

2.8b Later models – bolts go in from the rear and a locking clip (arrowed) is fitted to the securing nuts

9 Turn the steering to full left-hand lock, carefully pull the swivel hub assembly outwards, and withdraw the driveshaft outer constant velocity joint from the hub assembly. If necessary, the shaft can be tapped out of the hub using a soft-faced mallet.

10 Support the driveshaft, and then withdraw the inner constant velocity joint from the transmission, taking care not to damage the driveshaft oil seal. Remove the driveshaft from the vehicle. **Note:** *Do not allow the vehicle to rest on its wheels with one or both driveshafts removed, as damage to the wheel bearing(s) may result. If moving the vehicle is unavoidable, temporarily insert the outer end of the driveshaft(s) in the hub(s) and tighten the driveshaft nut(s). Support the inner end(s) of the driveshaft(s) to avoid damage.*

Right-hand driveshaft

11 Loosen the two intermediate bearing retaining bolt, then rotate the retaining plate anti-clockwise, so that it is clear of the bearing outer race **(see illustration)**.

12 Slacken and remove the two bolts securing the steering hub carrier to the base of the suspension strut. Pull the hub carrier outwards to free it from the strut. **Note:** *After releasing*

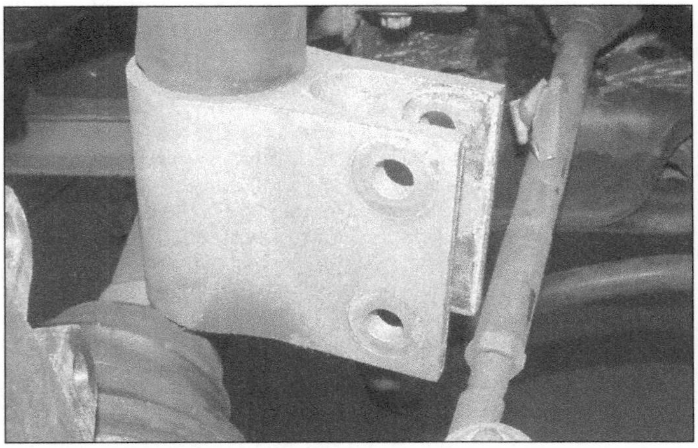

2.8c Rotate the base of the strut 90° towards the rear to minimise any chance of damaging the driveshaft gaiter

2.11 Slacken the two intermediate bearing retaining bolts (arrowed)

2.23a Tighten the driveshaft nut to the specified torque, then refit the locking cap ...

2.23b ... and secure it in position with the R-clip

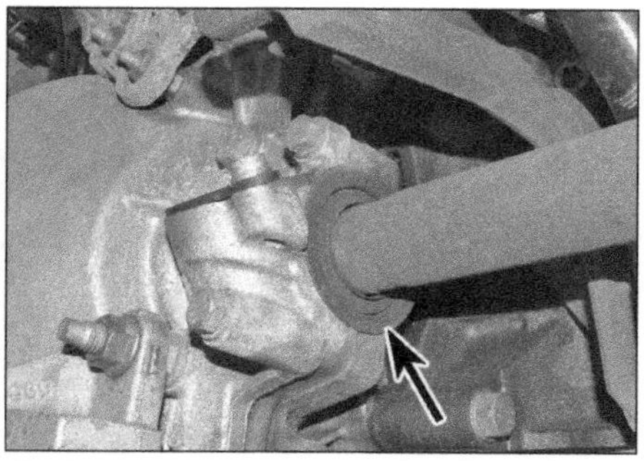

2.28 Locate the dust seal (where fitted) on the inner end of the right-hand driveshaft

*the hub carrier, rotate the base of the strut 90° towards the rear of the vehicle to minimise the chances of damaging the rubber driveshaft gaiter **(see illustrations 2.8a, 2.8b and 2.8c)**.*

13 Carefully pull the swivel hub assembly outwards, and withdraw the driveshaft outer constant velocity joint from the hub assembly. If necessary, the shaft can be tapped out of the hub using a soft-faced mallet.

14 Support the outer end of the driveshaft, then pull on the inner end of the shaft to free the intermediate bearing from its mounting bracket.

15 Once the driveshaft end is free from the transmission, slide the dust seal (where fitted) off the inner end of the shaft, noting which way around it is fitted, and remove the driveshaft from the vehicle. On automatic transmission models, the inboard end of the shaft fits over a splined shaft from the differential. Check the condition of the splined shaft O-ring. **Note:** *Do not allow the vehicle to rest on its wheels with one or both driveshafts removed, as damage to the wheel bearing(s) may result. If moving the vehicle is unavoidable, temporarily insert the outer end of the driveshaft(s) in the hub(s) and tighten the driveshaft nut(s). Support the inner end(s) of the driveshaft(s) to avoid damage.*

Refitting

16 Before installing the driveshaft, examine the driveshaft oil seal in the transmission for signs of damage or deterioration and, if necessary, renew it as described in Chapter 7A, Section 4 or Chapter 7B, Section 6. It is highly recommended that the seal be renewed, regardless of its apparent condition.

17 Thoroughly clean the driveshaft splines, and the apertures in the transmission and hub assembly. Apply a thin film of grease to the oil seal lips, and to the driveshaft splines and shoulders. Check that all gaiter clips are securely fastened.

Left-hand driveshaft

18 Offer up the driveshaft, and locate the joint splines with those of the differential sun gear, taking great care not to damage the oil seal. Push the joint fully into position.

19 Locate the outer constant velocity joint splines with those of the swivel hub, and slide the joint back into position in the hub.

20 Rotate the base of the strut 90° and align the hub carrier with the brackets on the strut. Insert the bolts and tighten them to the specified torque.

21 Refit the track rod end to the stub axle and tighten the retaining nut.

22 Refit the ABS wheel speed sensor wiring back into its retaining clips and refit the brake caliper as described in Chapter 9, Section 8.

23 Lubricate the inner face and threads of the driveshaft nut with clean engine oil, and refit it to the end of the driveshaft. Use the method employed on removal to prevent the hub from rotating (see paragraph 5), and tighten the driveshaft retaining nut to the specified torque. Check that the hub rotates freely then engage the locking cap with the driveshaft nut, so that one of its cut-outs is aligned with the driveshaft hole, and secure the cap in position with the R-clip **(see illustrations)**. Alternatively, depending on type of wheel fitted, lightly tighten the nut at this stage, and tighten it to the specified torque once the car is resting on its wheels again.

24 Refit the roadwheel, then lower the vehicle to the ground and tighten the roadwheel bolts to the specified torque. If not already done, tighten the driveshaft retaining nut to the specified torque then refit the locking cap, aligning its cut-outs with the driveshaft hole, and secure it in position with the R-clip.

25 Refill the transmission with the specified type and amount of oil, and check the level using the information given in Chapter 7A, Section 2.

Right-hand driveshaft

26 Check that the intermediate bearing rotates smoothly, without any sign of roughness or undue free play between its inner and outer races. If necessary, renew the bearing as described in Section 5. Examine the dust seal for signs of damage or deterioration, and renew if necessary. Check the condition of the differential splined shaft O-ring seal and renew if necessary.

27 Apply a smear of grease to the outer race of the intermediate bearing, and to the inner lip of the dust seal (where fitted).

28 Pass the inner end of the shaft through the bearing mounting bracket then, where necessary, carefully slide the dust seal into position on the driveshaft, ensuring that its flat surface is facing the transmission **(see illustration)**.

29 On manual transmission models, carefully locate the inner driveshaft splines with those of the differential sun gear, taking care not to damage the oil seal.

30 On automatic transmission models, located the end of the driveshaft over the differential splined shaft.

31 On all models, align the intermediate bearing with its mounting bracket, and push the driveshaft fully into position. If necessary, use a soft-faced mallet to tap the outer race of the bearing into position in the mounting bracket.

32 Locate the outer constant velocity joint splines with those of the swivel hub, and slide the joint back into position in the hub.

33 Ensure that the intermediate bearing is correctly seated, and then rotate its retaining plate back into position against the bearing outer race. Tighten the retaining bolts to the specified torque. Where necessary, ensure that the dust seal is tight against the driveshaft oil seal.

34 Carry out the operations described above in paragraphs 19 to 25.

3 Driveshaft rubber gaiters – renewal

Note: *There are three makes of driveshaft fitted to these models: GKN, PSA and NTN **(see illustration)**.*

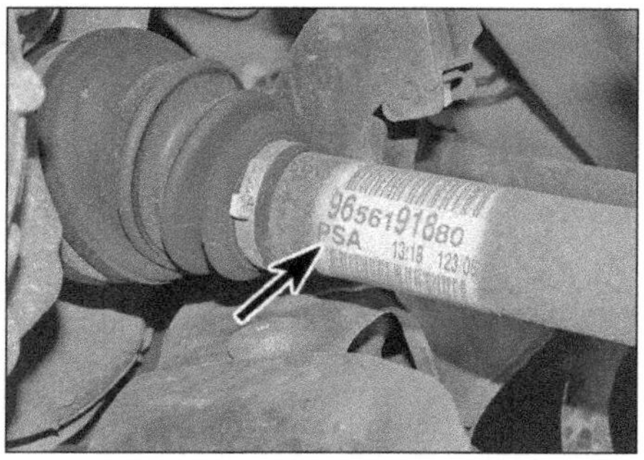

3.0 Make of driveshaft (PSA) written on label (arrowed)

3.3a Pull back the gaiter ...

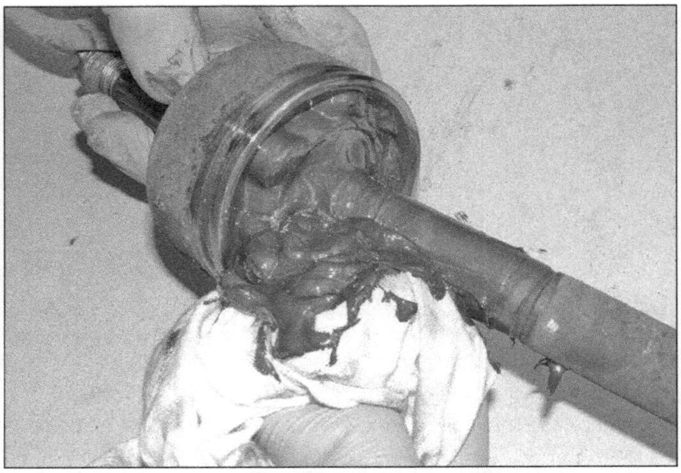

3.3b ... and clean out the old grease

Note: *The outer joint on GKN type driveshaft cannot be removed from the driveshaft; to renew the outer gaiter on this type, the inner joint will need to be removed and the gaiter fitted from that end.*

Note: *The inner tripod joint on PSA type driveshaft cannot be removed from the driveshaft; to renew the inner gaiter on this type, the outer joint will need to be removed and the gaiter fitted from that end.*

Outer joint (PSA and NTN type)

1 Remove the driveshaft from the vehicle as described in Section 2.

2 Secure the driveshaft in a vice equipped with soft jaws, and release the two outer gaiter retaining clips. If necessary, the gaiter retaining clips can be cut to release them.

3 Slide the rubber gaiter down the shaft, to expose the outer constant velocity joint. Scoop out the excess grease **(see illustrations)**.

4 Using a hammer and suitable soft metal drift, sharply strike the inner member of the outer joint to drive it off the end of the shaft **(see illustration)**. The joint is retained on the driveshaft by a circlip, and striking the joint in this manner forces the circlip into its groove, so allowing the joint to slide off.

5 Once the joint assembly has been removed, remove the circlip from the groove in the driveshaft splines, and discard it. A new circlip must be fitted on reassembly.

6 Withdraw the rubber gaiter from the driveshaft. Where applicable, slide the gaiter inner end plastic bush off the driveshaft **(see illustration)**.

7 With the constant velocity joint removed from the driveshaft, thoroughly clean the joint using paraffin, or a suitable solvent, and dry it thoroughly. Carry out a visual inspection of the joint.

8 Move the inner splined driving member from side-to-side, to expose each ball in turn at the top of its track. Examine the balls for cracks, flat spots, or signs of surface pitting.

9 Inspect the ball tracks on the inner and outer members. If the tracks have widened, the balls will no longer be a tight fit. At the same time, check the ball cage windows for wear or cracking between the windows.

10 If, on inspection, any of the constant velocity joint components are found to be worn or damaged, it will be necessary to renew the complete joint assembly (where available), or even the complete driveshaft (where no joint components are available separately). Refer to your Citroën dealer for further information on parts availability. If the joint is in satisfactory condition, obtain a repair kit consisting of a new gaiter, circlip, retaining clips, and the correct type and quantity of grease.

11 To install the new gaiter, perform the operations shown **(see illustrations)**. Be sure to stay in order, and follow the captions carefully. Note that the hard plastic rings and plastic bushes are not fitted to all gaiters, and the gaiter retaining clips supplied with the repair kit may be different to those shown in the sequence.

12 To secure the other type of clip in position, lock the ends of the clip together, and then remove any slack in the clip by carefully compressing the raised section of the clip using a pair of special pliers or side-cutters **(see illustration)**.

13 Check that the constant velocity joint moves freely in all directions, and then refit

3.4 Using a soft metal drift to release the outer joint

3.6 Where applicable, remove the plastic bush

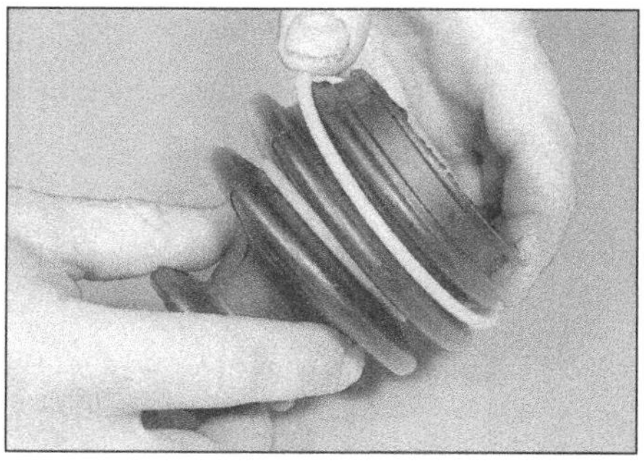

3.11a Where applicable, fit the hard plastic rings to the outer gaiter ...

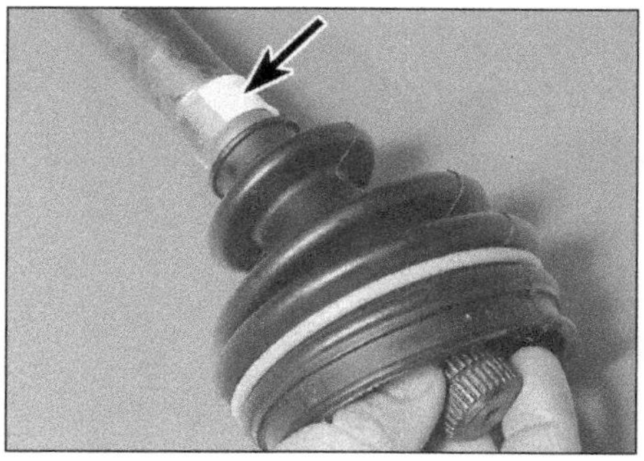

3.11b ... then slide on the new plastic bush (arrowed – where fitted), and seat it in its recess in the shaft. Slide the gaiter onto the shaft ...

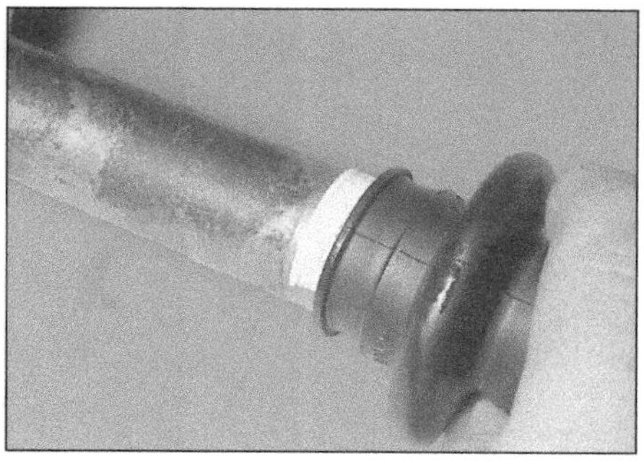

3.11c ... and seat the gaiter inner end on top of the plastic bush (as applicable)

3.11d Fit the new circlip to its groove in the driveshaft splines ...

3.11e ... then locate the joint outer member on the splines, and slide it into position over the circlip. Ensure that the joint is securely retained by the circlip

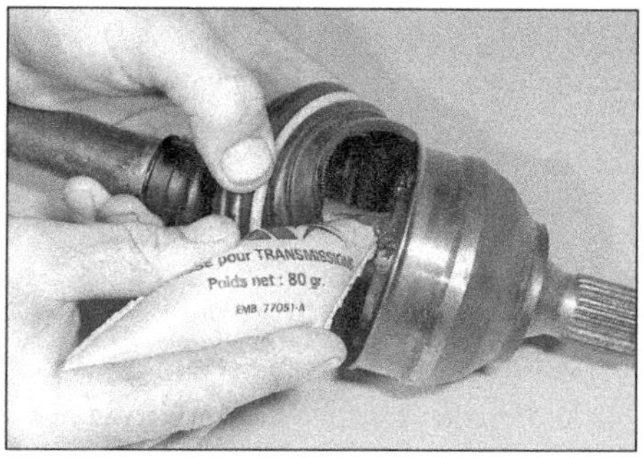

3.11f Pack the joint with grease, working it into the ball tracks while twisting the joint, then locate the gaiter outer lip in its groove on the outer member

3.11g Fit the outer gaiter retaining clip and, using a hook fabricated out of welding rod and a pair of pliers, pull the clip tight to remove all the slack

3.11h Bend the clip end back over the buckle, then cut off the excess

3.11i Fold the clip end underneath the buckle ...

3.11j ... then fold the buckle firmly down onto the clip to secure the clip in position

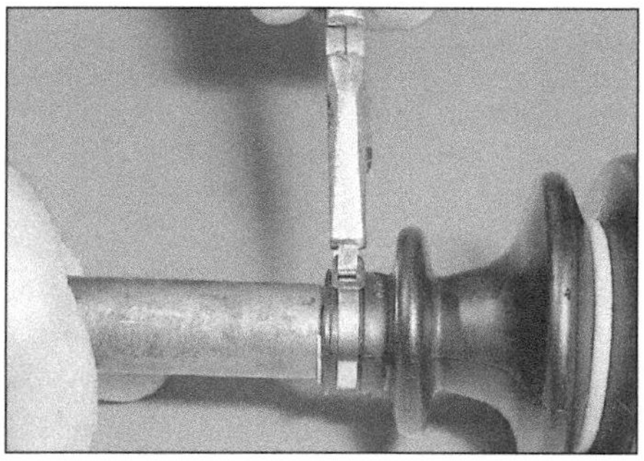

3.11k Carefully lift the gaiter inner end to equalise the air pressure in the gaiter, then secure the inner gaiter retaining clip in position using the same method

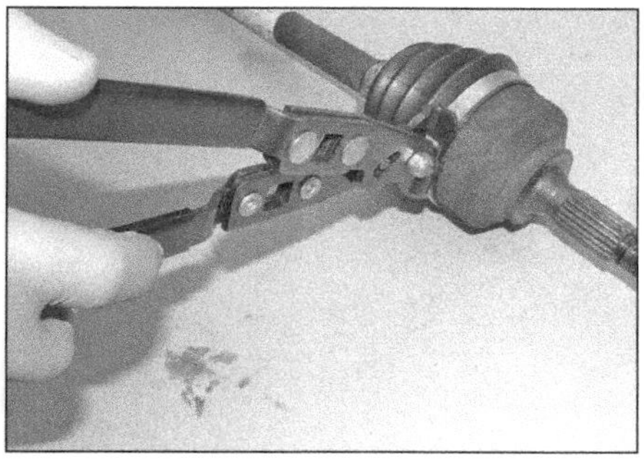

3.12 Using a pair of special pliers to secure the retaining clip

3.15a Cut the retaining clip ...

3.15b ... and remove the clip and gaiter

3.18a Slide the joint apart ...

3.18b ... and retrieve the spring (where applicable)

3.19a Release the circlip ...

3.19b ... and mark the position (arrowed) of the joint on the shaft

the driveshaft to the vehicle as described in Section 2.

Inner joint (GKN and NTN type)

14 Remove the driveshaft from the vehicle as described in Section 2.

15 Secure the driveshaft in a vice equipped with soft jaws, and release the two outer gaiter retaining clips. If necessary, the gaiter retaining clips can be cut to release them **(see illustrations)**. Take care not to damage the driveshaft when cutting the retaining clip.

16 Slide the rubber gaiter down the shaft to expose the outer constant velocity joint. Scoop out the excess grease.

17 If the gaiter is to be renewed, it can be cut off and removed from the driveshaft.

18 Slide the outer member off the tripod joint and remove the spring and/or cup from inside the outer member of the joint **(see illustrations)**.

19 Using circlip pliers, extract the circlip securing the tripod joint to the driveshaft **(see illustrations)**. Mark the position of the tripod in relation to the driveshaft, using a dab of paint or a punch.

20 The tripod joint can now be removed **(see illustration)**. If it is tight, draw the joint off the driveshaft end using a puller. Ensure that the legs of the puller are located behind the joint inner member and do not contact the joint rollers. Alternatively, support the inner member of the tripod joint, and press the shaft out using a hydraulic press, again ensuring that no load is applied to the joint rollers.

21 With the tripod joint removed, if not removed already, slide the gaiter off the end of the driveshaft.

22 Wipe clean the joint components, taking care not to remove the alignment marks made on dismantling. Do not use paraffin or other solvents to clean this type of joint.

23 Examine the tripod joint, rollers and outer member for any signs of scoring or wear. Check that the rollers move smoothly on the tripod stems. If wear is evident, check with your local dealer to see if the tripod joint and roller assembly can be renewed. Obtain a new gaiter, retaining clips and a quantity of the special lubricating grease.

24 Tape over the splines on the end of the driveshaft, then carefully slide the inner retaining clip and gaiter onto the shaft **(see illustration)**.

25 Remove the tape, then, aligning the marks made on dismantling, engage the tripod joint with the driveshaft splines **(see illustration)**. Use a hammer and soft metal drift to tap the

3.20 Slide the joint from the end of the shaft

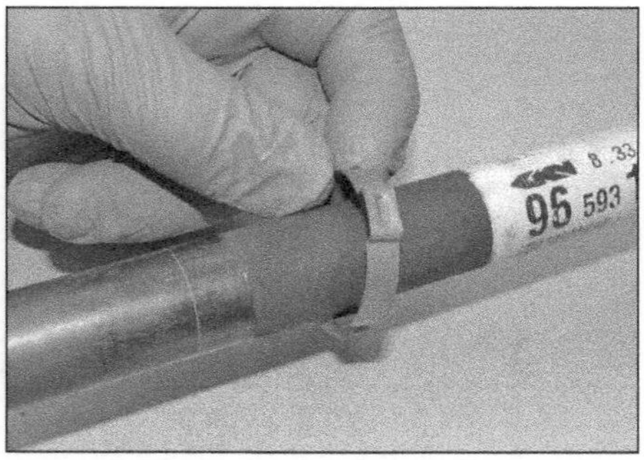

3.24 Make sure the inner retaining clip is put on the shaft

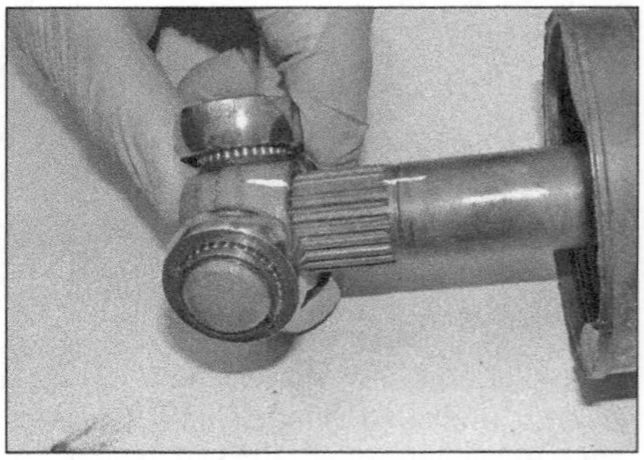

3.25 Align the marks up for refitting

3.26 Refit the circlip to secure the tripod joint

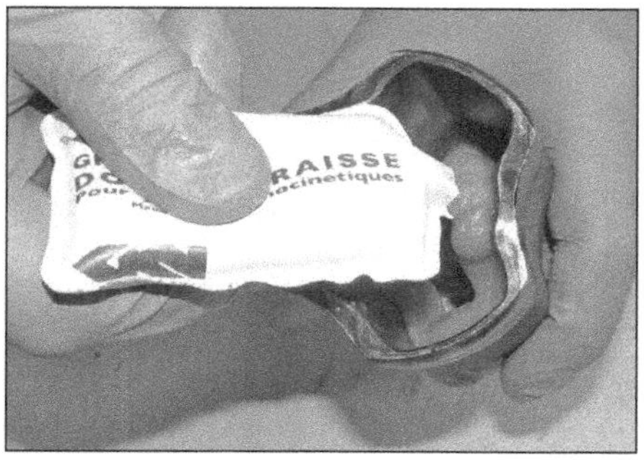

3.27a Pack the outer joint with grease ...

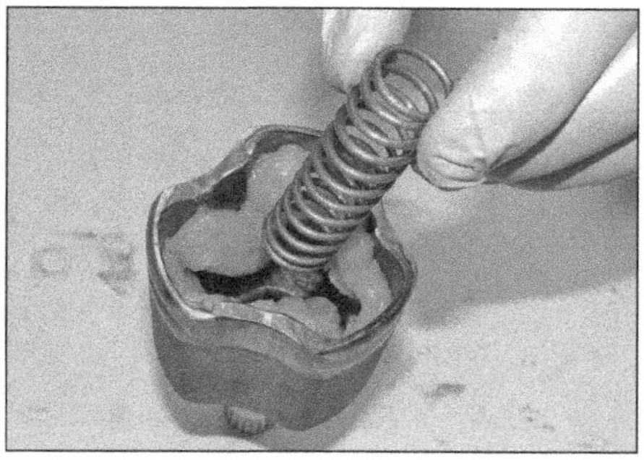

3.27b ... and insert the spring (where fitted)

joint onto the shaft, taking great care not to damage the driveshaft splines or joint rollers. Alternatively, support the driveshaft, and press the joint into position using a hydraulic press and suitable tubular spacer, which bears only on the joint inner member.

26 Secure the tripod joint in position with the circlip, ensuring that it is correctly located in the driveshaft groove **(see illustration)**.

27 Evenly distribute the grease contained in the repair kit inside the outer member, and then refit the spring and cup (where fitted) in the outer member **(see illustrations)**.

28 Pack the gaiter with the remainder of the grease and slide the two halves of the joint together **(see illustration)**.

29 Slide the gaiter up the driveshaft. Locate the gaiter in the grooves on the driveshaft and outer member.

30 Fit the inner retaining clip into place over the inner end of the gaiter.

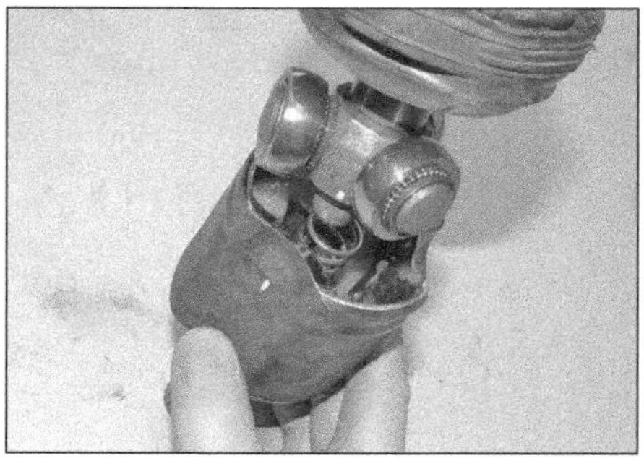

3.28 Refit the tripod joint into the outer joint

3.32 Secure the gaiter in position with the securing clips

31 Using a blunt rod, carefully lift the outer lip of the gaiter to equalise the air pressure.

32 Slip the new retaining clip into place to secure the outer lip of the gaiter to the outer member. Remove any slack in the gaiter retaining clip by carefully compressing the raised section of the clip (depending on type of clip supplied). In the absence of the special tool, a pair of pincers may be used **(see illustration)**. Secure the small retaining clip using the same procedure.

33 Check that the constant velocity joint moves freely in all directions, then refit the driveshaft as described in Section 2.

Inner gaiter (PSA type)

34 Remove the outer constant velocity joint as described above in paragraphs 1 to 5.

35 Tape over the splines on the driveshaft, and carefully remove the outer constant velocity joint rubber gaiter, and (where fitted) the gaiter inner end plastic bush. It is recommended that the outer joint gaiter be also renewed, regardless of its apparent condition.

36 Release the retaining clips, then slide the inner gaiter off the shaft and (where fitted) remove its plastic bush **(see illustration 3.6)**.

37 As the gaiter is released, the joint outer member will also be freed from the end of the shaft **(see illustrations)**.

38 Thoroughly clean the joint using paraffin, or a suitable solvent, and dry it thoroughly. Check the tripod joint bearings and joint outer member for signs of wear, pitting or scuffing on their bearing surfaces. Check that the bearing rollers rotate smoothly and easily around the tripod joint, with no traces of roughness.

39 If, on inspection, the tripod joint or outer member reveal signs of wear or damage, it will be necessary to renew the complete driveshaft assembly, since the joint is not available separately. If the joint is in a satisfactory condition, obtain a repair kit consisting of a new gaiter, retaining clips, and the correct type and quantity of grease.

40 On reassembly, pack the inner joint with the grease supplied in the gaiter kit. Work the grease well into the bearing tracks and rollers, while twisting the joint.

41 Clean the shaft, using emery cloth to remove any rust or sharp edges which may damage the gaiter, then slide the plastic bush (where fitted) and inner joint gaiter along the driveshaft. Locate the plastic bush in its recess on the shaft, and seat the inner end of the gaiter on top of the bush; where no bush is fitted, seat the inner end of the driveshaft in the recess on the shaft **(see illustration)**.

3.37a Release the inner gaiter retaining clips and remove the joint outer member

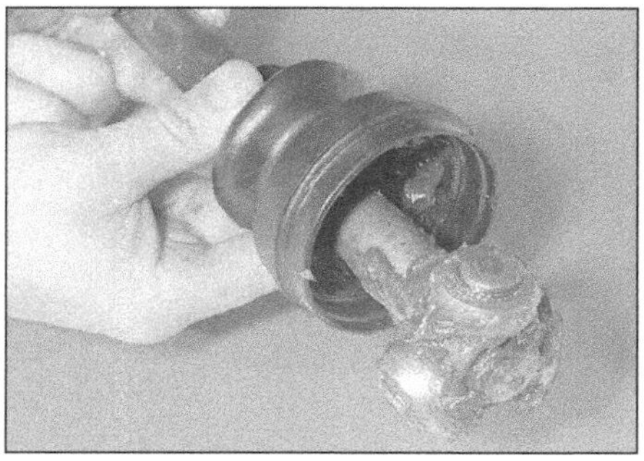

3.37b Slide the gaiter off the end of the driveshaft

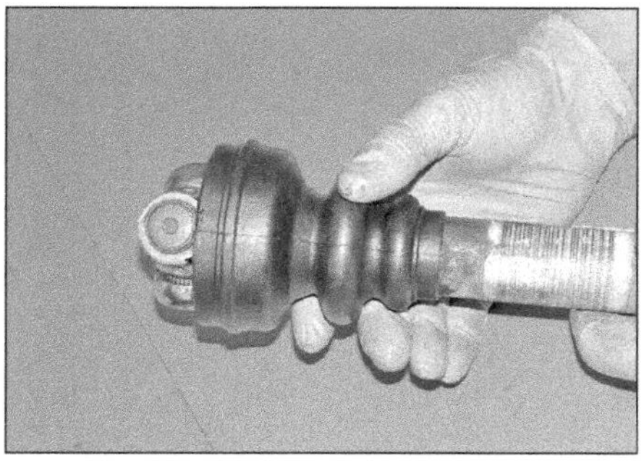

3.41 Locate the new gaiter in the groove on the driveshaft

42 Fit the outer member over the end of the shaft, and locate the gaiter in the groove on the joint outer member. Push the outer member onto the joint, so that it's spring-loaded plunger is compressed, then lift the outer edge of the gaiter to equalise air pressure in the gaiter. Fit both the inner and outer retaining clips, securing them in position using the information given in paragraph 11. Ensure that the gaiter retaining clips are securely tightened, and then check that the joint moves freely in all directions **(see illustration)**.

43 Refit the outer constant velocity joint components using the information given in paragraphs 11 to 13.

4 Driveshaft overhaul – general information

1 If any of the checks described in Chapter 1A, Section 5 or Chapter 1B, Section 6 reveal wear in any driveshaft joint, first remove the roadwheel trim or centre cap (as appropriate).

2 If the R-clip is still in position, the driveshaft nut should be correctly tightened; if in doubt, remove the R-clip and locking cap, and use a torque wrench to check that the nut is securely fastened. Once tightened, refit the locking cap and R-clip, and then refit the centre cap or trim. Repeat this check on the remaining driveshaft nut.

3 Road test the vehicle, and listen for a metallic clicking from the front as the vehicle is driven slowly in a circle on full-lock. If a clicking noise is heard, this indicates wear in the outer constant velocity joint. This means that the joint must be renewed; reconditioning is not possible.

3.42 Fit the new clips and crimp them into place

4 If vibration, consistent with roadspeed, is felt through the car when accelerating, there is a possibility of wear in the inner joints.

5 To check the joints for wear, remove the driveshafts, and then dismantle them as described in Section 3; if any wear or free play is found, the affected joint must be renewed. In the case of the inner joints (and on some models, the outer joints), this means that the complete driveshaft assembly must be renewed, as the joints are not available separately. Refer to your Citroën dealer for latest information on the availability of driveshaft components.

5 Right-hand driveshaft intermediate bearing – renewal

Note: *A suitable bearing puller will be required, to draw the bearing and collar off the driveshaft end.*

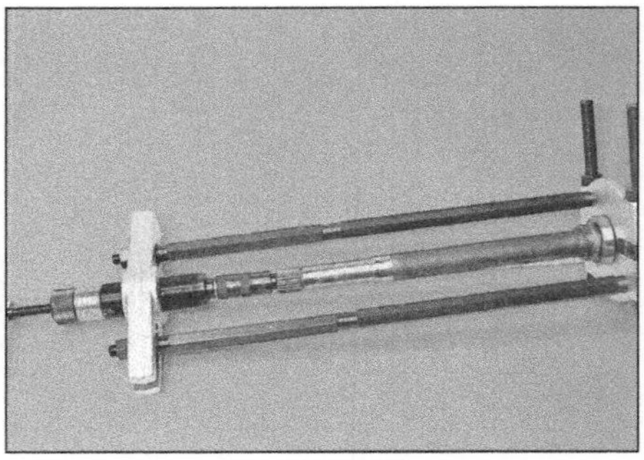

5.3 Using a long-reach bearing puller to remove the intermediate bearing from the right-hand driveshaft

1 Remove the right-hand driveshaft as described in Section 2 of this Chapter.

2 Check that the bearing outer race rotates smoothly and easily, without any signs of roughness or undue free play between the inner and outer races. If necessary, renew the bearing as follows.

3 Using a long-reach universal bearing puller, carefully draw the collar and intermediate bearing off the driveshaft inner end **(see illustration)**. Apply a smear of grease to the inner race of the new bearing, and then fit the bearing over the end of the driveshaft. Using a hammer and suitable piece of tubing which bears only on the bearing inner race, tap the new bearing into position on the driveshaft, until it abuts the constant velocity joint outer member. Once the bearing is correctly positioned, tap the bearing collar onto the shaft until it contacts the bearing inner race.

4 Check that the bearing rotates freely, then refit the driveshaft as described in Section 2.

Chapter 9
Braking system

Contents

Degrees of difficulty

Easy, suitable for novice with little experience	**Fairly easy,** suitable for beginner with some experience	**Fairly difficult,** suitable for competent DIY mechanic	**Difficult,** suitable for experienced DIY mechanic	**Very difficult,** suitable for expert DIY or professional

Specifications

Front brakes

Type	Vented disc, with single-piston sliding caliper
Caliper make:	
All models except 2.0 litre diesel	Bosch
2.0 litre diesel models	Teves
Piston diameter:	
Bosch calipers	54 mm
Teves calipers	57 mm
Disc diameter:	
All models except 2.0 litre diesel	266 or 283 mm
2.0 litre diesel models	302 mm
Disc thickness:	
266 mm diameter discs:	
New	22 mm
Minimum	20 mm
283 and 302 mm diameter discs:	
New	26 mm
Minimum	24 mm
Maximum disc run-out	0.05 mm
Brake pad friction material thickness:	
New	13.0 mm
Minimum	3.0 mm

Rear disc brakes

Type	Solid disc, with single-piston sliding caliper
Caliper make	Bosch or TRW Lucas
Piston diameter	38 mm
Disc diameter	249 mm
Disc thickness:	
New	9.0 mm
Minimum thickness	7.0 mm
Maximum disc run-out	0.05 mm
Brake pad friction material thickness:	
New	11.0 mm
Minimum	3.0 mm

Vacuum pump pressure (engine at idle)

VTi petrol engines (at 125°C):	
6 seconds	500 mbars
29 seconds	850 mbars
Diesel engines (at 80°C):	
4.5 seconds	500 mbars
18 seconds	800 mbars

Master cylinder

Make	Bosch
Diameter of cylinder:	
Petrol engines:	
Non-VTi	22.2mm or 23.8 mm
VTi	23.8 mm
Diesel engines:	
1.6 litre	22.2mm or 23.8 mm
2.0 litre	23.8 mm

Servo unit

Make	Bosch
Diameter of servo:	
Petrol engines:	
Non-VTi engine:	
1.4 litre	225 mm
1.6 litre	250 mm or 255mm
VTi engine	255mm
Diesel engines:	
1.6 litre	250 mm or 255mm
2.0 litre	255 mm

ABS hydraulic valve block

Make	Bosch
Type	ABS 8.1 (8.1 ESP)

Torque wrench settings

	Nm	lbf ft
ABS system components:		
Hydraulic hose/pipe union nuts:		
Without ESP	15	11
With ESP	18	13
Hydraulic/modulator unit mounting nuts	8	6
Hydraulic/modulator unit mounting bracket bolts	15	11
Wheel sensor retaining bolts	8	6
Gyrometer/accelerometer sensor nuts	8	6
Caliper bleed screws	10	7
Crossover linkage housing nuts and bolts (right-hand drive models)	25	18
Disc retaining screws	10	7
Front brake caliper:		
Hydraulic hose to caliper	18	13
Guide pin bolts (Bosch)	31	23
Guide pin bolts (Teves)	30	22
Mounting bracket bolts:*		
With washers:		
Stage 1	90	66
Stage 2	Angle-tighten a further 45°	
Without washers:		
Stage 1	33	24
Stage 2	Angle-tighten a further 45°	

Torque wrench settings (continued)

Torque wrench settings (continued)	Nm	lbf ft
Handbrake lever nuts	15	11
Master cylinder:		
Retaining nuts	20	15
Hydraulic hose/pipe union nuts:		
Without ESP	15	11
With ESP	18	13
Rear brake caliper:		
Hydraulic hose to caliper	18	13
Guide pin bolts*	30	22
Mounting bracket bolts:*		
Stage 1	30	22
Stage 2	Angle-tighten a further 35°	
Rear hub nut	300	221
Roadwheel bolts	90	66
Vacuum pump (diesel engine):		
Stage 1	5	4
Stage 2	18	13
Vacuum pump (petrol engine)	9	7
Vacuum servo unit mounting nuts	22	16

** Do not re-use.*

1 General information

The braking system is of the servo-assisted, dual-circuit hydraulic type. The arrangement of the hydraulic system is such that each circuit operates one front and one rear brake from a tandem master cylinder. Under normal circumstances, both circuits operate in unison. However, in the event of hydraulic failure in one circuit, full braking force will still be available at two wheels.

All models are equipped with disc brakes on all wheels. ABS is fitted as standard (refer to Section 18 for further information on ABS operation).

The disc brakes are actuated by single-piston sliding type calipers, which ensure that equal pressure is applied to each disc pad.

On all models, the handbrake provides an independent mechanical means of rear brake application. All models are fitted with rear brake calipers with an integral handbrake function. The handbrake cable operates a lever on the caliper that forces the piston to press the pad against the disc surface. A self-adjust mechanism is incorporated to automatically compensate for brake pad wear.

On VTi petrol engines and diesel engine models, there is a vacuum pump fitted to provide sufficient vacuum to operate the servo unit. The vacuum pump is mounted on the left-hand end of the cylinder head, and is driven directly off the end of the camshaft.

Note: *When servicing any of the system, work carefully and methodically; also observe scrupulous cleanliness when overhauling any of the hydraulic system. Always renew components (in axle sets, where applicable) if in doubt about their condition, and use only genuine Citroën parts, or at least those of known good quality. Note the warnings given in 'Safety first!' and at relevant points in this Chapter concerning the dangers of asbestos dust and hydraulic fluid.*

2 Hydraulic system – bleeding

Warning: Hydraulic fluid is poisonous; wash off immediately and thoroughly in the case of skin contact, and seek immediate medical advice if any fluid is swallowed or gets into the eyes. Certain types of hydraulic fluid are inflammable, and may ignite when allowed into contact with hot components; when servicing any hydraulic system, it is safest to assume that the fluid is inflammable, and to take precautions against the risk of fire as though it is petrol that is being handled. Hydraulic fluid is also an effective paint stripper, and will attack plastics; if any is spilt, it should be washed off immediately, using copious quantities of fresh water. Finally, it is hygroscopic (it absorbs moisture from the air) – old fluid may be contaminated and unfit for further use. When topping-up or renewing the fluid, always use the recommended type, and ensure that it comes from a freshly opened sealed container.

Caution: Ensure the ignition is switched off before starting the bleeding procedure, to avoid any possibility of voltage being applied to the hydraulic modulator before the bleeding procedure is complete. Ideally, the battery should be disconnected. If voltage is applied to the modulator before the bleeding procedure is complete, this will effectively drain the hydraulic fluid in the modulator, rendering the unit unserviceable. Do not, therefore, attempt to 'run' the modulator in order to bleed the brakes.

Note: *If difficulty is experienced in bleeding the braking circuit, this maybe due to air being trapped in the ABS modulator unit. If this is the case then the vehicle should be taken to a Citroën dealer or suitably-equipped specialist so that the system can be bled using special electronic test equipment.*

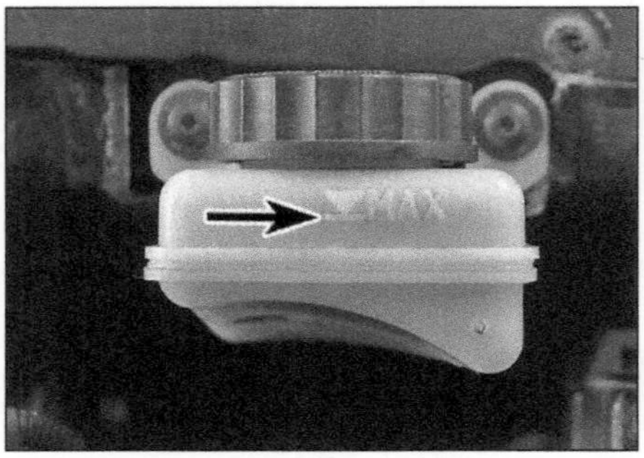

2.7 Fluid MAX level line

Note: *A hydraulic clutch shares its fluid reservoir with the braking system, and may also need to be bled (see Chapter 6, Section 2).*

General

1 The correct operation of any hydraulic system is only possible after removing all air from the components and circuit; this is achieved by bleeding the system.

2 During the bleeding procedure, add only clean, unused hydraulic fluid of the recommended type; never re-use fluid that has already been bled from the system. Ensure that sufficient fluid is available before starting work.

3 If there is any possibility of incorrect fluid being already in the system, the brake components and circuit must be flushed completely with uncontaminated, correct fluid, and new seals should be fitted to the various components.

4 If hydraulic fluid has been lost from the system, or air has entered because of a leak, ensure that the fault is cured before proceeding further.

5 Park the vehicle on level ground, switch off the engine and select first or reverse gear, then chock the wheels and release the handbrake.

6 Check that all pipes and hoses are secure, unions tight and bleed screws closed. Clean any dirt from around the bleed screws.

7 Unscrew the master cylinder reservoir cap, and top the master cylinder reservoir up to the MAX level line **(see illustration)**; refit the cap loosely, and remember to maintain the fluid level at least above the MIN/DANGER level line throughout the procedure, or there is a risk of further air entering the system.

8 There is a number of one-man, do-it-yourself brake bleeding kits currently available from motor accessory shops. It is recommended that one of these kits is used whenever possible, as they greatly simplify the bleeding operation, and also reduce the risk of expelled air and fluid being drawn back into the system. If such a kit is not available, the basic (two-man) method must be used, which is described in detail below.

9 If a kit is to be used, prepare the vehicle as described previously, and follow the kit manufacturer's instructions, as the procedure may vary slightly according to the type being used; generally, they are as outlined below in the relevant sub-section.

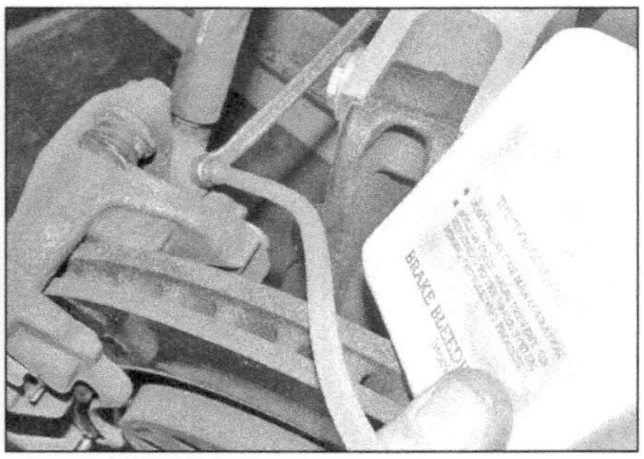

2.22 Connect the bleed kit to the bleed screw

10 Whichever method is used, the same sequence must be followed (paragraphs 11 and 12) to ensure that the removal of all air from the system.

Bleeding

Sequence

11 If the system has been only partially disconnected, and suitable precautions were taken to minimise fluid loss, it should be necessary only to bleed that of the system (ie, the primary or secondary circuit).

12 If the complete system is to be bled, then it should be done working in the following sequence:

a) Left-hand front brake.
b) Right-hand front brake.
c) Left-hand rear brake.
d) Right-hand rear brake.

Basic (two-man) method

13 Collect a clean glass jar, a suitable length of plastic or rubber tubing which is a tight fit over the bleed screw, and a ring spanner to fit the screw. The help of an assistant will also be required.

14 Remove the dust cap from the first screw in the sequence. Fit the spanner and tube to the screw, place the other end of the tube in the jar, and pour in sufficient fluid to cover the end of the tube.

15 Ensure that the master cylinder reservoir fluid level is maintained at least above the MIN/DANGER level line throughout the procedure.

16 Have the assistant fully depress the brake pedal several times to build up pressure, and then maintain it on the final downstroke.

17 While pedal pressure is maintained, unscrew the bleed screw (approximately one turn) and allow the compressed fluid and air to flow into the jar. The assistant should maintain pedal pressure, following it down to the floor if necessary, and should not release it until instructed to do so. When the flow stops, tighten the bleed screw again, have the assistant release the pedal slowly, and recheck the reservoir fluid level.

18 Repeat the steps given in paragraphs 16 and 17 until the fluid emerging from the bleed screw is free from air bubbles. If the master cylinder has been drained and refilled, and air is being bled from the first screw in the sequence, allow approximately five seconds between cycles for the master cylinder passages to refill.

19 When no more air bubbles appear, tighten the bleed screw securely, remove the tube and spanner, and refit the dust cap. Do not overtighten the bleed screw.

20 Repeat the procedure on the remaining screws in the sequence, until all air is removed from the system and the brake pedal feels firm again.

Using a one-way valve kit

21 As their name implies, these kits consist of a length of tubing with a one-way valve fitted, to prevent expelled air and fluid being drawn back into the system; some kits include a translucent container, which can be positioned so that the air bubbles can be more easily seen flowing from the end of the tube.

22 The kit is connected to the bleed screw, which is then opened **(see illustration)**. The user returns to the driver's seat, depresses the brake pedal with a smooth, steady stroke, and slowly releases it; this is repeated until the expelled fluid is clear of air bubbles.

23 Note that these kits simplify work so much that it is easy to forget the master cylinder reservoir fluid level; ensure that this is maintained at least above the MIN/DANGER level line at all times.

Using a pressure-bleeding kit

24 These kits are usually operated by the reservoir of pressurised air contained in the spare tyre. However, note that it will probably be necessary to reduce the pressure to a lower level than normal; refer to the instructions supplied with the kit.

25 By connecting a pressurised, fluid-filled container to the master cylinder reservoir, bleeding can be carried out simply by opening each screw in turn (in the specified sequence), and allowing the fluid to flow out until no more air bubbles can be seen in the expelled fluid.

26 This method has the advantage that the large reservoir of fluid provides an additional safeguard against air being drawn into the system during bleeding.

27 Pressure-bleeding is particularly effective when bleeding 'difficult' systems, or when bleeding the complete system at the time of routine fluid renewal.

All methods

28 When bleeding is complete, and firm pedal feel is restored, wash off any spilt fluid, tighten the bleed screws securely, and refit their dust caps.

29 Check the hydraulic fluid level in the master cylinder reservoir, and top-up if necessary (see *Weekly checks*).

30 Discard any hydraulic fluid that has been bled from the system; it will not be fit for re-use.

31 Check the feel of the brake pedal. If it feels at all spongy, air must still be present in the system, and further bleeding is required. Failure to bleed satisfactorily after a reasonable repetition of the bleeding procedure may be due to worn master cylinder seals.

3 Hydraulic pipes and hoses – renewal

Caution: Ensure the ignition is switched off before disconnecting any braking system hydraulic union and do not switch it on until after the hydraulic system has been bled. Failure to do this could lead to air entering the modulator unit requiring the unit to be bled using special Citroën test equipment (see Section 2).

Note: *Before starting work, refer to the note at the beginning of Section 2 concerning the dangers of hydraulic fluid.*

1 If any pipe or hose is to be renewed, minimise fluid loss by first removing the master cylinder reservoir cap, then tightening it down onto a piece of polythene to obtain an airtight seal. Alternatively, flexible hoses can be sealed, if required, using a proprietary brake hose clamp; metal brake pipe unions can be plugged (if care is taken not to allow dirt into the system) or capped immediately they are disconnected. Place a wad of rag under any union that is to be disconnected, to catch any spilt fluid.

2 If a flexible hose is to be disconnected, unscrew the brake pipe union nut before removing the spring clip that secures the hose to its mounting bracket **(see illustration)**.

3 To unscrew the union nuts, it is preferable to obtain a brake pipe spanner of the correct size; these are available from most large motor accessory shops. Failing this, a close-fitting open-ended spanner will be required, though if the nuts are tight or corroded, their flats may be rounded-off if the spanner slips. In such a case, a self-locking wrench is often the only way to unscrew a stubborn union, but it follows that the pipe and the damaged nuts must be renewed on reassembly. Always clean a union and surrounding area before disconnecting it. If disconnecting a component with more than one union, make a careful note of the connections before disturbing any of them.

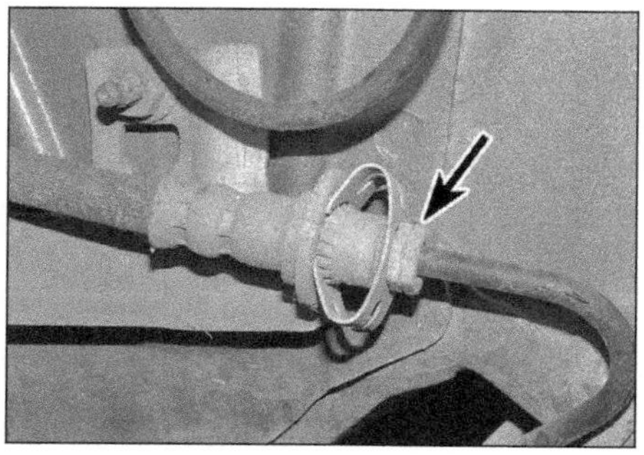

3.2 Slacken the union nut (arrowed) and then remove the spring clip

4 If a brake pipe is to be renewed, it can be obtained cut to length and with the union nuts and end flares in place, from Citroën dealers. All that is then necessary is to bend it to shape, following the line of the original, before fitting it to the car. Alternatively, most motor accessory shops can make up brake pipes from kits, but this requires very careful measurement of the original, to ensure that the new one is of the correct length. The safest answer is usually to take the original to the shop as a pattern.

5 On refitting, do not overtighten the union nuts. It is not necessary to exercise brute force to obtain a sound joint.

6 Ensure that the pipes and hoses are correctly routed, with no kinks, and that they are secured in the clips or brackets provided. After fitting, remove the polythene from the reservoir, and bleed the hydraulic system as described in Section 2. Wash off any spilt fluid, and then check the brake system carefully for fluid leaks.

4 Front brake pads – renewal

Warning: Disc brake pads must be renewed on both front wheels at the same time – never renew the pads on only one wheel, as uneven braking may result. Also, the dust created by wear of the pads may contain asbestos, which is a health hazard. Never blow it out with compressed air and don't inhale any of it. An approved filtering mask should be worn when working on the brakes. DO NOT use petroleum based solvents to clean brake parts. Use brake cleaner or methylated spirit only.

1 Apply the handbrake, slacken the front roadwheel bolts, then jack up the front of the vehicle and support it on axle stands. Remove the front roadwheels.

Bosch calipers

Note: *New guide pin bolts must be used on refitting.*

2 Push the piston back into its bore slightly, by pulling the caliper outwards.

3 Slacken and remove the caliper lower guide pin bolt **(see illustration)**. Discard the guide pin bolt – a new one must be used on refitting.

4 With the lower guide pin bolt removed, pivot the caliper away from the brake pads and mounting bracket, and tie it to the suspension strut using a suitable piece of wire **(see illustration)**.

5 Withdraw the two brake pads from the caliper mounting bracket; the shims (where fitted) should be bonded to the pad, but may have come unstuck in use **(see illustrations)**.

6 First measure the thickness of each brake pad's friction material **(see illustration)**. If

4.3 Remove the caliper lower guide pin bolt ...

4.4 ... then pivot the caliper upwards and away from the brake pads, and tie it to the suspension strut

4.5a Withdraw the brake pads from the caliper mounting bracket

4.5b Check the shim (where fitted) in the caliper piston

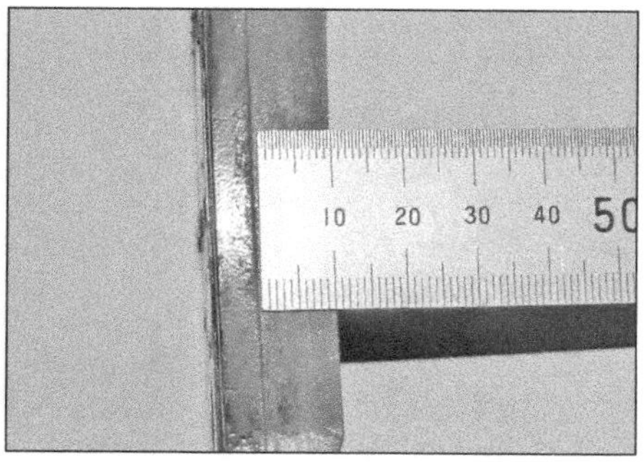

4.6 Measure the thickness of the pad's friction material

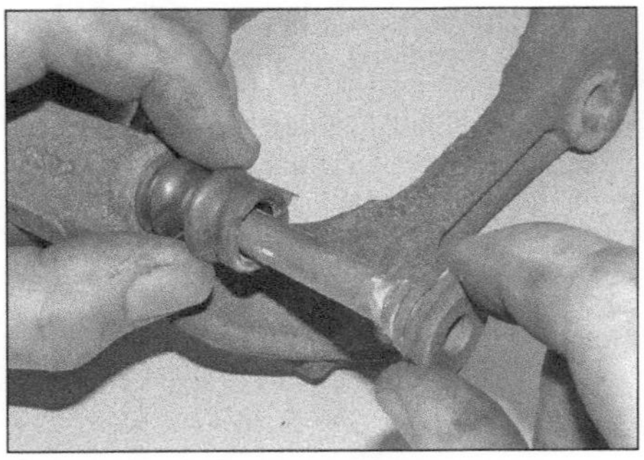

4.8a Check the condition of the guide pins ...

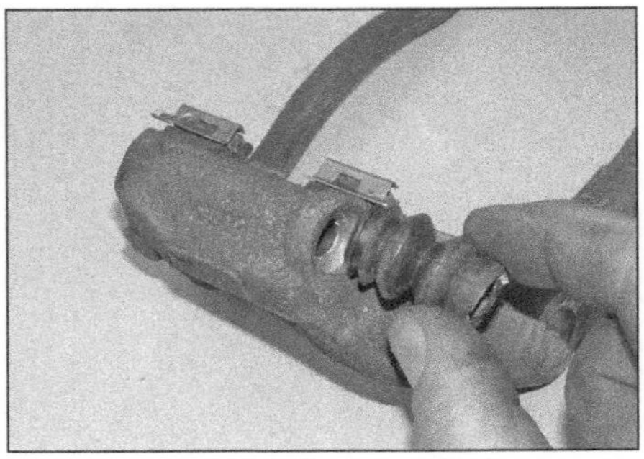

4.8b ... and the guide pin gaiters

4.8c Renew guide pins and gaiters, if required

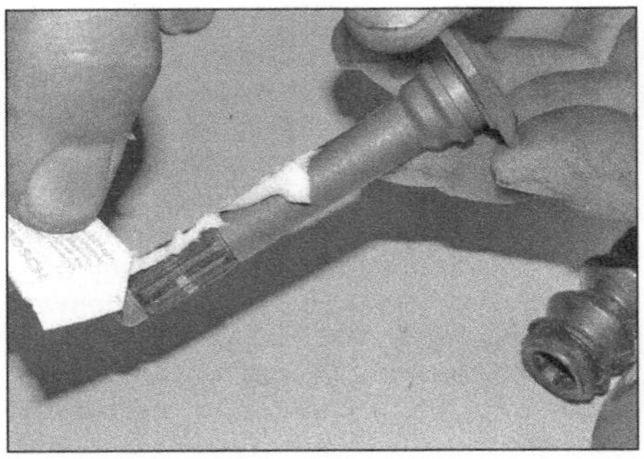

4.8d Use the special grease to lubricate the pins

4.10 Open the bleed nipple and push the piston back (piston retraction tool shown)

either pad is worn at any point to the specified minimum thickness or less, all four pads must be renewed. Also, the pads should be renewed if any are fouled with oil or grease; there is no satisfactory way of degreasing friction material, once contaminated. If any of the brake pads are worn unevenly, or are fouled with oil or grease, trace and rectify the cause before reassembly.

7 If the brake pads are still serviceable, carefully clean them using a clean, fine wire brush or similar, paying particular attention to the sides and back of the metal backing. Clean out the grooves in the friction material, and pick out any large embedded particles of dirt or debris. Carefully clean the pad locations in the caliper mounting bracket.

8 Prior to fitting the pads, check that the guide pins are free to slide easily in the caliper mounting bracket, and check that the rubber guide pin gaiters are undamaged **(see illustrations)**. If required a guide pin kit can be obtained, refit the pins noting their fitted position, using the grease provided.

9 Brush the dust and dirt from the caliper and piston, but do not inhale it, as it is a health hazard. Inspect the dust seal around the piston for damage, and the piston for evidence of fluid leaks, corrosion or damage. If attention to any of these components is necessary, refer to Section 8.

10 If new brake pads are to be fitted, the caliper piston must be pushed back into the cylinder to make room for them. Either use a G-clamp or similar tool, or use suitable pieces of wood as levers. Clamp off the flexible brake hose leading to the caliper then connect a brake bleeding kit to the caliper bleed nipple. Open the bleed nipple as the piston is retracted, the surplus brake fluid will then be collected in the bleed kit vessel **(see illustration)**. Close the bleed nipple just before the caliper piston is pushed fully into the caliper. This should ensure no air enters the hydraulic system. **Note:** *The ABS unit contains hydraulic components that are very sensitive to impurities in the brake fluid. Even the smallest particles can cause the system to fail through blockage. The pad retraction method described here prevents any debris in the brake fluid expelled from the caliper from being passed back to the ABS unit, as well as preventing any chance of damage to the master cylinder seals.*

11 Check to make sure the shims at the top and bottom of the caliper bracket are correctly fitted **(see illustration)**.

12 Ensuring that the friction material of each pad is against the brake disc, fit the pads to the caliper mounting bracket. If the shims (where fitted) have become detached, ensure that they are correctly positioned on each pads backing plate. If the pads have a chamfer at one edge, fit the pads so that the chamfer is at the top **(see illustration)**.

13 Pivot the caliper down into position over the pads. If the threads of the new guide pin bolt are not already pre-coated with locking compound, apply a suitable thread-locking compound to them (Citroën recommend Loctite Frenetanch – available from your Citroën dealer). Press the caliper into position, and then install the guide pin bolt, tightening it to the specified torque setting **(see illustration)**.

4.11 Ensure the shims at the top and bottom of the caliper mounting bracket are correctly fitted

4.12 Refit the pads, with the arrow (arrowed) in the direction of rotation

4.13 Pivot the caliper down and over the pads, then fit and tighten the new caliper guide pin bolt

4.15a Release the spring clips ...

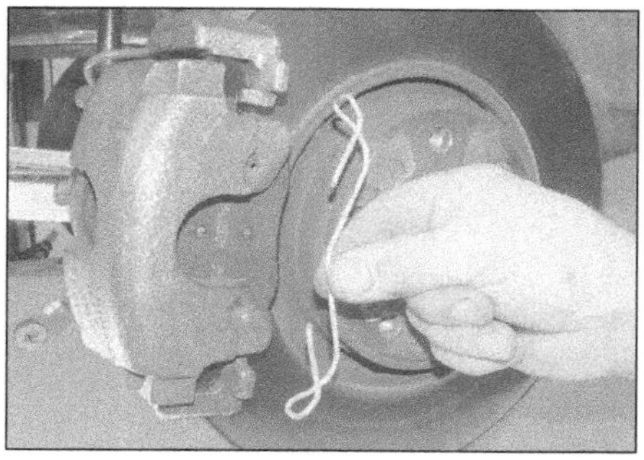

4.15b ... from the caliper and mounting bracket

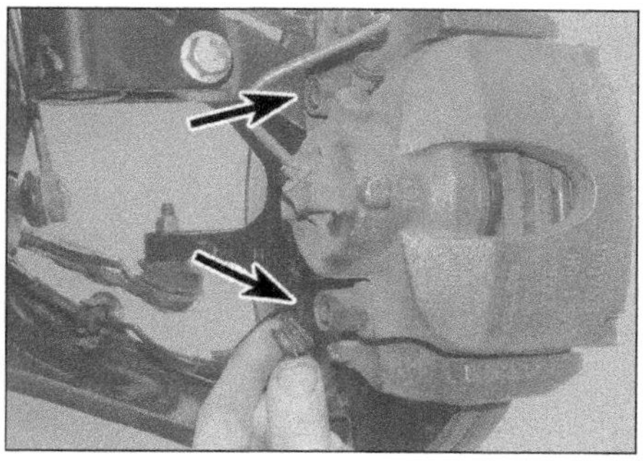

4.17 Unclip the two plastic caps (arrowed)

14 Refit the roadwheel, and then repeat the renewal procedure on the remaining front brake.

Teves calipers

15 Use a thin screwdriver to unclip and release the spring clip from the caliper mounting bracket **(see illustrations)**. Note the spring clips fitted position for refitting.

16 Unclip the brake hose from the mounting bracket on the lower part of the strut.

17 Unclip the two plastic plugs from the end of the guide pins **(see illustration)**.

18 Unscrew the two caliper guide pins from the rear of the caliper **(see illustration)**.

19 With the guide pins removed, lift the caliper away from the brake disc and move it to one side. The inner brake pad has a clip attached to it that locates in the caliper piston, so the pad will come away with the caliper **(see illustrations)**. Do not let the brake caliper hang on the brake hose; fasten it up using a piece of wire.

20 Withdraw the two brake pads, one from the carrier bracket and one from the caliper. If required, the thickness of the pads can be checked at this stage using a steel rule **(see illustration 4.6)**.

21 Before refitting the pads, check that the guide pins are free to slide in the caliper and check that the rubber dust excluders around the guide pins are undamaged. Brush the dust and dirt from the caliper and piston but do not inhale it, as it is injurious to health. Inspect the dust excluder around the piston for damage and inspect the piston for evidence of fluid leaks, corrosion or damage. If attention to any of these components is necessary, refer to Section 8.

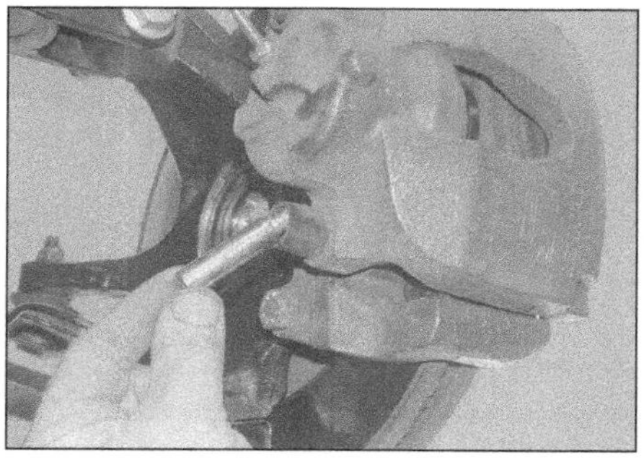

4.18 Unscrew the guide pins

4.19a Remove the caliper ...

22 Make sure that the caliper piston is fully retracted in its bore. If not, fit a bleed bottle and tube to the bleed screw, open the bleed screw and carefully push the piston in, preferably using a G-clamp or, alternatively, using a flat bar or screwdriver as a lever **(see illustration 4.10)**. As the piston is retracted, the fluid will be pushed out of the bleed screw and into the bleed bottle. Tighten the bleed screw, when the piston is fully retracted. **Note:** *The ABS unit contains hydraulic components that are very sensitive to impurities in the brake fluid. Even the smallest particles can cause the system to fail through blockage. The pad retraction method described here prevents any debris in the brake fluid expelled from the caliper from being passed back to the ABS unit, as well as preventing any chance of damage to the master cylinder seals.*

23 To refit the brake pads, place them in position on the carrier bracket and in the caliper piston **(see illustrations)**.

24 Position the caliper in place over the brake disc, then fit the guide pins starting with the lowest one first. Tighten the pins to the specified torque. Refit the two plastic plugs to the ends of the guide pins.

25 Reconnect the brake hose to the mounting bracket on the lower part of the strut. **Note:** *Make sure the brake hose and ABS sensor wiring are secure and will not foul any other components.*

26 Refit the spring clip to the caliper mounting

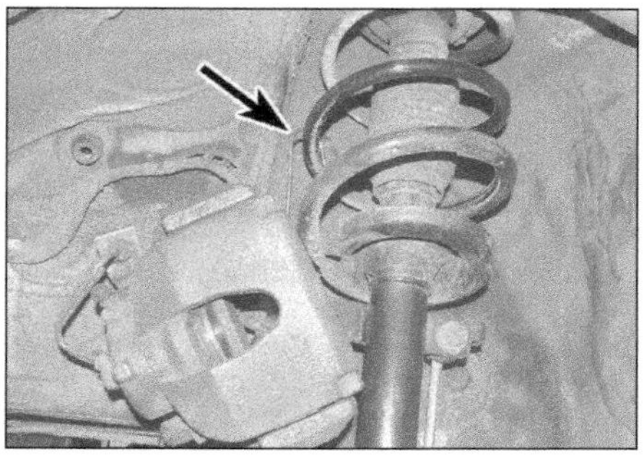

4.19b ... then tie it to the suspension strut

4.23a Fit the new brake pads ...

4.23b ... locating the inner one in the caliper piston

4.26 Make sure the spring clip is secure

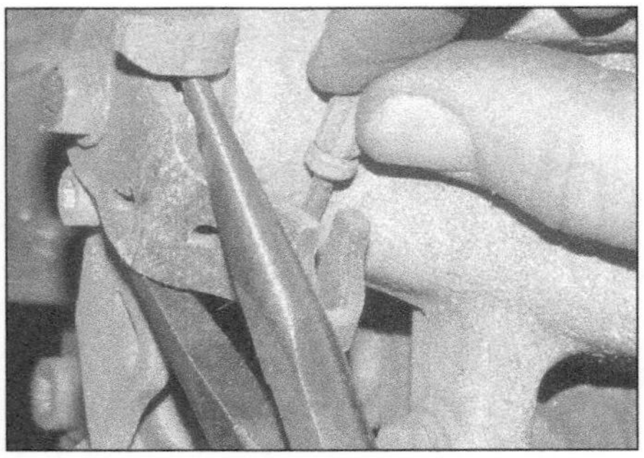

5.2a Disengage the handbrake cable from the caliper lever ...

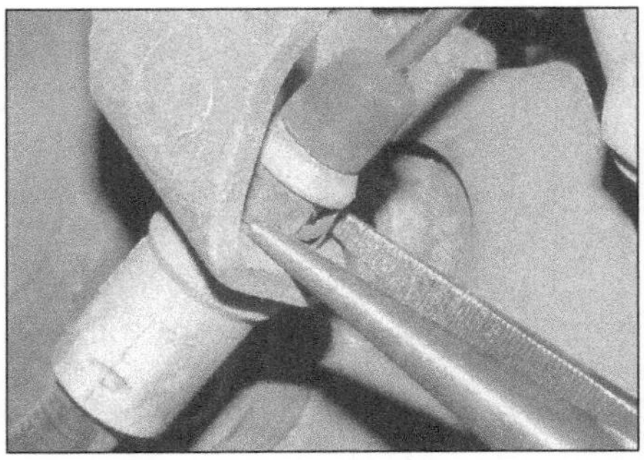

5.2b ... then squeeze the clip and pull the outer cable from the support bracket

bracket, making sure it is fitted correctly as noted on removal **(see illustration)**.

27 Refit the roadwheel, then repeat the renewal procedure on the remaining rear brake.

All calipers

28 Depress the brake pedal repeatedly, until the pads are pressed into firm contact with the brake disc, and normal (non-assisted) pedal pressure is restored.

29 if not already done, refit the roadwheels, and then lower the vehicle to the ground and tighten the roadwheel bolts to the specified torque.

30 On completion, check the fluid level in the reservoir, check the hydraulic fluid level as described in *Weekly checks*.

Caution: New pads will not give full braking efficiency until they have bedded-in. Be prepared for this, and avoid hard braking as far as possible for the first hundred miles or so after pad renewal.

5 Rear brake pads – renewal

Warning: Renew both sets of rear brake pads at the same time – never renew the pads on only one wheel, as uneven braking may result. Note that the dust created by wear of the pads may contain asbestos, which is a health hazard. Never blow it out with compressed air, and don't inhale any of it. An approved filtering mask should be worn when working on the brakes. DO NOT use petrol or petroleum-based solvents to clean brake parts; use brake cleaner or methylated spirit only.

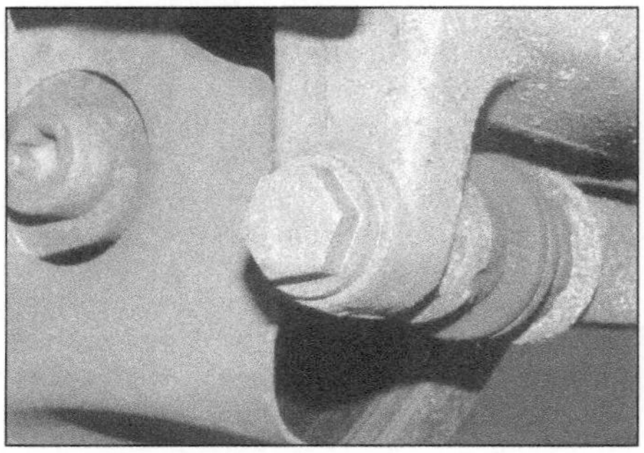

5.3 Remove the caliper lower guide pin bolt

5.4a Withdraw the inner ...

5.4b ... and outer pads

5.4c Note the fitted location of any shims fitted between the pads and caliper

Note: *New guide pin bolts must be fitted on reassembly*.

1 Chock the front wheels, slacken the rear roadwheel bolts, and then jack up the rear of the vehicle and support it on axle stands (see *Jacking and vehicle support*). Remove the rear roadwheels.

2 Using a pair of pliers, release the handbrake cable from the caliper lever. Compress the clip and pull the cable from the support bracket **(see illustrations)**.

3 Slacken and remove the caliper lower guide pin bolt, and swing the caliper up, pivoting around the top guide pin bolt, and tie it in place **(see illustration)**.

4 Withdraw the inner and outer pads from the caliper bracket, and note the location of any shims fitted between the pads and caliper **(see illustrations)**.

5 First measure the thickness of the friction material of each brake pad. If either pad is worn at any point to the specified minimum thickness or less, all four pads must be renewed. Also, the pads should be renewed if any are fouled with oil or grease; there is no satisfactory way of degreasing friction material, once contaminated. If any of the brake pads are worn unevenly, or fouled with oil or grease, trace and rectify the cause before reassembly. Examine the retaining pins for signs of wear and renew if necessary. New brake pads and retaining pin kits are available from Citroën dealers.

6 If the brake pads are still serviceable, carefully clean them using a clean, fine wire brush or similar, paying particular attention to the sides and back of the metal backing. Clean out the grooves in the friction material, and pick out any large embedded particles of dirt or debris. Carefully clean the pad locations in the caliper body/mounting bracket.

7 Prior to fitting the pads, check that the guide sleeves are free to slide easily in the caliper body, and check that the rubber guide sleeve gaiters are undamaged. Brush the dust and dirt from the caliper and piston, but do not inhale it, as it is a health hazard. Inspect the dust seal around the piston for damage, and the piston for evidence of fluid leaks, corrosion or damage. If attention to any of these components is necessary, refer to Section 9.

8 If new brake pads are to be fitted, the caliper piston must be pushed back into the

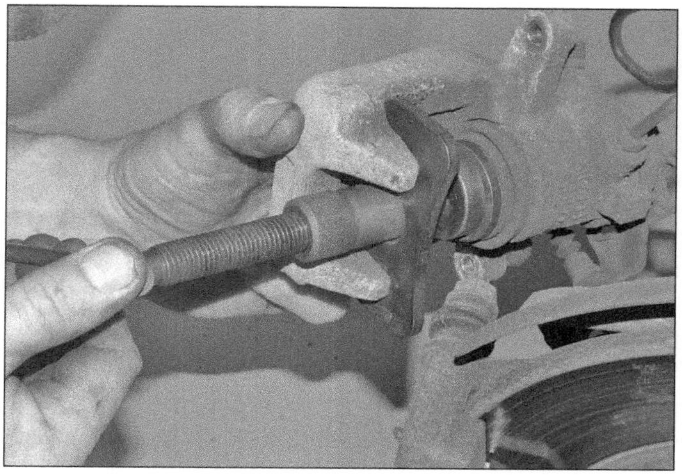

5.8 Use a retraction tool to rotate the piston whilst pushing at the same time

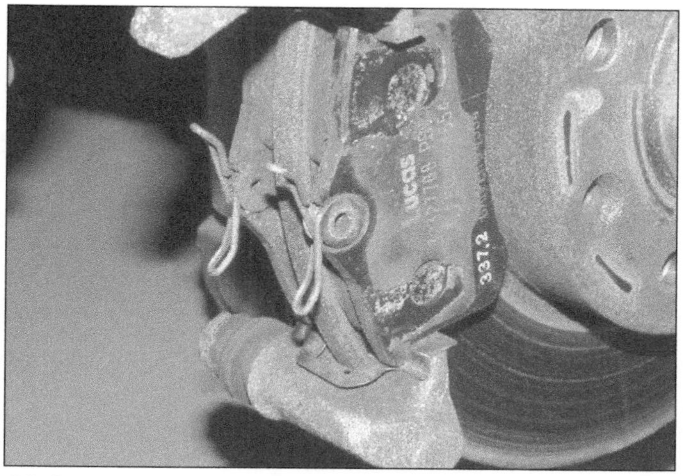

5.9 Ensure the pads are fitted with the friction material facing the brake disc

cylinder to make room for them. In order to retract the piston, the piston must be turned clockwise as it is pushed into the caliper. Citroën tool No DF61 is available to retract the pistons, as are several available from good accessory/parts retailers **(see illustration)**. Clamp off the flexible brake hose leading to the caliper then connect a brake bleeding kit to the caliper bleed nipple. Open the bleed nipple as the piston is retracted, the surplus brake fluid will then be collected in the bleed kit vessel. Close the bleed nipple just before the caliper piston is pushed fully into the caliper. This should ensure no air enters the hydraulic system. **Note:** *The ABS unit contains hydraulic components that are very sensitive to impurities in the brake fluid. Even the smallest particles can cause the system to fail through blockage. The pad retraction method described here prevents any debris in the brake fluid expelled from the caliper from being passed back to the ABS unit, as well as preventing any chance of damage to the master cylinder seals.*

9 Slide the brake pads into position in the caliper; ensuring each pad's friction material is facing the brake disc. If the shims (where fitted) have become detached, ensure that they are correctly positioned on each pad's backing plate **(see illustration)**.

10 Untie the caliper and lower it into position. Insert the new caliper lower guide pin bolt, and tighten it to the specified torque.

11 Slide the handbrake cable into the support bracket and reconnect the cable end fitting.

12 Depress the brake pedal repeatedly until the pads are pressed into firm contact with the brake disc, and normal (non-assisted) pedal pressure is restored.

13 Repeat the above procedure on the remaining rear brake caliper.

14 Check the operation of the handbrake, and if necessary, carry out the adjustment procedure as described in Section 14.

15 Refit the roadwheels, then lower the vehicle to the ground and tighten the roadwheel bolts to the specified torque setting.

16 Check the hydraulic fluid level as described in *Weekly checks*.

Caution: New pads will not give full braking efficiency until they have bedded-in. Be prepared for this, and avoid hard braking as far as possible for the first hundred miles or so after pad renewal.

6 Front brake disc – inspection, removal and refitting

Note: *Before starting work, refer to the note at the beginning of Section 4 concerning the dangers of asbestos dust.*

Inspection

Note: *If either disc requires renewal, BOTH should be renewed at the same time, to ensure even and consistent braking. New brake pads should also be fitted.*

1 Apply the handbrake, slacken the front roadwheel bolts, then jack up the front of the car and support it on axle stands (see Jacking and vehicle support). Remove the appropriate front roadwheel.

2 Slowly rotate the brake disc so that the full area of both sides can be checked; remove the brake pads if better access is required to the inboard surface. Light scoring is normal in the area swept by the brake pads, but if heavy scoring or cracks are found, the disc must be renewed.

3 It is normal to find a lip of rust and brake dust around the disc's perimeter; this can be scraped off if required. If, however, a lip has formed due to excessive wear of the brake pad swept area, then the disc's thickness must be measured using a micrometer. Take measurements at several places around the disc, at the inside and outside of the pad swept area; if the disc has worn at any point to the specified minimum thickness or less, the disc must be renewed **(see illustration)**.

4 If the disc is thought to be warped, it can be checked for run-out. Either use a dial gauge mounted on any convenient fixed point, while the disc is slowly rotated, or use feeler blades to measure (at several points all around the disc) the clearance between the disc and a fixed point, such as the caliper mounting bracket **(see illustration)**. If the measurements obtained are at the specified maximum or beyond, the disc is excessively warped, and must be renewed; however, it is worth checking first that the hub bearing is in good condition

6.3 Use a micrometer to measure the disc thickness

6.4 Check the disc run-out using a dial gauge

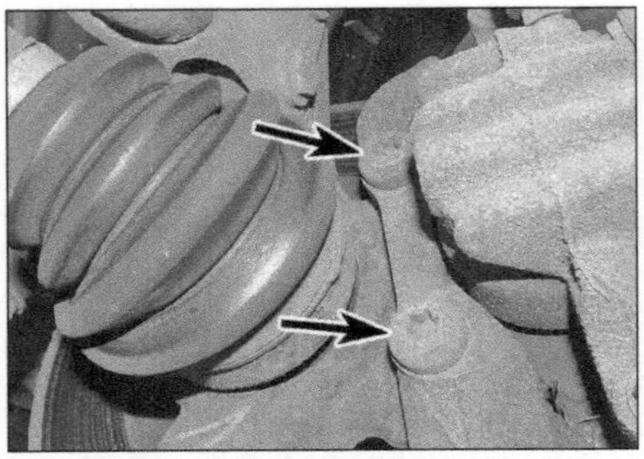

6.6a Undo the mounting bolts (arrowed) ...

6.6b ... and withdraw the caliper and bracket from over the disc

6.7 Undo the two Torx screws, and remove the disc

(Chapter 1A, Section 13 or Chapter 1B, Section 5). Also try the effect of removing the disc and turning it through 180°, to reposition it on the hub; if the run-out is still excessive, the disc must be renewed.

5 Check the disc for cracks, especially around the wheel bolt holes, and any other wear or damage, and renew if necessary.

Removal

6 Slacken and remove the two bolts securing the brake caliper mounting bracket to the hub carrier **(see illustrations)**, discard the bolts, as new ones will be required for refitting. Slide the assembly off the disc and tie it to the coil spring, using a piece of wire or string, to avoid placing any strain on the hydraulic brake hose.

7 Use chalk or paint to mark the relationship of the disc to the hub, then remove the screws securing the brake disc to the hub, and remove the disc **(see illustration)**. If it is tight, lightly tap its rear face with a hide or plastic mallet.

Refitting

8 Refitting is the reverse of the removal procedure, noting the following points:

a) Ensure that the mating surfaces of the disc and hub are clean and flat.

b) Align (if applicable) the marks made on removal, and tighten the disc retaining screws to the specified torque setting.

c) If a new disc has been fitted, use a suitable solvent to wipe any preservative coating from the disc, before refitting the caliper.

d) Fit new bolts to the caliper mounting bracket and tighten to the specified torque setting.

e) Refit the roadwheels, and then lower the vehicle to the ground and tighten the wheel bolts to the specified torque.

f) Apply the footbrake several times to force the pads back into contact with the disc before driving the vehicle.

7 Rear brake disc – inspection, removal and refitting

Note: *Before starting work, refer to the warning at the beginning of Section 5 concerning the dangers of asbestos dust.*

Inspection

Note: *If either disc requires renewal, BOTH should be renewed at the same time, to ensure even and consistent braking. New brake pads should also be fitted.*

1 Chock the front wheels, engage reverse gear (or P on models with automatic transmission) and release the handbrake. Jack up the rear of the vehicle and support it securely on axle stands (see *Jacking and vehicle support*). Remove the relevant roadwheel.

2 Inspect the rear brake discs, as described for the front brake discs in Section 6.

Removal

Note: *New hub/disc retaining nut must be fitted on reassembly.*

3 Remove the brake pads as described in Section 5.

4 Unscrew the two screws securing the brake caliper mounting bracket to the hub carrier, and move it clear of the disc **(see illustration)**.

5 Using a hammer and suitable chisel (or large flat-bladed screwdriver), carefully tap and prise the cap from the centre of the brake disc **(see illustration)**.

6 Using a socket and long bar, slacken and remove the rear hub nut – this will be very tight, so ensure that the car is well supported, and that only good quality, close-fitting tools are used **(see illustration)**. Discard the hub nut; a new one must be used on refitting

7 It should now be possible to withdraw the brake disc and hub bearing assembly from the stub axle by hand.

Refitting

8 If a new disc is being fitted, use a suitable solvent to wipe any preservative coating from the disc before refitting. Note that new discs may be supplied with new wheel bearings already fitted; see Chapter 10, Section 11, for further information on rear wheel bearings.

9 Before refitting the disc, carefully clean the

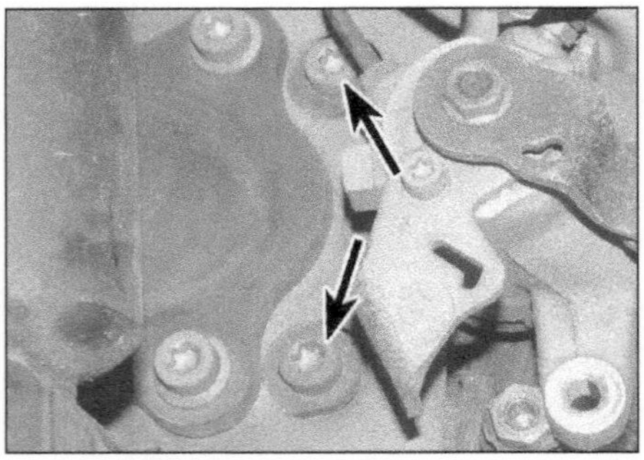

7.4 Slacken the two caliper mounting bracket Torx screws (arrowed)

7.5 Remove the cap from the disc/hub ...

7.6 ... and remove the rear hub nut

ABS magnetic ring on the back of the hub bearing **(see illustration)**.

10 Slide the disc back into position on the stub axle and fit the new rear hub nut; tighten it to the specified torque. Tap the cap back into place, in the centre of the disc (if the cap is in poor condition a new one should be fitted).

11 Apply a few drops of locking fluid onto the threads of the caliper mounting bracket bolts. Offer up the bracket and refit the bolts, tightening them to the specified torque.

12 Refit the brake pads as described in Section 5.

13 Refit the roadwheel, then lower the vehicle to the ground and tighten the roadwheel bolts to the specified torque.

14 On completion, depress the brake pedal several times to bring the brake pads into contact with the disc.

8 Front brake caliper – removal, overhaul and refitting

Caution: Ensure the ignition is switched off before disconnecting any braking system hydraulic union and do not switch it on until after the hydraulic system has been bled. Failure to do this could lead to air entering the modulator unit requiring the unit to be bled using special Citroën test equipment (see Section 2).

Note: *Before starting work, refer to the note at the beginning of Section 2 concerning the dangers of hydraulic fluid, and to the warning at the beginning of Section 4 concerning the dangers of asbestos dust.*

Note: *New caliper mounting bracket bolts will be required on reassembly.*

Note: *On Bosch calipers, new brake caliper guide pin bolts will be required on reassembly.*

Removal

1 Apply the handbrake, slacken the relevant front roadwheel bolts, then jack up the front of the vehicle and support it on axle stands (see *Jacking and vehicle support*). Remove the appropriate roadwheel.

2 Minimise fluid loss by first removing the master cylinder reservoir cap, and then tightening it down onto a piece of polythene, to obtain an airtight seal. Alternatively, use a brake hose clamp, a G-clamp or a similar tool to clamp the flexible hose **(see illustration)**.

3 Clean the area around the caliper hose union and place a wad of rag under the union, to catch any spilt fluid. On Teves calipers, slacken and remove the brake hose banjo bolt, and move the brake hose to one side. On Bosch calipers, it is only possible to slacken the brake hose fitting on the caliper at this point, as the hose will twist **(see illustration)**.

4 Slacken and remove the upper and lower caliper guide pin bolts or pins, refer to Section 4. Lift the caliper away from the brake disc, and then on Bosch type calipers, unscrew the caliper from the end of the brake hose. Note that the brake pads need not be disturbed, and can be left in position in the caliper mounting bracket. On Bosch calipers, discard the guide pin bolts; new ones must be used on refitting.

5 If required, the caliper mounting bracket can be unbolted from the hub carrier. Discard the bolts, as new ones must be fitted.

Overhaul

Note: *Check the availability of repair kits for the caliper before dismantling.*

6 With the caliper on the bench, wipe away all traces of dust and dirt, but avoid inhaling the dust, as it is a health hazard.

7 Withdraw the partially ejected piston from the caliper body, and remove the dust seal.

8 Using a small screwdriver, extract the piston hydraulic seal, taking great care not to damage the caliper bore.

9 Thoroughly clean all components, using only methylated spirit, isopropyl alcohol or clean hydraulic fluid as a cleaning medium. Never use mineral-based solvents such as petrol or paraffin, as they will attack the hydraulic system's rubber components. Dry the components immediately, using compressed air or a clean, lint-free cloth. Use compressed air to blow clear the fluid passages.

10 Check all components, and renew any that are worn or damaged. Check particularly the cylinder bore and piston; these should be renewed (note that this means the renewal of the complete body assembly) if they are scratched, worn or corroded in any way. Similarly check the condition of the guide pins and their gaiters; both pins should be undamaged and (when cleaned) a reasonably tight sliding fit in the caliper bracket. If there is any doubt about the condition of any component, renew it **(see illustrations 4.8a to 4.8d)**.

11 If the assembly is fit for further use, then obtain the appropriate repair kit; the components should be available from Citroën dealers in various combinations. All rubber seals should be renewed as a matter of course; these should never be re-used.

12 On reassembly, ensure that all components are clean and dry.

13 Soak the piston and the new piston (fluid) seal in clean brake fluid. Smear clean fluid on the cylinder bore surface.

14 Fit the new piston (fluid) seal, using only your fingers (no tools) to manipulate it into the cylinder bore groove.

15 Fit the new dust seal to the rear of the piston and seat the outer lip of the seal in the caliper body groove. Carefully ease the piston squarely into the cylinder bore using a twisting motion. Press the piston fully into position, and seat the inner lip of the dust seal in the piston groove.

16 If the guide pins are being renewed, lubricate the pin shafts with the special grease supplied in the repair kit, and fit the gaiters to the pin grooves. Insert the pins into the caliper bracket and seat the gaiters correctly in the bracket grooves.

Refitting

17 If previously removed, refit the caliper mounting bracket to the hub carrier, and tighten the new bolts to the specified torque.

18 On Bosch type calipers, screw the caliper body fully onto the flexible hose union.

19 Ensure that the brake pads are correctly fitted in the caliper mounting bracket and refit the caliper (see Section 4).

20 If the threads of the new guide pin bolts are not already pre-coated with locking compound, apply a suitable locking compound to them (Citroën recommend Loctite Frenetanch – available from your Citroën dealer). Fit the new lower guide pin bolt, then press the caliper into

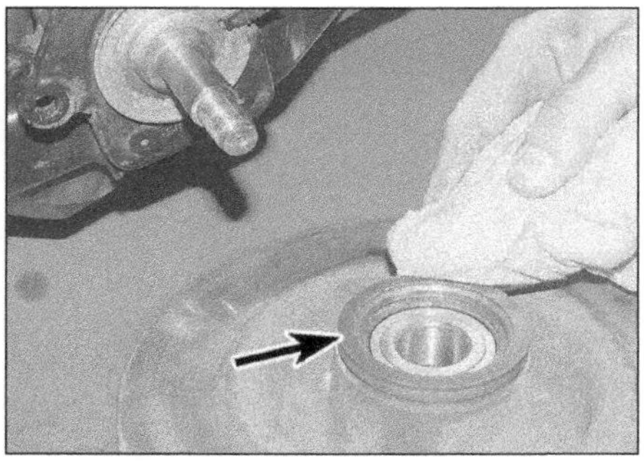

7.9 Clean around the ABS magnetic ring before refitting

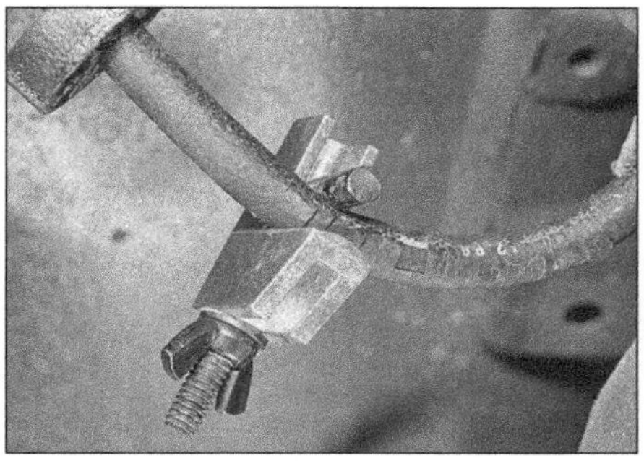

8.2 To minimise fluid loss, fit a brake hose clamp to the flexible hose

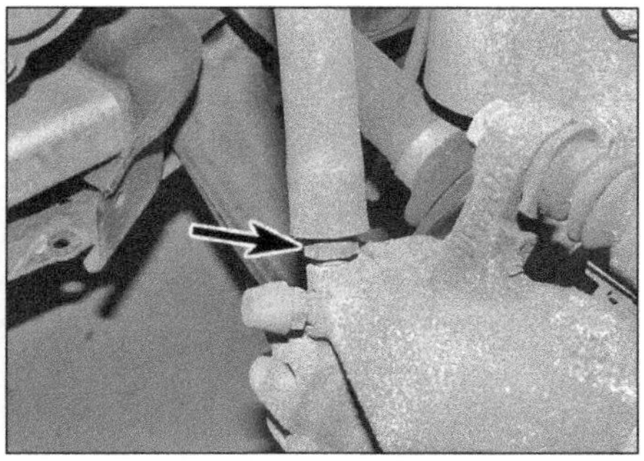

8.3 Slacken the brake hose nut (arrowed) – Bosch caliper

9.3 Unscrew the brake pipe union nut (arrowed)

position and fit the new upper guide pin bolt. Tighten both guide pin bolts to the specified torque.

21 On Teves calipers, refit the hydraulic brake hose to caliper and tighten the banjo bolt to the specified torque setting, then remove the brake hose clamp or polythene (where fitted).

22 On Bosch calipers, tighten the brake hose union nut to the specified torque, then remove the brake hose clamp or polythene (where fitted).

23 Bleed the hydraulic system as described in Section 2. Note that, providing the precautions described were taken to minimise brake fluid loss, it should only be necessary to bleed the relevant front brake.

24 Refit the roadwheel, then lower the vehicle to the ground and tighten the roadwheel bolts to the specified torque.

9 Rear brake caliper – removal, overhaul and refitting

Caution: Ensure the ignition is switched off before disconnecting any braking system hydraulic union and do not switch it back on until after the hydraulic system has been bled. Failure to do this could lead to air entering the modulator unit requiring the unit to be bled using special Citroën test equipment (see Section 2).

Note: *Before starting work, refer to the note at the beginning of Section 2 concerning the dangers of hydraulic fluid, and to the warning at the beginning of Section 5 concerning the dangers of asbestos dust.*

Note: *New caliper mounting bracket bolts and guide pin bolts when be required on reassembly.*

Removal

1 Chock the front wheels, slacken the relevant rear roadwheel bolts, then jack up the rear of the vehicle and support on axle stands (see *Jacking and vehicle support*). Remove the relevant rear wheel.

2 Minimise fluid loss by first removing the master cylinder reservoir cap, and then tightening it down onto a piece of polythene to obtain an airtight seal. Alternatively, use a brake hose clamp, a G-clamp or a similar tool to clamp the flexible hose at the nearest convenient point to the brake caliper **(see illustration 8.2)**.

3 Wipe away all traces of dirt around the brake pipe union on the caliper **(see illustration)**. Unscrew the union nut and disconnect the brake pipe from the caliper. Plug the pipe and caliper unions to minimise fluid loss and prevent dirt entry.

4 Remove the brake pads (see Section 5).

5 Slacken and remove the upper guide pin bolt, to remove the caliper from the vehicle. If required, the caliper mounting bracket can be unbolted from the hub carrier. Discard the bolts, as new ones must be fitted.

Overhaul

6 At the time of writing, no parts were available to recondition the rear caliper assembly, with the excepting of the guide pin bolts, guide pins and guide pin gaiters. Check the condition of the guide pins and their gaiters; both pins should be undamaged and (when cleaned) a reasonably tight sliding fit in the caliper bracket. If there is any doubt about the condition of any component, renew it **(see illustrations 4.8a to 4.8d)**.

Refitting

7 If previously removed, refit the caliper mounting bracket to the hub carrier, and tighten the new bolts to the specified torque.

8 Refit the brake pads as described in Section 5.

9 Refit the caliper and insert the new guide pin bolts, tightening them to the specified torque settings.

10 Reconnect the brake pipe to the caliper, and tighten the brake hose union nut to the specified torque. Remove the brake hose clamp or polythene (where fitted).

11 Bleed the hydraulic system as described in Section 2. Note that, providing the precautions described were taken to minimise brake fluid loss, it should only be necessary to bleed the relevant rear brake.

12 Refit the roadwheel, then lower the vehicle to the ground and tighten the roadwheel bolts to the specified torque.

10 Master cylinder – removal, overhaul and refitting

Caution: Ensure the ignition is switched off before disconnecting any braking system hydraulic union and do not switch it back on until after the hydraulic system has been bled. Failure to do this could lead to air entering the modulator unit requiring the unit to be bled using special Citroën test equipment (see Section 2).

Note: *Before starting work, refer to the warning at the beginning of Section 2 concerning the dangers of hydraulic fluid.*

Removal

1 Remove the battery and battery tray, as described in Chapter 5A, Section 4.

2 Remove the master cylinder reservoir cap and filter, and siphon the hydraulic fluid from the reservoir. **Note:** *Do not siphon the fluid by mouth, as it is poisonous; use a syringe or an old antifreeze tester. Alternatively, open any convenient bleed screw in the system, and gently pump the brake pedal to expel the fluid through a plastic tube connected to the screw until the reservoir is emptied (see Section 2).*

3 Undo the two retaining screws and remove the upper reservoir from the rear panel. Depress the release button and disconnect the plastic pipe from the upper reservoir and remove it from the engine compartment **(see illustration)**. Be prepared for some fluid spillage.

4 Disconnect the wiring connector from the brake fluid level sender unit in the left-hand rear of the reservoir **(see illustration)**.

5 Empty the lower reservoir by disconnecting the clutch master cylinder fluid supply pipe and draining the fluid into a container **(see illustration)**. Plug the pipe opening to prevent dirt ingress.

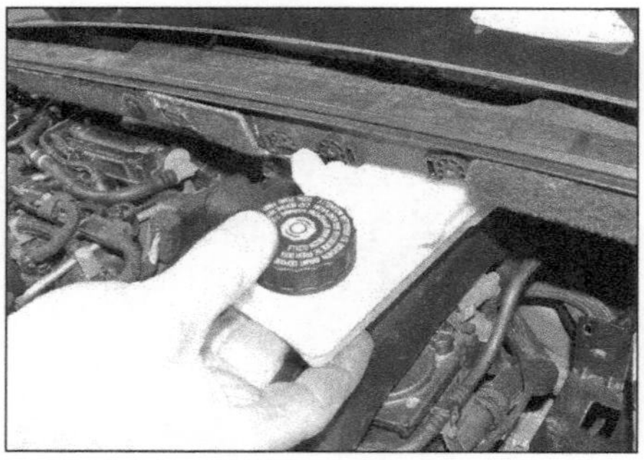

10.3 Undo the two screws securing the upper reservoir

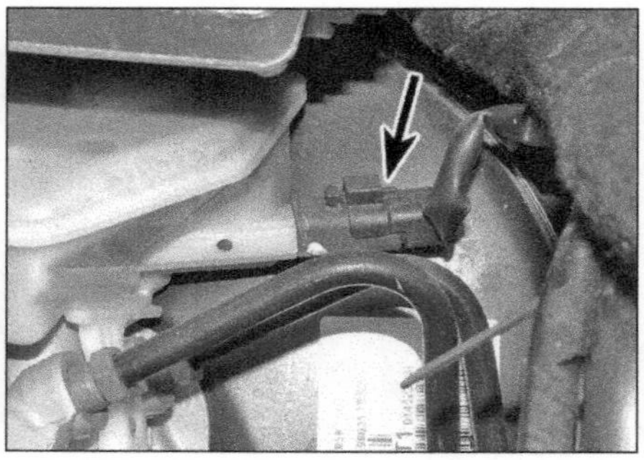

10.4 Disconnect the level sensor wiring plug (arrowed)

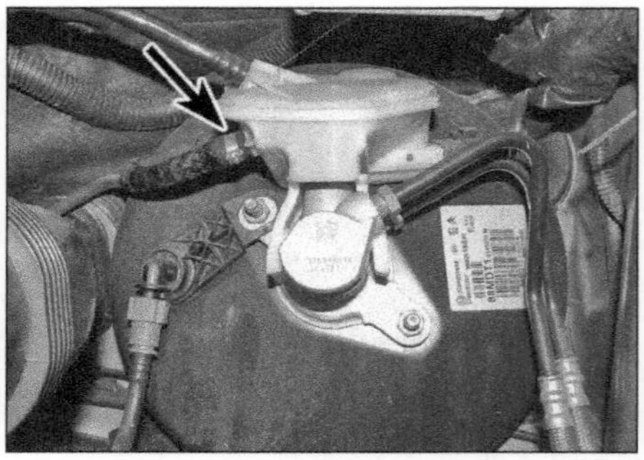

10.5 Clutch fluid supply pipe (arrowed)

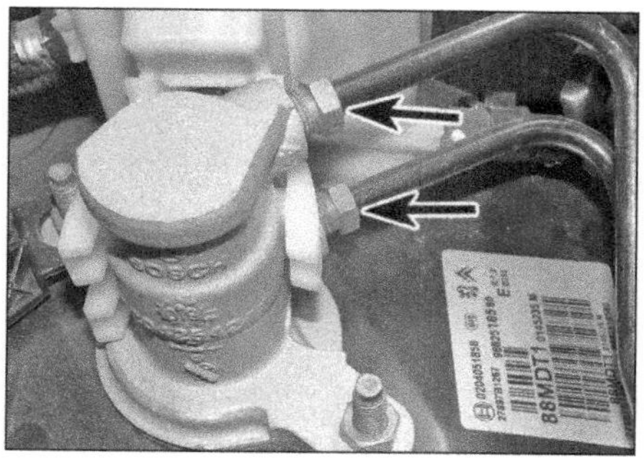

10.6 Slacken the brake fluid pipes (arrowed)

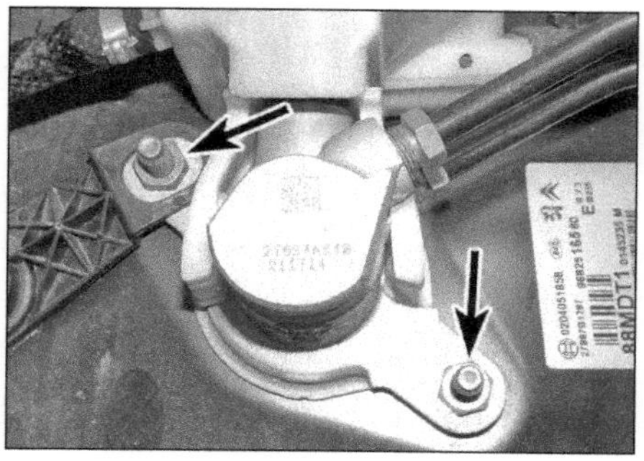

10.7 Master cylinder securing nuts (arrowed)

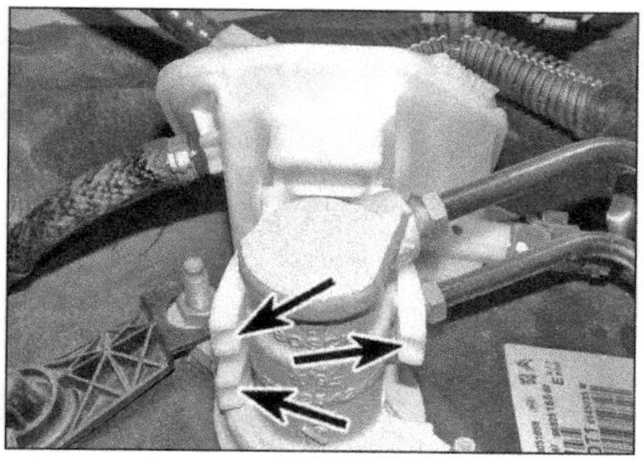

10.8 Release the plastic clips (arrowed) to remove the reservoir

6 Wipe clean the area around the brake pipe unions on the side of the master cylinder, and place absorbent rags beneath the pipe unions to catch any surplus fluid. Make a note of the correct fitted positions of the unions, then unscrew the union nuts and carefully withdraw the pipes **(see illustration)**. Plug or tape over the pipe ends and master cylinder orifices, to minimise the loss of brake fluid, and to prevent the entry of dirt into the system. Wash off any spilt fluid immediately with cold water.

7 Slacken and remove the two nuts securing the master cylinder to the vacuum servo unit **(see illustration)**. Release the plastic servo pipe clip from the mounting stud, and then withdraw the master cylinder from the engine compartment. If the sealing ring fitted to the rear of the master cylinder shows signs of damage or deterioration, it must be renewed.

8 If required, pull retaining lugs and separate the reservoir from the master cylinder **(see illustration)**.

Overhaul

9 The master cylinder may be overhauled after obtaining the relevant repair kit from a Citroën dealer. Ensure that the correct repair kit is obtained for the master cylinder being worked on. Note the locations of all components to ensure correct refitting, and lubricate the new seals using clean brake fluid. Follow the assembly instructions supplied with the repair kit.

Refitting

10 Remove all traces of dirt from the master cylinder and servo unit mating surfaces and ensure that the sealing ring is correctly fitted to the rear of the master cylinder.

11 If removed, press the mounting seals fully into the master cylinder ports then carefully ease the fluid reservoir into position. Secure it in position, making sure the retaining clips are correctly located.

12 Fit the master cylinder to the servo unit. Refit the master cylinder mounting nuts, and tighten them to the specified torque.

13 Wipe clean the brake pipe unions and refit them to the master cylinder ports, tightening them to the specified torque.

14 Reconnect the clutch master cylinder supply pipe (where applicable), and level sensor wiring plug.

15 Connect the fluid supply pipe to the upper reservoir, then fit the reservoir to the rear panel and tighten the retaining screws securely.

16 Refit the battery as described in Chapter 5A, Section 4.

17 Refit any other components removed to improve access then refill the master cylinder reservoir with new fluid. Bleed the complete hydraulic system as described in Section 2. **Note:** *A hydraulic clutch shares its fluid reservoir with the braking system, and may also need to be bled (see Chapter 6, Section 2).*

11 Brake pedal – removal and refitting

Removal

1 Prise up the centre pins, prise out the complete expanding plastic rivets, and remove the driver's side lower facia panel above the pedals **(see illustration)**. Disconnect the wiring connector from the footwell light as the panel is removed.

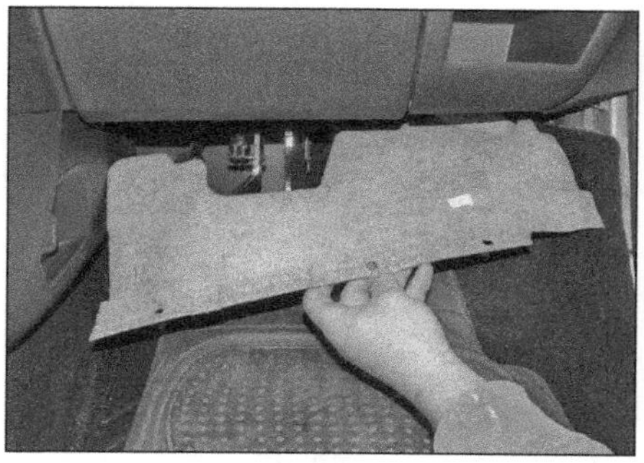

11.1 Remove the trim from under the facia panel

11.2b ... and remove it from the clevis pin

2 Slide off the retaining clip and withdraw the clevis pin securing the pedal crossover linkage pushrod to the pedal **(see illustrations)**. Discard the clevis pin; a new one must be fitted.

3 Slacken and remove the pivot bolt and nut **(see illustration)**, and remove the brake pedal from the vehicle. Slide the spacer and washer (where fitted) out from the pedal pivot. Examine all components for signs of wear or damage, renewing them as necessary.

Refitting

4 Apply a smear of multipurpose grease to the spacer and washer, and insert it into the pedal pivot bore.

11.2a Slide off the retaining clip (arrowed) ...

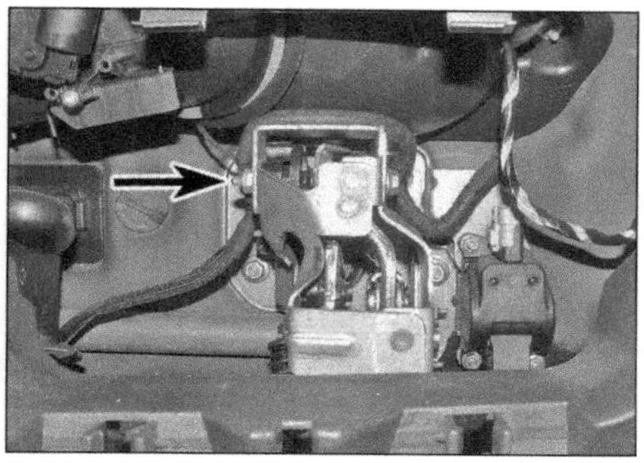

11.3 Slacken and remove the pivot bolt and nut (arrowed)

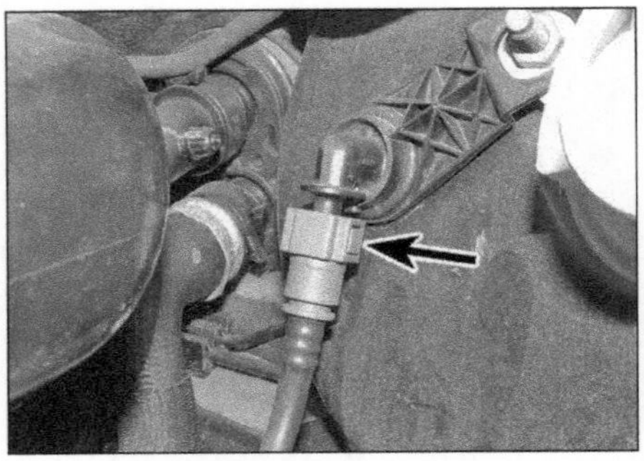

12.6 Depress the securing clip (arrowed)

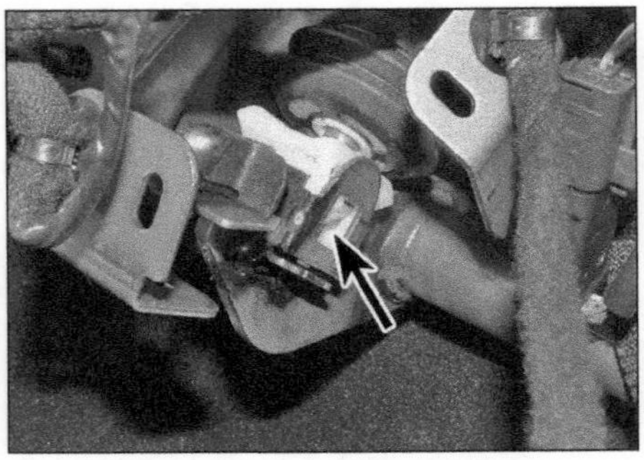

12.8 Release the securing tabs (arrowed) – one each side

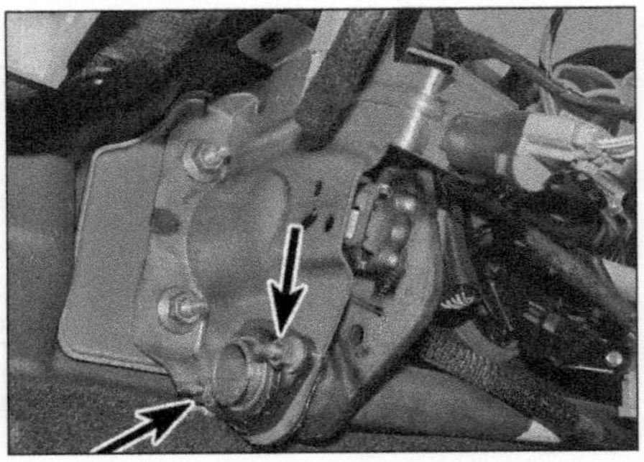

12.9 Undo the two crossover bar mounting nuts (arrowed)

5 Manoeuvre the pedal into position, making sure it is correctly engaged with the pushrod, and then insert the pivot bolt. Refit the nut to the pivot bolt and tighten it securely.
6 Align the pedal with the pushrod and insert the new clevis pin, securing it in position with the retaining clip(s).
7 Refit the driver's side lower trim panel to the lower part of the facia.

12 Vacuum servo unit – testing, removal and refitting

Testing

1 To test the operation of the servo unit, depress the footbrake several times to exhaust the vacuum, then start the engine whilst keeping the pedal firmly depressed. As the engine starts, there should be a noticeable 'give' in the brake pedal as the vacuum builds-up. Allow the engine to run for at least two minutes, and then switch it off. If the brake pedal is now depressed it should feel normal, but further applications should result in the pedal feeling firmer, with the pedal stroke decreasing with each application.
2 If the servo does not operate as described, first inspect the servo unit check valve as described in Section 13. On VTi petrol and diesel engine models, also check the operation of the vacuum pump as described in Section 21.
3 If the servo unit still fails to operate satisfactorily, the fault lies within the unit itself. Repairs to the unit are not possible – if faulty, the servo unit must be renewed.

Removal

4 Remove the master cylinder as described in Section 10.
5 Release the wiring harness adjacent to the servo from its retaining clips, and move it to one side.
6 Release the retaining clip, and then disconnect the vacuum pipe from the servo unit check valve **(see illustration)**.
7 Remove the glovebox assembly as described in Chapter 11, Section 27.
8 Release the securing tabs and then carefully disconnect the servo pushrod from the brake crossover shaft bracket **(see illustration)**.
9 Slacken and remove the two securing nuts from the end of the brake crossover bar **(see illustration)**.
10 Slacken and remove the securing nut from the upper support bracket at the top of the crossover bar mounting bracket **(see illustration)**.
11 Slacken and remove the four nuts securing the housing to the bulkhead **(see illustration)**.
12 Depress the two retaining clips (one to the top of the servo gaiter, and one to the bottom), then ease the mounting bracket away from the bulkhead **(see illustration)**.
13 With the mounting bracket away from the bulkhead, release the retaining plate from the securing clips on the lower left and upper right servo studs. The retaining plate can then be withdrawn from between the bulkhead and the crossover bar mounting bracket. Take care not to damage the gaiter on the servo as the retaining plate is removed.
14 Working back in the engine compartment, manoeuvre the servo unit out of position, along with its gasket which is fitted between the servo and housing. Renew the gasket if it shows signs of damage.

Refitting

15 Refitting is the reverse of removal, noting the following points.

a) Lubricate all crossover linkage pivot points with multipurpose grease.
b) Refit the retaining plate between the bulkhead and the mounting bracket, taking care not to damage the gaiter on the servo pushrod.
c) Tighten the servo unit and mounting bracket nuts and bolts to their specified torque settings, where applicable.
d) Make sure the servo pushrod locates correctly with the brake crossover bar linkage.
e) Refit the master cylinder as described in Section 10 and bleed the complete hydraulic system as described in Section 2.
f) Test the brakes and servo operation as described at the beginning of this Section.

12.10 Undo the support bracket lower mounting nut (arrowed)

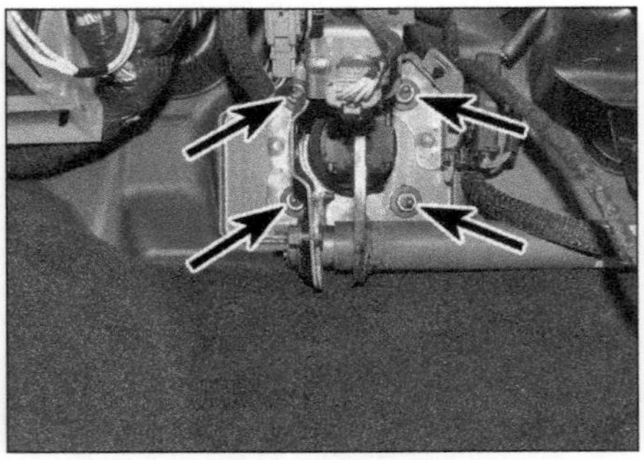

12.11 Undo the four servo mounting nuts (arrowed)

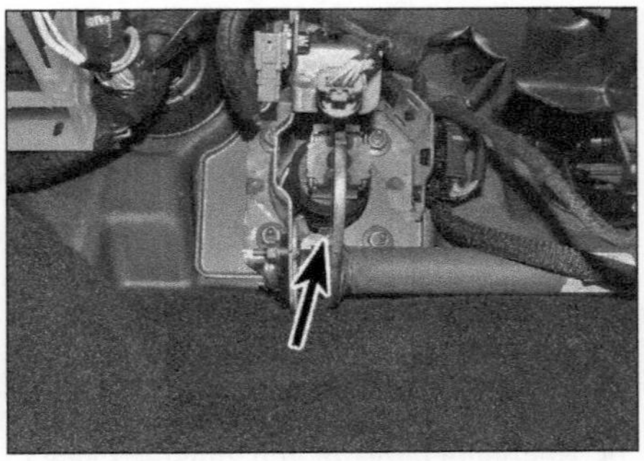

12.12 Release the servo retaining clips (lower one arrowed)

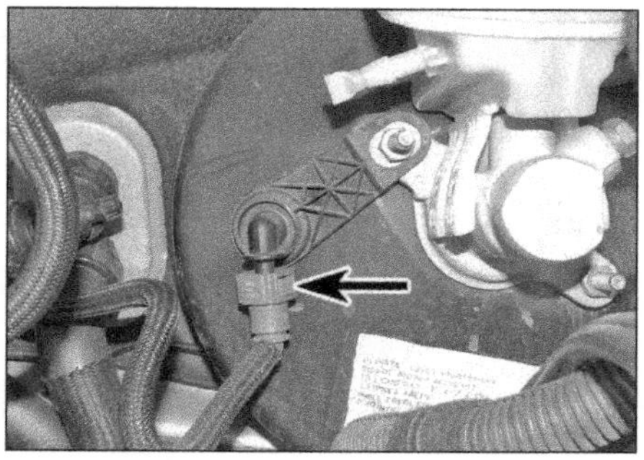

13.1 Depress the securing clip (arrowed) to disconnect the vacuum pipe

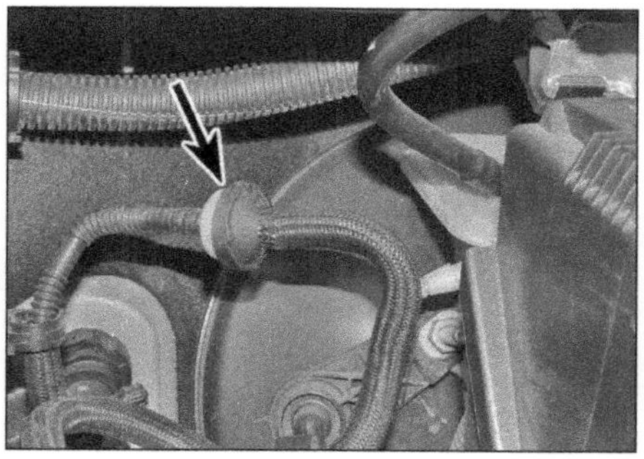

13.5 Vacuum pipe has an in-line valve (arrowed)

14.2 Remove the ashtray housing ...

13 Vacuum servo unit check valve – removal, testing and refitting

Removal

1 Release the retaining clip, and then disconnect the vacuum pipe from the servo unit check valve **(see illustration)**.

2 Withdraw the valve from its rubber sealing grommet in the servo, using a pulling and twisting motion. If required, remove the grommet from the servo and check its condition.

Testing

3 Examine the check valve for signs of damage, and renew if necessary. The valve may be tested by blowing through it in both directions. Air should flow through the valve in one direction only – when blown through from the servo unit end of the valve. Renew the valve if this is not the case.

4 Examine the rubber sealing grommet and flexible vacuum hose for signs of damage or deterioration, and renew as necessary.

5 On some models, there is also an in-line check valve fitted in the vacuum pipe from the pump to the servo **(see illustration)**. This can be tested in the same way as the check valve in the servo, see paragraph 3.

Refitting

6 Fit the sealing grommet into position in the servo unit.

7 Carefully ease the check valve into position, taking great care not to displace or damage the grommet. Reconnect the vacuum hose to the valve and, where necessary, securely tighten its retaining clip.

8 On completion, start the engine and check for air leaks from the check valve-to-servo unit connection.

14 Handbrake – adjustment

1 To check the handbrake adjustment, pull the handbrake lever to the fully applied position, applying normal moderate pressure, counting the number of clicks emitted from the handbrake ratchet mechanism. If adjustment is correct, there should be 2 clicks before the brakes begins to apply, and no more than 6 before the handbrake is fully applied. If this is not the case, adjust as follows.

2 Working at the rear of the centre console, pull open the lid, gently prise out the lower edge on each side and remove the ashtray **(see illustration)**. On models with centre armrests, remove the armrest as described in Chapter 11, Section 26. **Note:** *To make access easier it may be necessary to remove the centre console completely as described in Chapter 11, Section 26.*

3 Chock the front wheels, then jack up the rear of the vehicle and support it on axle stands (see *Jacking and vehicle support*).

4 Slacken the adjuster nut behind the equaliser plate on the rod from the lever **(see illustration)**.

5 Start the engine and depress the brake pedal approximately 20 times. Stop the engine.

6 Tighten the adjuster nut just enough to eliminate any free play in the cables, allowing a small gap (approx 2 mm) between the levers and stops on the brake calipers **(see illustration)**.

7 On some models, there may still be a plastic cable with a spacer on the end attached to the handbrake lever on the caliper. This will fit between the lever and stop on the brake caliper when the handbrake is released **(see illustration)**.

8 To settle the handbrake cables pull the handbrake lever on 10 times. On the last application, pull the lever up and stop after the second click is emitted.

9 Tighten the adjuster nut until the rear brake pads begin to make contact with the discs, rotate the wheels by hand to check.

10 Release the lever and check by hand that the rear wheels rotate freely, then check that no more than six clicks are emitted before the handbrake is fully applied.

11 Switch the ignition on and then pull the handbrake lever up 1 click, and then check that the warning light comes on the instrument panel.

12 Refit the ashtray, then lower the vehicle to the floor.

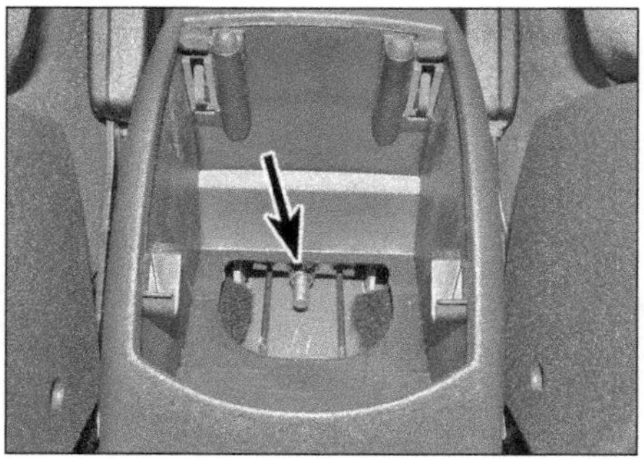

14.4 ... to access the handbrake adjusting nut (arrowed)

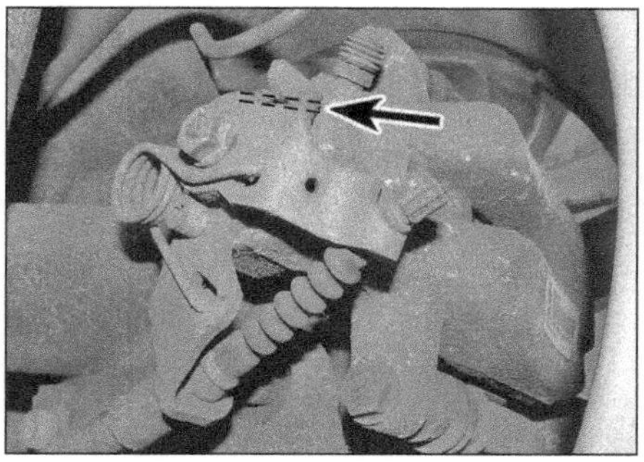

14.6 Allow a small gap (arrowed) between the lever and the stop

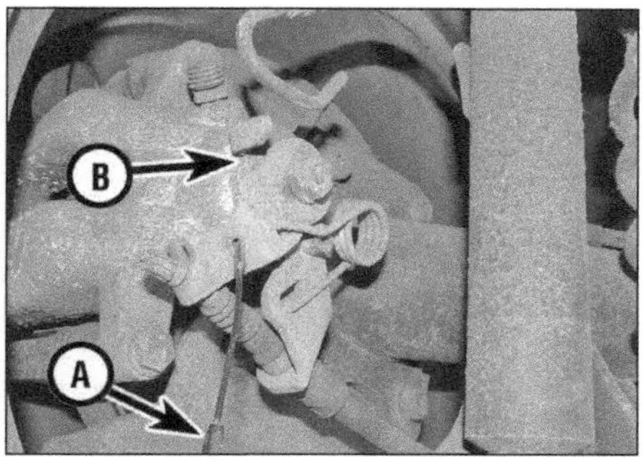

14.7 Fit plastic spacer (A), between the lever and the stop (B)

15.4a Disconnect the wiring connector ...

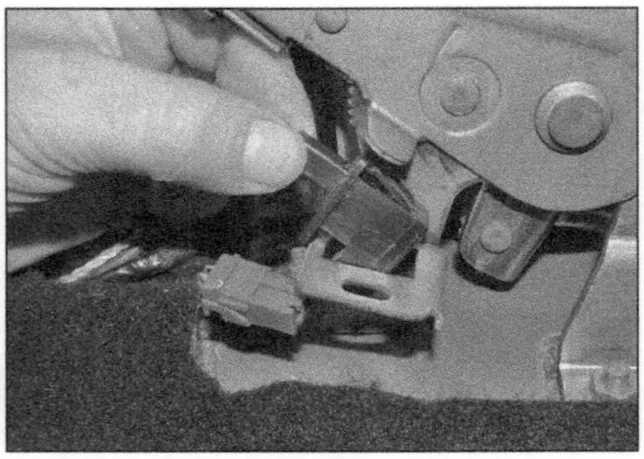
15.4b ... and remove the switch from the mounting bracket

15.5 Disengage the cable end fittings (arrowed) from the equaliser plate

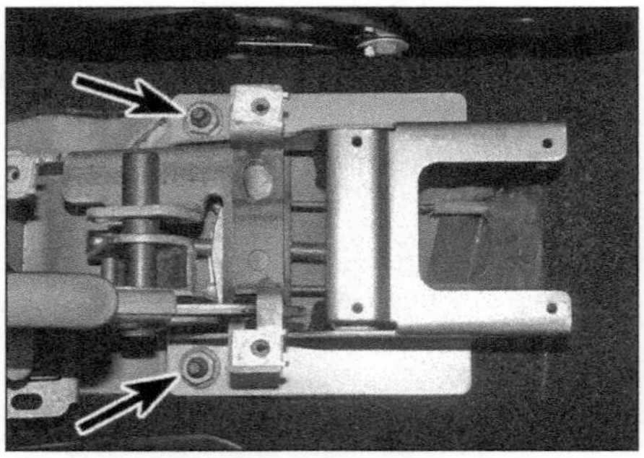
15.6 Undo the two support bracket retaining nuts (arrowed)

15.7 Undo the handbrake lever mounting nuts (arrowed)

15 Handbrake lever and switch – removal and refitting

Removal

1 Chock the front wheels then jack up the rear of the vehicle and support it on axle stands (see *Jacking and vehicle support*).

2 Referring to Section 14, release the handbrake lever and back off the adjuster nut to obtain maximum free play in the cables.

3 Remove the centre console as described in Chapter 11, Section 26.

4 Disconnect the wiring connector from the handbrake warning light switch, and then if required unclip the switch from the handbrake mounting bracket **(see illustrations)**.

5 Detach the two handbrake cables from the equaliser plate at the rear of the handbrake lever assembly **(see illustration)**, or completely remove the adjusting nut from the handbrake lever rod.

6 Where fitted undo the retaining nuts and remove the centre console mounting bracket from the top of the handbrake assembly **(see illustration)**.

7 Slacken and remove the lever mounting bracket retaining nuts, and remove the lever from the vehicle **(see illustration).**

Refitting

8 Refitting is a reversal of removal. Tighten the lever retaining nuts to the specified torque, and adjust the handbrake (see Section 14).

16 Handbrake cables – removal and refitting

Removal

1 The handbrake cable consists of a left-hand section and a right-hand section connecting the rear brakes to the adjuster mechanism on the handbrake lever rod. The cables can be removed separately.

2 Firmly chock the front wheels, slacken the relevant rear roadwheel bolts, and then jack up the rear of the vehicle and support it on axle stands (see *Jacking and vehicle support*).

3 Slacken the handbrake adjuster nut sufficiently to be able to disengage the relevant cable end fitting from the equaliser plate with reference to Section 14 **(see illustrations)**.

16.3a Disengage the cables (arrowed) ...

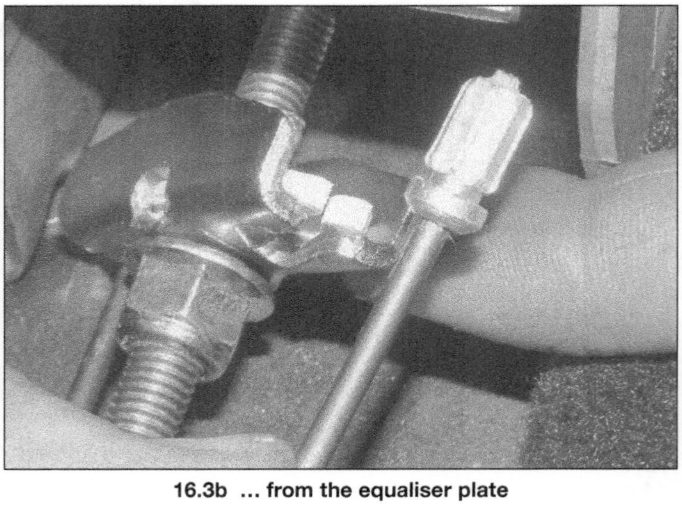
16.3b ... from the equaliser plate

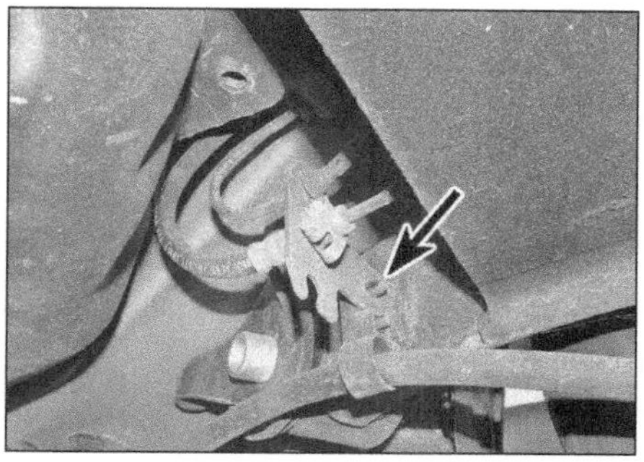

16.5a Release the handbrake cable securing clips (arrowed) ...

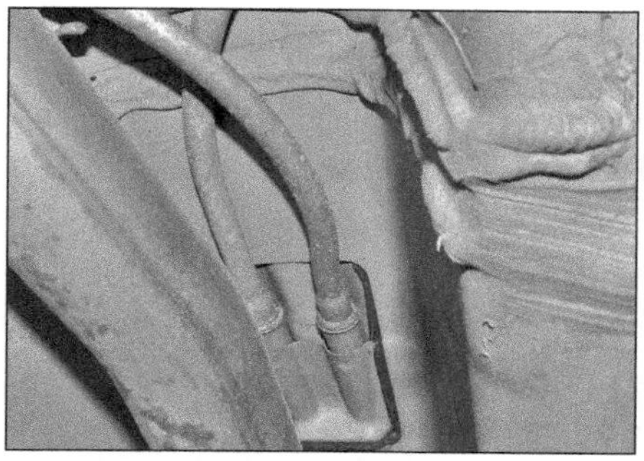

16.5b ... and then release the cable from the floor panel

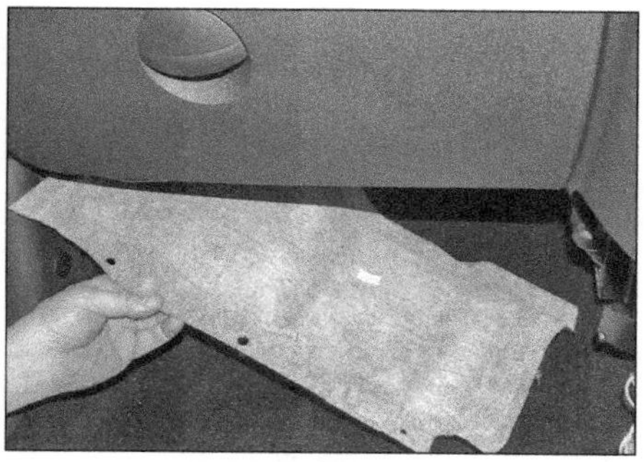

17.2 Remove the trim from under the facia panel

4 Release the cable end fitting from the lever on the brake caliper, and remove the cable from the support bracket **(see illustrations 5.2a and 5.2b)**.

5 Working underneath the vehicle, note its fitted location, then free the cable from the various retaining clips/brackets along its route, and pull the front end of the cable from the opening in the floor **(see illustrations)**. Withdraw the cable from underneath the vehicle.

Refitting

6 Refitting is a reversal of the removal procedure, adjusting the handbrake as described in Section 14.

17 Brake light switch – removal, refitting and adjustment

1 The brake light switch is located on the pedal crossover shaft bracket behind the passenger side of the facia. On models with automatic transmission or cruise control there are two switches fitted to the bracket – the brake light switch is the left-hand of the two.

Removal

2 Working in the passenger's footwell, prise up the centre pins, lever out the complete plastic expanding rivets, and remove the trim beneath the passenger's glovebox **(see illustration)**. Disconnect the wiring connector from the footwell light as the panel is removed.

3 Disconnect the wiring, then rotate the switch 90° anti-clockwise and remove it from the bracket **(see illustrations)**.

Refitting and adjustment

4 Check that the red locking latch is in line with the locating lug on the side of the switch **(see illustration)**.

5 Refit the switch back into position in the mounting bracket, and turn it 90° clockwise to lock it in position.

6 Reconnect the wiring connector, and check that the switch plunger is up against the brake pedal lever bracket.

7 Check the operation of the brake lights and refit the trim below the glovebox.

18 Anti-lock braking system (ABS) – general information

ABS is fitted to all models as standard; the system comprises a hydraulic valve block/modulator unit and the four roadwheel sensors. The hydraulic/modulator unit contains the electronic control unit (ECU); the hydraulic solenoid valves and the electrically driven return pump. The purpose of the system is to prevent the wheel(s) locking during heavy braking. This is achieved by automatic release of the brake on the relevant wheel, followed by re-application of the brake.

The solenoid valves are controlled by the ECU, which itself receives signals from the four wheel speed sensors (front sensors are fitted to the swivel hubs, and the rear sensors are fitted to the rear hubs), which monitor the speed of rotation of each wheel. By comparing these signals, the ECU can determine the speed at which the vehicle is traveling. It can then use this speed to determine when a wheel is decelerating at an abnormal rate, compared to the speed of the vehicle, and therefore predicts when a wheel is about to lock. During normal operation, the system functions in the same way as a non-ABS braking system.

If the ECU senses that a wheel is about to lock, it closes the relevant outlet solenoid valves in the hydraulic unit, which then isolates the relevant brake(s) on the wheel(s) which is/are about to lock from the master cylinder, effectively sealing-in the hydraulic pressure.

If the speed of rotation of the wheel continues to decrease at an abnormal rate, the ECU opens the inlet solenoid valves on the relevant brake(s), and operates the electrically-driven return pump which pumps the hydraulic fluid back into the master cylinder, releasing the brake. Once the speed of rotation of the wheel returns to an acceptable rate, the pump stops; the solenoid valves switch again, allowing the hydraulic master cylinder pressure to return to the caliper, which then re-applies the brake. This cycle can be carried out many times a second.

The action of the solenoid valves and return pump creates pulses in the hydraulic circuit.

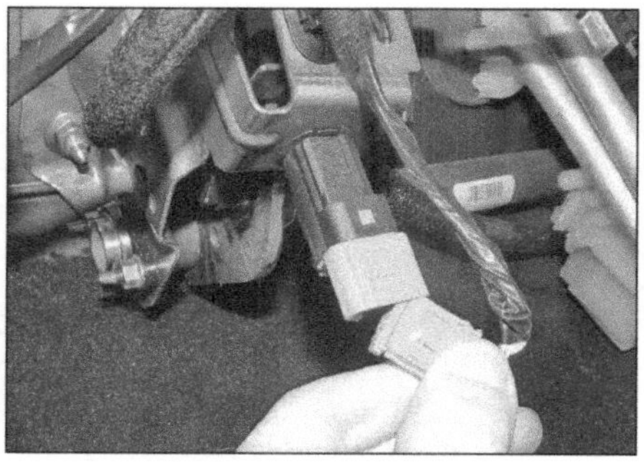

17.3a Disconnect the wiring connector from the switch

17.3b Rotate the brake light switch 90° anti-clockwise, and pull it from the bracket

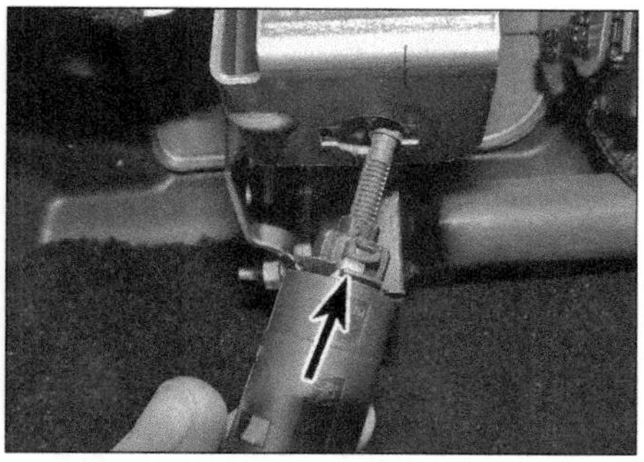

17.4 Align the locking catch (arrowed) with the centering lug

When the ABS system is functioning, these pulses can be felt through the brake pedal.

The operation of the ABS system is entirely dependent on electrical signals. To prevent the system responding to any inaccurate signals, a built-in safety circuit monitors all signals received by the ECU. If an inaccurate signal or low battery voltage is detected, the ABS system is automatically shut-down, and the warning light on the instrument panel is illuminated, to inform the driver that the ABS system is not operational. Normal braking should still be available, however.

The Citroën C4 (depending on model) is also equipped with additional safety features built around the ABS system. These systems are EBFD (electronic brake force distribution), which automatically apportions braking effort between the front and rear wheels, EBA (emergency brake assist) which guarantees full braking effort in the event of an emergency stop by monitoring the rate at which the brake pedal is depressed, and ESP (electronic stability program) which monitors the vehicle's cornering forces and steering wheel angle, then applies the braking force to the appropriate roadwheel to enhance the stability of the vehicle.

If a fault does develop in the any of these systems, the vehicle must be taken to a Citroën dealer or suitably-equipped specialist for fault diagnosis and repair.

19 Anti-lock braking system (ABS) components – removal and refitting

Hydraulic valve block/modulator and ECU

Caution: Disconnect the battery (see Chapter 5A, Section 4) before disconnecting the modulator hydraulic unions, and do not reconnect the battery until after the hydraulic system has been bled. Also ensure that the unit is stored upright (in the same position as it is fitted to the vehicle) and is not tipped onto its side or upside down. Failure to do this could lead to air entering the modulator unit, requiring the unit to be bled using special Citroën test equipment on refitting (see Section 2).

Note: *Before starting work, refer to the warning at the beginning of Section 2 concerning the dangers of hydraulic fluid.*

1 Disconnect the battery (see Chapter 5A, Section 4).

2 The hydraulic valve block assembly is located in the front left-hand corner of the engine compartment, behind the bumper, and below the left-hand headlight unit **(see illustration)**. Jack up the front of the vehicle and support it securely on axle stands (see *Jacking and vehicle support*).

3 Remove the front bumper as described in Chapter 11, Section 6.

4 Remove the left-hand front headlight unit as described in Chapter 12, Section 7.

5 Use a brake pedal depressor tool, or length of wood jammed between the steering wheel and the brake pedal to firmly depress the brake pedal. This will prevent any flow of fluid when the brake pipes are disconnected.

6 Release the retaining clips and remove the plastic cover from around the hydraulic unit **(see illustration)**

7 Lift off the plastic cover, release the securing clip and disconnect the main wiring connector from the hydraulic valve block ECU **(see illustrations)**.

8 Mark the locations of the hydraulic fluid pipes to ensure correct refitting, then unscrew the union nuts, and disconnect the pipes from the modulator assembly **(see illustration)**. Be prepared for fluid spillage, and plug the open ends of the pipes and the modulator to prevent dirt ingress and further fluid loss.

9 Slacken and remove the modulator mounting bracket bolts and remove the assembly from the engine compartment **(see illustration)**.

10 If necessary, slacken the three mounting nuts on the hydraulic unit, and then it can be removed from the mounting bracket **(see**

19.2 Location of ABS hydraulic valve block unit (arrowed)

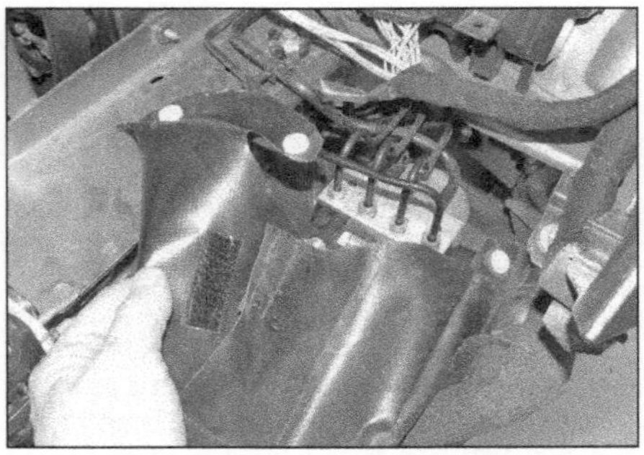

19.6 Remove the plastic weather cover from the unit

19.7a Unclip the plastic cover ...

19.7b ... and release the wiring plug locking lever (arrowed)

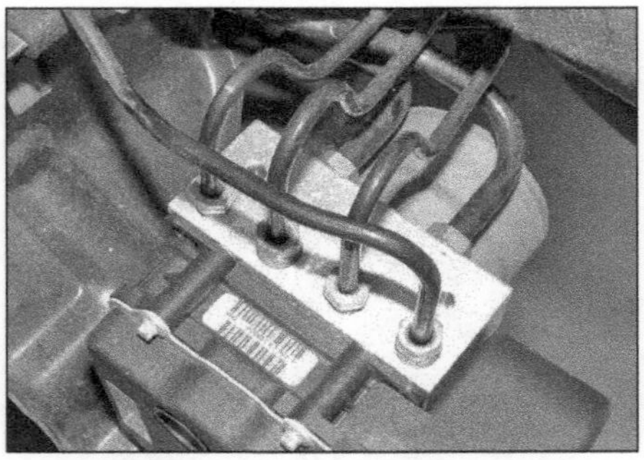

19.8 Mark the location of the various brake pipes before disconnecting them from the modulator

19.9 Undo the mounting bracket retaining bolts (arrowed)

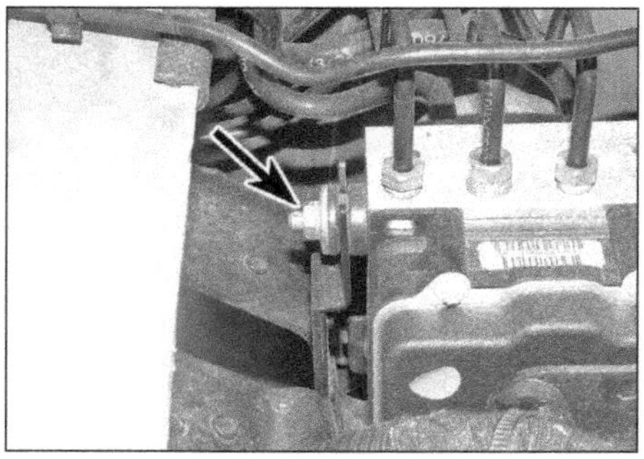

19.10a Upper mounting securing nut (arrowed) ...

19.10b ... and two lower mounting securing nuts (arrowed)

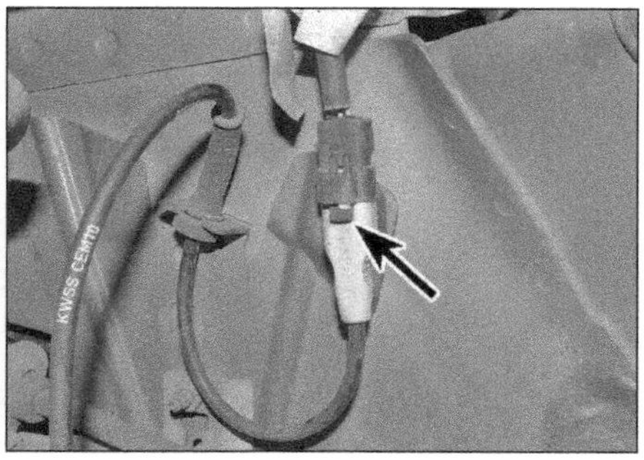

19.15 Disconnect the front sensor wiring connector (arrowed)

illustrations). Renew the rubber mountings if they show signs of wear or damage.

11 Refitting is a reversal of removal, bearing in mind the following points:

a) *New valve blocks/modulator are supplied pre-filled with fluid – remove the plugs prior to connecting the fluid pipes.*

b) *New ECUs must be initialised and programmed using Citroën dedicated diagnostic equipment. Entrust this task to a Citroën dealer or suitably-equipped specialist.*

c) *Tighten the hydraulic pipes and mounting bolts to the specified torque, where applicable.*

d) *On completion, bleed the brake hydraulic system as described in Section 2.*

e) *Make sure the plastic cover is placed around the hydraulic unit, to prevent dirt and water ingress.*

Electronic control unit (ECU)

12 The ECU is integral with the hydraulic valve block assembly, and is not available separately. See paragraphs 1 to 11 for further information.

Front wheel sensor

13 Ensure the ignition is turned off.

14 Apply the handbrake, slacken the appropriate front roadwheel bolts, then jack up the front of the vehicle and support securely on axle stands (see *Jacking and vehicle support*). Remove the relevant front wheel.

15 Trace the wiring back from the sensor, releasing it from all the relevant clips and ties on the inner wing panel, whilst noting its correct routing, then disconnect the wiring connector **(see illustration)**.

16 Slacken and remove the retaining bolt and withdraw the sensor from the rear of the hub carrier **(see illustration)**.

17 Ensure that the mating faces of the sensor and the swivel hub are clean, and apply a little anti-seize grease to the swivel hub bore before refitting.

18 Make sure the sensor tip is clean and ease it into position in the swivel hub.

19 Clean the threads of the sensor bolt and apply a few drops of thread-locking compound (Citroën recommend Loctite Frenetanch – available from your Citroën dealer). Refit the retaining bolt and tighten it to the specified torque.

20 Work along the sensor wiring, making sure it is correctly routed, and securing it in position with all the relevant clips and ties. Reconnect the wiring connector.

21 Refit the roadwheel, lower the vehicle to the ground and tighten the wheel bolts to the specified torque.

Rear wheel sensor

22 Ensure the ignition is turned off.

23 Chock the front wheels, slacken the relevant rear roadwheel bolts, and then jack up the rear of the vehicle and support it on axle stands (see *Jacking and vehicle support*). Remove the relevant roadwheel.

24 Trace the wiring back from the sensor, releasing it from all the relevant clips and ties whilst noting its correct routing, and disconnect the wiring connector **(see illustration)**.

25 Working through one of the wheel bolt holes, using an Allen key, slacken the retaining bolt and withdraw the sensor **(see illustrations)**.

26 Ensure that the mating faces of the sensor and the hub are clean, and apply a little anti-seize grease to the hub bore before refitting.

27 Make sure the sensor tip is clean and ease it into position in the rear of the hub.

28 Clean the threads of the sensor bolt and

19.16 Undo the wheel speed sensor bolt (arrowed)

19.24 Disconnect the rear sensor wiring connector (arrowed)

19.25a Insert the Allen key through one of the roadwheel bolt holes ...

19.25b ... to undo the speed sensor retaining bolt (arrowed)

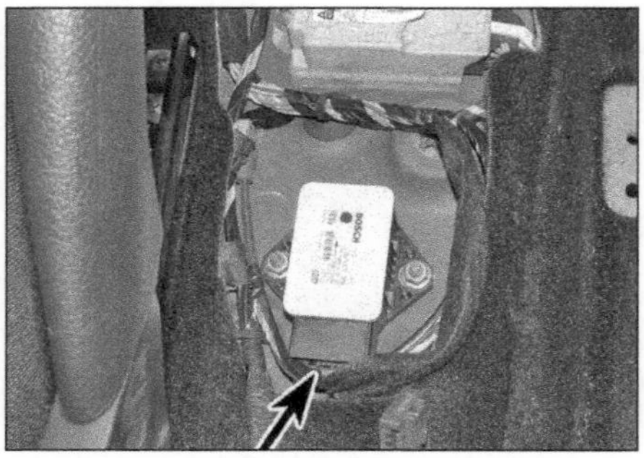

19.32 Disconnect the sensor wiring plug connector (arrowed)

20.3a Release the clip (arrowed) and disconnect the vacuum pipe – VTi petrol engines

20.3b Release the clip (arrowed) and disconnect the vacuum pipe – 1.6 litre diesel engines

apply a few drops of thread-locking compound (Citroën recommend Loctite Frenetanch – available from your Citroën dealer). Refit the retaining bolt and tighten it to the specified torque.

29 Work along the sensor wiring, making sure it is correctly routed, and securing it in position with all the relevant clips and ties. Reconnect the wiring connector.

30 Refit the roadwheel, lower the vehicle to the ground and tighten the wheel bolts to the specified torque.

20.3c Release the clip (arrowed) and disconnect the vacuum pipe – 2.0 litre diesel engines

Gyrometer/accelerometer sensor

31 Remove the centre console as described in Chapter 11, Section 26.

32 Release the retaining clip, and then disconnect the wiring plug **(see illustration)**.

33 Undo the two nuts and remove the sensor.

34 Refitting is a reversal of removal, ensuring the arrow on the top of the sensor points to the front of the vehicle.

20.4a Unclip the wiring loom ...

20 Vacuum pump – removal and refitting

Removal

1 The pump is located at the left-hand end of the cylinder head and is fitted to VTi petrol and diesel engine models.

2 To access the vacuum pump, remove the air cleaner ducting and pipes from the left-hand side of the cylinder head. Refer to Chapter 4A, Section 2 or Chapter 4B, Section 4 for further information.

3 Depress the retaining clip button and disconnect the vacuum hose from the pump **(see illustrations)**.

4 On 2.0 litre diesel engines unclip the wiring loom retaining clips and remove the bracket from below the vacuum pump **(see illustrations)**.

5 Also on 2.0 litre diesel engines, undo the retaining nut and remove the pipe bracket from the top of the vacuum pump **(see illustration)**. Then remove the pillar stud, which the bracket was attached to, from the top of the pump. Move the retaining clip from the pillar stud and move it to one side.

20.4b ... and unbolt the mounting bracket

20.5 Undo the upper bracket securing nut (arrowed)

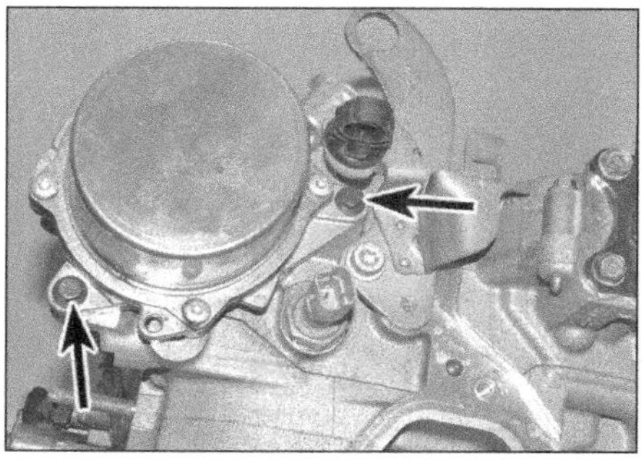
20.6a Vacuum pump mounting bolts (arrowed) – VTi petrol engines

20.6b Vacuum pump mounting bolts (arrowed) – 1.6 litre diesel engines

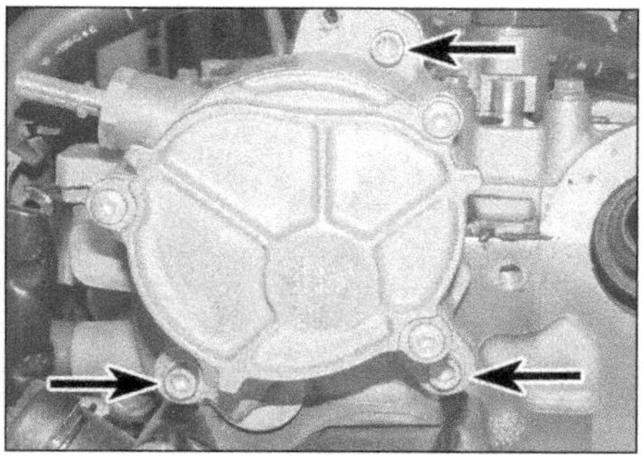
20.6c Vacuum pump mounting bolts (arrowed) – 2.0 litre diesel engines

6 Slacken and remove the retaining bolts/nut (as applicable) securing the pump to the left-hand end of the cylinder head, then remove the pump **(see illustrations)**. Discard the sealing rings – new ones must be used on refitting. On diesel engines one of the pump retaining bolts acts as a locating stud for the air intake ducting.

Refitting

7 Fit new sealing ring(s) to the pump recess, then align the drive dog with the slot in the end of the camshaft, and refit the pump to the cylinder head, ensuring that the sealing ring(s) remain correctly seated **(see illustrations)**.
8 Refit the pump mounting bolts/nut (as applicable) and tighten them securely.
9 Reconnect the vacuum hose to the pump, ensuring its retaining clip engages correctly, and (where necessary) refit the air cleaner duct.

21 Vacuum pump - testing

1 The operation of the braking system vacuum pump can be checked using a vacuum gauge.
2 Start the engine and get it up to temperature, then allow it to idle.
3 Disconnect the vacuum pipe from the pump **(see illustrations 20.3a, 20.3b or 20.3c)**, and connect the gauge to the pump union using a suitable length of hose.
4 Measure the vacuum created by the pump; refer to specifications at the beginning of this Chapter. If the vacuum registered is significantly less than specified, it is likely that the pump is faulty. However, seek the advice of a Citroën dealer before condemning the pump.
5 Overhaul of the vacuum pump is not possible, since no components are available separately for it. If faulty, the complete pump assembly must be renewed.

20.7a Renew the vacuum pump O-ring seals

20.7b Some pumps may have two O-ring seals (arrowed)

20.7c Ensure the pump drive dog engages with the slot in the end of the camshaft (arrowed)

Chapter 10
Suspension and steering

Contents

Section number

Degrees of difficulty

Easy, suitable for novice with little experience	**Fairly easy,** suitable for beginner with some experience	**Fairly difficult,** suitable for competent DIY mechanic	**Difficult,** suitable for experienced DIY mechanic	**Very difficult,** suitable for expert DIY or professional

Specifications

Wheel alignment and steering angles

Front wheels:	
Tracking (toe setting)	-0°11' ± 0°04'
Camber:	
Left-hand wheel	0° (+ 0°36' – 0°24')
Right-hand wheel	0° (+ 0°24' – 0°36')
Castor	+5° 12' ± 0°30'
Pivot angle (king pin inclination – KPI):	
Left-hand wheel	11°42' (+ 0°24' – 0°36')
Right-hand wheel	11°42' (± 0°36' – 0°24')
Rear wheels:	
Tracking (toe setting)	+0° 28' ± 0°04'
Camber	-1° 42' ± 0°30'

Front anti-roll bar

Diameter:	
White (colour identification)	22.0 mm
Blue (colour identification)	22.5 mm

Roadwheels

Type	Pressed-steel or aluminium alloy (depending on model)
Tyre pressures	See *Lubricants, fluids and tyre pressures*

Torque wrench settings

	Nm	lbf ft
Front suspension		
Anti-roll bar:		
Connecting link nuts*	50	37
Mounting clamp bolts:		
Rear bolt	104	77
Front nut	110	81
Driveshaft retaining nut	325	240
Hub carrier to strut*	90	66
Lower arm-to-subframe bolts	111	82
Lower balljoint:		
Balljoint to hub carrier	230	170
Retaining nut*	42	31
Lower crossmember mounting bolts:		
Vertical bolt	70	52
Horizontal bolt	51	38
Subframe mounting bolts	98	72
Suspension strut:		
Upper mounting plate nut	72	53
Upper spring seat nut	72	53
Rear suspension		
Axle hub nut:*		
Stage 1	70	52
Stage 2	Angle-tighten a further 45°	
Rear axle mounting bracket-to-body bolts	62	46
Rear axle-to-mounting bracket nut/bolt	76	56
Shock absorber:		
Lower mounting nut*	60	44
Upper mounting bolts	60	44
Stub axle bolts	63	46
Vibration damper (bolted on rear axle)	25	18
Steering		
High-pressure pipe-to-steering rack retaining bolt	20	15
High-pressure union on power steering pump	20	15
High-pressure union on steering rack/ram	10	7
Power steering pump mounting bolts:		
Lower mounting nut	22	16
Upper mounting nuts	23	17
Steering column mounting bolts	22	16
Steering column-to-steering rack pinch-bolt	22	16
Steering rack mounting nuts*	80	59
Steering rack mounting stud	10	7
Steering wheel housing to steering column nuts	22	16
Steering wheel retaining bolt	22	16
Track rod:		
Balljoint-to-hub carrier nut*	38	28
Balljoint locknut	55	41
Inner balljoint to steering rack	70	52
Roadwheels		
Wheel bolts	90	66

* *Do not re-use*

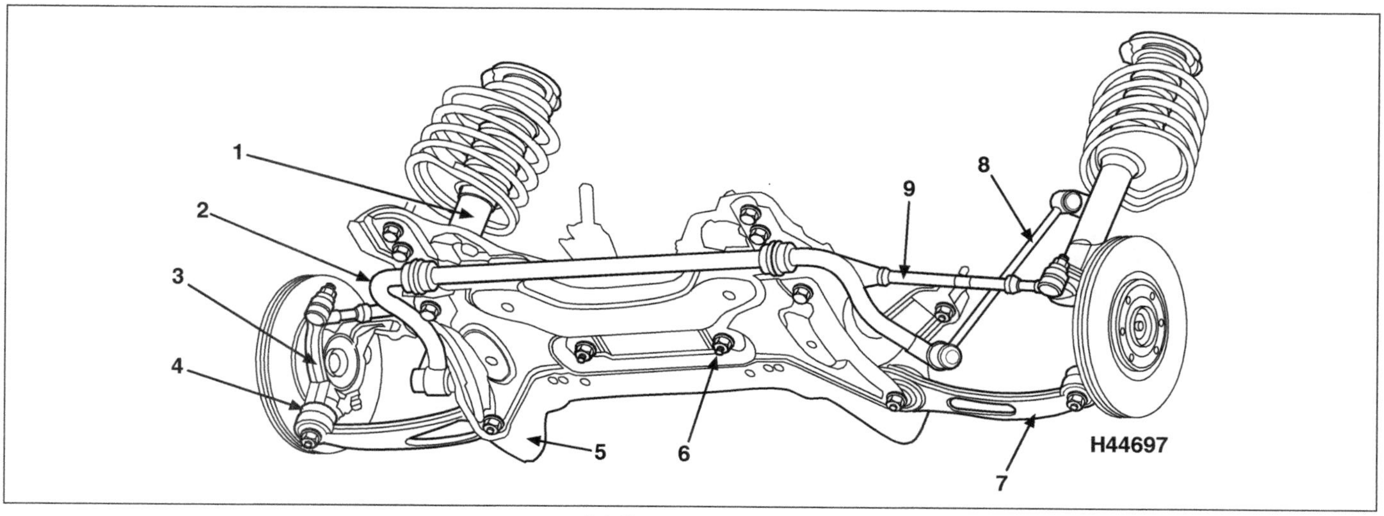

1.1 Front suspension

1 MacPherson strut
2 Anti-roll bar
3 Hub carrier
4 Lower balljoint
5 Subframe
6 Steering rack mounting nuts
7 Lower pivot arm
8 Anti-roll bar link
9 Track rod

1 General information

The independent front suspension is of the MacPherson strut type, incorporating coil springs and integral telescopic shock absorbers. The MacPherson struts are located by transverse lower suspension arms, which utilise rubber inner mounting bushes. The front hub carriers, which carry the wheel bearings, the brake calipers, the hub/disc assemblies and the lower balljoints, are bolted to the MacPherson struts, and connected to the lower arms via the balljoints. A front anti-roll bar is fitted to all models. The anti-roll bar is rubber-mounted onto the subframe, and is connected to the front suspension struts by link rods **(see illustration)**.

The rear suspension has separate telescopic shock absorbers and coil springs fitted between the beam axle and the vehicle body. The rear beam axle has an integral anti-roll bar, and pivots around rubber bushes that are bolted to the front mounting brackets **(see illustration)**.

The steering column has a universal joint fitted to its lower end, which is connected to the steering rack pinion by means of a clamp bolt.

The steering rack is mounted onto the front subframe, and is connected by two track rods, with balljoints at their outer ends, to the steering arms projecting rearwards from the hub carriers. The track rod ends are threaded, to facilitate adjustment.

A variable power steering system is fitted. The hydraulic pump alters the hydraulic pressure supplied to the steering rack to suit all conditions, ie, supplies high pressure when the vehicle is being driven slowly/parked and lower pressure when the vehicle is being driven at speed. The hydraulic steering system is powered by an electrically operated pump, which is controlled by the engine management ECU.

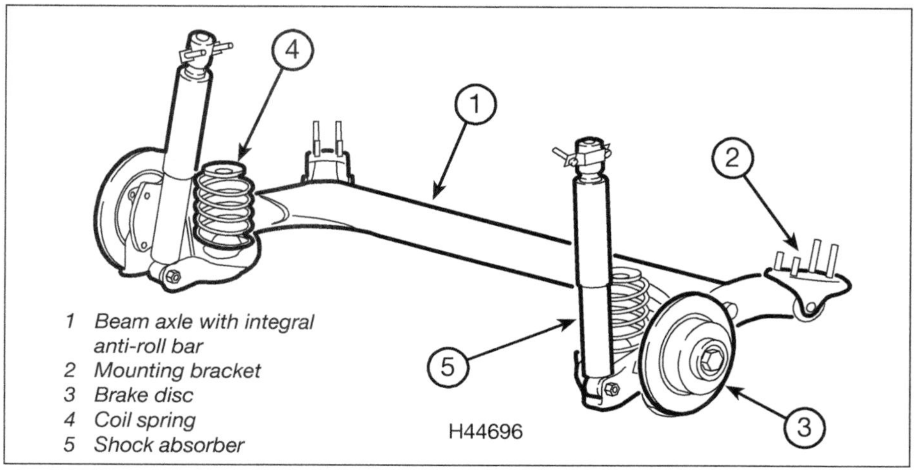

1.2 Rear suspension

2 Front hub carrier assembly – removal and refitting

Note: *A new track rod balljoint nut, lower balljoint nut, brake caliper mounting bracket bolts, and strut-to-hub carrier nuts will be required on refitting.*

Removal

1 Remove the wheel trim/hub cap (as applicable) then withdraw the R-clip and remove the locking cap from the driveshaft retaining nut. Slacken the driveshaft nut with the vehicle resting on its wheels **(see illustration)**. Also slacken the wheel bolts.

2 Chock the rear wheels of the car, firmly

2.1 Prise out the R-clip, remove the locking collar and slacken the driveshaft nut

2.4 Using a fabricated tool to hold the front hub stationary whilst the driveshaft nut is slackened.

2.7a Undo the lower balljoint retaining nut (arrowed) ...

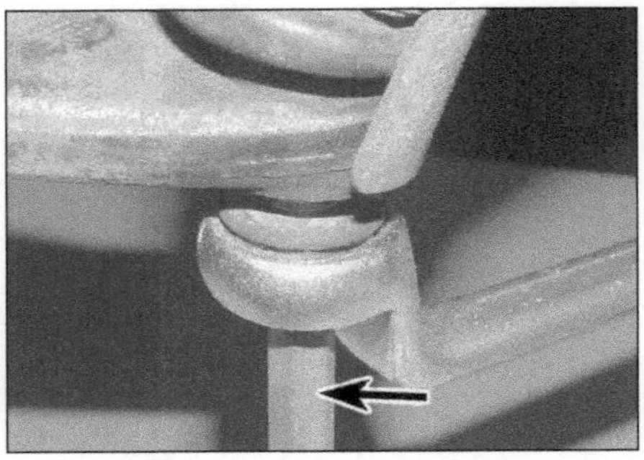

2.7b ... use a Torx bit (arrowed) in the balljoint end to counterhold the nut

apply the handbrake, and then jack up the front of the car and support it on axle stands (see *Jacking and vehicle support*). Remove the appropriate front roadwheel.

3 Unbolt the wheel sensor and position it clear of the hub assembly (see Chapter 9, Section 19). Note that there is no need to disconnect the wiring.

4 Slacken and remove the driveshaft retaining nut. If the nut was not slackened with the wheels on the ground (see paragraph 1), withdraw the R-clip and remove the locking cap. Refit at least two roadwheel bolts to the front hub, tightening them securely, then have an assistant firmly depress the brake pedal to prevent the front hub from rotating whilst you slacken and remove the driveshaft retaining nut. Alternatively, a tool can be fabricated to hold the hub stationary **(see illustration)**.

5 Slacken and remove the nut securing the steering rack track rod to the hub carrier then free the balljoint from the hub. If the balljoint is tight, use a universal balljoint separator to free it. Discard the nut; a new one should be used on refitting.

6 If the hub bearings are to be disturbed, remove the brake disc as described in Chapter 9, Section 6. If not, unscrew the two bolts securing the brake caliper mounting bracket assembly to the hub carrier, and slide the caliper assembly off the disc. Using a piece of wire or string, tie the caliper to the front suspension coil spring, to avoid placing any strain on the hydraulic brake hose.

7 Slacken and remove the lower balljoint nut and free the balljoint shank from the lower arm, if necessary, using a universal balljoint separator **(see illustrations)**. Use a Torx bit in the end of the threaded part of the balljoint to counterhold the nut. Discard the nut and lift off the protector plate (if loose).

8 Undo the nut and withdraw the hub carrier-to-suspension strut bolts, noting that the bolts on early models are inserted from the front of the vehicle. On later models, they are inserted from the rear of the vehicle, with a locking clip fitted to secure the retaining nuts **(see illustrations)**.

9 Free the hub carrier assembly from the end of the strut, then release it from the outer constant velocity joint splines, and remove it from the vehicle. Suspend the driveshaft by string from the suspension strut to prevent any damage to the constant velocity joints.

Refitting

10 Ensure that the driveshaft outer constant velocity joint and hub splines are clean, and then slide the hub fully onto the driveshaft splines.

11 Slide the hub assembly fully into the suspension strut bracket. On early models, insert the bolts from the front using new nuts, and tighten them to the specified torque. On later models, the bolts are inserted from the rear and a clip secures the nuts at the front.

12 Refit the protector plate (where removed) to the lower balljoint. Align the balljoint with the lower arm and fit the new retaining nut, tightening it to the specified torque.

13 Engage the track rod balljoint in the hub carrier, then fit the new retaining nut and tighten it to the specified torque.

14 Where necessary, refit the brake disc to the hub, referring to Chapter 9, Section 6 for further information. Slide the caliper into position, making sure the pads pass either side of the disc, and tighten the new caliper bracket bolts to the specified torque setting.

15 Refit the wheel sensor as described in Chapter 9, Section 19.

16 Lubricate the inner face and threads of the driveshaft retaining nut with clean engine oil, and refit it to the end of the driveshaft. Use the method employed on removal to prevent the hub from rotating (see paragraph 4), and tighten the driveshaft retaining nut to the specified torque. Check that the hub rotates freely then engage the locking cap with the driveshaft nut, so that one of its cut-outs is aligned with the driveshaft hole, and secure the cap in position with the R-clip. Alternatively, lightly tighten the nut at this stage and tighten it to the specified torque once the vehicle is resting on its wheels again.

17 Refit the roadwheel, then lower the vehicle to the ground and tighten the roadwheel bolts to the specified torque. If not already done, tighten the driveshaft retaining nut to the specified torque then refit the locking cap, aligning its cut-outs with the driveshaft hole, and secure it in position with the R-clip.

2.8a On early models the bolts go in from the front, with nuts and washers to the rear

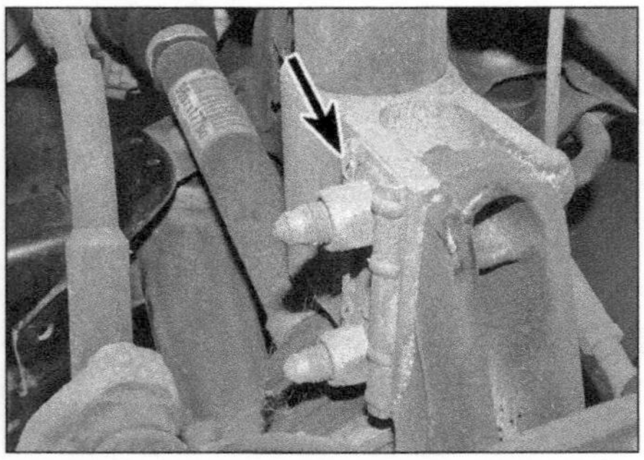

2.8b On later models the bolts go in from the rear and a locking clip (arrowed) is fitted to the securing nuts

3 Front hub bearings – renewal

Note: *The bearing is a sealed, pre-adjusted and pre-lubricated, double-row roller type, and is intended to last the car's entire service life without maintenance or attention. Never overtighten the driveshaft nut beyond the specified torque wrench setting in an attempt to 'adjust' the bearing.*

Note: *A press will be required to dismantle and rebuild the assembly; if such a tool is not available, a large bench vice and spacers (such as large sockets) will serve as an adequate*

3.2 Press the hub flange from the bearing

3.3 Extract the circlip from the inner side of the hub carrier

3.7 Take great care not to damage the seal in the bearing (arrowed) – it contains the encoder for the wheel speed sensor

substitute. The bearing's inner races are an interference fit on the hub; if the inner race remains on the hub when it is pressed out of the hub carrier, a knife-edged bearing puller will be required to remove it. A new bearing retaining circlip must be used on refitting.

1 Remove the hub carrier assembly as described in Section 2.

2 Support the hub carrier securely on blocks or in a vice. Using a tubular spacer, which bears only on the inner end of the hub flange, press the hub flange out of the bearing **(see illustration)**. If the bearing's outboard inner race remains on the hub, remove it using a bearing puller (see note above).

3 Extract the bearing retaining circlip from the inner end of the hub carrier assembly **(see illustration)**.

4 Where necessary, refit the inner race back in position over the ball cage, and securely support the inner face of the hub carrier. Using a tubular spacer, which bears only on the inner race, press the complete bearing assembly out of the hub carrier.

5 Thoroughly clean the hub and hub carrier, removing all traces of dirt and grease, and polish away any burrs or raised edges that might hinder reassembly. Check both for cracks or any other signs of wear or damage, and renew them if necessary. Renew the circlip, regardless of its apparent condition.

6 On reassembly, apply a light film of oil (Citroën recommend Molykote 321R – available from your Citroën dealer) to the bearing outer race and hub flange shaft, to aid installation of the bearing.

7 Securely support the hub carrier, and locate the bearing in the hub. Press the bearing fully into position, ensuring that it enters the hub squarely, using a tubular spacer which bears only on the bearing outer race. Note that the bearing is equipped with a magnetic encoder on its inboard face. When fitting the bearing, ensure this face is inboard adjacent to the ABS wheel speed sensor **(see illustration)**. Take care not to damage this encoder, or place it adjacent to a magnetic source. Ensure the encoder face is clean.

8 Once the bearing is correctly seated, secure the bearing in position with the new circlip, ensuring that it is correctly located in the groove in the hub carrier. **Note:** *Align the gap between the ends of the circlip with the gap for the ABS wheel speed sensor.*

9 Securely support the outer face of the hub flange, and locate the hub carrier bearing inner race over the end of the hub flange. Press the bearing onto the hub, using a tubular spacer that bears only on the inner race of the hub bearing, until it seats against the hub shoulder. Check that the hub flange rotates freely, and wipe off any excess oil or grease.

10 Refit the hub carrier assembly as described in Section 2.

4 Front strut – removal and refitting

Note: *Always renew any self-locking nuts when working on the suspension/steering components.*

Removal

1 Chock the rear wheels, apply the handbrake, slacken the appropriate front roadwheel bolts, then jack up the front of the car and support on axle stands (see *Jacking and vehicle support*). Remove the appropriate roadwheel.

2 Unclip the plastic wiring retaining clip and unscrew the nut securing the anti-roll bar connecting link to the strut **(see illustration).** Position the link clear of the strut; if necessary, retain the balljoint shank with a Torx bit to prevent rotation whilst the nut is slackened. Refer to Section 9 for further information; discard the nut, a new one should be used on refitting.

3 Undo the bolts and pull the hub carrier away from the lower end of the strut **(see illustration)**, prevent the hub carrier assembly

4.2 Undo the anti-roll bar link upper nut (arrowed)

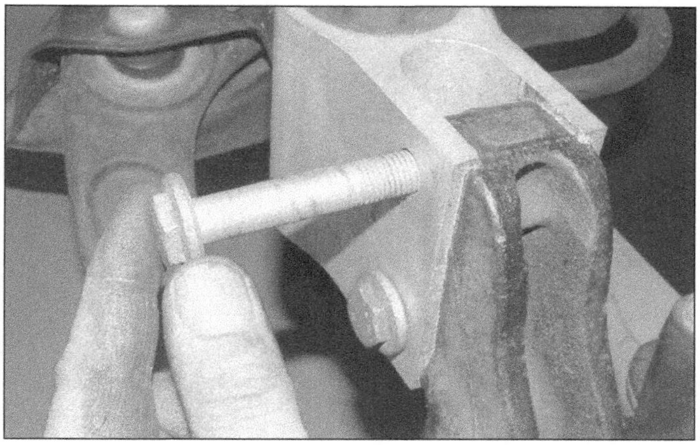

4.3 Remove the strut-to-hub carrier bolts – noting their fitted position

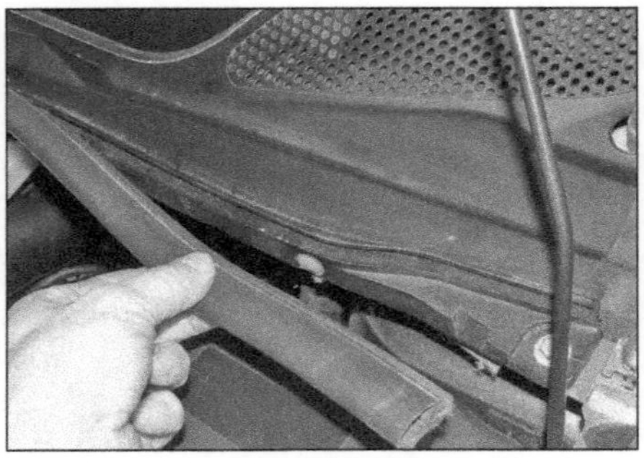

4.5a Pull up the seal ...

4.5b ... and remove the plastic scuttle panels

4.6a Undo the strut upper mounting nut ...

4.6b ... and use an Allen key in the end of the rod to counterhold whilst slackening the nut

dropping whilst the strut is removed by supporting the lower arm. Take care not to strain the brake hose and the wiring attached to the brake caliper and the hub carrier. Note that the bolts on early models are inserted from the front of the vehicle. On later models they are inserted from the rear of the vehicle, with a locking clip fitted to secure the retaining nuts **(see illustrations 2.8a and 2.8b)**.

4 Remove both wiper arms as described in Chapter 12, Section 13.

5 Unclip the plastic scuttle panel from below the windscreen, remove the rubber weather seal from the rear of the front of the scuttle panel trim and then pull up the ends of the scuttle panel to release it from the lower securing clips at the base of the windscreen **(see illustrations)**.

6 Working in the scuttle aperture, slacken and remove the strut upper mounting nut, counterholding the strut rod with an Allen key located in the end of the rod. Withdraw the strut from under the wheel arch **(see illustrations)**.

Caution: As soon as the upper mounting nut is removed, the strut will be unsupported.

Refitting

7 Manoeuvre the strut assembly into position, ensuring that the end of the strut rod is correctly located in the corresponding hole in the inner wing. Fit the upper mounting nut and tighten it to the specified torque.

8 Engage the lower end of the strut with the hub carrier, on early models insert the bolts from the front and tighten them to the specified torque. On later models, the bolts are inserted from the rear and a clip secures the nuts.

9 Refit the scuttle plastic trim, and the wiper arms.

10 Reconnect the anti-roll bar connecting link to the strut. Do not forget the wiring support bracket. Tighten the nut to the specified torque.

11 Refit the roadwheel, then lower the vehicle to the ground and tighten the roadwheel bolts to the specified torque.

5 **Front strut** - overhaul

Warning: Before attempting to dismantle the front suspension strut, a suitable tool to hold the coil spring in compression must be obtained. Adjustable coil spring compressors are readily available, and are recommended for this operation. Any attempt to dismantle the strut without such a tool is likely to result in damage or personal injury.

Note: *Always renew any self-locking nuts when working on the suspension/steering components.*

1 With the strut removed from the car (as described in Section 4), clean away all external dirt, and then mount it upright in a vice. Fit the spring compressor and compress the coil spring until tension is relieved from the spring seats **(see illustration)**.

2 Slacken and remove the upper spring seat nut whilst retaining the shock absorber piston with a suitable Allen key **(see illustration)**.

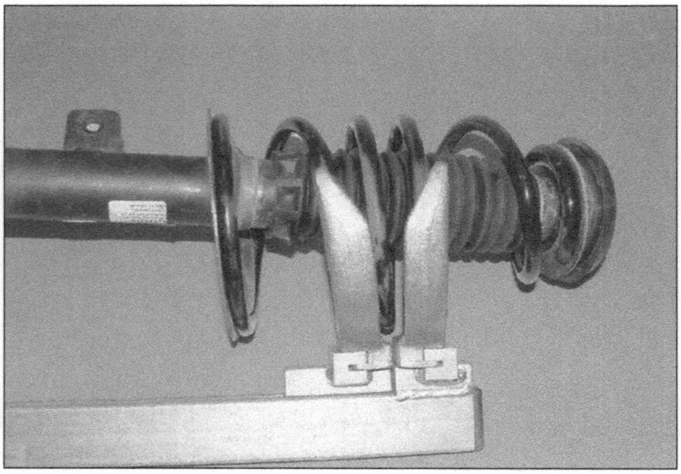

5.1 Fit the coil compressors to the springs

5.2 Slacken the top nut whilst retaining the rod with an Allen key

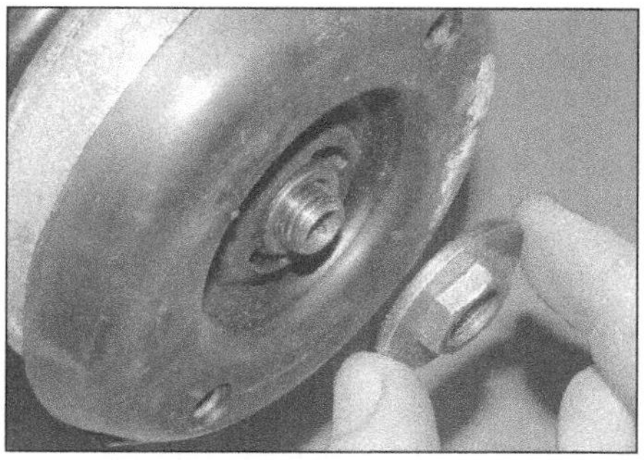

5.3a Remove the nut ...

5.3b ... the thrust bearing ...

5.3c ... the spring seat ...

3 Remove the nut then lift off the thrust bearing followed by the spring seat **(see illustrations)**.

4 Lift off the coil spring and remove the cap, dust gaiter and rubber bump stop from the shock absorber piston **(see illustrations)**.

5 Examine the shock absorber for signs of fluid leakage. Check the piston for signs of pitting along its entire length, and check the shock body for signs of damage. While holding it in an upright position, test the operation of the shock absorber by moving the piston through a full stroke, and then through short strokes of 50 to 100 mm. In both cases, the resistance felt should be smooth and continuous. If the resistance is jerky, or uneven, or if there is any visible sign of wear or damage to the shock absorber, renewal is necessary.

6 Inspect all other components for signs of damage or deterioration, and renew any that are suspect.

7 Slide the rubber bump stop onto the piston. Fit the dust gaiter and cap, making sure the lower end of gaiter is correctly positioned over the shock absorber end.

8 Refit the coil spring; making sure its lower end is correctly seated against the spring seat stop. Fit the upper spring seat, aligning its stop with the spring end, then the thrust bearing **(see illustration)**.

9 Fit the new nut. Retain the shock absorber piston and tighten the upper spring seat nut to the specified torque.

6 Front lower arm – removal, overhaul and refitting

Note: *Always renew any self-locking nuts when working on the suspension/steering components.*

Removal

1 Remove the relevant driveshaft as described in Chapter 8, Section 2.

2 Slacken and remove the nut, then free the lower balljoint shank from the lower arm, if necessary, using a universal balljoint separator. Discard the nut and lift off the protector plate (if loose). Use a Torx bit in the end of the balljoint shank to counterhold the nut.

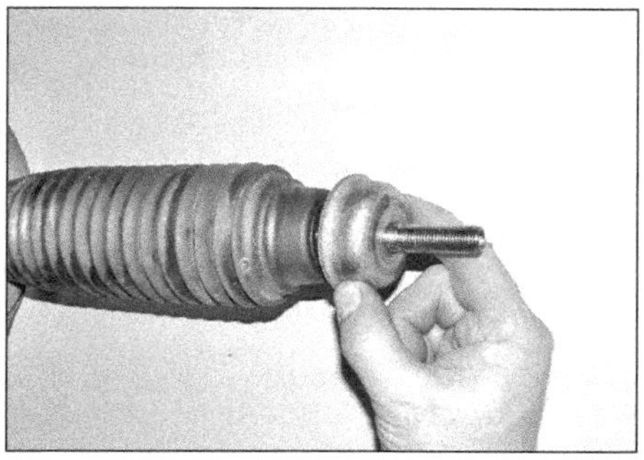

5.4a ... followed by the cap ...

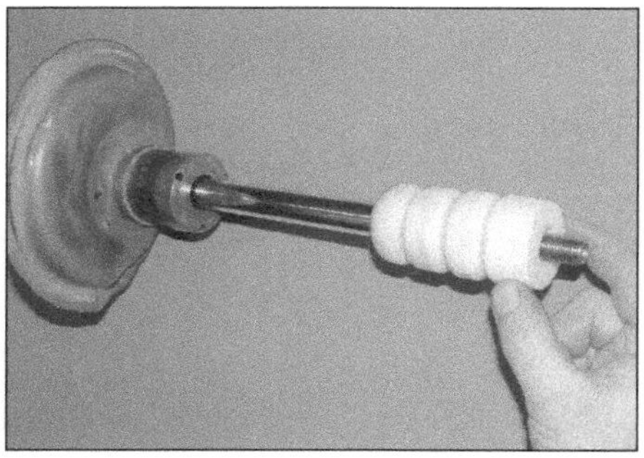

5.4c ... and the bump stop

3 Slacken and remove the lower arm front pivot bolt and nut **(see illustration)**.

4 Slacken and remove the rear pivot bolt and nut **(see illustration)**.

5 Manoeuvre the lower arm assembly out from underneath the vehicle.

6.3 Undo the lower arm front pivot bolt (arrowed) ...

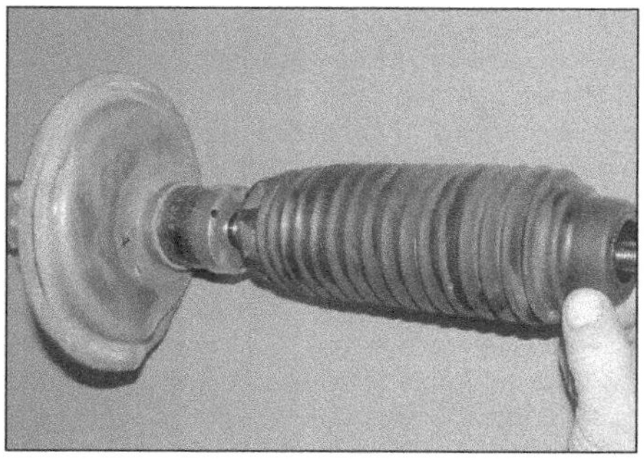

5.4b ... the dust gaiter ...

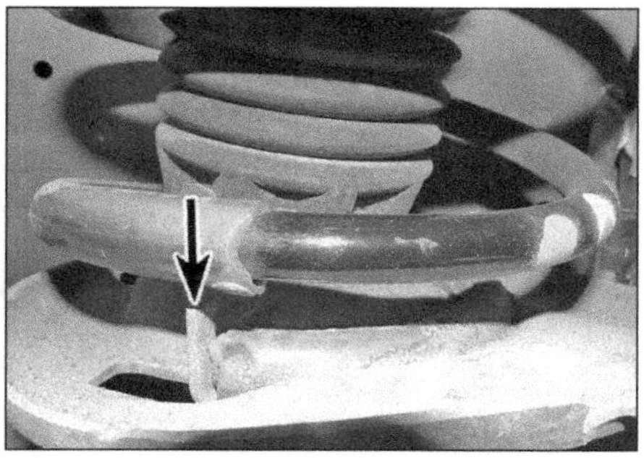

5.8 Ensure the lower end of the spring locates against the stop (arrowed)

Overhaul

6 Thoroughly clean the lower arm and the area around the arm mountings, removing all traces of dirt and underseal if necessary, then check carefully for cracks, distortion or any other signs of wear or damage, paying

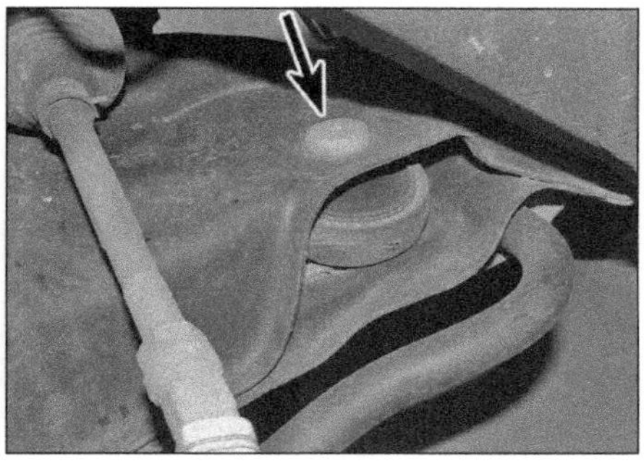

6.4 ... and rear pivot bolt (arrowed)

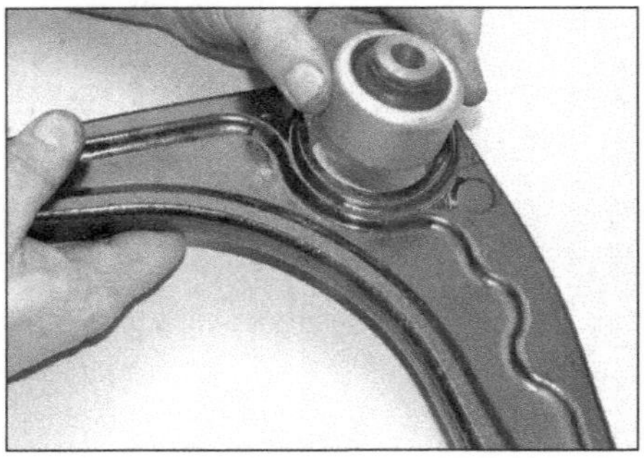
6.7a Press the bushes into the lower arm ...

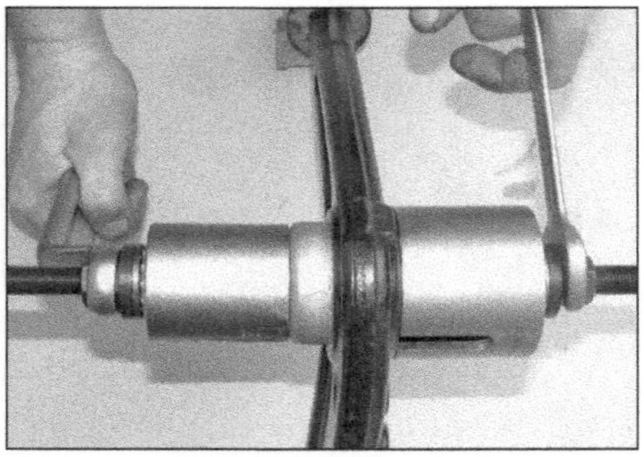
6.7b ... by using spacers and a threaded rod

particular attention to the pivot bushes, and renew components as necessary.

7 Renewal of the front and rear pivot bushes will required the use of a hydraulic press, a bearing puller and several spacers, and should therefore be entrusted to a Citroën dealer or specialist with access to the necessary equipment. Depending how tight the bushes are in the lower arm, it may be possible, to remove and refit the bushes using an assortment of spacers and a threaded bar **(see illustrations)**.

Refitting

8 Manoeuvre the lower arm assembly into position, and refit the front pivot bolt and nut, tightening it finger-tight only.

9 Refit the rear pivot bolt and nut, and then tighten them to the specified torque.

10 Refit the protector plate (where removed) to the lower balljoint, and then locate the balljoint shank in the lower arm. Fit the new retaining nut and tighten it to the specified torque.

11 Refit the driveshaft (see Chapter 8, Section 2).

12 Refit the roadwheel, then lower the vehicle and tighten the roadwheel bolts to the specified torque. Rock the car to settle the disturbed components in position, and then tighten the lower arm front pivot bolt to the specified torque.

13 Check and, if necessary, adjust the front wheel alignment as described in Section 25.

7 Front lower balljoint – removal and refitting

Removal

1 Remove the hub carrier assembly as described in Section 2.

7.2 Release the clips and remove the balljoint protector plate

7.3 Use a chisel or a punch to unstake the balljoint

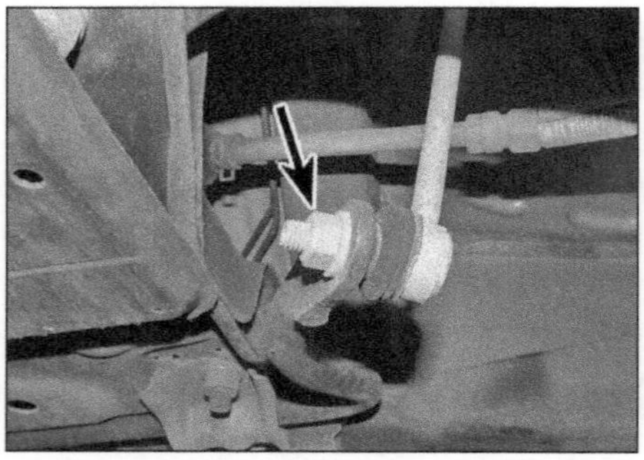
8.2 Undo the anti-roll bar link lower nut (arrowed)

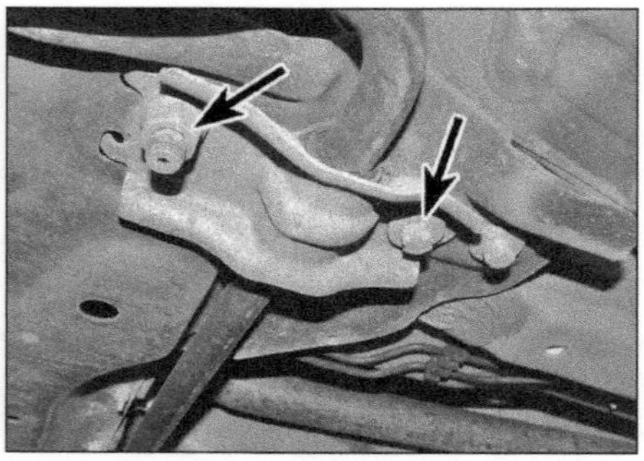
8.3 Undo the anti-roll bar clamp bolt/nut (one side shown)

2 Remove the protector plate from the balljoint and mount the assembly securely in a vice **(see illustration)**.

3 Using a hammer and pointed-nose chisel, tap up the staking securing the balljoint in position **(see illustration)**.

4 Fit a deep socket to the balljoint, then unscrew it and remove it from the hub carrier.

Refitting

5 Screw the balljoint into the hub carrier assembly. Fit the special tool, taking care not to damage the balljoint gaiter, and tighten the balljoint to the specified torque. Secure the balljoint in position by firmly staking it into one of the hub carrier notches using a hammer and punch.

6 Fit the new protector plate to the balljoint and secure it in position by staking it into the one of the balljoint notches.

7 Refit the hub carrier (see Section 2).

8 Front anti-roll bar – removal and refitting

Note: *Always renew any self-locking nuts when working on the suspension/steering components.*

Removal

1 Chock the rear wheels, firmly apply the handbrake, slacken the front roadwheel bolts, then jack up the front of the vehicle and support on axle stands (see *Jacking and vehicle support*). Remove both front roadwheels.

2 Slacken and remove the nuts securing the left- and right-hand connecting links to the anti-roll bar **(see illustration)**, and position the links clear of the bar. If necessary, retain the balljoint shank with a Torx bit to prevent rotation whilst the nut is slackened. Refer to Section 9 for further information; discard the nut, a new one should be used on refitting.

3 Slacken the two anti-roll bar mounting clamp retaining bolts and nuts, and remove both clamps from the top of the subframe **(see illustration)**.

4 Manoeuvre the anti-roll bar out from underneath the vehicle, and remove the mounting bushes from the bar.

5 Carefully examine the anti-roll bar components for signs of wear, damage or deterioration, paying particular attention to the mounting bushes. Renew worn components as necessary, noting the fitted position of the bushes if they are removed.

Refitting

6 Fit the rubber mounting bushes to the anti-roll bar. Position each bush so that the internal two flat surfaces are at the top and bottom and are correctly engaged with the flats on the anti-roll bar.

7 Offer up the anti-roll bar, and manoeuvre it into position on the subframe. Refit the mounting clamps, ensuring that their ends are

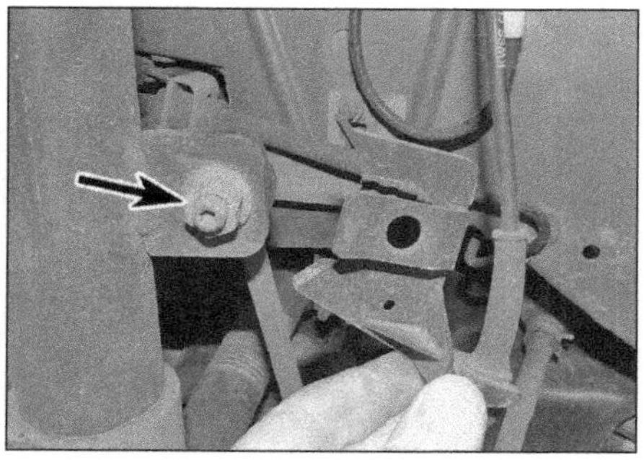

9.2a Undo the anti-roll bar link upper nut (arrowed) ...

correctly located in the hooks on the subframe, and refit the retaining bolts and nuts. Engage the connecting links with the ends of the bar then tighten the mounting clamp retaining bolts to the specified torque.

8 Fit the new retaining nuts to the connecting links and tighten them to the specified torque setting.

9 Refit the roadwheels then lower the vehicle to the ground and tighten the wheel bolts to the specified torque.

9 Front anti-roll bar connecting link – removal and refitting

Note: *New connecting link nuts will be required on refitting.*

Removal

1 Chock the rear wheels, firmly apply the handbrake, slacken the relevant roadwheel bolts, then jack up the front of the vehicle and support on axle stands (see *Jacking and vehicle support*). Remove the relevant roadwheel.

2 Unclip the plastic ABS wiring retaining clip from around the mounting bracket, and then undo the upper balljoint where it secures to the suspension strut **(see illustrations)**. If necessary, retain the balljoint shank with a Torx bit to prevent rotation whilst each nut is slackened.

3 Undo the lower balljoint where it secures to the end of the anti-roll bar **(see illustration)**; if necessary, retain the balljoint shank with a Torx bit to prevent rotation whilst each nut is slackened.

9.2b ... using a Torx bit to prevent rotation whilst the balljoint nut is undone

4 Inspect the link for signs of wear or damage and renew if necessary.

Refitting

5 Refitting is the reverse of removal, using new nuts and tightening them to the specified torque setting.

10 Front subframe – removal and refitting

Note: *Always renew any self-locking nuts when working on the suspension/steering components.*

Removal

1 Chock the rear wheels, firmly apply the handbrake, slacken the front roadwheel bolts, and then jack up the front of the vehicle and support it on axle stands (see *Jacking and vehicle support*). Remove both front roadwheels.

2 Remove the anti-roll bar as described in Section 8.

3 Slacken and remove the engine/transmission rear lower mounting bolt and nut, then undo the nut and bolt securing the link rod to the subframe and remove the link **(see illustration)**.

4 Slacken and remove the left-hand lower balljoint nut and free the balljoint shank from the lower arm, if necessary, using a universal balljoint separator. Discard the nut. Repeat the procedure on the right-hand side.

5 Slacken and remove the steering rack mounting nuts and washers **(see illustration)**. Discard the nuts, as new ones must be fitted.

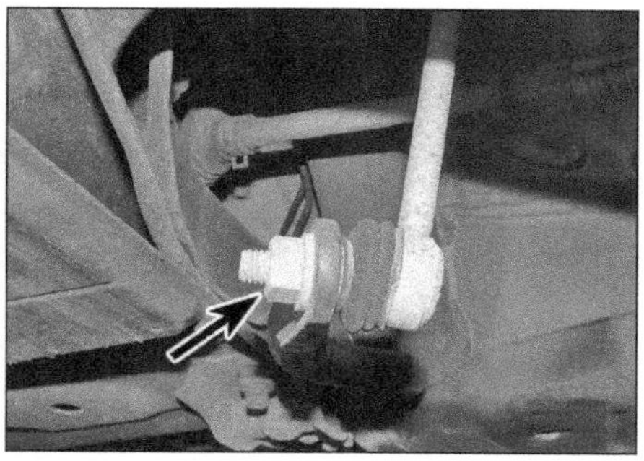

9.3 Undo the anti-roll bar link lower nut (arrowed) ...

6 Unclip the heat shield from the steering rack, then (where applicable) undo the bolt securing the power steering pipe bracket to the subframe.

7 Make a final check that all control cables/hoses that are attached to the subframe have been released and positioned clear so that they will not hinder the removal procedure.

8 Place a jack and a suitable block of wood under the subframe to support the subframe as it is lowered.

9 Slacken and remove the subframe mounting bolts then carefully lower the subframe assembly out of position and remove it from underneath the vehicle, taking great care to ensure that the subframe assembly does not catch the power steering pipes as it is lowered out of position. Recover the washers between the steering rack and the subframe **(see illustrations)**.

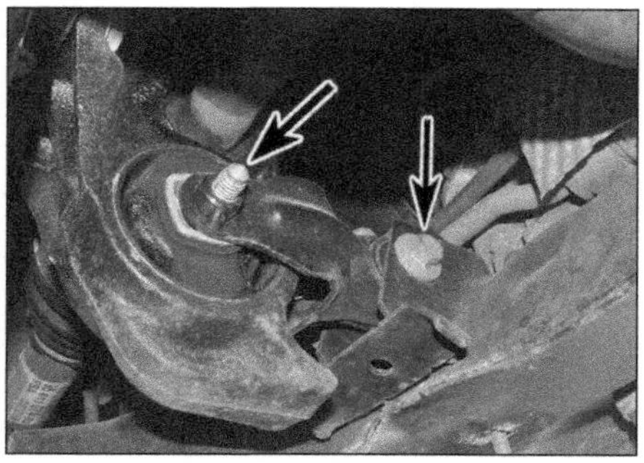

10.3 Undo the bolts (arrowed) securing the rear engine link rod

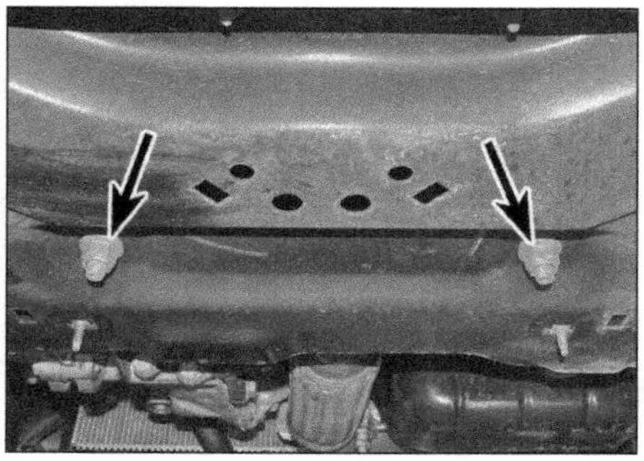

10.5 Steering rack mounting nuts (arrowed)

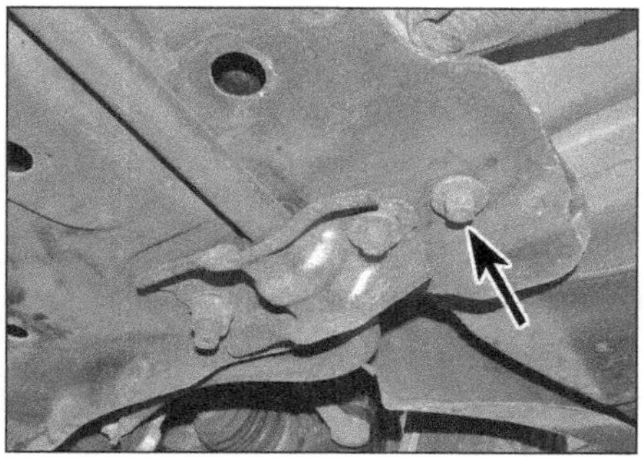

10.9a Undo the front subframe rear mounting bolts (arrowed) ...

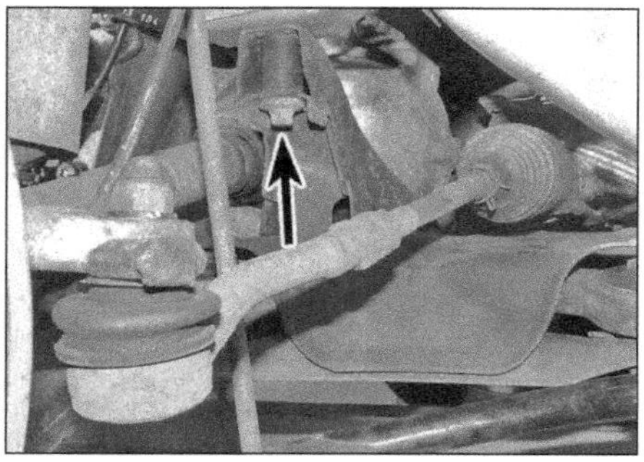

10.9b ... and front mounting bolts (arrowed)

Refitting

10 Refitting is a reversal of the removal procedure, noting the following points:

a) Use new connecting link and lower balljoint nuts, and steering rack nuts.

b) Tighten all nuts and bolts to the specified torque settings (where given).

c) On completion check and, if necessary, adjust the front wheel alignment as described in Section 25.

11 Rear hub bearings – checking and renewal

Note: *The bearing is a sealed, pre-adjusted and pre-lubricated, double-row ball type, and is intended to last the car's entire service life without maintenance or attention. Do not attempt to remove the bearing unless absolutely necessary, as it will be damaged during the removal operation. Never overtighten the hub nut in an attempt to 'adjust' the bearing. A press will be required to remove the bearing; if such a tool is not available, a large bench vice and suitable spacers (such as large sockets) will serve as an adequate substitute.*

Checking

1 Wear in the rear hub bearings can be checked for as described in Chapter 1A, Section 13 or Chapter 1B, Section 5. However, the most common first symptom of bearing wear is a rumbling noise, noted at a particular roadspeed, or when the offending wheel is loaded-up during cornering. In this case, besides rocking the wheel, spin it and listen carefully to distinguish between the sound of the brake pads rubbing the disc, and the rumble of bearing wear. Compare the sound with the other rear wheel to confirm.

2 Wheel bearings do not have to be renewed in pairs. However, if the bearing on one side has worn, it may only be a short while before the other one needs renewal.

Removal

3 Remove the rear brake disc as described in Chapter 9, Section 7. **Note:** *New rear discs supplied by Citroën dealers may come with new wheel bearings already fitted, but separate wheel bearing kits should also be available. Check for the availability of parts before stripping.*

11.4a insert a pair of circlip pliers into the holes ...

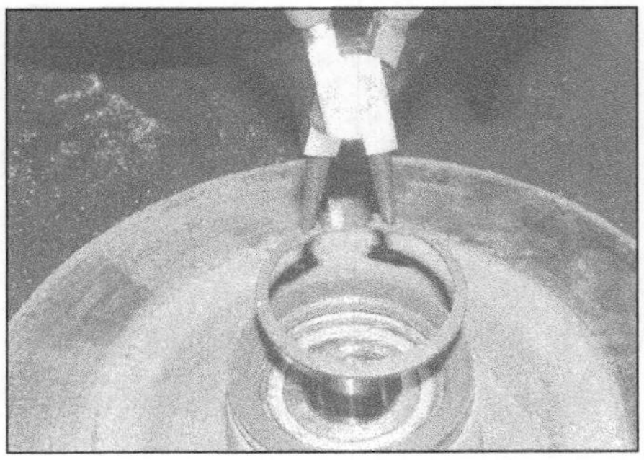

11.4b ... then compress the circlip to remove

4 To remove the bearing, the retaining circlip must first be removed, which requires the use of a sturdy pair of circlip pliers **(see illustrations)**. A new circlip should be used when refitting – one is usually supplied in the bearing kits supplied by Citroën dealers.

5 Care must be taken during bearing renewal, as there is an ABS target ring fitted to the rear of the disc which must not be damaged. Mount the disc over the open jaws of a sturdy bench vice, with the target ring facing upwards **(see illustration)**.

6 After applying a generous amount of spray lubricant, we were able to pull the bearing out, using two blocks of wood, together with a large nut and bolt, and several washers/spacers **(see illustration)**.

7 Tighten the nut and bolt to apply pressure to the bearing – this, and a few hammer blows, should be enough to get the bearing moving and extract it **(see illustration)**.

Refitting

8 Using emery paper, clean off any burrs or raised edges from the hub, which might stop the components going back together – take care not to damage the ABS target ring. Clean and lightly lubricate the bearing location in the hub.

9 Offer the bearing into position, and using a suitable spacer, tap it gently around its edge to start it squarely into the disc/hub **(see illustrations)**.

10 Using the same nut/bolt and spacers as

11.5 Mount the disc over the open jaws of a vice ...

11.6 ... then fit a large bolt, nut, spacers and two blocks of wood ...

11.7 ... to extract the bearing

11.9a Offer the bearing into place ...

11.9b ... then tap it gently to start it into the hub

11.10a Fit the same nut, bolt and spacers used for removal ...

11.10b ... then tighten the nut/bolt to press the bearing into place

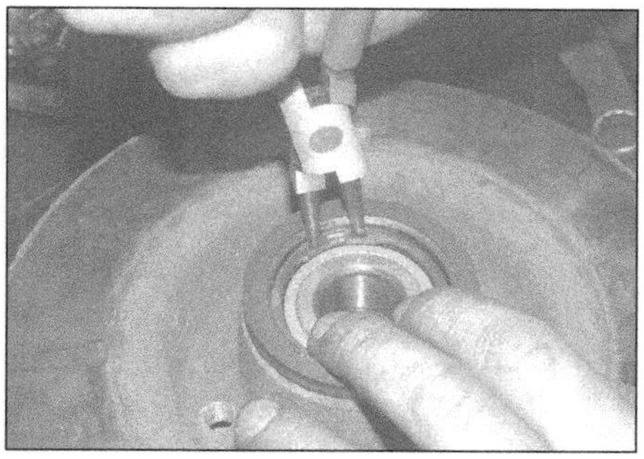

11.11 Fit the new bearing retaining clip

for removal, tighten the nut and bolt to press the bearing into place **(see illustrations)**.

11 The bearing is fully seated when the circlip groove is visible. Fit the new circlip using suitable circlip pliers to retain the bearing **(see illustration)**.

12 Refit the brake disc/hub and wheel speed sensor as described in Chapter 9, Section 7.

12 Rear shock absorber – removal, testing and refitting

Note: *Always renew any self-locking nuts when working on the suspension/steering components.*

Removal

1 Chock the front wheels, slacken the relevant rear roadwheel bolts, and then jack up the rear of the vehicle and support it on axle stands (see *Jacking and vehicle support*). Remove the relevant rear roadwheel.

2 Using a trolley jack positioned under the spring cup, raise the lower arm until the rear suspension coil spring is slightly compressed.

3 Working in the wheel arch, undo the two shock absorber upper mounting bolts **(see illustration)**.

4 Slacken and remove the lower mounting bolt and nut, then manoeuvre the shock absorber out of position **(see illustration)**.

Testing

5 Examine the shock absorber for signs of fluid leakage or damage. Test the operation of the shock absorber, while holding it in an upright position, by moving the piston through a full stroke and then through short strokes of 50 to 100 mm. In both cases, the resistance felt should be smooth and continuous. If the resistance is jerky, or uneven, or if there is any visible sign of wear or damage, renewal is necessary. Also check the rubber mountings for damage and deterioration. Renew worn components as necessary. Inspect the shank of the mounting bolt for signs of wear or damage, and renew as necessary. The self-locking nuts should be renewed as a matter of course.

Refitting

6 Prior to refitting the shock absorber, mount it upright in the vice, and operate it fully through several strokes in order to prime it. Apply a smear of multipurpose grease to the lower mounting bolt and contact face of the new nut (Citroën recommend Molykote G Rapide Plus – available from your Citroën dealer).

7 Fully extend the piston and manoeuvre the assembly into position. Refit the upper mounting bolts, and tighten them to the specified torque.

8 Align the shock absorber lower mounting with the lower arm and refit the mounting bolt. Fit the new nut, tightening it lightly only at this stage.

9 Refit the rear roadwheel then lower the vehicle to the ground and tighten the wheel bolts to the specified torque. Rock the vehicle to settle the shock absorber in position then tighten the shock absorber lower mounting to the specified torque setting.

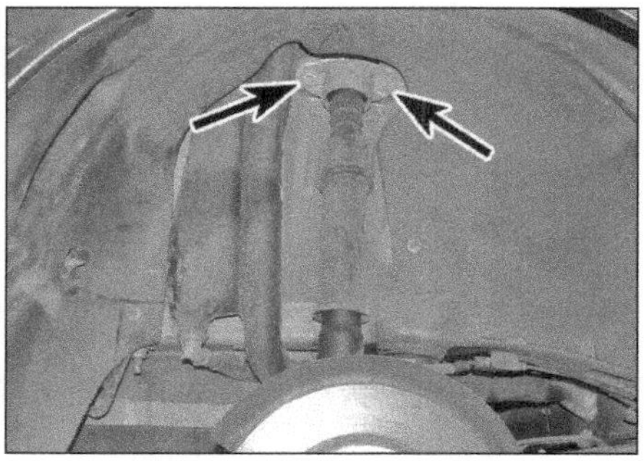

12.3 Undo the two shock absorber upper mounting bolts

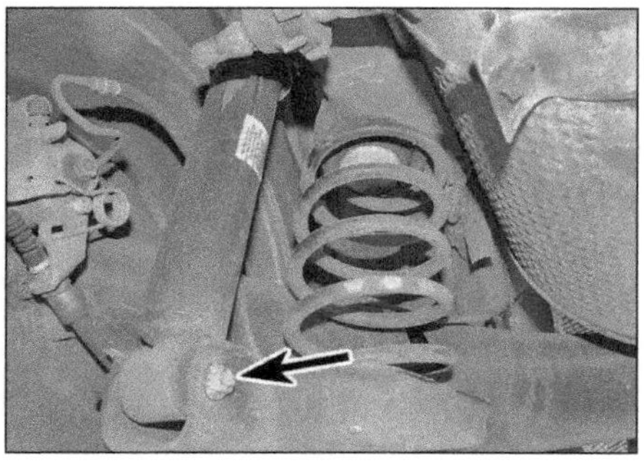

12.4 Remove the lower shock absorber mounting bolt (arrowed)

13 Rear coil spring – removal and refitting

Note: *Always renew any self-locking nuts when working on the suspension/steering components.*

Removal

1 Chock the front wheels, slacken the rear roadwheel bolts, and then jack up the rear of the vehicle and support it on axle stands (see *Jacking and vehicle support*). Remove the rear roadwheels.

2 Position a trolley jack underneath one of the lower arms spring cup and raise the arm until the rear suspension coil spring on that side is slightly compressed.

3 Unscrew the shock absorber lower mounting bolt/nut and withdraw the bolt. Discard the nut; a new should be used on refitting.

4 Slowly lower the jack as far as the lower arm will go, then position the jack under the lower arm spring cup on the other side, and raise the arm until the coil spring on that side is slightly compressed.

5 Slacken and remove the shock absorber lower mounting bolt. Again, discard the nut a new one must be fitted.

6 Lower the jack until all tension in the springs is released, then remove the springs.

7 Inspect the coil spring and its seats for signs of wear or damage and renew if necessary.

Refitting

8 Fit the lower spring seat in position on the lower arm, and seat the upper seat on top of the coil spring. Lubricate the shanks of the shock absorber and lower arm bolts and the contact faces of the new nuts with multipurpose grease (Citroën recommend Molykote G Rapide Plus – available from your Citroën dealer).

9 Manoeuvre the springs into position and carefully raise one lower arm with the jack, ensuring that the coil spring ends are correctly

13.9 Ensure the ends of the coil springs align correctly with the seats (arrowed)

aligned with both seats, and point to the front of the vehicle **(see illustration)**.

10 Align the shock absorber with the lower arm and refit its mounting bolt. Fit the new nut to the bolt, tightening it lightly only at this stage.

11 Remove the jack from underneath the lower arm, and position it under the lower arm spring cup on the remaining side.

12 Raise the jack and align the lower mounting of the shock absorber with the arm. Insert the bolt, and fit a new nut, tightening it lightly only at this stage.

13 Refit the rear roadwheel then lower the vehicle to the ground and tighten the wheel bolts to the specified torque. Rock the vehicle to settle the lower arm in position then tighten the shock absorber lower mounting bolts/nuts to their specified torque settings.

14 Rear stub axle – removal, overhaul and refitting

Note: *Always renew any self-locking nuts when working on the suspension/steering components.*

Removal

1 Chock the front wheels, slacken the relevant rear roadwheel bolts, and then jack up the rear of the vehicle and support it on axle stands (see *Jacking and vehicle support*). Remove the relevant roadwheel.

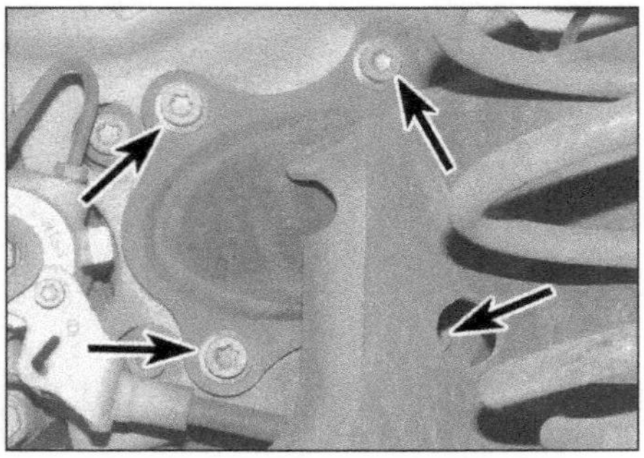

14.5 Undo the four bolts (arrowed) securing the stub axle to the lower arm

2 Unbolt the wheel sensor and position it clear of the stub axle (see Chapter 9, Section 19). Note that there is no need to disconnect the wiring.

3 Remove the disc/hub assembly as described in Chapter 9, Section 7. **Note:** *If the stub axle is to be renewed, there is no need to remove the disc/hub assembly, as the act of removal may destroy the bearing, necessitating its renewal.*

4 Undo the two rear brake caliper mounting bracket retaining bolts, and slide the caliper and bracket assembly from the disc. There is no need to disconnect the handbrake cable or caliper hose.

5 Undo the four bolts securing the stub axle to the lower arm and remove it, complete with disc backplate **(see illustration)**.

6 Inspect the stub axle for signs of wear or damage. If the stub axle shaft is worn or damaged then the assembly must be renewed.

Refitting

7 Obtain all the new nuts required and lubricate the shanks of the pivot bolts and contact faces of the new nuts with multipurpose grease (Citroën recommend Molykote G Rapide Plus – available from your Citroën dealer).

8 Offer up the stub axle and backplate, insert the bolts and tighten them to the specified torque.

9 Fit the brake disc/hub assembly as described in Chapter 9, Section 7.

10 Refit the wheel speed sensor to the stub axle (see Chapter 9, Section 19).

11 Slide the brake caliper and bracket assembly over the edge of the disc, and tighten the mounting bracket bolts to the specified torque.

12 Refit the rear roadwheel then lower the vehicle to the ground and tighten the wheel bolts to the specified torque.

15 Rear beam axle – removal, overhaul and refitting

Note: *Always renew any self-locking nuts when working on the suspension/steering components.*

Removal

1 Remove the coil springs as described in Section 13.

2 Trace the ABS wheel speed sensor wiring back to its connector, and unplug it **(see illustration)**. Free the sensor harness from any retaining clips on the axle.

3 Clamp the flexible brake hose, and undo the hose union where the flexible hose connects to the rigid hose **(see illustration)**. Plug the end of the hose/pipe to prevent dirt ingress. Repeat this procedure on the remaining side.

4 Release the handbrake cables from the retaining clips along the axle, then release the ends of the cables from the caliper levers and support brackets (see Chapter 9, Section 16). Repeat the procedure on the remaining side.

5 Make alignment marks between the axle mounting brackets and the vehicle body to aid refitment. Undo the 4 bolts each side securing the mounting brackets to the vehicle body, and lower the axle to the floor **(see illustration)**. If the axle is to be renewed, remove the brake caliper (Chapter 9, Section 9), and the stub axle (Section 14).

Overhaul

6 Thoroughly clean the axle and the area around the axle mountings, removing all traces of dirt and underseal if necessary, then check carefully for cracks, distortion or any other signs of wear or damage, paying particular attention to the pivot bushes.

7 Renewal of the pivot bushes will require

15.2 Disconnect the ABS sensor wiring connector (arrowed)

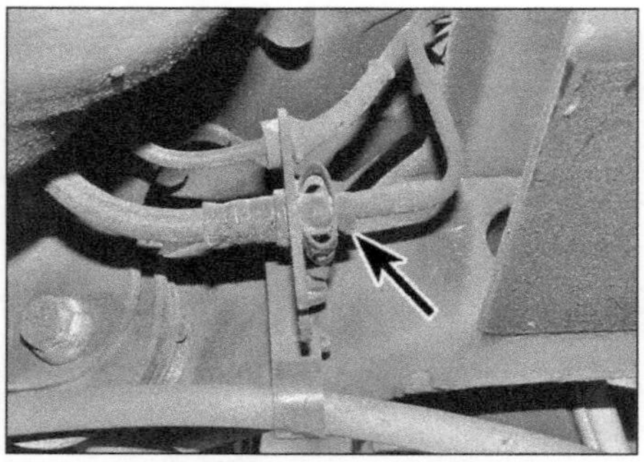

15.3 Disconnect the brake hose union (arrowed)

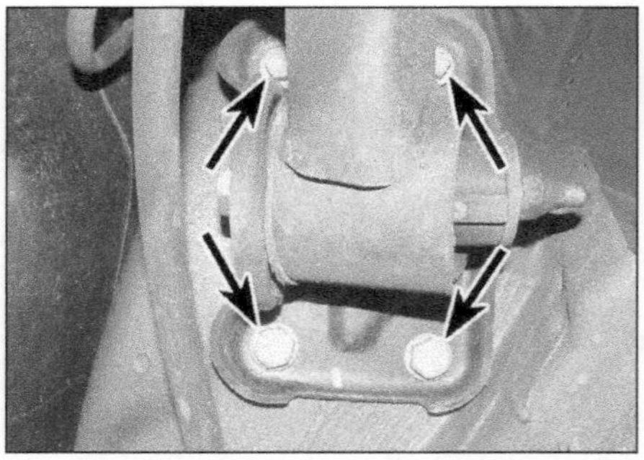

15.5 Undo the four bolts each side (arrowed) securing the axle brackets to the vehicle body

the use of a hydraulic press and several spacers, and should therefore be entrusted to a Citroën dealer or specialist with access to the necessary equipment.

Refitting

8 Lubricate the shanks of the axle mounting bracket bolts with multipurpose grease (Citroën recommend Molykote G Rapide Plus – available from your Citroën dealer).

9 Offer up the axle and mounting brackets, aligning the previously-made marks, and insert the retaining bolts. Tighten them to the specified torque.

10 Refit the handbrake cables to their retaining clips on the axle, and reconnect the cable ends to the caliper levers (see Chapter 9, Section 16).

11 Reconnect the rear brake flexible hoses, tightening the hose/pipe unions securely. Remove the hose clamps.

12 Refit the coil spring with reference to Section 13. On completion bleed the brakes as described in Chapter 9, Section 2.

16 Steering wheel – removal and refitting

Warning: Refer to the precautions given in Chapter 12, Section 21 before proceeding.

Removal

1 Remove the airbag unit as described in Chapter 12, Section 22.

2 Undo the retaining screws and remove the upper and lower steering column cowlings, as described in Chapter 11, Section 27.

3 Trace the wiring back from the lower right-hand side of the steering wheel and disconnect the two wiring connectors from the steering column wiring loom and the rear of the switch assembly **(see illustrations)**.

4 Slacken and remove the steering wheel retaining bolt, note the alignment marks on the steering wheel for alignment when refitting **(see illustrations)**. If no alignment marks are obvious, then mark the steering wheel and steering column shaft in relation to each other.

5 With the steering in the straight ahead position, insert two bolts into the upper recesses of the steering wheel to secure the fixed centred controls in the steering wheel **(see illustrations)**. Citroën use a special tool (No. 9702-T) to secure the controls in place.

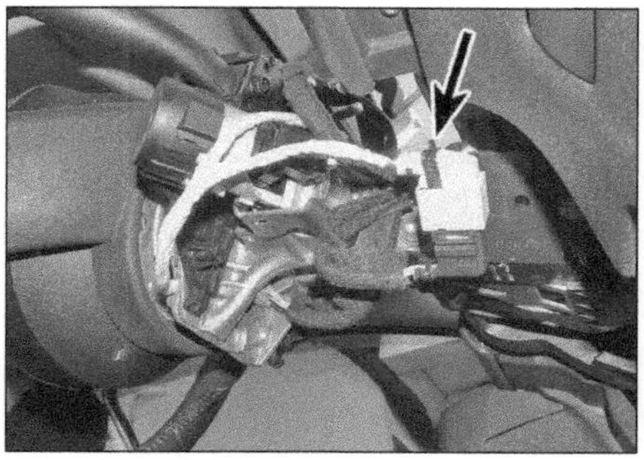

16.3a Disconnect the wiring connector (arrowed) ...

16.3b ... and the wiring connector at the rear of the switch assembly

16.4a Undo the steering wheel retaining bolt ...

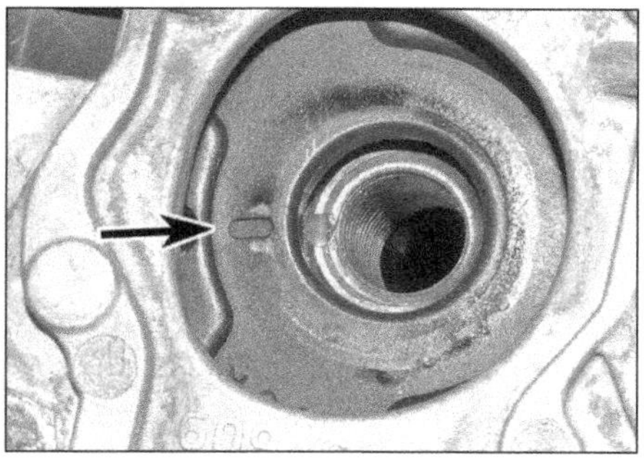

16.4b ... noting the alignment marks (arrowed) for refitting

16.5a Insert bolts into the steering wheel centre ...

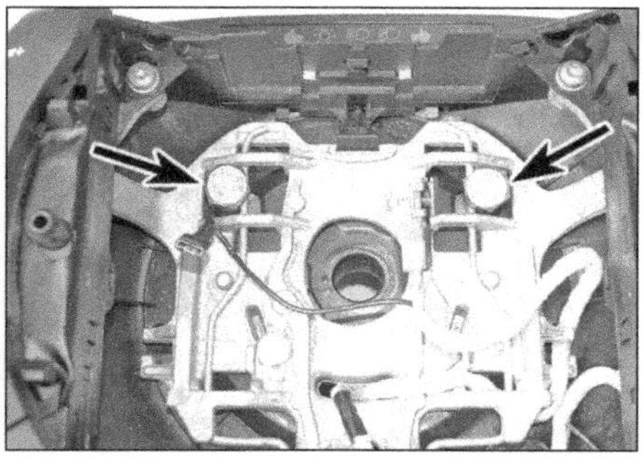

16.5b ... to lock it in position (two bolts arrowed)

6 Slacken and remove the three steering wheel housing retaining nuts **(see illustrations)**.

7 Withdraw the steering wheel assembly off the top of the steering column **(see illustration)**, making sure the wiring is

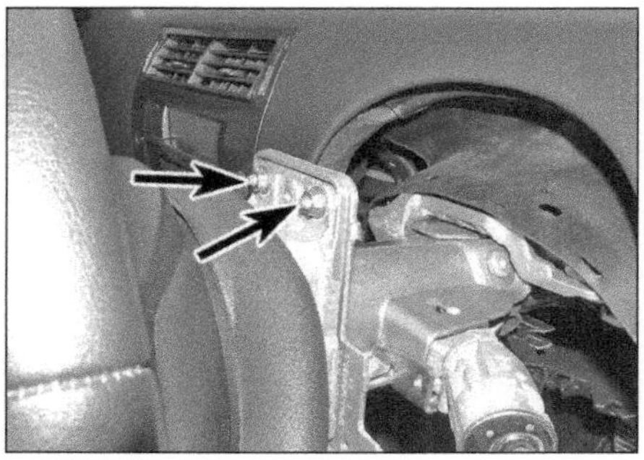

16.6a Undo the two upper retaining nuts (arrowed) ...

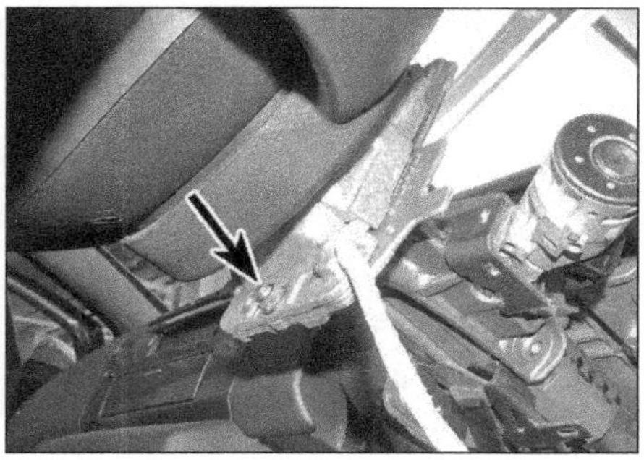

16.6b ... and lower retaining nut (arrowed)

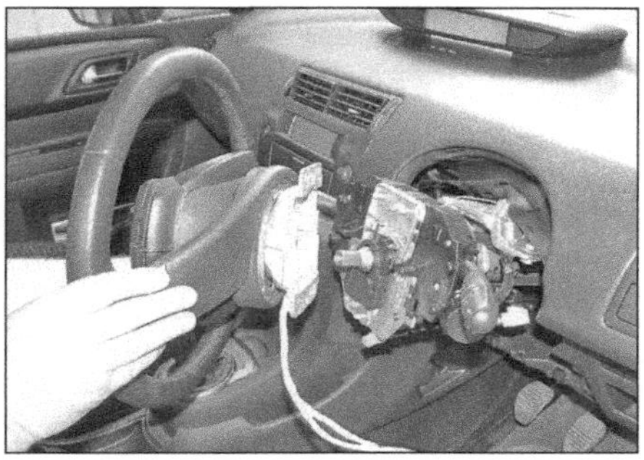

16.7 Remove the steering wheel assembly from the top of the column

released from any retaining clips as it is withdrawn.

Refitting

8 Prior to refitting the steering wheel, ensure that the front wheels are still in the straight-ahead position.

9 Refitting is a reversal of removal, noting the following points:

a) On refitting, align the master spline or the marks made on removal, taking great care not to damage the wiring loom, then tighten the retaining bolt/nuts to the specified torque.

b) Make sure the Citroën special tool (or bolts) for locking the central controls are removed before refitting the airbag unit.

c) On completion, refit the airbag unit as described in Chapter 12, Section 22.

17 Steering column – removal, inspection and refitting

Note: *As all models are equipped with a driver's airbag, refer to the precautions given in Chapter 12, Section 21 before proceeding.* **Note:** *A new pinch-bolt nut will be needed on refitting.*

Removal

1 Remove the steering wheel as described in Section 16.

2 Move the driver's seat as far back as possible.

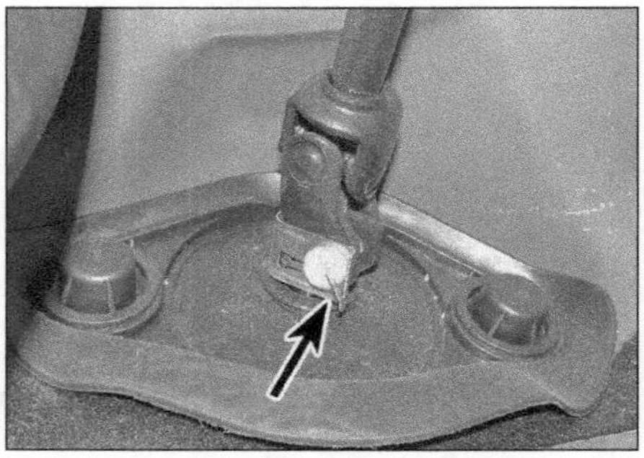

17.3a Release the retaining clip (arrowed) ...

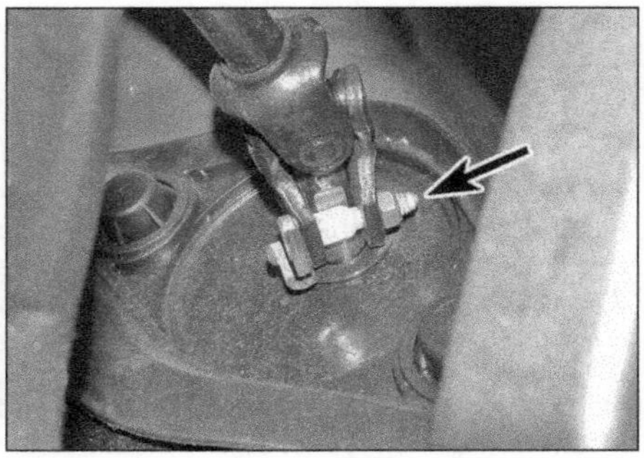

17.3b ... then remove the column lower pinch-bolt/nut (arrowed)

3 Working in the driver's footwell, make alignment marks between the universal joint and the steering rack pinion, release the retaining clip, then undo and remove the pinch-bolt/nut from the joint at the base of the column **(see illustrations)**.

4 Remove the combination switches from the top of the steering column as described in Chapter 12, Section 4.

5 Release the retaining clips and remove the lower facia panels above the driver's pedals **(see illustrations)**.

6 Disconnect the wiring connector at the rear of the ignition switch **(see illustration 18.5)**.

7 Note its fitted position, then release the wiring loom from its retaining clips and position it clear so that it does not hinder column removal **(see illustration)**.

8 Slacken and remove the four mounting bolts from the top of the column **(see illustrations)**. Slide the column assembly upwards and free from the steering rack pinion, and remove it from the vehicle.

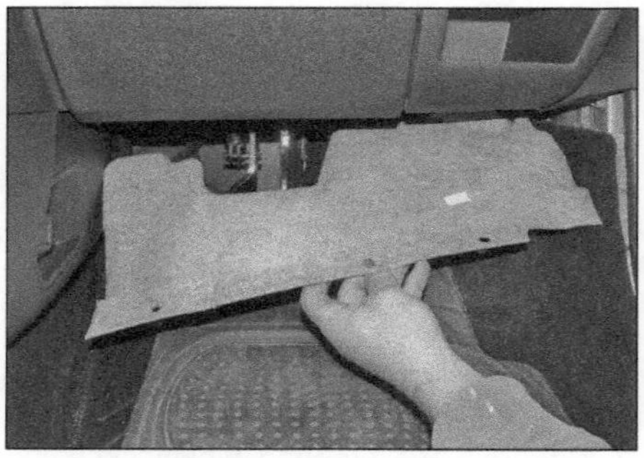

17.5a Remove the trim panel from under the facia

17.5b Unclip the plastic cover from the lower part of the facia

Inspection

9 Before refitting the steering column, examine the column and mountings for signs of damage and deformation, and renew as necessary. Check the steering shaft for signs of free play in the column bushes, and check the universal joints for signs of damage or roughness in the joint bearings. If any damage or wear is found on the steering column universal joint or shaft bushes, the column must be renewed as an assembly.

Refitting

10 Align the marks made prior to removal and engage the column universal joint with the steering rack pinion.

11 Slide the column assembly into position making sure its mounting bracket is correctly engaged with the facia bracket. Refit the column mounting bolts and tighten them to the specified torque setting.

12 Refit the universal joint pinch-bolt and nut, tighten them to the specified torque setting, and then refit the retaining clip.

13 The remainder of refitting is a reversal of the removal procedure, noting the following.

a) Ensure that all wiring is correctly routed and retained by all the necessary clips and ties.

b) Refit the steering wheel as described in Section 16.

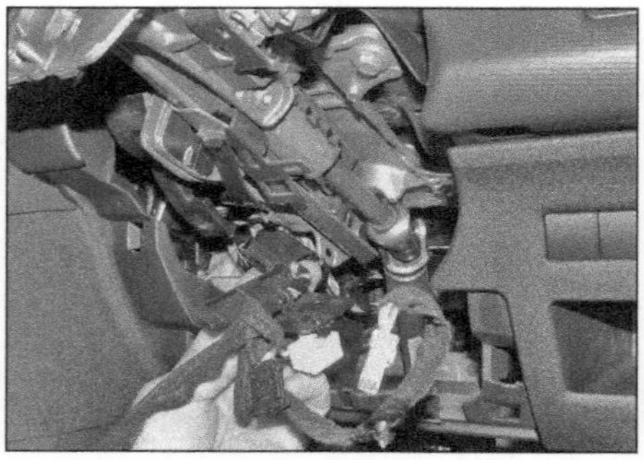

17.7 Unclip the wiring loom (arrowed) from the steering column

17.8a Undo the mounting bolts (arrowed) ...

17.8b ... and withdraw the steering column from the facia

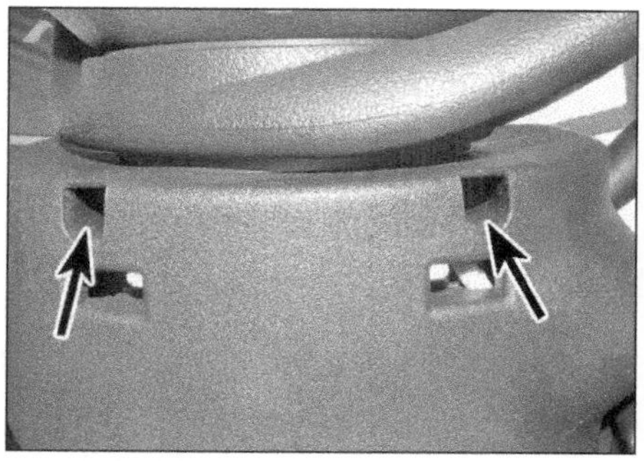

18.2a Undo the two retaining screws (arrowed) ...

18.2b ... and unclip the upper shroud ...

18.2c ... and then the lower shroud

18 Ignition switch/steering lock – removal and refitting

Removal

1 Disconnect the battery (refer to precautions in Chapter 5A, Section 1).

2 Undo the retaining screws securing the steering column lower shroud in position, then unclip the upper shroud, and release it from the retaining clips at its front edge **(see illustrations)**.

3 Trace the wiring back from the transponder and release the connector from the rear of the steering column combination switches **(see illustration)**.

4 Carefully lift the two plastic retaining clips and withdraw the transponder immobiliser unit to release it from the ignition switch housing **(see illustrations)**. Take care not to damage the transponder assembly.

5 Disconnect the wiring connector from the rear of the ignition switch **(see illustration)**.

6 Use a centre punch to mark the centre of the lock housing retaining screw then, using a drill and an extractor, remove the screw **(see illustrations)**. Obviously, a new screw will be required for refitting.

7 Insert the key into the steering lock and turn it to the first position, and then using a small screwdriver, depress the locating peg and slide the ignition switch from the steering column housing **(see illustration)**.

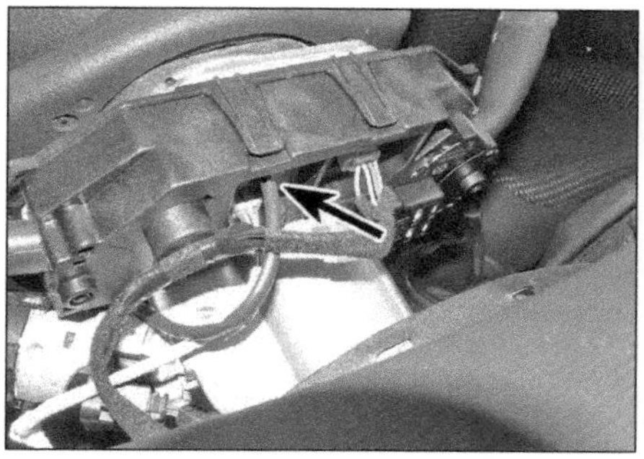

18.3 Disconnect the transponder wiring connector (arrowed)

18.4a Lift the transponder ring securing clips (upper shown) ...

18.4b ... and slide it from around the ignition switch

18.5 Disconnect the switch wiring connector

18.6a Drill out the centre of the shear bolt ...

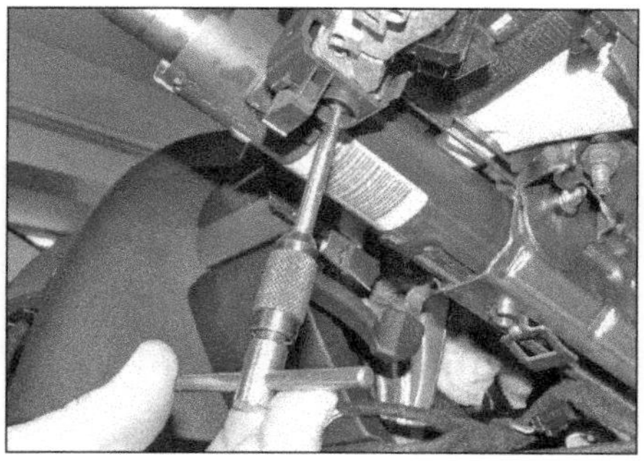

18.6b ... and use an extractor to remove the bolt

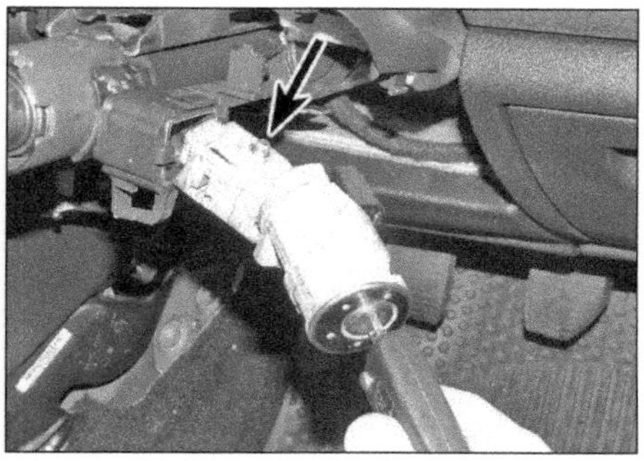

18.7 Depress the locating peg (arrowed) and slide the switch from the steering column

18.8 Fit the new shear bolt – tighten until the head shears off

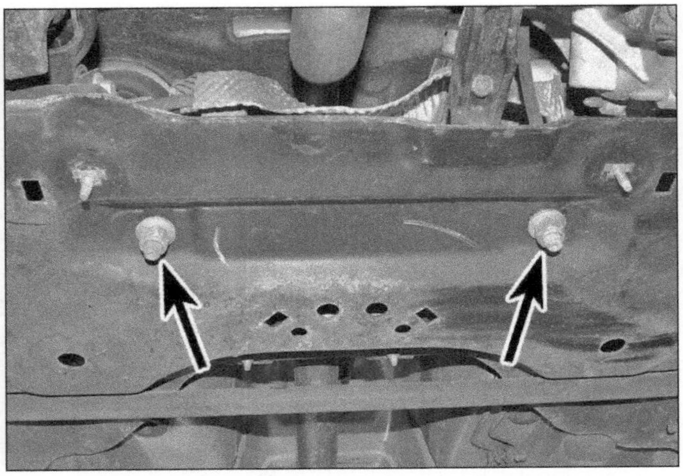

19.3 Steering rack mounting nuts (arrowed)

Refitting

8 Refitting is a reversal of removal, noting the following points:

a) *Ensure all wiring is correctly routed, and securely clipped back into its original positions.*

b) *Refit the steering lock housing with a new retaining/shear bolt* ***(see illustration)****. Tighten the bolt until the head shears off, leaving the threaded part securing the lock.*

19 Steering rack assembly – removal, overhaul and refitting

Note: *Always renew any self-locking nuts when working on the suspension/steering components***.**

Removal

1 Firmly apply the handbrake, slacken the front roadwheel bolts, and then jack up the front of the vehicle and support it on axle stands (see *Jacking and vehicle support*). Remove both front roadwheels.

2 Slacken and remove the nuts securing the steering rack track rod balljoints to the hub carriers. Release the balljoint tapered shanks using a universal balljoint separator, see Section 23. Discard the nuts; new ones will be needed on refitting.

3 Working underneath the vehicle, undo the remove the rack mounting nuts and studs **(see illustration)**. Recover the washers (where fitted) between the rack and the subframe, noting their positions. Discard the rack mounting studs and nuts, as new ones must be fitted.

4 Unclip the heat shield from the steering rack, then undo the bolt securing the steering rack pipe's bracket to the front of the subframe **(see illustration)**.

5 Position a jack under the centre of the front subframe. Remove the four subframe mounting bolts **(see illustrations 10.9a and 10.9b)**.

6 Undo the retaining nuts and detach the exhaust rubber mountings from the rear of the subframe **(see illustration)**.

7 Undo the bolt and detach the rear engine-mounting link from the bracket on the rear of the cylinder block **(see illustration 10.3)**. Lower the subframe approximately 60 mm to allow for the steering rack to be removed.

8 Clean the area around the rack pinion housing, then undo the nuts securing the fluid pipes to the rack pinion housing **(see illustration)**, release the pipes from the retaining clamp, and drain the fluid into a container. To completely drain system, remove fluid reservoir cap and turn the steering wheel from lock-to-lock to assist the draining process; remember to recentre the steering wheel afterwards. Discard the pipes O-ring seals, new ones must be fitted. Plug the ends of the pipes to prevent dirt ingress.

9 Working in the driver's footwell, using paint or a suitable marker pen, make alignment marks between the steering column universal joint and the steering rack pinion, then slacken and remove the universal joint pinch-bolt, and release the retaining clip **(see illustrations 17.3a and 17.3b).**

10 Still in the driver's footwell, undo the two retaining nuts and remove the seal around the steering rack pinion.

11 Free the steering rack pinion from the column universal joint and manoeuvre it out through the driver's side wheel arch aperture.

Overhaul

12 Examine the steering rack assembly for signs of wear or damage, and check that the rack moves freely throughout the full length of its travel, with no signs of roughness or excessive free play between the steering rack pinion and rack. Inspect all the steering rack fluid unions for signs of leakage, and check that all union nuts are securely tightened.

13 It is possible to overhaul the steering rack assembly housing components, but this task

19.4 Steering rack pipe's bracket (arrowed)

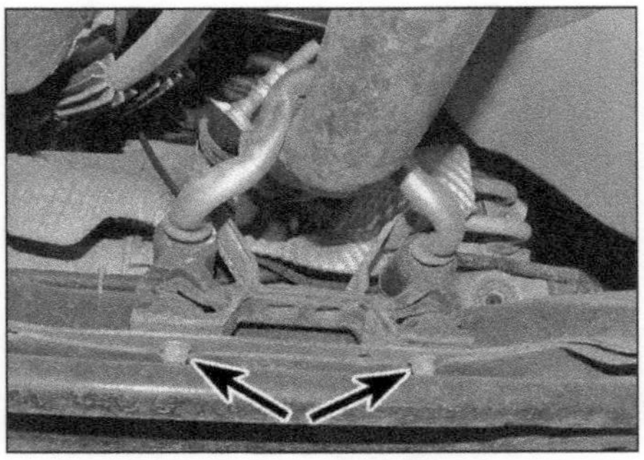

19.6 Exhaust mounting retaining nuts (arrowed)

19.8 Undo the fluid pipes unions

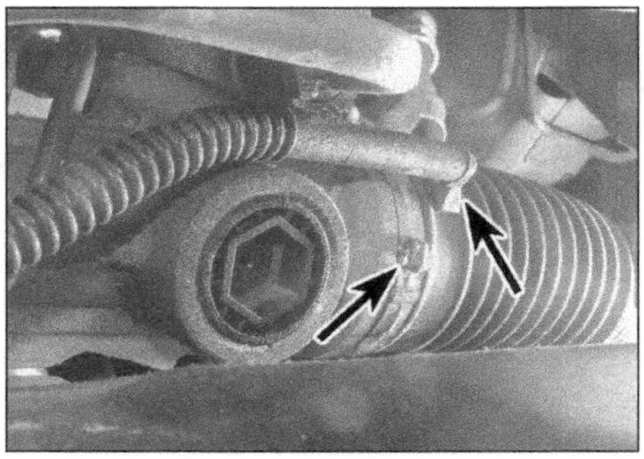

20.2 Rack gaiter breather pipe and inner clip (arrowed)

20.3 Rack gaiter outer retaining clip (arrowed)

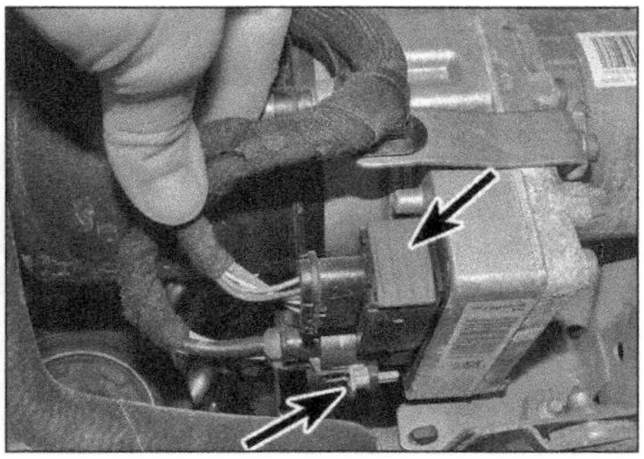

22.2 Release the securing clips (arrowed) and disconnect the wiring connectors

should be entrusted to a Citroën dealer or specialist. The only components that can be renewed easily by the home mechanic are the steering rack gaiters, the track rod balljoints and the track rods, which are covered elsewhere in this Chapter.

Refitting

14 Manoeuvre the steering rack into position and engage it with the column universal joint, aligning the marks made prior to removal.
15 Slide the washers into position between the subframe and steering rack. Insert the new mounting studs, and tighten the nuts to the specified torque.
16 The remainder of refitting is a reversal of removal, noting the following points:
a) Top-up the fluid reservoir and bleed the hydraulic system as described in Section 21.
b) On completion check and, if necessary, adjust the front wheel alignment as described in Section 25.

20 Steering rack rubber gaiters - renewal

1 Remove the track rod balljoint as described in Section 23.
2 Disconnect the breather pipe from the gaiter **(see illustration)**.
3 Mark the correct fitted position of the gaiter on the track rod, then release the retaining clips and slide the gaiter off the steering rack housing and track rod end **(see illustration)**.
4 Thoroughly clean the track rod and the steering rack housing, using fine abrasive paper to polish off any corrosion, burrs or sharp edges which might damage the new gaiter's sealing lips on installation. Scrape off all the grease from the old gaiter, and apply it to the track rod inner balljoint. (This assumes that grease has not been lost or contaminated as a result of damage to the old gaiter. Use fresh grease if in doubt.)
5 Carefully slide the new gaiter onto the track rod end, and locate it on the steering rack housing. Align the outer edge of the gaiter with the mark made on the track rod prior to removal, and then secure it in position with new retaining clips (where fitted).
6 Reconnect the breather pipe to the gaiter.
7 Refit the track rod balljoint as described in Section 23.

21 Power steering system - bleeding

1 This procedure will only be necessary when any of the hydraulic system has been disconnected.
2 Referring to *Weekly checks*, remove the fluid reservoir filler cap, and top-up with the specified fluid to the upper level mark.
3 Start the engine and allow it to idle for 3 minutes without moving the steering wheel. Check the fluid level frequently during this period and top it up if necessary.
4 Slowly move the steering from lock-to-lock several times to purge out the trapped air, then top-up the level in the fluid reservoir. Repeat this procedure until the fluid level in the reservoir does not drop any further.
5 Turn the engine off and allow the system to cool. Once cool, check that fluid level is up to the upper mark on the power steering fluid reservoir, topping-up if necessary.

22 Power steering pump - removal and refitting

Removal

1 Remove the windscreen washer fluid reservoir from inside the right-hand front wheel arch as described in Chapter 12, Section 16.
2 Release the locking clips and disconnect the power steering pump wiring plug connectors **(see illustration)**. Unclip the wiring loom from the pump bracket and move it to one side.
3 Release the retaining clips and disconnect the fluid hose and fluid pipe from the power steering pump **(see illustration)**. Be prepared for fluid spillage, and plug the pump and pipe/hose openings to prevent dirt ingress.
Caution: Do not bend the rigid power steering fluid pipe.
4 Undo the two upper and two lower pump mounting bolts, then remove the pump from the wheel arch **(see illustrations)**.
5 If the power steering pump is faulty it must be renewed. The pump is a sealed unit and cannot be overhauled.

22.3 Disconnect the fluid pipe and hose (arrowed) from the pump

22.4a Undo the upper pump mounting bolts (arrowed) ...

22.4b ... and lower mounting bolts (arrowed)

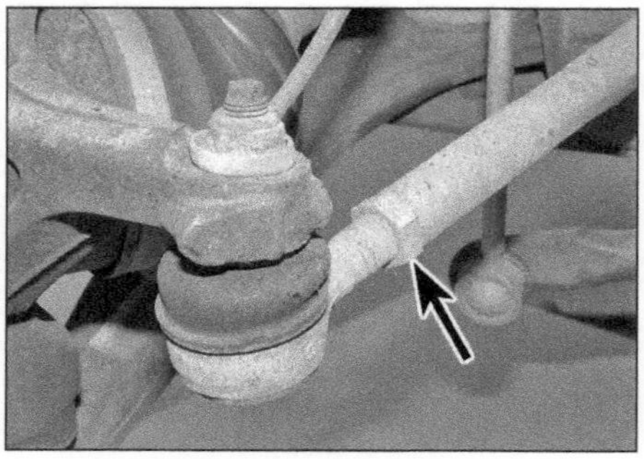

23.3 Slacken the track rod end locknut (arrowed)

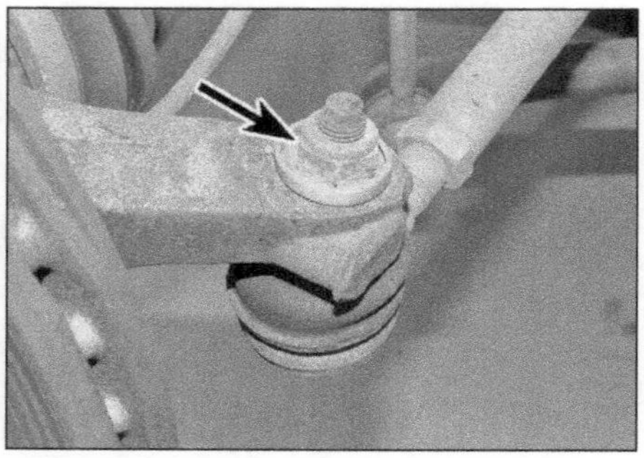

23.4a Undo the balljoint nut (arrowed) ...

23.4b ... then use a balljoint separator to release the tapered shank

Refitting

6 Manoeuvre the pump into position, then refit its mounting bolts and tighten them to the specified torque.

7 Reconnect the feed pipe to the pump and securely tighten the union bolt. Refit the supply pipe to the pump, and secure it with a new clip.

8 Refit the windscreen washer fluid reservoir as described in Chapter 12, Section 16.

9 On completion, bleed the hydraulic system as described in Section 21.

23 Track rod balljoint – removal and refitting

Note: *A new balljoint retaining nut will be required on refitting.*

Removal

1 Apply the handbrake, slacken the appropriate front roadwheel bolts, then jack up the front of the vehicle and support it on axle stands (see *Jacking and vehicle support*). Remove the appropriate front roadwheel.

2 If the balljoint is to be re-used, use a straight-edge and a scriber, or similar, to mark its relationship to the track rod.

3 Hold the track rod, and unscrew the balljoint locknut by a quarter of a turn **(see illustration)**. Do not move the locknut from this position, as it will serve as a handy reference mark on refitting.

4 Slacken and remove the nut securing the track rod balljoint to the hub carrier; discard the nut; a new one will be needed on refitting. Release the balljoint tapered shank using a universal balljoint separator **(see illustrations)**.

5 Counting the exact number of turns necessary to do so, unscrew the balljoint from the track rod end.

6 Count the number of exposed threads between the end of the balljoint and the locknut, and record this figure. If a new balljoint is to be fitted, unscrew the locknut from the old balljoint.

7 Carefully clean the balljoint and the threads. Renew the balljoint if its movement is sloppy or too stiff, if excessively worn, or if damaged in any way; carefully check the stud taper and threads. If the balljoint gaiter is damaged, the complete balljoint assembly must be renewed; it is not possible to obtain the gaiter separately.

Refitting

8 If a new balljoint is to be fitted, screw the locknut onto its threads, and position it so that the same number of exposed threads are visible, as was noted prior to removal.

9 Screw the balljoint into the track rod by the number of turns noted on removal. This should bring the balljoint locknut to within a quarter of a turn of the alignment marks that were made on removal (if applicable).

10 Ensure that the protector plate is in position then locate the balljoint shank in the hub carrier. Fit a new retaining nut and tighten it to the specified torque.

11 Refit the roadwheel, then lower the vehicle to the ground and tighten the roadwheel bolts to the specified torque.

12 Check and, if necessary, adjust the front wheel alignment as described in Section 25, then securely tighten the balljoint locknut.

24 Track rod arm – removal and refitting

Note: *A special wrench (Citroën number 0721-A) will be required to remove/refit the track rod inner balljoint from the end of the steering rack. Without the clamp, damage to the assembly is likely. The special wrench engages with the balljoint housing allowing the track rod to be easily slackened/tightened without the risk of damage. Note that without access to the special tool, track rod removal will be difficult, especially without causing damage.*

Note: *A new balljoint retaining nut will be required on refitting.*

Removal

1 Remove the relevant steering rack rubber gaiter as described in Section 20.

2 Using the special wrench (see note at the start of the Section), unscrew the track rod inner balljoint from the steering rack end. Take great care not to place excess strain on the rack, as the joint is unscrewed, if necessary, prevent the steering rack from turning by holding it carefully with a pair of grips. Take great care not to mark the surfaces of the rack and balljoint. To eliminate the possibility of damage, a Citroën special tool (0721-B) is available to prevent the rack from twisting.

3 Remove the track rod assembly. Examine the track rod inner balljoint for signs of slackness or tight spots, and check that the track rod itself is straight and free from damage. If necessary, renew the track rod; it is also recommended that the steering rack gaiter/dust cover is renewed.

Refitting

4 Screw the balljoint into the steering rack, and tighten it to the specified torque. If necessary, retain the steering rack with a pair of grips or the special Citroën tool, again taking great care not to damage or mark the track rod balljoint or steering rack.

5 Carefully slide on the new gaiter, and locate it on the steering rack housing. Turn the steering fully from lock-to-lock, to check that the gaiter is correctly positioned on the track rod, then secure it in position with new retaining clips (where fitted).

6 Refit the track rod balljoint as described in Section 23.

25 Wheel alignment and steering angles – information, checking and adjustment

Definitions

1 A car's steering and suspension geometry is defined in four basic settings – all angles are expressed in degrees (toe settings are also expressed as a measurement); the steering axis is defined as an imaginary line drawn through the axis of the suspension strut, extended where necessary to contact the ground.

2 Camber is the angle between each roadwheel and a vertical line drawn through its centre and tyre contact patch, when viewed from the front or rear of the car. Positive camber is when the roadwheels are tilted outwards from the vertical at the top; negative camber is when they are tilted inwards. The camber angle is not adjustable.

3 Castor is the angle between the steering axis and a vertical line drawn through each roadwheel's centre and tyre contact patch, when viewed from the side of the car. Positive castor is when the steering axis is tilted so that it contacts the ground ahead of the vertical; negative castor is when it contacts the ground behind the vertical. The castor angle is not adjustable.

4 Toe is the difference, viewed from above, between lines drawn through the roadwheel centres and the car's centre-line. 'Toe-in' is when the roadwheels point inwards, towards each other at the front, while 'toe-out' is when they splay outwards from each other at the front.

5 The front wheel toe setting is adjusted by screwing the track rod in or out of its balljoints to alter the effective length of the track rod assembly.

6 Rear wheel toe setting is not adjustable.

Checking and adjustment

7 Due to the special measuring equipment necessary to check the wheel alignment and steering angles, and the skill required to use it properly, the checking and adjustment of these settings is best left to a Citroën dealer or similar expert. Note that most tyre-fitting shops now possess sophisticated checking equipment. The following is provided as a guide, should the owner decide to carry out a DIY check.

Front wheel toe setting

8 The front wheel toe setting (tracking) is checked by measuring the angle of the wheels in relation to the longitudinal axis of the vehicle. Proprietary toe measurement gauges are available from motor accessory shops.

9 Adjustment is made by screwing the balljoints in or out of their track rods, to alter the effective length of the track rod assemblies.

10 Before starting work, check first that the tyre sizes and types are as specified, then check the tyre pressures and tread wear, the roadwheel run-out, the condition of the hub bearings, the steering wheel free play, and the condition of the front suspension components (see *Weekly checks* and Chapter 1A, Section 13 or Chapter 1B, Section 5). Correct any faults found.

11 Park the vehicle on level ground, check that the front roadwheels are in the straight-ahead position, then rock the rear and front ends to settle the suspension. Release the handbrake, and roll the vehicle backwards 1 metre, then forwards again, to relieve any stresses in the steering and suspension components.

12 Follow the tracking gauge manufacturer's instructions and measure the toe setting.

13 If adjustment is necessary, apply the handbrake, then jack up the front of the vehicle and support it securely on axle stands. Turn the steering wheel onto full-left lock, and record the number of exposed threads on the right-hand track rod end. Now turn the steering onto full-right lock, and record the number of threads on the left-hand side. If there are the same number of threads visible on both sides, then subsequent adjustment should be made equally on both sides. If there are more threads visible on one side than the other, it will be necessary to compensate for this during adjustment. **Note:** *It is most important that after adjustment, the same number of threads are visible on each track rod end.*

14 First clean the track rod threads; if they are corroded, apply penetrating fluid before starting adjustment. Release the rubber gaiter outboard clips (where necessary), and peel back the gaiters; apply a smear of grease to the inside of the gaiters, so that both are free, and will not be twisted or strained as their respective track rods are rotated.

15 Use a straight-edge and a scriber or similar to mark the relationship of each track rod to its balljoint then, holding each track rod in turn, unscrew its locknut fully.

16 Alter the length of the track rods, bearing in mind the note made in paragraph 13. Screw them into or out the balljoints, rotating the track rod using an open-ended spanner fitted to the flats provided on the track rod. Shortening the track rods (screwing them into their balljoints) will reduce toe-in/increase toe-out.

17 When the setting is correct, hold the track rods and tighten the balljoint locknuts to the specified torque setting. Check that the balljoints are seated correctly in their sockets, and count the exposed threads to check the length of both track rods. If they are not the same, then the adjustment has not been made equally, and problems will be encountered with tyre scrubbing in turns; also, the steering wheel spokes will no longer be horizontal when the wheels are in the straight-ahead position.

18 If the track rod lengths are the same, lower the vehicle to the ground and recheck the toe setting; re-adjust if necessary. When the setting is correct, tighten the track rod balljoint locknuts to the specified torque. Ensure that the rubber gaiters are seated correctly, and are not twisted or strained, and secure them in position with new retaining clips (where necessary).

Chapter 11
Bodywork and fittings

Contents

Degrees of difficulty

Easy, suitable for novice with little experience	**Fairly easy,** suitable for beginner with some experience	**Fairly difficult,** suitable for competent DIY mechanic	**Difficult,** suitable for experienced DIY mechanic	**Very difficult,** suitable for expert DIY or professional

Specifications

Torque wrench setting	**Nm**	**lbf ft**
Seat belt mountings	30	22

1 General information

The bodyshell is made of pressed-steel sections, and is available in a three-door Coupe or five-door Hatchback model. Most components are welded together, but some use is made of structural adhesives. The front wings are bolted on, and are made of a plastic material.

The bonnet, doors and some other vulnerable panels are made of zinc-coated metal, and are further protected by being coated with an anti-chip primer prior to being sprayed.

Extensive use is made of plastic materials, mainly in the interior, but also in exterior components. The front and rear bumpers and the front grille are injection-moulded from a synthetic material, which is very strong, yet light. Plastic components such as wheel arch liners are fitted to the underside of the vehicle, to improve the body's resistance to corrosion.

2 Maintenance – bodywork and underframe

The general condition of a vehicle's bodywork is the one thing that significantly affects its value. Maintenance is easy, but needs to be regular. Neglect, particularly after minor damage, can lead quickly to further deterioration and costly repair bills. It is important also to keep watch on those parts of the vehicle not immediately visible, for instance the underside, inside all the wheel arches, and the lower part of the engine compartment.

The basic maintenance routine for the bodywork is washing – preferably with a lot of water, from a hose. This will remove all the loose solids that may have stuck to the vehicle. It is important to flush these off in such a way as to prevent grit from scratching the finish. The wheel arches and underframe need washing in the same way, to remove any accumulated mud, which will retain moisture and tend to encourage rust. Paradoxically enough, the best time to clean the underframe and wheel arches is in wet weather, when the mud is thoroughly wet and soft. In very wet weather, the underframe is usually cleaned of large accumulations automatically, and this is a good time for inspection.

Periodically, except on vehicles with a wax-based underbody protective coating, it is a good idea to have the whole of the underframe of the vehicle steam-cleaned, engine compartment included, so that a thorough inspection can be carried out to see what minor repairs and renovations are necessary. Steam cleaning is available at many garages, and is necessary for the removal of the accumulation of oily grime, which sometimes is allowed to become thick in certain areas. If steam-cleaning facilities are not available, there are one or two excellent grease solvents available, which can be brush-applied; the dirt can then be simply hosed off. Note that these methods should not be used on vehicles with wax-based underbody protective coating, or the coating will be removed. Such vehicles should be inspected annually, preferably just prior to winter, when the underbody should be washed down, and any damage to the wax coating repaired using underseal. Ideally, a completely fresh coat should be applied. It would also be worth considering the use of wax-based protection for injection into door panels, sills, box sections, etc, as an additional safeguard against rust damage, where such protection is not provided by the vehicle manufacturer.

After washing paintwork, wipe off with a chamois leather to give an unspotted clear finish. A coat of clear protective wax polish will give added protection against chemical pollutants in the air. If the paintwork sheen has dulled or oxidised, use a cleaner/ polisher combination to restore the brilliance of the shine. This requires a little effort, but such dulling is usually caused because regular washing has been neglected. Care needs to be taken with metallic paintwork, as a special non-abrasive cleaner/polisher is required to avoid damage to the finish. Always check that the door and ventilator opening drain holes and pipes are completely clear, so that water can be drained out. Brightwork should be treated in the same way as paintwork. Windscreens and windows can be kept clear of the smeary film that often appears, by the use of proprietary glass cleaner. Never use any form of wax or other body or chromium polish on glass.

3 Maintenance – upholstery and carpets

Mats and carpets should be brushed or vacuum-cleaned regularly, to keep them free of grit. If they are badly stained, remove them from the vehicle for scrubbing or sponging, and make quite sure they are dry before refitting. Seats and interior trim panels can be kept clean by wiping with a damp cloth and proprietary upholstery cleaner. If they do become stained (which can be more apparent on light-coloured upholstery), use a little liquid detergent and a soft nail brush to scour the grime out of the grain of the material. Do not forget to keep the headlining clean in the same way as the upholstery. When using liquid cleaners inside the vehicle, do not over-wet the surfaces being cleaned. Excessive damp could get into the seams and padded interior, causing stains, offensive odours or even rot. If the inside of the vehicle gets wet accidentally, it is worthwhile taking some trouble to dry it out properly, particularly where carpets are involved.

Caution: Do not leave oil or electric heaters inside the vehicle for this purpose.

4 Minor body damage – repair

Scratches

If the scratch is very superficial, and does not penetrate to the metal of the bodywork, repair is very simple. Lightly rub the area of the scratch with a paintwork renovator, or a very fine cutting paste, to remove loose paint from the scratch, and to clear the surrounding bodywork of wax polish. Rinse the area with clean water.

Apply touch-up paint to the scratch using a fine paintbrush; continue to apply fine layers of paint until the surface of the paint in the scratch is level with the surrounding paintwork. Allow the new paint at least two weeks to harden, and then blend it into the surrounding paintwork by rubbing the scratch area with a paintwork renovator or a very fine cutting paste. Finally apply wax polish.

Where the scratch has penetrated right through to the metal of the bodywork, causing the metal to rust, a different repair technique is required. Remove any loose rust from the bottom of the scratch with a penknife, and then apply rust-inhibiting paint, to prevent the formation of rust in the future. Using a rubber or nylon applicator, fill the scratch with bodystopper paste. If required, this paste can be mixed with cellulose thinners, to provide a very thin paste that is ideal for filling narrow scratches. Before the stopper-paste in the scratch hardens, wrap a piece of smooth cotton rag around the top of a finger. Dip the finger in cellulose thinners, and quickly sweep it across the surface of the stopper-paste in the scratch; this will ensure that the surface of the stopper-paste is slightly hollowed. The scratch can now be painted over as described earlier in this Section.

Dents

When deep denting of the vehicle's bodywork has taken place, the first task is to pull the dent out, until the affected bodywork almost attains its original shape. There is little point in trying to restore the original shape completely, as the metal in the damaged area will have stretched on impact, and cannot be reshaped fully to its original contour. It is better to bring the level of the dent up to a point, which is about 3 mm below the level of the surrounding bodywork. In cases where the dent is very shallow anyway, it is not worth trying to pull it out at all. If the underside of the dent is accessible, it can be hammered out gently from behind, using a mallet with a wooden or plastic head. Whilst doing this, hold a suitable block of wood firmly against the outside of the panel, to absorb the impact from the hammer blows and thus prevent a large area of the bodywork from being 'belled-out'.

Should the dent be in a section of the bodywork that has a double skin, or some other factor making it inaccessible from behind, a different technique is called for. Drill several small holes through the metal inside the area – particularly in the deeper section. Then screw long self-tapping screws into the holes, just sufficiently for them to gain a good purchase in the metal. Now the dent can be pulled out by pulling on the protruding heads of the screws with a pair of pliers.

The next stage of the repair is the removal of the paint from the damaged area, and from an inch or so of the surrounding 'sound' bodywork. This is accomplished most easily by using a wire brush or abrasive pad on a power drill, although it can be done just as effectively by hand, using sheets of abrasive paper. To complete the preparation for filling, score the surface of the bare metal with a screwdriver or the tang of a file, or alternatively, drill small holes in the affected area. This will provide a really good 'key' for the filler paste.

To complete the repair, see the Section on filling and respraying.

Rust holes or gashes

Remove all paint from the affected area, and from an inch or so of the surrounding 'sound' bodywork, using an abrasive pad or a wire brush on a power drill. If these are not available, a few sheets of abrasive paper will do the job most effectively. With the paint removed, you will be able to judge the severity of the corrosion, and therefore decide whether to renew the whole panel (if this is possible) or to repair the affected area. New body panels are not as expensive as most people think, and it is often quicker and more satisfactory to fit a new panel than to attempt to repair large areas of corrosion.

Remove all fittings from the affected area, except those, which will act as a guide to the original shape of the damaged bodywork (eg, headlight shells etc). Then, using tin snips or a hacksaw blade, remove all loose metal and any other metal badly affected by corrosion. Hammer the edges of the hole inwards, in order to create a slight depression for the filler paste.

Wire-brush the affected area to remove the powdery rust from the surface of the remaining metal. Paint the affected area with rust-inhibiting paint; if the back of the rusted area is accessible, treat this also.

Before filling can take place, it will be necessary to block the hole in some way. This can be achieved by the use of aluminium or plastic mesh, or aluminium tape.

Aluminium or plastic mesh, or glass-fibre matting, is probably the best material to use for a large hole. Cut a piece to the approximate size and shape of the hole to be filled, then position it in the hole so that its edges are below the level of the surrounding bodywork. It can be retained in position by several blobs of filler paste around its periphery.

Aluminium tape should be used for small or very narrow holes. Pull a piece off the roll, trim it to the approximate size and shape required, then pull off the backing paper (if used) and stick the tape over the hole; it can be overlapped if the thickness of one piece is insufficient. Burnish down the edges of the tape with the handle of a screwdriver or similar, to ensure that the tape is securely attached to the metal underneath.

Filling and respraying

Before using this Section, see the Sections on dent, minor scratch, rust holes and gash repairs.

Many types of bodyfiller are available, but generally speaking, those proprietary kits, which contain a tin of filler paste and a tube of resin hardener, are best for this type of repair; some can be used directly from the tube. A wide, flexible plastic or nylon applicator will be found invaluable for imparting a smooth and well-contoured finish to the surface of the filler.

Mix up a little filler on a clean piece of card or board – measure the hardener carefully (follow the maker's instructions on the pack), otherwise the filler will set too rapidly or too slowly. Using the applicator, apply the filler paste to the prepared area; draw the applicator across the surface of the filler to achieve the correct contour and to level the surface. As soon as a contour that approximates to the correct one is achieved, stop working the paste – if you carry on too long, the paste will become sticky and begin to 'pick-up' on the applicator. Continue to add thin layers of filler paste at 20-minute intervals, until the level of the filler is just proud of the surrounding bodywork.

Once the filler has hardened, the excess can be removed using a metal plane or file. From then on, progressively finer grades of abrasive paper should be used, starting with a 40-grade production paper, and finishing with a 400-grade wet-and-dry paper. Always wrap the abrasive paper around a flat rubber, cork, or wooden block – otherwise the surface of the filler will not be completely flat. During the smoothing of the filler surface, the wet-and-dry paper should be periodically rinsed in water. This will ensure that a very smooth finish is imparted to the filler at the final stage.

At this stage, the 'dent' should be surrounded by a ring of bare metal, which in turn should be encircled by the finely 'feathered' edge of the good paintwork. Rinse the repair area with clean water, until all of the dust produced by the rubbing-down operation has gone.

Spray the whole area with a light coat of primer – this will show up any imperfections in the surface of the filler. Repair these imperfections with fresh filler paste or bodystopper, and once more smooth the surface with abrasive paper. If bodystopper is used, it can be mixed with cellulose thinners, to form a really thin paste that is ideal for filling small holes. Repeat this spray-and-repair procedure until you are satisfied that the surface of the filler, and the feathered edge of the paintwork, are perfect. Clean the repair area with clean water, and allow to dry fully.

The repair area is now ready for final spraying. Paint spraying must be carried out in a warm, dry, windless and dust-free atmosphere. This condition can be created artificially if you have access to a large indoor working area, but if you are forced to work in the open, you will have to pick your day very carefully. If you are working indoors, dousing the floor in the work area with water will help to settle the dust, which would otherwise be in the atmosphere. If the repair area is confined to one body panel, mask off the surrounding panels; this will help to minimise the effects of a slight mismatch in paint colours. Bodywork fittings (e.g. chrome strips, door handles etc) will also need to be masked off. Use genuine masking tape, and several thicknesses of newspaper, for the masking operations.

Before commencing to spray, agitate the aerosol can thoroughly, and then spray a test area (an old tin, or similar) until the technique is mastered. Cover the repair area with a thick coat of primer; the thickness should be built up using several thin layers of paint, rather than one thick one. Using 400-grade wet-and-dry paper, rub down the surface of the primer until it is really smooth. While doing this, the work area should be thoroughly doused with water, and the wet-and-dry paper periodically rinsed in water. Allow to dry before spraying on more paint.

Spray on the top coat, again building up the thickness by using several thin layers of paint. Start spraying at the top of the repair area, and then, using a side-to-side motion, work downwards until the whole repair area and about 2 inches of the surrounding original paintwork is covered. Remove all masking material 10 to 15 minutes after spraying on the final coat of paint.

Allow the new paint at least two weeks to harden, then, using a paintwork renovator or a very fine cutting paste, blend the edges of the paint into the existing paintwork. Finally, apply wax polish.

Plastic components

With the use of more and more plastic body components by the vehicle manufacturers (e.g. bumpers. spoilers, and in some cases major body panels), rectification of more serious damage to such items has become a matter of either entrusting repair work to a specialist in this field, or renewing complete components. Repair of such damage by the DIY owner is not really feasible, owing to the cost of the equipment and materials required for effecting such repairs. The basic technique involves making a groove along the line of the crack in the plastic, using a rotary burr in a power drill. The damaged part is then welded back together, using a hot air gun to heat up and fuse a plastic filler rod into the groove. Any excess plastic is then removed, and the area rubbed down to a smooth finish. It is important that a filler rod of the correct plastic is used, as body components can be made of a variety of different types (e.g. polycarbonate, ABS, polypropylene).

Damage of a less serious nature (abrasions, minor cracks etc) can be repaired by the DIY owner using a two-part epoxy filler repair material. Once mixed in equal proportions, this is used in similar fashion to the bodywork filler used on metal panels. The filler is usually cured in twenty to thirty minutes, ready for sanding and painting.

If the owner is renewing a complete component himself, or if he has repaired it with epoxy filler, he will be left with the problem of finding a suitable paint for finishing which is compatible with the type of plastic used. At one time, the use of a universal paint was not possible, owing to the complex range of plastics encountered in body component applications. Standard paints, generally speaking, will not bond to plastic or rubber satisfactorily. However, it is now possible to obtain a plastic body parts finishing kit, which consists of a pre-primer treatment, a primer and coloured top coat. Full instructions are normally supplied with a kit, but basically, the method of use is to first apply the pre-primer to the component concerned, and allow it to dry for up to 30 minutes. Then the primer is applied, and left to dry for about an hour before finally applying the special coloured top coat. The result is a correctly coloured component, where the paint will flex with the plastic or rubber, a property that standard paint does not normally possess.

5 Major body damage – repair

Where serious damage has occurred, or large areas need renewal due to neglect, it means that complete new panels will need welding-in, and this is best left to professionals. If the damage is due to impact, it will also be necessary to check completely the alignment of the bodyshell, and this can only be carried out accurately by a Citroën dealer, or accident repair specialist, using special jigs. If the body is left misaligned, it is primarily dangerous, as the car will not handle properly, and secondly, uneven stresses will be imposed on the steering, suspension and possibly transmission, causing abnormal wear, or complete failure, particularly to such items as the tyres.

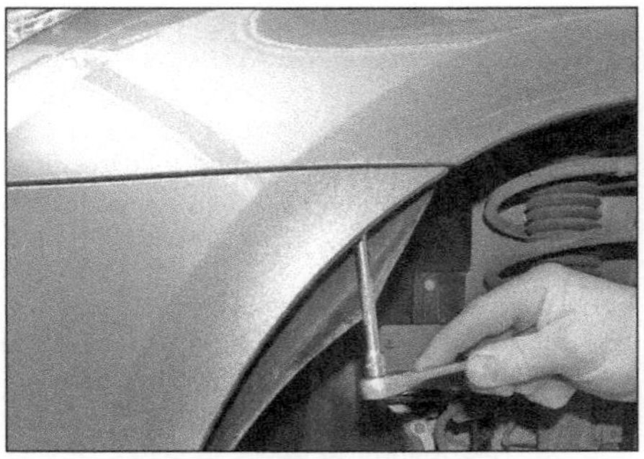

6.3 Undo the bumper-to-wing securing screws

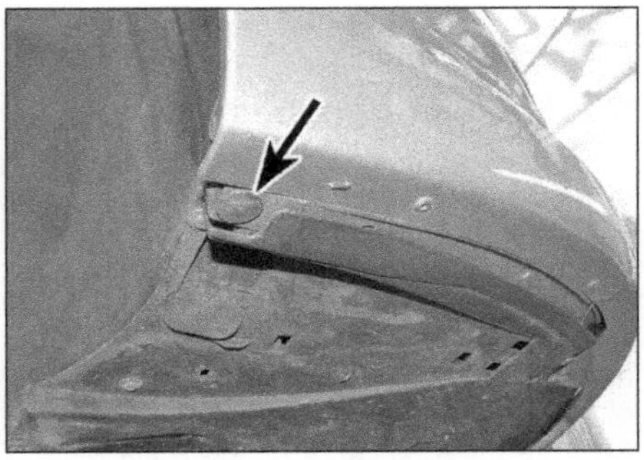

6.4 Remove the lower securing clip (arrowed)

6 Front bumper – removal and refitting

Note: *The help of an assistant is useful to support the bumper during the removal and refitting procedure.*

Removal

1 Firmly apply the handbrake, and then jack up the front of the vehicle and support it securely on axle stands (see *Jacking and vehicle support*). To improve access to the bumper fasteners, remove both front roadwheels.

2 Release the retaining clips, and then pull back the inner wheel arch liners on both sides of the vehicle to access the screws securing the bumper to the front wings.

3 Remove the screws (one each side) securing the upper edge of the bumper to the underside of the wing **(see illustration)**.

4 Release the retaining clips (one each side) from the lower outer edge of the bumper to the inner wheel arch liner **(see illustration)**.

5 Working under the front lower edge of the bumper undo the three retaining screws and release the lower edge of the bumper from the engine undershield **(see illustrations)**.

6 The upper part of the bumper is secured by six plastic rivets. Use a small screwdriver to release the centre of the plastic rivets, and then lever the complete rivets from place **(see illustration)**. **Note:** *The four plastic rivets at the rear of the upper bumper panel are a different size from the two front ones.*

7 Reach up behind the bumper at each end and disconnect the wiring connectors for the foglights, headlamp washers and/or parking sensors (depending on model) **(see illustration)**.

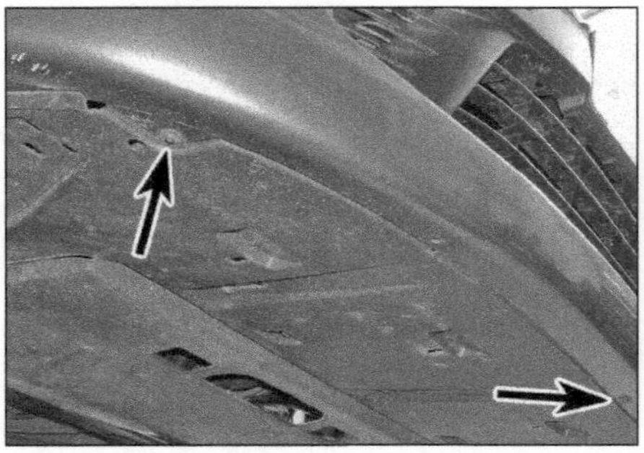

6.5a Undo the right and centre securing screws (arrowed) ...

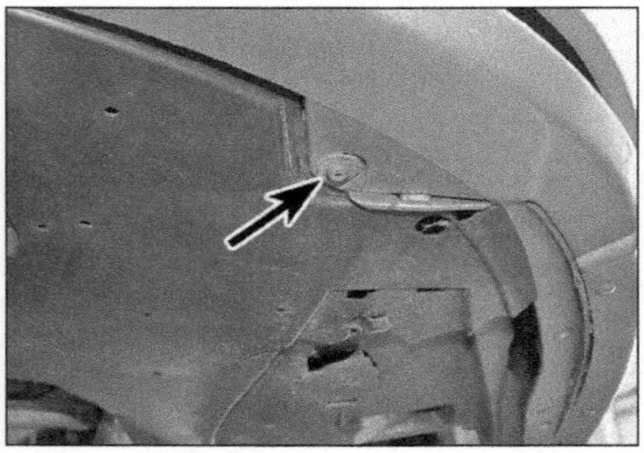

6.5b ... and the screw (arrowed) at the left-hand side

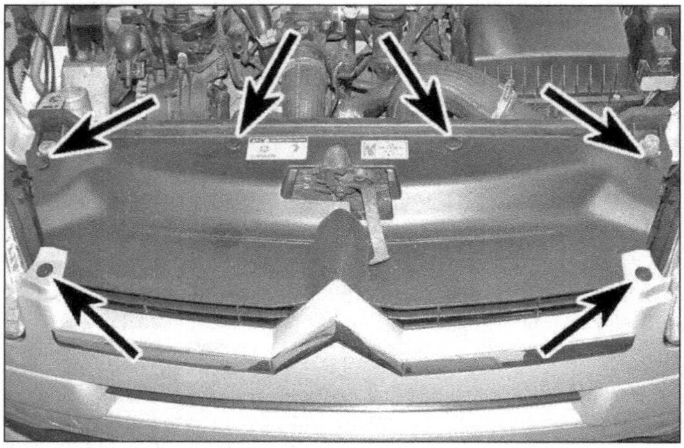

6.6 Release the securing clips (arrowed) along the upper part of the bumper

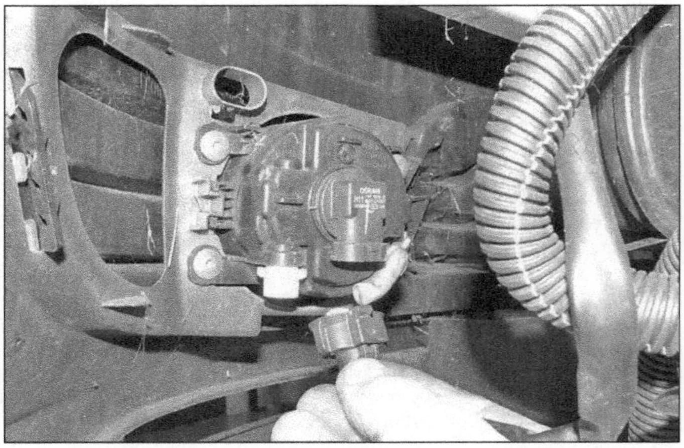

6.7 Disconnect the foglight wiring connector

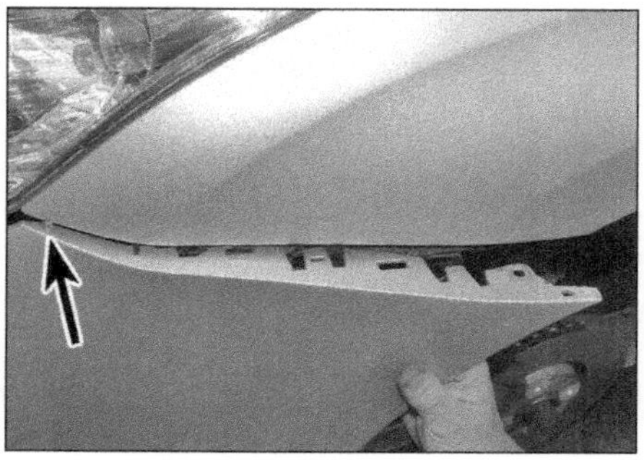

6.8 Release the bumper at each side, noting the locating peg (arrowed)

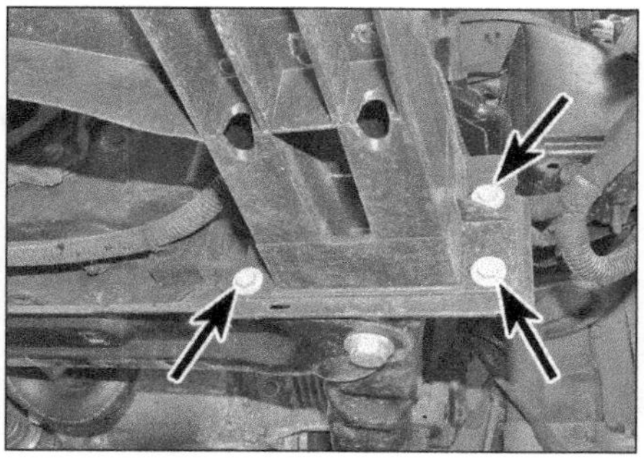

6.9 Undo the lower plastic bumper bar bolts (arrowed)

6.10 Undo the upper aluminium bumper bar bolts (one side shown)

8 With the help of an assistant, carefully unclip the bumper outer edges from the front wings **(see illustration)**, and then carefully pull the bumper forward to remove it from the vehicle. **Note:** *As the bumper is withdrawn from the vehicle, check for any wiring that may be still secured or connected to the bumper.*

9 If required, undo the retaining bolts (three each side) and remove the lower plastic impact absorber from across the front of the vehicle **(see illustration)**.

10 To remove the alloy bumper bar, undo the eight bolts (four bolts each side) and remove the upper bumper bar from across the front of the vehicle **(see illustration)**.

Refitting

11 Refitting is a reversal of removal, ensuring that the bumper correctly engages with the retaining clips along the upper edge and at each side as it is located in position at the wing panel.

7 Rear bumper – removal and refitting

Note: *The help of an assistant is useful to support the bumper during the removal and refitting procedure.*

Removal

1 Chock the front wheels, then jack up the rear of the vehicle and support securely on axle stands (see *Jacking and vehicle support*).

2 Remove the rear light cluster on both sides as described in Chapter 12, Section 7.

3 Working inside the luggage compartment, lift up the floor panel/carpet and disconnect the wiring connector for the number plate lights and rear parking sensors (depending on model) **(see illustration)**.

4 Working inside the rear wheel arch, undo the retaining screws (one at each side) to release the bumper from the rear wing panel **(see illustration)**.

5 At each end of the underside of the bumper, there are plastic expanding rivets (two at each side). Release the centre pins, and prise out the plastic rivets **(see illustration)**.

6 Undo the retaining bolt at the centre underside of the bumper **(see illustration)**.

7 On models fitted with rear plastic undertray, there are also two plastic securing clips at the lower edge of the bumper **(see illustration)**.

8 With the help of an assistant, carefully unclip the outer edges of the bumper from the rear wing panels **(see illustration)**.

9 Working inside the lower part of the rear

7.3 Disconnect the wiring block connector (arrowed)

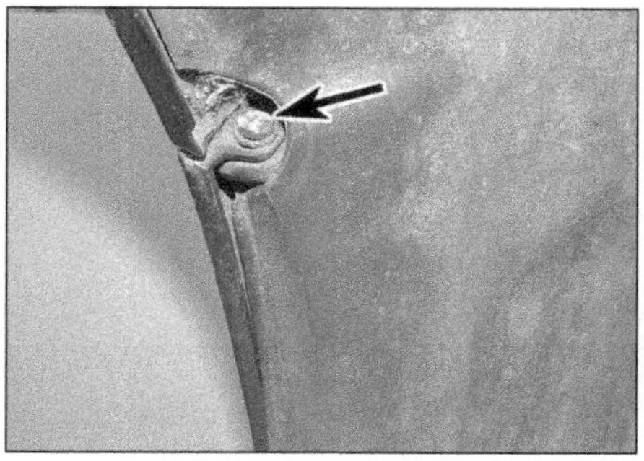

7.4 Undo the bumper-to-wing securing screw (arrowed)

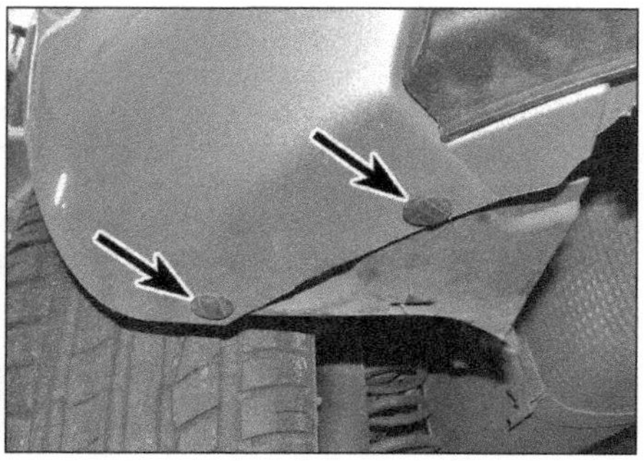

7.5 Remove the two lower securing clips (arrowed)

7.6 Undo the centre retaining bolt (arrowed) ...

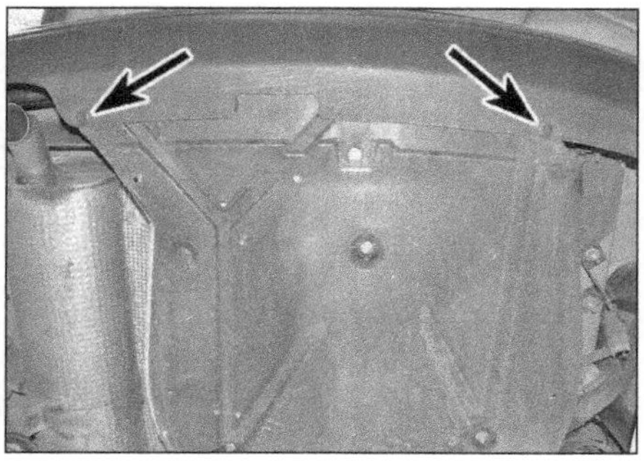

7.7 ... and release the outer retaining clips (arrowed) – where fitted

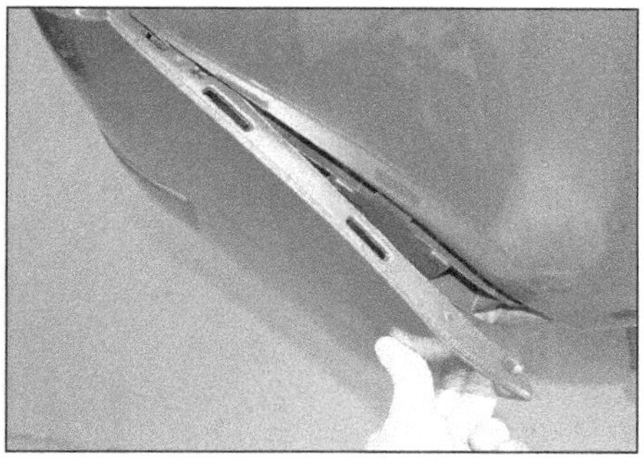

7.8 Release the sides of the bumper from the rear wing panels ...

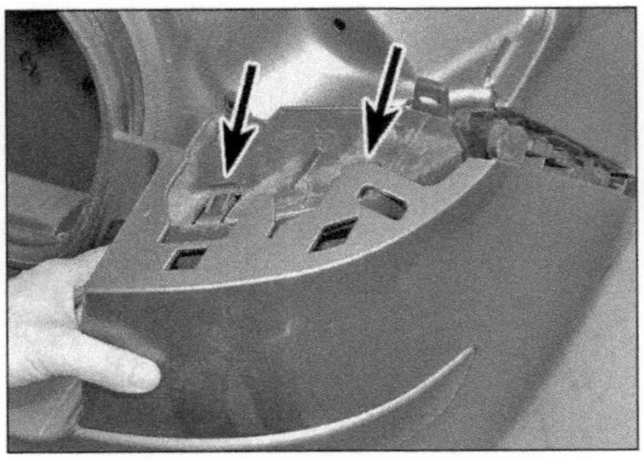

7.9 ... and from the retaining clips (arrowed) in the light apertures

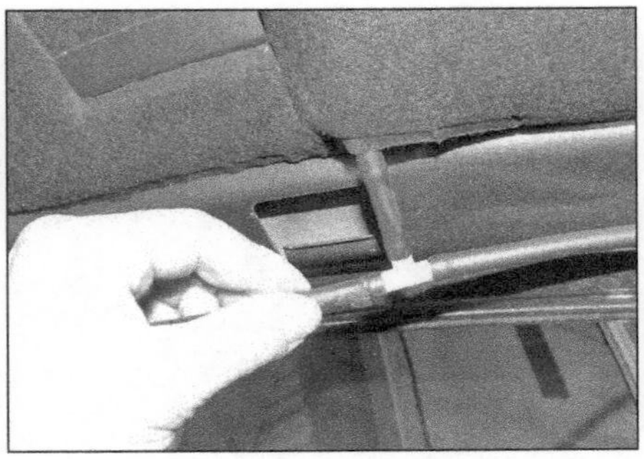

8.2a Disconnect the washer hose at the T connector ...

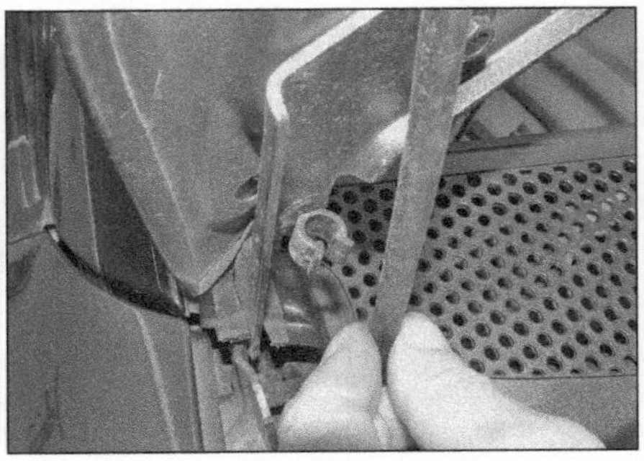

8.2b ... and unclip the washer hose from the retaining clip

light aperture, release the upper part of the bumper from the rear panel and carefully pull the bumper away from the rear of the car **(see illustration)**.

Refitting

10 Refitting is a reversal of removal.

8 Bonnet - removal, refitting and adjustment

Note: *The help of an assistant is useful to support the bonnet during the removal and refitting procedure.*

Removal

1 Open the bonnet and have an assistant support it, then using a pencil or felt tip pen, mark the outline of each bonnet hinge relative to the bonnet, to use as a guide on refitting.

2 Release the washer tubing from the washer jet hose connector, and then release it from any retaining clips **(see illustrations)**.

3 With the help of the assistant to support the bonnet, unscrew the bonnet-to-hinge retaining bolts at each side **(see illustration)**. Carefully lift the bonnet from the vehicle and store it out of the way in a safe place.

4 If required the bonnet insulation panel can be removed from the underside of the bonnet. Prise up the centre pins a little, lever out the plastic expanding rivets, and remove the insulation panel **(see illustrations)**.

Refitting and adjustment

5 With the aid of an assistant, offer up the bonnet, and engage the retaining bolts. Align the hinges with the marks made on removal, and then tighten the retaining bolts securely.

6 Close the bonnet, and check for alignment with the adjacent panels. If necessary, slacken the hinge bolts and re-align the bonnet to suit. When correctly aligned, tighten the hinge bolts securely.

7 Once the bonnet is correctly aligned, check that the bonnet fastens and releases in a satisfactory manner. If adjustment is necessary, slacken the bonnet lock retaining bolts, and adjust the position of the lock to suit. Once the lock is operating correctly, securely tighten its retaining bolts.

8 Reconnect the washer jet tubing and if removed refit the bonnet insulation panel.

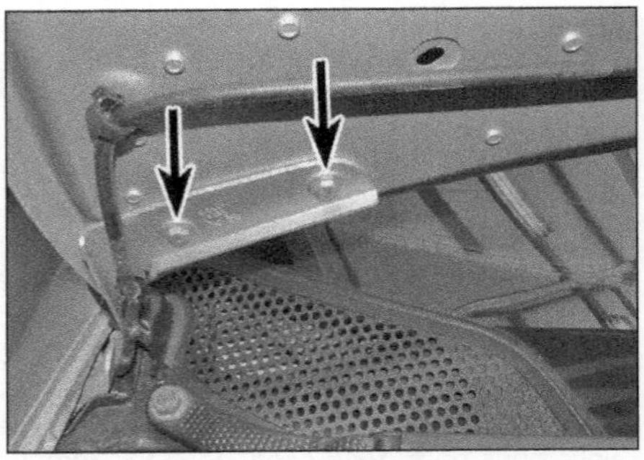

8.3 Bonnet hinge retaining bolts (arrowed)

9 Bonnet release cable - removal and refitting

Removal

1 Disconnect the battery (refer to precautions in Chapter 5A, Section 1).

2 Remove the front bumper, as described in Section 6.

3 Working at the front of the engine compartment, undo the two retaining nuts and

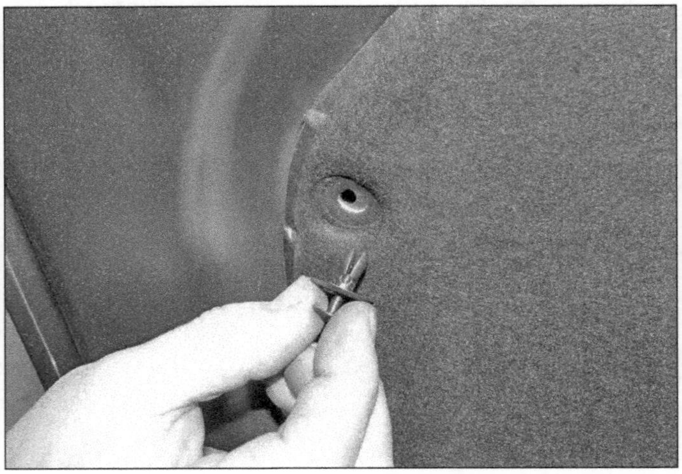

8.4a Prise up the centre pin and lever out the plastic rivet ...

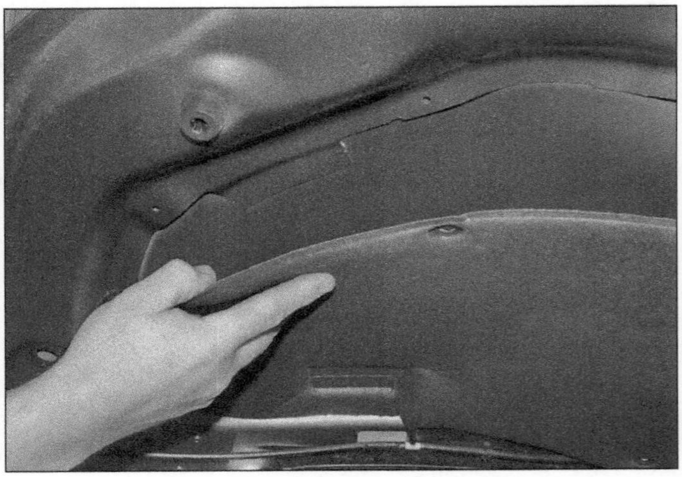

8.4b ... then remove the insulation

9.3 Undo the two retaining nuts and remove the plastic cover

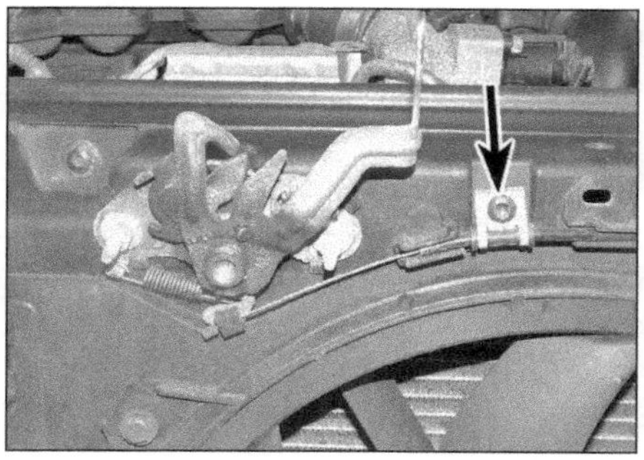

9.4a Undo the retaining screw (arrowed) ...

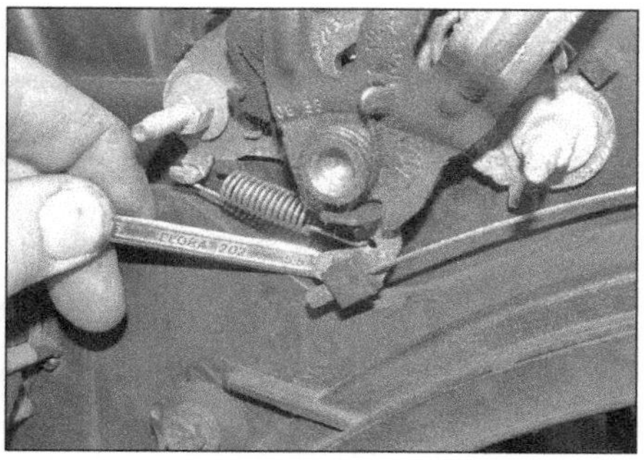

9.4b ... and use a ring spanner ...

unclip the plastic shield (where fitted) from the bonnet lock assembly **(see illustration)**.

4 Undo the retaining screw from the outer cable along the front edge of the upper crossmember, then using a small ring spanner, release the securing clips and disconnect the end of the cable from the lock lever **(see illustrations)**.

5 Work along the length of the cable in the engine compartment **(see illustrations)**, and release the cable from its retaining clips (noting their fitted positions). It may be necessary to remove the battery (see Chapter 5A, Section 4), and the engine compartment fusebox to make removal of the cable possible.

6 Remove the glovebox assembly as described in Section 27.

7 Working inside the vehicle footwell, release the securing clips and remove the sill trim panel from around the bonnet release lever **(see illustrations)**.

8 Pull the release lever downwards and out from the A-pillar to withdraw it from its location **(see illustration)**.

9 Carefully withdraw the cable bulkhead grommet into the passenger compartment. The cable is located around the rear of the facia built-in systems interface/fusebox assembly. If required slacken the fusebox assembly retaining nuts and pull it away from the bulkhead to allow the cable to be withdrawn.

10 Tie a length of string to the end of the cable in the engine compartment, note its routing, then carefully pull the cable through into the passenger compartment. Untie the string from the end of the cable, and leave the string in position to aid refitting.

Refitting

11 Locate the cable in position in the passenger compartment and tie the end of the new cable to the string, and pull it through into the engine compartment.

12 Check that the bulkhead grommet is securely seated, then remove the string and connect the cable to the bonnet lock lever.

13 Secure the release lever in place, making sure it is located securely in the retaining slots in the A-pillar.

14 Secure the cable in place with its retaining clips and refit the end of the cable to the lock assembly. Check the lock operates satisfactorily before proceeding.

15 If removed, refit the built-in systems interface/fusebox.

16 Refit the battery as described in Chapter 5A, Section 4.

17 Refit the front bumper as described in Section 6.

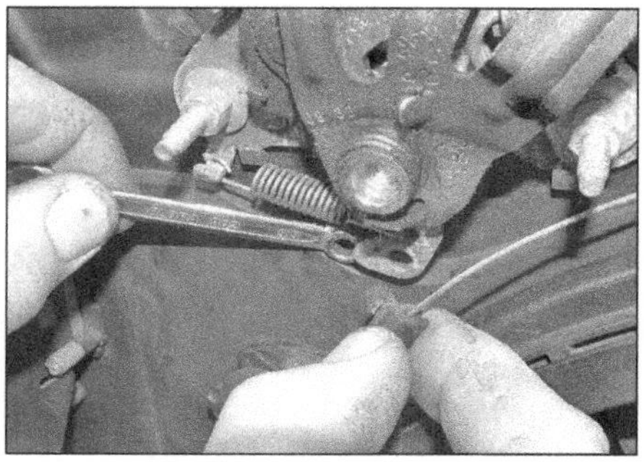

9.4c ... to release the cable retaining clip

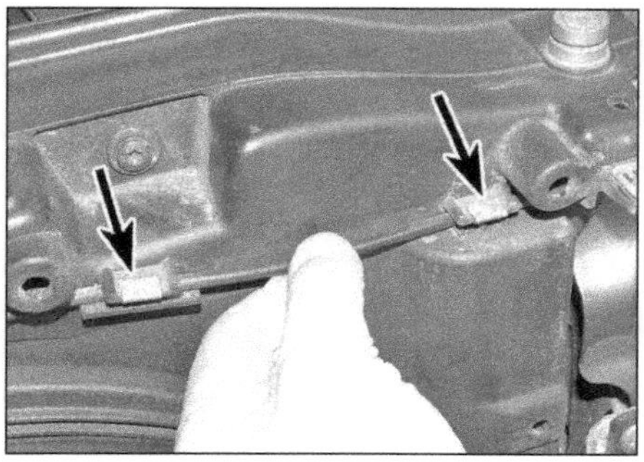

9.5a Release the cable from the two securing clips (arrowed) ...

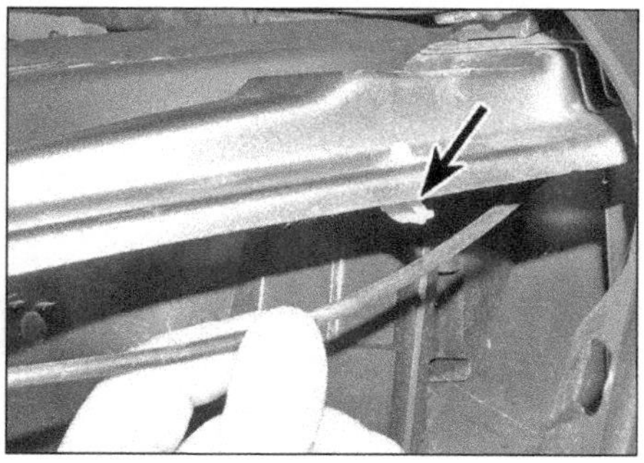

9.5b ... and any retaining clips (arrowed) along its length

9.7a Prise out the securing clip ...

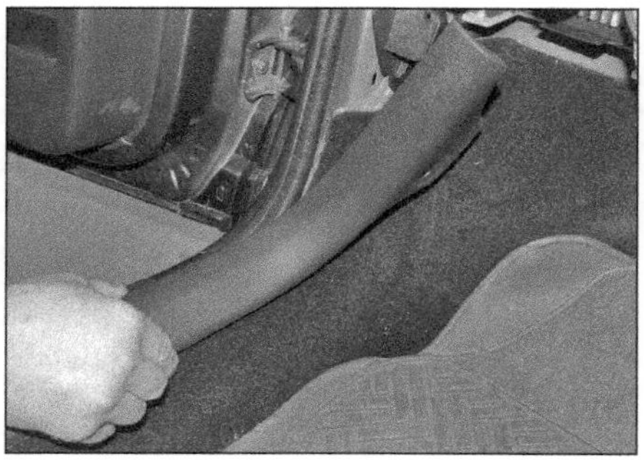

9.7b ... and unclip the trim panel from around the lever

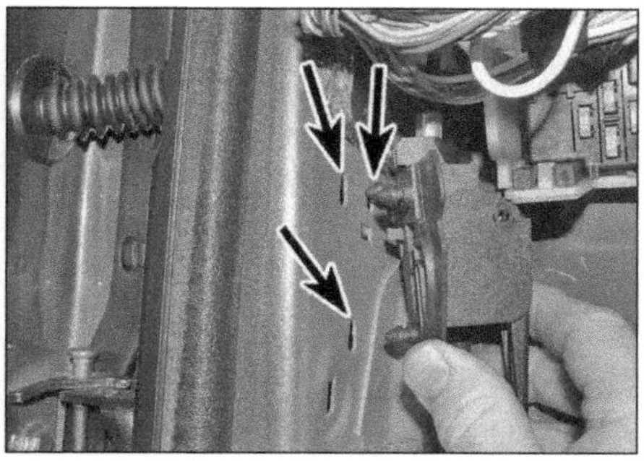

9.8 Slide the lever bracket downwards to release it from the locating holes (arrowed)

10.3 Bonnet lock retaining nuts/studs (arrowed)

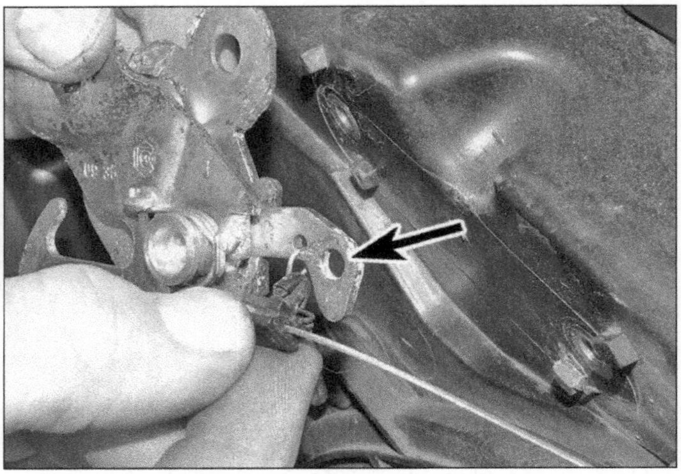

10.4 Unclip the cable from the operating lever

10 Bonnet lock – removal and refitting

Removal

1 Remove the front bumper and front impact absorber, as described in Section 6.

2 Working at the front of the engine compartment, undo the two retaining nuts and unclip the plastic shield from the bonnet lock assembly **(see illustration 9.3)**.

3 Unscrew the two bolts/studs securing the lock assembly to the front upper crossmember **(see illustration)**.

4 Withdraw the lock and disconnect the bonnet release cable from the lock lever **(see illustration)**.

Refitting

5 Refitting is a reversal of removal. On completion, check the operation of the lock and, if necessary, adjust the position of the lock to achieve satisfactory operation prior to closing the bonnet.

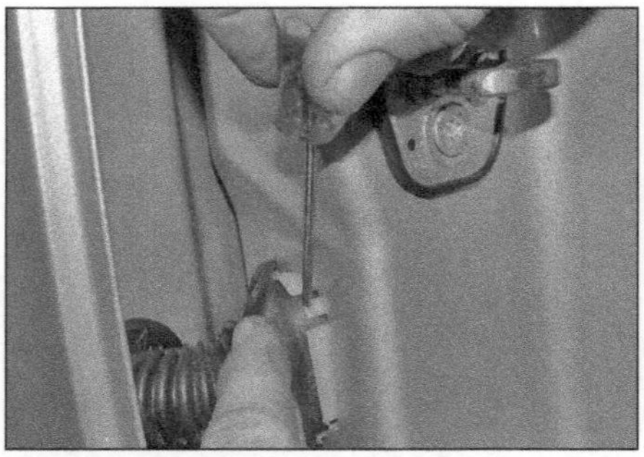

11.1 Prise out the wiring harness guide

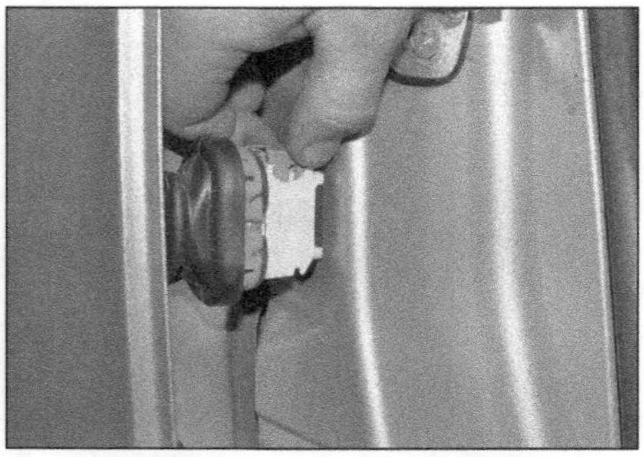

11.2 Release the locking catch and disconnect the wiring plug

11 Door – removal, refitting and adjustment

Note: *The help of an assistant is useful to support the door during the removal and refitting procedure.*

Removal

1 Using a small screwdriver, release the wiring harness guide retaining clips, and pull the harness and guide from the door pillar **(see illustration)**.

2 Prise up the locking catch and disconnect the door wiring connector **(see illustration)**.

3 Unscrew the securing bolt, and disconnect the door check strap from the door pillar **(see illustration)**.

4 With the help of an assistant, ensure that the door is adequately supported.

5 Slide out the hinge pin retaining clips, and then remove the upper and lower hinge pins **(see illustrations)**. Carefully lift the door from the vehicle.

Refitting

6 Refitting is a reversal of removal. Once the door is fitted, adjust the striker plate so that

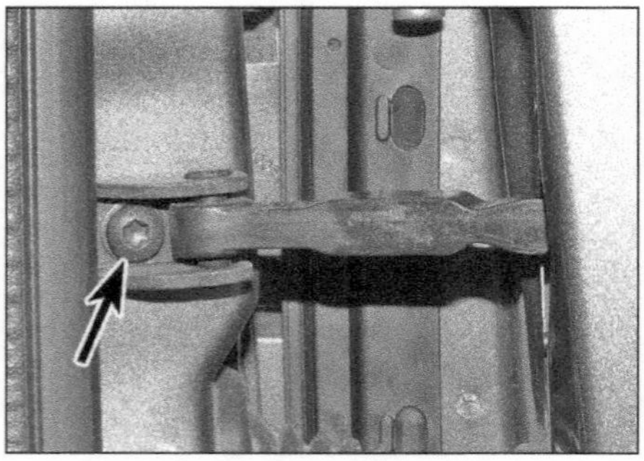

11.3 Undo the door check strap bolt (arrowed)

11.5a Release the upper hinge pin retaining clip (arrowed) ...

11.5b ... and lower hinge pin retaining clip (arrowed)

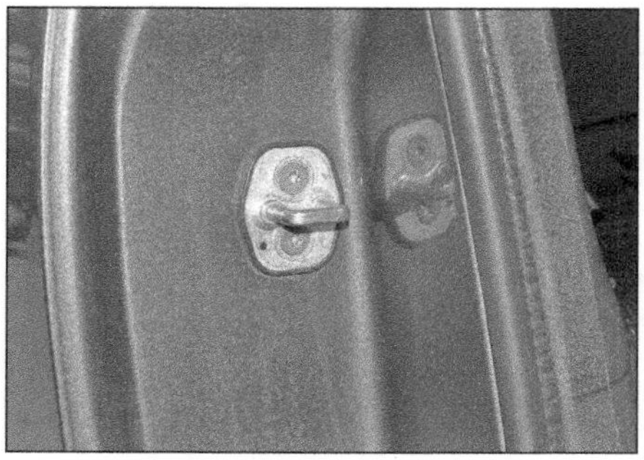

11.6 Door lock striker plate

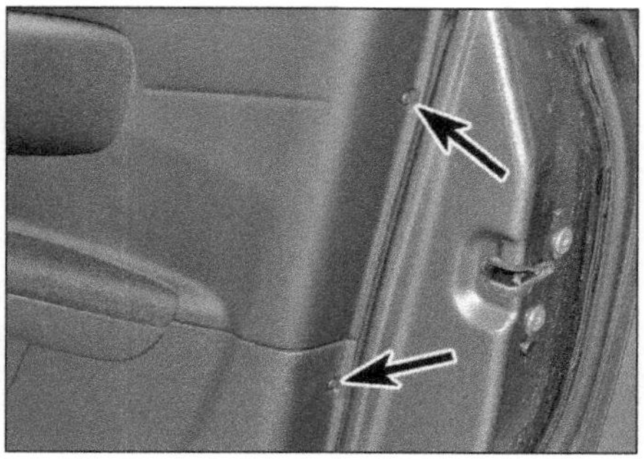

12.1a Undo the two retaining screws (arrowed) ...

12.1b ... and the lower front retaining screw (arrowed)

the door opens and closes easily but firmly. With the door handle pulled out, shut the door and check that the lock slides over the striker plate without scraping **(see illustration)**.

12 Door inner trim panel – removal and refitting

1 On the front doors, undo the two screws located at the rear edge of the door trim panel and the one located at the front lower end of the trim panel **(see illustrations)**.

2 On the rear doors, undo the three screws located at the front edge of the door trim panel **(see illustration)**.

3 Undo the retaining screw from inside the switch panel/grab handle recess **(see illustration)**.

4 Using a suitable lever, prise up the rear of the switch panel/grab handle assembly and withdraw it from the door trim panel. Disconnect the wiring plug connector(s) from the base of the switch panel as it is removed **(see illustrations)**.

5 Carefully unclip the plastic trim from around the release handle, and then remove it from the door trim panel **(see illustrations)**.

6 On rear doors with manual window winders, use a piece of cloth and move it side-to-side to release the securing clip. Then pull the window winder handle from the window

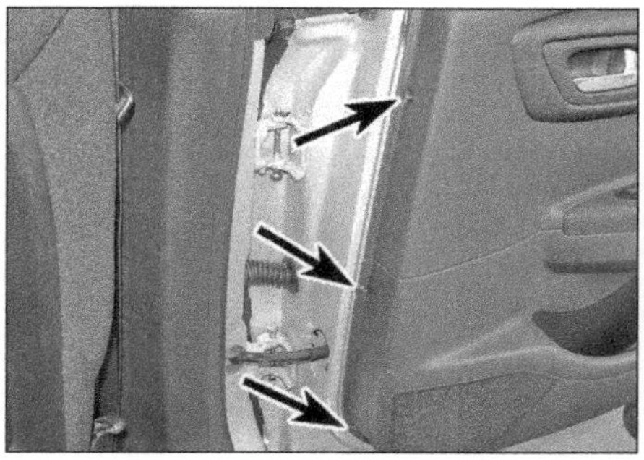

12.2 Undo the three retaining screws (arrowed) ...

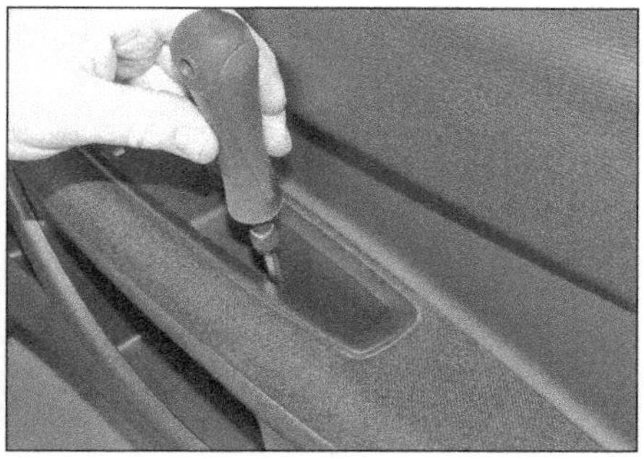

12.3 Undo the retaining screw inside the grab handle

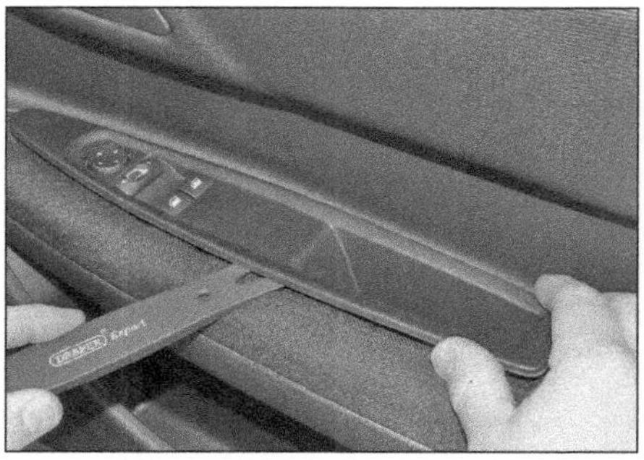

12.4a Carefully unclip the grab handle/ switch trim ...

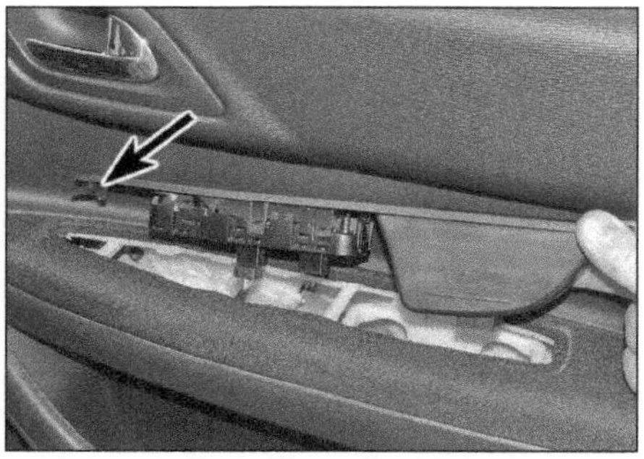

12.4b ... unclipping the front edge (arrowed) from the door trim ...

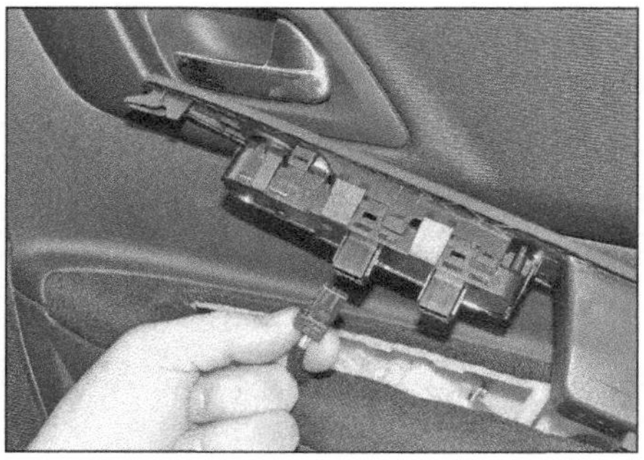

12.4c ... and then disconnect the wiring connectors

12.5a Carefully unclip the trim ...

12.5b ... from around the inner door release handle

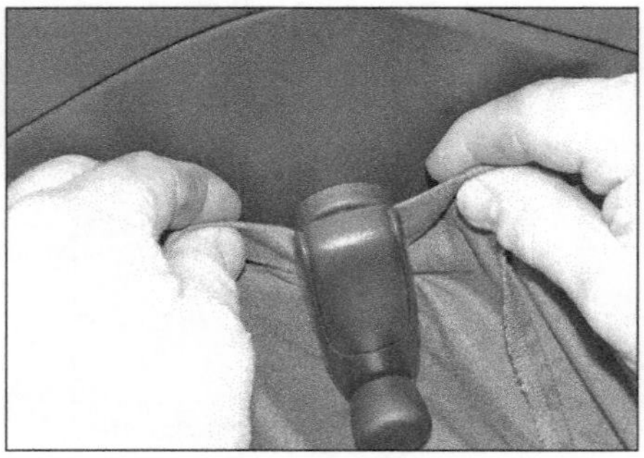
12.6a Using a piece of cloth ...

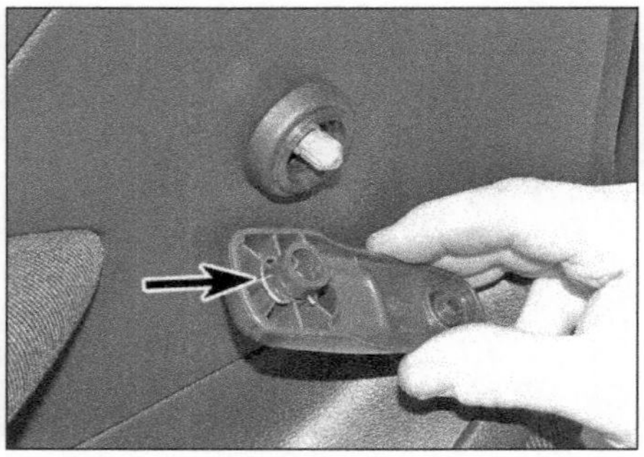
12.6b ... to release the securing clip (arrowed) in the window winder handle

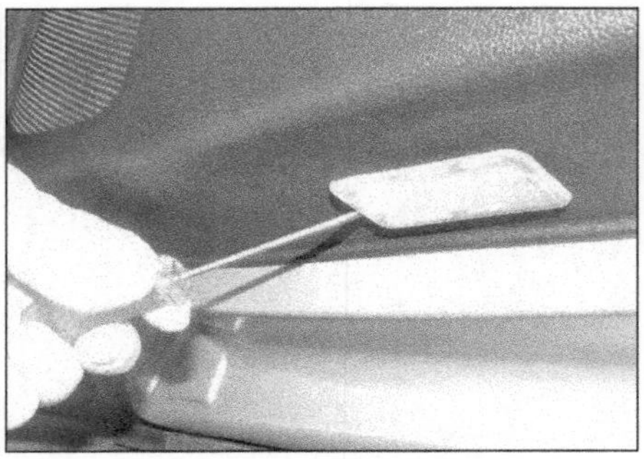
12.7 Unclip the courtesy light from the bottom of the door panel

regulator driveshaft and remove the spacer trim **(see illustrations)**. Make sure the spring clip is fitted correctly into the winder handle before refitting.

7 Where fitted, unclip the courtesy light from the bottom of the door panel and disconnect the wiring plug connector **(see illustration)**.

8 Using a suitable forked tool, work around the edge of the trim panel, and release the securing clips **(see illustration)**.

9 Pull the panel outwards, and then lift it up and remove it from the door **(see illustration)**.

10 Before refitting, check whether any of the trim panel retaining studs/clips where broken on removal. Renew the panel retaining studs/ clips as necessary, and then refit the panel using a reversal of removal.

Door sealing sheet

Note: *A new door sealing sheet may be required on refitting, if damaged/torn on removal.*

Note: *There is an interior switch panel/grab handle mounting bracket riveted to the inside of the door. Ensure that new rivets of the correct size are available for refitting.*

11 Remove the door inner trim panel, as described previously in this Section.

12 On front doors, drill out the two rivets from the handle mounting bracket, and then remove it from the inside of the door **(see illustrations)**.

13 On rear doors, drill out one rivet from the handle mounting bracket, and then unclip it from the inside of the door **(see illustrations)**.

14 Using a sharp knife, carefully release the sealing sheet from the adhesive bead and remove the sheet from the area to access the door lock/window mechanism **(see illustration)**. If care is taken, it may be possible to remove the sheet in one piece and re-use it when refitting.

15 Refitting is a reversal of removal; fit a new sealing sheet to the door if the original was damaged in any way during removal.

12.8 Using a forked tool, release the retaining clips around the door trim

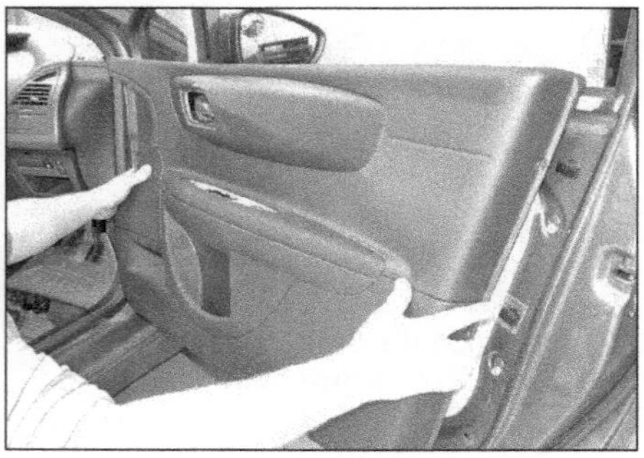
12.9 Lift and remove the trim panel from the door

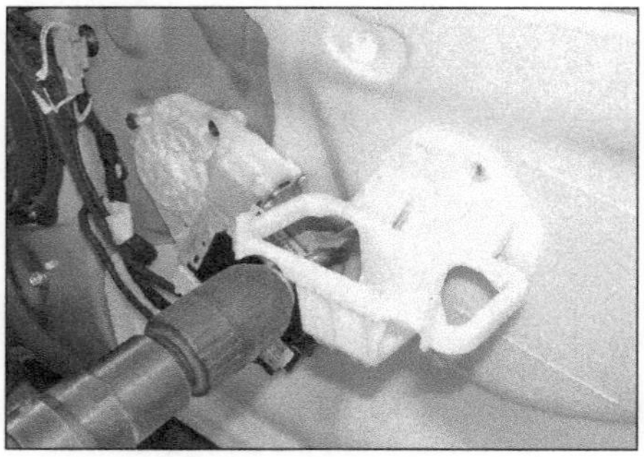
12.12a Drill out the two rivets ...

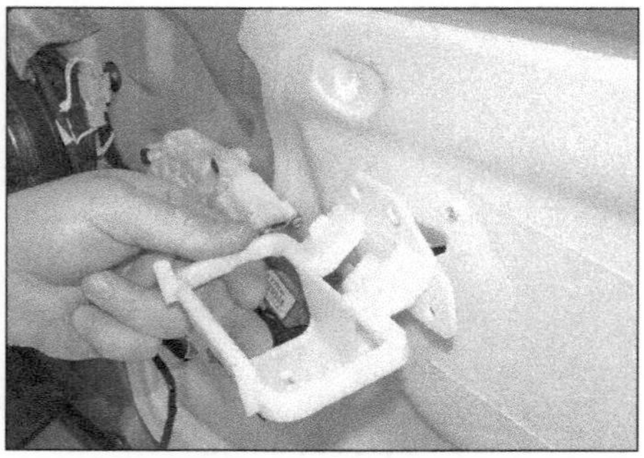
12.12b ... and remove the mounting bracket – front door

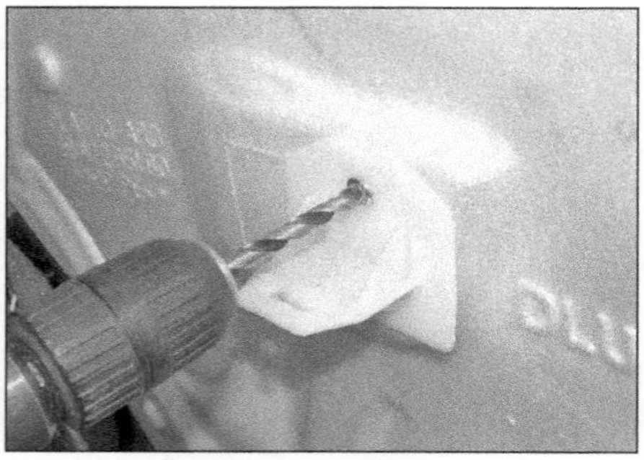
12.13a Drill out the single rivet ...

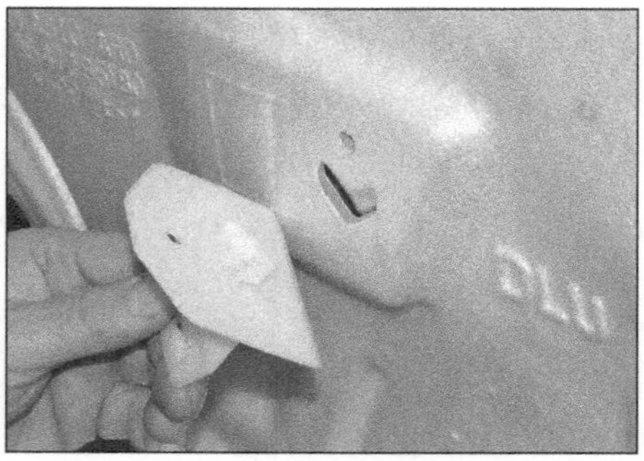
12.13b ... and remove the mounting bracket – rear door

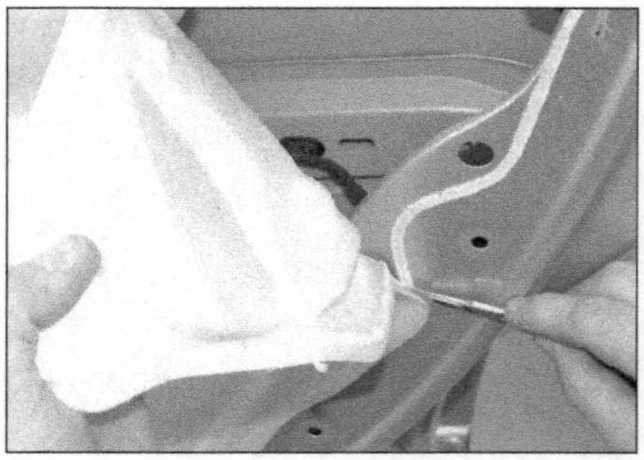
12.14 Using a knife to remove the sealing sheet

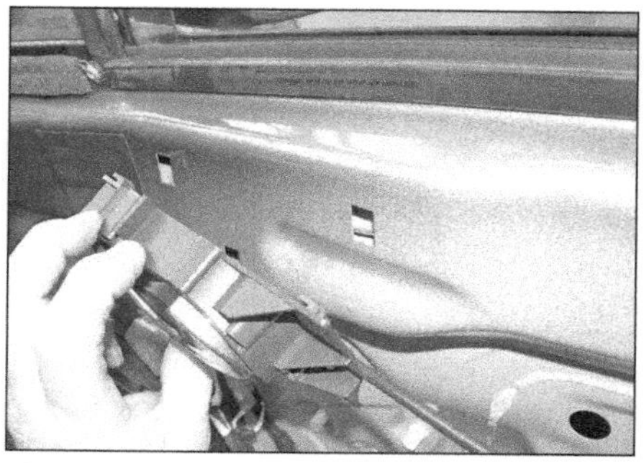

13.2 Release the inner release handle from the door

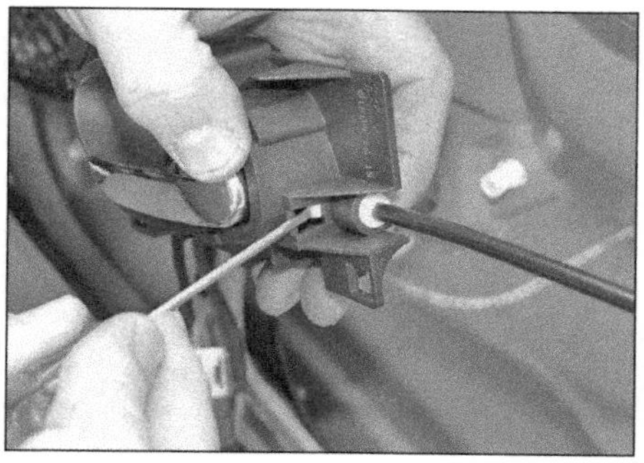

13.3a Release the retaining clip ...

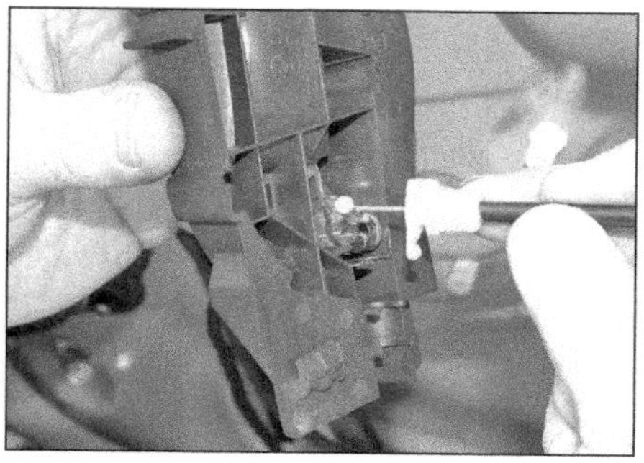

13.3b ... and disconnect the operating cable

13 Door handle and lock components – removal and refitting

Interior door release lever

1 Remove the door inner trim panel, as described in Section 12.

2 Remove the inner release lever by sliding the housing towards the rear edge of the door and then unclip it from the locating slots in the door **(see illustration)**.

3 Release the outer cable retaining clip from the housing and then disconnect the inner cable from the back of the release lever **(see illustrations)**.

4 Refitting is a reversal of removal, but ensure that the operating cable is correctly fitted to the release lever. Refit the inner trim panel as described in Section 12.

Exterior door handle

5 Open the door and remove the rubber grommet/plastic blanking cover at the rear edge of the door to access the retaining screw. On front doors on 3-door models and the rear doors on 5-door models, it will be necessary to pull back the door seal on the rear edge of the door, and then peel back the blanking cover seal to access the screw **(see illustrations)**.

6 Slacken the retaining screw until it cannot be turned no further and comes to a stop (DO NOT force the screw when it reaches the stop). The screw does not come completely out from the door panel. Carefully withdraw the push button/lock cylinder out from the door handle assembly **(see illustration)**. Take care not to damage the paintwork as it is removed.

7 Detach the handle by sliding it to the rear of the door, and then pulling it out from the handle recess **(see illustration)**.

8 Refitting is a reversal of removal, but ensure that the handle locates securely inside the door lock housing. When fitting the rear of the door handle, make sure the leg on the rear of the handle is positioned behind the lever on the support bracket inside the door panel **(see illustration)**.

Door lock assembly

9 Make sure the window glass is in the fully closed position and remove the door trim panel and inner sealing sheet, as described in Section 12.

10 On front doors, slacken the two retaining

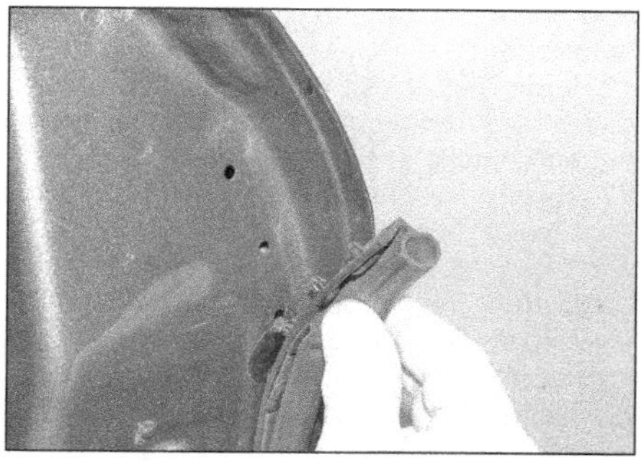

13.5a On 3-door models and the rear doors on 5-door models, pull back the door seal ...

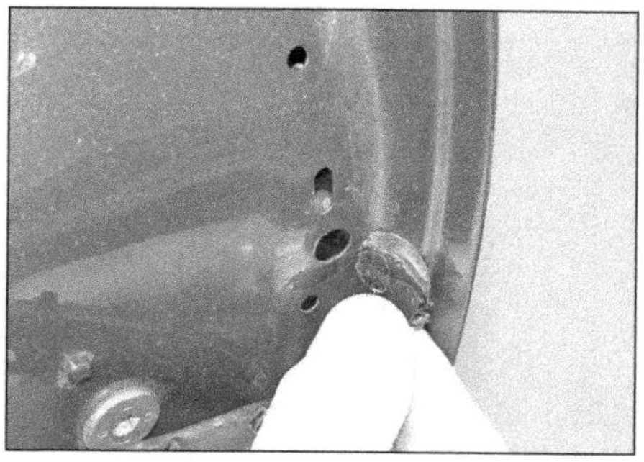

13.5b ... and remove the piece of tape covering the access hole

13.5c On the 5-door model front doors, remove the rubber grommet

13.6 Slacken the retaining screw and withdraw the lock cylinder/push button

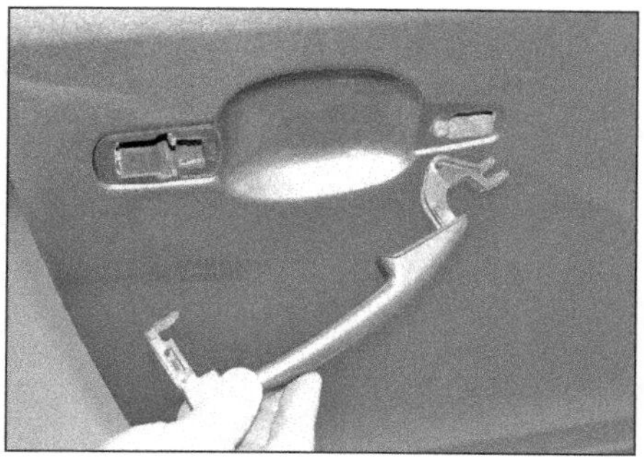

13.7 Slide the handle to the rear and pull it out to disengage it from the door

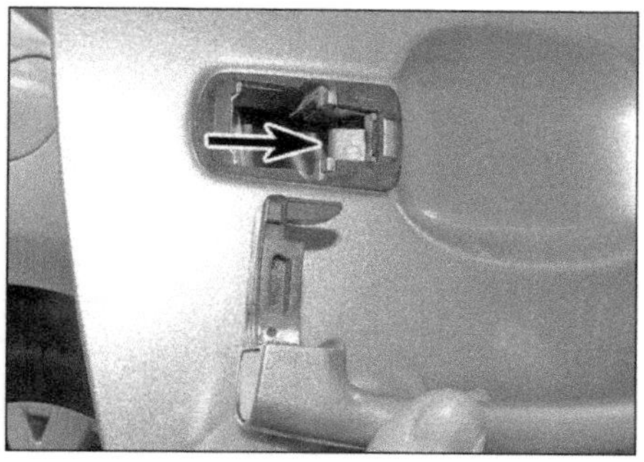

13.8 Make sure the handle hooks around the door lock lever (arrowed)

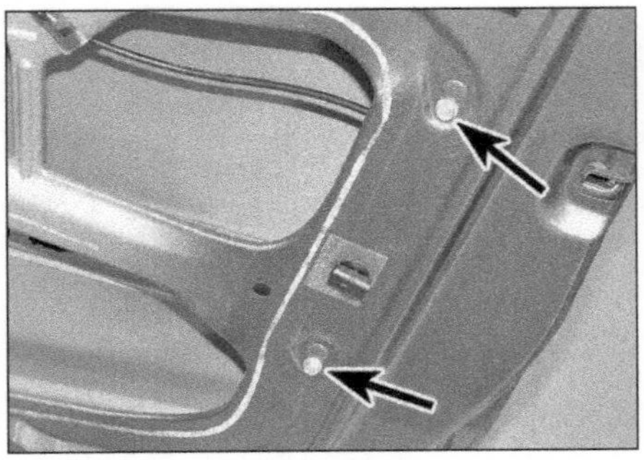

13.10a Slacken the two retaining bolts (arrowed) ...

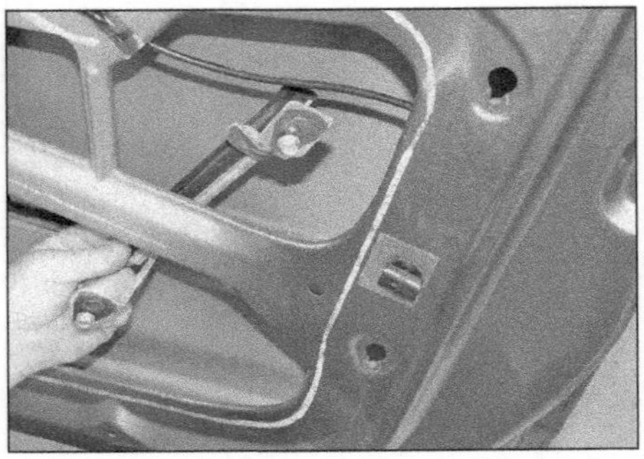

13.10b ... and remove the door glass rear guide

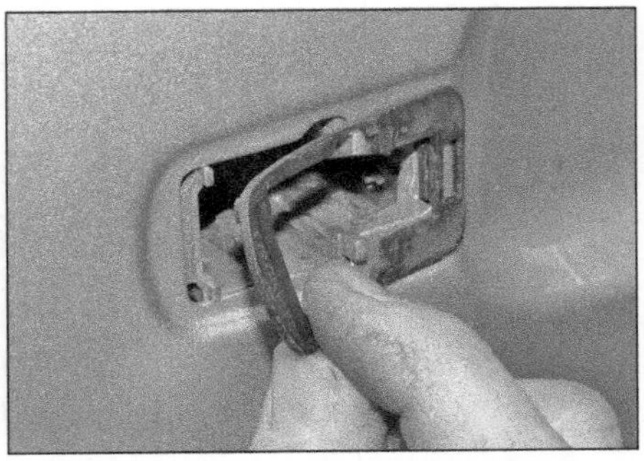

13.12a Remove the seal from the door aperture ...

bolts and slide the rear window channel upwards and remove it from inside the door panel **(see illustrations)**.

11 Remove the interior door release lever as described previously in this Section.

12 Remove the exterior door handle as described previously in this Section, and then remove the seal and slacken the retaining screw (do not remove completely) for the door handle housing from the outside of the door **(see illustrations)**.

13 Undo the two screws securing the lock assembly to the rear edge of the door **(see illustration)**.

14 Release the interior handle operating cable from the grommet in the door, then lower the lock assembly and manipulate it out through the door aperture **(see illustrations)**.

15 Disconnect the locking motor wiring plug, and then remove the lock assembly **(see illustration)**.

16 If required, unclip the lock operating outer cable from the lever on the exterior handle support bracket **(see illustration)**.

17 To remove the operating cable from the door lock assembly, release the securing clips and open the plastic cover. Release the outer cable from the housing and then unclip the inner cable from the operating lever inside the lock assembly **(see illustration)**.

18 Refitting is a reversal of removal. Fit a new sealing sheet to the door if the original was damaged in any way during removal. On completion, refit the door inner trim panel as described in Section 12.

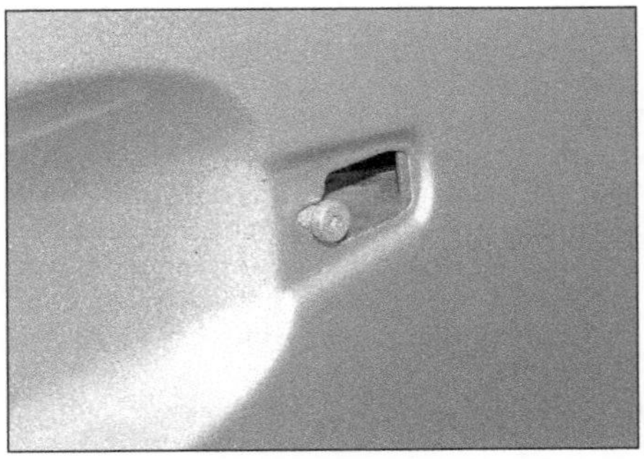

13.12b ... and undo the outer retaining screw from the handle support

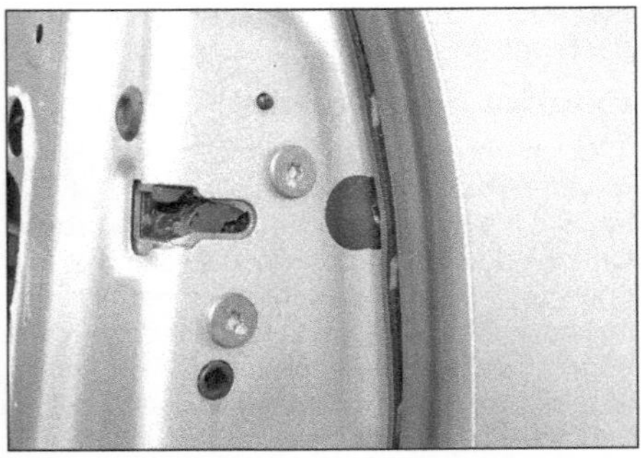

13.13 Undo the two screws securing the lock to the edge of the door

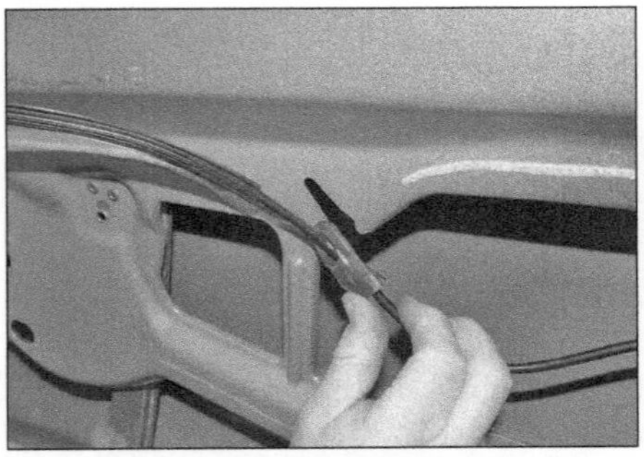

13.14a Release the operating cable from the door panel ...

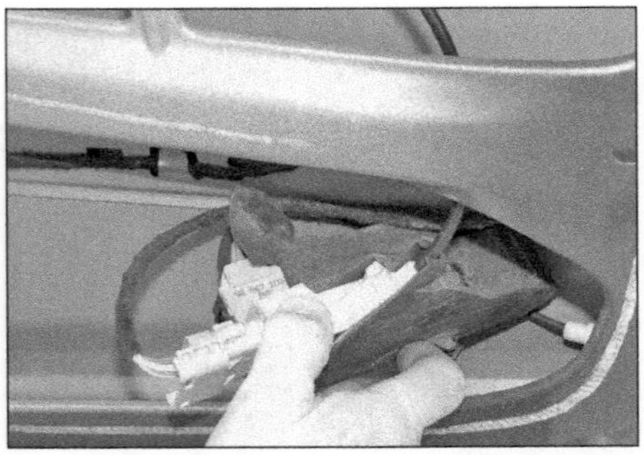

13.14b ... withdraw the lock assembly out from inside the door

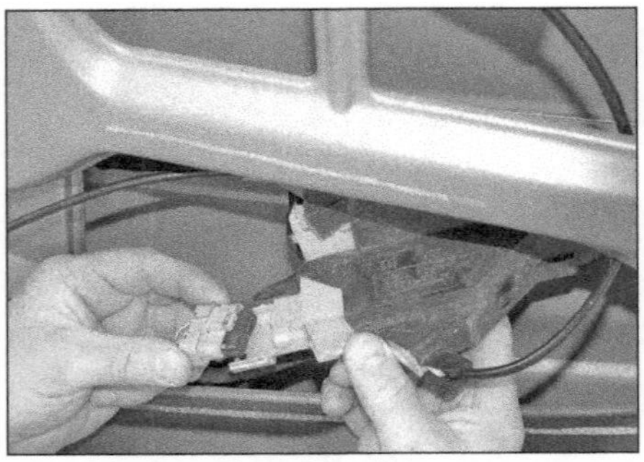

13.15 Disconnect the wiring connector from the door lock assembly

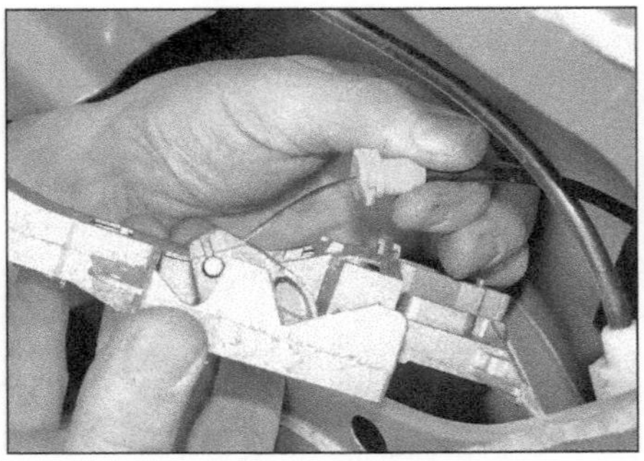

13.16 Release the operating cable from the handle support

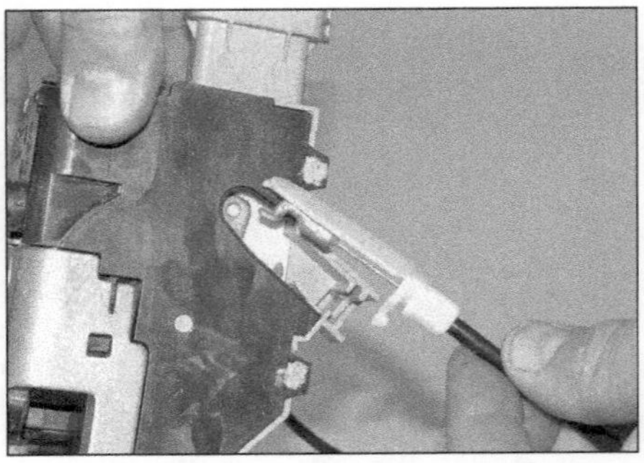

13.17 Release the outer cover and disconnect the inner handle operating cable

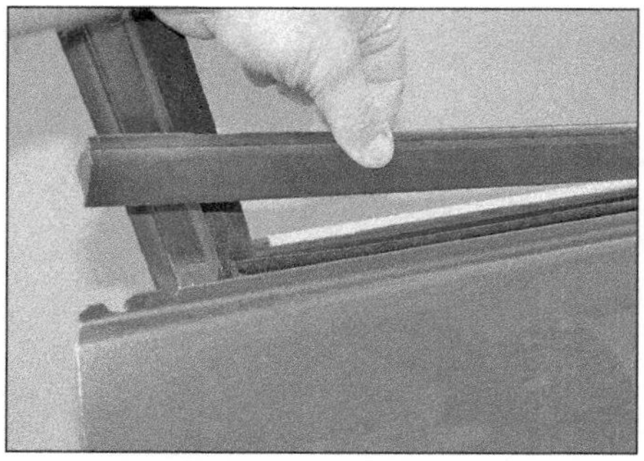

14.1 Carefully prise up the outer door seal

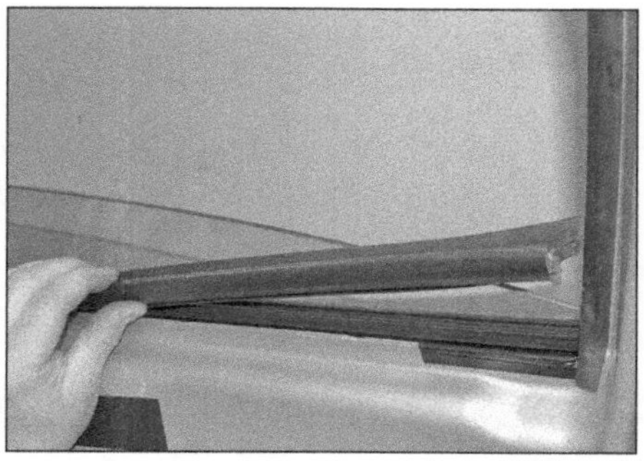

14.3 Carefully prise up the inner door seal

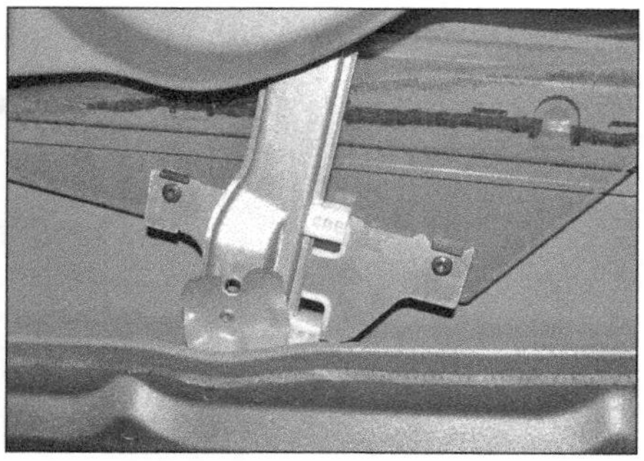

14.4a Undo the two window clamp screws ...

14 Door window glass, regulator and quarter light – removal and refitting

Front door window glass

1 Lower the window, and carefully remove the outer seal from the bottom of the window aperture **(see illustration)**.
2 Remove the door trim panel and inner sealing sheet, as described in Section 12.
3 Carefully unclip the inner seal from the top of the door panel **(see illustration)**.
4 Undo the two window glass clamp screws, and remove the window glass up through the aperture and out of the door **(see illustrations)**.
5 Refitting is a reversal of removal, but fit a new sealing sheet to the door if the original was damaged in any way during removal. On completion, refit the inner trim panel as described in Section 12.

Front door window regulator

Note: *The window regulator is riveted to the inside of the door frame, ensure that new rivets of the correct size are available for refitting.*
6 Remove the door trim panel and inner sealing sheet, as described in Section 12.
7 Undo the two window glass clamp screws **(see illustration 14.3a)**.
8 Slide the window glass up in its runners to the fully closed position and secure it in this position with masking tape over the top of the door frame.
9 Disconnect the wiring plug connectors from the window motor **(see illustration)**.
10 Undo the three retaining screws and remove the window motor from the inner door frame and regulator assembly **(see illustrations)**.
11 Drill out the three rivets securing the regulator bracket to the door frame **(see illustration)**.
12 Release the securing clips, then lift the regulator assembly upwards and disengage it from the door panel **(see illustration)**. Lower the regulator assembly, and manoeuvre it from the door aperture.
13 Refitting is a reversal of removal, but fit a new sealing sheet to the door if the original was damaged in any way during removal. On completion, refit the inner trim panel as described in Section 12.

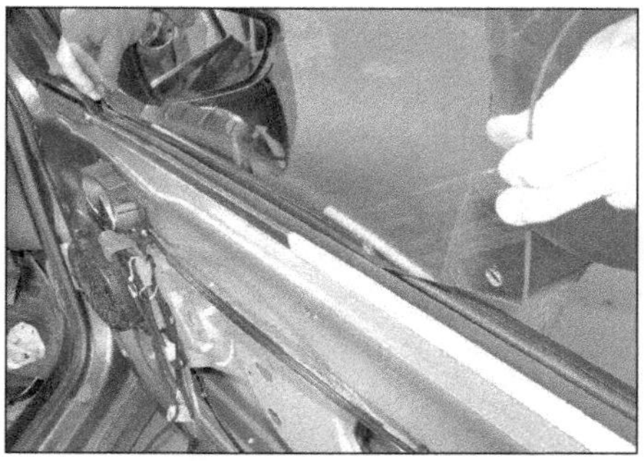

14.4b ... and withdraw the window glass out from the door

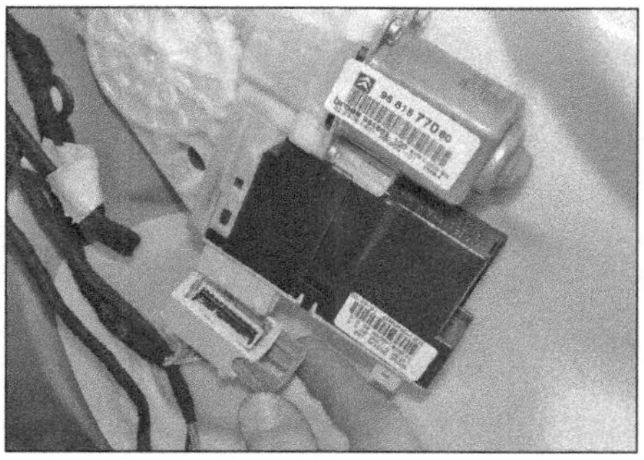

14.9 Release the securing clip and disconnect the wiring connector

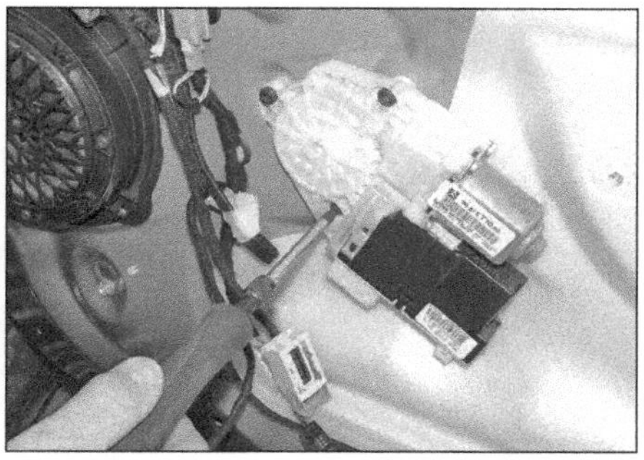

14.10a Undo the window motor retaining screws ...

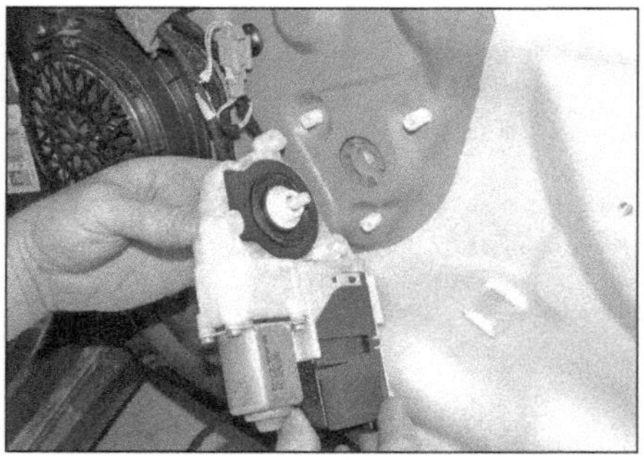

14.10b ... and remove the window motor from the door

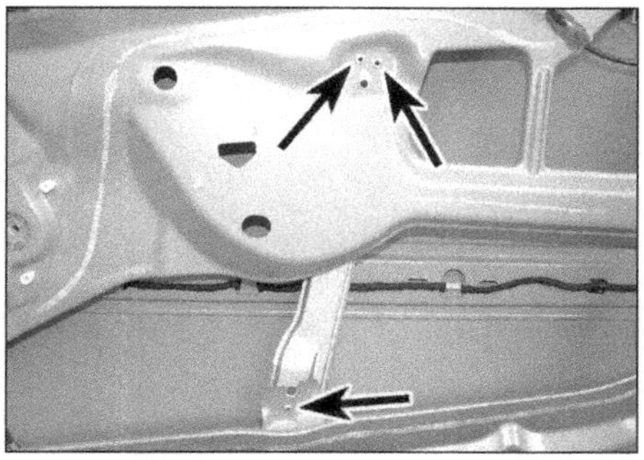

14.11 Drill out the three rivets (arrowed)

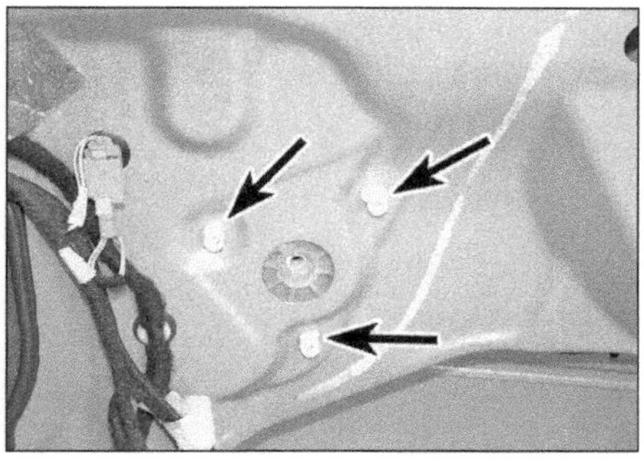

14.12 Unclip the regulator locating pegs (arrowed) from the door panel

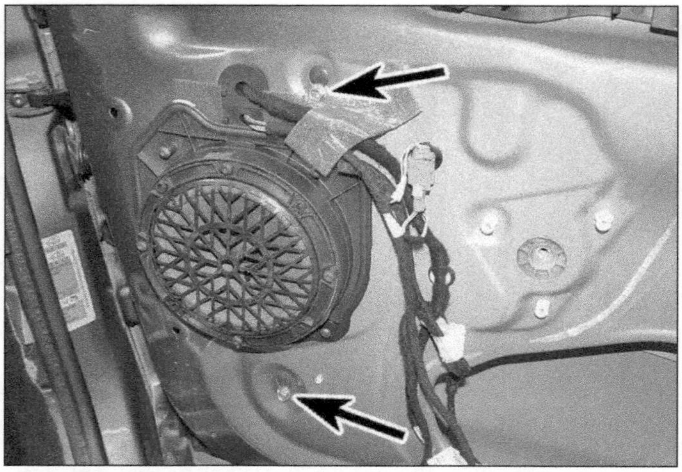
14.15 Slacken the front window guide retaining bolts (arrowed)

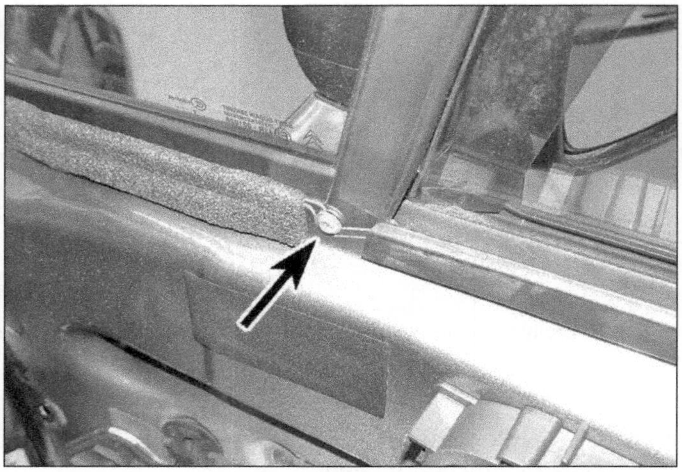
14.16 Undo the front window guide retaining screw (arrowed)

Front door quarter light

14 Remove the front door window glass and regulator, as described previously in this Section.

15 Slacken the two retaining bolts and slide the rear window channel upwards and remove it from inside the door panel **(see illustration)**.

16 Undo the window guide retaining screw from the top of the door panel **(see illustration)**.

17 Carefully pull back the quarter light rubber seal at the front of the glass and remove the retaining screw from the door frame **(see illustration)**.

18 Working on the outside of the door, carefully pull back the window channel rubber and drill out the rivet from the top of the window frame **(see illustrations)**.

19 Carefully unclip the plastic door seal and window channel rubber from around the window aperture. This door glass seal/ channel rubber is in one piece and can easily be damaged, take care on removal.

20 Pull the top of the quarter light pillar to the rear, and manoeuvre the quarter light from the door.

21 Refitting is a reversal of removal.

Rear door window glass

22 Lower the window, and carefully remove the outer seal from the bottom of the window aperture **(see illustration)**.

23 Remove the door trim panel and inner sealing sheet, as described in Section 12.

24 Carefully remove the interior seal from the bottom of the window aperture **(see illustration)**.

25 Undo the two window glass clamp screws **(see illustration)**.

26 Carefully unclip the upper part of the door seal from the window frame and then withdraw

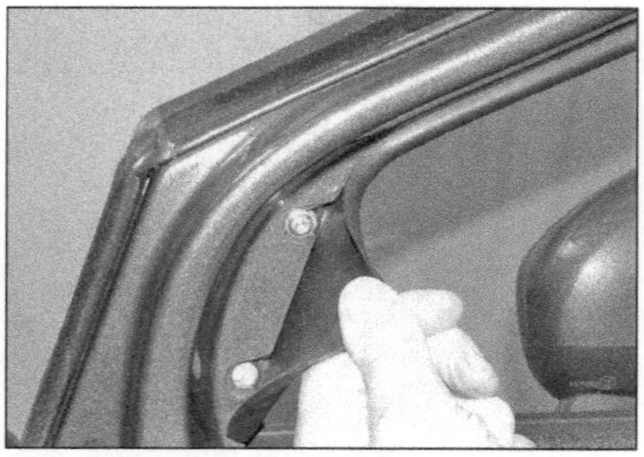
14.17 Pull back the rubber seal and undo the retaining screw

14.18a Pull the rubber seal from the front window guide ...

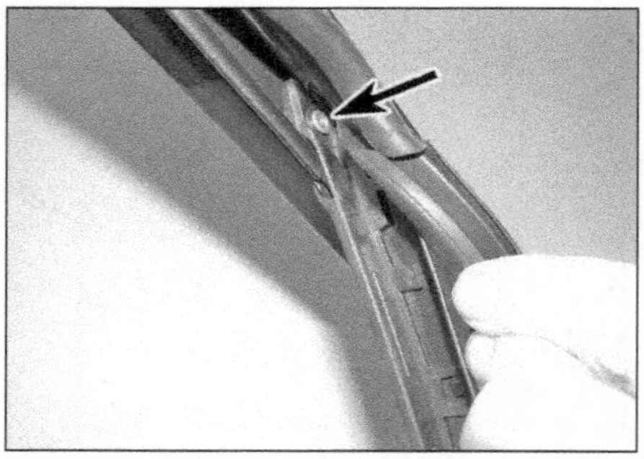
14.18b ... and drill the rivet (arrowed) at the top of the window guide

14.22 Carefully prise up the outer door seal

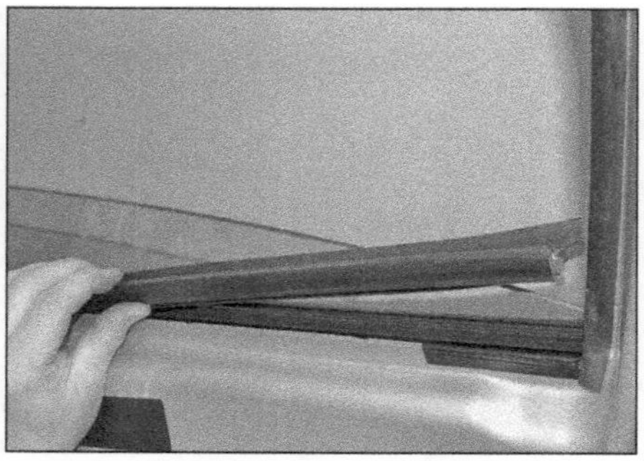
14.24 Carefully prise up the inner door seal

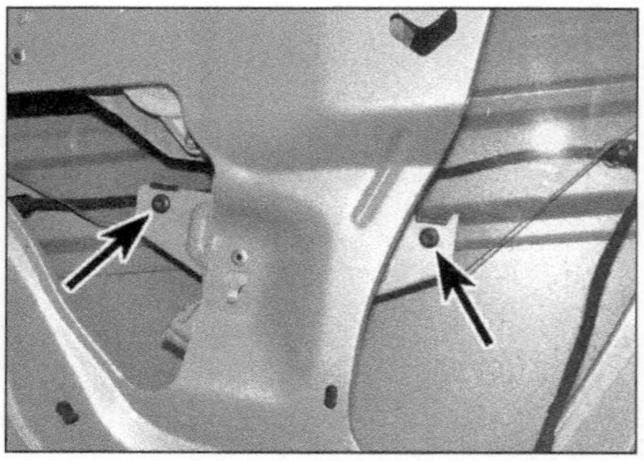
14.25 Undo the two window clamp screws (arrowed) ...

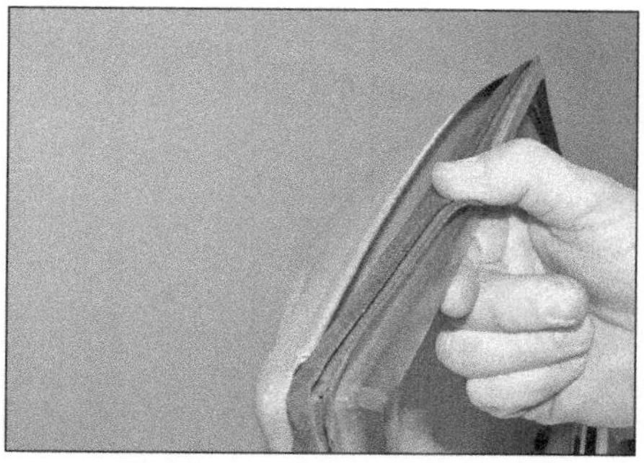

14.26a Carefully unclip the door seal from the top of the door frame

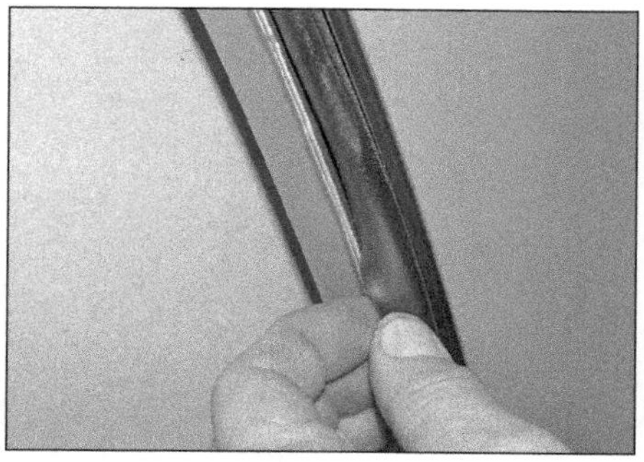

14.26b Pull the rubber seal from the front window guide ...

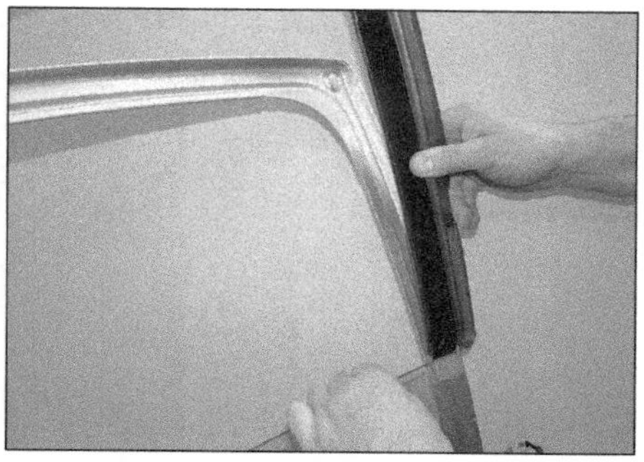

14.26c ... and slide it upwards and out from the door frame

14.27 Withdraw the window glass out from the door

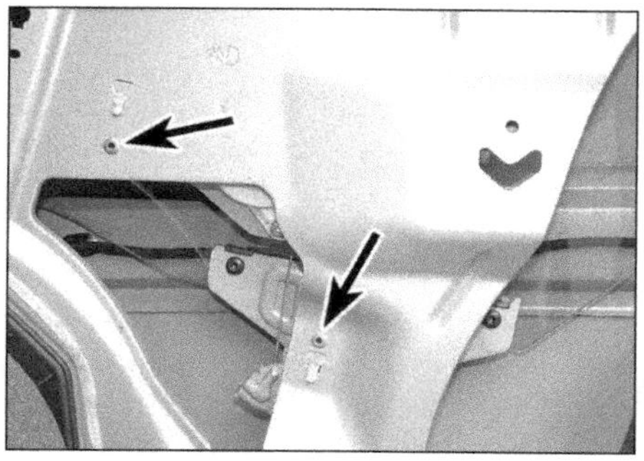

14.33a Drill out the two lower rivets (arrowed) ...

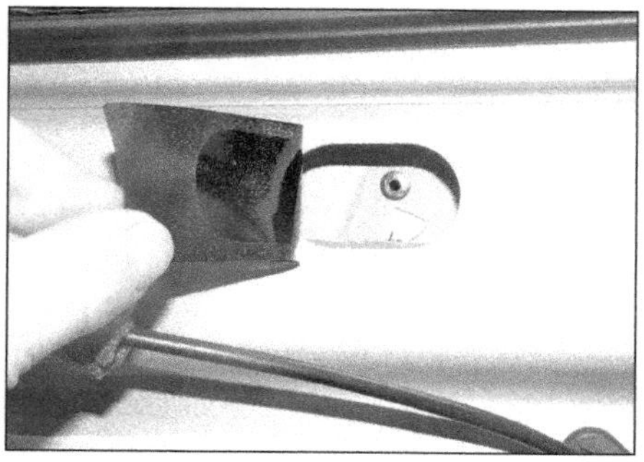

14.33b ... and the upper rivet

the seal complete with channel rubbers out from the window frame **(see illustrations)**. This door glass seal/channel rubber is in one piece and can easily be damaged, take care on removal.

27 Lift the window glass upwards and remove it from the outside of the door **(see illustration)**. Take care not to damage the paintwork on the door as it is withdrawn.

28 Refitting is a reversal of removal, but fit a new sealing sheet to the door if the original was damaged in any way during removal. On completion, refit the inner trim panel as described in Section 12.

Rear door window regulator

29 Remove the door trim panel and inner sealing sheet, as described in Section 12.

30 Undo the window glass clamp screw **(see illustration 14.25)**.

31 Slide the window glass up in its runners to the fully closed position and secure it in this position with masking tape over the top of the door frame.

32 On doors with manual window winders, undo the three retaining bolts (or drill out the rivets) to release the winder mechanism from the door frame.

33 Drill out the two rivets from the lower part of the window regulator, and peel back the seal and drill out the rivet in the upper part of the door frame **(see illustrations)**.

34 Release the regulator assembly from the door panel by lifting the regulator assembly upwards and disengage it from the door panel **(see illustration)**.

35 Lower the window regulator, and manoeuvre it from the door aperture. Disconnect the wiring plug connector as it is removed.

36 Refitting is a reversal of removal, but fit a new sealing sheet to the door if the original was damaged in any way during removal. On completion, refit the inner trim panel as described in Section 12.

15 Tailgate and support struts – removal and refitting

Tailgate

1 Remove the tailgate trim panels as described in Section 25.

2 Disconnect the wiring harness connectors at the tailgate internal components. Release the grommet from the tailgate and withdraw the wiring harness **(see illustration)**.

3 With the aid of an assistant, suitably support the tailgate, prise out the support strut spring clips, and pull the struts from the balljoints on the tailgate.

4 Unscrew the two nuts each side securing the hinges to the tailgate **(see illustration)**,

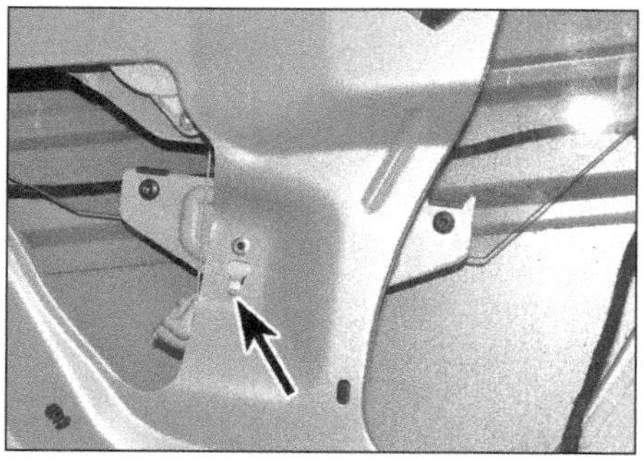

14.34 Unclip the regulator locating pegs (one arrowed) from the door panel

15.2 Unclip the wiring grommet (arrowed)

15.4 Undo the hinge retaining nuts

15.8 Prise out the clip and pull the strut from the lower balljoint

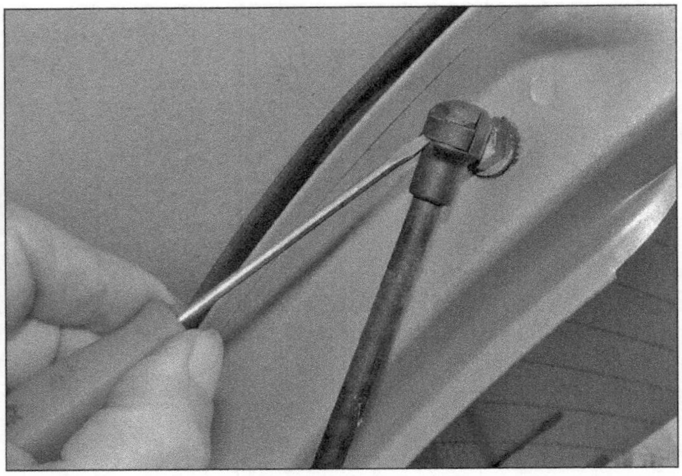

15.9 Prise out the clip and pull the strut from the upper balljoint

and carefully lift the tailgate from the vehicle.

5 If a new tailgate is to be fitted, transfer all serviceable components (lock mechanism, wiper motor, etc) to it.

6 Refitting is a reversal of removal, bearing in mind the following points:

a) *If necessary, adjust the rubber buffers to obtain a good fit when the tailgate is shut.*

b) *If necessary, adjust the position of the tailgate lock and/or hinge bolts within their elongated holes to achieve satisfactory lock operation.*

Support struts

7 Support the tailgate/glass hatch in the open position, with the help of an assistant, or using a stout piece of wood.

8 Using a small screwdriver, release the spring clip, and pull the support strut from its balljoint on the body **(see illustration)**.

9 Similarly, release the strut from the balljoint on the tailgate, and withdraw the strut from the vehicle **(see illustration)**.

10 Refitting is a reversal of removal, but ensure the spring clips are correctly engaged.

16.2 Undo the two bolts and remove the lock

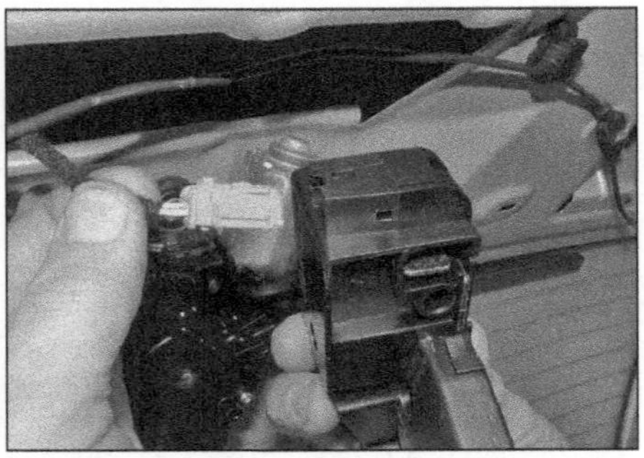

16.3 Disconnect the lock wiring plug

16.6 Undo the two bolts and remove the lock striker

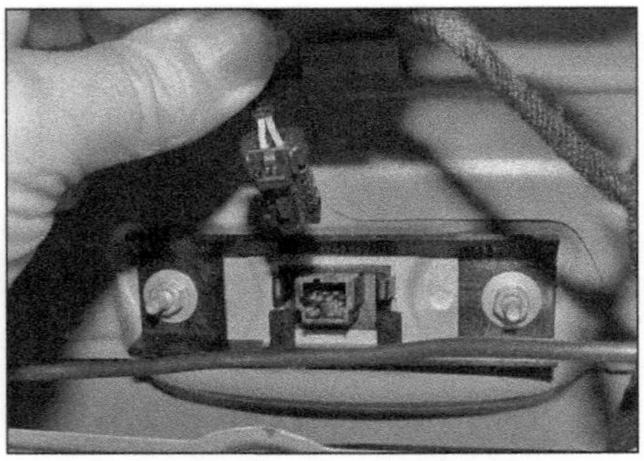

16.9 Disconnect the wiring plug connector ...

16 Tailgate lock components – removal and refitting

Tailgate lock

1 Remove the tailgate lower trim panel as described in Section 25.

2 Undo the two lock retaining screws and withdraw the lock from inside the tailgate **(see illustration)**.

3 Disconnect the wiring connector from the lock as it is removed **(see illustration)**.

4 Refitting is a reversal of removal, but adjust the tailgate lock striker as necessary to obtain satisfactory closure.

Tailgate lock striker

5 Release the retaining clips and fasteners, and remove the tailgate aperture lower panel (see Section 25) for access to the striker plate retaining bolts.

6 Mark the position of the striker on the body, for use when refitting. Unscrew the two securing bolts, and remove the striker from the body **(see illustration)**.

7 Refitting is a reversal of removal. Before tightening the securing bolts, the position of the striker should be altered (the securing bolt holes are elongated) until satisfactory lock operation is obtained. Use the marks made prior to removal, if appropriate.

Tailgate exterior switch/handle

5-door models

8 Remove the tailgate lower trim panel as described in Section 25.

9 Reach inside the tailgate and disconnect the wiring connector from the switch **(see illustration)**.

10 Undo the two switch retaining nuts, remove

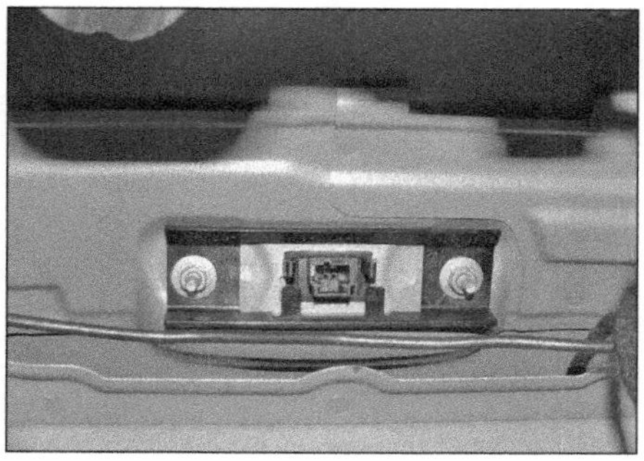
16.10a ... undo the two retaining nuts ...

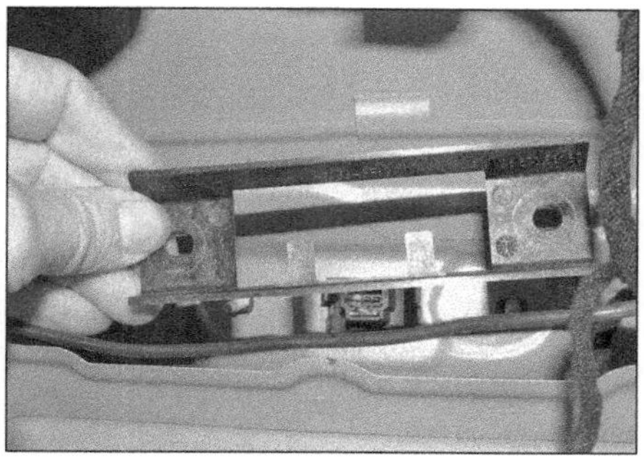
16.10b ... remove the mounting plate ...

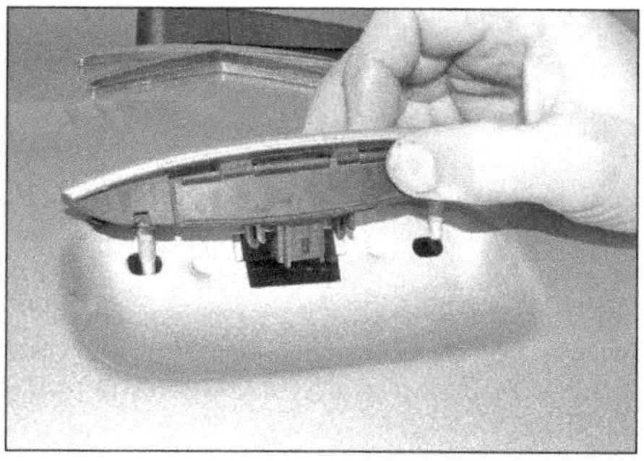
16.10c ... and remove the switch/handle from the tailgate

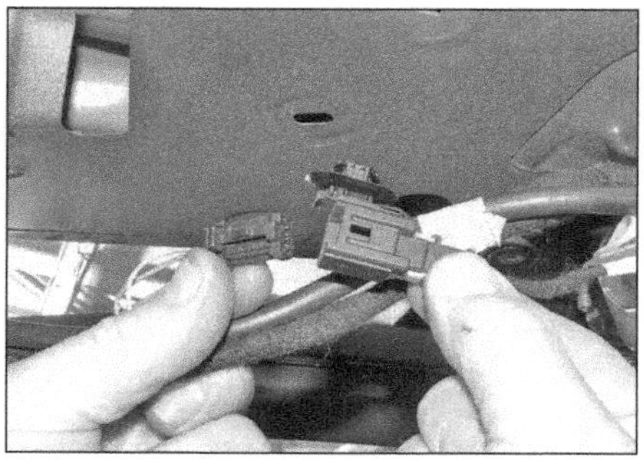
16.13 Disconnect the two switch wiring plug connector

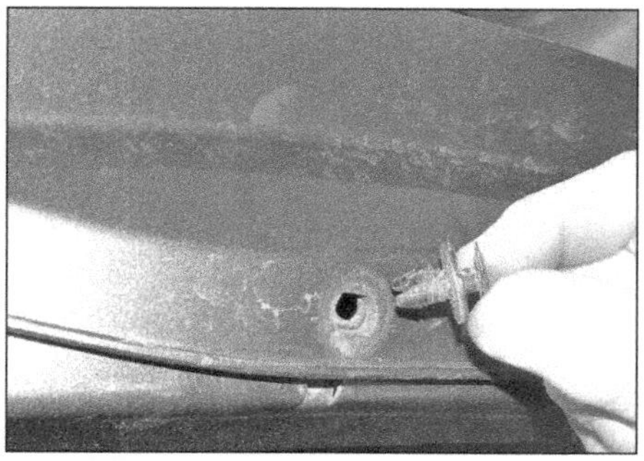
16.14a Release the retaining clips ...

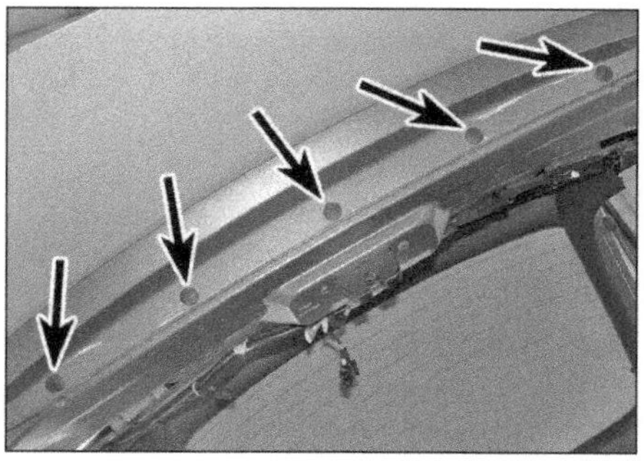
16.14b ... along the lower edge of the tailgate (arrowed)

the mounting plate and withdraw the lock from outside the tailgate **(see illustrations)**.

11 Refitting is a reversal of removal.

3-door models

12 Remove the tailgate lower trim panel as described in Section 25.

13 Disconnect the wiring connector for the switch and release the securing clip from the tailgate **(see illustration)**.

14 Working along the lower edge of the tailgate trim, pull out the centre peg and release the retaining clips **(see illustrations)**.

15 Working inside the tailgate, undo the retaining bolts securing the outer rear trim panel to the tailgate **(see illustrations)**.

16 With the bolts and clips removed, unclip the outer trim panel from the tailgate. Withdraw the wiring and rubber grommet from through the tailgate as the trim panel is removed **(see illustrations)**.

17 To remove the switch from the trim panel, disconnect the wiring connector, undo the two retaining nuts and unclip the switch from outside the trim panel **(see illustration)**.

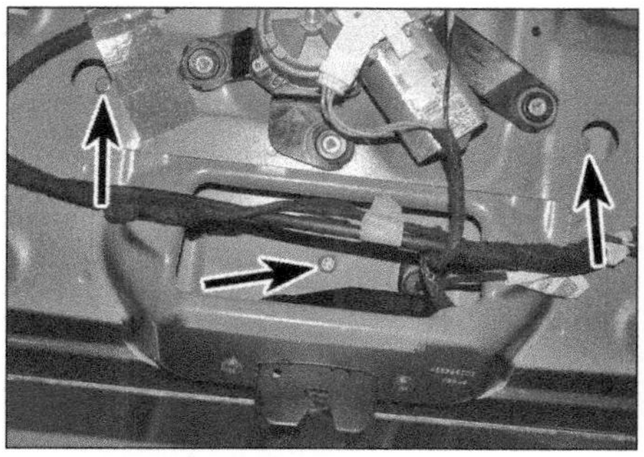
16.15a Undo the retaining nuts (three arrowed) ...

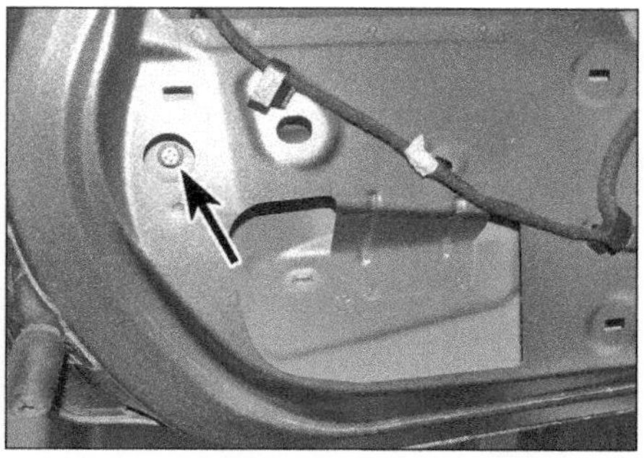
16.15b ... and one at each side (arrowed)

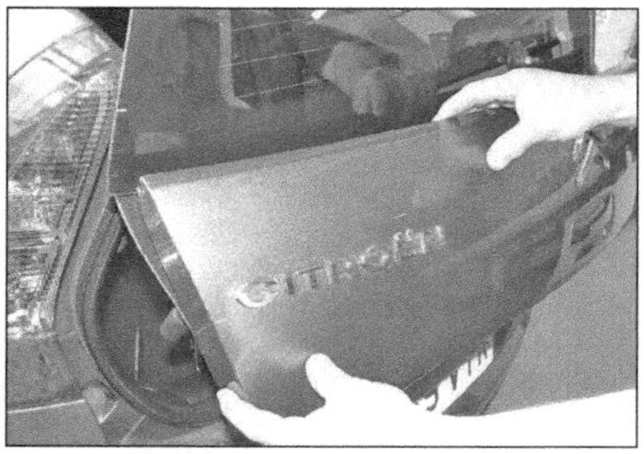
16.16a Remove the rear trim cover ...

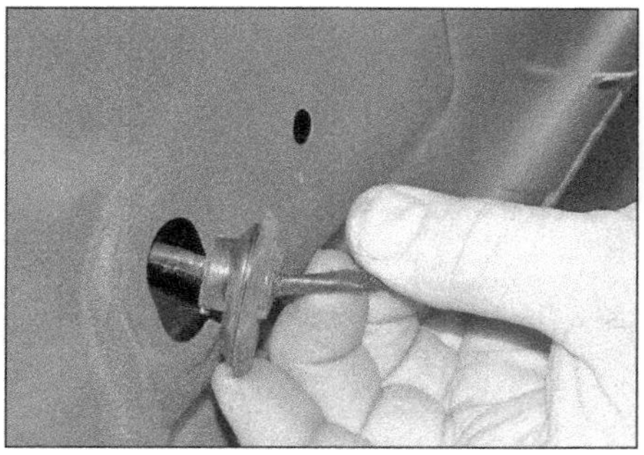
16.16b ... and withdraw the wiring grommet from the tailgate

16.17 Tailgate switch/handle retaining nuts (arrowed)

17 Central locking components – removal and refitting

Control unit

1 The central locking system is controlled by the built-in systems interface (BSI) which is the vehicle central computer controlling the main body electrical system functions. The unit is located behind the glove compartment on the left-hand side of the facia. Refer to Chapter 12, Section 23 for further information.

2 Should any problems be experienced with the operation of the central locking system or any of the other functions controlled by the BSI, the vehicle should be taken to a Citroën dealer for diagnostic investigation.

Door lock motor

3 The motor is integral with the door lock assembly. Removal and refitting of the lock assembly is described in Section 13.

Tailgate lock motor

4 Removal of the tailgate lock motor is described as part of the tailgate lock removal and refitting procedure described in Section 16.

Remote control transmitter

Battery renewal

5 When the remote control transmitter battery is nearing the end of its life, an audible signal will be emitted from within the vehicle, accompanied by a message on the instrument panel multifunction screen. The battery should then be renewed with a type CR 1620 (3 volt) battery.

6 Using a small coin in the slot at the upper end of the key, carefully prise the two halves of the transmitter apart **(see illustrations)**

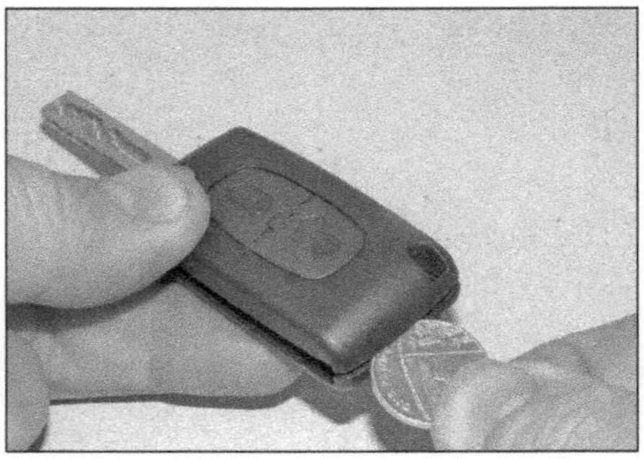

17.6a Twist the coin in the slot provided ...

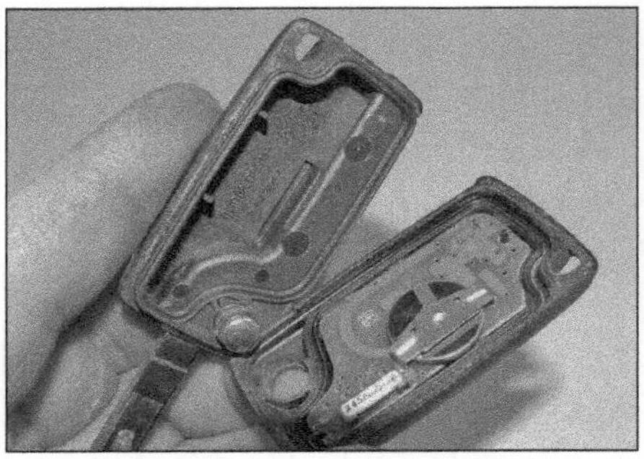

17.6b ... and unclip the cover from the key

7 Remove the printed circuit board and slide the battery out from its location in the circuit board, noting its fitted position **(see illustrations)**.

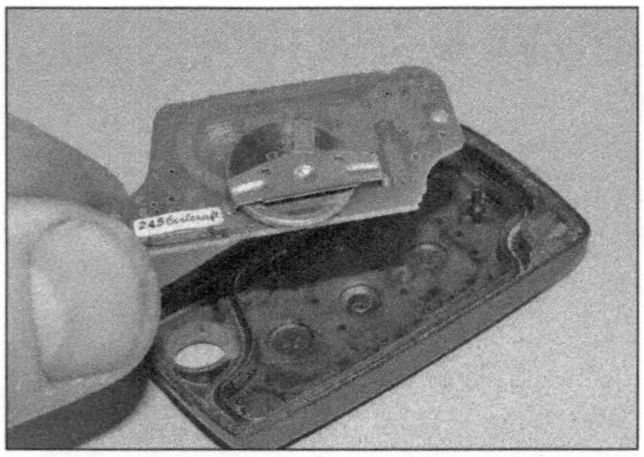

17.7a Remove the circuit board from the cover

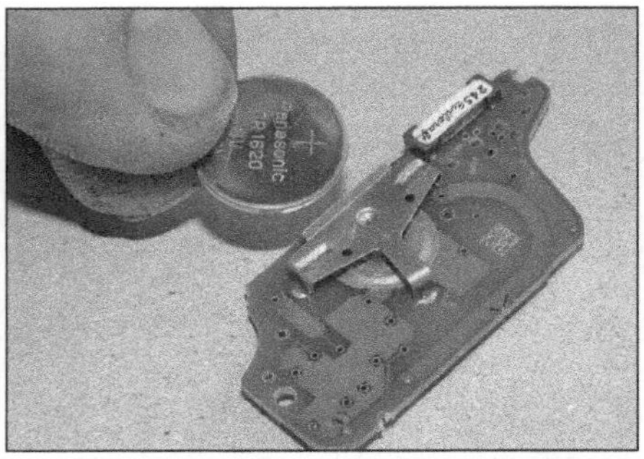

17.7b Slide the new battery into its location on the circuit board

8 Fit the new battery and reassemble the transmitter.

Initialisation

9 To initialise the unit after renewing the battery, put the key in the ignition and leave it in the off position. Then switch on the ignition (without starting) and immediately press the locking button on the key for 10 seconds. Then switch off the ignition and remove the key from the ignition lock. The key remote should now be fully operational.

18 Mirrors and mirror glass – removal and refitting

Exterior mirror assembly

1 Ensure the ignition is turned off.

2 Remove the door inner trim panel, as described in Section 12.

3 Remove the door loudspeaker, as described in Chapter 12, Section 18.

4 Disconnect the mirror wiring plug(s) at the front lower part of the door, and remove the grommet from the door panel **(see illustrations)**.

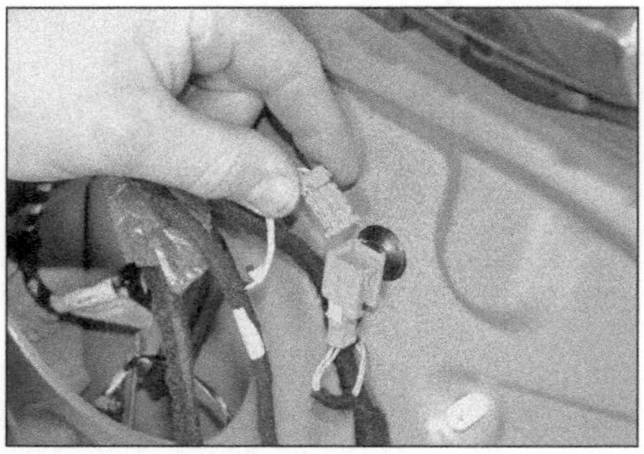

18.4a Disconnect the wiring connector ...

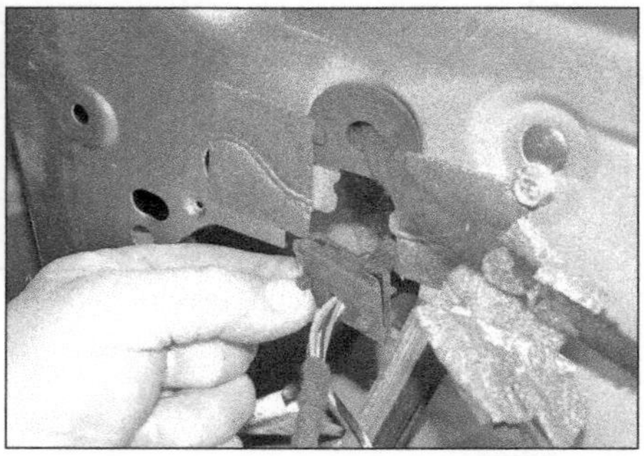

18.4b ... and unclip the grommet from the door panel

5 Uncover the access hole in the inner door panel and undo the two mirror retaining bolts **(see illustrations)**, whilst supporting the mirror assembly from the outside of the door.

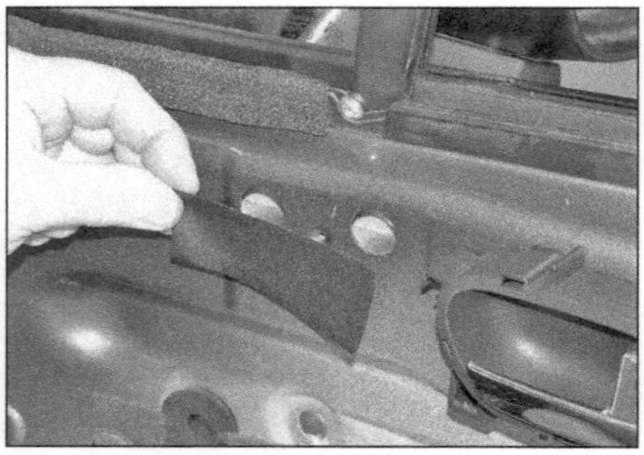

18.5a Peel off the piece of tape ...

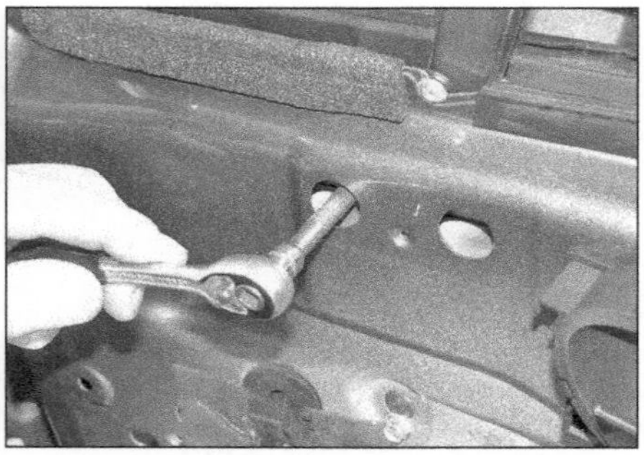

18.5b ... and undo the two securing bolts

6 Remove the mirror from the outside of the door. Withdraw the wiring loom releasing it from any retaining clips inside the door as the mirror is removed **(see illustration)**.

7 Refitting is a reversal of removal.

Exterior mirror glass

8 Carefully press the mirror glass in at the inner edge, and then working through the gap at the outside edge of the mirror glass, use a lever to release the clips that secure the mirror glass to the mirror body **(see illustration)**.

9 Withdraw the glass, and (where applicable) disconnect the heating element wiring connectors **(see illustration)**.

10 To refit, carefully push the mirror glass evenly until the securing clips lock into position on the mirror adjuster base.

Warning: It is advisable to wear gloves to protect your hands, even if the glass is not broken, due to the risk of glass breakage.

Exterior mirror shell

11 Remove the mirror glass as described previously in this Section.

12 Working from inside the mirror housing, release the retaining clips that secure the mirror shell to the mirror body **(see illustration)**.

13 To refit, carefully push the mirror shell onto the mirror body until the securing clips lock into position.

Interior mirror

14 Using a small flat-bladed screwdriver, carefully prise apart the two plastic covers over the mirror base housing **(see illustration)**.

15 Disconnect the wiring plug connector at the rear of the mirror base **(see illustration)**.

16 The mirror can now be pulled sharply downwards, to release it from the mounting base on the windscreen **(see illustration)**.

17 To refit the interior mirror to the base, offer it up and slide it upwards back into place. Reconnect the wiring connector and refit the plastic trim covers.

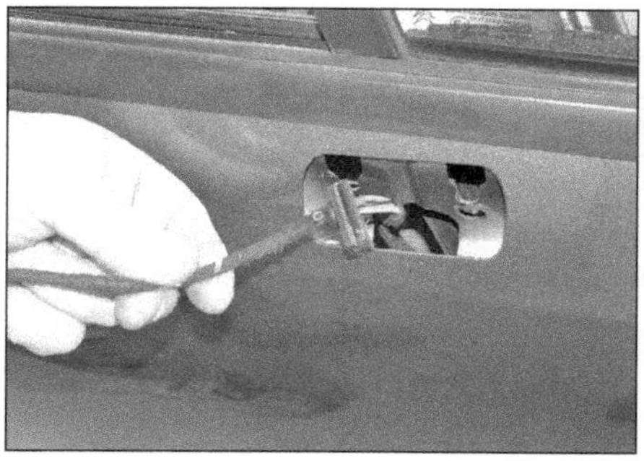

18.6 Withdraw the wiring loom out through the door aperture

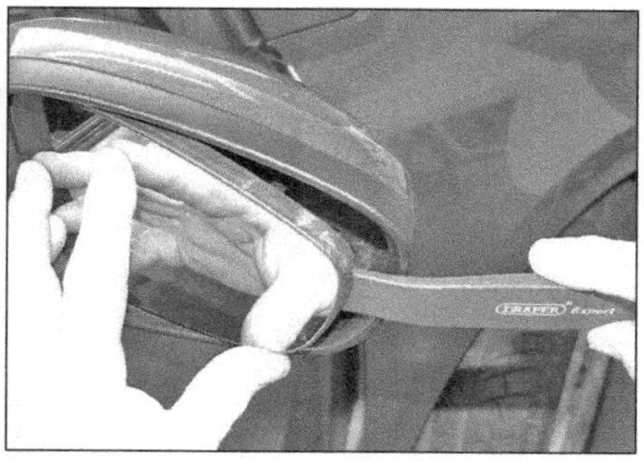

18.8 Carefully lever the outer edge of the mirror glass ...

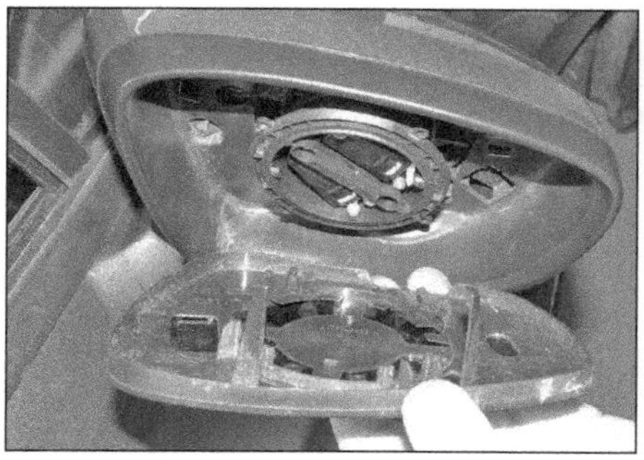

18.9 ... and unclip it from the mirror base

18.12 Release the retaining clips and remove the mirror outer shell

19 Windscreen, tailgate and fixed/hinged side window glass – general information

These areas of glass are secured by the tight fit of the weatherstrip in the body aperture, and are bonded in position with a special adhesive. Renewal of such fixed glass is a difficult, messy and time-consuming task, which is considered beyond the scope of the home mechanic. It is difficult, unless one has plenty of practice, to obtain a secure, waterproof fit. Furthermore, the task carries a high risk of breakage; this applies especially

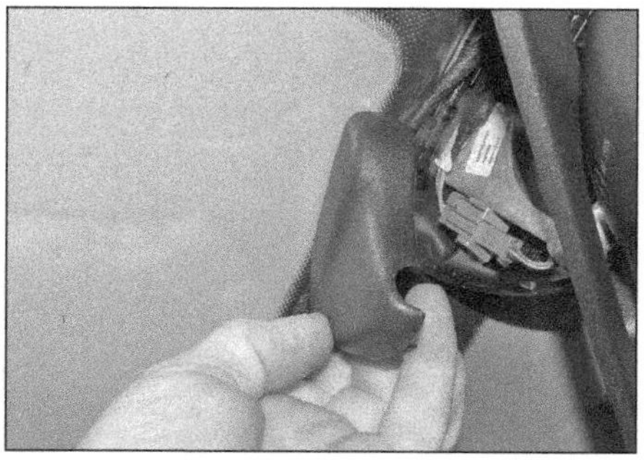

18.14 Prise apart the plastic cover

18.15 Disconnect the wiring connector

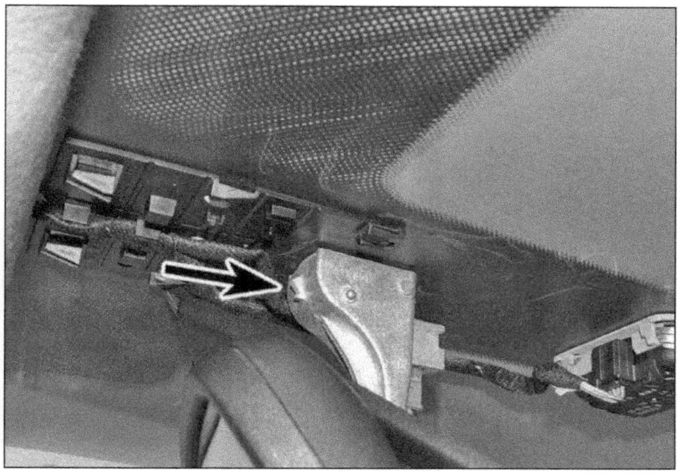

18.16 Slide the mirror base downwards (arrow) to remove

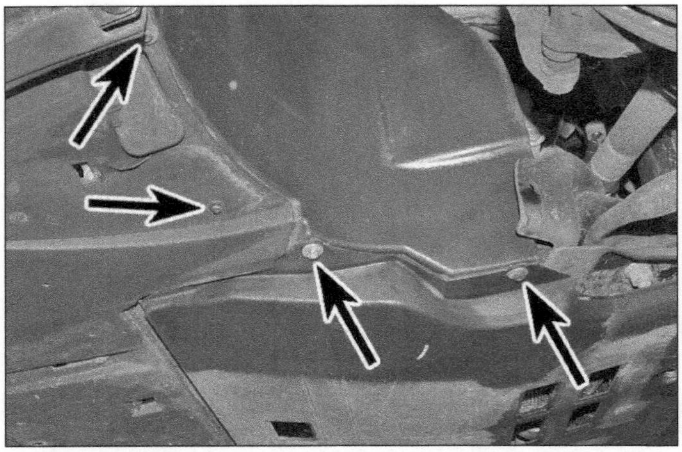

21.3a Undo the two retaining screws and the two retaining bolts (arrowed) ...

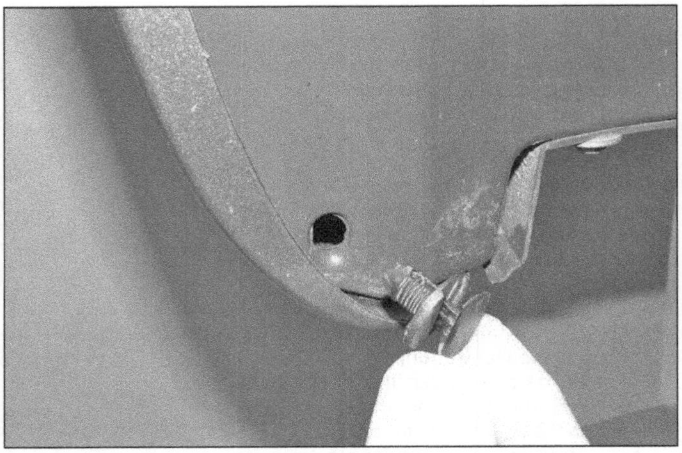

21.3b ... release the plastic securing clips ...

21.3c ... and remove the inner wheel arch liner

to the laminated glass windscreen. In view of this, owners are strongly advised to have this sort of work carried out by one of the many specialist windscreen fitters.

20 Sunroof - general information

Due to the complexity of the sunroof mechanism, considerable expertise is required to repair, renew or adjust the sunroof components successfully. Removal of the roof first requires the headlining to be removed, which is a tedious operation, and not a task to be undertaken lightly. Any problems with the sunroof should be referred to a Citroën dealer.

Initialising

After battery connection the sunroof will need to be initialised. Refer to Chapter 5A, Section 4.

21 Body exterior fittings - removal and refitting

Wheel arch liners/mud shields

1 The wheel arch liners are secured by expanding plastic rivets, screws, nuts or bolts.

2 Firmly apply the handbrake, and then jack up the vehicle and support it securely on axle stands (see *Jacking and vehicle support*). To improve access to the fasteners, remove roadwheel(s).

3 To remove the front liners, release the centre pins, and then prise the complete plastic rivet from place. Undo the retaining screws from under the front edge of the liner, and if the engine undershield is fitted undo the two retaining bolts. With all the fasteners removed, manoeuvre the liner from the wheel arch **(see illustrations)**.

4 On rear liners undo the retaining nuts inside the wheel arch, then release the centre pin and prise out the plastic rivets from the lower part of the liner. With all the fasteners removed, manoeuvre the liner from the wheel arch **(see illustrations)**.

Body trim strips and badges

5 The various body trim strips and badges are held in position with a special adhesive membrane. Removal requires the trim/badge to be heated to soften the adhesive, and then cut away from the surface. Due to the high risk of damage to the vehicle paintwork during this operation, it is recommended that this task should be entrusted to a Citroën dealer.

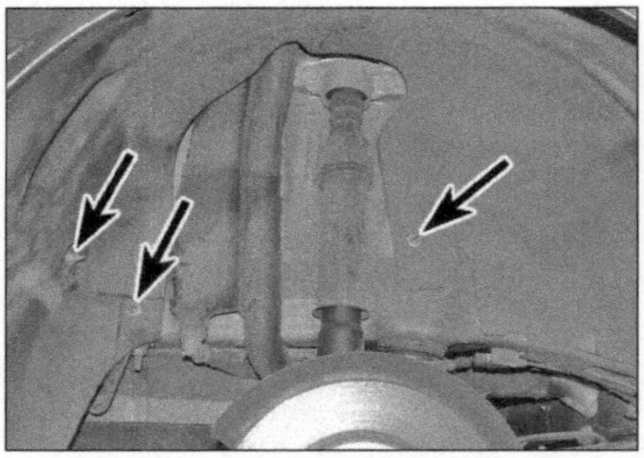

21.4a Undo the retaining nuts (three arrowed) ...

21.4b ... release the plastic securing clip ...

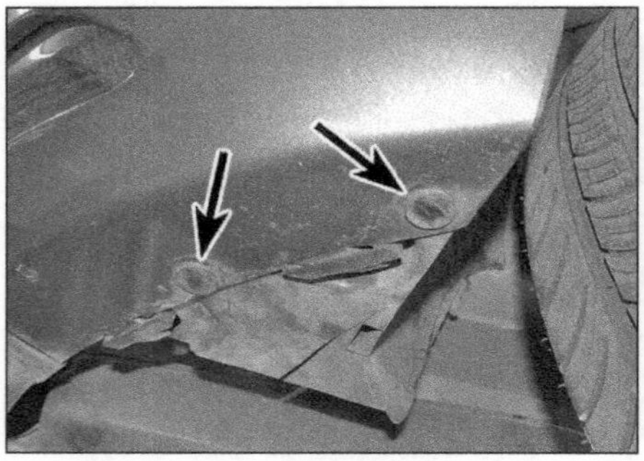

21.4c ... and lower securing clips (arrowed) ...

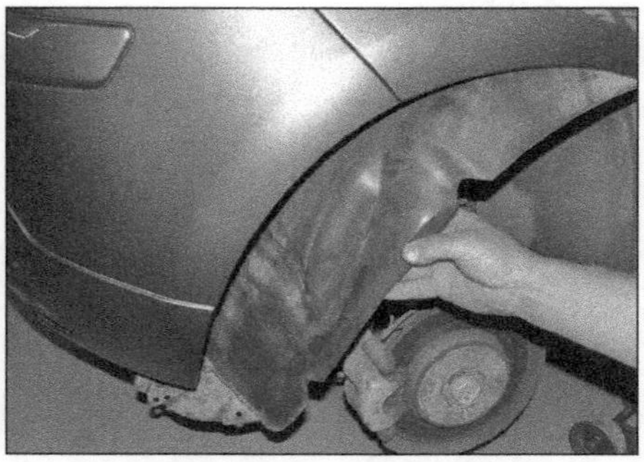

21.4d ... then remove the inner wheel arch liner

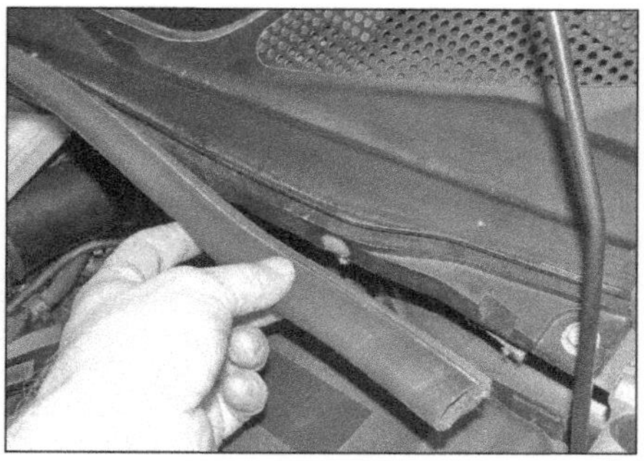

22.3 Pull the seal upwards to remove

22.4 Remove the brake/clutch reservoir from the bulkhead

22.5a Prise out the plastic rivet (arrowed) ...

22 Scuttle grille panel – removal and refitting

Removal

1 Open the bonnet and support it in the highest position.

2 Remove the windscreen wiper arms as described in Chapter 12, Section 13.

3 Pull the rubber sealing strip upwards and peel it from across the front of the scuttle panel **(see illustration)**.

4 Undo the two screws securing the brake/clutch master cylinder reservoir to the crossmember, and move it to one side. There is no need to disconnect the reservoir hose **(see illustration)**.

5 Prise up the centre pin and then remove the plastic rivet securing the centre of the upper scuttle panel to the scuttle crossmember **(see illustrations)**.

6 Pull the scuttle panel up at each end to release it from around the bonnet hinges, and then unclip it from the securing clips at the lower edge of the windscreen **(see illustrations)**.

7 Prise out the plastic rivets securing the sound insulation material to the lower part of the scuttle crossmember **(see illustrations)**.

8 Undo the bolt at the left-hand end of the scuttle crossmember, and then lift the

22.5b ... from the centre of the scuttle panel

22.6a Release the scuttle trim from around the hinge (arrowed) ...

22.6b ... and slide it downwards ...

22.6c ... to release it from the lower part of the windscreen

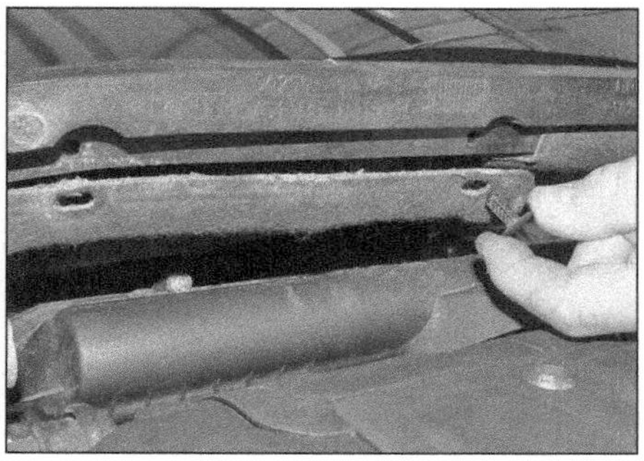

22.7a Prise out the retaining clips ...

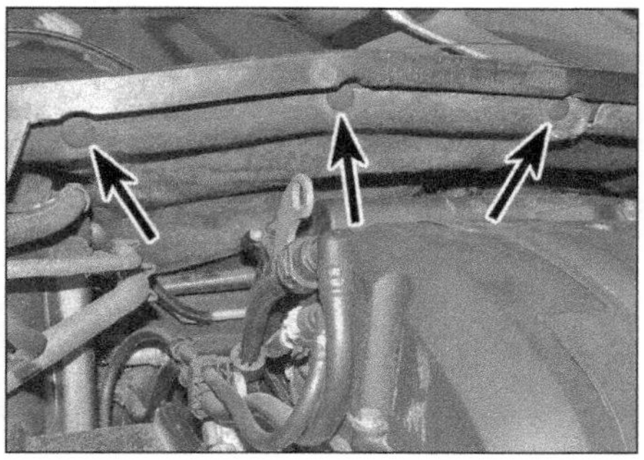

22.7b ... remove the clips (arrowed) from along the front edge of the panel ...

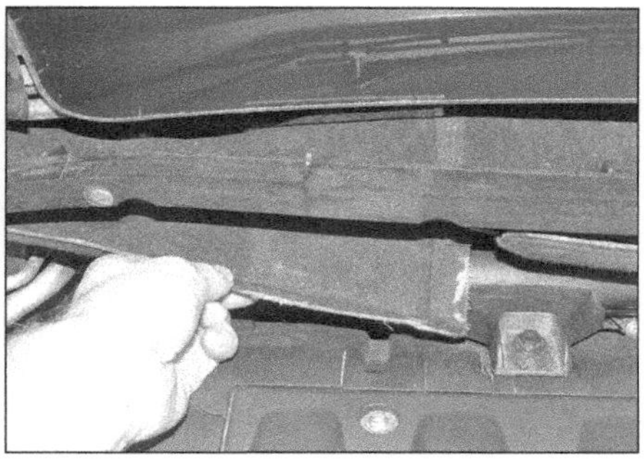

22.7c ... and remove the insulation material

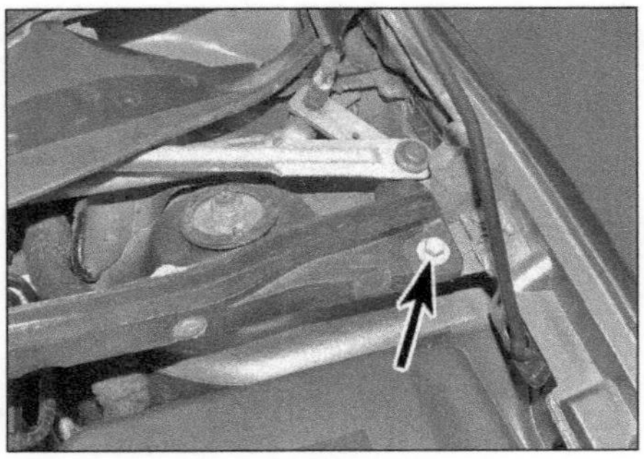
22.8a Undo the retaining bolt (arrowed) ...

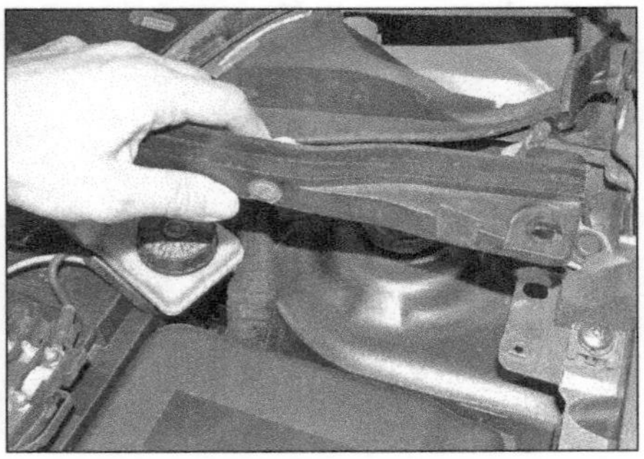
22.8b ... lift up the crossmember ...

22.8c ... and unclip the other end from the inner wing panel (arrowed)

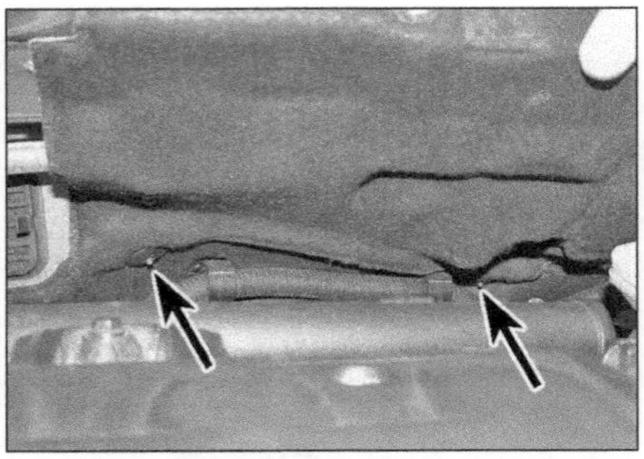
22.9a Unscrew the plastic fasteners (arrowed) ...

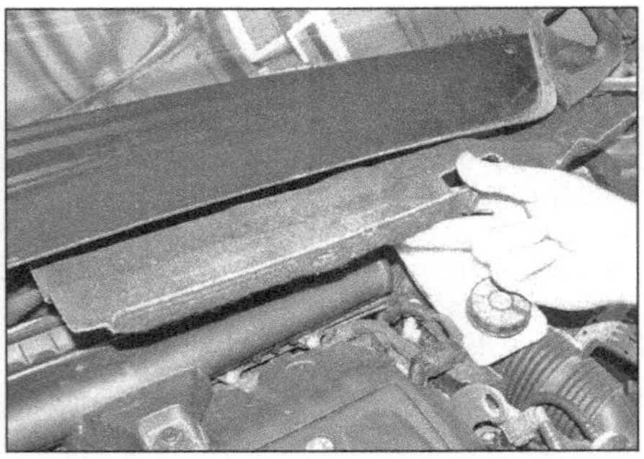
22.9b ... and withdraw the insulation material

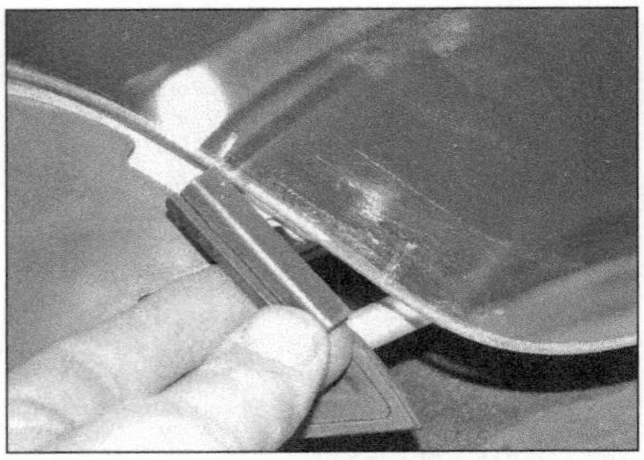
22.10a Make sure the securing clips are correctly located ...

crossmember upwards, releasing the securing clips at the right-hand end, then remove it from the rear of the engine compartment **(see illustrations)**.

9 Unscrew the plastic fasteners and withdraw the sound insulation material from the bulkhead at the rear of the engine compartment **(see illustrations)**.

Refitting

10 Refitting is a reversal of removal. Making sure that the securing clips along the lower edge of the windscreen are located correctly to secure the scuttle grille panel **(see illustrations)**

23 Seats – removal and refitting

Front seats

Warning: The front seats are equipped with side airbags built into the outer sides of the seats. Refer to Chapter 12, Section 21 for the precautions that should be observed when dealing with an airbag system. Do not tamper with the airbag unit in any way, and do not attempt to test any airbag system components. Note that the airbag is triggered if the mechanism is supplied with an electrical current (including via an ohmmeter), or if the assembly is subjected to a temperature of greater than 100°C.

1 De-activate the airbag system (see Chapter 12, Section 21) before attempting to remove the seat.

2 Move the seat fully forwards and remove the bolts (one on each side) securing the rear of the seat rails to the vehicle floor **(see illustration)**.

3 Move the seat fully rearwards and remove the bolts (one bolt on each side) securing the front of the seat frame to the floor **(see illustration)**.

4 Release the fasteners from the plastic trim

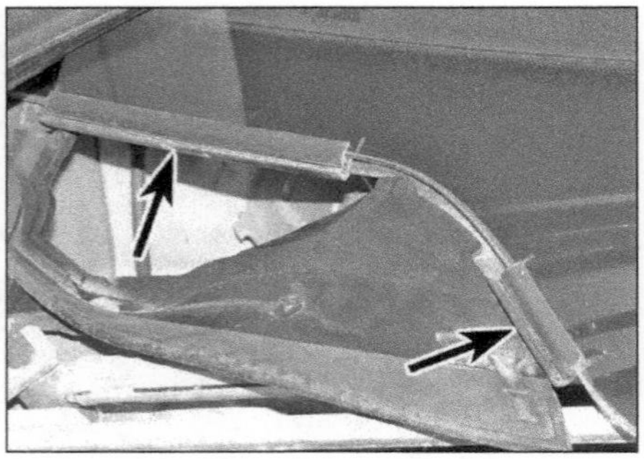
22.10b ... at each end of the windscreen

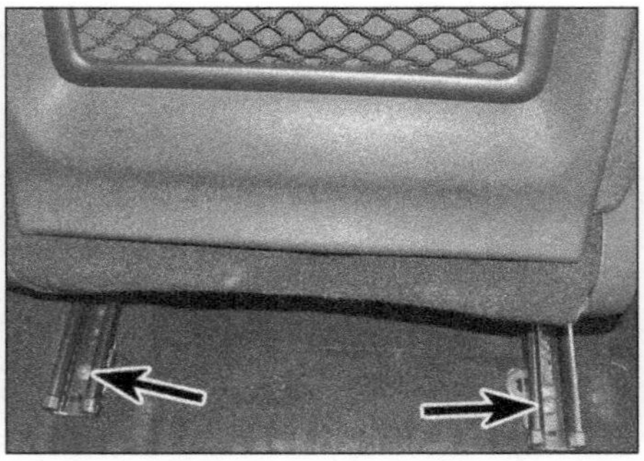
23.2 Undo the two bolts (arrowed) at the rear of the seat rails

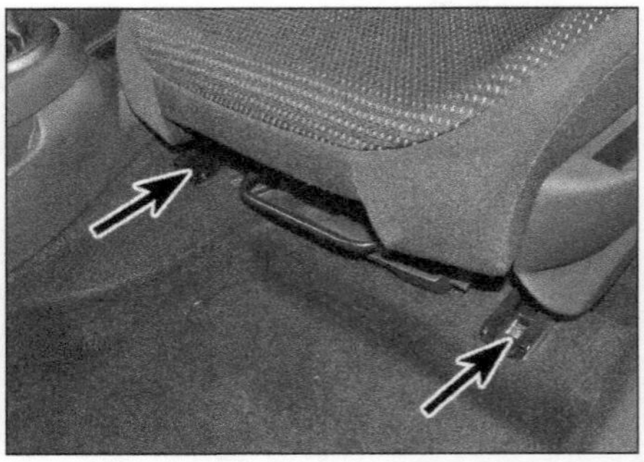
23.3 Undo the two bolts at the front of the seal rails (arrowed)

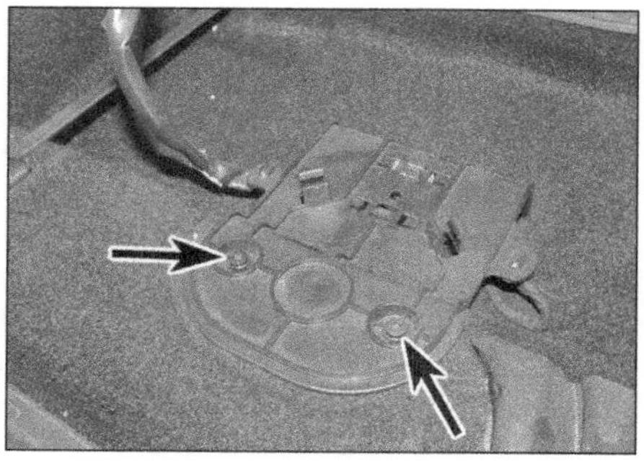

23.4a Release the two fasteners (arrowed) ...

23.4b ... lift up the plastic cover ...

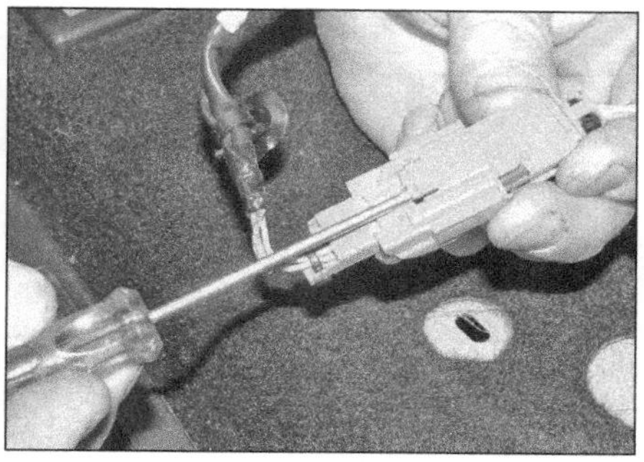

23.4c ... and disconnect the seat wiring plug

panel under the seat and disconnect the seat wiring plugs **(see illustrations)**.

5 Remove the headrest from the top of the seat back and then remove the seat from the passenger compartment.

6 Refitting is a reversal of removal, but observe the following precautions before reconnecting the battery.

a) Ensure that there are no occupants in the vehicle, and that there are no loose objects around the vicinity of the seats.

b) Ensure that the ignition is switched off and the keys removed from the vehicle, and then reconnect the airbag ECM and the battery.

c) Open the driver's door and switch on the ignition. Check that the airbag warning light illuminates briefly then extinguishes.

d) Switch off the ignition.

e) If the airbag warning light does not operate as described in paragraph c), consult a Citroën dealer before driving the vehicle.

Rear seats

Seat cushion

7 Lift the front edge first, followed by the rear edge, and tilt the seat cushion forwards. Push the hinge bracket stays inwards to release the ends from the mounting brackets on the floor panel. Then lift the seat cushion upwards and remove it from the passenger compartment **(see illustrations)**.

8 Refitting is a reversal of removal.

Seat backs

9 With the seat cushions lifted up and folded forward, undo the hinge bracket bolt at the join of the two seat backs **(see illustration)**.

10 Fold both the seat backs forward and undo the nut securing the rear part of the hinge bracket to the vehicle floor panel **(see illustration)**.

11 Starting with the right-hand smaller seat back, lift it up at the centre hinge bracket, then disengage the outer hinge peg and remove it from the vehicle **(see illustrations)**.

12 The left-hand larger seat back can now

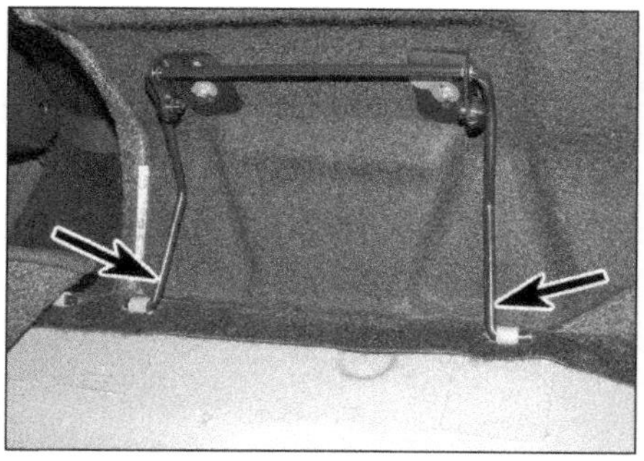

23.7a Push the hinge metal rod in the direction of the arrows ...

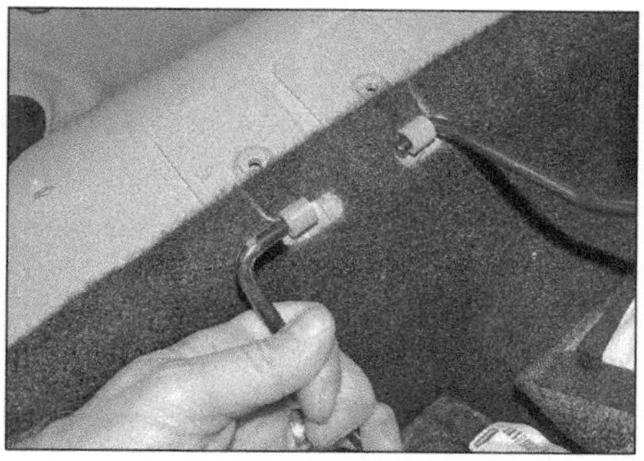

23.7b ... to release the lower end from the floor panel

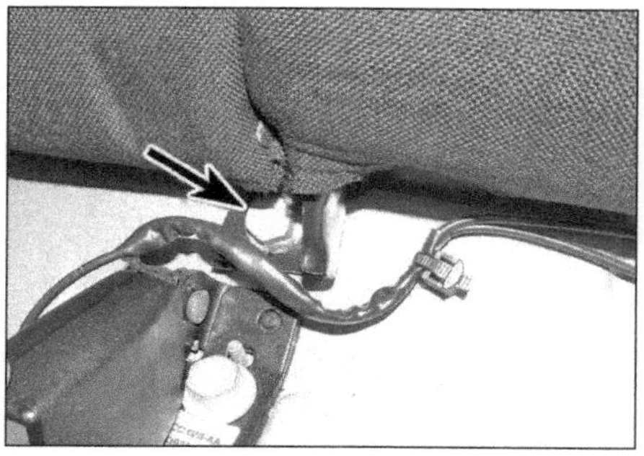

23.9 Undo the hinge front retaining bolt (arrowed)

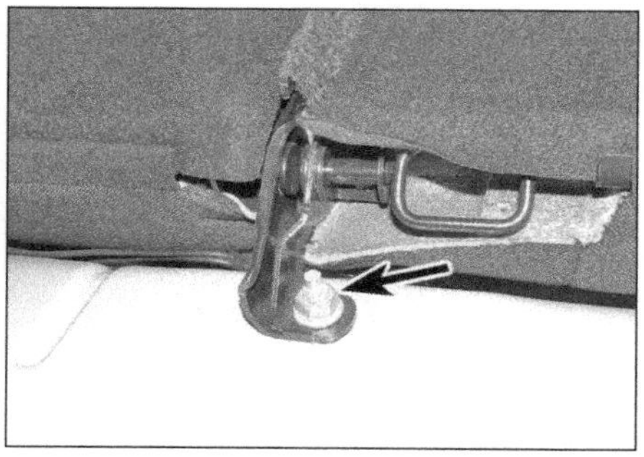

23.10 Undo the hinge rear retaining nut (arrowed)

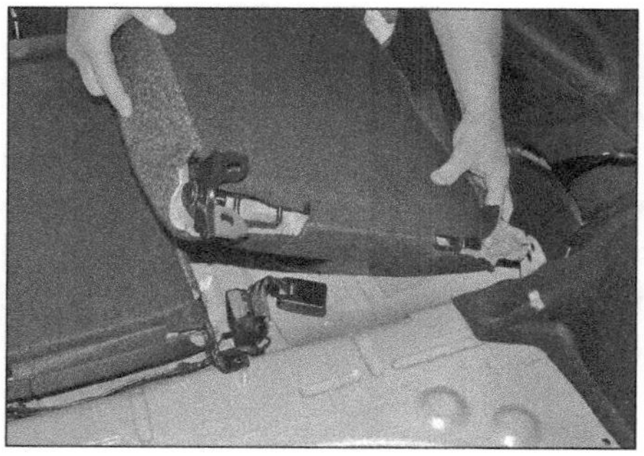

23.11a Withdraw the seat ...

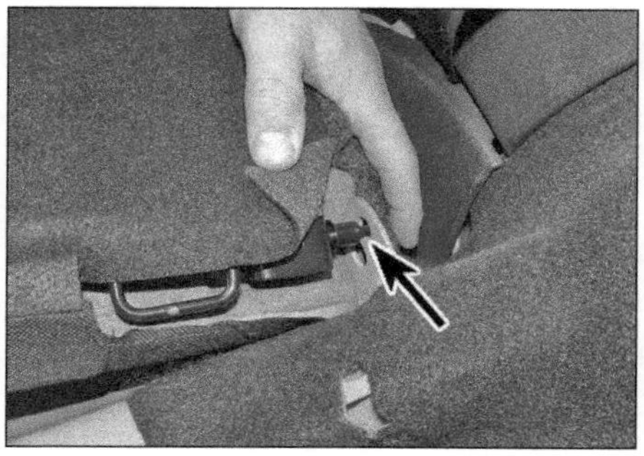

23.11b ... releasing the outer hinge locating peg from the floor bracket ...

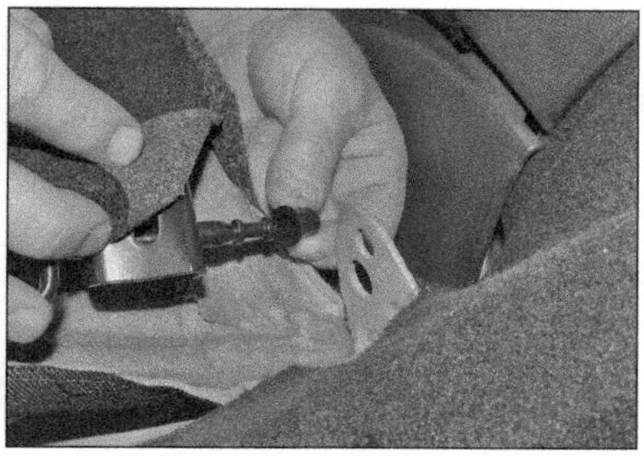

23.11c ... making sure the plastic bush is still located on the locating peg

be removed, as described in the previous paragraph for the right-hand seat back.

13 Refitting is a reversal of removal, tightening the hinge bolt/nut securely.

Seat catch

14 To remove the seat catch, the seat back cover must be partially removed. Remove the seat back as described in paragraphs 9 to 12.

15 Unclip the plastic trim panel from around the seat catch button at the top of the seat back **(see illustration)**.

16 Unclip the lower and side edges of the seat cover from the seat frame **(see illustrations)**.

17 Pull back the seat cover and foam cushion, then undo the two securing bolts and manoeuvre the seat catch from the seat frame **(see illustration)**.

18 Refitting is a reversal of removal.

19 Refit the seat backs as described previously in this Section.

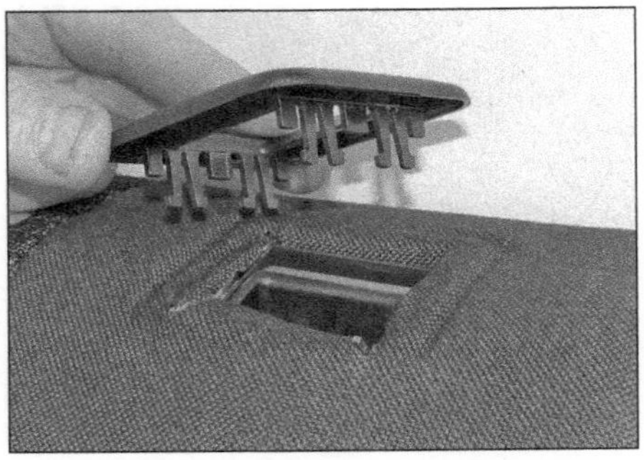

23.15 Unclip the seat catch trim from the top of the seat

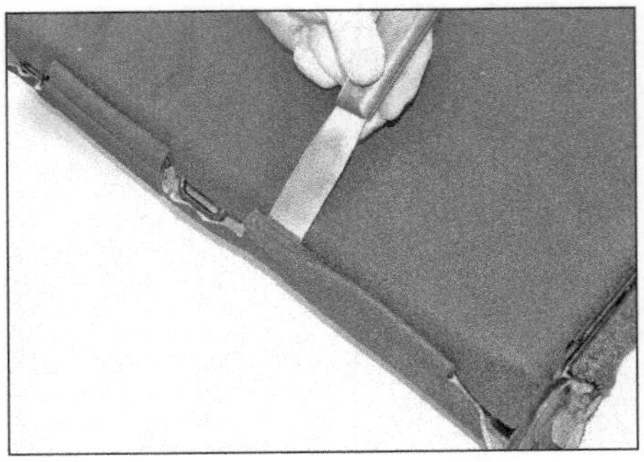

23.16a Unclip the lower ...

23.16b ... and side edges of the seat back cover ...

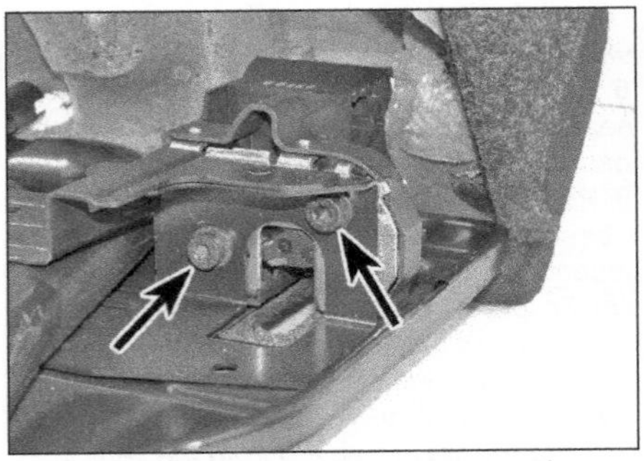

23.17 ... to expose the seat catch securing bolts (arrowed)

24 Seat belt components – removal and refitting

Note: *Record the positions of the washers and spacers on the seat belt anchors, and ensure they are refitted in their original positions.*

Front seat belt

Warning: The front seat belt inertia reels are equipped with a pyrotechnic pretensioner mechanism. Refer to the airbag system precautions contained in Chapter 12, Section 21, which apply equally to the seat belt pretensioners. Do not tamper with the inertia reel pretensioner unit in any way, and do not attempt to test the unit. Note that the unit is triggered if the mechanism is supplied with an electrical current (including via an ohmmeter), or if the assembly is subjected to a temperature of greater than 100°C.

24.4 Release the wiring connector from the inertia reel

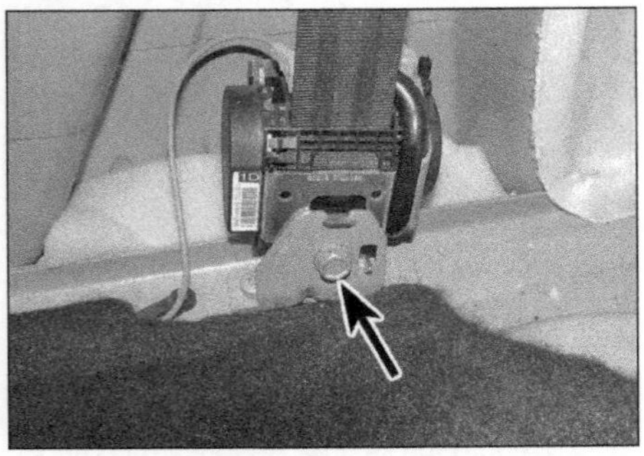

24.5a Undo the seat belt reel mounting bolt (arrowed) ...

1 De-activate the airbag system (which will also de-activate the pyrotechnic pretensioner mechanism) as described in Chapter 12, Section 21 before attempting to remove the seat belt.

2 If desired, to improve access, remove the relevant front seat as described in Section 23.

3 Remove the B-pillar trim panels as described in Section 25.

4 Release the locking clip (where applicable) and then disconnect the wiring connector from the inertia reel pretensioner unit **(see illustration)**.

5 Undo the seat belt lower anchor bolt and the inertia reel anchor bolt, and recover the washers **(see illustrations)**.

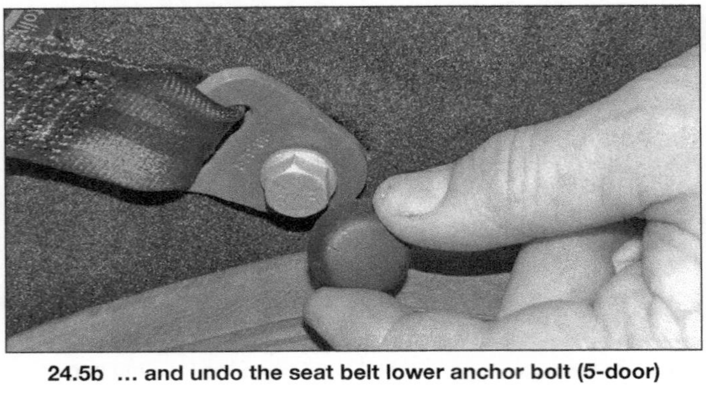

24.5b ... and undo the seat belt lower anchor bolt (5-door)

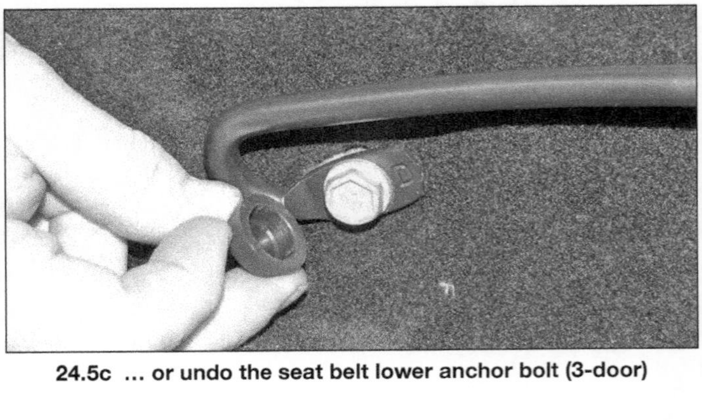

24.5c ... or undo the seat belt lower anchor bolt (3-door)

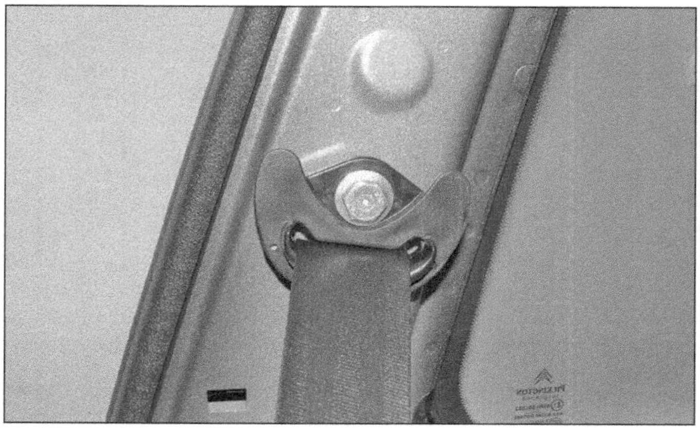

24.6a Undo the seat belt upper anchor bolt ...

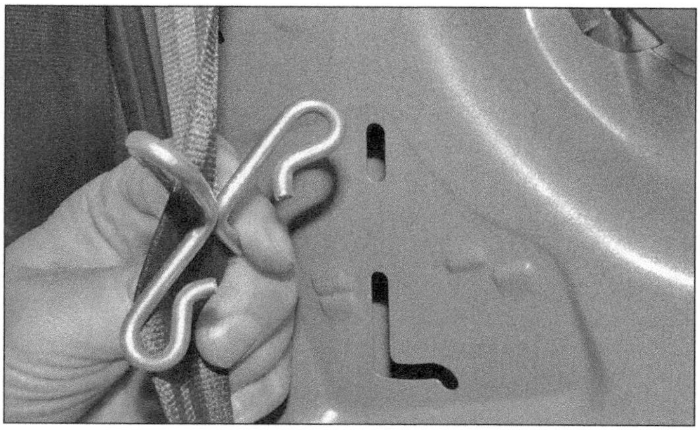

24.6b ... and release the guide clip from the pillar

6 Undo the seat belt upper anchor bolt and release the belt from its guide clip on the door pillar **(see illustrations**. Withdraw the inertia reel from the door pillar and remove the seat belt assembly from the vehicle.

7 Refitting is a reversal of removal, but observe the following precautions before reconnecting the battery.

a) Ensure that there are no occupants in the vehicle, and that there are no loose objects around the vicinity of the seats.

b) Ensure that the ignition is switched off and the keys are removed from the vehicle, and then reconnect the battery.

c) Open the driver's door and switch on the ignition. Check that the airbag warning light illuminates briefly then extinguishes.

d) Switch off the ignition.

e) If the airbag warning light does not operate as described in paragraph c), consult a Citroën dealer before driving the vehicle.

f) Tighten the seat belt mountings to the specified torque.

Front seat belt catch/stalk

8 Remove the front seat as described in Section 23. Disconnect the wiring connector from under the seat, and then undo the bolt securing the seat belt stalk to the seat frame **(see illustrations)**.

9 Refitting is a reversal of removal. Tighten the mounting bolt/nut to the specified torque.

Rear side seat belts

10 Remove the C-pillar trim panels, as described in Section 25.

11 Remove the insulated foam cover and undo the nut securing the seat belt inertia reel to the vehicle body **(see illustrations)**.

12 Unclip the plastic cover (where applicable) and undo the bolt securing the seat belt anchor to the vehicle body **(see illustration)**.

13 Refitting is a reversal of removal. Tighten the mounting bolt/nut to the specified torque.

Rear centre seat belts

14 To remove the centre seat belt inertia reel, the seat back cover must be partially removed. Remove the seat back as described in Section 23.

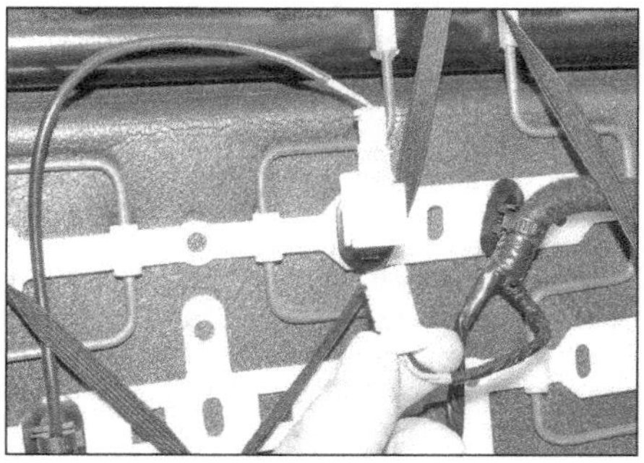

24.8a Disconnect the wiring connector ...

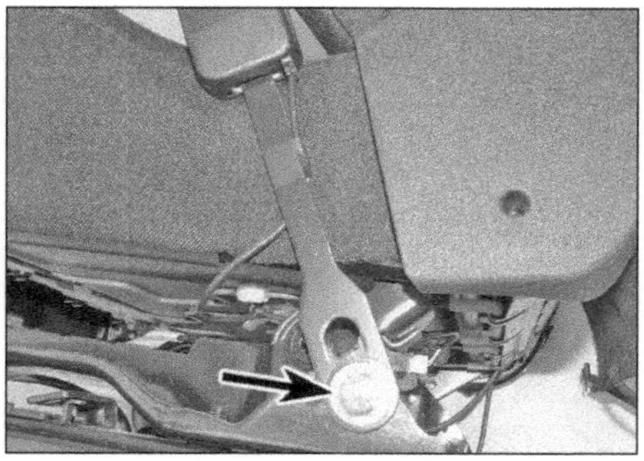

24.8b ... and undo the seat belt stalk retaining bolt (arrowed)

24.11a Remove the insulated cover ...

24.11b ... and undo the seat belt reel mounting nut (arrowed) – 3-door models

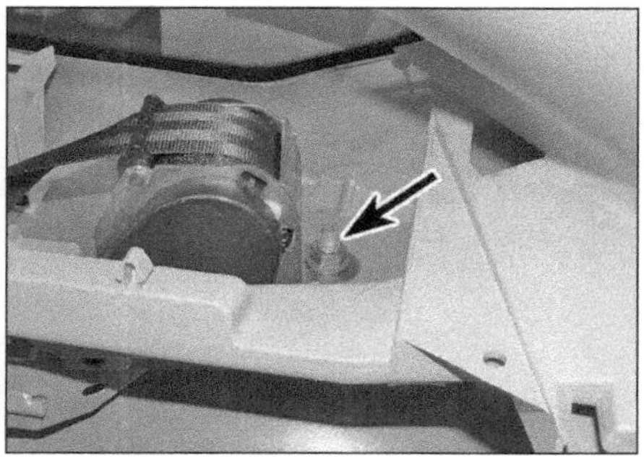

24.11c Seat belt reel mounting nut (arrowed) – 5-door models

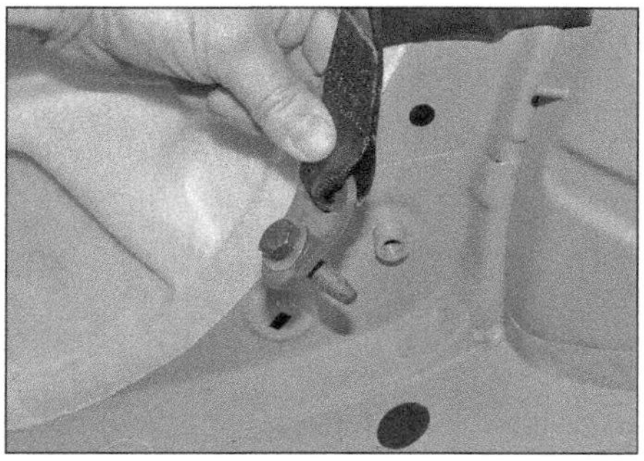

24.12 Undo the seat belt lower anchor bolt

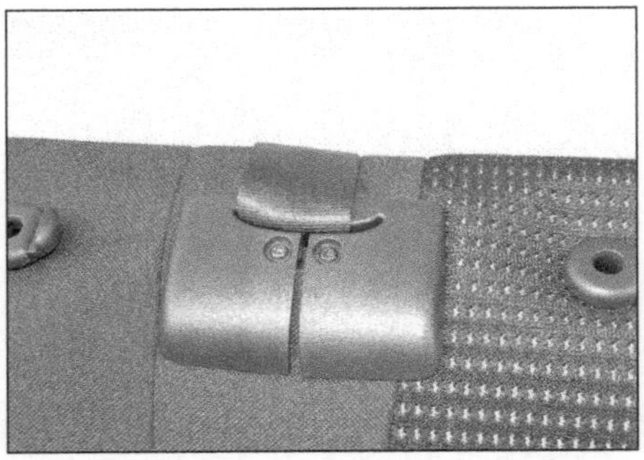

24.15a Undo the two retaining screws ...

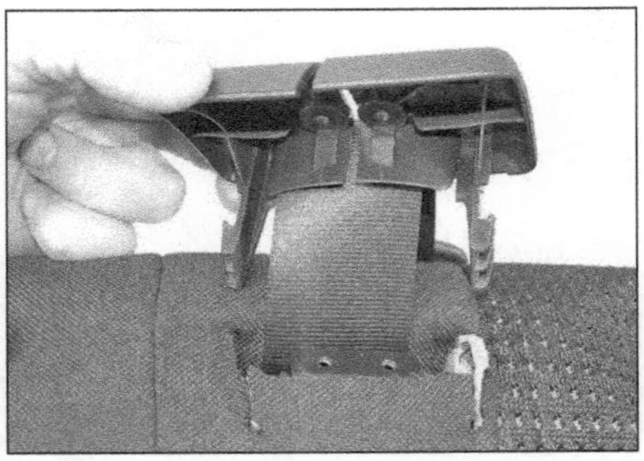

24.15b ... and unclip the plastic trim from the top of the seat

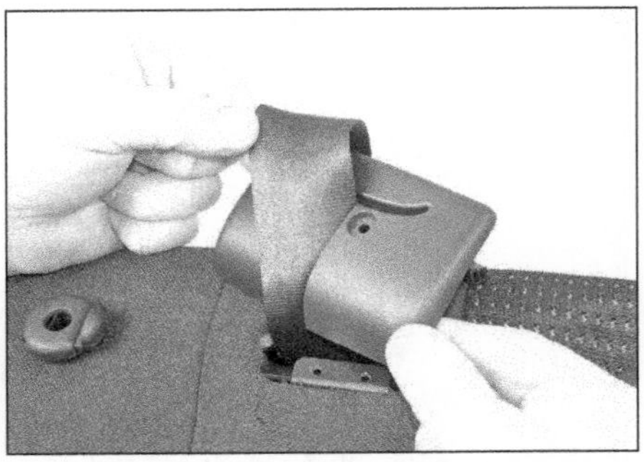

24.15c Unclip the seat belt from the plastic trim

15 Undo the two retaining screws and unclip the plastic trim panel from around the seat belt in the top of the seat back **(see illustrations)**.

16 Unclip the lower and side edges of the seat cover from the seat frame **(see illustrations)**.

17 Pull back the seat cover and foam cushion, then undo the nut securing bolts and manoeuvre the seat catch from the seat frame **(see illustration)**.

18 If required, with the headrests removed from the seat, release the retaining clips and withdraw the headrest guides from the top of the seat back **(see illustrations)**

19 Refitting is a reversal of removal. Tighten the mounting bolt/nut to the specified torque.

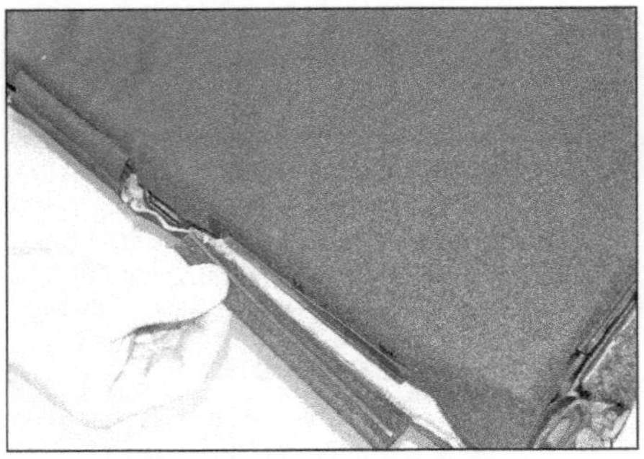

24.16a Unclip the lower ...

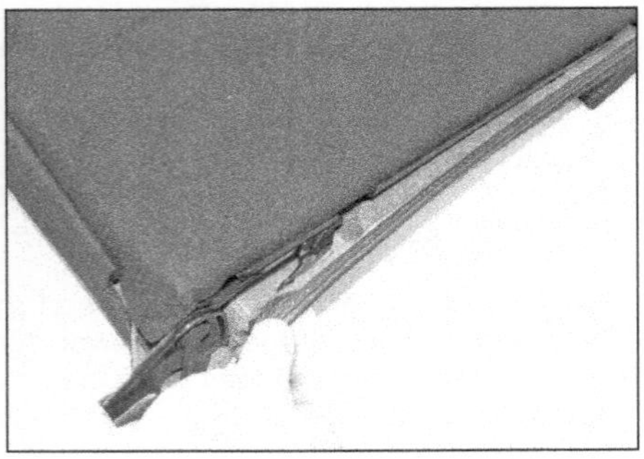

24.16b ... and side edges of the seat back cover ...

Rear seat belt catch/stalk

20 Lift up the rear of the seat cushion and fold it forwards. Disconnect the wiring connector, and then undo the bolt securing the seat belt stalk to the vehicle body **(see illustrations)**.

21 Refitting is a reversal of removal. Tighten the mounting bolt/nut to the specified torque.

25 Interior trim – removal and refitting

Door inner trim

1 Refer to Section 12.

A-pillar trim

2 Prise the weather seal from the front door aperture in the vicinity of the pillar trim.

3 Pull the trim away from the pillar starting at the top, then work down the trim panel and release it from behind the facia panel. Note that when removing the trim panel, the wiring loom may travel up the pillar and can make it awkward to disengage the bottom of the A-pillar trim panel from the facia, take care not to damage the wiring loom.

4 Refitting is a reversal of removal, but ensure that all retaining clips are fully engaged, and that the weatherstrip is fully seated.

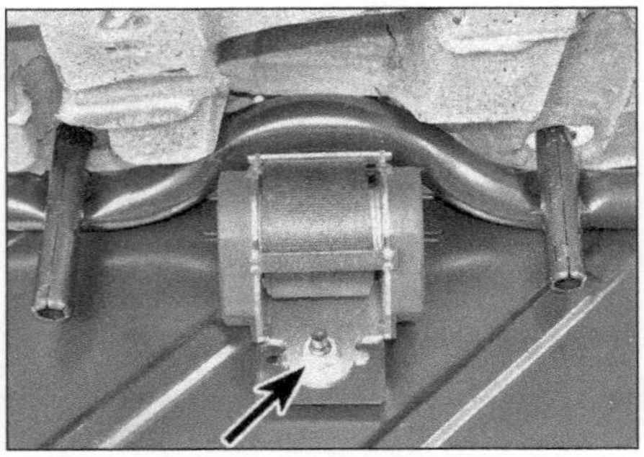

24.17 ... to expose the seat belt reel securing nut (arrowed)

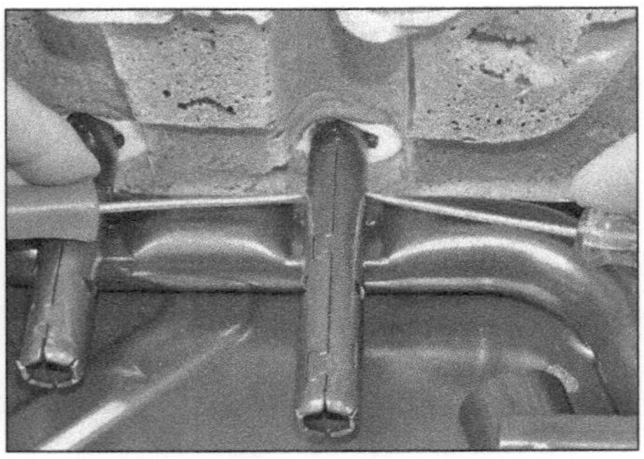

24.18a Release the securing clips ...

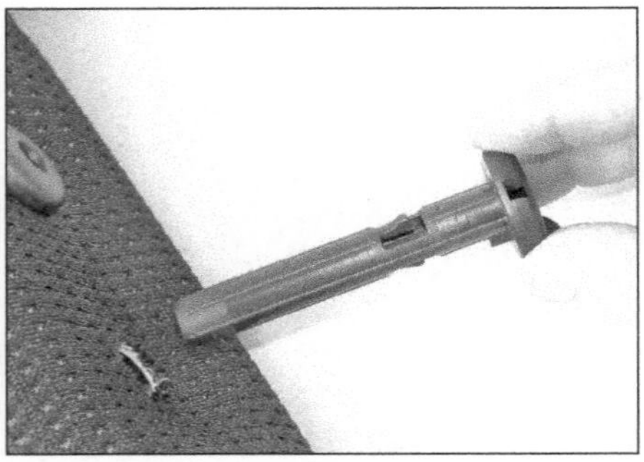

24.18b ... and withdraw the headrest guides from the top of the seat

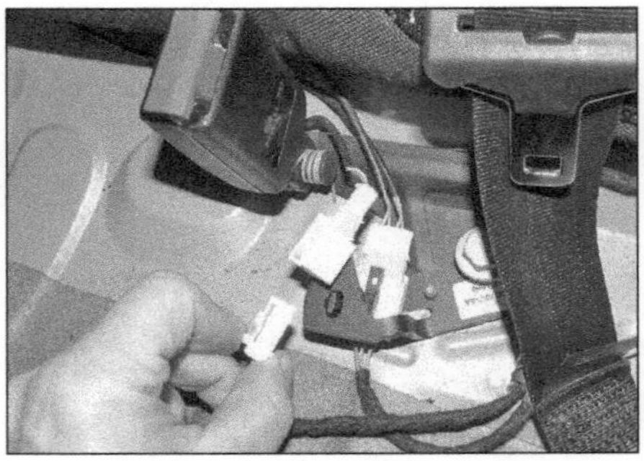

24.20a Disconnect the wiring connector ...

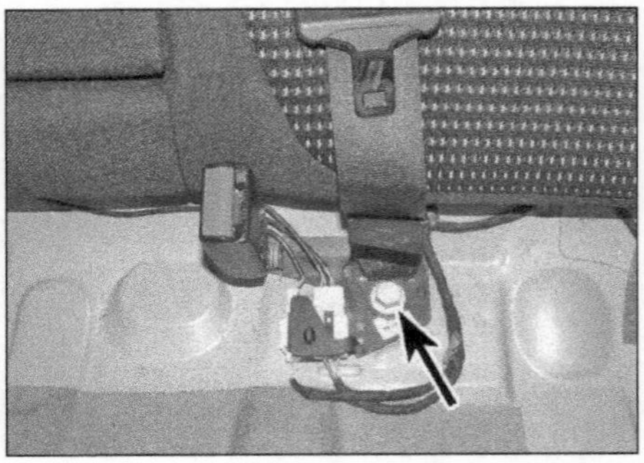

24.20b ... and undo the seat belt stalk retaining bolt (arrowed)

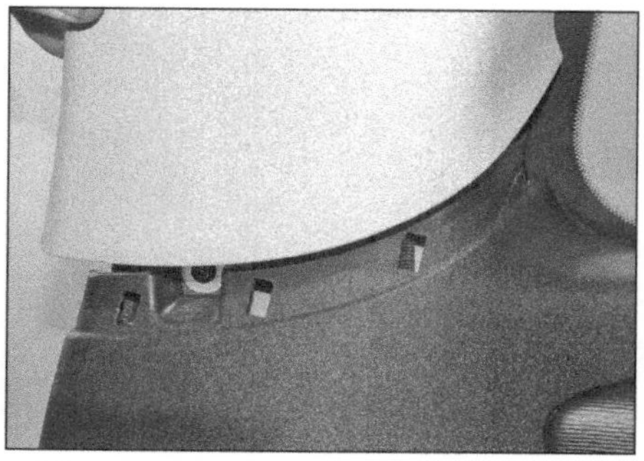

25.5a Unclip the lower part of the pillar trim panel

Upper B-pillar trim

Coupe

5 Unclip the lower part of the upper trim panel from the top of the lower panel, then withdraw it downwards from the headlining **(see illustrations)**.

6 To remove the upper panel completely, the lower B-pillar trim panel will need to be removed (see following procedures) to access the seat belt lower anchor bolt.

7 Undo the seat belt lower anchor bolt, and then withdraw the seat belt through the panel **(see illustration)**.

8 Refitting is a reversal of removal, but ensure that all retaining clips are fully engaged.

Hatchback

9 Remove the B-pillar lower trim panel, as described in the following procedures.

10 Undo the retaining screw from the lower part of the upper trim panel.

11 Unclip the lower part of the upper trim panel from the pillar, then withdraw it downwards from the headlining.

12 Undo the seat belt lower anchor bolt, and then withdraw the seat belt through the panel to completely remove the panel from the vehicle.

13 Refitting is a reversal of removal, but ensure that all retaining clips are fully engaged.

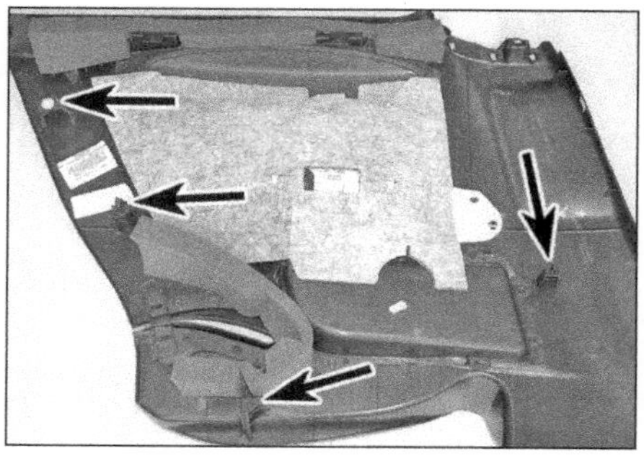

25.17a Rear side trim panel retaining clips (arrowed)

25.5b Unclip the upper part of the pillar trim panel

Lower B-pillar trim

Coupe

14 Remove the upper pillar trim as previously described.

15 Undo the retaining screw from the top of the trim panel **(see illustration)**.

16 Carefully pull the sill trim upwards to release its retaining clips and release the rear edge from its retaining clips **(see illustration)**.

17 Pull the lower end of the trim from its retaining clips, then working your way around the trim panel release it from the locating clips. Disengage the seat belt as the trim panel is removed **(see illustrations)**.

18 Refitting is a reversal of removal, but ensure that all retaining clips are fully engaged.

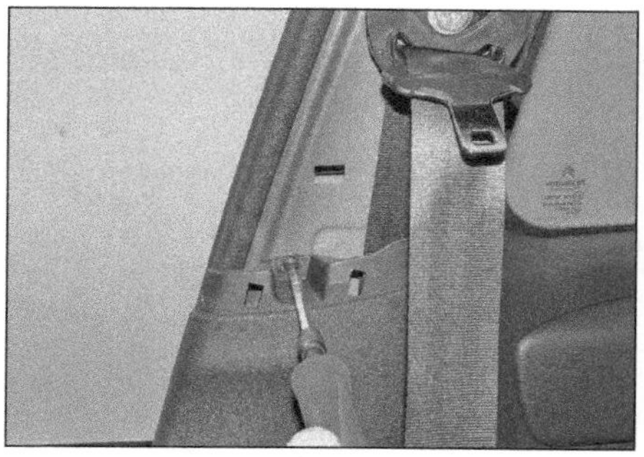

25.15 Undo the lower panel retaining screw

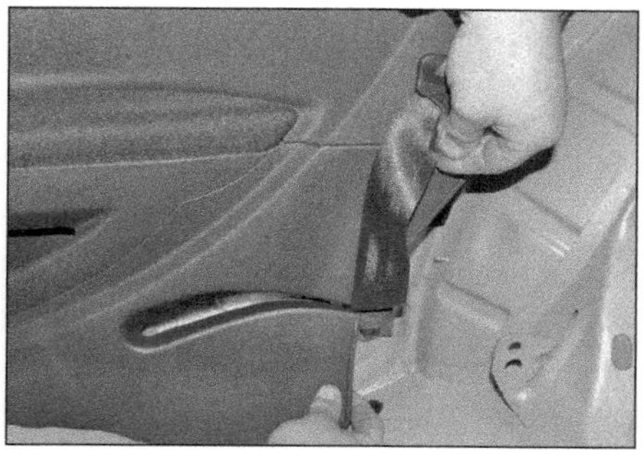

25.17b Pass the seat belt through the trim on removal

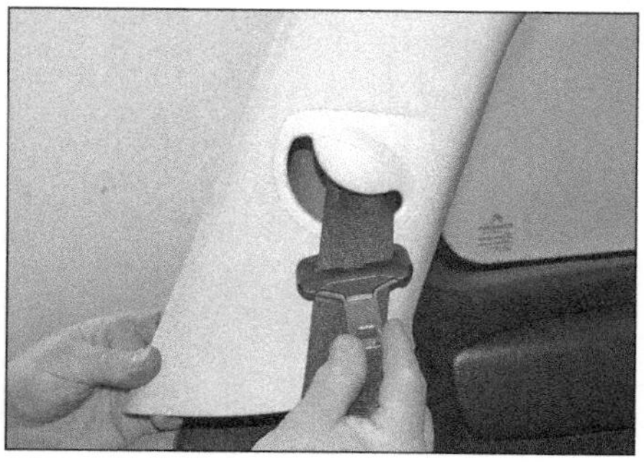

25.7 Pass the seat belt through the trim on removal

Hatchback

19 Carefully pull the front and rear sill trims upwards to release their retaining clips from the lower part of the B-pillar trim panel **(see illustration)**.

20 Pull away the rubber weatherstrip from each side of the B-pillar.

21 Carefully pull the trim from its retaining clips, and release it from the B-pillar.

22 Refitting is a reversal of removal, but ensure that all retaining clips are fully engaged.

Upper C-pillar trim

Coupe

23 Pull away the rubber weatherstrip from the tailgate and door aperture adjacent to the C-pillar trim.

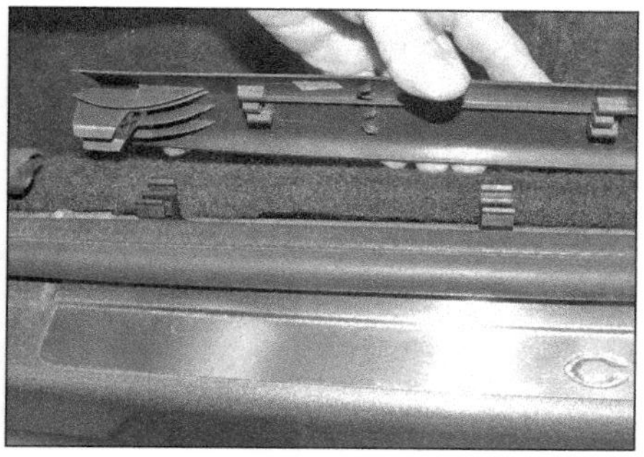

25.16 Unclip the rear sill trim

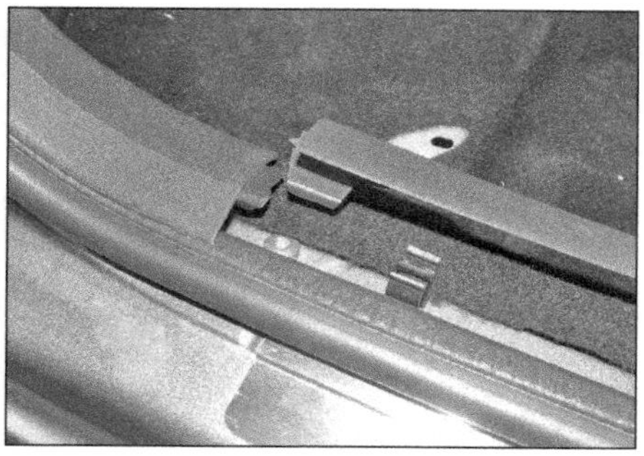

25.19 Unclip the front sill trim

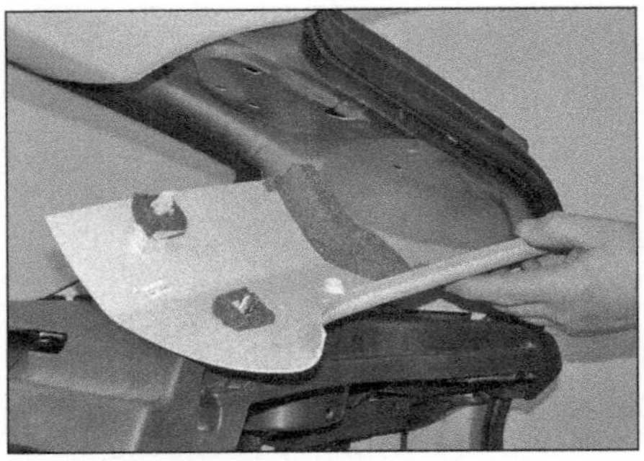
25.24 Unclip the upper trim from the rear pillar

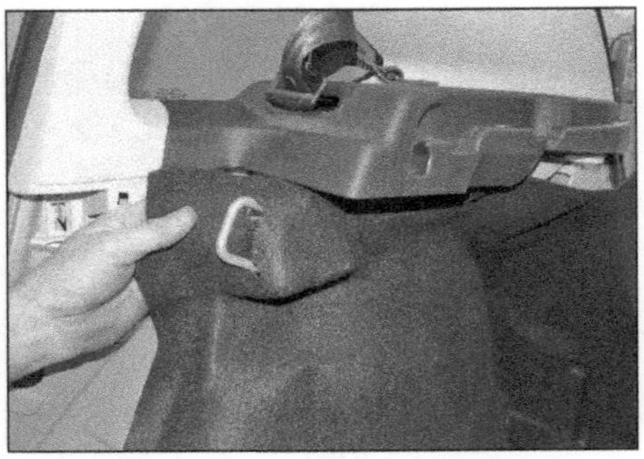
25.27 Unclip the rear side carpet from the around the seat catch

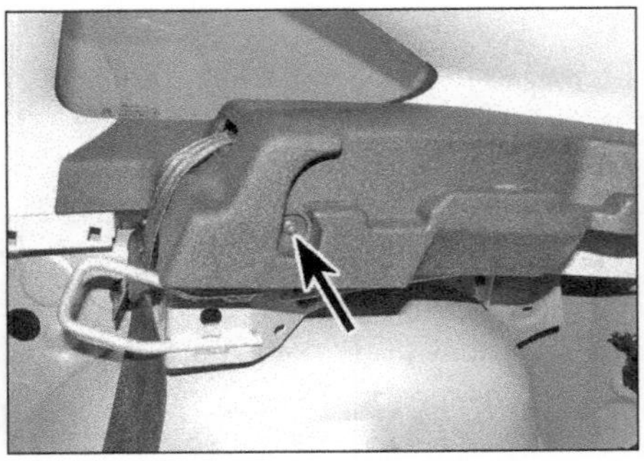
25.28a Undo the retaining screw (arrowed) ...

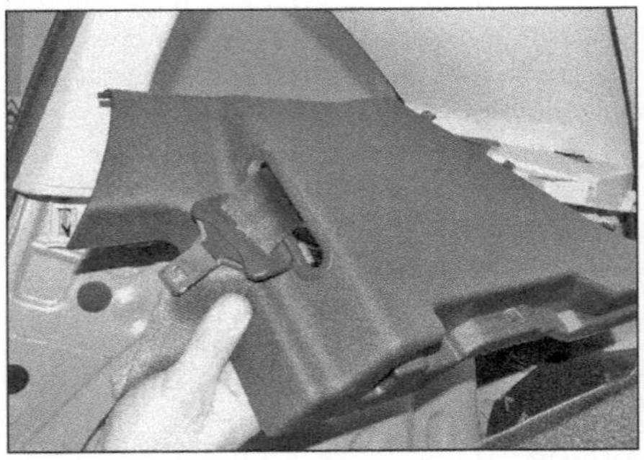
25.28b ... remove the upper shelf trim panel

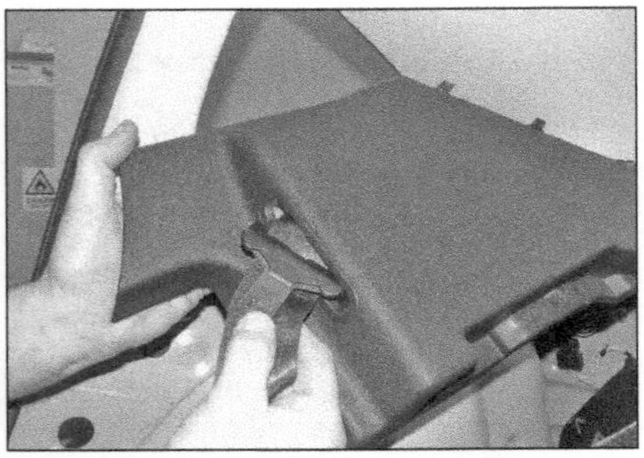
25.29 Pass the seat belt through the trim on removal

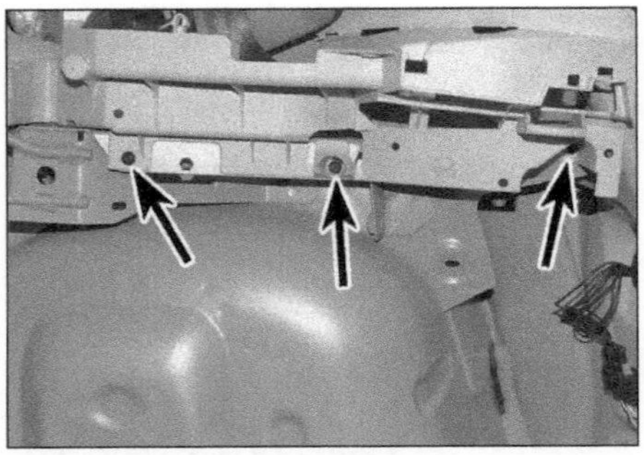
25.30a Undo the side shelf lower retaining screws (arrowed) ...

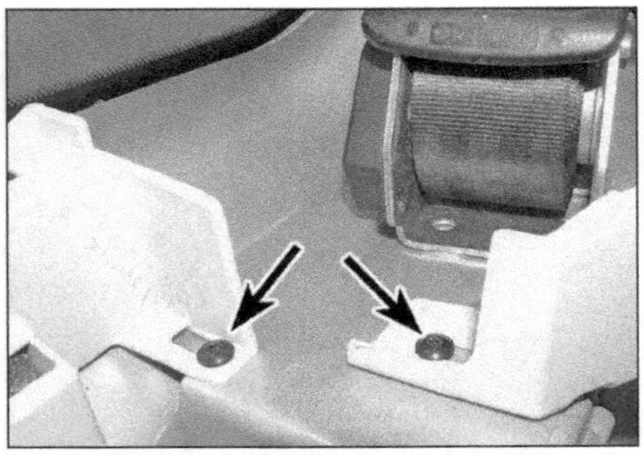
25.30b ... upper retaining screws (arrowed) ...

24 Carefully pull the pillar trim from the vehicle body to release its retaining clips **(see illustration)**.

25 Refitting is a reversal of removal, but ensure that all retaining clips are fully engaged.

Hatchback

26 Remove the C-pillar lower trim panel, as described in the following procedures.

27 Unclip the luggage compartment side carpet from around the seat catch bracket **(see illustration).**

28 Undo the retaining screw and unclip the parcel shelf support panel from the pillar upper trim **(see illustrations)**.

29 To remove the shelf panel completely, undo the seat belt lower anchor bolt, and then withdraw the seat belt through the panel **(see illustration)**.

30 Undo the retaining screws and carefully pull the upper pillar trim from the vehicle body to release its retaining clips **(see illustrations)**.

31 Refitting is a reversal of removal, but ensure that all retaining clips are fully engaged.

Lower C-pillar trim

Hatchback

32 Lift the seat cushion and fold it forward, then release the seat catch and tilt the seat back forwards to access the trim panel.

33 Carefully pull the front of the trim panel upwards to release its retaining clips from the lower part of the B-pillar trim panel **(see illustration).**

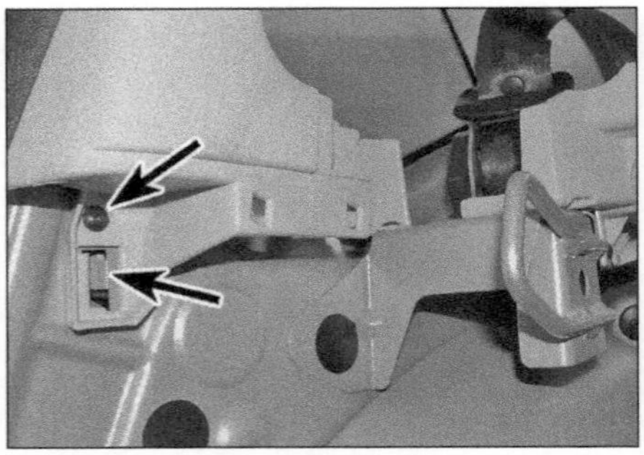
25.30c ... and front retaining screw and securing clip (arrowed)

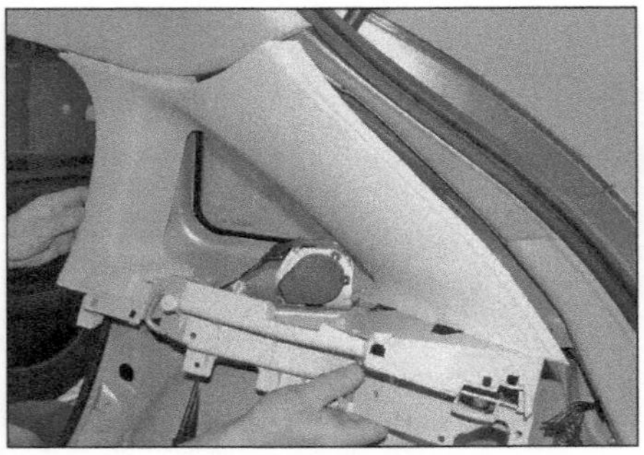
25.30d Unclip the upper trim from the rear pillars

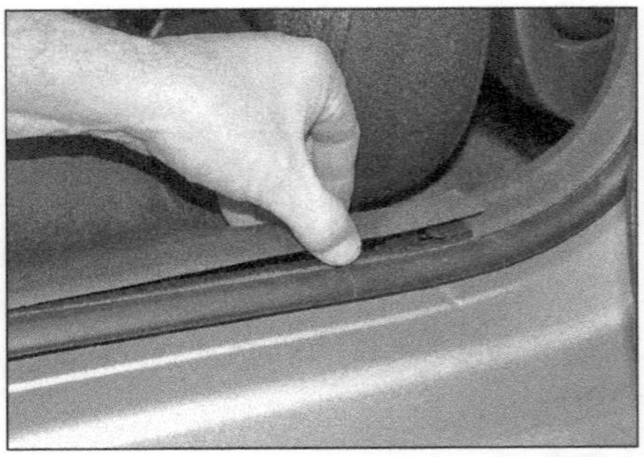
25.33 Unclip the front of the rear sill trim

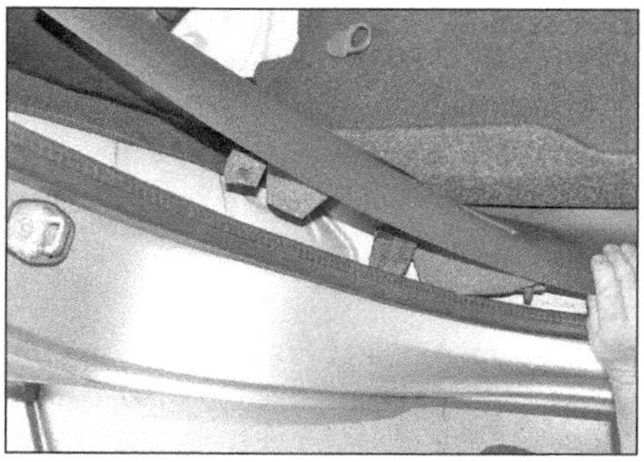

25.34a Unclip the trim panel from the C-pillar ...

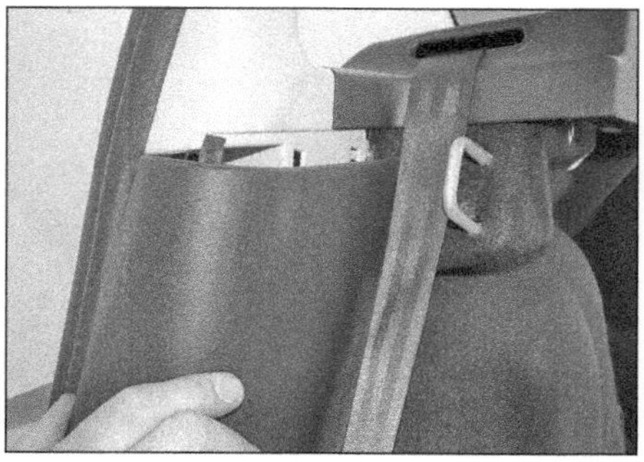

25.34b ... unclipping it from the upper trim panel

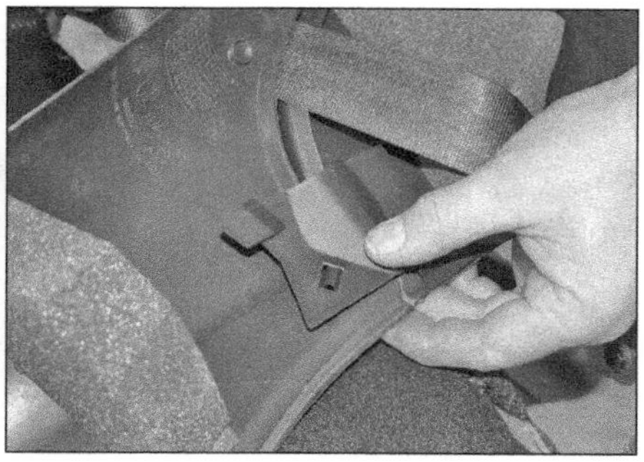

25.34c Release the trim retaining clip ...

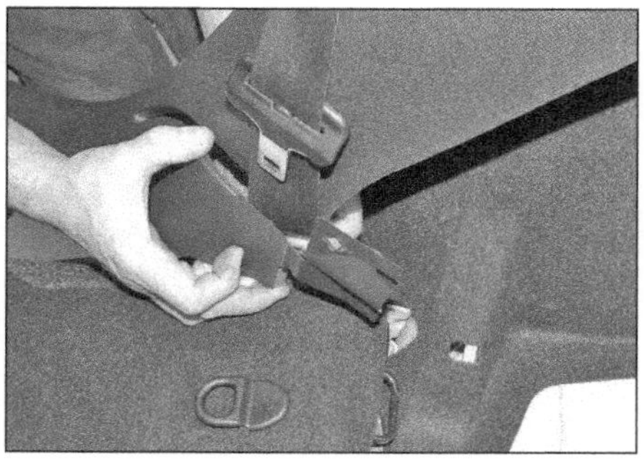

25.34d ... pass the seat belt through the trim on removal

25.38 Unclip the rear side carpet from the around the seat catch

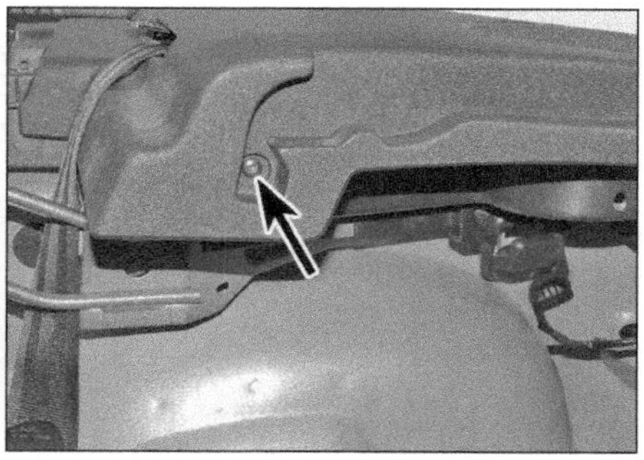

25.39a Undo the retaining screw (arrowed) ...

34 Working your way along the length of the trim panel release it from the locating clips, and then disengage the top of the lower trim from the upper trim. Disengage the seat belt as the trim panel is removed **(see illustrations)**.

35 Refitting is a reversal of removal, but ensure that all retaining clips are fully engaged.

Parcel shelf support panel

Coupe

36 Remove the B-pillar lower trim panel, as described previously in this Section.

37 Remove the C-pillar upper trim panel, as described previously in this Section.

38 Unclip the luggage compartment side carpet from around the seat catch bracket **(see illustration)**.

39 Undo the retaining screw, release the retaining clip and remove the parcel shelf support panel from the rear panel **(see illustrations)**.

40 To remove the shelf panel completely, undo the seat belt lower anchor bolt, and then withdraw the seat belt through the panel **(see illustration)**.

25.39b ... release the retaining clip ...

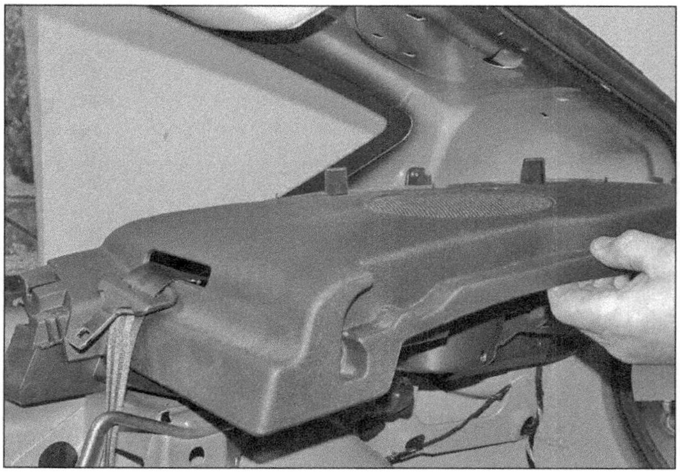

25.39c ... and remove the upper shelf trim panel

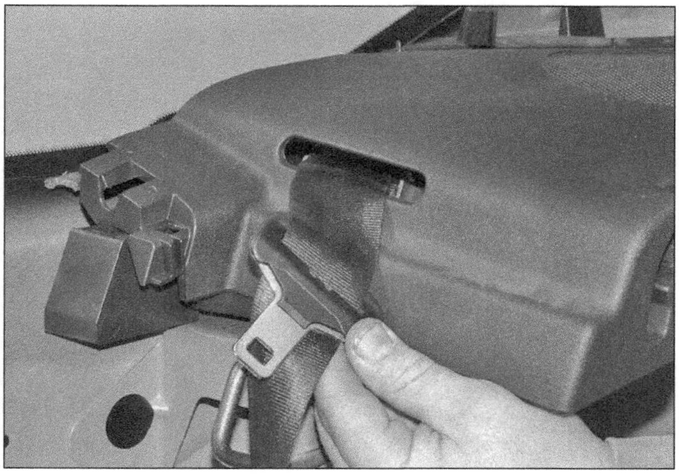

25.40 Pass the seat belt through the trim on removal

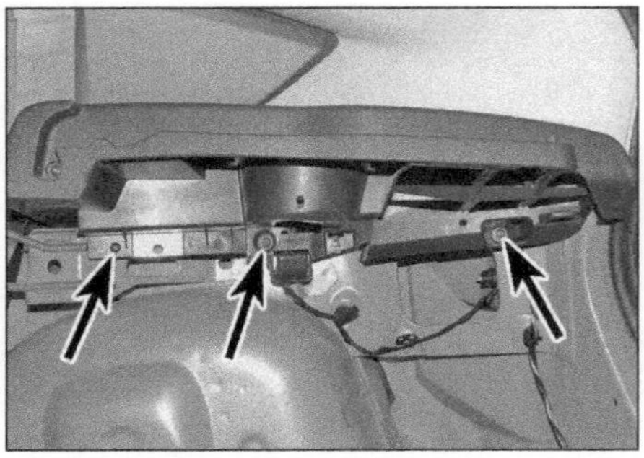

25.41a Undo the side shelf lower retaining screws (arrowed) ...

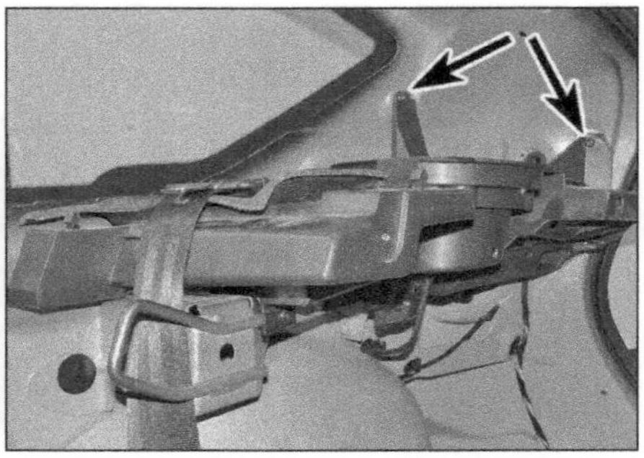

25.41b ... and upper retaining screws (arrowed)

41 Remove the shelf panel speaker housing, undo the retaining screws and withdraw the speaker housing from the rear panel, disconnect the wiring connector from the speaker as it is removed **(see illustrations)**.

42 Refitting is a reversal of removal, but ensure that all retaining clips are fully engaged.

Hatchback

43 See upper C-pillar trim removal, as described in paragraphs 29 and 30. The parcel shelf support panel needs to be removed to access the upper C-pillar trim.

Luggage area lower side trim

44 Lift the rear seat cushions and fold them forward, then release the rear seat catches and tilt the seat backs forward to access the lower side trim panels.

45 Remove the luggage compartment floor panel/carpet, withdraw the plastic compartment panels and then release the securing clips **(see illustrations)**.

46 Drill out the rivet securing the luggage eye to the floor panel, unclip the front edge of the carpet from around the seat catch bracket and remove the carpet side trim panels from the luggage compartment **(see illustrations)**.

47 Refitting is a reversal of removal, using a new rivet to secure the luggage eye to the floor panel **(see illustration)**.

Tailgate trims

Coupe

48 Open the tailgate and unhook the parcel shelf straps from the tailgate.

49 Undo the two screws in the handle recesses in the lower panel, one at each side of the tailgate **(see illustration)**.

50 Carefully pull the lower panel away from

25.45a Slide the plastic compartment out from the side carpet

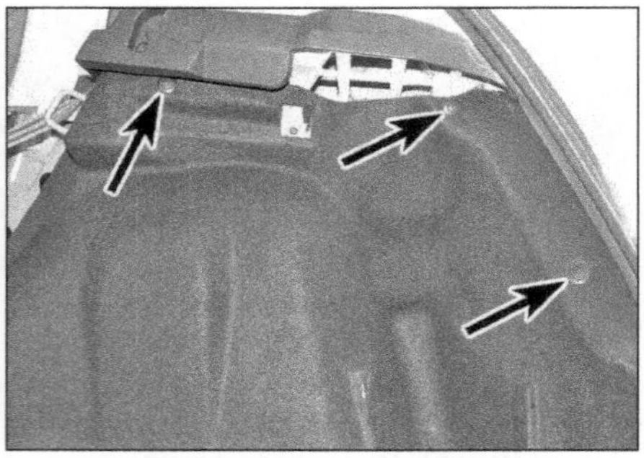

25.45b Release the securing clips (arrowed) – 5-door models

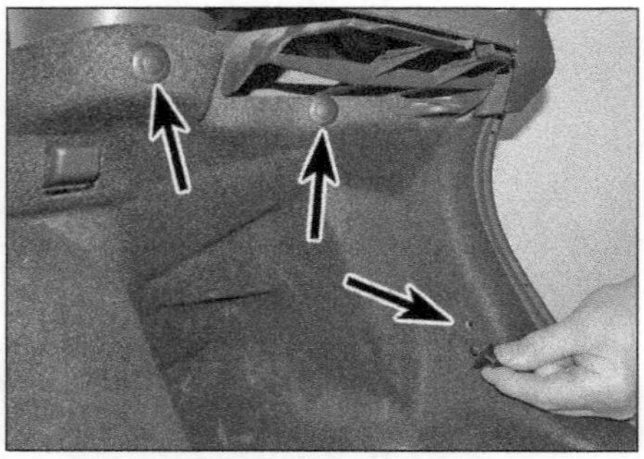

25.45c Release the securing clips (arrowed) – 3-door models

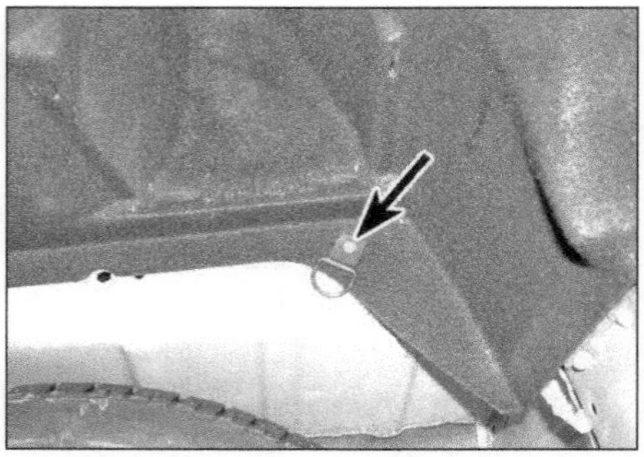

25.46a Drill out the luggage eye securing rivet (arrowed)

25.46b Unclip the rear side carpet from around the seat catch ...

25.46c ... and remove the side carpet from the luggage compartment

25.47 Fit a new rivet to the luggage securing eye

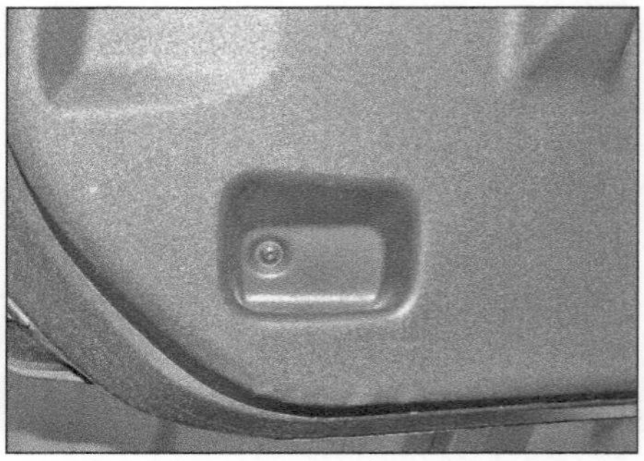

25.49 Undo the retaining screws in the handle recess

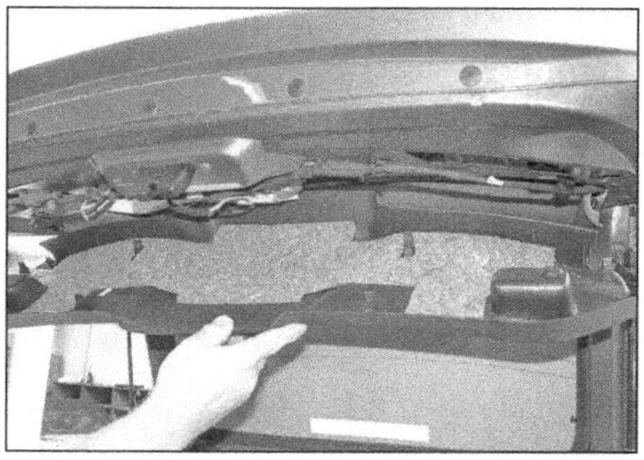

25.50 Unclip the lower trim panel from the tailgate

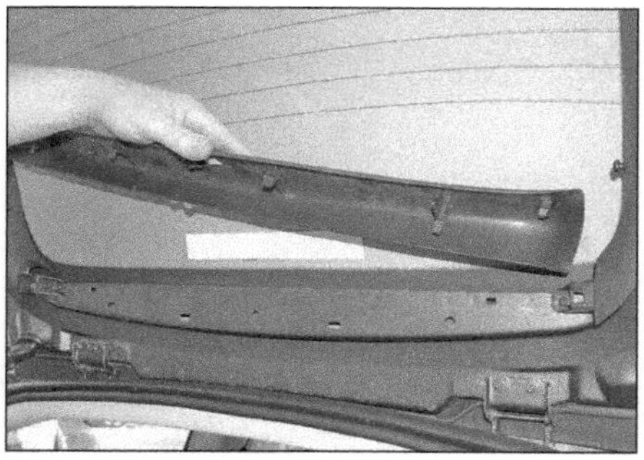

25.51 Carefully lever the upper trim panel from the tailgate

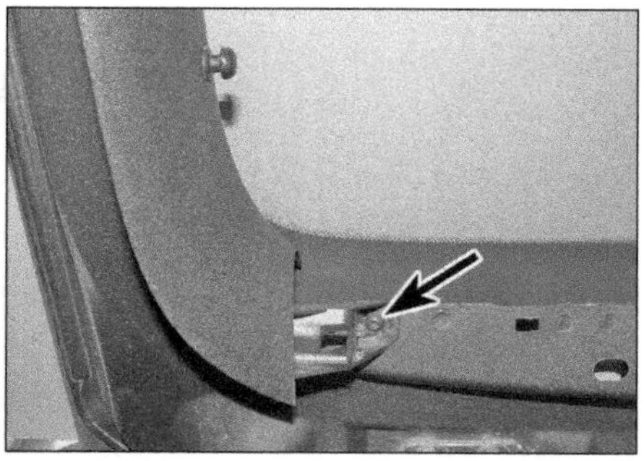

25.52a Undo the side trim retaining screw (arrowed) ...

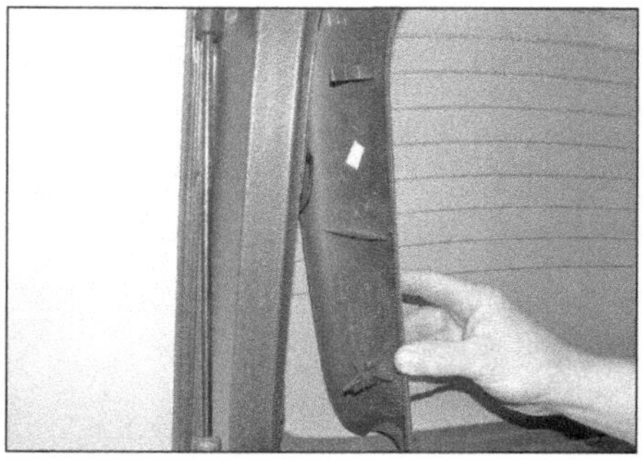

25.52b ... and unclip It from the tailgate

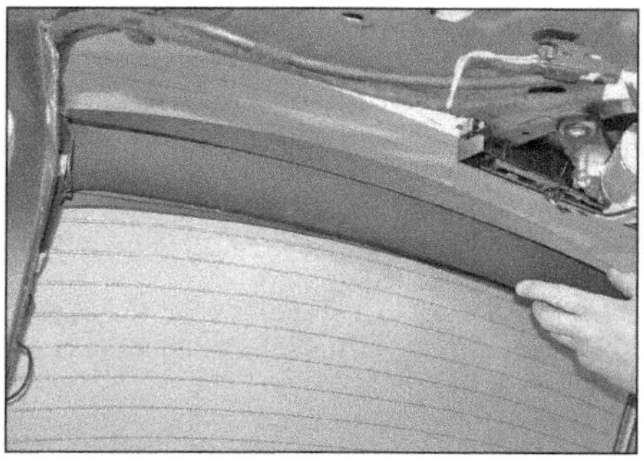

25.53 Carefully lever the centre trim panel from the tailgate

25.56a Unclip the trim panels ...

the tailgate, releasing the retaining clips **(see illustration)**.

51 Carefully lever the panel away from the tailgate at the top edge to release the retaining clips, then remove the panel from the tailgate **(see illustration)**.

52 Undo the two screws (one for each trim) and unclip the panels from each side of the rear screen **(see illustrations)**.

53 Carefully pull the centre trim from between the two rear screens, releasing the retaining clips to remove **(see illustration)**.

54 Refitting is a reversal of removal, but ensure that all retaining clips are fully engaged.

Hatchback

55 Open the tailgate and unhook the parcel shelf straps from the tailgate.

56 Carefully unclip the trim panels from each side of the rear screen **(see illustrations)**.

57 Undo the two screws (one at each end of the trim) and unclip the upper trim panel from the top of the tailgate **(see illustrations)**.

58 Undo the two screws in the handle recesses in the lower panel, one at each side of the tailgate **(see illustration 25.49)**.

59 Carefully pull the lower panel away from the tailgate, releasing the retaining clips **(see illustration 25.50)**.

60 Refitting is a reversal of removal, but ensure that all retaining clips are fully engaged.

Headlining

Note: *Headlining removal requires considerable skill and experience if it is to be carried out without damage, and is therefore best entrusted to a Citroën dealer or bodywork specialist. A general overview of the procedure is given below for those with the expertise to attempt the operation on a DIY basis.*

61 The headlining is clipped and glued to the roof, and can be withdrawn only once all fittings such as the grab handles, courtesy lights, sunvisors, sunroof (if fitted), pillar trim panels, and associated additional panels have been removed. The door, tailgate and sunroof aperture weatherstrips will also have to be prised clear and any additional screws and clips removed. Once the headlining attachments are released, the adhesive bonding in the centre panels must be broken using a hot air gun and spatula, starting at the front and working rearwards.

62 When refitting, a coat of neoprene adhesive (available from Citroën dealers) must

25.56b ... from both sides of the tailgate

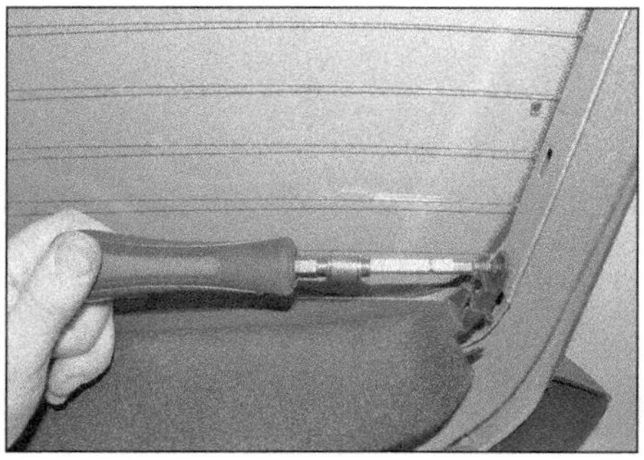

25.57a Undo the upper trim retaining screws (arrowed) ...

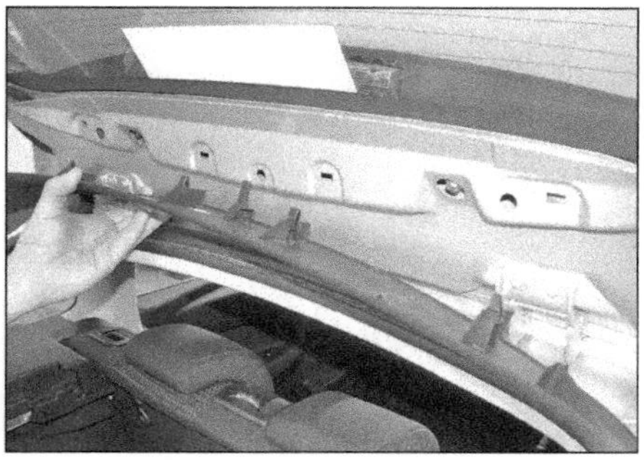

25.57b ... and remove the upper trim panel

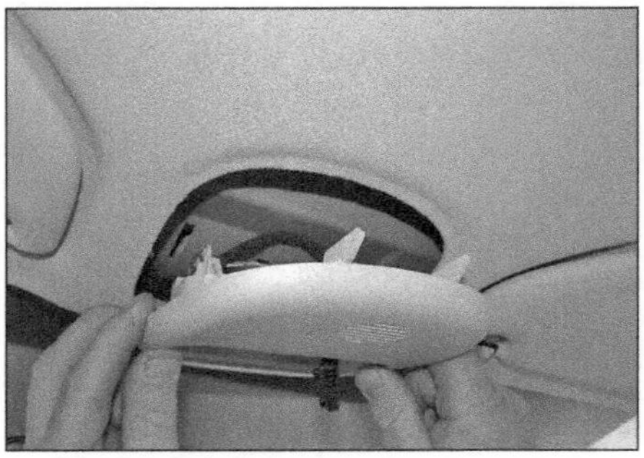

25.63 Pull down at the front of the console to unclip it from the headlining

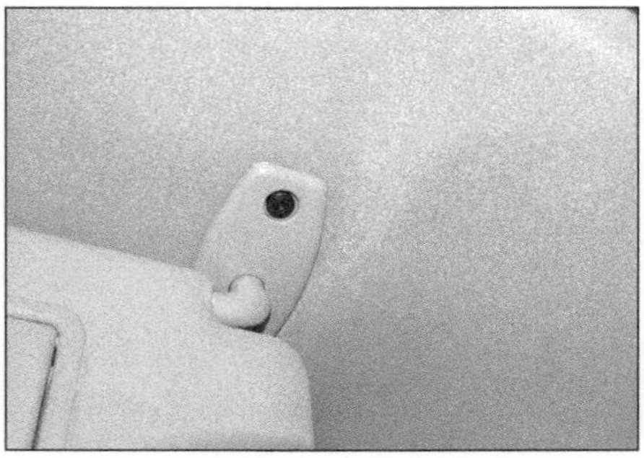

25.67 Undo the retaining screw and remove the sunvisor

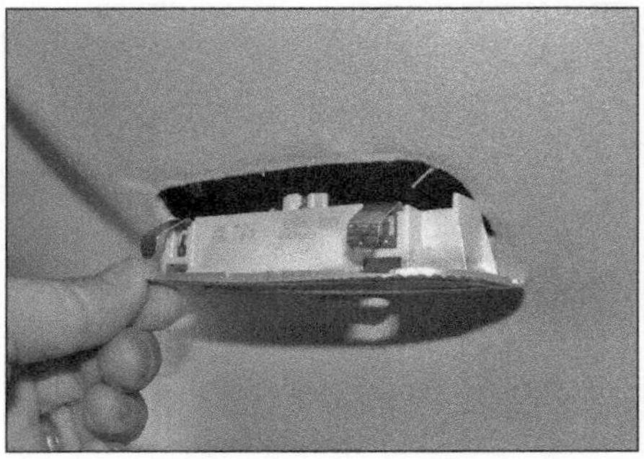

25.70 Unclip the light unit from the headlining

be applied to the centre panels in the locations noted during removal. Position the headlining carefully and refit all components disturbed during removal. Clean the headlining with soap and water or white spirit on completion.

Overhead console

63 Carefully pull down on the front of the console to release the retaining clips from the roof panel **(see illustration)**.

64 Disconnect the wiring plugs as the console is removed.

65 Refitting is a reversal of removal.

Sunvisor

66 The sunvisor is retained by a single screw. Prior to removing the sunvisor on models with lights fitted to the vanity mirror, remove the overhead console as described previously, and disconnect the wiring plugs.

67 Remove the sunvisor retaining screw and unclip the mounting from the headlining **(see illustration)**. Where applicable, identify the sunvisor vanity light wiring plug at the overhead console, and tie a length of string to it. Withdraw the sunvisor, pulling the string through the interior light aperture. When the string emerges at the sunvisor mount aperture, untie it from the wiring plug.

68 Tie the length of string to the visor wiring, and pull it through to the interior light aperture. Reconnect the wiring plug.

69 Refit the sunvisor mount to the headlining, and tighten the retaining screw securely.

70 If required the sunvisor retaining clip can be removed from the headlining. Undo the retaining screw and remove the clip from the headlining **(see illustration).**

Grab handle/ storage compartment

71 Pull the handle down and prise the plastic covers up at each end of the grab handle **(see illustration)**.

72 Undo the retaining screws and remove the handle **(see illustration)**.

73 Refitting is a reversal of removal.

26 Centre console – removal and refitting

Removal

1 Remove the audio unit from the facia, as described in Chapter 12, Section 17.

2 Carefully unclip the two trim panels from each side of the heater control panel and undo the retaining screws **(see illustrations)**.

3 On manual transmission models, unclip the gaiter and trim from the top of the console **(see illustrations)**. If required, pull the gaiter

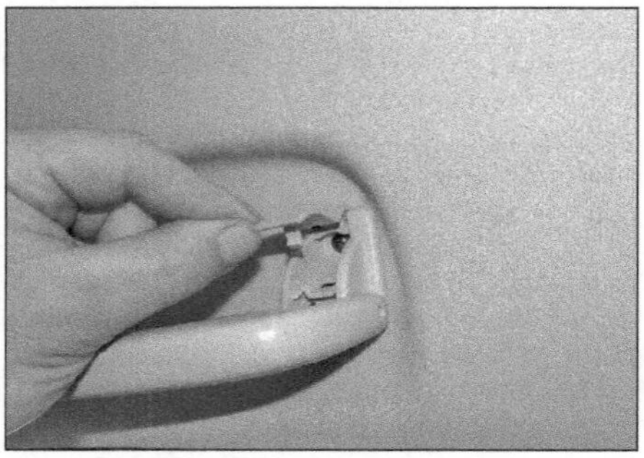

25.71 Unclip the plastic covers ...

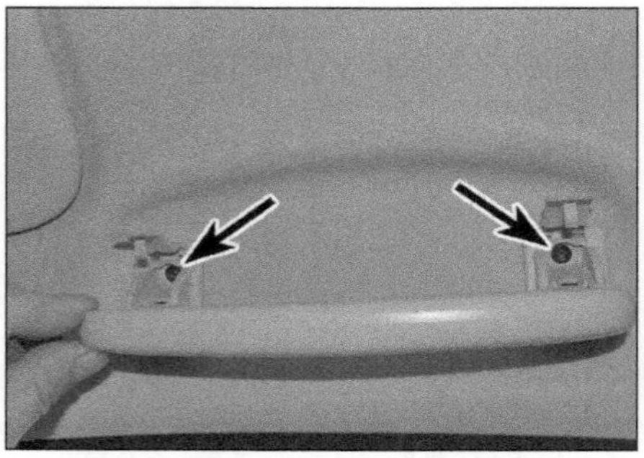

25.72 ... to access the grab handle retaining screws (arrowed)

26.2a Unclip the trim covers ...

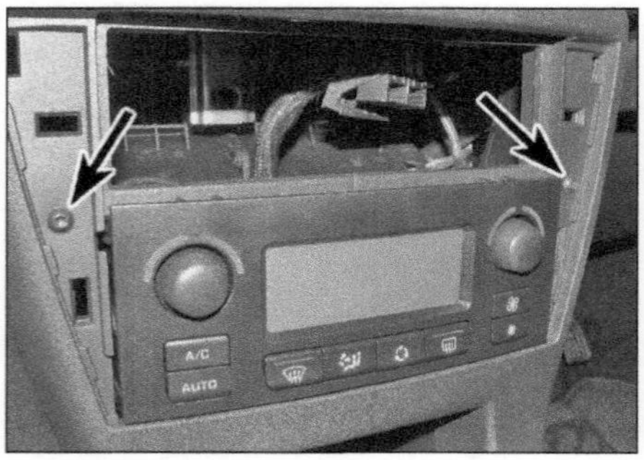

26.2b ... and remove the retaining screws (arrowed)

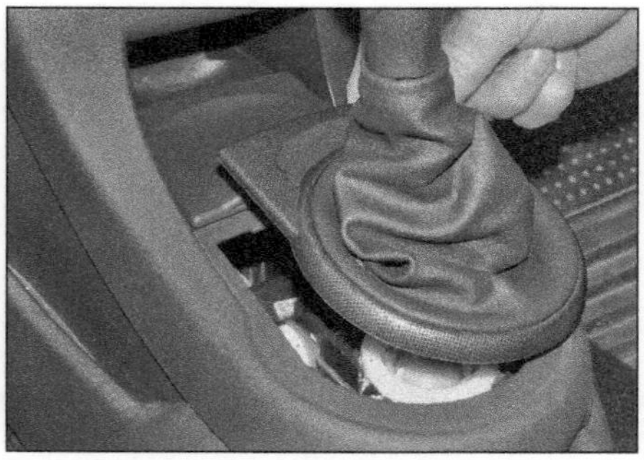

26.3a Unclip the trim from around the gear lever – manual models

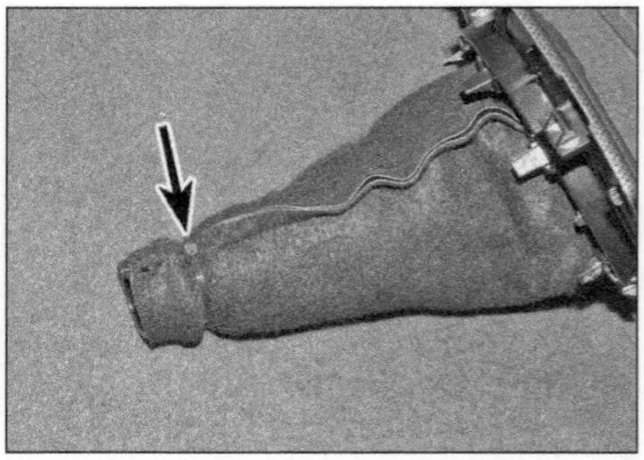

26.3b Release the cable-tie (arrowed) to remove the gear lever gaiter

26.4 Unclip the trim from around the gear lever – automatic models

26.5 Pull the gear knob upwards to remove it from the lever

26.6 Remove the ashtray

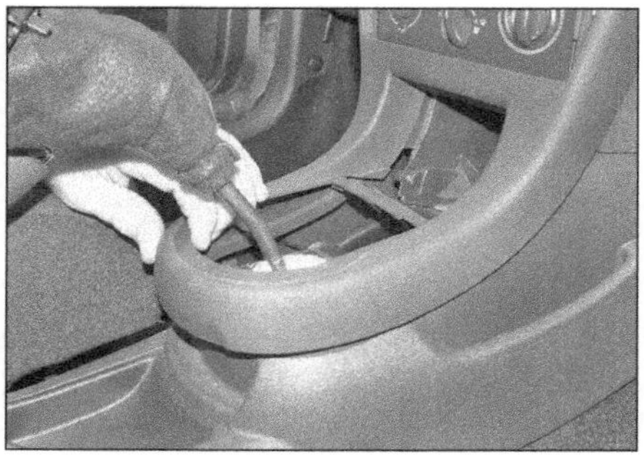

26.7a Unclip the lower part of the trim ...

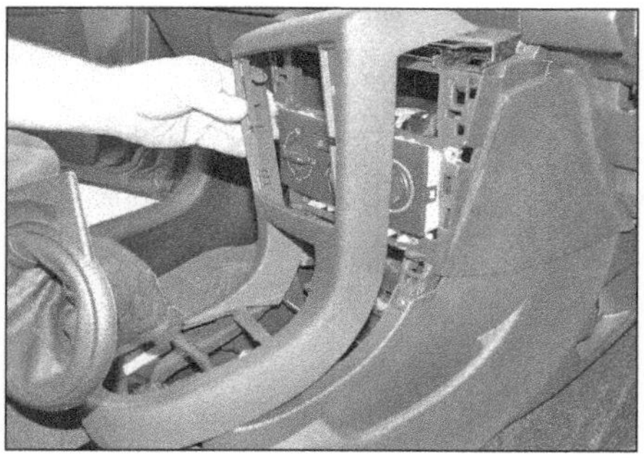

26.7b ... and then release the trim from the centre of the facia

26.8 Undo the retaining screws (arrowed) from the front of the centre console

upwards and release the securing clip to remove the gaiter from over the gear lever.

4 On automatic transmission models, unclip the selector gate outer trim from the top of the console **(see illustration)**.

5 If required, pull the gear knob from the top of the lever and unclip the trim panel/gaiter from the top of the gear lever **(see illustration)**. Note the gear knob is a very tight fit on the lever; take care of injuries when removing, as the plastic sleeve on the lever has sharp edges.

6 Unclip the ashtray from the front of the centre console **(see illustration)**.

7 Carefully unclip the lower part of the front trim panel and remove it from the front of the centre console and around the heater control panel **(see illustrations)**.

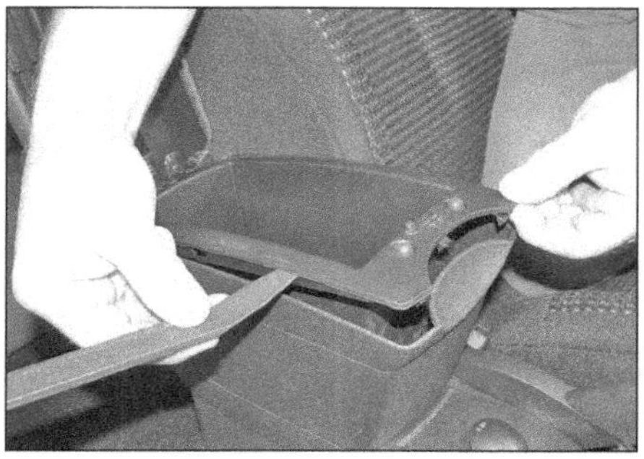

26.9a Unclip the storage tray from the armrest

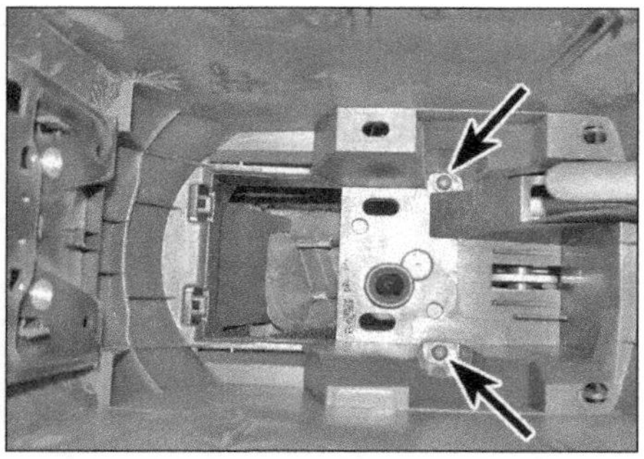

26.9b Undo the two retaining screws (arrowed)

8 Undo the two retaining screws from the front upper edge of the console **(see illustration)**.

9 On models with centre armrest, open the armrest and remove the storage compartment, and then undo the retaining screws **(see illustrations)**.

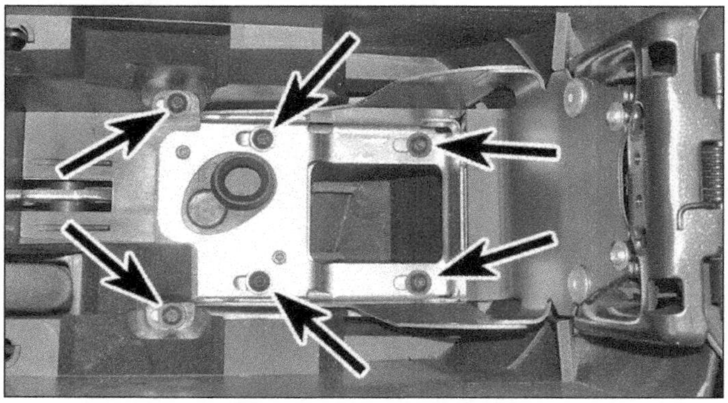

26.9c Undo the six retaining screws (arrowed) – models with strengthening plate

26.9d Pull up the armrest/storage tray from the rear of the console

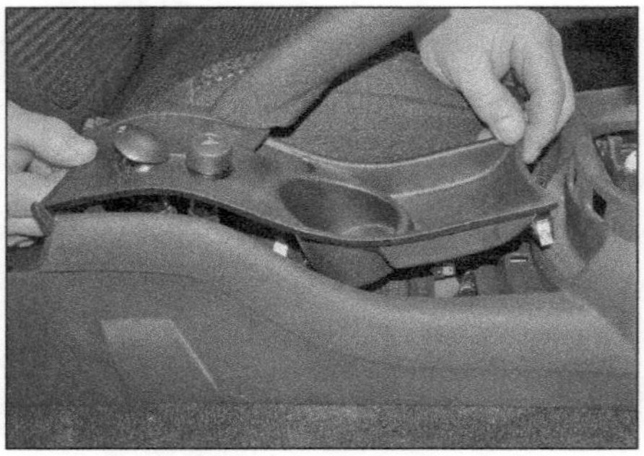

26.10a Unclip the upper trim panel from the centre console – model with armrest

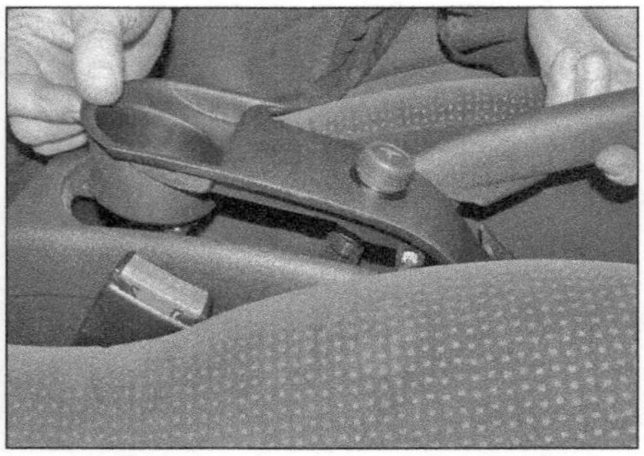

26.10b Unclip the upper trim panel from the centre console – model without armrest

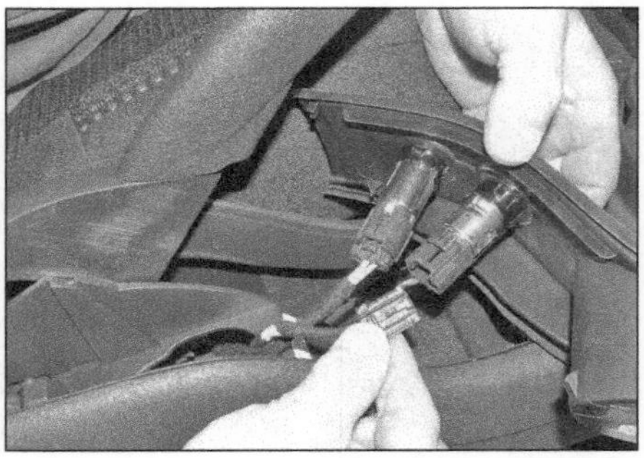

26.11 Disconnect the wiring connector(s) as the panel is removed

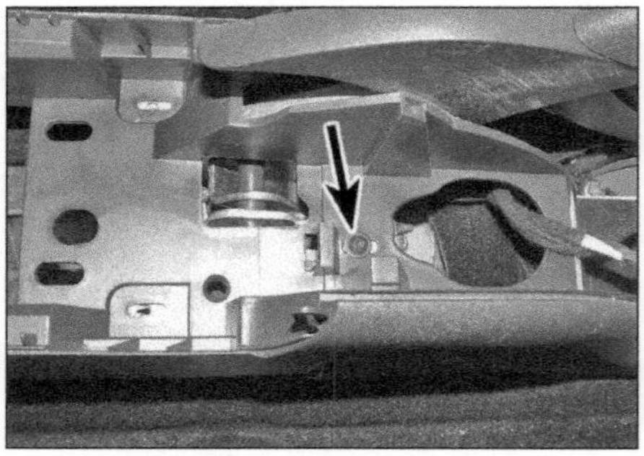

26.12a Undo the retaining screw (arrowed) – model with armrest

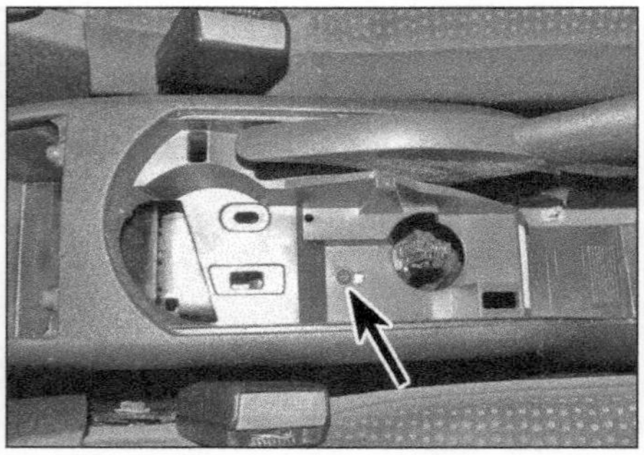

26.12b Undo the retaining screw (arrowed) – model without armrest

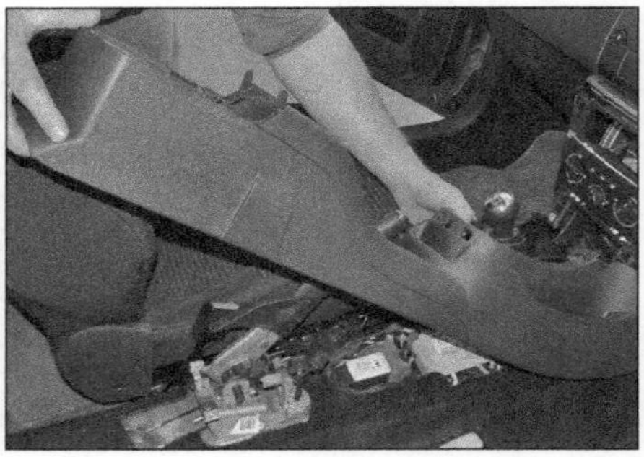

26.13 Remove the centre console from the vehicle

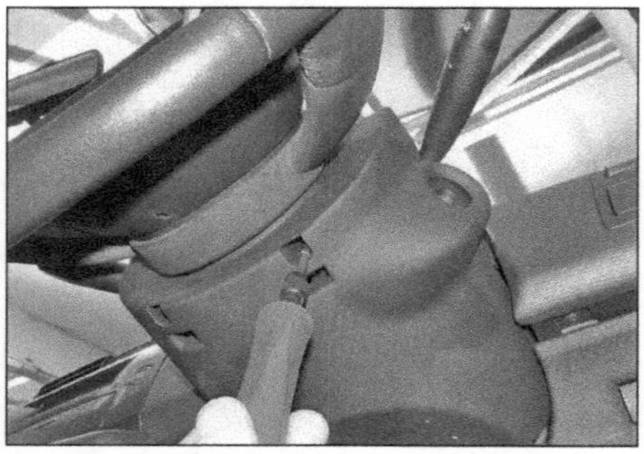

27.2 Undo the two retaining screws ...

10 Carefully release the upper trim cover from the top of the console, taking care not to break the securing clips **(see illustrations)**.

11 As the trim is removed, disconnect any wiring connectors **(see illustration)**.

12 Undo the retaining screw from the centre of the console **(see illustrations)**.

13 Lift up the rear of the console and withdraw it away from the facia, check for any wiring still connected to the console, and then lift it over the handbrake lever, and out of the passenger compartment **(see illustration)**.

Refitting

14 Refitting is a reversal of removal.

27 Facia panel components – removal and refitting

Steering column shrouds

1 Lower the steering column and pull it upwards to allow more room for removal of the shrouds.

2 Unscrew the two lower steering column shroud securing screws **(see illustration)**.

3 Unclip and lift off the upper shroud, disengaging it from the rubber trim attached to the facia **(see illustrations)**.

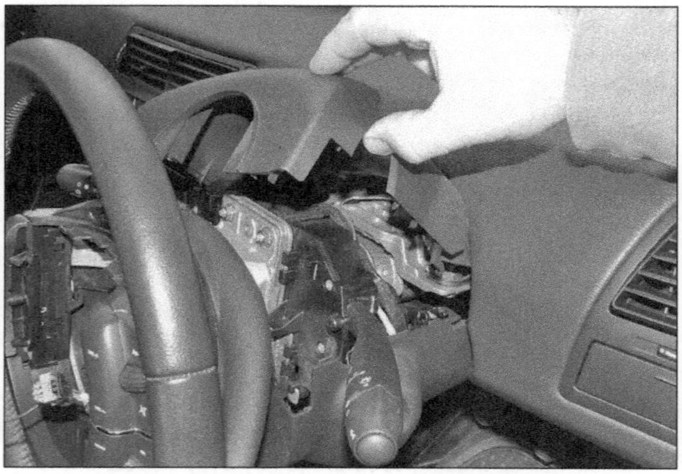

27.3a ... and remove the upper shroud ...

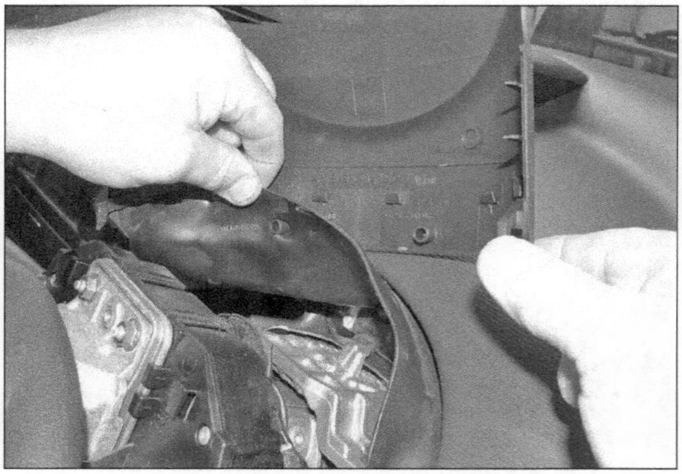

27.3b ... unclipping it from the rubber trim

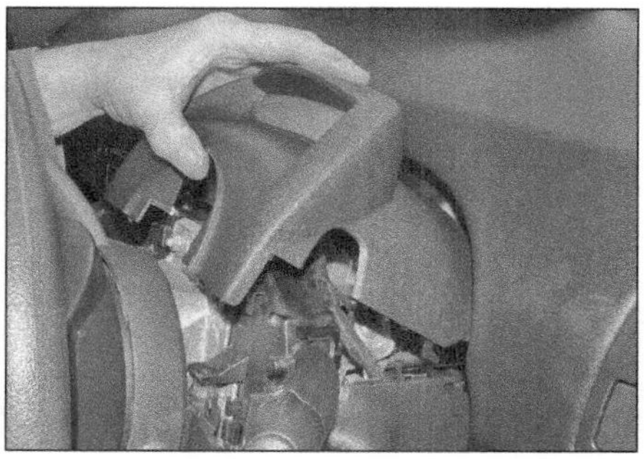
27.4a Unclip the upper shroud complete with digital rev. counter ...

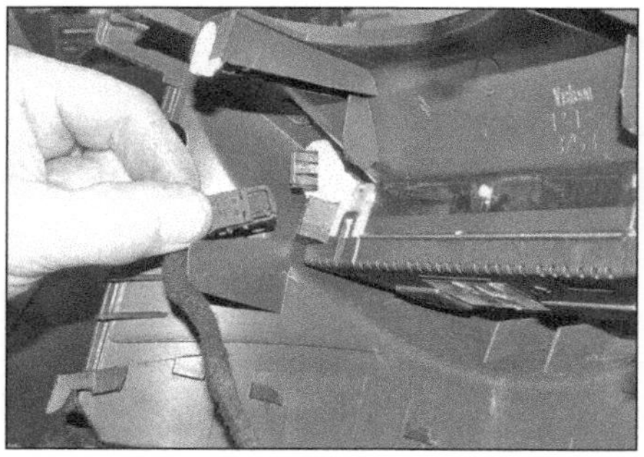
27.4b ... and disconnect the wiring connector

27.5 Remove the steering column lower shroud

27.7 Unclip and remove the lower trim panel

27.8a Undo the retaining screw ...

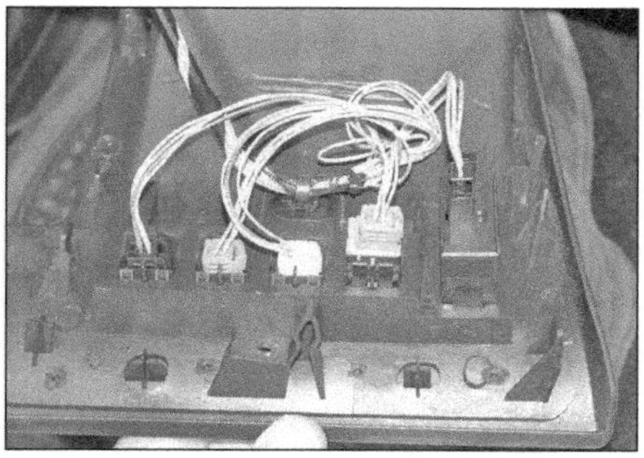
27.8b ... lower the switch panel ...

4 On early models (up to 2007), disconnect the wiring connector from the digital rev. counter built into the upper shroud **(see illustrations)**.

5 Unclip the lower shroud from under the steering column **(see illustration)**.

6 Refitting is a reversal of removal.

Lower facia panels

7 Carefully unclip the lower part of the facia panel on the driver's side below the steering column, pulling it free from its retaining clips **(see illustration)**.

8 The switch trim panel to the right of the steering column is secured by a screw. Undo the retaining screw and unclip the trim panel from the facia **(see illustrations)**. Disconnect the wiring connectors and retaining clip as it is removed.

9 The trim panels above the driver's pedals and passenger footwell are secured by expanding plastic rivets. Prise out the centre pins, and then lever the complete rivets from place **(see illustrations)**. Disconnect the wiring connector (where fitted) from the footwell light as the trim is removed. When refitting, ensure the front edge of the panel engages with the support bracket.

10 The trim panels at each side of the front footwells, in front of the centre console, are

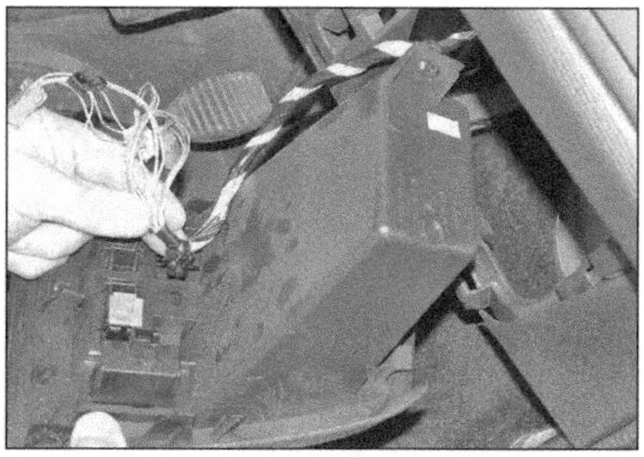
27.8c ... and disconnect the wiring

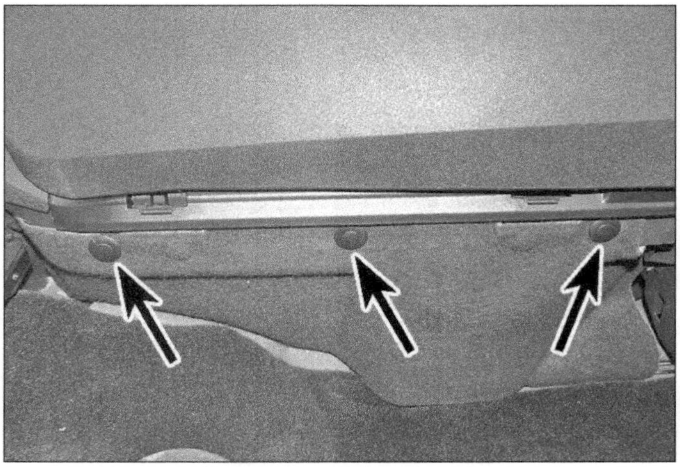
27.9a Release the plastic rivets ...

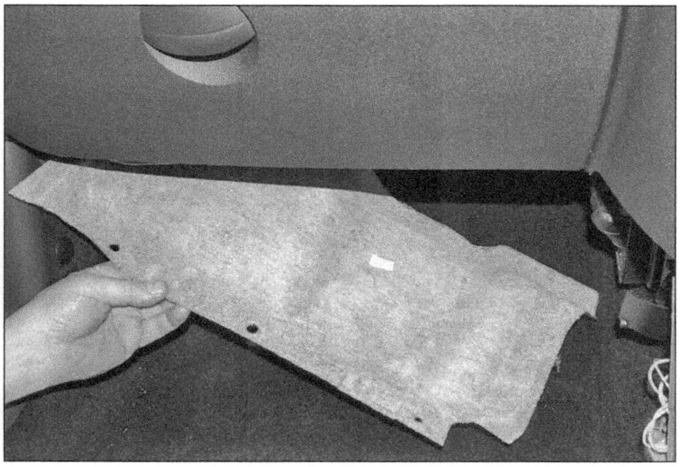
27.9b ... and remove the lower trim panel

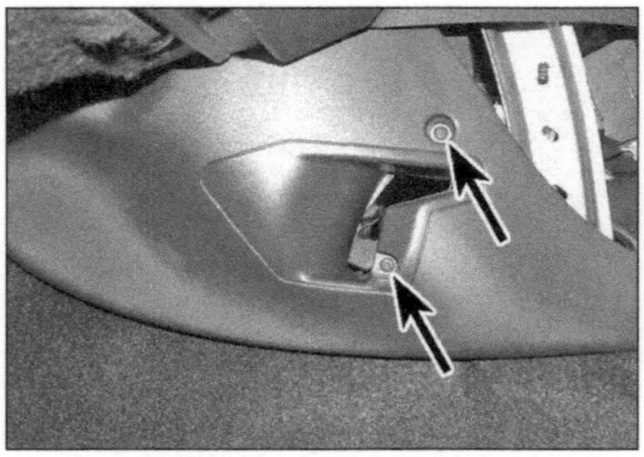

27.10a Undo the two retaining screws (arrowed) ...

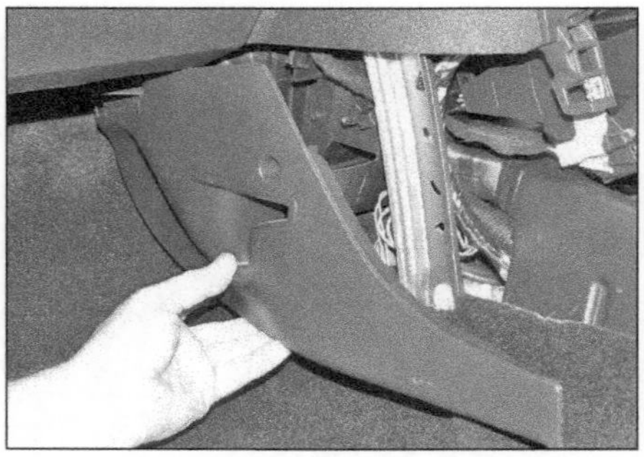

27.10b ... and remove the footwell trim panel

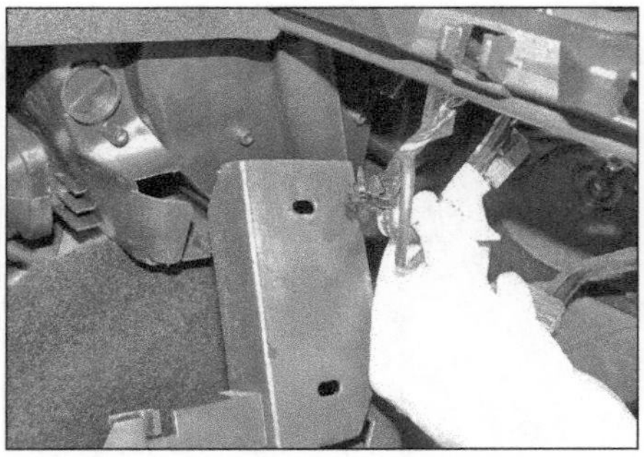

27.10c Unclip the wiring loom from the driver's side trim panel

27.12a Unclip the trim from the right-hand end of the facia

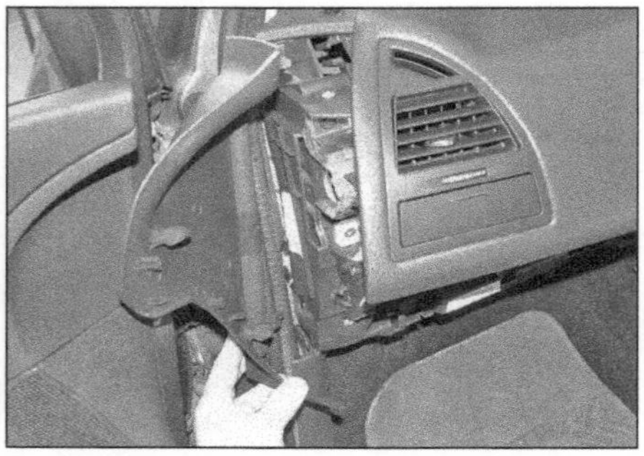

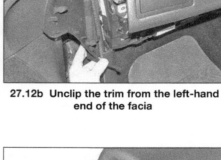

27.12b Unclip the trim from the left-hand end of the facia

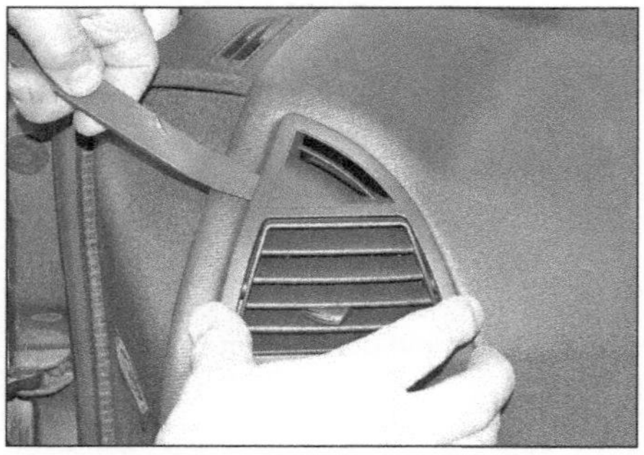

27.14a Carefully unclip the air vent ...

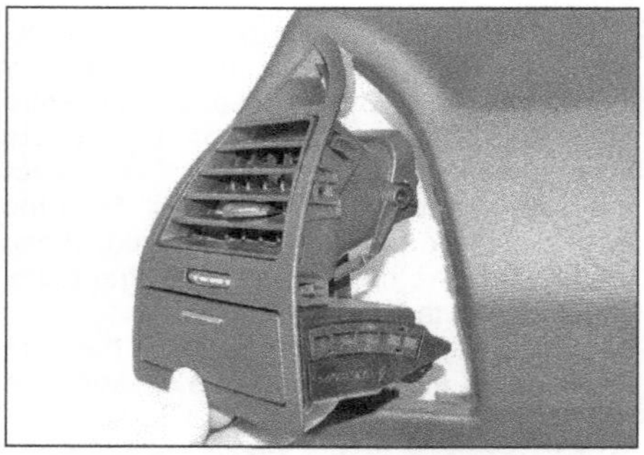

27.14b ... from the front of the facia

secured by screws. Undo the retaining screws and remove the trim panels from the front footwells **(see illustrations)**. Disconnect the wiring securing clip from the right-hand trim panel as it is removed.

11 Refitting is a reversal of removal.

Facia end panels

12 Carefully unclip the trim panels from each end of the facia, pulling them free from their retaining clips **(see illustrations)**.

13 Refitting is a reversal of removal.

Facia side air vents/ compartments

14 Carefully unclip the side air vents/ compartment from each end of the facia, pulling them free from their retaining clips **(see illustration)**. **Note:** *There are two clips at each side, and two clips along the lower edge.*

15 Refitting is a reversal of removal.

Passenger side glovebox

16 Release the three clips, and remove the trim beneath the facia **(see illustrations 27.9a and 27.9b)**. Where applicable, disconnect the wiring connector from the footwell light as the trim is removed.

17 Undo the two screws securing the lower part of the glovebox to the facia **(see illustration)**.

18 Open the glovebox lid, and undo the screws securing the upper part of the glovebox to the facia **(see illustrations)**.

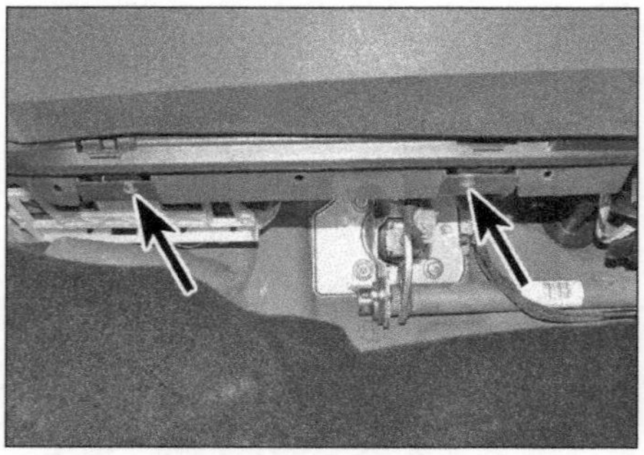

27.17 Undo the lower retaining screws (arrowed)

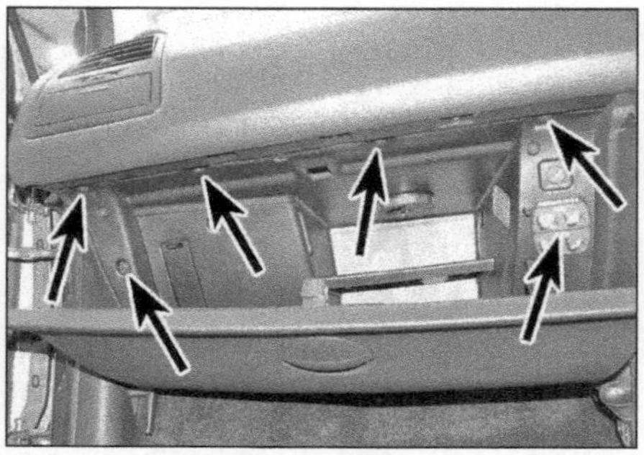

27.18a Undo the glovebox inner retaining screws (arrowed) ...

27.18b ... including the screw positioned behind the airbag sticker

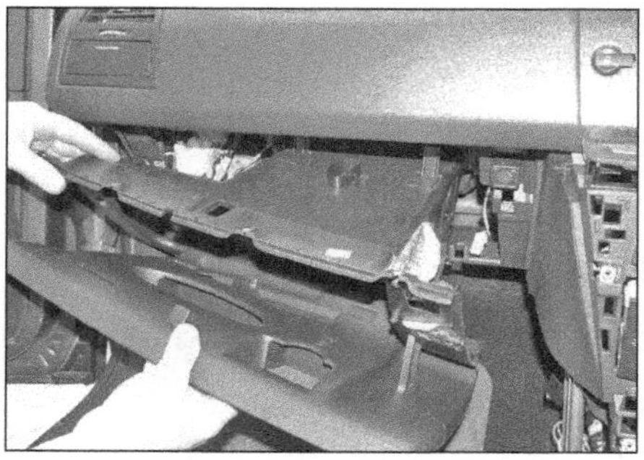

27.19 Withdraw the glovebox from the facia

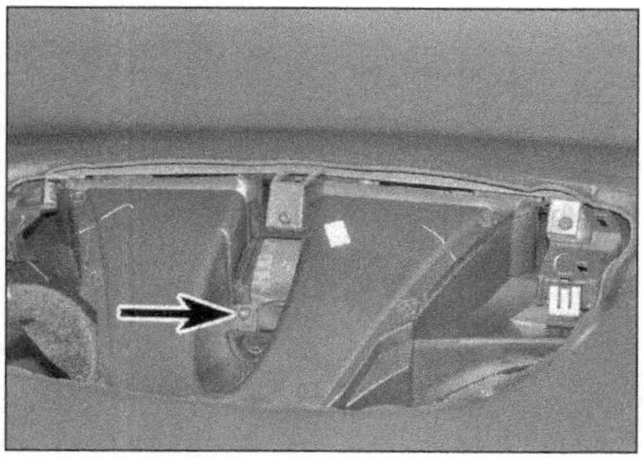

27.33 Undo the upper centre retaining screw (arrowed)

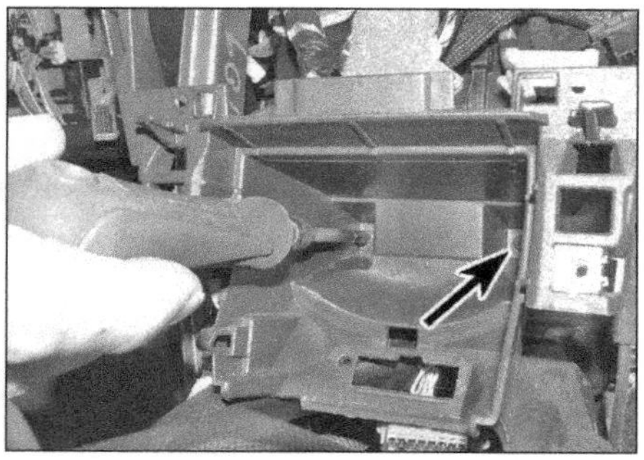

27.34 Undo the lower centre retaining screws (arrowed)

19 Release the retaining clips on the outer edge of the glovebox and slide the assembly out from the facia. Disconnect the wiring connectors from the light unit as the glovebox is removed **(see illustration)**.

20 Refitting is a reversal of removal.

Instrument panel

21 Refer to Chapter 12, Section 9.

Multifunction display

22 Refer to Chapter 12, Section 10.

Complete facia assembly

Note: *This is an involved operation entailing the removal of numerous components and assemblies, and the disconnection of a multitude of wiring connectors. Make notes or take pictures of the location of all disconnected wiring, or attach labels to the connectors, to avoid confusion when refitting.*

23 Disconnect the battery (refer to precautions in Chapter 5, Section 1).

24 Move the front seats as far back as possible. Set the steering wheel in the straight-ahead position, and engage the steering lock.

25 Remove the centre console as described in Section 26.

26 Remove the following facia panels as described previously in this Section:

a) Steering column shrouds.
b) Lower facia panels – driver's side.
c) Front footwell trim panels
d) Passenger side glovebox.
e) Facia end panels.

27 Remove the steering wheel and steering column, as described in Chapter 10, Section 16 and 17.

28 Remove the instrument panel and multifunction display, as described in Chapter 12, Section 9 and Section 10.

29 Remove the audio unit from the facia, as described in Chapter 12, Section 17.

30 Remove the heater/climate control panel, as described in Chapter 3, Section 10.

31 Remove the facia switches, as described in Chapter 12, Section 4.

32 Unclip the speakers/tweeters from top of the facia panel (one at each end), and disconnect the wiring connector.

33 Undo the retaining screw from the facia panel inside the instrument panel aperture and unclip the wiring loom **(see illustration)**.

34 Undo the two retaining screws from inside the lower part of the facia at the centre **(see illustration)**.

35 Undo the two retaining bolts from inside the audio unit player aperture **(see illustration)**.

36 Disconnect the wiring connector for the passenger side airbag unit **(see illustration)**. Note that the airbag will stay attached to the back of the facia panel as it is removed.

37 Disengage the ashtray/oddment tray bulbholder and wiring from the left-hand lower part of the facia **(see illustration)**.

38 Unclip the diagnostic plug from the lower centre of the facia panel **(see illustration)**.

39 Undo the retaining bolt at the lower left-hand side of the heater unit **(see illustration)**.

40 Working through the apertures above the steering column mounting bracket,

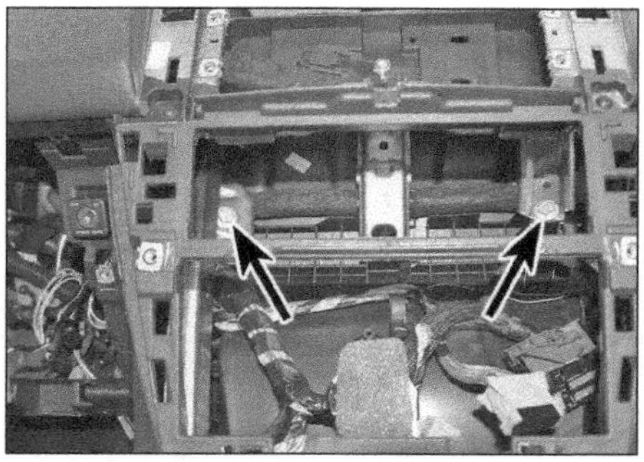

27.35 Undo the facia centre retaining bolts (arrowed)

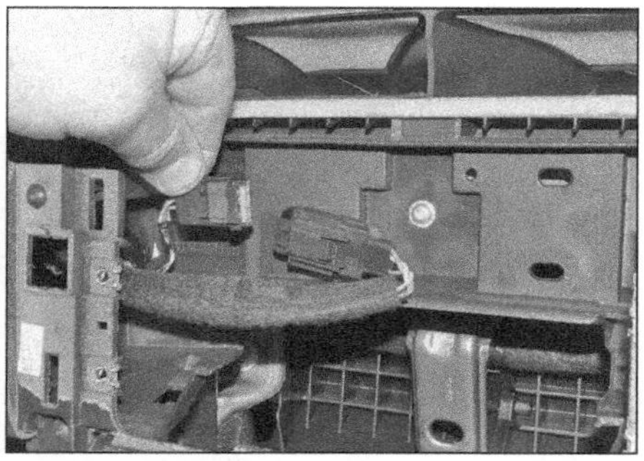

27.36 Disconnect the wiring connector for the passenger airbag

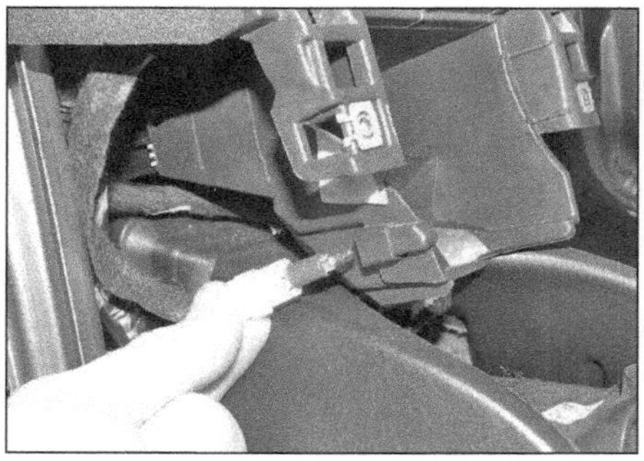

27.37 Unclip the ashtray illumination bulb from the facia

27.38 Unclip the diagnostic connector from the facia panel

27.39 Undo the centre mounting bracket bolt (arrowed)

27.40a Working through the front of the facia ...

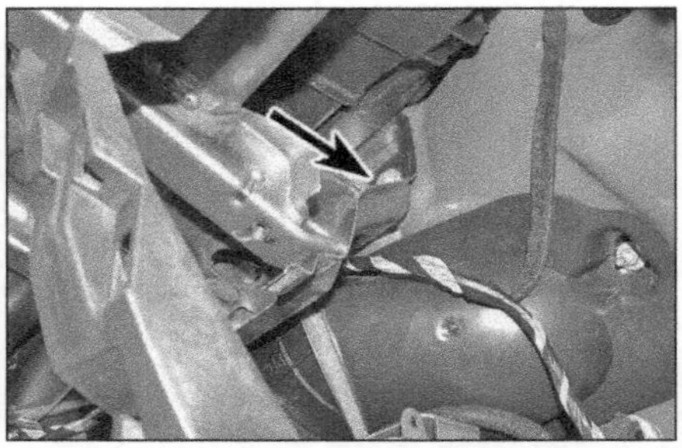

27.40b ... undo the retaining bolt (arrowed) above the facia crossmember

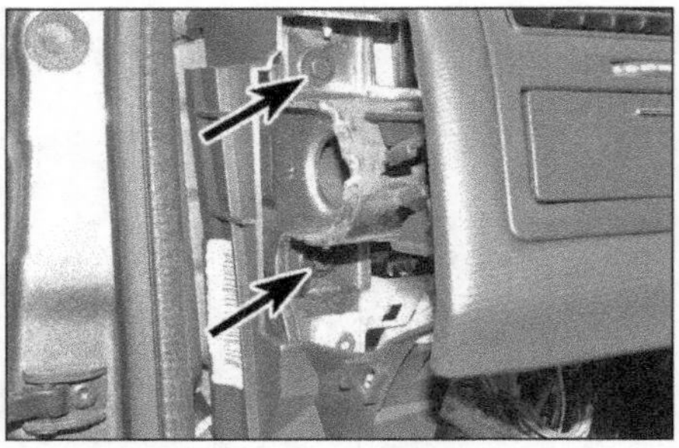

27.41a Undo the mounting bolts (arrowed) from inside the left-hand side ...

27.41b ... and right-hand side of the facia panel

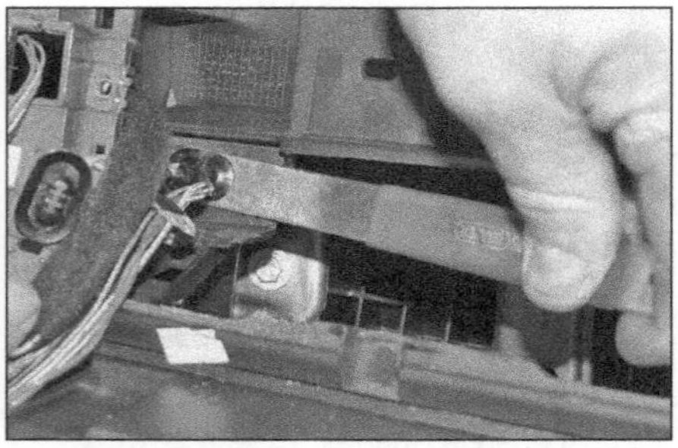

27.42a Release the wiring retaining clips inside the centre of the facia ...

27.42b ... from inside the glovebox aperture ...

undo the retaining bolt above the facia crossmember screwing into the bulkhead **(see illustrations)**.

41 Working through the apertures at each end of the facia, unscrew the two bolts each side securing the facia crossmember **(see illustrations)**.

42 Note their fitted positions and harness routing, then disconnect the facia wiring plugs and retaining clips. Take note of the location of the various wiring harness retaining clips, to aid refitment **(see illustrations)**.

43 Check around the facia for any other fixings and then with the help of an assistant, lift the facia complete with bulkhead crossmember from place, and remove it from the vehicle.

44 Refitting is a reversal of removal ensuring that all wiring is correctly reconnected and all mountings securely tightened.

45 If required, the upper padded part of the facia can be removed from the lower plastic housing. Working your way around the panel, undo the retaining screws and remove the upper padded part of the facia **(see illustrations)**.

27.42c ... and attached to the facia crossmember

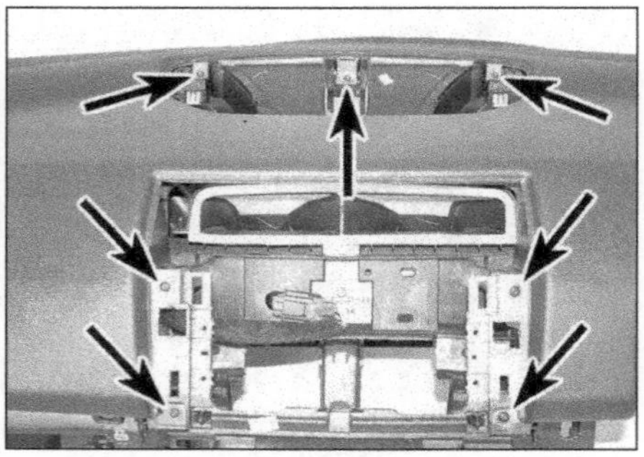

27.45a Undo the centre retaining screws (arrowed) ...

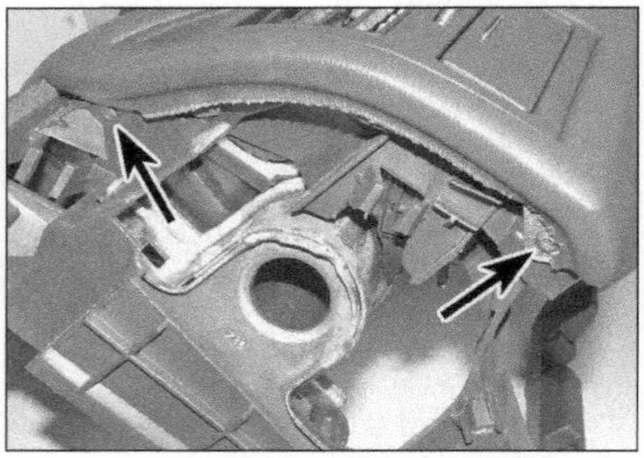

27.45b ... side retaining screw (arrowed) ...

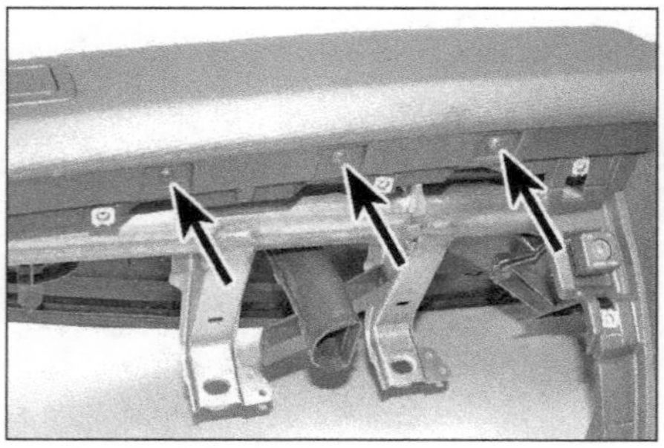

27.45c ... under the passenger side front ...

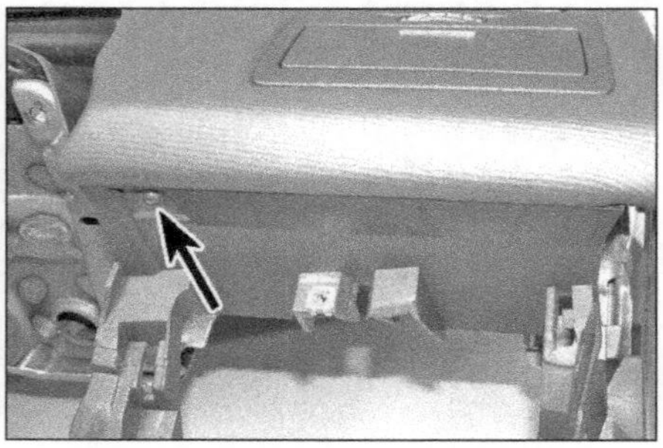

27.45d ... and driver's side front ...

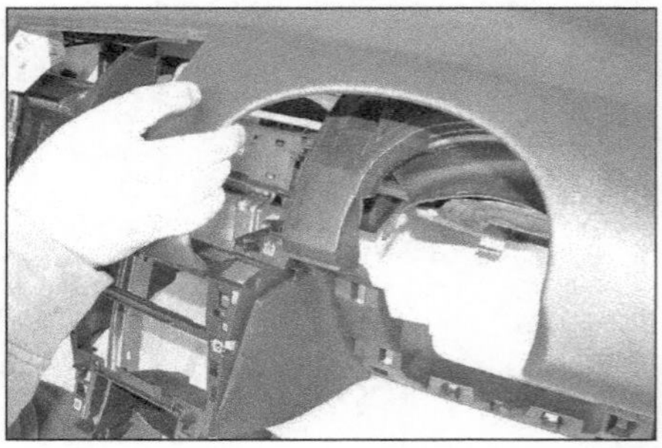

27.45e ... then lift the padded upper part of the facia to remove

Chapter 12
Body electrical systems

Contents

Degrees of difficulty

Easy, suitable for novice with little experience	**Fairly easy,** suitable for beginner with some experience	**Fairly difficult,** suitable for competent DIY mechanic	**Difficult,** suitable for experienced DIY mechanic	**Very difficult,** suitable for expert DIY or professional

Specifications

General

System type	12 volt negative earth

Bulbs

	Type	Wattage
Brake light	Bayonet	21
Direction indicator light	Bayonet	21
Direction indicator side repeater	Push-fit	5
Front ashtray light	Push-fit	1.2
Foglight:		
Front	H8	35
Rear	Bayonet	21
Front sidelights	Push-fit	5
Glovebox light	Push-fit	5
Headlights:		
Halogen:		
Main beam bulbs	H1	55
Dip beam bulbs	H7	55
Xenon:		
Dipped/main beam bulbs	D1S	35
Additional main beam bulbs	H1	55
High-level brake light:		
3-door models (5 bulbs)	Push-fit	5
5-door models	LED	
Interior/courtesy lights	Push-fit	5
Luggage compartment light	Push-fit	5
Number plate light	Push-fit	5
Reversing light	Bayonet	21
Tail light:		
3-door models	Bayonet	21/5
5-door models	Push-fit	5

Torque wrench setting

	Nm	lbf ft
Airbag control unit retaining nuts	8	6
Accelerometer sensor retaining bolts	8	6

1 General information

Warning: Before carrying out any work on the electrical system, read through the precautions given in 'Safety first!' at the beginning of this manual, and in Chapter 5A, Section 1.

The electrical system is of 12 volt negative earth type. Power for the lights and all electrical accessories is supplied by a lead-acid type battery, which is charged by the alternator.

Many of the body electrical systems are controlled by individual electronic control units (ECUs), these are in turn controlled by a main ECU known as a built-in systems interface (BSI). The various ECUs and the BSI exchange data with each other via a multiplex network. The multiplex network is a two-wire system linking the BSI with the system ECUs and is termed by Citroën as CAN (controlled area network) and VAN (vehicle area network). Essentially this means that the BSI and the ECUs controlling the 'comfort' systems, safety systems, security systems, and entertainment systems in the vehicle, are all interconnected via vehicle area networks.

An ECU connected to the multiplex network only receives some of the data needed for it to operate directly, with the remaining data being supplied by the other ECUs on the network. Because the ECUs share information via the network, several ECUs can control the operation of the same system. Also, one ECU can control several systems in an autonomous manner. The BSI is the manager of this information interchange as well as also being responsible for the control of certain vehicle systems itself. The BSI has a full diagnostic capability whereby any fault in any of the ECUs on the multiplex network can be traced using diagnostic equipment connected to the vehicle diagnostic connector, situated behind the centre console ashtray **(see illustration)**. Should any fault develop with a system on the network, have the self-diagnosis facility interrogated by a Citroën dealer or suitably-equipped specialist.

This Chapter covers repair and service procedures for the various electrical components not associated with the engine.

1.3 Vehicle diagnostic plug connector (arrowed)

Information on the battery, alternator and starter motor can be found in Chapter 5A.

It should be noted that, prior to working on any component in the electrical system, the battery should first be disconnected; to prevent the possibility of electrical short-circuits (see Chapter 5A, Section 4).

2 Electrical fault finding – general information

Note: *Refer to the precautions given in 'Safety first!' and in Chapter 5A, Section 1 before starting work. The following tests relate to testing of the main electrical circuits, and should not be used to test delicate electronic circuits (such as anti-lock braking systems), particularly where an electronic control unit (ECU) or multiplexing is used (see Section 1).*

General

1 A typical electrical circuit consists of an electrical component; any switches, relays, motors, fuses, fusible links or circuit breakers related to that component, and the wiring and connectors which link the component to both the battery and the chassis. To help to pinpoint a problem in an electrical circuit, wiring diagrams are included at the end of this Chapter.

2 Before attempting to diagnose an electrical fault, first study the appropriate wiring diagram, to obtain a more complete understanding of the components included in the particular circuit concerned. The possible sources of a fault can be narrowed down, by noting whether other components related to the circuit are operating properly. If several components or circuits fail at one time, the problem is likely to be related to a shared fuse or earth connection.

3 Electrical problems usually stem from simple causes, such as loose or corroded connections, a faulty earth connection, a blown fuse, a melted fusible link, or a faulty relay (refer to Section 3 for details of testing relays). Visually inspect the condition of all fuses, wires and connections in a problem circuit before testing the components. Use the wiring diagrams to determine which terminal connections will need to be checked, in order to pinpoint the trouble spot.

4 The basic tools required for electrical fault finding include a circuit tester or voltmeter; an ohmmeter (to measure resistance); a battery and set of test leads; and a jumper wire, preferably with a circuit breaker or fuse incorporated, which can be used to bypass suspect wires or electrical components. Before attempting to locate a problem with test instruments, use the wiring diagram to determine where to make the connections.

5 To find the source of an intermittent wiring fault (usually due to a poor or dirty connection, or damaged wiring insulation), a 'wiggle' test can be performed on the wiring. This involves wiggling the wiring by hand, to see if the fault occurs as the wiring is moved. It should be possible to narrow down the source of the fault to a particular section of wiring. This method of testing can be used in conjunction with any of the tests described in the following sub-Sections.

6 Apart from problems due to poor connections, two basic types of fault can occur in an electrical circuit – open-circuit, or short-circuit.

7 Open-circuit faults are caused by a break somewhere in the circuit, which prevents current from flowing. An open-circuit fault will prevent a component from working, but will not cause the relevant circuit fuse to blow.

8 Short-circuit faults are caused by a 'short' somewhere in the circuit, which allows the current flowing in the circuit to 'escape' along an alternative route, usually to earth. Short-circuit faults are normally caused by a breakdown in wiring insulation, which allows a feed wire to touch either another wire, or an earthed component such as the bodyshell. A short-circuit fault will normally cause the relevant circuit fuse to blow. **Note:** *As an aid to economy and to prevent battery discharge, certain functions of the electrical system can only be used for 30 minutes after the engine has been stopped. Bear this in mind when tracing power supply faults on these systems. After this period the BSI (built-in systems interface) cuts the power to these circuits. To restore power, start the engine. It is also possible for the BSI to turn off certain functions (heater blower, heated rear window) depending on the state of charge of the battery. When tracing a fault, ensure the battery is in a good state of charge.*

Functions affected

- *Windscreen wipers.*
- *Electric windows.*
- *Sunroof.*
- *Courtesy lights.*
- *Audio equipment.*

Finding an open-circuit

9 To check for an open-circuit, connect one lead of a voltmeter to either the negative battery terminal or a known good earth.

10 Connect the other lead to a connector in the circuit being tested, preferably nearest to the battery or fuse.

11 Switch on the circuit, bearing in mind that some circuits are live only when the ignition switch is moved to a particular position.

12 If voltage is present (indicated either by the tester bulb lighting or a voltmeter reading, as applicable), this means that the section of the circuit between the relevant connector and the battery is problem-free.

13 Continue to check the remainder of the circuit in the same fashion.

14 When a point is reached at which no voltage is present, the problem must lie between that point and the previous test point with voltage. Most problems can be traced to a broken, corroded or loose connection.

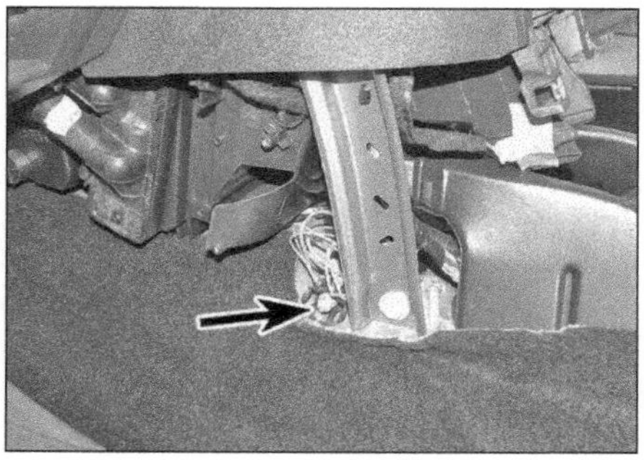

2.20a Earth connection inside passenger compartment ...

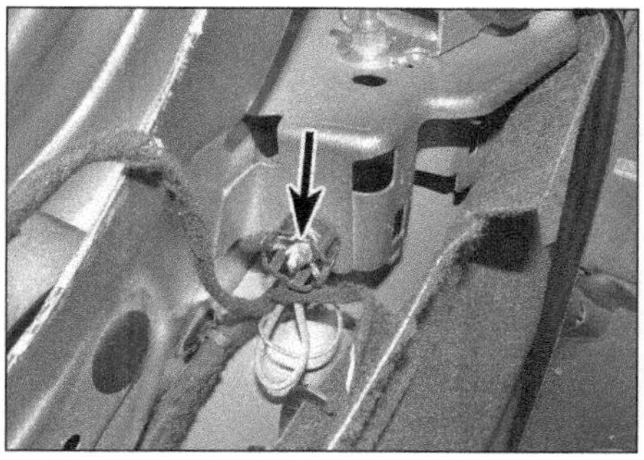

2.20b ... in rear luggage compartment ...

2.20c ... on the top of the transmission (arrowed)

Finding a short-circuit

15 To check for a short-circuit; first disconnect the load(s) from the circuit (loads are the components which draw current from a circuit, such as bulbs, motors, heating elements, etc).

16 Remove the relevant fuse from the circuit, and connect a circuit tester or voltmeter to the fuse connections.

17 Switch on the circuit, bearing in mind that some circuits are live only when the ignition switch is moved to a particular position.

18 If voltage is present (indicated either by the tester bulb lighting or a voltmeter reading, as applicable), this means that there is a short-circuit.

19 If no voltage is present, but the fuse still blows with the load(s) connected, this indicates an internal fault in the load(s).

Finding an earth fault

20 The battery negative terminal is connected to 'earth' – the metal of the engine/transmission and the car body – and most systems are wired so that they only receive a positive feed, the current returning via the metal of the car body. This means that the component mounting and the body form part of that circuit. Loose or corroded mountings can therefore cause a range of electrical faults, ranging from total failure of a circuit, to a puzzling partial fault. In particular, lights may shine dimly (especially when another circuit sharing the same earth point is in operation), motors (eg, wiper motors or the radiator cooling fan motor) may run slowly, and the operation of one circuit may have an apparently unrelated effect on another. Note that on many vehicles, earth straps are used between certain components, such as the engine/transmission and the body, usually where there is no metal-to-metal contact between components, due to flexible rubber mountings, etc **(see illustrations)**.

21 To check whether a component is properly earthed, disconnect the battery, and connect one lead of an ohmmeter to a known good earth point. Connect the other lead to the wire or earth connection being tested. The resistance reading should be zero; if not, check the connection as follows.

22 If an earth connection is thought to be faulty, dismantle the connection, and clean back to bare metal both the bodyshell and the wire terminal or the component earth connection mating surface. Be careful to remove all traces of dirt and corrosion, and then use a knife to trim away any paint, so that a clean metal-to-metal joint is made. On reassembly, tighten the joint fasteners securely; if a wire terminal is being refitted, use serrated washers between the terminal and the bodyshell, to ensure a clean and secure connection. When the connection is remade, prevent the onset of corrosion in the future by applying a coat of petroleum jelly or silicone-based grease, or by spraying on (at regular intervals) a proprietary ignition sealer or water-dispersant lubricant.

3 Fuses and relays – general information

Fuses

1 Fuses are designed to break a circuit when a predetermined current is reached, in order to protect the components and wiring, which could be damaged by excessive current flow. Any excessive current flow will be due to a fault in the circuit, usually a short-circuit (see Section 2).

2 The majority of fuses are located behind the glovebox lid on the passenger's side of the facia. Additional fuses (including the larger, higher-rated fuses) are located in the fuse/relay box on the left-hand side of the engine compartment.

3 To gain access to the facia fuses, open the glovebox, rotate the cover fastener through 90 degrees then remove the cover from the facia **(see illustrations)**.

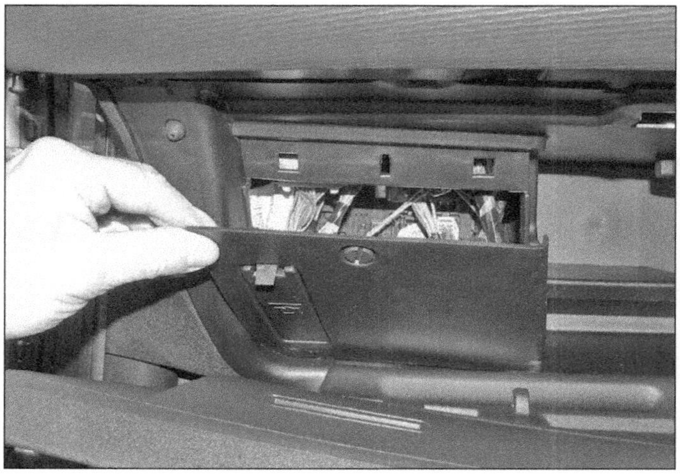

3.3a Rotate the fastener 90°and pull down the cover ...

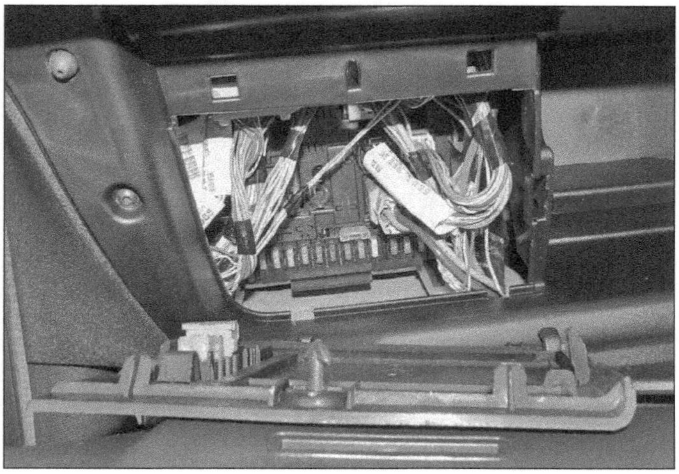

3.3b ... to access the fusebox

3.4a Lift up the plastic cover ...

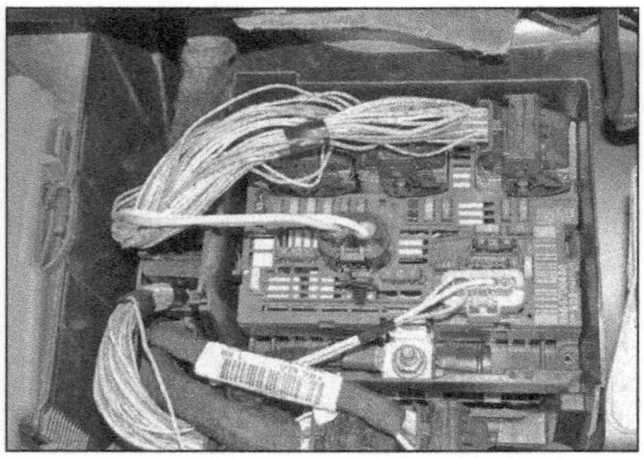

3.4b ... to access the fuses and relays ...

3.4c ... additional fused links on top of battery – VTi petrol engines

4 To gain access to the fuses in the engine compartment, simply unclip the cover from the fuse/relay box **(see illustrations)**. On VTi petrol models, additional fuses are under the red cover on top of the battery cover.

5 To remove a fuse, first switch off the circuit concerned (or the ignition), and then pull the fuse out of its terminals **(see illustrations)**. The wire within the fuse should be visible; if the fuse has blown it will be broken or melted.

6 Always renew a fuse with one of the correct rating; never use a fuse with a different rating from that specified. The fuse rating is stamped on the top of the fuse; the fuses are also colour-coded as follows. Refer to the wiring diagrams for details of the fuse ratings and the circuits protected.

Colour	Rating
Orange	5A
Red	10A
Blue	15A
Yellow	20A
Clear or white	25A
Green	30A

7 Never renew a fuse more than once without tracing the source of the trouble. If the new fuse blows immediately, find the cause before renewing it again; a short to earth as a result of faulty insulation is most likely. Where a fuse protects more than one circuit, try to isolate the fault by switching on each circuit in turn (where possible) until the fuse blows again. Always carry a supply of spare fuses of each relevant rating on the vehicle; a spare of each rating should be clipped into the fusebox.

3.5a Pull the fuse from its position in the fusebox

3.5b The removal tool is on the inside of the fusebox cover with spare fuses

Relays

Note: *The BSI unit is located on the passenger's side of the facia where it is situated directly behind the glovebox (see Section 23)*.

8 The majority of relay functions are incorporated into the built-in system interface (BSI) unit (see Section 23). Other relays are located in the fuse/relay box in the engine compartment and the ABS and pre/post-heating system (diesel models) relays are located in front of the engine compartment fusebox housing **(see illustration)**.

9 If a circuit or system controlled by a relay develops a fault and the relay is suspect, operate the system. If the relay is functioning, it should be possible to hear it 'click' as it is energised. If this is the case, the fault lies with the components or wiring of the system. If the relay is not being energised, then either the relay is not receiving a main supply or a switching voltage, or the relay itself is faulty.

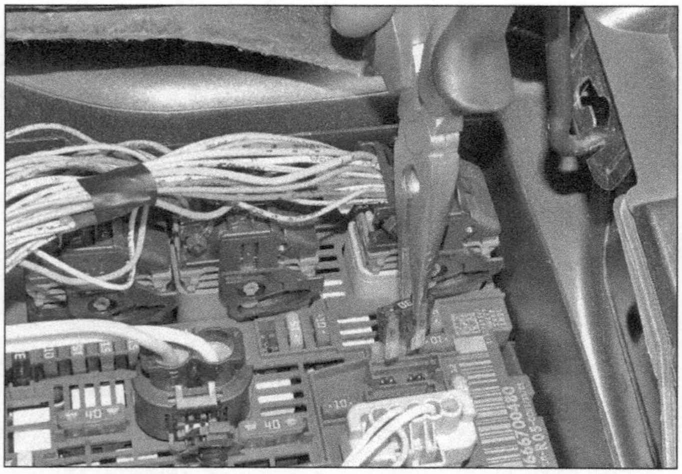

3.5c Using a pair of long-nose pliers to remove the fuses

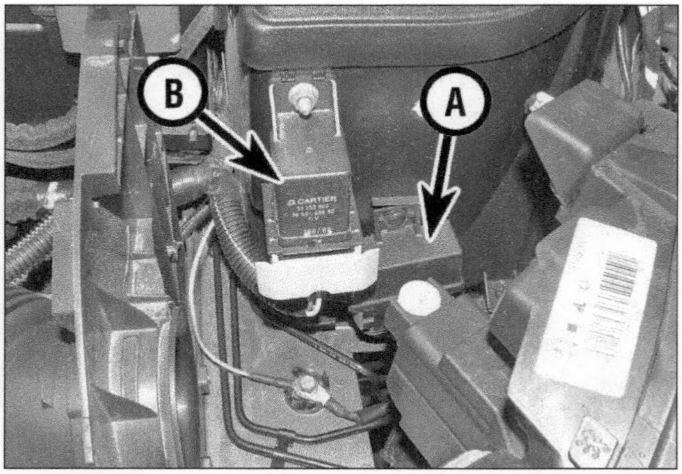

3.8 The ABS relay (A) and the diesel pre/post-heating relay (B) located in front of fusebox

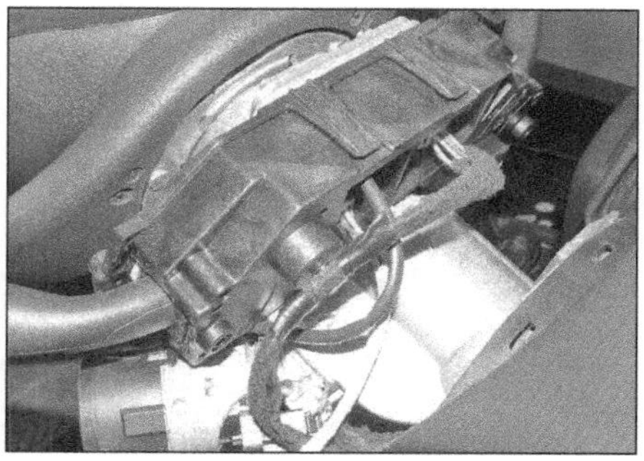

4.3 Disconnect the wiring connectors at the rear of the switch

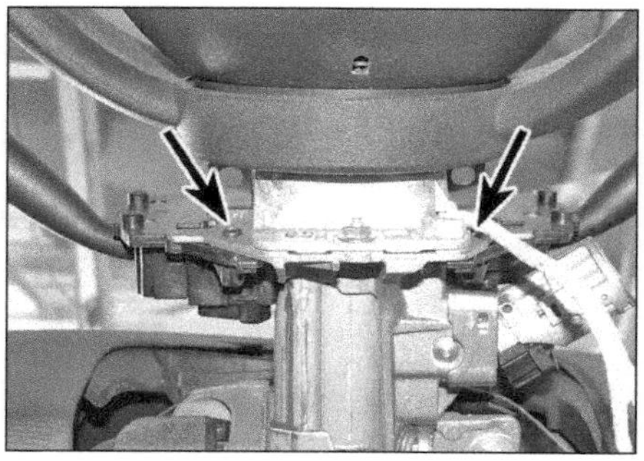

4.4a Undo the two switch assembly retaining screws (arrowed) ...

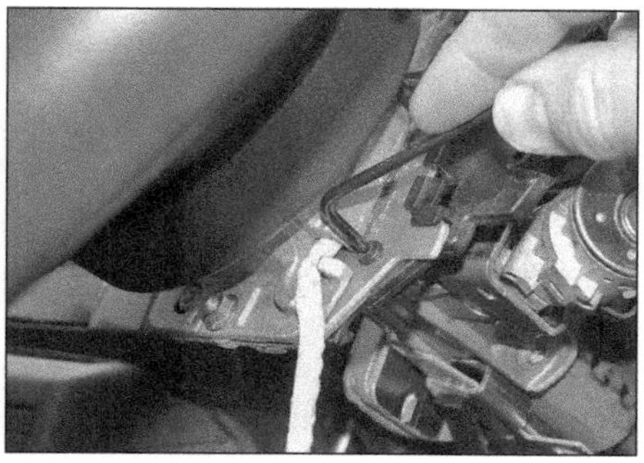

4.4b ... using a Torx head key

Testing is by the substitution of a known good unit, but be careful – while some relays are identical in appearance and in operation, others look similar but perform different functions.

10 To remove a relay, first ensure that the relevant circuit is switched off. The relay can then simply be pulled out from the socket, and pushed back into position.

4 Switches – removal and refitting

Note: *Disconnect the battery before removing any switch, and reconnect the lead after refitting the switch (see Chapter 5A, Section 4).*

Ignition switch

1 Refer to Chapter 10, Section 18.

Steering column switches

2 Remove the steering column lower and upper shrouds as described in Chapter 11, Section 27.

3 Disconnect the wiring plugs from the rear of the switch assembly **(see illustration)**.

4 Using a Torx key, undo the two retaining screws from the lower part of the steering housing **(see illustrations)**.

5 Slide the complete switch assembly upwards and away from the column **(see illustration)**.

6 Refitting is the reversal of removal.

Steering wheel switches

7 Remove the driver's airbag as described in Section 22.

8 Using a Torx screwdriver, undo the three retaining screws from inside the airbag aperure in the steering wheel **(see illustration)**.

9 Withdraw the switch assembly upwards and away from the steering wheel **(see illustration)**.

10 Disconnect the wiring plug(s) from the rear of the switch assembly as it is removed **(see illustration)**.

11 Refitting is the reversal of removal.

ESP, parking assist, lane warning and alarm switches

12 The switch trim panel to the right of the steering column houses the ESP, parking assistance, lane departure warning and anti-intrusion alarm switches.

13 Undo the retaining screw and unclip the trim panel from the lower part of the facia **(see illustrations)**.

14 Disconnect the wiring connector from the

4.5 Slide the switch assembly upwards to remove from the steering column housing

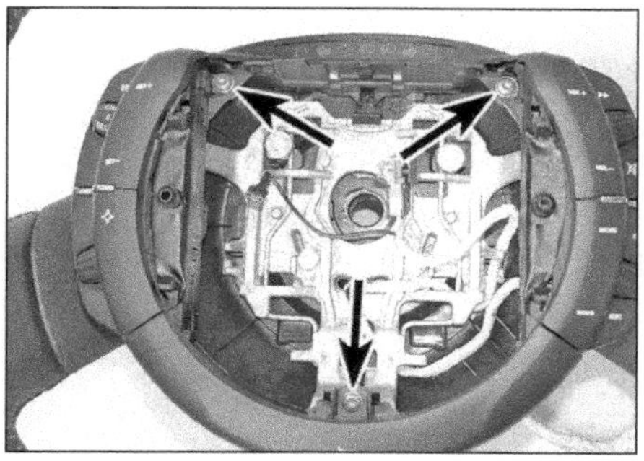

4.8 Undo the three switch assembly retaining screws (arrowed) ...

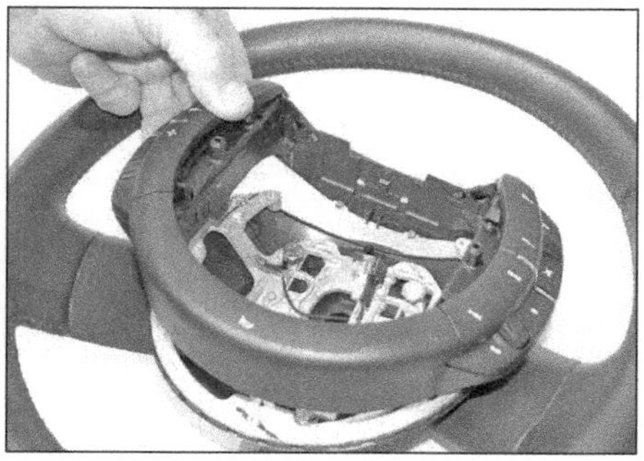

4.9 ... and withdraw it from the steering wheel

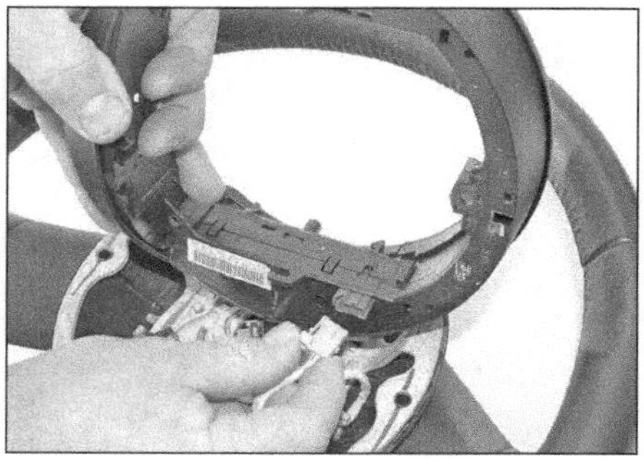

4.10 Disconnect the wiring plug connector

4.13a Undo the retaining screw ...

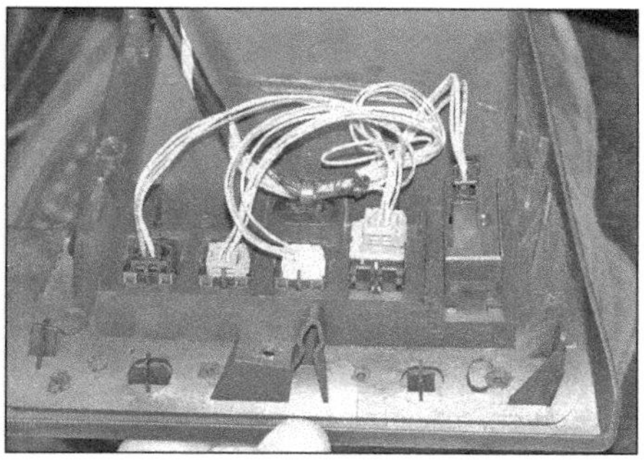

4.13b ... and unclip the panel from the facia

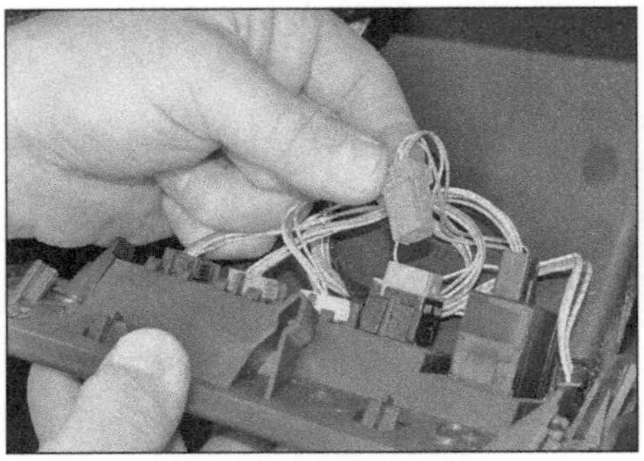

4.14a Disconnect the wiring connector ...

4.14b ... and unclip the switch from the panel

4.16 Carefully unclip the headlight switch from the facia ...

relevant switch and press the switch out from the front of the trim panel **(see illustrations)**.

15 Refitting is the reversal of removal.

Headlight height adjustment

16 Using a small screwdriver, carefully unclip the switch from the lower trim panel **(see illustration)**.

17 Disconnect the wiring plug from the rear of the switch as it is removed **(see illustration)**.

18 Refitting is the reverse of removal.

Hazard warning and central locking switches

19 Remove the multifunction display unit as described in Section 10.

20 Press the switch out from the facia panel and disconnect the wiring connector **(see illustrations)**.

21 Refitting is the reversal of removal.

Passenger airbag on/off switch

22 Using a small screwdriver, carefully unclip the switch from inside the glovebox **(see illustration)**.

23 Disconnect the wiring plug from the rear of the switch as it is removed **(see illustration)**.

24 Refitting is the reverse of removal.

Audio unit control and cruise control switches

25 The audio unit and cruise control switches are built into the steering wheel switches and are supplied as a complete unit. See paragraphs 7 to 11 for the removal and refitting procedure.

Heating/ventilation control and heated rear window switch

26 The switches are an integral part of the heater/ventilation control panel, and cannot be renewed separately. If any switch is faulty, the complete control panel must be renewed – refer to Chapter 3, Section 10 for details.

Brake light switch

27 Refer to Chapter 9, Section 17.

Handbrake warning light switch

28 Remove the centre console as described in Chapter 11, Section 26.

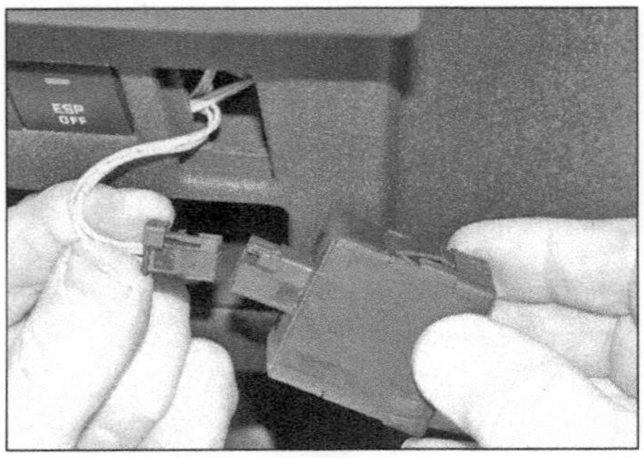

4.17 ... and disconnect the wiring connector

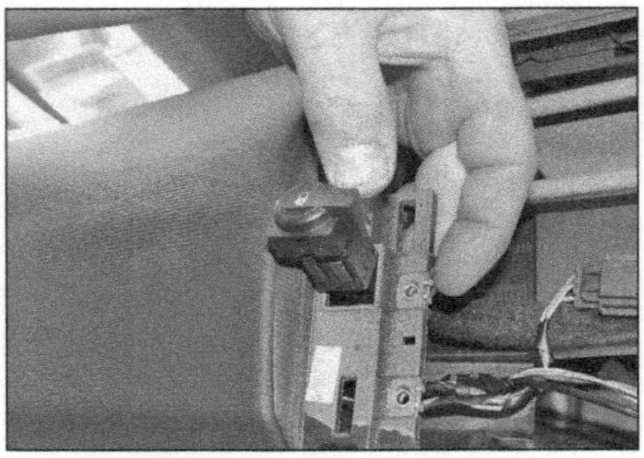

4.20a Unclip the door locking switch from the facia ...

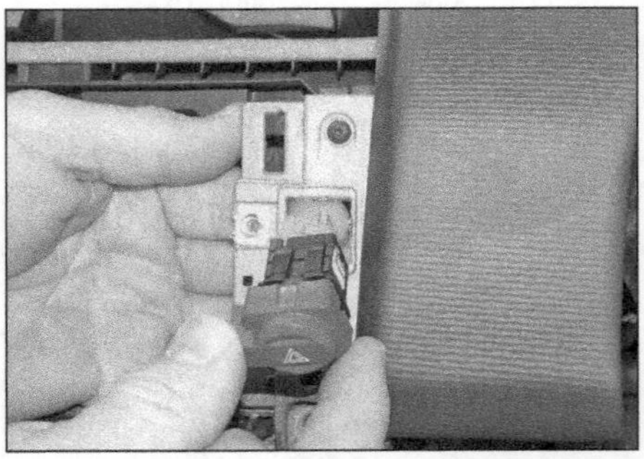

4.20b ... and hazard warning switch ...

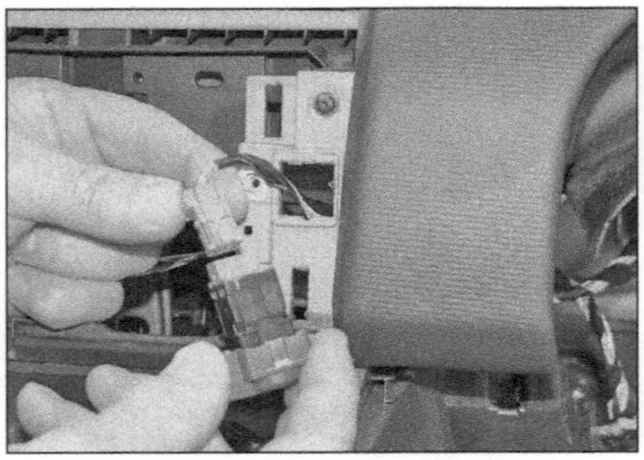

4.20c ... then disconnect the wiring connector

4.22 Carefully unclip the airbag switch from the facia ...

4.23 ... and disconnect the wiring connector

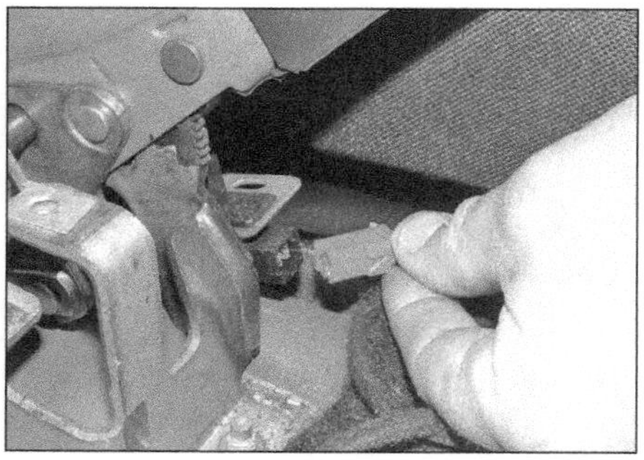

4.29 Disconnect the wiring connector ...

4.30 ... and unclip the switch from the handbrake bracket

5.2 Unclip the air intake ducting cover – 1.6 litre diesel engines

29 Pull the handbrake fully on and disconnect the switch wiring connector **(see illustration)**.

30 Release the retaining clips and remove the switch from the handbrake mounting bracket **(see illustration)**.

31 Refitting is the reverse of removal.

Courtesy light switch

32 The courtesy light switches are an integral part of the door lock assemblies. Refer to Chapter 11, Section 13 for door lock removal and refitting details.

Luggage area light switch

33 The luggage compartment light switch function is integral with the tailgate lock assembly. For tailgate lock removal, refer to Chapter 11, Section 16.

Glovebox illumination switch

34 The switch is integral with the light. Remove the light as described in Section 6.

Sunlight sensor

35 The sunlight sensor is built into the rear of the vehicle instrument panel; refer to Section 9 for the removal and refitting procedure.

Rain sensor

36 The rain sensor is covered in the heater/ventilation control system; refer to Chapter 3, Section 10, for the removal and refitting procedure.

Caution: Do not touch the rain sensor lens or the windscreen glass in the area of the sensor. These areas must be kept spotlessly clean if the sensor is to function correctly.

5 Bulbs (exterior lights) – renewal

General

1 Whenever a bulb is renewed, note the following points:

a) *Remember that, if the light has just been in use, the bulb may be extremely hot.*

b) *Always check the bulb contacts and holder, ensuring that there is clean metal-to-metal contact between the bulb and its live(s) and earth. Clean off any corrosion or dirt before fitting a new bulb.*

c) *Wherever bayonet-type bulbs are fitted (see Specifications), ensure that the live contact(s) bear firmly against the bulb contact.*

d) *Always ensure that the new bulb is of the correct rating, and that it is completely clean before fitting it; this applies particularly to headlight/foglight bulbs (see below).*

Headlight

2 Depending on model, to improve access to the left-hand headlight, remove the plastic cover from the air intake ducting **(see illustration).**

3 When handling the new bulb, use a tissue or clean cloth to avoid touching the glass with the fingers; moisture and grease from the skin can cause blackening and rapid failure of this type of bulb. If the glass is accidentally touched, wipe it clean using methylated spirit.

Main beam

Note: *Some vehicles are fitted with xenon bulbs (D1S); it is recommended that a Citroën dealer or specialist changes these.*

4 Reach behind the headlamp, and unclip the main beam's protective cover and remove it **(see illustration)**.

5 Disconnect the wiring plug from the bulb **(see illustration)**.

6 Release the bulb retaining clip, and withdraw the bulb **(see illustrations)**.

7 Install the new bulb, ensuring that its locating tabs are correctly seated in the light cut-outs, and secure it in position with the retaining clip.

8 Reconnect the wiring plug, and refit the protective cover.

5.4 Unclip the headlight bulb protective cover

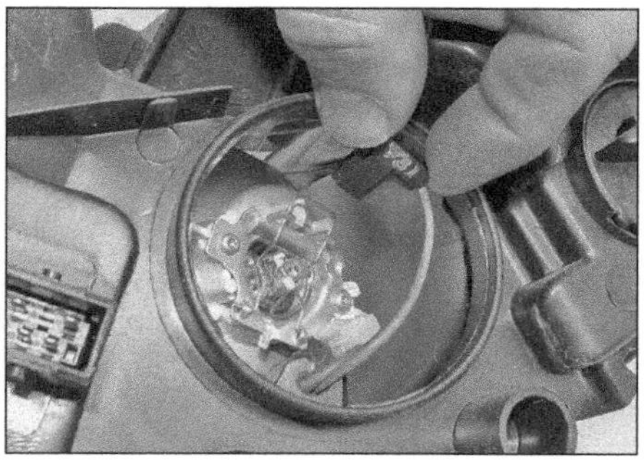

5.5 Disconnect the headlight bulb wiring plug

5.6a Release the retaining clip ...

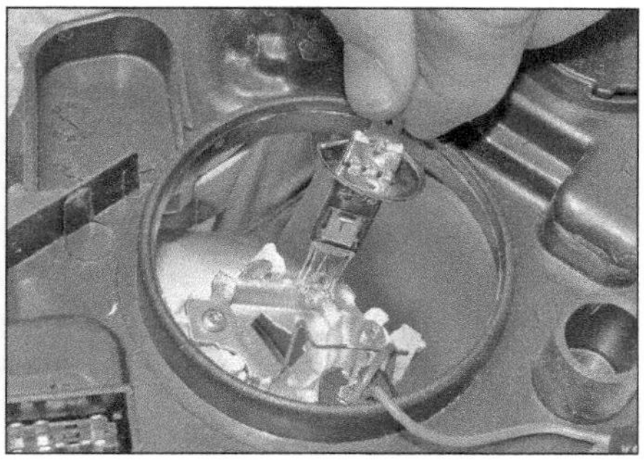

5.6b ... and remove the bulb

5.9 Unclip the headlight bulb protective cover

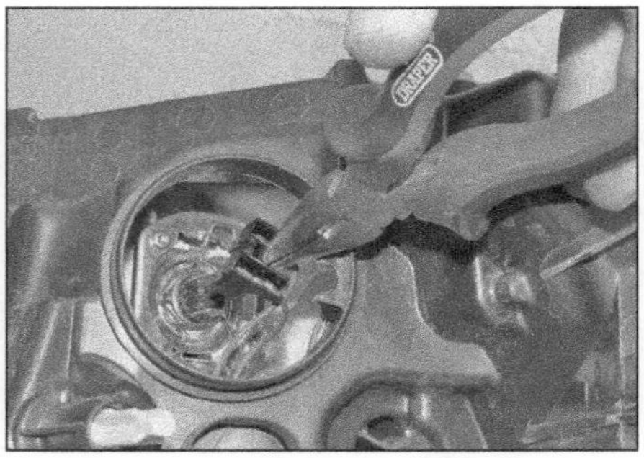
5.10 Using long-nose pliers to disconnect the wiring plug

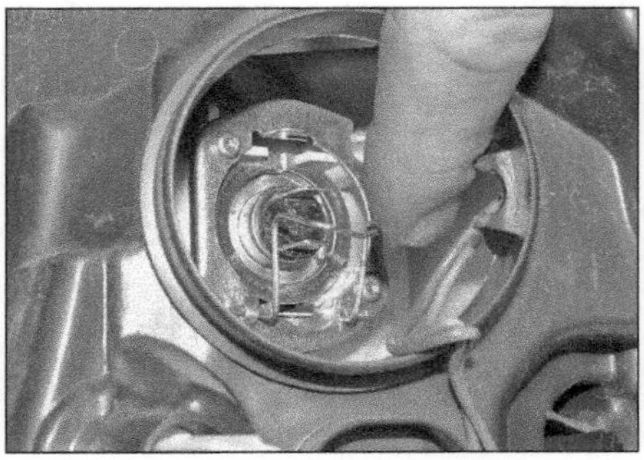
5.11a Release the retaining clip ...

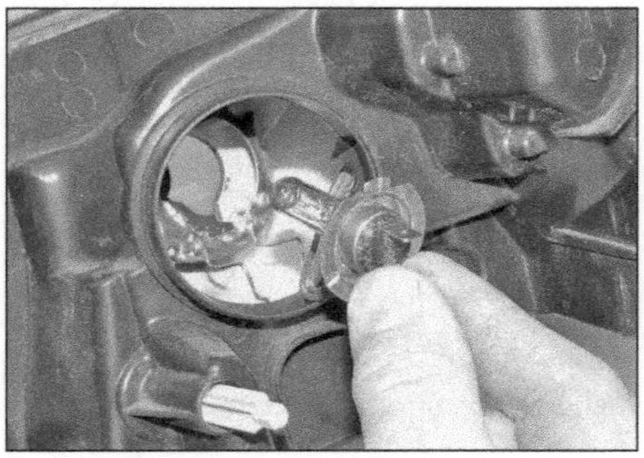
5.11b ... and remove the bulb

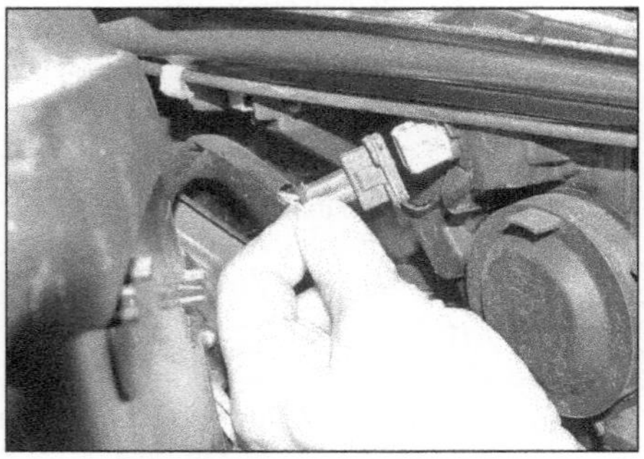
5.14 Disconnect the wiring plug

5.15 Rotate the bulbholder to remove ...

Dipped beam

9 Reach behind the headlamp, and unclip the dipped beam's protective cover and remove it **(see illustration)**.

10 Disconnect the wiring connector from the bulb **(see illustration)**. This may be a tight fit, if required, use a pair of long-nose pliers to pull the connector off the terminals.

11 Release the bulb retaining clip, and withdraw the bulb **(see illustrations)**.

12 Install the new bulb, ensuring that it's located correctly in the light unit cut-out, and secure it in position with the retaining clip.

13 Reconnect the wiring plug, and refit the protective cover.

Sidelight

14 Reach behind the headlamp and disconnect the wiring connector from the light unit **(see illustration)**.

15 Rotate the bulbholder 90° and then pull it from the rear of the light unit **(see illustration)**

16 The bulb is a capless (push-fit) type, and can easily be removed by pulling it out of the bulbholder **(see illustration)**.

17 Refitting is the reverse of the removal procedure.

Front foglight

18 The front foglights are located in the front bumper. Chock the rear wheels then jack up the front of the vehicle and support it on axle stands (see *Jacking and vehicle support*). For access to the foglight, it is necessary to release the front of the wheel arch liner by removing the fasteners.

19 Reach up under the front bumper and disconnect the wiring from the foglight bulbholder **(see illustration)**.

20 Turn the bulbholder 90° anti-clockwise and withdraw it from the rear of the foglight, then remove the bulb **(see illustration)**.

21 When handling the new bulb, use a tissue or clean cloth to avoid touching the glass with the fingers; moisture and grease from the skin can cause blackening and rapid failure of this type of bulb. If the glass is accidentally touched, wipe it clean using methylated spirit.

22 Fit the new bulb using a reversal of the removal procedure.

Front direction indicator

23 Depending on model, to improve access to the left-hand headlight, remove the air

5.16 ... then pull the bulb from its holder

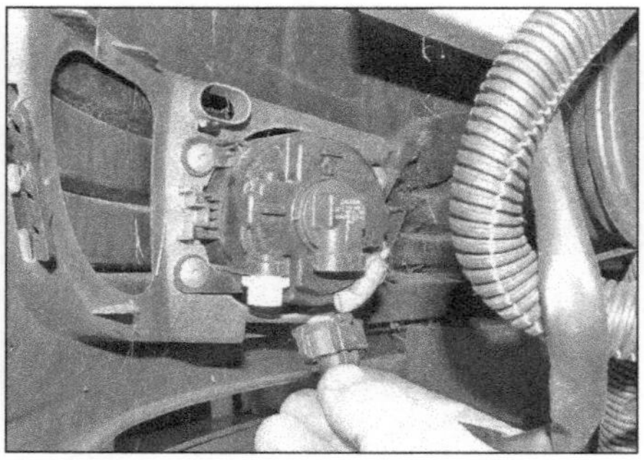
5.19 Disconnect the foglight wiring plug

5.20 Rotate the bulbholder anti-clockwise to remove

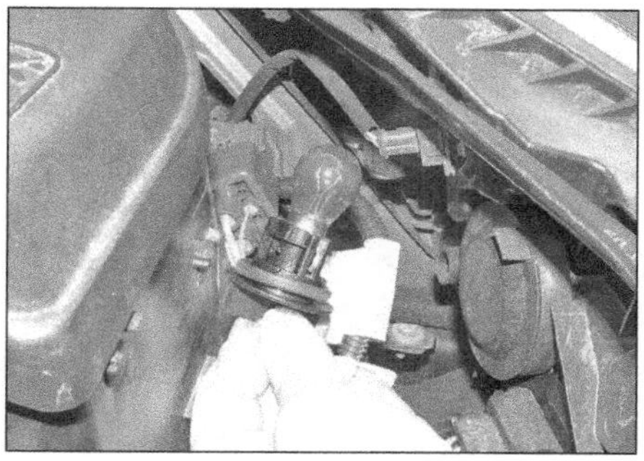

5.24 Rotate the bulbholder anti-clockwise to remove ...

5.25 ... then press in the bulb and rotate it anti-clockwise to remove it

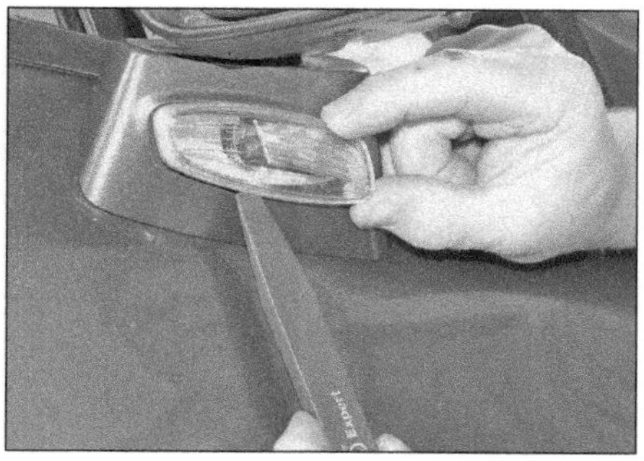

5.27 Unclip the light unit ...

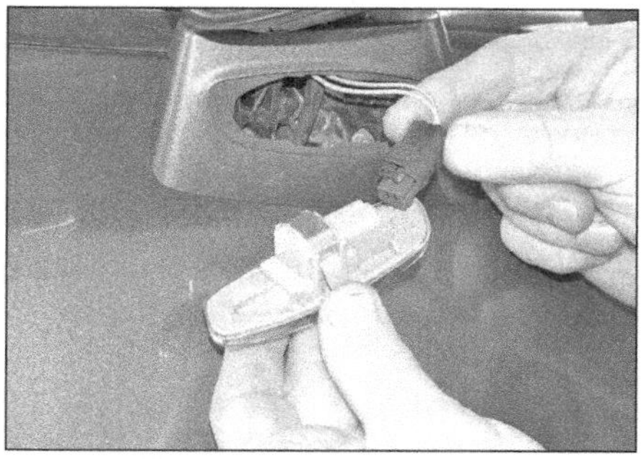

5.28 ... and disconnect the wiring connector

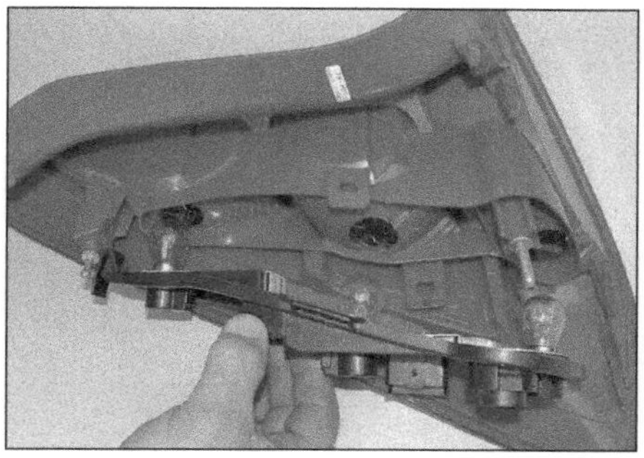

5.31 Release the retaining clips and pull the bulbholder from the light unit – 3-door models

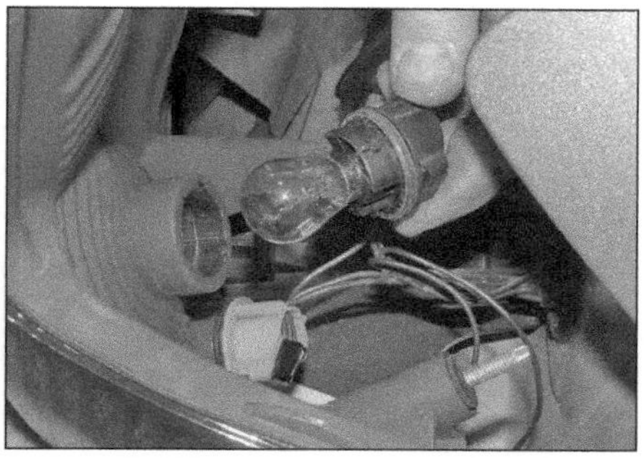

5.32 Rotate the bulbholders anti-clockwise to remove – 5-door models

intake plastic cover from the rear of the headlight unit **(see illustration 5.2)**.

24 Rotate the bulbholder 90° and free it from the rear of the headlight unit **(see illustration)**.

25 The bulb is a bayonet-fit in the holder, and can be removed by pressing it in and rotating it anti-clockwise **(see illustration)**.

26 Refitting is the reverse of the removal procedure, ensuring that the bulbholder seal is in good condition.

Side repeater

27 Release the retaining clips and remove the light unit from the base of the door mirror housing **(see illustration)**.

28 Disconnect the wiring connector from the light unit **(see illustration)**. The bulb is part of the light unit; the side repeater will need to be renewed as a complete unit.

29 Refitting is a reversal of the removal procedure.

Rear light cluster

30 Remove the relevant rear light unit as described in Section 7.

31 On 3-door models, release the retaining tabs and remove the bulbholder assembly from the rear of the light unit **(see illustration)**.

32 On 5-door models, rotate the bulbholder 90° and free it from the rear of the light unit **(see illustration)**.

33 All the bulbs (except sidelight bulbs on 5-door models) have bayonet fittings. The relevant bulb can be removed by pressing it in and rotating it anti-clockwise **(see illustrations)**.

34 On 5-door models the sidelight bulb is a capless (push-fit) type, and can easily be removed by pulling it out of the bulbholder **(see illustration)**.

35 Refitting is the reverse of removal, ensuring the light unit and bulbholder seals are in good condition.

High-level brake light

Note: *On 5-door models, the high-level brake light unit has LEDs fitted and can only be renewed as a complete unit.*

36 Remove the high level light unit as described in Section 7.

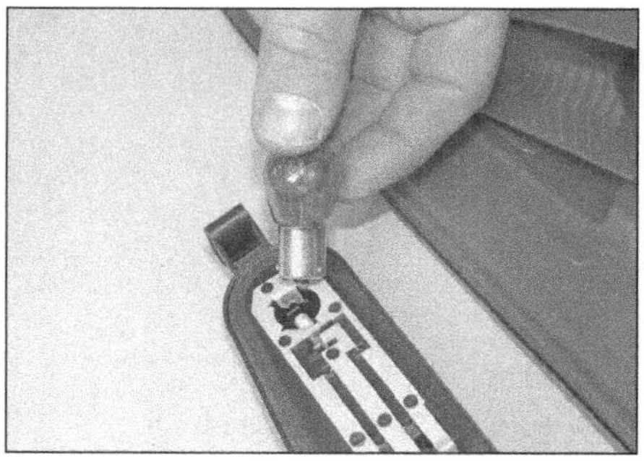

5.33a Press in the bulb and rotate it anti-clockwise to remove it – 3-door models

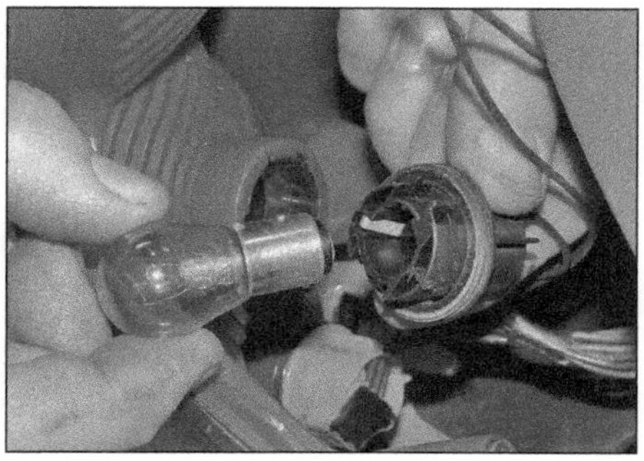

5.33b Press in the bulb and rotate it anti-clockwise to remove it – 5-door models

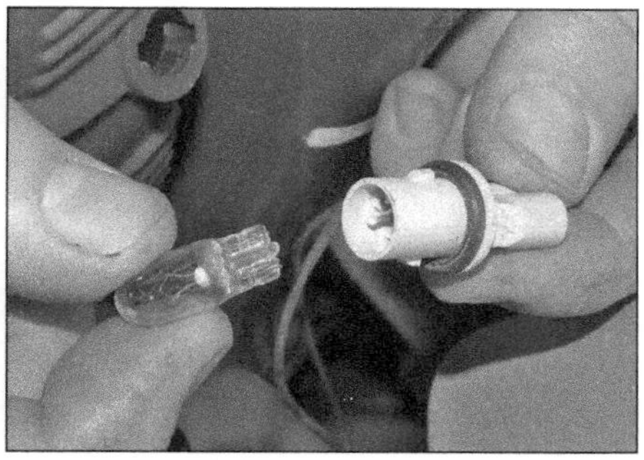

5.34 Pull the sidelight bulb from the bulbholder – 5-door models

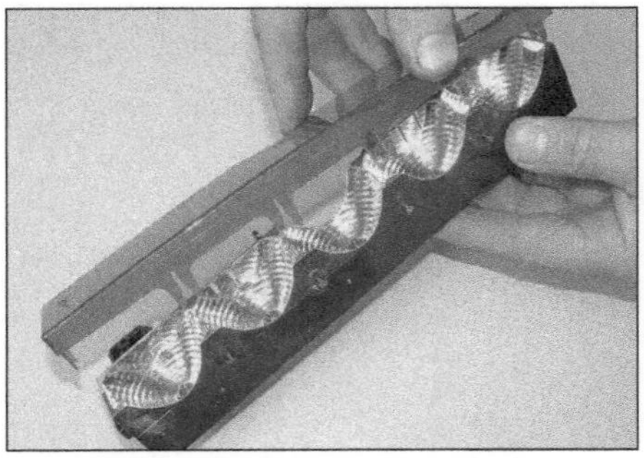

5.37a Carefully prise the light lens from place ...

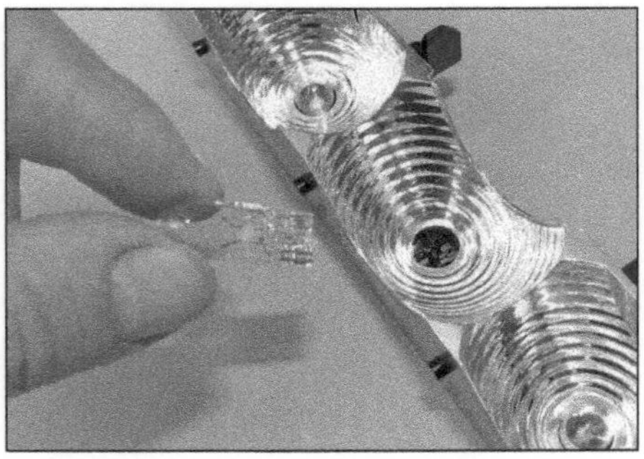

5.37b ... and pull the bulb(s) from the holder – 3-door models

5.39a Using a thin screwdriver ...

37 On 3-door models, release the retaining clips and detach the red light lens from the rear of the light unit, each bulb is of the capless (push-fit) type, and can easily be removed by pulling it out of the bulbholder **(see illustrations)**.

5.39b ... to carefully prise the light lens from place ...

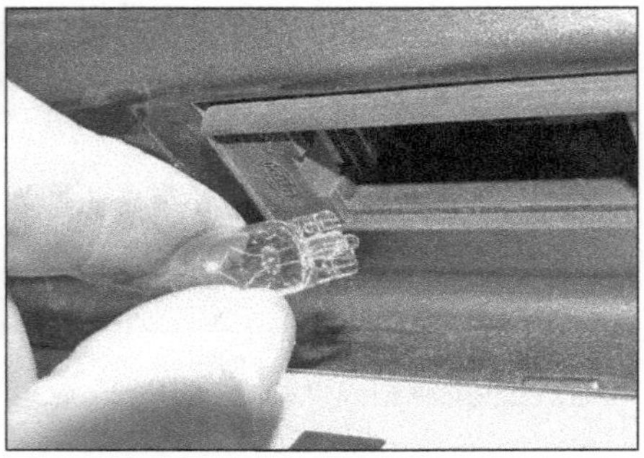

5.39c ... then pull the bulb from the holder

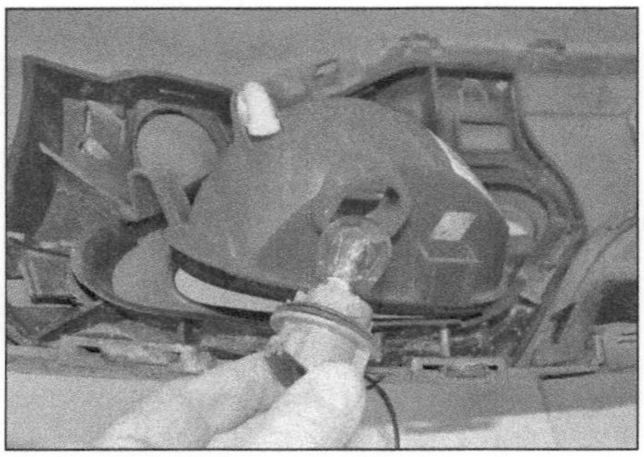

5.42 Rotate the bulbholder to remove ...

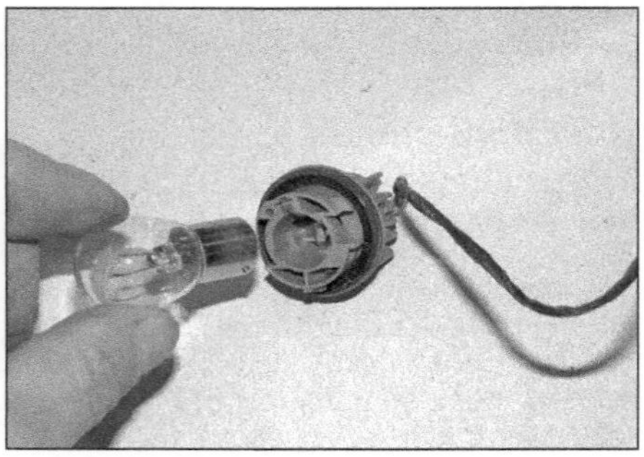

5.43 ... and rotate the bulb anti-clockwise to remove from holder

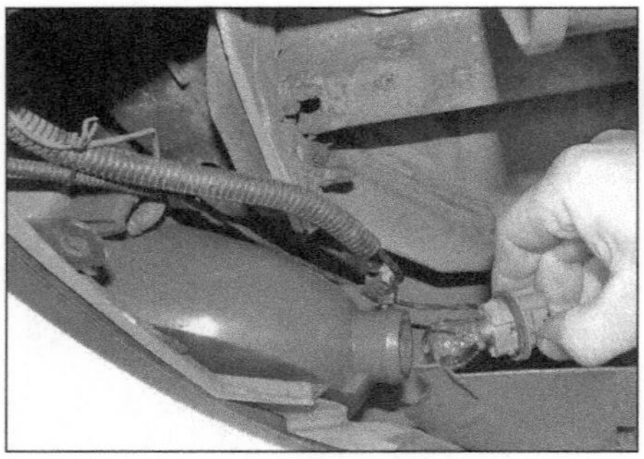

5.46 Rotate the bulbholder to remove ...

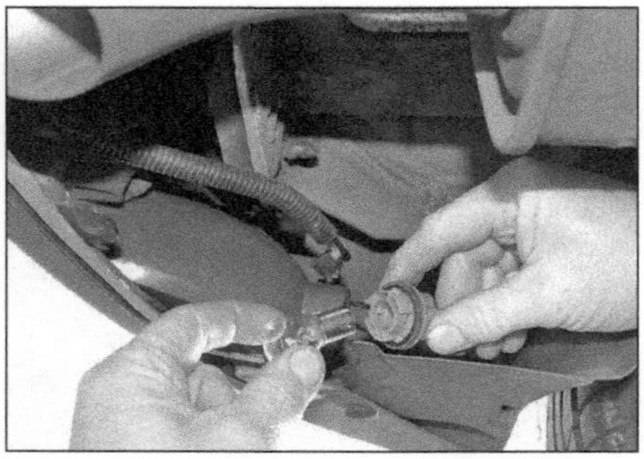

5.47 ... and rotate the bulb anti-clockwise to remove from holder

38 Refitting is the reverse of removal.

Number plate light

39 Using a small flat-bladed screwdriver, carefully prise out the end of the lens and remove it. The bulb is of the capless (push-fit) type, and can be removed by simply pulling it out of the light unit **(see illustrations)**.

40 Refitting is the reverse of the removal procedure, ensuring that the lens is securely clipped in position.

Rear foglights

41 Chock the rear wheels then jack up the rear of the vehicle and support it on axle stands (see *Jacking and vehicle support*).

42 Rotate the bulbholder and remove it from the rear of the light unit **(see illustration)**. To make access to the bulb easier it may be necessary to remove the light unit as described in Section 7.

43 The bulb is a bayonet-fit in the holder, and can be removed by pressing it in and rotating it anti-clockwise **(see illustration)**.

44 Refitting is a reversal of removal.

Reversing lights

5-door models

45 Chock the rear wheels then jack up the rear of the vehicle and support it on axle stands (see *Jacking and vehicle support*).

46 Reach up behind the rear bumper and rotate the bulbholder to remove it from the rear of the light unit **(see illustration)**.

47 The bulb is a bayonet-fit in the holder, and can be removed by pressing it in and rotating it anti-clockwise **(see illustration)**.

48 Refitting is a reversal of removal.

6 Bulbs (interior lights) – renewal

General

1 Refer to Section 5, paragraph 1.

Passenger compartment lights

2 Using a flat bladed-screwdriver, carefully

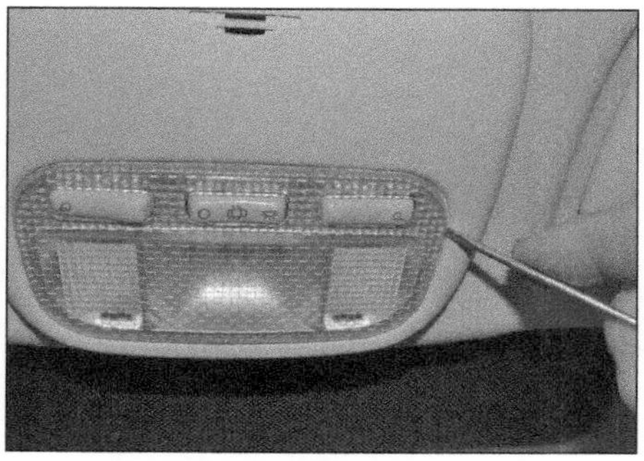

6.2a Using a thin screwdriver ...

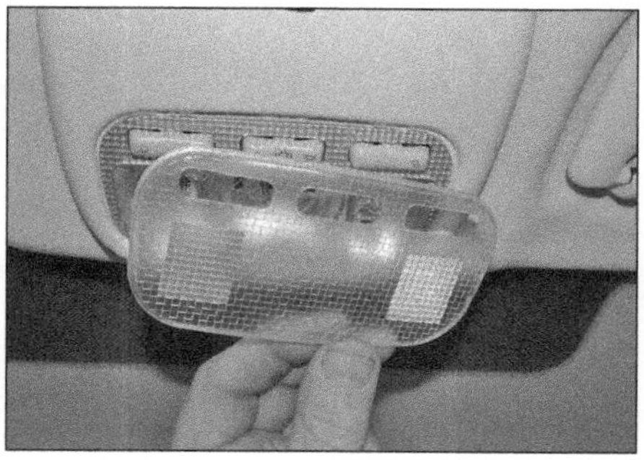

6.2b ... to unclip the front interior light lens ...

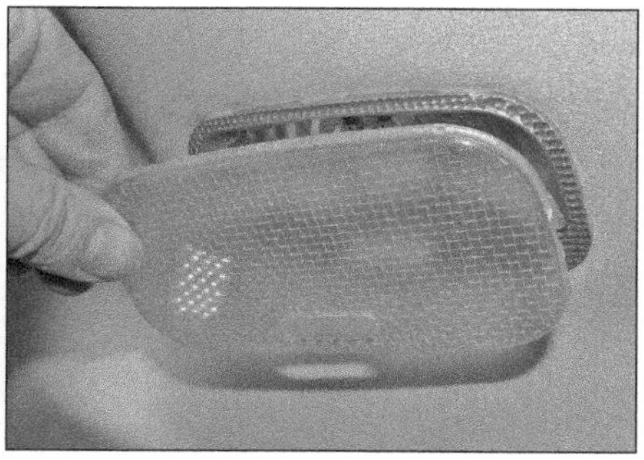

6.2c ... and the rear light lens

unclip the plastic lens cover from the light unit **(see illustrations)**.

3 The bulbs are of the capless (push-fit) type, and can be removed by simply pulling it out of the bulbholder **(see illustrations)**.

4 If required, release the securing clips and carefully remove the light unit from the headlining **(see illustrations)**. Disconnect the wiring from the rear of the unit as it is removed.

5 Refitting is the reverse of the removal procedure

Instrument panel lights

6 The instrument panel and warning lights are illuminated by integral LEDs. It is not possible to renew them independently of the panel. Instrument panel renewal is described in Section 9.

Heating/ventilation control illumination

Note: *The following procedure is for models with manually operated heater controls. On models with automatic climate control, the heater control panel is illuminated by integral LEDs. It is not possible to renew them independently of the panel.*

7 Remove the heater control panel as described in Chapter 3, Section 10.

8 Using a pair of long-nose pliers, twist the bulbholder and remove it from the rear of the heater control panel **(see illustrations)**.

9 Refitting is the reverse of the removal procedure

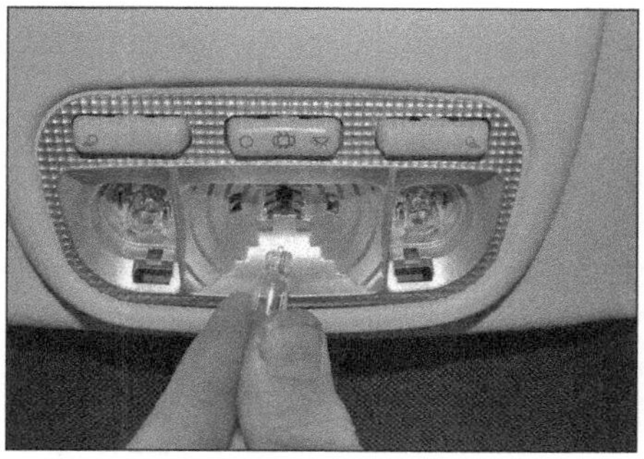

6.3a Pull the bulb from the front light unit ...

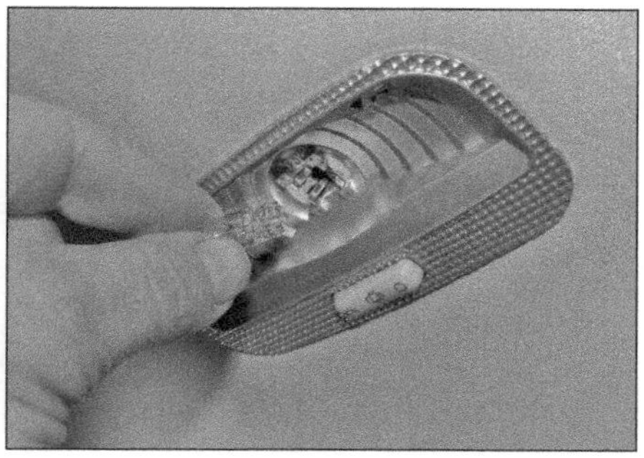

6.3b ... and the rear light unit

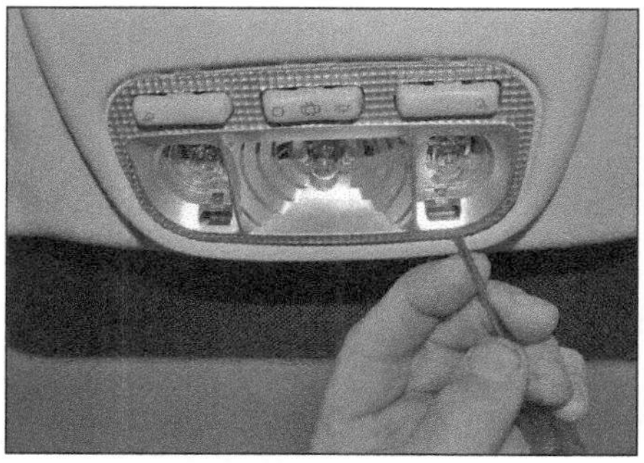

6.4a Using a thin screwdriver ...

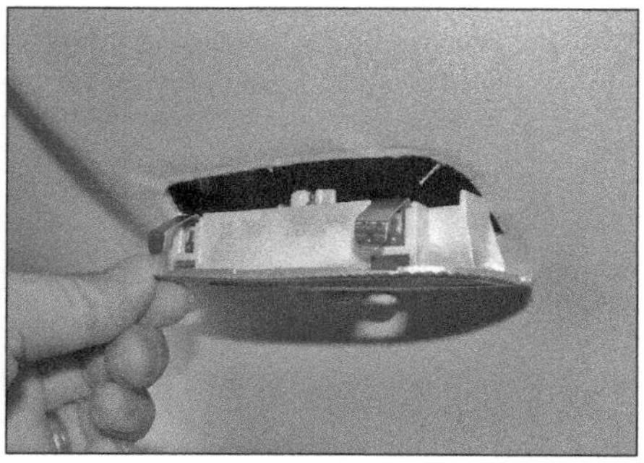

6.4b ... to release the two retaining clips ...

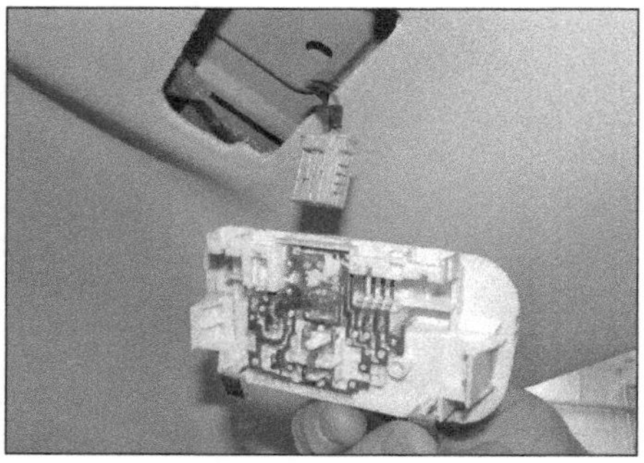

6.4c ... then disconnect the wiring plug

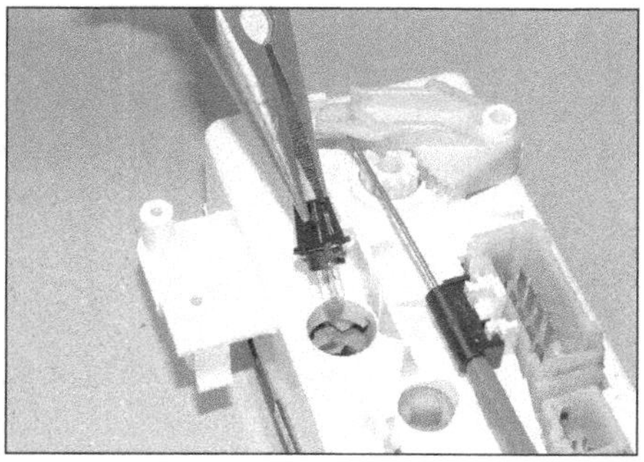

6.8a Rotate the bulbholder to remove ...

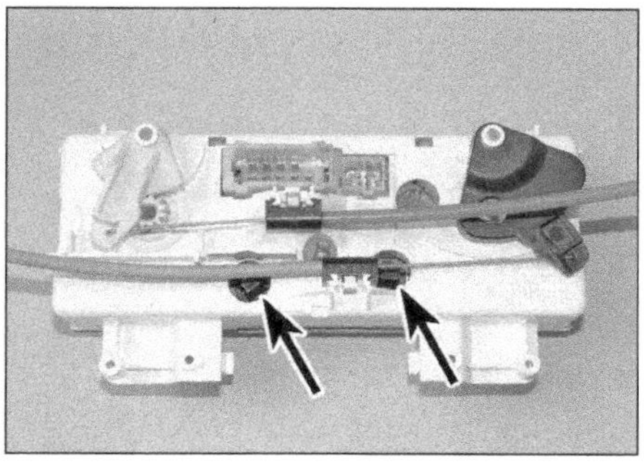

6.8b ... the two control panel bulbs (arrowed)

6.12a Unclip the light unit from the inside the glovebox ...

6.12b ... and withdraw the light complete with switch

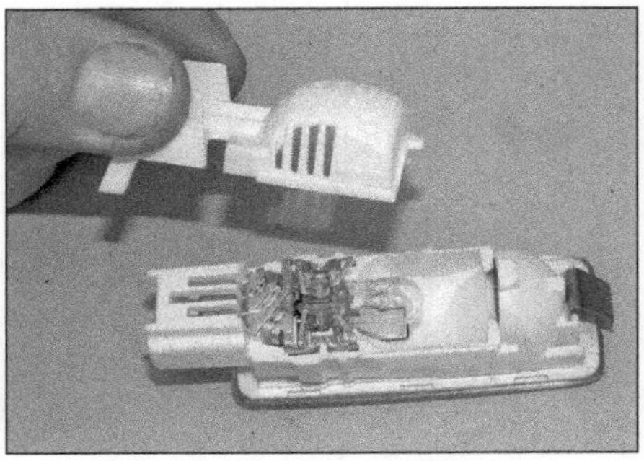

6.13a Unclip the plastic cover ...

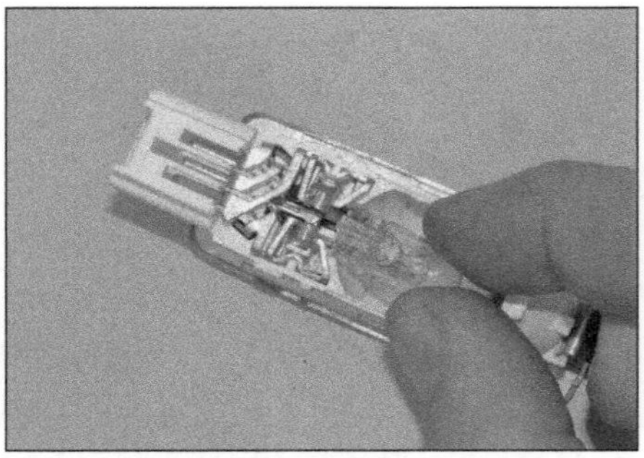

6.13b ... and pull the bulb from the holder

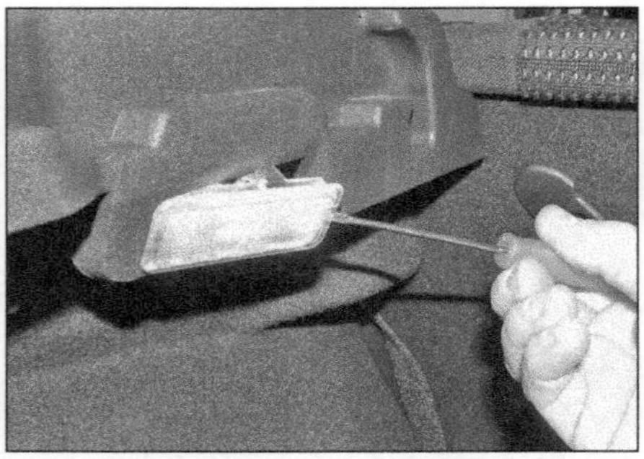

6.15 Unclip the light unit from the luggage compartment side trim panel ...

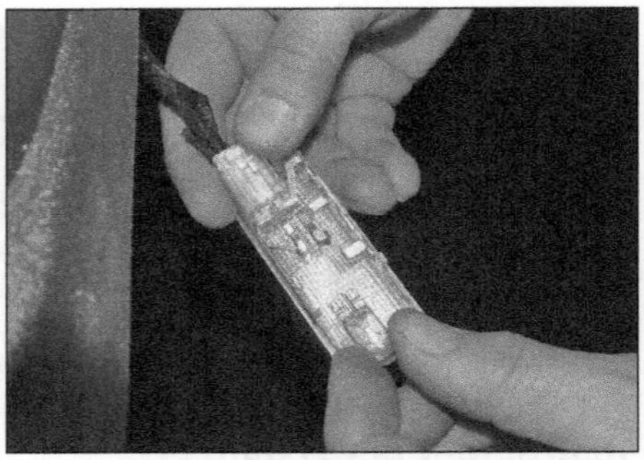

6.16 ... and pull the bulb from the holder

Multifunction display illumination

10 The multifunction display is illuminated by integral LEDs. It is not possible to renew them independently of the display. Remove the multifunction display as described in Section 10.

Switch illumination

11 All of the switches that are illuminated are done so by LEDs. These LEDs are an integral part of the switch and cannot be renewed separately. Renewal will therefore require renewal of the complete switch assembly (see Section 4).

Glovebox illumination

12 Open the glovebox, and unclip the light unit from inside the glove compartment. Remove the light unit, and disconnect the wiring plug as it is withdrawn **(see illustrations)**. Note that the switch is integral with the light.

13 Carefully unclip the plastic cover from the rear of the light unit. The bulb is of the capless (push-fit) type, and can be removed by simply pulling it out of the bulbholder **(see illustrations)**.

14 Refitting is the reverse of the removal procedure

Luggage area illumination

15 Open the tailgate, and unclip the light unit from inside the luggage side trim panel. Remove the light unit, and disconnect the wiring plug as it is withdrawn **(see illustrations)**.

16 The bulb is of the capless (push-fit) type, and can easily be removed by pulling it out of the bulbholder **(see illustration)**.

17 Refitting is the reverse of the removal procedure

Door courtesy illumination

18 Open the door, and unclip the light unit from the underside of the door trim panel. Remove the light unit, and disconnect the wiring plug as it is withdrawn **(see illustration)**.

19 Carefully unclip the plastic cover from the rear of the light unit. The bulb is of the capless (push-fit) type, and can be removed by simply pulling it out of the bulbholder **(see illustrations)**.

20 Refitting is the reverse of the removal procedure.

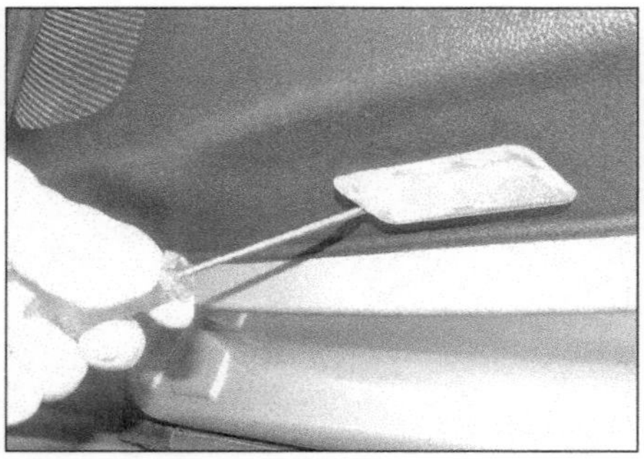

6.18 Unclip the light unit from the lower door trim panel

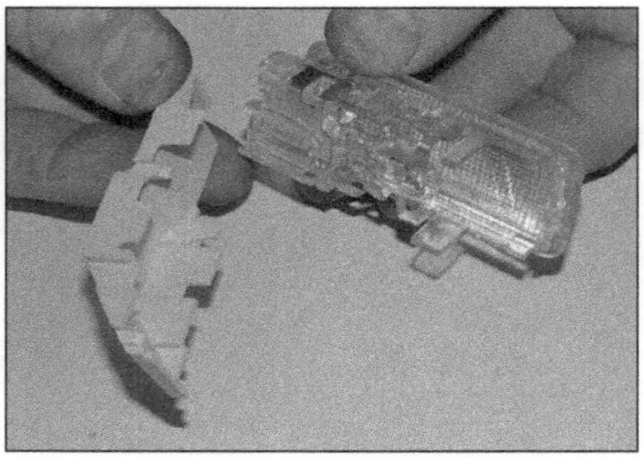

6.19a Unclip the plastic cover ...

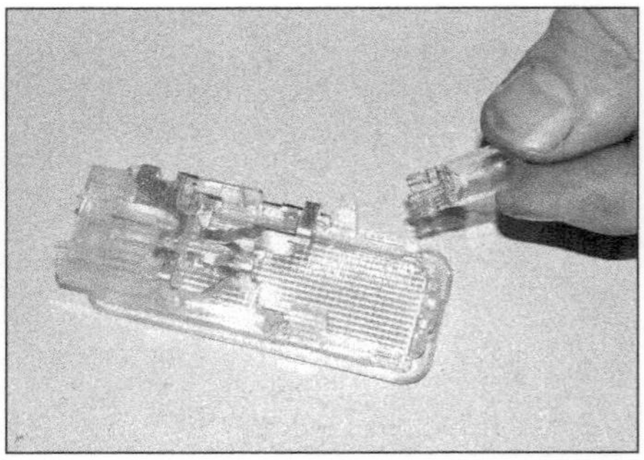

6.19b ... and pull the bulb from the holder

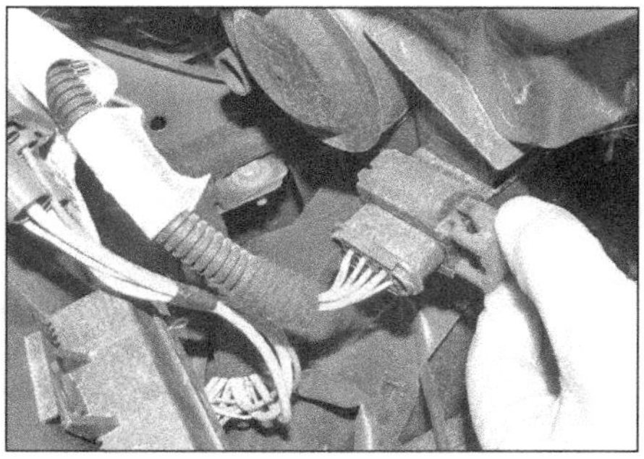

7.2a Release the locking clip to disconnect the wiring connector ...

7.2b ... also disconnect the sidelight wiring connector (arrowed)

7.3a Undo the two upper headlamp mounting bolts (arrowed) ...

7.3b ... and lower mounting bolt (arrowed)

7.11a Slide out the plastic compartment cover ...

7.11b ... release the side trim retaining clips and pull back the carpet

7 Exterior light units – removal and refitting

Headlight

1 Remove the front bumper (see Chapter 11, Section 6).

2 Reach behind the headlight, release the locking clip and disconnect the wiring connector from the rear of the headlight unit. Also disconnect the wiring connector for the sidelight at the top of the headlight unit **(see illustrations)**.

3 Slacken and remove the three mounting bolts and free the headlight unit from its mounting, then manoeuvre the unit out of position **(see illustrations)**.

4 When refitting, offer up the headlight unit and securely reconnect its wiring connectors.

5 Position the headlight in its aperture, and then refit and tighten the headlight mounting bolts.

6 Check the operation of the headlight, then refit the front bumper.

7 Check the headlight beam alignment using the information given in Section 8.

Front indicator side repeater

8 Release the retaining clips and remove the light unit from the base of the door mirror housing **(see illustration 5.27)**.

9 Disconnect the wiring connector from the light unit **(see illustration 5.28)**.

10 Refitting is a reversal of the removal procedure.

Rear light unit

3-door models

11 Remove the plastic compartment panel, release the retaining clips and pull out the carpet trim panel from behind the light unit **(see illustrations)**.

12 Undo the plastic retaining nut from the back of the light unit, then pull the light unit away from the body of the vehicle, releasing its locating peg **(see illustrations)**

13 Disconnect the wiring connector from the light unit as it is removed from the vehicle **(see illustration)**.

14 Refitting is the reverse of removal,

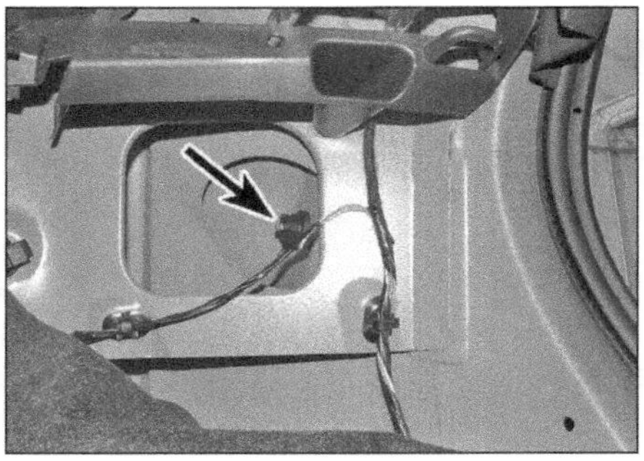

7.12a Undo the rear light unit plastic nut (arrowed)

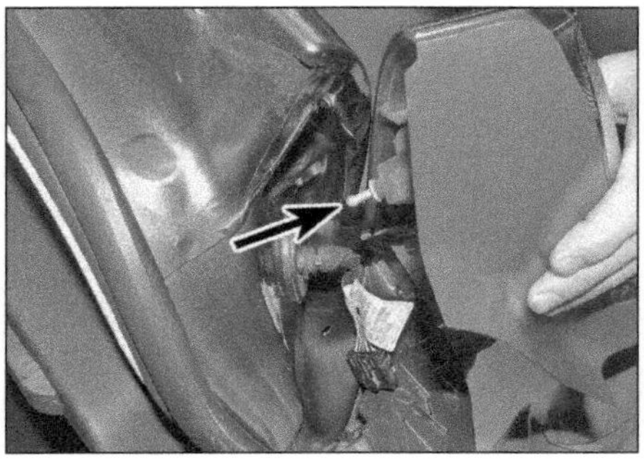

7.12b Pull the light unit to release the locating peg (arrowed)

7.13 Disconnect the wiring connector

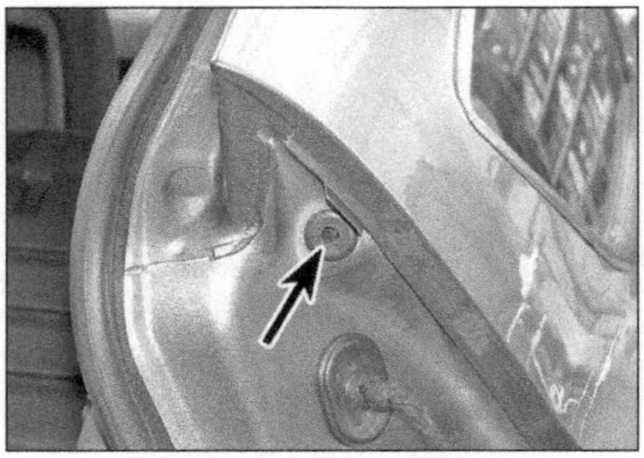

7.14 Make sure the peg locates in the grommet (arrowed)

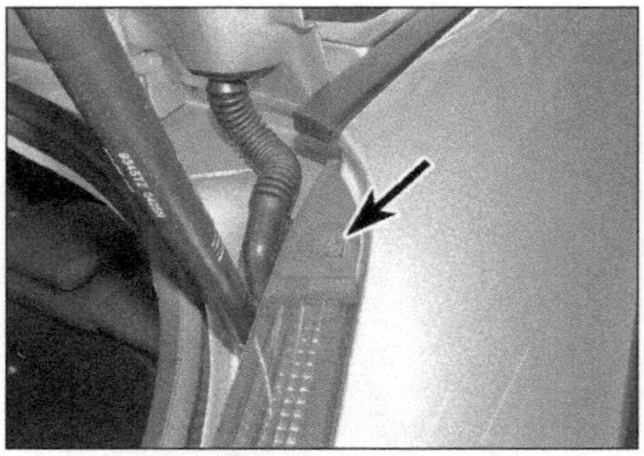

7.17a Undo the retaining screw (arrowed) ...

ensuring the light unit locating peg is fitted in the rear panel correctly **(see illustration)**.

5-door models

15 Remove the plastic compartment

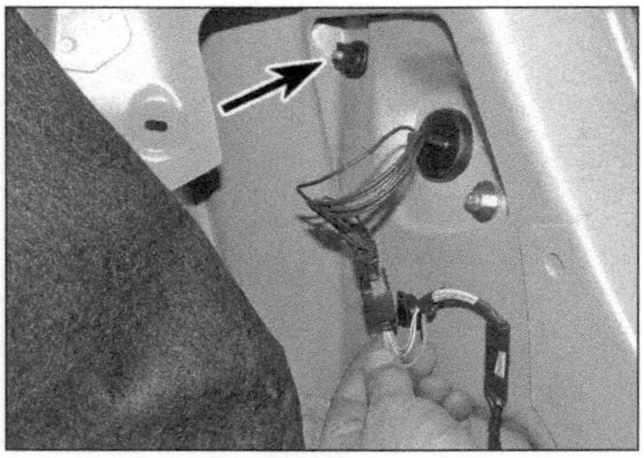

7.16 Disconnect the wiring connector and undo the plastic nut (arrowed)

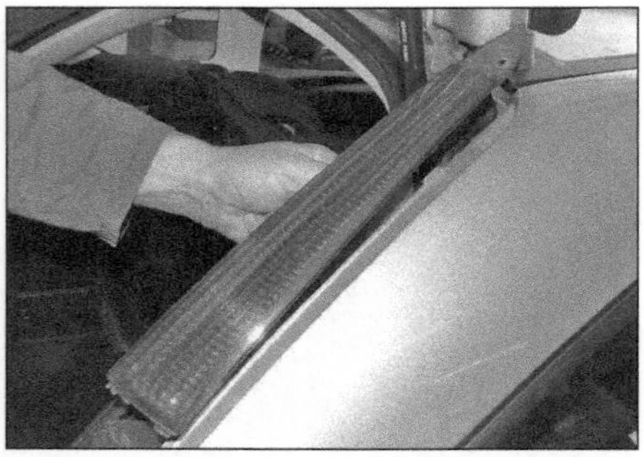

7.17b ... and remove the upper part of the light unit

panel, release the retaining clips and pull out the carpet trim panel from behind the light unit **(see illustrations 7.11a and 7.11b)**.

16 Undo the plastic retaining nut from the back of the light unit, and disconnect the wiring block connector **(see illustration)**.

17 Undo the retaining screw and remove the upper part of the light unit from the rear of the vehicle **(see illustrations)**.

18 Pull the lower part of the light unit away from the body of the vehicle, releasing the grommet from the body panel to withdraw the wiring connector as the light unit is removed **(see illustrations)**.

19 Refitting is the reverse of removal.

High-level brake light

3-door models

20 Open the tailgate and remove the lower tailgate trim panel as described in Chapter 11, Section 25.

21 Disconnect the wiring connector from the light unit **(see illustration)**.

22 Release the two retaining clips and slide the light unit out from the tailgate panel **(see illustrations)**.

23 Refitting is the reverse of removal.

5-door models

24 Open the tailgate and remove the upper tailgate trim panel as described in Chapter 11, Section 25.

25 Unscrew the nuts securing the upper rear spoiler to the top of the tailgate **(see illustration)**.

7.18a Withdraw the lower part of the light unit ...

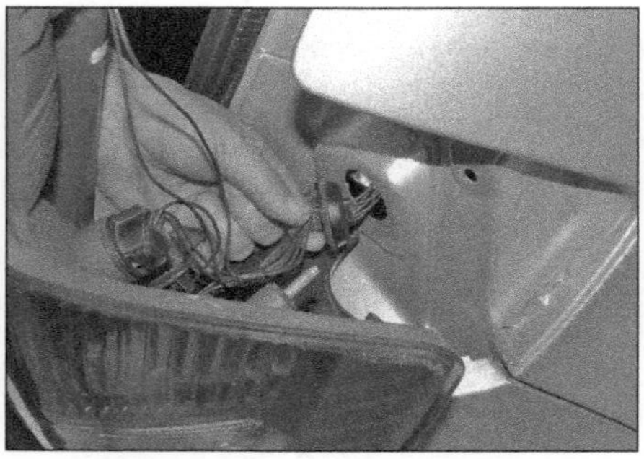

7.18b ... and unclip the wiring loom grommet from the body panel

7.21 Disconnect the wiring connector

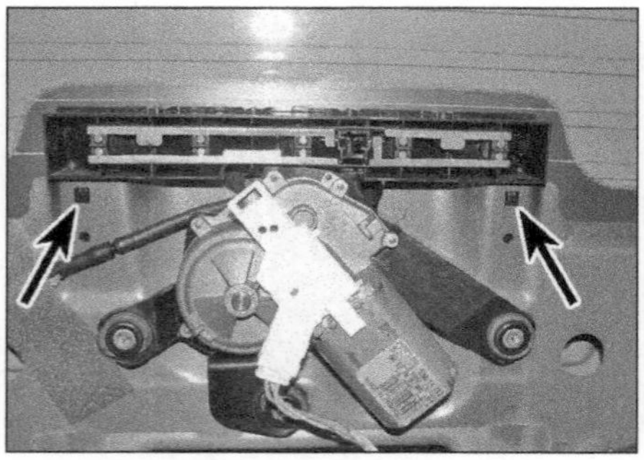

7.22a Release the securing clips (arrowed) ...

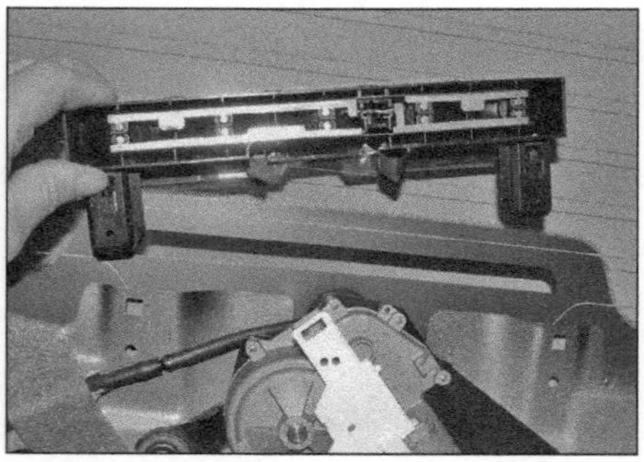

7.22b ... and slide the light unit from the tailgate

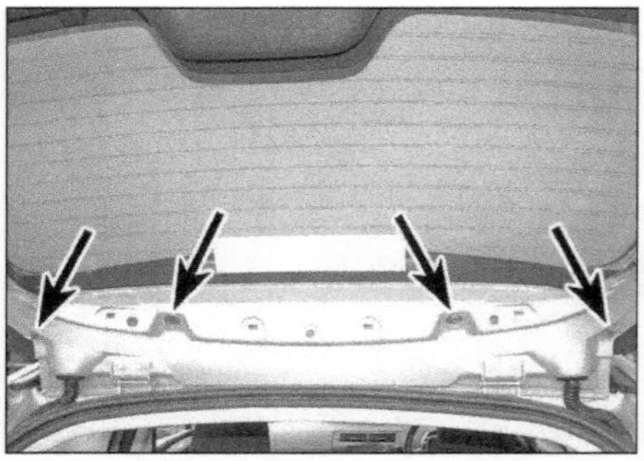

7.25 Undo the retaining nuts (arrowed) ...

7.26 ... and unclip the upper trim/spoiler panel from the tailgate

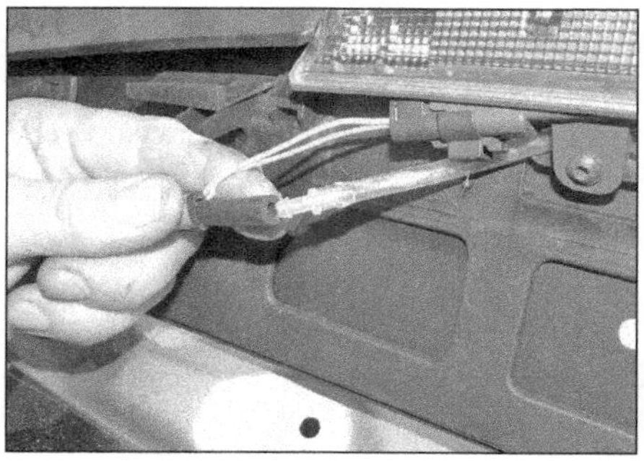

7.27a Disconnect the rear washer hose ...

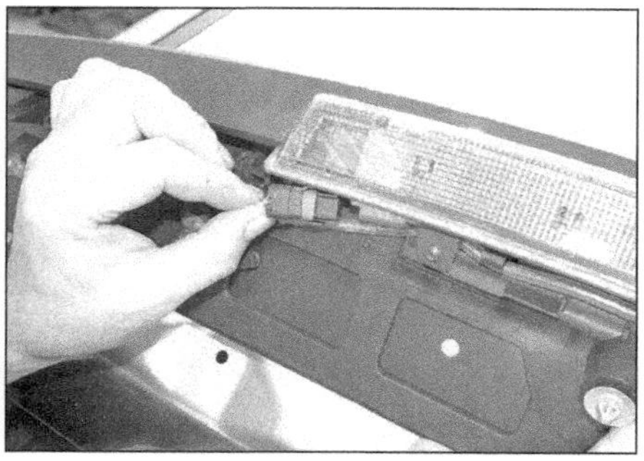

7.27b ... and wiring connector

26 Close the tailgate and unclip the spoiler from the top of the tailgate **(see illustration)**.

27 Disconnect the washer tube and wiring connector from the light unit **(see illustrations)**.

28 Undo the two retaining screws and withdraw the light unit from the spoiler **(see illustrations)**.

29 If required, the washer jet can be removed from the end of the light unit, as described in Section 16.

30 Refitting is the reverse of removal, noting the following points:

a) Make sure the wiring terminal is fitted securely.

b) Make sure the washer tube is fitted securely.

c) Do not overtighten the spoiler retaining nuts, as the plastic is easily broken.

Number plate light

Note: *it is possible to remove the light unit without removing the bumper, but damage to the light unit securing clip is possible. The following procedure shows the removal of the light unit with the bumper fitted.*

31 If required remove the rear bumper (see Chapter 11, Section 7).

32 Carefully push the relevant light unit to one side, and ease it from the bumper cover **(see illustrations)**.

33 Disconnect the wiring plug as the light unit is withdrawn from the bumper **(see illustration)**.

34 Refitting is a reversal of removal.

Front foglights

35 Chock the rear wheels then jack up the front of the vehicle and support it on axle stands (see *Jacking and vehicle support*). Remove the front roadwheel to give better access.

36 Release the front of the wheel arch liner by removing the fasteners **(see illustration)**.

37 Reach up under the front bumper and disconnect the wiring from the foglight bulbholder **(see illustration 5.19)**.

38 Using a pair of long-nose pliers release the securing clips at the rear of the light unit, and

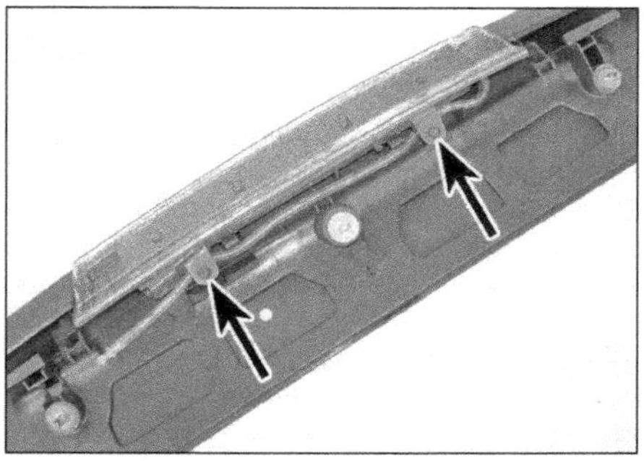

7.28a Undo the two retaining screws (arrowed) ...

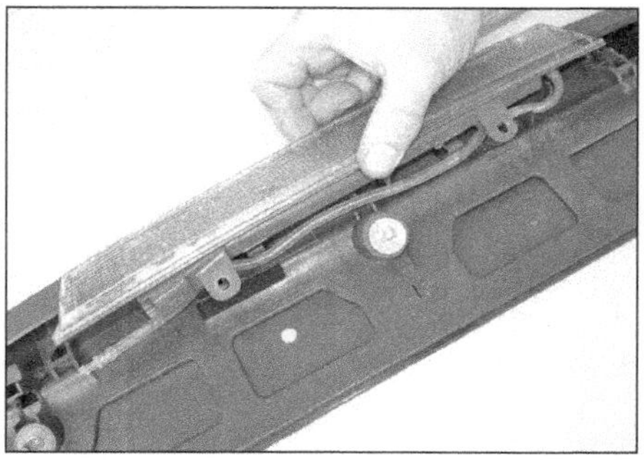

7.28b ... and remove the light unit from the spoiler

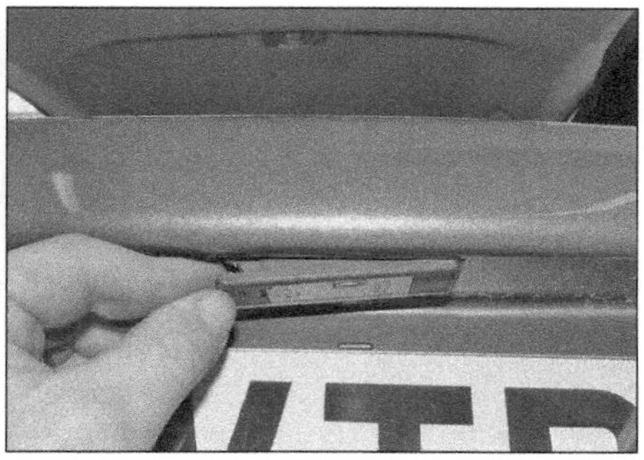

7.32a Push the light unit to one side ...

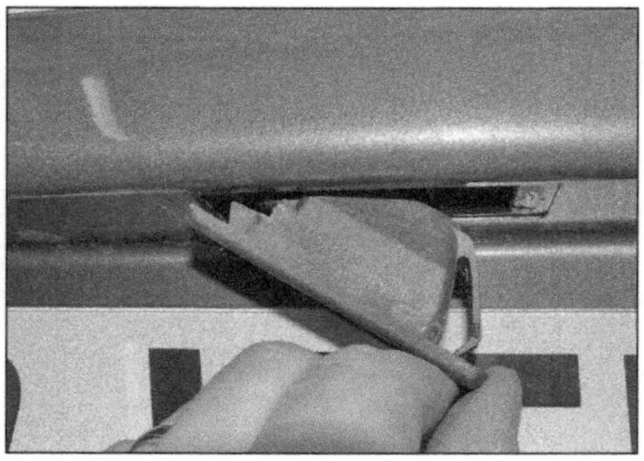

7.32b ... and release it from the rear bumper

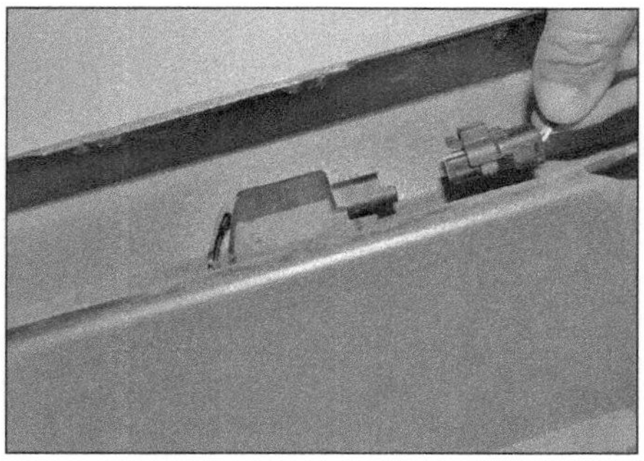

7.33 Disconnect the wiring connector (viewed from behind the bumper)

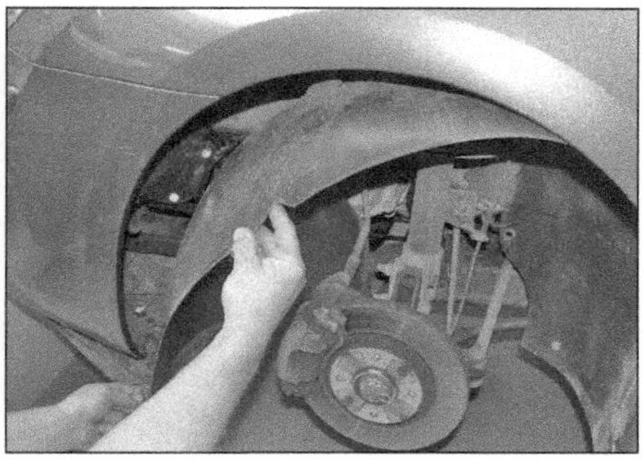

7.36 Pull back the inner wheel arch liner

7.38a Release the retaining clips (arrowed) ...

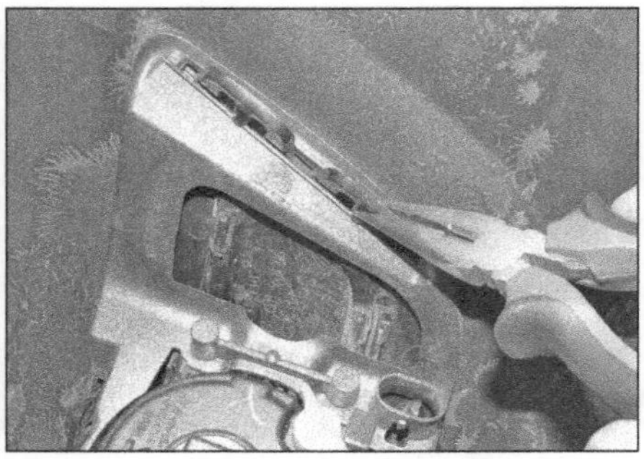

7.38b ... using a pair of long-nose pliers ...

7.38c ... to remove the front foglight surround

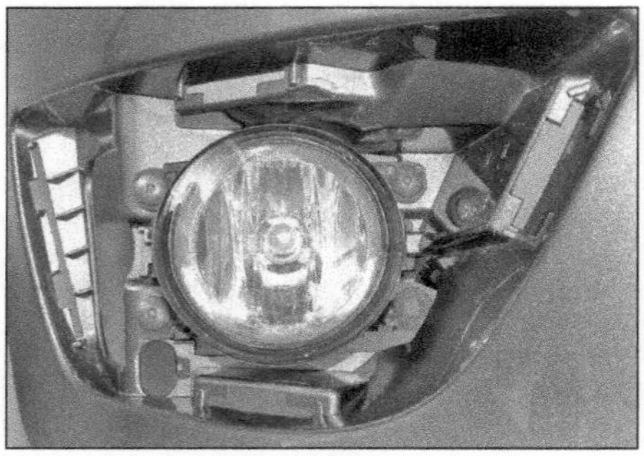

7.39 Foglight retaining screws

7.42 Release the securing clip (arrowed) ...

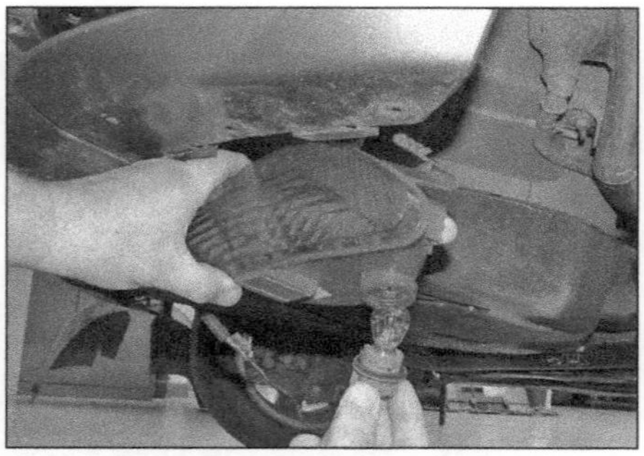

7.43 ... withdraw the light unit and remove the bulbholder

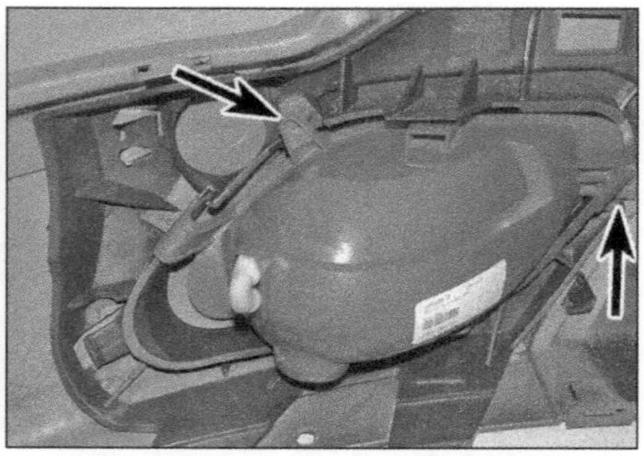

7.44 Make sure the locating pegs (arrowed) are located correctly

then withdraw the trim panel from around the front of the foglight unit **(see illustrations)**.

39 Undo the mounting screws and withdraw the foglight unit from the front of the bumper **(see illustration)**.

40 Refitting is a reversal of removal.

Rear foglights

41 Chock the rear wheels then jack up the rear of the vehicle and support it on axle stands (see *Jacking and vehicle support*).

42 Release the securing clip and withdraw the foglight from under the rear bumper **(see illustration)**.

43 Rotate the bulbholder and remove it from the rear of the light unit as it is removed **(see illustration)**.

44 Refitting is a reversal of removal, ensuring that the locating pegs are fitted to the rear of the bumper correctly **(see illustration)**.

Reversing lights

45 Chock the rear wheels then jack up the rear of the vehicle and support it on axle stands (see *Jacking and vehicle support*).

46 Release the securing clip and withdraw the reversing light from under the rear bumper **(see illustration)**.

47 Rotate the bulbholder and remove it from the rear of the light unit **(see illustration)**.

48 Refitting is a reversal of removal, ensuring that the locating peg is fitted to the bumper correctly **(see illustration)**.

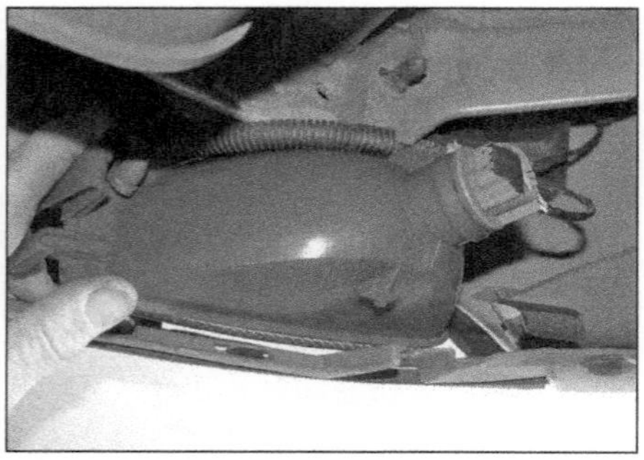

7.46 Remove the reversing light from the bumper ...

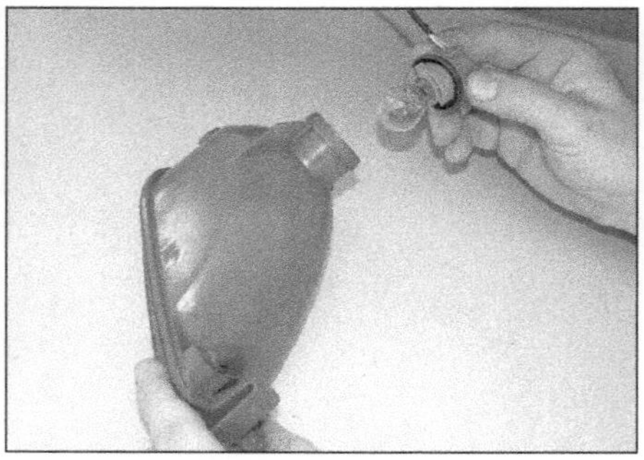

7.47 ... and remove the bulbholder

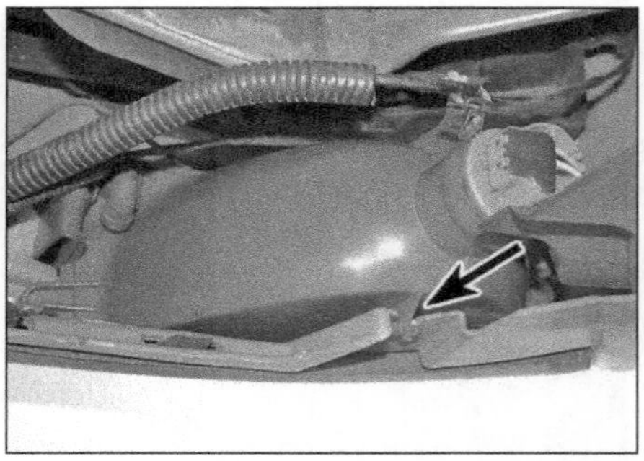

7.48 Make sure the locating peg (arrowed) is located correctly

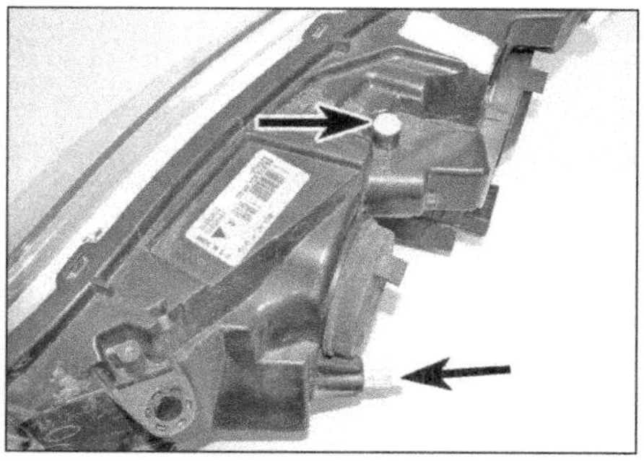

8.2 Headlight alignment adjusters (arrowed)

8 Headlight beam alignment – general information

1 Accurate adjustment of the headlight beam is only possible using optical beam-setting equipment, and this work should therefore be carried out by a Citroën dealer or suitably-equipped workshop.

2 For reference, the vertical and horizontal alignment of the headlights can be adjusted by rotating the adjuster assemblies, which are accessible at the rear of the headlight casing **(see illustration)**.

3 On models equipped with headlight leveling, ensure the adjuster switch on the facia panel inside the vehicle is set to position 0 before the headlights are adjusted.

8.4 Using an Allen key to adjust the front foglight alignment

4 On models with front foglights, these can be adjusted by using an Allen key at the rear of the light unit. Reach up behind the wheel arch liner to gain access **(see illustration)**.

9 Instrument panel – removal and refitting

Removal

1 Disconnect the battery (refer to precautions in Chapter 5A, Section 1.

2 Using two thin screwdrivers, insert them into the rear of the instrument panel and release the two outer retaining clips **(see illustrations)**.

3 Carefully lever the front of the instrument panel (nearest the windscreen) upwards to release the retaining clips along the front edge of the instrument panel **(see illustration)**.

4 With all the clips released, pull the instrument panel upwards and withdraw it from the top of the facia. Release the locking clip and disconnect the wiring plug(s) as the unit is withdrawn **(see illustrations)**.

5 Should the instrument panel develop a fault, have the vehicle's self-diagnosis facility interrogated by a Citroën dealer or suitably-equipped specialist. No parts are available separately for the instrument panel, if faulty, the complete assembly must be renewed.

Refitting

6 Refitting is a reversal of removal, ensuring that the wiring connectors are securely fitted and the retaining clips engage correctly when the instrument panel is pressed into position in the top of the facia.

10 Multifunction display unit – removal and refitting

Removal

1 Ensure the ignition is switched off.

2 Remove the front section of the centre console as described in Chapter 11, Section 26 (paragraphs 1 to 7).

3 Carefully unclip the pen tray from the front of the display unit **(see illustration)**.

4 Lever around the outer edge of the display

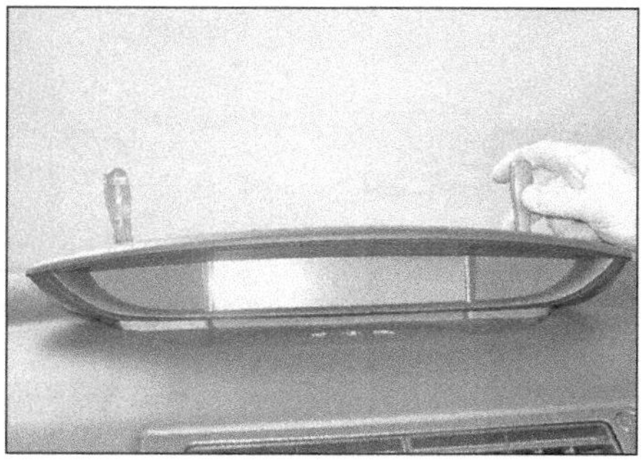

9.2a Insert two thin screwdrivers/pins ...

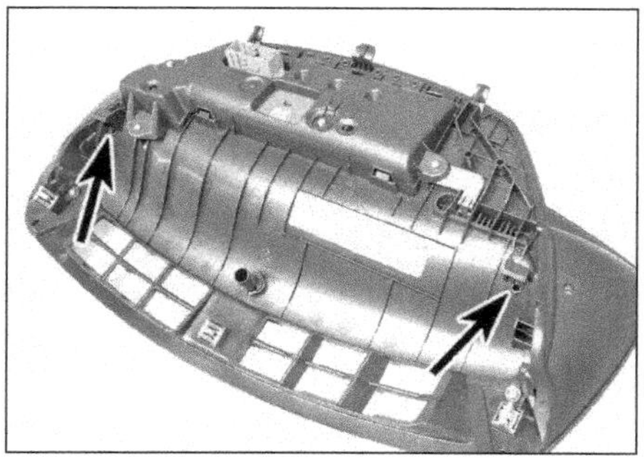

9.2b ... through the holes in the panel (arrowed)

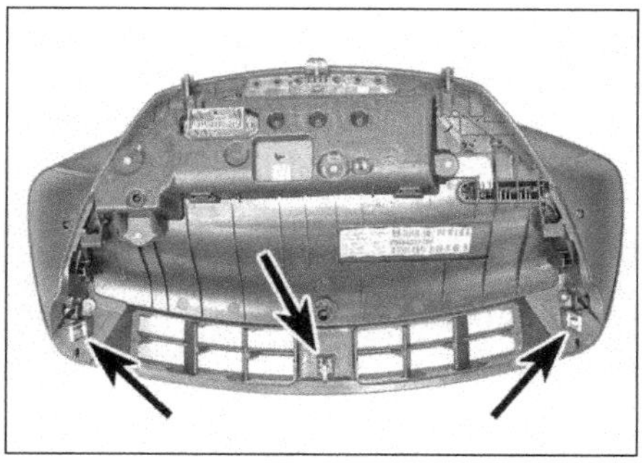

9.3 Release the three retaining clips ...

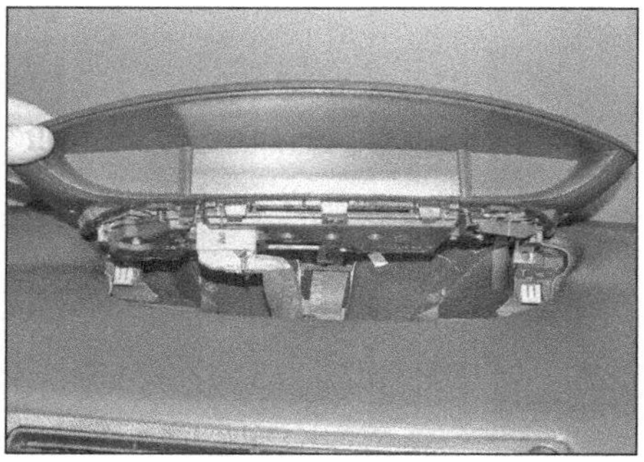

9.4a ... lift up the instrument panel ...

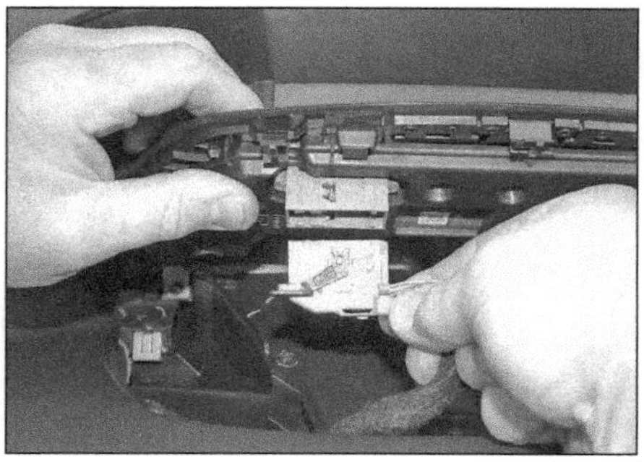

9.4b ... and disconnect the wiring connector

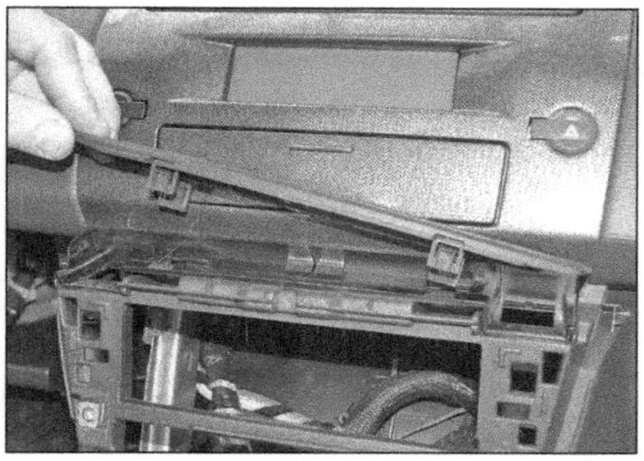

10.3 Unclip the pen tray from the facia ...

unit, and release it from the facia **(see illustration)**.

5 Depending on model, it may be necessary to undo the retaining screws to remove the display unit from the facia.

6 Release the locking clip and disconnect the wiring plug from the rear of the display unit as it is withdrawn from the facia **(see illustration)**.

Refitting

7 Refitting is a reversal of removal.

11 Cigarette lighter/accessory socket – removal and refitting

Removal

1 Remove the centre console as described in Chapter 11, Section 26.

2 Where illumination is fitted to the socket, carefully release the retaining clips and slide the light assembly off the base of the socket, taking great care not to break its electrical contacts.

3 Pull out the lighter element then release the tangs and push out the metal insert/accessory socket. The plastic outer section can then be removed from the console **(see illustrations)**.

Refitting

4 Align the plastic outer section tab with the cut-out then insert it into the console.

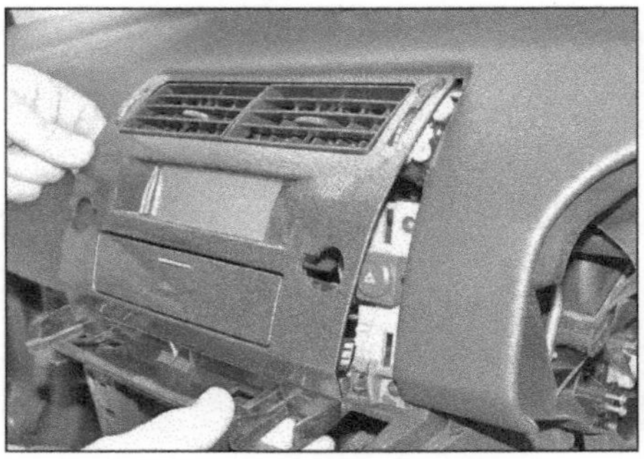

10.4 ... then unclip the display unit and surround from the facia

5 Align the bulbholder contact on the metal insert with the holder tangs on the plastic outer then clip the insert into position.

6 Slide the illumination light assembly onto the metal insert and clip it securely onto the plastic outer.

7 Ensure the cigarette lighter is correctly assembled then refit the centre console and/or trim panels.

12 Horn – removal and refitting

Removal

1 The horns are located behind the front bumper, on the right-hand side **(see illustration)**.

10.6 Disconnect the wiring connector from the display unit

2 Unclip the inner wheel arch liner in front of the left-hand side front wheel, and then reach in to access the horns. To make access easier, remove the front bumper as described in Chapter 11, Section 6.

3 Disconnect the wiring connector, then slacken the mounting bracket bolt and remove from under the front crossmember **(see illustrations)**.

4 To remove the horns individually from the mounting bracket, unplug the wiring connectors that join the two horns together, then undo the retaining nut and remove the horn from the bracket.

Refitting

5 Refitting is a reversal of removal.

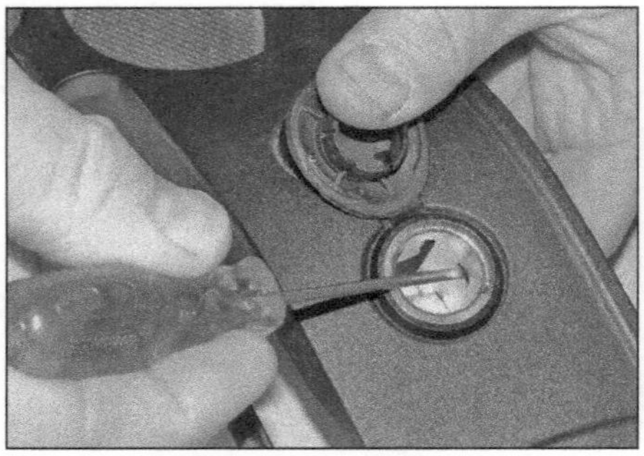

11.3a Release the retaining clips ...

11.3b ... slide out the inner metal sleeve ...

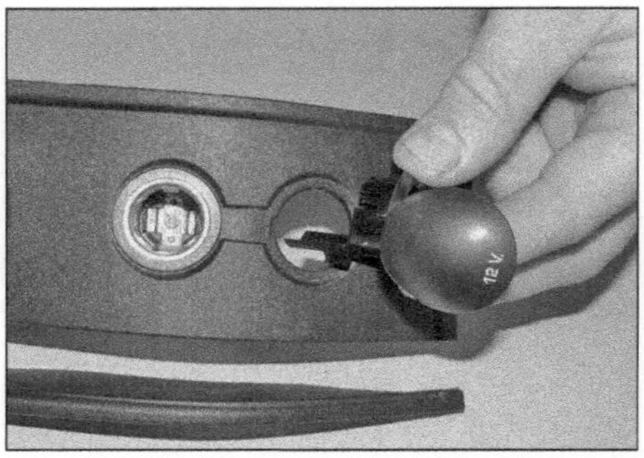

11.3c ... then unclip the plastic surround

12.1 Location of the horns behind right-hand side of bumper

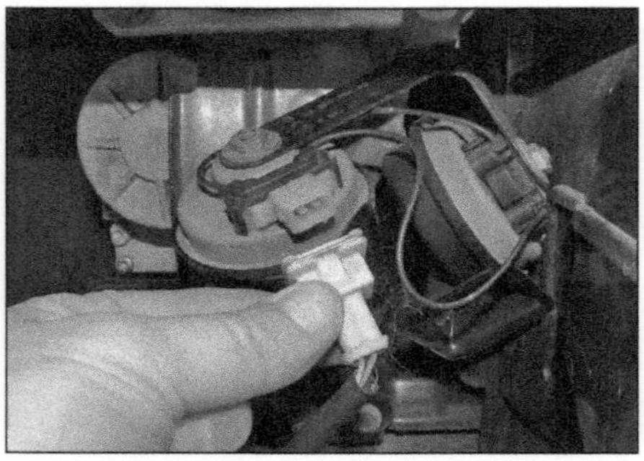

12.3a Disconnect the wiring connector ...

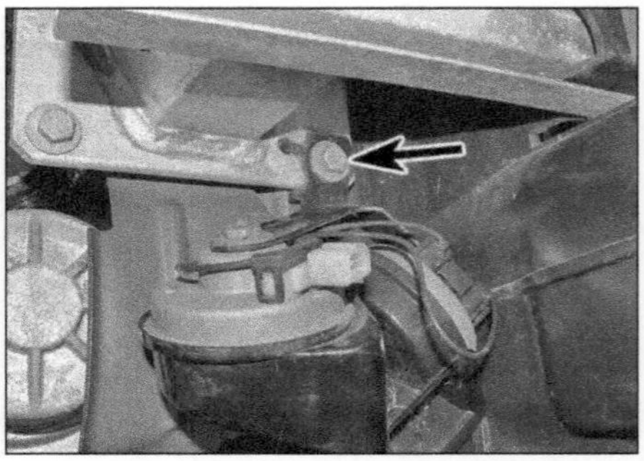

12.3b ... and undo the horn mounting bracket bolt (arrowed)

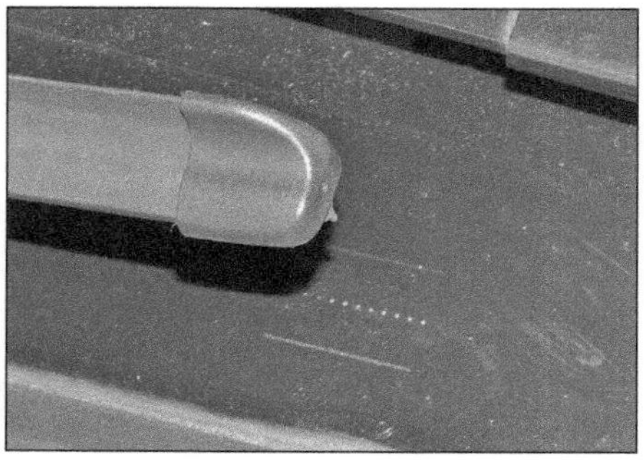

13.1 Wiper blade alignment mark on screen

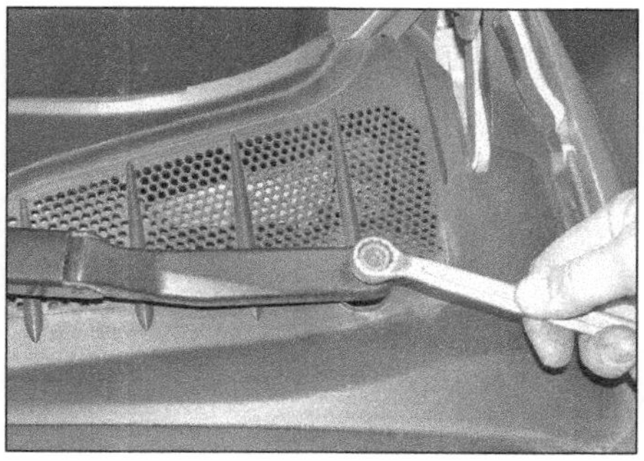

13.2 Undo the wiper arm spindle nut

13.3a Remove the wiper arm ...

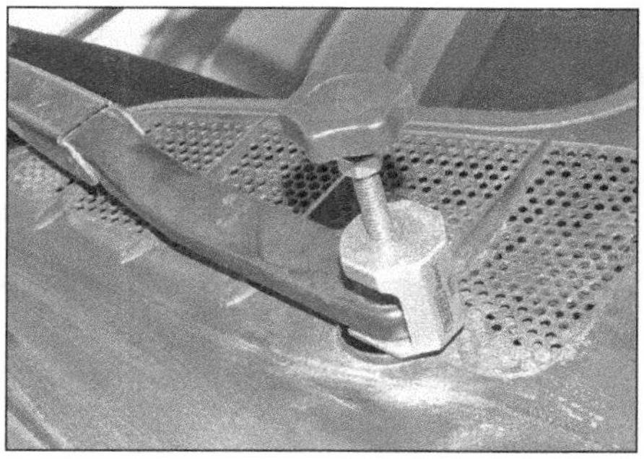

13.3b ... if it is tight on the spindle, use a puller

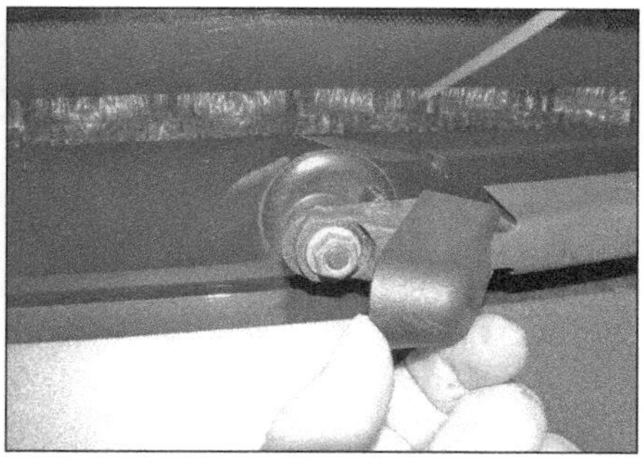

13.7 Lift up the trim cover and undo the wiper arm spindle nut

13 Wiper arm - removal and refitting

Note: *The wiper arms are a very tight fit on their spindles and it is likely that a puller will be needed to remove them safely and without damage.*

Front wiper

1 Operate the wiper motor, then switch it off so that the wiper arm returns to the at-rest position. Stick tape to the screen alongside the wiper blade to ensure correct refitment. There is also an alignment mark provided on the windscreen **(see illustration)**.

2 Lift up the wiper arm spindle nut cover (where fitted) then slacken and remove the spindle nut **(see illustration)**.

3 Lift the blade off the glass, and pull the wiper arm off its spindle. If the arm is very tight, free it from the spindle using a suitable puller **(see illustrations)**.

4 Ensure that the wiper arm and spindle splines are clean and dry, then refit the arm to the spindle, aligning the wiper blade with the tape fitted on removal, or the alignment marks provided.

5 Refit the spindle nut, tightening it securely, and clip the nut cover (where fitted) back into position.

Rear wiper

6 Operate the wiper motor, then switch it off so that the wiper arm returns to the at-rest position. Stick tape to the screen alongside the wiper blade to ensure the correct position for refitting.

7 Lift up the wiper arm spindle nut cover, then slacken and remove the spindle nut **(see illustration)**.

8 Remove the wiper arm spindle nut, lift the blade off the glass, and pull the wiper arm off its spindle **(see illustrations)**. If the arm is very tight, free it from the spindle using a suitable puller.

9 If required, the washer jet can be removed from the wiper spindle grommet, as described in Section 16.

10 Ensure that the wiper arm and spindle splines are clean and dry, then refit the arm to the spindle, aligning the wiper blade with the tape fitted on removal.

11 Refit the spindle nut, tightening it securely, and clip cover back into position.

14 Windscreen wiper motor and linkage - removal and refitting

Removal

1 Disconnect and remove the battery as described in Chapter 5A, Section 4.

2 Remove the wiper arms (see Section 13).

3 Remove the scuttle panel lower grille panel as described in Chapter 11, Section 22.

4 Depending on model, it may be necessary to remove the air cleaner upper housing to gain better access. Refer to Chapter 4A, Section 2 or Chapter 4B, Section 4 as required.

5 Release the retaining clip and disconnect the wiring connector from the wiper motor **(see illustration)**.

6 The wiper linkage assembly is secured by

13.8a Using a puller to release the wiper from the spindle

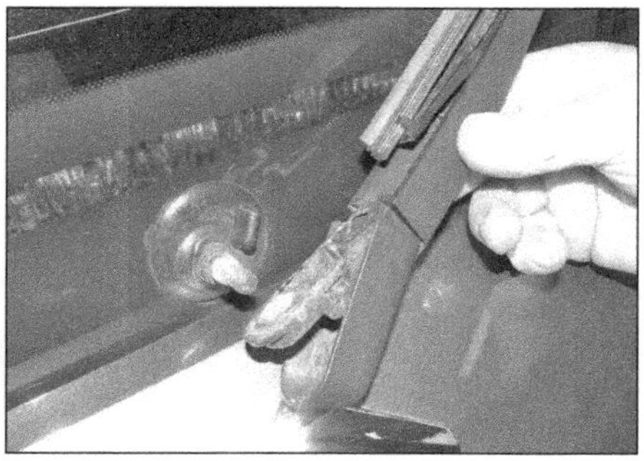

13.8b Remove the wiper arm from the spindle

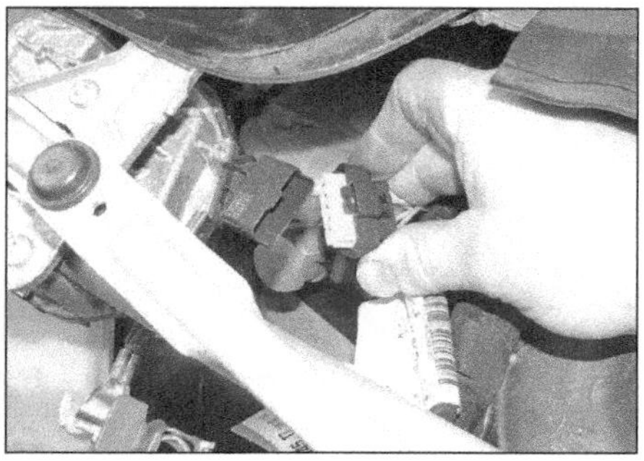

14.5 Disconnect the wiper motor wiring plug

14.6a Wiper linkage right-hand bolt (arrowed) ...

14.6b ... left-hand bolt (arrowed) ...

14.6c ... and central nut (arrowed)

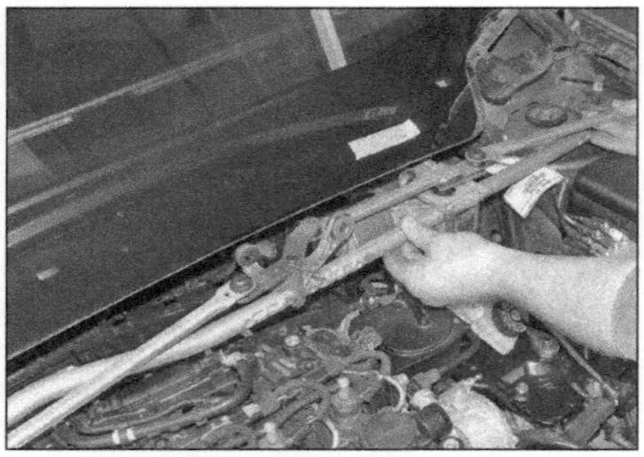

14.7 Remove the wiper linkage from the bulkhead

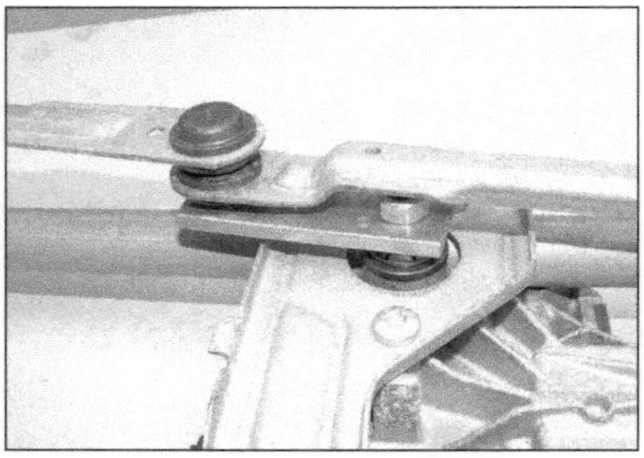

14.8a Remove the wiper linkage rods and arm retaining nut ...

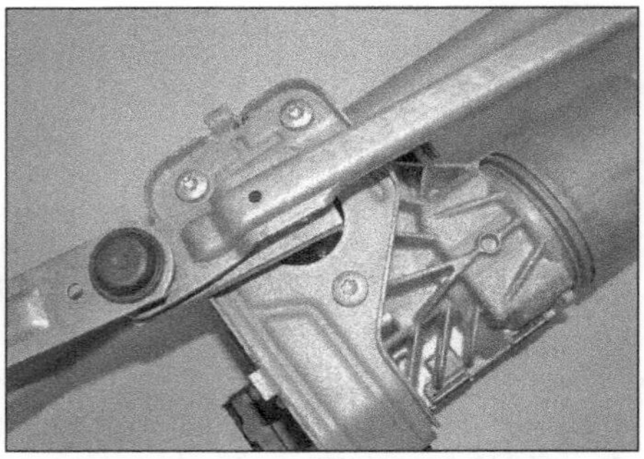

14.8b ... then undo the three retaining screws to remove the motor

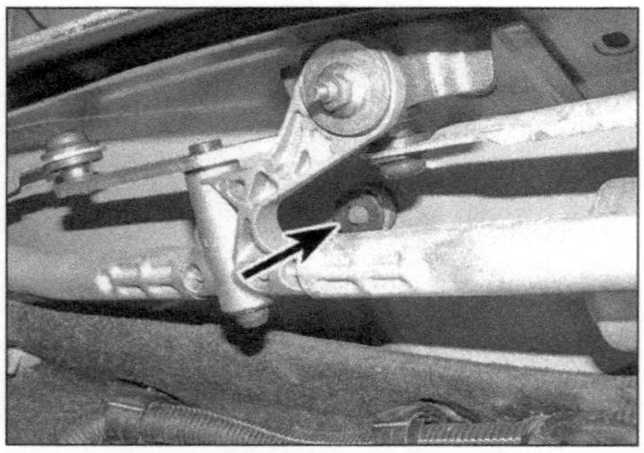

14.9 Locating dowel on bulkhead (arrowed) for wiper linkage

a bolt at each end of the linkage and a central nut **(see illustrations)**.

7 Undo the bolts/nut, and then lift the assembly from the locating pin on the bulkhead, then manoeuvre it from the engine compartment **(see illustration)**. **Note:** *Depending on engine type fitted, access to the wiper linkage assembly may be poor – patience will be required to manoeuvre the linkage from place. Take great care not to damage the windscreen or the vehicle paintwork.*

8 If required, disconnect the linkage rods from the wiper motor spindle arm by levering them from their balljoints. Undo the retaining nut to remove the arm from the wiper spindle, noting its fitted position. To remove the wiper motor from the linkage bracket, undo the three retaining screws **(see illustrations)**.

Refitting

9 Refitting is a reversal of removal, ensuring all fasteners are securely tightened. Note that before tightening the linkage mounting nut/bolts, ensure the assembly is correctly fitted over the locating dowel on the bulkhead **(see illustration)**.

15 Tailgate window wiper motor – removal and refitting

Note: *The wiper motor is held in place with special large rivets **(see illustrations)**, new ones will be required for refitting.*

Removal

1 Ensure the ignition is turned off.

2 Remove the tailgate lower trim panel as described in Chapter 11, Section 25.

3 Remove the wiper arm (see Section 13).

4 Disconnect the wiring connector from the wiper motor **(see illustration)**.

5 Drill out the three rivets securing the wiper

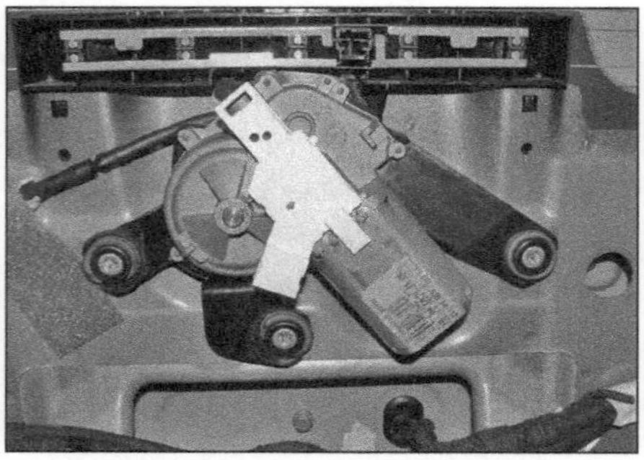

15.0a Wiper motor – 3-door models

15.0b Wiper motor – 5-door models

15.4 Disconnect the wiring plug connector

15.5a Drill out the wiper motor securing rivets ...

15.5b ... removing the old rivet from inside the tailgate

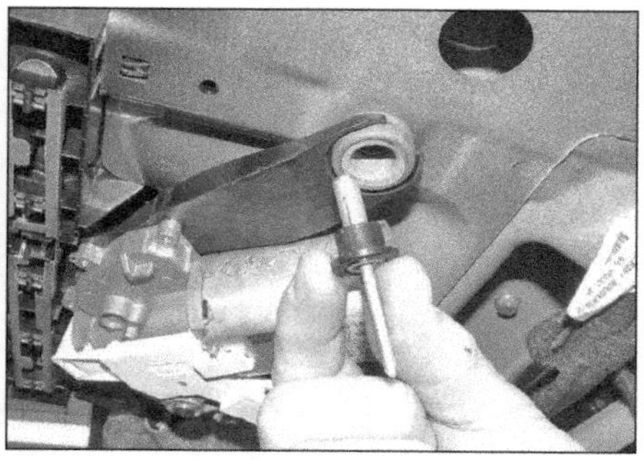

15.10 Fit new special rivet to secure motor

motor to the tailgate **(see illustrations)**. Retrieve the end of the old rivet from inside the tailgate to prevent any rattles when reassembled.

6 Remove the wiper motor from the tailgate and withdraw the spindle out from the sealing grommet in the tailgate glass.

Refitting

7 Prior to refitting check the sealing grommet and rubber mountings for signs of damage or deterioration and renew as necessary.

8 On 3-door models, ensure the washer jet is correctly fitted in the rubber grommet in the tailgate glass.

9 Make sure that any rubber mountings and collars (where fitted) are correctly positioned in the wiper motor mounting bracket.

10 Manoeuvre the wiper motor into position and secure it in position with new rivets **(see illustration)**.

11 Reconnect the wiring connector to the motor then refit the trim panel to the tailgate. Turn on the ignition, then operate the wiper and allow it to stop in the park position.

12 Refit the wiper arm as described in Section 13.

16 Washer system components – removal and refitting

Note: *Before working on the reservoir or pump, it is advisable to drain as much fluid out of the reservoir as possible, to prevent any spillage.*

1 The washer reservoir is located behind the right-hand side of the front bumper **(see illustration)** and supplies both the windscreen and tailgate washers via the same pump. On models equipped with headlight washers, the reservoir also supplies the headlight washer jets via an additional pump.

Washer fluid reservoir

2 Remove the front bumper as described in Chapter 11, Section 6.

3 Remove the right-hand headlight unit as described in Section 7.

4 Unclip the top of the reservoir filler neck from the bracket behind the headlight **(see illustration)**.

5 Note the correct fitted location of the washer hoses (if necessary, mark them for identification purposes) then disconnect the hoses from the washer pump(s) **(see illustration)**. Position a container beneath the reservoir to catch any washer fluid from the pump and hoses.

6 Disconnect the wiring connector(s) from the washer pump(s) **(see illustration)**.

7 Slacken and remove the retaining nut from the upper part of the reservoir, then undo the bolt at the lower front part of the reservoir and remove the mounting bracket **(see illustrations)**.

16.1 Location of washer reservoir behind right-hand side of bumper

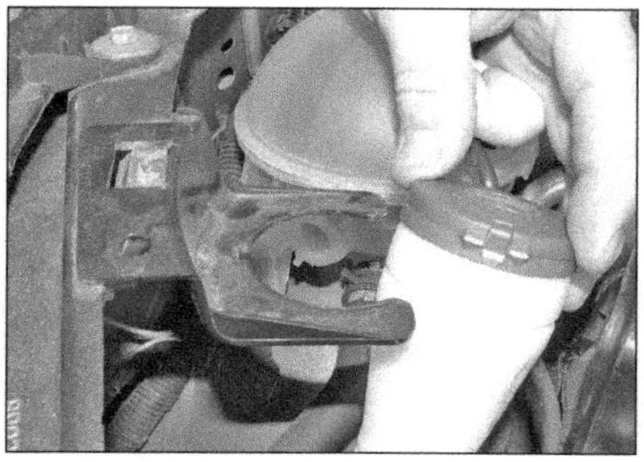

16.4 Unclip the top of the filler neck from the securing clip

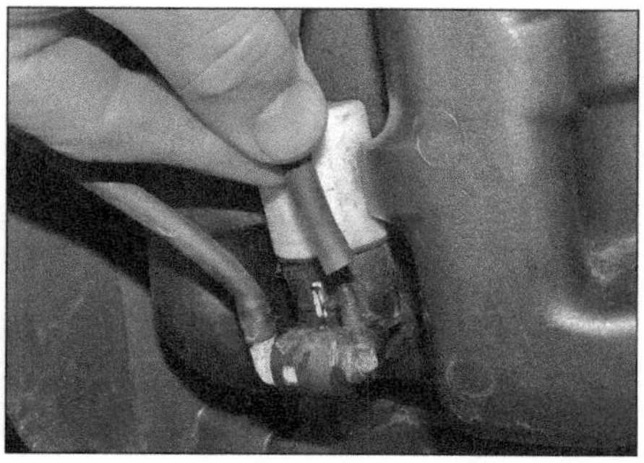

16.5 Disconnect the hoses from the washer pump

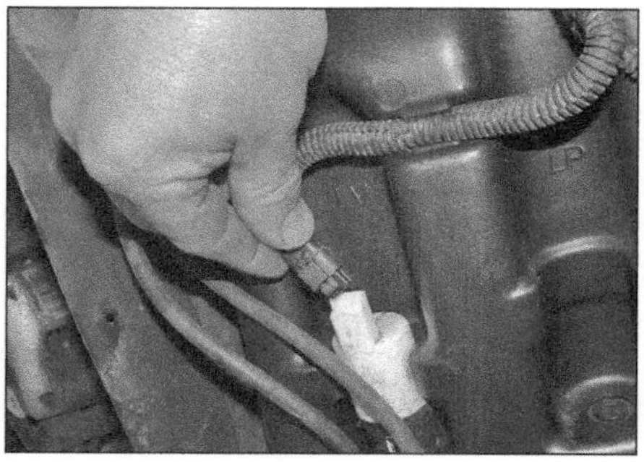

16.6 Disconnect the washer pump wiring plug connector

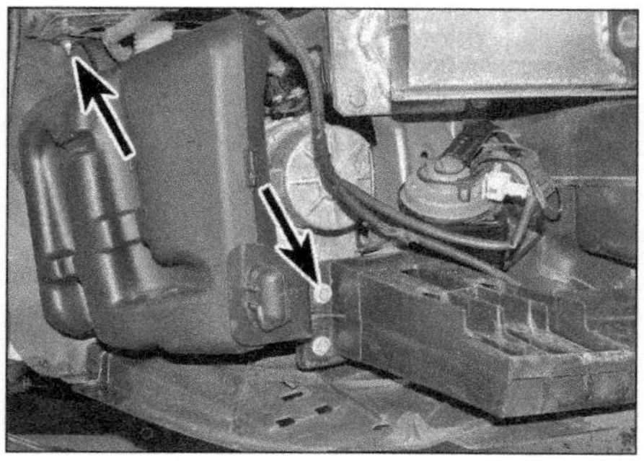

16.7a Undo the retaining nut and bolt (arrowed) ...

16.7b ... remove the mounting bracket ...

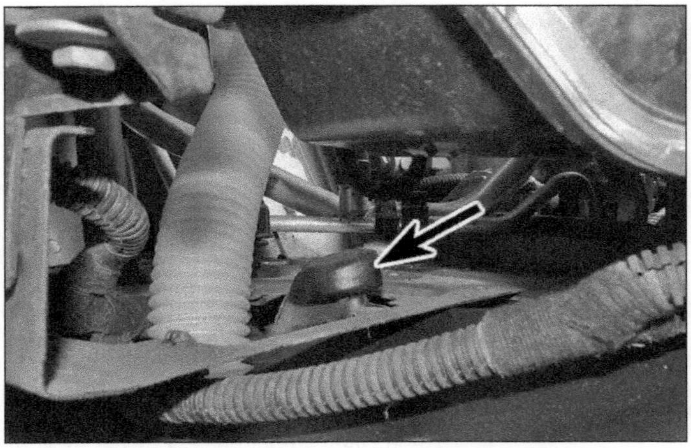

16.8a ... unclip the top of the reservoir (arrowed) from inner wing panel ...

16.8b ... then remove the washer reservoir

8 Release the upper part of the reservoir from the inner wing panel. Manoeuvre it out of position, releasing the wiring and hoses from the locating clips in the side of the reservoir **(see illustrations)**.

9 Refitting is the reverse of removal, ensuring that the hoses are securely reconnected. Refill the reservoir and check for leaks.

Washer pump

10 Slacken the right-hand front roadwheel bolts. Jack up the front of the vehicle, and support it securely on axle stands (see *Jacking and vehicle support*). Remove the right-hand roadwheel.

11 Remove the front right-hand wheel arch liner. The liner is secured by several expanding plastic rivets. Release the centre pins, then prise the complete rivets from place, and manoeuvre the front section of the liner out from underneath the wing.

12 Position a container beneath the reservoir to catch the washer fluid as the pump is removed.

13 Disconnect the washer fluid hoses and wiring connector from the washer pump.

14 Carefully ease the pump out from the reservoir, and recover its sealing grommet **(see illustrations)**. Wash off any spilt fluid with cold water.

15 Refitting is the reverse of removal, using a new sealing grommet if the original shows signs of damage or deterioration. Refill the reservoir and check the pump grommet for leaks on completion.

Windscreen washer jet

16 Open the bonnet. Prise up the centre pins a little, lever out the complete plastic expanding rivets, and remove the bonnet insulation panel to gain access to the base of the windscreen washer jets **(see illustrations)**.

17 Disconnect the washer hose(s) from the relevant jet, then depress the retaining clips and ease the jet out of position **(see illustrations)**.

18 On refitting, clip the jet into the bonnet and make sure the hose is reconnected securely; check the operation of the washer jet.

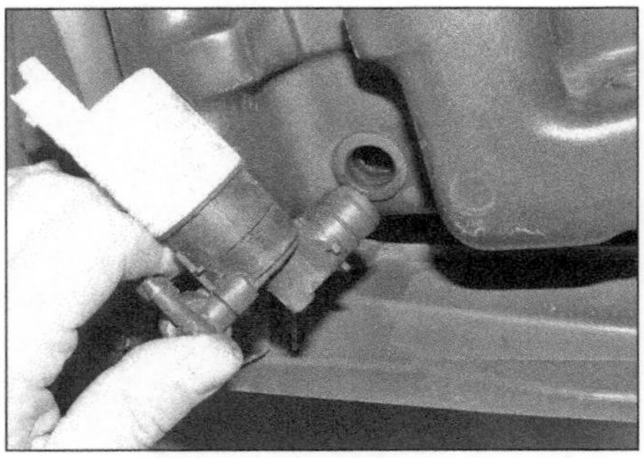

16.14a Ease the washer pump from the reservoir ...

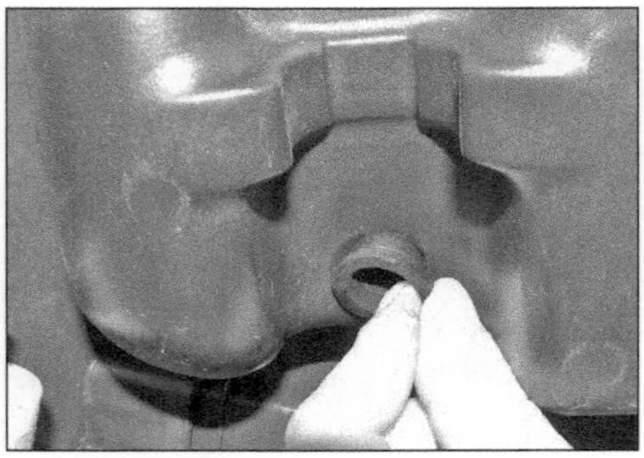

16.14b ... and remove the rubber grommet

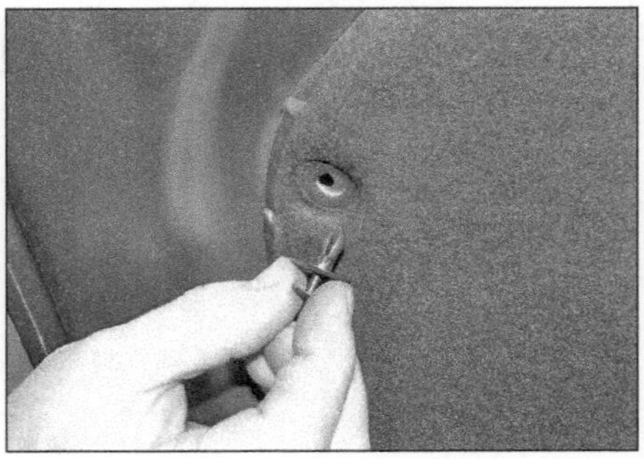

16.16a Release the securing clips ...

16.16b ... and remove the bonnet insulation

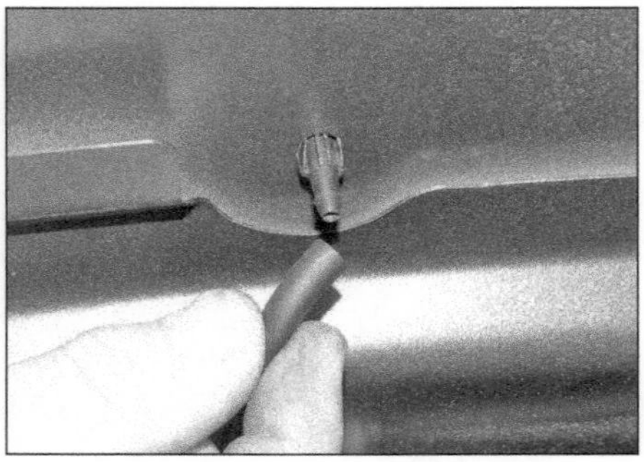

16.17a Disconnect the washer hose ...

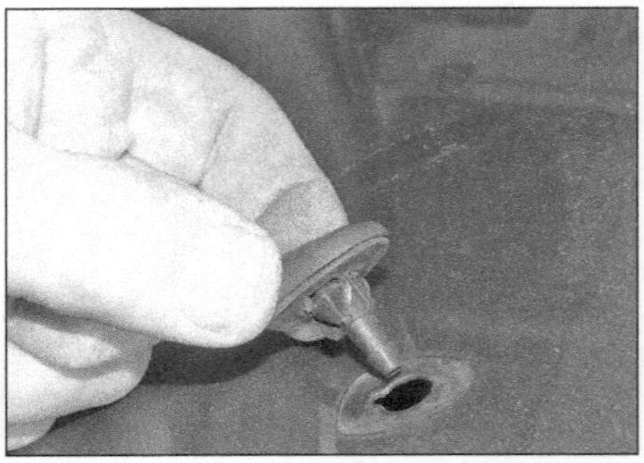

16.17b ... and squeeze together the clips to ease the jet from bonnet

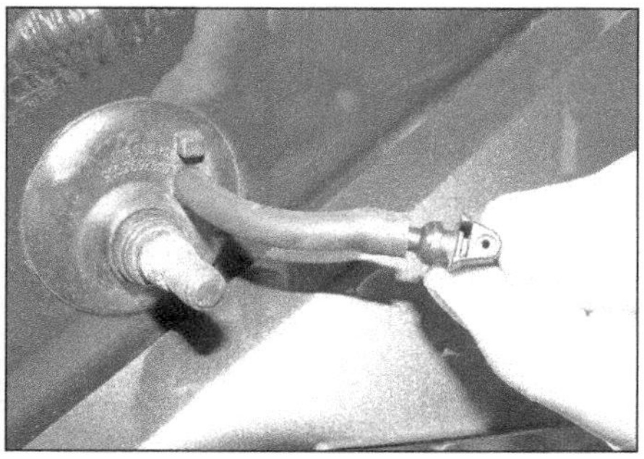

16.20a Pull the washer jet and hose from the grommet (3-door models) ...

16.20b ... if required, disconnect hose (arrowed) on the inside of the tailgate

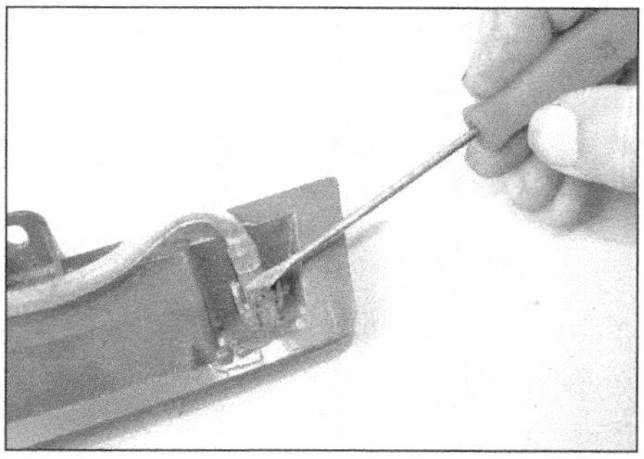

16.23 Release the clips and remove the washer jet – 5-door models

Tailgate washer jet

3-door models

19 Remove the rear wiper arm as described in Section 13.

20 Withdraw the washer jet hose from the wiper motor spindle grommet in the rear screen, then remove the rear washer jet from the end of the washer hose **(see illustrations)**. To access the washer hose inside the tailgate, remove the inner tailgate trim panel as described in Chapter 11, Section 25.

21 Refitting is the reverse of removal. Make sure the hose is reconnected securely and check the operation of the washer jet.

5-door models

22 Remove the high-level brake light unit as described in Section 7.

23 Disconnect the washer hose from the jet, then carefully release the retaining clips and unclip the washer jet from the end of the light unit **(see illustration)**. Where applicable, recover the jet O-ring.

24 Refitting is the reverse of removal. Make sure the hose is reconnected securely and check the operation of the washer jet.

Headlight washer jet

25 Carefully prise the jet cover from the bumper, and pull the assembly out to its full extent. To prevent any damage to the paintwork around the washer jet, use masking tape on the front bumper.

26 Have an assistant grip the washer jet tube with a pair of grips, then depress the retaining clips and pull the jet from the tube.

27 To remove the washer cylinders, remove the front bumper as described in Chapter 11, Section 6, then disconnect the washer tubing, and unclip the cylinders.

28 Refitting is the reverse of removal.

17 Audio unit – removal and refitting

Note: *The following procedure is typical for the range of equipment fitted by Citroën. There are many types of audio unit fitted depending on model; the type of removal clips (radio keys) will vary also.*

Removal

1 Ensure the audio unit and ignition is switched off.

2 Insert the removal clips (radio keys) into the holes at the sides of the unit until they release the retaining clips. Push the clips outwards to release the unit from the facia **(see illustration)**. If the removal clips are not available, insert a small screwdriver/punch into the holes on each side of the unit to release the clips.

3 Once both retaining clips have been released, slide the audio unit out of position. Disconnect the wiring connections and aerial lead, then remove the unit from the vehicle **(see illustrations)**.

17.2 Insert two pins into each side of the audio unit to release the clips, then pull the unit from place

Refitting

4 Prior to refitting, reset the unit retaining clips.

5 Securely reconnect the aerial lead and wiring connectors, then slide the unit back into position, taking care not to trap any wiring.

18 Loudspeakers – removal and refitting

Removal

Door speakers

1 Remove the door inner trim panel as described in Chapter 11, Section 12.

2 Remove the foam insulation from around the speaker housing **(see illustration)**

17.3a Disconnect the wiring plug connectors ...

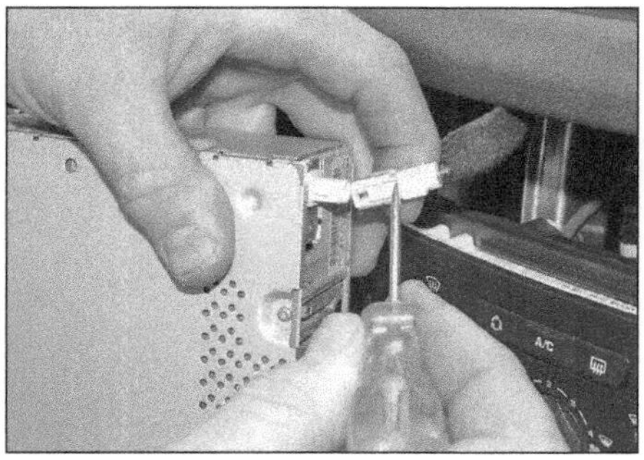

17.3b ... and release the clip for the aerial lead

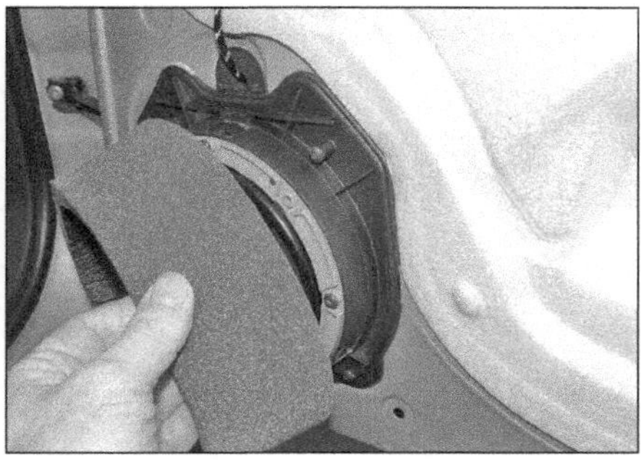

18.2 Remove the foam insulator from around the front door speaker

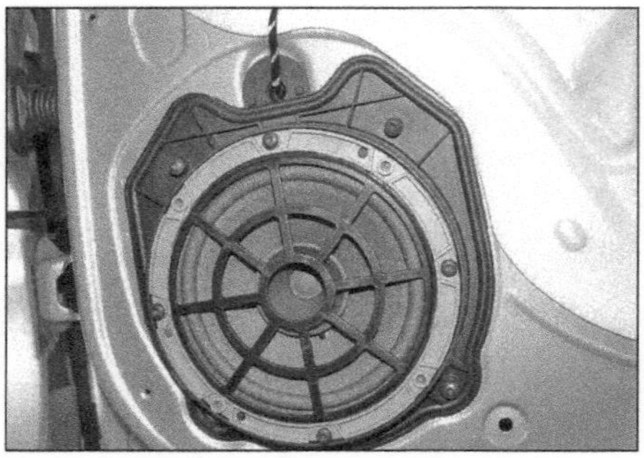

18.3a Undo the screws and remove the speaker ...

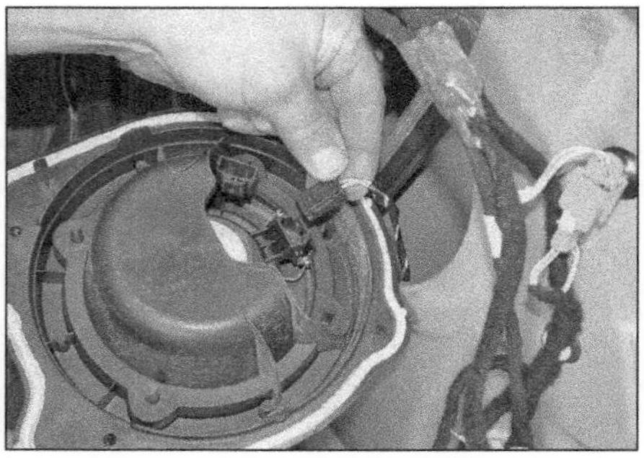

18.3b ... then disconnect the wiring connector

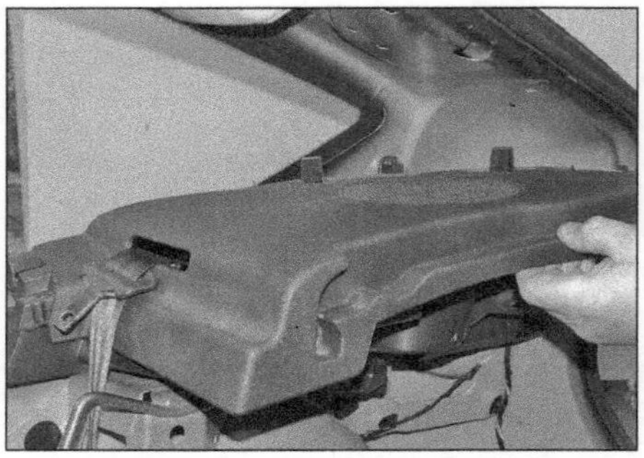

18.4 Remove the upper side shelf trim

18.5a Undo the speaker retaining screws ...

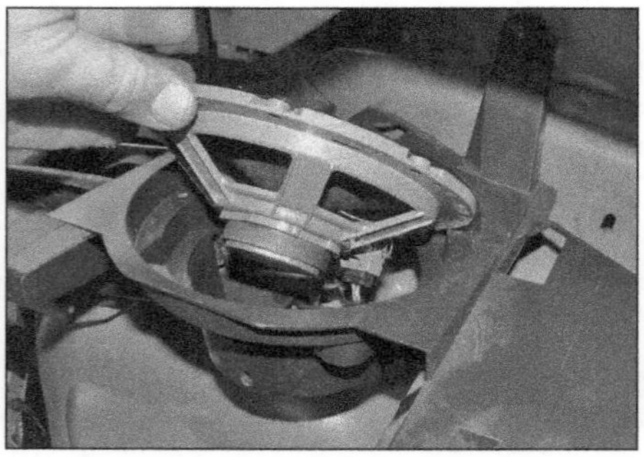

18.5b ... and remove the speaker

18.6 Carefully prise the tweeter/speaker from the facia

3 Undo the screws and remove the speaker from the door **(see illustrations)**, disconnecting the wiring plug as it becomes accessible.

Rear parcel shelf speakers

4 Remove the rear side shelf trim panel **(see illustration)**, as described in Chapter 11, Section 25.

5 Undo the retaining screws then remove the speaker from the plastic mounting bracket, disconnecting the wiring connector as it becomes accessible **(see illustrations)**.

Front tweeter

6 Carefully prise the tweeter from the upper corner of the facia **(see illustration)**.

7 Disconnect the wiring plug connector from the tweeter is withdrawn. Secure the wiring connector to the top of the facia, to prevent losing the wiring inside the facia.

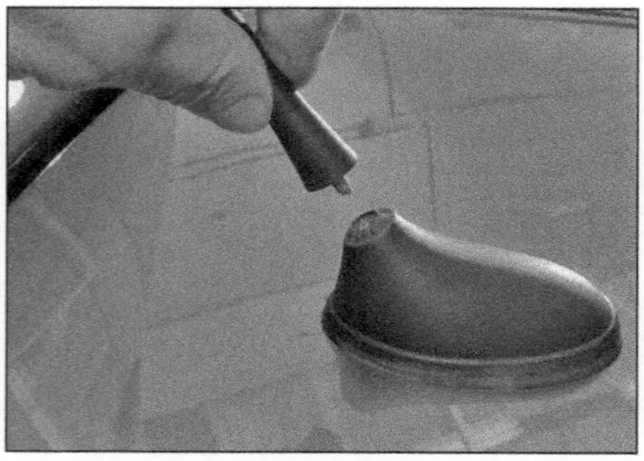

19.1 Unscrew the aerial mast from the base

Refitting

8 Refitting is a reversal of removal. Making sure that all wiring connectors are secure and the trim panels are clipped securely in position, with reference to Chapter 11, Section 12.

19 Radio aerial – removal and refitting

Removal

1 The aerial mast is a screw-fit in its base and is easily removed **(see illustration)**.

2 Remove the interior light unit from the rear of the headlining, as described in Section 6.

3 Undo the retaining nut, disconnect the aerial cable and remove the aerial base out from the roof panel **(see illustration)**.

19.3 Remove the interior rear light unit to access the aerial retaining nut

4 To remove the aerial cable, trace it back through the headlining and behind the trim panels, then disconnect the wiring plug connector from the control box on the rear pillar. Refer to Chapter 11, Section 25 for information on removal of trim panels.

Refitting

5 Refitting is the reverse of removal.

20 Engine immobiliser and anti-theft alarm system – general information

Note: *This information is applicable only to the systems fitted by Citroën as standard equipment.*

Engine immobiliser

1 An engine immobiliser system is fitted as standard to all models and the system is operated automatically every time the ignition key is inserted/removed.

2 The immobiliser system ensures the vehicle can only be started using the original Citroën ignition key. The key contains an electronic chip (transponder), which is programmed with a code. When the key is inserted into the ignition switch it uses the current present in the sensor ring (which is fitted to the ignition switch housing) to send a signal to the immobiliser electronic control unit (ECU). The ECU is incorporated into the built-in systems interface (BSI) unit (see Section 23). The ECU checks this code every time the ignition is switched on. If the key code does not match the ECU code, the ECU will disable the starter, fuel and ignition (as applicable) to prevent the engine being started.

3 When the vehicle is new, a confidential security card is supplied along with the other vehicle documentation. This card contains the security code which your Citroën dealer requires when carrying out any work on the immobiliser system. Keep this card in a safe place at home; never store it in the vehicle. If the ignition key is lost, a new one can be obtained from a Citroën dealer. Take the confidential security card and all the existing keys along to your Citroën dealer who will supply a new key and reprogramme all the keys with a new security code; this will render the lost key useless.

Caution: Without the confidential security card, it will not be possible to have the keys and immobiliser system reprogrammed.

4 Any problems with the engine immobiliser system should be referred to a Citroën dealer.

Anti-theft alarm system

5 Most models covered in this were also equipped with an anti-theft alarm system as standard equipment. The system was available as an option on all other models. The alarm is automatically armed when the deadlocking is set using the remote central locking transmitter and is disarmed when the doors are unlocked using the remote transmitter. The alarm system has switches on the bonnet, tailgate and each of the doors, and also has ultrasonic sensing, which detects movement inside the vehicle via sensors mounted on either side of the vehicle interior.

6 When the system is activated, the direction indicators will flash continuously for two seconds. **Note:** *If the bonnet, tailgate or one of the doors are not properly closed when the alarm is set, the siren will sound briefly. If the bonnet/tailgate/door (as applicable) is properly closed within 45 seconds the alarm will be armed. If not the alarm will remain disarmed.*

7 If for some reason the remote central locking transmitter fails whilst the alarm is armed, the alarm can be disarmed using the key. To do this, open the door with the key, and then enter the vehicle, noting that the alarm will sound as the door is opened. Insert the key and switch on the ignition, the immobiliser will recognise the key and will switch off the alarm.

8 Depending on model, the ultrasonic sensing facility of the alarm can be switched off, whilst retaining the switched side of the system. With the ignition switched off, depress the alarm switch (mounted on the driver's side of the facia) until the alarm indicator light on the switch is continuously lit. Get out of the vehicle and operate the deadlocking function using the remote transmitter to arm the alarm. The direction indicators will flash as normal but only the switched (door, tailgate and bonnet) side of the alarm system will be operational. This facility is useful as it allows you to leave the windows/sunroof open, and still arm the alarm. If the windows/sunroof are left open with the ultrasonic sensing not switched off, the alarm may be falsely triggered by a gust of wind.

9 Prior to disconnecting the battery, the alarm system should be disabled; this will prevent the alarm sounding when the battery is disconnected/reconnected. To do this, switch on the ignition then immediately depress and hold the alarm switch for two seconds; the indicator light on the switch should then flash rapidly for approximately three seconds indicating the alarm has been disabled. Switch off the ignition and disconnect the battery.

10 Once the battery has been reconnected, operate the deadlocking with the remote transmitter then unlock the vehicle. The alarm will be set as normal; the next time the deadlocking is set.

11 Should the alarm system become faulty, the vehicle should be taken to a Citroën dealer for examination.

21 **Airbag system** – general information and precautions

1 All models in the range are fitted with a driver's airbag, passenger's airbag, side front airbags, and side curtain airbags.

2 The airbag system is triggered in the event of a heavy frontal impact above a predetermined force, depending on the point of impact. The airbag is then inflated within milliseconds, and forms a safety cushion between the cabin occupants and the vehicle interior. This prevents contact between the upper body and vehicle interior, and therefore greatly reduces the risk of injury. The airbag then deflates almost immediately. The control unit also operates the front seat belt tensioner mechanisms at the same time.

3 The side airbags are fitted to the seat back of each front seat. Each airbag unit has its own lateral acceleration sensor, which is mounted onto the vehicle body on the outside of each front seat **(see illustration)**. The side airbags are not linked in any way and operate individually.

4 The curtain airbags are fitted behind the windscreen pillars and headlining on each side of the passenger cabin.

5 Every time the ignition is switched on, the airbag control unit performs a self-test. The self-test takes approximately six seconds and during this time the warning light in the instrument panel will be illuminated. After the self-test is complete, the warning light will go out (unless the passenger airbag unit has been deactivated – see paragraph 6). If the warning light fails to come on, remains illuminated after the self-test period, or comes on at any time when the vehicle is being driven, there is a fault in the airbag system. The vehicle should be taken to a Citroën dealer for examination at the earliest possible opportunity.

6 Most vehicles with a passenger airbag are equipped with a disabling switch fitted inside the right-hand side of the glovebox **(see illustration)**. The switch is operated using the ignition key and switches off the passenger airbag (it is not possible to disable the driver's or side/curtain airbags) to enable a rear-facing child seat to be installed in the passenger seat. Whilst the passenger airbag is disabled, the airbag warning light on the instrument panel will remain illuminated all the time.

Warning: Before carrying out any operations on the airbag system, disconnect the battery (see Chapter 5A, Section 4) and wait at least five minutes. Remove the centre console (see Chapter 11, Section 26), and then release the retaining clip and disconnect the wiring connector(s) from the airbag control unit. When the operations are complete, securely reconnect the control unit then refit the centre console. Make sure no one is inside the vehicle when the battery is reconnected then, with the driver's door open, switch the ignition on from outside vehicle and check the operation of the airbag warning light.

Warning: Do not subject the area of the body around the control unit to any form of shock, which could trigger the system.

Warning: Note that the airbags must not be subjected to temperatures in excess of 100°C. When the airbag is removed, ensure that it is stored the correct way up (padded surface uppermost) to prevent possible inflation.

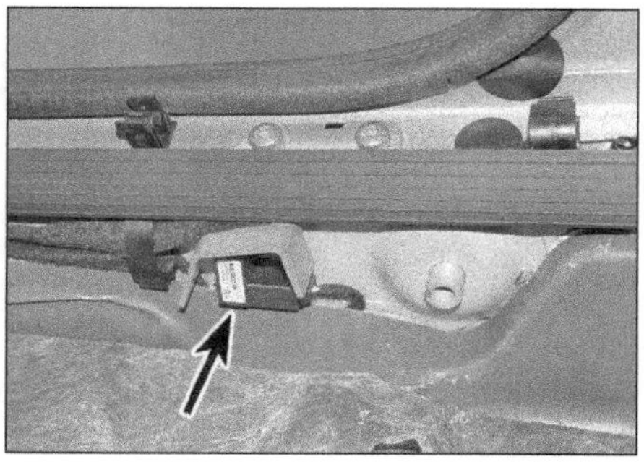

21.3 Location of lateral accelerator sensor (arrowed)

21.6 Location of passenger airbag disabling switch (arrowed)

Warning: Do not allow any solvents or cleaning agents to contact the airbag assemblies. They must be cleaned using only a damp cloth.

Warning: The airbags and control unit are both sensitive to impact. If either is dropped or damaged they should be renewed.

Warning: Disconnect the airbag control unit wiring connector prior to using arc-welding equipment on the vehicle.

Warning: Never fit a rear-facing child seat to the front passenger seat unless the passenger airbag has been disabled (paragraph 6).

Warning: Citroën recommend that the airbag units be renewed every ten years.

22 Airbag system components – removal and refitting

Warning: Refer to the precautions given in Section 21 before carrying out the following operations.

Driver's airbag

1 Disconnect the battery (see Chapter 5A, Section 4) and wait at least five minutes.

2 With the wheel in the straight-ahead position and the steering lock engaged, insert a screwdriver (or round punch) into the hole in the lower part of the steering wheel boss, and push it upwards to release the retaining clips **(see illustrations)**.

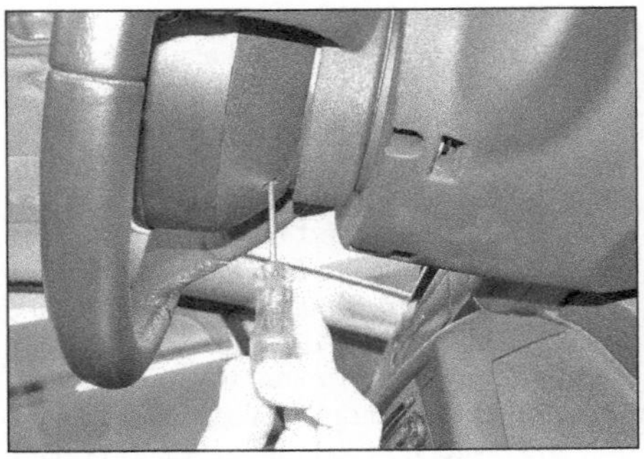

22.2a Insert a thin screwdriver/punch ...

22.2b ... in through the hole in the lower part of the steering wheel ...

3 Carefully lift the airbag unit away from the wheel, disconnecting the wiring connectors as they become accessible **(see illustrations)**.

Warning: Do not knock or drop the airbag unit and store it with its padded surface uppermost.

4 Securely reconnect the wiring connectors then seat the airbag unit in the steering wheel, ensuring the wiring does not become trapped.

5 Fit the airbag unit; press it into place in the steering wheel until the retaining clips engage.

6 Make sure no one is inside the vehicle then reconnect the battery. With the driver's door open, switch the ignition on from outside vehicle and check the operation of the warning light.

Passenger's airbag

7 Disconnect the battery and wait at least five minutes.

8 Remove the multifunction display unit as described in Section 10, then release the retaining clip and disconnect the wiring connector for the passenger airbag **(see illustration)**.

9 Unclip the trim panels from each end of the facia panel **(see illustration)**.

10 Remove the passenger side glovebox

22.2c ... to release the clips (arrowed) which secure the airbag

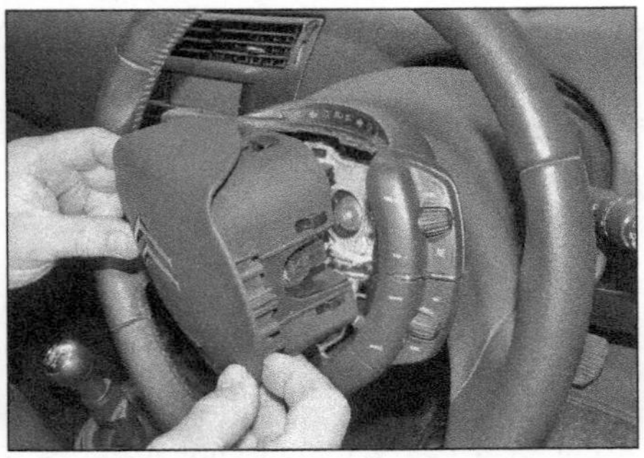

22.3a Remove the airbag ...

22.3b ... disconnect the earth wire (arrowed) ...

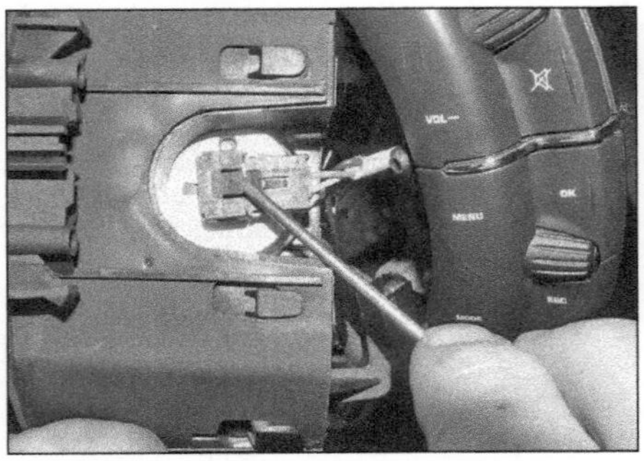

22.3c ... lift up the locking clip ...

22.3d ... and disconnect the wiring connector from the airbag

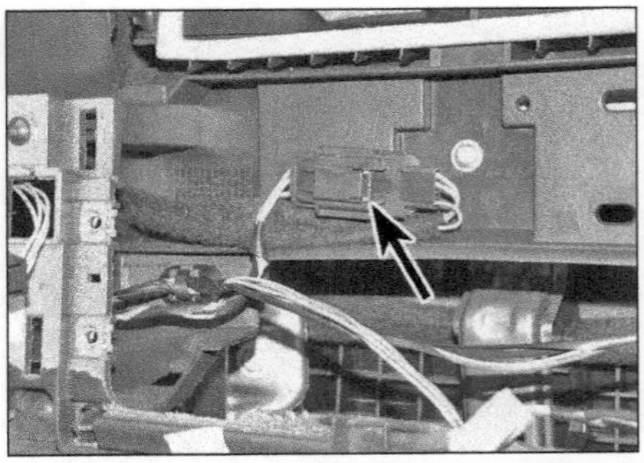

22.8 Disconnect the wiring connector (arrowed) for the passenger airbag

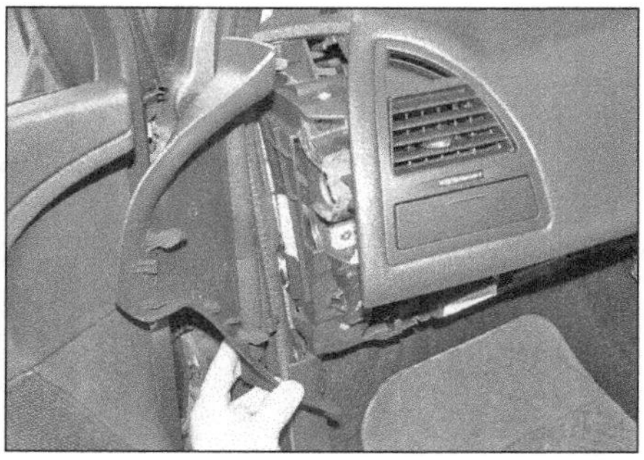

22.9 Unclip the left-hand trim from the end of the facia

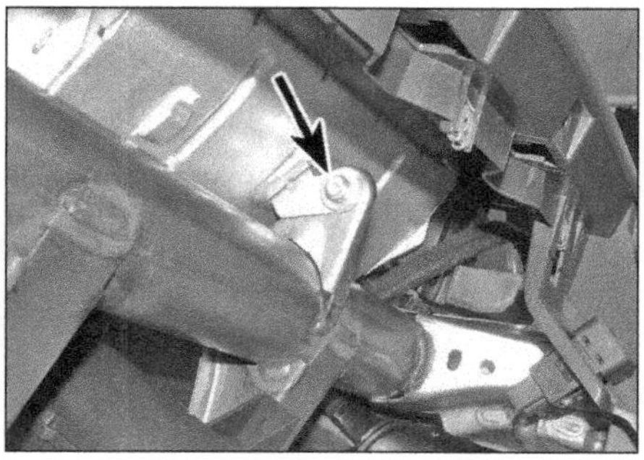

22.11 Undo the airbag bracket retaining screw (arrowed)

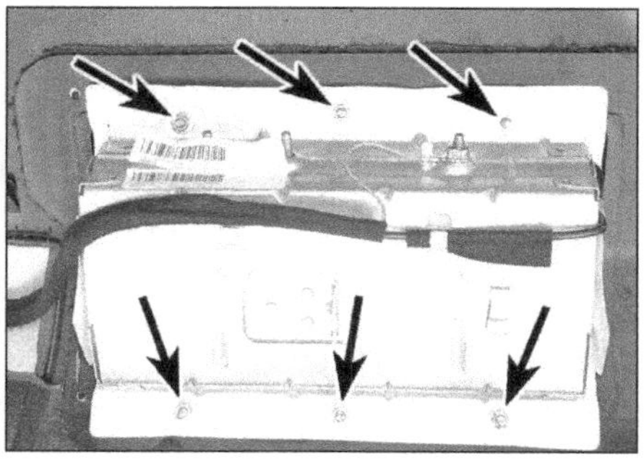

22.14 Undo the six airbag retaining nuts (arrowed)

assembly from the facia, as described in Chapter 11, Section 27.

11 Working through the glovebox aperture, slacken and remove the retaining screw from the support bracket on the airbag unit **(see illustration)**.

12 Remove the instrument panel, as described in Section 9,

13 Remove the upper part of the facia with reference to Chapter 11, Section 27, paragraph 45.

14 Undo the six retaining nuts, and remove the airbag from the rear of the facia panel **(see illustration)**.

15 Refit the airbag unit to the rear of the facia trim, ensuring the wiring is correctly connected and routed, and the nuts are securely tightened.

16 The remainder of refitting is the reverse of removal. On completion, make sure no one is inside the vehicle then reconnect the battery. With the driver's door open, switch the ignition on from outside vehicle and check the operation of the warning light.

Airbag control unit

17 Disconnect the battery (see Chapter 5A, Section 4) and wait at least five minutes. Remove the centre console (see Chapter 11, Section 26) then release the retaining clip and disconnect the wiring connectors from the airbag control unit **(see illustrations)**.

18 Unscrew the control unit retaining nuts, and then remove the control unit from the floor of the vehicle.

19 Refit the control unit, making sure the arrow on the top of the unit is pointing towards the front of the vehicle **(see illustration)**. Refit the control unit retaining nuts and tighten them to the specified torque.

20 Securely reconnect the airbag control unit wiring connectors.

21 Refit the centre console (see Chapter 11, Section 26). Make sure no one is inside the vehicle then reconnect the battery. With the driver's door open, switch the ignition on from outside vehicle and check the operation of the warning light.

Gyrometer/accelerometer sensor

22 The sensor is located under the centre console in front of the handbrake assembly. Remove the centre console as described in Chapter 11, Section 26.

23 Release the retaining clip, and then disconnect the wiring plug **(see illustration)**.

24 Undo the two nuts and remove the sensor.

25 Refitting is a reversal of removal, ensuring the arrow on the top of the sensor points to the front of the vehicle.

Lateral accelerometer sensor

26 Remove the relevant front seat, as described in Chapter 11, Section 23.

27 Remove the B-pillar lower trim panel, as described in Chapter 11, Section 25.

28 Pull back the carpet to gain access to the side airbag sensor **(see illustration 21.3)**.

29 Disconnect the wiring connector then undo the retaining bolt and remove the sensor from the inner sill panel **(see illustration)**.

30 Refitting is a reversal of removal, ensuring the bolt is tightened to the specified torque.

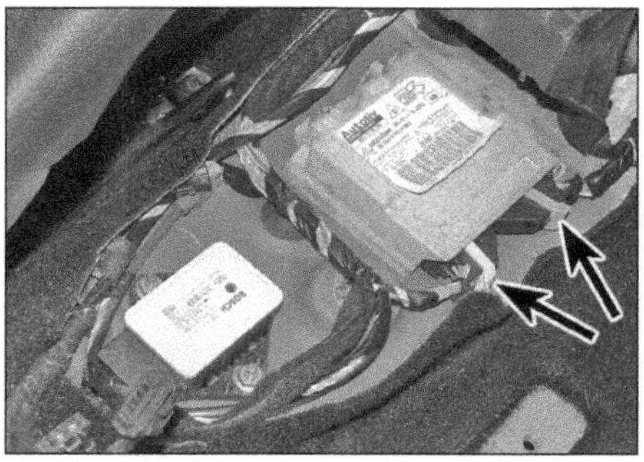

22.17a Release the locking catches (arrowed) ...

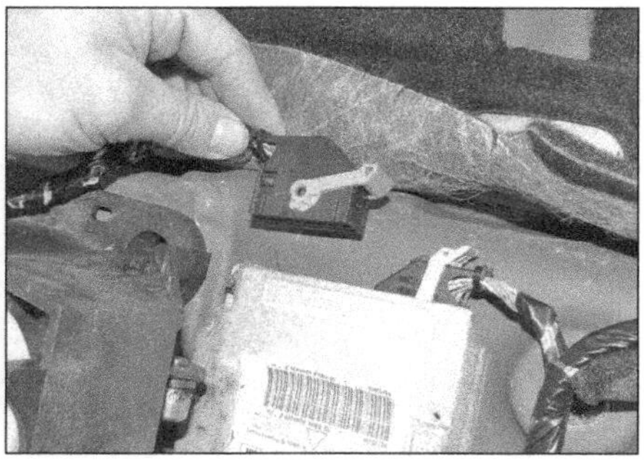

22.17b ... and disconnect the airbag ECU wiring plugs

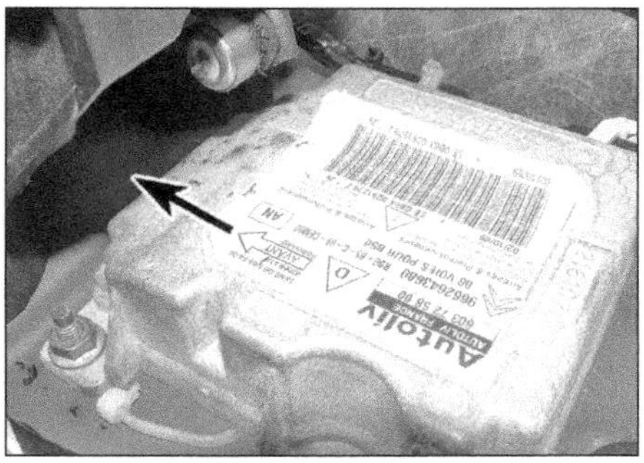

22.19 Make sure the arrow on the top of the unit is facing forwards

22.23 Location of gyrometer/ accelerometer sensor

22.29 Disconnect the wiring connector and undo the sensor retaining bolt

Side airbag

31 Removal and refitting of the side airbag units should be entrusted to a Citroën dealer. The seat must be dismantled to enable the airbag unit to removed/refitted.

Curtain airbag

32 Removal and refitting of the curtain airbag units should be entrusted to a Citroën dealer. The headlining must be partially removed to enable the airbag unit to removed/refitted.

23 Built-in systems interface (BSI) unit/fusebox – general, removal and refitting

General information

1 The built-in systems interface (BSI) unit is an electronic control unit which controls a variety of functions normally controlled by individual control units and relays. The BSI unit is located behind the facia panel on the passenger's side of the facia where it is situated directly behind the glovebox **(see illustration)**. The BSI unit controls the following functions (not all functions are fitted to all models).

- *Direction indicator/hazard warning lights.*
- *Windscreen/tailgate wiper motors.*
- *Rear window heating element.*
- *Immobiliser system.*
- *Anti-theft alarm system.*
- *Lights-on/ignition key warning buzzer.*

23.1 Built in system interface (BSI) unit, behind glovebox

- *Central locking/deadlocking, including the remote central locking receiver.*
- *Door open indicator.*
- *Courtesy light delay timer.*
- *Automatic transmission audible warning system.*

2 Should any of the above functions become faulty, first check the condition of the fuses. If this fails to locate the problem, take the vehicle to a Citroën dealer for testing. The only satisfactory way to test the BSI unit is by substitution with another unit that is known to be functioning correctly.

Removal

3 Disconnect the battery (see Chapter 5A, Section 4).

4 Remove the passenger side glovebox as described in Chapter 11, Section 27.

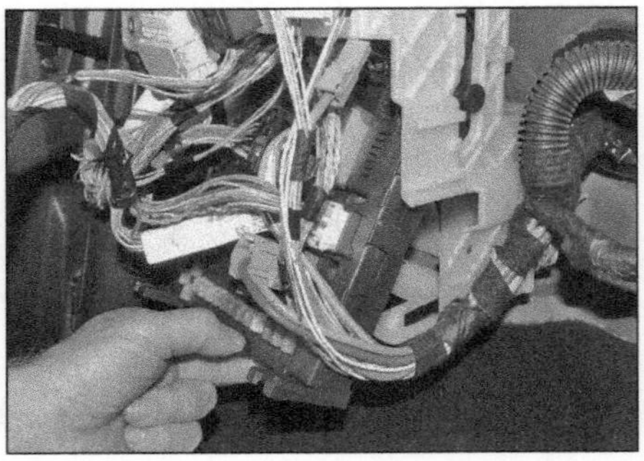

23.6a Pull the lower part of the unit out from the housing ...

5 Release the lower retaining clips and pull the lower part of the BSI unit outwards.

6 Pull the BSI unit downwards and then slide it out from its position in the white plastic housing **(see illustrations)**.

7 Note their fitted positions, then release the retaining clips, disconnect all the wiring connectors and remove the BSI unit from the vehicle. Note that there are several different designs of locking catches for the various connectors. Take your time to study the wiring connectors, and release them without using excessive force as they are easily damaged.

Refitting

8 Refitting is the reverse of removal, ensuring the wiring connectors are all securely reconnected and the BSI unit is secured **(see illustrations)**.

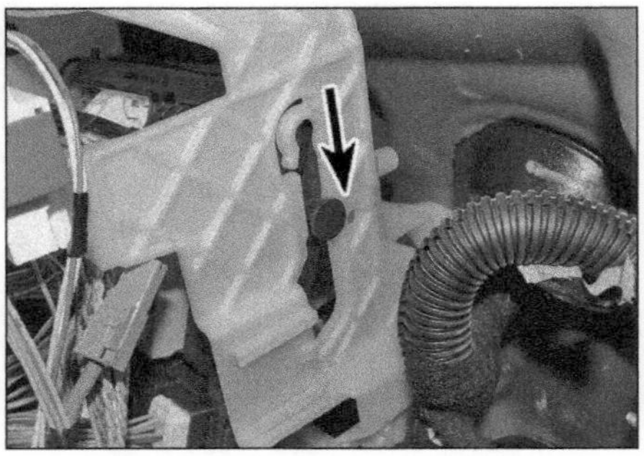

23.6b ... and then slide the unit downwards (arrow)

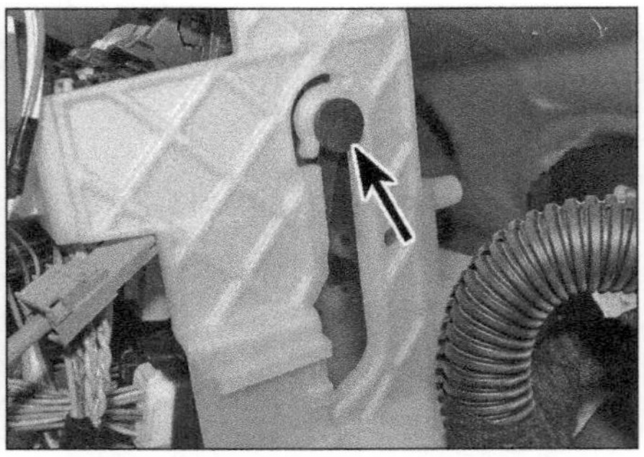

23.8a Make sure the locating peg (arrowed) is secure ...

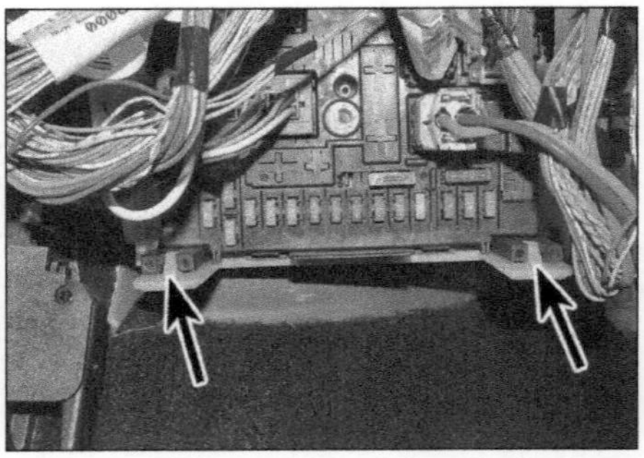

23.8b ... and also the two lower retaining clips (arrowed)

Citroen C4 wiring diagrams

Diagram 1

At the time of writing, certain wiring diagram technical information was unavailable. As a result these diagrams are intended as a representative set covering most major electrical systems typically encountered on this model range.

WARNING: This vehicle is fitted with a supplemental restraint system (SRS) consisting of a combination of driver (and passenger) airbag(s), side impact protection airbags and seatbelt pre-tensioners. The use of electrical test equipment on any SRS wiring systems may cause the seatbelt pre-tensioners to abruptly retract and airbags to explosively deploy, resulting in potentially severe personal injury. Extreme care should be taken to correctly identify any circuits to be tested to avoid choosing any of the SRS wiring in error.

For further information see airbag system precautions in body electrical systems chapter.

Note: The SRS wiring harness can normally be identified by yellow and/or orange harness or harness connectors.

The prime method of wire identification is by the number code printed on each wire. Additionally, the wires can be identified by using the terminal pin numbers (moulded into each component or connector and shown in the diagrams).

To relate each diagram to the vehicle wiring, locate the relevant component or connector illustrated and find the wire(s) connected to the terminal pin(s) as shown in the diagram.

Caution: Whilst a number (indicating the function of that wire) may be printed on each wire, this is not always the case, and in such instances, this is reflected by the absence of such wire numbering on our diagrams. Similarly, numbering of the connector/component terminal pins is not always available from the manufacturers' source information and may also be missing from our diagrams.

Key to symbols

Solenoid actuator

Earth point (E7)

Wire identification — MC50A

Connecting wires

Dashed outline denotes part of a larger item, containing in this case an electronic or solid state device. (16GR, 5, 9)
16GR - 16 pin grey connector, pins 5 & 9

Bulb

Switch

Fuse (F26)

Maxifuse fusible link (MF1)

Resistor

Variable resistor

Variable resistor

Wire splice, soldered joint, or unspecified connector

Diode

Light-emitting diode

Item number (12)

Motor/pump (M)

Heating element

Battery fusebox 9

Fuse	Rating	Circuit protected
F1	-	Not used
F2	30A	Electronic manual/auto. gearbox
F3	-	Spare
F4	-	Spare
F5	80A	Power steering pump
F6	70A	Diesel heating unit
F7	100A	Switching & protection unit
F8	-	Spare
F9	30A	Electronic manual gearbox
F10	30A	Valvetronic electric motor

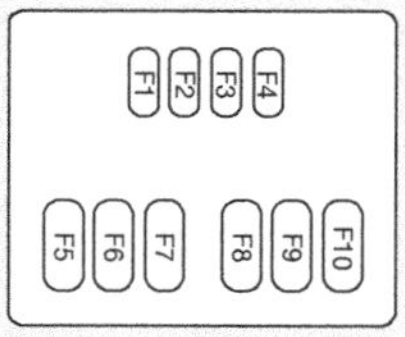

Maxi-fuses

Fuse	Rating	Circuit protected
MF1	30/50A	Engine cooling fan
MF2	30A	ABS/ESP pump supply
MF3	50A	ABS/ESP control unit
MF4	80A	Built-in systems interface
MF5	80A	Built-in systems interface
MF6	80A	Passenger compartment fusebox
MF7	20A	Diagnostic connector/additive pump
MF8	-	Spare

Engine fusebox 4

Fuse	Rating	Circuit protected
F1	20A	Engine management
F2	15A	Horn
F3	10A	Front/rear screen wash/wipe
F4	20A	Headlight washer
F5	15A	Engine management
F6	10A	Automatic gearbox, xenon & directional headlights
F7	10A	Power steering, ABS/ESP control unit
F8	25A	Starter
F9	10A	Diesel additional heater, engine coolant level switch
F10	30A	Engine management
F11	40A	Heater blower motor
F12	30A	Front wiper
F13	40A	Built-in systems interface
F14	-	Spare
F15	10A	RH main beam
F16	10A	LH main beam
F17	15A	LH dip beam
F18	15A	RH dip beam
F19	15A	Engine management
F20	10A	Engine management
F21	5A	Engine management

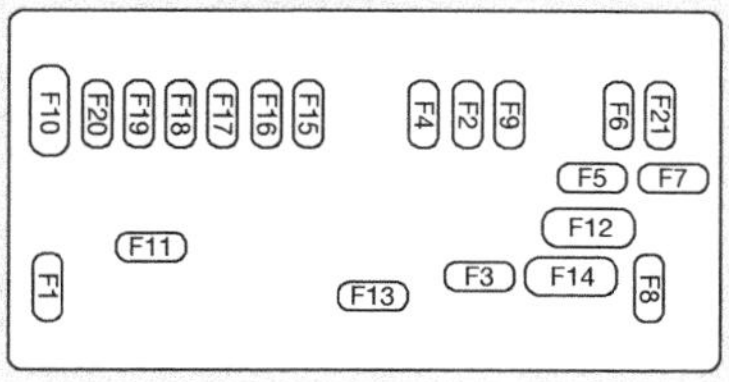

Built-in systems interface 6

Fuse	Rating	Circuit protected
F1	15A	Rear wiper
F2	30A	Central locking
F3	5A	Airbags
F4	10A	Clutch & brake pedals, rear view mirror, diagnostic connector, Diesel additive
F5	30A	Electric windows, heated mirrors
F6	30A	Rear electric windows
F7	5A	Interior lighting
F8	20A	Audio, 12v socket, multifunction display, alarm, steering wheel controls
F9	30A	Rear 12v socket, cigar lighter
F10	15A	Tyre pressure monitor auto. gearbox, STOP switch
F11	15A	Ignition switch, diagnostic connector, particle filter
F12	15A	Lane departure, parking assistance, memory seat
F13	5A	Rain/light sensor, electronic gearbox, engine relay unit
F14	15A	Air cond., instrument cluster, tachometer, airbags, trailer, telephone
F15	30A	Central locking
SH	-	Shunt
F17	40A	Heated rear screen

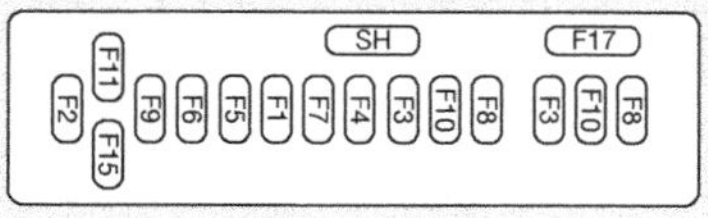

H47523

Diagram 2

Colour codes

BA	White	**OR**	Orange
BE	Blue	**RG**	Red
BG	Beige	**RS**	Pink
GR	Grey	**VE**	Green
JN	Yellow	**VI**	Mauve
MR	Brown	**VJ**	Green/Yellow
NR	Black		

Key to items

1 Battery
2 Starter motor
3 Alternator
4 Engine fusebox
5 Ignition switch
6 Built-in systems interface
7 Instrument cluster
8 Horn
9 Steering column control unit
10 Steering wheel boss control unit
11 Engine cooling fan control unit
12 Engine cooling fan

H47524

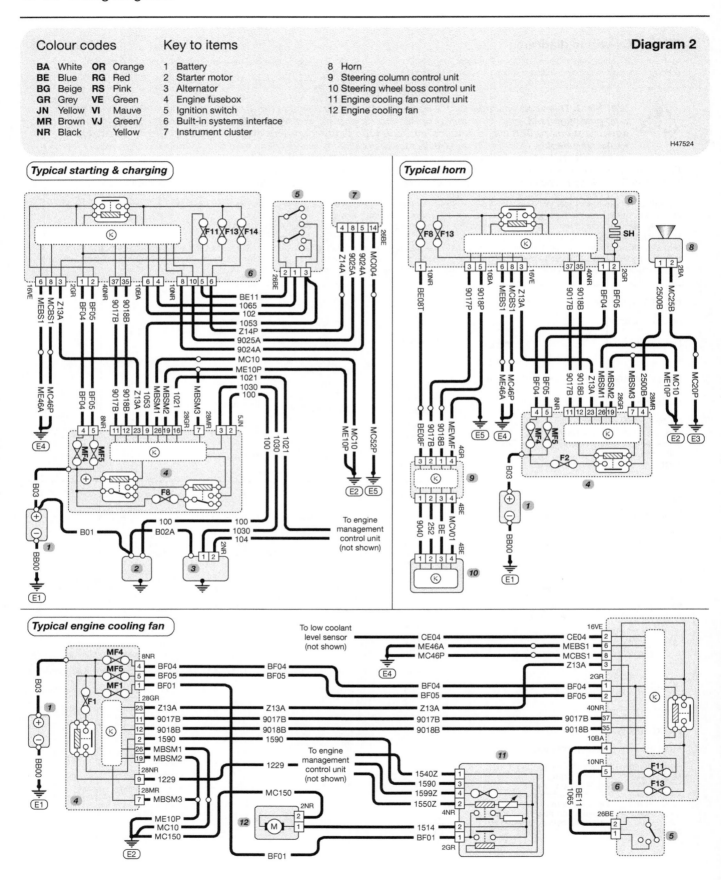

Typical starting & charging

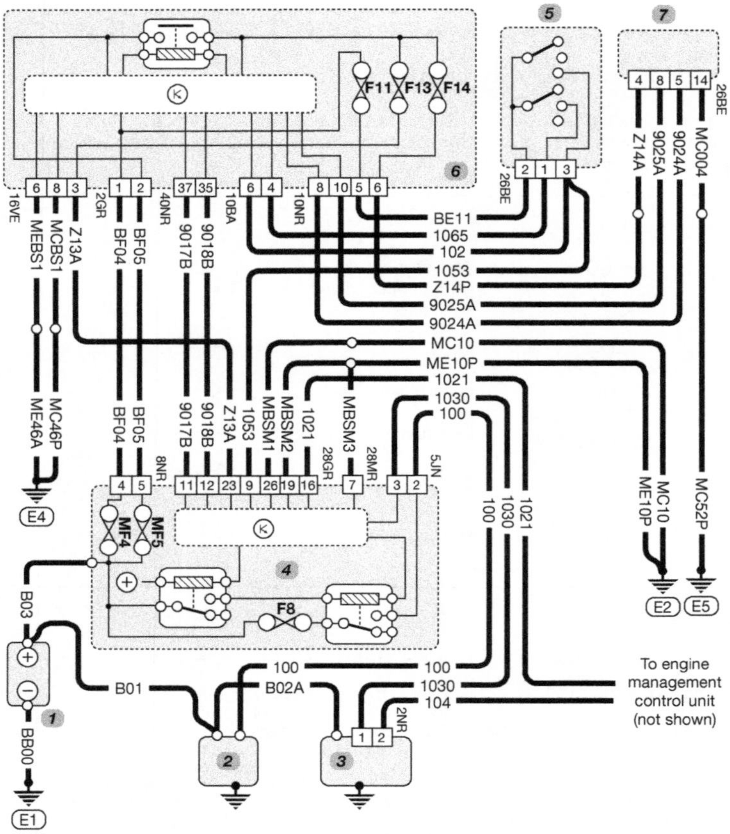

Typical horn

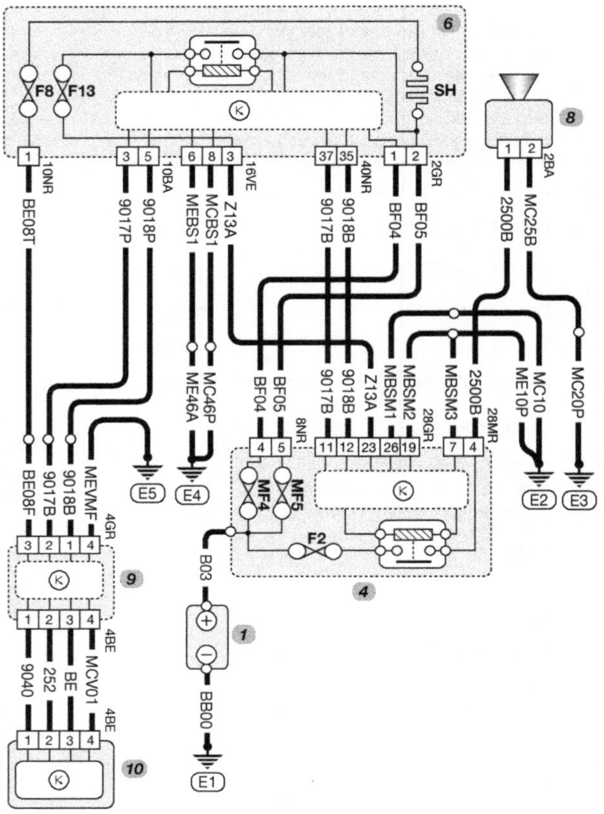

Typical engine cooling fan

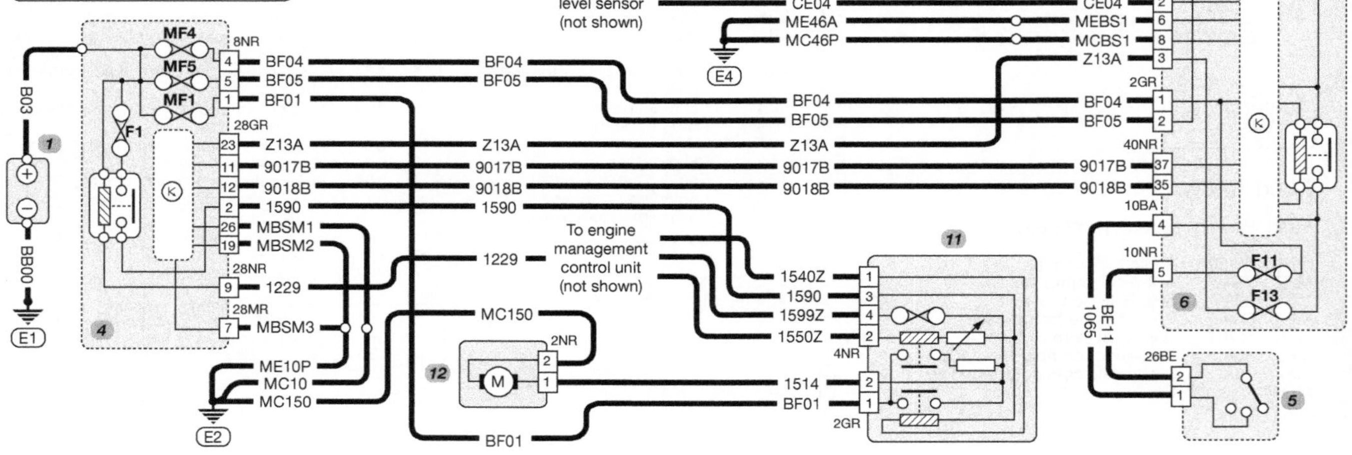

Diagram 3

Colour codes

BA	White	**OR**	Orange
BE	Blue	**RG**	Red
BG	Beige	**RS**	Pink
GR	Grey	**VE**	Green
JN	Yellow	**VI**	Mauve
MR	Brown	**VJ**	Green/Yellow
NR	Black		

Key to items

1 Battery
4 Engine fusebox
5 Ignition switch
6 Built-in systems interface
7 Instrument cluster
9 Steering column control unit
10 Steering wheel boss control unit
14 High level brake light
15 Stop light switch
16 Reversing light switch
17 LH rear light unit
 a = stop light
 b = reversing light
 c = tail light
18 RH rear light unit
 (a to c as above)
19 LH number plate light
20 RH number plate light
21 LH headlight unit
 a = main beam
 b = dip beam
 c = sidelight
22 RH headlight unit
 (a to c as above)
23 Rear foglight (5 door)
24 Light/rain sensor

H47525

Typical stop & reversing lights

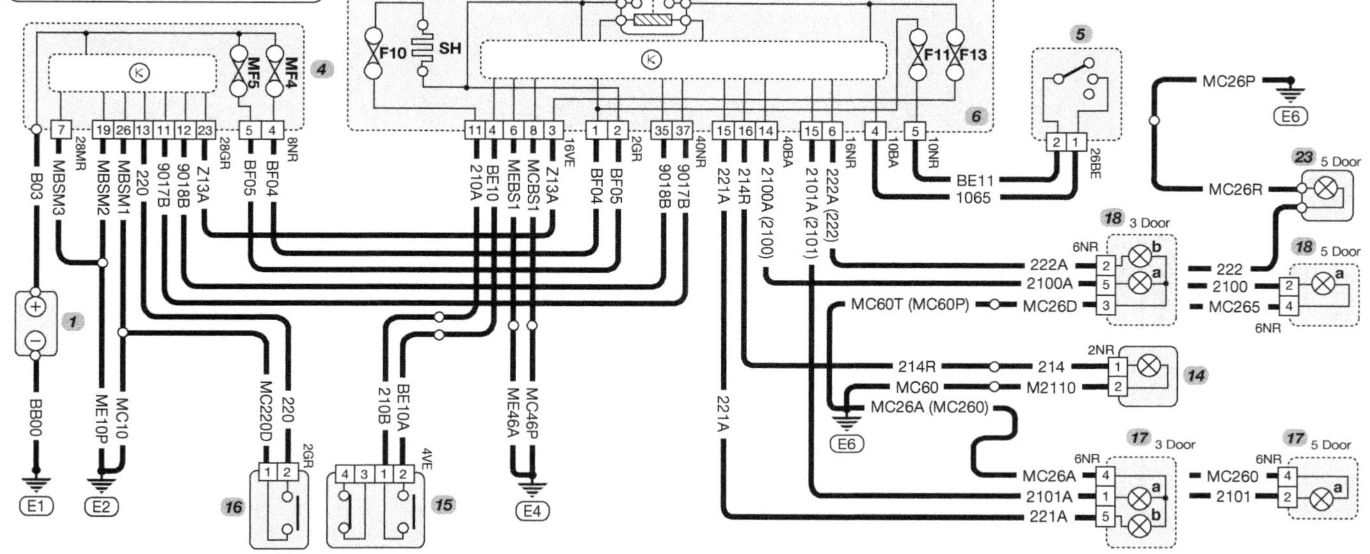

Typical side, tail, number plate & dip/main beam headlights lights

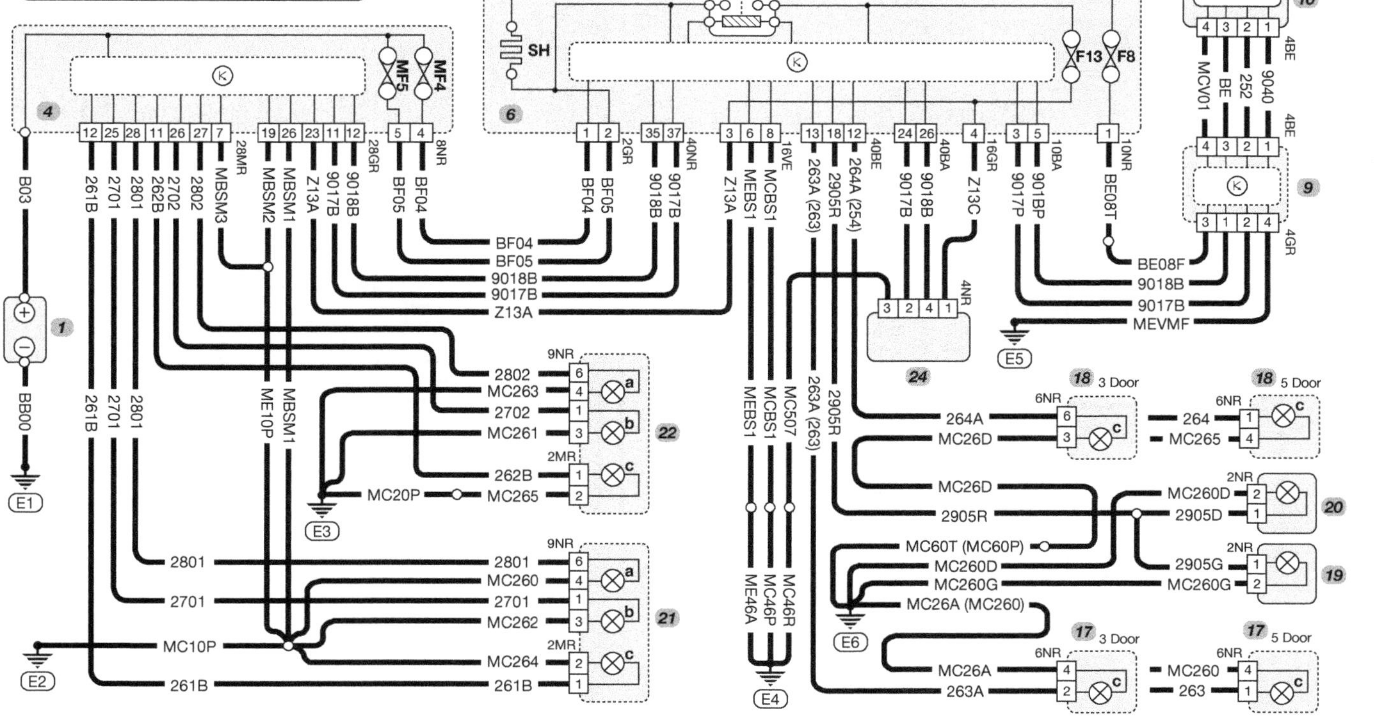

Diagram 4

Colour codes

BA	White	**OR**	Orange
BE	Blue	**RG**	Red
BG	Beige	**RS**	Pink
GR	Grey	**VE**	Green
JN	Yellow	**VI**	Mauve
MR	Brown	**VJ**	Green/ Yellow
NR	Black		

Key to items

1 Battery
4 Engine fusebox
5 Ignition switch
6 Built-in systems interface
7 Instrument cluster
9 Steering column control unit
10 Steering wheel boss control unit
17 LH rear light unit
  d = direction indicator
18 RH rear light unit
  (d as above)
21 LH headlight unit
  d = direction indicator
22 RH headlight unit
  d = direction indicator
27 Hazard warning switch
28 LH door mirror assembly
  a = LH indicator side repeater
29 RH door mirror assembly
  a = RH indicator side repeater
32 LH front fog light
33 RH front fog light
34 LH rear fog light (3 door)
35 RH rear fog light (3 door)
36 Rear fog light (5 door)

H47526

Typical fog lights

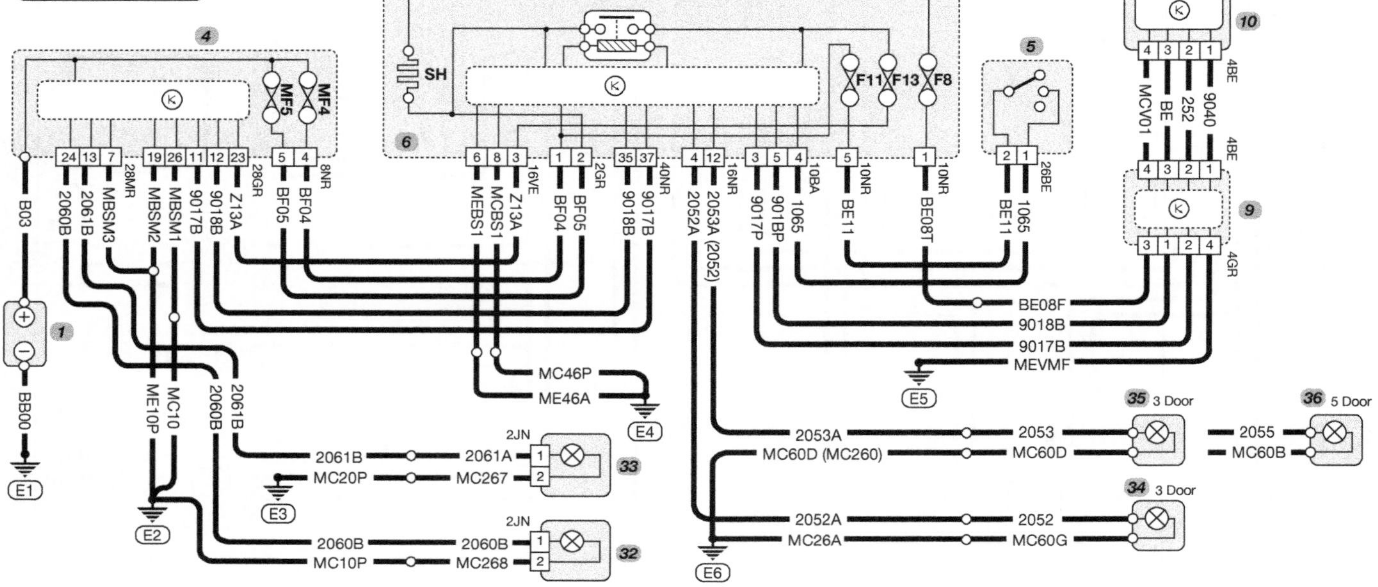

Typical direction indicators & hazard warning lights

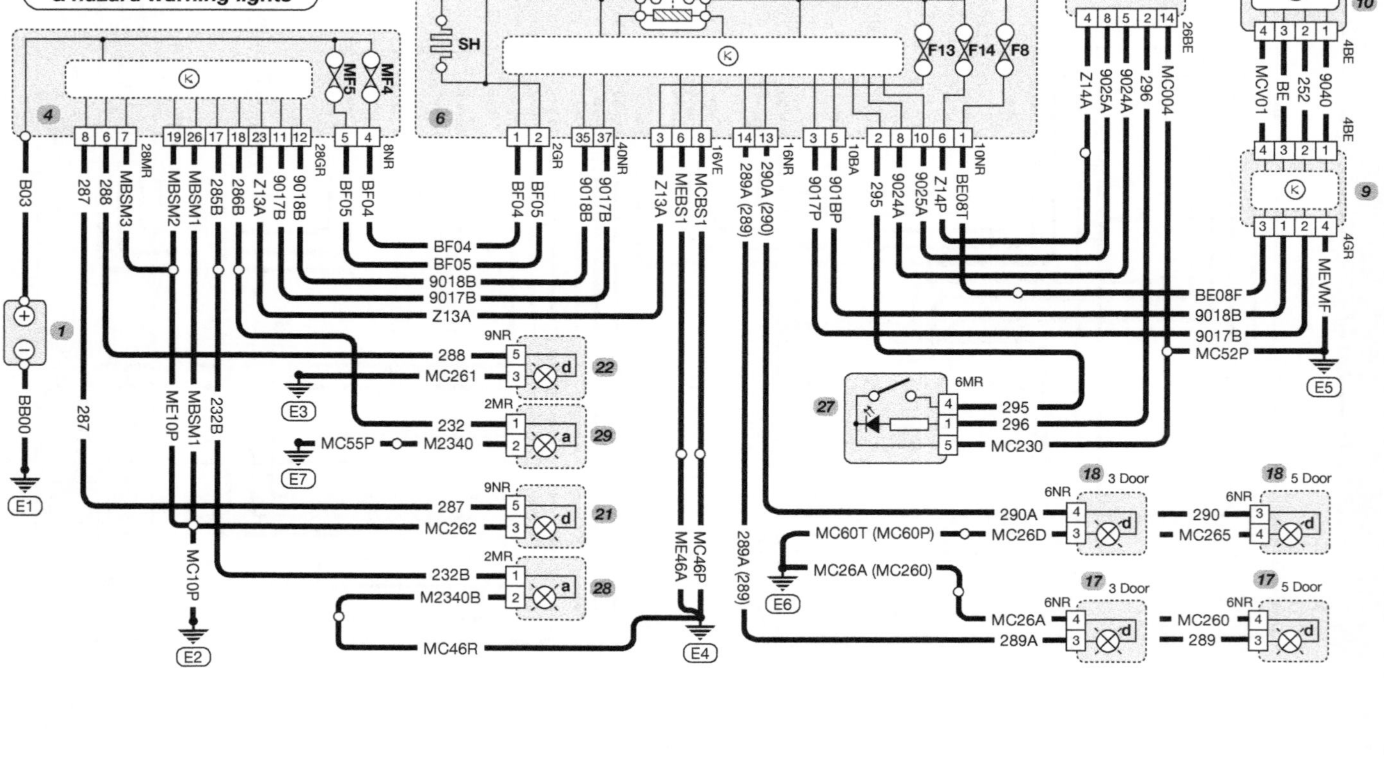

Diagram 5

Colour codes

BA	White	**OR**	Orange
BE	Blue	**RG**	Red
BG	Beige	**RS**	Pink
GR	Grey	**VE**	Green
JN	Yellow	**VI**	Mauve
MR	Brown	**VJ**	Green/ Yellow
NR	Black		

Key to items

1 Battery
4 Engine fusebox
5 Ignition switch
6 Built-in systems interface
7 Instrument cluster
24 Light/rain sensor
40 Air conditioning control panel
41 Evaporator sensor
42 Inlet air control motor
43 Heater blower motor
44 Heater blower resistors
45 Compressor
47 Washer pump
48 Wiper motor
49 Wash/wipe switch
50 Rear wiper motor

H47527

Typical air conditioning

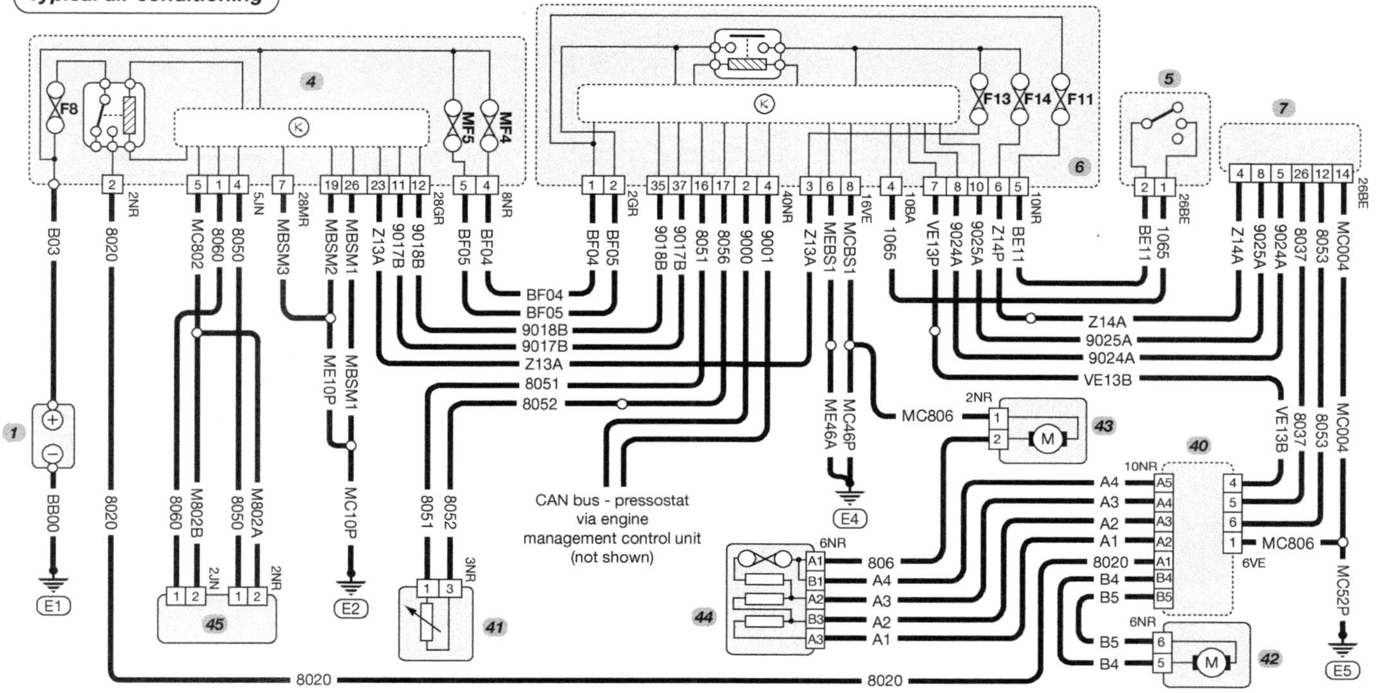

Typical wash/wipe

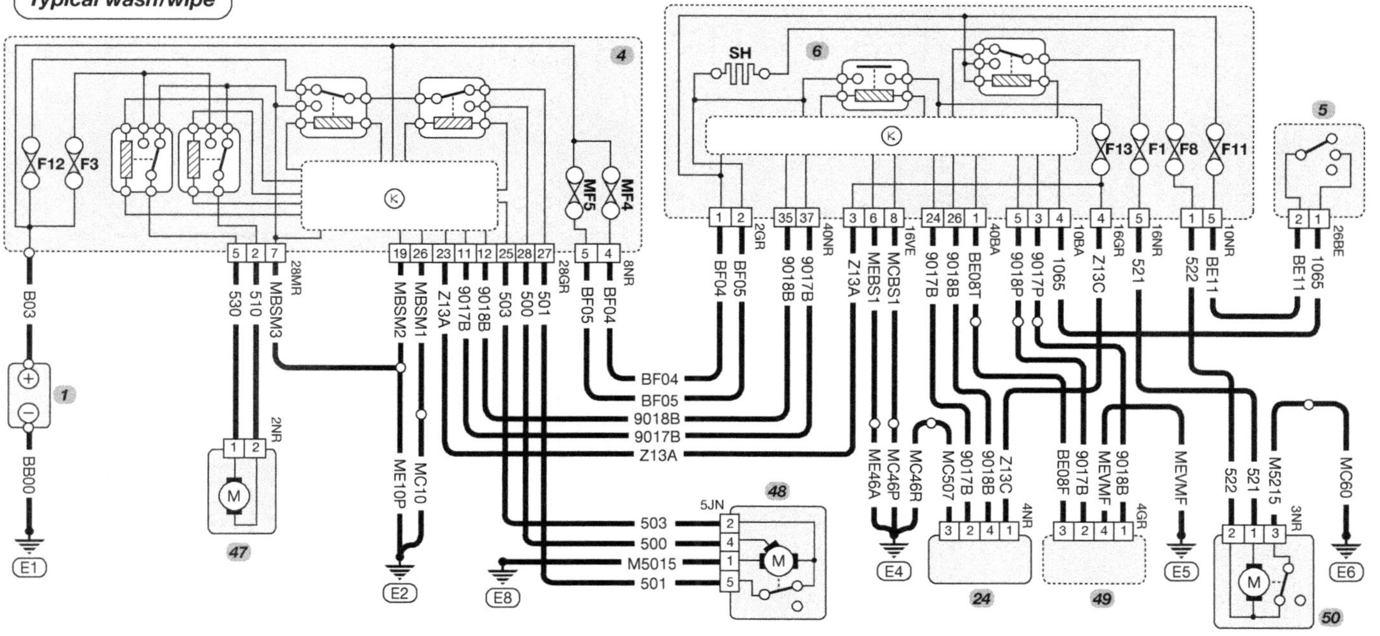

Colour codes

BA	White	**OR**	Orange
BE	Blue	**RG**	Red
BG	Beige	**RS**	Pink
GR	Grey	**VE**	Green
JN	Yellow	**VI**	Mauve
MR	Brown	**VJ**	Green/ Yellow
NR	Black		

Key to items

1 Battery
4 Engine fusebox
5 Ignition switch
6 Built-in systems interface
27 LH door mirror assembly
   b = mirror retraction motor
   c = mirror position sensor
   d = mirror adjustment motor
28 RH door mirror assembly
   (b to d as above)
52 Main window/mirror switch
53 Passenger's window motor/door control unit
54 Driver's window motor/door control unit
55 Passenger's window door switch

Diagram 6

H47528

Typical electric windows

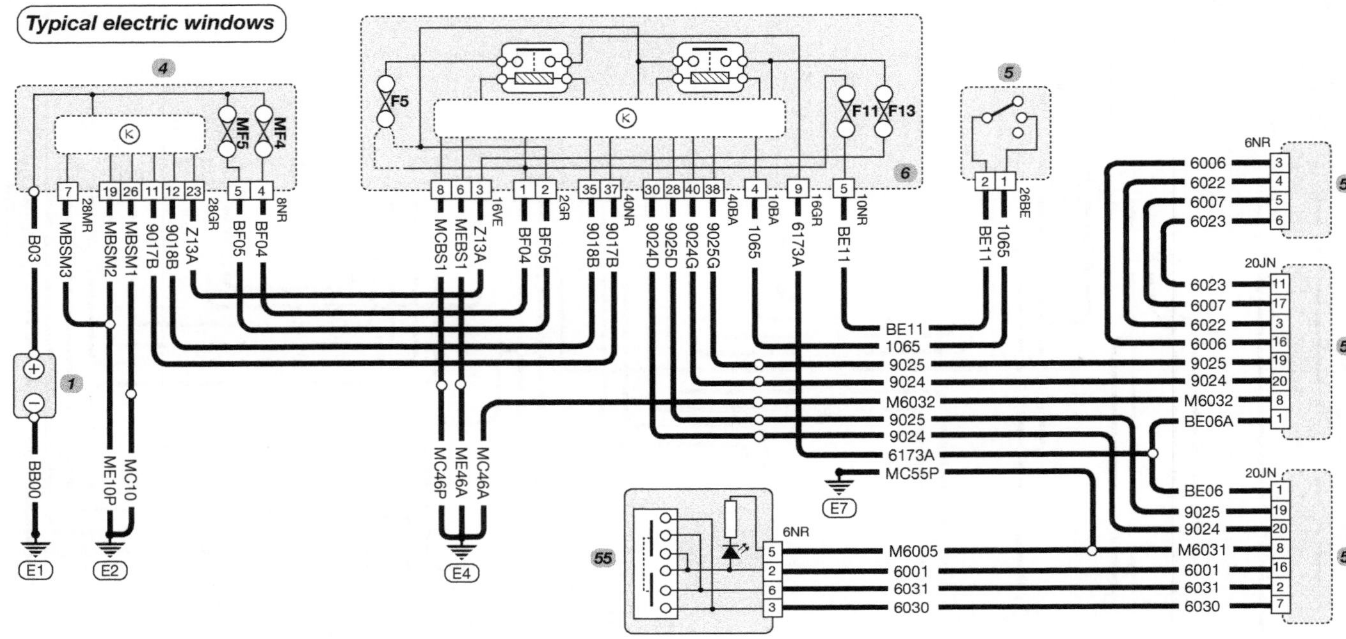

Typical electric mirrors

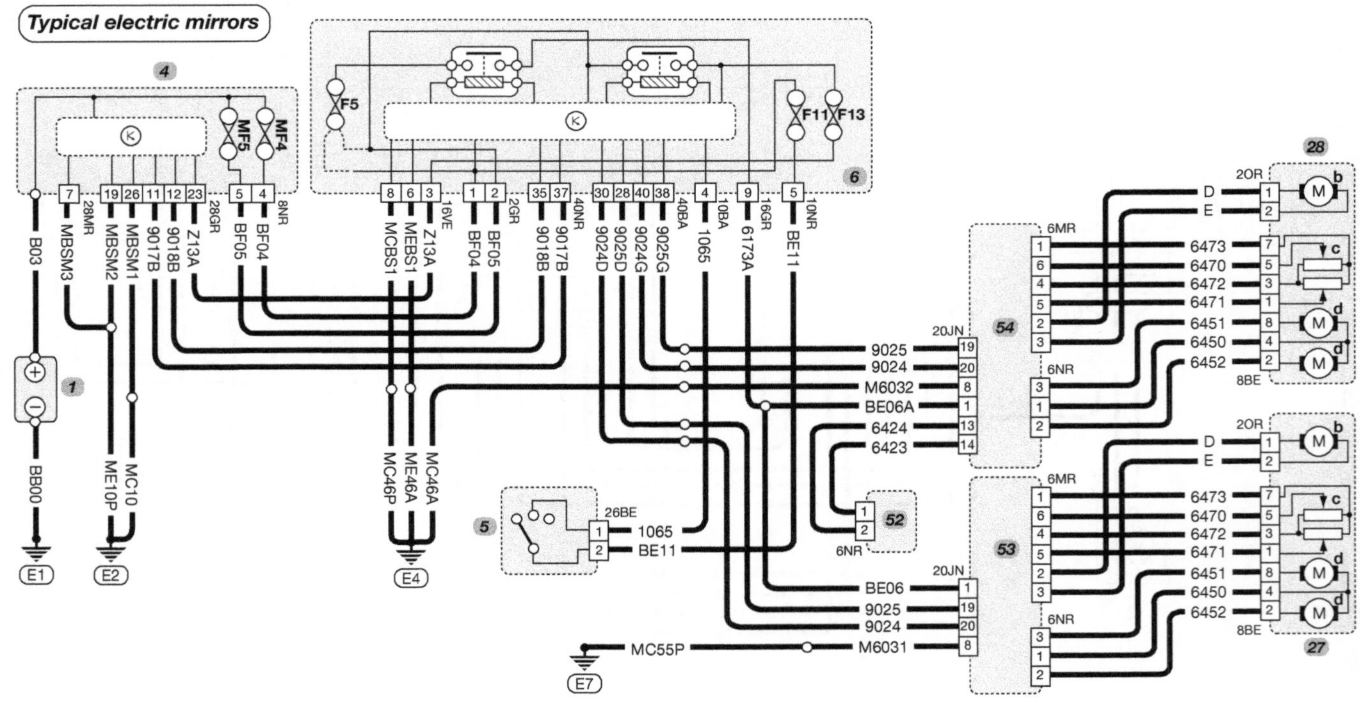

Colour codes

BA	White	**OR**	Orange
BE	Blue	**RG**	Red
BG	Beige	**RS**	Pink
GR	Grey	**VE**	Green
JN	Yellow	**VI**	Mauve
MR	Brown	**VJ**	Green/ Yellow
NR	Black		

Key to items

1 Battery
4 Engine fusebox
5 Ignition switch
6 Built-in systems interface
7 Instrument cluster
9 Steering column control unit
10 Steering wheel boss control unit
60 Central locking master switch
61 Driver's door lock
62 Passenger's door lock
63 LH rear door lock
64 RH rear door lock
65 Tailgate lock motor
66 Tailgate release switch

Diagram 7

H47529

Typical central locking

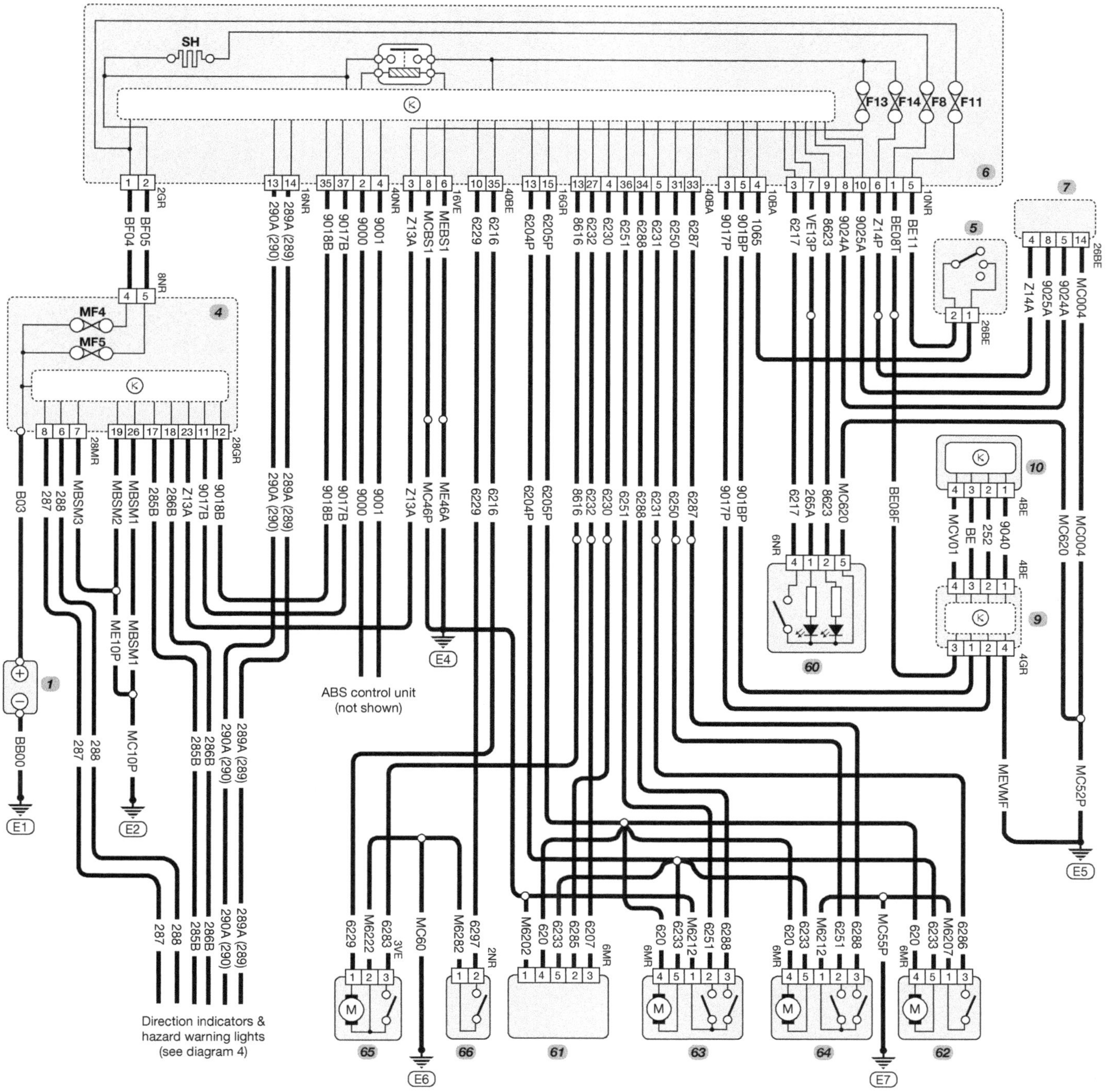

Dimensions and weights

Note: *All figures are approximate, and may vary according to model. Refer to manufacturer's data for exact figures.*

Dimensions

	Hatchback	Coupe
Overall length	4260 mm	4273 mm
Overall width (excluding mirrors)	1773 mm	1769 mm
Overall height (unladen)	1471 mm	1456 mm
Wheelbase	2608 mm	2608 mm

Weights

	Hatchback	Coupe
Unladen weight		
Petrol engine models:		
1.4 litre engine	1182 kg	1181 kg
1.6 litre engine:		
Manual transmission	1200 kg	1200 kg
Automatic transmission	1274 kg	1278 kg
Diesel engine models:		
1.6 litre engine:		
Without particulate filter	1270 kg	1269 kg
With particulate filter	1280 kg	1279 kg
2.0 litre engine:		
Manual transmission	1381 kg	1379 kg
Automatic transmission	1461 kg	1485 kg
Maximum gross vehicle weight*		
Petrol engine models:		
1.4 litre engine	1702 kg	1701 kg
1.6 litre engine:		
Manual transmission	1732 kg	1720 kg
Automatic transmission	1794 kg	1798 kg
Diesel engine models:		
1.6 litre engine:		
Without particulate filter	1800 kg	1790 kg
With particulate filter	1800 kg	1799 kg
2.0 litre engine:		
Manual transmission	1849 kg	1835 kg
Automatic transmission	1880 kg	1880 kg
Maximum gross train (vehicle and trailer) weight*		
Petrol engine models:		
1.4 litre engine	2902 kg	2901 kg
1.6 litre engine:		
Manual transmission	2932 kg	2920 kg
Automatic transmission	2994 kg	2998 kg
Diesel engine models:		
1.6 litre engine:		
Without particulate filter	3100 kg	3090 kg
With particulate filter	3100 kg	3099 kg
2.0 litre engine		
Manual transmission	3349 kg	3335 kg
Automatic transmission	3450 kg	3450 kg

	Hatchback	Coupe
Maximum towing weight**		
Braked trailer:		
Petrol engine models:		
1.4 litre engine	1200 kg	1200 kg
1.6 litre engine:		
Manual transmission	1200 kg	1200 kg
Automatic transmission	1200 kg	1200 kg
Diesel engine models:		
1.6 litre engine:		
Without particulate filter	1300 kg	1300 kg
With particulate filter	1300 kg	1300 kg
2.0 litre engine		
Manual transmission	1500 kg	1500 kg
Automatic transmission	1570 kg	1570 kg
Unbraked trailer:		
Petrol engine models:		
1.4 litre engine	628 kg	628 kg
1.6 litre engine:		
Manual transmission	637 kg	637 kg
Automatic transmission	674 kg	628 kg
Diesel engine models:		
1.6 litre engine:		
Without particulate filter	672 kg	672 kg
With particulate filter	677 kg	677 kg
2.0 litre engine:		
Manual transmission	728 kg	727 kg
Automatic transmission	740 kg	740 kg

* *Refer to the Vehicle Identification Plate for the exact figures for your vehicle – see 'Vehicle identification numbers'*
** *Ensure the combined weight of the trailer and vehicle never exceeds the gross train weight when towing.*

Fuel economy

Although depreciation is still the biggest part of the cost of motoring for most car owners, the cost of fuel is more immediately noticeable. These pages give some tips on how to get the best fuel economy.

Working it out

Manufacturer's figures

Car manufacturers are required by law to provide fuel consumption information on all new vehicles sold. These 'official' figures are obtained by simulating various driving conditions on a rolling road or a test track. Real life conditions are different, so the fuel consumption actually achieved may not bear much resemblance to the quoted figures.

How to calculate it

Many cars now have trip computers which will display fuel consumption, both instantaneous and average. Refer to the owner's handbook for details of how to use these.

To calculate consumption yourself (and maybe to check that the trip computer is accurate), proceed as follows.

1. Fill up with fuel and note the mileage, or zero the trip recorder.
2. Drive as usual until you need to fill up again.
3. Note the amount of fuel required to refill the tank, and the mileage covered since the previous fill-up.
4. Divide the mileage by the amount of fuel used to obtain the consumption figure.

For example:

Mileage at first fill-up (a) = 27,903
Mileage at second fill-up (b) = 28,346
Mileage covered (b - a) = 443
Fuel required at second fill-up = 48.6 litres

The half-completed changeover to metric units in the UK means that we buy our fuel in litres, measure distances in miles and talk about fuel consumption in miles per gallon. There are two ways round this: the first is to convert the litres to gallons before doing the calculation (by dividing by 4.546, or see Table 1). So in the example:

48.6 litres ÷ 4.546 = 10.69 gallons
443 miles ÷ 10.69 gallons = 41.4 mpg

The second way is to calculate the consumption in miles per litre, then multiply that figure by 4.546 (or see Table 2).

So in the example, fuel consumption is:

443 miles ÷ 48.6 litres = 9.1 mpl
9.1 mpl x 4.546 = 41.4 mpg

The rest of Europe expresses fuel consumption in litres of fuel required to travel 100 km (l/100 km). For interest, the conversions are given in Table 3. In practice it doesn't matter what units you use, provided you know what your normal consumption is and can spot if it's getting better or worse.

Table 1: conversion of litres to Imperial gallons

litres	1	2	3	4	5	10	20	30	40	50	60	70
gallons	0.22	0.44	0.66	0.88	1.10	2.24	4.49	6.73	8.98	11.22	13.47	15.71

Table 2: conversion of miles per litre to miles per gallon

miles per litre	5	6	7	8	9	10	11	12	13	14
miles per gallon	23	27	32	36	41	46	50	55	59	64

Table 3: conversion of litres per 100 km to miles per gallon

litres per 100 km	4	4.5	5	5.5	6	6.5	7	8	9	10
miles per gallon	71	63	56	51	47	43	40	35	31	28

Maintenance

A well-maintained car uses less fuel and creates less pollution. In particular:

Filters

Change air and fuel filters at the specified intervals.

Oil

Use a good quality oil of the lowest viscosity specified by the vehicle manufacturer (see *Lubricants and fluids*). Check the level often and be careful not to overfill.

Spark plugs

When applicable, renew at the specified intervals.

Tyres

Check tyre pressures regularly. Under-inflated tyres have an increased rolling resistance. It is generally safe to use the higher pressures specified for full load conditions even when not fully laden, but keep an eye on the centre band of tread for signs of wear due to over-inflation.

When buying new tyres, consider the 'fuel saving' models which most manufacturers include in their ranges.

Driving style

Acceleration

Acceleration uses more fuel than driving at a steady speed. The best technique with modern cars is to accelerate reasonably briskly to the desired speed, changing up through the gears as soon as possible without making the engine labour.

Air conditioning

Air conditioning absorbs quite a bit of energy from the engine – typically 3 kW (4 hp) or so. The effect on fuel consumption is at its worst in slow traffic. Switch it off when not required.

Anticipation

Drive smoothly and try to read the traffic flow so as to avoid unnecessary acceleration and braking.

Automatic transmission

When accelerating in an automatic, avoid depressing the throttle so far as to make the transmission hold onto lower gears at higher speeds. Don't use the 'Sport' setting, if applicable.

When stationary with the engine running, select 'N' or 'P'. When moving, keep your left foot away from the brake.

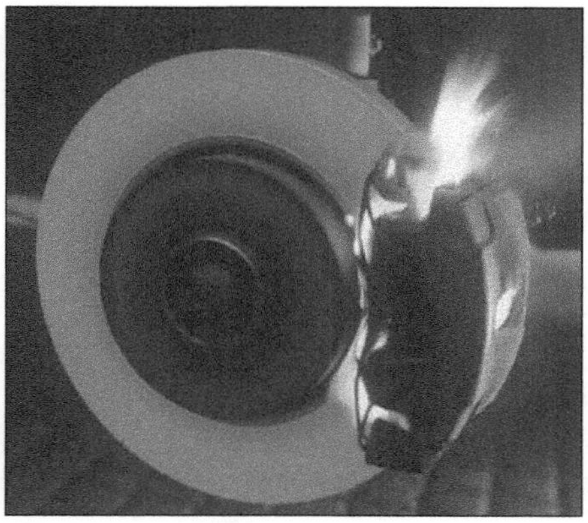

Braking

Braking converts the car's energy of motion into heat – essentially, it is wasted. Obviously some braking is always going to be necessary, but with good anticipation it is surprising how much can be avoided, especially on routes that you know well.

Carshare

Consider sharing lifts to work or to the shops. Even once a week will make a difference.

Electrical loads

Electricity is 'fuel' too; the alternator which charges the battery does so by converting some of the engine's energy of motion into electrical energy. The more electrical accessories are in use, the greater the load on the alternator. Switch off big consumers like the heated rear window when not required.

Freewheeling

Freewheeling (coasting) in neutral with the engine switched off is dangerous. The effort required to operate power-assisted brakes and steering increases when the engine is not running, with a potential lack of control in emergency situations.

In any case, modern fuel injection systems automatically cut off the engine's fuel supply on the overrun (moving and in gear, but with the accelerator pedal released).

Gadgets

Bolt-on devices claiming to save fuel have been around for nearly as long as the motor car itself. Those which worked were rapidly adopted as standard equipment by the vehicle manufacturers. Others worked only in certain situations, or saved fuel only at the expense of unacceptable effects on performance, driveability or the life of engine components.

The most effective fuel saving gadget is the driver's right foot.

Journey planning

Combine (eg) a trip to the supermarket with a visit to the recycling centre and the DIY store, rather than making separate journeys.

When possible choose a travelling time outside rush hours.

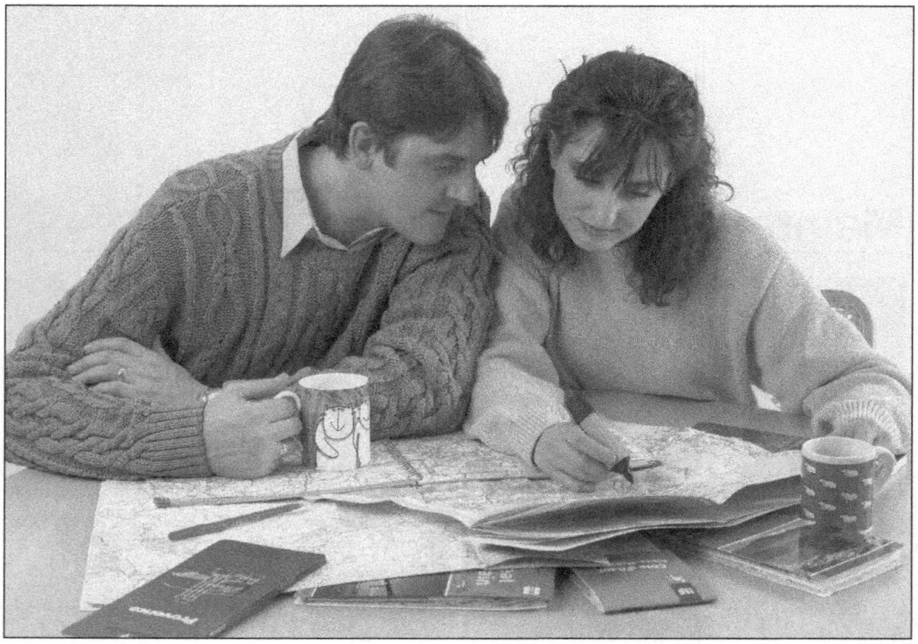

Load

The more heavily a car is laden, the greater the energy required to accelerate it to a given speed. Remove heavy items which you don't need to carry.

One load which is often overlooked is the contents of the fuel tank. A tankful of fuel (55 litres / 12 gallons) weighs 45 kg (100 lb) or so. Just half filling it may be worthwhile.

Lost?

At the risk of stating the obvious, if you're going somewhere new, have details of the route to hand. There's not much point in achieving record mpg if you also go miles out of your way.

Parking

If possible, carry out any reversing or turning manoeuvres when you arrive at a parking space so that you can drive straight out when you leave. Manoeuvering when the engine is cold uses a lot more fuel.

Driving around looking for free on-street parking may cost more in fuel than buying a car park ticket.

Premium fuel

Most major oil companies (and some supermarkets) have premium grades of fuel which are several pence a litre dearer than the standard grades. Reports vary, but the consensus seems to be that if these fuels improve economy at all, they do not do so by enough to justify their extra cost.

Roof rack

When loading a roof rack, try to produce a wedge shape with the narrow end at the front. Any cover should be securely fastened – if it flaps it's creating turbulence and absorbing energy.

Remove roof racks and boxes when not in use – they increase air resistance and can create a surprising amount of noise.

Short journeys

The engine is at its least efficient, and wear is highest, during the first few miles after a cold start. Consider walking, cycling or using public transport.

Speed

The engine is at its most efficient when running at a steady speed and load at the rpm where it develops maximum torque. (You can find this figure in the car's handbook.) For most cars this corresponds to between 55 and 65 mph in top gear.

Above the optimum cruising speed, fuel consumption starts to rise quite sharply. A car travelling at 80 mph will typically be using 30% more fuel than at 60 mph.

Supermarket fuel

It may be cheap but is it any good? In the UK all supermarket fuel must meet the relevant British Standard. The major oil companies will say that their branded fuels have better additive packages which may stop carbon and other deposits building up. A reasonable compromise might be to use one tank of branded fuel to three or four from the supermarket.

Switch off when stationary

Switch off the engine if you look like being stationary for more than 30 seconds or so. This is good for the environment as well as for your pocket. Be aware though that frequent restarts are hard on the battery and the starter motor.

Windows

Driving with the windows open increases air turbulence around the vehicle. Closing the windows promotes smooth airflow and reduced resistance. The faster you go, the more significant this is.

And finally . . .

Driving techniques associated with good fuel economy tend to involve moderate acceleration and low top speeds. Be considerate to the needs of other road users who may need to make brisker progress; even if you do not agree with them this is not an excuse to be obstructive.

Safety must always take precedence over economy, whether it is a question of accelerating hard to complete an overtaking manoeuvre, killing your speed when confronted with a potential hazard or switching the lights on when it starts to get dark.

Conversion factors

Length (distance)

Inches (in)	x 25.4	= Millimetres (mm)	x 0.0394	= Inches (in)
Feet (ft)	x 0.305	= Metres (m)	x 3.281	= Feet (ft)
Miles	x 1.609	= Kilometres (km)	x 0.621	= Miles

Volume (capacity)

Cubic inches (cu in; in^3)	x 16.387	= Cubic centimetres (cc; cm^3)	x 0.061	= Cubic inches (cu in; in^3)
Imperial pints (Imp pt)	x 0.568	= Litres (l)	x 1.76	= Imperial pints (Imp pt)
Imperial quarts (Imp qt)	x 1.137	= Litres (l)	x 0.88	= Imperial quarts (Imp qt)
Imperial quarts (Imp qt)	x 1.201	= US quarts (US qt)	x 0.833	= Imperial quarts (Imp qt)
US quarts (US qt)	x 0.946	= Litres (l)	x 1.057	= US quarts (US qt)
Imperial gallons (Imp gal)	x 4.546	= Litres (l)	x 0.22	= Imperial gallons (Imp gal)
Imperial gallons (Imp gal)	x 1.201	= US gallons (US gal)	x 0.833	= Imperial gallons (Imp gal)
US gallons (US gal)	x 3.785	= Litres (l)	x 0.264	= US gallons (US gal)

Mass (weight)

Ounces (oz)	x 28.35	= Grams (g)	x 0.035	= Ounces (oz)
Pounds (lb)	x 0.454	= Kilograms (kg)	x 2.205	= Pounds (lb)

Force

Ounces-force (ozf; oz)	x 0.278	= Newtons (N)	x 3.6	= Ounces-force (ozf; oz)
Pounds-force (lbf; lb)	x 4.448	= Newtons (N)	x 0.225	= Pounds-force (lbf; lb)
Newtons (N)	x 0.1	= Kilograms-force (kgf; kg)	x 9.81	= Newtons (N)

Pressure

Pounds-force per square inch (psi; lbf/in^2; lb/in^2)	x 0.070	= Kilograms-force per square centimetre (kgf/cm^2; kg/cm^2)	x 14.223	= Pounds-force per square inch (psi; lbf/in^2; lb/in^2)
Pounds-force per square inch (psi; lbf/in^2; lb/in^2)	x 0.068	= Atmospheres (atm)	x 14.696	= Pounds-force per square inch (psi; lbf/in^2; lb/in^2)
Pounds-force per square inch (psi; lbf/in^2; lb/in^2)	x 0.069	= Bars	x 14.5	= Pounds-force per square inch (psi; lbf/in^2; lb/in^2)
Pounds-force per square inch (psi; lbf/in^2; lb/in^2)	x 6.895	= Kilopascals (kPa)	x 0.145	= Pounds-force per square inch (psi; lbf/in^2; lb/in^2)
Kilopascals (kPa)	x 0.01	= Kilograms-force per square centimetre (kgf/cm^2; kg/cm^2)	x 98.1	= Kilopascals (kPa)
Millibar (mbar)	x 100	= Pascals (Pa)	x 0.01	= Millibar (mbar)
Millibar (mbar)	x 0.0145	= Pounds-force per square inch (psi; lbf/in^2; lb/in^2)	x 68.947	= Millibar (mbar)
Millibar (mbar)	x 0.75	= Millimetres of mercury (mmHg)	x 1.333	= Millibar (mbar)
Millibar (mbar)	x 0.401	= Inches of water (inH_2O)	x 2.491	= Millibar (mbar)
Millimetres of mercury (mmHg)	x 0.535	= Inches of water (inH_2O)	x 1.868	= Millimetres of mercury (mmHg)
Inches of water (inH_2O)	x 0.036	= Pounds-force per square inch (psi; lbf/in^2; lb/in^2)	x 27.68	= Inches of water (inH_2O)

Torque (moment of force)

Pounds-force inches (lbf in; lb in)	x 1.152	= Kilograms-force centimetre (kgf cm; kg cm)	x 0.868	= Pounds-force inches (lbf in; lb in)
Pounds-force inches (lbf in; lb in)	x 0.113	= Newton metres (Nm)	x 8.85	= Pounds-force inches (lbf in; lb in)
Pounds-force inches (lbf in; lb in)	x 0.083	= Pounds-force feet (lbf ft; lb ft)	x 12	= Pounds-force inches (lbf in; lb in)
Pounds-force feet (lbf ft; lb ft)	x 0.138	= Kilograms-force metres (kgf m; kg m)	x 7.233	= Pounds-force feet (lbf ft; lb ft)
Pounds-force feet (lbf ft; lb ft)	x 1.356	= Newton metres (Nm)	x 0.738	= Pounds-force feet (lbf ft; lb ft)
Newton metres (Nm)	x 0.102	= Kilograms-force metres (kgf m; kg m)	x 9.804	= Newton metres (Nm)

Power

Horsepower (hp)	x 745.7	= Watts (W)	x 0.0013	= Horsepower (hp)

Velocity (speed)

Miles per hour (miles/hr; mph)	x 1.609	= Kilometres per hour (km/hr; kph)	x 0.621	= Miles per hour (miles/hr; mph)

Fuel consumption*

Miles per gallon, Imperial (mpg)	x 0.354	= Kilometres per litre (km/l)	x 2.825	= Miles per gallon, Imperial (mpg)
Miles per gallon, US (mpg)	x 0.425	= Kilometres per litre (km/l)	x 2.352	= Miles per gallon, US (mpg)

Temperature

Degrees Fahrenheit = (°C x 1.8) + 32

Degrees Celsius (Degrees Centigrade; °C) = (°F - 32) x 0.56

** It is common practice to convert from miles per gallon (mpg) to litres/100 kilometres (l/100km), where mpg x l/100 km = 282*

The jack supplied with the vehicle should only be used for changing the roadwheels – see Wheel changing at the front of this manual. When carrying out any other kind of work, raise the vehicle using a hydraulic (or 'trolley') jack, and always supplement the jack with axle stands at the vehicle jacking points.

When using a hydraulic jack or axle stands, always position the jack head or axle stand head under one of the relevant jacking points; the jacking point is the area below the arrow head mark on the sill **(see illustration)**. Use a block of wood between the jack or axle stand and the sill – the block of wood should have a groove cut into it, into which the welded flange of the sill will locate.

Do not attempt to jack the vehicle under the front crossmember, rear axle, engine, transmission or any of the suspension components.

The jack supplied with the vehicle locates at the jacking points on the underside of the sills – see *Wheel changing*. Ensure that the jack head is correctly engaged before attempting to raise the vehicle.

Never work under, around, or near a raised vehicle, unless it is adequately supported in at least two places.

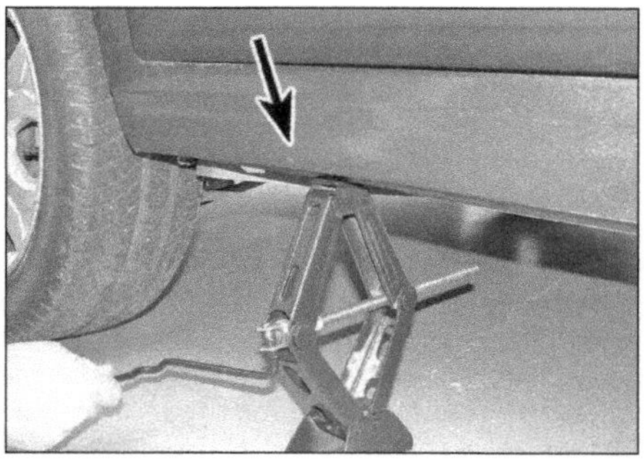

The jacking point is below the arrow head marking on the side of the sill

Buying spare parts

Spare parts are available from many sources, including maker's appointed garages, accessory shops, and motor factors. To be sure of obtaining the correct parts, it will sometimes be necessary to quote the vehicle identification number. If possible, it can also be useful to take the old parts along for positive identification. Items such as starter motors and alternators may be available under a service exchange scheme – any parts returned should be clean.

Our advice regarding spare parts is as follows.

Officially appointed garages

This is the best source of parts which are peculiar to your car, and which are not otherwise generally available (eg, badges, interior trim, certain body panels, etc). It is also the only place at which you should buy parts if the car is still under warranty.

Accessory shops

These are very good places to buy materials and components needed for the maintenance of your car (oil, air and fuel filters, light bulbs, drivebelts, greases, brake pads, touch-up paint, etc). Components of this nature sold by a reputable shop are usually of the same standard as those used by the car manufacturer.

Besides components, these shops also sell tools and general accessories, usually have convenient opening hours, charge lower prices, and can often be found close to home. Some accessory shops have parts counters where components needed for almost any repair job can be purchased or ordered.

Motor factors

Good factors will stock all the more important components which wear out comparatively quickly, and can sometimes supply individual components needed for the overhaul of a larger assembly (eg, brake seals and hydraulic parts, bearing shells, pistons, valves). They may also handle work such as cylinder block reboring, crankshaft regrinding, etc.

Engine reconditioners

These specialise in engine overhaul and can also supply components. It is recommended that the establishment is a member of the Federation of Engine Re-Manufacturers, or a similar society.

Tyre and exhaust specialists

These outlets may be independent, or members of a local or national chain. They frequently offer competitive prices when compared with a main dealer or local garage, but it will pay to obtain several quotes before making a decision. When researching prices, also ask what extras may be added – for instance fitting a new valve, balancing the wheel and tyre disposal all both commonly charged on top of the price of a new tyre.

Other sources

Beware of parts or materials obtained from market stalls, car boot sales, on-line auctions or similar outlets. Such items are not invariably sub-standard, but there is little chance of compensation if they do prove unsatisfactory. In the case of safety-critical components such as brake pads, there is the risk not only of financial loss, but also of an accident causing injury or death.

Second-hand components or assemblies obtained from a car breaker can be a good buy in some circumstances, but this sort of purchase is best made by the experienced DIY mechanic.

Whenever servicing, repair or overhaul work is carried out on the car or its components, observe the following procedures and instructions. This will assist in carrying out the operation efficiently and to a professional standard of workmanship.

Joint mating faces and gaskets

When separating components at their mating faces, never insert screwdrivers or similar implements into the joint between the faces in order to prise them apart. This can cause severe damage which results in oil leaks, coolant leaks, etc upon reassembly. Separation is usually achieved by tapping along the joint with a soft-faced hammer in order to break the seal. However, note that this method may not be suitable where dowels are used for component location.

Where a gasket is used between the mating faces of two components, a new one must be fitted on reassembly; fit it dry unless otherwise stated in the repair procedure. Make sure that the mating faces are clean and dry, with all traces of old gasket removed. When cleaning a joint face, use a tool which is unlikely to score or damage the face, and remove any burrs or nicks with an oilstone or fine file.

Make sure that tapped holes are cleaned with a pipe cleaner, and keep them free of jointing compound, if this is being used, unless specifically instructed otherwise.

Ensure that all orifices, channels or pipes are clear, and blow through them, preferably using compressed air.

Oil seals

Oil seals can be removed by levering them out with a wide flat-bladed screwdriver or similar implement. Alternatively, a number of self-tapping screws may be screwed into the seal, and these used as a purchase for pliers or some similar device in order to pull the seal free.

Whenever an oil seal is removed from its working location, either individually or as part of an assembly, it should be renewed.

The very fine sealing lip of the seal is easily damaged, and will not seal if the surface it contacts is not completely clean and free from scratches, nicks or grooves. If the original sealing surface of the component cannot be restored, and the manufacturer has not made provision for slight relocation of the seal relative to the sealing surface, the component should be renewed.

Protect the lips of the seal from any surface which may damage them in the course of fitting. Use tape or a conical sleeve where possible. Where indicated, lubricate the seal lips with oil before fitting and, on dual-lipped seals, fill the space between the lips with grease.

Unless otherwise stated, oil seals must be fitted with their sealing lips toward the lubricant to be sealed.

Use a tubular drift or block of wood of the appropriate size to install the seal and, if the seal housing is shouldered, drive the seal down to the shoulder. If the seal housing is unshouldered, the seal should be fitted with its face flush with the housing top face (unless otherwise instructed).

Screw threads and fastenings

Seized nuts, bolts and screws are quite a common occurrence where corrosion has set in, and the use of penetrating oil or releasing fluid will often overcome this problem if the offending item is soaked for a while before attempting to release it. The use of an impact driver may also provide a means of releasing such stubborn fastening devices, when used in conjunction with the appropriate screwdriver bit or socket. If none of these methods works, it may be necessary to resort to the careful application of heat, or the use of a hacksaw or nut splitter device. Before resorting to extreme methods, check that you are not dealing with a left-hand thread!

Studs are usually removed by locking two nuts together on the threaded part, and then using a spanner on the lower nut to unscrew the stud. Studs or bolts which have broken off below the surface of the component in which they are mounted can sometimes be removed using a stud extractor.

Always ensure that a blind tapped hole is completely free from oil, grease, water or other fluid before installing the bolt or stud. Failure to do this could cause the housing to crack due to the hydraulic action of the bolt or stud as it is screwed in.

For some screw fastenings, notably cylinder head bolts or nuts, torque wrench settings are no longer specified for the latter stages of tightening, "angle-tightening" being called up instead. Typically, a fairly low torque wrench setting will be applied to the bolts/nuts in the correct sequence, followed by one or more stages of tightening through specified angles.

When checking or retightening a nut or bolt to a specified torque setting, slacken the nut or bolt by a quarter of a turn, and then retighten to the specified setting. However, this should not be attempted where angular tightening has been used.

Locknuts, locktabs and washers

Any fastening which will rotate against a component or housing during tightening should always have a washer between it and the relevant component or housing.

Spring or split washers should always be renewed when they are used to lock a critical component such as a big-end bearing retaining bolt or nut. Locktabs which are folded over to retain a nut or bolt should always be renewed.

Self-locking nuts can be re-used in non-critical areas, providing resistance can be felt when the locking portion passes over the bolt or stud thread. However, it should be noted that self-locking stiffnuts tend to lose their effectiveness after long periods of use, and should then be renewed as a matter of course.

Split pins must always be replaced with new ones of the correct size for the hole.

When thread-locking compound is found on the threads of a fastener which is to be re-used, it should be cleaned off with a wire brush and solvent, and fresh compound applied on reassembly.

Special tools

Some repair procedures in this manual entail the use of special tools such as a press, two or three-legged pullers, spring compressors, etc. Wherever possible, suitable readily-available alternatives to the manufacturer's special tools are described, and are shown in use. In some instances, where no alternative is possible, it has been necessary to resort to the use of a manufacturer's tool, and this has been done for reasons of safety as well as the efficient completion of the repair operation. Unless you are highly-skilled and have a thorough understanding of the procedures described, never attempt to bypass the use of any special tool when the procedure described specifies its use. Not only is there a very great risk of personal injury, but expensive damage could be caused to the components involved.

Environmental considerations

When disposing of used engine oil, brake fluid, antifreeze, etc, give due consideration to any detrimental environmental effects. Do not, for instance, pour any of the above liquids down drains into the general sewage system, or onto the ground to soak away. Many local council refuse tips provide a facility for waste oil disposal, as do some garages. You can find your nearest disposal point by calling the Environment Agency on 08708 506 506 or by visiting www.oilbankline.org.uk.

Note: It is illegal and anti-social to dump oil down the drain. To find the location of your local oil recycling bank, call 08708 506 506 or visit www.oilbankline.org.uk.

Modifications are a continuing and unpublicised process in vehicle manufacture, quite apart from major model changes. Spare parts manuals and lists are compiled upon a numerical basis, the individual vehicle identification numbers being essential for correct identification of the part concerned.

When ordering spare parts, always give as much information as possible. Quote the car model, year of manufacture, body and engine numbers, but most importantly, the after sales replacement parts number (referred to as RPO number: Replacement Parts Organisation number).

The vehicle production code number is on a label on the driver's door A-pillar **(see illustration)**. The code provides Citroën dealers with details of the exact build date, model and where it was made. The first five numbers are the RPO number and then the next two letters/numbers are the factory code (eg, 88 is Mulhouse factory). The vehicle paint code is also given here (eg, EZR is Arctic Steel), along with the tyre prssures.

The vehicle identification number (VIN) is stamped onto right-hand upper strut inner wing panel, in the engine compartment **(see illustration)**.

The vehicle identification number (VIN) is also on a plate/label on the right-hand inner wing engine mounting bracket. The plate carries the VIN and vehicle weight information **(see illustration)**. The vehicle identification number is also stamped onto a plate visible through the base of the windscreen **(see illustration)**.

The engine number is situated on the front face of the cylinder block, and can be found in the following locations:

- *On petrol engines the code is stamped on a plate attached to the front of the cylinder block, or stamped directly onto the front face of the cylinder block lower casing, on the machined surface located just below the oil filter.*
- *On diesel engines the engine number is stamped on the base of the cylinder block at the front. On 1.6 litre engines, it is on the flat surface located on the right- hand side of the oil filter/cooler. On 2.0 litre engines to the left-hand side of the oil filter/cooler.*

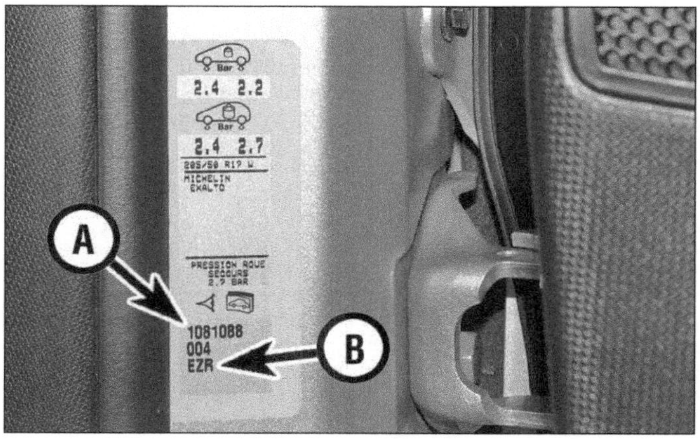

Vehicle parts and production code (A) and paint code (B) on driver's A-pillar

The vehicle identification number (VIN) is stamped on the right-hand inner wing panel

The vehicle identification number (VIN) is also on a label on the right-hand engine mounting bracket ...

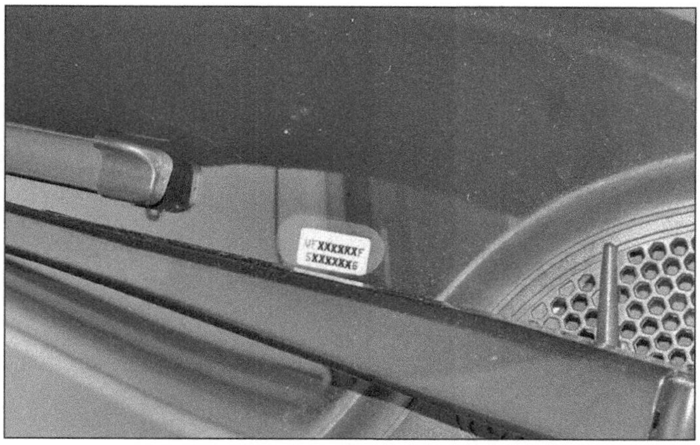

... and on a plate visible through the base of the windscreen

Introduction

A selection of good tools is a fundamental requirement for anyone contemplating the maintenance and repair of a motor vehicle. For the owner who does not possess any, their purchase will prove a considerable expense, offsetting some of the savings made by doing-it-yourself. However, provided that the tools purchased meet the relevant national safety standards and are of good quality, they will last for many years and prove an extremely worthwhile investment.

To help the average owner to decide which tools are needed to carry out the various tasks detailed in this manual, we have compiled three lists of tools under the following headings: *Maintenance and minor repair, Repair and overhaul*, and *Special*. Newcomers to practical mechanics should start off with the *Maintenance and minor repair* tool kit, and confine themselves to the simpler jobs around the vehicle. Then, as confidence and experience grow, more difficult tasks can be undertaken, with extra tools being purchased as, and when, they are needed. In this way, a *Maintenance and minor repair* tool kit can be built up into a *Repair and overhaul* tool kit over a considerable period of time, without any major cash outlays. The experienced do-it-yourselfer will have a tool kit good enough for most repair and overhaul procedures, and will add tools from the *Special* category when it is felt that the expense is justified by the amount of use to which these tools will be put.

Maintenance and minor repair tool kit

The tools given in this list should be considered as a minimum requirement if routine maintenance, servicing and minor repair operations are to be undertaken. We recommend the purchase of combination spanners (ring one end, open-ended the other); although more expensive than open-ended ones, they do give the advantages of both types of spanner.

- ☐ *Combination spanners:*
  Metric - 8 to 19 mm inclusive
- ☐ *Adjustable spanner - 35 mm jaw (approx.)*
- ☐ *Spark plug spanner (with rubber insert) - petrol models*
- ☐ *Spark plug gap adjustment tool - petrol models*
- ☐ *Set of feeler gauges*
- ☐ *Brake bleed nipple spanner*
- ☐ *Screwdrivers:*
  Flat blade - 100 mm long x 6 mm dia
  Cross blade - 100 mm long x 6 mm dia
  Torx - various sizes (not all vehicles)
- ☐ *Combination pliers*
- ☐ *Hacksaw (junior)*
- ☐ *Tyre pump*
- ☐ *Tyre pressure gauge*
- ☐ *Oil can*
- ☐ *Oil filter removal tool (if applicable)*
- ☐ *Fine emery cloth*
- ☐ *Wire brush (small)*
- ☐ *Funnel (medium size)*
- ☐ *Sump drain plug key (not all vehicles)*

Repair and overhaul tool kit

These tools are virtually essential for anyone undertaking any major repairs to a motor vehicle, and are additional to those given in the *Maintenance and minor repair* list. Included in this list is a comprehensive set of sockets. Although these are expensive, they will be found invaluable as they are so versatile - particularly if various drives are included in the set. We recommend the half-inch square-drive type, as this can be used with most proprietary torque wrenches.

The tools in this list will sometimes need to be supplemented by tools from the *Special* list:

- ☐ *Sockets to cover range in previous list (including Torx sockets)*
- ☐ *Reversible ratchet drive (for use with sockets)*
- ☐ *Extension piece, 250 mm (for use with sockets)*
- ☐ *Universal joint (for use with sockets)*
- ☐ *Flexible handle or sliding T "breaker bar" (for use with sockets)*
- ☐ *Torque wrench (for use with sockets)*
- ☐ *Self-locking grips*
- ☐ *Ball pein hammer*
- ☐ *Soft-faced mallet (plastic or rubber)*
- ☐ *Screwdrivers:*
  Flat blade - long & sturdy, short (chubby), and narrow (electrician's) types
  Cross blade – long & sturdy, and short (chubby) types
- ☐ *Pliers:*
  Long-nosed
  Side cutters (electrician's)
  Circlip (internal and external)
- ☐ *Cold chisel - 25 mm*
- ☐ *Scriber*
- ☐ *Scraper*
- ☐ *Centre-punch*
- ☐ *Pin punch*
- ☐ *Hacksaw*
- ☐ *Brake hose clamp*
- ☐ *Brake/clutch bleeding kit*
- ☐ *Selection of twist drills*
- ☐ *Steel rule/straight-edge*
- ☐ *Allen keys (inc. splined/Torx type)*
- ☐ *Selection of files*
- ☐ *Wire brush*
- ☐ *Axle stands*
- ☐ *Jack (strong trolley or hydraulic type)*
- ☐ *Light with extension lead*
- ☐ *Universal electrical multi-meter*

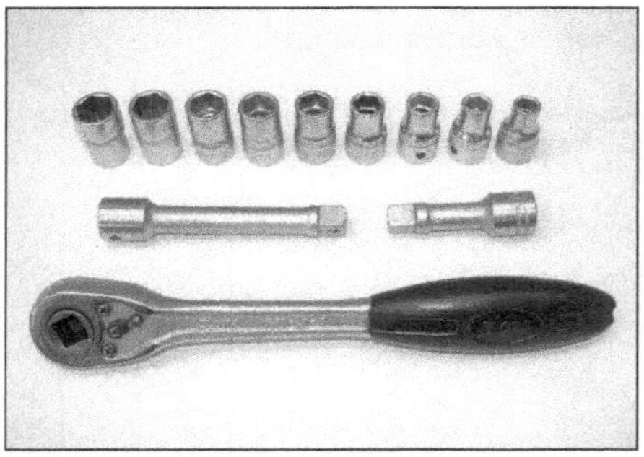

Sockets and reversible ratchet drive

Brake bleeding kit

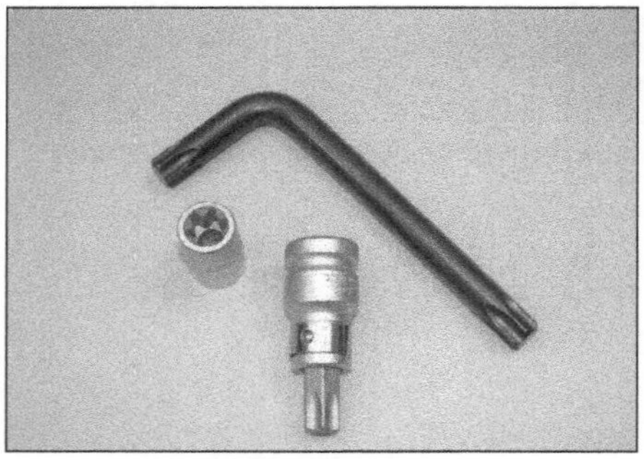

Torx key, socket and bit

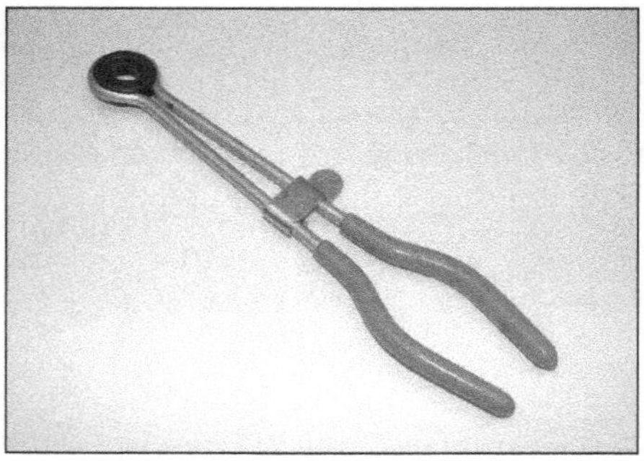

Hose clamp

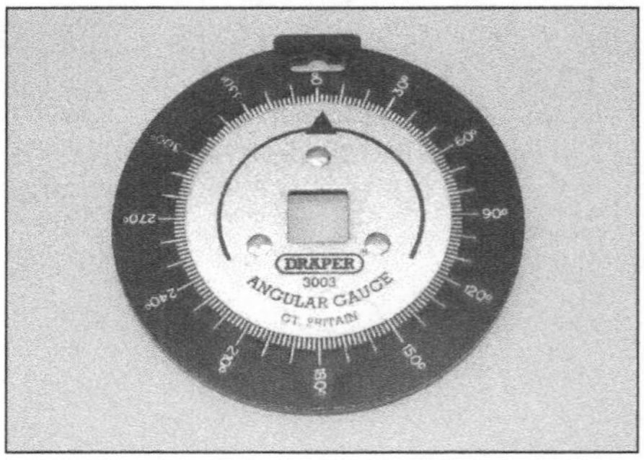

Angular-tightening gauge

Special tools

The tools in this list are those which are not used regularly, are expensive to buy, or which need to be used in accordance with their manufacturers' instructions. Unless relatively difficult mechanical jobs are undertaken frequently, it will not be economic to buy many of these tools. Where this is the case, you could consider clubbing together with friends (or joining a motorists' club) to make a joint purchase, or borrowing the tools against a deposit from a local garage or tool hire specialist.

The following list contains only those tools and instruments freely available to the public, and not those special tools produced by the vehicle manufacturer specifically for its dealer network. You will find occasional references to these manufacturers' special tools in the text of this manual. Generally, an alternative method of doing the job without the vehicle manufacturers' special tool is given. However, sometimes there is no alternative to using them. Where this is the case and the relevant tool cannot be bought or borrowed, you will have to entrust the work to a dealer.

- ☐ *Angular-tightening gauge*
- ☐ *Valve spring compressor*
- ☐ *Valve grinding tool*
- ☐ *Piston ring compressor*
- ☐ *Piston ring removal/installation tool*
- ☐ *Cylinder bore hone*
- ☐ *Balljoint separator*
- ☐ *Coil spring compressors (where applicable)*
- ☐ *Two/three-legged hub and bearing puller*
- ☐ *Impact screwdriver*
- ☐ *Micrometer and/or vernier calipers*
- ☐ *Dial gauge*
- ☐ *Tachometer*
- ☐ *Fault code reader*
- ☐ *Cylinder compression gauge*
- ☐ *Hand-operated vacuum pump and gauge*
- ☐ *Clutch plate alignment set*
- ☐ *Brake shoe steady spring cup removal tool*
- ☐ *Bush and bearing removal/installation set*
- ☐ *Stud extractors*
- ☐ *Tap and die set*
- ☐ *Lifting tackle*

Buying tools

Reputable motor accessory shops and superstores often offer excellent quality tools at discount prices, so it pays to shop around.

Remember, you don't have to buy the most expensive items on the shelf, but it is always advisable to steer clear of the very cheap tools. Beware of 'bargains' offered on market stalls, on-line or at car boot sales. There are plenty of good tools around at reasonable prices, but always aim to purchase items which meet the relevant national safety standards. If in doubt, ask the proprietor or manager of the shop for advice before making a purchase.

Care and maintenance of tools

Having purchased a reasonable tool kit, it is necessary to keep the tools in a clean and serviceable condition. After use, always wipe off any dirt, grease and metal particles using a clean, dry cloth, before putting the tools away. Never leave them lying around after they have been used. A simple tool rack on the garage or workshop wall for items such as screwdrivers and pliers is a good idea. Store all normal spanners and sockets in a metal box. Any measuring instruments, gauges, meters, etc, must be carefully stored where they cannot be damaged or become rusty.

Take a little care when tools are used. Hammer heads inevitably become marked, and screwdrivers lose the keen edge on their blades from time to time. A little timely attention with emery cloth or a file will soon restore items like this to a good finish.

Working facilities

Not to be forgotten when discussing tools is the workshop itself. If anything more than routine maintenance is to be carried out, a suitable working area becomes essential.

It is appreciated that many an owner-mechanic is forced by circumstances to remove an engine or similar item without the benefit of a garage or workshop. Having done this, any repairs should always be done under the cover of a roof.

Wherever possible, any dismantling should be done on a clean, flat workbench or table at a suitable working height.

Any workbench needs a vice; one with a jaw opening of 100 mm is suitable for most jobs. As mentioned previously, some clean dry storage space is also required for tools, as well as for any lubricants, cleaning fluids, touch-up paints etc, which become necessary.

Another item which may be required, and which has a much more general usage, is an electric drill with a chuck capacity of at least 8 mm. This, together with a good range of twist drills, is virtually essential for fitting accessories.

Last, but not least, always keep a supply of old newspapers and clean, lint-free rags available, and try to keep any working area as clean as possible.

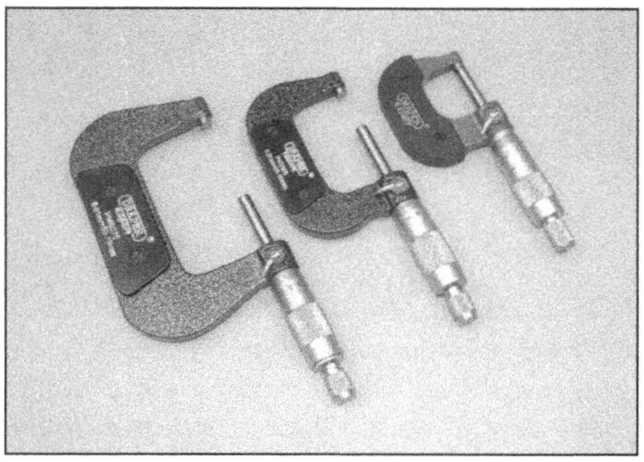

Micrometers

Dial test indicator ("dial gauge")

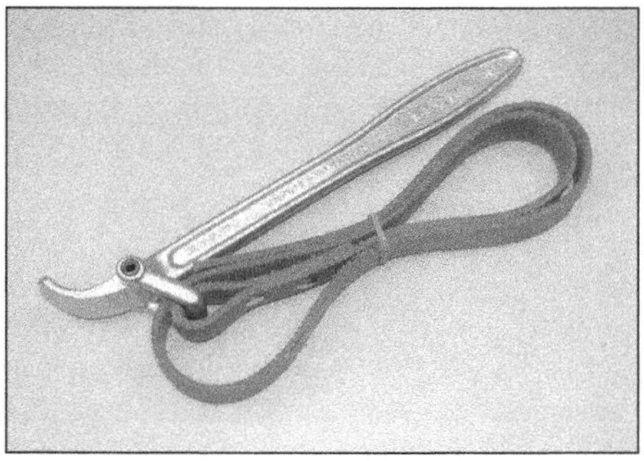

Oil filter removal tool (strap wrench type)

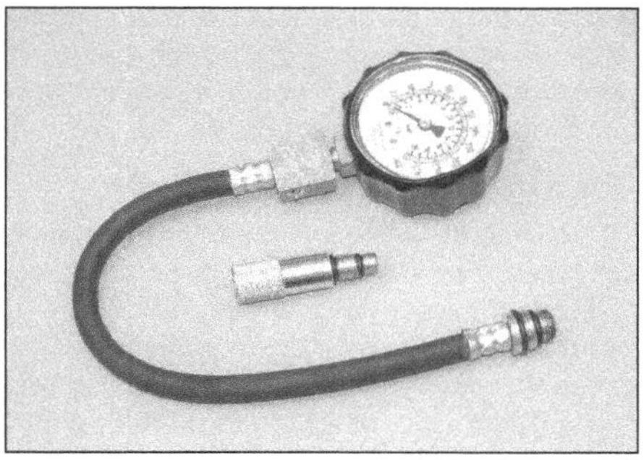

Compression tester

Bearing puller

MOT test checks

This is a guide to getting your vehicle through the MOT test. Obviously it will not be possible to examine the vehicle to the same standard as the professional MOT tester. However, working through the following checks will enable you to identify any problem areas before submitting the vehicle for the test.

It has only been possible to summarise the test requirements here, based on the regulations in force at the time of printing. Test standards are becoming increasingly stringent, although there are some exemptions for older vehicles.

An assistant will be needed to help carry out some of these checks.

The checks have been sub-divided into four categories, as follows:

1 Checks carried out **FROM THE DRIVER'S SEAT**

2 Checks carried out **WITH THE VEHICLE ON THE GROUND**

3 Checks carried out **WITH THE VEHICLE RAISED AND THE WHEELS FREE TO TURN**

4 Checks carried out on **YOUR VEHICLE'S EXHAUST EMISSION SYSTEM**

1 Checks carried out FROM THE DRIVER'S SEAT

Handbrake (parking brake)

☐ Test the operation of the handbrake. Excessive travel (too many clicks) indicates incorrect brake or cable adjustment.

☐ Check that the handbrake cannot be released by tapping the lever sideways. Check the security of the lever mountings.

☐ If the parking brake is foot-operated, check that the pedal is secure and without excessive travel, and that the release mechanism operates correctly.

☐ Where applicable, test the operation of the electronic handbrake. The brake should engage and disengage without excessive delay. If the warning light does not extinguish when the brake is disengaged, this could indicate a fault which will need further investigation.

Footbrake

☐ Depress the brake pedal and check that it does not creep down to the floor, indicating a master cylinder fault. Release the pedal, wait a few seconds, then depress it again. If the pedal travels nearly to the floor before firm resistance is felt, brake adjustment or repair is necessary. If the pedal feels spongy, there is air in the hydraulic system which must be removed by bleeding.

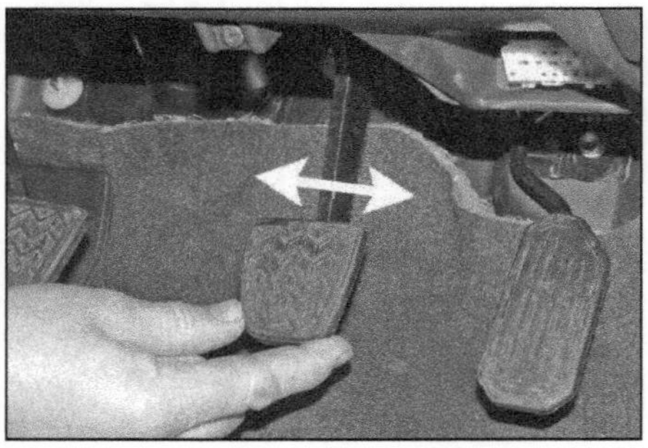

☐ Check that the brake pedal is secure and in good condition. Check also for signs of fluid leaks on the pedal, floor or carpets, which would indicate failed seals in the brake master cylinder.

☐ Check the servo unit (when applicable) by operating the brake pedal several times, then keeping the pedal depressed and starting the engine. As the engine starts, the pedal will move down slightly. If not, the vacuum hose or the servo itself may be faulty.

Steering wheel and column

☐ Examine the steering wheel for fractures or looseness of the hub, spokes or rim.

☐ Move the steering wheel from side to side and then up and down. Check that the steering wheel is not loose on the column, indicating wear or a loose retaining nut. Continue moving the steering wheel as before, but also turn it slightly from left to right.

☐ Check that the steering wheel is not loose on the column, and that there is no abnormal movement of the steering wheel, indicating wear in the column support bearings or couplings.

☐ Check that the ignition lock (where fitted) engages and disengages correctly.

☐ Steering column adjustment mechanisms (where fitted) must be able to lock the column securely in place with no play evident.

Windscreen, mirrors and sunvisor

☐ The windscreen must be free of cracks or other significant damage within the driver's field of view. (Small stone chips are acceptable.) Rear view mirrors must be secure, intact, and capable of being adjusted.

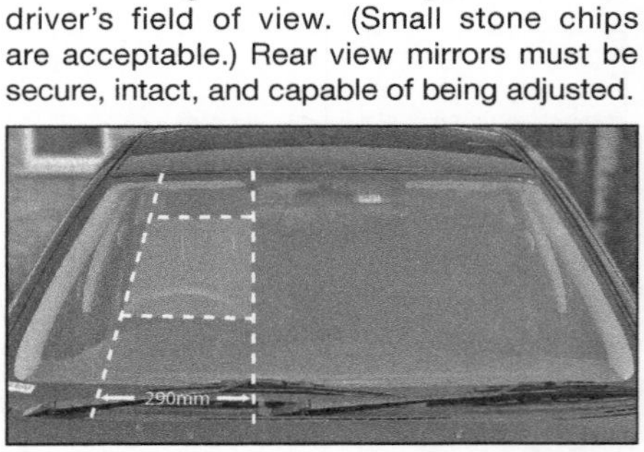

☐ The driver's sunvisor must be capable of being stored in the "up" position.

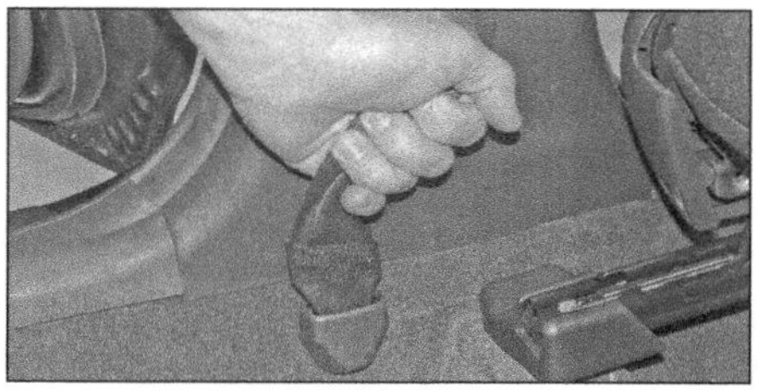

Seat belts and seats

Note: *The following checks are applicable to all seat belts, front and rear.*

□ Examine the webbing of all the belts (including rear belts if fitted) for cuts, serious fraying or deterioration. Fasten and unfasten each belt to check the buckles. If applicable, check the retracting mechanism. Check the security of all seat belt mountings accessible from inside the vehicle, ensuring any height adjustable mountings lock securely in place.

□ Seat belts with pre-tensioners, once activated, have a "flag" or similar showing on the seat belt stalk. This, in itself, is not a reason for test failure.

□ The front seats themselves must be securely attached and the backrests must lock in the upright position.

Doors

□ Both front doors must be able to be opened and closed from outside and inside, and must latch securely when closed.

Bonnet and boot/tailgate

□ The bonnet and boot/tailgate must latch securely when closed.

2 Checks carried out WITH THE VEHICLE ON THE GROUND

Vehicle identification

□ Number plates must be in good condition, secure and legible, with letters and numbers correctly spaced – spacing at (A) should be 33 mm and at (B) 11 mm. At the front, digits must be black on a white background and at the rear black on a yellow background. Other background designs (such as honeycomb) are not permitted.

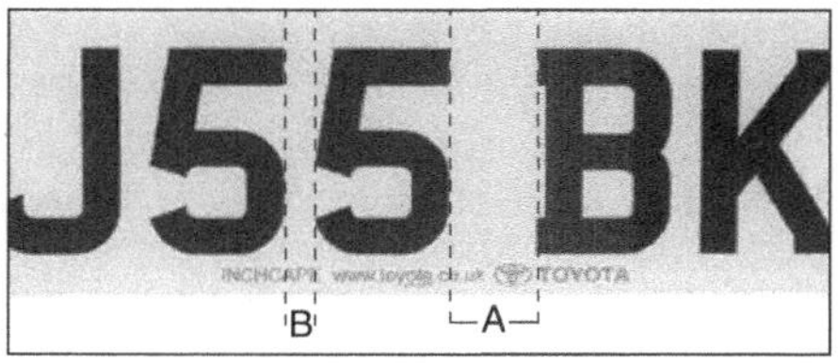

□ The VIN plate and/or homologation plate must be permanently displayed and legible.

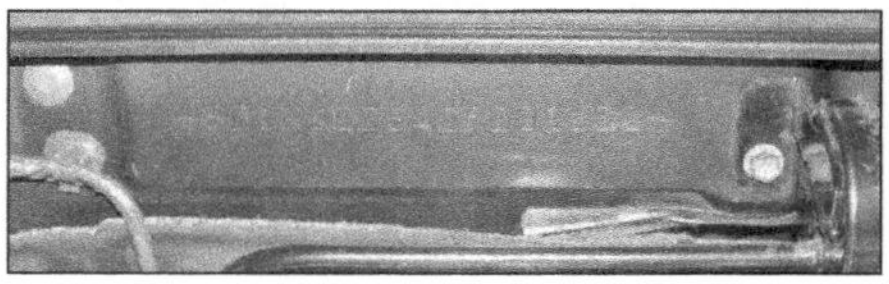

Electrical equipment

□ Switch on the ignition and check the operation of the horn.

□ Check the windscreen washers and wipers, examining the wiper blades; renew damaged or perished blades. Also check the operation of the stop-lights.

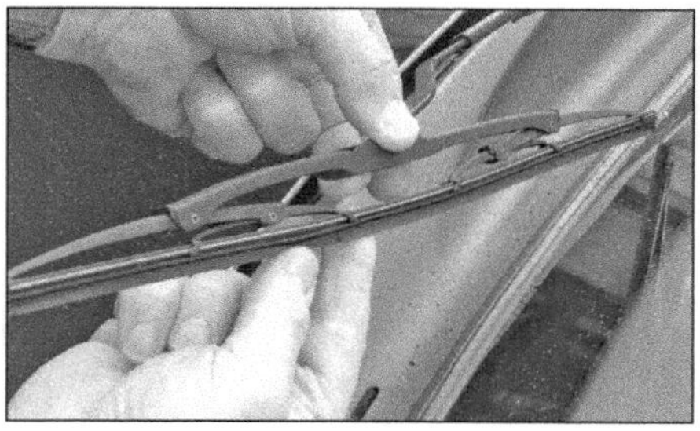

□ Check the operation of the sidelights and number plate lights. The lenses and reflectors must be secure, clean and undamaged.

□ Check the operation and alignment of the headlights. The headlight reflectors must not be tarnished and the lenses must be undamaged.

□ Switch on the ignition and check the operation of the direction indicators (including the instrument panel tell-tale) and the hazard warning lights. Operation of the sidelights and stop-lights must not affect the indicators - if it does, the cause is usually a bad earth at the rear light cluster. Indicators should flash at a rate of between 60 and 120 times per minute – faster or slower than this could indicate a fault with the flasher unit or a bad earth at one of the light units.

□ Check the operation of the rear foglight(s), including the warning light on the instrument panel or in the switch.

□ The warning lights must illuminate in accordance with the manufacturer's design. For most vehicles, the ABS and other warning lights should illuminate when the ignition is switched on, and (if the system is operating properly) extinguish after a few seconds. Refer to the owner's handbook.

Footbrake

□ Examine the master cylinder, brake pipes and servo unit for leaks, loose mountings, corrosion or other damage. If ABS is fitted, this unit should also be examined for signs of leaks or corrosion.

□ The fluid reservoir must be secure and the fluid level must be between the upper (**A**) and lower (**B**) markings.

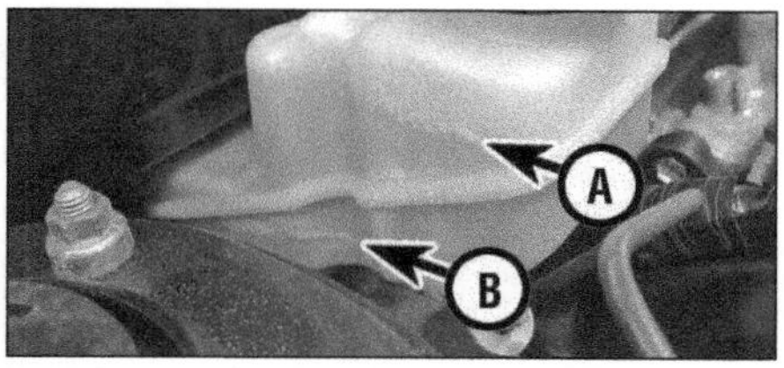

□ Inspect both front brake flexible hoses for cracks or deterioration of the rubber. Turn the steering from lock to lock, and ensure that the hoses do not contact the wheel, tyre, or any part of the steering or suspension mechanism. With the brake pedal firmly depressed, check the hoses for bulges or leaks under pressure.

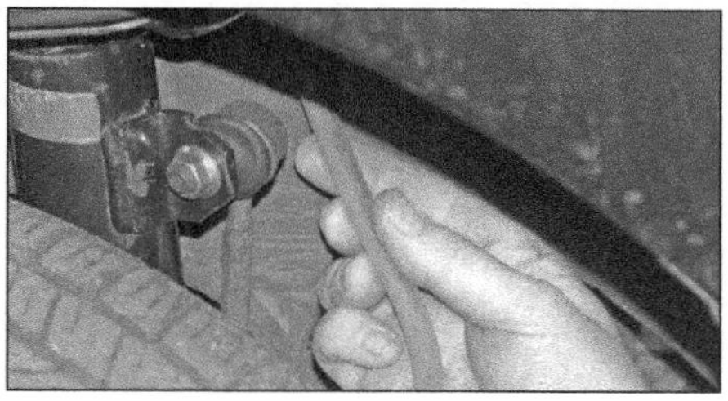

Steering and suspension

□ Have your assistant turn the steering wheel from side to side slightly, up to the point where the steering gear just begins to transmit this movement to the roadwheels. Check for excessive free play between the steering wheel and the steering gear, indicating wear or insecurity of the steering column joints, the column-to-steering gear coupling, or the steering gear itself.

□ Have your assistant turn the steering wheel more vigorously in each direction, so that the roadwheels just begin to turn. As this is done, examine all the steering joints, linkages, fittings and attachments. Renew any component that shows signs of wear or damage. On vehicles with power steering, check the security and condition of the steering pump, drivebelt and hoses.

□ Check that the vehicle is standing level, and at approximately the correct ride height.

Shock absorbers

□ Depress each corner of the vehicle in turn, then release it. The vehicle should rise and then settle in its normal position. If the vehicle continues to rise and fall, the shock absorber is defective. A shock absorber which has seized will also cause the vehicle to fail.

Exhaust system

☐ Start the engine. With your assistant holding a rag over the tailpipe, check the entire system for leaks. Repair or renew leaking sections.

3 Checks carried out **WITH THE VEHICLE RAISED AND THE WHEELS FREE TO TURN**

Jack up the front and rear of the vehicle, and securely support it on axle stands. Position the stands clear of the suspension assemblies. Ensure that the wheels are clear of the ground and that the steering can be turned from lock to lock.

Steering mechanism

☐ Have your assistant turn the steering from lock to lock. Check that the steering turns smoothly, and that no part of the steering mechanism, including a wheel or tyre, fouls any brake hose or pipe or any part of the body structure.

☐ Examine the steering rack rubber gaiters for damage or insecurity of the retaining clips. If power steering is fitted, check for signs of damage or leakage of the fluid hoses, pipes or connections. Also check for excessive stiffness or binding of the steering, a missing split pin or locking device, or severe corrosion of the body structure within 30 cm of any steering component attachment point.

Front and rear suspension and wheel bearings

☐ Starting at the front right-hand side, grasp the roadwheel at the 3 o'clock and 9 o'clock positions and rock gently but firmly. Check for free play or insecurity at the wheel bearings, suspension balljoints, or suspension mount-ings, pivots and attachments.

☐ Now grasp the wheel at the 12 o'clock and 6 o'clock positions and repeat the previous inspection. Spin the wheel, and check for roughness or tightness of the front wheel bearing.

☐ If excess free play is suspected at a component pivot point, this can be confirmed by using a large screwdriver or similar tool and levering between the mounting and the component attachment. This will confirm whether the wear is in the pivot bush, its retaining bolt, or in the mounting itself (the bolt holes can often become elongated).

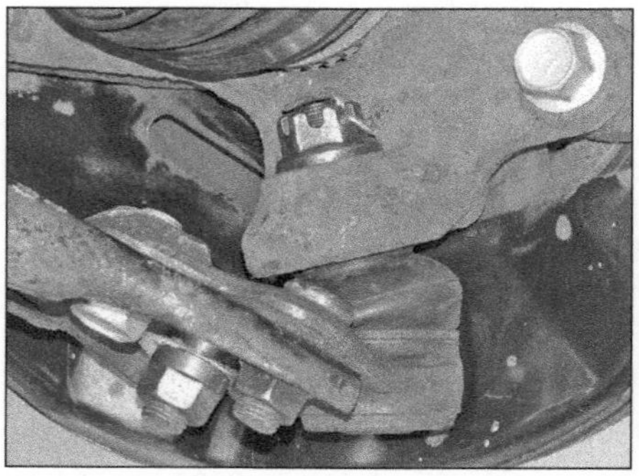

☐ Carry out all the above checks at the other front wheel, and then at both rear wheels.

Springs and shock absorbers

☐ Examine the suspension struts (when applicable) for serious fluid leakage, corrosion, or damage to the casing. Also check the security of the mounting points.

☐ If coil springs are fitted, check that the spring ends locate in their seats, and that the spring is not corroded, cracked or broken.

☐ If leaf springs are fitted, check that all leaves are intact, that the axle is securely attached to each spring, and that there is no deterioration of the spring eye mountings, bushes, and shackles.

☐ The same general checks apply to vehicles fitted with other suspension types, such as torsion bars, hydraulic displacer units, etc. Ensure that all mountings and attachments are secure, that there are no signs of excessive wear, corrosion or damage, and (on hydraulic types) that there are no fluid leaks or damaged pipes.

☐ Inspect the shock absorbers for signs of serious fluid leakage. Check for wear of the mounting bushes or attachments, or damage to the body of the unit.

Driveshafts (fwd vehicles only)

☐ Rotate each front wheel in turn and inspect the constant velocity joint gaiters for splits or damage. Also check that each driveshaft is straight and undamaged.

Braking system

☐ If possible without dismantling, check brake pad wear and disc condition. Ensure that the friction lining material has not worn excessively, (A) and that the discs are not fractured, pitted, scored or badly worn (B).

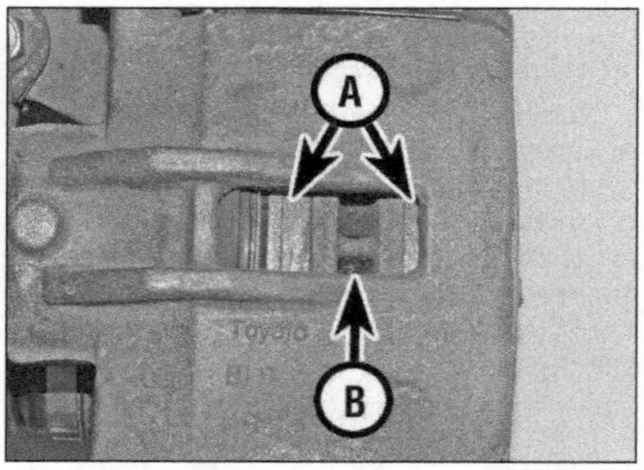

☐ Examine all the rigid brake pipes underneath the vehicle, and the flexible hose(s) at the rear. Look for corrosion, chafing or insecurity of the pipes, and for signs of bulging under pressure, chafing, splits or deterioration of the flexible hoses.

☐ Look for signs of fluid leaks at the brake calipers or on the brake backplates. Repair or renew leaking components.

☐ Slowly spin each wheel, while your assistant depresses and releases the footbrake. Ensure that each brake is operating and does not bind when the pedal is released.

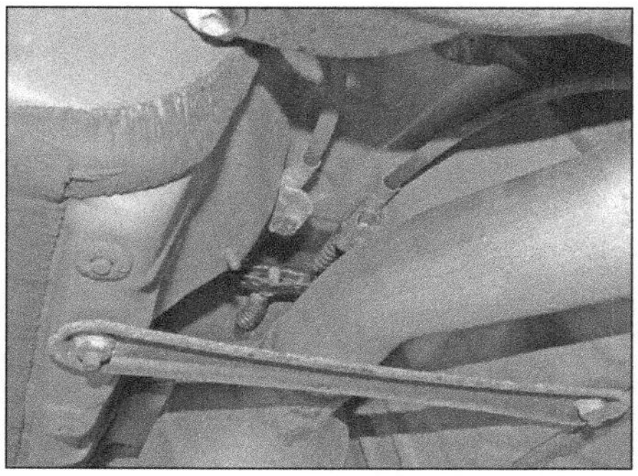

☐ Examine the handbrake mechanism, checking for frayed or broken cables, excessive corrosion, or wear or insecurity of the linkage. Check that the mechanism works on each relevant wheel, and releases fully, without binding.

☐ It is not possible to test brake efficiency without special equipment, but a road test can be carried out later to check that the vehicle pulls up in a straight line.

Fuel and exhaust systems

☐ Inspect the fuel tank (including the filler cap), fuel pipes, hoses and unions. All components must be secure and free from leaks. Locking fuel caps must lock securely and the key must be provided for the MOT test.

☐ Examine the exhaust system over its entire length, checking for any damaged, broken or missing mountings, security of the retaining clamps and rust or corrosion.

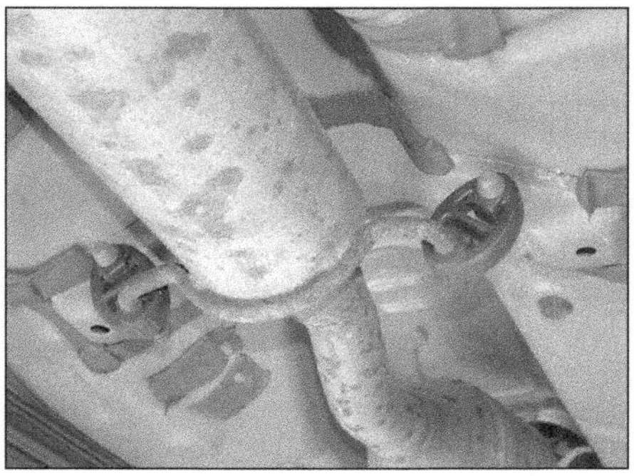

Wheels and tyres

☐ Examine the sidewalls and tread area of each tyre in turn. Check for cuts, tears, lumps, bulges, separation of the tread, and exposure of the ply or cord due to wear or damage. Check that the tyre bead is correctly seated on the wheel rim, that the valve is sound and properly seated, and that the wheel is not distorted or damaged.

☐ Check that the tyres are of the correct size for the vehicle, that they are of the same size and type on each axle, and that the pressures are correct.

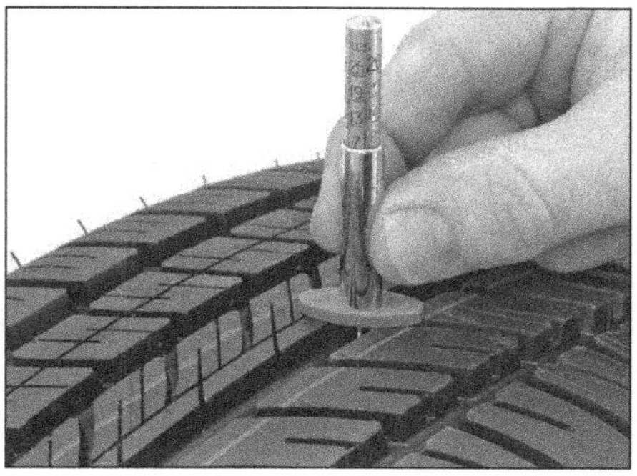

☐ Check the tyre tread depth. The legal minimum at the time of writing is 1.6 mm over the central three-quarters of the tread width. Abnormal tread wear may indicate incorrect front wheel alignment or wear in steering or suspension components.

☐ If the spare wheel is fitted externally or in a separate carrier beneath the vehicle, check that mountings are secure and free of excessive corrosion.

Body corrosion

☐ Check the condition of the entire vehicle structure for signs of corrosion in load-bearing areas. (These include chassis box sections, side sills, cross-members, pillars, and all suspension, steering, braking system and seat belt mountings and anchorages.) Any corrosion which has seriously reduced the thickness of a load-bearing area (or is within 30 cm of safety-related components such as steering or suspension) is likely to cause the vehicle to fail. In this case professional repairs are likely to be needed.

☐ Damage or corrosion which causes sharp or otherwise dangerous edges to be exposed will also cause the vehicle to fail.

Towbars

☐ Check the condition of mounting points (both beneath the vehicle and within boot/ hatchback areas) for signs of corrosion, ensuring that all fixings are secure and not worn or damaged. There must be no excessive play in detachable tow ball arms or quick-release mechanisms.

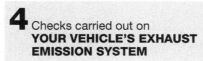

4 Checks carried out on **YOUR VEHICLE'S EXHAUST EMISSION SYSTEM**

Petrol models

☐ The engine should be warmed up, and running well (ignition system in good order, air filter element clean, etc).

☐ Before testing, run the engine at around 2500 rpm for 20 seconds. Let the engine drop to idle, and watch for smoke from the exhaust. If the idle speed is too high, or if dense blue or black smoke emerges for more than 5 seconds, the vehicle will fail. Typically, blue smoke signifies oil burning (engine wear); black smoke means unburnt fuel (dirty air cleaner element, or other fuel system fault).

☐ An exhaust gas analyser for measuring carbon monoxide (CO) and hydrocarbons (HC) is now needed. If one cannot be hired or borrowed, have a local garage perform the check.

CO emissions (mixture)

☐ The MOT tester has access to the CO limits for all vehicles. The CO level is measured at idle speed, and at 'fast idle' (2500 to 3000 rpm). The following limits are given as a general guide:

At idle speed – Less than 0.5% CO
At 'fast idle' – Less than 0.3% CO
Lambda reading – 0.97 to 1.03

☐ If the CO level is too high, this may point to poor maintenance, a fuel injection system problem, faulty lambda (oxygen) sensor or catalytic converter. Try an injector cleaning treatment, and check the vehicle's ECU for fault codes.

HC emissions

☐ The MOT tester has access to HC limits for all vehicles. The HC level is measured at 'fast idle' (2500 to 3000 rpm). The following limits are given as a general guide:

At 'fast idle' – Less then 200 ppm

☐ Excessive HC emissions are typically caused by oil being burnt (worn engine), or by a blocked crankcase ventilation system ('breather'). If the engine oil is old and thin, an oil change may help. If the engine is running badly, check the vehicle's ECU for fault codes.

Diesel models

☐ The only emission test for diesel engines is measuring exhaust smoke density, using a calibrated smoke meter. The test involves accelerating the engine at least 3 times to its maximum unloaded speed.

Note: *On engines with a timing belt, it is VITAL that the belt is in good condition before the test is carried out.*

☐ With the engine warmed up, it is first purged by running at around 2500 rpm for 20 seconds. A governor check is then carried out, by slowly accelerating the engine to its maximum speed. After this, the smoke meter is connected, and the engine is accelerated quickly to maximum speed three times. If the smoke density is less than the limits given below, the vehicle will pass:

Non-turbo vehicles: 2.5m-1
Turbocharged vehicles: 3.0m-1

☐ If excess smoke is produced, try fitting a new air cleaner element, or using an injector cleaning treatment. If the engine is running badly, where applicable, check the vehicle's ECU for fault codes. Also check the vehicle's EGR system, where applicable. At high mileages, the injectors may require professional attention.

Engine

- Engine fails to rotate when attempting to start
- Engine rotates, but will not start
- Engine difficult to start when cold
- Engine difficult to start when hot
- Starter motor noisy or excessively-rough in engagement
- Engine starts, but stops immediately
- Engine idles erratically
- Engine misfires at idle speed
- Engine misfires throughout the driving speed range
- Engine hesitates on acceleration
- Engine stalls
- Engine lacks power
- Engine backfires
- Oil pressure warning light on with engine running
- Engine runs-on after switching off
- Engine noises

Cooling system

- Overheating
- Overcooling
- External coolant leakage
- Internal coolant leakage
- Corrosion

Fuel and exhaust systems

- Excessive fuel consumption
- Fuel leakage and/or fuel odour
- Excessive noise or fumes from exhaust system

Clutch

- Pedal travels to floor – no pressure or very little resistance
- Clutch fails to disengage (unable to select gears)
- Clutch slips (engine speed rises, with no increase in vehicle speed)
- Judder as clutch is engaged
- Noise when depressing or releasing clutch pedal

Manual transmission

- Noisy in neutral with engine running
- Noisy in one particular gear
- Difficulty engaging gears
- Jumps out of gear
- Vibration
- Lubricant leaks

Automatic transmission

- Fluid leakage
- Transmission fluid brown, or has burned smell
- General gear selection problems
- Transmission will not downshift (kickdown) on full throttle
- Engine won't start in any gear, or starts in gears other than P or N
- Transmission slips, shifts roughly, is noisy, or has no drive in forward or reverse gears

Driveshafts

- Clicking or knocking noise on turns (at slow speed on full-lock)
- Vibration when accelerating or decelerating

Braking system

- Vehicle pulls to one side under braking
- Noise (grinding or high-pitched squeal) when brakes applied
- Excessive brake pedal travel
- Brake pedal feels spongy when depressed
- Excessive brake pedal effort required to stop vehicle
- Judder felt through brake pedal or steering wheel when braking
- Brakes binding
- Rear wheels locking under normal braking

Suspension and steering systems

- Vehicle pulls to one side
- Wheel wobble and vibration
- Excessive pitching and/or rolling around corners, or during braking
- Wandering or general instability
- Excessively-stiff steering
- Excessive play in steering
- Lack of power assistance
- Tyre wear excessive

Electrical system

- Battery will not hold a charge for more than a few days
- Ignition/no-charge warning light stays on with engine running
- Ignition/no-charge warning light fails to come on
- Lights inoperative
- Instrument readings inaccurate or erratic
- Horn inoperative, or unsatisfactory in operation
- Windscreen/tailgate wipers failed, or unsatisfactory in operation
- Windscreen/tailgate washers failed, or unsatisfactory in operation
- Electric windows inoperative, or unsatisfactory in operation
- Central locking system inoperative, or unsatisfactory in operation

Introduction

The vehicle owner who does his or her own maintenance according to the recommended service schedules should not have to use this section of the manual very often. Modern component reliability is such that, provided those items subject to wear or deterioration are inspected or renewed at the specified intervals, sudden failure is comparatively rare. Faults do not usually just happen as a result of sudden failure, but develop over a period of time. Major mechanical failures in particular are usually preceded by characteristic symptoms over hundreds or even thousands of miles. Those components that do occasionally fail without warning are often small and easily carried in the vehicle.

With any fault-finding, the first step is to decide where to begin investigations. Sometimes this is obvious, but on other occasions, a little detective work will be necessary. The owner who makes half a dozen haphazard adjustments or replacements may be successful in curing a fault (or its symptoms), but will be none the wiser if the fault recurs, and ultimately may have spent more time and money than was necessary. A calm and logical approach will be found to be more satisfactory in the long run. Always take into account any warning signs or abnormalities that may have been noticed in the period preceding the fault – power loss, high or low gauge readings, unusual smells, etc – and remember that failure of components such as fuses or spark plugs may only be pointers to some underlying fault.

The pages that follow provide an easy-reference guide to the more common problems, which may occur during the operation of the vehicle. These problems and their possible causes are grouped under headings denoting various components or systems, such as Engine, Cooling system, etc. The general Chapter that deals with the problem is also shown in brackets; refer to the relevant part of that Chapter for system-specific information. Whatever the fault, certain basic principles apply. These are as follows:

Verify the fault. This is simply a matter of being sure that you know what the symptoms are before starting work. This is particularly important if you are investigating a fault for someone else, who may not have described it very accurately.

Don't overlook the obvious. For example, if the vehicle won't start, is there fuel in the tank? (Don't take anyone else's word on this particular point, and don't trust the fuel gauge either!) If an electrical fault is indicated, look for loose or broken wires before digging out the test gear.

Cure the disease, not the symptom. Substituting a flat battery with a fully charged one will get you off the hard shoulder, but if the underlying cause is not attended to, the new battery will go the same way. Similarly, changing oil-fouled spark plugs (petrol models) for a new set will get you moving again, but remember that the reason for the fouling (if it wasn't simply an incorrect grade of plug) will have to be found and corrected.

Don't take anything for granted. Particularly, don't forget that a 'new' component may itself be defective (especially if it's been rattling around in the boot for months), and don't leave components out of a fault diagnosis sequence just because they are new or recently fitted. When you do finally diagnose a difficult fault, you'll probably realise that all the evidence was there from the start.

Engine

Engine fails to rotate when attempting to start

- ☐ Battery terminal connections loose or corroded (*Weekly checks*).
- ☐ Battery discharged or faulty (Chapter 5A).
- ☐ Broken, loose or disconnected wiring in the starting circuit (Chapter 5A).
- ☐ Defective starter motor (Chapter 5A).
- ☐ Starter pinion or flywheel/driveplate ring gear teeth loose or broken (Chapter 2A, 2B, 2C or 2D and 5A).
- ☐ Engine earth strap broken or disconnected (Chapter 5A).

Engine rotates, but will not start

- ☐ Fuel tank empty.
- ☐ Battery discharged (engine rotates slowly) (Chapter 5A).
- ☐ Battery terminal connections loose or corroded (*Weekly checks*).
- ☐ Worn, faulty or incorrectly-gapped spark plugs – petrol models (Chapter 1A).
- ☐ Preheating system faulty – diesel models (Chapter 5C).
- ☐ Engine management system fault – petrol models (Chapter 4A).
- ☐ Air in fuel system – diesel models (Chapter 4B).
- ☐ Fuel injector/injection pump fault – diesel models (Chapter 4B).
- ☐ Low cylinder compressions (Chapter 2A, 2B, 2C or 2D).
- ☐ Major mechanical failure (eg, camshaft drive) (Chapter 2A, 2B, 2C or 2D).

Engine difficult to start when cold

- ☐ Battery discharged (Chapter 5A).
- ☐ Battery terminal connections loose or corroded (*Weekly checks*).
- ☐ Worn, faulty or incorrectly-gapped spark plugs – petrol models (Chapter 1A).
- ☐ Preheating system faulty – diesel models (Chapter 5C).
- ☐ Engine management system fault – petrol models (Chapter 4A).
- ☐ Fuel injector/injection pump fault – diesel models (Chapter 4B).

Engine difficult to start when hot

- ☐ Engine management system fault – petrol models (Chapter 4A).
- ☐ Fuel injector/injection pump fault – diesel models (Chapter 4B).
- ☐ Low cylinder compressions (Chapter 2A, 2B, 2C or 2D).

Starter motor noisy or excessively rough in engagement

- ☐ Starter pinion or flywheel/driveplate ring gear teeth loose or broken (Chapter 2A, 2B, 2C or 2D and 5A).
- ☐ Starter motor mounting bolts loose or missing (Chapter 5A).
- ☐ Defective starter motor (Chapter 5A).

Engine (continued)

Engine starts, but stops immediately

- ☐ Vacuum leak at the throttle housing/intake manifold – petrol models (Chapter 4A).
- ☐ Engine management system fault – petrol models (Chapter 4A).
- ☐ Air in fuel system – diesel models (Chapter 4B).
- ☐ Fuel injector/injection pump fault – diesel models (Chapter 4B).

Engine idles erratically

- ☐ Vacuum leak at the throttle housing/intake manifold – petrol models (Chapter 4A).
- ☐ Worn, faulty or incorrectly-gapped spark plugs – petrol models (Chapter 1A).
- ☐ Engine management system fault – petrol models (Chapter 4A).
- ☐ Air in fuel system – diesel models (Chapter 4B).
- ☐ Fuel injector/injection pump fault – diesel models (Chapter 4B).
- ☐ Uneven or low cylinder compressions (Chapter 2A, 2B, 2C or 2D).
- ☐ Camshaft lobes worn (Chapter 2A, 2B, 2C or 2D).
- ☐ Timing belt/chain incorrectly fitted (Chapter 2A, 2B, 2C or 2D).

Engine misfires at idle speed

- ☐ Worn, faulty or incorrectly-gapped spark plugs – petrol models (Chapter 1A).
- ☐ Vacuum leak at the throttle housing/intake manifold – petrol models (Chapter 4A).
- ☐ Engine management system fault – petrol models (Chapter 4A).
- ☐ Faulty injector(s) – diesel models (Chapter 4B).
- ☐ Uneven or low cylinder compressions (Chapter 2A, 2B, 2C or 2D).
- ☐ Disconnected, leaking, or perished crankcase ventilation hoses (Chapter 4C).

Engine misfires throughout the driving speed range

- ☐ Fuel filter blocked (Chapter 1A or 1B).
- ☐ Fuel pump faulty (Chapter 4A or 4B).
- ☐ Fuel tank vent blocked, or fuel pipes restricted (Chapter 4A or 4B).
- ☐ Worn, faulty or incorrectly-gapped spark plugs – petrol models (Chapter 1A).
- ☐ Vacuum leak at the throttle housing/intake manifold – petrol models (Chapter 4A).
- ☐ Engine management system fault – petrol models (Chapter 4A).
- ☐ Fuel injector/injection pump fault – diesel models (Chapter 4B).
- ☐ Faulty ignition HT coil – petrol models (Chapter 5B).
- ☐ Uneven or low cylinder compressions (Chapter 2A, 2B, 2C or 2D).

Engine hesitates on acceleration

- ☐ Worn, faulty or incorrectly-gapped spark plugs – petrol models (Chapter 1A).
- ☐ Vacuum leak at the throttle housing/intake manifold – petrol models (Chapter 4A).
- ☐ Engine management system fault – petrol models (Chapter 4A).
- ☐ Fuel injector/injection pump fault – diesel models (Chapter 4B).

Engine stalls

- ☐ Fuel filter blocked (Chapter 1A or 1B).
- ☐ Fuel pump faulty (Chapter 4A or 4B).
- ☐ Fuel tank vent blocked, or fuel pipes restricted (Chapter 4A or 4B).
- ☐ Worn, faulty or incorrectly-gapped spark plugs – petrol models (Chapter 1A).
- ☐ Vacuum leak at the throttle housing/intake manifold – petrol models (Chapter 4A).
- ☐ Engine management system fault – petrol models (Chapter 4A).
- ☐ Fuel injector/injection pump fault – diesel models (Chapter 4B).

Engine lacks power

- ☐ Timing belt/chain incorrectly fitted (Chapter 2A, 2B, 2C or 2D).
- ☐ Fuel filter blocked (Chapter 1A or 1B).
- ☐ Fuel pump faulty (Chapter 4A or 4B).
- ☐ Uneven or low cylinder compressions (Chapter 2A, 2B, 2C or 2D).
- ☐ Worn, faulty or incorrectly-gapped spark plugs – petrol models (Chapter 1A).
- ☐ Vacuum leak at the throttle housing/intake manifold – petrol models (Chapter 4A).
- ☐ Engine management system fault – petrol models (Chapter 4A).
- ☐ Fuel injector/injection pump fault – diesel models (Chapter 4B).
- ☐ Brakes binding (Chapter 1A or 1B and 9).
- ☐ Clutch slipping (Chapter 6).

Engine backfires

- ☐ Timing belt/chain incorrectly fitted (Chapter 2A, 2B, 2C or 2D).
- ☐ Vacuum leak at the throttle housing/intake manifold – petrol models (Chapter 4A).
- ☐ Engine management system fault – petrol models (Chapter 4A).

Oil pressure warning light on with engine running

- ☐ Low oil level, or incorrect oil grade (*Weekly checks*).
- ☐ Faulty oil pressure warning light switch (Chapter 5A).
- ☐ Worn engine bearings and/or oil pump (Chapter 2E).
- ☐ High engine operating temperature (Chapter 3).
- ☐ Oil pressure relief valve defective (Chapter 2A, 2B, 2C or 2D).
- ☐ Oil pick-up strainer clogged (Chapter 2A, 2B, 2C or 2D).

Engine runs-on after switching off

- ☐ Excessive carbon build-up in engine (Chapter 2E).
- ☐ High engine operating temperature (Chapter 3).
- ☐ Engine management system fault – petrol models (Chapter 4A).
- ☐ Fuel injection pump fault – diesel models (Chapter 4B).

Engine noises

Pre-ignition (pinking) or knocking during acceleration or under load

- ☐ Engine management system fault – petrol models (Chapter 4A).
- ☐ Incorrect grade of spark plug – petrol models (Chapter 1A).
- ☐ Incorrect grade of fuel – petrol models (Chapter 4A).
- ☐ Vacuum leak at the throttle housing/intake manifold – petrol models (Chapter 4A).
- ☐ Excessive carbon build-up in engine (Chapter 2E).

Whistling or wheezing noises

- ☐ Leaking intake manifold or throttle housing gasket – petrol models (Chapter 4A).
- ☐ Leaking vacuum hose (Chapter 4A or 4B and 9).
- ☐ Blowing cylinder head gasket (Chapter 2A, 2B, 2C or 2D).

Tapping or rattling noises

- ☐ Worn valve gear or camshaft (Chapter 2A, 2B, 2C or 2D).
- ☐ Ancillary component fault (coolant pump, alternator, etc) (Chapter 3, 5A, etc).

Knocking or thumping noises

- ☐ Worn big-end bearings (regular heavy knocking, perhaps less under load) (Chapter 2E).
- ☐ Worn main bearings (rumbling and knocking, perhaps worsening under load) (Chapter 2E).
- ☐ Piston slap (most noticeable when cold) (Chapter 2E).
- ☐ Ancillary component fault (coolant pump, alternator, etc) (Chapter 3, 5A, etc).

Cooling system

Overheating

- ☐ Insufficient coolant in system (*Weekly checks*).
- ☐ Thermostat faulty (stuck closed) (Chapter 3).
- ☐ Radiator core blocked, or grille restricted (Chapter 3).
- ☐ Electric cooling fan or sensor faulty (Chapter 3).
- ☐ Pressure cap faulty (Chapter 3).
- ☐ Inaccurate temperature gauge/sensor (Chapter 3).
- ☐ Airlock in cooling system (Chapter 1A or 1B).
- ☐ Engine management system fault (Chapter 4).

Overcooling

- ☐ Thermostat faulty (stuck open) (Chapter 3).
- ☐ Inaccurate temperature gauge/sensor (Chapter 3).

External coolant leakage

- ☐ Deteriorated or damaged hoses or hose clips (Chapter 1A or 1B).
- ☐ Radiator core or heater matrix leaking (Chapter 3).
- ☐ Pressure cap faulty (Chapter 3).
- ☐ Coolant pump leaking (Chapter 3).
- ☐ Boiling due to overheating (Chapter 3).
- ☐ Core plug leaking (Chapter 2E).

Internal coolant leakage

- ☐ Leaking cylinder head gasket (Chapter 2A, 2B, 2C or 2D).
- ☐ Cracked cylinder head or cylinder bore (Chapter 2A, 2B, 2C, 2D or 2E).

Corrosion

- ☐ Infrequent draining and flushing (Chapter 1A or 1B).
- ☐ Incorrect coolant mixture or inappropriate coolant type (Chapter 1A or 1B).

Fuel and exhaust systems

Excessive fuel consumption

- ☐ Air filter element dirty or clogged (Chapter 1A or 1B).
- ☐ Engine management system fault (Chapter 4).
- ☐ Faulty injector(s) (Chapter 4).
- ☐ Tyres under-inflated (*Weekly checks*).
- ☐ Brakes binding (Chapter 1A or 1B and 9).

Fuel leakage and/or fuel odour

- ☐ Damaged or corroded fuel tank, pipes or connections (Chapter 4A or 4B).

Excessive noise or fumes from exhaust system

- ☐ Leaking exhaust system or manifold joints (Chapter 1A or 1B and 4A or 4B).
- ☐ Leaking, corroded or damaged silencers or pipe (Chapter 1A or 1B and 4A or 4B).
- ☐ Broken mountings causing body or suspension contact (Chapter 1A or 1B and 4A or 4B).

Clutch

Pedal travels to floor – no pressure or very little resistance

- ☐ Air in hydraulic system/faulty master or slave cylinder (Chapter 6).
- ☐ Broken clutch release bearing or fork (Chapter 6).
- ☐ Broken diaphragm spring in clutch pressure plate (Chapter 6).

Clutch fails to disengage (unable to select gears)

- ☐ Air in hydraulic system/faulty master or slave cylinder (Chapter 6).
- ☐ Clutch disc sticking on gearbox input shaft splines (Chapter 6).
- ☐ Clutch disc sticking to flywheel or pressure plate (Chapter 6).
- ☐ Faulty pressure plate assembly (Chapter 6).
- ☐ Clutch release mechanism worn or incorrectly assembled (Chapter 6).

Clutch slips (engine speed rises, with no increase in vehicle speed)

- ☐ Faulty hydraulic release system (Chapter 6).
- ☐ Clutch disc linings excessively worn (Chapter 6).
- ☐ Clutch disc linings contaminated with oil or grease (Chapter 6).
- ☐ Faulty pressure plate or weak diaphragm spring (Chapter 6).

Judder as clutch is engaged

- ☐ Clutch disc linings contaminated with oil or grease (Chapter 6).
- ☐ Clutch disc linings excessively worn (Chapter 6).
- ☐ Faulty or distorted pressure plate or diaphragm spring (Chapter 6).
- ☐ Worn or loose engine or gearbox mountings (Chapter 2A, 2B, 2C or 2D).
- ☐ Clutch disc hub or gearbox input shaft splines worn (Chapter 6).

Noise when depressing or releasing clutch pedal

- ☐ Worn clutch release bearing (Chapter 6).
- ☐ Worn or dry clutch pedal bushes (Chapter 6).
- ☐ Faulty pressure plate assembly (Chapter 6).
- ☐ Pressure plate diaphragm spring broken (Chapter 6).
- ☐ Broken clutch disc cushioning springs (Chapter 6).

Manual transmission

Noisy in neutral with engine running

- [ ] Input shaft bearings worn (noise apparent with clutch pedal released, but not when depressed) (Chapter 7A).*
- [ ] Clutch release bearing worn (noise apparent with clutch pedal depressed, possibly less when released) (Chapter 6).

Noisy in one particular gear

- [ ] Worn, damaged or chipped gear teeth (Chapter 7A).*

Difficulty engaging gears

- [ ] Clutch fault (Chapter 6).
- [ ] Worn or damaged gear selection cables (Chapter 7A).
- [ ] Worn synchroniser units (Chapter 7A).*

Jumps out of gear

- [ ] Worn or damaged gear selection cables (Chapter 7A).
- [ ] Worn synchroniser units (Chapter 7A).*
- [ ] Worn selector forks (Chapter 7A).*

Vibration

- [ ] Lack of oil (Chapter 1 and 7A).
- [ ] Worn bearings (Chapter 7A).*

Lubricant leaks

- [ ] Leaking differential output oil seal (Chapter 7A).
- [ ] Leaking housing joint (Chapter 7A).*
- [ ] Leaking input shaft oil seal (Chapter 7A).

** Although the corrective action necessary to remedy the symptoms described is beyond the scope of the home mechanic, the above information should be helpful in isolating the cause of the condition, so that the owner can communicate clearly with a professional mechanic.*

Automatic transmission

Note: *Due to the complexity of the automatic transmission, it is difficult for the home mechanic to properly diagnose and service this unit. For problems other than the following, the vehicle should be taken to a Citroën dealer service department or suitably-equipped specialist.*

Fluid leakage

- [ ] Automatic transmission fluid is usually dark in colour. Fluid leaks should not be confused with engine oil, which can easily be blown onto the transmission by airflow.
- [ ] To determine the source of a leak, first remove all built-up dirt and grime from the transmission housing and surrounding areas using a degreasing agent, or by steam-cleaning. Drive the vehicle at low speed, so airflow will not blow the leak far from its source. Raise and support the vehicle, and determine where the leak is coming from.

Transmission fluid brown, or has burned smell

- [ ] Transmission fluid level low, or fluid in need of renewal (Chapter 1A and 7B).

General gear selection problems

- [ ] Chapter 7B deals with checking and adjusting the selector cable on automatic transmissions. The following are common problems, which may be caused by a poorly adjusted cable:

    a) Engine starting in gears other than Park or Neutral.
    b) Indicator panel showing a gear other than that being used.
    c) Vehicle moves when in Park or Neutral.
    d) Poor gear shift quality or erratic gear changes.

- [ ] Refer to Chapter 7B for the selector cable adjustment procedure.

Transmission will not downshift (kickdown) at full throttle

- [ ] Low transmission fluid level (Chapter 1A).
- [ ] Incorrect selector cable adjustment (Chapter 7B).

Engine won't start in any gear, or starts in gears other than Park or Neutral

- [ ] Incorrect multi-function switch adjustment (Chapter 7B).
- [ ] Incorrect selector cable adjustment (Chapter 7B).

Transmission slips, shifts roughly, is noisy, or has no drive in forward or reverse gears

- [ ] There are many probable causes for the above problems, but the home mechanic should be concerned with only one possibility – fluid level. Before taking the vehicle to a dealer or transmission specialist, check the fluid level as described in Chapter 1A. Correct the fluid level as necessary, or change the fluid. If the problem persists, professional help will be necessary.

Driveshafts

Clicking or knocking noise on turns (at slow speed on full-lock)

- ☐ Lack of constant velocity joint lubricant, possibly due to damaged gaiter (Chapter 8).
- ☐ Worn outer constant velocity joint (Chapter 8).

Vibration when accelerating or decelerating

- ☐ Worn inner constant velocity joint (Chapter 8).
- ☐ Bent or distorted driveshaft (Chapter 8).
- ☐ Worn intermediate bearing (Chapter 8).

Braking system

Note: *Before assuming that a brake problem exists, make sure that the tyres are in good condition and correctly inflated, that the front wheel alignment is correct, and that the vehicle is not loaded with weight in an unequal manner. Apart from checking the condition of all pipe and hose connections, any faults occurring on the anti-lock braking system should be referred to a Citroën dealer for diagnosis.*

Vehicle pulls to one side under braking

- ☐ Worn, defective, damaged or contaminated brake pads on one side (Chapter 9).
- ☐ Seized or partially-seized front brake caliper (Chapter 9).
- ☐ A mixture of brake pad materials fitted between sides (Chapter 9).
- ☐ Brake caliper mounting bolts loose (Chapter 9).
- ☐ Worn or damaged steering or suspension components (Chapter 1A or 1B and 10).

Noise (grinding or high-pitched squeal) when brakes applied

- ☐ Brake pad material worn down to metal backing (Chapter 1A or 1B and 9).
- ☐ Excessive corrosion of brake disc. May be apparent after the vehicle has been standing for some time (Chapter 9).
- ☐ Foreign object (stone chipping, etc) trapped between brake disc and shield (Chapter 9).

Excessive brake pedal travel

- ☐ Faulty master cylinder (Chapter 9).
- ☐ Air in hydraulic system (Chapter 9).
- ☐ Faulty vacuum servo unit (Chapter 9).

Brake pedal feels spongy when depressed

- ☐ Air in hydraulic system (Chapter 9).
- ☐ Deteriorated flexible rubber brake hoses (Chapter 1A or 1B and 9).
- ☐ Master cylinder mounting nuts loose (Chapter 9).
- ☐ Faulty master cylinder (Chapter 9).

Excessive brake pedal effort required to stop vehicle

- ☐ Faulty vacuum servo unit (Chapter 9).
- ☐ Disconnected, damaged or insecure brake servo vacuum hose (Chapter 9).
- ☐ Primary or secondary hydraulic circuit failure (Chapter 9).
- ☐ Seized brake caliper (Chapter 9).
- ☐ Brake pads incorrectly fitted (Chapter 9).
- ☐ Incorrect grade of brake pads fitted (Chapter 9).
- ☐ Brake pads contaminated (Chapter 9).

Judder felt through brake pedal or steering wheel when braking

- ☐ Excessive run-out or distortion of discs (Chapter 9).
- ☐ Brake pads worn (Chapter 1A or 1B and 9).
- ☐ Brake caliper mounting bolts loose (Chapter 9).
- ☐ Wear in suspension or steering components or mountings (Chapter 1A or 1B and 10).

Brakes binding

- ☐ Seized brake caliper (Chapter 9).
- ☐ Incorrectly-adjusted handbrake mechanism (Chapter 9).
- ☐ Faulty master cylinder (Chapter 9).

Rear wheels locking under normal braking

- ☐ Rear brake pads contaminated (Chapter 1A or 1B and 9).
- ☐ ABS system fault (Chapter 9).

Suspension and steering

Note: *Before diagnosing suspension or steering faults, be sure that the trouble is not due to incorrect tyre pressures, mixtures of tyre types, or binding brakes.*

Vehicle pulls to one side

- ☐ Defective tyre (*Weekly checks*).
- ☐ Excessive wear in suspension or steering components (Chapter 1A or 1B and 10).
- ☐ Incorrect front wheel alignment (Chapter 10).
- ☐ Damage to steering or suspension components (Chapter 1A or 1B).

Wheel wobble and vibration

- ☐ Front roadwheels out of balance (vibration felt mainly through the steering wheel) (Chapter 1A or 1B and 10).
- ☐ Rear roadwheels out of balance (vibration felt throughout the vehicle) (Chapter 1A or 1B and 10).
- ☐ Roadwheels damaged or distorted (Chapter 1A or 1B and 10).
- ☐ Faulty or damaged tyre (*Weekly checks*).
- ☐ Worn steering or suspension joints, bushes or components (Chapter 1A or 1B and 10).
- ☐ Wheel bolts loose (Chapter 1A or 1B and 10).

Excessive pitching and/or rolling around corners, or during braking

- ☐ Defective shock absorbers (Chapter 1A or 1B and 10).
- ☐ Broken or weak spring and/or suspension part (Chapter 1A or 1B and 10).
- ☐ Worn or damaged anti-roll bar or mountings (Chapter 10).

Wandering or general instability

- ☐ Incorrect front wheel alignment (Chapter 10).
- ☐ Worn steering or suspension joints, bushes or components (Chapter 1A or 1B and 10).
- ☐ Roadwheels out of balance (Chapter 1A or 1B and 10).
- ☐ Faulty or damaged tyre (*Weekly checks*).
- ☐ Wheel bolts loose (Chapter 1A or 1B and 10).
- ☐ Defective shock absorbers (Chapter 1A or 1B and 10).

Excessively-stiff steering

- ☐ Lack of power steering fluid (Chapter 10).
- ☐ Seized track rod end balljoint or suspension balljoint (Chapter 1A or 1B and 10).
- ☐ Incorrect front wheel alignment (Chapter 10).
- ☐ Steering rack or column bent or damaged (Chapter 10).
- ☐ Power steering pump fault (Chapter 10).

Excessive play in steering

- ☐ Worn steering column universal joint (Chapter 10).
- ☐ Worn steering track rod end balljoints (Chapter 1A or 1B and 10).
- ☐ Worn steering rack (Chapter 10).
- ☐ Worn steering or suspension joints, bushes or components (Chapter 1A or 1B and 10).

Lack of power assistance

- ☐ Incorrect power steering fluid level (*Weekly checks*).
- ☐ Restriction in power steering fluid hoses (Chapter 1A or 1B).
- ☐ Faulty power steering pump (Chapter 10).
- ☐ Faulty steering rack (Chapter 10).

Tyre wear excessive

Tyre treads exhibit feathered edges

- ☐ Incorrect toe setting (Chapter 10).

Tyres worn in centre of tread

- ☐ Tyres over-inflated (*Weekly checks*).

Tyres worn on inside and outside edges

- ☐ Tyres under-inflated (*Weekly checks*).

Tyres worn on inside or outside edges

- ☐ Incorrect camber/castor angles (wear on one edge only) (Chapter 10).
- ☐ Worn steering or suspension joints, bushes or components (Chapter 1A or 1B and 10).
- ☐ Excessively-hard cornering.
- ☐ Accident damage.

Tyres worn unevenly

- ☐ Tyres/wheels out of balance (*Weekly checks*).
- ☐ Excessive wheel or tyre run-out (Chapter 1A or 1B).
- ☐ Worn shock absorbers (Chapter 1A or 1B and 10).
- ☐ Faulty tyre (*Weekly checks*).

Electrical system

Note: *For problems associated with the starting system, refer to the faults listed under 'Engine' earlier in this Section.*

Battery won't hold a charge for more than a few days

- ☐ Battery defective internally (Chapter 5A).
- ☐ Battery terminal connections loose or corroded (*Weekly checks*).
- ☐ Auxiliary drivebelt broken, worn or incorrectly adjusted (Chapter 1A or 1B).
- ☐ Alternator not charging at correct output (Chapter 5A).
- ☐ Alternator or voltage regulator faulty (Chapter 5A).
- ☐ Short-circuit causing continual battery drain (Chapter 5A and 12).

Ignition/no-charge warning light stays on with engine running

- ☐ Auxiliary drivebelt broken, worn, or incorrectly adjusted (Chapter 1A or 1B).
- ☐ Internal fault in alternator or voltage regulator (Chapter 5A).
- ☐ Broken, disconnected, or loose wiring in charging circuit (Chapter 5A).

Ignition/no-charge warning light fails to come on

- ☐ Warning light bulb blown (Chapter 12).
- ☐ Broken, disconnected, or loose wiring in warning light circuit (Chapter 12).
- ☐ Alternator faulty (Chapter 5A).

Lights inoperative

- ☐ Bulb blown (Chapter 12).
- ☐ Corrosion of bulb or bulbholder contacts (Chapter 12).
- ☐ Blown fuse (Chapter 12).
- ☐ Faulty relay (Chapter 12).
- ☐ Broken, loose, or disconnected wiring (Chapter 12).
- ☐ Faulty switch (Chapter 12).

Instrument readings inaccurate or erratic

Fuel or temperature gauges give no reading

- ☐ Faulty gauge sensor unit (Chapter 3 or 4).
- ☐ Wiring open-circuit (Chapter 12).
- ☐ Faulty gauge (Chapter 12).

Fuel or temperature gauges give continuous maximum reading

- ☐ Faulty gauge sensor unit (Chapter 3 or 4).
- ☐ Wiring short-circuit (Chapter 12).
- ☐ Faulty gauge (Chapter 12).

Horn inoperative, or unsatisfactory in operation

Horn operates all the time

- ☐ Horn push either earthed or stuck down (Chapter 12).
- ☐ Horn cable-to-horn push earthed (Chapter 12).

Horn fails to operate

- ☐ Blown fuse (Chapter 12).
- ☐ Cable or cable connections loose, broken or disconnected (Chapter 12).
- ☐ Faulty horn (Chapter 12).

Horn emits intermittent or unsatisfactory sound

- ☐ Cable connections loose (Chapter 12).
- ☐ Horn mountings loose (Chapter 12).
- ☐ Faulty horn (Chapter 12).

Windscreen/tailgate wipers failed, or unsatisfactory in operation

Wipers fail to operate, or operate very slowly

- ☐ Wiper blades stuck to screen, or linkage seized or binding (Chapter 1A or 1B and 12).
- ☐ Blown fuse (Chapter 12).
- ☐ Cable or cable connections loose, broken or disconnected (Chapter 12).
- ☐ Faulty built-in system interface (BSI) unit (Chapter 12).
- ☐ Faulty wiper motor (Chapter 12).

Wiper blades sweep over too large or too small an area of the glass

- ☐ Wiper arms incorrectly positioned on spindles (Chapter 12).
- ☐ Excessive wear of wiper linkage (Chapter 12).
- ☐ Wiper motor or linkage mountings loose or insecure (Chapter 12).

Wiper blades fail to clean the glass effectively

- ☐ Wiper blade rubbers worn or perished (*Weekly checks*).
- ☐ Wiper arm tension springs broken, or arm pivots seized (Chapter 12).
- ☐ Insufficient windscreen washer additive to adequately remove road film (*Weekly checks*).

Windscreen/tailgate washers failed, or unsatisfactory in operation

One or more washer jets inoperative

- ☐ Blocked washer jet (*Weekly checks*).
- ☐ Disconnected, kinked or restricted fluid hose (Chapter 12).
- ☐ Insufficient fluid in washer reservoir (*Weekly checks*).

Washer pump fails to operate

- ☐ Broken or disconnected wiring or connections (Chapter 12).
- ☐ Blown fuse (Chapter 12).
- ☐ Faulty washer switch (Chapter 12).
- ☐ Faulty washer pump (Chapter 12).

Electric windows inoperative, or unsatisfactory in operation

Window glass will only move in one direction

- ☐ Faulty switch (Chapter 12).

Window glass slow to move

- ☐ Regulator seized or damaged, or in need of lubricant (Chapter 11).
- ☐ Door internal components or trim fouling regulator (Chapter 11).
- ☐ Faulty motor (Chapter 11).

Window glass fails to move

- ☐ Blown fuse (Chapter 12).
- ☐ Broken or disconnected wiring or connections (Chapter 12).
- ☐ Faulty motor (Chapter 11).
- ☐ Faulty built-in systems interface (BSI) unit (Chapter 12).

Central locking system inoperative, or unsatisfactory in operation

Complete system failure

- ☐ Blown fuse (Chapter 12).
- ☐ Broken or disconnected wiring or connections (Chapter 12).
- ☐ Faulty built-in system interface (BSI) unit (Chapter 12).

Door/tailgate locks but will not unlock, or unlocks but will not lock

- ☐ Broken or disconnected link rod(s) (Chapter 11).
- ☐ Faulty lock motor (Chapter 11).

One lock fails to operate

- ☐ Broken or disconnected wiring or connections (Chapter 12).
- ☐ Faulty lock motor (Chapter 11).
- ☐ Broken, binding or disconnected link rod(s) (Chapter 11).

Note: *References throughout this index are in the form* "Chapter number" • "Page number". *So, for example, 2C•15 refers to page 15 of Chapter 2C.*

A

B

C

Note: *References throughout this index are in the form* "Chapter number" • "Page number"*. So, for example, 2C•15 refers to page 15 of Chapter 2C.*

D

E

F

G

H

I

Note: *References throughout this index are in the form* "Chapter number" • "Page number". *So, for example, 2C•15 refers to page 15 of Chapter 2C.*

Note: *References throughout this index are in the form* "Chapter number" • "Page number". *So, for example, 2C•15 refers to page 15 of Chapter 2C.*

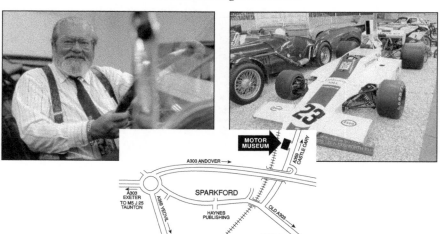